ML
421
.B4
N65
2005

MU

Chicago Public Library

W9-APD-530

Shout! : The Beatles in their generation

DAMAGE NOTED prior 4/19/23

CHICAGO PUBLIC LIBRARY
VISUAL AND PERFORMING AI
400 S. STATE ST.   60605

CHICAGO PUBLIC LIBRARY
VISUAL AND PERFORMING ARTS
400 S. STATE ST. _____ 60605

THE BEATLES
IN THEIR GENERATION

REVISED AND UPDATED

PHILIP NORMAN

A FIRESIDE BOOK
Published by Simon & Schuster
New York   London   Toronto   Sydney

FIRESIDE
Rockefeller Center
1230 Avenue of the Americas
New York, NY 10020

Copyright © 1981, 1993, 2003
All rights reserved,
including the right of reproduction
in whole or in part in any form.

This revised and updated edition first published in Great Britain in 2003 by Sidgwick & Jackson, an imprint of Pan Macmillan Ltd.

This Fireside Edition 2005

FIRESIDE and colophon are registered trademarks of Simon & Schuster, Inc.

We would like to thank Northern Songs Ltd. for the three lines from the LP *Abbey Road*, "The love you take, / Is equal to the love, / You make"; and for the line "All the lonely people" from "Eleanor Rigby."

Photo credits can be found on page 526

For information regarding special discounts for bulk purchases, please contact Simon & Schuster Special Sales at 1-800-456-6798 or business@simonandschuster.com

Designed by Jaime Putorti

Manufactured in the United States of America

10   9   8   7   6   5   4   3   2

Library of Congress Cataloging-in-Publication Data is available

ISBN 0-7432-3565-7

R0404529733

John alone seemed to get it right, back in the seventies' bleary dawn when everyone around him was mourning the end of an era, the disintegration of a movement, the extinction of a culture, the death of a dream. "It's just a rock group split up," he said with his usual withering bluntness. "It's not important."

And, surely, that's what it all comes down to in the end. However talented, innovative, famous—magical, even—the Beatles were fundamentally just a rock group that split up.

Oh, were they?

MUSIC INFORMATION CENTER
VISUAL & PERFORMING ARTS
CHICAGO PUBLIC LIBRARY.

CONTENTS

PART THREE
Having

PART FOUR
Wasting

PART FIVE
Lasting

SEPTEMBER 2001: ACROSS THE UNIVERSE

More than two decades have passed since John Lennon died at the hands of a deranged former fan outside his New York apartment. Even those with no special feelings for him or the Beatles recognized the event as a milestone, a moment when craziness and murder moved into previously uncharted terrain. He was only a pop musician, for Christ's sake, coming home late from the recording studio. What cause could possibly be advanced, or grievance assuaged, by blowing him away?

Now, in the city that sheltered John but could not protect him, another such milestone has been reached. Like nothing else in the long history of human cruelty, it will be forever defined and its horrors recalled simply by numbers, like the innocent reading on a digital clock face: 9/11.

Whereas Lennon's end came near midnight on a dimly lit sidewalk, witnessed only by his wife and a handful of chance bystanders, this new kind of annihilation happens at peak commuter time on a glorious autumn morning and is viewed in its entirety on live television. Millions of people, not just in New York but across America—across the world—see those two airliners hijacked by Muslim terrorists fly straight at the twin towers of the World Trade Center. They see the dark lizard shape of each plane merge seamlessly into its chosen satin-silver column, and the blossoming of black smoke on the opposite side. They see the victims—just brokers and financial planners and secretaries, for Christ's sake!—craning from the windows of summit floors beyond any hope of rescue. They see the plunging bodies of those who prefer to jump eighty and more stories to their death (some in pairs, holding hands) rather than face the holocaust within. It is a real-life disaster movie beyond the worst paranoia of the Cold War years or the most lurid dreams of Hollywood. Less than two hours later, each tower in turn collapses in a billowy gray cascade, engulfing scores of firefighters and rescue workers, including a priest administering the last rites. The world's greatest skyline is defiled by the hideous semblance of a nuclear mushroom cloud. Where the uttermost symbols of its power and wealth and pride stood half an hour ago, there is now only a charred, Hiroshima-like wilderness.

Armageddon has not come to sunny Manhattan alone. In Washington, another hijacked airliner has plowed into a ground-floor sector of the Pentagon, the nation's military nerve center, incinerating hundreds of service and civilian staff. A fourth plane has been diverted from its kamikaze course, thanks to heroic resistance by its passengers, and has crashed in open country near Pittsburgh, killing everyone on board.

It is America's darkest day since November 22, 1963, when President John F. Kennedy was assassinated in Dallas—the very first of those modern milestones backward to Hell. And, incredibly, in an equivalent national trauma thirty-eight years later, Americans turn to the very same voices their parents and even grandparents once did for consolation. For hope.

On October 20, a bevy of U.S. and British rock stars give a charity concert in New York for the families of September 11's victims, now finally tallied at close to three thousand. The roster onstage at Madison Square Garden includes Mick Jagger, Eric Clapton, Bon Jovi, Billy Joel, and The Who, supported by Hollywood names like Robert de Niro, Leonardo DiCaprio, Harrison Ford, and Meg Ryan, plus the city's doughty mayor, Rudolph Giuliani, and representatives of the fire and medical services who have lost their bravest and best.

But the headliner, as always and everywhere, is Paul—now Sir Paul—McCartney. Nearing sixty he may be, a widower with grown-up children and a grandchild, but there is still no other performer on earth with a presence to equal his. Wearing a firefighter's T-shirt, he performs a new song, "Freedom," written in the aftershock of the atrocity, which now becomes New York's defiant response to the mass murderers from the sky. More poignant still is his rendition of "Yesterday," not with his traditional sad, puppy dog look but genuinely in tears for the young widows and fatherless children who now "long for yesterday." As the show's finale, performers and audience join in the most emollient and prayerful of his Beatles anthems, "Let It Be." "And in my hour of darkness, there is still a light that shines on me . . ."

Even at a moment like this, it seems, Paul and John can't stop competing. To mark the twenty-first anniversary of John's death in two months' time, TNT television had planned a tribute concert, "Come Together," at Radio City Music Hall, featuring its own cast of fellow musoes and Beatles-addicted Hollywood names, with its proceeds to be donated to the apposite cause of gun control. But with September 11, "Come Together" turns into a fund-raiser—in MC Kevin Spacey's words "to keep John's memory alive and help rebuild New York." There are reverential cover versions of Lennon tracks, in and out of the Beatles, plus those familiar film clips of him holding forth on long-ago chat shows and loping around Central Park. Dave Stewart and Nelly Furtado duet on "Instant Karma." Lou Reed sings "Jealous Guy." John's widow, Yoko, and their son, Sean, harmonize with Rufus Wainwright in "Across the Universe." The most touching moment is relayed live from the corner of the park that has been renamed Strawberry Fields in his memory. Cyndi Lauper performs "Strawberry Fields Forever," with candles flickering on the mosaic pavement that bears his one-word epitaph, "Imagine." The thoughts of Lennon are written once more on enormous billboards, but this time no one looks exasperated or snickers behind their hand: IMAGINE ALL THE PEOPLE, LIVING LIFE IN PEACE.

For weeks afterward, the world's media are consumed by September 11 and its political and economic fallout. America's new president, George W. Bush, declares a "war on terrorism," raging against his unseen enemy and vowing revenge like Shakespeare's King Lear: "I will do such things . . . what they are yet I know not . . . but they shall be the terrors of the earth." The Saudi millionaire Osama bin Laden and his Al Qaeda organization are named as the perpetrators of the atrocity, and Afghanistan's fundamentalist Taliban government is accused of giving them shelter. Supported by Britain, Russia, and a string of uneasy Muslim nations, the world's last superpower sets about bombing Afghanistan, a country scarcely emerged from feudal times. Anti-Americanism sparks riots in Israel's Palestinian territory and Pakistan, and convulses the liberal enclaves of Europe. Across the whole "civilized" West, stock markets dip, big business panics, airport departure lounges are deserted; every type of negative commercial trend, from a drop in mineral-water sales to a depletion of hotel business in the Lake District, is blamed on "9/11." With bin Laden reportedly bent on germ warfare, people grow afraid even to open their morning mail lest it contain spores of lethal anthrax. In New York, the ghastly pit of World Trade Center rubble now known as Ground Zero has not ceased smouldering yet.

Against such a news agenda, there is only one non–9/11 story with the power to lead every TV news bulletin and wipe clean every front page.

On November 29, George Harrison dies in America after a long battle against cancer, aged fifty-eight. The headlines are as monumental as if some statesman on the scale of a Churchill or a de Gaulle has quitted the world—as monumental, indeed, as they were after John Lennon's death in 1980. Even the London *Times* splashes the story, reporting that the Queen has added her voice to the chorus of worldwide grief. Po-faced British broadsheets employ the same treatment as red-top tabloids: In the *Daily Telegraph,* as in the *Mirror* and the *Sun,* the whole front page is a single picture—mustached George in a rare smile from the *Let It Be* period and, below, simply a caption: "George Harrison 1943–2001."

It is not long since the thirtieth anniversary reissue of *All Things Must Pass*, his triumphant 1970 solo triple album, with additional tracks including a new version of its globally successful single, "My Sweet Lord." The song that brought George greatest acclaim, and greatest humiliation, is now released in Britain as a "tribute" single, its earnings pre-donated to charities he supported. It enters the UK Top Ten at number one. The premier spot on BBC TV's *Top of the Pops* is a thirty-one-year-old film clip of George playing it live at the concert for Bangladesh, all white suit and earnest beard and hallelujah and Hare Krishna.

And all over the world, the same bleak little thought comes to old and young alike, in many languages, across countries and cultures with not a single other thing in common:

Only two of them left.

I began researching *Shout!* in 1978 when the newspaper for which I then worked was shut down for a year by industrial troubles. Colleagues and friends did their best to talk me out of choosing the Beatles as subject matter. Don't waste your time, they said. The story has been told too many times. Everyone already knows all there is to know.

Despite being a Beatles fan and a writer on London's most chic Sunday color supplement, I had never considered them to be remotely "my" subject. Fleet Street, when I arrived in the mid-sixties, was stuffed with Beatles experts, churning out millions of words each year between them. On such an overloaded bandwagon, how could there possibly be room for me? When, in 1969, an American magazine asked me to write about Apple Corps and its troubles, I almost turned down the assignment on grounds of being underqualified. However, I decided to brazen it out. The Beatles' press officer, Derek Taylor, liked some pieces I'd written on nonpop subjects and so let me hang around their Apple house for several weeks that summer. I talked to John and Yoko, sat in on photo shoots with George, overheard Ringo on the telephone to Asprey's, the jewelers, even got to have breakfast with the terrifying Allen Klein. Without knowing it, I was watching the Beatles break up under my very nose. My article made the cover of *Show* and the *Sunday Times* magazines, was syndicated in various other publications abroad, and also begat a short story in my 1972 collection, *Wild Thing*. Then, thinking that was that, I put my notes into storage and moved on to other things.

In 1978, I had published three works of fiction, but never attempted a biography. I chose the Beatles for my debut on a simple basis: Which nonfiction story exerted the greatest fascination over the whole human race? It came down to Jesus, Kennedy's assassination, and them. I also was tempted to set down a marker in a field where the overwhelming majority of books were shoddily produced paperbacks retailing the same stale facts in half-literate prose. Pop fans were supposed incapable of reading "real" books. Nonfans were not supposed to read books about pop. I wanted to have a shot at changing that.

I started my research during Britain's infamous "Winter of Discontent," when public sector strikes paralyzed the nation and the Sex Pistols were an all-too-fitting soundtrack to abandoned schools and hospital wards and piles of uncollected garbage in the streets. Amid the press hoo-ha over punk, there would still be an occasional rumor of the ex-Beatles putting their solo careers on hold and getting back together. Their old American promoter, Sid Bernstein, kept up his annual full-page advertisement in the *New York Times*, offering them more and yet more millions for a single reunion concert. But no one any longer believed it could ever happen—or would have much relevance if it did. For young pop fans in the late seventies, life was no longer about love and peace and hedonism, but urban decay, hyperinflation, and unemployment lines. Although the Beatles' music was still ubiquitously played and enjoyed, their day was believed to have gone for ever.

From the outset I knew that there was little chance of interviewing the former Beatles themselves—doing so, I mean, in the forensic detail required by a biography. The handouts from their respective press people had been the same since 1971: What concerned them now was their growth as individuals, not delving back into the past. In reality (as we had not yet learned to say in the late seventies) they were all in denial. Talking about their Beatles years was almost impossible, even on the shallow level of a television talk show. The same symptoms showed in each of them, even John—the look that still did not quite comprehend; the glib, throwaway lines camouflaging the inexpressible or unthinkable. They were less like superstars than shell-shocked veterans of some terrible war.

At the George V Hotel in Paris, I spent half an hour with Ringo as he drank Mumm champagne (it was his heaviest drinking period) and fulminated about British income tax. At a London press reception for Paul and Linda McCartney's Wings group, I managed to buttonhole Paul and ask for his cooperation. He promised vaguely to "sit down" with me, but his PR man later conveyed a formal refusal, ending with the words "fuck off." Letters to George's home, record label, and film company, Hand-Made, produced no reply. My best hope seemed to be John in New York, despite the unexplained withdrawal from public life that had followed his *Rock 'n' Roll* album in 1975. There were rumors that he was terminally ill—even that, horror of horrors!, he had gone completely bald. I found out that he was living at the Dakota apartment building (a fact not then generally known) and wrote to him there, suggesting I might personally deliver a supply of his favorite Chocolate Oliver biscuits. A polite turndown came back, signed by Frederick Seaman, "assistant to John and Yoko."

I therefore had no alternative but to fall back on the methods of the investigative reporter, piecing the story together like a mosaic from the myriad viewpoints of those caught up in it. I also wanted to use the faculties I had developed as a novelist in evoking the times the Beatles lived through and the social and political forces that helped create the phenomenon they become. At the outset, I made two rules for myself: first, never to believe anything I read in a newspaper clipping; second, to follow up every lead, however unpromising. I was fortunate early on in securing the help of a young man named Mark Lewisohn, then rejoicing in the title "Beatles Brain of Europe." Mark's combination of encyclopedic knowledge and scrupulous accuracy—not to mention his humorous tough-mindedness toward his idols—would sustain me in an otherwise solitary, unnerving ordeal. I, on my side, take some small credit for discovering the future author of definitive Beatles reference books.

After only a few weeks' digging it became clear to me that my colleagues and friends were wrong. They didn't know everything there was to know about the Beatles. They knew almost nothing that there was to know. Over time, the story had become like some ancient Norse myth, reduced to a string of worn-smooth legends and half-truths by endless fireside telling and retelling. Yet the whole truth had been out there for anyone who wanted to find it: more unbelievable than the myth; more exciting, more charming, more hilarious, more tragic.

I also realized that fascinating though the ex-Beatles' input to my book would have been, it was not essential. The fact was that throughout their career, from scruffy obscurity to stupefying fame, they had only the haziest idea of what was happening to them or why. From the moment Brian Epstein started to manage them, he put them inside a protective bubble that afforded security greater than any band ever enjoyed, or ever will, but also kept them largely in ignorance of what was being done in their name. They had no idea how Epstein fiddled and finessed them into the British charts with the weakest of all their A-sides, "Love Me Do," nor how, later, he finessed and fiddled them into top billing on the *Ed Sullivan Show,* on a night that changed the course of American culture. They had no idea about the millions that were lost through botched contracts for Beatles merchandising, nor about Epstein's tortured private life on the wilder shores of the gay world. And after Epstein's death, somehow that obscuring, anesthetizing bubble remained unbroken. Even John, with all his angry honesty, never got near to the bottom of his Beatles past. Paul preferred—and still prefers—the glossy showbiz version of myth.

Gaining access to the key background figures was no pushover either. All had been interviewed countless times already: It took the persuasiveness of a cold-calling double-glazing salesman on my part to convince them this book would be different and that I could prompt them to say anything new. I had illuminating talks with George Martin, the Beatles' nonpareil record producer; with Bob Wooler, the Cavern Club disk jockey who gave them crucial early tips about stage presentation; with Pete Best, the drummer they brutally dumped on the threshold of their success. I drank tea with John's aunt and childhood guardian, Mimi

Smith, and Irish coffee with Michael McCartney, Paul's younger brother. Brian Epstein's mother, Queenie, and his brother, Clive, gave me their blessing, as did Millie Sutcliffe, mother of the gifted, tragic "fifth Beatle," Stuart, and his sister, Pauline. I flew to New York to see Epstein's former close friend Nat Weiss, and to Los Angeles to see his old lieutenant, and near clone, Peter Brown. I traveled to Hamburg to explore the dives and strip clubs where the Beatles cut their teeth as performers, and to track down Astrid Kirchherr, whose photographs gave them their most durable as well as classiest image.

I also unearthed dozens of minor players in the drama who had never been interviewed before, whose stories were still fresh and undistorted by repetition. There was Joe Flannery, the gently hilarious man who had provided Brian Epstein's one and only happy, stable gay relationship. There was Nicky Byrne, the dapper Chelsea wheeler-dealer who had presided over the merchandising fiasco in America, and Byrne's former business partner Lord Peregrine Eliot, heir to the Cornish earldom of St. Germans. There was "Lord Woodbine," the calypso singer who had accompanied the Beatles on their first trip to Hamburg; Paddy Delaney, the guardsmanlike former doorman of the Cavern Club; Tommy Moore, who briefly became the Beatles' drummer although old enough to be their father, but then decided he preferred his former job on a forklift truck. Time and again, my research took me back to Liverpool to stay at the Adelphi Hotel, then still glorious, writing up my notes in its *Titanic*-sized Palm Court, going to sleep at night under blankets bearing the insignia of the old London–Midland Railway. I grew to love the city: its sumptuous Victorian architecture, its scabrous, surreal humor. Listen to almost any Scouser [Liverpudlian] on the street and you understand all about the Beatles and why they captured the planet. Nowhere else can you be told, as a term of affection, that you are "as useful as a one-legged man in an arse-kicking contest."

Writing a biography is impossible without obsession. And I became obsessed, talking about nothing but the Beatles, thinking about nothing but the Beatles, puzzling and worrying at night over tiny missing links in the narrative, developing one muscle in my brain to an inordinate degree while other muscles grew slack. Wasn't it going the tiniest bit too far to list all the stallholders and amusements at Woolton church fete where Paul met John in 1957? Would anyone really care exactly how many steps led down from Mathew Street into the Cavern Club? F. Scott

Fitzgerald's comparison of writing with swimming underwater returned to me often in those days, as the seventies staggered toward their end. Like others of my generation I remembered how very different the last months of the previous decade had felt, how the joss-scented sunshine, with *Abbey Road* playing through every open window, had promised to go on and on forever. We hated to leave the sixties, but everyone seemed to want out of the seventies: to forget flares and platform heels, sideburns and socialism, and stride boldly into the new high-tech Tory utopia of the eighties promised by Margaret Thatcher.

Ironically, the cusp of the eighties brought the strongest ever speculation about a Beatles reunion. In Kampuchea, formerly Cambodia, millions of refugees were fleeing the war between the country's Vietnamese invaders and Pol Pot's genocidal Khmer Rouge. Over Christmas 1979, it was announced that Paul McCartney would headline a series of concerts at London's Hammersmith Odeon cinema to aid the Red Cross and UNICEF relief effort. When George and Ringo indicated willingness to join Paul onstage, feverish excitement broke out in newsrooms across the hemispheres. But John in New York quickly stamped on any idea that he might complete the reincarnation. Even a personal plea from the United Nations' secretary-general, Kurt Waldheim, could not move him. "We [the Beatles] gave everything for ten years," he said. "We gave *ourselves*. If we played now, anyway, we'd only be four rusty old men."

A few months later a song came on the radio that sounded vaguely like John—and *was* John, though you had to listen twice to recognize the voice, purged of anger and wrapped in a relaxed early-sixties-ish, Motown-ish beat. And soon afterward, there he was in the flesh, neither ill nor bald, revealing how he had decided to opt out of the rat race and had spent the past five years as Yoko's "househusband," caring for their new son, Sean. Despite the New Man aura, here was the old John, as dry, droll, and helplessly honest as ever. Here he was describing how a sudden urge to create music again had sent him back into the studio to make *Double Fantasy*, an album with Yoko, celebrating their later life together; here he was being photographed with her in the nudity that had seemed grotesque ten years earlier, but now seemed only natural and rather touching. Here he was age forty, seemingly reborn and "starting over" as the song said, celebrating the first step into middle age, the end of the seventies, the joys of parenthood, the rediscovery of his art, and the continuing freshness and interest of a love affair that, against the whole world's wishes, seemed to have lasted.

I delivered my manuscript to my British publisher in late November 1980, with a warning that there might be more to come. With John so accessible and talkative again, I had high hopes of persuading him to see me before the book went to press. That hope disappeared with a phone call from a friend in New York in the early hours of December 8.

The scale of the grief after John's murder was—and remains—something unique in modern times. Unlike the mourning for John F. Kennedy seventeen years earlier, it was not confined largely to the victim's own homeland. Unlike that for Diana, Princess of Wales, seventeen years later, it had no taint of hype or media manipulation; no sense, as in the Diana aftermath, that people were reacting in a distorted, even dysfunctional way. It was an utterly spontaneous and genuine outpouring of misery across continents by those who felt they had lost an intimate, inspirational friend. I particularly remember the broken voice of a young New Yorker during the candlelit vigil outside the Dakota: "I can't believe John's dead . . . he kept me from dying so many times . . ." In a supreme irony that the old truant, rebel, and blasphemer would have appreciated, he had become an instant twentieth-century saint.

Millions of fans were now forced to accept, as they never quite had in the preceding nine years, that the Beatles' career really was now over. The result was a refocus on an oeuvre that had for so long been taken for granted: a new, objective appreciation of its energy and variety, its poetry and humor, its astounding seven-league leaps from aural primitive painting to Michelangelo masterpiece.

All this, of course, was an outcome I had never dreamed of when I began my book against such heavy discouragement two years earlier. Immediately after December 8, my concerns were the anesthetizing ones of journalism: I had to write a five-thousand-word tribute to John for the front of the *Sunday Times* Review section as well as advise on a rushed memorial issue of its magazine. I filed my five thousand words in the since outmoded Fleet Street manner, dictating it into the telephone as a copy taker at the office typed it. Not until the very end did full comprehension strike me: This was the boy whose life I had lived vicariously from Menlove Avenue and Quarry Bank High School to the London Palladium, Ed Sullivan, Shea Stadium, Savile Row, and Central Park West. My final half-dozen words of dictation were checked by an involuntary sob.

Shout! was published in Britain in April 1981, and in the United States a couple of months later. It became a best seller in both countries and was translated into a variety of languages, including Estonian. While I was in New York doing promotion Yoko saw me talking about John on the *Good Morning America* program and invited me to visit her at the Dakota. So I did get there after all, albeit five months too late. My conversation with Yoko became an epilogue to the mass market paperback edition of *Shout!* It included many surprising sidelights on the Lennons' relationship, and also her observation—made sadly rather than with any bitterness or malice—that "John used to say no one ever hurt him the way Paul hurt him."

When Paul read the quote in the British press he took the unusual step of bypassing his usual PR screen and telephoning me personally at my London flat (having presumably obtained my number from the PR man who, some months earlier, bade me "Fuck off"). Unfortunately, I was out when he phoned, and he left no number for me to call him back. I never did find out what he'd wanted, whether to argue with Yoko's assertion or, more likely, to give me an earful for repeating it.

So that was that, I thought: I'd "done" the Beatles and proved my point that for a biographer the most banally obvious ideas are generally the best ones. Again I put my notes into storage and made plans to move on to other things.

Since 1981, I have written three other music biographies (of the Rolling Stones, Elton John, and Buddy Holly), two works of fiction, an autobiography, and television and stage drama as well as journalism on subjects ranging from Tony Blair's government to World War II. But, try as I might, there has been no moving on from the Beatles.

More than thirty years after their breakup, they dominate the headlines almost as much as in their mid-sixties high noon. Every month or so brings some page-leading fresh twist in the story—a distant cousin of John's now claiming to have been his closest childhood confidant, a Hamburg matron alleging long-forgotten amours with Paul or George, a Sotheby's auction of freshly unearthed memorabilia; a lost letter, a doodled lyric, a fragment of reel-to-reel tape. Books on the Beatles, ranging from muck-raking "revelations" to scholarly analyses, now run into the hundreds, and go on multiplying all the time. Their old recording studios on Abbey Road, north London, is a shrine rivaling Elvis

Presley's Graceland, perennially setting some kind of record for how much mourning graffiti can be crammed onto a single wall. To feed this insatiable appetite I myself must have written the equivalent of another couple of biographies in newspaper and magazine articles, commentaries, reviews, reconstructions, and obituaries, and spoken at least a further one aloud in radio and television interviews. Like it or not, I am tagged as a Beatles "expert" for good and all. I have come to dread the light that springs into people's eyes at parties when the only alternative to clamlike rudeness on my part is to admit I've written a book about the Beatles. I know that from here on I shall be allowed to talk about nothing else.

They are, after Winston Churchill, the twentieth century's greatest standard-bearer for Britain. When we look back over that lowering and ugly hundred years, only two moments give rise to genuine collective national pride: the one in 1940 when we stood alone against Hitler, and the one in the barely formed sixties when four cheeky-faced boys from Liverpool recolonized the world in our name. At times, indeed, they seem to be all we have left as everything once valued about this country slides deeper into neglect and anarchy. Our streets may be overrun by muggers and carjackers, our public transportation a homicidal mess, our hospitals uncaring Third World slums, our schools devalued, our legal system a joke, our police force in retreat, our royal family in ruins. But nothing, it seems, can ever tarnish the glory that was John, Paul, George, and Ringo.

At the start of their career they were mocked for choosing a name that suggested an insect. Perhaps the ultimate sign of their fame is that now in the English language, wherever spoken, a small black creepy-crawlie is, by a long way, only the second image the word "beetle" calls to mind.

Their longevity testifies, of course, to the residual power of the generation that grew up with them: the Chelsea-booted boys and Biba-frocked girls who would one day metamorphose into presidents, prime ministers, captains of industry, television bosses, and newspaper editors. Virtually every Briton and American now in their fifties looks back to the same goldenly privileged mid-sixties youth and cherishes the same clutch of Lennon-McCartney songs, above all, as mementoes of that gorgeous time. Forty years on, shapeless, wrinkled, and balding though they may be, they still find it inconceivable that any other generation could embody the state of being young more perfectly than themselves. Hence, the post-sixties culture that compels no one to yield to *anno Domini*, where even old-age pensioners can still cling to their bath-shrunk Levis and ponytails and miniskirts. To this worldwide realm of eternal teenagerdom, there is no more instantaneous passport than a Beatles tune.

Yet, immense though the nostalgia market is, it represents only a part of their global constituency. Billions adore them who had no share in their radiant heyday—who, in many cases, were not even born when they ceased to exist as a band. First-generation fans may well smile to recollect how furiously they rejected the pop idols of their own parents; how being a Beatles fan in the early days meant facing a constant barrage of adult disapproval and contempt. Back in the early sixties it would have been extraordinary for a young pop addict to share his or her grandparents' fondness for some hit-maker of three decades before, like Harry Roy or Debroy Somers and the Savoy Orpheans. Yet today, grandparents and grandchildren listen to *Revolver,* say, or *Sgt. Pepper's Lonely Hearts Club Band* with the same unreserved delight.

Most potently of all, perhaps, the Beatles are the so-called "Swinging Sixties" incarnate. Britain has a long tradition of spinning history into fantasy worlds—theme parks of the mind, one might call them—from the knights and damsels of Henry V and the lute-playing buccaneers of Good Queen Bess through the posthorns and stagecoaches of Dickens to the Naughty Nineties, the Roaring Twenties, the "blitz spirit" of World War II. But none of these yearningly recollected, endlessly redramatized epochs even begins to compare with what came over stuffy, staid old London between 1964 and 1969. Although every last trace vanished decades ago, millions of foreign tourists annually still come seeking it. You can see them any day of the week, in their drab blue denim crocodiles, from France, Germany, Scandinavia, Japan—everywhere—picking over the souvenir rubbish that now swamps Carnaby Street, treading the no longer motley pavements of Chelsea and Knightsbridge, or lurching purposelessly amid the garbage and beggars of the modern West End.

Liverpool, which took so long to recognize its most priceless civic asset, now has a John Lennon Airport and a permanent exhibition, *The Beatles Story,* housed in the new Albert Dock development and attracting millions of visitors, that—along with Paul McCartney's Liverpool

Institute for the Performing Arts—have set the seal on the city's recent renaissance. Recent donations to *The Beatles Story* have included the orange-tinted glasses John Lennon wore when writing and first recording "Imagine," now valued at one million pounds. Echoing Scott Fitzgerald's *The Great Gatsby,* there is also a giant replica of the glasses, their lenses showing images of John's major creative influences, the Vietnam War, the peace movement, the "beautiful people" in robes and beads who are now grandparents and retirees.

Other vivid decades seemed grotesque and embarrassing to the ones immediately following. But the swinging Britain of the Beatles grows more modish the further it recedes into history. When Tony Blair brought the Labour Party back to power as New Labour in 1997, he was marketed as the figurehead of a youthful dynamism, creativity, and lightheartedness that evoked the mid-sixties in almost eerie detail. The jaded and broken-down nation Blair's claque had inherited was rebranded overnight with the sixties-speak imprimatur of "Cool Britannia." As in the days of his Old Labour predecessor Harold Wilson, 10 Downing Street thronged with pop stars, painters, designers, and couturiers, all eager to hobnob with a premier more hopelessly starstruck and camera-hungry even than the shameless Harold.

The concurrent "Britpop" movement consisted almost wholly of bands in Beatley haircuts playing Beatley songs with Beatley harmonies and enacting shadow plays from Beatles history, one quartet even being shown skipping over a zebra crossing like on the cover of the *Abbey Road* album. The supposed rivalry between the two leading Britpop bands, Oasis (working-class northern lads) and Blur (middle-class southern lads), was portrayed in exactly the same terms as that between the Beatles and the Rolling Stones thirty-odd years earlier. Psychedelic colors, microskirts, long-pointed shirt collars, Union Jack designs on tote bags . . . suddenly they were all in business again. Never had there been so virulent an outbreak of what psychologists have come to define as "nostalgia without memory."

It is often said that "if you can remember the sixties, you can't have been there." But to the vast majority of the decade's survivors whose brains were unaddled by pot or Scotch and coke, it never felt quite so dreamily enchanted as it is portrayed in retrospect. The age of so-called love and peace saw the world almost as rife as today with natural disaster and human cruelty. As well as free rock festivals, kipper ties, fun furs, and white lipstick, it brought the Vietnam War, the Arab–Israeli Six-Day War, the assassinations of John F. Kennedy, Robert Kennedy, and Martin Luther King, cataclysmic race riots across America, famine in Bihar, and genocide in Biafra. Even as Britain "swung" with such apparent careless joy, it had to deal with horrors and tragedies like the Aberfan disaster, the Moors murders (to this day still unmatched for depraved child cruelty), and the opening shots of Northern Ireland's later bloodbath. Being a sixties teenager had sunburst moments, certainly, but also involved long stretches of workaday dullness, unrelieved by modern diversions like mobile phones, text messaging, personal stereos, video games, or the Internet.

If we are honest we must accept the extent to which the heady new freedoms of youth in the sixties paved the way for the frightening, ungovernable world we see about us today. From the happy high of pot and pills and the cozy hallucinations of *Sgt. Pepper's Lonely Hearts Club Band* grew the drug menace that now saturates the most respectable, most rural communities, turns once bright and happy children into black-and-blue-punctured suicides, litters public thoroughfares and parks with the same foul stew of broken ampules and needles. From the sexual freedom granted to sixties boys and girls by the contraceptive pill came the long breakdown in the age-old, civilizing influence of the family, the freedom of sixties children's children in their turn to thieve and vandalize without the slightest fear of parental retribution.

From the great discovery of sixties youth through the example of the Beatles—that, with a bit of cheek, you could get away with anything— evolved the whole ghastly panoply of modern contempt for convention and self-restraint that encompasses urban terrorism at one extreme and supermarket "shopping cart rage" at the other. Just as John Lennon realized he could get away with teasing his blue-blooded audience at the 1963 Royal Command performance, so the IRA realized they could get away with blowing up innocent women and children; so successive governments realized they could get away with allowing the national infrastructure to fall into decay; so the police found they could get away with abandoning whole communities; so hospitals found they could get away with ceasing to accord patients basic human dignity; so the legions of murderers, child molesters, muggers, and celebrity stalkers found they could become ever more arrogantly audacious in their predatory activities; so egotism, viciousness, and disregard for others grew to the point where bin Laden and his fanatics found they could get away with the vileness of September 11, 2001. If you seek to pinpoint the exact place in the twentieth century where civilization ceased moving steadily forward and began taking quantum leaps backward, there can be no other culprit but the sixties.

Yet, at the same time, one cannot gainsay the decade's many positive, if illusory and short-lived, qualities: its vigor and optimism; its belief that idealism could move the grimmest, rockiest old mountains; its abounding creativity; its ready assimilation of the wildest originality and eccentricity; its childlike sense of discovering the whole world anew. Such are the echoes that sixties nostalgics, with or without memory, seek most avidly and find most abundantly in the music of the Beatles.

Weary though I may be of discussing the subject, heartsick as I am at the prospect of writing anything further about it (including this prologue), I cannot pretend that my interest has waned over two decades. For this is the greatest show business story ever told; one whose fascination only deepens as our collective obsession with the joys and horrors of celebrity grows. As a moral tale it is both utterly emblematic (be careful what you wish for lest your wish come true) and utterly unique. If it were presented as fiction, with its web of extraordinary accidents, conjunctions, and coincidences, no one would believe it. A modern Dickens or Tolstoy would be needed to create such a cast of characters, such a cavalcade of mold-shattering events, such a shading of comedy into tragedy, such a sweeping panorama of social evolution and transformation—though not even Dickens or Tolstoy had the nerve to make any of their heroes actually change the world.

From the moment the Beatles realized they need not fear being overtaken by Dave Clark and the "Tottenham Sound" there has been no dispute about their being the greatest pop act of all time. No matter how pop's sound and look may develop, or regress, they remain the ideal, the exemplar, the summit to which all performers aspire, whether male or female, singular or plural; their name the ultimate turn-on in the language of promotion, huckstering, and hype. There is not a single hopefully seminal attraction of the past three decades, from seventies glam- and snob-rockers, through punk, disco, and new romantics, to today's zombie-strutting boy- and girl- and boy-girl "bands," whose keepers have not staked their claim to greatness by announcing they have sold more singles or more albums than the Beatles, played to larger combined audiences than the Beatles, had more consecutive hits than the Beatles, stormed the charts more quickly than the Beatles, been mobbed at airports more hysterically than the Beatles, generated more obsessive media coverage than the Beatles. Perhaps the only group to have approached the worldwide stir they created were the Spice Girls in the middle and late nineties. The highest accolade Ginger, Scary, Posh, and Sporty received, or desired, was to be called "female Beatles."

The truth is that in purely statistical terms many later performers can legitimately make one or another of these claims. The Beatles, after all, rose to fame in a music industry as different from the modern one as the Stone Age from *Star Wars*. Plenty of other acts have shifted more product, counted more heads on their tours, and certainly earned more money than the Beatles did. Plenty have mimicked their milestone moments—like U2's simulation of their Apple rooftop concert. But none has ever been or could ever hope to be so much loved. Love was what took them to their unbeatable heights but also destroyed them; the terrible, mindless love that ultimately enwrapped them squeezed the vitality from them, like a giant boa constrictor. That is the power, above all, that endures in those recordings from long-ago Abbey Road in long-ago London. Play any Beatles song (except maybe "Revolution No. 9") to any group of toddlers in any country and of whatever culture: They will instantly love it.

Britain thus far has produced only one equivalent object of mass adoration and fascination. From the early eighties to the late nineties, the beautiful, brave, batty Diana, Princess of Wales, rivaled the Beatles—at times even threatened to overtake them—as the world's favorite icon; no longer pop stars as royalty but royalty as a pop star. In 1995, the reunion that millions had longed for since 1971 actually did happen. Their long-dormant Apple company announced plans to release the definitive film record of their career that their former roadie, Neil Aspinall, had been compiling for more than a quarter of a century, plus a collective text autobiography. Paul, George, and Ringo reconvened at Abbey Road under their old producer, now Sir George Martin, to provide instrumental and vocal backup to some Lennon vocal tracks unearthed by Yoko among his archives at the Dakota. But, although the headlines befitted a second Second Coming, they did not shout quite as loudly or last quite as long as they might normally have done. For this happened also to be the moment when Diana chose to give a television interview, exposing the sham of her supposed "fairy-tale" marriage to Britain's future king. A changed world, indeed, when the Fab Four played second fiddle to a royal broadcast!

Now Dianamania flickers fitfully on and off like faulty neon while Beatlemania blazes stronger than ever. In 2001 an album was released titled simply *1*, a collection of twenty-seven number-one Beatles singles from three decades earlier. It topped the album charts in Britain and America and around the world, selling twice as many copies as their concept masterpiece *Sgt. Pepper's Lonely Hearts Club Band*, and making them *Billboard* magazine's best-selling act of the year above contemporary giants like Britney Spears and J-Lo.

A year later came perhaps the ultimate instance of nostalgia with and without memory as well as delicious full-circle irony. The Queen's Golden Jubilee celebrations reached their climax with a marathon pop concert in the seldom seen rear grounds—actually, front garden—of Buckingham Palace, featuring every major British pop act of the past half-century, including Shirley Bassey and Atomic Kitten. Its twofold purpose was to celebrate Britain's most consistently successful export over fifty years and demonstrate how switched-on and accessible the monarchy had become after its near-fatal bout with "the People's Princess."

For the almost-one-million-strong crowd that seethed down The Mall like some weird, blue-lit cornfield there was no contest as to the top of the night's bill. One could almost see them on the giant TV monitors like black-and-white ghosts, swaggering in to collect their MBE medals in 1965 and, afterward, boasting of puffing joints in a palace washroom. It was bizarre to remember what national outrage greeted the award of even so modest an honor to grubby hit-paraders. Tonight, the stage thronged with pop musical knights, all of whom had received their dubbing without the smallest public controversy—Sir Cliff Richard, Sir Elton John, and, of course, Sir George Martin, the man who made Beatles music possible, today as beloved a national institution as a great statesman or philanthropist.

The whole night belonged to the old Fab Four as surely as it did to the new Fab Windsors. Here were Joe Cocker and his glorious throat-ripping cover version of "With a Little Help from My Friends" from *Sgt. Pepper*. Here was Eric Clapton, paying tribute to his friend George Harrison with "While My Guitar Gently Weeps" from the *White Album*. And here, to close the show, was Sir Paul again, at yet another uncharted high-water mark of fame and national prestige. Here was the billionaire megastar showing what a simple working musician he is at heart as he provided backup piano and vocals for Clapton in the Harrison number. Here he was, leading a million born-again royalists in a mass version of "Hey Jude" whose "La-la-la-lalala-la" chorus rolled through the floodlit human seas, both with and without memory, as familiarly as their own heartbeat.

John Lennon was there too, in spirit, albeit more than likely turning a bit in his grave. The concert's closing number—indeed, the backing track for the whole jubilee—was "All You Need Is Love," a song even more achingly true of today's world than that of 1967. But now John's countercultural mantra had become an anthem of loyalty to tradition and the status quo, "God Save the Queen" in all but name: an alternative "Rule Britannia."

The original *Shout!* ended in 1970, a year before the Beatles' official breakup. There are thus more than three decades to be covered of their respective post-Beatles lives, a story fully as bizarre, if not as light-hearted, as their collective one. Also, since 1981 I have collected much new information about their life together, from both original and new sources and from researching subsequent books, particularly my biography of the Rolling Stones. Hence this revised edition in the fortieth year since Beatlemania descended on Britain.

How different a book would I write if I were starting out now? Some critics felt I gave too much credence to an explanation for Brian Epstein's death never previously raised: that he was murdered by a contract killer in reprisal for the vast sums lost in America through his botched deals on Beatles merchandise. It was a line I could hardly ignore, faced as I was with a source who claimed not only to have heard a murder threat made against Epstein but also to have been informed by phone after the contract had been carried out. Significantly, none of the ex-Beatles ever regarded the theory as too far-fetched. Nor did Epstein's own family, though in their case it may have been preferable to subsequent unsubstantiated claims that he died as a result of a sex game that went wrong. With hindsight, I think it more likely his death was by "misadventure," as the coroner recorded.

I must also admit to having suppressed one crucial fact. After Epstein's death two suicide notes were found shut away in his desk drawer at Chapel Street. They had apparently both been written some little time previously, either for attempts on his own life that he never carried through or as a way of getting attention from his long-suffering associates. Both his brother, Clive, and his mother, Queenie, begged me not to mention these notes. At one point I had both of them on the phone at once saying, "Please, Philip . . . *please.*" They were nice, decent people whom I had no wish to hurt. So I agreed.

Others felt that my judgments of Paul McCartney were too harsh, perhaps even motivated by personal dislike. In the Beatles subculture one inevitably finds oneself tagged either as a "John" person or a "Paul" person. I cannot pretend to be other than the former. Just the same, it was wrong of me—though it won me my initial access to Yoko—to say, as I did on an American TV news program, that "John was three-quarters of the Beatles." I would not question McCartney's huge talent or deny that, like all of them, he was far nicer than he ever needed to be.

Any writer would hope to have improved over a span of more than twenty years. Looking back from here at the original *Shout!* I see all too many examples of clumsiness and imprecision; indeed, my first instinct was to rewrite the whole book. But its various imperfections do not seem to have stopped people from enjoying it. Apart from updating and correcting, therefore, I've limited myself to toning down the more garish purple passages and sharpening what was too fuzzy before. I was also criticized for dwelling too little on the Beatles' music and that, too, I have tried to rectify.

For all its faults, I do not think any other Beatles book has overtaken it. Peter Brown's *The Love You Make* (1983) was marketed as the sensational revelations of a Beatles "insider," yet proved curiously uninformative in a large number of areas. The late Albert Goldman's *The Lives of John Lennon* was a jumble of the ordurous untruths and crass misunderstandings peculiar to that author, often contradicting itself ludicrously from one page to the next. Paul McCartney's authorized biography, *Many Years From Now,* was exhaustively informative—but mainly about Paul. The three ex-Beatles' collective "autobiography"—in fact just unedited transcripts of their interviews for the *Anthology* TV documentary—featured much fascinating reminiscence, especially from George, but was grossly slanted and selective (every first-generation Beatle wife, for instance, having been firmly airbrushed out of the narrative).

It is said that even the most fortunate journalist meets only one truly smashing story in his or her career. The main thing I have learned about biography writing is that it is even more a matter of pure luck. Lucky me to have lit on what the Beatles' irreplaceable publicist, Derek Taylor, rightly called "the twentieth century's greatest romance."

PART ONE

WISHING

ONE

"HE WAS THE ONE I'D WAITED FOR"

John Lennon was born on October 9, 1940, during a brief respite in Nazi Germany's bombing of Liverpool. All summer, after tea, people would switch on their radios at low volume, listening, not to the muted dance music but to the sky outside their open back doors. When the music cut off, before the first siren went, you knew that the bombers were returning.

Liverpool paid a heavy price for its naval shipyards, and for the miles of docks where convoys stood making ready to brave the North Atlantic. The city was Britain's last loophole for overseas food supplies. Night after night, with geometric accuracy, explosions tore along the seaming of wharves and warehouses and black castle walls, and over the tramlines into streets of friendly red back-to-back houses, of pubs and missions and corner dairies with cowsheds behind. During the worst week so many ships lay sunk along the Mersey there was not a single berth free for incoming cargo. But on Lime Street the Empire theater carried on performances as usual. Sometimes the whole audience would crowd out into the foyer and look across the black acropolis of St. George's Hall to a sky flashing white, then dark again as more bombs pummeled the port and the river.

Mimi Stanley had always worried about her younger sister, Julia. She worried about her especially tonight with more Luftwaffe raids expected and Julia in labor in the Oxford Street maternity home. When news of the baby came by telephone Mimi set out on foot from the Stanley house on Newcastle Road. "I ran two miles. I couldn't stop thinking, 'It's a boy, it's a boy. He's the one I've waited for.'"

She held John in her arms twenty minutes after he was born. His second name, Julia said—in honor of Britain's inspirational prime minister, Winston Churchill—would be Winston. Just then a parachute-borne land mine fell directly outside the hospital. "But my sister stayed in bed," Mimi said, "and they put the baby under the bed. They wanted me to go into the basement, but I wouldn't. I ran all the way back to Newcastle Road to tell Father the news. 'Get under shelter,' the wardens were shouting. 'Oh, be quiet,' I told them. Father was there, and I said, 'It's a boy and he's beautiful, he's the best one of all.' Father looked up and said, 'Oh heck, he *would* be.' "

Mimi's and Julia's father was an official with the Glasgow and Liverpool Salvage Company. He was aboard the salvage tug that tried to raise the submarine *Thetis* from her deathbed in Liverpool Bay. He had five daughters and brought them up strictly, though he was often away from home salvaging ships. "We loved Father," Mimi said, "but we liked it when he went away to sea and we girls could kick over the traces a bit. If ever there was a boy I had my eye on, I used to pray at night, 'Please God, let no one be hurt but let there be a wreck.' "

Mimi was slender, brisk, and dark, with fine cheekbones like a Cherokee. Julia was slim, auburn-haired, more conventionally pretty. Both loved laughter, but Mimi insisted there should be sense in it. "Oh, Julia," she would endlessly plead, "be *serious*." Julia could never be serious about anything.

Her marriage to Freddy Lennon in 1938 had been the least serious act of her life. She met Freddy one day in Sefton Park, and commented on the silly hat he wore. To please her, Freddy sent it skimming into the lake. She started bringing him home, to her whole family's great dismay. He was only a ship's waiter, erratically employed; he preferred, in the nautical term for malingering, to "swallow the anchor." Julia married him on an impulse at Mount Pleasant Register Office, putting down her occupation as "cinema usherette" because she knew how it would annoy her father. "I'll never forget that day," Mimi said. "Julia came home, threw a piece of paper on the table and said, 'There, that's it. I've married him.' "

Within little more than a year, World War II had broken out, sending Freddy to sea on a succession of merchant ships and condemning Julia to a life of alternating grim boredom and terror in the Liverpool Blitz. Freddie was doing war work requiring as much courage and self-sacrifice as any other. But he also loved shipboard life, where he was always the star turn in amateur concerts, "blacking up" like Al Jolson or singing torrid ballads like "Begin the Beguine."

After John was born, in 1940, Freddie's spells of shore leave became increasingly more erratic. His longest absence was a bizarre eighteen-month odyssey that saw him variously arrested for deserting his ship in

New York and stranded in Bône, North Africa, while, back home in Liverpool, his family presumed him dead and payment of his wages to Julia was suspended. When eventually he arrived home, it was to find Julia pregnant by another man, a Welsh soldier stationed in Liverpool. The baby, a girl, baptized Victoria Elizabeth, was born in 1945, a few weeks after the war's end. Freddie was willing to forgive Julia, adopt Victoria, and bring her up alongside John. But Julia's family, fearing a public disgrace, insisted that the baby must be put out for adoption.

Though his marriage was clearly on the rocks, Freddie was unwilling to relinquish John. In April 1946, hearing that Julia had acquired a new man friend, he abducted John and fled with him to the seaside resort of Blackpool, planning vaguely for the two of them to emigrate to New Zealand. Before he could take the scheme further, however, Julia turned up in Blackpool and announced she was taking John home to Liverpool. The six-year-old was then faced with an agonizing choice: "Do you want to go with Mummy or Daddy?" He chose Julia. A crushed Freddie made no move to keep them from going off together.

All Julia's sisters lent a hand in caring for John. But one sister cared specially—the one who, having no babies of her own, ran through the air raid to hold him. From the moment John could talk, he would say, "Where's Mimi? Where's Mimi's house?"

"Julia had met someone else, with whom she had a chance of happiness," Mimi said. "And no man wants another man's child. That's when I said I wanted to bring John to Menlove Avenue to live with George and me. I wouldn't even let him risk being hurt or feeling he was in the way. I made up my mind that I'd be the one to give him what every child has the right to—a safe and happy home life."

The fires ceased falling on Liverpool. The city, though cratered like a Roman ruin, returned to its old, majestically confident commercial life. St. George's Hall, badly scarred, still stood within its columns, between equestrian statues of Victoria and Albert. Along the docks, the overhead railway remained intact, passing above the funnels and warehouses and branching masts, the horse-drawn wagons and clanking, shuffling "Green Goddess" Liverpool trams. Business resumed in the streets lined by statues and colonnades and Moorish arches and huge public clocks. At the Pier Head, that broad riverfront, congregations of trams drew up between the Mersey and its three gray waterside temples: the Cunard

Company, the Docks and Harbour Board, and the Royal Liver Insurance Company. The "Liver building" was still there, its twin belfries soaring higher than the seagulls and crowned with the skittish stone silhouettes of the "Liver birds."

Liverpool was still business and banking and insurance—and ships. From the southern headland, under rings of tall cranes, came the rhythmic clout of Cammell Laird's yard where they built the *Alabama,* the *Mauretania,* the *Ark Royal,* the *Thetis.* Across from Birkenhead, brisk river ferries crossed the path of ocean liners, warships, merchantmen, and the smaller fry of what was still Europe's busiest shipping pool. Ever and again, from a slipway on the broad river bend, some fresh ungarnished hull would slide backward, and ride there, free of drag chains, while tug whoops mingled with cheers from the bank.

Liverpool was docks and ships and as such indistinguishable in Britain's northern industrial fogs but for one additional, intermittent product: Liverpool was where music-hall comedians, such as Tommy Handley, Arthur Askey, and Robb Wilton, came from. Some elixir in a population mixed from Welsh and Irish, and also lascar and Chinese, and uttered in the strange glottal dialect that simultaneously seems to raise derisive eyebrows, had always possessed the power to make the rest of the country laugh.

Liverpool "comics" were always preferred by the London theatrical agents. But there was a proviso. It was better for them to lose their Liverpool accents, and omit all references to the city of their origin. No one in London cared about a place so far to the northwest, so gray and sooty and old-fashioned, and above all, so utterly without glamour as Liverpool.

Woolton, where John grew up, is a suburb six miles to the southeast, but further in spirit, from the Liverpool of docks and Chinatown and pub signs pasted round every street corner. From Lime Street you drive uphill, past the grand old Adelphi Hotel, past the smaller backstreet hotels with no pretense at grandeur, past the Baptist temples and Irish meeting halls and grassed-over bomb sites turned into eternal temporary parking lots, lapping against some isolated little waterworks or church. Eventually you come to a traffic circle known by the name of its smallest tributary, Penny Lane. Woolton lies beyond, in wide dual carriageways with grass verges and mock Tudor villas whose gardens adjoin parks, country clubs, and golf courses.

Woolton, in fact, is such a respectable, desirable, and featureless suburb as grows up close to any British industrial city. Until 1963, it had only one claim on history. A lord of the same name was Britain's wartime minister of food and inventor of the "Woolton Pie," which boasted total, if unappetizing, nourishment for only one old shilling a portion.

The country village that Woolton used to be is still distinguishable in narrow lanes winding up to its red sandstone parish church, St. Peter's. In the early 1940s, it was still more villagelike. It even had its own small dairy farm, to which people would go for fresh milk ladled straight from the churn. The farm and dairy belonged to George Smith, the quiet kindhearted man whom high-spirited Mimi Stanley had married.

George and Mimi lived at "Mendips," a semidetached house on Menlove Avenue, round the corner from the dairy, almost opposite Allerton golf course. Built in 1933, it was a semidetached villa designed for the aspirational lower middle class, with mock Tudor half-timbering, windows inset with Art Nouveau stained glass, and the tiny living room beside the kitchen grandly described as a "morning room." In the years before Mimi and George brought their little nephew, John Lennon, to live here, the house had even had live-in domestics. The untold million future acolytes of the self-styled "working-class hero" never dreamed he actually grew up in a house with a morning room, Spode and Royal Worcester plates displayed on ledges around its quasi-baronial front hall, and servants' bells in its kitchen.

Julia had settled only a short bus journey away, at Springwood. Her man friend, John Dykins, was headwaiter at the splendiferous Adelphi Hotel. Every afternoon, she came across to her sister's to see John. He called her "Mummy"; his aunt he called plain "Mimi." "John said to me once when he was little, 'Why don't I call *you* Mummy?' I said, 'Well—you couldn't very well have *two* Mummies, could you?' He accepted that."

From the moment Julia gave him to her, Mimi devoted her life to John. "Never a day passed when I wasn't with him—just that one time a year when he went up to Scotland to stay with his cousins. And at night, for ten years, I never crossed the threshold of that house. As I came downstairs I'd always leave the light on on the landing outside his room. This little voice would come after me, "Mimi! Don't waste light."

"I brought him up strictly. No sweets—just one barley sugar at night—and no sitting around in picturedomes. He never wanted it. He'd play for hours in the garden in summer, in his little swimming shorts. I'd go to the butcher's for pheasants' feathers and I'd make him up like an Indian with gravy browning, and put lipstick for war paint on his cheeks. And when he said his friends were dead, they *were* dead.

"He never had a day's illness. Only chicken pox. 'Chicken pots,' he called it. And he loved his uncle George. I felt quite left out of that. They'd go off together, just leaving me a bar of chocolate and a note saying: 'Have a happy day.' "

Mimi, for all her briskness, liked nothing better than laughter. Julia had always known how to get her going so that she threw her head back and guffawed, slapping her knee. "I was very slim in those days. Julia would come in in the afternoon and dance up to me, singing, 'O dem bones, dem bones—' She'd only got to lift her eyebrow and I'd be off.

"John was the same. I'd be battling with him. I'd send him out of the room, then I'd flop down exhausted in the big armchair next to the morning-room window. He'd crawl round on the path and pull faces at me through the window. He'd come at me like a monster, going, 'Woooo!' He could get me off just the same way Julia could."

When Mimi took charge of John she sent him to Dovedale Primary School, near Penny Lane. She took him there each morning, and each afternoon met him at the bus stop, near the Penny Lane traffic circle. In his class at Dovedale Primary was a boy named Peter Harrison whose younger brother George sometimes came with their mother to meet the three-thirty outpouring from school.

John did well at Dovedale, learning to read and write with precocious speed. He liked sport, especially running and swimming, but was inept at soccer. The discovery was made that he had chronically poor eyesight. His teachers thought that must be what made his English compositions so unusual. He changed almost every word into another one like it. Instead of "funds," he would write "funs." He loved reading, especially Richmal Crompton's Just William stories about a lawless eleven-year-old. He loved writing and drawing and crayoning. He could amuse himself for hours with books or pencils in the tiny bedroom above the front door that had little space for anything but its red-quilted single bed, undersized wardrobe, and one-bar electric heater. Each Christmas, when Mimi took him to the pantomime at the Liverpool Empire, he would endlessly retell the experience in stories, poems, and drawings. At the age of seven he began writing books of his own. One of them was called *Sport and Speed Illustrated;* it had cartoons and drawings and a serial story ending: "If you liked this, come again next week. It'll be even better."

One day, while playing in a nearby field, John encountered another seven-year-old with a pale pink-and-white face and fuzzy blond hair. The boy's name was Peter Shotton; his mother kept a small needle-woman's and grocery shop in Woolton village. The encounter quickly turned into combat. "I'd found out his name was Winston," Shotton says. "I was calling out to him, 'Winnie, Winnie . . .' He got me down on the ground with his knees on my shoulders. I said: 'OK, go ahead and hit me. Get it over with.' But he couldn't. He said: 'OK, I'll let you off. Just don't call me that name again.' I walked away, then I turned round and shouted, 'Winnie, Winnie.' He was so angry, he couldn't speak. Then I saw his face break into a smile."

Pete Shotton and John Lennon became inseparable friends. Pete lived on Vale Road, just round the corner from Menlove Avenue. The addition of another Vale Road boy, a mutual acquaintance, named Nigel Walley, added a new dimension. Three of them made enough for a gang.

Nigel went to school with Pete Shotton in Mosspits Lane. He also sang in the choir with John at St. Peter's, Woolton. He had often sat in the choirstalls in his white surplice, wriggling with laughter at things which the white-surpliced John dared to do. "He'd steal the Harvest Festival fruit. And every time the Rector, Old Pricey, climbed into the pulpit, John used to say, 'He's getting on his drums now.' "

The gang grew to four with the arrival of another Dovedale boy, Ivan Vaughan. Thus constituted, it embarked on its career as the terror of Woolton. One of the earliest games was to climb a tree over the busy main road and dangle a leg down in front of an approaching double-decker bus, then yank it back to safety in the nick of time. If your foot scraped the bus roof, that counted as extra points.

"John was always the leader," Nigel Walley says. "He was always the one to dare you. He never cared what he said or did. He'd think nothing of putting a brick through the glass in a street lamp. He'd dare us to go with him and play on the Allerton golf course, trying to hit golf balls across Menlove Avenue. Once, the police came and chased us off. We'd pick up these great clods of earth to chuck at the trains when they went into the tunnel at Garston. Something else was putting stuff on the tram rails to try to derail the trams.

"Shoplifting was another thing. We'd go into a sweet shop run by this little old lady. John'd point to things he said he wanted on the top shelf and, all the time, he'd be filling his pockets from the counter. He did the same at a shop that sold Dinky cars, in Woolton—opposite the Baths. He'd put a tractor or a little car in his pocket while the bloke was looking the other way. We went back to that same shop later on, but this time John hadn't got his glasses on. He couldn't understand why his fingers couldn't get at the Dinky cars. He couldn't see that the bloke had covered them over with a sheet of glass.

"We'd go to all the garden fetes in the summer, get under tents, and pinch stuff. People would come in looking for their trays of cakes and buns that we'd eaten. We went to one fete organized by the nuns, and somehow John got hold of this robe and dressed himself up as a monk. He was sitting with some other monks on a bench, talking in all these funny words while we were rolling about under the tent, in tucks.

"Pete was a bit of a bully, always picking on me, so John used to look after me. Whatever he told me to do, I'd do it. 'Walloggs,' he used to call me."

Aunt Mimi approved of Nigel Walley. His father was a senior police officer. Mimi thought him a wholesome influence.

At the age of twelve, John left Dovedale Primary and started at Quarry Bank High [i.e., grammar] School, on Harthill Road, a mile or so from Menlove Avenue. Mimi, distrusting the school outfitter, got his uncle George's tailor to make his new black blazer with its red-and-gold stag's head badge and motto, *Ex Hoc Metallo Virtutem* (From This Rough Metal We Forge Virtue). On his Raleigh "Lenton" bicycle he would toil up the long hill to school, past old sandstone quarries, long emptied and overgrown. Woolton sandstone built the Anglican cathedral, as well as the many mock Elizabethan mansions in which Liverpool merchants indulged themselves at the height of their Victorian prosperity.

It was in a local timber baron's mock-gothic "folly" that Quarry Bank High School was founded in 1922. Despite its newness it was, by the time John arrived in 1952, as steeped in academic lore as any of Liverpool's ancient grammar schools. There was a house system; there were masters in gowns; there were prefects and canings. In later years, after it had produced two Labour cabinet ministers—William Rodgers and Peter Shore—Quarry Bank came to be nicknamed "The Eton of the Labour Party."

John's Dovedale friend, Ivan Vaughan, had gone on to Liverpool Institute High School. Nigel Walley was now at the Bluecoat School near Penny Lane. Pete Shotton was the only one of the Woolton gang who accompanied him to Quarry Bank. "We went through it together like Siamese twins," Pete says. "We started in our first year at the top and gradually sank together into the subbasement.

"I remember the first time we both went to be caned. I was really terrified. John wasn't—or if he was, he didn't show it. We were both waiting outside the headmaster's study. John started telling me the cane would be kept in a special case, with a velvet lining and jewels all round it. I was in tucks, even though I was so scared.

"John went in first for the cane. I could hear it—swipe, swipe. Then he came out. What I didn't realize was that there was a little vestibule you had to go through before you got into the head's study. John came out through this little vestibule—though I didn't know it—crawling on all fours and groaning. I was laughing so much when I went in that I got it even worse than he had."

In 1955 Mimi's husband, Uncle George, died suddenly after a hemorrhage. It was a shock to the whole family to lose the quiet, hardworking dairy farmer who got up every morning without complaint to do the milking and whose only unusual demand of Mimi was his two breakfasts a day. Uncle George had been John's ally when he was in disgrace, smuggling buns upstairs to him behind Mimi's back. Uncle George had bought him the mouth organ John carried in his blazer pocket and tinkered on for hours when he ought to have been doing homework.

Mimi was left alone to cope with a boy whose will was now almost the equal of hers and who seemed to glory in idleness and lawlessness and wasting the opportunities he had been given. From his first moderately virtuous year at Quarry Bank, he gravitated, in Pete Shotton's company, to the bottom of the C stream, and made no attempt to rise again thereafter. The two were perpetually in detention or being sent to the headmaster's study for a caning. Frequently, their exploits were serious enough to be reported to their homes. "I used to dread the phone going at ten in the morning," Mimi said. "A voice would come on, 'Hello, Mrs. Smith. This is the secretary at Quarry Bank . . .' 'Oh Lord,' I'd think. 'What's he done now?' "

"It was mostly skiving," Pete Shotton says. "Not doing the things the others did. We were like wanted men. We were always on the run."

Rod Davis, a studious boy in the A stream, had watched John and Pete's double act since they were seven-year-olds sitting in a ring at St. Peter's Sunday school and John had managed to put a piece of chewing gum into the teacher's hand so that all her fingers stuck together. "I'd always known him and Pete as the school thugs, dragging on a cigarette they'd got behind their backs, or running into Marks & Spencers and shouting 'Woolworths!' "

"John used to turn Religious Knowledge into chaos," Pete Shotton says. "One day he cut out all the shiny white cardboard bits from a lot of Weetabix packets and made dog collars for the whole class. When the teacher, McDermott, came in, he was so angry, he couldn't speak. Then he had to start laughing. He made us wear them for the rest of the class."

The school punishment book records for what diversity of crime J. Lennon and P. Shotton were beaten: "failing to report to school office"; "insolence"; "throwing blackboard duster out of window"; "cutting class and going awol"; "gambling on school field during house match."

"We were in detention once, clearing up the sports field," Pete Shotton says. "I found this big envelope full of dinner tickets. You used to pay a shilling a day for a ticket to have your school dinner. These were the used ones that somebody had accidentally dropped. When John and I counted them, we found we'd got the whole school's dinner tickets— about fifteen hundred of them. And they were worth a shilling each. We sold them off for sixpence each. We were rich. We even gave up shoplifting while that was going on."

Even John's talent for writing and drawing failed to earn him any good marks or exam distinctions. Only in the last forty minutes of every day, in the unsupervised prep period, would he show what ability he was relentlessly wasting. He would fill old exercise books and scraps of paper with his cartoons and word play and verse. His nonsense sagas, "The Land of the Lunapots," and "Tales of Hermit Fred," were passed to Pete Shotton first, then enjoyed wide under-the-desk circulation. "He'd do all these caricatures of the masters," Pete says. "We'd stick them on bits of cereal packets and make a stall at the school fete where people could throw darts at them. We handed in more money than any other stall—and we still had five times as much in our pockets."

Often they would cut school altogether. They would go on the bus to see Julia, John's mother—now living with the nervous waiter the boys called "Twitchy," by whom she had two small daughters. "Julia didn't mind if we'd sagged off school," Pete Shotton says. "She used to wear these old woollen knickers on her head while she did the housework. She'd open the door to us with the knicker legs hanging down her back. She didn't care. She was just like John."

John, as he grew older, grew more and more fascinated by this pretty auburn-haired woman, so much more like an elder sister than a mother. For Julia did not echo the dire warnings given by Aunt Mimi and Quarry Bank. Julia encouraged him to live for the present, as she did, and for laughter and practical jokes. "She'd do these tricks just to make us laugh," Pete says. "She'd put on a pair of glasses with no glass in the frames. She'd stand talking to a neighbor and suddenly stick her finger through where the lens ought to have been, and rub her eye."

Julia thought as John and Pete did, and said the things they wanted to hear. She told them not to worry about school or homework or what their lives might have in store.

Jim McCartney was no stranger to female admiration. During the 1920s he led the Jim Mac Jazz Band, dapperly outfitted in dinner jackets, paper shirt fronts, and detachable cuffs that could be bought then for a penny per dozen. A photograph taken at the time shows a group of girls in silver shoes and stockings, their hair pertly fringed and bobbed, re-clining with formal abandon on a dance floor around the Jim Mac drum set. Among them sits the bandleader with his formal wing collar and close-cropped hair, and his so familiar looking big brown eyes.

Jim was a cotton salesman working for Hannay's of Chapel Street, Liverpool, an old established firm of cotton brokers and purveyors to the Manchester mills. His position, for a working-class boy, was a good one; he had risen to it by neatness, diligence, and a genuine flair for selling, though he lacked the ruthlessness that might have taken him higher. He had taught himself to play the piano by ear, as any young man did who wished for social grace. The Jim Mac Jazz Band performed at socials and works dances, occasionally even in cinemas. Their biggest engagement was providing incidental music for a silent Hollywood epic, *The Queen of Sheba*. When a chariot race began on the screen Jim Mac and the boys played "Thanks for the Buggy Ride." During the Queen of Sheba's death scene they played "Horsy, Keep Your Tail Up."

Perhaps there were too many of those girls in silver shoes and stockings around the drum set. At all events, Jim McCartney went through his thirties as a bachelor, working at the Cotton Exchange, playing his spare-time dance music, content for his family to be the hospitable reflection of his married sisters, Millie and Jin.

At the very point where he seemed resigned to bachelorhood, and the impending war seemed to confirm it, Jim McCartney proposed marriage to Mary Mohin. She, like Jim, was of the Liverpool's medical services, a slender and gently spoken woman employed by Liverpool Corporation as a district health visitor. Herself in her early thirties, Mary could override the faint objection that Jim did not share her membership in the Catholic Church. They were married in 1941, shortly before Jim's fortieth birthday.

Exempted from military service by partial deafness, he had been transferred from Hannay's to munitions work with Napier's, the firm that produced the Sabre aircraft engine. On June 18, 1942, while Jim was fire watching, Mary gave birth to a son in Walton General Hospital. She had worked there once as nursing sister in charge of the maternity ward, and so received the luxury of a private room. The baby was perfect, with a placid, impish smile and big eyes just like his father's. Such was Mary's love for Jim that the more famous saint's name did not receive precedence. The baby was christened James Paul.

His first home was furnished rooms in Anfield, not far from the mass graves where the dead from the dockland blitz had been buried. Jim, no longer needed for munitions work, had left Napier's and become an inspector in the local authority's cleansing department. His job was to follow the garbagemen, seeing that they did not skimp their round. The work was badly paid, and to supplement Jim's earnings, Mary returned to her former job as a health visitor. After her second son, Michael, was born in 1944, she took up full-time midwifery.

The process had already begun that was to gouge out the old, shabby, vibrant heart of Liverpool, flattening its bombed streets and scattering their inhabitants wide across an arid suburban plain. Communities that Hitler could not displace were now induced, by the hundreds of thousand, to migrate to new housing projects, dumped down amid transplanted industry and isolated by walls of dingy open air.

Mary McCartney became a domiciliary midwife on one of the several projects built around Speke's new industrial parks. The rent-free public housing on Western Avenue helped to reduce the strain on Jim's small wage. The disadvantage was that Mary had to be available twenty-four hours a day. Her kindness and patience became a legend among people already suspecting they may have been forgotten by the authorities. Little gifts of plaster ornaments or somebody's sugar ration were always being brought to the McCartneys' back door, or left shyly outside on the step.

Her own children, despite the constant pressure, received immaculate care. Jim, who had been somewhat unprepared for fatherhood—and somewhat dismayed by Paul's redness as a newborn baby—could only marvel at the ingenuity with which Mary found time, and money enough, to dress the boys beautifully and feed them with imaginative good sense. Her special concern was that they should speak well, not in broad Liverpudlian like other children in the housing project.

Paul came to consciousness in an atmosphere of worship. His aunts and the neighbors loved him for his chubbiness, his large eyes and amiable, undespotic disposition. The arrival of a little brother, and potential rival, showed him the importance of maintaining popularity. He soon discovered that he possessed charm, and learned early how to put it to use. Though the boys did things together, and were together in normal boyish scrapes, it would invariably be Michael, the more impetuous and turbulent one, who received punishment. Jim McCartney, for all his mildness, was of the generation that believed in hitting children. Michael remembers being chastised by Jim while Paul, who had escaped, stood by, shouting, "Tell him you didn't do it and he'll stop." Where Michael would shout and cry, Paul, if his father hit him, showed no emotion. Later he would go into his parents' bedroom and tear their lace curtains imperceptibly at the bottom.

Though Mary was a Catholic, she preferred to entrust the boys' education to Protestant schools. Paul started in Speke, at Stockton Road Primary. Michael joined him there, and when the classes became overcrowded, both were transferred to Joseph Williams Primary, Gateacre. Here the same contrast was revealed between them. Paul was quiet and law abiding, and Michael, hotly argumentative. Where Michael found it difficult to absorb learning, Paul came out on top in almost every lesson with ease. He was especially good at English composition and art. His handwriting received praise for its clear regularity.

Money remained a difficulty, though the boys never knew it. Jim McCartney had left his job with the Cleansing department and gone back to selling cotton. This, however, was not the secure trade it had been in prewar days with Hannay's. After a hard week's traveling Jim would be lucky to find six pounds in his wage packet. Mary took a second domiciliary job on the Speke estate, necessitating a move from Western Avenue to another council house, on Ardwick Road. Her husband, worried at the long hours she worked, was relieved when she decided to give up midwifery and return to regular nursing. She became a school nurse, making rounds with school doctors in the Walton and Allerton district.

Bella Johnson met Mary at the central clinic from which both of them worked. A round, little, jolly woman, Bella too was finding it difficult to make ends meet. She had been widowed at the age of thirty-six, with two small daughters to educate. This she had done so spectacularly well that one of them, Olive, now worked for the Law Society in Liverpool. The Law Society's offices were only a street away from the Cotton Exchange. On her way to work, Olive used to pass the time of day with Jim McCartney, not knowing that his wife and her mother were colleagues and friends.

Mrs. Johnson and Olive got to know the McCartneys well. Bella remembered a family contented and normal, suffused by Mary's gentleness and strength. "She was a beautiful person: it came from something deep inside her," Olive says. "Jim adored her. I remember how he'd sometimes tell us a story he'd picked up from the businessmen at the Cotton Exchange. If it was a bit off-color, Mary used to look at him and say, '*Husband!*'"

Olive had a small car in which they would all go on weekend trips into the Cheshire countryside. She became a big sister to Paul and Michael, joining in their games, rowing them in a skiff across the lake at Wilmslow. "Mary always made us a special treat at tea time," Mrs. Johnson said. "I'll never forget them. Apple sandwiches with sugar."

On Coronation Day 1953, the Johnsons and McCartneys celebrated together at Ardwick Road. The boys had received their commemorative mugs and spoons, and Paul, in addition, had won a book as a coronation essay prize. They watched, as people did all over Britain in one another's front parlors, the ceremonial flickering over a tiny, bluish television screen.

Michael McCartney sat at his mother's feet, as ever. "He was the one you always felt you wanted to love and protect," Olive says. "With Paul, you loved him, but you knew you'd never have to protect him."

•   •   •

Paul passed the eleven plus examination without difficulty, and with sufficient distinction to receive a place at Liverpool Institute, the city's oldest grammar school. The honor entailed a long bus journey each day from Speke into Liverpool and up behind the Anglican Cathedral to Mount Street, where the institute's square portico jutted out into steeply plunging pavement. Founded in the 1830s as a Mechanics Institute for deserving artisans, the building had been later divided to form the grammar school and the college of art. Behind the heavy wrought-iron gates was an interior unchanged since Victorian times, save that the gas lamps over each classroom door were no longer lit on winter afternoons. *Non nobis solum*, the school motto runs, *sed toti mundo nati:* "Not for ourselves only but for the good of all the world."

Among hundreds of boys, swarming through the green-distempered school thoroughfares, Paul McCartney was not conspicuous, nor wished to be. His black blazer was neat and his hair slicked flat with Brylcreem; he belonged to that cooperative species from which are recruited the collectors of exercise books and operators of window poles; he was, more or less permanently, head boy in his grade. With his classmates he was popular, if a little reserved. They called him not by his surname or a nickname—just Paul. His close friend Ivan Vaughan was an exception to this attitude of noticeable deference.

He had been put into the A stream, tending as he moved higher to specialize in history and languages. He found most lessons easy, and could get high marks even in Latin if he bothered to apply his mind. He was nonchalant about homework, an embarrassing obligation in a housing project where other boys could do what they pleased at night. On the morning bus into Liverpool, he could churn out an essay still impressive enough to receive commendation from his English master, "Dusty" Durband. Mr. Durband, even so, was aware of the extent to which Paul relied on facility and bluff to see him through. It sometimes failed him, as when he had been given the task of preparing a talk about the Bodley Head edition of Stephen Leacock's works. Paul delivered an impromptu stream of nonsense about the Bodley Head's Elizabethan logo.

He knew what he wanted and even then would be satisfied with nothing less. When the institute put on Shaw's *St. Joan* as its end-of-term play, Paul auditioned keenly for the part of Warwick. He did not get it, and had to be content with the minor role of an inquisitor in the trial scene. The disappointment made him unusually fractious: Mr. Durband, the play's producer, remembers shouting in exasperation at the medievally hooded figure that persisted in disrupting rehearsals.

In 1955, when Paul was thirteen, the McCartneys left Speke and its pallid factory smog. Jim had managed to get a council house in Allerton, one of Liverpool's nearer and better suburbs. It was a definite step up for the family to move into 20 Forthlin Road, a double row of semi-detached houses small and neat enough to pass for privately owned villas. Mimi Smith's home in Woolton was only a mile or so away, if you cut across the golf course.

For some time, Mary had been troubled by a slight pain in her breast. She did not like to trouble the doctor for fear he would dismiss it as nurse's hypochondria. As she was now in her mid-forties, she and Jim philosophically concluded that "the change" must be to blame for the small lump that had appeared. The pain was not great but would not seem to go away.

Paul and Michael were camping with the Boy Scouts that summer. The weather was very wet and cold, and Mary told Bella Johnson, her friend at the school clinic, that she was worried about the boys sleeping under canvas. So one afternoon, Olive took Mary and Jim in her car to visit them. On the way home Mary was in such pain that she had to lie down on the back seat.

"When she got home, she went straight to bed," Olive says. "I went up later and found her crying. 'Oh, Olive,' she said to me, 'I don't want to leave the boys *just* yet.' "

After a few days' rest she felt so much better that she began to think that, after all, the trouble was simply overwork. Then the pain returned so severely that, at last, she consulted a specialist. He sent her at once into hospital—not Walton General but the old city Northern, so that he could keep a close eye on her. Breast cancer was diagnosed. She went into surgery for a mastectomy, which was not carried out: The cancer had already spread too far. A few hours later Bella and Olive Johnson received the news that Mary had died.

Jim McCartney's predicament was one calculated to crush a younger as well as wealthier man. At the age of fifty-three he found himself bereft of a loving, capable wife and faced with the task of caring for two adolescent boys, all on a wage that still had need of the extra Mary had earned. That, indeed, was the first thing fourteen-year-old Paul blurted out in the shock of his mother's loss: "What are we going to do without her money?"

Mary was buried as a Catholic—the wish she had expressed to Jim on her deathbed. Paul and Michael were taken to stay with their auntie Jin at Huyton to spare them the funeral and the sight of their father's devastation. Mrs. Johnson and Olive moved in to Forthlin Road to be with Jim and to prepare him for the boys' return. Their task, at first, seemed hopeless. All he wanted, he kept saying, was to be with Mary.

"QUARRY MEN, STRONG BEFORE OUR BIRTH"

Nineteen fifty-six was a worrying year for English parents. It seemed that something had gone seriously wrong with the Victorian age. The generation born before 1941, despite exterior differences, lived by much the same rules and values as their parents and their grandparents. It boiled down to a single phrase, the base of Victorianism: They "had respect." They had respect for their elders and their betters. They had respect for their country with its Empire, now Commonwealth, its God-given right to be called "Great" Britain. Having just survived a world war, they had respect for politicians and soldiers. They had respect also for clergymen, policemen, schoolteachers, and the Queen. And suddenly, in 1956, they realized that their children did not have respect for them.

The year was one of unparalleled national humiliation. It was the year that the British engaged with France in a ludicrous plan to invade Egypt and were foiled by, of all people, the Egyptians. After Suez, the world would never again function at the behest of British gunboats. We had become overnight a second-class power, barely noticed in the new, harsh glare of America and Russia's nuclear cohabitation.

The British language, meanwhile, had been invaded by certain bewildering new words. Of these, the most bewildering was "teenager." In Britain before 1956 there were no such things as teenagers. There were only children and grown-ups. Transition took place at sixteen when boys put on tweed jackets like their fathers' and girls turned into matrons with "twinsets" and "perms." Conscription, or national service, for two years completed the male maturing process. The only remission was given to university students, a minority, who were still largely upper class and thus permitted to behave like hooligans on boat race night and other fixed ceremonial occasions.

But there now stalked the streets of Britain young men in clothes as outlandish as they were sinister. The costume, of velvet-trimmed drape jackets, frilled shirts, and narrow trousers, was inspired partly by Edwardian fashion—hence the name "Teddy Boy"—and partly by gunslingers and riverboat gamblers in Hollywood movies. Amid the drab uniformity of postwar Britain they seemed utterly freakish. Their hair, in a land still army-cropped, was scarcely believable. A greasy cockade flopped over the forehead, swept back past the ears with constant combing to form two flaps like the posterior of a duck. Their socks were luminous pink or orange. Their shoes had soles three inches thick. They were believed to carry weapons such as switchblades, razors, and bicycle chains. Their other, scarcely less threatening, predilection was for coffee bars and "rock 'n' roll."

Coffee bars, to the British of 1956, might just as well have been opium dens. They had sprung up all at once out of the country's Italian population, and also the sudden fifties' craze for "contemporary" design. They were dark and filled with basket chairs and foliage; they had names like La Lanterna or La Fiesta; they dispensed, from huge silver machines, a frothy fluid barely recognizable as the stuff which the British were accustomed to boiling with milk in saucepans. They were the haunt of Teddy Boys and Teddy Girls, and of jukeboxes. Their jukeboxes united the Teddy-Boy contagion with that of rock 'n' roll.

Rock 'n' roll, as every sensible Briton knew, was American madness such as one saw as a novelty item at the end of the weekly cinema newsreel. Sometimes it was flagpole sitting, sometimes dance marathons, sometimes pie-eating contests. Now it was a young singer who did not sing but merely writhed about, pretending to play a guitar, and yet who aroused American female audiences to transports of ecstasy greater even than had Valentino, the screen lover, or Frank Sinatra, the crooner. His songs, or lack of them, and his suggestive movements, had scandalized America. When he appeared on American television he was shown only from the waist up. His name was Elvis Presley. That, too, the British thought, could only happen in America.

Yet the madness seemed to be drifting this way. In 1955, a song called "Rock Around the Clock" had caused riots in several British cinemas during shows of a film called *The Blackboard Jungle*—significantly, a study of juvenile crime. The singer, Bill Haley, and his group, the Comets, had afterward visited Britain, arriving in London by boat train amid mob scenes unequaled since VE night or the coronation.

That had seemed to be a freak occurrence. The country settled back again to its former dull diet of Anglicized American dance-band music—of "light orchestras," crooners named Dennis Lotis and Dickie Valentine, and novelty songs about Italy or little Dutch dolls. Here, at least, there was a powerful guardian of morality and taste. The British Broadcasting Corporation, with its monopoly of all radio, continued to ensure that nothing was played save that in its own image and of its own cold custard consistency.

In February 1956, an Elvis Presley record called "Heartbreak Hotel" was released in Britain, on the hitherto respectable HMV label. Within days, it had smashed through the crooners and light orchestras and little Dutch dolls to first place in the Top Twenty records chart. It remained there for eighteen weeks. Another by the same singer followed it, bearing the ludicrous title "Blue Suede Shoes"; then another, even surpassing that in ludicrousness, called "Hound Dog."

Britain's parents listened, so far as they were able, to the lyric, so far as it could be understood. The vocalist was exhorting some bystander, endlessly and incoherently, not to tread on his blue suède shoes. He was accusing the same bystander, with equal, mumbling persistence, of being a "hound dog." A few people over twenty enjoyed the music, and even recognized it for what it was: an adaptation of American blues, sharing the same honorable origins as jazz. Presley was simply applying blues intonation and phrasing to songs in the white cowboy, or country and western, idiom. He was, in other words, a white man who sang like a black man. The charges of obscenity were ironic. All Presley's blues songs had been purged of their sexual and social content for the white audience's sensitive ears.

To Britain, as to America, the idea that a white man could sing like a black man was intrinsically lewd. It confirmed the malignant power of rock 'n' roll music to incite young people, as jungle drums incited primitive peoples, to their newly evidenced violence, promiscuity, disobedience, and disrespect. To Britain, as to America, there was only one consolation. A thing so grotesque as Elvis Presley could not possibly last. They said of rock 'n' roll what was said in 1914, when the Great War started: In six months, it would all be over.

The headmaster of Quarry Bank High School, Liverpool, considered John Lennon and Peter Shotton to be the worst Teddy Boys among the pupils in his charge. Detentions, canings, even temporary expulsion seemed to have no effect on the insolent-faced, bespectacled boy and his fuzzy-haired companion, whose clothes conformed less and less to school regulation, and who now overtly gloried in their power to cause disturbance. A typical Lennon–Shotton incident occurred when the whole school went into Liverpool to see the film *Henry V* at the Philharmonic Hall. By ill luck, this had been preceded by a Donald Duck cartoon. One did not have to guess from whom, in the tittering auditorium, had come those cries of, "There he is! There's old King Henry!"

For John, as for most fifteen-year-olds, rock 'n' roll began as a curiosity manifest among slightly older boys. Pete Shotton and he, on their truant-playing days, would often hang around Liverpool gaping at the full-dress Teddy Boys—mostly seamen on leave from the big ships—whose disregard for authority was on a scale far more gorgeous than theirs. When *Rock Around the Clock*, the first Bill Haley film, reached Liverpool, John went to see it, but to his disappointment, no riot happened. There was just this fat man in a tartan jacket with a kiss curl on his forehead, and saxophones and double basses just like any dance band.

Then, at the beginning of 1956, a friend played "Heartbreak Hotel" for him. "From then on," his Aunt Mimi said, "I never got a minute's peace. It was Elvis Presley, Elvis Presley, Elvis Presley. In the end I said, 'Elvis Presley's all very well, John, but I don't want him for breakfast, dinner, *and* tea.'"

Mimi had been struggling for months to keep her charge from turning into a Teddy Boy. She still sent John to school in blazers that were tailor-made, and saw no reason why these should not do for all social occasions. "Drainpipe" trousers and drape jackets were, as Mimi constantly affirmed, no kind of dress for a boy who went to Quarry Bank. The trouble was that John now spent more and more time out of Mimi's sight with her sister, Julia, his real mother. Julia, as Mimi knew, was too easygoing to worry what John wore. Julia bought him colored shirts and gave him money to have school trousers "taken in." He would leave Menlove Avenue a nice Quarry Bank schoolboy and then, at Julia's, turn into a Teddy Boy as bad as any to be seen around the docks.

The stunning music that went with the clothes was available only with equal deviousness. John listened to it, as thousands did, under the bedclothes, late at night. Since the BBC would not broadcast rock 'n' roll, the only source was Radio Luxembourg, a commercial station, beamed from the Continent with an English service after 8:00 P.M. The Elvis records came through, fading and blurred with static, like coded messages to an occupied country. Now there were other names and other songs that split open the consciousness with disbelieving joy. There was Little Richard's "Tutti Frutti"; Bill Haley's "Razzle Dazzle"; Freddy Bell and the Bellboys' "Giddy-up-a-Ding-Dong." The sound came from beyond comprehension; it played, then died out again. You could not catch it, nor sing it nor write it down.

Then, late one night over the hidden radios, a new message came. A banjo player with the Chris Barber Jazz Band had formed his own small group to record "Rock Island Line," an American folk song dating back to the Depression, or earlier. The number was played in what jazz audiences knew already as skiffle, a style originating in the poor Southern states where people would hold rent parties to stave off the landlord, playing music on kazoos, tin cans, and other impromptu instruments. The banjoist, Tony—or "Lonnie"—Donegan, sang in a piercing pseudo-blues wail, set about by elementary rhythm of which the main component was an ordinary kitchen washboard, scraped and tapped by thimble-capped fingers.

"Rock Island Line" began a national craze. For anyone could form a skiffle group simply by stealing his mother's washboard and fixing a broom handle to a tea chest, then stringing it with wire to make a rudimentary double bass. The biggest craze of all, thanks to Elvis Presley, was for guitars. A straitlaced instrument long muffled in orchestral rhythm sections found itself suddenly the focus of all adolescent desire.

As boys pestered throughout Britain, so did John Lennon pester his aunt Mimi to buy him a guitar. Each afternoon, when Julia paid her daily visit to Menlove Avenue, she, too, would be entreated to give—even lend—him the money. For Julia, as it happened, could play the banjo a little. John's father, Freddy, had taught her before disappearing overseas. And Freddy's father, so he had always said, used to play professionally in America with a group of Kentucky minstrels.

It was, however, not Julia but Mimi who eventually gave in. One Saturday morning, she put on her coat, checked the money in her purse, and told John unceremoniously to come along.

Hessy's, the music shop in Whitechapel, central Liverpool, had an abundant stock of guitars. Frank Hessy, the owner, was sending a van regularly down to London to buy up every one to be found in the Soho street markets. Jim Gretty, his showroom manager, was selling roughly one guitar a minute from the hundreds festooned along the narrow shop wall. Jim was himself a guitarist, western-style, and each week held a beginners' class in an upstairs room, chalking huge elementary chord-shapes on the wall.

It was Jim who sold Aunt Mimi the guitar that John said he wanted—a little Spanish model with steel strings and a label inside: "Guaranteed not to split." "It cost me seventeen pounds, I think," Mimi said. "I know I resented paying that, even though I'd been giving twelve pounds each for his school blazers."

From that moment, John was—as they say in Liverpool—"lost." Nigel Walley, calling round at Mendips, would find him up in his bedroom, oblivious to time or the first soreness of fingertip split by the steel strings. "He'd sit on his bed, just strumming," Nigel says. "Strumming the banjo chords Julia had shown him, and singing any words that came into his head. After about ten minutes, he'd have got a tune going."

When Mimi could no longer stand the noise, or the foot beating time through her ceiling, she would order John out of the house, into the little front porch with its walls of Art Nouveau–patterned glass. "He stood there leaning against the wall so long, I think he wore some of the brickwork away with his behind," Mimi said. "To me, it was just so much waste of time. I used to tell him so. 'The guitar's all very well, John,' I told him, 'but you'll never make a *living* out of it.' "

The first skiffle group he formed had only two members: himself on guitar and his crony Pete Shotton on kitchen washboard, crashing its glass ridges with thimble-capped fingers as the two of them tried out "Cumberland Gap," "Rock Island Line," "Don't You Rock Me," "Daddy-O," and other skiffle classics. They named themselves, in rough-hewn skiffle style, the Quarry Men, after the sandstone quarries dotted around Woolton, and also in unwilling recognition of the school they both attended. The school song contains a reference to "Quarry men old before our birth"—a sentiment chorused lustily by John and Pete, since it invariably figured in the final assembly of term.

The Quarry Men grew in the image of the gang that had formerly terrorized St. Peter's Sunday school. Nigel Walley, now a Bluecoat Grammar School boy, and Ivan Vaughan, from the Liverpool Institute, divided the role of tea-chest bass player amicably between them. Nigel's first Teddy-Boy clothes had been seized by his policeman father and thrown on the fire, so now he kept all his choicer garments down the road at Ivan's house. Each played bass with the Quarry Men when the other could not be bothered.

Quarry Bank High School supplied a further recruit in Rod Davis, the earnest, bespectacled boy in 4A whose parents had just bought him a banjo. Another Woolton boy named Eric Griffiths came in on the strength of his new guitar, and because he claimed to know someone on King's Drive who owned a full-size set of drums. He took the others to meet Colin Hanton, an apprentice upholsterer who had just begun installment plan payments on a thirty-eight-pound set from Hessy's. Colin was two years older than the others but, as he was extremely small, it didn't matter. He was so small, he carried his birth certificate in his pocket to prove to suspicious pub landlords that he was old enough to be served with beer.

In the group, as in the gang, John was the undisputed leader. His plaid shirt collar turned up, Teddy Boy style, scowling like Elvis, he monopolized the foreground and the microphone, if there chanced to be one. "He always used to beat hell out of his guitar," Rod Davis says. "He'd always be busting a string. Then he'd hand his guitar to me, take my banjo, and carry on on that while I knelt down in the background and tried to fix the string.

"We did all the skiffle numbers that Lonnie Donegan recorded. Right from the start, John wanted to play rock 'n' roll as well; I can remember him singing "Blue Suede Shoes." I'd got some Burl Ives records, so we did "Worried Man Blues." The only way you could learn the words was by listening to the radio—or buying the record. Records were six bob (30p) each, and none of us could afford that. So John always used to make up his own words to the songs that were popular. "Long, black train" was one of them. Another one went "Come, go with me, down to the Penitentiar-ee." They weren't any worse than the words you were supposed to sing."

Skiffle contests were happening all over Liverpool, at ballrooms like the Rialto and the Locarno as a cheap way of filling the intervals. In ten minutes between regular band spots three or four groups would hurry onstage and patter out their brief, invariable repertoire. The Quarry Men entered numerous such competitions, without notable success. One of the groups that continually beat them had as its chief attraction a midget named Nicky Cuff, who actually stood on the tea-chest bass while plucking at it.

Rod Davis's father had a big old Austin Hereford car in which he would occasionally chauffeur them to a skiffle contest. For most of the time, they traveled on buses, with tea chest, drum set, and all.

On Saturday afternoons they met to practice at Colin Hanton's house since his father, a Co-op shop manager, was guaranteed to be absent. Least practicing of all was done at Mimi's, for the boys were somewhat in awe of her sharp tongue. Instead, they would go to Julia's house, where they were always certain of a welcome and a laugh. Sometimes Julia would take Rod's banjo and demonstrate chords and little runs for John and Eric Griffiths to copy on their guitars. Both as a result learned to play in banjo style, leaving the two bass strings untuned. "We used to practice standing in the bath at Julia's," Rod Davis says. "You could get more of an echo that way."

In 1956, a new headmaster, William Edward Pobjoy, took charge of Quarry Bank High School. At thirty-five, he was young for such a post, and seemed younger with his boyish quiff of hair and quiet, sardonic manner. Since the new head resorted neither to shouting nor sarcasm, the Quarry Bank heavies believed they were in for an easy time.

Among the information passed on by his predecessor to Mr. Pobjoy was that John Lennon and Pete Shotton were the school's leading criminals. "I was told there was even one master whom they not only used to terrorize, but whom Lennon had actually thumped. The poor man was so ashamed, he begged for the matter not to be reported."

Mr. Pobjoy, in his unobtrusive way, seems to have got the measure of Lennon and Shotton. The punishment book shows that John was caned by him only once. On another occasion, he and Pete were each suspended for a week.

Mr. Pobjoy, they discovered with some astonishment, did not disapprove of skiffle. Nor did he try, on the strength of their other crimes, to stamp out the Quarry Men. He encouraged them to do anything more positive than smoking and slacking. Now when John entered the head-master's office—the timber merchant's circular book room, with finely inlaid shelves, where he had been caned so many times—it would not be defiantly, as before, but to ask Mr. Pobjoy, in all humility, if the Quarry Men could play for ten minutes during the interval at the sixth form dance.

Another source of engagements was St. Peter's parish church, Woolton. John had sung in its choir and disrupted its Sunday school, and he and Pete Shotton still belonged to its youth club, which met in the hall across the road for badminton and ping-pong. The Quarry Men would play at the youth club "hops," unpaid and glad of an opportunity to use a stage, and experience acoustics larger than those of John's mother's bathroom. When John broke a guitar string he was reimbursed from church funds.

The group existed on the most casual basis, expanding and shrinking according to members available. Already there was some dissent between Rod Davis, who wished to play pure folk music, and John with his passion for Elvis. Pete Shotton was in it only for laughs, as he strove to make clear on all occasions. Little Colin Hanton, drumming irregularly, with his birth certificate in his top pocket, was more interested in pubs and pints of Black Velvet. Fights sometimes broke out between the musicians as they were performing, or with members of the audience whose criticisms were untactfully voiced. Fights broke out also if a spectator believed a Quarry Man to be ogling his girlfriend, and clambered up among them to take revenge. John Lennon, for some reason, was always the principal target of such attacks, and was seldom averse to using his fists. "Except if it was a *really* big bloke," Nigel Walley says. "Then John'd be as meek as a mouse. He'd always manage to talk his way out."

"There were these two particular big Teds," Rod Davis says. "Rod and Willo their names were. They were the terror of Woolton. Rod and Willo were always looking for us and threatening to do us over. One night when we got off the bus—with all our gear, and the tea chest as well—Rod and Willo were there, waiting for us. They came chasing after us in their long coats, and we scattered. I know we left the tea chest behind on the pavement."

The tea chest, which Rod's mum had covered with wallpaper, remained a prominent feature of Woolton village for about a week afterward. Sometimes it would be standing on the pavement; sometimes it would have migrated to the middle of the road.

The role of bass player was transferred after this to Len Garry, another Liverpool Institute boy whom Ivan Vaughan had introduced into the Lennon circle. Nigel Walley, whose consuming interest was golf not skiffle, assumed the duties of manager. With his sun-tanned complexion and shining white teeth, "Walloggs" was amply suited to a diplomatic role. He took bookings for the Quarry Men and prevailed on local shop-keepers to put advertisements in their windows for no fee. He gave out formal visiting cards that read:

> Country. Western. Rock 'n' Roll. Skiffle
> The Quarry Men
> OPEN FOR ENGAGEMENTS

Summer was just beginning when the Quarry Men played at an open-air party in Rosebery Street. A printer friend of Colin Hanton, who had designed the label on their bass drum, was helping to orga-nize festivities to celebrate Liverpool's 750th anniversary as a city. Though the engagement lay some distance from Woolton—and in a rough district of Liverpool 8—it was welcomed for the beer it promised, and the girls. The Quarry Men played standing on the tail-gate of a truck, which had to be moved because somebody was ill in the bedroom above. They played in the afternoon, then again in the evening, after strings of colored bulbs had come alight on the back-to-back houses.

Colin Hanton had, as usual, preceded the engagement by going to a pub, producing his birth certificate, and downing several pints of Black Velvet. By himself at the end of the trailer, he played his drums in happy disregard for what John and Eric Griffiths were singing. Pete Shotton, cradling his washboard, wore a long jacket, draped against his bony frame. Rod Davis, on banjo, looked serious, as always.

"I suddenly heard these two blokes talking, next to the trailer," Colin Hanton says. " 'Let's get that Lennon,' they said. I told John, and we all jumped off the back of the wagon and ran into my mate's house: the printer. His mum sat us down and gave us all salad. These blokes that were after us stayed outside, shouting and thumping on the windows. I'd met a girl at the party, so I took my drums and stayed the night at her house. The other lads had to have a policeman to see them to the bus stop."

In Paul McCartney's home, there had always been music. His father, Jim, never tired of recalling those happy prewar days when he had led his own little group, the Jim Mac Jazz Band. The McCartneys still had what all families once used to—a piano in the living room. Jim had bought it long ago, when money was easier, from the North End Music Stores on Walton Road. Whenever he had a spare moment—which was not very often—he would move the piled-up newspapers off a chair, sit down at the piano, open its lid, and play. He liked the old tunes, like "Charmaine" and "Ramona" and, his favorite of all, "Stairway to Paradise."

Jim's recovery had been marvelous to see. It was as if Mary's quiet competence had somehow been handed on to him. From the engulfing anguish following her death he had suddenly clicked into a calm resolution that for Paul's sake and for young Michael's home life must go on.

Though housekeeping was mysterious to him he applied himself doggedly to mastering its every department. He taught himself to cook and sew, to wash and to iron. Each day, after finishing work at the Cotton Exchange, he would hasten to the grocer's and the butcher's, then home to Allerton to tidy the house and cook Paul and Michael their evening meal. His sisters, Jin and Millie, each came in one full day a week to give the house a thorough cleaning. Bella Johnson and her daughter Olive also remained close at hand. When Paul and Michael came in from school, even if the house chanced to be empty, there would be notes left for them about where to find things, and sticks and paper laid for a fire in the grate.

Like Mimi Smith, Jim McCartney did his utmost to prevent there being a Teddy Boy in the family. The trouble was that, being at work all day, he had no alternative but to trust Paul and Michael to go to the barber's on their own and choose clothes for themselves with the money he gave them. In genuine perplexity he wondered how Paul, in particular, was able to return from the barber's seemingly with more hair than when he went, piled up in a cascading sheaf. There were battles, too, over trousers, which, Jim insisted, must not be "drainies" but of conventional and respectable cut. Paul would bring home a satisfactory pair and show them to his father; then he would smuggle them out again to one of the tailors who specialized in tapering. If Jim noticed anything Paul was ready to swear that the fourteen-inch drainies clinging to his ankles were the same pair that his father had sanctioned.

In 1956, Lonnie Donegan and his Skiffle Group arrived in Liverpool to appear at the Empire theater. Paul and some friends from the Institute waited outside during their lunch hour, hoping to catch a glimpse of the star when he arrived for rehearsal. He was slightly delayed and, with great consideration, wrote out notes for the factory workers who had waited to see him, explaining to their foremen why they were late back on shift. This testament of how nice a star could be always stayed in Paul McCartney's mind.

It was after seeing Lonnie Donegan that Paul began clamoring for a guitar. He was lucky in having a father only too glad to encourage him to take up any musical instrument. Already in the house, along with Jim's piano, there was a battered trumpet that Paul had tried to learn, but had discarded on being told it would make a callus on his upper lip. For he had now begun to sing—or, at least, to sing in public—without embarrassment. He had always sung to himself in bed at night, not knowing that Jim and Olive Johnson were often listening to him from the bottom of the stairs.

Despite the money shortage Jim brought home a 'cello guitar with F-holes, sunburst coloring, and a white scratch plate that cost him fifteen-pounds. Olive Johnson remembers how eagerly he set about trying to teach Paul to play by giving him chords from the living-room piano. "He'd sit there for hours, shouting, 'Come on, Paul. Now try this one!' "

Paul, strangely, made little initial progress. His left-hand fingers found it irksome to shape the patterns of black dots shown in the instruction book, and his right hand, somehow, lacked the bounce necessary for strumming. Then he discovered he could play far better if he fingered the fretboard with his right hand and strummed with his left. He took the guitar back to the shop and had its strings put on in reverse order. The white scratch plate, which carries the strummer's hand down after each chord, could not be moved; it was uselessly upside-down in the way that Paul now held the guitar.

From that moment, he too was lost. The guitar became a passion overruling all else in his life. It was the first thing he looked at on waking each morning; at night, after the lights were out, his eyes searched the darkness for the glow of its sunburst face. School lessons, games, bus journeys, the meals his father set in front of him—all were things to be endured and rushed through for the sake of that moment when he could pick up the guitar again and hear the hollow bump it made, and discover if the chord he had been practicing came out clearly this time. He played the guitar in his bath, even while sitting on the lavatory.

From an assortment of "Play in a Day" tutors he learned enough chords to play all the skiffle hits. Skiffle bored him after a time: What he really wanted to play were the guitar solos on rock 'n' roll records—the interludes so magically shrill and blurred that one could not analyze them but only listen as they shivered and wailed around the voice of Little Richard, Carl Perkins, or Elvis. "All Shook Up" was his favorite Elvis record. He played it over and over on the gramophone, his voice in vain pursuit of the wonderful, mumbling incantation, his acoustic guitar strumming in a different key, and universe.

He also bought every new record by the Everly Brothers, a newly popular American act from whom he made the discovery that rock 'n' roll could be performed at a lesser volume, in close, even subtle harmony. For a time, he and another boy, Ian James, modeled their lives on the Everlys: They combed their hair alike, wore matching white jackets, and hung around fairgrounds where the fast roundabouts always played the latest American hits. Paul's voice was like Phil Everly's, the higher of the duo, although he would torture it with impersonations of Little Richard, the shrieking exponent of "Tutti Frutti," "Rip it Up," and "Good Golly Miss Molly."

He even made one or two desultory attempts to involve his younger brother, Michael, in an Everly-style rock 'n' roll act. Michael McCartney, to add to their father's difficulties, currently had an arm in plaster after an accident at Boy Scout camp. It was a serious fracture that paralyzed his fingers for several months and forced him to give up learning the banjo Jim had bought him to equal Paul's guitar.

That summer of 1957—the first after Mary's death—Jim took Paul and Michael for a week's vacation at Butlin's holiday camp in Filey, Yorkshire. There, Paul roped Michael into joining him in an amateur talent contest. They sang an Everly Brothers song that was rather spoiled by Michael's plaster-encased arm. They didn't win the talent contest. "But after that, we had our first fan," Michael McCartney says. "I remember because it was me she fancied and not our kid."

The skiffle craze had by now seeped into the ancient precincts of Liverpool Institute grammar school. Paul, however, joined none of the newly formed groups, even though his friend Ivan Vaughan repeatedly enthused about one over in Woolton to which Ivan and another institute boy, Len Garry, belonged. Ivan Vaughan offered to take Paul to meet the leader—a "great fellow," so Ivan said. But Paul did not commit himself; nor, for that matter, did Ivan. He prided himself on taking only other "great fellows" to meet John Lennon.

The big event in Woolton each summer was a garden fete organized by St. Peter's parish church. They made a proper carnival of it, with fancy dress and a procession of decorated floats, representing all the church organizations, that wound through the streets of the old village, gathering up followers for the subsequent gala in the field at the top of Church Road.

The fete planned for July 6, 1957, was to have a particularly elaborate program. It included, as well as the customary Rose Queen ceremony, the band of the Cheshire Yeomanry and a team of trained police dogs from the City of Liverpool force. This year, too, for the first time, the teenagers of the parish were to be catered to. That Lennon boy had been asked to bring his group, the Quarry Men, to take part in the procession and to perform afterward at the fete.

The Quarry Men's fortunes were currently at a low ebb. A few days earlier, in common with dozens of other skiffle groups, they had gone into Liverpool to audition for a Carroll Levis *Discoveries* show at the Empire theater. The great star-maker Levis had been there in person, selecting local talent for what was presumed to be instant international fame. The Quarry Men had won their audition heat, and then found themselves matched in the final with the group that featured Nicky Cuff, the midget. This other group had played two numbers to the Quarry Men's one and had, on audience response, been declared the winner. "They were miles better than we were, anyway," Rod Davis says. "They all leapt about all over the place. We were the purists. We stood still and didn't even smile."

Early the next Saturday afternoon the Quarry Men climbed aboard the gaily bedecked coal merchant's wagon that was to carry them through the Woolton streets. It had been decided that their float should bring up the rear of the procession, to allay any clash of rhythms with the band of the Cheshire Yeomanry. In between, on vehicles borrowed from other local tradesmen, were tableaux representing the Boy Scouts, Girl Guides, Wolf Cubs, and Brownies, and the motorized throne on which the thirteen-year-old Rose Queen sat, in white lace and pink velvet, surrounded by miniature soldiers and attendants.

Just as had been hoped, the Quarry Men brought a large influx of teenagers into Woolton to see the parade. Among them was Paul Mc-Cartney. Ivan Vaughan, his classmate at the Institute, had asked him over, although Len Garry, not Ivan, was playing the tea-chest bass in the group that afternoon. Another strong inducement to Paul was the possibility of picking up girls. He cycled over from Allerton, balancing his piled-up hair carefully against the wind.

It was a warm, sunny, Saturday garden party afternoon. Liverpool, its ship towers and grime, seemed remote from the village decked in faded flags, and from the little red sandstone church up the hill, in whose square tower the gold clock hands seemed to point to perpetual summer.

Beside the churchyard, a rough track led into the two small parish-owned fields. Of these, the smaller one, on upland near the Boy Scouts' hut, was too uneven for anything but the refreshment marquee. On the lower, larger field were set out stalls purveying handkerchiefs, hardware, homemade cakes, fruit and vegetables, and sideshows including bagatelle, egg-hoopla, quoits, and shilling-in-the-bucket. Beyond the Scouts' airborne kiddy ride a blackened stone wall formed the boundary with another of Woolton's worked-out quarries. A constant patrol of stewards was necessary to ensure that no child climbed over and fell into the deep, overgrown pit.

That Saturday had begun badly for John Lennon. In the morning, coming downstairs at Mendips, he had revealed himself to his aunt Mimi as a full-blown Teddy Boy. His toppling hair, his plaid shirt, and drainpipes seemed to Mimi to be a repudiation of all her care, self-sacrifice, and sense. There had been a furious row, after which John had stalked out of the house to find Pete Shotton. In between leaving Mimi and climbing aboard the coalman's wagon he had contrived—in his own estimation at least—to get roaring drunk. The parade, the stalls, the Rose Queen, the opening prayers by the Reverend Maurice Pryce-Jones, all reached John through the gaseous mist of several illicit light ales.

Mimi, before she arrived at the fete, seems not to have known of the Quarry Men's existence. "I'd just got there, and was having a cup of tea in the refreshment tent. Suddenly, in the midst of everything, came this—this eruption of noise. Everyone had drained away from where I stood, into the next-door field. And there on the stage I saw them—John, and that Shotton."

"John saw me standing there with my mouth open. He started to make words up about me in the song he was singing. 'Mimi's coming,' he sang. 'Oh oh, Mimi's coming down the path . . .' "

The Quarry Men's big numbers that afternoon were "Cumberland Gap," "Railroad Bill," and "Maggie May," a Liverpool waterfront song in which the references to a famous tart and her beat along Lime Street were, fortunately, incomprehensible to the ladies of the church committee. The whole performance was watched keenly by Paul McCartney, standing with Ivan Vaughan next to the little outdoor stage. Paul noticed the tinny banjo chords that the leading Quarry Man played, and how, while singing, he stared about him, as if sizing up or challenging the rest of the world.

While the police dogs were performing obedience trials Ivan Vaughan took Paul across the road to the Church Hall, where the Quarry Men had made a small encampment of chairs and their coats. They were due to perform again, at a dance that evening, in alternation with the George Edwards band.

Introductions were made, Pete Shotton remembers, a little stiffly. " 'This is John.' 'Hi.' 'This is Paul.' 'Oh—hi.' Paul seemed quite cocky, sure of himself, but he and John didn't seem to have much to say." The ice positively splintered when Paul revealed a brilliant accomplishment. "He actually knew how to *tune* a guitar," Pete Shotton says. "Neither John nor Eric Griffiths had learned how to do that yet. Whenever their guitars went out of tune, they'd been taking them round and asking a fellow in King's Drive to do it."

It impressed John further that Paul knew the lyrics of rock 'n' roll songs all the way through. He himself could never remember words, which was partly why he preferred to make up his own. Paul was even prepared, in his neat hand, to write out all the verses of "Twenty Flight Rock," which Eddie Cochran had sung in the film *The Girl Can't Help It*. Then, with equal obligingness, he wrote out the words of Gene Vincent's "Be Bop a Lula."

As church committee ladies washed up in the scullery nearby, Paul borrowed a guitar and launched into his full Little Richard act—"Long Tall Sally," "Tutti Frutti," and the rest. As he played, he became aware of someone getting uncomfortably close to him and breathing a beery smell. The Quarry Men's chronically nearsighted leader was paying him the compliment of watching the way he shaped his chords.

Paul was not immediately asked to join the Quarry Men. His obvious ability, if anything, weighed against him. He was so good, they reasoned, he would hardly want to throw in with them. John in particular gave the idea what was, for John, prolonged thought. Up to that point he had been the Quarry Men's undisputed leader. By admitting Paul, he would be creating a potential threat to that leadership. The decision was whether to remain strong himself or make the group stronger. A week after the Woolton fete Paul was cycling to Allerton across the golf course when he met Pete Shotton. Pete told him that John wanted him in.

Pete's own skiffle career ended soon afterward at a party when John took away his washboard and smashed it over his head. "All of us were pissed and larking around. It didn't hurt me. I just sat there, framed by the washboard, with tears of laughter running down my face. I'd known for a long time that I was no good at music—I was only in the group through being a mate of John's. I was finished with playing, but I didn't want to say so, nor did John. This way let me out and it let John out."

If Pete had not left the Quarry Men at that point it is doubtful whether Paul and John would have become the close friends they subsequently did. For no two temperaments could have been more unalike. John, dour and blisteringly direct, fought against authority and inhibition in any form. Paul, baby-faced and virtuous, hated to be on anybody's wrong side. Not least of the differences in them was their attitude to the money they earned by playing. Whereas John would—and frequently did—give away his last sixpence, Paul showed noticeable signs of thrift. One of his first suggestions on joining the Quarry Men was that Nigel Walley should not receive equal shares since, as manager, he did not actually play onstage.

What Paul and John had in common was their passion for guitars. They began to spend hours in each other's company, practicing, usually at Paul's. John would even let himself be seen in his hated spectacles, the better to understand the chords that Paul showed him. Whole afternoons would pass in the living room at Forthlin Road, where Jim Mc-Cartney had papered the walls with a design of Chinese pagodas. Paul's younger brother Mike would often be there, too, taking photographs of them as they played. One of Mike's pictures records the moment when both were able to play a full six-string chord with the left-hand index finger barring the keyboard. Their faces, as they hold up their two guitars, are rigid with pride and pain.

The other Quarry Men did not take quite so strongly to Paul. "I always thought he was a bit big-headed," Nigel Walley says. "As soon as we let him into the group, he started complaining about the money I was getting them, and saying I should take less as I didn't do any playing. He was always smiling at you, but he could be catty as well. He used to pick on our drummer, Colin—not to his face, making catty remarks about him behind his back. Paul wanted something from the drums that Colin didn't have it in him to play."

"Paul was always telling me what to do," Colin Hanton says. 'Can't you play it this way?' he'd say, and even try to show me on my own drums. He'd make some remark to me. I'd sulk. John would say, 'Ah, let him alone, he's all right.' But I knew they only wanted me because I'd got a set of drums."

Even Pete Shotton—still a close friend and ally—noticed a change in John after Paul's arrival. "There was one time when they played a really dirty trick on me. I knew John would never have been capable of it on his own. It was so bad that he came to me later and apologized. I'd never known him to do that before for *anyone*."

It was shortly after Paul joined the Quarry Men that they bought proper stage outfits of black trousers, black bootlace ties, and white cowboy shirts with fringes along the sleeves. John and Paul, in addition, wore white jackets; the other three played in their shirtsleeves. Eric Griffiths, though also a guitarist, did not have the jacket-wearing privilege. A cheerful boy, he did not recognize this for the augury it was.

Their main engagements were still at church halls like St. Peter's in Woolton or St. Barnabas's, off Penny Lane. A step up came when a local promoter named Charlie McBain booked them to play at regular dances at the Broadway Conservative Club and at the Wilson Hall in Garston. The latter was in a district renowned for its toughness and the size of its Teddy Boys, among whom the fashion had lately arisen of going to skiffle dances with leather belts wrapped round their hands. At Wilson Hall one night a gigantic Ted terrified the Quarry Men by clambering onto the stage in the middle of a number. But it was only to request Paul quite politely to do his Little Richard impersonation.

Nigel Walley had left school and become an apprentice golf professional at the Lee Park course. He continued to act as the Quarry Men's manager and, despite Paul's protests, to draw equal shares: His wallet packed with their visiting cards, he would cycle assiduously with news of a booking from one member's house to the next. Through Nigel, they were even once invited to play at Lee Park golf club. "They did it for nothing, but they got a slap-up meal, and the hat was passed round for them afterward. They ended up making about twice what they would have done if they'd been getting a fee."

At the golf course, Nigel got to know a doctor named Sytner whose son, Alan, had recently opened a jazz club in the center of Liverpool. Nigel arranged for the Quarry Men to appear there, too, late in 1957. The club was in Mathew Street, under a row of old warehouses, and fully deserved its name, the Cavern. It was strictly for jazz; it allowed skiffle but absolutely barred rock 'n' roll. "We started doing Elvis numbers when we played there," Colin Hanton says. "While we were on stage, someone handed us a note. John thought it was a request. But it was from the management, saying: 'Cut out the bloody rock.' "

THREE

"IF I'D JUST SAID A FEW MORE WORDS, IT MIGHT HAVE SAVED HER"

John was to leave Quarry Bank school at the end of July 1957. He had taken his GCE ordinary-level examination and had failed every subject by one grade—a clear enough sign to Mr. Pobjoy, the headmaster, that with a little exertion he could have passed every one. Art, his outstanding subject, had been squandered with the rest. The question paper asked for a painting to illustrate the theme "travel." John, for the amusement of his exam-room neighbors, drew a wart-infested hunchback.

He sat out that last summer term, stubbornly resistant to all ideas of soon having to make his way in the world. The panoramic school photograph shows him, slumped behind his Slim Jim tie, conspicuous among a fifth form (junior class) with faces otherwise expectant and purposeful. Rod Davis, the Quarry Men's banjo player, was to enter the sixth (senior year) to do advanced-level Spanish, Latin, and history. Even Pete Shotton, John's old partner in crime, had, to his teachers' and possibly to his own great surprise, been accepted as a cadet at the police college on Mather Avenue.

Aunt Mimi's great fear was that, like his father Freddy thirty years before, John would just drift away to sea. "I remember him bringing home this boy with hair in a Tony Curtis, they called it, all smoothed back with grease at the sides. 'Mimi,' John whispered to me in the kitchen, 'this boy's got *pots* of money. He goes away to sea.' I said, 'Well, he's no captain and he's no engineer—what is he?' 'He waits at table,' John said. 'Ha!' I said. 'A fine ambition!'"

Mimi afterward stumbled on a plot between John and Nigel Walley to run away to sea as ship's stewards. Nigel says they had got as far as buying their rail tickets to the catering college. "I was rung up by this place at the Pier Head," Mimi said, ". . . some sort of seaman's employment office. 'We've got a young boy named John Lennon here,' they said. 'He's asking to sign up.' 'Don't you even *dream* of it,' I told them."

Mimi was called to Quarry Bank to discuss with Mr. Pobjoy what John might do with his life. Reviewing his meager school achievements, there seemed only one possibility—his talent for painting, design, and caricature. "Mr. Pobjoy said to me, 'Mrs. Smith, this boy's an artist, he's a bohemian. If I can get him into the art college are you prepared to keep him on for the next twelve months?' " Mimi said that she was.

Quarry Bank's valediction was, in the circumstances, quite kind. "He has been a trouble spot for many years in discipline, but has somewhat mended his ways. Requires the sanction of 'losing a job' to keep him on the rails. But I believe he is not beyond redemption and he could really turn out a fairly responsible adult who might go far."

Aunt Mimi went with him for his interview at the art college on Hope Street. "Otherwise," Mimi said, "he'd never have been able to find it. He'd only ever been into Liverpool on the one sort of bus, to the shop opposite the bus stop where he used to buy his Dinky cars."

On that day, John managed to make himself a relatively unalarming figure, submitting to both white shirt and tie and an old tweed suit that had once belonged to his uncle George. When he presented himself for enrollment, however, it was in his Teddy-Boy jacket and lilac shirt and the drainpipe jeans Aunt Mimi had forbidden him to wear. He put them on under normal trousers that he stripped off as soon as he was out of Mimi's sight.

Hope Street bisects the old, elegant, upland part of Liverpool where cast-iron letters on street corners enshrine the great shipping dynasties of Canning, Rodney, Roscoe, and Huskisson. In 1957, the whole district round the art college was a haunt of painters, sculptors, poets, and writers, sharing the faded Georgiana in amity with small businesses, guest houses, junk shops, and West Indian drinking clubs. The Anglican cathedral being still unfinished, the principal aesthetic attraction was the Philharmonic Dining-Rooms, a pub fashioned by Cunard shipwrights in crystal and mahogany, where even the Gents' urinals were carved of rose-colored marble.

Whatever hopes John may have had of a wild bohemian existence were confounded in his first week at college. He had been accepted for the intermediate course of two years' general study, followed by specialization in the third and fourth years. To his disgust, he found himself in a classroom again, obliged to study a set curriculum including figure drawing, lettering, and architecture. It was, in other words, little different from the school he had just left.

His Teddy-Boy clothes estranged him instantly from his fellow students in their duffel coats, suede shoes, and chunky Shetland sweaters with sleeves pushed up to the elbow. At art college in 1957 no one liked Elvis or rock 'n' roll: What everyone liked was traditional jazz, played in cellars flickering with beer-bottle candlelight. Indeed, the most famous Liverpool group of the moment was the Merseysippi Jazz Band, frequently to be heard on radio as well as at the Cavern Club on Mathew Street. John hated the jazz crowd, with their sweaters and their GCE passes.

His tutor on the intermediate course was Arthur Ballard, a balding, soft-spoken man who had once been a middleweight boxing champion. Himself an abstract painter of some reputation, Ballard had no great love for formal teaching and, in fact, held most of his seminars in a tiny pub called Ye Cracke, on Rice Street, where the back room was dominated by gigantic etchings of Wellington greeting Marshal Blücher and Nelson's death at Trafalgar.

Ballard noticed John Lennon first merely as an ill-at-ease Teddy Boy whose clothes were officially disapproved of and whose posture was less defiant than dejected. "The students would pin their work up, and we'd all discuss it. John's effort was always hopeless—or he'd put up nothing at all. He always struck me as the poor relation in the group. The rest used to cover up for him.

"Then one day in the lecture room I found this notebook full of caricatures—of myself, the other tutors, the students—all done with descriptions and verse, and it was the wittiest thing I'd ever seen in my life. There was no name on it. It took me quite a long time to find out that Lennon had done it.

"The next time student work was being put up and discussed, I brought out this notebook and held it up, and we discussed the work in it. John had never expected anyone to look at it, let alone find it funny and brilliant. Afterward I told him, 'When I talk about interpretation, boy, *this* is the kind of thing I mean as well. *This* is the kind of thing I want you to be doing.' "

Around the windy corner, in Mount Street, Paul McCartney still daily climbed the steps to the Institute High School. That summer he had taken two O-levels, passing in Spanish but failing Latin; in 1958, he was due to take six further subjects and then go into the sixth form. The ultimate plan, ardently supported by his father, was that Paul should go on to teacher training college. His English master, "Dusty" Durband, thought this a feasible course. He could imagine Paul one day appearing in the Institute's own staff room, or driving a modest saloon car to and from some small college of adult education.

But Paul's school career, previously so unexceptionable, now grew unsettled and erratic. The presence of John Lennon, literally beyond the classroom wall, affected both his work and his hitherto blameless conduct. More than ever, Mr. Durband noticed, he relied on charm and facility to compensate for skimped or unfinished preparation. He had even, unknown to Mr. Durband, begun to cut certain classes. There was an internal way from the Institute into the art college, across a small courtyard beside the school kitchens. John would have told him which lecture room was empty and available for guitar practice. No one in the college thoroughfares looked twice at the big-eyed youth with his black raincoat buttoned up to the neck to hide his institute tie.

The Quarry Men had been hard hit by the flux of the final school year. Rod Davis was too busy in the Quarry Bank sixth to have any time for banjo playing. Nigel Walley had contracted tuberculosis—the consequence, he thinks, of overwork in the cause of skiffle and his golf pro job. Soon afterward, Len Garry, the bass player, fell ill with meningitis and joined Nigel at the sanatorium at Fazakerley. "The other lads used to come and see us on a Sunday. They'd bring their guitars with them, and we'd have a singsong at the end of the ward."

The skiffle era was by now definitely over. Last year's big names, the Vipers, Chas McDevitt, Bob Cort, even Lonnie Donegan himself, had all dropped the word "skiffle" discreetly from their billing. In Liverpool, as all over Britain, broom handles were being restored to their brushes, thimbles returned to maternal work baskets, and tea chests, decorated with musical notes, left outside for reluctant refuse men. But if thousands of skiffle groups broke up, there were hundreds more with a taste—even a talent—for performing who decided to try their luck with rock 'n' roll.

They had the consolation of knowing that, however bad they might sound at the beginning, they did not sound much worse than professional English rock 'n' rollers. Tommy Steele, launched in 1956 as

Britain's "answer" to Elvis Presley, had set the pattern of clumsy mimicry. Since then, there had arisen numerous other "answers" to Presley as well as to the Everly Brothers, Bill Haley, the Platters, and Little Richard. There had been Marty Wilde, the Most Brothers, Russ Hamilton, Tony Crombie, and the Rockets. Some found hit records and a large following that, for all that, regarded them much as an earlier generation had regarded British films. They were poor substitutes for the real elixir, pumped from its only true source: America.

Liverpool stood closer to America than any other place in Britain. There was still, in 1957, a transatlantic passenger route, plied by ships returning weekly to tie up behind Dock Road's grim castle walls. With them came young Liverpudlian deckhands and stewards whom the neighbors called "Cunard Yanks" because of their flashy New York clothes. As well as Times Square trinkets for their girlfriends and panoramic lampshades of the Manhattan skyline for their mothers' front rooms, the Cunard Yanks brought home records not available in Britain. Rhythm and blues, the genesis of rock 'n' roll, sung by still obscure names such as Chuck Berry and Ike Turner, pounded through the back streets of row houses each Saturday night as the newly returned mariners got ready to hit the town.

The Quarry Men knew no friendly Cunard Yank who would bring them American records to copy. They had no money, either, for the new electric guitars and amplifiers now thronging Hessy's shop window. They could not even change their name, as all the other groups were doing. The Alan Caldwell Skiffle Group had become Rory Storm and the Raving Texans. The Gerry Marsden Skiffle Group now called themselves Gerry and the Pacemakers. The Quarry Men stayed the Quarry Men because that was the name lettered on Colin Hanton's drums.

In late 1957, American rock 'n' roll gave struggling ex-skiffle groups in Britain their first friend. His name was Buddy Holly, although at the beginning he figured anonymously in a group called the Crickets. Among the new performers thrown up after Presley, Buddy Holly was unique in composing many of the songs he recorded, and also in showing ability on the guitar, rather than using it merely as a prop. He gave hope to British boys because he was not pretty, but thin and bespectacled, and because his songs, though varied and inventive, were written in elementary guitar chords, recognizable to every beginner.

Paul McCartney had always used his guitar to help him make up tunes. His main objective in the Quarry Men, however, was to oust Eric Griffiths from the role of lead guitarist. One night at the Broadway Conservative Club he prevailed on the others to let him take the solo in a number. He fluffed it and, later, in an attempt to redeem himself, played over to John a song he had written, called "I Lost My Little Girl." John, though he had always tinkered with lyrics, had never thought of writing entire songs before. Egged on by Paul—and by Buddy Holly—he felt there could be no harm in trying. Soon he and Paul were each writing songs furiously, as if it were a race.

Sometimes, when the Quarry Men played at Wilson Hall, they would be watched by a boy whose elaborate Teddy-Boy hair stood up around a pale, hollow-cheeked, unsmiling face. The others knew him vaguely as a schoolfriend of Paul's and a would-be guitarist, though he played with no group regularly. His name, so Paul said, was George Harrison, and, in Paul's opinion, he would be extremely useful as a recruit to the Quarry Men. No one, to begin with, took very much notice. For Paul's friend was so silent and solemn and, at fourteen, so ridiculously young.

Paul had gotten to know him years before, when the McCartneys still lived at Speke and George used to catch the same bus to school each morning from the stop near Upton Green. Among the shouting, satchel-swinging crowd George Harrison was known as the boy whose dad actually drove one of these pale green Corporation buses. When Paul, one morning, was short of his full fare, George's mother gave him extra pennies, enough to travel all the way into Liverpool.

The Harrisons, Harry and Louise, had married in 1929 when she worked in a greengrocer's shop and he was a seaman on ships of the White Star line. The thin, dapper, thoughtful young shipboard waiter proved a perfect match with the jolly, warm-hearted young woman whose mother had been a lamplighter during the Great War. In 1931, a daughter, Louise, was born to them and, in 1934, their first son, Harold Junior. Harry quit the sea soon afterward, braving the worst of the Depression to be nearer his wife and children. After fifteen months on the dole he managed to get a job with the corporation, initially as a bus conductor. A third child, Peter, was born in 1940, at the height of the Liverpool Blitz.

The family lived then at Wavertree, in the tiny row house in Arnold

Grove that Harry and Louise had occupied since their marriage. It was here, on February 25, 1943, that Louise gave birth to her fourth child and third son, George. When Harry came upstairs to see the new baby, he was amazed at its likeness to himself. Louise, too, noticed the dark eyes that, even then, cautiously appraised the world.

Though Harry earned little on the buses, he made sure his large family lacked for nothing. Louise was a capable and also a happy mother, whose laughter rang constantly through the house. George, as the baby of the family, was petted by everyone, from his big sister Lou downward. Accustomed to being the center of attention, he was, at the same time, independent, solitary, and thoughtful. Even as a toddler he forbade Louise to go with him to school, for fear she would get mixed up with "all those nosy mothers." It horrified him to think they might ask her what he did and said at home.

The wartime baby "bulge" had brought in its wake an acute shortage of space at primary schools. George—like his mother—had been baptized a Catholic, but could be fitted in only at an Anglican nursery school, Dovedale Primary, near Penny Lane. He was there at the same time as John Lennon. Though the age-gap was too great for them ever to become friendly.

In 1954, George went on to Liverpool Institute, where he was put into the form below Paul McCartney. Unlike Paul, however, he soon began to do extremely badly. Alert and perceptive, with an unusually good memory, he developed a hatred of all lessons and school routine. Detentions, even beatings, could not lift the firmly shut barriers of his indifference, and soon his teachers found it less fatiguing to leave him alone.

He acquired further disreputability by coming to school in clothes that did not conform to the Institute's regulation gray and black. Already, in admiration of the dockland Teds, his hair was piled so high that a school cap could only cling on precariously at the back. He would sit in class, his blazer buttoned over a canary yellow waistcoat borrowed from his brother Harry, his desk-top hiding trousers secretly tapered on his mother's sewing machine. His shirt collar, socks, and shoes growing pointed all uttered the defiance still hidden in his gaunt face while some master or other, like "Cissy" Smith, was sarcastically making fun of him.

In 1956, his mother noticed him drawing pictures of guitars on every scrap of paper he could find. He had heard Lonnie Donegan, and seen Donegan's guitar. Soon afterward, he came to Louise and asked her to give him three pounds to buy a guitar from a boy at school. She did so, but when George brought it home, he accidentally unscrewed the neck from the body, then found he couldn't put them back together. The guitar lay in a cupboard for weeks until his brother Peter took it out and mended it.

Learning to play even the first simple chords in the tuition book was an agonizing process for George. Unlike Paul, he had no inherited musical ability; nor was he, like John, a born adventurer. All he had was his indomitable will to learn. His mother encouraged him, sitting up late with him as he tried and tried. Sometimes he would be near to tears with frustration and the pain of his split and dusty fingertips.

His brother Peter had taken up the guitar at about the same time, and together they formed a skiffle group, the Rebels. Their first and only engagement was for ten shillings each at the Speke British Legion Club. At George's insistence, they left the house one at a time, ducking along under the garden hedge so that "nosy neighbors" wouldn't see.

The family had moved by now to a new council house, in Upton Green, Speke. It was on his bus journey into Liverpool each morning that George met Paul McCartney. Though Paul was a year older and in a higher grade at school, their passion for guitars drew them together. Paul would come across from Allerton to practice in George's bedroom, bringing with him his 'cello guitar with the upside-down scratch plate. George now had a guitar that his mother had helped him buy for thirty pounds—a far better one than Paul's, with white piping and a cutaway for reaching the narrow frets at the bottom of the neck.

To pay back his mother George did a Saturday morning delivery round for a local butcher, E. R. Hughes. One of the houses on his round belonged to a family named Bramwell, whose son Tony had met Buddy Holly during the star's recent British tour. Tony Bramwell would lend George his Buddy Holly records to listen to and copy. Confidence came from the songs built of easy chords, like E and B_7; the changes he could do now from one chord to the other; the solo bass runs that, painfully, unsmilingly, he was learning to pick out for himself.

Paul introduced him to the other Quarry Men one night late in 1957, in the suburb of Liverpool called Old Roan. "It was at a club we used to go to, called the Morgue," Colin Hanton says. "It was in the cellar of this big old derelict house. No bar or coffee or anything, just a cellar with dark rooms off it, and one big blue lightbulb sticking out of the wall."

The others crowded round George, interested in what they could see of his guitar with its cutaway body. They listened while George played all he had been carefully rehearsing. He played them "Raunchy," an eight-note tune on the bass strings; then he played the faster and more tricky "Guitar Boogie Shuffle."

George was not asked to join the Quarry Men that night. Indeed, they never asked him formally to join. He would follow them with his guitar around the halls where they played, and in the interval stand and wait for his chance to come across and see Paul. Generally, he would have some newly mastered chord to show them, or yet another solemn-faced bass string tune. If another guitarist had failed to arrive, George would be allowed to sit in.

No one other than Paul took him very seriously. John Lennon in particular, from the pinnacle of seventeen years, considered him just a funny little eager white-faced lad who delivered the weekend meat. Even George's ability as a guitarist became a reason for John to tease him. "Come on, George," he would say. "Give us 'Raunchy.' " George played "Raunchy" whenever John asked him to, even sitting on the top deck of the number 500 bus to Speke.

The great benefit of letting George tag along was that it brought the Quarry Men another safe house in which to practice. At weekends or on truant days they could always find refuge at George's. Mr. Harrison would be out on the buses, but Louise always welcomed them, never minding the noise. She developed a soft spot for John Lennon, in whom she recognized much of her own scatty humor. She used to say that John and she were just a pair of fools.

Aunt Mimi, by contrast, did not like John to associate with someone who was, after all, a butcher's errand boy, and whose accent was so thickly Liverpudlian. George called at Mendips one day to ask John to go to the cinema, but John, still thinking him just a "bloody kid," pretended to be too busy. "He's a real whacker, isn't he?" Mimi said bitterly when George had gone. "You always go for the low types, don't you, John?"

To Mimi, in her innocence, George—and even Paul—were the bad influences: If John had not met *them* he would still be happy in ordinary clothes. "Paul used to wear these *great* long winklepicker things, with buckles on the sides. And as for *George*! Well, of course you couldn't wish for a quieter lad. But one day when I came into the house, there was George with his hair in a crew cut, and wearing this *bright* pink shirt. I told him, '*Never* come into this house with a shirt like that on again.' "

With George sitting in more and more, the Quarry Men now found themselves with a glut of guitarists. For, as well as John and Paul, there was still Eric Griffiths, the chubby-faced boy who had been a founder member, and who did not realize his growing superfluousness. At length, the others decided that Eric must be frozen out. Colin Hanton, his best friend in the group, was visited by Nigel Walley and asked to go along with the plan. They still needed Colin or, rather, his drum set that cost thirty-eight pounds.

"We didn't tell Eric we were going to Paul's house to practice," Colin says. "He rang up while we were there. The others got me to talk to him and explain how things stood. Eric was pretty upset. He couldn't understand why they'd suddenly decided to get rid of him. I told him there wasn't a lot I could do about it. I could tell that if they wanted somebody out, he was out."

Between John and Aunt Mimi, the atmosphere had grown increasingly turbulent. Mimi had to support him at art college for a full year until he qualified for a local authority grant; she therefore felt doubly entitled to pronounce adversely on his clothes, his silly music, and the friends who were, in Mimi's opinion, so very ill-attired and unsuitable. Pete Shotton was only one of John's friends who witnessed memorable fights between him and the aunt who so resembled him in strength of will and volatile spirits. "One minute," Pete says, "they'd be yelling and screaming at each other; the next they'd have their arms round each other, laughing."

Behind Mimi's briskness and sarcasm lay the real dread of losing John. She was only a substitute, as she well knew, for his real mother, her sister Julia. And John, in his teenage years, had grown adept at playing on that fear. After a row at Mendips, he would storm out and go straight to Julia's house, remaining there for days, sometimes weeks on end. With Julia, life was always pleasant and carefree. Having made no sacrifice for him, she bore no grudge against his indolence: she pampered him, bought him unsuitable clothes, and made him laugh. Her man friend, John Dykins, would frequently press on him a handful of the evening's restaurant tips.

Mimi, aware that she was being exploited, sometimes took dramatic measures to call John's bluff. "They used to keep a little dog called Sally," Pete Shotton says. "John really thought the world of her. One time, when he'd walked out and gone off to Julia's, Mimi got rid of Sally, saying there'd be no one left in the house to take her for walks. That was the only time I ever saw John really heartbroken and showing it—when he came home to Menlove Avenue and didn't find Sally there."

On the evening of July 15, 1958, Nigel Walley left his house on Vale Road and took the short cut over the stile into Menlove Avenue to call for John. At Mendips, he found Mimi and Julia talking together by the front garden gate. John was not there, they said—he had gone to Julia's for the whole weekend. Julia, having paid her daily visit to Mimi, was just leaving to catch her bus.

"We'd had a cup of tea together," Mimi said. "I said, 'I won't walk to the bus stop with you tonight.' 'All right,' Julia said, 'don't worry. I'll see you tomorrow.' "

Instead, it was Nigel Walley who walked with John's mother through the warm twilight down Menlove Avenue toward the big road junction. "Julia was telling me some jokes as we went," Nigel remembers. "Every time you saw her, she'd have a new one she'd been saving up to tell you." About two hundred yards from Mimi's house, they parted. Nigel continued down Menlove Avenue and Julia began to cross the road to her bus stop.

Old tram tracks, concealed by a thin hedgerow, ran down the middle of the busy divided highway. As Julia stepped through the hedge into the southbound lane, a car came suddenly out of the twilight, swerving inward on the steep camber. Nigel Walley, across the road, turned at the scream of brakes to see Julia's body tossed into the air.

"I can picture it to this day. I always think to myself, 'If only I'd said just one more sentence to her, just a few words more, it might have saved her.' "

There was first the moment, parodying every film melodrama John had ever seen, when a policeman came to the back door at Springwood and asked if he was Julia's son. The feeling of farce persisted in the taxi ride with Twitchy to Sefton General Hospital; in the sight of the faces waiting to meet them there. For Julia had died the instant the car had struck her. The shock was too much for Twitchy, who broke down with grief and dread of what would now become of him and his children by Julia.

Even in the moment of her death it must have seemed to John that his mother was someone else's property.

The anguish was drawn out over several weeks. The car that killed Julia had been driven by an off-duty policeman. Pete Shotton was working on attachment from police college in the local CID department that investigated the case. The inquest exonerated the driver of any blame. "I went as a witness," Nigel Walley says, "but me being only a boy, they didn't give much weight to what I'd seen. Mimi took it very hard—shouting at the fellow who'd driven the car; she even threatened him with a walking stick."

John, in the weeks after Julia's death, reminded Pete Shotton of the times they would be caned at Quarry Bank, when John used to fight with all his strength not to let out a single sound of pain. Few people knew the extent of his grief since few understood his feeling for the happy, careless woman who had let her life become separate from his. At college, he would sit for hours alone in the big window at the top of the main staircase. Arthur Ballard saw him there once, and noticed that he was crying.

Elsewhere, if his desolation showed, it would be in manic horseplay with his crony Jeff Mohamed, both in college and at the student pub, Ye Cracke, where John was increasingly to be found. "They'd come back to college pissed in the afternoon," Arthur Ballard says. "I caught John trying to piss into the lift shaft." Ballard was human enough to understand the reason for such behavior. But even Pete Shotton was shocked to see how much of the time John now spent anesthetized by drink. "I remember getting on a bus once and finding John on the top deck, lying across the backseat, pissed out of his mind. He'd been up there for hours with no idea where he was."

He had never been short of girlfriends, though few were willing to put up for long with the treatment that was John Lennon's idea of romance. His drinking, his sarcasm, his unpunctuality at trysts, his callous humor, and most of all, his erratic temper drove each of them to chuck him, not infrequently with the devastating rejoinder that is the specialty of Liverpool girls. "Don't take it out on me," one of them screamed back at him, "just because your mother's dead."

Not long after Julia's death his eye fell on Cynthia Powell, an intermediate student in a group slightly ahead of his. Cynthia was a timid, bespectacled girl with flawless white skin. Hitherto, if John had noticed her at all, it was merely to taunt her for living in Hoylake, on the

Cheshire Wirral, where primness and superiority are thought to reign. "No dirty jokes please—it's Cynthia," he would say while she blushed, knowing full well that dirty jokes would inevitably follow.

This was the girl who, nevertheless, found herself drawn to John Lennon with a fascination entirely against her neat and cautious nature. She dreaded, yet longed for, the days when John would sit behind her in the lettering class and would pillage the orderly pattern of brushes and rulers she had laid out for the work. She remembers, too, a moment in the lecture hall when she saw another girl stroking John's hair, and felt within herself a confusion that she afterward realized was jealousy.

They first got talking one day between classes, after some of the students had been testing one another's eyesight and Cynthia discovered John's vision to be as poor as hers, despite his refusal to be seen in glasses. Encouraged by this, she took to loitering about the passages in the hope of meeting him. She grew her perm out, dyed her mousy hair blonde, exchanged her usual modest outfit for a white duffel coat and black velvet trousers, and left off her own spectacles, with frequently catastrophic results. The bus she caught each day from Central Station regularly carried her past Hope Street and the college stop and on into Liverpool 8.

John approached her formally at an end-of-term dance at lunchtime in one of the college lecture rooms. Egged on by Jeff Mohamed, he asked her to dance. When he asked her for a date Cynthia blurted out that she was engaged—as was true—to a boy back home in Hoylake. "I didn't ask you to marry me, did I?" John retorted bitterly.

In the autumn term of 1958, amid much local astonishment, they began going steady. Cynthia's friends—especially those who had already passed through the John Lennon experience—warned her strongly against it. Equally, in John's crowd no one could understand his interest in a girl who, although nowadays had somewhat improved in looks, still had nothing in common with John's ideal woman, Brigitte Bardot. Even George Harrison forgot his usual shyness in John's company to declare that Cynthia had teeth "like a horse."

Against these defects there was about her a gentleness, a malleability that John, brought up among frolicsome and strong-willed aunts, had not met in a female before. To please him, she began to dress in short skirts, fishnet stockings, and garter belts that shocked her to her suburban soul as well as giving her much anxiety while she waited for him outside Lewis's department store, terrified of being mistaken for a "totty," or Liverpool tart. For him, each night, she braved the last train out to Hoylake, and its cargo of hooligans and drunks.

She was, even then, terrified of John—of his reckless humor no less than the moods and sudden rages and the ferocity with which he demanded her total obedience. He was so jealous, Cynthia says, he would try to beat up anyone at a party who so much as asked her to dance. He would sit for hours with her in a pub or coffee bar, never letting go her hand. It was as if something stored up in him since Julia's death could be exorcised, or at least quieted, through her.

Elvis was tamed. The gold-suited figure whose lip had curled on behalf of all British adolescence, whose defiant slouch had altered the posture of a generation, could now be seen meekly seated in a barber's chair preparatory to serving two years in the United States Army. No one yet quite comprehended how much this repentance was a stroke of incomparable showmanship by his manager, "Colonel" Tom Parker, a one-time huckster at fairs and carnivals. It mattered less to America than to Britain, which Elvis had not yet visited, although rumors of his coming were continually rife. As the colonel beamed fatly and Elvis shouldered arms, showing what a decent kid he had been all along, England's rockers vowed that, in their eyes at least, "the King" would never abdicate.

There was some consolation in an upsurge of British rock 'n' roll, and a television show capable of reflecting it. *Oh Boy!* every Saturday night, on the solitary commercial channel, filled a dark stage, as in some Miracle play, with major American performers like Eddie Cochran and Gene Vincent, and their British counterparts, Marty Wilde, Dickie Pride, Duffy Power, Vince Eager, and Tony Sheridan. There was also a new young Elvis copy, Cliff Richard, whose lip unfurled at the corner like a faulty window blind, and whose backing group, the Shadows, featured in equal prominence around him, stepping to and fro with their guitars in unison. Their first single, "Move It," was the first successful British version of American rock 'n' roll, with its junglelike bass rhythm and clangorous lead guitar.

Up in Liverpool, the three guitarists in a group still called the Quarry Men watched *Oh Boy!* every Saturday night, crawling close to the television screen when the Shadows came on, to try to see how they did that stupendous "Move It" intro. Paul worked it out first and at once jumped onto his bike with his guitar to hurry over to John's.

Of all the original, top-heavy skiffle group, apart from John himself, only one member remained. They still had Colin Hanton, the little upholsterer, and the drum set he was paying thirty-eight-pounds for in installments. They only kept him on, as Colin well knew, for the sake of those drums. Having a drummer, however unsatisfactory, made the difference between a *real* group and three lads just messing around with guitars.

Without Nigel Walley to manage them, their playing was on a haphazard basis, at birthday parties, youth club dances, or social clubs, where they would perform for a pie and a pint of ale. To Colin, the ale was consolation for knowing they only wanted him for his drums, and for the increasingly acid remarks made by Paul about his playing.

Both John and George now owned electric guitars. John's was a fawn-colored Hofner "Club 40," semisolid, with two knobs on it, while George had persuaded his mother to help him raise thirty pounds for a Hofner "Futurama," a cheap version of Buddy Holly's two-horned Fender Stratocaster. But neither could yet afford to buy an amplifier. Better-equipped groups would usually lend them an amp for their orphan guitar leads. Failing that, George the trainee electrician would wire both his and John's instruments to the club or dance hall's public address system.

In mid-1958, they scraped up £5 between them to make a demonstration record that, they hoped, might act as a more impressive calling card than the printed ones in Nigel's wallet. The "studio" they chose was in the back room of a private house in Kensington, Liverpool, owned by an elderly man named Percy Phillips. The group that day comprised John, Paul, George, Colin Hanton, and a temporary recruit named John Lowe. Their money bought them a two-sided shellac disk, its A-side a cover version of the Crickets' "That'll Be the Day" with John singing lead and George rather tinnily reconstructing Buddy Holly's guitar licks. Of far more individuality was John's B-side vocal, a country-ish ballad called "In Spite of All the Danger," written by Paul with help from George. However, the first duty of all amateur groups in 1958 was to mimic hot sounds in the charts. Their Crickets cover was what they played and replayed, to themselves and anyone else who would listen.

Colin Hanton was still with them when a second chance arrived to become Carroll Levis "Discoveries." Again, with every other local group, they presented themselves at the Empire theater to be auditioned by the great man—this time for his Granada Television talent show. They got through the Liverpool heats, and were booked to appear in the semifinals at the Hippodrome Theater studios in Manchester. Before they left they changed their name to Johnny and the Moondogs.

The journey to Manchester was overshadowed by their general poverty. "We hadn't worked out in advance how much it would cost us to get there by train and by bus," Colin Hanton says. "When we got on the bus in Manchester Paul discovered he hadn't got enough money to get home again. He was panicking all over the place. 'What am I going to *do*? This is *serious*.' A bloke stood up at the front to get off and, as he passed Paul, he stuck a two-shilling piece (10p) into his hand. Paul got up and yelled down the bus stairs after him, 'I love you.' "

Poverty robbed them of their opportunity to appear on television with Carroll Levis' infant ballerinas and players of musical saws. The final judging, on the strength of the audience applause for each act, did not take place until late evening, after the last bus and train back to Liverpool had gone. Johnny and the Moondogs, with no money to spend on an overnight hotel stay, had to leave before the finale.

Colin Hanton appeared with them as drummer for the last time one Saturday night at the Picton Lane busmen's social club. They had got the engagement through George Harrison's father, who acted as MC there and, with Mrs. Harrison, ran a learners' ballroom dancing class. From George's dad had come the important news that a local cinema manager would be dropping in to see whether Johnny and the Moondogs were suitable to put on in the interval between his Sunday picture shows.

"At the beginning, that night went really well," Colin Hanton says. "We were all in a good mood—pulling George's leg and saying, 'There's George's dad; where's his bus?' It was a real stage they'd put us on, with a curtain that came up and down. The curtain got stuck, so we played six numbers, not five, in our first spot. The busmen and clippies were all cheering, they really dug us.

"In the interval, we were told, 'There's a pint for you lads over at the bar.' That pint turned into two pints, then three. When we went on for the second spot, we were *terrible*. All pissed. The bloke from the Pavilion never booked us. There was a row about it on the bus going home, and I thought, 'Right. That's it. I'll not bother playing with them again.' " At the next stop, even though it was before his destination, Colin hauled his drum set off the bus and did not turn up for any further gigs.

For some time afterward Johnny and the Moondogs, or the Quarry Men, or whatever they felt like calling themselves, remained poised on the edge of extinction. They would still get together and play, but only at small events like birthday parties, where the lack of a drummer did not count as much. One night, when they all arrived in different colored shirts, they called themselves the Rainbows. John and Paul would sometimes work as a duo, the Nurk Twins. George regularly sat in with a more stable group, the Les Stewart Quartet, at a club in West Derby called the Lowlands.

A short distance away, in the quiet thoroughfare of Hayman's Green, stood a large Victorian house belonging to a family named Best. Johnny Best had originally been Liverpool's main promoter of boxing matches in the city's six-thousand-seat stadium. He had lately separated from his wife, Mona, leaving her the big old house with her bedridden mother, her two sons, Peter and Rory, a collection of paying guests, and assorted Eastern mementoes including a Hindu idol that flexed its many arms in the front hall.

Peter, her elder son, was then eighteen, and in the sixth form (senior year) at Liverpool Collegiate Grammar School. An outstanding scholar and athlete, he was also unusually handsome, in a wry, brooding way, with neat, crisp, wavy hair that gave him more than a look of the film star Jeff Chandler. If, in addition, he was somewhat modest and slow to push himself, then "Mo," as he called his mother, would always be there to do it for him.

Under the house were extensive cellars, used for storage and the boys' bicycles. Pete and Rory, fatigued by the long summer holiday of 1958, asked Mona Best if they could make a den down there for themselves and their friends. There were so many friends that Mrs. Best suggested making the cellar into a real club, like the Lowlands and city espresso bars. For the rest of that year, she, her two sons, and a team of potential members redecorated the cellar, installing bench seats and a counter above which, as a final touch, Mrs. Best painted a dragon on the ceiling. Her favorite film being *Algiers*, with Charles Boyer, she decided to call the new club the Casbah.

There then arose the question of finding a group to play on club nights. One of the girl helpers mentioned Ken Browne, who played at the Lowlands in Les Stewart's quartet. Ken Browne paid the Casbah a visit while redecorations were still in progress, bringing with him another quartet member, George Harrison. "George didn't seem to show too much enthusiasm for what we were doing," Mona Best said, "but Ken Browne threw himself heart and soul into it. He'd come over and help us with the work at weekends."

When George came back he brought with him two other musicians for the Casbah's resident group. "John Lennon walked in with Paul McCartney, and John's girlfriend, Cyn. We were still painting—trying to get ready for our opening night. John got hold of a paint brush to help us, but he was without his glasses and as blind as a bat. He started putting paint on surfaces which didn't require paint. And all in gloss when I'd told him to use undercoat. On opening night, some of the paint still wasn't quite dry."

In sedate West Derby, the Casbah Coffee Club caught on with teenagers at once. Mona Best ran it in person, selling coffee, sweets, and soft drinks behind the miniature bar. John, Paul, George, and Ken Browne played, without a drummer and using Ken Browne's 10-watt amplifier, for three pounds a night among the four of them. They all grew friendly with the Bests, especially with Pete, the handsome, taciturn elder son who, despite his plan to become a teacher, was keenly interested in rock 'n' roll and show business. The group proved such an attraction that, at weekends, Mrs. Best would hire a doorman to keep out the rougher element.

"It all went fine," Mona Best said, "until this one night when Ken Browne turned up with a heavy cold. I could see he wasn't well enough to play. I said to him, 'Look, you go upstairs and sit with Mother'—he often did that; she was bedridden, you see, and he'd sit and talk to her. I said, 'I'll bring a hot drink up to you.' But Ken said no, he'd stay down in the club and watch. Just John, Paul, and George played, and at the end, I gave them 15s (75p) each. There was a bit of murmuring; then they said, 'Where's the other 15s?' 'I've given it to Ken,' I told them.

"They didn't like that. They wanted the full three pounds. But it was too late. I'd already given Ken his fifteen shillings. There was a bit of arguing, and Ken said, right, that was it, he'd finished with them. The other three walked out of the club there and then.

"Pete, my elder boy, had been getting more and more interested, watching the others play. I remember Ken Browne saying to him, 'Right. I'm out of that lot. Come on, Pete: Why don't you and I get a group up now?' "

Twice each week, Arthur Ballard would leave the college of art on Hope Street to conduct a private tutorial with the student he considered the most gifted of all under his charge. The student, a white-faced, tiny boy named Stuart Sutcliffe, refused to work in college; he had his own cramped studio, in the basement of a house in Percy Street, where Ballard would visit him, bringing a half-bottle of Scotch whisky for refreshment. The tutorial was a morning's talk, during which Sutcliffe never stopped painting. "He worked with large canvases, which wasn't at all fashionable then," Arthur Ballard says. "He was so small, he almost had to jump with his brush to reach the top."

Among the students, Stu Sutcliffe was something of a cult. His pale, haunted face, topped by luxuriantly swept-back hair, gave him a more than passing resemblance to James Dean, the Hollywood star who had become legendary to that generation for the hectic fame and shortness of his life. Stu was aware of the resemblance, cultivating it with dark glasses and an air of brooding far from his true personality.

He was born of Scottish parents in Edinburgh in 1940. His father, Charles, a marine engineer, moved to Liverpool on wartime attachment to Cammell Laird's shipyard and subsequently went to sea as a ship's engineer. The rearing of Stuart and his two younger sisters was left to their mother, Millie, a preschool teacher. Charles and Millie had a volatile relationship, veering from intense mutual affection to passionate rows, generally on the eve of his departure back to sea. From the earliest age, Millie Sutcliffe said, Stu strove to take on the role of her protector. "I'd sometimes be sitting in my chair with my head in my hands. Stuart would sit at my feet, looking up at me. 'You're tired,' he'd say. 'Come on, we'll put the little ones to bed, then you and me must have a talk.' "

He had entered art college from Prescot Grammar School, below the normal admittance age, and had quickly revealed a talent of dazzling diversity. His first terms, in addition to prosaic curriculum work, produced notebooks thronging with evidence of a facility to reproduce any style from Matisse to Michelangelo. Derivative as his student work was, it had a quality that excited Arthur Ballard—a refusal to accept or transmit anything according to convention. "Stu was a revolutionary," Ballard says. "Everything he did crackled with excitement."

Early in 1959, the path of Hope Street's most promising student crossed that of its most uninspired and apathetic one. At Ye Cracke, the student pub in Rice Street, beneath the etchings of Wellington greeting Blücher at Waterloo and Nelson's death at Trafalgar, Stu Sutcliffe fell into conversation with John Lennon.

The intermediary was a friend of Stu's named Bill Harry, a curly-haired boy who had won his way from a poor childhood on Parliament Street to become the college's first student of commercial design. Bill was a prolific amateur journalist, a writer and illustrator of science fiction "fanzines," and, like Stu himself, an omnivorous reader. They would sit for hours in Ye Cracke, discussing Henry Miller and Kerouac and the "beat" poets, Corso and Ferlinghetti.

In Bill Harry, John found someone not standoffish and superior as he had thought all his fellow students to be, but down-to-earth, friendly, humorous, and encouraging. Bill knew already of John's interest in writing, and one lunchtime at Ye Cracke, asked if there was anything of John's that he could read. He remembers with what embarrassment John dragged some scraps of paper from his jeans pocket and handed them over. Instead of the Ginsberg or Corso pastiche he had expected, Bill Harry found himself reading a piece of nonsense about a farmer that made him gurgle with laughter.

Stu Sutcliffe's effect on John was more complex. For Stu, in 1959, resembled neither Teddy Boy nor jazz cellar habitué. He had evolved his own style of skin-tight jeans, pink shirts with pinned collars, and pointed boots with high, elasticized sides. His dress, in fact, was disapproved of by the art college far more than John's but was tolerated because of his brilliance as a student.

Stu's passionate commitment to his painting, and to art and literature in all young and vital forms, communicated itself to John in a way that no formal teaching had been able to do. From Stu, he learned of the French Impressionists, whose rebellion against accepted values made that of rock 'n' roll seem marginal. Van Gogh, even more than Elvis Presley, now became the hero against whom John Lennon measured the world.

John's sudden enthusiasm for his college studies to some extent benefited Paul also. Paul, still revising for O-levels at the institute, was only too glad to join in intellectual discussions, passing himself off as a student from the nearby university. For George Harrison, it was more arduous, since John among his art college cronies was even more inclined to be witty at George's expense. But he was fifteen now, and not such a kid, and learning to answer John back.

This new era revived the group, which had been languishing again since the dispute at Mrs. Best's. Stu and Bill Harry both sat on the Students' Union committee, and were thus able to get bookings for John, Paul, and George to play at college dances. The trouble was, although John and George had electric guitars, they no longer had Ken Browne and his 10-watt amplifier. On Stu Sutcliffe's recommendation, the Students' Union agreed to buy an amplifier for them to use, on the understanding, of course, that it should not be taken away from college.

Stu's interest in rock 'n' roll was a purely aesthetic one. He passionately wanted to join a group as an adjunct to the personal image he had created for himself. As John and he became closer friends, the idea grew that Stu, in some or other capacity, should join John's group. That he possessed no ability on any instrument was not considered a disqualification. If he were to buy a guitar—or, better still, some drums—he surely would be able to learn in the way the other three had. Unfortunately, Stu, with his small grant and his straitened family circumstances, had no money to spend at Hessy's music shop.

In 1959, the biennial John Moores Exhibition took place at Liverpool's illustrious Walker Art Gallery. Mr. Moores was the city's commercial patriarch, deriving fortunes from football pools, shops, and mail-order catalogs, of which a sizable part was philanthropically devoted to encouraging the arts on Merseyside. This was the second Moores Exhibition, offering four thousand pounds in prize money and attracting some two thousand entries from all over the British Isles. A canvas submitted by Stu Sutcliffe was one of the handful selected for hanging.

Aunt Mimi remembered John's unfeigned pleasure in Stu's achievement. "He came *rushing* in to tell me. . . . 'You'll never guess; it's the Moores Exhibition. You must come and see it. And look *nice!*'

"We went to the Walker Art Gallery and John took me up to this enormous painting. It seemed to be all khaki and yellow triangles. I looked at it and I said, 'What *is* it?' Well! John got hold of my arm and hustled me outside; I wasn't allowed to see another picture in the show.

'How could you *say* a thing like that, Mimi?' He gave his chest a big thump, and bellowed, 'Art comes from in here!' "

As well as hanging in one of Europe's principal galleries, Stu's painting was bought, by the great John Moores himself, for sixty-five pounds. "He'd never really had any money before," Millie Sutcliffe said. "I knew he'd got one or two little debts he needed to pay. The rest would see him right, I thought, to buy his paints and canvases for a few weeks.

"His father was home, and went up to Stuart's room while he wasn't there. It was his father who found this thing that Stuart had spent *all* the John Moores prize money on. 'That's right, Mother,' he said. 'It's a bass guitar. I'm going to play with John in his group.' "

FOUR

"THE BASS DRUM USED TO ROLL AWAY ACROSS THE STAGE"

In Slater Street, on the edge of Chinatown, there was a little coffee bar, with copper kettles in its window, called the Jacaranda. John Lennon, Stu Sutcliffe, and their art college friends went there almost every day, between classes or in place of them. The coffee was cheap, toast with jam cost only fivepence a slice, nor was the management particular about the time its customers spent wedged behind the little kidney-shaped tables. Whole days could be spent, over one cold coffee cup, looking through the window steam at passing Chinese, West Indians, dockers, and men going to and from the nearby unemployment office.

To the Jacaranda's black-bearded owner, Allan Williams, John and his friends were "a right load of layabouts." Williams had studied them at length while passing coffees and toasted sandwiches through from the back kitchen where his Chinese wife, Beryl, cooked and kept accounts. He had particularly noticed the slightly built boy in dark glasses whom the others teased for carrying art materials round with him in a carrier bag. He could not but notice the one called John, who expertly dredged money from the purse of the blonde girl who sat next to him, and could even cajole free drinks and snacks from the more susceptible waitresses.

"The Jac" was not Williams's sole enterprise. He had, in his time, pursued many trades, among them plumber, artificial jewelry–maker, and door-to-door salesman. Being a Welshman, naturally he had a voice. Indeed, he had almost trained for the operatic stage. His Welsh tenor was heard, instead, in the Victorian pubs and West Indian shebeens round Liverpool 8, where Williams pursued an energetic but as yet unspecific career as a bohemian and entrepreneur.

At intervals, his curly haired, stocky figure would swagger back along Slater Street to the tumbledown house where, on a capital of a hundred pounds, he had opened his Jacaranda coffee bar. The "right load of layabouts" would still be there. Prying their coffee cups away, Allan

Williams would remark with heavy sarcasm that *they* were never going to make him his fortune.

In the world outside Liverpool unabated disapproval of rock 'n' roll had worn it into a more acceptable shape. The word was "rock" no longer, but "pop." The taste—again dictated by America—was for clean-cut, collegiate-looking youths whose energy had left their pelvic regions and gone into their ingratiating smiles. The British idol of the hour was a former skiffler named Adam Faith, with the looks of a haunted Cassius and a voice that all the artifice of recording engineers could not rid of its heavy adenoids. A ballad called "What Do You Want?"—or, as Adam Faith enunciated it, "Puwhat Do Yuh Pwant?"—went to number one late in 1959, using an arrangement of pizzicato violins unashamedly copied from Buddy Holly. Holly lodged no suit for plagiarism, having died in an air crash eight months earlier.

But while Britain listened to Adam Faith and pop, Liverpool listened to rhythm and blues. The Cunard Yanks were bringing over records by a new young black performer still confined by his own country to the low, indecent level of "race" music. His name was Chuck Berry; the songs he sang were wry and ragged, vividly pictorial eulogies to girls and cars, the joys and neuroses of American urban life. His verbal felicity and subversive wit had instant appeal for young men who, although white, felt themselves hardly less segregated in their own land from the more privileged and glamorous south. All over Merseyside, in ballrooms, town halls, church meeting houses, even swimming baths and ice-skating rinks, there were amateur R&B groups pumping out Berry's repertoire along with that of other kindred black performers such as Little Richard and Fats Domino.

By far and away Liverpool's most adulated group in those days were Rory Storm and the Hurricanes. Rory, a blond, amiable youth known by day as Alan Caldwell, was afflicted by a stammer that, fortunately, vanished when he opened his mouth to sing. He had been an outstanding athlete and swimmer, and would enliven his stage performance by feats of acrobatics and climbing. At the Majestic ballroom in Birkenhead he would shin up a pillar from the stage to the promenade balcony. At the Tower Ballroom, downriver in New Brighton, he would crawl about inside the one-hundred-foot-high dome. His occasional falls increased his drawing power. His group had lately acquired a new drummer—a slightly built boy from the Dingle, with mournful eyes, prematurely graying side-whiskers, and a habit of burdening his fingers with cheap rings. This drummer's name was Richard Starkey, but he preferred, in emulation of his Wild West heroes, to be known as Ringo Starr.

After Rory Storm in popularity came Cass and the Casanovas, a four-man group whose drummer, Johnny Hutch, was the most powerful on Merseyside. They said of Johnny Hutch—as, indeed, he said of himself—that he could take his brain out and lay it on the table and his drumsticks would still go on hitting in time.

The Saturday dances over, most of the groups would drive back from the suburbs into Liverpool to congregate at Allan Williams's Jacaranda coffee bar. At night in the basement there was dancing to a West Indian steel band. Though no alcohol could be served legally, much was drunk in spiked coffee and soft drinks.

Rory Storm, Brian Casser, and Duke Duval were personalities whom John Lennon and his followers held in awe. For John's group, such as it was, figured nowhere in the leagues of local favoritism. No less an authority than Johnny Hutch, the Casanovas' drummer, had given his opinion that they "weren't worth a carrot."

To begin with, they still lacked a drummer. This wouldn't have mattered so much with a strong undercurrent of bass guitar. But Stu Sutcliffe had only just begun learning to play the big Hofner "President" bass he had bought with his John Moores prize. The President hung heavy on Stu's slight frame; his slim fingers found difficulty in stretching to the simplest chord shapes. He would stand turning half-away so the audience could not see how little and how painfully he was playing.

They had had, and lost, one good opportunity at the Casanova Club, a Sunday afternoon jive session in a room above the Temple restaurant on Dale Street. The promoter, Sam Leach, agreed to try them out in support of his resident group, Cass and the Casanovas. But the club members had little time for a group with no drummer and only one small tinkling amp—a group that did not go in for suits and step dance routines like Cliff Richard's Shadows, but instead wore strange, scruffy, arty black crewneck sweaters and tennis shoes, and jumped and leapt in wild asymmetry. And when Paul McCartney began to sing in his high, almost feminine voice, there were titters of amusement from some of the girls.

They did little better at Lathom Hall, out at Seaforth where the Mersey broadens against the rim of Albert Dock. The night's main group were the Dominoes, featuring Kingsize Taylor, a vast youth visible by day cutting up meat in a local butcher's shop. Paul, John, George, and Stu had been hired merely to play during the interval. They were so bad that the management ordered them offstage after their second song. When the Dominoes came on again, Kingsize Taylor saw John, Paul, and George standing near the stage, each scribbling furiously on a piece of paper. "They were writing down the words of the songs as we sang them. They'd take turns to scribble down a line each of 'Dizzy Miss Lizzie.' "

They still practiced for hours on end, at George's or Paul's house, using a tape recorder of the old-fashioned sort that grew warm after a couple of hours' use. They had no idea of the way they wanted to be. They knew only that they wanted to be nothing like Cliff Richard's neat, smiling, step-dancing Shadows. A tape has survived of a long, rambling blues sequence with George on lead guitar, his fingers stumbling frequently over half-learned phrases, John and Paul strumming along, and Stu Sutcliffe keeping up on bass by playing as few notes as possible. At one point, Paul's voice breaks in impatiently with a kind of impromptu jazz scat-singing. Later there are attempts at various rhythms, first rockabilly, then Latin American, then a note-for-note copy of the Eddie Cochran song "Hallelujah I Love Her So." Suddenly they break into a song that was among the first ever written by John Lennon—"The One After 909." The beat lifts; their voices coalesce: For a moment they are recognizable as what they were to become. Then they go back to sitting round while George, painfully, tries to learn the blues.

From the same period there is a letter drafted by Paul in his scholarly hand, soliciting a mention in some local newspaper after a chance encounter with one of the journalists. The letter claims group accomplishments as much academic as musical; it makes great play with the fact that John goes to art college, and confers on Paul himself a fictitious place "reading English at Liverpool University." Paul's songwriting partnership with John is said to have produced "more than 50 numbers," among them "Looking Glass," "Thinking of Linking," "Winston's Walk," and "The One After 909." To cover every option, the group is credited with a "jazz feel" and a repertoire of "standards" such as "Moonglow," "Ain't She Sweet," and "You Are My Sunshine." "The group's name," Paul wrote, "is . . ." They still had not been able to make up their minds.

Stu Sutcliffe had lately been evicted from his basement in Percy

Street for painting all the furniture white. He suggested to John that they both move into their friend Rod Murray's flat in Gambier Terrace, a big, windswept Victorian promenade overlooking the Anglican cathedral. The flat was principally floorboards, strewn with records, stolen traffic signs, and the mattresses used by various seminomadic tenants. Bill Harry, a frequent sleeper in the bath, remembers all-night talk sessions in which he and Stu elaborated their plan to write a book that would give Liverpool the same cultural identity that Kerouac and the beat poets had given America. John Lennon's chief contributions were word games and charades of elaborate craziness.

Though John soon left Gambier Terrace, his friendship with Stu continued. The two were together most of the day, when Paul and George could not escape class at the Institute. They would sit for hours in the Jacaranda, Stu sketching and crayoning while John, with his wolfish smile, cadged coffees from the softer-hearted waitresses. So it came about that Allan Williams, with his talent for using people, discovered a way of using even two penniless art students.

Williams was currently engaged in his first major venture as an entrepreneur. He had hired St. George's Hall, Liverpool's chief public building, as the venue for a gala modeled on the Chelsea Arts Ball in London. John and Stu found themselves roped in to design and build the decorated carnival floats whose ritual destruction was the best-known feature of the London event. On the day of the ball Williams used them as a laboring gang to manhandle the floats across St. George's piazza, under the disapproving eye of Victoria and Albert, and into the Great Hall with its mosaic floor, its marble busts of Peel and George Stephenson, and its towering pipe organ.

The 1959 Liverpool Arts Ball was an event prophetic of Allan Williams's career as an impresario. The comedian Bruce Forsyth was among VIP guests who watched, not only the ritual destruction of the carnival floats, but also flour and fire extinguisher fights and intermittent attempts to play rock 'n' roll on the Civic organ. At midnight, balloons came down from a web of football goal nets suspended in the ceiling. After that, owing to employee error, the heavy, greasy nets themselves fell onto the heads of the crowd.

Among the promoters of British pop music in the late 1950s, none had so potent a reputation as Larry Parnes. It was Parnes who, in 1956, metamorphosed Tommy Steele, Britain's first rock 'n' roller, from a Cockney merchant seaman he had spotted strumming a guitar in a Soho drinking club. Tommy Steele's colossal success with British teenagers was due largely to his youthful manager's intuitive brilliance as an agent and image-builder and the jealous care with which, following Colonel Tom Parker's example, he guarded his money-spinning protégé. Though Tommy Steele had now somewhat diminished as a pop attraction, the enterprises of Larry Parnes had prospered and multiplied.

By 1959, Parnes controlled what he himself liked to call a stable of the leading British male pop singers. Most were ingenuous youths from unknown provincial cities who had somehow found their way to London and the 2i's coffee bar in Old Compton Street, hallowed as the place where Larry Parnes had spotted Tommy Steele. Whether they could sing or not Parnes fashioned them into lucrative teen idols by giving them stage names that combined the homely with the exotic: Billy Fury, Marty Wilde, Vince Eager, Duffy Power, Dickie Pride, Johnny Gentle. A closet homosexual who made extensive use of the casting couch, he styled his protégés to reflect his own private fantasies, equipping them all with virtually identical blow-waved hair, tight jeans, and pointy cowboy boots. It was wonderfully ironic, therefore, that the adult anti–rock 'n' roll lobby should have complained so vociferously about their sexual power over teenage *girls*. Several of them actually lived at Parnes's flat on London's Cromwell Road, directly opposite Baden Powell House, the headquarters of the Scout movement. When not coaching his charges in deportment or stagecraft Parnes would produce a pair of powerful binoculars and gaze longingly through them at the Boy Scouts across the road.

As well as furnishing the cast of early TV pop shows such as *Oh Boy!* and *Drumbeat,* Parnes used his stable to create self-contained traveling shows that for British fans in places far from London represented the sole chance to see live rock 'n' roll music. Larry Parnes shows played at theaters and cinemas, but also at town halls and rural corn exchanges (grain markets that had been turned into cultural and community venues). No audience was too far-flung or insignificant to be visited by the glossy-haired, unflappable young man whom the music business— believing money to be his sole preoccupation—had nicknamed Mister Parnes Shillings and Pence.

Early in 1960, Larry Parnes promoted a tour headed by two imported American stars, Eddie Cochran and Gene Vincent. Cochran, whose "Summertime Blues" had sold a million copies in 1958, was a twenty-one-year-old Oklahoman with the hulking pout of an Elvis run to fat. Vincent was a twenty-five-year-old ex-sailor famous for his wailing voice, his group the Bluecaps, and a classic piece of rock 'n' roll gibberish called "Be Bop a Lula." Partly disabled from a motorcycle accident, he performed anchored to the stage by a leg iron and irradiating depravity and ill health. Nor was this present tour destined to build up his constitution.

In Liverpool, as in every city along its route, the Cochran-Vincent show was a sellout. Larry Parnes himself was at the Empire theater to watch the wild welcome his artists received, even in this remote corner of the land. Elsewhere, amid the shouting and stamping, three would-be rock 'n' rollers from a group last known as Johnny and the Moondogs strained their eyes to try to see the fingering of Eddie Cochran's guitar solo in "Hallelujah I Love Her So." In yet another seat, the proprietor of the Jacaranda coffee bar suddenly perceived that there might be easier ways to a fortune than by attempting to bring the Chelsea Arts Ball to Liverpool. In Allan Williams's own words, "I could smell money. Lots of it."

Afterward, Williams sought out Larry Parnes and, as one impresario to another, invited him back to the Jacaranda. By the end of the night Parnes had been talked into bringing back Eddie Cochran and Gene Vincent for a second concert, promoted in partnership with Allan Williams at the city's boxing stadium. Half the program would consist of Parnes acts; the other half would be provided by Williams from among local groups like Rory Storm and the Hurricanes and Cass and the Casanovas. The concert, lasting several hours, was fixed to take place after Eddie Cochran and Gene Vincent had finished their current tour.

At the very last minute, however, there was a hitch. Cochran and Vincent had appeared at the Hippodrome theater, Bristol, and were returning to London by road. Near Chippenham, Wiltshire, their rental car skidded and struck a tree. Eddie Cochran—who, by one of those bilious musical ironies had just recorded a song called "Three Steps to Heaven"—suffered fatal injuries. Gene Vincent and another passenger, the songwriter Sharon Seeley, were both seriously hurt.

A telephone call to Larry Parnes confirmed the news that Allan

Williams had heard over the radio. Eddie Cochran would not be able to appear at Liverpool boxing stadium. Gene Vincent, despite fresh injuries added to his residual ones, might be fit, Parnes thought; just the same, it would be wiser to cancel the promotion. Williams, having sold most of the tickets, and feeling death to be insufficient as an excuse to a Liverpool audience, insisted the show should go ahead, and feverishly went in search of more local groups to pad out the program.

His search took him, among other places, to Holyoake Hall, near Penny Lane, and one of the better run local jive dances. The hall, unlike most, had its own regular emcee and disk jockey, Bob Wooler. A clerk in the railway dock office at Garston, Wooler possessed an encyclopedic knowledge of local bands and their personnel. On his earliest recommendation Allan Williams booked Bob Evans and the Five Shillings and Gerry and the Pacemakers, the latter an up-and-coming quartet whose leader, Gerry Marsden, worked on the railway also, as a van delivery boy.

The Gene Vincent boxing stadium show, jointly promoted by Larry Parnes and Allan Williams, thus inadvertently became the first major occurrence of a brand of teenage music indigenous to Liverpool and the Mersey. By an inscrutable irony the three individuals destined to carry that music into undreamable galaxies of fame were not then considered competent enough to take part. John Lennon, Paul McCartney, and George Harrison had to be content with ringside seats and watching Rory Storm, Cass and the Casanovas—even their old rivals, the group that featured the midget Nicky Cuff.

The concert proceeded on a note of rising pandemonium, at the height of which Rory Storm was sent out with his incapacitating stammer to appeal for calm. The show's best performance was unanimously felt to be that of Gerry and the Pacemakers, singing "You'll Never Walk Alone" from Rodgers and Hammerstein's *Carousel.* No more inappropriate introduction could have been given to the infirm, black leather–clad figure of Gene Vincent himself, who was at last propelled through the ropes into the boxing ring. As the ringside spectators made a rush to join him, Larry Parnes and Allan Williams trotted round briskly, stamping on their hands.

It was shortly after this memorable night that John Lennon sidled up to Williams at the Jacaranda's kitchen door and muttered, "Hey, Al, why don't you do something for us?" John had been there with George and

Stu Sutcliffe after the boxing stadium show when Williams brought the great Larry Parnes back to discuss further copromotions. Parnes, impressed by the Liverpool music, had hinted at the possibility of using local groups to back solo singers from his stable when touring brought them northward.

Allan Williams, while thinking no more highly of John's group than anyone else, felt he owed them a favor in return for the arts ball floats. Though not prepared to offer them to Larry Parnes, he did agree to help Johnny and the Moondogs become better organized. They, in return, would do such small general jobs as Allan Williams required.

Williams further promised to try to find them the drummer they so chronically lacked. From Cass, of Cass and the Casanovas, he heard of a man named Tommy Moore who sometimes sat in on drums at Sam Leach's club and who, despite owning his own full set, belonged to no group permanently. Within the week, Tommy Moore had been persuaded by Allan Williams to throw in his lot with Johnny and the Moondogs.

The new recruit was a small, worried-looking individual of thirty-six, whose daytime job was driving a forklift truck at the Garston Bottle-making Works. For all that, in his audition at Gambier Terrace, he proved to be a better drummer than any who had ever sat behind Johnny and the Moondogs. When he showed himself able to produce the slow, skipping beat of the Everly Brothers' song "Cathy's Clown," even Paul McCartney seemed satisfied.

Tommy Moore began practicing with them downstairs at the Jacaranda, in preparation for the work that Allan Williams had promised them when they were good enough. Williams, meantime, used them as odd-job men to redecorate the Jac's primitive ladies' lavatory. John and Stu Sutcliffe were also encouraged to cover the brick walls of their rehearsal room with voodooish murals.

Tommy soon noticed what peculiar tensions were at work within Johnny and the Moondogs. "John and Paul were always at it, trying to outdo each other. It was them at the front and the rest of us way behind. George used to stand there, not saying a word. And didn't they used to send up that other lad, Stuart! Oh, they never left off teasing him. They said he couldn't play his bass—and he couldn't, though he tried."

To begin with, Allan Williams would allow them to play to the Jacaranda customers only when his regular attraction, the Royal

Caribbean Steel Band, had the night off. Since the cellar had no microphone stands, two girls had to be persuaded to kneel in front of John and Paul, holding up hand mikes attached to a mop handle and broom. "I could have retired on what we used to get for playing at the Jac,'" Tommy Moore said. "A bottle of Coke and a plate of beans on toast."

The great Larry Parnes, meanwhile, had contacted Allan Williams again about the possibility of using Liverpool musicians as backing groups for the solo singers in his stable. It happened that Mister Parnes Shillings and Pence was experiencing difficulty in finding London bands willing to go on tour in the north and Scotland for the rates of pay he offered. When Parnes contacted Allan Williams again, it was with a request that Williams should marshal some local groups for audition as possible sidemen for Parnes's biggest male pop star, Billy Fury.

The news caused a particular stir in Liverpool because Billy Fury was himself a Liverpudlian. Born Ronnie Wycherley in the tough Dingle area, he had been a Mersey tugboat hand until two years earlier, when his girlfriend had sent Larry Parnes some of the songs he had written. Parnes had worked the usual transformation with a tempestuous stage name, a brooding persona, and a series of hit records sung in an Elvis-like mumble. Billy Fury, it was further announced, would be coming up to Liverpool with his manager to attend the auditions in person.

Every group that frequented the Jacaranda was agog for what seemed a heaven-sent opportunity. Williams, in the end, narrowed the field down to Rory Storm and the Hurricanes, Cass and the Casanovas, Derry Wilkie and the Seniors, and Johnny and the Moondogs. In Allan Williams's opinion, Johnny and the Moondogs were now ready for something more than decorating the ladies' lavatory.

One pressing requirement, before Larry Parnes saw them, was for a change of name. What they needed was something spry and catchy, like Buddy Holly's Crickets. On an empty page in his sketch-book, Stu Sutcliffe wrote "The Beetles." He was not thinking of small black insects but the motorcycle gang led by Marlon Brando in America's prototype youth rebellion film, *The Wild One*. Although *The Wild One* had been banned by the timorous British film censor, pop culture–vultures like Stu and his circle would undoubtedly have known all about it. Coincidentally, Buddy Holly's own group had made the same connection a couple of years earlier and almost named themselves the Beetles before deciding on the Crickets.

"Crickets" were one thing, but "Beetles," even allowing the Brando precedent, were quite another. No group that wished to be taken seriously in the late fifties could possibly identify itself with so lowly and unattractive a form of life. Still, the idea was kicked around, undergoing various barely serious mutations along the way. John, unable to resist any pun, turned it into "Beatles," as in beat music. Stu himself took to spelling it "Beatals" in the sense of beating all competition. Nonetheless, he is the one who must go down in history as the only true begetter.

However it might be spelled, the name was greeted with the same disbelieving scorn by both their supporters and rivals at the Billy Fury audition. Allan Williams pleaded with them to think of something—anything—else if they didn't want the great Larry Parnes to laugh them into extinction. This opposition had the predictable effect of making John determined now to go on as the "Beetles," "Beatles" or "Beat-als." A more persuasive voice, however, was that of Brian Casser, lead singer with Cass and the Casanovas: If they had to ally themselves with bugs, Casser urged, then at least stick to the conventional formula of such-and-such and the so-and-so's. Prompted by memories of R. L. Stevenson's *Treasure Island*, he suggested "Long John and the Silver Beatles." Though John jibbed at calling himself Long John, the Silver Beatles won the vote.

The place fixed for the auditions was a small workingmen's club, the Wyvern, in Seel Street, just round the corner from the Jacaranda. Allan Williams had recently acquired the premises with the object of turning it into a plushy London-style night spot. Punctual to the minute, in through the half-demolished foyer walked Larry Parnes, silk-suited and affable, accompanied by the nervy-looking ex–tugboat hand, currently the biggest name in British pop music, who cared rather less for stardom than for the dog and tortoise he was permitted to keep at his manager's London flat.

Down in the basement the Silver Beatles viewed the competition with dismay. Every group was locally famous, smartly suited, and luxuriously equipped. Derry and the Seniors had been well known in Liverpool for years as an authentic rhythm-and-blues group featuring a black singer, Derry Wilkie, an electric keyboard, and a real live saxophone. Johnny Hutch of Cass and the Casanovas was already setting up the sequined drum set that he was said to be able to play in his sleep. Rory Storm was there, deeply tanned, with his Italian-suited Hurricanes.

Rory's drummer, the little sad-eyed, bearded one, came from the Dingle also, and had been in Billy Fury's class at school. Neither John nor Paul in those days much liked the look of Ringo Starr.

Parnes, sitting with Billy Fury at a small table in the twilight, was impressed by the power and variety of the music. Derry and the Seniors and Rory Storm's Hurricanes were both marked down as strong contenders for the prize. Parnes also favored Cass and the Casanovas, thanks mainly to their bass player, Johnny Gustafson, a black-haired, extremely good-looking boy. "Johnny Gus," in fact, was later called down to London to experience the Parnes star-making process on his own.

The Silver Beatles, when their turn came, made rather less of an impression. "They weren't a bit smart," Larry Parnes remembered. "They just wore jeans, black sweaters, tennis shoes—and lockets." There was a delay as well, owing to the nonarrival of Tommy Moore, who had gone in search of some stray pieces of drum equipment at the Casanova Club. At length, when Tommy still had not appeared, Johnny Hutch had to be persuaded to sit in with them.

A snapshot, taken in mid-audition, shows the Silver Beatles exactly as Larry Parnes saw them that day at the Wyvern social club. John and Paul occupy the foreground, back to back madly bucking and crouching over their cheap guitars. To the right stands George, his sole concession to rhythm a slight hanging of the head. Stu Sutcliffe, to the rear with his overburdening bass guitar, turns away as usual to hide his inadequate playing. In the background, Johnny Hutch sits at his magnificent drums, showing a great deal of patterned ankle sock and, very clearly, bored to death.

As to what Larry Parnes thought of them, there are conflicting eyewitness accounts. Allan Williams's version is that both Parnes and Billy Fury were knocked out by the Silver Beatles, excepting Stu Sutcliffe. Parnes would have signed them at once, at one hundred pounds per week, provided they would agree to drop Stu. It was John Lennon's curt refusal to betray his friend, so Williams says, that robbed them of their first big chance.

Parnes himself, unfortunately, had no recollection of finding fault with Stu's bass playing. To Parnes, the eyesore of the group was the worried, rather elderly-looking man who arrived halfway through the audition and took over from Johnny Hutch on drums. Tommy Moore had finally made it across town from Dale Street. "I thought the boys in front were great," Parnes said. "The lead guitar and the bass, so-so. It was the *drummer*, I told them, who was wrong."

What Larry Parnes really wanted, it transpired, were cut-rate musicians to accompany his lesser-known artists on tour to Scotland. Cass and the Casanovas were first to be so engaged, as the backing group for a gravel-voiced Parnes singer named Duffy Power.

The next letter from Larry Parnes to Allan Williams concerned the Silver Beatles. In mid-May, Parnes was sending another of his stable, Johnny Gentle, on a two-week Scottish tour. The Silver Beatles could have the job of backing him, for the same as Cass and the Casanovas had received: eighteen pounds each per week.

The offer sent the Silver Beatles into transports of elation. Since the Wyvern social club audition they had thought they'd lost any chance of finding stardom via Larry Parnes. That Johnny Gentle was the least-known of all Parnes's singers did not diminish the excitement of being offered their first work as professionals, of going on tour the way the big names did, of performing in real cinemas and theaters and staying in hotels the whole night.

All five immediately set about disentangling themselves from their everyday commitments in mid-May. For Stu and John it was simply a matter of cutting college for two weeks. It was less simple for Tommy Moore, whose girlfriend set great store by his weekly wage packet from Garston bottle works. Tommy pacified her with visions of the wealth he would bring back from across the border.

George Harrison, too, was now a working man. He had left the Institute grammar school at sixteen, without O-levels and, for want of anything better, had applied for a job as a window dresser at Blackler's department store. That vacancy had been filled, but there was another one for an apprentice electrician. To be an apprentice, as his two elder brothers were, represented both a safe and an honorable course. But the only way he could get time off to go to Scotland was to take his summer holiday early.

The greatest ingenuity was shown, as usual, by Paul McCartney. He had to find a method of extricating himself from the Institute sixth form where, supposedly, he was deep in revision for his forthcoming A-level exams in English and art. His friend Ivan Vaughan told him he would be mad to risk those A-levels for the sake of the Scottish tour.

Somehow he managed to convince his father that two weeks off in term time would aid his revision by giving his brain a rest.

Before they set off they decided that to be real pop musicians they must all adopt stage names. Paul took to calling himself Paul Ramon, thinking it had a hothouse 1920-ish sound. George, whose idol was Carl Perkins, called himself Carl Harrison, and Stu became Stu de Stael, after the painter. John Lennon and Tommy Moore decided not to bother.

They embarked by train from Lime Street, wearing the jeans and black sweaters and tennis shoes that were also their stage outfits, and carrying a selection of borrowed amplifiers that Tommy Moore viewed with deep mistrust. "The amps got by—just. George was the sparks if anything went wrong. I'd always stand well back while he was fiddling with the plugs. My drums didn't have everything they ought to have had either. I hadn't got a spur to hold the bass drum down. When Paul and John got going in one of their fast Chuck Berry numbers, the bass drum used to go rolling away across the stage."

The tour struck complications from the start. Duncan McKinnon, Parnes's Scottish intermediary, did not like the look of the Silver Beatles. They liked even less the look of the small van in which they and Johnny Gentle were expected to travel through the Highlands. Nor was there any time to rehearse with Johnny, a handsome young hunk who not long previously had been a merchant seaman putting into Birkenhead.

This particular member of Parnes's stable suffered chronically from stage nerves, which he would attempt to calm by drinking large quantities of lager. Even so, he insisted on taking his turn at the driving because that was the most comfortable seat. On about the second day, somewhat the worse for lager, he drove the vehicle, not at all gently, into the rear of a parked Ford Popular car with a couple of old ladies sitting in it. The impact dislodged all the luggage and equipment from the interior suitcase rack and hurled it on top of Tommy Moore.

Tommy was taken away in an ambulance, badly concussed, with his front top and bottom teeth loosened. That night, as he lay in the hospital—it was in Banff, he thought—wearing borrowed night clothes and heavily sedated, the others arrived and hauled him out of bed for the night's performance. He remembers playing the drums, still groggy, with a bandage round his head.

Tommy Moore, with most of his teeth loose and some pain-killing drugs the hospital had given him, climbed back into the van next morning for the journey onward, to Stirling, Nairn, and Inverness. "I hadn't much idea where we were. I looked out once and saw the big distillery. That's how I knew we'd got to the Highlands."

According to Larry Parnes, the Silver Beatles went down better than any other backing group he had sent to Scotland. Parnes said that Johnny admitted they were getting more applause than he was, and urged his manager to sign them up without delay. Parnes, however, found the management of solo singers strenuous enough. "Maybe it sounds silly, but I just didn't want the worry of a five-piece group."

Johnny and the Silver Beatles traveled as far north as Inverness, arriving too early in the morning to go to their hotel. "We had to walk the streets, and all around the harbor next to the fishing boats," Tommy Moore said. "That was the finish as far as I was concerned. I'd had enough of them all—especially Lennon. And I was hungry."

Their money did not get through to them until the very end of the fortnight. Tommy Moore remembered that on the train journey back to Liverpool he had a couple of pounds in his pocket. "I went and sat with Stuart on the journey. He was the only one of them I could stand by that time."

At Lime Street, Tommy said good-bye rapidly and went to his flat in Smithdown Lane where his girlfriend awaited him. "She said, 'How much have you brought back then?' I told her, 'A couple of quid.' 'A couple of *quid*!' she said. 'Do you realize how much you could have earned in two weeks at Garston bottle works?' "

For the Silver Beatles the most important consequence of the Scottish tour was that Allan Williams had at last begun to take them seriously as a group. The Welshman, through his company Jacaranda Enterprises, now looked after several bands, booking them out to dance promoters in Liverpool and "over the water" on the Cheshire Wirral. The Silver Beatles were added to the portfolio Williams hawked around, in Birkenhead, New Brighton, and Wallasey, using the big Jaguar that was well known to the Mersey Tunnel Police.

The Grosvenor ballroom in Wallasey was run by Les Dodd, a small, brisk stationery retailer with bright blue eyes and a back as straight as a slow foxtrot. Les Dodd had promoted strict tempo ballroom dancing at the Grosvenor since 1936, resisting the successive contagions of swing, bebop, skiffle, and rock 'n' roll, but by 1960, even he had begun to realize that his customers wanted something more untamed than his regular musicians, The Ernie Hignett Quartet.

For his first reluctant "Big Beat" dance, on June 6, 1960, Les Dodd paid Allan Williams ten pounds for a group whose name—if Mr. Dodd understood aright—was the Silver Beetles. So he advertised them, together with Gerry and the Pacemakers, as "jive and rock specialists." The same display advertisement carried a reassurance that on Tuesday the Grosvenor's strict tempo night would take place as usual.

Not long after Les Dodd began booking them, Tommy Moore decided he had had enough. He had continued as drummer after the Scottish tour, despite the loss of his front teeth, existing on a weekly share-out that, as his girlfriend constantly reminded him, could be bettered by almost any type of laboring work. One evening, when the Silver Beatles met before crossing the river to Wallasey, Tommy Moore was not among them. He had gone back to his former, more lucrative occupation of driving a forklift truck.

The Silver Beatles, knowing too well the disgrace of being drummerless, tried hard to win back their elderly colleague. En route for Wallasey they called at the Garston bottle works, found Tommy in the yard on night shift, and pleaded with him not to quit. Tommy Moore's only reply was to swivel his forklift away in the opposite direction. Another night, when Tommy was at home, they went to his flat on Smithdown Road and shouted up at his window. His girlfriend, resentful of what had been done to her loved one's income and teeth, requested the Silver Beatles to fuck off.

Though Tommy Moore had gone, his drums remained behind. Each week, when they set out for the Grosvenor or for Neston Institute, the drum set would be taken along. Before the first number John Lennon would announce half-facetiously that anyone in the audience who fancied himself as a drummer was welcome to come up and have a try. The joke misfired badly one night at the Grosvenor when a huge Wallasey Ted named Ronnie accepted the invitation, sat in on Tommy's drums, and produced a din that would have been no worse if he had thrown the set from the top of a high building. An SOS call brought Allan Williams to the Grosvenor just in time to dissuade the beaming tough from electing himself to permanent membership.

Williams was now booking them into Liverpool halls where gang warfare—between girls no less than boys—was considered essential to a full night's entertainment. At Hambledon Hall or Aintree Institute there always came a point in the evening, just after the pubs had closed, when up to fifty Teds would come in at once and pass along the jivers, slit-eyed with beer and hope of "bother." Most notorious of all were Garston Swimming Baths, known locally as "the Blood Baths," so violent and gory were the battles fought over the floor that concealed the pool. The gangs, which bore tribal names such as The Tiger or The Tank, would sometimes forget their enmities in a common assault on the no less frightening squads of bouncers, equipped with bloodlust and weapons to rival theirs. One legendary bouncer was of such size that he never needed to use his fists. A single jog from his stomach could send an assailant flying. Another, more imaginative promoter employed no stewards other than one little old lady to issue tickets. If a Ted cut up rough the little old lady would shriek at him, "You stop that or I'll tell your mum." These were words to cow the most ruthless Teddy Boy.

Musicians were not immune from attack, particularly if they hailed from a part of Liverpool held in local disfavor, if they played Chuck Berry when the gang preferred Little Richard, or if one of them, however unwittingly, attracted the attention of a local patron's "judy." Guitars and drums were frequently smashed and microphone stands turned into clubs and lances if the stage seemed likely to be carried by storm.

The Silver Beatles witnessed their share of violence. At the Grosvenor in Wallasey a regular uproar took place as local Teds clashed with invading cohorts from New Brighton or Birkenhead. At Neston Institute one night a sixteen-year-old boy was booted to death during one of their performances. Even John, who fancied himself as a fighter, now cared more for protecting his guitar when the chairs and beer bottles began to fly or girls rolled into view on the dance floor, scratching and spitting.

Their luck held until one night in June or July, when Williams had sent them to Litherland Town Hall, a low-lying municipal building in the north of Liverpool. During or after their performance something was said or implied that upset a faction in the audience. An ambush was laid for the Silver Beatles as they made their way through the car park back to their van. In the ensuing scuffle, Stu Sutcliffe went down and received a kick in the head.

Millie Sutcliffe had waited up for Stu that night. She found him in his room with blood still pouring from the gash in his head. He told her it had happened after the Litherland dance and that John and Pete Best had come to his rescue, John "mixing it" so ferociously with the attackers that he broke one of his own fingers.

"There was blood all over the rug—everywhere," Mrs. Sutcliffe said. "I was going to get the doctor but Stuart wouldn't allow me to do it. He was so terribly adamant. 'Mother,' he said, 'if you touch that phone, I go out of this house and you'll never see me again.' "

FIVE

THE GREAT FREEDOM

The Silver Beatles hit their lowest point in the summer of 1960. Still drummerless, they had given up trying to persuade dance promoters like Les Dodd and Sam Leach to book them. Their only regular engagement was at a strip club part-owned by Allan Williams, off Liverpool's Upper Parliament Street. Williams paid them ten shillings each to strum their guitars while a stripper named Janice grimly shed her clothes. At Janice's request, the musicians stuck to standards such as "Moonglow" and the "Harry Lime Theme," and they even gamely attempted "The Gipsy Fire Dance" from sheet music.

The New Cabaret Artistes Club was run for Williams by a West Indian named Lord Woodbine. Born in Trinidad, Woody earned a varied living as a builder and decorator, steel band musician, and freelance barman. His ennoblement—after the fashion of calypso singers—derived from a certain self-possessed grandeur as much as from the Woodbine cigarette permanently hinged on his lower lip.

Lord Woodbine ran his own club, the New Colony, in the attic and basement of a semiderelict house in Berkeley Street. The Silver Beatles played there, too, sometimes in the afternoons, while merchant seamen danced against hard-faced whores, and occasional troublemakers were pacified by the sight of the cutlass that Lord Woodbine kept under the bar.

Williams promised he would make something better happen for them soon. And Williams, by a sequence of cosmic blunders into 1,000-to-1 chances, did exactly that.

It all started when Williams returned to his coffee bar, the Jacaranda, one night and heard silence when he expected to hear the Royal Caribbean Steel Band. The entire band, he was told, had been lured away by a German theatrical agent to appear at a club in Hamburg. Down in the basement, set about by Stu Sutcliffe's voodoo murals, not a single 40-gallon steel drum remained.

To Williams, as to most Englishmen of that era, Hamburg, more than London or even Paris, was a city of breathtaking wickedness. British soldiers stationed after World War II in Germany brought back extraordinary tales of entertainments purveyed by the Reeperbahn, Hamburg's legendary cabaret district—of women wrestling in mud and sex displays involving pythons, donkeys, and other animal associates. Such things could only be whispered about in a Britain where the two-piece bathing suit was still considered rather daring.

Evidently, along with everything else, there were music clubs along the Reeperbahn. Williams's curiosity was further aroused by letters from various members of the Royal Caribbean Steel Band, showing no remorse at their sudden disappearance but telling Williams guilelessly what a great place Hamburg was and urging him to come across with some of his Liverpool beat groups to share it.

His first idea was to take the Silver Beatles with him to Hamburg on an exploratory trip, but chronic shortage of cash prevented this. Instead, he got them to make a tape recording of their music, in company with Cass and the Casanovas and a local trad jazz band, the Noel Lewis Stompers, to be played to the Hamburg impresarios.

The journey that Williams made was in every sense characteristic. Wearing a top hat and accompanied by Lord Woodbine, he took a cheap charter flight to Amsterdam, intending to proceed to West Germany by train. In one eventful night in the Dutch capital, he succeeded in drinking champagne from a chorus girl's shoe; passing Lord Woodbine off as a genuine English aristocrat; and being thrown into the street after making matador passes at a flamenco dancer with his coat.

The next evening found him in a similar state, temporarily parted from Lord Woodbine and dazzled by the overarching lights of the Grosse Freiheit, that small but crowded tributary of the Hamburg Reeperbahn, whose name in English means "The Great Freedom."

Halfway down the Grosse Freiheit, opposite a Roman Catholic church, Williams stumbled into a downstairs club called the Kaiserkeller. He found it to be decorated in confusedly nautical style, with booths like lifeboats, barrels for tables, and a mural depicting life in the South Sea Isles. On a tiny central space several hundred people danced while an Indonesian group performed Elvis Presley songs in German.

Williams demanded to speak to the proprietor and, after some delay, was shown into the presence of a short, broad-chested man with a quiff of sandy hair, a turned-up nose, and a disabled leg that little inhibited his movements. Before the conversation had progressed far a waiter came in to report a disturbance in the club area. Williams, through the open door, saw a squad of waiters systematically working over a solitary customer. Snatching from his desk drawer a long ebony cosh, the proprietor left the room with an agile, hopping gait, to lend them a hand.

The talk then resumed on amiable lines. Allan Williams introduced himself as the manager of the world's best rock 'n' roll groups. The Kaiserkeller's owner, whose name was Bruno Koschmider, inquired if they were as good as Tommy Steele. Williams assured him they were better than Elvis Presley. For proof he brought out the tape he had made of the Silver Beatles and others. But when it was played on Herr Koschmider's tape recorder, nothing could be heard but scrabble and screech. Somebody back in Liverpool had blundered.

Having failed, as he thought, to convert Hamburg's Reeperbahn to Liverpool beat music, Allan Williams returned to being a functionary of the great Larry Parnes. The Silver Beatles—or plain Beatles, as they now defiantly called themselves—receded somewhat in Williams's mind. His chief property was the rhythm-and-blues group Derry and the Seniors, which Parnes had promised work in a summer show at Blackpool. The entire band, in expectation of this, gave up their jobs to turn professional. Then, at the last minute, a letter arrived on elaborately crested Parnes notepaper canceling the engagement.

An enraged deputation led by Howie Casey, the Seniors' sax player, confronted Williams at his Blue Angel Club in Seel Street. Casey was a youth of powerful build, and Williams promised hastily to find them some alternative work. In sheer desperation, he packed the entire five-piece group and their equipment into his Jaguar and headed for the only place he could think of where work for a rock 'n' roll band might magically exist. He was taking them, he said, to the famous 2i's coffee bar in London. There, in the home of skiffle, where Tommy Steele had first been discovered, something or other must surely turn up.

Fortune now smiled upon the agitated Welshman to the ludicrous, implausible extent that Fortune sometimes does. Upon entering the 2i's, whom should he see first but a small, barrel-chested West German gentleman with a quiff of sandy hair, a turned-up nose, and a disabled leg not at the moment noticeable. It was Herr Bruno Koschmider, proprietor of the Kaiserkeller club in Grosse Freiheit, Hamburg.

Koschmider, it transpired, had been deeply impressed by Williams's visit to his establishment, playing unintelligible tapes and boasting of rock 'n' roll groups better than Elvis. Not long after Williams's dispirited return to Liverpool, Herr Koschmider had decided to visit England and hear these wonderful groups for himself. Naturally, however, it was not Liverpool he visited, but London, and the famous 2i's coffee bar.

He had already paid one visit to the 2i's and had signed up a solo singer, Tony Sheridan, to appear at the Kaiserkeller. Sheridan in fact was a gifted performer, temporarily down on his luck. At the Kaiserkeller, he had been such a sensation that Bruno Koschmider had decided to sack his Indonesian Elvis impersonators and go over completely to English rock 'n' roll. He was thus at the 2i's a second time, hoping to hire another English group. He had not yet done so when Derry and the Seniors walked in.

It was the work of a few minutes for Williams to get Derry and the Seniors up and playing on the 2i's stage. Despite having had nothing to eat but some stale cake, they performed so well that Bruno Koschmider booked them for his Kaiserkeller club on the spot. They would receive thirty marks each per day—about twenty pounds a week—with travel expenses and accommodation found. A contract was drafted with the help of a German waiter from the adjacent Heaven and Hell coffee bar.

Derry and the Seniors set off by train from Liverpool to Hamburg with five pounds between them and no work permits. If challenged, Allan Williams said, the four tough-looking Liverpool boys and their black lead singer should pretend to be students on vacation. The story did not convince German frontier officials, and at Osnabruck the entire group was ordered off the train and held in custody until Bruno Koschmider could be contacted to vouch for them.

The next news to reach Williams was a great deal better. Derry and the Seniors, together with Tony Sheridan and his band, were a hit at Herr Koschmider's Kaiserkeller. Together with rapturous postcards from various musicians, a letter arrived from Koschmider himself, asking Williams to send across a third group to play in another of Koschmider's clubs, the Indra.

The group Williams wanted to send was Rory Storm and the Hurricanes. They, however, were already committed to a summer season at

Butlin's Skegness holiday camp. Gerry and the Pacemakers, his second choice, did not fancy going abroad. So Allan Williams, rather reluctantly, wrote to Bruno Koschmider, telling him to expect a group called the Beatles.

Shortly afterward, a letter of protest arrived from the Seniors' lead singer, Derry Wilkie. It would spoil things for everyone, Derry said, if Allan Williams sent over "a bum group like the Beatles."

The offer came when John Lennon's art college career was approaching the point of collapse. He had recently sat—or rather half-sat—the exam by which his past three years' work would be assessed. The test paper in lettering, his weakest subject, was supposed to have been completed in May, while the Beatles were touring Scotland with Johnny Gentle. Cynthia, John's girlfriend, had risked her own college career by doing the paper for him, racked by pains from a grumbling appendix, under a single lightbulb at the Gambier Terrace flat.

And yet, for all John's inexhaustible laziness, there were still glimpses of brilliance, in his cartoons and poster designs, which made Arthur Ballard, his tutor, think him worth defending. In Ballard's view, the only logical place for John was the newly opened faculty of design: unfortunately, however, he could not convince the relevant department head. "I had a row with the fellow in the end," Ballard says. "I told him if he couldn't accept an eccentric like John, he ought to be teaching in Sunday school. Then I heard from Cyn that it didn't matter because John was going to Hamburg. He'd told everyone he'd be getting a hundred pounds a week."

For Stu Sutcliffe the break with college was more serious, coming as it did at the start of a year's postgraduate teacher training. Stu at first turned down the Hamburg trip; then John and the others talked him into it. The college subsequently indicated it was willing to accept him on the teaching course as a late entrant.

Paul McCartney obtained his father's consent with typical diplomacy and circuitousness. With A-level exams now past, he technically had no further school commitments. His English teacher, Dusty Durband, was in fact one of the first to hear of the Hamburg offer, just before the Institute broke up for the summer. Mr. Durband was skeptical. "As far as I knew, Paul was going on, as his father wished, to teacher-training college. When he told me about Hamburg, I said, 'Just who do you want to be, Paul? Tommy Steele?' He just grinned and said, 'No, but I feel like giving it a try.' "

Jim McCartney, when told the big news at last, faced a united front consisting of Paul, his brother Michael, and Allan Williams, who came up to Forthlin Road to assure him the arrangements were all above-board. Though full of misgivings, Jim felt that if Paul were allowed this one jaunt he might the sooner return to his senses, and to college. He let Paul go at the price of only a minimal pep talk about being careful and eating regular meals.

George Harrison, though even now only just seventeen, encountered the least opposition from his family. With his father and elder brothers he had achieved the status of working man, and was as such entitled to command of his own affairs. The quiet, hardworking Harrison family, besides, had produced its share of travelers. As well as Harry and his sea voyages, there was Louise, George's grown-up sister, now married to an American and living in St. Louis. Germany, by contrast, seemed not too distant; if the Harrisons knew of the Reeperbahn's reputation, they were prepared to trust in George's level head. His mother made him promise to write, and baked him a tin of homemade scones for the journey.

One big worry spoiled the collective excitement. It was the same old plaguing worry—they still had no drummer. What would do as backing for a stripper in Upper Parliament Street would not do, Allan Williams told them forcefully, for a big-time, luxurious Hamburg nightspot like the Indra Club. The contract with Herr Koschmider specified a full in-strumental complement. If the Beatles could not provide one, the gig must be given to someone else.

They had been searching, in fact, ever since Tommy Moore had de-serted them to return to his forklift truck at Garston bottle works. The only replacement they had been able to find was a boy called Norman Chapman whom they had overheard one night, practicing on Slater Street in a room above the National Cash Register Company. Norman played a few dates with them, happily enough, but then had to join one of the last batches of young Britons drafted into the Army.

Lately, for want of anything better, the Beatles had gone back to play-ing at the Casbah, Mona Best's cellar club in Hayman's Green. They had not been there since they were called the Quarry Men and had walked out over the docking of fifteen shillings from their night's fee.

To their surprise, they found the Casbah thriving. Ken Browne, the bespectacled ex–Quarry Man, now led his own group, the Black Jacks, with Mrs. Best's son, Peter, on drums. The Black Jacks were among the most popular groups in that district, drawing even larger crowds to the Casbah than did big names like Rory Storm and the Hurricanes.

Pete Best had just left Liverpool Collegiate Grammar School with abundant GCE passes and athletic distinctions but not so clear-cut a plan as hitherto to go on to teacher-training college. The taciturn, good-looking boy, to his mother's surprise, announced instead that he wanted to become a professional drummer. Mrs. Best, ever ready to encourage and invigorate, helped him raise the deposit on a brand-new drum set that he had long been admiring in the music department at Blackler's.

That decision taken, nothing much seemed to happen. The Black Jacks were due to disband because Ken Browne was about to move away from Liverpool. No other group had offered Pete a job as drummer, nor was he one to push himself. For several weeks, he sat around at home all day, and at night went downstairs into the club to watch this other group Mo was now booking. Whenever he came in, a little desperate sigh used to run around the girls on the nearer benches.

The Beatles, too, had noticed Pete Best. More specifically, they had noticed his glittering new drum set. Five weeks after leaving school Pete was rung up by Paul McCartney and asked if he would like to join them for a two-month club engagement in Hamburg. The question, really, was superfluous. Pete Best said he would.

They were to travel to Hamburg by road. Allan Williams had offered to drive them there himself, not in his Jaguar but in a battered cream-and-green Austin minibus that he had acquired for his Liverpool enterprises. Williams, thinking he might as well make a party of it, invited also along his Chinese wife, Beryl, his brother-in-law, Barry Chang, and his West Indian business associate, Lord Woodbine. On their way through London they were to pick up a tenth passenger, the waiter from the Heaven and Hell coffee bar, who was returning to Hamburg to become Bruno Koschmider's interpreter.

None of the five Beatles had ever been abroad before. John Lennon, indeed, only acquired a passport within a few days of setting off. Their preparations, even so, were not elaborate. Williams advanced them fifteen pounds to buy new black crewneck sweaters from Marks and Spencer and some extra pairs of tennis shoes. For a stage uniform they now had little short high-buttoning jackets of houndstooth check. Their luggage was the family type, hauled out from under spare-room beds. Paul also brought along a new, very cheap, solid guitar and a tiny Elpico amplifier to go with the one that, strictly speaking, still belonged to the art college. George had the tin of homemade scones his mother had baked for him.

Only one parent was outside the Jacaranda to see them off. Millie Sutcliffe, having said good-bye to Stu at home, followed him down to Slater Street secretly and stood in a shop doorway, watching while the van was loaded and its sides were embellished with a legend, THE BEATLES, in cutout paper letters stuck on with flour and water paste. For some reason, Mrs. Sutcliffe could not stop herself from crying.

At Newhaven, where they were to embark for the Hook of Holland, the dockers at first refused to load the top-heavy conveyance aboard its appointed cross-Channel steamer. John talked them into it just a few moments before sailing time. The English coast receded amid a chorus of "Bye Bye Blackbird" from the Anglo-Chinese party clustered at the stern rail.

In Holland next morning the minibus surfaced among crowds of students on bicycles, some of whom leaned against its tattered sides for support. Williams shared the driving with Lord Woodbine while Beryl, perched on the overheating gearbox, acted as navigator. The five Beatles, Barry Chang, and the German waiter, Herr Steiner, occupied the rear, cut off by a wall of luggage and utensils for cooking along the way. As they headed off across Europe, some more fitful singing broke out.

Like Derry and the Seniors before them, the Beatles were without the necessary German work permits. At the frontier, they, too, planned to pose as students on vacation. They had not proceeded far into Holland before Williams began to doubt if they would get even that far. During a brief stop at Arnhem John emerged from a shop with a mouth organ that, in Lord Woodbine's words, "he'd picked up to look at and forgotten to put back."

The halt is commemorated by a snapshot that Barry Chang, Williams's Chinese brother-in-law, took at the Arnhem Memorial to the dead of World War II. Paul, in a turned-up lumberjack collar, sits with Pete Best and George in front of a marble plinth inscribed with the epitaph "Their Names Liveth For Ever More." John is missing from the group; he had refused to get out of the van.

• • •

They expected a city like Liverpool, and this, in a sense, they found. There was the same river, broad like the Mersey but, unlike the Mersey, crowded with ships and with shipyards beyond that seemed to grow out of lush forests. There was the same overhead railway that Liverpool had recently lost, although nothing resembling the same tired cityscape beneath. Not the bomb sites and garbage, but tree-lined boulevards, seamless with prosperity; chic shops and ships' chandlers and cafés filled with well-dressed, unscarred, confident people. There was a glimpse of the dark-spired City Hall, and of the Alster lake, set about by glass-walled banks and press buildings, and traversed by elegant swans. What was said inside Allan Williams's minibus that August evening would be echoed many times afterward in varying tones of disbelief: Wasn't this the country that had *lost* the war?

The journey from the West German frontier had been rich in incident. At one point, they were almost run down by a tram, in whose rails Lord Woodbine had accidentally jammed the minibus's front wheels. Allan Williams, taking over as driver on the outskirts of Hamburg, had immediately rammed a small sedan.

They arrived on the Reeperbahn just as neon lights were beginning to eclipse the fairground palings of the nightclubs and their painted, acrobatic nudes. Spotting the narrow road junction, where an *imbiss* belched out fumes of *frikadellen* and *currywurst*, Allan Williams remembered where he was. They turned left into Grosse Freiheit, welcomed by overarching illuminations and the stare of predatory eyes.

Even John Lennon, with his fondness for human curiosities, had not expected an employer quite like Bruno Koschmider. The figure that hopped out of the Kaiserkeller to greet them had begun life in a circus, working as a clown, fire-eater, acrobat, and illusionist with fifty small cage-birds hidden in his coat. His dwarfish stature; his large, elaborately coiffured head; his turned-up nose and quick, stumping gait, all made even John not quite like to laugh. Bruno, for his part, was unimpressed by the look of his new employees: "They were dressed in bad clothes—cheap shirts, trousers that were not clean. Their fingernails were dirty."

If Bruno was somewhat disconcerting, his Kaiserkeller club brought much reassurance. The exterior portico bore, in large letters, the name DERRY AND THE SENIORS VON LIVERPOOL. A glimpse inside, on the way to Koschmider's office, showed what seemed a vast meadow of tables and side booths, shaped like lifeboats, around the stage and miniature dance floor. The Beatles, their spirits reviving, began to laugh and cuff one another, saying this was all right, wasn't it? Allan Williams reminded them that they were not booked to play here but in one of Herr Koschmider's other clubs, the Indra.

Further along the Grosse Freiheit, beyond St. Joseph's Catholic church, the illuminations dwindled into a region of plain-fronted bordellos interspersed with private houses where elderly *hausfraus* still set potted plants on the upper window ledges. Here, under a neon sign shaped like an elephant, was to be found the Indra Club. Bruno Koschmider led the way downstairs into a small cellar cabaret, gloomy, shabby, and at that moment occupied by only two customers. Down here, for the next eight weeks, the Beatles would be expected to play for four and a half hours each weeknight and six hours on Saturdays and Sundays.

Koschmider next conducted them to the living quarters provided under the terms of his contract with Allan Williams. Across the road from the Indra he operated a small cinema, the Bambi Kino, that varied the general diet of flesh by showing corny old gangster movies and Westerns. The Beatles' lodgings were one filthy room and two windowless cubbyholes immediately behind—and in booming earshot of the cinema screen. The only washing facilities were the cinema toilets, from the communal vestibule of which an old woman attendant stared at them grimly over her saucer of tips.

It was some consolation to meet up with Derry and the Seniors and to learn that, despite munificent billing outside the Kaiserkeller, Liverpool's famous R&B group were also having to sleep rough. "Bruno gave us one little bed between five of us," Howie Casey, the sax player, says. "I'd been sleeping on that, covered by a flag, and the other lads slept on chairs set two together. The waiters used to lock us inside the club each night."

The Bambi Kino was not a great deal worse than the cellar of Lord Woodbine's New Colony Club or the Gambier Terrace flat back home in Liverpool. Paul and Pete Best took a cubbyhole each while John, Stu, and George flopped down in the larger room. All five were soon asleep, untroubled by the sounds of gunfire and police sirens that wafted through the grimy wall from the cinema screen.

Their first night's playing at the Indra was a severe letdown. Half a dozen people sat and watched them indifferently from tables with red-shaded lamps. The clientele, mainly prostitutes and their customers, showed little enthusiasm for Carl Perkins's "Honey Don't" or Chuck Berry's "Too Much Monkey Business." The club also bore a curse in the form of an old woman living upstairs who continually phoned police headquarters on the Reeperbahn to complain about the noise. Bruno Koschmider, not wishing for that kind of trouble, hissed at them to turn even their feeble amplifiers down.

Allan and Beryl Williams, Barry Chang, and Lord Woodbine remained in Hamburg throughout that inaugural week. Williams, himself comfortably ensconced in a small hotel, did what he could to improve the Beatles' living quarters—it was at his urgent insistence that Bruno provided blankets for their beds. Beryl shopped in the city center with her brother, and Lord Woodbine, as usual, remained worried by nothing. He sang calypsos at the Kaiserkeller and, one night, grew so affected by its libations that he attempted to dive into the South Sea Islands mural.

Williams, in his conscientious moments, worried about the club he had committed his charges to, and about their plainly evinced hatred of it. On their opening night they had played the entire four-and-a-half-hour stretch mutinously still and huddled-up. "Come on, boys!" Williams exhorted them from the bar. "Make it a show, boys!" Bruno Koschmider took up the phrase, clapping his large, flat hands. "Mak show, boys," he would cry. "Mak show, Beatles! Mak show!"

John's answer was to launch himself into writhings and shimmyings that were a grotesque parody of Gene Vincent at the Boxing Stadium show. Down the street at the Kaiserkeller word began to spread of this other group *von* Liverpool who leapt around the stage like monkeys and stamped their feet deafeningly on the stage. They were stamping out the rhythm to help their new drummer, Pete Best, and also to goad the old woman upstairs.

Before long, the rival groups from the Kaiserkeller had come up to the Indra to see them. Howie Casey was astonished at the improvement since their audition as the Silver Beatles in front of Larry Parnes. "That day, they'd seemed embarrassed about how bad they were," Howie says. "You could tell something had happened to them in the meantime. They'd turned into a good stomping band."

Derry and the Seniors brought with them a wide-eyed, curly-haired youth whom all the Beatles—George especially—regarded with awe. Born Anthony Esmond Sheridan McGinnity, he was better known as Tony Sheridan, a singer and inspired solo guitarist with many appearances to his credit on the *Oh Boy!* television show. His talent, however, was accompanied by habits too blithely erratic to suit the rock 'n' roll star-makers. When Bruno Koschmider hired him he had been sacked from *Oh Boy!* and most other engagements, and was playing at the 2i's coffee bar for one pound a night. Even now, the British police were hard on his trail due to various installment plan irregularities.

Anthony Esmond steered the Beatles, past beckoning doorway touts, for an insider's tour of the Reeperbahn's peculiar delights. They saw the women who grappled in mud, cheered on by an audience tied into a protective communal bib. They visited the Roxy Bar and met ravishing hostesses with tinkling laughs and undisguisably male biceps and breastbones. Two streets away, where a wooden fence forbade entry to all under eighteen, their companions steered them through the Herbertstrasse, past red-lit shop windows containing whores in every type of fancy dress, all ages from nymphet to scolding granny, smiling or scowling forth, gossiping with one another, reading, knitting, listlessly examining their own frilly garters or spooning up bowls of soup.

The other initiation was into beer. For beer, damp gold, foam piling under thin metal bar taps, had never been more plentiful. Derry and the Seniors, when they first opened at the Kaiserkeller, had been allowed beer ad lib in breaks between performing. Though Koschmider had hastily withdrawn this privilege, the nightly allowance still seemed vast to five boys who, at home in Liverpool, had often been hard put to scrape up the price of a half-pint each. Then there were the drinks pressed on them by customers at the Indra, the drinks that would be sent up to them onstage while they played. It became nothing unusual for a whole crate of beer to be shoved at their feet by well-wishers whose size and potential truculence underlined the necessity of finishing every bottle.

Sex was easily available. Here you did not chase it, as in Liverpool, and clutch at it furtively in cold shop doors. Here it came after you, putting strong arms round you, mincing no words; it was unabashed, expert—indeed, professional. For even the most cynical whores found it piquant to have an innocent boy from Liverpool—to lure and buy as a change from being, eternally, bait and merchandise.

The Freiheit provided an abundance of everything but sleep. Sheridan and the other musicians already knew a way to get by without it, just as the barmaids and whores and bouncers and pickpockets did. Someone in the early days had discovered Preludin, a brand of German slimming tablet that, while removing appetite, also roused the metabolism to goggle-eyed hyperactivity. Soon the Beatles—all but Pete Best—were gobbling "Prellys" by the tubeful each night. As the pills took effect they dried up the saliva, increasing the desire for beer.

Now the Beatles needed no exhortation to "mak show." John, in particular, began to go berserk onstage, prancing and groveling in imitation of any rock 'n' roller or movie monster his dazzled mind could summon up. The fact that their audience could not understand a word they said provoked John into cries of *"Sieg Heil!"* and "Fucking Nazis!" to which the audience invariably responded by laughing and clapping. Bruno Koschmider, who had spent the war in a panzer division, was not so amused.

At 5:00 or 6:00 A.M.—according to subsequent adventures—they would stagger back along the sunny Freiheit, past doorway touts unsleepingly active. Behind the Bambi Kino they would collapse into their squalid beds for the two or three hours' sleep that were possible before the day's first picture show. Sometimes it would be gunfire on the screen that jolted them awake, or the voice of George Raft or Edward G. Robinson.

Hounded into consciousness, they would dash to the cinema toilets while the basins were still clean. Rosa, the female custodian, for all her outward grimness, kept clean towels for them, and odds and ends of soap. "She thought we were all mad," Pete Best says. "She'd shout things at us—*verrucht* [wicked] and *beknaakt*—but she'd be laughing. We called her 'Mutti.' "

There were now five or six hours to be disposed of before they began playing and drinking again. At the Gretel and Alphons or Willi's Bar, the Freiheit's two most tolerant cafés, they would breakfast on cornflakes or chicken soup, the only food that their dehydrated frames could endure. They would then drift round the corner, through the stench of *frikadelli* and last night's vomit, to the shop on the main Reeperbahn that fascinated John Lennon especially with its display of switchblades, bayonets, coshes, swords, brass knuckle-dusters, and teargas pistols.

If not too devastatingly hung over they might catch a tram into central Hamburg and stroll on the elegant boulevards, looking at the clothes and the perfumes, the elaborate bakers and confectioners, the radios and tape recorders and occasional displays of imported American guitars, saxophones, and drums. Since their wages, paid out by Bruno on a Thursday, seldom lasted more than twenty-four hours, such expeditions were usually limited to gazing and wishing. John, however, blew every pfennig he had on a new guitar, an American Rickenbacker "short arm."

The daylight hours improved considerably after someone, walking on the dockside, discovered Hamburg's long-established branch of the British Sailors' Society, a refuge for mariners ashore in foreign ports. Jim Hawke, the resident manager, was a hefty Londoner who had entered Hamburg with the first invading Allied troops and had subsequently done duty as a guard at the Nuremberg trials. In 1960, he and his German wife, Lilo, had been in charge of the Hamburg branch only a few months. Already, as it happened, they had met Stu Sutcliffe's father, still then a second engineer with the Booth shipping line.

Hawke, a tenderhearted man under his stern exterior, granted the same privileges to Liverpool musicians as to sailors far from home. Most attractive from the Beatles' point of view were the English breakfasts, cooked by an elderly German woman, Frau Prill, who knew the secret of frying real English chips. "They never seemed to have any money," Hawke said. "You could see them carefully counting out the coins. They always had what was the cheapest—steak, egg, and chips, which I put on for two marks 80 (about twenty-five pence). And big half-liter tankards of milk. Some days they'd have an Oxo cube beaten up in milk.

"They were never any trouble—I wouldn't have stood for it in any case. Just nice, quiet, well-behaved lads, they seemed. They didn't even smoke then. They'd sit and play draughts [checkers] or go upstairs for a game of ping-pong with my daughter, Monica. In the room through the bar we had an old piano that had come from the British forces. They used that, or John and Paul did, to help them write their songs. We had a library as well. I'd leave a bag of books for them on the table in front of the settee they always used. They liked reading, but they never took any of the books away. They said they couldn't read very easily where they were staying.

"They'd come in about eleven in the morning and stay until three or four in the afternoon. They'd be quite subdued. I'd look over from the bar and see the five of them, always round that same table, not talking— just staring into space. I've seen the same look on men who've been away at sea in tankers for a long time. Not with it, if you know what I mean."

One bleary-eyed morning when they emerged from the Bambi Kino, a piece of good news awaited them. Bruno Koschmider, bowing at last to the complaints of his customers and the old woman upstairs, was moving them out of the Indra and into his larger, better club, the Kaiserkeller.

The Kaiserkeller, at first, threatened to eclipse even John Lennon in noise and spectacle. The noise came from an audience several hundred strong, frequently containing entire ships' companies from English and American naval craft visiting the port. The spectacle was provided by Bruno Koschmider's white-aproned waiters, converging on any outbreak of trouble and quelling it with a high-speed ruthlessness that made Garston Blood Baths look like a game of pat-a-cake. If the troublemaker were alone he might find himself propelled not to the exit but into the office of Willi, the undermanager, there to be worked over at leisure with coshes and brass knuckles. Finally, as the victim lay prostrate, Bruno himself would weigh in with the ebony nightstick from his desk drawer.

Bruno's chief bouncer, a tiny, swaggering youth named Horst Fascher, epitomized the breed. Horst had started life as a featherweight boxer and had represented both Hamburg and the West German national team before being banned from the ring for accidentally killing a sailor in a street fight. His squad, nicknamed locally Hoddel's gang, recruited from his friends at the Hamburg Boxing Academy, were held among the Freiheit's other strong-arm gangs in profound respect.

Horst took the Liverpool musicians—fortunately for them—to his heart. It became an unwritten rule at the Kaiserkeller that if a musician hit trouble Hoddel's gang would swoop unquestioningly to his aid. Horst showed them the Reeperbahn's innermost haunts and its choicest pleasures; he also took them home to Neuestadt to meet his mother and brothers and taste Frau Fascher's bean soup. All he asked in return was the chance, sometime after midnight, to get up with the group on stage and bellow out an Eddie Cochran song.

"The Beatles were not good musicians at the beginning," Horst Fascher says. "John Lennon was a very poor rhythm guitarist. I remember Sheridan telling me in amazement that John played chords with only three fingers. And always they are funny—never serious. But they steal from Sheridan, from the Seniors, all the time with their eyes. And all the time the bass drum is beating like your foot when you stamp.

"That John Lennon—I loved him, he was mad. A fighter. He is *zyniker* [a cynic]. You say to him, 'Hey, John . . .' He would say, 'Ah, so fuckin' what.' Paul was *lustig*, the clown. He gets out of trouble by making a laugh. George was *schuchtern*, the baby one. I could never get to know Stu. He was too strange. And Pete—he was *reserviert*. You had to pull words out through his nose."

Soon after the Beatles reached the Kaiserkeller, Derry and the Seniors finished their engagement there. The replacement group, brought out from Liverpool by Allan Williams, was Rory Storm and the Hurricanes. When Rory, relaxed and suntanned from Butlin's, saw the Hamburg living quarters, his stammer totally overcame him. Nor did his drummer, the little bearded one with rings on his fingers, show great delight at having to sleep on chairs covered with old flags. Ringo Starr, like all the Hurricanes, was used to a little more luxury. "You want to see what the Beatles have got to put up with," Williams retorted.

Rory Storm's flashiness and acrobatic feats increased the wildness of the Kaiserkeller nights. A contest developed between the Beatles and Hurricanes to see which group could first stamp its way through the already old and half-rotten timbers of the stage. Rory did it at last, vanishing from sight in the middle of "Blue Suede Shoes." A case of junk champagne was the prize, washed down with more "Prellys" at their favorite bar, the Gretel and Alphons.

Bruno Koschmider fumed and fulminated—but they got away with it, as they got away with most things. John got away with standing out in the Freiheit in a pair of long woolen underpants, reading the *Daily Express*. George got away with it time after time in the *Polizei Stunde*, or midnight curfew hour when all under eighteen were supposed to have left the club. For their drinking, swearing, fighting, whoring, even vandalizing, Grosse Freiheit pardoned them all forms of retribution but one. Williams, the self-styled "little pox doctor of Hamburg," received many a worried confidence in a back room at the Gretel and Alphons, and like a connoisseur, held many a beer glass of urine speculatively up to the light.

Pete Best figured in only a couple of shady Beatles exploits on the Reeperbahn. One night, chronically short of cash, John enlisted his help as the group's most seasoned hard man in mugging a drunken sailor and stealing his wallet. Pete himself later confirmed John's account of how the two followed the sailor from a club and managed to put him on the ground. As they started to go through his pockets, however, their victim pulled out a handgun. In fact, the weapon fired only tear-gas cartridges, but neither John nor Pete realized this and, empty-handed, ran for their lives.

Pete played drums well enough—or so it then seemed—hitting his bass pedal in the hard, stomping "mak show" beat, yet somehow always in a world apart from the unending frontal contest between John and Paul. He was, and knew it, the most handsome Beatle, with his athlete's physique, his dark eyes, wry smile, and neat, crisp Jeff Chandler hair. Like the girls back home in West Derby, the Kaiserkeller girls were mad about him. Craning their necks to see past John and George, past even Paul, they would scream at Pete Best in English and German to give them a smile.

Being able to speak the most German increased Pete's independence, and he was often away from the Freiheit in the daytime, sunbathing alone or buying new parts for his drums. His fellow Beatles grew accustomed to his absence. They had plenty afoot with Tony Sheridan and Rory Storm and the drummer from Rory's group, whom they were growing to like more and more. Ringo Starr, in contrast with Pete Best, was friendly, simple, straightforward, and in his slow, big-eyed way, as funny as even John. They also liked the way he played drums. They were happy with Pete Best's drumming until they began to notice Ringo's.

When Allan Williams next hit town Paul and John met him, clamoring for his help to find a studio in which they could record. They wanted to try out some numbers with a member of Rory Storm's group, a boy named Wally, whose prodigious vocal range went from bass to falsetto. Pete Best would not be involved. They had also fixed up to borrow Ringo Starr.

The studio Williams found for them was a record-your-voice booth at the rear of Hamburg's main railway station. There, John, Paul, and George, with Ringo on drums, backed the talented Wally through two numbers, "Fever" and "Summertime." The man who cut the acetate for their recording mistakenly handed back to Williams first an old-fashioned 78-rpm disk with a commercial message for a local handbag shop on its reverse. Eventually some 45-rpm discs were made, on the booth's "Arnstik" label, of *The Beatles mit Wally*. Just for a few moments—subtracting Wally—the right four had found each other.

Astrid Kirchherr was born in 1938 into a solid, respectable middle-class Hamburg family. Her grandfather, a manufacturer of fairground slot machines, still owned the factory he had twice seen wrecked by war, and twice painstakingly built up again. Her father was a senior executive in the West German division of the Ford Motor Company. Three generations of Kirchherrs lived together in Altona, a comfortable Hamburg suburb. To Altona people, the dockyard and St Pauli, the Reeperbahn and Grosse Freiheit might as well be on another planet: They are mentioned only to warn children sternly never to stray in that direction.

Astrid Kirchherr was never like other children. At the age of four or five she would protest when her mother decked her out in the flounces and hair ribbons expected of little German girls. She preferred to wear plain black. She knew that best became her white skin, her large, dark eyes, and the blanched-gold hair she would shake free of all encumbrances. Frau Kirchherr visited the nursery school to confirm that the child must have her curious wish.

Already, she had a strongly marked talent for drawing and painting; as she grew older, she would design and make clothes for herself. When the family assembled, as was traditional, to decide her future, her grandfather agreed that there was only one sensible course. Astrid should go to college and study dress design. Possibly that would encourage her to forsake her eccentric ideas for styles more widely acceptable.

She went not to the state art college but to a private academy, the Meister Schule. There she met an elegant boy of equally good family, a doctor's son named Klaus Voorman. Klaus, a talented illustrator, passionately loved rock 'n' roll music and wanted to be a designer of pop record covers. He became Astrid's boyfriend, also moving in as a lodger at the hospitable Kirchherr house. Their friends were a set known as *exis*—from "existentialist": intellectual, beautiful, ascetic, and avant-garde. Astrid and Klaus were the most beautiful, ascetic, and avant-garde of them all.

At the Meister Schule Astrid also struck up a friendship with Rhein-hardt Wolf, tutor on the photographic course and a well-known con-tributor to various Hamburg-based magazines. The perceptiveness with which she commented on his work led Wolf to suggest that Astrid should herself try taking some pictures. These proved so impressive that, at Rheinhardt Wolf's insistence, she changed courses from dress design to photography. After leaving the Meister Schule she was taken on by Wolf as his assistant.

One late summer evening in 1960, Astrid and Klaus Voorman had quarreled, and Klaus went off to the cinema on his own. Afterward, walking about aimlessly, he found himself in Grosse Freiheit. A blast of rock 'n' roll music was issuing from the open door into the Kaiserkeller club. Klaus decided, against all the instincts of his upbringing, to go in and have a look.

The group on stage at the time was Rory Storm and the Hurricanes. Klaus sat down nervously in the tough crowd, and was at once swept away with excitement and delight. He had never been in a club before, and certainly never seen rock 'n' roll played with such crazy ebullience. At a table next to his some more English musicians, in houndstooth check jackets, with wondrously piled-up, greased-back hair, were wait-ing their turn to play. In due course this group was announced as the Beatles. Klaus stayed on to watch the whole of their four-hour perfor-mance.

Astrid, when he told her about it, was a little disgusted to hear that Klaus had been hanging around dives in St. Pauli. He could not per-suade her to go back with him to the Kaiserkeller and be shown the amazing music. He went again on his own, determined to talk to the Beatles if he could. Shy and unsure of his English, he took with him a sleeve he had designed for an American single, the Ventures' "Walk Don't Run." In a break between sessions he went over to the leader—so he had already identified John Lennon—and in halting English tried to explain about the design. John only muttered, "Show it to Stu—he's the artist round here," indicating the one who had interested Klaus most with his pointed shoes, dark glasses, and brooding James Dean face.

By the time Astrid did agree to go to the Kaiserkeller, Stu and Klaus Voorman had become good friends. Klaus brought her in at last one night, dressed in her black leather *exi* coat, white-faced, crop-headed, and spectrally cool. When the Beatles began playing she, too, was instantly won over. "I fell in love with Stuart that very first night. He was so tiny but perfect, every feature. So pale, but very, very beautiful. He was like a character from a story by Edgar Allan Poe."

The Beatles, in their turn, were flattered by the interest of this in every way beautiful, ghost-eyed girl, so different from the usual Freiheit scrubber. They were still more flattered when, with her few words of English, Astrid asked if she could take their photograph. She met all five of them on the Reeperbahn next day and took them into Der Dom, the city park, where the twice-yearly fun fair was in progress. Astrid posed them with their guitars and Pete Best's snare drum on the side of a fairground wagon, then on the broad bonnet of a traction engine.

The photographing over, she asked the five Beatles back to Altona for tea at her home. Pete Best declined; he said he had some new drum skins to buy. The other four readily piled into Astrid's little car. "They met my Mum—she was as knocked out by them as I was. Directly she saw them, she wanted to start feeding them."

Astrid took them upstairs to the black-and-white studio bedroom she had designed for herself. "I wanted to talk to them, but I knew hardly any English then," Astrid says. "John seemed very hard—cynical, sarcastic, but something more than that. Paul smiled—he always smiled and was diplomatic. George was just a baby boy, with his piled-up hair and his ears sticking out.

"I wanted to talk to Stuart. I tried to ask him if I could take his picture, but he didn't understand. I knew I would have to ask Klaus to help me speak better English."

The flattery of being photographed by a beautiful blonde German girl was nothing to the flattery bestowed by the photographs themselves. These were not the usual little snapshots knocked off by some bystander, usually at the least flattering possible moment. These were big, grainy prints, conjured by the girl herself from the recesses of her black satin room and showing the five Beatles as they had never imagined themselves before. Astrid's lens, in fact, captured the very quality that attracted intellectuals like Klaus and her—the paradox of Teddy Boys with child faces; of would-be toughness and all-protecting innocence. The blunt, heavy fairground machines on which they sat seemed to symbolize their own slight but confident perch on grown-up life. John, with his collar up, hugging his new Rickenbacker; Paul, with the pout he knew suited him; George, uneasy; Pete Best, self-contained, a little apart—each image held its own true prophecy. In one shot, Stu Sutcliffe stood with his back to the others, the long neck of his guitar pointing into the ground.

It was the first of many photographic sessions with Astrid in the weeks that followed. Each time she would pose them, with or without their guitars, against some part of industrial Hamburg—the docks or the railway sidings. She was lavish with the prints she gave them and with invitations to meals at her house. "I'd cook them all the things they missed from England: scrambled eggs, chips." All the time, with Klaus Voorman's help, her English was improving.

At the Kaiserkeller, a part of the audience now were *exis* brought in by Astrid and Klaus. It became a fad among them to dress, like the rockers, in leather and skin-tight jeans. The Beatles' music belonged to the same intellectual conversion. Soon the *exis* had their own small preserve of tables next to the stage. And always among them the girl who followed no style but her own sat with Klaus Voorman, or without him, waiting for the moment, late at night, when John and Paul stood aside and Stu Sutcliffe stepped forward with his heavy bass to sing the Elvis ballad, "Love Me Tender."

Astrid made no secret of the pursuit, and Stu, for his part, was shyly fascinated. Her elfin beauty, combined with big-breasted voluptuousness, her forthright German ways mingled with a yielding softness, were more than sufficient to captivate any young, inexperienced heterosexual male. Across the barrier of language, they found their passionate artistic and literary beliefs to be one. The talks by candlelight on Astrid's black coverlet quickly led to other delights unenvisaged by a schoolteacher's son from Sefton Park, Liverpool.

Astrid was the initiator and teacher, and Stu the willing pupil. With the skills of the artist and the practicality of the *hausfrau* she began to model him into an appearance echoing and complementing her own. She did away first with his Teddy-Boy hairstyle, cutting it short like hers, then shaping it to lie across the forehead in what was then called a French cut, although high-class German boys had worn a similar style since the days of Bismarck.

When Stu arrived at the Kaiserkeller that night John and Paul laughed so much that he hastily combed his hair back into its old upswept style. Next night, he tried the new way again, ignoring the others' taunts. Strangely enough, it was George, the least adventurous or assertive one, who next allowed Astrid to unpick the high sheaf of black hair that had previously so emphasized his babyish ears. Paul tried it next, but temporarily—he was waiting to see what John would do. John tried it, so Paul tried it again. Only Pete Best's hair stayed as before, a crisp, unflappable cockade.

Astrid also began to design and make clothes for Stu. She made him first a suit of shiny black leather jerkin and sheath-tight trousers like the ones she wore herself. The other four Beatles so admired it that they at once ordered copies from a tailor in St. Pauli. Theirs, however, were of less fine workmanship, baggy-waisted and with seams that kept coming apart. At that point, for the moment, Astrid's influence over them stopped. They laughed at Stu for wearing, as she did, a black corduroy jacket without lapels, based on Pierre Cardin's current Paris collections. "What are you doing in Mum's suit then, Stu?" became the general taunt.

Astrid's mother, horrified to learn of Stu's living conditions, insisted on giving him his own room, as Klaus Voorman had formerly had, at the top of the Kirchherr house. In November 1960, two months after their first meeting, they became engaged. They bought each other rings, in the German fashion, and went in Astrid's car for a drive beside the river Elbe. "It was a real engagement," Astrid says. "We knew from the beginning that it was inevitable we should marry. And so it should have been."

Stu, despite his quietness and gentleness, was not always an easy person. At times he could be moody and jealously suspect Astrid of being in love with someone else. His emotion, when angry or passionate, could reach an intensity that was almost like a mild seizure. He suffered, too, from headaches, sudden and violent, that shut his eyes in agony behind the dark glasses that were not, she discovered, entirely for show. Then, with equal suddenness, the fit of pain would pass.

Even Astrid could not affect Stu's life as the downtrodden butt of the other Beatles' humor. On stage, they teased and taunted him continually, for his smallness, for his outrageous new clothes, above all for the bass playing that never seemed equal to their needs. John inflicted the worst treatment of all, even though, as Astrid well knew, a deep friendship still existed between Stu and him. It was in Paul's more bantering tone that the true arrows came. For Paul wanted Stu's job as bass guitarist. "When John and Stu had a row," Astrid says, "you could still feel the affection that was there. But when Paul and Stu had a row, you could tell Paul hated him."

A few yards up the Reeperbahn stood a large, semiunderground arena called the Hippodrome. In former days, it had been a circus, featuring horses ridden by naked girls. By 1960, such entertainments having grown unfashionable, the Hippodrome stood, behind its heavy iron portcullis, dark and in decay. Its owner, a certain Herr Eckhorn, decided to hand it on to his son, Peter, who had recently come home from the sea and was anxious to start a music club in competition with Bruno Koschmider's Kaiserkeller.

Young Peter Eckhorn wasted no time in hitting at his intended rival. First, he suborned Koschmider's chief bouncer, Horst Fascher. While still employed at the Kaiserkeller, Horst was helping Eckhorn convert the old Hippodrome, putting in a stage and dance floor and makeshift wooden booths painted the cheapest color, black. Fascher, in addition, began to sow discontent at the Kaiserkeller, telling Bruno's musicians of the better pay and conditions that Eckhorn's club—the Top Ten—would offer. "I showed Tony Sheridan out of the back door right away," Horst recalls with pride. "That Koschmider went crazy, but what could he do to me? He had too great a fear."

The Top Ten club opened in November 1960, with music by Tony Sheridan and his original Soho-levied group, the Jets. Eckhorn also wanted Derry and the Seniors, but they were by now so poverty-stricken that they had applied to the British consul in Hamburg for an assisted passage home to Liverpool.

The Beatles stayed on at the Kaiserkeller, although in a mood of increasing restlessness. The Top Ten, with its circuslike dimensions and higher rates of pay, was infinitely more attractive than Bruno Koschmider's nautically inspired basement. Their employer, moreover, stung by Horst Fascher's and Tony Sheridan's defection, grew rabidly proprietorial. With a stubby forefinger he drew their attention to the clause in their contract that forbade them to play in any other club within a twenty-five-mile radius of the Kaiserkeller. It had reached Bruno's ears that when visiting the Top Ten they would sometimes get up and jam with Tony Sheridan on stage.

Before long, Peter Eckhorn had persuaded them to forget the residue of their contract with Koschmider and come across to play for him at the Top Ten. Koschmider, according to Pete Best, hinted that if the Beatles joined Eckhorn, they might not be able to walk with complete safety after dark.

Retribution of a different sort overtook them, however, possibly with some help from Bruno Koschmider. They were about to open at the Top Ten when the *Polizei*, conducting a belated examination of George Harrison's passport, discovered that he was only seventeen, and too young to be in a club after midnight. For plainly flouting this rule George was ordered out of Germany. Stu and Astrid put him on the train home, dismayed and lost-looking, with some biscuits and apples for the journey.

The others played a few nights at the Top Ten, with John taking the lead guitar part, or leaving it out, and Paul doubling on a piano that was there. Astrid, Klaus, and the *exi*s had followed them from the Kaiserkeller; so had Akim Reichel, a dockside waiter who had discovered them first at the Indra. Akim remembers how tired and dispirited the four survivors seemed. They had been on the Reeperbahn, after all, nearly four months. "They would play sometimes a whole hour," Akim says, "sitting on the edge of their amplifiers."

Peter Eckhorn, as well as paying ten marks a day more than Koschmider, provided sleeping accommodation above the club, in an attic fitted with bunk beds. Though far from luxurious, and shared with Tony Sheridan's group, it was still a vast improvement on the Bambi Kino. Rosa, the WC lady—who had also forsaken the Kaiserkeller for the Top Ten—was prevailed upon by John Lennon to bring coffee and shaving water up to them when they woke in the early afternoon.

In their haste to desert Koschmider Paul and Pete Best had left most of their belongings in the rooms behind the Bambi. They nerved themselves to go back a few days later, walking in through the cinema foyer without opposition, and finding their property all intact behind the screen. Coming out again, down the dark corridor from their respective cubbyholes, Paul struck a match in order to see. "There were some filthy old drapes on the wall, like sacking," Pete Best says. "Paul caught a bit of that stuff with the match. It wasn't anything like a fire. It just smouldered a little bit." Paul's version is that, in a spirit of half-hearted vandalism, they set fire to a condom.

Early the next morning, policemen entered the Top Ten club,

pounded upstairs to the attic, hauled Pete Best and Paul out of bed, hustled them off to the Reeperbahn's Station 15, and placed them under lock and key. Between them, using their O-level German, they elicited the fact that they were being held on suspicion of trying to burn down the Bambi Kino. "They only kept us there a few hours," Pete Best says. "Afterward they admitted it never should have happened."

No charges were pressed—according to Bruno Koschmider, a magnanimous gesture on his part. Even so, Paul and Pete were both immediately deported. The next day found them on a flight to England, minus most of their clothes and luggage and Pete Best's drum set.

For John and Stu there was no alternative but to follow the others home. Stu made the journey by air, with a ticket paid for by the Kirchherrs. John went on the train alone, carrying his guitar and the amplifier he had not yet paid for, and terrified he wouldn't find England where he had left it.

SIX

"HI, ALL YOU CAVERN-DWELLERS. WELCOME TO THE *BEST* OF CELLARS"

He reached home in the early hours of a December morning and threw stones at his aunt Mimi's bedroom window to wake her. Mimi opened the front door and, as John lurched past, enquired sarcastically what had happened to his hundred pounds a week. And if he thought he was going around Woolton in those cowboy boots, Mimi added, he had better think again. John collapsed into bed, not stirring out of doors for a week afterward. In a little while there came a timorous knock at the door of the outer porch. It was his ever faithful, long-suffering girlfriend, Cynthia Powell.

At Forthlin Road Paul found waiting for him a single GCE A-level certificate—in art—and a father who, luckily, was not the type to crow. Even so, Jim McCartney pointed out, it was time to think about getting a proper job. Paul gave in and registered at the local Labor Exchange. The two weeks before Christmas he spent helping to deliver parcels around the docks on the back of a truck belonging to the Speedy Prompt Delivery Company.

He didn't contact John again until just before Christmas, by which time, to add to the gloom, snow was falling. Snow is never pretty in Liverpool. The two ex-Hamburg desperados, with watering eyes and fingers huddled in their pockets, met down in the city for a drink. They could feel through their boot soles, too, the chill damp of dead-end failure.

Together, they sought out their erstwhile manager, Allan Williams, and found him in equally deflated spirits. Returning from Hamburg the last time he had decided to open the first Liverpool version of a Reeperbahn beat music club. He had taken over an old bottle-washing shop in Soho Street, and employed Lord Woodbine to effect a brief renovation. The new club was to be called the Top Ten and run by Bob Wooler, the railway clerk and spare-time disk jockey who had helped Williams recruit attractions for his Boxing Stadium concert. Wooler, on the strength of Williams's offer, had even resigned his steady job with the docks office.

Liverpool's Top Ten club opened on December 1, 1960. Six days later, it burned to the ground. Local opinion suspected a "torch job."

Only the cellar club in West Derby run by Pete Best's mother remained as a potential gig for Williams's unlucky protégés. Derry and the Seniors had played the Casbah following their own Hamburg disaster, and had good-naturedly plugged the Beatles' name. When Mona Best gave them their first return booking a poster was put on the cellar door loyally proclaiming the "Fabulous Beatles" had returned. George was then contacted—lying low in Speke, he had not realized that John and Paul were home. Stu Sutcliffe, however, remained out of touch with the others until well into the following January.

That first night back at the Casbah showed what a transformation Hamburg had wrought. The months of sweated nights at the Kaiser-keller had given their music a prizefighter's muscle and power; each number was stamped through as if against a Reeperbahn brawl, or in one last attempt to break through Bruno Koschmider's stage. They literally rocked the little club under the Victorian house, where nothing more wicked than Pepsi Cola was drunk, nothing popped more potent than peanuts, and where no fracas arose that could not be quelled by Mrs. Best's vigorous, dark-eyed stare.

A few days later they were, once more, sitting round Allan Williams's Jacaranda coffee bar. So was Bob Wooler, the disk jockey who had quit his railway job in the expectation of running a beat club for Williams. That job having gone up in smoke, Wooler was now working for a promoter named Brian Kelly who ran regular dances at Litherland Town Hall, Lathom Hall, and Aintree Institute.

"They were moaning to me about how little was happening," Wooler said. "I'd never heard them before, but I said I'd try to get Kelly to put them on. In fact, I rang him up from the Jacaranda. I asked for eight pounds for them. Kelly offered four; we settled on six."

Brian Kelly, a somewhat melancholy man employed by the Mersey Docks and Harbour Company, had no overwhelming enthusiasm for rock 'n' roll music. To Kelly, it was a question of simple mathematics. You hired a hall for five pounds, and by filling it with jivers at three shillings (fifteen pence) each you showed a profit. As a dance promoter he possessed one major asset—he did not mind clearing up vomit. Much tended to appear midway in the evening as late-comers arrived from the pubs.

At Litherland Town Hall, on December 27, 1960, Brian Kelly stood in his usual place on one side of the dance area, waiting to go forth with mop bucket and disinfectant. A large crowd was there, curious more than anything to see the group that Bob Wooler had billed dramatically as "Direct from Hamburg." Because of this, many people thought they must be German. Among the spectators was Pete Best's young brother, Rory, and a friend of his called Neil Aspinall, an accounting student who lodged with the Bests. Neil, a thin, serious boy with an impressive cache of O-levels, had never been much interested in rock 'n' roll. He was here tonight only because Rory had said it would be good.

Brian Kelly did not think so. He had booked the Beatles before, in their pre-Hamburg days, and remembered them as very ordinary. He was astonished, when Bob Wooler announced them and the terrible noise started, to see what effect it had on his customers. "Everyone—the whole lot—surged forward towards the stage. The dance floor behind was completely empty. 'Aye aye,' I said to myself. 'I could have got twice the numbers in here.'"

After their performance, the Beatles emerged into the parking lot where, a few months earlier, Stu Sutcliffe had been knocked down and kicked in the head. Once again, there was an ambush waiting—but of girls this time, squealing and asking for autographs. Their van had been covered with lipstick messages. Some of the girls who mobbed them still thought they were German and complimented them on speaking such good English.

Amid the general acclaim they had made two important new friends. One was Bob Wooler, the disk jockey. The other was Neil Aspinall, the accounting student for whom Fate had ordained a future very different from sitting his finals.

Wooler became the intermediary for further six-pound bookings at Brian Kelly's other weekly dances at Lathom Hall and Aintree Institute. He also became the means of spreading the Beatles' name over wider and wider areas of Liverpool. As a disk jockey he was an unlikely figure, with his round face, his earnest politeness and devotion to wordplay and puns. He loved to draft elaborate posters and handbills in which, for example, the initial letters of Litherland Town Hall served additionally to spell "Lively Time Here," and all the bus routes to the hall would be microscopically detailed. "Jive Fans!" a Wooler handbill would say, "This is It!" In neat capital letters he would draft the evening's running order, murmuring to himself such cautionary slogans as "Horses for courses. Menus for venues." Somehow, in the shabby jive halls, he maintained the gravitas of a Roman senator, wagging his large forefinger as he strove to impress on beer-crazed seventeen-year-olds that punctuality and politeness were the primary virtues of life. Yet his voice, through the microphone, was as rich and relaxed as the best to be heard on Radio Luxembourg.

The Beatles were not interested in punctuality or politeness. But they respected Bob Wooler and recognized that his wagging forefinger often conveyed a valuable point. It was Wooler who advised them to begin playing even before the curtains opened, and who delved among his own record collection for the "William Tell Overture" and suggested using its opening fanfare as their signature tune.

Their other strong supporter was Mona Best. They always met first at the Casbah, setting off on dates in a van driven by Mrs. Best's part-time doorman, and usually accompanied by Neil Aspinall, ever ready to leave his accounting studies to help unload and set up the drums and amplifiers.

Mona Best made forceful efforts on behalf of "Pete's group," as she considered them. She took their bookings over the telephone, when Pete was not at home to do it: She became, as much as anyone was, their agent and manager. She wrote on their behalf to the BBC in Manchester, requesting a radio audition. The BBC's answer was not discouraging. The Beatles' name would be kept on file.

In Bob Wooler's eyes, too, Pete Best was their principal asset. At Aintree or Litherland, as the first bars of the "William Tell Overture" died away and the crash of guitars began behind still-closed curtains, that shriek of ecstasy, that rush to the front of the stage, was mainly for Pete. At a dance on St. Valentine's Day, 1961, Wooler offered the novel idea of moving Pete's drums forward to a rank equal with the other three. That night, the girls all but dragged him off his stool and off the stage.

One evening just after Christmas Mrs. Best rang up the Cavern Club on Mathew Street and asked to speak to the owner, Ray McFall. It happened to be a big trad jazz night at the Cavern, starring Humphrey Lyttleton, and, what with the noise, McFall had to press his ear close to the receiver. "Look here, Mr. McFall," insisted the dulcet voice that sounded both a little Indian and a little Scouse, "there's this group called the Beatles—you should have them at the Cavern, you know." McFall replied politely that he'd think about it.

When Alan Synter started the Cavern as a jazz club in 1957, Ray McFall had been the family accountant. In 1959, Synter decided to get out, and McFall took over the lease. It was he, in fact, who had booked John Lennon and the Quarry Men the night they gave offense by playing rock 'n' roll. Orders to desist were relayed to them from the man who still looked like an accountant, with his light gray suit, his close-shaven cheeks and carefully manicured hands, and the small fur hat he wore during winter.

Mathew Street is among the warren of cobbled lanes that once carried goods traffic up from Liverpool docks to their hinterland of dark Victorian warehouses. By day, the lanes were alive with heavy goods trucks, unstacking and loading in the squeak of airborne hoists. By night, they were empty but for cartons and cabbage leaves and the occasional meandering drunk.

Underneath the warehouse at 10 Mathew Street, in 1960, could be found the Cavern Jazz Club. Its entrance was a hatchway, under a single naked lightbulb. A flight of eighteen stone steps turned at the bottom into three arched, interconnecting brick tunnels. The center tunnel was the main club area, with a stage against the inner wall and school-like rows of wooden chairs. In the nearer tunnel, the money was taken; in the further one, beyond obscuring pillars, you danced. The best British jazz bands had performed down there, in an atmosphere pervaded by damp and mold and the aroma of beer slops and small, decaying mammals and the cheeses that were kept in the cellar next door.

Ray McFall, though a passionate jazz fan, was aware of rock 'n' roll's growing popularity. The call from Mona Best only confirmed what he had heard about huge and profitable beat dances in out-of-town halls. The short craze for trad was now definitely over, and modern attracted only the earnest, intellectual few. McFall, therefore, decided to let pop into his jazz stronghold, gradually at first so as not to enrage the existing clientele. His first regular group, the Blue Genes, occupied a curious middle ground, playing both rock and jazz, with banjo and stand-up bass. Tuesdays, the Blue Genes' Guest Night, became the first break in the Cavern's all-jazz program.

McFall had noticed how many young office workers in central Liverpool spent their lunch hour hanging round music shops like Hessy's and the record department in NEMS, the electrical shop in Whitechapel, round the corner from Mathew Street. It suddenly occurred to him that he could just as easily open the Cavern for dancing at midday as at night. So he began to put on lunch-hour sessions, featuring trad jazz bands in alternation with a beat group called the Metronomes whose singer, Tommy Love, worked in a city insurance office. Derry and the Seniors also got a lunchtime booking after their return from Hamburg.

Bob Wooler, visiting the Cavern one lunchtime, was persuaded by Johnny Hutch of the Big Three to say something into the stage microphone. "I did it just as the people were going out. I said, 'Remember, all you cave-dwellers, the Cavern is the best of cellars.' I'd prepared that little pun on Peter Sellers' album *The Best of Sellers*. Ray McFall came across. I thought I was going to get a lecture, but instead he offered me the job of compering the lunchtime sessions."

Wooler lost no time in urging McFall to hire the Beatles. Paddy Delaney, the club doorman and an accomplished mimic, would from then on impersonate Wooler's voice and wagging forefinger as he told McFall they would bring in a following of sixty, at least.

Delaney, a huge, straight-backed, kindhearted Irishman, had seen service both in the Guards and the Liverpool Parks Police. He was equally immaculate in his spare-time profession of helping to dissuade Teddy Boys from entering Liverpool's premier dance halls, the Locarno and the Grafton Rooms. In 1959, to oblige his brother-in-law, he agreed to put in one night on the door of the Cavern Club. "I thought it was a proper place, like the Grafton Rooms, so I turned up smart. I had three dinner suits in those days. I put one of them on with a maroon bow tie, a matching cummerbund with a watermark in it, and three diamond studs in my shirt. I walked up and down Mathew Street three times before I could even *see* the Cavern."

Paddy Delaney was still there—still in evening dress complete with studs and cummerbund—when the Beatles first played at the Cavern in January 1961. Ray McFall had booked them, tentatively, to appear on a Tuesday, midway through the Blue Genes' Guest Night.

"I'm standing there under the light and I see this lad coming along in a leather jacket, a black polo-necked jersey. I remember thinking to myself, 'That's the youngest tramp *I've* ever seen.' 'Are you a member, pal?' I said to him. He said, 'I'm George Harrison. I'm in the Beatles.' I let him go in; then Paul McCartney came along; then John. Then a taxi came with Pete Best and the drums and their two amplifiers. Just chipboard, those were, no paint or anything, with the speakers nailed up inside."

Bob Wooler's prophecy was fulfilled. The Beatles brought in at least sixty extra customers, in contingents from Aintree, Litherland, and West Derby. The Blue Genes, supposedly the main event of the evening, were totally eclipsed. Paddy Delaney witnessed the furious row upstairs on Mathew Street between Ray McFall and his outraged regular musicians.

McFall was impressed by the door receipts but shocked to the depths of his jazz-pure soul by the Beatles' unkempt appearance. He had thought, after seeing Cliff Richard's Shadows, that groups wore suits. He told Bob Wooler that if the Beatles wanted to play the Cavern again, they must not wear jeans. To this the Beatles replied that Ray McFall could get stuffed. Wooler interceded on their behalf, pointing out to McFall the advantage of block-booking a group that, being "professional"—that was to say, unemployed—would be available to play lunchtimes on any day of the week. "The Beatles," Wooler said with pride, "were what I called the first rock and *dole* group."

So it came about that, on three or four days each week, the deliverymen and warehouse checkers in Mathew Street witnessed the unprecedented sight of scores of young girls, from city center shops and offices, in beehive hair and stiletto heels, picking their way down the alleys among the delivery trucks and cast-off fruit crates. By noon, when the session began, a queue would stretch from the corner leading to Whitechapel to the doorway, like a ship's hatch, that would be unnoticeable but for the bouncer who stood there, blocking it with his arm. As the city clocks struck noon that queue would start to move forward, by degrees, into the hatchway and down the eighteen steps to the table where Ray McFall sat, surrounded by soup bowls full of money. Admission cost 1s (5p) to members or 1s 6d (7p) to nonmembers. Beyond McFall's table was a microscopic cloakroom, tended by a girl named Priscilla White during her lunch break from a neighborhood typing pool.

Under the gloomy arches Bob Wooler's voice would gravely resound in what had become each session's inaugural catechism. "Hi, all you

Cavern-dwellers—welcome to the *best* of cellars." Wooler broadcast, not from the stage but from behind it, in a tiny recess that served also as a changing room for the bands. The sole ventilation came from the next-door cellar, via a grille that became gradually blocked by a mounting pile of drum sets. A single cupboard served to accommodate the DJ's amplifier and record-playing deck. Between each live session Wooler sat in this reeking priest hole, playing records from his own large personal collection.

Ray McFall paid the Beatles 25s (£1.25) each per day. For this they did two forty-five-minute spots at the end of the center tunnel, on the tiny stage with dead rats under it, and positively no acoustics. The low-arched brick, and the wall of impacted faces and bodies, so squeezed out all empty air that Pete Best's drumbeats rebounded an inch in front of him, making the sticks jump like pistols in his hand. A single Chuck Berry number, in that heat, caused even tidy Paul to look as if his head had been plunged into a water barrel. The bricks sweated with the music, glistening like the streams that coursed from their temples and sending a steady drip of moisture over equipment in which there were many naked wires. Each breath they took filled their lungs with each other's hot scent, mingling uniquely with an aroma of cheese rinds, damp mold, disinfectant, and the scent of frantic girls.

For their lunchtime audience they poured out the vast Hamburg repertoire that could switch crazily from American blues to maudlin country-and-western; from today's Top Twenty hit to some sentimental prewar dance-band tune. It seemed to Bob Wooler that they took a per-verse delight in playing what no rival group would dare to. "They had to let you know they were different. If everyone else was playing the A-side of a record, they'd be playing the B-side. If the others jumped around, they'd decide to stand still like zombies." Wooler himself possessed a number of rare American singles that he would play as surprise items over the Cavern loudspeakers. One of these, Chan Romero's "Hippy Hippy Shake," besotted Paul McCartney, who begged to be allowed to borrow it and copy down the words. "Hippy Hippy Shake" became the climax of their catalog of sheer stage-stamping rock. A moment later, they would change to the cocktail-lounge tempo of "Till There Was You," from the stage show *The Music Man*, crooned by Paul with the sweat drying on him.

Stu Sutcliffe was back with them on bass guitar, although little

more proficient than he had been before the Hamburg trip. "He'd bop around like the others," Bob Wooler said. "But he seemed to know that the others were carrying him." Stu was hardly noticed by John and Paul in their perpetual contest to be the cynosure of all eyes. They in turn failed to notice how often those eyes would pass over their bobbing heads, to settle on Pete Best. George, on the right, took no part in the clowning, but waited solemnly, biting his lower lip, for the moment when his solo arrived. To his mother, Louise, he explained that he had no time to horse around—it was up to him to keep the music together.

In the intervals, they would go across Mathew Street to the Grapes, a marine-looking pub with scrubbed wooden tables much frequented by postmen from the GPO in North John Street. There they would sit as long as possible over a fivepenny half of bitter each. The landlady complained they took up seats that might have been more profitably occupied by postmen drinking pints of draft Guinness.

The Cavern provided lunch of a sort—hot soup with mysterious lumps in it; meat pies and rolls and soft drinks. "Paul borrowed a halfpenny off me once," Paddy Delaney, the doorman, said. "He wanted a Coke and a cheese roll; it came to sevenpence halfpenny, and he'd only got sevenpence. 'There you are, Paul,' I said to him. 'Remember me when you're up there, famous.'"

Paul's father, Jim McCartney, was the first of their parents to investigate this new epoch. He had noticed the state in which Paul came home from the Cavern, with clothes stinking of mold and a shirt so drenched it could be wrung out over the kitchen sink. Jim was still in the cotton business, working at the Cotton Exchange just round the corner from Mathew Street. Venturing into the Cavern on his own lunch hour, Jim could not get near enough to the stage to speak to Paul. When he came after that it would usually be to drop in some meat he had bought to cook for Paul and Michael that evening. Above the din in the band room he would give Paul careful instructions about when, and at what number, to switch on the electric cooker.

John's aunt Mimi was less easily placated. Ray McFall, sitting behind his soup-bowl exchequer, was dismayed to be confronted by a lean and angry woman demanding the whereabouts of John Lennon. For Mimi, up to that point, still believed John to be studying at art college. He was on stage at the time, doing a song whose lyrics suddenly changed—as at

the Woolton fete—to: "Oh, oh, Mimi's coming. Mimi's coming." In the break, when he reeled into the band room, he found waiting for him, as well as faithful Cynthia, an extremely grim-faced aunt. "I said to him, 'This is very nice, John, isn't it? This is *very* nice!' "

George's mother also happened to be at the Cavern that day, but in the audience. She would go along and shout and scream for George as loudly as any girl. She saw Mimi going out one day, and shouted exuberantly, "Aren't they great?" "I'm glad somebody thinks so," was Mimi's tart reply.

Allan Williams, although busy with his Blue Angel club, was still the sole exporter of Liverpool groups to Hamburg. Early in 1961, he booked Gerry and the Pacemakers to play a two-month session for Peter Eckhorn at the Top Ten Club. It was a well-deserved chance for Gerry Marsden, the smiley little delivery boy from Menzies Street, who had made such a success at the Boxing Stadium show by singing "You'll Never Walk Alone."

Gerry and his group were quiet boys, intent on saving their Hamburg money to buy new equipment. Even so, they brought home enough stories—of Willi's Café, the Gretel and Alphons, and Jim Hawke's Seaman's Mission—to reawaken the Beatles' addiction to Reeperbahn life. Peter Eckhorn had told them they could go back to the Top Ten any time, subject to police and immigration approval. Pete Best's drums were still there, together with the clothes that he and Paul had been compelled to leave behind in the attic.

Pete, with the approval of the other four, rang up Eckhorn from Mona Best's house in Hayman's Green. Eckhorn instantly gave them a booking, to begin in April, at forty pounds each per week—exactly twice as much as they had been paid by Bruno Koschmider. Nor would they have to pay Williams his 10 percent agent's commission, having fixed the engagement without his help. Williams, unaware of this decision, applied to the German consulate in Liverpool for work permits on their behalf, explaining the circumstances of the Bambi Kino fire and rendering heartfelt assurances as to their reliability and good character.

Stu Sutcliffe originally had no intention of accompanying them. Guilty at having traded on John's loyalty for so long, he was now perfectly prepared to hand over the role of bass player in the band to Paul, as Paul so desperately wanted. He was even more full of guilt at having so long neglected his art studies for a career as musician that clearly would never lead anywhere. His intention was to accede to his mother's wishes and return to Liverpool Art College to take his teacher-training diploma. On the strength of his previous brilliant record as a student, the college had indicated that he could go back whenever he liked. But now they informed him that he could not be readmitted. When Millie Sutcliffe made enquiries she learned Stu was suspected of having stolen the Student's Union amplifier that the Beatles had appropriated months before.

This unexpected about-face plunged the sensitive Stu into a depression so intense that, for a time, he feared he might never pick up a paintbrush again. His one desire was to get away from Liverpool, with what he saw as its constricting narrow-mindedness, and back to the freedom of Hamburg and the arms of his beautiful fiancée. In exchange for that, a little more humiliation on stage with the Beatles seemed a small price to pay.

The Beatles' Top Ten engagement started in April 1961. Thanks to Allan Williams they had proper work permits this time, and proper train tickets, purchased with money sent across by Peter Eckhorn. They arrived at Hamburg Station to be greeted by Astrid in her black leather trouser suit. Even the bashful George did not hesitate to fling his arms around her.

The hours at the Top Ten were, if anything, more punishing than at the Kaiserkeller. They went on at 7:00 P.M. each night, playing in alternation with Tony Sheridan's band, until 2:00 or 3:00 A.M. The club's barn-like size meant they must "mak show" even more obviously and violently to be seen out in the remoter parts. Now, too, along the front of the stage, there would often be photographers—friends of Astrid and Klaus Voorman—training their long lenses upward and shouting, "More sveat, boys! More sveat."

Most of their Kaiserkeller friends had forsaken Bruno Koschmider to work at the new Top Ten. There was Horst Fascher, the Reeperbahn's champion bouncer, just released from another prison sentence and ready, in the Liverpool phrase, to "worship the bones of their bodies." There was Rosa, the WC attendant, and her big sweet jar of Prellys. There were three bold-eyed, powerful barmaids with whom almost everyone had explored the delights of "muff-diving," "finger pie," and "yodeling up the canyon," and who signified when a song had gone down well by setting all the lampshades above the bar counter swinging and jogging.

Astrid continued her flattering habit of photographing the Beatles at every opportunity. She produced studies of them, lounging on the docks or in railway yards, complementing their beardless menace with tugboats, freight wagons, or other specimens of German industrial design. She did studio portraits, too, using a technique pioneered by the American Richard Avedon, which gave drama to the face by halving it between shadow and light. George and John were photographed in this way, but not Pete Best—who was genuinely unconceited about his appearance—and, strangely, not Paul. Astrid tended to be with George, whom she mothered, and John, because, as well as being Stu's closest friend, he fascinated her.

It was no coincidence, perhaps, that Stu persuaded John to allow his own steady girlfriend, Cynthia Powell, to come out to visit him in Hamburg. Paul's steady, a girl named Dot Rhode who worked in a Liverpool chemist's shop, was also invited. The two girls had become friends in their common purdah, squeezing themselves into photography booths for snapshots to send to their lords and masters, or laboriously transcribing the words of the newest Chuck Berry song.

The visit took place in Cynthia's Easter college vacation, and passed off happily, against all the odds. For most of the fortnight she stayed with the hospitable Kirchherr family. Astrid was nice to her, lent her stunning clothes, and drove her down to the Reeperbahn each evening to see the Beatles play. Some nights, she stayed behind, heroically sharing John's bunk in the Top Ten attic, while George snored in the bunk below. Paul and Dot stayed, with Tony Sheridan and other itinerant lodgers, on a harbor barge lent to them by Rosa, the club's lavatory attendant. Most of the meals, as usual, were provided by Jim and Lilo Hawke at the Seaman's Mission. Rosa, walking through the early morning fish market, would steal extra rations for Paul, slipping bananas or sardines into her coat pockets or up her sleeves.

Relations between Stu Sutcliffe and Paul McCartney, meanwhile, grew steadily worse. Paul made no secret of his contempt for Stu's bass playing, and his own conviction that he could do it better. There were rows on the Top Ten stage, behind John's back; one night, Paul's taunts even goaded Stu to physical violence. "Paul had made some remark about Astrid," Tony Sheridan says. "Stu went for him, but he was only a little guy. Paul started beating the shit out of him."

Stu spent the club intermissions talking wistfully to *exis*, like Peter Markmann and Detlev Birgfeld, who were students at the Hamburg State Art College. They and Astrid urged him to try to enroll there as a student. Things were especially good just now, they said, as the college had appointed the famous sculptor Edouardo Paolozzi—one of Stu's longtime idols—to run a course of painting and sculpture master classes. Eventually, he was persuaded to go and meet Paolozzi, taking some samples of his Liverpool College work.

A brief glance was enough for Edouardo Paolozzi. He promised to use his influence, not only to admit Stu to the state art college but also to get him a grant from the Hamburg City Council.

In Paolozzi's class, and in an attic studio that Frau Kirchherr gave him, Stu nerved himself to paint again. And once he had started, he could not stop. His Liverpool work, though accomplished, had always been derivative, slipping in and out of identities that caught his fancy. Hamburg, and the Reeperbahn's dark, sleazy colors, gave him his own line at last. Huge swirling abstracts, like crushed Rio carnivals, like cities crumbling into impacted seas, thronged the canvases that, once again, were almost too tall for him to reach the top. Each one, completed in a day or a night, was impatiently stacked aside. Life now seemed too short for the miles his brush had to travel.

For the first month he led a dual life, both studying under Paolozzi and playing at the Top Ten club. At 2:00 or 3:00 A.M., he would go into his attic and work there until it was time for class. He existed for days without sleep, borne up by pills and drink and the feverish excitement of his work. The headaches, which had intermittently troubled him, began to increase, in frequency and ferocity. Sometimes the pain would send him into a kind of fit, in which he would smash his head against the wall or scream at Astrid for some supposed infidelity—then, equally without warning, the anguish would disappear.

He quit the Beatles gradually, without rancor, glad to see how easily they closed ranks behind him. Paul, as Paul had so long wanted, took over bass guitar, borrowing Stu's Hofner President until he could get one of his own. When it came, it was a bizarre new Hofner model, shaped like a violin. Once or twice, for old times' sake, Stu sat in with the Beatles, playing bass alongside Paul. A photograph taken at one such moment shows him half in shadow, his eyes frowning, sightless, as in some study taken a hundred years ago. It was a look that his college tutor, Edouardo Paolozzi, found especially disturbing. "I felt there was a desperate thing about Stuart. I was afraid of it. I wouldn't go down to that club."

Though Stu was a Beatle no longer, he allowed himself to be deputized for the job that none of the others fancied. He wrote to Allan Williams in Liverpool, informing Williams of the decision to withhold his 10 percent commission. It was shabby treatment for a man who, for all his shortcomings, had made genuine efforts on their behalf. Williams wrote back a long and aggrieved letter, threatening to have them blacklisted among theatrical agents, if not deported from Germany all over again. He seems, for once, to have been too hurt to exact retribution. All his written agreements with the Beatles had been destroyed in the fire at his own short-lived Top Ten club. So Williams let the Beatles go.

In Hamburg, meanwhile, a new Messiah had appeared, in Bert Kaempfert, a well-known West German orchestra leader and producer for the German label Polydor. Kaempfert had been to the Top Ten to see Tony Sheridan and immediately put him under contract to Polydor. As a backing group—largely on Tony Sheridan's recommendation—Bert Kaempfert hired the Beatles.

They had gone to bed as usual, Pete Best remembers, just after dawn. At eight sharp, taxis arrived to take them and Tony Sheridan to the recording studio. This, despite Kaempfert's eminence, proved to be no more than the hall of the local nursery school. They recorded on the stage, with the curtains closed.

Bert Kaempfert's idea of rock 'n' roll was to put a drumbeat behind tunes familiar to a German audience from their nights of beer and boomps-a-daisy. He had chosen for Sheridan and his backing group material that included two of the world's most boring songs, "My Bonnie Lies over the Ocean" and "When the Saints Go Marching In." Tony Sheridan sang them in a voice still wide-eyed with last night's Prellys, while the "Beat Brothers"—as Kaempfert had renamed them—rattled off two versions of the same non-arrangement.

The Beat Brothers, thrilled just to be in the proximity of disc-making equipment, were content with their subordinate role. They did prevail on Kaempfert, however, to listen to a handful of Lennon-McCartney songs. The great man's verdict was one to which John and Paul were growing accustomed—their songs did not sound enough like the hits of the moment. But Kaempfert was impressed enough to let them cut a disk in their own right. They did "Ain't She Sweet," one of the standbys from their all-night club act, with John taking the vocal and the old jazz chords rearranged in a style strongly reminiscent of Paul. Kaempfert also liked an instrumental that George had worked out as a parody of Cliff Richard's group, the Shadows. This, too, was taped under the ironic title "Cry for a Shadow."

The tracks chosen by Polydor for release were, as might have been feared, "My Bonnie Lies over the Ocean" coupled with "When the Saints Go Marching In." The Beat Brothers had played for a flat fee of three hundred marks each (about twenty-six pounds), and so could expect no royalty on the disk's quite healthy German sales. "Ain't She Sweet" and "Cry for a Shadow" were still in the Polydor vaults in June 1961, when John, Paul, George, and Pete caught the train back to Liverpool.

Stu Sutcliffe did not go with them. He had decided to settle in Hamburg, marry Astrid, and continue at the state art college. His mother shortly afterward received a photograph of him taken by Astrid in his attic studio, in jeans and gumboots, standing before the easel bearing some new work in headlong progress. The technique was the same that she had used on George and John, splitting the face between light and shadow. In this portrait of Stu the effect was eerie, his features the palest glimmer against what seemed an encroaching dark.

In Liverpool now, beat music raged like a fever. From Mathew Street it had seeped up between the warehouses onto Dale Street and through the studded gates of the Iron Door, another longtime jazz stronghold gone over to evening or all-night pop sessions in overt rivalry with the Cavern. The same had happened all over the city, in clubs like the Downbeat and the Mardi Gras, in dance halls formerly dedicated to quicksteps and Veletas. The Riverside Ballroom and the Orrel Park Ballroom, the Rialto Ballroom, the Avenue cinema, even the Silver Blades Ice Rink clamored for beat groups to fill their Saturday nights. New groups sprang up by the dozen, mutating from older ones, then splitting like amoebas into newer groups still. Now, as rivals to the Beatles at the Cavern, there were the Searchers at the Iron Door. There were Ian and the Zodiacs; Kingsize Taylor and the Dominoes; Faron and the Flamingoes; Earl Preston and the TTs; Lee Curtis and the All-Stars; Dale

Roberts and the Jaywalkers; Steve Day and the Drifters; the Remo Four; the Black Cats; the Four Jays. Hessy's music store thronged each day with eager customers for new guitars, new basses and drum sets to be paid for far into a future that had no relevance compared with the finger-sliding, tom-tomming excitement of tonight.

Bill Harry knew every group and every place there was to play. The curly-haired design student from Parliament Street was always to be seen in the clubs and jive halls, talking to the musicians between numbers and scribbling on bits of paper. He kept notes on every new group that was formed and every new venue opened. For him, as for John Lennon, beat music disrupted an art college course, though in Bill's case, poor family circumstances dictated that even a hobby should be a matter of feverish hard work. He earned extra money by designing stationery for a local printer, and by writing and drawing anything, anywhere, for anyone.

Bill, an inveterate compiler of sci-fi fanzines, had long cherished an ambition to start his own music newspaper. For a time, he planned one called *Storyville and 52nd Street,* to cover jazz. Then in 1961, with details of 350 beat music venues in his notebook, another idea occurred to him. He had noticed, on his trips around clubs and ballrooms, how parochial each one was, how little each audience knew of the sheer size and variety of the beat craze. The musicians, too, often had no idea where their friends or their rivals were performing. Bill Harry conceived the idea of a fortnightly beat music newspaper that would serve both as a guide to clubs and halls and an insight for the fans into the lives of their favorite groups.

The paper, launched on July 6, 1961, was christened *Mersey Beat.* A local civil servant named Jim Anderson provided its fifty pounds starting capital. Bill Harry was editor, designer, chief reporter, sub editor, and advertisement and circulation manager, all while ostensibly studying at the art college. Each lunch hour, he would sprint out of college, down the hill to the *Mersey Beat* office, a single room above a wine merchant's shop in Renshaw Street. His girlfriend, Virginia, who typed and took telephone calls, was the only other member of staff.

John Lennon's former Gambier Terrace flatmate could naturally be counted on to give the Beatles plenty of space in his new paper. When Bill asked them for photographs they handed over a pile of the ones Astrid had taken in Hamburg, together with some informal snapshots of John in his underwear, standing on the Grosse Freiheit and reading the *Daily Express*. John's was precisely the kind of Goon Show humor Bill Harry wanted to flavor the *Mersey Beat* editorial. He had never forgotten the nonsense verses that John had shown him during student lunchtime sessions at Ye Cracke. For *Mersey Beat*'s first issue he asked John to write his own personal account of the Beatles' beginnings as a group. This was produced, Billy Harry remembers, on scraps of paper, with a hangdog, half-embarrassed air. John clearly did not expect his words to be suitable for publication.

Issue number one of *Mersey Beat* had a print run of five thousand copies. Bill Harry, as well as writing the entire paper, delivered bundles of it personally to twenty-eight Liverpool newsstands. Further stocks went on sale at local dances, at Hessy's music shop, and on the record counters of major city stores like Blackler's. One of Bill's best contacts had proved to be NEMS, the electrical appliance shop in Whitechapel that had a record department run by the owner's elder son, Brian Epstein. He showed keen interest in *Mersey Beat*, giving Bill Harry a firm order for a dozen copies.

The first issue carried on its front page a picture of Gene Vincent, the American rock 'n' roll star who had visited Liverpool, as the caption admitted, "earlier in the year." Bill Harry, unable to afford to make photographic blocks, was compelled to borrow what he could from a local weekly newspaper. Underneath, a story headed "Swinging Cilla" told how Cilla Black, the Cavern Club's part-time cloakroom attendant, better known along Scotland Road as Priscilla White, had begun to gain confidence as a singer by afterhours appearances on stage with Rory Storm's group and the Big Three.

The right-hand column was given over to John Lennon's article. Bill Harry had printed it complete under its author's heading "a short diversion on the dubious origins of Beatles, translated from the John Lennon." What followed revealed little of those origins but much about the boy whose fascination with words coexisted with utter disregard of all normal punctuation and spelling. "Many people ask what are Beatles? Why Beatles? Ugh, Beatles, how did the name arrive? So we will tell you. It came in a vision—a man appeared on a flaming pie and said unto them: 'From this day on you are Beatles.' 'Thank you, Mister Man,' they said, thanking him.'"

Mersey Beat was an immediate sellout. At NEMS in Whitechapel, all twelve copies went within minutes of their appearance in the record department, and Brian Epstein telephoned Bill Harry with an order for two dozen more. The next day, he requested a further hundred. For issue two, published on July 20, Epstein's order was twelve dozen copies.

Prominent in the first issue, and every one that followed, was a large display advertisement for the Cavern Club, giving details of its lunchtime, evening, and, occasionally, all-night sessions. Here, the Beatles' name, varying in type-size from the garish to the microscopic, rotated week by week with that of Gerry and the Pacemakers, Rory Storm and the Hurricanes, Kingsize Taylor and the Dominoes, and also the traditional jazz bands that Ray McFall stubbornly continued to hire.

Though conscientiously filled with news about all groups and their doings, *Mersey Beat* made no secret of its overriding preference. Issue two, when it reached the counter of NEMS record store in Whitechapel, banner-headlined the retrospective hot news of the "Beatles'" recording session and contract with Bert Kaempfert in Hamburg. Only now did their Liverpool following learn of the existence of the Beatles' music on disk, albeit a little-known foreign label. The story was illustrated by Astrid's photograph of them, with Stu Sutcliffe, on the traction engine at Der Dom. Paul's surname was given, in one of its several *Mersey Beat* versions, as "McArtrey."

The paper soon became known not merely for news about the Beatles but as an extension of the comedy and clowning in their Cavern Club stage act. John, at Bill Harry's encouragement, contributed more nonsense verses and an irregular column called "Beatcomber," called after the Beachcomber column in the *Daily Express*. He also wrote and paid for comic small ads, filling a section that would otherwise have been empty, and prolonging Beatle in-jokes for weeks at the modest cost of fourpence a word. "HOT LIPS, missed you Friday—Red Nose." "RED NOSE, missed you Friday—Hot Lips." "Whistling Jock Lennon wishes to contact HOT NOSE."

Mersey Beat flourished, thanks to its thorough coverage and the sprinting energy of its editor. Anyone who placed a large ad could expect a large story to be written about them. If the advertiser could write his own copy, so much the better. It was on this principle that *Mersey Beat*, in its early August issue, published a short article by one of its best customers, Brian Epstein of the NEMS electrical shop, reviewing the new records NEMS currently had for sale. Mostly, he recommended ballads from musical shows like *West Side Story* and *The Sound of Music*. A cursory reference was made to Chubby Checker's "Let's Twist Again," and the Streamliners' "Frankfurter Sandwiches." The closing paragraph was devoted to new John Ogden piano recitals of works by Liszt and Busoni.

Bob Wooler, the Cavern disk jockey, also wrote regularly for *Mersey Beat*. His debut column on August 31 dealt entirely with the Beatles: They were, said Wooler, "the biggest thing to hit the Liverpool rock 'n' roll set up in years." Among hundreds of groups playing roughly the same R&B material, Wooler pinpointed accurately the novelty in musicians with equal appeal to both sexes—to the boys through their dress and manner; to girls, in Wooler's view, chiefly through the "mean, moody magnificence" of their drummer Pete Best. Pete, indeed, was the only Beatle singled out by name. Wooler summed them up, with true alliterative relish, as "rhythmic revolutionaries . . . seemingly unambitious yet fluctuating between the self-assured and the vulnerable. Truly a phenomenon—and also a predicament to promoters. Such are the fantastic Beatles. I don't think anything like them will happen again." The only other item on the page was the brief column by "Brian Epstein of NEMS" recommending new releases by Frank Sinatra, the Shadows, and the George Mitchell Singers.

Bob Wooler's endorsement in *Mersey Beat* was backed up by ceaseless plugging of their Polydor record, over the Cavern microphone and in the halls where Wooler ran regular dances for Brian Kelly. Such was their drawing power now that Kelly would post bouncers outside their changing room to stop rival promoters from offering them more than ten pounds per night.

Between the groups, by contrast, there was little competition, save in the sinking of pints and the attracting of girls. Bob Wooler's strict running-order would frequently be confounded by a hybrid semi-orchestra formed of two, or more, groups who felt like jamming together. At Litherland Town Hall one night the Beatles merged with Gerry and the Pacemakers to form the "Beatmakers." Gerry wore George's leather outfit, George wore a hood, Paul wore a nightdress, and Gerry's brother Fred and Pete Best played one drum each.

Three or four nights a week at the Cavern the queue would move, past Ray McFall's soup bowls, into heat barely describable by those who ever experienced it. "You could feel it as you went down those eighteen steps, climbing up your legs," Paddy Delaney, the doorman, said. "The lads used to faint as well as the girls." In the glue of bodies the only space, apart from the stage, was an area at the opposite end of the center tunnel where the boys would go and urinate. A girl wishing to get to the ladies' room could often make the journey only by being passed over the heads of the crowd.

For all the "kicks and kudos," as Bob Wooler alliteratively phrased it, the summer of 1961 ended on a note of anticlimax. The Beatles seemed to have progressed as far as any group could outside the mystic sphere of London. Other local idols, like Rory Storm with his Butlin's holiday camp dates, seemed to be forging far ahead.

John Lennon took out his boredom in writing for *Mersey Beat*, and in letters to Stu Sutcliffe in Hamburg—long letters in pencil on exercise book paper, full of scribble and doodles, poems that started seriously but petered out into self-conscious obscenity and anguished cries about the "shittiness" of life. The correspondence could not be shown to Aunt Mimi or Millie Sutcliffe, teeming as it did with swear words and a running joke whereby Stu took the character of Christ and John, that of John the Baptist. It seemed that Stu, by staying on in Hamburg, had done the adventurous and enviable thing.

One letter from Stu mentioned that Jurgen Vollmer, a photographer friend of Astrid's, was soon going to be in Paris on vacation. John and Paul decided on the spur of the moment to use some money John's Scottish aunt had given him to go across to Paris and meet Jurgen. They went without a word to George or Pete Best, and despite the imminence of several important bookings. For almost a week they lived in Montmartre and hung around the Flea Market, looking for sleeveless jackets like the one Jurgen wore. They also persuaded Jurgen to cut their hair in the "French" style that Astrid had given Stu and George. They returned to Liverpool to find George and Pete Best disgusted with them; for a time, it seemed that the Beatles were finished. Bob Wooler and Ray Mc-Fall persuaded them to continue, each lecturing John and Paul sternly on the need to be reliable.

What did it matter anyway? The Cavern was always there, with another nightlong session to trap them underground. Up on Mathew Street, where Paddy Delaney stood in his evening dress, a cloud of steam from the close-packed bodies below drifted out under the solitary light.

PART TWO

GETTING

SEVEN

"WHAT BRINGS MR. EPSTEIN HERE?"

Each Wednesday night in the late 1930s little Joe Flannery would be dressed in his nightclothes and taken to spend the evening at the house of his father's best customer, Harry Epstein. Joe's father, Chris Flannery, was a cabinetmaker specializing in the heavy sideboards sold at Epstein's Walton Road shop. "Mr. Harry" was a stickler for quality, refusing to accept any piece whose drawers did not slide in as easily upside-down. But on Wednesday evenings formality relaxed. The Flannerys and the Epsteins drove into Liverpool together to attend the weekly wrestling bouts. Seven-year-old Joe would wait for his parents at Mr. Harry's house, playing upstairs in the nursery with the Epsteins' son, Brian.

This other boy was not like Joe. He was slender and delicate; he had a nanny to look after him in his own softly lit upstairs domain. He did not speak like Joe, nor like any Liverpool child. And he had many beautiful toys. Joe, in particular, loved the model coach that Brian had been given to mark the 1937 coronation of George VI. It was the state coach in miniature, made of tin but magnificently gilded, drawn by a dozen plumed tin horses, spurred on by liveried tin postillions and grooms.

Brian knew how much Joe loved the coronation coach. To grant, or arbitrarily refuse, permission to play with it gave him a sensation he slowly recognized as power over someone older and stronger. Though he himself cared little for the coach, he worried that Joe, because of loving it so much, would somehow gain possession of it. So one night while Joe was there, he stamped on it until he had broken it.

In 1933, the wedding took place of eighteen-year-old Malka Hyman to twenty-nine-year-old Harry Epstein. The match was approved of, uniting as it did two highly respectable Jewish families and two comparably thriving furniture firms. Harry's father, Isaac, owned the Liverpool shop he had founded as a penniless Lithuanian immigrant at the turn of the century. The Hymans, Malka's people, owned the Sheffield Cabinet

Company, mass producing such items as The Clarendon, a bedroom suite that, in the twenties and early thirties, graced many a suburban English home.

Malka received a comfortable upbringing and a boarding-school education. In 1933, she was a slender, rather refined and artistic girl whose only serious complaint against the world was the way it had Anglicized her given name. Malka is the Hebrew word for queen. So Queenie was what her family, and her new husband, called her.

Her first child was born on September 19, 1934, at a private nursing home on Rodney Street, Liverpool. It was a boy, and as such a cause for rejoicing to grandparents concerned with the perpetuity of business. To Queenie, the baby in her arms was something more beautiful than she had dared to imagine. She called him Brian because she liked the name, and Samuel for the sake of the family and the scriptures.

The new baby was brought home to substance and comfort. Queenie's dowry from her parents was a handsome modern town house in Childwall, one of the smartest Liverpool suburbs. One ninety-seven Queens Drive was a five-bedroom residence with bay windows and a sunrise design on the glass over the front door, which a uniformed maid would open to visitors. A nanny became necessary when, in 1935, Queenie gave birth to her second son, Clive John.

The Epstein family shop occupied a prominent place on Walton Road. A row of tall display windows, extending around the corner onto Royal Street, offered a range of furniture and home requisites, from sideboards to standard lamps, whose appearance was not especially chic but whose quality and durability could always be relied on. Next door stood the North End Music Stores, a little double-fronted shop that had been there since the days when young men and women bought sheet music to sing around the parlor piano. Jim McCartney's was one of the many local families that bought pianos from NEMS on the installment plan. Subsequently, Epstein's had taken over the little shop, extending its stock to phonographs and radios.

Harry Epstein worked hard, but enjoyed his pleasures and sharing them with his wife. They were keen bridge players, fond of films and the theater, well known, in a hospitable community, for the generosity and style of their entertaining. Once a week, they would drive into Liverpool to dine in the Sefton Restaurant at the Adelphi, a hotel then at its splendid apogee. In Ranelagh Place, next to Lime Street, the polished auto-

Earliest known picture of John Lennon's Quarry Men, playing at the Rosebery Street centenary party, summer 1957. 'I could hear these blokes whispering that they were going to get Lennon . . . the lads had to have a policeman to see them to the bus stop.'

John in garden

Julia

Mimi Smith

Michael and Paul

GROWING UP

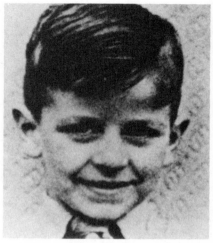

Ringo as a boy

Mary McCartney

Ringo's parents

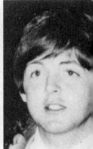

Four faces metamorphosed by fame: from Liverpool scufflers to conventional Pop idols; from sleek millionaires to psychedelic bandsmen; from lank-haired hippies to trinket-bedecked Caesars, their Em dissolving around them.

Rory Storm (*centre*) the blithe, blond Liverpool Rock 'n' Roll showman who, in mid-performance, would athletically shin up a pillar at New Brighton Tower ballroom. His occasional falls increased his drawing power. Extreme right in his group, The Hurricanes, is the sad-eyed drummer still known as Ritchie Starkey, soon to be transformed into Ringo Starr.

Rooftop cowboys in Hamburg. Their silver-embossed boots and Gene Vincent caps caused a sensation among polite West German boys.

John waltzes with George at the Queen's Hall, Aldershot, December 1960, after playing for two hours to 18 people.

Stu Sutcliffe in 1961. Astrid produced this disturbing double image at a time when Stu's headaches were growing worse, his black-outs more frequent.

A rare photograph by Astrid of herself in a mirror, showing the beauty so often kept back behind her camera lens.

At the Top Ten Club, Hamburg, 1961;
Paul still on rhythm guitar, George still
using the cheap Hofner he saved for, John
still uncertain how to comb his hair.

John and Paul at a boulevard cafe during
their truant trip to Paris in 1961, when
Jurgen Vollmer cut their hair as Beatles for
keeps. Back in Liverpool, George and
Pete almost quit in disgust.

On the beach near Hamburg, 1961: Stu (*right*) the creator and initiator, works on a collage, helped by John, his admirer and disciple.

1961: Stu and Astrid on the beach near Hamburg. The uneasy figure in the background is John's then girl friend, Cynthia Powell.

Mathew Street in the heyday of the Cavern Club's lunch-time sessions, the queues stretching back from an entrance that would be unnoticed but for the bouncer's blocking arm. In foreground, right, is Paddy Delaney, the ex-Guardsman who nightly stood watch in cummerbund and pearl-studded shirt.

Cavern Club interior: walls reeking of cheese rind, streaming with condensation. 'The lads used to faint as well as the girls.'

Paul, John, Pete and George, in the dank days and steamy nights of Cavern Club stardom –
a local supremacy chiefly attributed to Pete Best's 'mean, moody magnificence'.

Clowning at the Cavern between sessions:
a mock funeral for a still-smoking Paul.

With new hair, and Hamburg leathers, in
full flood on the Cavern stage with its
heavily-autographed and graffiti-ed back
wall.

Above: the Beatles photographed on Brian's instructions, by a leading Liverpool wedding portraitist. When Brian mentioned his 'group', the photographer thought it was a family group. Dissatisfied with the Hamburg leather image, Brian had them re-photographed (*below*) disgruntled in their new stage suits.

Recording Love Me Do, 4 September 1962, under George Martin's critical eye. George Harrison still had the black eye he had received in the Pete Best riots. Before taping PS I Love You they broke for tea in the EMI canteen.

The Star-Club, Hamburg, 1962; a postcard view omitting the fights, upturned tables, bludgeoned customers and Ali, the drop-kicking waiter.

Back from Scandinavia, to the astonishing London Airport welcome. 'Is all this meant for someone else?'

mobiles slid up the ramp. Doormen hastened out to welcome them into the majestic, shiplike interior of the entrance hall.

To their two small sons Harry and Queenie Epstein gave the security, not only of Jewish family life but also of a middle class untroubled, as yet, by any social guilt. For Merseyside, in that time, was racked by unemployment. A few miles from Childwall, on gray and unknown dockyard streets, the men massed at dawn, like livestock, for the favor of even half a day's work at four and sixpence. Only a mile or so away ragged children played barefoot on flinty cobblestones. But in Childwall, the nursery lights glowed softly; there was Auntie Muriel or Uncle Mac on the radio, and thin bread and butter for tea.

Brian left babyhood rapidly, learning to walk by the age of eleven months and to talk soon after that, clearly and interrogatively. In looks he was like his father, dark-eyed and round-faced, with wavy, light-brown hair. His temperament was Queenie's, most notably in his love of refinement, and a feeling for style manifest even as a toddler. He would stand in his mother's bedroom while she got ready to go out, and gravely confer with her about which dress and accessories she should wear. Like Queenie he loved the theater, its world of romance, strange light, and make-believe. *The Wizard of Oz*, the first film he ever saw, left him astounded with its wistful fantasy for days. At the same time he seemed normally robust, hammering wooden shapes into a plywood board at his first kindergarten school, Beechanhurst on Calderstones Road.

In 1940, during the bombing of Liverpool, Harry Epstein moved his family to relative safety in Southport on the West Lancashire coast. Brian attended Southport College, but hated it so much that Queenie transferred him to a smaller prep school. Despite his obvious intelligence and alertness he did not seem to do well there either. But now it was 1944, and safe to move back to Liverpool. Ten-year-old Brian was arrayed in a new black blazer and sent to Liverpool College, the most exclusive and expensive of the city's fee-paying academies.

Before he had reached his eleventh birthday the college asked Harry and Queenie to remove him. It was alleged that he had done a dirty drawing in the mathematics class. According to Brian, this had been a design for a theater program, legitimately adorned by the figures of dancing girls. Privately the headmaster told Queenie that in other respects, too, Brian had proved to be a "problem child." He himself was never to forget the shame of sitting on a sofa at home and hearing his father say, "I don't know *what* we're going to do with you." The words produced one of the furious blushes by which Brian betrayed even the smallest discomfiture.

He had not sat for the eleven-plus exam, and so could not be sent to any of Liverpool's excellent grammar schools. His parents were forced to settle for another small private academy that Brian, predictably, loathed. Queenie by now had begun to suspect that the fault might not be entirely on his side. Anti-Semitism was a habit in which many otherwise agreeable British people still overtly and comfortably indulged. The nation that had recently pitted itself against the Nazi Holocaust saw no harm in using words like "Yid" or "Jewboy" and in passing such expressions on to its children.

The Epsteins decided to try a school that actually welcomed Jewish boys. The nearest that could be found was Beaconsfield, near Tunbridge Wells in Kent. There, despite Queenie's forebodings, Brian seemed to do a little better. He took up horseback riding and was encouraged to paint and draw. He made a friend of another Liverpool boy, Malcolm Shifrin, also the son of furniture people. The experiment was so successful that his younger brother, Clive, came to Beaconsfield to join him.

He continued to show a precocious love of luxury and refinement. Even when quite small, his greatest treat was to go with his mother and father for dinner at the Adelphi. Throughout the boy's infancy Harry and Queenie sacrificed vacations abroad in favor of annual seaside visits to Llandudno in North Wales, or St. Anne's. One wet summer in Llandudno, when Brian was eleven, as a change from variety shows, Queenie took him to a concert by the Liverpool Philharmonic Orchestra. From that moment he began to love and learn about classical music. Another year, at St. Anne's, the family struck up acquaintanceship with Geraldo, a bandleader famous for his BBC radio shows. Brian was invited to go into Blackpool to watch Geraldo make a recording. Queenie remembers how he sat spellbound in the studio when the red light went on for silence.

His formal education had yet again run into squalls. Shortly to leave Beaconsfield, he was busily engaged in failing the entrance exams for major private schools such as Rugby, Repton, and Clifton. At last he was able to satisfy the requirements of Clayesmoore, a small private school still further away, in Dorset. "As soon as he got there, he started to grumble," Queenie Epstein remembered. "Oh, those grumbles of his were enormous."

Clive, his younger brother, a placid, conscientious, practical boy, had passed through prep school without trouble or complaint. Clive was good at exams, and so easily got into Wrekin College, a private school of the higher echelon in Shropshire. On the strength of Clive's performance, the Wrekin head agreed to accept Brian also.

Wrekin was his eighth school. He stayed there for two years, in a torpor faithfully described in his school reports. His only aptitudes seemed to be for art and—he discovered—acting. He found that he could face an audience without blushing, and that he enjoyed speaking lines. School dramatics brought him friends, at times even won him official commendation. But some worm of reticence, nurtured by all his previous scholastic failures, prevented him from sharing this new success with his parents. Queenie Epstein always remembered driving down to Wrekin to see a school play about Christopher Columbus, and failing to spot Brian where she expected to see him, among the supporting cast. He had not told her, so she did not realize, that he *was* Christopher Columbus.

He left school at fifteen, without sitting for his school certificate. He had written home that exams were not needed in the career he had chosen. Throughout his final terms he had come top of his class in art and design. He wanted to go to London and become a dress designer.

Few enough people in 1950 would have wished to see their sons make such a choice of profession. To a northern Jewish family, with its age-old view of filial duty, no more disturbing or wounding suggestion could have emanated from an elder son. Harry Epstein was outraged and made no secret of it; Queenie, though more sympathetic, could see no means of granting Brian's wish within convention. The great scheme was buried quickly, before it could reach the ears of relations.

Another idea, that he might study art, languished as quickly under his father's remorseless practicality. With no exams behind him, no aptitude save that of upsetting his parents, there was nothing left for Brian but to submit to heredity. In September 1950, shortly after his sixteenth birthday, he started work as a furniture salesman in the family's Walton Road shop.

A woman came in to Epstein's that day to buy a mirror. Brian was allowed to deal with her under the critical eye of his parental superiors. By the time the customer left he had persuaded her that what she really needed was a dining-table that cost twelve-pounds.

He was, he discovered, a born salesman. Walton Road was not a grand thoroughfare, nor were they grand people who shopped for furniture at I. Epstein & Sons. This young man who served them, with his dapper suit, solicitous manner, and upper-class voice, was decidedly an asset to the shop. Salesmanship awoke in him what eight costly schools could not—the will to work hard and be organized and efficient. He found he enjoyed arranging things for display, and window dressing. And he was doing something that did not disappoint, but actually pleased, his father.

To his grandfather, he was less pleasing. Isaac Epstein still directed the firm he had founded, arriving on the premises each morning as early as 6:00 A.M. Isaac, having dictated matters for half a century, looked askance on a grandson who boldly arranged dining-room chairs in the shop window with their back to the street, claiming it was "more natural."

Upsets with his grandfather became so frequent that, in 1952, his father and Uncle Leslie judged it wiser to remove him temporarily from Isaac Epstein's sight. For six months that year Brian worked as a trainee with the Times Furnishing Company at their Lord Street, Liverpool, branch. Reports on his progress were consistently favorable. As a salesman, he was smart and efficient; he dressed windows with flair and taste. When his stay with the branch ended he received a parting gift of a Parker pen and pencil set.

To outward appearances, his position was an enviable one. The son of wealthy parents, adored by his mother, indulged by a father glad to see this newfound business zeal, he seemed, in 1952, the very acme of provincial young bachelorhood. Ample pocket money supplemented his salesman's pay, enabling him to dress with an elegance beyond his eighteen years. His suits came from the best Liverpool tailors; his ties were half-guinea silk foulards; he had his hair cut in the salon at Horne Brothers' shop. He belonged to a sophisticated young set that congregated at tennis clubs and cocktail parties, and in fashionable Liverpool haunts such as the Adelphi Palm Court lounge and the Basnett oyster bar. Among this circle he was popular, witty, generous, and charming. Girls found him attractive, with his wavy hair, his snub nose and delicate mouth, and the large soft eyes that did not always look directly into theirs.

But by the time Brian was eighteen, he realized that, much as he enjoyed female company, he had no wish to share his life with any of the young women whom Queenie and his Adelphi set steered into his path. He must face the fact that he was homosexual.

It was a discovery calculated to fill any young British male of that era with unmitigated horror. In the 1950s, and up to the end of the following decade, homosexual acts between males were still a crime punishable by imprisonment. Only in rarified and enclosed worlds such as show business and couture could homosexuals yet find a measure of tolerance under the humanizing term "gay." In the everyday world they were loathed, feared, and mocked as "queers," "bum-boys," "nancies," "gingers," "fruits," "arse-bandits," and innumerable other heartless synonyms, abused and even attacked with impunity if they betrayed themselves in the smallest detail. For the son of respectable, religious Jewish parents in Liverpool's lingering Victorian twilight, the predicament was infinitely worse. There was never any question of Brian "coming out," even—or especially not—to his own family. His father was simply unable to grasp such a concept; his more sensitive, intuitive mother may have known the truth even before Brian did, but she feared to breathe a word about it to anyone.

In 1952, he became eligible for national service. He was put into the army—not the RAF as he had wished—and sent south to do his basic training in Aldershot. He had hopes of being picked as officer material, but instead became a clerk in the Royal Army Service Corps. He was posted to London, to the RASC depot at Albany Barracks, Regent's Park.

His army life was mitigated by plentiful pocket money from home and comparative liberty after 6:00 P.M. His mother's sister, his aunt Frieda, lived in Hampstead, only a mile or so away; he was also within easy reach of the West End. He took to going around like a young Guards officer, with bowler hat, pinstripe suit, and rolled umbrella. Driving back into barracks one night he was mistakenly saluted by the gate sentry, and next morning was put on a charge of impersonating an officer.

The army's reaction to this seemingly trivial escapade was draconian. Brian was confined to barracks and subjected to lengthy medical and psychiatric examinations without ever being told their purpose. His superiors may well have discovered his homosexuality, which needless to say was absolutely barred from all armed forces in those days. A close business associate would also later suggest that the incident at the barrack gate was no innocent misunderstanding, but that Brian habitually posed as an officer to gain entrance to service clubs like the "In and Out" in Piccadilly. Whatever the cause, he was declared psychologically unfit for military service and discharged after less than half his two-year term. Although the army could not be rid of him fast enough, it still provided a character reference describing him as "sober, conscientious . . . at all times utterly trustworthy."

Within a few months he was once more a dapper and purposeful young man-about-Liverpool, working hard in the family business—and now with some real empathy and enjoyment. The little NEMS music shop in Harry Epstein's empire had lately widened its stock from pianos and radios to phonograph records. Harry gave Brian the job of organizing and running the new record department.

The success he made of it reflected his passion for classical music as well as his newfound business efficiency. Even as a schoolboy he had had his own impressive record collection, housed in a cabinet made specially for him at his Hyman grandparents' Sheffield factory. With his schoolfriend Malcolm Shifrin he was an ardent supporter of the "Liverpool Phil." "Brian's knowledge of music really was impressive even then," Shifrin says. "So was his knowledge of the related arts, like ballet. He always *knew* music people—John Pritchard, the Philharmonic's conductor, was a friend of his. We drove up twice to the Edinburgh Festival, and Brian introduced me to people there. But I always had the feeling he was a lonely person."

He was still as addicted to the theater as he had been in his school days. Liverpool's two main theaters, the Playhouse and the Royal Court, were surrounded in those days by half a dozen smaller but flourishing professional repertories. Behind the Royal Court was a genuine stage-door district of pubs and hotel bars that resounded to extravagant greetings in London accents. Brian haunted both the theaters and their adjacent bars in the hope of getting to know stage people. He himself appeared in one or two local amateur productions and, like an actor, acquired the habit of giving away signed photographs of himself to his friends.

Among the actors who befriended him was Brian Bedford, then, at the start of his career, starring in *Hamlet* at the Liverpool Playhouse. To Bedford, Brian confided one night that he hated shop work and Liverpool, and that he, too, wanted to become an actor. Bedford encouraged him to try for an audition at the Royal Academy of Dramatic Art in London. RADA's director, John Fernald, as it happened, had formerly run the Liverpool Playhouse. Brian auditioned with Fernald and, to his astonishment, was accepted.

The news filled his parents with dismay. In provincial Jewish business circles "going on the stage" was hardly less deplorable than becoming a dress designer. All the stability Brian seemed to have acquired was now put away, with his formal suits and ties. "He'd made up his mind," Queenie said, "he was going to be a duffel-coated student. He wouldn't even take his car. We'd given it to him for his twenty-first birthday. A beautiful little cream and maroon Hillman Californian."

Under John Fernald at RADA Brian was a more than adequate pupil, sensitive and gentle. "He didn't have a spectacular talent," Fernald says, "but it was a pleasing one. If you think in terms of typecasting, he would have played the second male lead—the best friend in whom the hero can always confide."

At RADA he acquired—or seemed to—a steady girlfriend. Her name was Joanna Dunham; she wore a fur coat dyed red. "Brian always seemed older than the rest of us," Joanna says. "Even though he was only twenty-one. And he drank. That was something hardly anyone at RADA did then, although everyone smoked. Brian would say, just like an older person would, 'I *must* have a drink.'

"I never thought he had any particular acting talent. There was one time, though, when he *did* surprise me. We had to do a test together for Fernald—a scene from *The Seagull*. We chose the scene between Konstantin and his mother, where Konstantin is adoring to his mother first, then flies into a terrible rage and tears the bandage off his head. The words must have had some special meaning for Brian. As he spoke the lines I could feel he was getting out of control. When he started tearing the bandage off, I really felt frightened. It was almost as if he were having a nervous breakdown there on stage."

Brian seems to have tried to make one last stab at heterosexuality by having an affair with Joanna. One night at a party he got drunk and started to confide in her some of the secrets of his school days. "I felt he seriously wanted to have a relationship with me, and that he was trying to tell me something. He was very pissed and threatened to drive me home. I behaved very badly, I'm afraid. I just ran away."

Worse was soon to come. At the end of RADA's 1957 Easter term Brian returned to Liverpool to be with his family during Passover, then returned to London, where he'd arranged to spend the rest of the vacation working in a bookshop. One night, as he returned home to his North London flat after seeing a play at the Arts Theatre Club, he exchanged glances and a few words with a young man in the men's lavatory at Swiss Cottage underground station. His interlocutor was a policeman, waiting there to entrap homosexuals in the act of cottaging, or seeking sex around public bathrooms. Despite having committed no offense Brian was arrested and charged with "persistently importuning." When he appeared at Marylebone Magistrates Court later, officers persuaded him to plead guilty, assuring him he'd get nothing worse than a fine or conditional discharge. Only when he'd done so did he realize he was up on a charge of "importuning seven men."

A letter, apparently written to his lawyer in the midst of this ordeal, reveals how desperately he had tried to join the sexual mainstream. "I do not think I am an abnormally weak-willed person—the effort and determination with which I have tried to rebuild my life these last few months have, I assure you, been no mean effort. I believed that my own will-power was the best thing with which to overcome my homosexuality. And I believe my life may have become contented and may even have attained a public success. . . ."

In fact, it now seems that Harry and Queenie Epstein did not hear about the case, which would have been unlikely even to figure in any newspaper of wider circulation than the *Hampstead and Highgate Express*. But London was now poisoned for Brian, seemingly forever. On the eve of his fourth RADA term, over a family dinner at the Adelphi Hotel, he told his parents what they had so much longed to hear: He'd had enough of being a duffel-coated student. He was ready to come home to Liverpool and become a businessman.

For this apparent sacrifice he was given even further independence within the family firm. His father had bought a small shop in Hoylake, on the Cheshire Wirral, to be stocked with the more exclusive modern furniture that Brian favored, and run by him on his own. It was his idea that the opening should be performed by a celebrity, "Auntie Muriel," his childhood radio favorite from *BBC Children's Hour*.

There now began Brian's uneasy and painful double life. By day, managing Clarendon Furnishings, he was a smart young executive. By night, he was a furtive and self-loathing lawbreaker, cruising the Liverpool darkness in search of others like himself, in constant fear of the police and of no less vigilant "queer-bashing" gangs. Though the city could not dare harbor anything like a modern gay bar, there were two acknowledged rendezvous under the sheltering wing of the Royal Court theater. A pub called the Magic Clock (or "Magic Cock") and an old hotel named the Stork (more usually pronounced "Stalk") both attracted an exclusively male clientele, dressed always with severe understatement, semaphoring their forbidden brotherhood only with the faintest flicker of eyes or mouths.

But this precarious refuge was not enough for Brian. It was his further misfortune not to be attracted to other middle-class young men like himself, with whom he might have enjoyed discreet and—in that pre-AIDS era—relatively safe physical relationships. His taste was for heterosexual men of the artisan class: the very dockers, laborers, and merchant seamen who hated "queers" the most, and most actively sought to do them physical harm. For all their detestation there were many who habitually posed as "rough trade," first leading a gay male on, then beating him up in simulated amazed outrage—and later, more often than not, blackmailing him with the threat of exposure to his family or the police.

Some time around 1958 Brian began his first, and probably last, happy emotional affair. One night in the Stork Hotel he met a tall, dark-haired young man whose evident nerves were kept in check by a quiet, measured Liverpool voice. With mutual astonishment, Brian and he recognized one another. The tall young man was Joe Flannery, the cabinetmaker's son who used to be left in the nursery with Brian every Wednesday night.

The two began a relationship that from the beginning was more companionable than passionate. Joe hungered for glamour and refinement, and was as dazzled by Brian's sophistication as he once had been by his beautiful toy coronation coach. The two would go to the theater and smart restaurants in Liverpool or sometimes further afield in Manchester. As Joe quickly discovered, Brian still treated his many expensive playthings with utter cavalierness. "Whenever he was parking his car between two other ones, he never cared if he bumped the one in front or the one behind. 'What are bumpers for?' he used to say."

Driven from home by a homophobic father, Joe had opened a small bric-a-brac shop on Kirkdale Road and taken a flat in Alexander Terrace. Brian would come and have lunch with him in the shop or stay overnight at the flat. Joe bought a "bed settee" on the installment plan for them to share that, out of respect for Brian's family, he did not get from Epstein's furniture shop but from nearby Gerard Kelly's. He still treasures the payments book for it to this day.

He was head over heels in love with Brian, but always accepted that his feelings were not returned with the same intensity. He recognized, too, that Brian still had an insatiable need to go downtown and seek the life-threatening thrills of rough trade. Their flat increasingly became a refuge when these encounters left Brian in no shape to go home to his family. "He'd sometimes come back at night with his face all bruised and cut and his beautiful Peter England white shirt soaked with blood. 'Joe,' he'd say to me, 'put it straight into the bin.' "

His shy, fastidious flatmate came to understand that the danger, the humiliation, the physical pain—even the engulfing shame and self-disgust—of Brian's night forays gave him an excitement he could not live without, try as he might. A horrible excitement lingered even from his worst disaster—the one that finally unmasked him to his family circle and much of Liverpool.

He described it all to Joe in quiet moments, as they lay together on the bed settee. A few months earlier one of his sexual partners had threatened to go to his family unless he paid a substantial sum. But the blackmail had not stopped there; it had gone on increasing until there was no alternative but to tell the police. In return for a guarantee of anonymity Brian had agreed to help snare the blackmailer by inviting him to the NEMS shop after hours, where concealed police officers could hear him incriminate himself out of his own mouth. The man had been caught and brought to trial—with Brian giving evidence as "Mr. X"—and had gone to prison, vowing vengeance.

It was evident that Brian derived some queasy thrill from the idea of a convict with a festering grudge against him. "He used to tell me all the time that somebody was out to get him," Joe remembers, "and how his life wouldn't be safe when this person was free again."

The Epstein electrical retail business continued to expand. In 1958, with the start of the television boom, Harry was ready to move into central

Liverpool. His first city shop was on Great Charlotte Street, near the Adelphi, and called NEMS after the North End Music Stores. Brian ran the record department and his younger brother, Clive, the household electrical side. Once again, at Brian's prompting, there was a celebrity opening, by singer Anne Shelton, the "Forces Sweetheart."

The next year, an even bigger singing star, Anthony Newley, opened a second, greatly extended NEMS city center shop. This one was in Whitechapel, close to Liverpool's banking and insurance district, a narrow street recently developed by a row of contemporary shops. The Whitechapel NEMS had three sales floors, with a fourth for stock rooms and offices.

Brian had worked hard enough and produced profits enough at the Great Charlotte Street NEMS to convince his father that the new shop should have a greatly extended record department. In the event it had two: the classical on the ground floor, popular in the basement. The Whitechapel street window displayed records with a flair developed in Brian's table and chair arrangements for the Times Furnishing Company. Another of his ideas was to cover the ceiling of the ground-floor department with hundreds of LP sleeves.

Before long, NEMS in Whitechapel, rather than Lewis's or Blackler's department stores, advertised "The Finest Record Selection in the North." The policy, instituted by Brian, was that no request by a customer must ever be turned away. If the record were not in stock, it must be ordered. An ingenious system of cardboard folders with colored strings kept Brian constantly abreast of which records were in stock and which had sold out and needed reordering.

He was now twenty-seven, but looked older, with his dark suit and his conservative haircut. His staff called him "Mr. Brian"; behind his back they called him "Eppy." They laughed a little at his slightly pompous executive airs. But they respected him as a decent and considerate employer, though a niggling perfectionist. If some small things were not right, he could fly into a red-faced tantrum, shouting and stamping his foot. Then, in a minute, he would again be his usual, quiet, charming, courteous self.

If there were occasional whispers about men's lavatories and blackmail and court cases and "Mr. X," they were no more than whispers. Few who saw him by day in Whitechapel could visualize him in circumstances other than driving out to some smart Cheshire restaurant, accompanied by an equally smart young woman. He liked female company and had several passing girlfriends. Once, to please Queenie, he even got engaged. The young woman involved was evidently mad about him. Somehow, his mother had noticed, that was always the point when Brian would grow nervous and evasive.

His adventures had brought him the benefit of certain good, long-standing male friends. There was Geoffrey Ellis, a recent Oxford graduate, now working in Liverpool for the Royal Insurance Company. There was also Peter Brown, who had originally run the record department at Lewis's department store, and had afterward taken over from Brian as manager of the Great Charlotte Street NEMS. A slender, sensitive young man, rejected by his Catholic family in Bebington, Peter was to model his whole existence on Brian's.

By the summer of 1961 Brian was again growing restless. The Whitechapel shop, well established and smooth running, absorbed less and less of his attention and energy. The one small innovation that summer had been *Mersey Beat,* Bill Harry's new music paper, with its mutually advantageous record review column by "Brian Epstein of NEMS." The column lapsed when Brian went away, as he regularly did, for a long vacation in Spain. In October, the experience and his tan had faded; he was conscious of a vague dissatisfaction. He felt as if he were waiting for something to happen.

On Saturday, October 28, an eighteen-year-old Huyton boy named Raymond Jones strolled into the Whitechapel branch of NEMS. Brian, that morning, happened to be behind the counter, helping with the weekend rush. He himself stepped forward to serve Raymond Jones, whom he recognized vaguely as one of the crowd of printers' apprentices often to be seen in the shop during their lunch hour, sorting through the country-and-western stock. Like a good businessman he even remembered that Carl Perkins was this particular customer's favorite singing star.

Today, Raymond Jones did not as usual ask for anything new by Carl Perkins. He asked for a single called "My Bonnie," by the Beatles.

Brian had never heard of the single or the group whose name, in the busy shop, had to be repeated to him: Beatles, with an "a." No group of that name, certainly, appeared in the Top Ten chart currently posted on NEMS's front window. No such single had gone into a stock folder, marked by its appropriate colored string. Raymond Jones could provide no further details of the disk. He had heard about it, he said, at Hambleton Hall, where he and his mates always went on Friday night. The emcee, Bob Wooler, had urged them to be sure and ask their record shop for "My Bonnie" by the Beatles.

The only clue as to the record label was that it "sounded foreign." Brian asked if these Beatles were a foreign group. No, Jones replied, they were Liverpudlians, working abroad sometimes, but mainly playing at a cellar club not far from this very shop.

The NEMS policy, that any disk could be ordered, held sway no less on a busy Saturday for an eighteen-year-old in jeans and a leather jacket. Brian promised Jones he would investigate the mystery and on his executive notepad wrote, "The Beatles—check on Monday." His resolution to do so was strengthened by two further requests for "My Bonnie," from girls this time, before the shop closed that afternoon.

It was certainly a little odd that Brian had not heard of the Beatles until then. He was, after all, in charge of a shop thronging with their admirers and visited regularly, when at a loose end, by the very Beatles in question. He was contributing to a music paper that mentioned their name about a dozen times in every issue. The Cavern Club itself was only just across Whitechapel and round the corner.

But Brian was twenty-seven and therefore of an age, as well as social background, still untouched by rock 'n' roll music. His interest in it, like his *Mersey Beat* column, had been cultivated purely for business, and with some inner distaste by an ardent devotee of Sibelius and the Liverpool Phil. And none of his journeys, by day or night, in Liverpool would be likely to take him to Mathew Street.

He was, nevertheless, intrigued to learn of a homegrown group not only available on disk but also in demand by so discerning a customer as Raymond Jones. The following Monday, he began telephoning around NEMS's usual record wholesalers. None could find in its catalogs any record called "My Bonnie" by the Beatles.

By this stage, with so small a potential profit at stake, any record dealer would have been justified in abandoning the search. Brian, however, partly as a result of the boredom he had been feeling, seized on the challenge of tracking down Raymond Jones's request. If these Beatles truly were a Liverpool group, he reasoned, it would be quicker to go out and find them and ask which label had released their record. Jones, on his next visit, remembers Brian asking in all innocence, "Where *is* this Cavern Club everyone's talking about?" Only then did he discover it was less than two hundred yards away.

Brian's first visit to the Cavern, at lunchtime on Thursday, November 9, was arranged with typical formality and precision. He rang up Bill Harry, the editor of *Mersey Beat*; Bill then rang Ray McFall, the Cavern's owner, who in his turn instructed Paddy Delaney, the doorman, that Brian was to pass through without the required one-shilling membership card. Paddy remembers seeing Brian that day on his way up Mathew Street, picking his way around the fruit crates and squashed cabbage leaves. "He had a dark suit on, very smart. And a briefcase under his arm."

A few minutes later he bitterly regretted his decision. The warehouse cellar, with its dank archways, its dripping walls and dungeonlike aroma, bore no resemblance to any club in his understanding of the term. Equally discomfiting was the obvious gulf between him, at twenty-seven, and the teenage throng among which, luckily, the darkness hid his intrusion, all but the glimmer of his white business shirt. Bob Wooler's record session was still in progress, with no activity yet down the middle tunnel on what could be seen of the stage. His ears affronted only a little less than his nostrils, Brian decided to wait just a few minutes longer.

What he saw that day was the Beatles giving a routine lunchtime Cavern performance. The club and its audience had become as much a habit as the wild welcome that they scarcely acknowledged, pitching into song after song as if to use time up as fast as possible; in the intervals, talking to each other, wolfing the Cavern snacks that were part of McFall's payment, laughing at private jokes, pretending to cuff one another, at all times picking up and laying down the draggled cigarettes that smouldered dangerously on chairs and amplifier rims. Then, through the tomfoolery and indifference, would unexpectedly break the pounding, shining sound; the harmony of their grouped faces; the bass and guitars cutting knife-sharp.

On Brian Epstein, their effect was transfixing, but for quite another reason. It is doubtful whether, in those surroundings and with his conservative taste, he could even have begun to appreciate the freshness of the Beatles' music. Rather, it was the sight of four slim boys in form-fitting leather, sweat-drenched and prancing, that held him fascinated. It was a daydream, encountered at midday, a rearing up in public of his most covert fantasies. Most of all, the eye of his secret life watched the boy who seemed most aggressive and untidy, whose offhand manner and bad language would have affronted the daytime Mr. Epstein, but filled the nighttime Brian with a scarcely endurable excitement. Though he did not know it then, the one he could not take his eyes off was John Lennon.

At the interval, he pushed his way, briefcase and all, through the middle tunnel to try to speak to the Beatles as they came offstage. He still had no clear idea of why he wanted to meet them or what he might say. Bob Wooler had already mentioned him over the PA system and given a plug to NEMS as the shop where the Cavern bought its records. George Harrison, to whom Brian spoke first outside the band room, drily enquired, "What brings Mr. Epstein here?"

He stayed at the Cavern through the Beatles' second session, until 2:10 P.M. When he climbed the stairs into daylight again he had managed to speak to Paul as well as George, and to discover that the record they had made was only as a backing group, and on the Polydor label. He had done his duty, both to NEMS and to Raymond Jones. But by now, a different idea had begun to germinate in his mind.

He might have shown less reticence had he known how bored the Beatles themselves were at this moment, and how desperately they, too, were hoping for something to happen.

November 1961 found them in precisely the same position as after their return from Hamburg three months before. They were undisputed kings of the Cavern, and of *Mersey Beat*. They had had the satisfaction of seeing bands that used to condescend to them now avidly copying their R&B repertoire, their clothes, their hair, and even the types of instrument they played. They had been abroad; they had even made a record, albeit under an alias, which now, it appeared, was selling for actual money in the shops. These were achievements pleasant to contemplate, so long as they did not put their hands in their pockets, to feel the halfpence there, or look down at their shoes, or listen on Saturday morning to the BBC Light Program, when the Top Twenty was beamed to Liverpool from places still a million miles away.

The one bright spot had been meeting up again with Sam Leach, the promoter who formerly ran the Sunday afternoon sessions at the

Casanova Club in Temple Street. They liked Sam, as everyone did, for the scope, if not the invariable success, of his concert enterprises. He now ran many—some said, too many—dances all over Liverpool, apparently relishing the continual uncertainty as to whether his door receipts would cover costs. He was a pleasant, big-eyed, scatterbrained youth, always nudging people and laughing.

Sam, even so, was the first local impresario to look beyond the northwest, to London. Realizing that no London agent would ever come up to Liverpool, he was planning to start his own record label, and had already booked Gerry and the Pacemakers to cut some demonstration disks in a studio in Crosby. His plan for the Beatles was no less audacious. He would get them on in a hall down south, and lure the big London impresarios to see them.

Sam Leach's choice of a southern venue was Aldershot, Hampshire. That glum military settlement, more adjacent to Stonehenge than London, had a dance hall called the Queen's that Sam Leach hired for five consecutive Saturday nights. It wasn't exactly the West End, as he conceded, but it was roughly in that direction. If the Beatles could hit Aldershot in a big enough way, the word might easily spread.

Sam and a photographer friend of his named Dick Matthews made the nine-hour journey from Liverpool to Hampshire in a hired Ford Classic. Following them down the highway came a van containing the Beatles and driven by one of Sam's bouncers, Terry McCann.

They reached the Queen's Hall, Aldershot, to find four people waiting. "I'd meant to put an ad in the paper," Sam says. "But it hadn't got out. Maybe I forgot. We went round all the local cafés, telling people, 'Hey, there's a dance on up the road.' We said we'd let them in for nothing if they came."

Eventually, eighteen customers had been rounded up. "The lads said it wasn't worth playing at first, but Paul persuaded them. "Come on," he said. "Let's show we're professionals."

The Beatles gave those eighteen people a two-and-a-half-hour all-out nonstop session. When they showed signs of flagging, Paul revived them with his Little Richard act, played to the limit. Dick Matthews, a learned-looking man in a tweed sports jacket, photographed them on the little stage with its wallpapered proscenium, and the half-dozen couples, not all very youthful, jiving under a mirror globe that the management felt it not worthwhile to illuminate. Sam Leach also went among the dancers, pleading with them to look more numerous by spreading out.

Helped by Southern Watney's bottled pale ale and Sam's irrepressible spirits, the evening had its measure of jollity. When the last of the few dancers had gone John and George, in their thin shortie overcoats, danced a ritual slow foxtrot together. "Then we had a game of football [soccer] over the dance floor with ping-pong balls," Sam says. "When we finally got outside there was a great wagon-load of bobbies waiting for us. "Get out of town," they said, "and don't come back." The next Saturday, 210 people came to the dance, just to see the Beatles—but they weren't there."

Despite the Aldershot fiasco, bright ideas still rocketed around inside Sam's tousled head. He despised promoters like Brian Kelly for the meanness of their dances, with one group only onstage and a finish well before midnight. Sam dreamed of marathon jive sessions, like they were in America, with half a dozen groups or more on a bill lasting into the early hours. Groups were there in abundance all around: Sam needed only an outside sporting chance of being able to pay them.

Earlier that year, he had negotiated with Tommy McArdle the wintertime hire of the New Brighton Tower Ballroom. This gargantuan relic of Victorian seaside splendor—and of an actual tower, higher than Blackpool's—was the largest dance venue anywhere on Merseyside. Its use for rock 'n' roll was spasmodic, ceasing arbitrarily when violence threatened its gilded fabric, or when Rory Storm, climbing up inside the dome, fell to the stage and almost broke through it to the one-thousand-seat theater underneath.

"Operation Big Beat," as Sam Leach called his inaugural Tower night, took place on November 10, 1961, the day after Brian Epstein had walked into the Cavern Club. The Beatles shared the bill with Gerry and the Pacemakers, Rory Storm and the Hurricanes, Kingsize Taylor and the Dominoes, and the Remo Four. Special buses were provided to transport the Liverpool fans through the tunnel and downriver to New Brighton's bleak, unfrequented sea promenades.

"It was a real foggy night," Sam says. "The Beatles were on at another dance as well, at Knotty Ash Village Hall. They went on at half-seven in the Tower, then over to Knotty Ash, then they came back later for their second spot at half-eleven." Neil Aspinall, Pete Best's friend, drove them and their equipment in a secondhand van he had recently bought. He had forsaken his accounting studies to become their road manager for a fee of 5s (25p) from each of them per night.

Operation Big Beat attracted a crowd of 3,500. "I was that scared," Sam Leach says. "I thought maybe I'd not sell any tickets at all. There were hundreds there, even when the Beatles played first at half-seven. When they came back for the half-eleven spot, the kids went wild." Tommy McArdle, the Tower's general manager, was somewhat less entranced. "I was ready to ban the Beatles there and then. I caught them behind the stage, poking their fingers through the backcloth. All starry it was, and beautiful, and Lennon and them just sticking their fingers through it."

As Operation Big Beat wore on, and the empty pint glasses formed regiments on the two licensed bars, the Birkenhead faction expressed itself in the customary way. "I was in the big downstairs bar," Sam Leach says, "and I see this fellow get hold of a table and pick it up. He threw it straight at the mirror behind the bar. It went within just a few inches of Paul McCartney."

Sam rose to the Birkenhead challenge by hiring bouncers in quantities outnumbering the biggest gang. When fifty Teds from Birkenhead paid the Tower a visit, Sam Leach and a hundred bouncers were waiting. One of his regular helpers, a barrel-shaped youth named Eddie Palmer, later grew famous in Liverpool gangland as "The Toxteth Terror."

"I got so that I could feel trouble coming," Sam says. "There were these four big yobboes in one night that I knew were out to give the Beatles a good thumping. They were up near the stage, all pissed and whispering to each other. I'd got a bouncer behind each one of the four of them. The first moment one of them pulled his arm back, all my four lads pounced at once."

A few days later at the Cavern Club word was passed to the Beatles that Brian Epstein had come in again. He watched them play and, as before, spoke to them when they came off stage at the break. They still had no idea what he wanted, and so were as inclined as any other Cavernite to laugh at his dark suit and tie and briefcase, and the blush that spread over his face when any of them, especially John, looked him directly in the eye. Even so, they were vaguely flattered to number among their followers this obviously prosperous businessman whose car, it quickly became known, was a new Ford Zodiac.

His aura grew still more impressive when he took to arriving with a personal assistant. Alistair Taylor, an employee in the Whitechapel record shop, had found himself elevated to this mutually flattering post.

All through November, in a roundabout way, Brian was enquiring about the Beatles: about where they played, for whom, and at what fee. The idea that he should manage them was one he had not yet articulated, even to himself. It was in a purely theoretical way that he questioned the record company reps, and contacts in London at the big HMV Oxford Street store, about groups and managers and the relationship of one to another. And everyone whom he quizzed unconsciously reiterated the same discouraging fact: People of his age and social background played no noticeable part in British pop music.

Meanwhile, Polydor Records had dispatched his order of two hundred copies of "My Bonnie," an event loyally noted by *Mersey Beat*. The record sold moderately well among the Beatles' following, though some—Raymond Jones included—were disappointed to find them only a backing group to Tony Sheridan and billed as "the Beat Brothers."

Bob Wooler, the Cavern disk jockey, was one of the first to discover Brian's interest in managing the Beatles, even though his overtures were still muffled by his own embarrassment and uncertainty, and by the Beatles' own elaborate indifference to all outsiders. Wooler, as a close adviser, went with them to the first formal meeting suggested by Brian, early in December. It was to take place on a Wednesday afternoon, directly following their Cavern lunchtime show. Wooler and the Beatles stopped off for beers at the Grapes first, and possibly the White Star, and so did not reach Whitechapel until well after the appointed time. It was early-closing day, and they found Brian waiting for them on the darkened ground floor, among displays of home appliances. "He hated to be kept waiting," Wooler said. "That was his first introduction to many hours of being kept waiting by the Beatles. He was quite open by that time about wanting to manage them, but they still wouldn't commit themselves. It was left at, 'well, we'll see what happens.' "

Equally little encouragement came from those in Brian's own circle to whom he confided his plan. He had already consulted his family's lawyer, E. Rex Makin, hoping for some legal help on the kind of contract he might offer the Beatles. Makin lived next door to the Epsteins on Queens Drive and had known Brian and Clive since their boyhood. He poured scorn on what he termed "just another Epstein idea."

The other person Brian sought out was Allan Williams. He had discovered that Williams used to have a contract of some kind with the Beatles, and had been responsible for sending them to work in Hamburg. Visiting the Welshman at his Blue Angel Club, Brian found him still resentful about the commission the Beatles owed him. Williams said he wanted nothing more to do with them, and that Brian was at liberty to take them over. His advice, however, was not to touch the Beatles "with a barge-pole."

At another afterhours meeting at the NEMS shop Brian, blushing furiously, succeeded at last in coming to the point. He told the Beatles that they needed a manager; he was willing to do it; did they want him to? A silence ensued, broken by John Lennon's gruff "Yes." Paul then asked if being managed by Brian would make any difference to the music they played. Brian assured him that it would not. There was a second uneasy silence, again broken by John. "Right then, Brian," he said. "Manage us."

Harry and Queenie Epstein, who had been away to London for a week, returned home to find their elder son in a state of high excitement. He sat them down in the drawing room and insisted that they listen to "My Bonnie," telling them all the time to pay no attention to the voice, only to the backing. From Brian's hectic chatter, and the din on a normally well-mannered phonograph, Harry at last extracted the displeasing news that shop business was about to be let slide again. Brian assured his father this was not so: Managing the Beatles would require only two half-days each week.

On the Beatles' side the news spread as rapidly as news in Liverpool generally does. Sam Leach heard it direct from Paul. "He said there was this millionaire who wanted to manage them." Sam, though he had been putting the Beatles on regularly at New Brighton Tower, had no contract with them and did not attempt to manufacture one. Nor did Pete's mother, Mona, who had helped to get them on at the Cavern, and had pushed them in other ways. She was satisfied Brian knew, as everyone did, that Pete was the Beatles' leader.

Not all the parents were quite so content. Olive Johnson, the McCartney family's close friend, received a call from Paul's father in a state of some anxiety over his son's proposed association with a "Jew boy." Since Olive knew the world so well, Jim asked her to be at Forthlin Road on the evening that Brian called to outline his intentions for Paul. "He turned out to be absolutely charming," Olive says. "Beautifully mannered but completely natural. He and Jim got on well at once."

John Lennon's Aunt Mimi was less easily placated. What worried Mimi about Brian was precisely what impressed the other parents—his charm and position and affluence. "I used to tackle Brian about that," Mimi said. "'It's all right for you,' I told him, 'if all this group business turns out to be just a flash in the pan, it won't matter. It's just a hobby to you. If it's all over in six months, it won't matter to you, but what happens to *them*?'"

"Brian said to me, 'It's all right, Mrs. Smith. I promise you, John will never suffer. He's the only important one. The others don't matter, but I'll always take care of John.'"

EIGHT

"ELVIS'S MANAGER CALLING BRIAN EPSTEIN IN BIRKENHEAD"

Brian, at the outset, foresaw no great difficulty in getting the Beatles a recording contract. As a retailer, he was in regular touch with all the major London companies: Decca, EMI, Phillips, and Pye. He had given them all good business in building up "The Finest Record Selection in the North." Any of them, surely, would be only too glad to oblige so large and reliable a wholesale customer as NEMS Ltd.

There was a further promising augury. Each week, the old-fashioned broadsheet *Liverpool Evening Echo* published a record review column signed with the pseudonym "Disker." Brian, soon after meeting the Beatles, had written to Disker, soliciting a mention for them. It turned out that Disker was not based with the *Echo* but was a freelance journalist named Tony Barrow, Liverpool-born but now living in London. As well as his journalism, Barrow worked regularly as a writer of album-sleeve notes for the Decca label.

Tony Barrow wrote back to Brian, saying that as the Beatles had not made a record yet, he could not mention them in Disker's column. What he could do, as a fellow Merseysider, was to recommend them to Decca's "Artists and Repertoire" department. The ensuing conversation, strangely enough, was much as Brian had imagined it. "When I mentioned Brian Epstein," Barrow says, "everybody asked 'Who?' But when I mentioned NEMS, it was quite different. 'Oh, yes—NEMS of Liverpool. *Very* big retailers for us in the northwest.'"

The word reached Decca's Head of A&R, Dick Rowe. A large northern record retailer had a pop group he wanted auditioned. It would be tactful, for business reasons, to say "Yes." The job was given to a new young assistant in the A&R department named Mike Smith. However, in fairness, the gesture was more than perfunctory. Mike Smith offered to come up to Liverpool to hear the group to best advantage in the club where they usually played. And so, Brian, several weeks before the

Beatles had agreed to be managed by him, was able to give them an astounding piece of news. Someone from Decca—from the company that had Tommy Steele, and Buddy Holly, and Little Richard, and the Everly Brothers, and Duane Eddy and Bobby Vee—was coming into town to audition *them*.

Mike Smith arrived and, after an expensive dinner with Brian, was conducted to Mathew Street, past Paddy Delaney and down the eighteen cellar steps to witness the Beatles in their stifling habitat. Their playing impressed the A&R man, not enough to sign them there and then but certainly enough to arrange a further audition for them as soon as possible in London, at Decca's West Hampstead studios. This second test was quickly confirmed for New Year's Day, 1962.

On New Year's Eve, in cold snowy weather, the participants made their separate ways south. Brian traveled down by train to stay overnight with his aunt Frieda in Hampstead. The Beatles set off at midday by road, packed with their equipment in the freezing rear of Neil Aspinall's van. Neil had never been to London before and, striking blizzards near Wolverhampton, lost his bearings altogether. Not until ten hours later did they arrive in Russell Square, near King's Cross, where Brian had booked them into a small hotel, the Royal. For the rest of New Year's Eve they wandered round, watching the drunks in Trafalgar Square and trying to find a place to eat. On Charing Cross Road they met two men who offered them something called "pot" on condition they could "smoke" it together in Neil's van. The Liverpool boys fled.

At Decca's studios the next morning they had to wait some time for Mike Smith to arrive. Brian, as ever punctual to the second, reddened at this implied slight, just because they were unknown and from Liverpool. The Beatles, already nervous, became more so when Smith rejected the amplifiers they had dragged with them from Liverpool and made them plug their guitars into a set of studio speakers.

Brian believed that the way to impress Smith was not by John and Paul's original songs, but by their imaginative, sometimes eccentric, arrangements of standards. Among the fifteen numbers heard by Mike Smith—and preserved for posterity on bootleg singles, stolen later from the master tape—are Paul's versions of "Till There Was You" and "September in the Rain"; "Sheik of Araby," sung by George with jokey Eastern effects; and semihumorous versions of "Three Cool Cats" and "Your Feet's Too Big." From scores of Lennon-McCartney songs the only three selected were "Hello Little Girl," "Like Dreamers Do," and the recently written "Love of the Loved."

The Beatles were far from happy with their performance. Paul's voice had cracked with anxiety several times; George's fingers were stickier than usual; at certain points in Chuck Berry's song "Memphis" John as lead vocalist seemed to have been thinking of something else. And Pete Best kept up the same drum rhythm, patient rather than cohesive. Only on "Love of the Loved" had the elements coalesced: Paul's voice at its most appealing within an arrangement both neat and dramatic.

Mike Smith, however, reassured them that the session had gone well. So enthusiastic did the young A&R man seem that when the Beatles and Brian walked out into the snow that evening the contract seemed as good as signed. Before their hideous van journey with Neil back to Liverpool, Brian took them to a restaurant in Swiss Cottage and allowed them to order wine.

At Decca, meanwhile, Smith was beginning to have second thoughts. The main reason was another group, Brian Poole and the Tremeloes, that had also auditioned that day and had put up a much better show. His boss, Dick Rowe, was prepared to let Smith have his head only to the extent of signing one new group.

"I told Mike he'd have to decide between them," Dick Rowe remembered. "It was up to him—the Beatles or Brian Poole and the Tremeloes. He said, 'They're both good, but one's a local group, the other comes from Liverpool.' We decided it was better to take the local group. We could work with them more easily and stay closer in touch, as they came from Dagenham."

On January 4, issue number 13 of *Mersey Beat* published the results of a poll among its five thousand readers to find Liverpool's most popular group. The Beatles were first, followed by Gerry and the Pacemakers, the Remo Four, Rory Storm and the Hurricanes, Kingsize Taylor and the Dominoes, and the Big Three. The whole front page was devoted to a photograph of the winners in their black leather, cropped to conceal their scruffy shoes, and captioned by the hand that always rendered Paul's surname as "McArtrey." In all four Beatles' homes lay piles of December *Mersey Beat*s minus the voting coupon on which, like everyone involved, they had voted for themselves.

Mersey Beat knew nothing, however, of the test for Decca in London.

Brian would not risk announcing it until the contract had been definitely awarded. The only mention was in Disker's *Liverpool Echo* column, filed by Tony Barrow from inside Decca, where the signs still seemed good. "I said it was only a matter of weeks before they came down to record their first single."

Barrow then learned to his astonishment from Dick Rowe's office that the Beatles were to be turned down. The reasons given were that they sounded "too much like the Shadows," and that groups with guitars were "on the way out."

Brian fought Decca's decision as hard as he could. He traveled to London alone to reason, unavailingly, with Dick Rowe and another Decca man, Beecher Stevens. He also went back to the salespeople, reminding them of his position in the retail world. "I heard afterward that he'd guaranteed to buy three thousand copies of any single we let the Beatles make," Dick Rowe says. "I was never told about that at the time. The way economics were in the record business then, if we'd been sure of selling three thousand copies, we'd have been forced to record them, whatever sort of group they were."

Someone at Decca suggested to Brian the possibility of hiring a studio and a freelance A&R man to supervise a session for the Beatles. He went so far as to contact Tony Meehan, formerly the Shadows' drummer, and now an independent producer. But Meehan proved offhand; besides, the studio hire would have cost at least a hundred pounds. Brian was not yet prepared to go that far. He walked out of Decca having made the grand pronouncement that his group would one day be "bigger than Elvis." The Decca men smiled. They had heard that one so many times.

On January 24, seven weeks after first approaching them, Brian was finally able to tie the Beatles down to a formal agreement. He had sent away for a sample management contract, and had modified and rewritten the terms in a praiseworthy attempt to make them fairer. The final document, though portentously worded and stuck with sixpenny postage stamps, had no legal validity. Since Paul and George were still under twenty-one, their signatures ought to have been endorsed by their fathers. And Brian forgot to sign his own name.

The four still slightly skeptical and uneasy Liverpool scruffs thus found themselves contracted to a real live organization. It had been Brian's impressive idea to form a limited company, with his brother,

Clive, to administer his new charges. He called it NEMS Enterprises, after the family business. Over the Whitechapel branch was a suite of offices that his father allowed him to use, mainly because that would enable him to continue running the record shop downstairs. Harry was determined Brian should keep his promise that managing the Beatles would take only two afternoons each week.

His brisk executive efficiency foundered the moment he first tried to fix the Beatles a booking. Only then did he realize he had no idea how to talk to the rough, tough Liverpool dance promoters on whom they depended for regular work. Tommy McArdle, the ex–middleweight boxer who ran New Brighton Tower Ballroom, was one of many puzzled local impresarios whom Brian suggested should "come across and have lunch."

The first booking he managed to arrange was at a tiny seaside café on the Dee Estuary over in Cheshire. The profit to NEMS Enterprises, after paying for posters and Neil Aspinall's gas and sundry expenses, and giving each Beatle his share, was slightly over one pound.

Nor had Brian yet realized the quality for which the Beatles were notorious up and down the Mersey—their dedicated unreliability and unpunctuality. He realized it one day when Ray McFall rang up to say that only three Beatles had turned up for the Cavern lunchtime session. Freda Kelly, who worked for NEMS Enterprises as wages clerk and fan club organizer, saw Brian go into one of many subsequent transports of fury. "There's only *three* of them!" he kept saying. "Gerry Marsden's singing with them, standing on an orange box so they needn't bother to let the microphone down to his height."

At night he would drive in his Ford Zodiac to wherever the Beatles were playing—to Neston Women's Institute Hall, to Birkenhead, Wallasey, or New Brighton. Since everyone wore dark suits and white shirts to dances in those days, he was not too conspicuous as he walked in. Approaching the Beatles still threw him into a ferment of embarrassment—a circumstance that John Lennon was quick to spot. The more John stared at him, the more Brian would blush and stammer his way into some shaming faux pas. Sam Leach, all innocence, advised John to accept Brian's proposal that they should fly together for the weekend to Copenhagen. "John nudged me in the ribs," Sam says. 'Shut up,' he went. 'Can't you see he's after me!' "

All the time, he was regularly traveling to London to try to interest other record companies in the Beatles. He now had a dozen of their songs on tape from the Decca audition—"Sheik of Araby," "Hello Little Girl," "Three Cool Cats," "Red Sails in the Sunset," "Your Feet's Too Big."

Decca, at least, had given them two auditions. At Pye, at Phillips, at EMI's two prestige labels, Columbia and HMV, interest did not even extend to that. The fad now was for solo singers—Helen Shapiro, Jimmy Justice, Frank Ifield. Often, the mere mention of Liverpool was sufficient to glaze over the A&R man's eye. "You've got a good business, Mr. Epstein," one of them said with a show of kindness. "Why not stick to it?"

The Beatles would be waiting for him when he got off the train at Lime Street, tired and deflated by yet another supercilious turndown. He would break the latest disappointing news to them over coffee at the nearby Punch and Judy cafeteria or at Joe's, an all-night greasy spoon where Brian kept a reserved table as grandly as if it were the Ritz. The boys did not reproach him for his continued lack of success; on the contrary, they did their best to lift his spirits and reassure him that next time he was bound to get lucky. John Lennon would joke that, if no one else wanted them, they'd have to settle for Embassy, the despised cheapo label sold only by Woolworth's. Then John would pump up the other four with a time-honored routine, performed in the cheesey American accents of some 1940s showbiz movie starring Judy Garland and Mickey Rooney:

"Where we goin', fellas?"

"To the top, Johnny!"

"And where's that?"

"To the *toppermost* of the *poppermost*, Johnny!"

One night, as Brian drank with the Beatles at the Iron Door Club, a tall, dark-haired man came over and shyly introduced himself. It was Joe Flannery, his companion in the nursery and in the later, brief relationship that Joe, at least, had never forgotten. He had not seen Brian since their amicable breakup in 1957, and initially presumed him to be "downtown" seeking rough trade, as of yore. That definition certainly seemed to apply to at least one of the boys Brian had with him: the slant-eyed, abrasive one who instantly turned the name Joe Flannery into "Flo Jannery."

As sympathetic a listener as ever, Flannery soon elicited the fact that Brian now managed a pop group and that all was going far from smoothly. They adjourned for a private drink at the Beehive pub in Paradise Street, where Brian poured out the dual frustration of canvassing London record labels and trying to do business with small-time dance promoters on the Cheshire Wirral. "He told me he was really cheesed off with everything," Joe says. "He was thinking of chucking it all in and going back to learning to act at RADA."

Joe, as it happened, was managing his younger brother's beat group, Lee Curtis and the All Stars. He offered to work unofficially for NEMS Enterprises, talking to promoters on the Beatles' behalf and negotiating fees. He did it simply out of love for Brian. "I liked the way Brian spoke on the telephone. He never said 'Hello'—just, 'Joe . . .' I always liked hearing that."

The kindly, hospitable Flannery even let them use his pin-neat house as a base camp when gigs ended too late for them to return to their own homes. "I'd cook them beans on toast or cheese on toast, then they'd go to sleep all around my living room. Even then, I noticed there was a peck order. John always took the couch while Paul had the two armchairs pushed together. George didn't seem to need as much sleep as the others, so I'd take him out in my car in the early hours of the morning and teach him to drive."

On a side table in Flannery's living room stood a hand-colored photograph of his mother, taken in the 1920s, her bobbed hair forming a glossy helmet with bangs above her eyes. Flannery remembers how fascinated John used to be by the photograph, and remains convinced that his mother, not Astrid or Jurgen Vollmer, was the genesis of the Beatle Cut.

With all these mundane management chores lifted from his shoulders, Brian was free to concentrate on matters he did understand. He understood, for example, how to design a poster, tastefully yet with an impact maximizing the Beatles' meagre achievements. When they were booked to play at the Institute hall in Barnston, a small Cheshire village, Brian's posters blazed the advent of MERSEY BEAT POLL WINNERS! POLYDOR RECORDING ARTISTS! PRIOR TO EUROPEAN TOUR!

On the Beatles themselves, Brian began to effect the same transformation—against much the same resistance—as on the display windows of the family's Walton Road shop. He rearranged the four black-leather, draggle-headed, swearing, prancing Hamburg rockers to reflect his own idea of what a successful pop group ought to be.

To begin with, and most important of all, he told them, they must be punctual. They must not go onstage as a three-piece group, backing Gerry Marsden on an orange box. They must play to a program, not just as they pleased. They must not shout at their friends, and foes, in the audience. They must not eat or drink beer or wrestle and cuff each other onstage, or make V-signs or belch into the microphone. And if they must smoke, let it not be Woodbines, the workingman's cigarette, but some sophisticated brand like Senior Service.

The black *exis* suits they had bought in Hamburg, and worn and slept in for more than a year, were Brian's next concern. Black leather, to most people in 1962, still signified Nazis. He suggested an alternative that John Lennon, at first, doggedly refused to consider. Paul agreed with Brian that they should try it. Paul sided with Brian throughout the whole smartening process. George and Pete Best seemed not to mind, so John reluctantly gave way to the majority. On March 24, when they arrived for their twenty-five-pound date at Barnston Institute, each carried a bag from Burton's, the chain-store tailor. That night, they took the stage in shiny gray lounge suits with velvet collars, cloth-covered buttons, and pencil-thin lapels.

Joe Flannery, having special knowledge, guessed at once what underlay Brian's devotion. He had fallen in love with John Lennon. He was besotted, not by the pretty-faced Paul or Pete but by the boy whose facade of crudeness and toughness touched the nerve of his most secret rough trade fantasies. Joe recognized the look in Brian's eye as he blushed and writhed under John's pitiless sarcasm: "I've sat for hours with him in the car while he's been crying over the things John's said to him."

Harry and Queenie Epstein, meanwhile, worried over the time and money Brian was spending, and his neglect of record-shop business in pursuit of his mad idea. To add to their anxiety, he had forsaken his smart lounge suits and white shirts and Horne Brothers ties, and taken to going around Liverpool dressed, like the Beatles, in a leather jacket and black polo-neck sweater. He even came to the Cavern dressed that way, not realizing that everyone was laughing at him. "He was champing a lot, too, that night," Bob Wooler recalled. "They'd got him on the pep pills, the ones that dried up the saliva."

Yet for all his efficiency, his headed notepaper, his expenditure on new lounge suits, his typewritten memoranda to the Beatles concerning punctuality and cleanliness, he still could not move them outside the same old drab hemisphere of Merseyside. No one in London had heard of them, save through a brief mention in the music newspaper *Record Mirror*—and that was through a fan's letter, not through Brian. The *Record Mirror* afterward sent up a photographer to see them. His name was Dezo Hoffman; he was a middle-aged Hungarian freelancer. To the Beatles, he seemed godlike. They all had a bath before they came to Whitechapel to meet him. He shot rolls of film of them around Sefton Park, and lent them a movie camera so that they could film each other, leaping up and down in the spring sunshine and driving round town in Paul's green Ford Classic.

The only excitement on their horizon, after Hoffman had gone, was returning to Hamburg. On April 13, they were to open a new Reeperbahn attraction, the Star-Club. That was the European Tour grandly billed by Brian outside Barnston Institute. Another very grand thing was that they were to go to Hamburg this time by air. Brian insisted on it, knowing what an effect the news would have on *Mersey Beat*'s readership.

He would go to any lengths to convince them that, despite all appearances, a big, wonderful moment was only just around the corner. In Birkenhead, sitting around in the pub next to the Majestic ballroom, he whispered to Joe Flannery to go out of the room, then come back in and say that Colonel Tom Parker, Elvis Presley's manager, was trying to reach him on the telephone. "They believed it," Flannery says. "They really believed that Colonel Parker had been trying to ring up Brian Epstein in Birkenhead."

That Christmas of 1961, while Brian was still wooing the Beatles, their old bass player Stu Sutcliffe had come over from Hamburg with his German fiancée, Astrid. Stu's friends at the Cavern, like Bill Harry, were shocked by his thinness and translucent pallor. Allan Williams, with typical forthrightness, told him that he looked "at death's door."

Stu admitted to his mother that, since settling in Hamburg, in his studio in the Kirchherr house, he had been suffering severe headaches, even occasional blackouts. He had fainted once at art college, during Edouardo Paolozzi's master class. The news had already reached Mrs. Sutcliffe via worried letters from Astrid to Stu's younger sister, Pauline. Astrid feared he was working too hard. For days at a time, she said, he would not come down from his attic to sleep or eat. And the headaches were sometimes so violent, they seemed more like fits. Millie Sutcliffe had described the symptoms, so far as she understood them, to the dean of Liverpool University Medical School. He told her that she *did* have grounds for concern.

Stu still refused to believe that the headaches were a consequence of anything more than overwork and his and Astrid's round-the-clock Hamburg life. He did agree, for his mother's sake, to see a specialist in Liverpool. The specialist instantly sent him for an X-ray. No appointment could be made for three weeks: By that time, Stu and Astrid had returned to Hamburg.

From January to April the only news Mrs. Sutcliffe received was in Astrid's photographs. One of these showed Stu seated, stiff as a wax-work, in a bentwood rocking chair next to a marble-topped table crowded with liquor bottles. Another was a close-up of Stu and Astrid together. The face, next to the dark-eyed, ravishing girl, was haunted and brittle. "When I looked at that," Millie Sutcliffe remembered, "something told me that my son was dying."

In February, Stu again collapsed during an art school class. This time, he did not return. Astrid's mother forced him to leave his attic and be properly nursed by her in a bedroom downstairs. The Kirchherr family doctor, suspecting a brain tumor, sent him for X-rays. No tumor showed itself. Two further doctors who examined Stu were equally baffled. "We tried everything," Astrid says. "One treatment was a kind of special massage under water. When Stu came home in the afternoon from his massage he told my mother he'd been looking in an undertaker's window and seen a beautiful white coffin. 'Oh, Mum,' he said, 'buy it for me. I'd *love* to be buried in a white coffin.' "

By March, the headaches brought with them spells of temporary blindness. The pain grew so intense at times that Astrid and her mother had to hold Stu down to stop him from throwing himself out of the window. Yet on other days, he could appear quite normal. Astrid would come home from work to find him sitting up in bed reading, sketching, or writing another long letter to John in Liverpool. He was looking forward eagerly to the Beatles' arrival and the opening of the Star-Club on April 13.

On April 10, Astrid, at work in her photographic studio, received a call from her mother to say that Stu was much worse, and that she was sending him to the hospital. It was the day that three of the Beatles—

John, Paul, and Pete Best—flew out from Manchester Ringway Airport. George had the flu and was to follow with Brian Epstein a day later.

Stu died in the ambulance, in Astrid's arms. "At half past four," Millie Sutcliffe said, "I was in my bedroom at home in Liverpool. I felt as if a great strong cold wind came through that house, lifted me up, and laid me across the bed. For fifteen or twenty minutes not a muscle in my body was capable of movement. That was the time, I discovered later, when Stuart was dying."

The news came in two telegrams from Astrid, out of sequence. The first said he had died, the second that he was seriously ill.

Stu's father was away at sea. Mrs. Sutcliffe faced alone the ordeal of breaking the news to her two daughters, getting leave from the school where she was teaching, and booking herself on the first available flight to Hamburg. By chance, it was the one on which Brian Epstein and George Harrison were traveling to join the other Beatles. Brian gave her a lift to Manchester and sat with her on the flight.

At Hamburg Airport, Astrid was waiting with John, Paul, and Pete Best. Paul and Pete were red-eyed, but John showed no emotion. With unintended harshness then, the Beatles' and Millie Sutcliffe's paths diverged. Theirs lay to the Star-Club, where they were to open in a few hours. Hers lay to the mortuary, the formal identification of Stu, the receipts to be signed for his clothes, his watch, and his signet ring.

Cause of death was given officially as cerebral paralysis due to bleeding into the right ventricle of the brain. "The doctors told us," Astrid says, "that Stu's brain was actually expanding—getting too big for the space it floated in. It's a very rare medical condition, but it can happen. Even if Stuart had lived, he would have been blind and probably paralyzed. He wouldn't have been able to paint. He would have preferred to die."

From the mortuary Millie Sutcliffe was taken to the Kirchherr house, to see the room that had been Stu's last home, and the attic where he had worked. Scores of canvases, stacked against every wall, showed with what desperate energy his last months were spent. Mrs. Sutcliffe picked up, and never afterward let out of her sight, the palette on which Stu had mixed his final brilliant colors.

The shock expressed by such eminent figures as Edouardo Paolozzi bore witness to the tragedy that such a talent should be so brutally extinguished. At twenty-two, Stu left behind a body of work in which mere promise already yielded to virtuosity. Those last visions, torn between agony and exhilaration, the blue and crimson carnivals, now left the city whose squalor and glamour had inspired them. So did a sketch of himself Stu had made at a time when the attacks were getting worse. Both his hands are pressed to a head that is almost a nuclear mushroom cloud of pain and confusion.

Millie Sutcliffe bequeathed Stu's brain for scientific research at the hospital that had been treating him. Eighteen months later, a set of German X-ray plates, taken after his death, were brought across to Liverpool by Astrid. These revealed, for the first time, the presence of a small brain tumor. The Hamburg radiologist had attached a note in English: "Note the depressed condition of the skull." Studying the tumor's small shadow, and the cranial depression that seemed to press down on it, Mrs. Sutcliffe remembered a night, some three years before, when Stu had been playing bass with the Beatles, and she had found him in his room late at night with blood pouring from his head after being kicked in a scuffle outside Litherland Town Hall.

The Beatles were devastated by Stu's death. Neither George nor Pete Best could stop crying. Paul felt especially bad, remembering his fights with Stu in the past. He tried to find words of consolation for Mrs. Sutcliffe but, unfortunately, they did not come out quite right. "My mother died when I was fourteen," he told her, "and I'd forgotten all about her in six months."

John alone showed no outward emotion, even though he felt the loss as badly as Stu's own family. To the end of her days, Millie Sutcliffe would bitterly remember his failure to shed a single tear or show his feelings apart from one small detail. He asked for, and was given, the long woolen scarf that Stu used to wear in their winters together among the cold Liverpool streets and alleys.

In fact, John's toughness and pragmatism helped others through the tragedy. "It was John who saved me," Astrid says. "He convinced me, after Stu was gone, that I couldn't behave as if I were a widow. He pretended to be heartless, but I knew what he said came from a heart. 'Make up your mind,' he told me. 'You either live or die. You can't be in the middle.' "

Thanks to the efforts of his mother and, after Millie Sutcliffe's death in 1983, his younger sister Pauline, Stu would eventually achieve international renown as a painter who only incidentally happened to have invented the Beatles' name and most abiding image. His work would be shown in prestigious galleries all over the world and form an exhibit at the Rock and Roll Hall of Fame in Cleveland, Ohio; his drawings and sketchbooks would feature in the same blue-chip auctions as handwritten Lennon or McCartney lyrics. He would be the subject of numerous books, academic treatises, and TV documentaries and, in the mid-1990s, of a British-made film, *Backbeat*, although in a loutish and foul-mouthed incarnation that few of his contemporaries can have recognized.

In 2001, Pauline Sutcliffe would come forward with further information bearing on her brother's death. She said that while John and Stu were together in Hamburg in May 1961, John had flown into a sudden rage over his friend's poor musicianship, knocking Stu to the ground, then kicking him repeatedly in the head as he lay there. The depression found in Stu's skull after his death was consistent with such an attack— as much, Pauline believes, as that earlier fight outside Litherland Town Hall when John and Pete Best came to Stu's rescue. She said Stu himself had told her of John's assault, and that, many years afterward, John himself had owned up to it. To the end of his life, Pauline believes, he remained troubled by the thought of possibly having been an unwitting factor in Stu's death.

Awful as the tragedy was for all of them, the Beatles could not stay miserable around the clock. They were, after all, the main attraction at the largest and newest of the Reeperbahn beat clubs. It stood in Grosse Freiheit, next door to St. Joseph's Catholic Church, in the bowels of what had formerly been a movie theater, the Stern Kino. As the Star-Club, it put Koschmider's Kaiserkeller and Eckhorn's Top Ten in the shade. Not that Koschmider or Eckhorn attempted serious competition. The Star-Club's owner, Manfred Weissleder, a huge man with a dusting of golden hair, was the biggest strip-club owner on the Freiheit: His sex shows thrived owing to the particular predilection Weissleder had for filming naked girls under water.

During the Star-Club's hours, from 4:00 P.M. to 6:00 A.M., as many as fifteen thousand customers could pass through it, most staying long enough to hear their favorite band, moving on to other bars or clubs, then returning later to hear the band's second, third, fourth, and fifth spot. After midnight, the place would be swollen by the Freiheit's own population of whores, pimps, strippers, and transvestites. To maintain order, Weissleder had recruited Horst Fascher, the Kaiserkeller's old chief bouncer who, luckily for the Beatles, "worshipped the bones of their bodies." For the Star-Club Fascher recruited a new and even more deadly "Hoddel's Gang," including a much feared one-armed doorman and a waiter named Ali who would instantly floor any troublemaker with a wrestler's dropkick.

However exploitative—and frightening—Weissleder was a good employer, whose evident power in the Hamburg underworld protected his young British employees from the Reeperbahn's darker perils. Each was issued with a small gilt Star-Club badge that acted as a potent shield in cases of difficulty or danger. "The usual thing was that you'd be walking along and someone would try to pull you into a doorway and rob you or rip you off," Liverpool musician Kingsize Taylor remembers. "But as soon as they saw that badge, and realized you worked for Weissleder, they'd back off straight away."

The bands were given accommodation in a block of flats above Maxim's Club where Weissleder's strippers and mud wrestlers also recuperated between shows. "We were all pretty rough and ready," Kingsize says, "but the Beatles were the worst of all. Theirs was the only flat where, if the toilet was occupied, they'd go on the floor, then cover it up with newspaper. When they moved out, Weissleder had to have the whole place fumigated."

The ringleaders in all the maddest and most pointlessly offensive escapades were John Lennon and Adrian Barber, the Big Three's guitarist who later took a management job with Weissleder. It developed into a kind of contest to see who could be the most outrageous. Barber would walk along the Reeperbahn, dragging a hairbrush behind him on a dog lead. John would come onstage at the Star-Club, goose-stepping and *Sieg Heil*–ing, or naked, with a lavatory seat round his neck. Barber bought a pig at the fish market, brought it back to the flats, and threw it onto a bed where a fellow musician named Buddy Britten was sleeping. Kingsize Taylor remembers Britten's terrified shrieks and the "shit coming out of the pig's arse like a flamethrower."

But even Barber could not match John in the acts of sacrilege that seemed to spring from some profound loathing of his own churchgoing past. On Sunday mornings, he would stand on the balcony of the Beatles' flat shouting abuse at people walking to services at nearby St.

Joseph's. In yet another misuse of his art school training, he carved a wooden effigy of Christ on the Cross and attached a water-filled condom to represent an erection. One Easter Sunday, he urinated from the balcony onto the heads of a party of nuns.

"That was the sort of crazy thing you did, full of drink and pills," Johnny Hutch of the Big Three remembers. "Before we started playing at night, we'd shake Preludin down our throats by the tubeful. I've seen John Lennon foaming at the mouth, he's got so many pills inside him."

The Beatles were still in Hamburg when, toward the end of April, Brian set off from Liverpool for one last try with the London record companies. As his train rattled south he could not even be sure with whom that try should be made. Every label he could find in the NEMS stock catalog had by now turned the Beatles down. The only hope really did seem to be Embassy, the one everyone laughed at because it was stocked by Woolworth's.

Someone had suggested that, instead of offering the Beatles on tape he should have a proper "demo" disk to play to the A&R men. That was what brought Brian, in his smart dark overcoat, to the teeming HMV record shop in Oxford Street. Above the shop was a small recording studio where, for a fee of one pound, a tape spool could be converted to an acetate demo.

Brian's luck finally began to change when the studio engineer, a man named Jim Foye, looked up from processing the disk to remark that the music on it was "not at all bad." The studio in fact belonged to a firm of music publishers named Ardmore and Beechwood who were in turn a subsidiary of EMI, the record giant from whom Brian and the Beatles had already suffered multiple rejections. So enthused was Foye that he took the demo up to Ardmore and Beechwood, one floor above the studio, and played it to the company's boss, Syd Coleman. Coleman in turn saw "something" in the demo, asked to see Brian, and offered to publish two of the numbers on it, "Love of the Loved" and "Hello Little Girl." He also asked whether the Beatles were signed with a record label, to which Brian's diplomatic answer was "not yet." In fact, he nurtured one final hope and had seriously been on the point of auditioning the Beatles with Embassy, the despised "Woolies" label.

Coleman's deputy at Ardmore and Beechwood, a former singer named Kim Bennett, was so taken with their demo that he suggested recording them as an independent production in the studio below. According to Bennett, Coleman put this idea to EMI's recording head, Len Wood, but the company's rigid internal protocol could not permit its publishing arm to start dabbling in recording. Instead, Coleman sent Brian to yet another EMI subsidiary, the Parlophone label, whose A&R head, George Martin, happened to be a personal friend. According to Kim Bennett, a "gentlemen's agreement" was made between Coleman and Brian that if the Beatles proved successful, Ardmore and Beechwood would handle their song publishing.

At that time, the only George Martin known outside Tin Pan Alley was a cockney radio comedian specializing in domestic monologues. Nothing could have been more unlike the Parlophone label boss who shook Brian's hand a few days after that chance visit to the HMV shop. This George Martin was tall and gauntly elegant, with a clipped BBC newsreader's accent and the air, Brian himself later said, "of a stern but fair-minded schoolmaster."

Martin listened politely to Brian's claim that the Beatles would one day be "bigger than Elvis." Like everyone else in the business he had heard that many times before. Playing the acetate, he could understand why a group partial to "Sheik of Araby" and "Your Feet's Too Big" might not be considered an instantly commercial proposition. But, unlike everyone else, he found things to praise. He said he liked Paul's voice and some of the guitar playing, and the jaunty harmony in "Hello Little Girl." He was not excited, merely interested. "There was an unusual quality—a certain roughness. I thought to myself, 'There might *just* be something there.' "

Martin agreed to give the Beatles a recording test in June, after their return from Hamburg. It would only be a test, a studio audition like the one they had failed at Decca, and for a label not much in prestige above Embassy. But Brian was never one to downplay things, least of all now. "Congratulations, boys," ran the telegram he at once sent to Hamburg. "EMI request recording session. Please rehearse new material."

NINE

"SOMEBODY HAD TO PAY FOR THOSE 10,000 RECORDS BRIAN BOUGHT"

When George Martin joined EMI in 1950 people still played "gramophones" cranked up by handles, and records were heavy black objects one foot in diameter that broke if you dropped them. Record studios were drab institutional places supervised by men in white coats, and so rigidly formal that not even a jazz drummer could take his jacket off during the recording session.

Young George Martin had joined EMI's Parlophone label as assistant to the head of A&R, Oscar Preuss. He was, even then, suave, elegant, and polite. His superiors, in the trade jargon, said he was "very twelve inch." They little realized he came from a humble North London background and that his father had once sold newspapers on a street corner.

He taught himself to play piano by ear, and at school ran his own little dance band, George Martin and the Four Tune Tellers. In 1943, aged seventeen, he joined the Fleet Air Arm. It was his navy service that gave him a large social leg up and also allowed him later to attend the London Guildhall School of Music, to continue his piano studies and take up the oboe. His first job, before joining Parlophone, was with the BBC Music Library. A little of the BBC manner and accent stuck.

EMI in 1950 was a corporation not much different in size and spirit from the BBC. Founded in 1931 as The Gramophone Company, its name changed, as its field diversified, to Electrical and Mechanical Industries. EMI invented the first practicable British television system: It manufactured television sets, medical equipment, and weapons systems under contract to the then War Office.

It also made records on a series of labels ingested mostly during the prewar years. Its pride was HMV, the definitive label of wistful dog staring into a gramophone trumpet. An HMV dealership in the retail world was as prized as one in Rolls-Royce cars.

No one ever prized the dealership for Parlophone. EMI had bought it in the 1930s as the German Lindstrom label—hence the L label logo that was one day to be mistaken for a £ sterling sign. Within EMI in the fifties it was known derisively as the "junk" label. To Oscar Preuss and his assistant George Martin were left the despised light music catalog— Sidney Torch and his Orchestra; Bob and Alf Pearson; Roberto Inglez, "the Latin American Scot." A sale of only a few hundred copies made any artist viable; to sell a thousand was spectacular. It happened in 1954 when a crooner named Dick James went to number two in the Top Twenty with the theme song from the *Robin Hood* television show.

That year, as it happened, EMI was in deep trouble. Its chief product, the heavy wooden cabinet TV set, was fast growing obsolete against the new, light, plastic sets coming from Japan. Decca, EMI's great rival, had just introduced the long-playing record, for which EMI's technicians predicted no future other than passing novelty.

In 1954, the EMI chairmanship passed to Joseph Lockwood—not a showbiz man, like his predecessor, but a successful industrialist, big in engineering and flour milling. Lockwood was appalled by the decay of the organization he had inherited. He also quickly decided where the future lay. He ended the production of cabinet TV sets and ordered twenty of the new LP record presses. A year later, in what was considered a foolhardy enterprise, he paid 3 million pounds for an established American record company, Capitol.

It was in the flurry of Lockwood's first year as chairman that Oscar Preuss, Parlophone's head of A&R, retired. By oversight more than any-thing, George Martin became, at twenty-nine, the youngest boss of an EMI label, at a salary of £1,100 per year.

Parlophone, to EMI's bureaucratic mind, remained the junk label. It was simply junk of a different, not unsuccessful kind. Martin, in the late fifties, went in heavily for comic dialogue records like Peter Ustinov's *Mock Mozart* and Peter Sellers's *Songs for Swinging Sellers*. One of his coups was to recognize what potential cult followings lay in the new generation of London comedy stage revues. He produced live album versions of Flanders and Swann's *At the Drop of a Hat*, and of a four-man undergraduate show, destined to influence comedy throughout the next decade, called *Beyond the Fringe*.

When rock 'n' roll arrived George Martin shared in the general detes-tation felt by all trained musicians. It was his duty, however, as an A&R man, to tour the Soho coffee bars for talent. He auditioned and turned down Tommy Steele, preferring to sign up Steele's backing skiffle group, the Vipers. Significantly, in six years up to 1962, Parlophone's only Top Ten hit was a comedy number, "You're Driving Me Crazy," by the Temperance Seven.

On EMI's Columbia label, the A&R head Norrie Paramour meanwhile enjoyed virtually unbroken success and gigantic sales with his discovery, Cliff Richard and the Shadows. George Martin did not particularly like the echoey guitar sound that the Shadows had made all the rage. But he did envy Paramour his golden, effortless protégés. Each comedy success for Parlophone was the result of an endless search for new original material. With a pop group the product was all the same, so Martin thought: You simply sat back and let it happen.

Such was Martin's frame of mind that April day in 1962 when Brian Epstein walked in and played the Beatles' demo. After all their efforts to be otherwise, they would have been enraged by Martin's first idea. Perhaps, he thought, he had found his very own Cliff Richard and the Shadows.

On Wednesday, June 6, 1962, the Beatles arrived at EMI's Abbey Road studios in the leafy north London suburb of St. John's Wood. Today, the place still looks very much as it did back then: the very last imaginable location for an international record company's creative nerve center. Within an expansive front drive stands a plain-fronted late Victorian town house, painted plain white, with a steep flight of stone steps ascending to its front door. The espionage world could hardly have created a more innocent front for the labyrinth of state-of-the art studios, technical departments, and offices that lay—and still lie—behind.

The Beatles followed their manager up the front steps in a state of high excitement largely induced by Brian's failure to explain precisely what was to happen today. They believed—as did everyone in Liverpool—that the test was the merely routine preamble to recording for Parlophone on the basis of a contract already promised. *Mersey Beat* had said so, even giving July as the month of their first record release and inviting readers to suggest possible titles for issue. They were, in any case, still dazed after Hamburg, the Star-Club, and six virtually sleepless weeks.

At Abbey Road studios that day, something entirely unexpected happened. George Martin, that elegant BBC-accented A&R man and the four scruffily shod Liverpool boys took a liking to one another. Early in their conversation George Martin happened to mention he had worked with Peter Sellers and Spike Milligan, the founding members of the radio *Goon Show.* "Goon" humor is dear to most Liverpudlians: In John Lennon's eyes, especially, Martin was instantly raised to near divinity by his connection with the man who had sung the "Ying-Tong Song." He was, besides, agreeably plainspoken, neither ingratiating nor condescending. John and Paul—and especially George—were soon plying him with questions about the studio and its equipment. Only Pete Best remained, as usual, silent. George Martin does not remember exchanging a word with him all afternoon.

Brian had already sent down a neatly typewritten list of songs that the Beatles could play if required. A large portion were standards, like "Besame Mucho," since these, Brian thought—mistakenly—had impressed Martin most on the demo tape. There was also the batch of new songs they had written in Hamburg, mostly round the battered piano at Jim Hawke's Seaman's Mission on the docks.

Despite everything else on George Martin's mind, the test he gave the Beatles was exhaustive. Ringed by their puny amps they stood in the well of the huge studio, attacking song after song, then waiting, in sudden silence, for the verdict of the polite, unexcited voice over the control-room intercom. What they did not realize was that Martin was putting each of them on test individually, to try to see which might be the Cliff Richard he still hoped to find. He could not decide between Paul, whose voice was more melodious, and John, whose personality had greater force. George, and his rather strained, adenoidal voice, figured little in these computations. "I was thinking that on balance I should make Paul the leader," Martin says. "Then I realized that if I did, I'd be changing the whole nature of the group. Why not keep them as they were?"

The question of material remained vexing. Martin still felt that "Red Sails in the Sunset," "Your Feet's Too Big," and "Besame Mucho" were "too corny." Nor did he particularly like the songs they had written for themselves. He listened patiently but without inner animation to the one that, plainly, they hoped he would choose as the A side of their record. Called "Love Me Do," it was a simple and very brief Lennon and McCartney composition whose loping rhythm served mainly as a showcase for Pete Best's drumming. Its chord structure was basic; its harmony unambitious; its lyric the kind that any tin-eared beginner might have jotted on an envelope: "Love, love me do . . . you know I love you . . . I'll always be true . . ." Its only virtue was that at least it sounded glancingly like other 1962 pop songs. But Martin still decided to reserve judgment.

One thing he did know, right from the beginning, was that he didn't want Pete Best. "At the end of the test I took Brian on one side and said, 'I don't know what you intend to do with the group as such, but this drumming isn't at all what I want. If we do make a record, I'd prefer to use my own drummer—which won't make any difference to you because no one will know who's on the record anyway.' " Brian did not protest. Nor did he mention it to Pete, who was packing up his gear as excitedly as the other three.

"If we make a record" was still as far as Martin would commit himself. He liked the Beatles, and felt there was definitely "something" there. At the same time he knew that in signing so offbeat and potentially uncommercial a group, he could well risk his own small position within EMI. Besides, he had a full program of recording celebrities such as Bernard Cribbins, and a live LP to make at London's first satirical night club, the Establishment.

Not until late July did Brian receive a definite offer. Martin agreed to record the Beatles on Parlophone, subject to the most niggardly contract that EMI's penny-pinching caution could devise. In an initial one-year period Parlophone would record four titles at a royalty, to Brian and the Beatles together, of one penny per double-sided record. Four further one-year options were open to Martin, each bringing a royalty increment per record of one farthing, or a quarter of an old penny.

A few days after the audition someone said a curious thing to Pete: "They're thinking of getting rid of you, you know—but they don't dare do it. They're too worried about losing all your fans."

At about the same time Bob Wooler, the Cavern disk jockey, making his rounds of Liverpool after dark, came into Danny English's pub to join a meeting in progress between Brian, Paul, and George. Wooler, as a long-time confidant, had been specially invited, though for what reason Brian would not say. It soon became clear that Paul and George were both urging that Pete Best be sacked.

Brian himself held out for some time against sacking Pete. At first, he seems to have thought he could appease all sides by keeping Pete on for live dates but using a substitute drummer on record, as George Martin had suggested. Brian had nothing against Pete—indeed, he relied heavily on him as the group's most punctual and businesslike member. Pete's home in West Derby, and the little coffee club downstairs, continued to be the Beatles' main rendezvous and base camp. An added complication existed in Neil Aspinall, their indispensable van driver and bodyguard, who was Pete's closest friend. There would also, in the event of unpleasantness, be Pete's mother to contend with. Mona Best, as Brian already knew, was a force one did not lightly provoke.

All through June and July, before word came from George Martin at Parlophone, the plots simmered against a still unsuspecting Pete. The Beatles—already billed by Brian as "Parlophone Recording Artists"—were back at their old ballroom haunts, the Grafton, the Majestic in Birkenhead, and the New Brighton Tower. It was after a radio appearance in Manchester, on the BBC Light Program *Northern Dance Orchestra Show*, where he had been literally mobbed by girls, that someone dropped the first hint to Pete: "They're thinking of getting rid of you, you know." The thought amused Pete; he even mentioned it jokingly to Brian, who responded by blushing and spluttering "how ridiculous." Just the same, when Martin wrote to him in late July, and the Parlophone contract became real at last, Brian took care not to let Pete Best know.

John stayed out of the plot, having a far more urgent worry on his mind. His girlfriend, Cynthia, in one of her rare utterances, had informed him that her monthly "friend" had failed to pay her a visit. Since John and she were virtually living together, in equal innocence of birth control methods, this crucial friend's arrival had long been in jeopardy. Now it was certain, confirmed by a woman doctor whose harshness drove the mild, shortsighted girl to tears. Cyn was going to have a baby.

John bowed to the inevitable as fatalistically as any north country workingman. In that case, he told Cynthia, there was nothing else for it; they'd have to get married. With Cyn's mother away in Canada the only family member to be reckoned with was John's aunt Mimi. They put off breaking it to Mimi until the eve of their hastily arranged wedding. Mimi's response was a hollow and heartfelt groan. She had groaned in exactly that way in 1938, when John's mother, Julia, came home and threw a marriage certificate casually on the table. "I told them," Mimi remembered, "'I'll say one thing only, then I'll hold my peace. You're *too young*! There now, I've said it. Now I'll hold my peace forever.'"

August began, and still Pete Best knew nothing of the contract with Parlophone. The Beatles, en route for the Grafton on West Derby Road, were all in Mona Best's sitting room, waiting for Pete to come downstairs. He did so in high spirits, full of the Ford Capri car he had almost decided to buy. Mrs. Best remembered that Paul, in particular, showed unease over the price Pete intended to pay for the car. "He went all mysterious, suddenly. He told Pete, "'If you take my advice, you won't buy it, that's all. You'd be better saving your money.'"

On Wednesday, August 15, they were on at lunchtime in the Cavern. The next night was the first of four major bookings at the Riverpark Ballroom in Chester. Pete had decided to make his own way there, giving John a lift. They both came out of the Cavern and Pete asked John what time he should pick him up tomorrow night. John muttered, "Don't bother," and walked away in a hurry. Later, at home, Pete got a call from Brian in his Whitechapel office. "He said he wanted to see me there tomorrow morning at 11:30. That was nothing unusual. He'd often ask me things about halls or bookings that I knew from the time when I'd been handling the dates."

Pete's friend Neil Aspinall drove him into the city to see Brian the next morning. "I went bouncing into Brian's office," Pete says. "As soon as I saw him, I could tell there was something up. He said: 'The boys want you out of the group. They don't think you're a good enough drummer.' I said, 'It's taken them two years to find out I'm not a good enough drummer.' While I was standing there the phone rang on Brian's desk. It was Paul, asking if I'd been told yet. Brian said, 'I can't talk now. Peter's here with me in the office.' "

"I went outside and told Neil. He said, 'Right then, that's it. I'm out as well.' Brian followed me and asked me if I'd still play the dates in Chester, as they wouldn't be able to get a replacement drummer in time. I said, OK, I would. We went outside, and Neil went straight away to ring home and tell Mo about it. I just went off and had a few pints—numb. I'd been cut and dried and hung out on the line."

Luck had very seldom favored the boy who was born Richard Starkey on July 7, 1940, at number 9 Madryn Street, deep in the Liverpool Dingle. The baby was one month late and had to be induced with forceps; as his mother, Elsie, lay upstairs recovering, the sirens sounded Germany's first aerial visitation. The densely packed Dingle houses had no bomb shelter other than the coal hole under the stairs. As Elsie, with Ritchie, and three neighbors crouched there, she could not understand why the baby on her shoulder was screaming. Then she realized she was holding him upside-down.

The sad-eyed child they named Ritchie after his father came to consciousness on the tailboard of a moving van as it carried his mother's few possessions from Madryn Street around the corner to a new, even smaller row house in Admiral Grove. His father, Ritchie senior, a bakery worker, had by now moved away from home but continued conscientiously to support his wife and child. He could only send 30s (£1.50) a week, so Elsie herself took work as a barmaid in a pub. Young Ritchie thus spent much of his early childhood at the home of his grandfather Starkey, a boilermaker in the Mersey shipyards. He was a solitary boy, but philosophical and happy with the little that he had. His only reproach to Elsie was the lack of any brothers and sisters, "so there'd be someone to talk to when it's raining."

His education was dogged from the beginning by chronic ill health. At the age of six, after only a year at primary school, he was rushed to the hospital with a burst appendix. Surgeons operated in the nick of time to save his life, but he remained in a coma for several weeks. Elsie would come in late, after work at the pub, to peep at the little figure in its hospital cot. He recovered, became his old cheerful self, and was about to come home when he fell out of bed while showing a toy to someone. This first absence from school eventually dragged out to a full year.

At eight, consequently, he was unable to read or write. A neighbor's daughter, Mary Maguire, did her best to help him catch up by encouraging him to spell out words from magazines. The operation had left his stomach in a delicate state from which it was never to recover fully. When there was lamb scouse—stew—for dinner, Mary would sit beside Ritchie, carefully picking the onions out of his portion.

When he was eleven his mother began to keep company with Harry Graves, a Liverpool Corporation house painter, originally from London. Harry and Elsie married in 1953, when Ritchie was not quite thirteen. He had begun to attend Dingle Vale Secondary School, but was still greatly handicapped by all the lessons he had missed. That same year, he caught a cold that turned to pleurisy and affected one of his lungs. They took him to the big children's sanatorium at Heswall on the Wirral; he remained there for the next two years.

When eventually discharged he was fifteen and of graduation age. No one remembered him at Dingle Vale Secondary when he went back there for a reference. He could read and write only with difficulty, and the months in a hospital had left him thin, weak, and sallow. Patches of premature gray were starting to show in his hair and his left eyebrow. His nature, against all the odds, continued to be cheerful.

The Youth Employment Officer, well accustomed to such lost causes, eventually found him a job with the railway as a messenger boy. He left after six weeks because they wouldn't give him a uniform, and took casual work as a barman on the ferryboats plying slantwise over the Mersey between Liverpool and New Brighton. Then, thanks to his stepfather, he was taken on by Hunt's, a local engineering firm, as apprentice to a carpenter. The overalls, the slide-rule, the contract binding for years ahead all promised security for life.

A fellow Hunt's apprentice was a boy named Eddie Miles who lived near the Starkeys in Admiral Grove. When the skiffle craze began in 1956 Eddie and Ritchie started a group to amuse the other apprentices in the dinner hour. Ritchie, who had always banged and beaten on things, took the role of drummer. Harry Graves bought him his first full set, paying ten pounds for it down in London and carrying it valiantly back to Lime Street on the train.

The Eddie Clayton Skiffle Group, as they called themselves, played around the same church hall network as John Lennon's original Quarry Men. Ritchie by now was using brand-new drums for which his grandfather Starkey had lent him the fifty-pound deposit. The set was his passport, around 1959, into Liverpool's most successful amateur group. He joined the Ravin' Texans, afterward the Hurricanes, the quartet that played while Rory Storm sang and, occasionally, shinned up ballroom pillars. The others nicknamed him "Rings," because he wore so many, then Ringo as it sounded more cowboyish. Starkey was first abbreviated to Starr at Butlin's summer camp, so that his solo drumming spot could be billed on a poster as "Starr Time."

Until 1961, Ringo belonged to a group far more glamorous and successful than the Beatles. He only got to know them in Hamburg when Rory Storm came over to play the Kaiserkeller and from then on he got to know them well, in many an uproarious bedroom and bar. The Beatles liked him for his droll, harmless humor; for being, in those unreal neon nights, as homely as a Pier Head pigeon. And he was, undoubtedly, a better drummer than Pete Best. The plot to oust Pete dates right back to 1961, when Ringo joined the Beatles as a backing group for Wally in the record booth at the Hamburg railway station.

After Hamburg, Rory Storm's fortunes became somewhat mixed. At one point, he even signed on at his local unemployment office as "rock 'n' roll pianist." Ringo had by now given up his apprenticeship; and he, too, spent several weeks on the dole, sitting out vacant days at the Cavern, the Jacaranda, or the *Mersey Beat* office upstairs on Renshaw Street. Late in 1961, while sorting through some records, he noticed an LP by Lightnin' Hopkins that gave the singer's birthplace as Houston, Texas. Ringo, who had always adored the Wild West, conceived the idea of emigrating to America. He even wrote to the Houston Chamber of Commerce enquiring about job prospects in that area. The chamber wrote back helpfully enough, but Ringo lost heart at the sight of the registration forms.

Early in 1962, Peter Eckhorn appeared in Liverpool to recruit musicians for his Top Ten Club. When Brian Epstein priced the Beatles out of his reach Eckhorn persuaded Ringo to go back to Hamburg with him and join Tony Sheridan's resident band. Eckhorn thought highly enough of Ringo to offer him a permanent job at thirty pounds per week, with a flat thrown in. He was also the special favorite of Jim and Lilo Hawke at the Seaman's Mission. But Ringo felt homesick for Liverpool, Admiral Grove, and his mother.

In August, he had rejoined Rory Storm and the Hurricanes and gone south to Skegness with them for their regular summer gig at Butlin's camp. Back in Liverpool, his mother opened the front door one day to George Harrison's pale, unsmiling face. Mrs. Graves told him that Ringo wasn't at home. "Tell him we're trying to get him to join us," was George's message.

It was John who finally got through to Ringo, ringing up Butlin's and then waiting until Ringo could be found and brought to the camp office phone. The pay as a Beatle, John said, would be twenty-five pounds per week. In return, Ringo would have to comb his hair forward and shave off his beard. His "sidies," however, could remain.

Rory Storm was magnanimous over the theft of his drummer. The only stipulation Rory made was that when Ringo left the Hurricanes to join the Beatles his pink stage suit was passed on to sixteen-year-old Gibson Kemp, who had not yet left school and who was so small that the jacket had to be pinned at the back with pins to make it fit him.

Mersey Beat broke the news in its issue of August 23. Pete Best was out of the Beatles and Ringo Starr had replaced him. According to *Mersey Beat,* the change had been mutually and amicably agreed. The story went on to announce that George Martin was ready at last for the Beatles to go to London and record their first single for Parlophone. They would be flying down with their new drummer for a session on September 4.

The uproar among Pete Best fans was on a scale far greater than even Bob Wooler had predicted. Petitions signed by hundreds of girls poured into the *Mersey Beat* office, protesting at their idol's banishment. For Ringo's debut as a Beatle the venue was fortunately quiet and far from Liverpool—the annual dance of Port Sunlight Horticultural Society. But when he first took the stage with them at the Cavern, there were hostile chants of "Pete Best for ever! Ringo never!" The more besotted of Pete's fans kept a nightlong vigil outside the Best family home. When Mona Best opened the front door to pick up her morning milk she found girls with tear-smudged eye makeup asleep all over her yard.

The following day, in chaos compounded of Pete Best's firing and several pneumatic road drills, John Lennon married Cynthia Powell at Mount Pleasant Register Office. It was the same place where, in 1938, his mother Julia had married Freddy Lennon, putting her occupation down as cinema usherette for a joke. As on that earlier occasion, no parents were present. Cynthia's mother had come from Canada but gone again; and Aunt Mimi could not bear to see history repeat itself so exactly. Cynthia was given away by her brother, Tony, and Brian Epstein— who had obtained the special marriage license—acted as John's best man. With insufficient money to buy herself a new wedding outfit, Cynthia went before the registrar wearing some of Astrid's cast-off clothes. Paul and George were there also, torn between embarrassment and giggles. Much of the service was inaudible, owing to road drills. Afterward, in the pouring rain, they ran across the road for a chicken lunch at Reece's restaurant. Since Reece's had no alcohol license, the toast to the newlyweds was drunk with water.

Brian had expected the Pete Best storm to fizzle out after a day or so, but he was wrong. When the Beatles turned up at the Cavern Club almost a week later there were still angry pickets outside. In a stage-door scuffle involving Pete himself—tough nut for all his good nature—George received a black eye that ripened spectacularly in the course of the evening's performance. Brian, after this, refused to go to the Cavern unless Ray McFall provided him with a bodyguard. But, being Brian, he did not wholly dislike the notion of being "the most hated man in Liverpool."

Pete's mother had already paid Brian the first of many wrathful and accusing visits. Mona Best was—and remained—convinced that Pete's sacking was due simply to the jealousy of John, Paul, and George. "He'd given them so much with his beat and everything. To a lot of the fans, he *was* the Beatles. I knew that Brian hadn't wanted to do it; he respected Peter too much. None of the others was introduced to Brian's parents; now why was that? Why was Peter the only one?"

The worst affected, after Pete himself, was Neil Aspinall, the Beatles' by now indispensable roadie, whose links with the Best family were now closer than most of their combined circle ever dreamed. Mona Best was still an extremely attractive and vibrant woman and, somehow in the past year, she and her older son's friend, the serious young would-be accountant, had had an affair that had resulted in Mrs. Best's becoming pregnant. Just a few weeks before Pete's sacking, on July 21, she had given birth to Neil's son, whom she named Roag and brought up as a Best, along with Pete and his brother Rory. In an almost Gilbert and Sullivan twist, the Beatles' driver/bodyguard was also the father of their sacked drummer's half-brother.

Pete understood Neil's conflict of loyalties and had no wish for his friend to suffer on his account. When Neil considered walking out on the Beatles Pete urged him to stay with them for a few more months at least, to see where they might end up. For a time, the Beatles even continued using the Casbah as a meeting place before engagements, though they were careful to keep out of Mrs. Best's way. "Then one day Paul knocked on the door and asked me if he could leave his car in the drive. I managed to keep my peace but Kathy, Pete's girlfriend, gave John and Paul a damned good talking-to."

Brian tried to soften the blow to Pete by offering to build a new group around him. What he eventually did was to fit Pete into Lee Curtis and the All Stars, the group managed by Brian's friend and helper Joe Flannery. Joe agreed to accept Pete despite misgivings that his good looks would clash with those of Lee Curtis, Joe's younger brother. The transfer was effected, he remembers, with subtlety typical of Brian. "First Brian got me to agree to have Pete. Then I had to talk to Pete and say: "I think I can arrange it with Mr. Epstein.'"

Pete, very naturally, failed to turn up for the first of the Chester Riverpark ballroom dates. Since Ringo had not yet arrived from Skegness, a substitute drummer had to be found at short notice. Brian solved the difficulty by borrowing Johnny Hutch from the Big Three.

The next big beat show at New Brighton Tower, on July 27, was presented, not by Sam Leach but by NEMS Enterprises. The star was Joe Brown, a popular Cockney rock 'n' roller whose song "Picture of You" was currently high in the charts. Second on the bill were the Beatles. In this way, Brian implanted the idea that Joe Brown, for all his big name, was only a line of type ahead of them. More big names followed, always with the Beatles second on the bill. "He'd watch the charts all the time and see who was selling the most records," Joe Flannery says. "When someone like Joe Brown or Bruce Channel came up, Brian would make a big day of it. There'd be an autograph-signing session at the shop, then the show in the evening. American stars used to think that was wonderful. They weren't used to getting that kind of treatment in England, not even in London."

On September 6, Brian took a full-page advertisement in *Mersey Beat* to announce a coup that any promoter might have envied. Little Richard, rock 'n' roll's baggy-suited and clamorous founding father, was currently touring Britain. Brian had negotiated with Richard's London promoters to bring him to New Brighton Tower for one night, on October 12. The Beatles were second on the program, together with more Liverpool groups than had appeared in one place since Allan Williams' Boxing Stadium show.

George Martin knew nothing of the Pete Best sacking. He expected Pete to be still with the others when, on September 11, they came back to the Abbey Road studios. Accordingly, down on the floor of Studio Two there waited an experienced session drummer named Andy White whom Martin had engaged to play on the record in place of Pete. When Ringo was introduced to him as Pete's replacement, he saw no reason to depart from his original plan. He knew nothing about Ringo as a drummer, he said, and preferred not to take any chances. White must play on the recording.

After this rather stern beginning, Martin tried to make amends by involving the Beatles in every facet of the recording process. He explained that due to the wonders of EMI science they could record their voices and instruments as separate tracks, to be "mixed" afterward for optimum texture and balance. He let them record a warm-up number, then took them into the control room to play it back. He asked them if there was anything they didn't like. George said, in his slow, gruff way, "Well, for a start, I don't like your tie." "Everyone fell about with laughter at that," Martin says. "The others were hitting him playfully, as schoolboys do when one of them has been cheeky to teacher."

Martin had decided, after all, to use Lennon-McCartney songs as both the A and B sides of the single. For the A side, after much deliberation, he chose "Love Me Do." The number had improved since he had last heard it, chiefly by the addition of a harmonica riff that John had copied from the Bruce Channel hit "Hey Baby." For the B side, to bring Paul to the fore, Martin chose "P.S. I Love You," liking the song for its harmonies, its switch from major to minor chords, and the way that John's voice chimed with Paul's on key words through the lyric.

During rehearsals that afternoon Martin somewhat relented in his attitude to Ringo's drumming. "He hit good and hard, and used the tom-tom well, even though he couldn't do a roll to save his life." Ringo himself did not know yet that there was a session drummer waiting to replace him. When it came time to record the "Love Me Do" instrumental track Ringo was handed a tambourine and instructed to hit it twice on every third beat. He looked so doleful that Martin relented a little. They would record two versions, Martin said: one with Andy White on drums and one with Ringo. The vocal track would be mixed with whichever version came out best.

The White and Ringo versions became indistinguishable in the quantity of "takes" that were needed before Martin was content with the instrumental track. The fifteenth attempt finally satisfied him, even though John Lennon's mouth had grown numb with sliding along the harmonica bars. There was a short break; then they returned to do the backing track for "P.S. I Love You." Andy White sat at the drums and Ringo, this time, was given maracas to shake. He later said that he thought the others were "doing a Pete Best" on him.

At EMI's next "supplement meeting," when each label head outlined his release plans for the coming month, Martin caused a ripple of amusement by announcing that Parlophone was putting out a single by a group called the Beatles. The general view was that it must be another comedy disk. Somebody even asked: "Is it Spike Milligan disguised?" "I told them, 'I'm serious. This is a great group, and we're going to hear a lot from them.' But nobody took much notice."

Up in Liverpool, Brian had begun to prepare the Beatles for impending stardom. Freda Kelly from the NEMS office had to go round to each one with a printed sheet for "Life Lines"—favorite food, favorite clothes, likes, dislikes, and so on—just as it was done in the *New Musical Express.* Next to "Type of car?" Paul wrote "Ford Classic (Goodwood green)"; next to "Dislikes?" he wrote "False and soft people," and next to "Ambition?" "Money etc." George gave his main dislike, ironically, as "Black eyes," his "Greatest musical influences?" as Carl Perkins, his "Ambition?" "To retire with a lot of money, thank you." John, using an italic fountain pen, gave his "Dislikes?" as "Thick heads, Trad Jazz," his favorite film director as Ingmar Bergman, his "Ambition?" as "Money and everything." Ringo's favorite food was "Steak and chips"; his "Likes?" "Everyone who likes me."

On October 2, a second contract was signed by the Beatles and Brian—a thoroughly legal document this time, and witnessed, as the law required, by Paul and George's fathers. The term of the agreement was five years. Brian's share of the earnings was 25 percent. A further clause—a slip on Clive Epstein's part, hastily rectified soon afterward—gave each side power to terminate the agreement at six months' notice.

On October 12, Little Richard and retinue arrived in Liverpool for his show at the New Brighton Tower. The legendary screamer of "Lucille" and "Good Golly Miss Molly" was by now slightly toned down in a conventional sharkskin suit, his former wild, greasy locks planed flat to the scalp. But his manner remained as outrageously camp and his mood as wildly unpredictable as ever. With him came his British agent, Don Arden, a stocky, belligerent man who lost no opportunity to stress what a great honor was being done to New Brighton and Merseyside.

Entrepreneurs who have put on Little Richard shows tell bloodcurdling stories of his temperament, his unreliability, his bizarre whims and fancies, his refusal in some cases to do anything for the audience but slowly remove his clothes. But on October 12, 1962, when Richard performed at New Brighton Tower Ballroom, something seemed to have happened to put him in a mood of perfect tractability and cooperativeness. "Brian seemed to be able to do anything with him," Joe Flannery says. "When Richard finished his act, something had gone wrong with the mike for the next group, Pete MacLaine and the Dakotas. Brian could even get Richard to walk across, nice as you please, and hand his personal microphone on to Pete MacLaine." It was rumored that Brian had won the volatile star over by spending the previous night with him in a room at the Adelphi Hotel. Richard himself firmly denies this, however. "I didn't even have so much as a *sandwich* with Brian," he says now.

The Beatles were initially so overcome with nerves at sharing a bill with their greatest soul hero that they couldn't even pluck up courage to ask him to do a photograph with them. Instead, while Richard was on stage, John stood watching him from the wings on one side and Paul photographed the two of them from the wings opposite.

After the show, he was just as seraphically amiable, telling local journalists how much he loved England and Liverpool, posing for pictures with John, Paul, George, and Ringo in a tickled-pink group around him. He even gave Paul instruction in the trademark scream he called his "little holler." For the rest of his erratic career he would always maintain, "The Beatles was my group. I taught 'em everything they knew."

So powerful was Brian's influence over Little Richard that he was able to bring him back to Liverpool for a second concert, at the Empire theater on October 28, to head the existing bill of Craig Douglas, Jet Harris and the Jetblacks, and the Beatles. Brian planned the entire event as a means of giving them their first professional booking at the Empire.

Because it was Sunday none of the groups were allowed to appear in costume, so they all took off their jackets. The Beatles played in pink, round-collared shirts. For a fan like Freda Kelly it was no less a miracle that they had crossed the gulf from underground clubs to this softly lit, luxurious realm of concert and Christmas pantomime. "I remember when the spotlight went on Paul in his pink shirt, and he started to sing "Besame Mucho." I thought, "This is *it*. Now they've *really* made it.""

"Love Me Do" was released on October 4, 1962, in a week when America's grip on the British Top Twenty had seldom been stronger. Carole King, Tommy Roe, Bobby Vee, Little Eva, Ray Charles, and Del Shannon all had new songs making, or about to make, their inevitable ascent. The sensation of the moment was "Let's Dance" by Chris Montez, prolonging the Twist dance craze that French students had imported into Britain during the summer. Among British artists, the continuing success of Helen Shapiro, Jimmy Justice, Kathy Kirby, and Shane Fenton seemed to bear out the Decca prophecy that solo singers were what the teenagers wanted, that guitar groups were "on the way out."

EMI themselves seemed to think so. After "Love Me Do" was released virtually no effort was made to plug the disk to the trade press or BBC radio, or even to EMI's own sponsored Radio Luxembourg show. Newspaper publicity was confined to a single printed handout, copied from the "Life Lines" that Freda Kelly had drawn up in Liverpool, vouchsafing to indifferent Fleet Street record columnists that Paul McCartney's favorite clothes were leather and suede, that Ringo Starr's favorite dish was steak and chips, that George Harrison's greatest musical influence was Carl Perkins, and that John Lennon's "type of car" was "bus."

After his experience with Decca Brian was taking no chances. He himself had ordered ten thousand copies of "Love Me Do" from Parlophone. He had been told that that was the quantity you had to sell to have a Top Twenty hit.

Though the Liverpool fans loyally bought "Love Me Do," and though *Mersey Beat*'s chart made it instantaneously number one, most of the ten thousand copies remained in unopened cartons in a back room of the Whitechapel NEMS shop. "Brian took me and showed me them," Joe Flannery says. "He even made up a little song about all the copies he hadn't been able to sell. 'Here we go gathering dust in May,' he'd sing." A few days later, in London, Flannery bumped into Paul McCartney. "Paul said he was hungry; he'd only had a cake to eat all day. I was amazed. I said, 'Paul—how?' Paul said, 'Someone had to pay for those ten thousand records Brian bought.' "

The first radio play was on Luxembourg, after hundreds of requests from Liverpool. George Harrison sat waiting for it next to the radio all evening with his mother, Louise. She had given up and was in bed when George ran upstairs, shouting, "We're on! We're on!" Mr. Harrison was angry at being disturbed; he had to be up early the next morning to drive his bus.

A few scattered plays followed on the BBC Light Program, where pop was beginning to creep into "general" music shows like the early evening *Roundabout*. The best exposure was secured by Kim Bennett of Ardmore and Beechwood, the publishers who had first steered Brian back to EMI and George Martin. By dint of repeatedly nagging a radio producer friend, Bennett got "Love Me Do" onto the playlist of *Two-Way Family Favourites*, a hugely popular Sunday-morning show playing record requests for British forces overseas. After two appearances there on consecutive Sundays, "Love Me Do" was shown at number fortynine in *Record Mirror*'s top 100. The *New Musical Express*, shortly afterward, showed it at number twenty-seven. Finally, on December 13, it reached number seventeen.

For a first record, especially on Parlophone, that was not at all a bad performance. If "Love Me Do" had not taken the country by storm, it had confirmed George Martin's instinct that the Beatles could be successful singing the right song. He reached that conclusion even before "Love Me Do" made its brief Top Twenty showing. The second single under their first year's contract was due to be recorded on November 26.

Though bound to EMI on record for five years, Brian had only a gentlemen's agreement with Syd Coleman of Ardmore and Beechwood that A&B would continue publishing John Lennon and Paul McCartney's song output. He felt disappointed with Ardmore and Beechwood's performance in publicizing "Love Me Do"—though, to be fair, the failure was all on EMI's side—and now confided to George Martin that he'd be seeking new publishers for the Beatles' follow-up single. His initial idea was to go to an American firm, Hill and Range, that held British rights on the Elvis Presley catalog. Martin's advice was to pick a small firm with a drive to succeed that would match Brian's own: "In other words, what I told Brian he needed was a hungry music publisher."

The hungriest music publisher George Martin knew was Dick James, a tubby, amiable, bald-headed man whose office was one first-floor room at the corner of Denmark and Old Compton Streets. Born Isaac Vapnik, James had begun his career as a crooner in the 1930s, as featured vocalist with Primo Scala's Accordion Band. He had sung with leading orchestras, including Henry Hall's and Cyril Stapleton's, and made several records, of which the most famous was the theme song for *Robin Hood*, a children's series on early commercial television. On losing his moderate female fan base along with his hair he had turned first to song plugging, then to publishing. In November 1962, he had been in business on his own for one year exactly. Everyone knew Dick James, everyone liked him, but no one yet mistook him for Tin Pan Alley's next millionaire.

In the early 1950s, as a newcomer to Parlophone, George Martin had produced Dick James on several minor hit records, including "Tenderly" and "Robin Hood." It was natural, therefore, that when EMI's own publishing company proved deficient, he should approach Dick James informally, both as a possible publisher for the Beatles and also in James's old capacity as a plugger of likely recording material. The first approach, when Martin mentioned "this Liverpool group," was not encouraging. James laughed his cuddly laugh and echoed, "Liverpool? So what's from Liverpool?"

The answer, by then, was a disk with at least a toe-hold in the *New Musical Express* Top 100. James heard "Love Me Do," liked the overall sound but agreed with Martin that the song was "just a riff." He promised to use his Tin Pan Alley contacts to find them a good "professional" song for their follow-up record. This he produced within days, on a demo disk that he played to Martin. The song was "How Do You Do It?" by a young composer named Mitch Murray. "As soon as Dick played it to me," Martin says, "I started jumping up and down. 'This is it,' I said. 'This is the song that's going to make the Beatles a household name.' "

He said the same to the Beatles themselves when Brian brought them back to Abbey Road studios on November 26. He played them the demo of "How Do You Do It?" accompanied by his own carefully thought-out ideas on how the song could be adapted to suit them. He was surprised, and not a little irritated, when John and Paul said flatly that they didn't like it, and wanted to do another of their own songs. This apparent willfulness in the face of an almost certain hit brought a stern lecture from Martin. " 'When you can write material as good as this I'll record it,' I said. 'But right now, we're going to record *this*.' "

His words sent them, chastened, into the studio, to produce a version of "How Do You Do It?" in which every note and nuance of John Lennon's lead voice made plain their lugubrious distaste. George Harrison, halfway through, produced a guitar solo not far removed in scale and ambition from the twanging of a rubber band. Even so, they could not stop a little charm and originality from creeping in.

The song they wanted to record was one of John and Paul's called

"Please Please Me," one fairly slow version of which had already been tried on Martin. Since then, they had worked on it, tidying up the lyric and making it faster. The revised version was now played by Paul and John on their acoustic Gibson guitars while Martin, perched on a musician's high stool, listened critically. Then, as their voices broke together on the "Whoa yeah" Martin recognized something. His objection was that the song as it stood lasted barely more than a minute. They could lengthen it with an intro on John's harmonica, and by repeating the first chorus at the end.

The first take of "Please Please Me" was so belligerently alive that George Martin decided to use it, even though Paul had forgotten the words in the first chorus and John, more obviously, had forgotten them in the finale. "The whole session was a joy," Martin says. "At the end, I pressed the intercom button and said, 'Gentlemen, you have just made your first number one.' "

He now had to break it to Dick James that the Mitch Murray song would not, after all, be out soon on Parlophone. "George rang me up," James says. "His words were, 'You know that song the Beatles *were* going to record . . .' " James held his head in Tin Pan Alley mock anguish, but agreed to meet Brian Epstein the next day with a view to publishing—and plugging—"Please Please Me." It was arranged that Brian would bring an early pressing of the single for James to hear at his Denmark Street office at 11:00 A.M.

Brian arrived, instead, at 10:20. He had had an earlier appointment with another music publisher, but the man he was supposed to meet had not bothered to keep the appointment. Instead, it was suggested that he play his demo disk to the office boy. He had walked out in fury and come straight on to Dick James Music. James, to his lasting benefit, was at work already, and able to greet the angrily blushing young man in person.

A single hearing of "Please Please Me" was enough for James. He loved the song, he told Brian; could he publish it? Brian, a little nonplussed by the shabby office, asked what James thought he could do for the Beatles that EMI's publicity department had not already done. James's answer was to pick up the telephone and call a friend of his named Philip Jones, the producer of the Saturday night television pop show *Thank Your Lucky Stars*. He told Jones to listen, then put "Please Please Me" onto his record player and held the telephone receiver near to it. Jones agreed that it was very good. He also agreed, at James's skillful prompting, to put the Beatles into *Thank Your Lucky Stars*. In five minutes, Dick James had guaranteed them exposure on what was—after BBC TV's *Juke Box Jury*—the show with the greatest influence over the record-buying public. "Now," he asked ingenuously, "can I publish the song?"

Another reason why George Martin had sent Brian to James was that he knew James to be very straight in financial matters. As a singer, he had himself frequently been done out of large earnings in the days when English artists received no royalty on American sales of their records. Twice in the early 1950s he had topped the American charts and yet received only seven pounds each time—the then standard studio fee. The deal he now offered Brian, while not actuated by pure benevolence, was both fair and imaginative.

Under the usual predatory publisher's contract James would have taken 10 percent of the *retail* price of sheet music, plus up to half of the royalties from radio play and cover versions. Instead, he proposed that a special company be formed within his own organization but exclusively publishing Lennon-McCartney songs. The company would be called Northern Songs and its proceeds split 50-50: half to Dick James, 20 percent each to John and Paul, and 10 percent to Brian. It sounded handsome, and it was, notwithstanding the clause that James's own company would take a percentage of Northern Songs' earnings "off the top." "Brian said to me, 'Why are you doing this for us?' " James recalled. "What I said to him then was the truth. I was doing it because I had such faith in the songs."

"Please Please Me" was not scheduled for release until January 1963. In the meantime, the Beatles were committed to return to Hamburg for a two-week engagement at Manfred Weissleder's Star-Club. The booking had been made back in the summer, before George Martin's advent, at rates of pay that no longer seemed attractive. All four, besides, felt they had had their fill of the Reeperbahn. Also, for the first time, they would be away from home during both Christmas and New Year's Eve. The clincher was an offer from Manfred Weissleder to Brian of one thousand deutschmarks in "brown bag money" that wouldn't have to be declared for income tax.

On December 2, a severe jolt was sustained by the Beatles' collective ego. Brian, through sheer effrontery, had managed to get them into what was then known as a package show of pop acts currently enjoying Top Twenty success. He had discovered the private telephone number of Arthur Howes, the country's biggest tour promoter, and had rung up Howes one Saturday afternoon at home in Peterborough. Arthur Howes, a veteran at the agency game, smiled a bit when he heard the name of the group on offer, but was fair-minded enough not to refuse them without a trial. He offered to put them on for one night only at the Embassy cinema, Peterborough, in a show headed by Frank Ifield, the Australian yodeler.

The appearance was an unmitigated flop. The staid East Anglian audience had come to see Frank Ifield, not four unknowns from the north; they had come to worship suntan and upswept hair, not eccentric bangs, and to hear sentimental ballads, not Chuck Berry and Carl Perkins music. Total silence followed every perversely loud number. But something about them appealed to Arthur Howes; he told Brian that the disaster was not all their fault, and even made a small offer for the option of using them in future package shows.

On December 18, with the worst possible grace, they set off for Hamburg and what would be their farewell performance at the Star-Club. "Please Please Me" was just beginning to show in the Top Twenty; rather than vanishing abroad they felt they should be on home territory, taking every possible opportunity to promote the single. It was not much consolation that sharing the Star-Club's Christmas bill would be Carl Perkins, one of their earliest rock 'n' roll idols, whose easygoing numbers, like "Honey Don't" and "Matchbox," had proved ideal for giving Ringo a stab at singing lead.

By now the Beatles' place as darlings of the Reeperbahn had been somewhat usurped by Kingsize Taylor and the Dominoes, the high-octane R&B band who had taught them so much at Merseyside gigs like Lathom Hall. Kingsize Taylor, the towering, throaty-voiced butcher's apprentice, was an uncomplaining workhorse for Weissleder and other German promoters, sometimes playing sets of up to twelve hours' duration with just fifteen minutes' break each hour. However, after several incidents with tear-gas guns in the flats above Maxim's Club, Weissleder had felt it safer to move all his British bands into a small hotel, the Pacific. There Kingsize and the Beatles celebrated their reunion by pelting one another with grapes.

The Star-Club's barnlike acoustics made it impossible for the bands to hear themselves while they played. To help him and his colleagues check their sound balance, Kingsize Taylor left a tape recorder running throughout much of that 1962 Christmas show. So was accidentally preserved for posterity the fullest and most vivid record of the Beatles' soon-to-disappear stage act. Audibly drunk, fluffing words and notes, shouting back to hecklers in pidgin German, they lurch through some twenty songs in their old, undisciplined mixture of rock 'n' roll classics, country songs, middle-of-the-road ballads, and show tunes—"Your Feet's Too Big," "Red Sails in the Sunset," "Besame Mucho," even Marlene Dietrich's "Falling in Love Again." Kingsize and the Dominoes had been featuring a new soul number, the Isley Brothers' "Twist and Shout," which—keeping up Lathom Hall tradition—the Beatles had instantly pirated, reproducing even the Dominoes' added guitar break.

On Ray Charles's "Hallelujah I Love Her So," the lead vocal is warbled by an unfamiliar voice that makes Ringo Starr sound Caruso-like by comparison. It is Horst Fascher, the Star-Club's lethal bouncer. They let Horst (and also his brother Freddy) have a go onstage in return for getting the beer in.

TEN

"FOUR FRENZIED LITTLE
LORD FAUNTLEROYS
EARNING 5,000 POUNDS A WEEK"

The winter of 1962–63 was Britain's worst for almost a hundred years. From December to mid-March the entire country disappeared and a snow-leveled tundra took its place, stretching from north to south, silent and motionless but for snowplows trying to locate the buried highways. With the blizzards came Siberian cold that froze the English Channel, annihilated old people and the Essex oyster beds, wiped out the zebra at Whipsnade Zoo, turned milk into cream-flavored sorbet, and caused beer to explode spontaneously in its bottles. Southwest England was completely cut off; indeed, there seemed at one point a sporting chance that Wales would never be seen again. As usual in Britain winter was the last thing anyone had expected and, as usual, the British responded to chaos with cheerfulness. A year of unprecedented uproar, of unparalleled outrage, thus began with a feeling that everything in Britain was much the way it had always been. Everyone talked, and talked, about the weather.

On January 12, the nation, still snowed into its homes, provided a bumper audience for ABC-TV's Saturday night pop show *Thank Your Lucky Stars*. The show was popular for two reasons: its teenage record critic Janice, and the imaginative studio sets that were built around singers and groups as they mimed, not always accurately, their latest Top Twenty disk. Janice's peculiar magic was a thick Birmingham accent in which, awarding some new release maximum points, she would invariably say: "Oi'll give it foive."

A certain act on *Lucky Stars* that night had caused some perplexity to the show's producer, Philip Jones, and his set designer. Jones had kept his promise to his friend Dick James to book the Beatles in the same week that "Please Please Me" was released. Jones had not met them until the afternoon they arrived at ATV's Birmingham studios, after driving straight down from a tour of Scottish ballrooms. "We'd no idea how to present them," Jones says. "In the end, we just gave up. We decided to put each one of them inside a big metal heart. It was obvious that the song, not our set, would be the thing that sold them."

The four metal hearts framed a pop group such as no British teenager south of Lancashire had ever seen before. Their hair was not blow-dried into a cockade; it fringed their eyes like the high fur hats of Grenadier guardsmen. Their suits buttoned up to the neck, completely concealing their ties. The front three figures did not, as was usual, step to and fro: They bounced and jigged with their guitar necks out of time. One, unprecedentedly, played a Spanish guitar; another held a bass guitar like a stretched-out violin, its skinny neck pointing leftward rather than rightward, in completely the wrong direction. All four compounded their eccentricity by refusing to look stern and moody, as pop stars should, but by grinning broadly at the cameras and each other. The song they performed was largely inaudible, owing to the screams of the studio audience—all but for the moment where, with one extra zesty "Whoa yeah," their voices toppled into falsetto. Then, six million snowbound British teenagers heard what George Martin, on his musician's stool, had heard; what Dick James in his Tin Pan Alley garret had heard; what Philip Jones had heard even over the telephone. It was the indefinable yet unmistakable sound of a number one.

The same week brought enthusiastic reviews of "Please Please Me" in the music trade press. Keith Fordyce, a leading Radio Luxembourg disk jockey, said in *New Musical Express* that "Please Please Me" was "a really enjoyable platter, full of vigour and vitality." The *World's Fair* thought the Beatles had "every chance of becoming the big star attraction of 1963." Brian Matthew, emcee of *Thank Your Lucky Stars* and BBC radio's *Saturday Club,* and the country's most influential commentator on pop music, delivered the ultimate accolade, calling them "musically and visually the most accomplished group to emerge since the Shadows."

The national press, however, still maintained an attitude of scornful indifference to teenagers and their music. One exception was the London *Evening Standard,* which on Saturdays published a full page by its young pop columnist, Maureen Cleave. A friend of Cleave's, the Liverpool-based journalist Gillian Reynolds, had been urging her for months to come up and write something about the Beatles and the Cavern Club. Late in January, just as "Please Please Me" was about to enter the Top Ten, Maureen Cleave traveled to Liverpool to interview them for her *Evening Standard* page. On the train she met Vincent Mulchrone, the *Daily Mail*'s chief feature writer, bound on the same assignment.

The Beatles were in Liverpool to play a one-nighter at the Grafton Ballroom before leaving on the Helen Shapiro package tour. Mulchrone and Cleave were taken by Brian to see the queues that, as usual, had formed outside the Grafton two hours in advance of opening time. Some of the girls told Cleave they hadn't bought "Love Me Do" when it first appeared for fear the Beatles would become famous, leave Liverpool, and never return.

The interview that followed was like none Maureen Cleave had ever done with a pop group. "The Beatles made me laugh immoderately, the way I used to laugh as a child at the Just William books. Their wit was just so keen and sharp—John Lennon's especially. They all had this wonderful quality—it wasn't innocence, but everything was new to them. They were like William, finding out about the world and trying to make sense of it."

"John Lennon," Cleave wrote, "has an upper lip which is brutal in a devastating way. George Harrison is handsome, whimsical and untidy. Paul McCartney has a round baby face while Ringo Starr is ugly but cute. Their physical appearance inspires frenzy. They look beat-up and depraved in the nicest possible way."

The piece caught the knockabout flavor of their conversation—John's threat, for instance, to lie down on the stage like Al Jolson during the Helen Shapiro tour, and Paul's rejoinder that he was too blind to see the audience anyway. In John, Cleave found a fellow devotee of the William stories. "After the piece came out, John said to me, 'You write like that woman who did the William books.' For me, it was like being told one wrote like Shakespeare."

They had been hired to tour with Helen Shapiro by Arthur Howes, the promoter who saw them die the death at Peterborough but who had, even so, kept an option with Brian to rebook them. This Howes now did, for a bottom-of-the-bill fee of eighty pounds per week. The tour was to last throughout February, visiting theaters as far south as Taunton, Shrewsbury, and, once again, Peterborough.

It was by no means one of Arthur Howes' major package tours. Helen Shapiro, who had enjoyed spectacular success as a fourteen-year-old schoolgirl, was now considered, at sixteen, to be somewhat past her best. The Beatles, at any rate, found her awesomely starlike with her chauffeur-driven car, her dressing-room TV set, and constant, ferocious chaperonage.

She was, as it happened, a friendly girl who preferred to dodge her chauffeur and chaperone and travel with the Beatles and other small fry on the bus. Her chief memory is of snow, and of John Lennon, next to her, pulling his cripple face at passersby through a clear patch in the frosted window. "He would never sit still—none of them could. They'd always be writing songs or fooling about or practicing their autographs. Paul, I remember, used to practice his a lot. They didn't have any give-away photographs of themselves, so they used to practice signing across pictures of me.

"Paul was the PR. He was the one who came up to me on the tour and said, very nervous, 'Er—we've written this song, we wonder if you'd like to do it.' It was 'Misery.'"

In Carlisle, after they had returned to their hotel, someone came up to Helen and invited her to a Young Conservatives dance in progress in the hotel ballroom. Feeling cold and bored she decided to accept. The Beatles also decided to accept. The Young Conservatives door steward saw them all coming down the corridor, taking long steps and snapping their fingers in chorus like a *West Side Story* "Jets" routine. They got past the door steward but were then, stiffly, asked to leave. The Beatles' leather jackets had caused offense and outrage.

Next morning, the *Daily Express* reported that the famous schoolgirl pop star Helen Shapiro had been ejected from a dance in Carlisle. Sympathy was entirely with the hotel, the Young Conservatives, and with the schoolgirl star herself, since the incident had obviously not been her fault. It was the leather jackets worn by her companions that gave the story the whiff of sordidness that was Fleet Street's only interest in printing stories about pop musicians.

On February 16, while they were still iced into the tour bus with Helen Shapiro, *Melody Maker*'s Top Twenty showed those reprehensible leather jacket wearers' record "Please Please Me" at number two. That meant another journey south through the snow, to appear a second time on *Thank Your Lucky Stars*, on BBC radio's *Saturday Club,* and on

EMI's own *Radio Luxembourg Show*. On March 2, the snows were beginning to melt. *Melody Maker*'s chart showed "Please Please Me" at number one. Brian spread the paper out on his desk in Liverpool, and Olive and Freda and everyone crowded round to look. It was true.

Liverpool could not believe it. Letters poured into the NEMS office, written on complete toilet rolls, on cardboard hearts four feet high, on cylinders of wallpaper. There were also celebratory offerings of life-size cuddly toys, "Good Luck" cakes from Sayer's, sacks of charm bracelets, brooches, eternity rings, jelly babies, even—from one fan with dockyard connections—a live tarantula in a specially ventilated box. "Luckily, I never opened it," Freda Kelly says. "I took one look inside the box and ran. Brian sent me out to find a home for it at the School of Tropical Medicine."

In his third-floor front office Brian sat, amid ringing telephones, with a pretense at coolness that, for once, deceived no one. "I'd never seen him so excited," Freda says. "It was the first thing he said to anyone who rang up. 'Have you heard about the boys?' If anyone came to see him it was the first thing out of his mouth: 'Have you heard about the boys?' "

George Martin heard the news with elation, but also deep thought. The Beatles were doing this week what the Kalin Twins had done in 1957, what the Allisons had done in 1960, and what the Brook Brothers had in 1961. Any A&R man could reel off a list of such one-hit wonders, raised to freakish fame on a single song, then instantly forgotten. Martin's concern was to capitalize on a success that, according to the statistics of the business, had only the smallest outside chance of happening twice.

The way you capitalized on a number-one single in 1962 was to rush-release an LP record of the same name. It was a simple, shameless catch-penny device to persuade the teenage public to buy the same song again, but at £1.50 instead of 62p. For few, if any, listened to the supporting tracks, knowing all too well what they would be. They would be standards, hastily recorded in an insincere attempt to pass off some perishable, new, blow-dried zombie as an "all-round entertainer.' "

Martin's instinct was that he could do something better with the Beatles' first LP. He was, after all, distinguished as a producer of live stage recordings. He considered, but abandoned, the idea of taping them live at the Cavern. His gamble was that they would be able to pour out the excitement anywhere. "What you're going to do," he told them on February 11 at Abbey Road studios, "is play me this selection of things I've chosen from what you do at the Cavern."

In one thirteen-hour session Martin pushed them through enough songs to complete the fourteen-track LP. The numbers were those, like "I Saw Her Standing There," that John and Paul had thrown together long ago to get them through a Hamburg night, mixed with American soul songs like "Chains" and "Baby It's You." Martin, once again, confined himself to editing, shaping, rearranging, and dovetailing. He added a piano intro—played by himself—to "Misery," and the double-tracking of Paul's voice through "A Taste of Honey." George and Ringo, in fairness, were given the lead vocal on one song each. George's was a new Lennon-McCartney composition called "Do You Want to Know a Secret?" He sang it in thick Liverpudlian, barely managing its falsetto line. Ringo, with even less of a voice, still managed to give an infectious joy to "Boys," the old Cavern show-stopper. The finale was "Twist and Shout," the Isley Brothers song with which their stage act always closed. "John absolutely screamed it," Martin says. "God knows what it did to his larynx, because it made a sound like tearing flesh. That *had* to be right on the first take."

It was the same performance they were giving each night in a different English town, on tour once again for the Arthur Howes Organization. Howes had booked them—before "Please Please Me" reached number one—for the same eighty pounds per week they had got for the Helen Shapiro tour. By now, any promoter would have paid ten times that fee. Brian Epstein would not renege on his agreement with Howes.

Two American singers, Chris Montez and Tommy Roe, were supposed to be the tour's joint stars. It soon became obvious to Arthur Howes that neither was getting applause on the same scale as the Beatles. Their wages did not increase but their billing did. The running order was changed so that they, and "Twist and Shout," closed the show each night.

On March 22, the release of their album, *Please Please Me,* provoked fresh interest from the music papers. Even the jazz-oriented *Melody Maker* welcomed what every reviewer agreed was not the usual cash-in LP dross but a run of songs each in its own way different and surprising. For the first time it became apparent that the Beatles were songwriters on a scale unknown among performers of pop music. Record buyers previously had cared little about who *wrote* the songs they liked. On the back of the *Please Please Me* sleeve were helpful notes (by Disker, the *Liverpool Echo* columnist) detailing which of the songs were the Beatles' own and also acknowledging their debt to American groups like the Shirelles and songwriters like Goffin and King. The front cover photograph showed four figures in burgundy-colored stage suits, grinning cheerfully down from a balcony in what seemed to be a housing project. No one seen in the Top Twenty since Tommy Steele had made so overt a declaration of being working class.

By now their personalities as well as their records were reaching a national public. Two BBC radio pop shows, *Saturday Club* and *Easy Beat*, brought them to London during the Tommy Roe tour to play in the studio what they were to play onstage that evening a hundred miles away through the sleet and slush. In London, their faces were still unknown: They could walk as they pleased, with Dezo Hoffman, their *Record Mirror* friend, around Shaftesbury Avenue and Berwick Market, and eat at Hoffman's favorite restaurant, the Budapest in Greek Street. Dezo also showed them how to work the new cameras he persuaded a Soho shop to give them in exchange for a signed photograph. Dezo Hoffman saw the same reaction everywhere that he had felt on his first trip up to Liverpool. The Beatles were something that pop musicians had never been before. They were witty, lively, intelligent; they charmed and tickled and excited all who met them. Brian Matthew, the *Saturday Club* emcee, strove in vain to keep up his usual BBC manner against John Lennon's devastating ad-libs. "I was introducing them on one show, going through the usual thing of asking them about the music. I'd just come back from holiday in Spain. As I was talking John leaned across and said into the microphone, 'Brian's nose is peeling, folks.'"

To George Martin, John was like a precocious child, only half-aware of the joltingly funny things he said. "I remember we were having dinner out one night, and the waiter brought *mange-tout* [snow] peas. John had very evidently never seen such a thing before, but I said he ought to try them. "All right then," he said, "but put them over there, not near the food."

Brian, too, was spending much of every week in London. His father could hardly object to that now. The Whitechapel record shop ran smoothly under Peter Brown's management, and the office upstairs in Olive Johnson's charge. Olive was the McCartney family friend whom

Paul's father had first consulted about Brian. She had afterward left her job with the Law Society to join NEMS Enterprises as his "personal assistant."

In London he still had no base other than his favorite hotel, the Grosvenor House. "He'd walk into my office," Dick James said, "and tell me he'd been offered this date for the Beatles at two hundred pounds. I'd say: 'Tell 'em to double it.' Brian would come back in amazement and say, 'It worked.' 'Next time,' I'd say, 'tell 'em to double that figure again.' "

In early 1963, a South London impresario could still book the Beatles for thirty pounds to play for dancing at Wimbledon Palais. Brian's chief concern seems to have been to ensure them a full summer's work, even if the follow-up single to "Please Please Me" did not make the charts. He struck up a regular business arrangement with Larry Parnes, still a leading impresario despite the virtual eclipse of Billy Fury and the rest of his stable by the Mersey tidal wave. Parnes and Brian had Jewishness as well as concealed homosexuality in common and became good friends, though their mutual intransigence thwarted Mr. Parnes Shillings and Pence's plan to build a series of Sunday concerts around the Beatles at the end of Great Yarmouth pier. "I was offering thirty pounds per show and Brian wanted seventy-five pounds," Parnes remembered. "He told me that if I'd meet his price I could have an option to do shows with the Beatles and all the other NEMS acts for the next five years. In the end, he came down from seventy-five pounds to thirty-five. I went up to thirty-two pounds. I wouldn't budge and neither would he."

The Beatles unquestioningly went wherever Brian told them, however small the fee or insignificant the venue. Perhaps the most bizarre was arranged after a pupil at Stowe, the Buckinghamshire private school, wrote and asked if they could perform for him and his schoolmates. It helped that the pupil was David Moores, a scion of Liverpool's Littlewoods stores family (and a future chairman of the Liverpool soccer club). For one hundred pounds, the Beatles performed two thirty-minute sets in the school's Roxburgh Hall, watched by boys and teachers seated in orderly rows as if listening to a visiting bishop on Speech Day. Afterward, they were given tea and a conducted tour of the school. This with one hit already behind them and another single ("From Me to You") due to be released the following week.

NEMS Enterprises, Brian decided, must have lawyers in London as well as Liverpool. Characteristically, he chose the most expensive and fashionable of West End law firms specializing in show business clients. The Beatles were now on the books of M. A. Jacobs of Pall Mall, in company with such illustrious past litigants as Marlene Dietrich and Liberace. The firm's senior partner, David Jacobs, was himself a fashionable figure, to be seen tirelessly ministering to his clients' needs at the Savoy or Dorchester. He was, like Brian, cultivated, immaculate, Jewish, and a homosexual.

Already, a bit of trouble had arisen that required urgent consultation with Jacobs. The owner of a Hamburg club was threatening to hold a Beatle responsible for making his daughter pregnant. Jacobs referred the matter to counsel, who advised a quick settlement. It was the first of countless such claims, consultations, visits to counsel, and recommendations to settle out of court. With David Jacobs, Brian formed a shield around the Beatles that would not be lifted so long as he or Jacobs remained alive.

Early in March, every national and provincial newspaper in Britain received a publicity handout announcing the recording debut of a second group managed by NEMS Enterprises. Journalists who bothered to read the handout learned that the group was called Gerry and the Pacemakers, that it recorded on EMI's Columbia label, that it shared the same management as another successful group, the Beatles, and that it came from the same city, Liverpool. For the first time since its birth in Britain's industrial dawn, Liverpool was deliberately invoked as a source of excitement, glamour, and novelty.

Brian Epstein was hardly the first to see potential in Gerry Marsden, the ex–messenger boy from Ringo Starr's neighborhood who had led a successful group on Merseyside since 1958. But no one before Brian had taken the trouble to harness Gerry's boundless energy, nor to dress him in a suit instead of sweaters and jeans, and stop him from smoking Woodbines, and tell him to project.

Gerry's first single was "How Do You Do It?" the song that the Beatles had rejected in favor of "Please Please Me." He and the Pacemakers came across from Hamburg to record it, in blissful unawareness that the mutinous John Lennon version was anything other than a helpful demo. Gerry's jaunty treatment confirmed what George Martin had said all along—the number was a natural hit. It reached number one on March 22. The music papers realized that two hits from the same source constituted a "sound." From now on there was constant reference to the Liverpool or the Mersey Sound.

The Beatles' third Parlophone single, "From Me to You," released on April 12, had a similarly stylish publicity send-off. The smallest local paper in Britain received the NEMS handout, written by Tony Barrow and designed much as Brian used to draw up his posters for dances at New Brighton Tower. Instead of the usual glossy studio pose the Beatles were shown with their instruments on the deck of a Mersey tugboat. Underneath was Brian Matthew's potent declaration that they were "visually and musically the most exciting group since the Shadows."

The song had been written by John and Paul on the bus during the Helen Shapiro tour. It was "Please Please Me," a little slower, with the falsetto repositioned, and its reviews proved no more than lukewarm. Most of the music papers thought they had gone off since "Please Please Me." Keith Fordyce said the new record was not even as interesting as "Love Me Do."

On April 27, "From Me to You" was number one, well on the way to selling half a million copies and earning a silver disk. "How Do You Do It?" by Gerry and the Pacemakers was still at number three. Everyone who watched television or listened to radio in Britain had heard of the Mersey Sound.

Four days earlier, in Sefton General Hospital, Liverpool, Cynthia Lennon had given birth to a son. The labor was long and painful; the delivery became complicated when the umbilical cord was found to be wrapped round the baby's neck. His father knew nothing of these anxieties, being still out on tour in the Chris Montez show. Not until a week later did John visit Cynthia, and even then he had to wear a crude disguise to avoid the fans waiting outside. He held his son in his arms, watched by a grinning crowd through the glass cubicle wall.

The baby was called Julian, the nearest John could get to his mother's name, Julia. His obvious delight at becoming a father encouraged Cynthia to visions of happy domesticity in Woolton, where they were to occupy the whole ground floor of Mimi's house. The visions evaporated when John told her that Brian had asked him to go away on a vacation to Spain. Cynthia, recognizing that she had no real say in the matter, assented with a show of cheerfulness.

This vacation, in May 1963, was Brian's first and only public declaration of his feelings toward John. It was made in the euphoria of seeing two of his groups in the Top Twenty, when all other impediments to happiness seemed to have been swept away; why not this last intractable one? Close friends like Olive Johnson advised against it, in vain. The two of them flew off to Brian's vacation haunts, leaving Liverpool to gossip as it pleased and Cynthia to take care of the baby. Years later, John as good as admitted that, in their Spanish hotel, Brian finally plucked up courage to make sexual advances to him and that, with his kind and resigned heart, he did not resist. But matters went no further than "a hand job."

Recently, Brian's attention had become focused on another, far more conventionally beautiful young man. Billy Ashton—or Kramer as he was known in the dance halls—led a group of Bootle boys called the Coasters, rated third in *Mersey Beat* newspaper's popularity league. Brian paid fifty pounds to acquire Billy from his original manager, an elderly gentleman named Ted Knibbs who had rehearsed the nervous Adonis by making him sing standing on a chair.

Billy J. Kramer, with the new suits and initial that Brian had bestowed on him, was then brought to London for a recording test by George Martin at Parlophone. Martin gave his opinion that for the first time Brian had made a mistake. Though the youth was undoubtedly good-looking, his voice was erratic and his personal magnetism rather slight. Brian, however, insisted that "my Billy" should be allowed to record.

Billy J. was duly taped, backed by a Manchester group, the Dakotas, singing the Lennon-McCartney ballad "Do You Want to Know a Secret?" If George Harrison's voice had cracked on the falsetto line, Billy J. Kramer's broke into smithereens. Martin concealed the worst of it by double-tracking the vocal and filling in the cracks with his own piano accompaniment. The record was released on April 26; by mid-May every Top Ten chart showed it at number two.

That Brian had no idea of what the Beatles were already becoming is amply shown by his activities with NEMS Enterprises during the summer of 1963. Formerly, his desire had been to become a Beatle; to merge his existence, if only spiritually, with theirs. Now he began to see them merely as brand leaders in an empire of Liverpool artists, founded and ruled over paternalistically by himself. One of the NEMS handouts, indeed, showed all of them, the Beatles, Gerry and Billy J., the Pacemakers and Dakotas, as disembodied heads encircling Brian's in a schoolmasterly mortarboard.

By June, he had signed up the Big Three and the Four Jays, another popular Cavern group, with twenty-two O-level passes between them, now renamed the Fourmost. He wanted a ballad singer to complement all the groups: Tommy Quigley, a freckle-faced boy he had seen at the Queen's Hall, Widnes, was even now being groomed, as Tommy Quickly, to fulfill that destiny. One group he was dissuaded from signing was Lee Curtis and the All Stars, even though their manager was his great friend Joe Flannery. The Beatles vetoed the idea, apparently because Lee Curtis, Joe's brother, was too handsome. When the two groups appeared together, Paul McCartney would never sing any songs that Lee had in his repertoire.

NEMS Enterprises now had a London office and the services of a full-time publicity man. Tony Barrow, in fact, had been industriously writing handouts for Brian since late 1962, still carrying on his PR work for Decca and his Disker column in the *Liverpool Echo*. Brian's offer of thirty-six pounds per week was exactly double what Barrow earned as a freelancer. Another young PR man gave him some journalists' names and addresses to copy out in exchange for a cheap lunch.

One of Barrow's first jobs was to reorganize the Beatles' Fan Club, which Freda Kelly still ran from the NEMS office in Liverpool. Freda could no longer cope with the applications for membership, running into tens of thousands, and the sacks of letters, inscribed toilet rolls, soft toys, and other Beatles-inspired greetings that poured daily into her office and her home. Barrow divided the club into a northern region, run by Freda in Liverpool, and a southern region, run from Monmouth Street by a girl named Bettina Rose. It was Barrow's idea to invent a national secretary, "Anne Collingham," whose duplicated signature appeared on every newsletter. To girls all over the British Isles "Anne Collingham" was real, and revered as an intermediary between their idols and them.

NEMS Enterprises also briefly encompassed a nineteen-year-old hustler of Anglo-Dutch parentage named Andrew Loog Oldham who had previously worked as a PR man for Larry Parnes, Don Arden, and the designer Mary Quant. Meeting Brian on the set of ABC-TV's *Thank Your Lucky Stars* show, Oldham wangled a twenty-five-pounds-per-month retainer as an additional publicist for NEMS. To his chagrin he found this did not mean working with the Beatles, merely with subordinate Epstein discoveries like Gerry and the Pacemakers and Billy J. Kramer.

In April 1963, unable to make further headway with NEMS, Oldham gave up his retainer and decided to strike out as a manager on his own. A tip-off from a friendly music journalist led him to the Station Hotel in Richmond, Surrey, where a band called the Rolling Stones played Chicago-style rhythm and blues, fronted by a sweater-clad sometime economics student then known as Mike Jagger. Scenting the odor of raw sex, Oldham offered to manage them despite having neither previous experience nor funds to back up such a venture. So he went back to Brian Epstein, offering 50 percent of the Stones in exchange for some office space and minimal cash investment. But Brian felt he already had more than enough bands and singers on his plate, and thus missed the chance to run both of the greatest supergroups of all time.

Oldham brought the Beatles to see the Stones at the Station Hotel, and introduced the two bands afterward. Despite their cultural differences, the homespun northerners and the more worldly, cynical southerners instantly struck up a rapport. In the Stones' rebelliousness and sartorial free choice the Beatles all too clearly saw themselves as they had been before Brian cleaned and tidied them up. John particularly admired the Stones' then leader Brian Jones for his multifaceted instrumental talent, especially on harmonica. "You really play that thing, don't you?" he said to Jones wistfully. "I just blow and suck."

The Beatles were now making their first-ever tour as top of the bill, headlining over Gerry and the Pacemakers and the American country star Roy Orbison. Orbison was such a hero of theirs that they felt almost guilty to see him take the subordinate slot on the bill, with his dark glasses, huge forelock of hair, and suboperatic arias like "In Dreams" and "Only the Lonely." Another new performing hazard derived from George's recent faux naif remark to a press interviewer that one of his major passions in life were children's jelly babies. As a result, the Beatles were welcomed on stage not only by demented feminine screams but also by lime, orange, or blackcurrant jelly babies in hails thicker than locusts that stung unpleasantly whenever they connected with human flesh.

Up until this point their solitary roadie had been Neil Aspinall, the one-time accounting student whom they had got to know through Pete

Best. For the first three tours Brian had left everything connected with the band's welfare to him. It was he who drove them from town to town, carried in their guitars and amplifiers, and saw that they had food, sleep, and stage suits, if necessary tending to the last with a portable iron. Brusque and hollow-cheeked, with hair already thinning, Neil—or "Nell" as the Beatles called him—was both friend and servant, their equal, yet their errand boy.

In May 1963, after overwork had reduced Neil's weight by forty-two pounds, Brian took on Mal Evans as assistant road manager. Mal was a hefty Liverpudlian, formerly employed as a post office engineer and part-time Cavern Club bouncer. Despite his size, he was gentle, amiable, and filled with the romance of rock 'n' roll. At twenty-eight he was noticeably older than the Beatles and Neil; he was also married, with a newborn baby son. "He had a lot of sleepless nights, wondering if he should go on with them," his widow, Lil Evans, says. "I didn't want him to. I told him, 'You're a person in your own right—you don't need to follow others.' But he was starstruck."

John's aunt Mimi, having been a seagoing pilot's daughter, did her best to cope with the growing chaos of life at Mendips. Though Cynthia and the baby were living downstairs, all Mimi had seen of John for weeks were the suitcases of sodden stage shirts he would leave for Cyn and her to wash. The telephone rang continuously; at the front gate there was a permanent picket of girls. "And if I left the back door open," Mimi said, "there wouldn't be a teacup or a saucer left in the kitchen."

In Speke, Harry and Louise Harrison faced similar problems in their low-income housing. The fans were there when Harry left for work in the morning; they lined up at the bus stop, hoping to stop his bus. In the Dingle, little Elsie Graves was frankly bewildered by what had happened to her Ritchie. One minute he was on the dole; the next, he had so much money his mother wondered if it was all quite honest. "I remember her coming to me in a terrible state," Olive Johnson says, "because she'd found pound notes left all over Ringo's dressing table. He didn't have a bank account until Brian opened one for him."

Because of the siege of fans at Forthlin Road, Paul's twenty-first birthday, on June 18, had to be celebrated at his auntie Jin's in Birkenhead. The large family party was augmented by John Lennon and Cynthia, Ringo and his girlfriend Maureen, George, Brian, and Bob Wooler. It was, as Paul had wanted, a typical Liverpool booze-up, riotous and noisy, with children underfoot and Jim McCartney's piano renditions of sentimental evergreen songs. Unfortunately, the hard-drinking, sharp-tongued Wooler chose the occasion to voice some caustic speculation about John's relationship with Brian, as apparently corroborated by their recent Spanish vacation. John flew into a rage and laid into Wooler with his fists, breaking the portly DJ's nose and bruising several of his ribs. The incident was smoothed over with profuse apologies and an ex gratia payment for damages to Wooler, though it still somehow managed to leak into the tabloid *Sunday Mirror*. But John and the Beatles were still too obscure in the adult world for it to generate much interest, let alone the deluge of follow-up stories that would have resulted today.

Liverpool was currently undergoing a hectic visitation by London A&R men, all eager to sign up their own Beatles and Pacemakers. In July, the Pye label released "Sweets For My Sweet" by the Searchers, long resident at the Iron Door Club. When "Sweets For My Sweet" went to number one, the A&R invasion of Liverpool became positively desperate. Any group would do so long as it talked Scouse, played rhythm and blues, buttoned its jackets high, and combed its hair forward. The man from Oriole signed Faron's Flamingoes, Rory Storm and the Hurricanes, Earl Preston and the TT's; the Fontana man took the Merseybeats and Howie Casey and the Seniors; the Pye man took the Undertakers and the Chants.

Merseyside's new modishness was not confined to pop, but affected every sphere of British entertainment. Comedians who had once been told to disguise their Scouse accents now used them as an irresistible schtick, notably Beatle-fringed young Jimmy Tarbuck, a former habitué of the Cavern Club and friend of the Beatles, and Ken Dodd, who poured out a never-ending stream of Liverpool goonery about "Diddy Men" and "tickling sticks" and a seemingly mythical place called Knotty Ash. Arty and poetic Liverpool also received a look-in when Paul McCartney's younger brother, Michael, joined with poets Roger McGough and John Gorman in a trio called the Scaffold, scoring hits with unlikely material like the Cub Scouts' campfire song "Gin-Gan-Goolie." The city that had once been the furthest possible point from all things fashionable had even inspired a "Mersey Look" for metropolitan dolly birds to complement the Mersey Sound—Lennon caps, wet-look PVC coats, and striped scarves marked "Liverpool" or "Everton."

The south's Merseymania brought salvation, at least, for Dick Rowe of Decca Records who had passed on the Beatles, albeit after two exhaustive auditions. In April 1963, Rowe agreed to judge a talent contest in Liverpool, hoping vainly it might produce some facsimile of the band he now so wished he hadn't turned down. To make him even more uncomfortable, one of his fellow judges turned out to be none other than George Harrison. But it was to prove a blessing in disguise. During the evening, George happened to tell him about the great R&B group that Andrew Loog Oldham had just found playing behind the Station Hotel in Richmond, Surrey. Dick Rowe left Liverpool there and then, dashed down to Richmond, and offered Oldham's discovery a contract, so winning dual immortality as The Man Who Turned the Beatles Down and The Man Who Signed the Rolling Stones.

Whatever new northern hit act came along, Brian Epstein's NEMS stable always seemed to take another giant leap ahead. In June, Gerry Marsden was again number one with "I Like It." In July, Billy J. Kramer did the same with "Bad To Me," another Lennon-McCartney song, skillfully doctored by George Martin. At one point, the first three Top Ten places were occupied by NEMS acts—Gerry, Billy J. Kramer, and the Beatles' "From Me to You." To this day, no other pop impresario has matched the achievement.

In August, to lessen disruption at the Whitechapel shop, Brian moved NEMS Enterprises to Moorfields, a couple of streets away, near the old Liverpool Exchange station. The new offices, situated above a joke shop, had a reception area decorated with blow-up photographs of all the NEMS acts. Freda Kelly's friend, a deep-voiced Irish girl named Laurie McCaffery, was taken on as receptionist and switchboard operator. Another new arrival was Tony Bramwell, George Harrison's childhood friend, as office boy.

The Beatles were doing what all pop groups hoped for in summer. They were at the south coast resort of Margate, appearing with Gerry and the Pacemakers at the Winter Gardens theater. Dezo Hoffman came down from London to photograph them in their swimming trunks and socks, sunbathing on the terrace of their modest seafront hotel. They did not look like a group with the country's best-selling single *and* album. Hoffman also filmed them, as he had in Liverpool, this time skylarking on the beach in striped Victorian bathing suits. Another visitor was the publisher of *Beat Monthly*. Brian had agreed to let him start a separate publication dealing exclusively with the Beatles and their fan club. "What are you going to find to write about us every month?" Paul McCartney asked him.

They had already been back to Abbey Road studios to record their fourth Parlophone single for George Martin. The song, "She Loves You," was in the Lennon-McCartney tough-tender mode that previously had been confined to B sides. For the first time in any British pop song by male vocalists its subject was not a girl but another boy—a friend who couldn't or wouldn't see how much his girl cared for him. Cupid's message, however, was not delivered by a quiet word in his ear but by an affirming shout of "She loves you, yeah, yeah, yeah!" that could have been heard from the top of the Liver Building. John and Paul played it over on their acoustic guitars and, as usual, Martin had an editorial suggestion—why not move the first verse back and start with the chorus? Once again, in their instinctive way, they had hit on melodic effects far outside the usual pop scale. The ringing last chord of "She Loves You," their producer informed them to their surprise, was a major sixth, reminiscent of forties big bands like Glenn Miller's. Martin even worried if the song's ending might be a little corny. But he had no such doubts about its beginning.

Britain, that wet and windy summer, had been enjoying a sex scandal unrivaled since the reign of Edward VII. A cabinet minister, John Profumo, holding no less an office than Conservative secretary of state for war, had been caught in a sexual liaison with a twenty-two-year-old model named Christine Keeler. The affair was enriched by Miss Keeler's extremely wide circle of men friends, which included sundry West Indians, a property racketeer, a seedy osteopath named Stephen Ward, and—most piquant of all—the naval attaché at the Russian embassy in London. It was the possibility that Britain's war minister shared the same courtesan as a Russian spy that drew Secret Service attention finally to Profumo's sexual habits. Questioned in Parliament, he at first denied the impropriety; then—faced with imminent police and press disclosures—he admitted that he had misled the House of Commons.

The Profumo affair provided Fleet Street with a saga of almost infinite dimensions. From the unhappy minister, an avenue of sleaze stretched in one direction to the Notting Hill slums, where Keeler's ex-lover, Peter Rachman, would set dogs on his uncooperative tenants; in the other direction, it implicated the cream of British aristocracy, the

Astor family, on whose Cliveden estate Profumo had made his fatal acquaintanceship. By midsummer, all Britain seethed with rumors of sexual perversion on every level of public life. It was variously claimed that another cabinet minister had been caught receiving fellatio in public; that up to eight high court judges had been involved in a sex orgy; and that at a fashionable dinner party one of the country's most eminent politicians had waited at table, naked and masked, with a placard around his neck reading: "If my services don't please you, whip me."

Months passed, the summer worsened, the Profumo affair ran on, and on. Christine Keeler disappeared, then reappeared. Profumo resigned in disgrace. Stephen Ward was arrested for living off immoral earnings. Every newspaper front page, day after day, steamed with the torrid, frequently horrid, doings of Christine Keeler and her associate, Mandy Rice-Davies. And gradually the surfeit of sex and scandal passed the limit that even the British public could absorb. Attention moved away from Profumo and on to the prime minister who had so indolently accepted the lie of his fellow aristocrat. Harold Macmillan, after eleven years in office, was reexamined in a new and searching light. What it revealed was scarcely credible as a twentieth-century politician. A dusty old man in a walrus moustache hummed and hawed in the accent that had ruled Britain for a thousand years, but which now signified only complacency, crassness, and the natural conspiracy between men who shared the same private school and club.

No newspaper will ever admit to there being too much news. But to Fleet Street, in the summer of 1963, that condition was perilously close. Stephen Ward committed suicide on the eve of his trial; then, five days later, a second colossal story broke. A mail train on its way from Scotland to London was waylaid and robbed of 2 million pounds, the largest haul in criminal history. The search for the gang was then pushed off the front pages by Macmillan's belated resignation and the struggle within the Tory party to choose his successor. By the end of September every editor in Fleet Street was longing for a diversion from this incessant heavy news—something light; something unconnected with the aristocratic classes; something harmless, blameless, and above all, cheerful.

The *Daily Mirror* found the answer first. The *Mirror* in those days belonged to the same publishing group as *Melody Maker*, Britain's oldest established music newspaper. On September 11, *Melody Maker* announced the results of a poll among its readers to find the year's most popular record artists. The Beatles—who had barely scraped into the 1962 poll—came out as top British group. Billy J. Kramer was named in the same poll as "Brightest Hope for 1964."

As well as a fraternal story about the poll, the *Mirror* ran a two-page profile of the Beatles by its acerbic show-business columnist, Donald Zec. Under the headline "Four Frenzied Little Lord Fauntleroys Who Are Earning £5,000 a Week" Zec described the scenes he had witnessed among young girls at a Beatles concert in Luton, Bedfordshire. He afterward had the Beatles to tea at his flat, an ordeal that they survived with high spirits enough to drain all vitriol from the columnist's pen. They were, Donald Zec said, "as nice a group of well-mannered music makers as you'll find perforating the eardrum anywhere."

Other papers, too, were awakening to the existence of a population whose chief interest was not oversexed cabinet ministers but a pop record whose wild "yeah, yeah, yeah" chorus kept piercing the summer static. For "She Loves You," having gone straight to number one on advance orders of half a million copies, was still there, almost two months after its release. Radio disk jockeys such as Brian Matthew no longer even bothered to announce it. "Do you realize," Matthew frequently enquired of his listeners, "how many songs in the current Top Ten are written by, if not sung by, the Beatles?"

To Brian Epstein, this was still no more than a facet of success on every front. Brian's big autumn project was the launch of NEMS Enterprises' first female artist. Priscilla White, the Cavern Club's gawky cloakroom girl, now renamed Cilla Black, was to be, not a discovery like the Beatles and Gerry but a *creation*, wrought by Brian's own feminine taste. For weeks, he had lavished attention on Cilla; on her clothes, her hair, her makeup. He had taken her to George Martin, and Martin—privately thinking her a "Cavern screamer"—had recorded her singing the Lennon-McCartney song "Love of the Loved." Tony Barrow, in Monmouth Street, was producing the usual stylish NEMS press release, describing Cilla's recherché taste for wearing men's jeans, and relaying Cavern Club slang such as "gear," "fab," and "endsville."

On October 13, the Beatles were due to appear on British television's top-rated variety program, *Sunday Night at the London Palladium*. The show went out live on Sunday nights from the famous old, gilt-encrusted theater, in Argyll Street, just off Oxford Circus. In form it was straight music hall, with jugglers, trampolinists, a "Beat the Clock" interlude in which members of the audience underwent ritual self-humiliation, and finally a top-of-the-bill act that was quite likely to be the pop singing sensation of the moment. At the end, the entire cast stood on a revolving platform among chorus girls and giant letters spelling out SUNDAY NIGHT AT THE LONDON PALLADIUM.

News of the engagement had circulated among Beatles fans and there were girls waiting on Argyll Street that Sunday morning when the Beatles arrived at the Palladium to rehearse. The photographer Dezo Hoffman, who accompanied them, counted "about eight girls. The car drew up—we went inside, no trouble." Since rehearsals lasted all day the Beatles were provided with a roast lamb lunch in their dressing room. While they were eating it a group of girls ran into the auditorium and had to be ejected.

The show that night broke all precedent by putting on its top-of-the-bill act first, for a few seconds only. Bruce Forsyth, the emcee, then appeared and stuck out his long chin. "If you want to see them again," Forsyth taunted, "they'll be back in forty-two minutes." That final, short, inaudible performance, before they hurried aboard the revolving stage, was watched by an audience of 15 million.

Next morning, every mass-circulation British newspaper carried a front-page picture and story of riots by Beatles fans outside the London Palladium. "Police fought to hold back 1,000 squealing teenagers," the *Daily Mirror* said, "as the Beatles made their getaway after their Palladium TV show." Both the *Daily Mail* and *Daily Express* had pictures of the four Beatles peeping out in supposed dread of a mob, this time said to number five hundred. "A Police motorcade stood by," the *Mirror* continued, "as the four pop idols dashed for their car. Then the fans went wild, breaking through a cordon of more than 60 Policemen" (20, the *Express* said). "With engines racing, the cavalcade roared down Argyll Street and turned into Oxford Circus, heading for a celebration party at the Grosvenor House hotel."

This official outbreak of Beatlemania in Britain has certain puzzling aspects. In every case, the published photograph of those "1,000 squealing teenagers" was cropped in so close that only three or four could be seen. The *Daily Mail* alone published a wide-angle shot—Paul McCartney and Neil Aspinall emerging from the Palladium, watched by one policeman and two girls.

"There were *no* riots," Dezo Hoffman says. "I was there. Eight girls we saw—even less than eight. Later on, the road managers were sent out to find the Beatles a girl each, and there were *none.*"

ELEVEN

"EVEN THE JELLY BABIES ARE SYMBOLIC"

In 1963, the simple fact was, Britain's population had become unbalanced by a vast surplus of people under eighteen. The decline in infant mortality, together with the mysterious nonappearance of a third world war, had allowed an entire generation to grow up virtually intact. They were the babies born after 1945 and raised in a Britain struggling to transform itself from postwar drabness to the material well-being so long observed and envied in America. Cars, radios, washing machines, all the luxuries still cherished by their parents were, to these young people, simply the mundane furniture of life. Television spread the whole world before them, to be casually viewed and judged. In 1960, the kindly Macmillan government abolished the two-year period of compulsory military service that had shaped young men's lives since the end of World War II. For those between sixteen and twenty-one no obligation remained save that of spending their ever-increasing pocket money on the amusements demanded by their ever-quickening glands.

Pop music was the most obvious sign of youth's growing economic power. What had begun in 1956 as a laughable, disreputable adolescent outburst was now an industry turning over 100 million pounds each year. The attitude toward teenagers remained largely unchanged: They were, as in 1956, a puzzling, fractious element of the population, endlessly deplored and advised by politicians, headmasters, and clergymen. They were also a market, undreamed of in size and potential, to be wooed and cajoled by the retail trade at every level.

The British teenage girl of early 1963 faithfully reflected the numerous boom industries who battled for her weekly pay packet. Her hair, teased up into a huge hollow bouffant, or "beehive," represented hours spent at the hairdressing salon and in arduous private back-combing and curling with heated rollers. Her face was deathly white but for two coal-black eyes embellished with false lashes like those popularized by the singer Dusty Springfield. She wore trousers, or "trews," with loops under each foot, but more usually a formal dress with a wasp-tight waist and a full skirt ballooned by starch-stiffened petticoats into the semblance of an outsized tea cosy. Her shoes, invariably matching her handbag, were white or beige with winklepicker points and the stiletto heels that had wrought destruction on polished dance floors across the land.

Her boyfriend was an even more interesting sight, for young males were gradually reviving the conventions of the fifteenth and sixteenth centuries in dressing as colorfully as females. He might be a mod, a faction of which went in for ostentatiously neat Italian suits and trilby hats and rode about on Vespa or Lambretta motor scooters. He might, on the other hand, be a rocker, the heirs of the fifties Teds, who favored the macho look of early Elvis rock 'n' roll, draped themselves in black leather, decorated themselves with tattoos, and aspired only to do a "ton" (100 mph) on their thunderous motorcycles. The mods and rockers had sprung up in 1963, simultaneously and with an instant mutual loathing of one another. All that summer, in innocent seaside resorts like Clacton and Margate, their set-piece battles had surged back and forth, trampling day-trippers, deck chairs, and children's sand castles.

In autumn, the mod–rocker war was eclipsed by a new kind of teenage excess that was not new but was louder and wilder than Britain had ever known it before. Television and cinema newsreels added live pictures to those appearing daily in all the national papers. The pictures showed girls in their hollow-spun bouffants and spectral make-up, their black eye make-up running in rivulets down their faces. The sound was of incessant screaming.

Girls had screamed for pop stars before, but never quite like this. Never—as they did at the Beatles' Cambridge concert—hunched into a fetal position, alternately punching their sides, covering their eyes, and stuffing handkerchiefs and fists into their mouths. Later, when the curtain had fallen and the last dazed girl had been led through the exits, a further difference from the screams that greeted Valentino became manifest. Hundreds of the cinema seats were wringing wet. Many had puddles of urine beneath them.

Such scenes had been commonplace for six months already: The difference now was that newspapers reported them. Fleet Street had realized that the Beatles were more than a momentary diversion—they were a running story of guaranteed reader interest. The riots faked on Argyll Street were to be seen, ten times more spectacularly, along the route of their current package tour. On October 26 in Carlisle—the small border town they had last seen as nobodies with Helen Shapiro—six hundred fans stood in line for thirty-six hours to buy tickets. When the box office opened, the line moved forward with such ardor that nine people were crushed and had to receive hospital treatment.

Fleet Street's initial line was simply reporting on the girls' hysteria. It changed the moment someone took the trouble to visit the Beatles' dressing room. There, in the tiny space hemmed in by teacups and stage-suit bags, the hacks found what every journalist craves and what he will distort the plainest fact to manufacture—good quotes. For when John and Paul got going no one had to invent the dialogue.

"How long do you think the group will last, John?"

"About five years."

"Are those wigs you're wearing?"

"If they are, they must be the only wigs with dandruff."

"What kind of guitar is that, Paul?"

"It's a Hofner violin bass. Here, take a look." The bass—now widely copied by other groups—would be tossed into the startled questioner's lap.

"Are they expensive?"

"Fifty-six guineas. I could afford a better one but I'm a skinflint."

Ringo, still unsure of himself, would be coaxed forward to say a mordant word or two. If asked why he wore so many rings on his fingers, he replied it was because he couldn't get them all through his nose. "I don't like talking," he explained. "Some people gab all day and some people play it smogo. I haven't got a smiling face or a talking mouth."

George, unless specially asked for, would remain apart, his hollow face cupped in a high black turtle neck, his eyes under the Beatle bangs not happy. He would tune guitars assiduously, John's as well as his own, despite knowing they had not the remotest chance of being heard. Even at this early stage, the fan uproar, the flailing screams and toys and jelly babies, were a source of detestation to him.

Certain journalists, on the strength of past favors, were exempt from the moments when Neil Aspinall, at a secret signal, would clear the Beatles' dressing room of the press. Maureen Cleave from the *Evening Standard* was one such: John Lennon called her "the Just William woman."

Another was Ray Coleman, from *Melody Maker*. The Beatles liked *MM* because it troubled to discuss their musicianship as well as the riots. Coleman, a quiet, clerkly figure, would stand in the wings, telling John the words of songs that, even though John himself had written them, he could barely remember from day to day. Usually, when he ran on stage, the words would be written on the back of his hand.

Peter Jones, of *Record Mirror*, found himself in the most difficult position. Jones had written the first article about the Beatles in a national publication; he was now contributor-in-chief to their fan magazine, *Beatles Monthly*. He was at once privy to their most intimate moments and sworn to secrecy concerning all that might have shown them not as cuddly toys but as ordinary, imperfect human beings.

The papers did not mind revealing that all four of these new national role models, especially George, were heavy smokers. But on other matters Peter Jones had to remain silent. He could say nothing about the hatred they already felt for performing night after night, and how Neil Aspinall sometimes literally chased them from their dressing room into the wings. Jones could not mention the rows they frequently had with one another, or with Brian. Nor could he make even the vaguest mention of what everyone in the Beatles' entourage called "the girl scene," the sexual encounters with young women, handpicked from their night's audience or stage-door crowd, that continually went on in hotel bedrooms or bathrooms or out-of-the-way theater passages or toilets.

"At times," Jones says, "they could pick on someone for a kind of corporate cruelty that was absolutely merciless. Down on the south coast there was this old journalist who went into the swimming pool with them while some photographs were being taken. All four of them really set on this quite elderly guy—pretending it was all fun, but it wasn't. They were so rough with him, they actually broke one of his toes."

Such stories, if written, would not have been printed. Fleet Street had settled on its view of the Beatles—the four happy-go-lucky Liverpool lads who looked absurd, but knew it, and whose salty one-line witticisms seemed to epitomize the honesty of the working classes, blowing through the seedy lies of the Profumo upper crust. "You *had* to write it that way," an ex–*Daily Mirror* man says. "You knew that if you didn't, the *Sketch* would and the *Express* would and the *Mail* and the *Standard* would. You were writing in self-defense."

Within a week of the London Palladium show, Britain's attitude toward the Beatles had completely changed. No longer were they just a silly pop group that incited teenagers to be even sillier than usual. They were also, unprecedently, endowed with wit and intelligence. The inclusion among their cover versions of several songs originally recorded by American girl groups—notably the Marvelettes' "Please, Mister Postman" and the Cookies' "Chains"—underscored their Liverpool toughness with appealingly paradoxical sensitivity. Whatever the prejudice engendered by their hair and clothes, it vanished as soon as their voices began to speak, in what was half-remembered, through ages of music hall and radio, as comedy's natural dialect:

"None of us has quite grasped wharrit's all about yet. It's washin' over our 'eads like a yuge tidal wave—"

"—I don't s'pose I think mooch about the future. Though, now we have made it, it would be a pity to get bombed—"

"I get spasms of being intellectual. I read a bit about politics. But I don't think I'd vote for anyone. No message from those phoney politicians is coomin' through to me."

"—We've always 'ad laughs. Sometimes we find ourselves gettin' hysterical, especially when we're tired. We laugh at soft things that other people don't get—we call it 'The Cruelies'—"

"Is it true that you were turned down by Decca?"

"A guy at Decca turned us down."

"He must be kicking himself now."

"I 'ope he kicks himself to death."

On October 16, an announcement was made that both confirmed their new status beyond any doubt and brought Fleet Street northward in a still more maddened pursuit. The Beatles had been chosen to appear in the Royal Command Variety Performance in London on November 4. Bernard Delfont, the organizer, told reporters he had picked them on the insistence of his ten-year-old daughter. Buckingham Palace, to which the list went for approval, offered no objection.

Late in October, Brian Epstein moved his entire organization from Liverpool to London. "It happened at about a week's notice," Tony Bramwell says. "Eppy walked in and said he was going south—were we coming?" Tony, Alistair Taylor, Laurie McCaffery the switchboard girl, immediately went home to pack. Freda Kelly's father refused to let her go, although she pleaded. Almost the entire staff managed to reassemble itself in London to greet Brian when he arrived, looking as if he had expected nothing else.

The new NEMS office was on Argyll Street, only a few doors away from the London Palladium. Brian drew great satisfaction from being so close to this famous old theatrical monument. He drew equal satisfaction from his new cable [telegram] address: Nemperor, London. It was Bob Wooler, the Cavern's pun-loving disk jockey, who had once said to him on the telephone, "Is that the Nemperor?"

Brian now had his own London flat, in a fashionable building in William Mews, Knightsbridge. One of the first people he took there was Brian Sommerville, an old friend of his who had recently left the Royal Navy and was now working in Fleet Street. "The flat was very Brian," Sommerville says, "all white walls and black leather cushions. While I was there, he showed me a proof of the Beatles' new LP cover. He was already starting to suggest that we might work together."

Once installed in the new flat Brian began to entertain lavishly. David Jacobs, his lawyer, had introduced him to many of the show business celebrities for whom Jacobs's firm also acted. He developed a particular friendship with Lionel Bart, the East End ex-skiffler who had won, and was rapidly losing, a fortune as a composer of West End musicals. He loved all show people, and in their cocktail chatter found a measure of security. Show people did not care who was, or was not, gay.

He had, as his success grew more hectic, placed increasing reliance on Jacobs and on his accountants, Bryce, Hanmer and Isherwood of Albemarle Street, Mayfair. Bryce, Hanmer were, in fact, a Liverpool firm whose London office made a speciality of theatrical clients. Dr. Walter Strach, one of the firm's senior members, a gaunt and melancholy Czech, thus found himself, in late 1963, charged with the responsibility of finding London accommodation for all four of the Beatles. Total secrecy was maintained, to evade the fans and to keep the rents within reason.

For John and Cynthia a flat was rented in Emperor's Gate, Kensington, just behind the Cromwell Road terminal where, in those days, one could check in for flights from Heathrow airport. Thanks to the almost psychic powers of detection bestowed on Beatles fans, the hideaway became instantly and universally known. Girls waited all day, as well as most of the night, around the pilastered front porch, even venturing into the hallway, if the front door was left open, to settle down with blankets, sleeping bags, and vacuum flasks. Across the road was a student hostel with a balcony that looked directly into the Lennons flat. Whenever Cyn looked, she would see figures hanging over the balcony and waving. Six flights up, without a lift, she spent days at a time, with baby Julian, in conscientious isolation.

George and Ringo moved together into a flat lower down in the William Mews block where Brian lived. Old ladies, carrying Pekinese dogs, looked askance at the girls who instantaneously took up stations on the front steps. Brian was torn between excitement at having two Beatles so closely under his wing and terror that George and Ringo might find out what, in any case, they had known about him for years. Even when he asked them to one of his gay parties he seems to have hoped they would view the all-male gathering as no more than coincidence. "Do you think they noticed?" he later anxiously asked a friend.

As to the living arrangements of Paul McCartney, not even the most tenacious journalist trying to get his foot in the door could hazard a guess. Whereas George and Ringo's address, like John's, would invariably be specified in newspaper reports, Paul, since leaving the President Hotel, could only be said ambiguously to be living at "an address in Central London."

Four months earlier, at a pop concert in the Albert Hall, the Beatles had met a young actress called Jane Asher, herself on the way to becoming a celebrity through her appearances on the BBC TV show *Juke Box Jury*. The Beatles crowded round her in their usual way, all four instantly proposing marriage. The others guessed at once that such a "classy" girl, red-haired and madonna-like, would appeal strongly to the socially ambitious Paul. They had asked her back to their hotel for a drink and, after some winking and nudging, had left her and Paul alone in the bedroom. It quickly transpired that Jane, as well as being only seventeen, was still a virgin. When the others came back she and Paul were sitting there, deep in discussion about their favorite kinds of food.

Jane's background, as much as her chaste beauty, fascinated Paul. Her father, Sir Richard Asher, was a noted psychiatrist. Her mother, a professional musician, had taught George Martin the oboe. Her brother, Peter, belonged—as did Jane herself—to a teenage top drawer that played its rock records in the studies of elegant town houses and formed the earliest clientele of the music clubs and boutiques now springing up in the West End and Chelsea. Since heeding his mother's plea not to talk like other children in the projects, Paul McCartney had dreamed of worlds like this.

The fans knew that Paul and Jane were often seen together, at parties or the theater. The Ashers' house in Wimpole Street was plagued by telephone gigglings and breathings that Sir Richard could not shut off because the line belonged to his medical practice. What few people knew, even within the Beatles' entourage, was that Paul now spent all his time in London with the Ashers. Returning from the Continent late one night he had missed his connection to Liverpool, and Jane's mother had offered him the spare room. That room was now permanently his.

To young men long used to staying out all night, London in 1963 offered many diversions. The old West End night spots, with their clientele of debutantes and Guards officers, were giving way to with-it clubs like Wips, whose advertisement promised "pirhanas in the dark above London's skyline . . . black velvet and new faces . . . music, strong, hard and moody." In Soho, for a brief season, flourished the Establishment Club, named for all the hapless official targets, from Royalty downward, flayed nightly by the satirists in its floor show. In Mayfair, handily close to George and Ringo's shared flat, was the super-posh Saddle Room, kept by the television personality Hélène Cordet, from which the two Beatles would often return home to Williams Mews by horse-drawn carriage. Just off Leicester Square was the Ad Lib—its very name a declaration of London's unlimited treats—where pop stars mingled with their own kind and excluded outsiders in the same way that Pall Mall gentlemen's clubs had for the past two centuries.

Newspaper acquaintances, like Ray Coleman, who ran into the Beatles after dark at the Ad Lib, could be sure both of an eventful night and of a large bill to be camouflaged among expenses. "None of them ever seemed to have any money," Coleman said. Peter Jones, the journalist in closest contact with them, received an impression, not so much of Liverpool thrift as of spasmodic insolvency. "If I was on my way to see them, I'd ring up first. Often they'd say, 'Here, pick up some food for us on the way, will you?' "

The fact is that, although the Beatles were Britain's biggest-selling pop group, their income was—and for a long time remained—astonishingly small. The records now selling in millions earned them, under their original Parlophone contract, a fourth of a penny per double-sided disc. Their concert appearances, richly profitable to promoters and cinema circuits, often realized barely enough to cover their travel and hotel expenses. For Brian was still letting them work at rates agreed to months previously.

At Bryce, Hanmer and Isherwood, Dr. Strach's first act—after sorting out certain small tax difficulties arising from their Hamburg days—was to form the Beatles into a limited company for which the grave Czech gentleman himself acted as both treasurer and secretary. It was to Strach that the bills for their flats and living expenses came. In those days, the doctor remembered, his main concern was to amass a reserve of money to pay income tax after—as must invariably happen—the Beatles had stopped earning money as pop stars. The residue of their earnings, therefore, simply lay in bank accounts, expecting that evil day. For meals, drinks, the suits and shirts and boots they wore once and then discarded, they turned to Neil Aspinall, their road manager, and the float Neil always carried. Larger expenditure was discouraged by the black-suited figure whom, without much conviction, the Beatles called "Uncle Walter."

Dr. Strach remembered how Brian Epstein strove at every step to make his dealings with the Beatles fair. "He always worried that he might be taking advantage of them. He came to me once and said he wanted to give them a piece of *his* company, NEMS Enterprises. He gave them 10 percent of it, so they would get back some of the 25 percent they paid him. Brian didn't have to do that, but he wanted to. He was a decent, honest, average human being."

Punctilious in small matters, and small amounts, Brian could not adjust his sights to the bigger and bigger commercial prospects now materializing on every side. At the same time his pride would not allow him to ask advice from older, more experienced people in the same business. Resolutely he did every deal for the Beatles in person, never revising a payment scale still based more on Liverpool's values than London's. And among his pursuers the word rapidly spread. Brian Epstein—in the American entrepreneurial phrase—was not streetwise.

In the autumn of 1963 he received an offer for the Beatles to appear in their first feature film. This was already a recognized way of capitalizing on pop music success—simple exploitation movies in which the thinnest background was given to the regurgitation of Top Twenty hits for a cinema audience. United Artists, the company that approached Brian, were at that stage chiefly interested in sales of a Beatles soundtrack album.

UA had already hired Walter Shenson, an independent American producer based in London with some reputation for making successful low-budget comedy films. Shenson agreed to meet Brian, together with Bud Orenstein, UA's office head in London, to discuss the terms under which the Beatles would be allowed to appear.

"I knew Bud Orenstein well," Walter Shenson said. "So I went over to his flat before Brian arrived to talk over the deal that we'd be prepared to make. I knew nothing about pop music or managers. I said: 'What do you think he's going to ask for?' The film was low budget, with not much to pay in advances. Bud and I agreed it would be fair to offer Brian and the Beatles 25 percent of the picture.

"Then Brian came in. He seemed very nice. We put to him the fee we'd thought of—the Beatles would get a salary of twenty-five thousand pounds to work on the picture—and he agreed to that. Then we asked him, 'Mr. Epstein, what would you consider a fair percentage of the picture?' Brian thought for a minute, then he said, 'I couldn't accept anything less than seven-and-a-half percent.' "

Uproar spilled over into the Beatles' first European tour—a series of concerts in Sweden from October 24–29. Self-possessed Swedish girls now jigged and shrieked as wildly as any Cavernite, and sensible Swedish boys wore their hair in what Scandinavian newspapers called the Hamlet style. At a concert in Stockholm fans rushed the stage, breaking through a forty-strong police cordon and trampling George Harrison momentarily underfoot. Between concerts, Paul wore a disguise so effective that not even the other Beatles could recognize him.

Their return to London on October 29 showed them for the first time the full extent of their British following. At Heathrow airport, as their aircraft taxied to a stop, a concerted scream broke out from hundreds of girls massed along the terminal's terraced roof. The invasion had thrown the whole airport into a chaos in which such other celebrities as Britain's prime minister, Sir Alec Douglas Home, and the newly elected Miss World passed by, totally unnoticed.

The Royal Command Variety Peformance is an institution dating back to Queen Victoria, whose little dour face masked a fondness for theatrical glamour and who would "command" all the latest entertainers, like Buffalo Bill Cody, to give private performances for her and her family at Windsor. From this had evolved an annual royal charity gala featuring a marathon bill of top entertainers that gave the West End its most glamorous night of the year and was later seen by the rest of the nation on TV. In 1963, the Queen could not attend, being heavily pregnant with her fourth child, the future Prince Edward, and her place in the royal box was to be jointly filled by Queen Elizabeth, the Queen Mother, and Princess Margaret. The Beatles were placed seventh on a nineteen-act program that included Marlene Dietrich; comedians Charlie Drake, Harry Secombe, and Eric Sykes; the self-styled Red-Hot Mama Sophie Tucker; and the dancing pig puppets Pinky and Perky.

But there was no question as to the night's real draw. Long before dusk, on that raw afternoon, five hundred policemen had been drafted to duty outside the Prince of Wales theater, off Leicester Square, where the usual crowd, assembled to glimpse the royals, was swollen by several thousand girls, screaming and chanting, "We want the Beatles." Marlene Dietrich, a legend of thirty years' standing, was able to enter the stage door, unrecognized. But when the Queen Mother herself appeared, waving and smiling, followed by Princess Margaret and her photographer husband, Lord Snowdon, a basic British instinct asserted itself: the screaming and chanting changed to applause and cheers.

Brian Epstein, in all the hurry and excitement, very nearly found himself without the evening clothes that are de rigueur at a royal performance: His dinner jacket, he remembered, too late, was hanging in the wardrobe at home in Liverpool. To add to the tension he was due to fly to America the next morning. His parents, Harry and Queenie, sitting in the audience, had almost resigned themselves to not seeing him when, just before curtain up, in his hastily fetched tuxedo, he lowered himself into the empty seat next to theirs.

The Beatles, cooped up with Neil and Mal Evans in a dressing room no more munificent than usual, were also evincing signs of strain. Their spot in the show was brief—four songs near the end, surrounded by carefully rehearsed bows. What Brian feared more than musical slipups was that, despite his entreaties for decorum, some ad-lib would be made, offensive to royal ears. John had already threatened one ghastly ad-lib if the audience proved unresponsive: "I'll just tell 'em to rattle their fuckin' jewelry."

Brian's fears proved groundless. The audience of stiff-shirted showbiz notables and their wives could not have been more susceptible to the Beatles' insouciant charm and the cheekiness that by instinct they measured out in precisely the right amount. Paul struck the exact note at once, surveying the dignified dark and saying, "How are yer—all right?" A joke between songs, about "Sophie Tucker, our favorite American group," produced a ripple of confirming laughter. Then it was John's turn, to announce the final number, "Twist and Shout." The line that had jangled Brian's nerves in the dressing room came out as a perfect mingling of impudence and deference: "Will people in the cheaper seats clap your hands? All the rest of you, if you'll just rattle your jewelry . . ."

The next day's papers were unanimous. "Beatles Rock the Royals," said the *Daily Express.* "Night of Triumph for Four Young Men," said the *Daily Mail,* roguishly adding, "Yes—the Royal Box was stomping." It was reported that the Queen Mother had listened to "Twist and Shout" with every appearance of enjoyment and that Princess Margaret had definitely leaned forward, "clapping on the off-beat." John's little joke was quoted everywhere, as was the banter overheard later when the Beatles stood in the royal receiving line. Asked by the Queen Mother where they were appearing next, they had together murmured "Slough." "Oh . . . that's near us," Her Majesty replied with such warmth as to suggest she might seriously consider popping over from nearby Windsor Castle to catch the gig.

The *Daily Mirror*'s coverage of scenes outside and inside the Prince of Wales theater bore the simple headline "Beatlemania!" The *Mirror* simultaneously gave the epidemic a name and offered its six million readers this deeply infected diagnosis:

YEAH! YEAH! YEAH!
You have to be a real sour square not to love the nutty, noisy, happy, handsome Beatles.
If they don't sweep your blues away—brother, you're a lost cause. If they don't put a beat in your feet—sister, you're not living.
How refreshing to see these rumbustious young Beatles take a middle-aged Royal Variety performance by the scruff of their necks and have them Beatling like teenagers.
Fact is that Beatle People are everywhere. From Wapping to Windsor. Aged seven to seventy. And it's plain to see why these four cheeky,

energetic lads from Liverpool go down so big.

They're young, new. They're high-spirited, cheerful. What a change from the self-pitying moaners, crooning their lovelorn tunes from the tortured shallows of lukewarm hearts.

The Beatles are whacky. They wear their hair like a mop—but it's WASHED, it's super clean. So is their fresh young act. They don't have to rely on off-colour jokes about homos for their fun.

To say that Britain, in November 1963, succumbed to an all-excluding obsession with a four-man pop group—even one that had made royalty smile—would be palpably absurd. The mania was Fleet Street's; it therefore appeared to blanket the land. In a single week after the royal variety performance, the *Daily Express* ran five front-page stories indicative of Beatlemania at every compass point. Its chief rival, the *Daily Mail*, soon afterward ceased bothering even to use the name "Beatles" in headlines. A small cartoon logo of four fringed heads gave all the identification that was needed.

Naturally, the press soon winkled out the fact which Brian had striven so to conceal—that John Lennon was married, with a baby son. The fans, however, far from resenting Cynthia, seemed to regard her as part of John's inexhaustible originality. She continued, nonetheless, to exist in the deepest hinterland, at the top of the Emperor's Gate flat or some sternly defined public corral, fenced off by a road manager's shoulder.

The scope of Fleet Street coverage was widening from theater sieges and screaming and the cheeky things they said. On November 10, the first school headmaster sent the first teenage boy into public martyrdom for sporting a Beatle haircut. On November 18, the first vicar invoked their name, requesting them to provide a tape of "Oh Come All Ye Faithful, Yeah Yeah Yeah" for his Christmas congregation. Two days later occurred the first parliamentary mention. A Labor MP in the House of Commons demanded that police protection for the Beatles should end. On the *Express* editorial page there appeared a prophetic cartoon. The prime minister, Sir Alec Douglas Home, genuflecting before the Beatles, asked: "Gentlemen—could we persuade you to become Conservative candidates?"

The quality papers, traditionally aloof from such proletarian topics, now weighed in with purportedly scientific analyses of the Beatles' effect on teenage girls. The *Observer* published a picture of a Cycladic fertility goddess that, it was maintained, "dates the potency of the guitar as a sex symbol to about 4,800 years before the Beatle era." The livelier-minded *Sunday Times* commended the Beatles for enriching the English language with words from their private slang—like "gear" and "fab"—that were now in fashionable use. The *Sunday Times* went on to examine Beatlemania in a style and vocabulary that were to be widely imitated. " 'You don't have to be a genius,' says a consultant at a London hospital, 'to see the parallels between sexual excitement and the mounting crescendo of delighted screams through a stimulating number like "Twist and Shout," but at the level it is taken, I think it is the bubbling, uninhibited gaiety of the group that generates enthusiasm.' "

The habit quickly spread of consulting the medical profession, especially its psychiatric branch, for opinions that would lend scientific weight to the orgies of chortling prose. And doctors and psychiatrists, sensing regular fees, were careful to pronounce nothing unfavorable. Not even the *News of the World* could find anything in Beatlemania against which to caution its credulous readership. Psychologists, the *NotW* said, in its usual comfortably inexplicit way, had been trying to discover why the Beatles sent teenage girls into hysteria. One of them had come up with this explanation:

> This is one way of flinging off childhood re-
> straints and letting themselves go. . . . The fact
> that thousands of others are screaming along
> with her makes the girl feel she is living life to
> the full with people of her own age. . . . [T]his
> emotional outlook is very necessary at her age. It
> is also innocent and harmless.
>
> The girls are subconsciously preparing for
> motherhood. Their frenzied screams are a re-
> hearsal for that moment. Even the jelly babies
> are symbolic.

EMI hastened to release the second Beatles LP, recorded by George Martin in mid-July and incubated through autumn until sales of the first album, and its spin-off singles, should finally subside. This second album, *With the Beatles*, appeared on November 22. Never before had a pop LP been released not to cash in on a Top Ten single but on the strength of its overall content. Advance orders alone totalled 250,000 copies—more than for Elvis Presley's biggest-selling album, *Blue Hawaii*.

By far the most striking thing about *With the Beatles* was its cover. Brian had for months been showing his proof copy to friends and asking anxiously what they thought. Gone was the look of the *Please Please Me* album—the cheap, cheeky faces, looking down from high-rise flats. A top London fashion photographer, Robert Freeman, had shot the Beatles, heads and shoulders only, in black and white. Faces halved by shadow, hemmed in by their bangs and high polo necks, they could have been a quartet of young actors or art students. It was the same technique Astrid had used to photograph Stu Sutcliffe three years before in Hamburg, in her black-and-silver room.

A week later came their fifth single, "I Want to Hold Your Hand," that advance orders of one million copies placed instantly at number one. The pre-Christmas air seemed to transmit little other than that loping, hand-clapping beat. The album, meanwhile, had its independent existence in the stunning combination of Lennon-McCartney songs like "All My Loving" and "It Won't Be Long," with Chuck Berry's "Roll Over Beethoven," Berry Gordy's "Money," and other R&B songs so little known to the general pop audience, it was thought the Beatles must have written those also.

Never again would pop music be considered the prerogative only of working-class boys and girls. *With the Beatles* was played not only in the projects but in West London flats, in young ladies' finishing schools, and in the blow-heated barns where country squires' daughters held their Christmas dances.

On November 5, the day after the Royal Command show, Brian Epstein flew to New York, accompanied by Billy J. Kramer, that handsome but awkward young man. Landing at the airport still called Idlewilde, they drove in a yellow cab toward the magic skyline that reveals itself at first in miniature like the crest on a souvenir ashtray. Brian, on the drive, was full of what Broadway plays they would see in between his several very important business meetings. These meetings, Billy J. gathered, were the merest preliminary to the Beatles' instant subjugation of the North

American continent. Even if Brian himself ever believed this, he ceased to do so as the cab entered Manhattan and the streets became sheer glass on every side.

America up to now had regarded the Beatles as it regarded every British pop performer—an inferior substitute for a product that, having been invented in America, could only be manufactured and marketed by Americans. The view was reinforced by the half-century in which American artists, through every musical epoch, had dominated the English market as against only one or two freakish incursions by English acts traveling the other way. In the same fashion now, American pop music dwarfed its English counterparts in size and wealth, in the complexity of its chart systems and the corollary role of hundreds of independent radio stations. Even so big a British name as Cliff Richard had attempted only one American tour, halfway down the bill, amid deafening indifference. The British, it was agreed in the boardrooms of Manhattan, should stick to the things they knew best, like whisky, woolen sweaters, and Shakespeare.

America in late 1963 had already ordained the new direction of teenage music. Three brothers from California, Brian, Carl, and Dennis Wilson, and their cousin Mike Love, known collectively as the Beach Boys, were already internationally famous for their close-harmony songs hymning the West Coast pleasures of surf riding, drag racing, and crew-cut, freckled sex. That surfing sound, like previous pop styles, reflected a nation still jingoistically confident in the perfection of all its values; whose new young president, John F. Kennedy, had precisely the same sun-healthy, college-fresh appeal.

George Martin had found the anti-British barrier impossible to penetrate, even though, thanks to Sir Joseph Lockwood's entrepreneurial drive, EMI owned the American Capitol label. When "Please Please Me" went to number one in Britain Martin had immediately sent it to Jay Livingstone, Capitol's boss in New York. Back from Livingstone came the reply, "We don't think the Beatles will do anything in this market."

Martin, to his great annoyance, was therefore obliged to hawk "Please Please Me" around other American labels in direct competition with Parlophone's own parent company. It was finally accepted by Vee Jay, a small Chicago-based firm. Released by Vee Jay in February, "Please Please Me" had instantly vanished without trace. The same happened in

May with "From Me to You." Martin offered it to Capitol, who gruffly refused it; issued by Vee Jay, it rose no higher than 116th in *Billboard* magazine's chart.

In August, when "She Loves You" began its eight-week blockade of the British charts, Martin appealed for the third time to Jay Livingstone, and was again told that in Capitol's opinion the Beatles had no prospects in America. Instead, "She Loves You" was issued by a small New York label, Swan. The sound engulfing the British Isles did not even penetrate the *Billboard* Hot 100.

One American entrepreneur at least—a tubby, sentimental New York agent named Sid Bernstein—disagreed with Capitol's prognosis. Bernstein worked for the General Artists Corporation, America's largest theatrical agency, but having a thirst for culture, spent his leisure time attending an evening course on the subject of Civilization. "Our teacher had told us to study the British way of life as a great democracy comparable with our own. He said the best way to study England was to read the British newspapers. That was how I first heard about what the Beatles were doing over in Europe."

Quite early in 1963, Bernstein says, he was telling his superiors at GAC that the mania he had read about in the British press could happen in New York City. "I could see what they were, and that they were going to be monsters here. I wanted them."

Brian arrived in New York, unaware that Sid Bernstein had been trying for several weeks to contact him by transatlantic phone. "I couldn't sell the idea to anyone at GAC," Bernstein says, "so I decided to make it my own independent promotion. I had already booked Carnegie Hall, the most famous auditorium in New York. You couldn't get Carnegie Hall unless you made the reservation months ahead. I chose February 12, 1964—Lincoln's birthday. The lady I dealt with at Carnegie Hall had a thick Polish accent. 'The Beatles?' she said, 'Vat are they?' I knew that Carnegie Hall would never allow a pop concert to happen in its famous auditorium. I said, 'They're a phenomenon.' 'Oh, a *phenomenon*,' she said, thinking that was maybe a type of string quartet."

Brian had only one friend in New York. Geoffrey Ellis, the Liverpool estate agent's son, was still working there for the Royal Insurance Society. Geoffrey had not seen Brian since he was home on vacation in 1962 and Mrs. Epstein confided to him that the family were "letting Brian get this group thing out of his system." Geoffrey was astonished to see what a *real* impresario Brian had made himself; how earnestly he dissuaded Billy J. Kramer from buying a cheap shirt, "because it's not your *image*, Billy."

Dick James, the music publisher, had recommended him to Walter Hofer, an attorney who already acted for James's company in New York. Hofer, hospitable and an Anglophile, at once invited Brian up to his office on West Fifty-seventh Street. "From the beginning he was full of questions," Hofer remembered. "How did American TV work? How did the radio stations work? While he was in town, I gave a cocktail party for him, which was a disaster. No one had ever heard of Brian Epstein. No one came but a few people from Liberty Records, because Billy J. Kramer was signing with them."

Similarly, no one at Capitol Records recognized the severely dapper young Englishman who came in to see their director of eastern operations, Brown Meggs. Brian had called in person to try to persuade Capitol to give the Beatles an American release. With him he had a demo of the song that John and Paul, working in the basement of Jane Asher's house, had striven to invest with "a sort of American spiritual sound." And, indeed, to Capitol's hypersensitive ears, the song did have something that three consecutive British number ones had lacked. Brown Meggs, after much corporate deliberation, agreed that Capitol would release "I Want To Hold Your Hand." Even so, it was made clear to Brian, the company did not expect a great response. The release date was January 13, 1964.

Brian's other appointment was to meet a little sharkskin-suited elderly man with heavy jowls, a gruff voice, and an air of misanthropy often detectable in those renowned as talent spotters and arbiters of the public taste. At the Delmonico Hotel, Brian Epstein, for the second time, found himself face to face with the great Ed Sullivan.

For fifteen years, Sullivan's CBS television show had been famous for breaking in new entertainers, not only in New York but across the whole American continent via hundreds of local stations served by the CBS network. Sullivan, a former sports journalist, combined an uncanny instinct for the sensational with an air of bewilderment that his fellow Americans could find such things remotely entertaining. It was Sullivan who had booked Elvis Presley to sing "Hound Dog" on condition that the cameras showed him only from the waist up. Sullivan's introduction then was simply a shrug and the words: "America, judge for yourselves."

Ed Sullivan had been aware of the Beatles since his recent talent-spotting trip to Europe, when he and Mrs. Sullivan were among many travelers at Heathrow airport inconvenienced by their homecoming from Sweden. He had asked to meet them, and been sufficiently impressed to offer Brian a tentative booking on his show early in 1964.

Sullivan's idea at that stage was to use the Beatles as a minor novelty item in a show constructed around some established American entertainer. Brian, however, insisted they should receive top billing. The Sullivan show's producer, Bob Precht—who happened also to be Ed Sullivan's son-in-law—remembers how surprised both he and the great man were by this unforeseen tactic. Top billing was conceded against a deal otherwise far from munificent. "I said that if we were going to pay the Beatles' airfares out here," Precht says, "we ought to get more than one appearance out of them." It was agreed that the Beatles should appear in two Ed Sullivan shows, on February ninth and sixteenth, and should record more songs to be used in a subsequent transmission. The fee for each appearance would be $3,500, plus $3,000 more for the taping. "Even for an unknown act," Bob Precht admits, "that was about the least we could pay."

If America had not fallen, it was at least prepared to listen. Brian had that much to comfort him when, a day or two afterward, he and Billy J. Kramer flew back to London. He had persuaded Capitol. He had persuaded Ed Sullivan. Short of the fatigue, the phoning back, the waiting, and the compromise, these would seem dazzling achievements. And halfway over the Atlantic, as he read the British papers, Beatlemania grew audible again.

America, if Brian had only known it, was already his—was moving nearer his unconscious grasp as, far away in Texas, the mechanism of a high velocity rifle was cleaned and checked, and a vantage-point selected. America fell to him on the morning in Dallas that the presidential motorcade set off on its route, supremely confident and open to the sunshine, and the curbside ciné-enthusiast turned his camera toward the limousine that carried a young man's unprotected head. This was November 22, the day the Beatles' second album went on sale in Britain. Late that afternoon, the news began to come through that, for every English person, hardly less than every American, would fix in the memory forever the exact time, place, and circumstances of hearing it.

•   •   •

For their winter tour, through the deepening blizzards of national dementia, Brian entrusted the Beatles to his friend Brian Sommerville, the ex–naval officer turned Fleet Street journalist. Tony Barrow, NEMS's original press officer, now had more work than he could handle alone. It was therefore fixed that Barrow should represent Gerry, Billy J. Kramer, Cilla, and the Fourmost while Sommerville—or rather, Sommerville's one-man PR company—acted exclusively for the Beatles. Small, plump, already balding, he had the aspect of a country squire and a quarterdeck brusqueness that did not at once endear him to his new charges.

The tour was the most arduous one yet—six weeks of one-night concerts at Gaumont, ABC, or Odeon cinemas in a zigzag course from Cambridge to Sunderland. At the same time they were rehearsing their pantomime sketches for a special NEMS Christmas show in London, at the Finsbury Park Astoria. In Liverpool in one twenty-four-hour period, as well as their two evening concerts, they taped appearances for two television shows and performed for a convention of the Beatles Northern Area Fan Club. John and Paul were also working on a dozen new songs for the film that Walter Shenson wanted to shoot the following spring.

In university city or Midland industrial town, the procedure was invariable. Mal Evans went in first, driving the van with their equipment through the blue avenues of waiting police. At dusk, by vainly circuitous routes, would come the Austin Princess limousine containing the Beatles, Neil Aspinall, and Brian Sommerville. They would go straight to the theater, remaining in the dressing room until the performance while Neil brought in food or pressed their stage clothes and Sommerville stood guard testily outside. As soon as the curtain fell Sommerville would shoo them, in their damp suits, out through the police ranks to their beleaguered car. By midnight, they would be trapped inside some provincial hotel that, more often than not, would have stopped serving dinner at 9:00 P.M. On many nights, all they could get to eat were dishes of cornflakes.

In Lincoln, Ringo developed an earache and had to be rushed to the hospital, disguised in an overcoat, hat, and spectacles that, as one reporter noted, "made him look like Brecht being smuggled out of Germany." Near Doncaster, their car ran out of petrol and they had to thumb a lift in a truck. In Sunderland, they escaped from the theater by running into the adjacent fire station, sliding down the firemen's pole, and escaping in a police car while one of the engines rushed out to create a diversion.

In Liverpool, the Empire theater had been commandeered by the BBC for a special edition of *Juke Box Jury* featuring all four Beatles as panelists. Disgruntled technicians, faced with this unprecedented journey outside London, were heard muttering that BBC must stand for "Beatle Broadcasting Corporation." Before the show, the Beatles mischievously rearranged their name cards so that George Harrison sat behind the one reading "John Lennon." As panelists, they were not only far funnier and livelier than the usual aging disk jockeys and empty-headed starlets; they also displayed a depth of musical knowledge seldom, if ever, heard on that show before. When the Swinging Blue Jeans' version of their old Cavern showstopper "Hippy-Hippy Shake" was played, George remarked what a big fan he was of the song's composer, Chan Romero. At that time, the only Chan most teenage record buyers had ever heard of was Charlie.

The advantage of Brian Sommerville as publicist was that he spoke in an upper-class voice, in a tone to which policemen, doormen, and other potential obstacles almost all automatically responded. The Beatles, hemmed in as tightly by authority figures as by screaming fans, recognized the need for someone, like Sommerville, peppery and abrasive. "I had a good relationship with John; he called me 'old baldy-something-or-other.' Paul and I got on well enough, though I always found him rather two-faced. Ringo was just Ringo. I did have one serious fight with George. He never regarded me with anything but muffled dislike."

Throughout the tour, Sommerville was left totally in charge to screen the press seeking interviews, sign the hotel bills, and negotiate strategy with theater managers and the police. Brian would appear at irregular intervals, in his overcoat and polka-dotted scarf. "He'd float into the dressing room, usually with a piece of paper for them to sign," Sommerville says. "But if there was any trouble, you could count on Brian to be miles away. He had this wonderful knack of being able to disappear during a crisis."

Backstage rows were frequent between Brian and Sommerville. It irked Brian to see anyone close to the Beatles but himself. He even suspected Sommerville of trying to usurp his own growing fame as their mentor and mouthpiece. "Brian already saw himself as a star in his own right," Sommerville says. "*He* wanted to do the things they did, like appearing on *Juke Box Jury*. He was hurt because he hadn't been asked to chair the special Mersey edition of *Thank Your Lucky Stars*. The worst rows we had were after I'd made some comment, and the press quoted me instead of Brian. 'You had no right to do that!' he'd say."

And yet, at times, Brian would seem unable to pluck up courage to go into the Beatles' dressing room, but would stand out in the auditorium, suddenly as distant from them as the farthest screaming girl. "I saw him once," Sommerville says, "in one of those northern ABCs, when the curtains opened and the scream went up. He was standing there with tears streaming down his face."

It had become clear at an early stage, to various sharp-eyed people, that the Beatles were capable of selling far more than phonograph records by the million. Beatlemania demonstrated as never before to what extent young people in Britain were a market, gigantic and ripe for exploitation. From October 1963 onward Brian Epstein carried in his wake a little trail of businessmen, coaxing, cajoling, sometimes begging to be authorized to produce goods in the Beatles' image.

Merchandising as a concept was largely unknown in mid-twentieth-century Britain, even though the Victorians had been adept at it. Walt Disney, that peerless weaver of dreams into plastic, was imitated on a small scale by British toy manufacturers, producing replicas of television puppets. Pop singers until now had lasted too short a time in public esteem to sell any but the most ephemeral goods.

No precedent existed, therefore, to warn Brian that there were billions at stake. He saw the merchandising purely as public relations—a way to increase audience goodwill and keep the fan club happy. He worried about the fan club and keeping it happy.

The first Beatles products catered simply for the desire, as strong in girls as in boys, to impersonate their idols. In Bethnal Green, East London, a factory was producing Beatles wigs at the rate of several thousand each week. The hairstyle that Astrid's scissors had shaped for Stu Sutcliffe became a best-selling novelty, a black, fibrous mop, hovering just outside seriousness, 30s (£1.50) apiece. A Midlands clothing firm marketed collarless corduroy Beatles jackets like the one Astrid had made for Stu, the one that the Beatles at the time despised as "Mum's jacket." Girls, too, wore the jackets, the tab-collar shirts, even the elastic-sided, Cuban heel "Beatles boots," obtainable by mail order at 75s 11d (£3.80), including shipping and handling.

Christmas 1963 signaled a fresh avalanche of Beatles products into the shops. There were Beatles guitars, of plastic, and miniature Beatles drums. There were Beatles lockets, each with a tiny quadruple photograph compressed inside. There were red and blue Beatles kitchen aprons, bespeckled with guitar-playing bugs. The four faces and four signatures, engraved, printed, or transferred, however indistinctly, appeared on belts, badges, handkerchiefs, jigsaw puzzles, rubber airbeds, record racks, bedspreads, "ottomans," shoulder bags, pencils, buttons, and trays. There was a brand of confectionery known as Ringo Roll, and of Beatles chewing gum, each sixpenny packet warranted to contain *seven* photographs. A northern bakery chain announced guitar-shaped "Beatles cakes" ("Party priced at 5s") and fivepenny individual Beatles "fancies."

Brian, in the beginning, personally examined the products of each prospective licensee. In no case, he ruled, would the Beatles directly endorse any article. Nor would they lend their name to anything distasteful, inappropriate, or overtly exploitive of their fans. And, indeed, parents who had scolded their children for buying trash were frequently surprised by the goods' quality and value. The Beatles jacket was smart, durable, and well-lined. The official Beatles sweater ("Designed for Beatles people by a leading British manufacturer") was 100 percent botany wool, hardly extortionate at 35s (£1.75).

Soon, however, unauthorized Beatles goods began to appear. Though NEMS Enterprises held copyright on the name Beatles, infringement could be avoided simply by spelling it "Beetles." The vaguest representation of insects, of guitars or little mop-headed men, had the power to sell anything, however cheap, however nasty. Even to spot the culprits, let alone bring lawsuits against them, meant a countrywide monitoring such as no British copyright holder had ever been obliged to undertake. NEMS Enterprises certainly could not undertake it. And so, after one or two minor prosecutions, the pirates settled down, unhampered, to their bonanza.

By late 1963, the merchandising had got into a tangle that Brian had not the time or the will to contemplate. He therefore handed the whole matter over to his lawyer, David Jacobs. It became Jacobs's job not only to prosecute infringements, where visible, but also, at his independent discretion, to issue new manufacturing licenses. Prospective licensees were referred from NEMS Enterprises to Jacobs's offices in Pall Mall.

Since Jacobs, too, was deeply preoccupied with social as well as legal matters, the task of appraising designs, production strategy, and probable income was delegated to the chief clerk in his chambers, Edward Marke.

Among the other cases currently being handled by M. A. Jacobs Ltd were several claims for damages by the relatives of passengers lost aboard a wrecked cruise ship, the *Lakonia*. The waiting-room where these bereaved litigants sat also served as a dumping ground for cascades of Beatles guitars, plastic windmills, and crayoning sets. Mr. Marke, though a conscientious legal functionary, knew little of the manufacturing business. So David Jacobs, in his turn, looked round for someone to take on this tiresome business of making millions.

His choice was Nicky Byrne, a man he had met at one of the numerous cocktail parties he attended. Byrne, indeed, was rather a celebrated figure at parties, of which he himself gave a great many at his fashionable Chelsea garage-cum-flat. Small, impishly dapper, formidably persuasive, he had been variously a country squire's son, a Horse Guard trooper, and an amateur racing driver. His true avocation, however, was membership of the Chelsea Set, the subculture of debutantes, bohemians, heiresses, and charming cads that, since the mid-fifties, had flourished along and around the King's Road.

Nicky Byrne was not a totally implausible choice, having in his extremely varied life touched the worlds of show business and popular retailing. In the fifties, he had run the Condor Club in Soho where Tommy Steele was discovered. His wife, Kiki—from whom he had recently parted—was a well-known fashion designer with her own successful Chelsea boutique.

The offer from Jacobs was that Byrne should administer the Beatles' merchandising operation in Europe and throughout the world. He was not, he maintains, very eager to accept. "Brian Epstein had a very bad name in the business world at that time. Nobody knew who was licensed to make Beatles goods and who wasn't. I got in touch with Kiki, my ex-wife, to see what she thought about it. I mentioned this company firm in Soho that was meant to be turning out Beatles gear. Kiki said, 'Hold on a minute.' She'd had a letter from a firm in the Midlands, asking her to design exactly the same thing for them."

Nicky Byrne was eventually persuaded. He agreed to form a company named Stramsact to take over the assigning of Beatles merchandise rights. A subsidiary called Seltaeb—Beatles spelled backward—would handle American rights, if any, when the Beatles went to New York in February to appear on the *Ed Sullivan Show*.

Five partners, all much younger than Nicky Byrne, constituted both Stramsact and Seltaeb. One of them, twenty-six-year-old John Fenton, had already been doing some merchandising deals of his own via David Jacobs. Two others, Mark Warman and Simon Miller-Munday, aged twenty and twenty-two, respectively, were simply friends of Nicky's who had been nice to him during his breakup with Kiki.

Nicky Byrne's most picturesque recruit after himself was twenty-three-year-old Lord Peregrine Eliot, heir to the Earl of St. Germans and owner of a six-thousand-acre estate in Cornwall. Lord Peregrine's qualification was that he had shared a flat with Simon Miller-Munday. Although extremely rich, he was eager to earn funds to recarpet his ancestral home, Port Eliot. For one thousand pounds cash, His Lordship received 20 percent of the company.

Only Malcolm Evans, the sixth partner, a junior studio manager with Rediffusion TV, had any definite professional ability of any kind. Evans had met the others at a Nicky Byrne party, the high spot of which was the pushing of a grand piano through the Chelsea streets. "Nicky had got the entire Count Basie Orchestra to play at his party," Evans says. "I remember that they were accompanied on the bagpipes by a full-dress pipe major from the barracks over the road."

The contract between Stramsact-Seltaeb and NEMS Enterprises was left to Jacobs to draw up, approve, even sign on Brian's and the Beatles' behalf. "I was at my solicitor's, just round the corner," Nicky Byrne says. "He told me, 'Write in what percentage you think you should take on the deal.' So I put down the first figure that came into my head—90 percent.

"To my amazement, David Jacobs didn't even question it. He didn't think of it as 90 percent to us, but as 10 percent to the Beatles. He said, 'Well, 10 percent is better than nothing.'

Christmas, far from diverting the mania, actually seemed to increase it. The Beatles *became* Christmas in their fancy dress, playing in the NEMS Christmas Show at Finsbury Park Astoria. One of the sketches was a Victorian melodrama in which George, as the heroine, was tied on a railway line by Sir Jasper (John) and rescued by "Fearless Paul the Signalman'" They had acted such plays and farces for years among themselves. Mal Evans, their second road manager, stood by, laughing, as all did, at the good-humored knockabout fun; Mal had just received a savage tongue-lashing from John for having lost his twelve-string acoustic guitar.

Beatles records made the December Top Twenty literally impassable. As well as "I Want to Hold Your Hand" at number one, it contained six songs from the *With the Beatles* LP—indeed, the album itself, with almost a million copies sold, qualified for entrance to the *singles* chart at number fourteen; the customary seasonal gimmick record was Dora Bryan's "All I Want for Christmas is a Beatle."

Two anxiously awaited messages that Christmas went out to the British nation. The first came from Queen Elizabeth, speaking on television from Balmoral Castle. The second came from four young men, unknown a year ago, speaking to their eighty thousand fan club members in a babble of excited voices. They sang "Good King Wenceslas" and wished their subjects "a very happy Chrimble and a gear Near Year."

"An examination of the heart of the nation at this moment," the London *Evening Standard* said, "would find the name 'Beatles' upon it." Under the heading "Why Do We Love Them So Much?" columnist Angus McGill said it was because "like well-bred children they are seen and not heard." Maureen Cleave, in another article, could only conclude that "everybody loves them because they look so happy."

In marketing terms, the figures they represented were still barely believable. "She Loves You" had sold 1.3 million copies; "I Want to Hold Your Hand" had sold 1.25 million. They had transformed the British music industry from complacent torpor to neurotic—though still unavailing—competitiveness. A tiny record label called Parlophone towered over the frantic A&R men with a run of success, unequaled to this day. For thirty-seven weeks out of the previous fifty-two, George Martin had had a record at number one. He was currently reading a memo from his EMI superiors explaining that he would not this year qualify for the staff Christmas bonus.

Pop music was legitimized—and not only socially. At the end of December a ballet, *Mods and Rockers*, was scored with Lennon and McCartney music. The *Times* published an article by its classical music critic, William Mann, who pronounced John and Paul to be "the outstanding English composers of 1963" for qualities of which they were probably unconscious. In their slow ballad "This Boy" Mann detected "chains of pandiatonic clusters," and in "Not a Second Time," "an Aeolian cadence—the chord progression which ends Mahler's 'Song of the Earth.'" He further noticed their "autocratic but not by any means ungrammatical attitude to tonality . . . the quasi-instrumental vocal duetting . . . the melismas with altered vowels." That one article raised for all time the mental portcullis between classical and pop; it also ushered in decades of sillier prose.

No Englishman, however cantankerous, could any longer profess ignorance on the subject. Not even Field Marshal Lord Montgomery, hero of El Alamein, who, speaking from the garden where he still kept Rommel's desert caravan, threatened to invite the Beatles for the weekend "to see what kind of fellows they are."

Nineteen sixty-four began on a note of post-Christmas acidity. In the Top Twenty "I Want to Hold Your Hand" yielded its number-one position to a non-Lennon-McCartney song, "Glad All Over" by the Dave Clark Five. Since the Five all came from the same north London suburb, they were greeted as harbingers of a "Tottenham Sound"; they had "crushed" the Beatles, several front-page headlines said. The *Daily Mail* published a cartoon in which a group of girls contemptuously regarded one of their number. "She must be really old," the caption ran, "she remembers the Beatles."

As a prelude to America, they were to visit Paris. Brian had booked them a three-week engagement at the Olympia theater, beginning on January 15. The crowd that massed at Heathrow to see them off descried only three Beatles being herded out to the aircraft. Ringo Starr, the newspapers said, was fogbound in Liverpool. Ringo, in fact, most unusually, was having a fit of temperament and had declared he wasn't fookin' coming. Across the Channel, further large and small hitches waited.

The Olympia, a wholly Parisian cross between cinema and music hall, was operated by a wily French promoter named Bruno Coquatrix. For three weeks of nightly Beatles shows Coquatrix was paying Brian Epstein a fee that did not cover their travel and hotel expenses—particularly since Brian, with typical expansiveness, had booked the entire entourage into the expensive George V hotel. To offset the loss Brian Sommerville did a publicity deal with British European Airways. The

Beatles were issued with special inflight bags lettered BEAtles. For carrying and prominently displaying these they and their guardians received three weeks' unlimited air travel between London and Paris.

Brian justified the low fee, once more, against the publicity value. France, until now, had remained noticeably indifferent to Beatlemania. He was determined that the Beatles should conquer Paris, and that Paris should be in no doubt concerning who had engineered that conquest. Before the journey, he asked Dezo Hoffman the photographer to print up five hundred giveaway pictures of himself. Hoffman persuaded him this was not a good idea.

A vast contingent of British journalists went to Paris to cover the event. This time, the *Daily Express* led the field, having signed up George Harrison to write a daily column. The writing was actually to be done by Derek Taylor, a Hoylake-born *Express* reporter, formerly the paper's northern dramatic critic. This cultural background, no less than his Italianate good looks, recommended Taylor to Brian for what was a deliberate attempt to give George a share of the limelight. "It will be *nice* for George," Brian told him. "John and Paul have their songwriting and Ringo is—ah—rather new."

The George V's foyer was thronged with expectant photographers, hungrily noting the comings and goings of various important stakeholders in the quartet. George Martin, their record producer, had flown over to supervise a German-language recording of "She Loves You." Dr. Strach, their accountant, was there; so was Walter Shenson, their prospective film producer, accompanied by Alun Owen, a Liverpool playwright whom the Beatles themselves had requested as scriptwriter. Nicky Byrne, of the Stramsact company, was there to arrange large deals, so he expected, for Beatles merchandise in France and throughout Europe.

As well as variety acts such as jugglers and acrobats, the Beatles shared the Olympia bill with two singers whose French followings greatly exceeded theirs. One was Sylvie Vartin, France's own turbulent pop chanteuse. The other, Trini Lopez, was an American with a huge Continental chart success called "Lemon Tree."

Lopez's manager, Norman Weiss, instantly sought out Brian at the George V. Weiss worked with the American General Artists Corporation, whose former associate, Sid Bernstein, had already booked Carnegie Hall in New York in the hope of being able to present the Beatles there. February 12, the date of Bernstein's booking, was only three days after their first *Ed Sullivan Show*. Weiss, therefore, concluded the deal at last on Sid Bernstein's behalf. Brian agreed that the Beatles would give two concerts at Carnegie Hall, each for a flat fee of $3,500.

They themselves were very different now from the four boys in George Martin's studio, earnestly doing everything their producer told them. Martin, waiting at EMI's Paris studio to supervise their German-language recording of "She Loves You" ("Sie Liebt Dich"), was coolly informed by telephone that the Beatles had decided not to come. He stormed over to the George V to find them lounging round their suite while Paul's girlfriend, Jane Asher, poured out tea. Such was Martin's schoolmasterly wrath that all four scattered in terror to hide under cushions and behind the piano.

On the eve of their first concert, while the French and English press jostled for position outside, John and Paul slept until 3:00 P.M. Dezo Hoffman in the end accepted the hazardous job of waking them. "I told John, '*Paris-Match* is waiting. They want to do a cover story.' '*Paris-Match*?' John said. 'Are they as important as the *Musical Express*?'"

Emerging into the Champs-Elysées in a circle of retreating lenses they found Paris rather less than ecstatic at their arrival. According to Hoffman, very few passersby even recognized them. The British press made a valiant attempt to stimulate Beatlemania, posing John and Paul at a sidewalk café and hedging them in among waiters and reporters. Vincent Mulchrone remarked on the prevailing apathy in his dispatch to the *Daily Mail*. "Beatlemania is still, like Britain's entry into the Common Market, a problem the French prefer to put off for a while."

Backstage at the Olympia the following night naked violence broke out after the French press had had the Beatles' dressing-room door slammed in their faces. French photographers, especially those who have served in theaters of war like Algeria and Indochina, are not so easily discouraged. A fierce scuffle followed in which Brian Sommerville received a rabbit punch and Brian—who tried to interpose himself with outstretched arms and a querulous, "No—not *my* boys!"—was shoved backward by a burly French pressman who was simultaneously treading on his toes.

The show ran late, as French shows invariably do, and the Beatles did not go onstage until well after midnight. Trini Lopez, who had closed the first half hours before, seemed much more like top of the bill. To add to their unease, a glimpse through the curtains showed the audience to be almost entirely male. "Where's all the bloody chicks then?" they kept asking in agitation.

During the performance their usually reliable Vox amplifiers broke down three times. George, enraged by his fading guitar, began to complain openly of sabotage. Neither John nor Paul made any attempt to speak French, and the audience, for its part, evinced boredom toward Lennon-McCartney songs. All they seemed to want were rock 'n' roll numbers like "Twist and Shout," which they greeted with cries of *"un autre, un autre."* At one point, a strange chant became audible. "Ring-o," it sounded like. "Ring-o, Ring-o."

The reviews next morning were tepid. *France-Soir* called them *zazous* (delinquents) and *vedettes démodées* (has-beens). According to Nicky Byrne the effect on merchandising prospects throughout Europe was swift and disastrous. Galeries Lafayette, the department store, decided, after all, not to fill an entire window with Beatles goods. Nor did Lambretta, the Italian motor scooter corporation, proceed with its plan to market a special model with a Beatles wig for a saddle.

The barbs of *France-Soir,* in common with everything French, had ceased to matter to the *zazous* and their entourage several hours earlier. Dezo Hoffman, eating dinner at a small restaurant with Derek Taylor, received an urgent summons back to the George V. Both returned, to find the Beatles' suite in a state of eerie quiet.

"Brian was there as well," Hoffman says. "He was sitting on a chair and the Beatles were sitting on the floor around him. He said the news had come through that 'I Want to Hold Your Hand' was number one in the American Top Hundred. The Beatles couldn't even speak—not even John Lennon. They just sat on the floor like kittens at Brian's feet."

TWELVE

"THEY'VE GOT EVERYTHING OVER THERE. WHAT DO THEY WANT *US* FOR?"

Early on February 7, 1964, when the New York streets were still empty but for snow and steam and fast-bouncing cabs, a disk jockey on station WMCA sounded the first note of impending madness. "It is now 6:30 A.M., Beatle time. They left London thirty minutes ago. They're out over the Atlantic Ocean, headed for New York. The temperature is 32 Beatle degrees."

America's interest, until the eleventh hour, had remained no more than cursory. The American press is at the best of times notoriously parochial, and these were the worst of times. Since November 22, there had been only one newspaper story in America; only one picture, on an amateur's movie film, endlessly replayed up to that same frozen frame. A young man, next to his wife in an open car, slumped sideways as the bullets tore into him.

Just before a Christmas holiday that very few Americans felt disposed to celebrate, Walter Hofer, the New York attorney, sat in his office on West Fifty-seventh Street. Hofer, like many New Yorkers, had the habit of perpetual work. It was one way, at least, to shut out the dull, slow, directionless feeling that, since President John Kennedy's assassination in Dallas, had shrouded Manhattan like a fog.

"Out of the blue, I got this call from Capitol Records. They wanted to know, was it right that I acted in New York for a British company called NEMS Enterprises? I told them, yes, I did. They said they were trying to find out who controlled the publishing on a song called 'I Want to Hold Your Hand' by this British group, the Beatles."

Capitol, prepared to release that unknown British group's record into the sluggish post-Christmas market, had received some puzzling news from out of town. A disk jockey in Washington, D.C., working on station WWDC, had somehow obtained a copy of "I Want to Hold Your

Hand" and was playing it on the air amid a commotion of interest from his listeners. The record had come not from Capitol but direct from London via the disk jockey's girlfriend, who was a stewardess with British Overseas Airways.

"Capitol wanted to get clearance on the publishing side, to be able to ship a few hundred copies into the Washington area," Walter Hofer remembers. "In fact, I had to tell them that the publishing rights had been sold to another company, MCA. Sold for almost nothing, it so happened, just to give the song any foothold that was possible over here."

While Capitol tried to resolve this trifling matter, a second, identical commotion was reported, from Chicago. A radio station was being besieged by enquiries after playing a song called "I Want to Hold Your Hand" by this British group, the Beatles. Apparently it had been sent on tape from a friend of the disk jockey's at WWDC, Washington. From Chicago, by the same fraternal taping process, it moved west again, to St. Louis.

In New York, as the sidewalk Santas pessimistically clanged their bells, a drastic change was ordered in the marketing strategy of Capitol Records. A week earlier, Brown Meggs and his colleagues had been uneasy about a prospective pressing for "I Want to Hold Your Hand" of two hundred thousand copies. Now three entire production plants—Capitol's own and that of CBS and RCA—were alerted to work through Christmas and New Year's to press one million copies.

By the time the news reached Brian Epstein in Paris, sales were closer to 1.5 million. The night disappeared, after speech had returned, in a wild spree of drinking and piggyback riding and a restaurant party, joined by George Martin and his wife-to-be, Judy Lockhart-Smith, when Brian so far forgot himself as to sit and be photographed with a chamberpot on his head.

Next morning, the American press were there en masse. *Life* magazine's London bureau chief, having planned to slip over to Paris merely for lunch, found himself, to his dismay, assigned to write the week's cover story. Equivalent responsibilities had suddenly devolved onto representatives of CBS, Associated Press, the *New York Times,* and the *Washington Post.* The Beatles, roused from sleep at 1:00 P.M., were brought in, still in their dressing gowns, to meet the first deputation.

The deputation, crop-haired and collegiate-looking as all good

American media types ought to be, saw at once what element in the story their readers would find of consuming but abhorrent fascination.

The *New York Times* tried to put it tactfully.

"Who does your hair while you're in Paris?"

"Nobody does it when we're in *London*."

"But where did those hairdo's . . ."

"You mean hairdon'ts," John said.

"We were coming out of a swimming bath in Liverpool," George said, amid earnest note-taking, "and we liked the way it looked." So the story went out on the AP and UPI agency wires.

The most celebrated journalistic visitor was Sheila Graham, F. Scott Fitzgerald's last love and one of America's most widely syndicated columnists. She waited an hour and a half while the Beatles underwent medical examinations for their forthcoming film.

At length, only George put his serious face around the door. "Why— hello, dear," Miss Graham said, rising. "Now tell me quickly—which one are you?"

Nicky Byrne and his Seltaeb partners were already in New York. They had gone ahead of the Beatles to set up merchandising deals according to the 90–10 percent contract in their favor. Nicky Byrne wore an overcoat with an astrakhan collar. Lord Peregrine Eliot wore a scruffy leather jacket belying his ancestral home with its 130 chimney stacks.

New York, by this time, late in January, made only one kind of sound. Every radio station every few seconds played a Beatles record. Capitol had now also released the *With the Beatles* LP—renamed *Meet the Beatles*—and, to their blank astonishment, had seen it go instantly to the top of the album charts.

Nicky Byrne and his Seltaeb young men stayed at the elegant Drake Hotel and worked out of offices on Fifth Avenue. Within hours, they were besieged by manufacturers seeking a part in what the American business world already recognized as the biggest marketing opportunity since Walt Disney had created Mickey Mouse.

The procedure was that Seltaeb, having satisfied themselves as to the suitable nature of the merchandise, issued a license in exchange for a cash advance against 10 percent manufacturing royalties. An early licensee, the Reliant Shirt Corporation, paid twenty-five thousand pounds up front for exclusive rights to produce Beatles T-shirts in three factories they had bought for the purpose. Three days after the T-shirts went on sale, a million had been sold.

At Seltaeb's Fifth Avenue office three or four presidents of major American corporations would obediently wait in line outside Nicky Byrne's door. With magnificent hauteur, Byrne refused to talk business with anyone below the rank of president. Not the least confusion among these urgent supplicants arose from the knowledge that one Seltaeb director they might deal with was an earl. Lord Peregrine Eliot, more than once, was buttonholed by an anxious, "Say, listen Earl—"

Within a week of setting up in New York Nicky Byrne received an offer of fifty thousand dollars for Seltaeb from Capitol Records. "They were willing to pay the money straight into the Bahamas," he remembers. "*And* they were willing to let us keep a half-interest in the company. But I turned them down. Part of the deal was that they were going to get me one of the top American merchandising men—a man who'd worked for Disney and who'd since retired. Then I found out that Capitol had no intention of persuading this man to work with us. I turned them down because they'd lied to me.

"Capitol wouldn't take no for an answer. They tried *everything* to get me to sell. They'd checked out my background and found out about my interest in motor racing. At our next meeting, when I said I still wouldn't sell, the Capitol man said, 'Just take a look out of the window, Nicky.' Down in the street there was one of the most exclusive Ferraris ever made—the 29. Only one had come into America, to be driven by the North American Racing Team. This was it—it had mechanics standing beside it. 'That's yours, Nicky,' I was told, 'if we can do this deal.'

"I said, 'But it's not as easy as that. I've got five partners.' The Capitol man turned round and said, 'Joe! Get five more of those.'"

At Capitol Records, $50,000 was hastily allocated for a crash publicity program leading up to the Beatles' arrival on February 7. Five million posters and car windshield stickers were printed with the cryptic message "The Beatles Are Coming." A four-page life story was circulated, with promotional records, to disk jockeys across the continent. Certain stations also received tapes of open-end interviews, prerecorded by the Beatles, with spaces left for the disk jockey's questions. Capitol executives, like so many repentant Scrooges, were photographed in Beatles wigs.

The *Ed Sullivan Show*, meanwhile, had received fifty thousand applications for the seven-hundred-odd seats at its broadcast on February 9. CBS had a greater number even than for Elvis Presley's first appearance in 1957. There was similar massive demand for the Beatles' second appearance for Sullivan, a week later, in a special show broadcast from the Hotel Deauville, Miami. Not a seat remained for their first American concert, at the Washington Coliseum, nor for Sid Bernstein's two concerts at Carnegie Hall. Mrs. Nelson Rockefeller was one of numerous celebrities whom Bernstein hoped to accommodate by putting extra seats on the stage.

And yet for all this brisk commercial activity, nothing had been done to connect the manifest excitement of American teenagers with the Beatles' physical presence on American soil. A film clip of them, shown on NBC's *Jack Paar Show*, brought confident predictions, notably from the *New York Times*, that although the Beatles might be coming, Beatlemania definitely was not. "For all Capitol and CBS cared," Nicky Byrne says, "they were just going to walk off the plane and go to their hotel. Nobody would even have known they were in America."

Byrne, as a merchandiser of Beatles goods, had his own reasons for desiring something more. "I kept ringing London to say, 'Look here, Capitol are hopeless, nobody's doing *anything* in the way of publicity.' I couldn't get hold of Brian Epstein at all. He'd completely disappeared. So had David Jacobs."

As February 7 drew near Nicky Byrne decided to take the initiative. He enlisted the help of a T-shirt manufacturer and of two New York radio stations, WMCA and WINS. "Every fifteen minutes, the same announcement was made over the air. A free T-shirt for every kid who went out to the airport to meet the Beatles."

The objects of all this ferocious maneuvering were seen off from Heathrow Airport by one thousand banner-waving fans whose screams Cynthia Lennon mistook, in her innocence, for the noise of their waiting Pan Am jet. Cynthia was to accompany the party and, such was the momentousness of the occasion, even received permission to be photographed by the press corps that packed the VIP lounge. No departure from Britain had so mingled national acclamation and hope since Neville Chamberlain's flight to Munich in 1938.

The greater part of Pan Am flight 101 was occupied by the Beatles and their entourage. They themselves sat in the first class cabin with Brian, Cynthia, and a new friend, the American record producer Phil Spector. Certain favored press friends also traveled first class, such as Maureen Cleave from the *Evening Standard* and a *Liverpool Echo* journalist, coincidentally blessed with the name George Harrison. Harrison, when he retired from Fleet Street in the 1950s, had thought himself out of the rat race. Now he found himself bound on the world's biggest assignment, with expenses, which, for the thrifty *Echo,* was equally phenomenal.

In the economy cabin sat Dezo Hoffman and the two road managers, Neil and Mal, already deep in their task of forging Beatle signatures on thousands of giveaway photographs. Scattered among the other press, and eyeing each other just as balefully, was a contingent of British manufacturers with ideas for new lines in Beatles merchandise. Unable to contact Brian Epstein on the ground, they hoped he would prove more accessible at thirty thousand feet. Notes were passed to Brian throughout the flight, and endorsed with a polite refusal.

The Beatles, though resolutely laughing and larking, all showed signs of terror at what lay ahead. None could be convinced they were any different from previous British entertainers who had taken on America, and lost. The example of Cliff Richard was frequently mentioned. George, on a visit to his elder sister in St. Louis, had seen Cliff's film *Summer Holiday* relegated to a drive-in second feature. Nor did the work permits Brian had obtained make them feel very special. The H2 classification allowed them to play, within a strict two-week period, "so long as unemployed American citizens capable of performing this work cannot be found."

Paul McCartney strapped himself tightly into his safety belt, not unbuckling it throughout the whole flight. To Maureen Cleave and Phil Spector he confessed the same unease that George did to his namesake from the *Liverpool Echo.* "He mentioned all the big American stars who'd come across to Britain," Harrison said. "He'd been across, unlike the others; he knew what the place was like. 'They've got everything over there,' he said. 'What do they want *us* for?' "

America, at first, presented only the normal aerial view of coast and long piers and the snow-flecked scrubland up to the runway edge. Even after the wheels struck tarmac, no particular welcome was visible save in the earmuffed men who walked backward, signaling with their small round bats. Then, as the terminal buildings came into view, the prospect dramatically changed. Five thousand people waited like a mural beyond the thick window glass. "The Beatles had no idea it was for them," Dezo Hoffman says. "They thought the president must be going to land in a minute."

The opening of the door let in a sound that made Heathrow and its cataclysms seem merely decorous. Not only were there more fans than the Beatles had ever seen before: They also made twice the noise. Screaming, they hung over balconies and retaining walls; screaming, they buckled against a one-hundred-man police cordon, oblivious to peril or pain. Blended with the shriek was the shout of photographers, equally possessed, who approached the aircraft clinging to a hydraulic crane. As the Beatles began to descend the steps, a girl on the terminal's third outside level flung herself into space and hung there on the arms of two companions, crying: "Here I am!" Near the bottom step stood the first intelligible New Yorker, a policeman. "Boy," he was heard to remark, "can they use a haircut."

Brian Sommerville, their press officer—who had arrived two days earlier—advanced through the uproar accompanied by Pan Am officials, not the least of whose concerns was to cover up the Beatles' BEAtle inflight bags. As the remaining passengers descended each received from Capitol Records a packet consisting of a photograph, an "I Like the Beatles" badge, and a Beatles wig. The Beatles had by now reached customs, where every item of their luggage was examined. In one direction, several hundred howling girls were chased back by police and security men; the other way, about one thousand more flung and flattened themselves like insects against the plate-glass wall.

On the first floor of the main terminal, where two hundred journalists waited, Brian Sommerville began to show his quarterdeck irascibility. The photographers, massed in front of reporters and TV crews, were making too much noise for any formal question to be heard. Sommerville, after several more or less polite injunctions, grabbed a microphone and snapped: "Shut up—just shut up." The Beatles concurred, "Yeah, shurrup." This produced spontaneous applause.

The New York press, with a few exceptions, succumbed as quickly as the fans. Within minutes, one svelte and sarcastic woman journalist was babbling into a telephone: "They are absolutely too cute for words. America is going to just *love* them." On another line, an agency reporter began his dispatch: "Not since McArthur returned from Korea . . ." Meanwhile, in the conference room, their 198 colleagues continued the interrogation that was supposed to have been ironic and discomfiting but that had produced anything but discomfiture. The Beatles were at their flash-quick, knockabout, impudent best.

"Are you going to have a haircut while you're in America?"

"We had one yesterday," John replied.

"Will you sing something for us?"

"We need money first," John said.

"What's your secret?"

"If we knew that," George said, "we'd each form a group and be managers."

"Was your family in show business?" John was asked.

"Well, me dad used to say me mother was a great performer."

"Are you part of a teenage rebellion against the older generation?"

"It's a dirty lie."

"What do you think of the campaign in Detroit to stamp out the Beatles?"

"We've got a campaign of our own," Paul said, "to stamp out Detroit."

Outside the terminal, four chauffeur-driven Cadillacs waited. The Beatles, ejected rather than emerging from the rear entrance, were each lifted bodily by two policemen and thrust into a Cadillac. Long after they had returned to England their arms would still bear the marks of this helpful assistance. Paul, in addition, had a handful of his hair wrenched by a photographer, to see if it was a wig. "Get out of here, buddy," a policeman told the leading chauffeur, "if you want to get out alive."

Outside the Plaza hotel on Fifth Avenue stretched a sea of screaming teenage humanity on which a squad of mounted policemen bobbed as ineffectually as corks. Reservations had been made a month earlier in the individual names of Lennon, McCartney, Harrison, and Starr, four "London businessmen." At the time, the hotel checked only as far as to ascertain their good financial status. Directly the true nature of their business became known, a Plaza representative went on radio, offering them to any other New York hotel that would take them.

As the four Cadillacs sped in from Kennedy Airport among their weaving and shouting and grimacing motorcade, the Plaza strove valiantly not to capitulate. The Palm Court served tea, as usual, with violin music, though the orchestra leader was vexed to receive requests for Beatles songs. Waiters moved among the pillars and heaped pastries, discreetly requesting the odd errant guest to remove his Beatles wig.

The Beatles and their party had been allocated the hotel's entire twelfth floor. A special force from the Burns Detective Agency was on duty around the clock to screen all arrivals and conduct periodic searches in the floors above, where some female fans had climbed several hundred fire stairs to lie in wait. A bevy of undermanagers ran around, fearful, as well they might be, for the hotel's cherished fabric. When a photographer asked John to lie down on a bed and show his boots, a Plaza man interrupted, "Oh no—*that's* not the image we want to project." "Don't worry," John reassured him. "We'll buy the bed."

Interconnecting suites, ten rooms in all, had been provided for the Beatles, their solitary wife, their two autograph-manufacturing road managers, and their overworked publicist. Only Brian had separate accommodations, on the Central Park side, far away from everyone else.

One of the first to get through the security was Geoffrey Ellis, Brian's old Liverpool friend, the Royal Insurance man. "The whole scene was extremely surrealistic," Ellis says. "The Beatles were all sitting round with transistor radios in their ears, listening to their records playing and watching themselves on television at the same time."

All the evening TV news bulletins carried the airport scenes as top story, though not all expressed unqualified delight. On NBC, Chet Huntley, the celebrated anchorman, quivered with bilious distaste. "Like a good little news organization, we sent three cameramen out this afternoon to cover the arrival of a group from England, known as the Beatles. However, after surveying the film our men returned with, and the subject of that film, I feel there is absolutely no need to show any of that film." A dissident radio station, WNEW, repeatedly observed that "I Want to Hold Your Hand" made some people want to hold their noses.

On every other pop frequency Beatles' voices could be heard, conversing in prerecorded form or as they had spoken a few minutes earlier, live from their hotel suite. Fast-talking disk jockeys found them an easy target, instantly friendly and funny and willing to endorse anything or anyone. The great success in this field was scored by Murray the K Kaufman of station WINS; having first interviewed the Beatles by telephone, he arrived in their suite, accompanied by an entire girl singing group, and was seldom, if ever, got rid of thereafter.

The strain was beginning to tell already on Brian. First, there was a furious dispute with Brian Sommerville over the room arrangements, which ended with Sommerville threatening to resign. Then Brian came into the Beatles' suite, crimson with anger. Among the products they had obligingly endorsed by telephone were several bootleg recordings of their own music, smuggled out of England and now on sale in the New York shops. "Brian screamed at them for what they had done," Dezo Hoffman says. "They listened to him like naughty children. He still had some authority with them then."

Shortly after their arrival George went to bed, complaining of a sore throat. He had been unwell in Paris, too, dictating his *Daily Express* column—as he was to continue to do—without mention of the disconcerting French habit of administering medicines in suppository form. His elder sister, Louise, who had just arrived from St. Louis, moved into the Plaza to nurse him.

The other three, despite the crowds outside, managed some limited after-dark movement. Paul visited the Playboy Club, leaving subsequently with a Playboy Bunny. The Lennons and Ringo, under Murray the K's garrulous protection, went to the Peppermint Lounge, finding it the home of the Twist no longer; its resident group were imitation Beatles. Later, John and Cynthia scuttled back past the photographers, their two heads covered by a coat. Ringo did not return; it was feared for a time that he might have been kidnapped. He returned in the early hours, unaware of the frenzied unease he had caused.

The next morning, it drizzled. Twelve floors below, the crowds and police horses still struggled together in a muted chant of "She Loves You." Brian, in his sequestered drawing room, made a series of urgent telephone calls. The first was to Walter Hofer, the attorney, on West Fifty-seventh Street. Hofer, at this time, was not sure if he was still NEMS's New York lawyer. "Brian told me, 'You're our attorney—we need you over here.' He gave me the job of dealing with all the Beatles' fan mail. I put my usual messenger service to work on it. Later on, I got this call from the messenger. 'Mister—I'm seventy-seven years old! There's thirty-seven sacks of mail here.'

"We set up a special department in another hotel to deal with it. One of the letters that was opened had come from Lyndon B. Johnson. Another was from the manager of the Plaza. 'When are you guys going to settle your check?' it said."

An urgent appeal went to Capitol Records for a temporary secretary to help Brian in New York and travel on with the British entourage to Miami. Through their classical music department Capitol found Wendy Hanson, an imposing blonde who had until recently been personal assistant to Leopold Stokowski. "I had to fight my way into the Plaza through all this pandemonium," Wendy says, "and there, absolutely cut off from it all, was this baby-faced young man, *drenched* in Guerlain. 'Hello, my dear,' were his first words. 'Would you like some tea?' "

The Beatles, meanwhile—minus George—sat in a limousine packed so close among keening girls the chauffeur could get in only by crawling across the roof. John Lennon, in dark glasses and Bob Cratchit cap, was asked if all this bothered him. "No," he replied in all innocence, "it's not our car."

At the Ed Sullivan Theatre on West 53rd Street, a set had been constructed of half a dozen inward-pointing white arrows. The program designer explained to a posse of journalists his desire "to symbolize the fact that the Beatles are *here*." Even for the rehearsal, with Neil Aspinall standing in for George, three high-ranking CBS executives were turned away at the door. Sullivan himself was all amiability, rebuking his musical director for having told the *New York Times* the Beatles would last no longer than a year, and threatening to put on a Beatles wig himself if George was not well enough for the broadcast. He became a little less affable when Brian approached him and said grandly: "I would like to know the exact wording of your introduction." "I would like you to get lost," Ed Sullivan replied.

The *Ed Sullivan Show* on February 9 was watched by an audience of 70 million, or 60 percent of all American television viewers. At the beginning, a congratulatory telegram was read from Elvis Presley. Conditioned as they were to hyperunreality, this event still gave pause to Liverpool boys who had listened to "Hound Dog" under the bedclothes, and struggled to learn the words of "All Shook Up" as it was beamed from its inconceivable heaven.

For a generation of young Americans, only weeks after the Dallas horror, it would be another—but infinitely happier—moment fixed forever in their memories. And, whether their destiny was to turn into famous pop stars, film directors, industrial magnates, politicians and even presidents, or simply suburban dads and moms, the same image would be eternally etched on their memories, its slightly distorted monochrome image and warbly sound quality somehow enhancing the rush of incredulous delight. Not only New York, the Bronx, Brooklyn, New Jersey, and Queens, but Chicago, Philadelphia, Washington, Pittsburgh, San Francisco, and Los Angeles, the snowbound Midwest, the Southern swamps and bayous, and the far-western prairies, all succumbed to the same instant, laughing adoration of those four little, jiggling figures with their shiny suits, preposterous hair, and indefatigable smiles. Like some rare entomological specimen, each Beatle was given a subtitle bearing his name. John's caption said "Sorry girls—he's married."

The *New York Herald Tribune*, next morning, called them "75 per cent publicity, 20 per cent haircut and 5 per cent lilting lament." The *Washington Post* called them "asexual and homely." The *New York Times* carried reviews by both the television and the music critic. The former judged the Beatles "a fine mass placebo" while the latter, anxious to out-obfuscate William Mann, discovered in "All My Loving" "a false modal frame . . . momentarily suggesting the mixolydian mode." Earl Wilson, the *New York Post* columnist, was photographed at the head of his afternoon's paragraphs in a bald wig. From UPI came the news that Billy Graham, the evangelist, had broken a lifetime's rule by watching television on the sabbath.

On that one night America's crime rate was lower than at any time during the previous half-century. Police precinct houses throughout New York could testify to the sudden drop in juvenile offenses. In all the five boroughs not one single car hubcap was reported stolen.

The nervous plans, the small-scale hopes, the little deals for cut-rate fees all coalesced in a moment that was miraculously right. America, three months earlier, had been struck dumb by a great and terrible event. America now found her voice again through an event that no psychiatrist could have made more therapeutically trivial. That voice was in itself therapeutic, reassuring a suddenly uncertain people that at least they had not lost their old talent for excess.

It was a moment when the potential existed for a madness that nothing indigenously American could unleash. It was a moment when all America's deep envy of Europe, and the eccentricity permitted to older established nations, crystallized in four figures whose hair and clothes, to American eyes, placed them somewhere near Shakespeare's Hamlet. It was a moment simultaneously gratifying America's need for a new idol, a new toy, a pain-killing drug, and a laugh.

On the morning after the *Ed Sullivan Show* the Beatles were brought to the Plaza Hotel's Baroque Room to give a press conference that was itself record-breaking, both in size and fatuousness. Even superior organs like *Time* magazine and *The New Yorker* stiffened themselves to the task of determining whether Beatle hair was correctly described as bangs and their footwear as pixie boots. The *Saturday Evening Post* had sent a photographer with one hundred thousand dollars' worth of equipment to shoot a cover. The *New York Journal-American* had sent Dr. Joyce Brothers, a psychologist with flicked-out blonde hair and her own television show. Dr. Brothers had her pulse humorously taken by the Beatles and afterward reminded her readers that "Beatles might look unappetizing and inconsequential, but naturalists have long considered them the most successful order of animals on earth."

However patronizing, insulting, or plain clueless the question, the answer would be the same disarming mixture of angel-faced politeness and needle-sharp wit. As well as new music, the Beatles were inventing what would one day be known as sound bites. "Either they're employing the most marvellous concealed gag man," Maureen Cleave cabled the *London Evening Standard*, "or Bob Hope should sign them up right away."

"What do you think of the Playboy Club?" Paul was asked.

"The Playboy and I are just good friends."

"Why aren't you wearing a tie?" a woman journalist snapped at George.

"Why aren't *you* wearing a hat?" he fired back.

The inquisition continued all day, without a break for lunch. Instead, some plates of hotel chicken were brought in. "I'm sorry to interrupt you while you're eating," a woman reporter said, "but what do you think you'll be doing in five years' time?"

"Still eating," John replied.

"Have you got a leading lady for your movie?"

"We're trying to get the Queen," George said. "She sells."

"When do you start rehearsing?"

"We don't," John said.

"—oh yes we do," Paul put in.

"We don't, Paul does," John amended. Some papers had already discovered the fact that among the other three, Paul was referred to as "the star."

The American press, in its wild scramble, paid little attention to the other young Englishman, in a polka-dotted foulard scarf, who stood at one side, observing the scene with what the *New York Times* described as "a look of hauteur." Even when Jay Livingstone—the same Capitol boss who had said, "We don't think the Beatles will do anything in this market"—stepped beamingly forward to present them with two million-sale gold records, Brian still did not allow himself the relaxation of a smile. "He had ice water in his veins before," another Capitol man remarked. "Now it's turned to vinegar."

Actually Brian's "hauteur"—like the seeming cool imperturbability with which he had greeted Wendy Hanson—was nothing but a front. A far more accurate index to his feelings were his frequent mysterious bursts of weeping or the furious, red-faced rows he kept having with Brian Sommerville. For the ever-increasing size and fury of the Beatles' American hurricane only made Brian more and more aware of his inability to manage it.

For example, he had presumed that the only Beatles records available to their new American fans would be the brand-new product on Capitol. But, inevitably, the other U.S. labels that had released Beatles' songs when they were nobodies now hastened to cash in on their success. The Chicago Vee Jay label, which had grudgingly put out "Please Please Me" a year earlier, rereleased it, and within a day saw it rocket to number three. The MGM label even got hold of "My Bonnie," which the Beatles had recorded long ago in Hamburg as "the Beat Brothers" with Tony Sheridan. These unauthorized, but genuine, Beatles releases were bad enough, blocking the ascent of official Capitol releases up the charts and earning almost nothing in royalties, but even worse were the number of counterfeit Beatles groups—known as "Beetles" or "Bugs"—already recording and being bought by fans by mistake for the genuine article. One unscrupulous producer had even talked his way into the Beatles' suite and tricked them into taping an endorsement for his particular poor facsimile of themselves.

Only now, too, was Brian starting to realize what a catastrophic deal had been made on his behalf with Nicky Byrne's Seltaeb merchandising company. In the aftermath of the *Ed Sullivan Show,* Beatles goods were pouring into the New York shops. REMCO industries had already produced one hundred thousand Beatles dolls. Beatles wigs were flopping off the production line at the rate of thirty-five thousand a day. The overindulged American child could choose from a range including Beatles masks, pens, bow ties, "Flip Your Wig" games, edible disks, and Beatle nut ice cream. Agreement was reportedly pending between Seltaeb and a major cola company. Woolworth's and Penney's were negotiating to put "Beatles counters" in hundreds of their stores, coast to coast. The *Wall Street Journal* estimated that by the end of the year $5 million worth of Beatles goods would have been sold in America.

Nor was it reassuring to observe the progress around New York of the man whose company's share of the profits would be 90 percent. For Nicky Byrne did business on a magnificent scale. His lunches took place at the Four Seasons or the New York Jockey Club. He had two chauffeur-driven limousines, on twenty-four-hour standby, and a private helicopter. His style quickly communicated itself to the five young men from Chelsea who were his partners. Lord Peregrine Eliot has pleasant memories of dropping into the Seltaeb office once or twice a week to draw a thousand-dollar bill from petty cash.

Nicky Byrne argued—and still argues—that it was the only way to do business with large American corporations. He is equally firm on a point later to be disputed—that as the money in manufacturers' advances poured into Seltaeb, the 10 percent due to Brian and the Beatles was paid over to them within seven days.

"When Brian arrived in New York, I'd just banked ninety-seven thousand dollars. So, of course, I handed a check to Brian for nine thousand seven hundred dollars. He was delighted at first. 'Now,' he said, 'how much of this do I owe you?' 'Nothing, Brian,' I said. 'That's your 10 percent.' He was amazed and furious all at the same time. 'But this is *marvelous*, Nicky,' he was saying—because he'd been told I'd fixed the airport business. 'How did you *do* it, Nicky—but you had no *right* to do it! But it was marvelous, Nicky.' "

Having proved his talents as a fixer with the Kennedy Airport crowds, Byrne remained on hand throughout the tour, pushing Beatles records on the radio—at one point, he claims, even buying off a photographer who had obtained some pictures of Brian in his secret gay life and was threatening to make them public.

"Brian said, 'You must work for *me*, Nicky—I'll make you a president, I'll give you a thousand a year.' I said, 'A thousand a year? Oh come *on*, Brian.' Then all of a sudden I realized he was crazy."

On February 11, the Beatles were to fly to Washington to give their first American concert, at the Coliseum sports arena. The booking had been made for Brian by Norman Weiss, of the General Artists Corporation, to help offset the loss on the overall trip. Brian had also accepted an invitation from the British ambassador to a function as yet unclearly defined. "Is it true," the press kept asking them, "that you're going to a masked ball?" By coincidence, Sir Alec Douglas Home, who had succeeded Macmillan as Britain's prime minister, was also due in Washington for talks with Kennedy's successor, Lyndon Johnson. On hearing of the Beatles' imminent arrival in D.C., Sir Alec wisely postponed his own until the day afterward.

The morning of their departure snow began falling thickly on New York. Led by George, the Beatles flatly refused to fly in a "fookin' blizzard." They were, however, amenable to traveling by train. A private carriage was sought, and miraculously appeared in the magnificent shape of an Edwardian sleeping car from the old Richmond, Fredericksburg, and Potomac Railroad. This equipment drew out of a shrieking Pennsylvania Station, carrying, with the Beatles and their entourage, dozens of journalists, several TV crews, and the egregious Murray the K. Cynthia Lennon, disguised by sunglasses and a brunette wig, was almost left behind on the platform.

At Washington's Union Station, three thousand teenagers flung themselves against the 20-foot-high wrought-iron platform gates. Seven thousand more filled the Coliseum, an arena with the stage in the center, like a boxing ring. While the Beatles performed Brian Sommerville had to keep running out to turn them in a different direction. The Washington fans, having read George Harrison's joke about liking jelly babies, resolutely pelted the stage with America's version, the jelly bean—often not troubling to remove them from the packet—as well as buttons, hair rollers, and spent flashbulbs. A policeman near the stage philosophically screwed a .38-caliber bullet into each of his ears. And Brian Epstein, once again, was noticed standing and weeping.

The British embassy visit had been arranged by Brian Sommerville, an old shipmate of the naval attaché there. The Beatles agreed to go only because Brian thought it would be good for the image. Upon arriving, they were greeted by the ambassador, Sir David Ormsby-Gore, pleasantly enough. What followed was extremely unpleasant, though not atypical of foreign office social life. Men in stiff collars and their gin and tonic wives pushed and struggled for autographs, at the same time exclaiming in patrician amusement, "Can they actually *write*?" One cawing female produced nail scissors and cut off a piece of Ringo's hair. The purpose of this visit, they discovered, was to announce the prizes in an embassy raffle. When John Lennon demurred, a group of young F.O. types formed threateningly around him. Ringo, touching his shoulder, said pacifically, "Come on—let's get it over with."

The story, when reported in the British press, caused a major parliamentary incident. A Conservative MP, Joan Quennell, called on the foreign secretary, R. A. Butler, to confirm or deny that the Beatles had been manhandled by embassy personnel. Mr. Butler replied that, on the contrary, the Beatles' manager had written to Lady Ormsby-Gore "thanking her for a delightful evening."

At the White House, meanwhile, Sir Alec Douglas Home had arrived for his talks with President Lyndon Johnson. The Beatles in fact largely helped break the ice between a big, folksy Texan and a tweedy, skeletal Scottish earl who otherwise might have found small talk difficult. "I like your advance guard," Johnson quipped. "But don't you think they need haircuts?"

And in New York, the promoter Sid Bernstein sat on the staircase at Carnegie Hall, listening to an uproar that made even the framed portraits of Schubert and Ravel jiggle slightly on the corridor wall. His phenomenon, mistaken by that Polish lady for a string quartet, had in one night recouped for Sid Bernstein the losses suffered in promoting the 1960 Newport Jazz Festival. Celebrities like David Niven and Shirley MacLaine had unsuccessfully begged him for tickets to the Beatles' Carnegie Hall concerts. Mrs. Nelson Rockefeller, with her two daughters, had waited half an hour just for a peep into the dressing room.

"After the second concert," Bernstein says, "I walked with Brian across to Madison Square Garden. We looked inside the old Garden arena. Seventeen thousand seats. I knew the Garden wanted the Beatles; they could have had tickets printed in twenty-four hours. I offered Brian twenty-five thousand dollars and a five-thousand-dollar donation to the British Cancer Fund. I knew he was tempted. But he gave me that little smile he had. 'Sid,' he said, 'let's save it for next time.'

Brian Epstein as he most wanted to be: urbane, relaxed, a successful leading man. His giveaway fan picture for 1964 gives no sign of what disquiet already gnawed at his dazzling success.

The first mad flush of Beatle merchandise, from socks and soap to crayons, rugs and Ringo Roll. In America, the bonanza was ten times larger, earning millions of dollars that the Beatles never saw.

The Beatles leap, yet again, for Press cameras during rehearsals for the Royal Variety Show. Brian, extreme right, waits on tenterhooks.

Beatlemania, 1964: a madness newly-diagnosed, with an underlying good humour that would last for several years.

Refined by Brian Epstein from a Liverpool Art student's clothes and a Hamburg girl's hairdressing scissors: the image that at last seized and besotted the world.

The fans wanted their heroes mapped inch by inch.

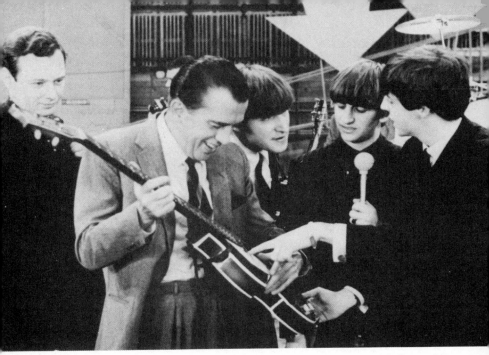

February 1964: with Ed Sullivan in New York. 'I would like you to get lost,' Sullivan told Brian.

March, 1964: with Harold Wilson – 'Mr Dobson', as John called him – at the Variety Club awards. The crafty Socialist has already hit on his vote-winning secret.

Allan Williams

Bob Wooler

Bruno Koschmider

Bill Harry

Cynthia Lennon

Tony Sheridan

Neil Aspinall

Mal Evans

Peter Brown

Derek Taylor

George Martin

Dick James

Jane Asher

David Jacobs

Maureen Starr

Pattie Harrison

Maharishi Mahesh Yogi

Linda Eastman

Yoko Ono

Allen Klein

Brian, ever the best man, at Ringo's wedding to Maureen Cox, and George's to Pattie
Boyd. He had done the same for John and Cynthia in 1962.

Brian, at unaccustomed ease, backstage during the '65 American tour that included the Shea Stadium triumph. 'It couldn't have happened that way for anyone else . . . it only happened because it was Brian Epstein's fantasy.'

Brian, in an airport lounge, draws up the playing-order. 'A fragile bond of memos and lists . . .

After the Investiture, 1965: the Beatles deliver MB quips, watched by Brian and their constant courtier Neil and Ma

John with Julian at Kenwood, 1966: the Nowhere Man, still afraid to break out of the palace.

John with George Martin listening to the Sergea Pepper playback: acid-drenched, sparkling visions fro his voyage through LS

1968: Pilgrims at Rishikesh with their mirthful guru. The group also includes Mia Farrow and Donovan. Daily competitions were held to see who could meditate longest.

George with his new master, Ravi Shankar: dazzled by India's mysticism, seeing none of its equally vast mundaneness.

3 Savile Row London W.1.

John and Yoko's last stand at Apple, the ground floor front office. Here Yoko said that when John showed a film of his penis, 'the critics wouldn't touch it.'

The Georgian town house where Apple's empire rose and rotted. The 'vibes' made it first glow rosily, then turn pale with fear.

April, 1969: Pipe-puffing, statesmanlike, Allen Klein tries to reassure the City about his involvement with the Beatles' Northern Songs takeover bid. The Press conference, one paper said, 'must have set some kind of record for unprintable language . . .'

Linda with Paul, Yoko with John: an infrequent, uneasy quartet. Ringo does his best to keep up the conversation.

1969: The Two Virgins, unashamed, unabashed, undefeated. John has found a partner he needs more than he needs Paul McCartney.

1969: Paul marries Linda on a bleak day for the young women of the western world.

January, 1969: The cold, chaotic Apple rooftop session. 'Four musicians playing as no four ever would again.

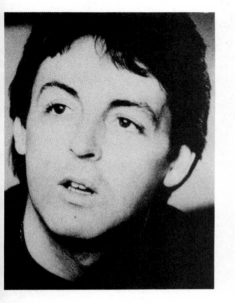

The aftermath: a multimillionaire businessman . . .' 'a landed gentleman hippy . . .'
'Ringo, invulnerably Ringo . . .'

Overleaf: John, with Yoko in New York two
weeks before his death: 'our love is still
special . . .'

Next morning, the police barricades were removed from the front of the Plaza Hotel; its elegant lobby grew quiet but for the headlines on the newsstand counter. "Britain's Boy Beatles Buzz By, Bomb Bobbysoxers." "Audience Shrieks, Bays and Ululates." A large sum of money, which CBS had paid into the hotel for the use of the Beatles party, was found to be untouched. Nobody even knew it was there.

The Beatles were aboard a National Airlines jet bound for Miami and their second *Ed Sullivan Show,* their course to the southwest plotted by a flight engineer in a Beatles wig. On landing, they were greeted by a crowd of seven thousand who smashed twenty-three windows and glass doors inside the terminal building.

At the hotel, each Beatle was decanted into his own lofty, luxurious, three-room prison cell. For the Deauville, like the New York Plaza, was in a state of screaming siege. Two enterprising girls had themselves wrapped in two parcels addressed to the Beatles, but were apprehended before they could be delivered.

George Martin, who happened to be in America on a business trip, came to see them in Miami, bringing his wife-to-be, Judy Lockhart-Smith. Martin watched the Beatles rehearse in bathing trunks in the hotel ballroom, and later repay Ed Sullivan's $3,500 with a performance destined to break every record in audience ratings for televised entertainment. So far as such things can ever be computed, 75 million Americans watched the *Ed Sullivan Show* that night. During the broadcast, from the hotel's Mau Mau Club, a girl next to George Martin broke off sobbing and bouncing to stare at him in surprise. "Do *you* like them, *too*, sir?" she asked.

Another widely oversubscribed photo opportunity took place at the 5th Street Gymnasium where Cassius Clay—still some years from renaming himself Muhammed Ali and embracing Islam—was in training for his impending World Heavyweight title fight against Sonny Liston. Even John could not compete with the loose-limbed young giant whose every word defied America's unwritten rule that even famous black people must conduct themselves with slavish self-effacement. The Beatles pretended to spar with Clay for the camera and smiled complicitly when he gave his so-quotable verdict that they might be "the greatest" but he was still "the prettiest." Long-suffering Ringo even found himself picked up and flourished aloft by the soon-to-be champ.

Their only escape from the crowds and press was a day spent at the beach-side mansion of a Capitol Records executive. Sergeant Buddy Bresner, a Miami cop who had befriended them, arranged for them to escape from the Deauville in the back of a butcher's truck while other policemen brought decoy guitar cases out through the front lobby.

George Martin and Judy joined them for that first real respite since they had sunbathed on the seafront at Margate. Brian was there, too, with his temporary assistant, Wendy Hanson. The householder, though absent, had left an armed bodyguard to look after them. Their protector barbecued steaks for them with a cigarette in his mouth, his shoulder holster clearly visible. "Brian was complaining about all the bootleg records that were coming out," George Martin remembers. "Suddenly, this tough-looking guy who was barbecuing our steaks leaned forward and said: 'You want we should take care of them for you, Mr. Epstein?' It was a *very* sinister moment."

PART THREE

HAVING

THIRTEEN

"ONE MORE STAGE, ONE MORE LIMO, ONE MORE RUN FOR YOUR LIFE"

The scene is an oak-paneled room deep in the hallowed precincts of an ancient and illustrious Oxford college. Before the open fire stands the principal, an elderly gentleman both scholar and diplomat, conversing in mellifluous undertone with his junior dons and one or two of his most favored students. A cold buffet supper, garnished by the rarest wines from the college cellars, is attended by white-jacketed servants. From a distance, through the historic courtyards and cloisters, a clock may be heard, civilly striking the hour.

The fifteenth-century oak door opens—to admit the Beatles. They are wearing, as always, dark suits, deep-collared shirts, and boots with elasticated sides. Their manner, as they meet the college principal, the tutors and undergraduates, is deferential yet impudent. A servant offers Paul McCartney champagne in a silver goblet: Paul says he would rather have milk. George Harrison surveys the spread of smoked salmon and beef filet buffet, then beckons to a retainer. "Have you got any jam butties?" he asks. "I'll trade you an autograph for a jam butty."

The scene comes not from *A Hard Day's Night* but from life. It happened at Brasenose College in March 1964 arranged by a still unknown self-publicist named Jeffrey Archer. It is recorded in the *Daily Mail*, in a vast picture spread and a story running to three columns. Nothing evokes more powerfully Britain's mood in early 1964 than the *Mail*'s hyperbolic triumph at this coup; its writer's mixture of jocular indulgence and history-witnessing earnestness.

The Beatles were no longer a teenage fad: They had become a national obsession. Far from self-destructing in the way everyone had predicted, their fame somehow fed on its own freakishness, passing more and still more previous limits of celebrity.

Anyone, in however unrelated and elevated a sphere, could command instant attention simply by mentioning their name. The usually rarified *New Statesman* published an editorial headed "The Menace of Beatledom." The literary peer Lord Willis denounced them as "a cheap candy-floss culture-substitute"—as if his own television creations such as *Dixon of Dock Green* had not been precisely that. In his regular Sunday soapbox orations at Hyde Park Corner, the Methodist cleric-peer Lord Soper asked, "In what aspect of the full life of the Kingdom of God can we find a place for the Beatles?" Even royalty was beginning to recognize them as a national asset on a par with—well, royalty. The Duke of Edinburgh, in an address to a youth conference, called them "good blokes." Buckingham Palace even let it be known that an American fan had written to the Queen, congratulating her on having John, Paul, George, and Ringo among her subjects. A lady-in-waiting had written back, regretting "that it is impossible for the Queen to tell you how to get in touch with them."

The Variety Club of Great Britain named them, collectively, Show Business Personality of the Year. Wax effigies of them in their round-collar shirts were put on show among world leaders and film stars at Madame Tussaud's. They became an entry in the *Encyclopaedia Britannica*. It was all like a game, played with the roguish connivance of ancient institutions, to see in what unlikely surroundings the Beatles would turn up next, unawed by any grandeur, disarming the pomp of ages with a request for a jam butty.

In April, a literary luncheon, more heavily subscribed than any that Foyle's bookshop had run since the age of Shaw and H. G. Wells, commemorated John Lennon's entry into authorship. The little drawings and verses he used to doodle under his Quarry Bank desk—and still did at odd moments backstage—appeared as a slim volume entitled *John Lennon In His Own Write*. It was, said the *Times Literary Supplement*, "worth the study of anyone who fears for the impoverishment of the English language." Other critics saw, in the book's myopically mispronounced, punning fragments, the influence of Edward Lear and James Joyce. "Do you," a radio interviewer asked John, "make conscious use of onomatopoeia?" "Automatic pier?" John echoed. "I haven't the faintest idea what you're talking about."

It was thought shocking, but forgivably so, when the Foyle's luncheon received no speech from the guest of honor. John, who arrived with Cynthia, deeply hungover after a night at the Ad Lib, had not realized he was supposed to say anything. Urged to his feet, he could only mumble, "Thank you. It's been a pleasure." An obliging press translated this into the more Beatlelike: "You've got a lucky face."

The Mersey Sound pumped out by George Martin from Abbey Road studios represented a mere fraction of the teen music from far-flung British locations that now filled the charts, sometimes under names that made "Beatles" look positively conventional. There was also a "Manchester Sound," spearheaded by the Hollies, whose spiraling harmonies were analyzed by musicologists with almost the same earnestness as the Beatles' own. There was a Tyneside Sound, spear-headed by the Animals and their epic-length version of an old bordello-blues number, "The House of the Rising Sun." There was a Birmingham Sound, spearheaded by the Applejacks, a Scottish Sound, spearheaded by Lulu and the Luvvers and the Poets, an Irish Sound, spearheaded by Them, featuring the young (but never youthful-looking) Van Morrison.

London and the south, meanwhile, fought back to regain their old cultural ascendancy with a Shepherds Bush Mod group called the High Numbers, soon to be transmogrified into The Who; with Soho blues stars like Georgie Fame; and with a thousand and one eager young R&B bands from which would eventually emerge Eric Clapton, Elton John, and Rod Stewart.

Ironically, the group destined to become the Beatles' greatest rivals owed their start to the Liverpudlians' native friendliness and generosity. On the day of their Variety Club awards back in 1963 John and Paul had been riding through Soho in a taxi when they spotted Brian's erstwhile teenage publicist, Andrew Loog Oldham, walking along with a preoccu-pied frown on his face. Oldham had gone on to manage his Richmond discoveries, the Rolling Stones, after Brian passed on them. But, to his disappointment, they had so far failed to make themselves—and him—rich by writing their own songs à la Beatles.

Their first release, a cover version of Chuck Berry's "Come On," had barely registered in the charts. At this very moment Oldham had just left them at a club in Great Newport Street, vainly arguing about what to record as a follow-up. Overcome with frustration and annoyance, their young manager had gone out for a breath of fresh air—and the first people he happened to meet were John Lennon and Paul McCart-ney. "The conversation really did go like this," Oldham recalls. "''ello, Andy. You're looking unhappy. What's the matter?' 'Oh, I'm fed up. The

Stones can't find a song to record.' 'Oh—*we've* got a song we've almost written. The Stones can have that to record if yer like.'"

The song was "I Wanna Be Your Man," a tongue-in-cheek blast of R&B destined to be sung by Ringo on the *With the Beatles* album. With an obligingness Oldham still marvels at to this day, John and Paul turned their taxi around, accompanied him back to the Stones' rehearsal room, and finished off the song so that the Stones could record it with minimum delay. One can read it as kindliness or as hard-hearted opportunism, since John and Paul at this point both saw their ultimate destiny as songwriters rather than performers. Like so many early Lennon-McCartney songs, "I Wanna Be Your Man" proved wonderfully adaptable to non-Beatles treatment, in this case providing a perfect frame for Mick Jagger's sneery punk voice and Brian Jones's palpitant slide guitar. By December 1963, it was headed for the U.K. Top Ten and the Stones were off the launchpad at last.

This huge glut of pop had long ago proved too much for the British Broadcasting Corporation, whose music radio output remained limited to a few strictly controlled slots on what it still rather condescendingly called the Light Programme. Now, that hitherto impregnable bastion of the Establishment was also to be challenged. The challenger was a young Irish entrepreneur named Ronan O'Rahilly, a colorful figure around the London scene well known to Brian Epstein and the Beatles. On Easter Day 1964, O'Rahilly's pirate station, Radio Caroline, began transmitting continuous pop, with slick American-style disk jockeys and jingles, from a small ship anchored outside Britain's territorial limits, beyond the jurisdiction of the Wireless Telegraphy Act that enshrined the BBC's radio monopoly. The public's response to getting what it, rather than the Light Programme, wanted was instantaneous. Radio Caroline won a huge listenership and gave the signal for a whole armada of rival pirate stations to begin operation from various offshore moorings as far north as the mouth of the River Clyde.

On pirate wavelengths, as everywhere, the Beatles were preeminent. Their new single, "Can't Buy Me Love," had become the first record ever to go to number one simultaneously in Britain and America, and that before a note of it had been heard. Advance orders from America alone exceeded three million copies.

Their first film had been shot during the six weeks between their return from America and their departure on a tour of Europe and the Far

East. Rather than confecting an artificial plot, their scriptwriter Alun Owen had sensibly opted to show them just as they were, four astonished lads perpetually on the run, with seasoned British comedy actors in supporting roles like Norman Rossington as Norm, their manager, and Wilfred Brambell, from television's top sitcom *Steptoe and Son*, as Paul's grandfather. Owen's script largely reproduced the four's own private badinage, with an unacknowledged steal from W. S. Gilbert in the running joke about Brambell being "a clean old gentleman." Location filming took place in north London, in installments rarely lasting longer than about ten minutes. "Wherever we set up, the word would instantly get out that the Beatles were there," director Richard Lester remembers. "After about three takes, we'd all have to run for our lives."

Within this simple formula Lester managed to give the film both the gritty honesty of working-class dramas like *Saturday Night and Sunday Morning* and the surreal artiness of something French or Italian. In its most memorable sequence, aboard an old-fashioned British Railways corridor train, the Beatles played "I Should Have Known Better" inside the guard's van's metal cage—first to an audience of glamorous gym-slipped schoolgirls, then as a soundtrack to their own private card game. Lester's history with the Goons' *Running, Jumping, Standing Still Film* also came to the fore in a speeded-up comedy sequence recalling Mack Sennett's silent-movie *Keystone Kops*. Escaping their pent-up life, the Beatles gamboled onto an open sports field and began to hold imaginary running and sack races. Not even Cliff Richard had presented so pure an image of pop-star innocence.

The film was supposed to have been called *Beatlemania*. Then, at the last minute, a far better and more Beatle-like title offered itself in a favorite phrase of Ringo Starr's. Whenever a round of performing, recording, partying, and fleeing from fans had been particularly crazy, Ringo, in an unconscious paraphrase of Eugene O'Neill, would say it had been "a hard day's night." The eponymous album that came with the film was the first to consist entirely of Lennon-McCartney compositions, including "If I Fell," "I'm Happy Just to Dance With You," "I Should Have Known Better" (with "yeah yeah yeah" mutating into "hey hey hey") and the title track with its gloriously long and irrelevant guitar coda. The material had mostly been written months earlier, between *crêpes flambées* at the George V. Yet the album evoked the film, just as the film caught Beatlemania at its maddest and happiest.

The film received a West End premiere in July, attended by Princess Margaret and her photographer husband, Lord Snowdon. "There was a big party afterward," Walter Shenson says. "Nobody thought that Princess Margaret would agree to come to it, so no one invited her. I said we should at least *ask*. It turned out that she and Lord Snowdon had an engagement for dinner but that they'd love to be asked to stop in for a drink first.

"We were all in the anteroom, having drinks before going in to the food. George Harrison gave me a look and whispered: When do we eat? I told him, We can't until Princess Margaret leaves." She and Lord Snowdon had this other engagement but they stayed longer and longer at the Beatles' party, having drinks, chatting. Finally George went across to Princess Margaret and said, 'Ma'am—we're starved, and Walter says we can't eat until you leave.' Princess Margaret just burst out laughing. 'Come on, Tony,' she called out. 'We're in the way.'"

A second premiere took place in Liverpool, accompanied by a civic welcome from the lord mayor. "The Beatles were nervous wrecks about that," Walter Shenson says. "Even though they'd just come back from a world tour, they were scared about that appearance in Liverpool. "Ah," they kept saying, "you don't know what people are like up there."

They drove in from Speke Airport, along the same Woolton avenues where Paul used to cycle with his guitar on his back, and where John would struggle along with the Quarry Men, carrying a tea chest. All the way, between bus stops, crowds stood waving and cheering. Paul, to his particular pleasure, recognized Dusty Durband, his English teacher from the Institute. And there, beyond what used to be Uncle George's dairy, was the red sandstone tower of St. Peter's, where the annual fete would soon be held.

There was a civic reception at the Town Hall, then the four former black-leather troglodytes from Mathew Street emerged onto the balcony with the lord mayor and other dignitaries to wave to the cheering throng below. Unbeknown to them, and the adoring media, the crowd was not composed entirely of well-wishers. A few hours earlier Brian Epstein had heard that leaflets were circulating throughout Liverpool naming a Beatle as the father of a young child recently born to one of their Cavern Club seraglio. Helped by his brother, Clive, Brian had tracked down the claimants and managed to buy their silence.

·   ·   ·

It was the year they conquered the world, but did not see it. For them the world shrank to a single dressing room, buried under continents of screaming. More than once, on their zigzag flight down back alleys between the hemispheres, they would ask which country this was. "It all looked the same to them," Tony Bramwell says. "One more stage, one more limo, one more run for your life."

In June they toured Scandinavia, Holland, the Far East, and Australasia. Ringo Starr was having his tonsils out and missed three-quarters of the journey; in his place sat Jimmy Nicol, a session drummer small and obscure enough to scotch any rumor of permanent change. Nicol drummed with them until Melbourne, where Ringo rejoined. History from then on relates nothing further of Jimmy Nicol.

Among the entourage for the tour's Far East and Australian segment was John's aunt Mimi. In Hong Kong, the police cleared a path for her, crying, "John Mama, John Mama." The sight of Adelaide and three hundred thousand fans, the largest Beatles crowd ever, proved too much for Mimi's nerves: After glimpsing New Zealand she flew home to Woolton. "I got into trouble," Mimi said, "for telling an Australian TV man that John used to be bad at arithmetic when he was at school. So, on TV, this man said to him, 'If you're bad at maths, how do you count all that money you're earning?' 'I don't count it,' John said. 'I weigh it.'"

In August, they returned to America to find Beatlemania so rampant as to make the British and European variety seem muted by comparison. At one point in April the first five places in *Billboard* magazine's Top 100 records were Beatles records. *A Hard Day's Night,* opening in five hundred cinemas across the country, had earned $1.3 million in its first week. Cinema showings were accompanied by as much screaming as a live concert.

The Beatles, traveling in their own private Lockheed Electra, performed in twenty-three cities, crossing and recrossing American air space on a journey totalling 22,441 miles, or more than 600 miles per day. At times they did not know if they were in Jacksonville, Baltimore, Denver, Cincinnati, Detroit, or Atlantic City. Everywhere, there were mayors and senators and senators' wives and sheriffs and deputies; there were the town's most exclusive call girls; there were handicapped children, lined up in wheelchairs near the stage, and later brought into the Beatles' dressing room as if to see or touch them might work a Lourdes-like miracle. The sight always filled John with horror, awakening the fear of disability and disfigurement he had always tried to sublimate by pulling village-idiot faces and shambling around like the hunchback of Notre Dame. In the four's private language, long before political correctness outlawed such words, "cripple" came to mean anyone in the dressing room who was making themself unwelcome. A murmur of "Cripples, Neil" to their roadie would be the signal for the room to be unceremoniously cleared, to their own seeming regret.

In San Francisco, at the Hilton Hotel, a woman guest was robbed and pistol-whipped, her cries unheard in the noise greeting the Beatles' motorcade. At Love Field, Dallas, fans broke through the police barrier, climbed onto the aircraft wings, and belabored the windows with Coke bottles. Later at the hotel a chambermaid was kidnapped and threatened with a knife unless she revealed the location of the Beatles' suite; other girls had to be rescued from the air-conditioning shaft. In Los Angeles, the postconcert escape plan featured an armored truck, all four tires of which proved to be flat. In Seattle, as the Beatles left the stage, a girl fell from an overhead girder, landing at Ringo's feet. In Cleveland, they were physically dragged offstage while mounted police charged the arena, lassoing two hundred fans together in a giant net. In New York, the whole of Riverside Drive was cordoned off for their passing; in Toronto, they came in from the airport at 3:00 A.M., past seventeen miles of continuous parked cars. Each day the madness differed yet remained the same. It was cops and sweat and jelly beans hailing in dreamlike noise; it was faces uglied by shrieking and biting fists; it was huge amphitheaters left littered with flashbulbs and hair rollers and buttons and badges and hundreds of pairs of knickers, wringing wet.

Out of the itinerary of chaos, a single figure came to personify that '64 American tour. His name was Charles O. Finley; he owned a baseball team, the Kansas City Athletics. He first approached Brian Epstein in San Francisco, offering one hundred thousand dollars if the Beatles would give an additional concert at his baseball stadium in Kansas City. He said he had promised Kansas City they would have the Beatles. Brian replied that the tour could not be extended.

Charles O. Finley did not give up. He reappeared in various other cities, increasing his offer by degrees to $150,000 if the Beatles would let him keep his promise to Kansas City. At length, in Seattle, as it became clear to Brian and Norman Weiss that the tour might not quite cover its gigantic overheads, Charles O. Finley and Kansas City took on a new significance. It was up to the Beatles, Brian said, and whether they were willing to sacrifice one of their few rest days. The Beatles, playing cards with George Harrison of the *Liverpool Echo,* said they would leave it up to Brian. So, at the rate of £1,785 per minute, Charles O. Finley and Kansas City were not disappointed.

In New York, a brisk sale was reported in canned Beatles' breath. In Denver, the bed linen they had used at two stopover hotels was bought by a business consortium and placed, unlaundered, in a maximum security bank vault. The sheets were cut into three-inch squares and sold at ten dollars per square, each one mounted on parchment and accompanied by a legal affadavit swearing it to have once formed part of a Beatle's bed.

John Lennon started to put on weight. The face, under the Beatles fringe and the mocking, shortsighted eyes, grew rounder—more contented, so Cynthia hopefully thought. Cyn did not know what happened on tour, nor did she want to know. When she read the letters John received from girls, she laughed them off as he did, doing her best to mean it. She hoped that between tours he would settle down to his unenforced obligations as husband and father. And for a time, that did seem to please him—just staying in at night after Julian was asleep, smoking, reading, doodling, endlessly playing the same Bob Dylan records.

Paul McCartney was more and more often to be seen escorting Jane Asher to Belgravia parties and West End first nights. It clearly gave him huge satisfaction that Jane was not only a classy bird but also now becoming a celebrity in her own right as a stage and film actress and a panelist on television's *Juke Box Jury.* With her tumbling red hair and his cheeky Beatles grin, they made a perfect couple and seemed totally wrapped up in each other—unless some big star appeared on the horizon to divert Paul's attention. "Paul and Jane came out to a dinner party with my wife and me one night," Walter Shenson said. "Joan Sutherland, the opera singer, just happened to be there. Paul zeroed in on her at once. He left Jane with me and my wife and stayed talking to Joan for the rest of the evening."

George Harrison had begun dating Patti Boyd, a nineteen-year-old model with a quirky, gap-toothed smile who had played one of the schoolgirl nymphets in *A Hard Day's Night.* Pale and waiflike, Patti was the archetype of 1964 high fashion. She now became an object of hatred to George's fans, who booed and jostled her, even once tried to beat her up.

Equally rough treatment was suffered in Liverpool by Maureen Cox, Ringo's steady since Cavern Club days. Maureen worked as a hairdresser: On many occasions, the very head she was shampooing would be uttering threats at her via the mirror. At last, Maureen, too, became public, visiting the hospital where Ringo was having his tonsils removed. A dark-haired, rather undernourished girl stood on the London pavement in bewilderment, clutching a carrier bag.

The Beatles gave entertainment also for the millions they were presumed to earn; for existing, like boy maharajahs, in clouds of spending money. George, it was reported, had changed his E-Type Jaguar for a white Aston Martin like Paul's. Ringo, fresh from his driving test, now drove an Italian Facel Vega. John, who had not yet learned to drive, owned a Rolls-Royce, a Ferrari, and a Mini Minor. Their adoption of such consumer status symbols gave vicarious pleasure; their verdict on unattainable luxury was earthily reassuring. An entire newspaper article was based on the revelation that George had tasted his first avocado. "I've had caviar and I like it," he told Maureen Cleave, "but I'd still rather have an egg sandwich."

All four spent with diminishing pleasure but at increasing speed, in the few seconds possible before the shop became a riot. John, while filming in Bond Street, ran into Asprey's silversmiths through one door and out through another, having managed to spend six hundred pounds. All day, wherever they were, they bought themselves presents, scarcely heeding the accumulation of presents behind them: the suits by the dozen; shirts by the hundred; the movie-cameras; projectors; watches; gold lighters; the Asprey's silverware and cocktail cabinets shaped like antique globes. Asprey's was as good as Woolworth's, Ringo said—they had everything spread out in the open so you could see it.

The clouds of ready money bought new homes for their families, according to pop star precedent. John's aunt Mimi left Woolton for a luxury bungalow near Bournemouth, overlooking Poole Harbor. Jim McCartney, now retired from the Liverpool Cotton Exchange, moved out on to the Cheshire Wirral to enjoy the house, the wine cellar, and the racehorse that Paul had given him. Harry and Louise Harrison gave up their Speke council house for a bungalow in the country near Warrington. Only Ringo's mother, Mrs. Graves, said she was happy where she was. She stayed in the Dingle at Admiral's Grove, and her husband, Ringo's stepfather, continued to paint the local authority's lampposts.

The acquisition of country houses and estates for the Beatles themselves took place in late 1964, in the spirit of yet another swift shopping trip. Again, the task devolved chiefly on Dr. Strach, their accountant. Strach lived in Esher, Surrey, and so concentrated his search around that semirural haven of accountants and stockbrokers.

For John and Cynthia, Dr. Strach found "Kenwood," a thirty-thousand-pound mock-Tudor mansion on the select St. George's Hill estate at Weybridge. "Sunny Heights," a similar, closely adjacent property, was earmarked for Ringo after his—as yet unannounced—marriage to Maureen Cox. The idea at that stage seems to have been for all four Beatles to live together in a mock-Tudor, topiary-encircled compound around a fifth property owned by Brian Epstein. It was one of Brian's more impossible dreams to have them in his sight for always, to know that John was literally at the far end of his garden.

For John, that location could not have been more unfortunate. A mile or so from Weybridge, in the kitchen of an Esher hotel, a 52-year-old dishwasher was even now working up courage to step forward and claim the leading Beatle as his son and heir. It was, indeed, Freddy Lennon, the father John had not laid eyes on since the age of six.

Aunt Mimi had always feared that Freddy might turn up again—though not in this terrible way, selling his life story to *Tit Bits* and *Weekend* magazine. "When they told me who it was," Mimi remembered, "I felt a shock run right through my body to my fingertips and the tips of my toes."

A meeting was arranged between John and Freddy that seemed to go well. But when Freddy called at Kenwood later he had the door slammed in his face. Subsequently, via the Beatles' accounts, he received a flat and a small pension. He resold his life story for diminishing fees, and even made a pop record entitled "That's My Life." Julian Lennon did not acquire a long-lost grandfather.

Nor at Weybridge did there materialize Brian's hoped-for village of Beatles mansions. George broke the pattern by buying a bungalow on a different stockbroker estate, at Esher. And Paul, though offered several properties in the district, refused to commit himself yet. The house that Paul bought, and everything in it, was to be the result of minute social calculation. "He telephoned me one night," Walter Shenson said, "but it was my wife he wanted to speak to. They talked for a long time. Paul was asking about a red velvet couch he'd seen at our house. He wanted to know where he could get one made exactly like it and how much it would cost."

Patti Boyd was discovering that to be a Beatle's girlfriend was like joining a cell of Resistance fighters. Her initiation had been when she and George and the Lennons attempted a weekend at a secluded hotel in Ireland, and awoke next morning to find the world's press all had their address and room number. Patti and Cynthia left the hotel disguised as chambermaids and concealed in two wicker laundry hampers.

That summer, in a bid to go on vacation, they split into two groups. Paul and Jane with Ringo and Maureen flew to the Virgin Islands by way of quick airline changes at Paris, Lisbon, and San Juan, Puerto Rico. The Lennons, George, and Patti were sighted variously in Amsterdam, Vancouver—where a radio station incited local teenagers to form "Beatles posses" to hunt them down—then Honolulu and Papeete, Tahiti. From Papeete they put to sea in a cabin cruiser stinking of diesel oil and largely provisioned with potatoes. The vessel at once ran into heavy seas, causing Cynthia to be sick in the nearest receptacle: her new flowered sun hat.

Drugs occurred, like everything else, in almost wearisome profusion. The need dated from Hamburg and the months without sleep; it remained, amid the dizzying fame, to prop their eyes open through each night's arduous pleasure. Now the pills were bright-colored, like new clothes and cars—French Blues, Purple Hearts, Black Bombers, and Yellow Submarines. The reflex grew in their growing boredom with everyday pleasures. More exciting than worship or sex, champagne or new toys, was to swallow a pill, just to see what would happen.

In 1964, in certain fashionable London circles, a curious after-dinner ritual was beginning to take place. A member of the party, upon a certain conspiratorial signal, would take out a small plastic bag, a cigarette-rolling machine such as previously used only by the poorest classes, and a packet of similarly proletarian Rizla cigarette papers. With much thumb twisting and paper licking, a meager, loosely packed cigarette would be made. It would be then passed round the table for each guest to puff, with a deep inhalation, then handed on to the next as reverently as if it were a portion of the Host.

Marijuana, resin of the Indian hemp or cannabis plant, had been used in England hitherto chiefly by West Indian immigrants to allay, with its languorous fumes, the misery of their Brixton tenements. Now, as "pot" or "hash," the ancient Oriental dream substance became the latest social accessory. That it was also strictly illegal, under laws that had cleansed the drug-crazy Victorian age, bothered no one very much at first.

The Beatles were initiated into pot smoking in 1964. The telltale medicinal fragrance of marijuana joints hung about the set of their second feature film, *Help!* "They were high all the time we were shooting," the director, Richard Lester, says. "But there was no harm in it then. It was a happy high."

It was a laugh, even better than earning millions, to watch the awkward little cigarette rolled; and to breathe down the sweetish smoke that made laughing even easier. It was a laugh to see what characters began to sidle up, their mouths twitching with the promise of even more sensational pleasures. "I saw it happen to Paul McCartney once," Richard Lester says, "the most beautiful girl I've ever seen, trying to persuade him to take heroin. It was an absolutely chilling exercise in controlled evil."

Early in 1965, George Harrison took John and Cynthia Lennon and Patti to a dinner party given by a friend of his. "I'll always remember," Cynthia says, "that when we walked into this man's drawing room, there were four lumps of sugar arranged along the mantelpiece. We all had a delicious dinner with lots of wine. When coffee came, one of the four sugar lumps was put into each of our cups.

"It was as if we suddenly found ourselves in the middle of a horror film. The room seemed to get bigger and bigger. Our host seemed to change into a demon. We were all terrified. We knew it was something evil—we had to get out of the house. But this man told us we couldn't leave. We got away somehow, in George's Mini, but he came after us in a taxi. It was like having the Devil following us in a taxi.

"We tried to drive to some club—the Speakeasy, I think it was. Four of us, packed into the Mini. Everybody seemed to be going mad. Patti wanted to get out and smash all the windows along Regent Street. Then we turned round and started heading for George's place in Esher. God knows how we got there. John was crying and banging his head against the wall. I tried to make myself sick, and couldn't. I tried to go to sleep, and couldn't. It was like a nightmare that wouldn't stop whatever you did. None of us got over it for about three days."

Their host had playfully dipped their coffee sugar into a substance that, although widely used in mental hospitals and on prisoners of war as a truth serum, was so new as a recreational drug that it had not yet been declared illegal. It was a man-made substance, odorless and colorless; its chemical name, lysergic acid diethylamide, was usually shortened to LSD.

Britain, meanwhile, had changed governments and prime ministers. The general election of October 1964 had swept the Conservatives from power after thirteen years and brought back the Labour party for only the fourth term in its history. Supreme power had passed from an obscure Scottish laird to a plump, white-haired man who smoked a pipe and vacationed in the Scilly Isles, and about whom little else was known other than that he represented the constituency of Huyton, near Liverpool.

Harold Wilson—Yorkshire-born, a Merseysider only by electoral accident—restored Labour to office largely with the pop idiom used by teenagers and would-be teenagers. "Let's Go With Labour!," the decisive campaign slogan, borrowed pop music's preeminent image—that of being galvanized, as by music, into keen and exhilarating life. Such was the New Britain that Mr. Wilson promised, in language as attuned to the mass mood as any juke-box hit—"a hundred days of dynamic action" . . . "a dynamic, expanding, confident, above all purposive Britain" . . . "forged in the white heat of the technological revolution."

There was, however, another side to Harold Wilson. It had become visible, though not yet diagnosable, the previous April when, as leader of the opposition, he had presented the Beatles with their Variety Club award at the Dorchester Hotel. It was perhaps the most astute act of his political career to telephone Sir Joseph Lockwood, chairman of EMI, and offer to grace the occasion as a fellow Merseysider. Not that the Beatles recognized Mr. Wilson as such—or, indeed, recognized him at all. John Lennon, mistaking him for the Variety Club's "chief barker or MC," and getting confused with Barker and Dobson toffee, mumbled: "Thank you, Mr. Dobson." But Mr. Dobson did not mind. His face, in the double-page newspaper spreads, wore the smile of one who had discovered a great secret.

Britons who had feared the socialist menace wondered how, for instance, such an apparition could possibly conduct his regular and necessary meetings with the Queen. Yet conduct them the apparition did, with every sign of confidence. And despite technology's white heat, the old familiar state apparatus went on functioning as before. Early in 1965, just as today, the Queen's official birthday was marked by a distribution of honors. Just as today, the Queen herself merely put a signature to the list drawn up by her prime minister.

On June 12, it was announced that the Beatles were each to receive the MBE—Membership of the Most Excellent Order of the British Empire. One northern newspaper headlined the story: "She Loves Them! Yeah! Yeah! Yeah!"

The Beatles, recuperating from their second European tour, awoke to find a throng of press eager to ascertain how they would feel at being entitled to walk in state processions behind peers of the realm and hereditary knights but in front of baronets' younger sons and "Gentlemen of Coat Armor."

They felt confused.

"I thought you had to drive tanks and win wars to get the MBE," John Lennon said.

"I think it's marvelous," Paul McCartney said. "What does that make my dad?"

"I'll keep it to dust when I'm old," Ringo Starr said.

"I didn't think you got that sort of thing," George Harrison said, "just for playing rock 'n' roll music."

In Harold Wilson's Britain, as would become abundantly clear, you did. The country had elected its first Beatle prime minister.

The Wilson Age, which had promised such starkness, such austere purpose, was to produce, instead, an interlude of frivolity unmatched since Charles II sat on the English throne. Newly socialist Britain in 1965 is remembered, not for white heat or driving dynamism but for short-sighted euphoria and featherheaded extravagance. It is remembered above all for a hallucination that descended on England's capital city, brilliant at first, but in quickly fading, tawdry colors—the hallucination of Swinging London.

Swinging London was born at a moment when government debts at home and abroad had brought the country to the edge of economic ruin. Yet the hard times, so earnestly promised by Mr. Wilson, were nowhere visible. All that could be seen was a spending boom registered on the now familiar gauge of teenage fashion. London girls, whey-faced and crop-headed, now tripped along in black-and-white Op Art dresses terminating scandalously far above the knee. The boys who queued outside the Marquee Club wore hipster trousers and spotted or flowered shirts. Opulence was the rage, and offered to all through Sunday color-supplement ads for "pure new wool," "real cream—pour it on thick," the "unashamed luxury" of sleekly packaged, though inexpensive, after-dinner mints. Magazines like *Town* and *Queen* mirrored the new preoccupation with taste and style, publishing extravagant picture stories on emergent arbiters of fashion whose extreme youth and humble backgrounds were invoked, almost unconsciously, as a parallel with the Beatles'. Fame, almost equaling that of pop stars, descended on the fashion model Jean Shrimpton, the photographer David Bailey, and the clothes designers Mary Quant and John Stephen, whose menswear shops were already transforming a West End backwater called Carnaby Street.

Swinging London was a look—of short skirts, floppy hats, white rabbit fur—it was also, at the beginning, an attitude. That attitude, to a great extent, came from the Beatles. As they had looked, wide-eyed, around the strange world of their celebrity, so young Londoners now looked round a capital whose ancient sedateness seemed suddenly hilarious. The essence of Swinging London was in its happening against a tolerant background of non-Swinging London—of black taxis, red buses, Grenadier Guardsmen, the sacred monuments and statues past which the young, outrageously dandified, zoomed laughingly in open-top Mini Mokes, the Union Jack itself translated to a novelty kitchen apron or tote bag. The essence was audacity, like the Beatles'; it was certainty that because they had gotten away with it everyone could.

Swinging London was also big business like none before or since. All summer, in the West End around Carnaby Street, in Chelsea around the King's Road, in formerly down-at-the-heel byways of Fulham and Kensington, there sprang up boutiques, as clothes shops were now called; there sprang up hairdressers offering the Beatles or Mary Quant bobs; bistros, serving newly fashionable cream-laden dishes; windows jumbled with the latest crazes in Victorian bric-a-brac. A rash of new clubs vied with the Ad Lib to attract those who, in the yearning terminology of that hour, were the with-it set, the new faces, the In crowd.

The innermost In crowd, the ultimate clique, continued to be the Beatles. Their hair now sculpted and razored, their clothes one jump ahead of Carnaby Street, they were the model, and their songs the background, for boutique shopping, bistro dining, feather boa wearing, Swinging London life. They, together with Union Jacks and wooden-headed dolls and Great War recruitment posters, were founding effigies in the Pop Art vogue, born of the period's childlike brilliance and bric-a-brac. *Queen* magazine reported in July that Peter Blake, London's leading pop artist, was employed on a major study of them, while the sculptor David Wynne was casting their heads in bronze for what was predicted to be "one of the most profound English philosophical portrait sculptures of the 20th century."

Their second film, *Help!*, is Swinging London personified—part music, part color-supplement travelogue, part Pop Art strip cartoon. Again the producer was Walter Shenson and the director, Richard Lester. Again the theme was the Beatles' private life—not real life this time, but a fantasy one such as their song lyrics and public clowning had led their fans to half-imagine. The opening sequence shows John, Paul, George, and Ringo each entering a front door in four identical row houses. Within is a communal pad equipped with vending machines, a sunken floor, a grass carpet, and a cinema organ.

Various writers, among them the dramatist Charles Wood, had labored on a plot that, in its final, much rewritten form, dealt with the efforts of a Hindu murder sect to recover a ring stuck on Ringo's finger. No less appropriate to the moment, the cast included character actors like Eleanor Bron and Roy Kinnear, well known from fashionable television satire shows. There being no restraint on budget now, the action moved from London to Salisbury Plain, where the Beatles performed inside a ring of Centurion tanks; then to Austria and the Bahamas.

The West End premiere, in Princess Margaret's by now almost inevitable presence, brought reviews hailing the Beatles as "modern Marx Brothers." They had, in fact, prepared for their roles by studying the Marx Brothers' classic *Duck Soup*. Ringo Starr received special praise for a Chaplinesque performance recognizable to everyone around him as just Ringo being Ringo on camera. On the sleeve of the soundtrack album, four ski-clad Beatles semaphored a title song that had been number one in Britain for most of the two preceding months.

Their evolution into national treasure received an extra boost through the growing notoriety of the band they'd helped find a first foothold in the charts. After initially trying to market the Rolling Stones as ersatz Beatles, Andrew Loog Oldham had hit on the brilliant idea of turning his discovery into anti-Beatles, shattering every convention of charm and family friendliness that John, Paul, George, and Ringo had laid down for all pop groups. The Stones did not smile, but sneered. Their hair was not barbered into neat bangs, but left to hang in Byronesque tangles over their ears and collars. They did not perform in shiny stage uniforms, but in the same unmatched, unpressed clothes they had worn to the gig. Their music was not tuneful and catchy like the Beatles', but charged with an animal fury and sexuality that goaded their audiences to violence and vandalism like nothing seen since the earliest days of rock 'n' roll.

Oldham realized that a huge segment of the teenage pop audience felt they had lost the Beatles to their parents, even their grandparents. Boys who attended school with Stones-style hair down to their shoulders were now being sent home with instructions to get it "cut neatly like the Beatles." From the five hitherto law-abiding Stones their teenage manager fashioned rebels and outlaws whose subliminal message was they'd never sell out in the same way. A series of publicity stunts staged by Oldham had turned the Stones into a national scandal that obsessed the media almost as noisily as Beatlemania once had. They were the bêtes noirs of every pulpit-thumping clergyman, youth leader, and columnist for a catalog of crimes that ranged from urinating in public to refusal to ride the revolving platform on TV's *Sunday Night at the London Palladium*. And, just as Oldham had predicted, the more the grown-up world mocked and reviled them, the more teenagers adored them.

Pop fans not just in Britain and America but the world over now polarized into two camps. It was the first question whenever one raver met another: "Are you Beatles or are you Stones?" To reply "Beatles" meant that one was essentially conventional and law-abiding; to reply "Stones" meant that one gloried in anarchy, subversion, and free love. "The Beatles want to hold your hand," famously wrote the New York journalist Tom Wolfe, "but the Stones want to burn your town." Wolfe, of course, had no idea that the squeaky clean Fab Four had been no less averse to a bit of town burning in their Liverpool and Hamburg days.

The Stones, too, had now conquered the States and were enjoying a run of huge hit singles, recently cowritten by their vocalist Mick Jagger and lead guitarist, then known as Keith Richard. Jagger, the former shy student, under Oldham's influence had become a star in his own right, focusing the band's insolence and provocativeness in his strutting, girlish body and enormous, rubbery lips. What few people outside the Ad Lib club realized was that, although polar opposites and deadly rivals in public, the Beatles and the Stones were privately the best of friends. John, in particular, admired Jagger and Richard as well as envying them their license to speak and behave as they chose. As time went on, the two bands would even cooperate, making sure they did not release a new single at the same time and so impede each other's progress up the charts.

The Beatles' investiture as MBEs was performed by the Queen on October 26, 1965. Swinging London was thus united with Buckingham Palace in a spectacle whose solemn pomp and hilarious incongruity spoke prophecies of the Wilsonian honors system. Mr. Wilson's idea had not been universally applauded. Several MBE holders, together with sundry OBEs and BEMs, had returned their decorations in protest that an honor hard won through war or subpostmastership should be given to what one outraged naval hero described as "a gang of nincompoops." Colonel Frederick Wagg announced his resignation from the Labour party and cancellation of a twelve-thousand-pound bequest to party funds. The general delight showed that Mr. Wilson had achieved his object: to reflect the Beatles' popularity upon himself. No single commentator expressed surprise that, despite achievements which nowadays would probably have taken him into the House of Lords, Brian Epstein received no honor of any kind.

Crowds even larger than those that await royal births and deaths collected along the palace railings and around the Victoria Monument's winged chariot to watch the Beatles take their place in the hierarchy of State. Once again, real life had exceeded any scriptwriter's fantasy—in the cries of "God save the Beatles" as they entered by the Privy Purse Door; in the Lord Chamberlain's official six feet three inches in knee breeches, who instructed them how and when to bow; and, finally, the white and gold State ballroom, and the long red carpet leading to the regal figure destined, on this occasion, to play only a bit part.

Later at a press conference, holding up their rose-ribboned silver crosses, they were asked their opinion of Buckingham Palace. Paul McCartney replied that it was a "keen pad." They had been to other palaces, of course—such as the San Francisco Cow Palace. And the Queen? They liked her, Paul said—she had been "like a mum." The Queen had asked how long they had been together and Ringo had replied, "forty years," at which Her Majesty had laughed. "Were you scared?" John was asked. "Not as much as some others in there," he replied. "What will you do with your medal?" "What do people usually do with medals?" Paul replied. Paul would later claim—or, at least, strongly hint—that they had been created Members of the Most Excellent Order of the British Empire in a happy haze of a marijuana joint, quickly puffed by turns in a mahogany-lined palace washroom.

In Birmingham that same day Princess Margaret was opening the new offices of the *Birmingham Post and Mail*. The first issue off the new presses had the Beatles' investiture as its lead story. Glancing at it, the princess made what seemed like a veiled comment on the most inexplicable absentee from her sister's Honors List: "I think MBE must stand for 'Mr. Brian Epstein.'"

At the end of 1964 a New York business syndicate had offered Brian 3 million pounds outright for the Beatles. He was also considering an offer for NEMS Enterprises from the powerful British Delfont Organization. "What shall I do? Shall I take it?" he would ask, resting his forefinger along his cheek as the paper millions danced around him.

The Beatles, though the most colossal element in Brian's success, were by no means the only one. Gerry and the Pacemakers had remained consistently popular and were themselves now making a feature film. Even greater had been the impact of Cilla Black, the Cavern Club's metamorphosed cloakroom girl. Strangely unsuccessful with Lennon-McCartney material, Cilla made her breakthrough with a song that Brian found for her in America: the Burt Bacharach ballad "Anyone Who Had a Heart." Hit records continued into 1965 for Cilla Black, as they did for Billy J. Kramer, the Dakotas, and the Fourmost.

Success beyond exaggeration had brought obvious personal wealth. Brian's suits came from Savile Row, his shirts—of pure monogrammed silk—from Jermyn Street: his presence had the crispness of new banknotes, the cool fragrance of cologne and triumphant deals. In Chapel Street, Belgravia, he had a Georgian house, furnished with fastidious taste, glittering with ceremonial silver, pale with white gold, and quiet with excellent art. There he maintained a domestic staff befitting a young lord, and entertained with a generosity and thoughtfulness that few of his guests have ever forgotten. He took pains, for instance, to notice which brand of cigarettes each visitor smoked, and to ensure that brand would be next to his or her place at dinner. When George Martin married Judy Lockhart-Smith, each table setting was marked by Brian's gift of "M" monogrammed silver napkin rings—not the conventional dozen but eleven, commemorating the number present.

It was the same solicitousness that Brian devoted to all his artists at the beginning—the finicking almost feminine perfectionism that chose Cilla's dresses and worried over Billy J.'s tendency to plumpness; that sent telegrams on first nights, placed flowers and fruit and champagne and portable TV sets in dressing rooms; that provided hairdressers, tailors, doctors, lawyers; that, in a thousand, almost unnoticed ways, eased gawky Liverpool boys and an even gawkier Liverpool girl into their roles as international celebrities.

The Beatles came first, and everyone knew it: the Beatles were not in Brian's head but his heart. Whatever desire he had once felt for John Lennon had changed, amid the world's worship, into a quadruple infatuation, an affair with an image he had created yet still doted uneasily on. To be with them, or a few paces behind them, represented his life's only absolute happiness. On their return from America late in 1964 he had gone up to Liverpool; he was in his old office, talking to Joe Flannery, his longtime friend and confidant. "We made an arrangement to meet for coffee the next morning," Flannery says. "That night, the Beatles flew into London airport. Next day, I was with Brian in his office, the television was on—and there was Brian with the Beatles on the screen. He'd driven all the way down to London to meet them at the airport, then all the way back up to Liverpool to keep his appointment with me. He had to be with them. He could never let go."

Yet he was never quite at ease with them, always a little nervous of going into their dressing room unless to impart some further astounding piece of news. Even after all this time, for all his triumphs, a barbed comment from John could still cut him to the heart. George Martin remembers such a moment, late one night at Abbey Road studios while the Beatles and Martin were working on a track that stubbornly refused to come out right. "Brian appeared in the control room with one of his boyfriends—and did something I'd never seen him do before. When John had finished a vocal track, Brian switched on the intercom and said, 'I don't think that sounded quite right, John.' John looked up at him and in his most cutting voice said, 'You stick to your percentages, Brian. We'll take care of the music.' "

The publicists he employed tended to bear the brunt of his possessiveness where the Beatles were concerned. Brian Sommerville's tenure came to a stormy end on the first American tour when he committed the sin of being quoted by name in a news story about the band. Brian screamed at him, then tried to make him sign a written oath of anonymity in all future dealings with the media. Sommerville refused, dissolved his freelance arrangement with NEMS, and went off to read for the bar.

In his place Brian took on Derek Taylor, the Hoylake-born *Daily Express* reporter who had ghostwritten George Harrison's articles from Paris. Among the Fleet Street scrimmage Taylor had caught Brian's eye with his Italianate good looks and droll, idiosyncratic speech. He joined NEMS in April 1964, initially as Brian's personal assistant. "I suppose it was because he fancied me that I got the job," Taylor admitted, "even though, in all the time I knew him, he never so much as laid a finger on my knee."

Earlier in 1964, Brian had agreed to write his autobiography for a London publisher, the Souvenir Press. Taylor's first NEMS job, even before he had quite left Fleet Street, was to ghostwrite Brian's life story on the basis of one weekend with him and a tape recorder at the Imperial Hotel, Torquay. The result was the evasive yet strangely honest self-portrait that he called *A Cellarful of Noise*, but those in his inner circle retitled *A Cellarful of Boys*.

As the Beatles' press officer, for the first of three terms, Taylor stood in the firing line of Brian's proprietorial obsession. "I'd been told he could be cruel. I only realized it when I came to organize a Fab Four press conference. Brian didn't want it to work. If I made a mess of it, even though the Beatles would be in that mess, he'd be happy—because I'd gained no control over them. He said, 'Go ahead—but this is doomed. I look forward to speaking to you about it afterward.' I joined in April; here he was in May, treating me with *massive* cruelty."

In 1964, during the Beatles' second American tour, Brian met Nat Weiss, a pale, cautious New Yorker who until then had earned his living as a divorce lawyer. Over the next three years, Weiss became to Brian what a few male friends, like Joe Flannery and Peter Brown, were—an adviser, a confidant, and with increasing frequency, a means of rescue.

The Brian who revisited Nat Weiss in 1965, however, was still the languid, immaculate young Englishman who loved New York and its arrant luxury, who bought clothes extravagantly up and down Fifth Avenue, who had a weakness for the Waldorf Hotel, French toast, and American chef's salads, and whose large intake of alcohol, especially cognac, seemed to produce only greater euphoria. "When he was high," Weiss says, "he'd pile the furniture up. He'd put chairs on top of tables and then more chairs on top, just to see the effect. Moving furniture was always a thing with Brian.

"But however high he was, he'd never talk about the Beatles. I've seen him at parties when people tried to broach the subject. Brian would suddenly change—it was as if an icy shutter had come down.

"Anything he ever told me was in the strictest confidence, over lunch or dinner. To Brian, the relationship with the Beatles was something mystical—he himself used that word. He believed there was a chemistry between the five of them that no one else could understand. They weren't a business to Brian: They were a vocation, a mission in life. They were like a religion to him."

Weiss came as close as anyone did to Brian in those three tumultuous years. His memory is deeply affectionate, admiring, and perplexed. For with Weiss, as with even his most intimate companions, Brian Epstein defied understanding. "He wasn't a Jekyll and Hyde character—he was Jekyll and Hyde and about twenty other people besides."

He was, on one hand, the ice-cool young tycoon who sat in Walter Hofer's office, saying nothing, only listening, while big brash New York promoters bludgeoned him with their bonhomie, but at the first inconsistency politely interrupting, "but I thought you said a minute ago. . . ." He was the businessman whose integrity seemed born of an earlier age, whose handshake was as good as a contract, who treated the unknown teenage masses of Denver or Cincinnati with the same scrupulous fairness as customers in his family's Liverpool shop. "He always insisted that concert promoters should never take advantage of the fans—that tickets always had to be kept as cheap as possible."

But always there was the other Brian, contradicting each strength with a weakness, each cool-headed triumph with a peevish, destructive temper tantrum, each provident care and precaution with a reckless and fearful risk.

There was the Brian who, with the whole world at his feet, spent time and energy in buying up *Mersey Beat*, the little Liverpool music paper, simply for the pleasure of settling old scores among local musicians and promoters. There was the Brian who, unable to adjust his mind from Liverpool shopkeeping values, attempted to woo people like Nicky Byrne and George Martin into his employment by promising them "a thousand a year." There was the Brian who, as paper millions whirled around him, hardly realized what tangible millions were slipping through his grasp.

The Beatles' 1964 American tour, though buoyed up on cash advances larger than any in entertainment history, had eventually done little more than cover its gigantic overheads. To make matters worse, the U.S. Internal Revenue Service had become uneasy about all the dollars that, reputedly, were to be removed from the country. Under a long-standing Anglo-American tax treaty, the Beatles' tour earnings were liable only for British income tax. The U.S. authorities nonetheless obtained a New York court order, freezing one million dollars in concert proceeds while "clarification" was sought.

Still worse was the position with Seltaeb, the American merchandising company of whose projected multimillion-dollar earnings from Beatles buttons, masks, ice cream, and more than 150 other items, NEMS Enterprises' share was fixed at 10 percent.

In August 1964, the original ludicrous Seltaeb-NEMS contract was renegotiated. The Beatles' royalty from goods in their image rose to 46 percent. Relations between NEMS and Seltaeb's English president, Nicky Byrne, deteriorated sharply in the process. They deteriorated still further when Byrne's lawyers informed him that some American manufacturers were turning out Beatles merchandise on licenses granted not by Seltaeb in New York but by NEMS direct from London.

As a further complication there was strife within Seltaeb among Byrne's young English partners. Lord Peregrine Eliot, after six months of "good lunacy" as he describes it, received a distinct impression that neither the Beatles nor Uncle Sam had been paid the sums due to them and that, under tax treaty law, Uncle Sam might seek to annex his Cornish ancestral home, Port Eliot. So, while Nicky Byrne was in London, Lord Peregrine and Malcolm Evans, another Seltaeb partner, instituted court proceedings against him. They claimed that Byrne had failed to pass on Beatles royalties while at the same time spending $150,000 for his own "comfort and benefit." The comforts alleged included hotel bills running into thousands of dollars, two Cadillacs and chauffeurs on twenty-four-hour standby, and charge accounts for his girlfriends at costly Fifth Avenue stores.

At the same time NEMS began a lawsuit against Seltaeb for alleged nonpayment of fifty-five thousand dollars in merchandise royalties. Nicky Byrne entered a countersuit claiming breach of contract and damages of five million dollars.

The NEMS-Seltaeb dispute entered the pretrial stage of a legal epic destined to last three years, accumulate three tons of documents, and dissipate fortunes that no one can ever accurately compute. For the confusion over licenses had caused panic among America's litigation-wary retailers. Woolworth's and Penney's instantly canceled orders together worth seventy-eight million dollars. The total of business lost among the lawsuits, in that one year alone, must be closer to one hundred million dollars.

NEMS Enterprises, meanwhile, had swollen to literally unmanageable size. For Brian, while on the one hand struggling to contain the Beatles phenomenon, continued to sign up any new act that caught his increasingly capricious fancy. Sounds Incorporated; Cliff Bennett and the Rebel Rousers; Paddy, Klaus and Gibson; and the Rustiks—each in turn received the now familiar NEMS treatment of new suits, stylish press handouts, and if fortunate, a Lennon-McCartney song. It did not occur to Brian that his eye could be at fault; that he mistook mere competence for Beatles-size talent; that often his new discoveries only obtained record contracts on the strength of what he had discovered before.

Nor did Brian now have the assiduous energy of eighteen months ago. The arrival of Peter Brown from Liverpool in 1965 allowed him to delegate much day-to-day routine to the slim young man who, in so many ways, became his surrogate presence. He had also persuaded his other Liverpool friend, Geoffrey Ellis, to quit the insurance business and join NEMS, ultimately as a director. The arrival of Vic Lewis, an established London agent, completed the transformation from one-man company to multifaced, impersonal organization.

The change was felt most keenly by the Liverpudlians who had followed Brian to London, and now found his attention withdrawn from all but the Beatles and Cilla. Tommy Quickly, his intended solo sensation, lost hope of ever seeing the Top Twenty. Billy J. Kramer put on weight, unreproached. The Fourmost bemoaned their lack of songs to record. The Big Three so hated the prissy image that Brian had given them, they were publicly threatening to beat him up. Gibson Kemp, of Paddy, Klaus and Gibson, supplemented his weekly fifteen pounds NEMS salary by working as an office cleaner.

It was partly this accumulating discontent that led Brian, during 1965, to move away from NEMS's Argyll Street offices to a small command post of his own on Stafford Street, near Piccadilly. There he planned to devote himself only to top-level management—in other words, the Beatles. The move was made with elaborate secrecy: Only Peter Brown and Geoffrey were supposed to know his new address. "Brian spoiled that," Geoffrey Ellis says, "by immediately ringing up his twenty closest friends and telling them where he was."

With him to Stafford Street he took Wendy Hanson, the high-powered, ebullient English girl whom he had wanted as his personal assistant since she had worked for him briefly in America the previous year. Wendy had subsequently come to Europe "because of a man in Paris"; the man having proved difficult, she found herself able to accept Brian's offer. She remained with him, despite many attempted resignations, until the end of 1966.

Her job in principle was to provide anything a Beatle wanted, from new Asprey's luggage for Ringo to a Coutt's bank account for Paul; from Jane Asher's birthday cake at Maxim's in Paris, to the whole of the Harrods store kept open after hours for the Beatles as had only been done hitherto for royalty. There was also the continuing job, for which Wendy's experience among turbulent operatic tenors and prima donnas had only half-prepared her, of trying to organize Brian.

"We were in Nassau while the boys were filming *Help!*; it had all got a bit dull, so Brian decided to go to New York for the weekend. Pan Am couldn't seat us together on the flight, which made Brian *furious*. There and then he wrote a letter to Pan Am, saying, 'The Beatles will never use this airline again.' When we got to New York there were, I promise you, twenty Pan Am officials, bowing and scraping on the tarmac.

"The next morning we were supposed to leave for London. Pan Am sent their own limo to the airport to fetch us. I was downstairs in the lobby with all my bags—no Brian. I waited and waited. Still no Brian. Eventually, I went up to his room. There he was, still in bed with not one of his thirteen suitcases packed.

"All the way to the airport the limo driver was in radio contact with Pan Am: 'We're just crossing the river,' I could hear him saying. 'We're five miles from Kennedy . . .' They got us on to the flight with literally seconds to spare—in fact, they threw our bags into the compartment after us. Then, as we were taxiing along the runway, Brian looked at his watch. 'Hm,' he said. 'Half a minute late in taking off. Typical.' "

The move to Stafford Street, far from concentrating Brian's mind, presaged a deterioration that, for the moment, only Wendy Hanson noticed. Wendy, increasingly, found herself left alone with the hot line the Beatles used to communicate their wishes and whims. When they asked for Brian she would have to admit he had not been in to the office that day.

The trouble was partly insomnia, inherited from his mother and fostered by London's extravagant night haunts. A relentless gambler, he was known to lose up to twelve thousand pounds in one roulette or chemin de-fer session at the Curzon Club. The price was a small one for the company of waiters, croupiers, the rolling ball, the click of cards from the shoe. At dawn or later, dosed with pills on top of the night's brandy, he might, if he was fortunate, fall asleep. The sleep became ever more difficult to penetrate from the office where, at 4:00 or 5:00 P.M., he would still have not made an appearance.

The trouble, above all, was an emotional life into which fame and money had brought no fulfillment. It was the helpless heart, still lost to any loutish rough trade boy: the beatings-up, the thefts and petty blackmail. It was the pimply young Guardsmen who left Chapel Street at dawn; the steel-hatted construction worker calling to see him at the New York Waldorf at 5:00 A.M. It was the fear, reborn each horrified morning, that the police, the press—but, most frightful of all, the Beatles—would find out.

That the Beatles had not yet found out remained a hallucination with Brian, despite grins exchanged behind his back, and despite John Lennon's occasional brutal puncturings of the masquerade. "What shall I call this book of mine?" he had wondered aloud after finishing *A Cellarful of Noise.* John, fixing him with a merciless eye, replied, "Queer Jew."

Despite this underlying malaise the Beatles' 1965 American tour seemed once more to confirm Brian's power to take the Beatles beyond even their wildest dreams. On both their previous two tours they had hoped to meet their idol Elvis Presley and thank him in person for his cordial welcoming telegram. But the visits had been too short and their schedule too insanely crowded for anything to be worked out. This time around it happened that when they hit the West Coast in August Elvis would be in Hollywood, shooting one of the three films he was obliged to make each year. All four entreated Brian to move heaven and earth, if necessary, to procure them an audience with the King.

A meeting was arranged between Brian and Presley's manager, Colonel Tom Parker, at the Colonel's permanent office at Paramount Studios, which was exotically furnished with mementoes of his personal symbol and totem, the elephant. The crafty old carnival huckster offered his pale young British visitor a lunch of pastrami sandwiches, little suspecting how many times his name had been taken in vain to spice up fictitious phone messages for Brian in Birkenhead pubs.

Colonel Parker being amenable to Elvis meeting the Beatles, their roadie Mal Evans was dispatched to finalize arrangements with Joe Esposito, Elvis's road manager and head honcho of his protective body-guard, the legendary Memphis Mafia. "Mal was a huge Elvis fan," Esposito remembers. "He turned up at the studios all dressed up in a suit and tie. When Elvis said 'Hi' to him and shook his hand, Mal was a nervous wreck.

"We sent cars to fetch the Beatles and bring them to the house in Bel Air where Elvis was living. I rode over in one car with George and Ringo; in the other one were John, Paul, and Brian. It was all supposed to have been a secret, but the Colonel had tipped off one of the radio stations, and when we arrived there were hundreds of screaming kids outside.

"When we showed the Beatles into the living room Elvis was in his bathrobe and playing a bass guitar. All four of them were tongue-tied to meet him . . . even John could hardly speak. Finally Elvis said, 'Well, if we're just going to sit here looking at each other all night, I'm going to bed.'"

"That broke the ice a little bit and they started playing roulette to-gether—all but for George, who got high as a kite on grass out beside the pool."

The '65 tour included the Beatles' greatest performing triumph—one that still found Brian apparently center stage and in full control. It oc-curred on August 23, when a helicopter containing the Beatles, Brian, and Tony Barrow tilted down through the New York twilight and the pilot pointed out Shea Stadium, though they could already hear the roar of it, and see the flashes of unnumbered cameras pointed hopefully into the sky.

Brian was there at the New York Mets' baseball field, to witness the concert that, though it grossed $300,000, earned only $7,000 for its promoter, Sid Bernstein. He is there in the film that was made, standing near the stage, nodding his head in time a little jerkily, looking out to the bleachers at fifty-five thousand people—in seats kept cheap at his insistence—then back to the four figures for whom fifty-five thousand voices are screaming, with their military-style khaki tunics, their hot foreheads, and still unwearied smiles.

"If he'd been an ordinary manager, Shea Stadium couldn't have happened," Nat Weiss says. "None of it could have happened the way it did. It all only happened that way because it was Brian Epstein's fantasy."

FOURTEEN

"THIS IS IT. THIS IS THE LAST ONE EVER"

At the beginning, two boys in travel-creased shirts would stand in front of George Martin, playing the new song they had scribbled in an old school exercise book. Martin even then saw two personalities at war. A song would be John's aggression held in check by Paul's decorum; it would be Paul's occasionally cloying sentiment cut back by John's unmerciful cynicism. Yet Paul loved all-out rock 'n' roll, just as John could be capable of brusque tenderness. Examples of total collaboration were rare. More often, one would write half a song and then come to the other for help with the chorus or "middle eight." The formula was established that whoever had written most of the song took the lead vocal, the other providing harmony. That harmony derived its freshness and energy from the contest being waged within it.

Collaboration was dictated, in any case, by close confinement in tour buses, dressing rooms, and later, aircraft; the pressure of songwriting to order in spaces cleared among newspapers, teacups, and the debris of "the road." From the early, simple yeah-yeah hits up to the *Hard Day's Night* album the songs, whether by John or Paul, are chiefly redolent of a common life on the run. Nor was it still absolutely certain that Lennon-McCartney songs were what the public wanted. Their next, and fourth, album, *Beatles for Sale*, reverted largely to their old Liverpool and Hamburg stage repertoire: Chuck Berry's "Rock and Roll Music"; Carl Perkins's "Honey Don't"; Little Richard's "Kansas City"; Buddy Holly's "Words of Love," a track on which their fans first discovered their almost uncanny powers of mimicry. By covering the songs of these and many others of their rock and soul idols, and openly acknowledging their creative debt, they had reactivated several careers previously in the doldrums, notably Berry's and Perkins's, and Holly's posthumous one. It was thanks to them also that knowing about pop history for the first time became cool.

The importance of George Martin cannot be overemphasized. First of all, he signed them. Second, he did not cheat them. Third, he did not adulterate them. It would have been easy for him, as all-powerful record producer, to insist that each release should carry a B side composed by himself. Martin happened to be of the rare breed who are content to use their talents in improving other people's work. To Lennon and McCartney he was the editor that all creative promise strikes if it is lucky. He took the raw songs, he shaped and pruned and polished them and, with scarcely believable altruism, asked nothing for himself but his EMI salary and the satisfaction of seeing the songs come out right. As the songs grew more complex, so did Martin's unsung, unsinging role.

Paul McCartney was, of the two, the more obviously natural musician. Much came from heredity, and the Jim Mac Jazz Band. He had an instinctive grasp of harmony, a gift of phrasing that raised the bass guitar in his hands to an agile, expressive lead instrument. Already proficient in guitar and drums, he was now taking formal piano lessons. Paul developed by following rules, a notion altogether repugnant to John Lennon. John's music was, like his drawing, bereft of obedience and straight lines, but honest and powerful in a way that Paul's never dared to be.

Innovators though they had become, they were still as wide open to outside influences and quick to absorb other people's good ideas as they had been in far-off days when they'd sit in Paul's front room copying Buddy Holly and Carl Perkins. They still looked as eagerly to America, where scores of new ensembles with round-collared suits and bangs now adopted Beatle-ish names (the Turtles, the Byrds, the Monkees) and used Beatle-ish harmonies and humor to claw back the Scouse-borrowed music of their native land. Even the new habit of calling the former groups "bands" came from John, George, Paul, and Ringo, who would often collectively sign themselves "The Beatles—a band," like tuba and triangle players from some Yorkshire mining village or the Salvation Army. Many American bands went so far as to adopt Liverpool accents and use Liverpool phrases, despite blissful ignorance as to their meaning. One Monkees song, for instance, was to come out in the United States as "Randy Scouse Git" (hastily changed to "Alternate Title" for its British release).

But the most significant of Britain's American converts to rock was Bob Dylan, formerly a folk-singing reincarnation of travelin' man Woody Guthrie and chief standard-bearer for the emergent protest movement. Then, one fateful day, on his car radio, Dylan heard the Animals' Newcastle-on-Tyne version of New Orleans' "The House of the Rising Sun." There and then Dylan abandoned acoustic protest songs like "Blowin' in the Wind" and "A Hard Rain's A Gonna Fall" for electric-powered rock, thereby instantly turning the form into one without limitations of subject, expression, or length.

Dylan had also been an early convert to the Beatles, although at the time crediting them with rather more daring than they possessed. When they first met him he told them how blown away he'd been by the "druggy" line in "I Want to Hold Your Hand"—"I get high, I get high!" John and Paul had to explain rather sheepishly that they'd actually sung "I can't hide, I can't hide!"

John, in particular, now waited for every new Dylan release, hungry for the next giant leap in experimentation it was bound to bring. He also kept a weather eye on the Beach Boys, whom Beatles records had prompted to abandon simple surfing chants for complex urban chorales, developing the harmonic genius of their leader, Brian Wilson. In 1965, too, there was a rising New York band, the Lovin' Spoonful, whose lead singer/songwriter John Sebastian worryingly seemed to possess the humor of Lennon and the romanticism of McCartney inside one Beatle-shaggy head.

The soundtrack album for *Help!* brought the disparate characters of John and Paul, for the first time, into open contrast. On the one hand, there were unmistakably "John" songs, like "You've Got to Hide Your Love Away," written under Bob Dylan's influence: sardonic and world-weary, idylls of the morning after. On the other hand there was Paul's solo performance of a ballad he had been playing around with for weeks under the provisional title of "Scrambled Eggs" but hadn't liked to bring to the studio because he couldn't believe its melody had never been used before. Now titled "Yesterday," it was performed by Paul alone, accompanied by a classical string quartet and no other Beatle vocal or instrumental embellishment whatever. It was immediately covered by a leading British ballad singer, Matt Monro, the first of some two thousand recorded versions.

Rubber Soul, their second album that year, reflected a widening schism belied by the four Carnaby-look Beatles, still barely distinguishable from each other, in its modish fish-eye lens sleeve. Paul and John were by now leading separate—and, as it proved—mutually inimical lives. John's was the dominant presence, through songs that were fragments of current autobiography—the boredom, in "Nowhere Man," of sitting at home in his Tudor mansion; the edgy lust of "Norwegian Wood," a description of infidelity in some London girl's flat. From Paul came "Michelle," a love song as sweet and untroubled as his affair with Jane and half its lyrics translated into French as if to impress the high-brow Asher family.

EMI's Abbey Road studios, whatever other amenities they lacked, were an ideal hideaway. London's northbound traffic sped in total indifference past the plain-fronted white house with its neat gravel driveway and high front steps. Only the doorman, eyeing the fan pickets posted respectively at the IN and OUT gateway, hinted at anything discordant with St. John's Wood, acacia bushes, retired publishers, and Austrian au pair girls.

In the house's rubber-silenced hinterland, Studio Two, that once strictly rationed Holy of Holies, was now consecrated almost exclusively to the Beatles' use. George Martin likewise no longer looked in his diary to see whether or not he could fit in a session. When the source of EMI's current three-million-pound profit felt an urge to record, Martin and his engineer, Norman Smith, obeyed the peremptory summons.

Gone, too, was the producer's old clock-watching authority. Studio Two at Abbey Road became in effect a rehearsal room where new Beatles songs took shape by methods increasingly prodigal of time and expense. Four-track recording, which had replaced two-track at Abbey Road in late 1963, altered the entire concept of an album session. Whereas *Please Please Me* had been blasted off in one thirteen-hour marathon, *Rubber Soul* grew over several weeks as a layering of rhythm, vocal, and instrumental tracks, any of which could be erased and rerecorded. Both John and Paul, in their different ways, embraced these new technical possibilities. Each built his own private studio where demo tapes could be produced as a guide to the final Abbey Road version. Both ran through George Martin's domain as through a toy shop, alighting with rapture on this or that novelty of sound. They must have *that* on the track, they would say. Martin, the trained musician, Norman Smith, the trained engineer, would reply that it couldn't work. Then they found it did work. Studio procedure was to be changed for all time by this whim of iron.

At a certain moment in each session Martin would leave John and Paul and cross the cable-strewn floor to George Harrison, waiting apart from the others, unsmiling with his Gretsch rehearsal guitar. George would then play to Martin whatever solo he had worked out for the song. If Martin did not like it he would lead George to the piano, tinkle a little phrase, and tell him to play that for his solo. Such was the origin of the guitar in "Michelle." "I was," Martin admits, "always rather beastly to George."

In George the world's ecstasy had as yet produced no answering lift of inspiration. He played lead guitar as he always had, earnestly, a little ponderously. He took his turn at lead singing in a voice whose thick Scouse seemed to mask an underlying embarrassment. Lately, goaded into action by John and Paul's stupendous output, he, too, had begun to write songs by himself rather than in partnership with either of the other two and with titles unwittingly echoing his rather testy and impatient nature: "Don't Bother Me"; "Think for Yourself." Each new album, in fairness, featured a song by George—just one. He was also learning the Indian sitar, an instrument that Richard Lester had added for comic purposes to a scene in *Help!* "Norwegian Wood" was the first Beatles song to benefit from the wiry whining and wailing of George's sitar.

As for Ringo, he sat patiently in a corner of the studio, waiting to be called to sing his song or drum as directed, whiling away hours when he was not needed in card games with Neil and Mal.

Their U.K. tour in the winter of 1965 included their last ever performance in Liverpool—though no one realized this at the time. They had intended to visit the Cavern Club and perform under its reeking stone arches, just for old time's sake, but Brian talked them out of the idea for their own safety. John felt particularly enraged at being unable to move about as he pleased even in his home city. He longed to meet Bill Harry and his other art college cronies again at Ye Cracke and have a quiet pint or two under the mural of Wellington greeting Marshal Blücher at the Battle of Waterloo.

Had they made it to Mathew Street they would have found the Cavern still much the same as when they'd played there, even though it was now world famous as the club that broke the Beatles, and to play there was the objective of every band seeking to follow in their footsteps. There were still the same stone steps, the same reeking arches, the same mingled odors of cheese rind and sweat. Outside, Paddy Delaney the doorman still stood in his dinner jacket and cummerbund, often now greeting celebrities such as Rex Harrison and Lionel Bart as they disembarked from chauffeur-driven limousines.

The Beatles' last Liverpool concert also was their last chance to revisit the Cavern. Its owner, Ray McFall, had gotten into financial difficulties and, a few weeks later, suddenly announced to Delaney that the bailiffs would be coming in the following morning. The members tried to prevent this by holding an all-night session, then blocking the steps with chairs and setting off all the fire extinguishers. Police sympathetically cleared the demonstrators, then escorted Delaney out in a guard of honor, his immaculate dinner jacket white with foam. The warehouse was demolished soon afterward, and the tunnels beneath, with all their Beatles echoes and memories, obliterated by a car park.

The Beatles' European and world tour of summer 1966 brought them another, slightly more satisfactory homecoming. The concerts included one in Hamburg, though this time they had to play for only thirty inaudible minutes at the city's Ernst March Halle sports arena rather than all night on the Reeperbahn. "Don't try to listen to us," John told the German support band. "We're terrible these days."

There were backstage reunions with old Hamburg friends like Bert Kampfaert and Bettina, the Star-Club barmaid whose friendly nails had raked so many pale young Liverpool backs. John even found his way to Jonhannasbollwerk to see Jim and Lilo Hawke at the Seaman's Mission and eat a nostalgic plate of Frau Prill's real English chips. To the disappointment of all four the visitors did not include Horst Fascher, the bouncer whose killer punch had protected them on so many bloodthirsty Star-Club nights, and was once again in a bit of trouble with the law. At their concert, the Beatles dedicated "Roll Over Beethoven" to him, remembering how he loved to step in as their ad hoc vocalist whenever John or Paul were too pissed.

There was also a reunion with Astrid Kirchherr, the woman who so crucially helped to create the image that now obsessed the world. Astrid's photographs of those tough-tender child rockers, sitting on the fairground traction engine, had appeared in newspapers and magazines throughout the world without any credit—or fee—to her. "It was one of a bundle of prints I'd sent over to Liverpool," Astrid says now. "Later on, when it turned up in the media, it was credited to UPI. I didn't sue them; what would have been the point? To me, it was just a photograph of some friends."

Astrid told the Beatles she'd now given up photography, thinking herself not good enough. She had taken a job in a female drag bar, dancing as required with the "men." In her black-draped bedroom there was still a blow-up portrait of Stu Sutcliffe above her head. Candles burned night and day in memory of the fifth Beatle whom no one but his mother and sisters in Liverpool now seemed to remember.

The tour's stop after Hamburg was Tokyo, via the polar route. Because of a typhoon warning their aircraft was forced to land in Anchorage, Alaska. Nat Weiss in New York was roused from sleep by Brian's voice on the telephone, demanding with some petulance, "Who *owns* Alaska, Nat? And can you recommend a nice place to stay?"

Their two Tokyo concerts, at the Nippon Budo Kan (Martial Arts Hall), were, not surprisingly, the best organized of the Beatles' performing career. The promoters explained to Brian that any riot would have brought dishonor upon themselves. Accordingly, the nine-thousand-strong audience had three thousand police to guard them. Backstage, the Beatles were provided with geisha girls, a perpetual tea ceremony, and a Japanese road manager for liaison. Between concerts, in the twenty-four-room Presidential Suite at the Tokyo Hilton, a private bazaar was spread, of radios, cameras, happi coats, and painting sets. The Beatles all bought inks and calligraphy brushes and, having nothing intelligible to watch on television, produced a garish mural on one huge sheet of paper that was later given to the Japanese fan club.

They expected something similar in the Philippines. They were charmed, as are all newcomers to Manila, by a miniature Texas set down among tropical islands, by the skyscrapers, specially earthquake-proofed, the shanties and juke boxes and brilliant jeep taxis, the jungle foliage reflected in a speed cop's Harley-Davidson. After dark, as the bats bounced like shuttlecocks against the rim of Manila Bay, shotgun blasts at random bespoke Southeast Asia's most uninhibited autocracy.

The Philippines in those days were still the fiefdom of President Ferdinand Marcos and his wife, Imelda, a woman long celebrated for her vanity, her enormous wardrobe, and unscrupulous use of her husband's absolute power. Herself a Beatles fan, Mrs. Marcos had arranged a lavish garden party at Malacanang, the presidential palace, to introduce them to three hundred handpicked government officials and their families. The invitation delivered to Tony Barrow, however, gave no hint of these elaborate preparations: Even Brian saw no particular necessity to attend.

Manila's English language newspapers next morning carried the banner headline "Beatles Snub President." When a president happens also to be a military dictator, his wounded feelings naturally evince widespread sympathy. The concert promoters sympathized by refusing to pay Brian Epstein the Beatles' concert fee. Other citizens sympathized by telephoning death threats to the British embassy.

Brian, horrified by the furor, did his best to make amends. He asked to appear on Manila television the following night to explain that no snub had been intended. The transmission was almost wiped out by heavy static that, coincidentally, vanished as soon as Brian's apology came to an end.

Departure from Manila Airport on July 5 was accompanied by ugliness unenvisaged even outside Litherland Town Hall. Deprived of all police protection the Beatles party dashed for the aircraft through a concourse of jeering customs officers; they were jostled, even punched and kicked. The KLM flight for New Delhi took off only after lengthy negotiations between Brian and a Philippines income tax official who refused to let them go until they had paid seven thousand pounds.

En route back from New Delhi to London, exhausted, disillusioned, bruised physically as well as mentally, the Beatles told Brian that was it, they'd had enough. When this tour finally wound its way to an end, there would be no more.

The news so devastated Brian that his whole body erupted in a painful case of hives. Suffering from total exhaustion he fled to a hotel in Portmeirion, the Welsh resort where he had always found a measure of relaxation and quiet. He had barely settled down there when Nat Weiss telephoned from New York to tell him that Beatles albums were being ritually burned in Nashville, Tennessee.

The previous February, in one of her regular Beatles reports for the London *Evening Standard,* Maureen Cleave had asked John his views, if any, on organized religion. His response gave little hint of a past life in the choir of St. Peter's Church, Woolton. "Christianity will go. It will vanish and shrink . . . we're more popular than Jesus now. I don't know which will go first—rock 'n' roll or Christianity." He had nothing against Jesus, he went on, but the disciples were "thick." "They're the ones that ruin it for me."

In Britain, the remark passed unchallenged—indeed, unnoticed. Such was not the case five months later when, on the eve of the Beatles' American tour, Maureen Cleave's interview with John was reprinted by a teenage magazine, *Datebook*. What in the *Evening Standard* piece had been merely an aside was headlined on *Datebook*'s cover: a stray ad-lib transformed to vaunting sacrilege. John Lennon was claiming that the Beatles were "bigger than Jesus Christ."

In cheerily godless Britain with its enfeebled Protestant Church—already reeling under the mockeries of young satirists like Peter Cook and Alan Bennett—the remark had seemed no more than flippant and rather foolish. But to the core of old-fashioned, literal-minded Christianity that runs through America, it was no more or less than outright blasphemy. In fundamentalist southern states even the most avid female Beatles fans had no doubt as to whom they owed greater loyalty. The Tennessee radio station that invited shocked and disillusioned teenagers to cast their Beatles albums onto public bonfires was just one of hundreds originating similar protests throughout the country. One outraged community installed rubbish bins labeled "Place Beatle Trash Here"; another brought in a tree-crushing machine to pulp the offending vinyl. Pastor Thurmond Babbs of Cleveland, Ohio, threatened to excommunicate any of his flock who attended a Beatles concert on the approaching tour. Their music was banned on thirty-five radio stations, from Ogdenburg, New York, to Salt Lake City, Utah.

The outcry added further fuel to what was already extreme disenchantment with the British Invasion of pop bands who had followed the Beatles' triumphal path across the Atlantic. Now, the product being offered to America's youth was no longer innocent and charming Hamlet bangs, pixie boots, and deft one-liners. It had become a seemingly unstoppable procession of shaggy-headed and unsmiling yahoos who seemed to compete with each other in the tunelessness of their music and the mayhem of their performance. It was The Who, led by their anarchic, windmill-armed leader Pete Townshend, who ended each set by smashing his guitar to smithereens as though urging his audience to do the same to the concert hall. It was a new three-man band named Cream, the first ever to lose the definite article, whose drummer, Ginger Baker, delighted in firing off sticks like guided missiles to hit watching police or security men. Above all, it was the Rolling Stones, whose shaggy hair was popularly supposed to be teeming with vermin, whose lyrics had to be bleeped on television, and whose recent U.S. smash, "Satisfaction," was apparently a hymn to the joys of playing with yourself.

Worse even than that was the new mood growing up among America's own young music makers, the singers and groups whom the Beatles had galvanized into new energy and experimentation barely two years earlier. Under the leadership of Bob Dylan American pop had ceased to be about high schools, drive-ins, and junior proms and become as much a medium of protest and ridicule as acoustic folk had ever been, but now reaching an infinitely wider audience. The hitherto unchallenged war in Vietnam, racial intolerance, white suburban snobbery, urban decay, even the prospect of impending nuclear destruction, all now found their way into the charts in songs that sold by the billion. Until this moment, every type of American mass culture had reassured its citizens that their country was infallibly the good guy. Now the mocking voices of Dylan, Joan Baez, the Byrds, and a hundred other insurrectionists broke the news that it had become the bad guy, not in folkies' harsh monotone but in seductive commercial hooks and harmonies, set about by electric pianos, wistful flutes, and zithery twelve-string guitars.

The Beatles were not in any sense political or subversive. But there was no doubt that they had changed, radically and disconcertingly, from the instant charmers on the *Ed Sullivan Show*. The single they released early in 1966—unconnected to any album, and a double A side—bore the unmistakable stamp of Bob Dylan, and many others besides. Paul's contribution was "Paperback Writer," a vague satire against hack journalism and the mass media, set about by Pete Townshendesque guitar chords and intricate harmonies with more than a nod toward the Beach Boys. "Rain" was by John, echoing the Byrds as they had sounded in their smash cover version of Dylan's "Mr. Tambourine Man," but with his own special air of being pressured and persecuted almost beyond endurance: "When the rain comes, you run and hide your head . . . you might as well be dead . . ." Its closing babble of gibberish was added late at night in his private studio, by drunkenly running the vocal chorus backward.

As usual, advance orders took "Rain/Paperback Writer" instantly to number one in Britain and America. Only after 1 million copies had been taken home and played did some little uncertainty arise. "Paperback Writer," which received the most radio play, frankly mystified

American fans with its allusions to a man named Lear and the *Daily Mail.* A suspicion formed, even if no one dared yet to say it, that the Beatles were not infallible.

A further bloody mess of controversy was just around the corner. To promote their American tour Capitol had issued a compilation album of songs from *Help!* and *Rubber Soul,* plus three from the new British album still awaiting release. The title of this hybrid, reflecting its most lyrical McCartney contribution, was *The Beatles—Yesterday and Today.* Any promise of gentle nostalgia was dispelled by a full-color sleeve on which the Beatles, wearing white butchers' overalls, nursed dismembered and decapitated toy dolls and brandished bloody joints of meat.

The "butcher sleeve," as it became known, was the Beatles' own art-directing concept. Sean O'Mahony, editor of their fan club magazine, had been present at the photographic session and had covered his eyes in dismay when the props were brought in. Such was their power by then that Brian's misgivings were overruled. The gruesome tableau appeared first in England, on the cover of *Disc* magazine. Capitol Records, cowed by their former lack of prescience, agreed that it would probably be a winner. Seven hundred and fifty thousand sleeves had been printed before the first calls came in from disk jockeys almost retching over their advance copies. The sleeve was then axed, together with all the promotional material, at a cost of two hundred thousand dollars. A special staff spent one weekend extracting each of the 750,000 discs from its butcher sleeve and inserting it into one hastily improvised round a picture of the Beatles leaning on a cabin trunk. In many cases, to save trouble, the new sleeve was simply pasted over the old.

As to which Beatle had proposed the bloody joints and limbless dolls, there was never any serious doubt. The banned cover, a bitterly resentful John Lennon said, was "as relevant as Vietnam." His tone, people noticed, was neither cheeky nor funny.

Meanwhile, John's "bigger than Jesus" remark continued to be denounced from pulpits across the world. Both the Spanish and South African governments issued official condemnations, though the latter, still ostracized for its racial policies, did not carry excessive moral weight. The Pope added his disapproval via the Vatican newspaper *L'Osservatore Romano,* which declared that "some subjects must not be dealt with profanely, even in the world of beatniks."

Though debilitated with hives as well as groggy from a bout of flu,

Brian flew to New York ahead of the tour party in an attempt to calm, at least, the American furor. Nat Weiss remembers how his anxiety and distress when he got off the plane were not just about the huge sum of tour earnings at stake. "He really cared most about the possibility that the Beatles would suffer abuse—that they might even be in danger," Weiss says. "The first question he asked me was: 'What will it cost to cancel the tour?' I said: 'A million dollars.' He said: 'I'll pay it. I'll pay it out of my own pocket, because if anything were to happen to any one of them, I'd never forgive myself.' "

Using all his powers of diplomacy, Brian assured the American press that John had intended no sacrilege, but only wished to express concern at the decline in spiritual values. It was announced that when the Beatles arrived on August 12, John himself would formally apologize. He did so at a press conference in Chicago, pale and nervous—for the hate mail that he had been receiving had badly shaken him. "I'm sorry I opened my mouth," he said. "I'm not anti-God, anti-Christ, or antireligion. I wouldn't knock it. I didn't mean we were greater or better."

So began the tour destined to be the worst, if not yet officially last, of all. To add to the general unease, a famous American clairvoyant had predicted that three of the four Beatles would die soon in an air crash. Though the prophecy was later retracted, it cast a lingering tremor over the constant shuttle flights. Mal Evans was convinced he would not survive the tour, and spent one journey between concerts composing a last letter to his wife, Lil, and his new baby daughter, Julie.

All four Beatles became conscious for the first time of a threat that had worried Brian since the American tours began—that some night, in some huge, oval human sea, someone might be hiding with a high-velocity rifle. In each big-city stadium, grinding out the numbers they could no longer hear, they felt themselves endangered now by something other than dangerous adoration. At Memphis, their first concert south of the Mason-Dixon Line, the backstage fear was as palpable as sweat. On television earlier that day a portly wizard of the Ku Klux Klan had promised that if they went onstage, the Klan would fully justify its name as a terror organization. Instead of jelly beans, rubbish began to land on the stage. Halfway through the performance, a firecracker exploded. Brian, for one hideous moment, thought it was a rifle shot.

Almost every major venue along the tour route seemed to bring its own peculiar curse. In Washington, D.C., the Beatles had to play in competition with a race riot a few blocks away. At the Los Angeles Dodger Stadium scores of innocent fans were manhandled by security staff and attacked by baton-wielding police. In Cincinnati, the concert promoter tried to economize by building a stage with no roof or canopy. Just before the Beatles went out to play a downpour of rain began. They could not have gone ahead without serious risk of electrocution. "The whole audience—thirty-five thousand screaming kids— had to be turned away," Nat Weiss says. "They all got passes for a show the next day but, for a while, it really looked ugly out there. All the Beatles were frightened. Paul, I know, was physically sick."

The final concert of the tour was on August 29 at Candlestick Park, San Francisco. "Brian told me it was the end in San Francisco," Nat Weiss says. "He was dejected. 'This is it,' he told me, 'this is the last one ever.'"

The day was to be even more terrible than Brian anticipated. For some months past he had been living with an American youth, but the relationship had proved too stormy, and physically violent, even for Brian's taste. Unlike previous partners, the youth proved recalcitrant when shown the door and had threatened to tell the whole story to the Beatles unless given a substantial sweetener. Through Nat Weiss, Brian had paid him three thousand dollars in exchange for a promise to stay off this present tour, when one single further word of bad publicity would have been disastrous.

By the time the tour party reached Los Angeles, however, Brian had started to hanker for his former lover again. Against Weiss's pleas, he was brought to L.A., put up in a bungalow at the Beverly Hills Hotel, and invited to the Beverly Hills house where Brian and Weiss were based.

On August 29, after the Beatles had left for San Francisco, the two returned to the house to discover that both their briefcases had been stolen. Weiss's merely contained business papers, but Brian's was a compendium of drugs, homosexual correspondence, and pornographic pictures, plus a hefty sum in cash skimmed off the tour's concert receipts, which he had intended to share among the Beatles as a bonus. While the money was of little consequence, the briefcase's other contents put a lethal blackmail weapon into any ill-wisher's hands. Brian was so convulsed with terror and dread that he dared not even leave the house.

So, to his lasting remorse, he missed the Beatles' last live concert. He never forgave himself for not being at Candlestick Park, on that night of all nights, to watch over the four boys in his charge.

Britain, that summer of 1966, had little cause to feel pleased with itself or the world. The year, barely half-expended, could already chalk up the varying torments of a general election and a national shipping strike. The pound ailed; inflation kept briskly on the ascent. The reelected Wilson government stood revealed, not as dynamic or purposeful but merely another set of politicians, with the usual capacity to bungle and vacillate. Rhodesia, having seceded from British rule a year earlier, still thumbed a derisive nose at her fuming mother country across the world. From still further afield came noises that penetrated even the age-old British indifference to what was still vaguely thought of as the Orient. America began bombing the North Vietnamese cities of Hanoi and Haiphong. A war hitherto faint and far-flung ceased to happen comfortably out of earshot.

There was, however, bright sunshine. The British, as they had in the past forgotten pestilence, famine, the Great War, Hitler's bombs, and the Suez Crisis, now just as easily forgot Mr. Wilson, Vietnam, and the pay freeze under the influence of weeks of unbroken summer. So 1966 was to pass into popular remembrance: not for crises, both present and promised, but for blue skies, soft breezes, and for two events—the only two—that fortified that ephemeral happiness.

On July 30, England won the World Football [Soccer] Cup, audaciously snatching the vital goal in the last seconds of the final against Germany. Old wartime animosities doubtless assisted the fervor with which, on another hot summer evening, the victorious team was welcomed home to London. Footballers looked like pop singers now; they grew their hair, wore trendy clothes, and received the approbation of great men. For Harold Wilson, naturally, was there, puffing his pipe as smugly as if England's winning goal had originated in a cabinet memorandum.

The second, even more potent source of national esteem owed its origin to America's *Time* magazine, which had only recently gotten around to noticing the Swinging London phenomenon that, in fact, had peaked more than a year earlier. On April 13, *Time* had devoted its cover and a breathless twelve-page report to London as "the Style Capital of Europe," a judgment with which other American mainstream magazines like *Life* and the *Saturday Evening Post* were quick to agree. As a result, London was experiencing an influx of American visitors unknown since World War II. Hitherto, crossing the Atlantic had always been prohibitively expensive, creating Britain's image of the American tourist as a cigar-chewing plutocrat with a guidebook. But now a coincidental drop in transatlantic air fares allowed thousands—millions—of American students, even schoolchildren, to come across under their own steam and experience the staid old capital's new short-skirted, strange-scented wonders. Almost without exception, the first question these visitors asked on touching down at Heathrow was "Where can I find the Beatles?"

On August 5, an album appeared in the record shops that, were it not for the fact that approximately one million copies had been ordered in advance, might have seemed to stand little chance of being noticed on the shelves. Its cover, amid its rivals' Carnaby colors, was plain black and white: a collage of photo fragments spiraling through what looked like palm fronds but proved on close inspection to be hair, encircling four silhouetted faces so instantly recognizable, it was not thought necessary to print their collective name. Who else in the world would announce themselves in graphics reflecting the smartest magazines? Who would call a record album simply *Revolver,* investing even that commonplace pun with the sleekness of some newly minted avant garde? Who but the Beatles would have confidence colossal enough to be so chastely downbeat?

Revolver was not presented in the usual patchwork album style but as a continuous, cohesive performance, as if they had chosen Abbey Road's Studio Two as a substitute stage. There was, first of all, to underline this, some stagey coughing and throat clearing. Then came "Taxman," not a love song but a bitter satire written as well as lead sung by a chronically bitter George Harrison, railing against the huge portion of the Beatles' earnings due in income tax under jolly Mr. Wilson. There was "Eleanor Rigby," sung by Paul alone with a string octet, a song more like a short story, evoking Paul's Irish Catholic roots, about a lonely woman picking up other people's wedding rice. There was John's "I'm Only Sleeping," answering back Paul's sentimental conscience with a paean to unrepentant apathy. There was the contrast of George's sitar-squibbly "Love You To" and the stunning, simple charm of Paul's latest Jane idyll, "Here, There and Everywhere." There was "Yellow Submarine," a song for children (as it seemed) perfectly suited to Ringo's happy drone, accompanied by slurpings and gurglings, ringing ships' bells, a subaqueous brass band, and commands from the bridge in a John Lennon funny voice; and then John's nonfunny voice, in "She Said She Said," among graffiti-like guitar phrases, saying "I know what it's like to be dead."

On side two, to glorify the weather, there was "Good Day Sunshine." There was "And Your Bird Can Sing," more lucid Lennon nonsense, and Paul's pretty, self-pitying "For No One." There was "Doctor Robert," the first of many in-jokes and concealed references to be planted in Beatles music: a sly dig at one of the upmarket medical men who kept them supplied with pills. There was George's "I Want to Tell You," with its wonderful message to pampered, unharassed, and fully employed 1966 teenagers that it was still okay to feel flat and dissatisfied (or "hung up") the way George did; and then Paul's "Got to Get You into My Life," a soul song as neat and brassy and rousing as ever came out of Memphis or Chicago.

The Beatles, in fact, were not the first to nail down Swinging London in sound. Four months earlier, the Rolling Stones' *Aftermath* album had created very much the same King's Road and Carnaby Street feel, thanks mainly to the multi-instrumental talent of Brian Jones, whose intuitive sitar playing made George by contrast sound as though his fingers were all thumbs. But no one looked to the Stones to catch the zeitgeist, whereas for the Beatles it was now almost a duty to be in step with the nation's destiny. Thus *Revolver* became the perfect aural snapshot of Britain's greatest triumph since 1940, a moment that would be still un-equaled and revisited as often as its soundtrack was replayed half a century later.

If they were not quite the first to distill the present, they made up for it by prophesying the future soon to dawn. It was there on *Revolver*'s seemingly aberrant closing track, "Tomorrow Never Knows," a Ringo saying transmuted by John into a weird mélange of backward-played tapes, his once exuberant lead voice flattened to near tunelessness. "Turn off your mind, relax and float downstream / Lay down all thought, surrender to the void / Or play the game Existence to the end. Of the beginning." Like England World Cup victories, the days of "She loves you, yeah, yeah, yeah" were over for good and all.

The four who stopped running, who stood still at last in 1966 looking curiously about them, were beings such as the modern world had never seen. Only in ancient times, when boy emperors and pharaohs were clothed, even fed, with pure gold, had very young men commanded an equivalent adoration, fascination, and constant, expectant scrutiny. Nor could anyone suppose that to be thus—to have such youth and wealth, such clothes and cars and servants and women, made for any state other than inconceivable happiness. For no one since the boy pharaohs, since the fatally pampered boy Caesars, had known, as the Beatles now knew, how it felt to have felt everything, done everything, tasted everything, had a surfeit of everything; to live on that blinding, deadening, numbing surfeit that made each, on bad days, think he was aging at twice the usual rate.

It was as little comprehensible that to command such fame as the Beatles might not be enough; that each, in the stupendous collective adoration, felt himself to be overlooked as an individual; that each on his own should long to test the reality, or otherwise, of his independent existence.

John Lennon seemed the most determined—and best qualified—to make an individual career. That autumn, with Neil Aspinall, he detached himself from the other three to appear in a new film, *How I Won the War*, directed by the now extremely fashionable and financable Richard Lester. It had been clear to Lester, even in the harmless knockabout of the two Beatles films, that John had serious possibilities as a screen actor. This view was confirmed when *How I Won the War* went on release and John's portrayal of Private Gripweed was singled out for critical praise. "I told him then he could do anything he wanted in films," Richard Lester says. "But he wasn't interested. It came too easily to him. He despised it."

The Beatle who had vanished into Private Gripweed was never to reemerge. He kept his hair cropped short—a renunciation already front-page news throughout the world. He took to wearing the glasses he had always hated, perversely choosing little owl-eyed frames like those prescribed for him at primary school in the 1940s.

Under the cropped hair, the granny glasses, the clothes that tended increasingly toward flowered scarves and loose waistcoats, much of the same old John remained. The same impossible vagueness still caused him to forget the words of his own songs, his unlisted telephone number, even his aunt Mimi's first name. The same impossible generosity would still press on anyone his last cigarette or whatever was in his pocket, whether sixpence or a thousand pounds. The same blistering sarcasm and silly puns kept those around him suspended between terror of his contempt and helpless, incredulous laughter.

When he came off the road in 1966 John's life seemed to hold so many possibilities. Publishers wanted him to write for them. Print engravers and greeting card companies urged him to draw for them. Art galleries—now springing up in London almost as rapidly as boutiques—begged him to attend their private views. Art seemed to engage his whole attention for a time. He would drive up from Weybridge two or three times a week in the rainbow-daubed Rolls-Royce whose Scottish chauffeur also used it as an occasional bed.

Newest of all the new little West End galleries was the Indica in Mason's Yard, run by Marianne Faithfull's ex-husband, John Dunbar. In November 1966, the Indica was hanging an exhibition called "Unfinished Paintings and Objects by Yoko Ono." The artist, a Japanese-born American, enjoyed minor notoriety in London for having recently exhibited her photographs of various unclothed human bottoms.

The night before the Indica exhibition opened, John arrived to look at it. He spent quite a long time over the Unfinished Paintings and Objects, particularly a painting attached to the ceiling with a ladder up to it and an apple unembellished but for a price ticket saying "£200." Later on, John Dunbar sent Yoko across to talk to him in hopes he might turn out a useful patron. She proved to be very small and dressed entirely in black, her face almost obscured by clouds of black hair. Instead of speaking, she handed John a card on which was written the single word "Breathe."

Next day, he was back in the small living room in one corner of the mansion that had taken nine months to decorate, folded up inside the small sofa he preferred to all his pastel-upholstered acres. He would lie there for hours, watching television or half-watching it, glancing at books and papers, then throwing them aside. He could lie there all day, not speaking to Cynthia, not seeming to notice Julian, his trance penetrable only by some scrap of nonsense from a TV quiz, some stray paragraph from the *Daily Express*, some costly and purposeless toy like his "nothing box," a black plastic cube in which red lights winked on and off at random. He could spend hours in trying to guess which of the red lights would wink on next.

Late at night, if no excursion was happening, he would unfold himself from the couch and wander away to his studio, the guitars, the Vox organ, the ten linked-up Brunel tape recorders. Cynthia knew she would not see him again that night. Next day, she would have to keep the house quiet until early afternoon, when she took up his breakfast tray.

Sitting downstairs with her drawing or her needlework, cowed by the feuding between Dot, the housekeeper, and the general factotum's wife, afraid to go outside the grounds in case some photographer saw Julian; thrifty, soft-spoken, eternally hoping for the best, Cyn was the same person she had always been.

Paul, the most committed performer, the most addicted to worship, the one who had worked the hardest at being a Beatle, now found himself at something of a loss. His first act, after the touring stopped, was to take a long and, for him, extravagant sabbatical. With Mal Evans—whose wife, Lil, still waited patiently at home in Sunbury-on-Thames—he set out on a long road safari across Africa.

His future, Paul announced on returning, would be concerned with all-round cultural self-improvement. He felt—as, indeed, both John and George did—that being a Beatle had been a form of missing life. The A-level Institute boy was excited, too, by London's increasing artistic bustle. "People are saying things and painting things and writing things that are great," he told the *Evening Standard*. "I must *know* what people are doing."

In this endeavor, as in all Paul's private life, his girlfriend Jane Asher was the main stimulus. Jane, unlike the other Beatles women, possessed complete independence: Now twenty-one, she had her own highly successful stage and film career. With her angelic looks went a strong mind and forthright manner that curtailed Paul's ego, deflated his superstar pomposities, and made her a companion altogether preferable to any of the brainless beauties who clustered adoringly round him. He made a point of seeing all Jane's plays, wherever the run happened to start. It was in Bristol, waiting to see Jane in a play, that a shopfront name gave him the idea for "Eleanor Rigby." His best love songs had been written for Jane: In the feather-light "Here, There and Everywhere" she is an almost tangible presence.

His first project apart from the other Beatles was the composition of theme music for a new British comedy film, *The Family Way*. *Newsweek* magazine—which otherwise would hardly have noticed such a minor piece—considered his score "neat and resourceful." He had already begun producing records—for Peter and Gordon, the duo featuring Peter Asher, Jane's brother; for a group called the Escourts; and for Cliff Bennett and the Rebel Rousers when they covered his song "Got to Get You into My Life."

He had chosen a house at last: not in stockbroker land with the other Beatles but on Cavendish Avenue, St. John's Wood. The district epitomized his cultural and social ambitions and was also conveniently close to the EMI studios. The house, discreetly large, was enclosed by high walls and protected by electronic security gates. With it, Paul acquired the accessory status symbols of a married couple: butler and cook. An Old English sheepdog named Martha roamed the extensive garden that, despite his family's protests, he resolutely neglected.

As far as the press and public were concerned, the most interesting thing about Paul's self-improvement program was the point in it when he and Jane Asher would announce their engagement. Jane had helped him to decorate and furnish the new house although, with a nicety characteristic of both, she did not officially live with him there.

Each of them had grown adept at fending off the same old, microphone-thrusting question. "I certainly would be most surprised," Jane said, "if I married anyone but Paul." And Paul himself, caught yet again outside his electronic gates, looked up from his Aston Martin with the geniality that never seemed to falter, listened to the question, considered, and replied: "Just say that when you asked me that, I smiled."

George, so it seemed, was even more at a loss. He had been a Beatle ever since the age of fifteen. All his adult life had been spent running or, with his gradually more magnificent guitar, his mop-top framing his pale, wary face, just standing there.

For the final year of touring, if not longer, George had actively hated his Beatle existence. On the outside, it might appear pure gold; on the inside, it bristled with snubs and slights—the patronizing air of George Martin in the studio; the overwhelming brilliance of John and Paul's partnership that allowed him, if he was lucky, one song per album; the realization that in their eyes he was still what he had been in Liverpool, the kid just tagging along.

His unvented rage he turned upon the adoring world. While Beatlemania was still a laugh to the others, to George it was an affront against the musicianship he had so laboriously taught himself. His fame seemed to have brought him only money and a terrible touchiness—a suspicion, already voiced in one song lyric, of "people standing round who screw you in the ground." His wife, Patti—they had married in January 1966—virtually gave up her modeling career lest, in George's eyes, people should try to exploit him through her.

It had been with the idlest curiosity, on the *Help!* film set, that George first heard Indian sitars playing a burlesque version of the Beatles' own song "A Hard Day's Night." *Help!* was, of course, a goonish romp about Eastern mystics in pursuit of a sacrificial jewel. The finale was a pitched battle between Beatles and dacoits in the surf along a Bahamas beach while a many-armed Hindu idol lolled in the offshore swell. As Richard Lester remembers, no one quite knew if it was part of the script or not when, in the midst of shooting, an Indian suddenly rode up on a bicycle and handed each Beatle a small religious book.

From the joke film property and the Indian on the bicycle grew the earnest passion that was to make George Harrison the least recognizable Beatle of all. He acquired a sitar of his own and began to play it, initially as if it was a guitar. Clumsy as his first experiments were, they gave him something he had never had before—a definite and distinctive contribution to what the Beatles did in the studio. For not even George Martin could be snooty about sitars. The sound tentatively used on *Rubber Soul* was one of the prime elements, and praised as such, in *Revolver*. Henceforward it was recognized that when a group of Indians walked in and squatted down, balancing their strange, giraffe-necked instruments against the ball of one bare foot, that was when George took over and gave orders. In 1966, at a dinner party, he met Ravi Shankar, the Indian sitar virtuoso who offered to visit his bungalow in Esher and give him private tuition.

He had already been to India once, briefly, on the run from the Philippines. In autumn 1966—after what he at least firmly regarded as the Beatles' last appearance—he returned there with Patti for two months' sitar study under Ravi Shankar. He also met Shankar's spiritual teacher, or guru, who explained to him the law of karma—the Buddhist principle of inevitability. He and Patti traveled to Kashmir, where they witnessed religious festivals and conversed with students and holy men.

Just as he had once obsessively applied himself to the guitar, George now devoted his life to sitar practice. In this period, indeed, he rarely touched a guitar outside the recording studio. He practiced day and night, sitting on the floor in his Indian tunic with Ravi Shankar's instructions playing on tape.

George, too, was now regularly taking LSD. For him, the mental landscape the drug produced was one he had already seen. It was the India of mystic sounds and mystic beings, able to levitate or lie on spikes or bury themselves; the India that, in sight and touch and voice and clamor and calm, was the furthest distance you could go from being a Beatle, wearing a suit, and singing, "Yeah, yeah, yeah." He who had always kept his mind shut tight against all schooling, now began to devour books about yoga and meditation. The books promised a state he had so far found unattainable—of perfect pleasure, "enlightenment," and peace. He need not worry then about the taxman and who was screwing him; about who recognized him, or failed to recognize him; about the girls who climbed into the garden he cultivated like a northern working man and broke the tops off his roses.

Only Ringo seemed to know for certain what he wanted. He wanted to stay at home with Maureen and their new baby, Zak. They called the baby Zak because it was the name Ringo had wished for when small. Life for Ringo was still that simple, even when he stood in the grounds of Sunny Heights, looking across his landscaped garden to the wall half-constructed by his own building company, and at his cars, the Facel Vega, the Land-Rover, the Mini Cooper, and at the house itself with its miles of soft furnishings, its white carpets, its six TV sets, its movie equipment, billiard table, and Las Vegas-style fruit machine. He would remember his childhood in the Liverpool Dingle and all those lonely hospital beds, and think: "What's a scruff like me doing with all this lot?"

Even as separate householders and individual millionaires, they could not stop being together. No wife, no girlfriend yet had broken the inexplicable bond among four individuals who had not only grown up together but also helped each other through an ordeal none but that four understood. The habit continued of doing things, wearing things, buying things, having crazes for things in unison. When John took to wearing glasses, the others did. Paul and John, during the New Delhi stopover, bought sitars like George's. All took simultaneously to baggy-sleeved flowered shirts, high-buttoning Prince Albert coats, wide-brimmed hats, and loosely tied scarves. And early in 1967, on the upper lips of all four, there appeared identical small curved mustaches.

Just as on tour, the people closest to them were the two fellow Liverpudlians who, as road managers, had so long formed their only bulwark against the world. Neil—or, as John called him, Nell—Aspinall, the nervous, clever former accounting student, and Mal Evans, the inoffensive ex-bouncer, continued to fill a role necessary to each Beatle and the four as a unit. Neil and Mal went where the Beatles went, wore what the Beatles wore, smoked what the Beatles smoked: For their not overlarge salaries they remained perpetually on call to provide any Beatle with any of life's necessities, from a transcontinental chauffeur to a tray of tea and toast. Mal's wife, Lil, in Sunbury, did not see him for weeks at a time. Neil—paradoxically in the service of such masters—was starting to lose his hair.

Similarly, the close friends each Beatle had tended to be friends acquired collectively, in Liverpool or Hamburg. There was Tony Bramwell, George's childhood acquaintance, who had progressed from NEMS office boy to stage manager of Brian's latest venture, the Saville theater. There was Terry Doran, another Brian friend, his partner in Brydor Cars, but welcome in every Beatles home for his willingness to go anywhere, fetch anything, and his talent to amuse. There was Klaus Voorman, their art student friend from Hamburg, the boy whom Astrid forsook for Stu Sutcliffe. Klaus now played bass guitar in the Manfred Mann group but had stayed close enough to his former Hamburg mates to design the *Revolver* album sleeve. There was also, intermittently, Pete Shotton, John Lennon's old school and skiffle crony, whom John had recompensed for the night he smashed Pete's washboard over his head by buying a supermarket for him to run in Hampshire.

Creatively, the band seemed to be coasting—little dreaming it was just the calm before the storm. Though committed to making a third film for United Artists, they could not agree with Walter Shenson, their producer, over a script. John, especially, complained that in *Help!* they had been "extras in our own film." One idea was that they should make a Western; another was that they should play the Three Musketeers; another—the one that Shenson thought most promising—visualized them as four living facets of the same personality. As with the previous two films, Shenson looked around for a quality writer. A script was commissioned from Joe Orton, the young working-class dramatist whose macabre comedies *Loot* and *Entertaining Mr. Sloane* had each been huge West End successes.

Orton visited Brian Epstein at Chapel Street to discuss the project. Paul, who had much admired *Loot*, was also there. "I'd expected Epstein to be florid, Jewish, dark-haired, and overbearing," Orton wrote in his diary. "Instead, I was face-to-face with a mousey-haired, slight young man. He had a suburban accent. Rather washed out. Paul was just as in the photographs. Only he'd grown a mustache. 'The only thing I get from the theatre,' Paul M said, 'is a sore arse' . . ."

Orton, typically, produced an outrageous script entitled *Up Against It* in which the Beatles were to be portrayed as anarchists, adulterers, and urban guerillas. After a long delay, the script was rejected without comment. "An amateur and a fool," wrote Orton angrily of Brian. "Probably he will never say Yes. Equally he hasn't the courage to say No. A thoroughly weak, flaccid type."

During November, the Beatles had returned to Abbey Road in what proved an abortive attempt to make an end-of-year follow-up to *Revolver*. All that appeared that Christmas was a cut-rate collection of Beatles oldies-but-goldies and the traditional zany recorded message to their fan club.

What with one thing and another these days, they seemed to see almost nothing of Brian. From various intermediaries like Peter Brown and Geoffrey Ellis they had heard that he seemed depressed. But at that moment the thought concerned them rather less than what in hell they were going to put out as their next album, if anything.

FIFTEEN

"I DON'T THINK THERE WAS ANY HOPE FOR HIM SINCE THE DAY HE MET THE BEATLES"

For those whose blessed good fortune it was to grow up in the 1960s, the year to be remembered above all is 1967. Already in the twentieth century, moments of especially purblind human delusion had been symbolized by summers—the long Edwardian summer before World War I; the hot summer of still trusting to Hitler's essential good intentions in 1939. But none of those could compare, nor ever will, to 1967's so-called Summer of Love.

Internationally, the world had probably never had less love in it. America's "limited" military intervention to support South Vietnam's friendly government against the communist north had swollen into an all-out conflict, demanding huge resources in machinery and men and remorselessly laying waste one of the most beautiful countries in Southeast Asia. It was the first war of the television age, and one in which America's military had yet to learn the most fundamental techniques of news management. European TV crews flocked to record a conflagration in which women and children, often of stunning beauty and grace, perished by the thousand. Horrific images were beamed into every Western living room: of helicopter gunships strafing rice paddies; of toddlers blistered from head to toe by a state-of-the art incendiary called napalm; of a U.S. Army spokesman declaring in all earnestness, "In order to save this village, it was necessary to destroy it."

America, for the first time in her history, found herself involved in a war she could not win, a war that, even more bewilderingly, was opposed by many Americans. A wave of pacifist feeling swept the country, not among cranks and beatniks only but among the ordinary teenagers now liable for military service. Protest as a concept left the lunatic fringe, spreading through formerly peaceable universities, spreading also into the black ghettos whose young men were impartially called on to fight for a system that still oppressed them. Pop music was a reflection—even aggravation—of the new rebellious mood. Bob Dylan's bitter mockery, the sweet reproaches of Joan Baez, became the spur to antiwar demonstrations and marches, and the ever-increasing numbers who fled "the military draft" to Canada or Europe.

So the American Dream began to dissolve. Yet that bitter awakening, ironically, produced its own short, golden reverie in a city harboring more American dreams than most. Like the first settlers and the gold-seekers, like the Zen Buddhists of the early sixties, like Kerouac and his "beat" poets, America's dissenting youth in 1967 turned their eyes to that side of the republic where the ocean began and, in particular, where the ocean's space and freedom seemed reflected in the city of San Francisco.

San Francisco's rundown Haight-Ashbury district had long ago been settled by a homespun and bewhiskered hippie community. That community now swelled with the arrival of draft dodgers, disaffected students, and social dropouts by the thousand. Fresh hippie colonies sprang up along the northern California coast, around the University of California at Berkeley, and in remote beach hamlets like Big Sur. The environment, with its natural beauty and leisurely policing, was ideally suited to resignation from all conventional American life. More and more came to share the hippie heaven: to grow their hair, put on flowing robes, and walk barefoot; to speak softly, behave meekly, offer each other flowers, and turn on by means of the small, limp cigarettes that somehow became more special the more mouths had previously dragged on them.

Marijuana was the badge of hippie brotherhood, the odor most common in hippie refuges, the initiator of the hippie belief that through drugs lay a path to higher wisdom and humaneness. A middle-aged university physicist, Dr. Timothy Leary, was already their leader—or guru—following his dismissal from Harvard for experiments into the psychedelic (literally, mind-expanding) properties of LSD. Leary and his academic converts led the awakening interest in drug-inspired literature, from Byron to Aldous Huxley, and of drug-sanctioning Eastern religions. Joss sticks were thus tentatively lit in California, and Buddhist prayers phonetically intoned. Astrology became a youth fad to rival the hula hoop. It was through astrology most of all that wisdom became available: an age-old wisdom settling, in the pot smoke, over woolly and impressionable minds. An entire new vocabulary evolved to distinguish the hippie from his persecutor, the beautiful from the short-haired and workaday, the divine souls who turned on, tuned in, freaked out, and blew their minds from the residue of unenlightened humanity.

Musicians, being natural converts, blew the hippie happening like pollen across America. By early 1967, San Francisco groups like Jefferson Airplane and the Grateful Dead were bringing the first rumors to British youth—of Haight-Ashbury and Big Sur and a huge outdoor concert at Monterey; of harsh new metal sounds and flashing lights; of a new dream world that young Britons, having no Big Sur, only Margate and Llandudno, supposed they must be content to experience at second hand.

On February 17, Parlophone released two new Beatles songs: "Penny Lane" and "Strawberry Fields Forever." The tracks had been recorded late in 1966 for the album that was to surpass *Revolver:* With a lightweight ditty called "When I'm Sixty-Four" they represented the sum of almost three months' work. Since a single was long overdue, George Martin had no choice but to sacrifice the two three-minute productions that, each in its own way, had involved more time and expense than most entire LPs. The double-A-side formula was less a boast than a political necessity, since one side was wholly John's and the other entirely Paul's: The weight of creativity packed into each only emphasized what a gulf lay between them.

Strawberry Field was the name of a Salvation Army children's home John remembered from his Liverpool boyhood. The song he had named after this childhood landmark began with the air of a nostalgia trip ("Let me take you down, 'cause I'm goin' . . .") then dissolved into LSD hallucinations, intensified still further by chronic myopic pun making ("Nothing is real. And nothing to get hungabout"). The lyric was a stream of semiconsciousness conjuring forth all the elements in John's character—now loftily philosophical, now angry, now fearful, now sarcastic, now despairing, now wearily resigned—seesawing between the surreal and the colloquial ("Er, yes but it's all right . . ."), in total adding up to nothing that remotely resembled a Salvation Army children's home nor a field of strawberries, yet destined to imprint each obscure image and clouded thought on the listener with the burning-brand indelibility of Blake's "Jerusalem."

Paul's "Penny Lane," by contrast, re-created with photographic clarity a part of Liverpool well known to all the Beatles, the place where Aunt Mimi used to see John off to Dovedale Primary and where the Quarry Men had played their earliest gigs at the little hall called Barney's. It mentioned the traffic circle, the fire station, the barber's with its shop-window portraits of satisfied customers; it had a cast of characters including the fireman with his loyal "picture of the Queen," and a "pretty nurse" like Paul's own much missed mother, "selling poppies from a tray." It evoked the "blue suburban skies" and "pouring rain" of their Liverpool childhood, the "four of fish" (i.e., four-pennyworth) they would order at their local fish 'n' chips, the "finger pie" (poking at a girl's crotch with a forefinger, then sniffing it) that was their ultimate sexual thrill before they were old enough to make love in earnest. It was surrealism from a rational mind, as recognizable yet mysterious as looking at someone else's family snaps.

As an arranger, Martin's only guide was Paul's enthusiasm for the piccolo trumpet passage in Bach's "Brandenberg Concerto." David Mason of the London Symphony Orchestra stood by in Studio Two with his piccolo trumpet while Paul hummed the notes he wanted and Martin inked them into a score.

"Strawberry Fields" proved an even greater test of the producer's ingenuity. The song, as John first played it on acoustic guitar, was a simple, reflective melody. With the other Beatles added, it changed to the heavy metal style they were already absorbing from the San Francisco psychedelic groups. John liked it that way at first but then, a few days later, asked Martin to produce a softer arrangement with trumpets and cellos. In the end, he could not decide between the two versions. He said he liked the beginning of one but preferred the ending of the other. Martin had to find a way of splicing half the heavy metal version with half the orchestral one. To his lasting credit, no one noticed the join.

With each song came a color film sequence designed to be shown on television pop shows in place of the band themselves. Rather than the usual straight performance shots, however, these were minifantasies heightening the mood of the music, with the Carnaby-colored Beatles appearing as actors rather than musicians. For "Strawberry Fields" they were shown romping through a landscape that was actually Knole Park, the Kentish stately home, playing tag around an oak tree, and seated around an open-air dinner table laid with candelabra, being waited on by footmen in stockings and powdered wigs (one of whom, in an un-witting moment of truth, was their roadie, Mal Evans). For "Penny Lane" they were seen riding white horses through cobbled streets that actually belonged to London's East End, with intercut shots of the real Penny Lane, still scarcely altered since their childhood. The age of pop video starts here.

Self-surpassing talent, given in double measure, resulted in the first Beatles single since 1962 that did not reach number one in the Top Twenty. It climbed to second place, but was just nosed out for the top spot by a middle-of-the-road ballad containing no innovation what-ever: Engelbert Humperdinck's "Release Me."

The fact was, the Beatles now had an influence no longer measurable by the Top Twenty alone. George Melly, the jazz singer and critic and a fellow Liverpudlian, reviewed "Penny Lane" as poetry: It was, he said, a true evocation of Liverpool in the 1950s with "great sandstone churches and the trams rattling past." The imagery worked with no less power on those who had never seen Liverpool and barely remembered the fifties, those for whom Penny Lane's blue suburban skies, like Strawberry Fields' acid-swirling bridle path, became a mirage eclipsing even that of San Francisco. You heard it even better, people said, when you were high.

Late in 1966, at his Belgravia home, Brian Epstein tried to commit sui-cide with an overdose of sleeping tablets. Fortunately, both his secretary, Joanne Newfield, and his chauffeur, Brian Barratt, were on hand to thwart him. Barratt broke down the double doors to his bedroom while Joanne telephoned for Dr. Norman Cowan, the physician who had been regularly treating him. The three managed to keep Brian conscious until they could get him to his usual clinic.

The attempt was kept secret among those, like Joanne or Peter Brown, who were privy to his homosexual life and so familiar with its leitmotif of despair. Doomed love affairs with brutal boys had driven him often to the brink before. But always before he had had the means to recover, to convince himself, as no rational argument could, that his life still held pleasure and purpose.

For Brian, that pleasure and purpose were extinguished on August 29, 1966, when the Beatles gave their last concert in Candlestick Park, San Francisco; when Brian, terrified and preoccupied as he was that day, would have given anything to unravel the years and the wealth and be back at Barnston Women's Institute, watching four boys arrive with their new stage suits in Burton's shopping bags.

On the homeward flight he had almost let his unhappiness show. "What am I going to do now?" he kept saying. "Shall I go back to school and learn something new?"

The Beatles, for five years, for the centuries contained in each of those years, had been his all-eclipsing passion. He had lived for them, and through them, with an intensity granted to few born under his unlucky star. He had loved them, not shamefully, not furtively, but with an idealism that millions found fit to share. That love was as the painter for his canvas, the parent for his children, the lost soul for its salvation. Having been hardly noticed, it was not rejected with any great show of regret.

He remained the Beatles' manager; a celebrity in that due proportion. He was, indeed, rather more often in the papers nowadays since their submersion in private projects and recording. Was it true they had started to break up? Quite untrue, Brian patiently said. They were simply resting. After what they had been through, who could blame them? Just before Christmas 1966, when a nursery school in the Welsh village of Aberfan was engulfed by a coal slag heap, several public voices as good as demanded that the Beatles do a live show to help raise funds for the bereaved families. The concept of the charity benefit pop concert was then an unknown one and, much as all four sympathized with Aberfan's plight, they rejected what seemed a further move to turn them into national public property. As ever, Brian was there to explain the position on their behalf and stop the media criticism from rising above a mutter.

He might convince the press, but he did not deceive himself. A bond was broken that had, in any case, been so fragile, composed of arrangements, schedules, timetables, and notes. Despite the years and miles he had traveled with them, despite a fame and reckless wealth to equal theirs, he had no point of communication with them but a contract. Once their talent outran his efficiency Brian Epstein had no further part to play. With all else that was to be heard in their brilliant new music, Brian could hear the sound of his own doom.

He was, to outward appearances, still the epitome of that youthful success associated with Swinging London. Not yet thirty-two, he controlled an entertainment organization that, as well as the Beatles, represented some of the best-known names in show business. His personal wealth was estimated, by the *Financial Times*, at seven million pounds. Outside 13 Chapel Street his red Rolls-Royce or his silver Bentley convertible stood in the mellow Belgravia sun.

NEMS Enterprises, though administered by many hands, still owed its main direction to Brian's personal business judgment, that strange mixture of rashness and prescience. In 1965, he had bought the Saville Theatre on Shaftesbury Avenue, impervious to objections that it was just a few yards on the wrong side of the West End. The building appealed to Brian with its Art Deco exterior, its boxes with private anterooms in which leopardskin couches stood. At the Saville, he planned to put on straight plays in alternation with Sunday night pop shows. "We brought the Four Tops over from America, on the Sunday before their big record, 'Reach Out, I'll Be There,' went to number one in Britain," Tony Bramwell says. "Brian paid them $32,000 for a £2,000 gross at the Saville. Then, of course, he was able to bring them back to do a seven-week British tour."

His passion for theater led Brian to subsidize the Saville through seasons of excellent, barely profitable productions, both drama and dance. He spent a fortune on the place, much of it unnecessarily—as with his insistence on taking out all the existing seats and replacing them with more comfortable ones. He had his own box there, and his own private bar. At the Saville, he could play theatrical impresario right to the borderline of his true desire, undimmed since his RADA days—that one night on the lit stage the leading man who entered left, through French windows, would be Brian himself.

The fantasy recurred in various projects with which, after August 1966, he attempted to fill his life. There was, for instance, his plan, in partnership with the disk jockey Brian Matthew, to build a new theater-cum-record studio in Bromley, Kent. He also dabbled in bullfighting, his other surreptitious passion. He put money into a film about El Cordobes and became a sponsor of the English matador Henry Higgins.

These ventures were not for profit, since he had more than enough money: They were symptoms of Brian's desperate wish to find some other role than entrepreneur and businessman. He wanted to be creative, as the Beatles were—to establish by any possible means that credential for reentry into their world. So he tried to produce a record, for the Liverpool singer Rory Storm. He had always felt guilty at having poached Ringo Starr from Rory's group. He even tried directing a play, *Smashing Day*, at the New Arts theater. John Fernald, his old RADA teacher, had been supposed to direct it but had fallen ill. "Brian took over and really threw himself into rehearsals," Joanne Newfield says. "He was totally involved, right up to the evening of the dress rehearsal. All the cast were waiting in their costumes—but no Brian. He'd forgotten all about it."

Joanne had joined NEMS originally as secretary to Brian's assistant, the high-powered Wendy Hanson. She inherited Wendy's job in late 1966, when Brian closed down his Stafford Street office and announced he would be working entirely from Chapel Street. Sitting upstairs, under two life-size David Bailey portraits of her employer, Joanne was first to see the marked change in Brian's dress and habits. His clothes grew more flamboyant, his gestures more overtly camp; it became a struggle for Joanne to keep him to his business engagements. "I'd find notes for me in the morning, asking me to get him out of appointments—meetings or lunches. I once had to cancel Bernard Delfont four times."

One business matter had so harried and tormented Brian that he now refused even to think about it. In New York, the lawsuit against Seltaeb, the merchandising company, was about to enter its third year. The huge delay—caused largely by Brian's failure to attend pretrial examinations—had seen Nicky Byrne's claim for allegedly lost revenues rise, as the Beatles grew still more famous, from five million to twenty-two million dollars. The Beatles themselves even now knew nothing of the millions that their name had generated but that Brian had been unable to catch.

His other NEMS artists—apart from "my Cilla"—had long ago ceased to absorb his energy. Gerry Marsden was in a West End musical; Billy J. Kramer and the Fourmost had gone to other agencies. Brian was in fact actively seeking a business partner who could ultimately take over the whole NEMS operation from him. He had already offered a controlling interest to Larry Parnes, which Parnes turned down because the deal would not include the Beatles. Instead, Brian turned to Robert Stigwood, a ruddy-faced Australian who, since his arrival in London, had built up an impressive roster of emergent pop acts. Stigwood became NEMS's joint managing director, pending his acquisition of a majority shareholding. Among the new clients he brought into the company were Cream, the Moody Blues, and Jimi Hendrix, a young blues guitarist from Seattle whose explosive virtuosity had turned even modern legends like Eric Clapton and George Harrison into besotted disciples. Also under Stigwood's wing three brothers from Australia called the Bee Gees, until then thought not to have a prayer because their name sounded too much like the Beatles.

Brian himself was now rarely to be seen in the daylight hours. Joanne Newfield, arriving at Chapel Street each morning, would find her day's instructions in the note pushed under his bedroom door—a note written at dawn in amphetamine wakefulness, before the antidote drug plunged him into sleep. Sometimes, pushed under the door, there would be a pile of money, won on his perpetual journey round the Mayfair gambling clubs. "Jo . . ." one note said, "Please bank my happiness . . ."

With luck, and a little extra dose, he would not have to open his eyes until mid-afternoon. Joanne knew he had surfaced when the intercom in his bedroom was switched on. "When he first got up, he always felt terrible—hung over from drink and pills. He'd take some uppers to get over that. At about five o'clock, he'd be full of life. He'd come in and say, "Right. Let's start work."

The mounting depression, the chemicals warring within him, produced fits of irrational anger that drove Joanne many times to the point of resignation. Like others before her, she could never quite bring herself to do it. "The smallest thing could send him half-crazy. I got him a wrong number once, and he literally went berserk. He threw a whole tea tray at me. Another time, it was my birthday: He was terrible to me all day. The next day, I found this note. 'Jo—good morning. Better late than never. Many happy returns of yesterday. Be a bit tolerant of me at my worst. Really, I don't want to hurt anyone . . .' "

Several times he made a determined attempt to pull himself together. He began seeing a psychiatrist and, on at least two occasions, went into a drying-out clinic in Putney. For one period of several weeks a doctor and a nurse took up residence at Chapel Street. The nurse went out one afternoon, and Brian escaped. He was missing for two days. No one thought of looking for him where he was more and more to be found— in the dismal trysting alleyways of Piccadilly Underground station.

At other times it seemed he could find satisfaction only by creating a bizarre facsimile of his own mother, or at least the all-encompassing security she had once given him. Among his secret ports of call was a dominatrix in Mayfair whose clients also included several senior figures in the Conservative party. Her main task was to gratify the almost conscious death wish that still remained a strong part of Brian's sexual makeup while simultaneously making him feel childishly coddled and secure. He would lie in a rubber coffin while she read the newspapers out loud to him.

Life could still return to normal, as when his mother came down from Liverpool for a visit. Paradoxically, spells of conventional illness put him back on the rails. "I looked after him when he had glandular fever," Joanne Newfield says. "He had a bout of jaundice as well, when Queenie came down to stay. Brian got into a good routine then and really seemed to enjoy it. I remember one Saturday afternoon how thrilled he was that he and Peter Brown had been out to Berwick Market to buy fruit. Brian thought this was wonderful. He'd done something normal—something just the same as other people did."

Early in 1967, he made a second attempt to kill himself with a drug overdose. The Beatles were by then deeply involved in recording their new album. Brian had let an early pressing of "Strawberry Fields" / "Penny Lane" be stolen from Chapel Street by one of his boyfriends. Shortly afterward, the words "Brian Epstein is a queer" were scrawled on the garage door in lipstick. "He did once confide in me how hopeless his private life was," Joanne says. "'I'm no good with women and I'm no good with men,' he told me. He was in absolute despair that day.

"The doctor told me once that Brian was like a collision course inside himself. He could only be terribly happy or terribly unhappy. If there was any depression or misery, Brian would be drawn helplessly into it. The Beatles caused that happiness, and they caused that unhappiness. I don't think there was any hope for him since the day he met the Beatles."

The sixties' increasingly tolerant atmosphere did little to ease his particular problems. In London at least, homosexuality had lost much of its Victorian stigma, thanks mainly to the fact that even ragingly hetero young men with their long hair, velvet suits, and ruffle-fronted shirts personified the traditional notion of "queers." Nineteen sixty-seven was to see the decriminalization of homosexuality per se, with sexual acts permitted between consenting adult partners in private. But Brian's tastes left him still miles on the wrong side of the law; besides, for someone in his public position and of his parentage and religious background, it remained as impossible as ever to come out of the closet.

America still held vestiges of happiness. With his lawyer friend Nat Weiss he had formed a separate company, Nemperor Artists, to represent NEMS acts in New York. Weiss had himself gone over to artist-management, handling groups like Cyrkle, whose song "Red Rubber Ball" Brian had correctly judged a million-selling U.S. single. Nemperor Artists had another new signing, of talents as yet unrealized—Brian Epstein. He virtually gave the company to Nat Weiss so that Weiss could become *his* agent.

The portly, rather strange New Yorker had become Brian's most loyal, long-suffering friend. There were difficulties in that city, too, after encounters with predatory boys around Times Square. One day, when Brian was due to be interviewed on radio WOR-FM, Nat Weiss found him drugged almost insensible with Seconal tablets. Weiss somehow revived him and delivered him to the studio.

That interview, with the longtime Beatles adherent Murray the K, has survived on an hour-long tape in Nat Weiss's possession. It is remarkable less for the subjects covered than for the tenacity with which Brian, once on the air, fought his way back from his Seconal coma. At the beginning, he can scarcely even speak. But slowly, his voice frees itself, his thoughts unstick. He can articulate what everyone—what he most of all—has hoped to hear. The Beatles and he remain as close as they have ever been. "There hasn't been so much as . . . a row.

"At the moment they're doing great things in the studio. They take longer nowadays, of their own volition, to make records. They're hypercritical of their own work. Paul rang me the other day and said he wanted to make just one small change to a track.

"I hope 'Penny Lane' and 'Strawberry Fields' are going to prove a thing or two. And certainly—*certainly*—the new album is going to prove more than a thing or two."

"So—there we go," are Murray the K's sign-off words. "It's good to know the Beatles are still together. Eppy is still together . . ."

There had been moments at Abbey Road studios during the previous four months when George Martin wondered whether the Beatles might have gone too far this time. There was, for instance, the time they asked him to provide farmyard noises, including a pack of foxhounds in full cry. There was the matter of the Victorian steam organs, the forty-one-piece orchestra with no score to play, and the hours spent searching for a note that only dogs could hear. At such times, the Beatles' record producer feared this new album would end, if it ended at all, merely by baffling its listeners.

Early 1967 had found them in the now familiar position of having to out-do the rivals they themselves had created. After *Revolver*, every other creative mind in pop was awakening to the possibilities of an album that was not just a compendium of past hits but a self-contained work on a definite theme, its tracks working interdependently like movements in a classical concerto. Two post-*Revolver* productions from across the Atlantic that had taken the Beatles' idea several notches further on were largely responsible for driving them back into the studio. One was the Beach Boys' *Pet Sounds*, an almost Mozartian montage of multidubbed harmonies and counterpoint, recorded almost single-handedly by Brian Wilson while the rest of the band were out on tour. The second, even sharper goad was *Freak-Out* by a new California group called the Mothers of Invention: one of the first ever "double" albums, pungent with the iconoclastic wit of their leader, Frank Zappa, and embellished with quasi-comical sound effects and scraps of conversation.

The Beatles had originally meant their answer to *Pet Sounds* and *Freak-Out* to be an album in the most literal sense, each track a snapshot of Liverpool as they remembered it from childhood. But, having completed "Penny Lane" and "Strawberry Fields Forever," they found their enthusiasm for the idea beginning to wane, and simply turned over those two unmatched pearls to Martin for release as their next single. Afterward they continued recording songs with no theme save the things they were currently doing, the newspapers they chanced to be reading, the London whose language and fashion they continued both to dictate and reflect. The newest London craze was for Victorian militaria, sold in shops with ponderously quaint names like I Was Lord Kitchener's Valet. So one night, the Beatles met to rehearse a new song, in that same vein of mustachioed whimsy, entitled "Sgt. Pepper's Lonely Hearts Club Band."

"It was Paul's number," Martin says. "Just an ordinary song, not particularly brilliant as songs go. When we'd finished it, Paul said: 'Why don't we make the whole album as though the Pepper band really existed, as though Sergeant Pepper was doing the record. We can dub in effects and things.' From that moment, it was as if Pepper had a life of its own."

That life stemmed at first from simple enjoyment. They relished the idea that the four most famous pop musicians in the world should create mock bandsmen as their alter ego, and present their music in the faux-naif setting of a children's circus and pantomime. Then, as the sessions progressed, there was born in both musicians and their producer that special life, that sensation comparable only with walking on water, that comes from the certain knowledge that one is making a masterpiece.

Its strength lay in the fact that to all four Beatles the vision was the same. All four were now converted to the LSD drug. Even Paul McCartney, the cautious, the proper, had finally given in. LSD is said to have beneficial effects only if used among close friends. In *Sgt. Pepper* it not only moved the Beatles to brilliant music, it also restored them to a closeness they had nearly lost in the numbness of being adored by the whole world. It would be remembered as their best record, and also their very best performance.

Martin had no idea about the LSD at the time. The Beatles, in deference to their schoolmasterly producer, kept even innocent joints out of his sight, puffing them furtively in the gent's toilets. Martin was, in any case, fully occupied with trying to reconcile an infinity of new ideas with his by now antiquated and inhibiting four-track recording machine. As the kaleidoscope blossomed and expanded Martin and his engineer, Geoff Emerick, cadged extra sound channels by dubbing one four-track machine over another.

Martin had taught the Beatles much: He learned a little, too, in reckless spontaneity. The song that set the circus atmosphere was "Being for the Benefit of Mr. Kite," a John Lennon composition suggested by the words of an old theater bill he had bought in an antique shop. Martin's instructions as arranger were to provide "a sort of hurdy gurdy effect." He did so by means of assorted steam organ sound-effect tapes cut into irregular lengths, thrown on the studio floor, then reedited at random. The result was a dreamlike cacophony, swirling about the Lennonesque big top where "summersets," rather than somersaults, are executed, and "tonight Henry the Horse dances the waltz."

Martin, indeed, found his last reserves melting in admiration of a song like John's "Lucy in the Sky with Diamonds," whose images—of "tangerine trees," "marmalade skies," "newspaper taxis," and "looking-glass ties"—were dazzling enough to a man with his middle-aged senses intact. It did occur to him sometimes that John looked rather strange, if not actually unwell. One night, in the aftermath of an acid trip, he looked so ill that Martin had to take him up onto the studio roof for air. Later, Paul took charge of him, driving him home to Weybridge and keeping him company in the hoped-for restorative of turning on yet again.

For Paul, *Sgt. Pepper* was a chance to experiment still further with the vein of narrative realism he had found in "Eleanor Rigby" and "Penny Lane." Among the treasures he brought to the table was "Lovely Rita," a cod love song to a meter maid, America's more seductive term for a female traffic warden, its tweeness diluted by the background of yearningly ironic "ooohs" and "aaahs" from John. "When I'm Sixty-Four" found Paul looking forward to barely conceivable old age, a Darby-and-Joan vision of "doing the garden," "renting a cottage in the Isle of Wight," and grandchildren named "Vera, Chuck, and Dave."

His most ambitious offering was "She's Leaving Home," the story of a young woman nerving herself to leave her dependent parents and elope with "a man in the motor trade." Introduced by a rippling harp, the song unfolded like one of the new, gritty working-class plays to be seen on black-and-white TV—the young woman stealing away from home at daybreak, "leaving the note that she hoped would say more," then her mother discovering her loss with a cry of "Daddy! Our baby's gone!" It was a small—perhaps not so small—masterpiece from a humane and understanding heart, only slightly marred by its composer's imperiousness when the moment came to cut it. As usual, Paul had produced a "head arrangement" that needed George Martin to turn it into a formal orchestral score. When Martin could not do the job on twenty-four hours' notice, as Paul wanted, he found himself summarily dropped in favor of an outside arranger.

Paul, at least, had no doubt that every song the Beatles were recording formed a link in the overall concept. "This is our *Freak-Out*," he kept saying. But Ringo was to have a different recollection. "After we'd done the original Sergeant Pepper song, we dropped the whole military idea. We just went on doing tracks."

If they were not quite following the original plan, they were working together with a harmony, unity, and enjoyment they had seldom known before, and never were to again. George, as usual, was given his moment of control when Indian musicians came in to help record his latest sitar epic, "Within You Without You." Ringo was called from the sidelines ("I learned to play chess during *Sgt. Pepper,*" he would later say) to do a vocal for "With a Little Help from My Friends," the song destined to be given the crucial place after the overture. The roadies Neil and Mal took an active part, helping to operate the numerous sound effects and even playing backup harmonicas. Martin watched beamingly from the control room, still convinced that all these dazzling pyrotechnics were fueled by no stimulant stronger than tea.

Indeed, the album's stand-out masterpiece, "A Day in the Life," represented a John-Paul collaboration like none since early Beatlemania. The idea had been suggested to John by the death in a car crash of Tara Browne, youthful heir to the Guinness fortune and a friend of both the Beatles and the Rolling Stones. When he first played Martin an acoustic guitar sketch of the song, with its references to "a lucky man who made the grade and blew his mind out in a car," Martin already felt the hairs prickle at the back of his neck. Unable to finish the lyric, John turned to Paul for something to fill its middle-eight. Paul provided a scrap of an unfinished song about getting up late and running for a bus, as cheery and everyday as the rest was bleak and apocalyptic. The bridge between the two parts was a long drawn-out cry of "I'd love to turn you on!" that they knew was asking for trouble. But there could be no pulling back now.

The song's finale, John told Martin, had to be, "a sound building up from nothing to the end of the world." That was the night Martin faced the forty-one-piece symphony orchestra and announced that what they were to perform had no written score. All he would tell them were the highest and lowest notes to play. In between, it was every man for himself.

The song, in its final form, was taped at Abbey Road amid a gala of pop aristocrats such as Mick Jagger and Marianne Faithfull. The orchestra wore full evening dress and also carnival disguises distributed by the Beatles. One noted violinist played behind a clown's red nose; another held his bow in a joke gorilla's paw. Studio Two thronged with peacock clothes, Eastern robes, abundant refreshments, and exotically tinted smoke. The four Beatles sat behind music stands playing trumpets, with

Brian leaning on a chair back among them. Their mustaches had aged them: It was Brian, in this last photograph with them, who suddenly looked like a boy.

As with every masterpiece, the hardest part was letting go. They had tailed as well as topped the album with *Sgt. Pepper*'s theme song, adding a reprise of the "Lovely Rita" backing vocal that left John's grin floating in the air like a bespectacled Cheshire cat's. Recognizing that "A Day in the Life" was something quite apart from even the most recherché of the other tracks, they had turned it into a devastating afterthought, followed by a multiple crash of piano chords—like the totaling of Tara Browne's car—that would slam the collection shut like a sarcophagus. They had worked from 7:00 A.M. to 3:00 P.M. simply to produce a brief snatch of gibberish to be heard from the record's normally mute play-out groove. As they stood around the microphone, a drug-dazzled Ringo suddenly remarked, "I think I'm going to fall over," and toppled forward, to be caught like a doll in Mal Evans's arms. The final touch was a note at 20,000 hertz frequency, audible only to the fine-tuned hearing of dogs.

The album sleeve, as much as its music, perfectly evoked the hour of its coming. The pop artist Peter Blake was commissioned to design a frontispiece as up-to-the-minute as its four subjects were, and as heedless of convention or expense. The Beatles, holding bandsmen's instruments and dressed in satin uniforms, pink, blue, yellow, and scarlet, stood mock solemn behind their own name spelled in flowers, set about by a collage of figures representing their numerous heroes. The group included Bob Dylan, Karl Marx, Laurel and Hardy, Aleister Crowley, Marlon Brando, Diana Dors, W. C. Fields—every fashionable face from the pantheon of Pop Art pseudo-worship. There were also private jokes, such as the Beatles' own ludicrous wax effigies from Madame Tussaud's, a stray Buddha, and a doll with a sign reading WELCOME ROLLING STONES. In one corner, next to Aubrey Beardsley, above Sonny Liston's head, the face of Stu Sutcliffe, the Beatle who was lost, peered out from a snapshot fragment of some long-forgotten Hamburg night.

EMI initially rejected the design, fearing that those among the assembly who were still alive would object to their likenesses being used in this way. The Beatles appealed directly to the company's chairman, Sir Joseph Lockwood, who informally consulted two of the country's most eminent lawyers, Lord Goodman and Lord Shawcross. "Both Shawcross and Goodman said the same," Sir Joseph recalled. " 'Don't touch it,' they said. '*Everyone* will sue.' "

"Paul McCartney talked me into allowing it. 'Ah, everyone'll love it,' he said. 'All right,' I said, 'but take Gandhi out. We need the Indian market. If we show Gandhi standing around with Sonny Liston and Diana Dors, they'll never forgive us in India.' So the Beatles agreed to take Gandhi out."

EMI further stipulated that the Beatles should indemnify them to the tune of some twenty million pounds against possible legal trouble. In addition, Brian had to undertake to get clearances from as many of the sixty-two celebrities as possible. Wendy Hanson, his former assistant, was brought back specially to undertake this marathon of the transatlantic telephone. As she later remembered, most of them were only too flattered and delighted to be asked.

Sgt. Pepper had taken four months and cost twenty-five thousand pounds—an unheard-of sum in those days, more than twenty times the cost of the Beatles' debut album. Its packaging also was something altogether new, reflecting that age of conspicuous consumption. Instead of the usual single envelope, it came in a double segment that opened like a book. On the back, replacing the traditional leaden sleeve notes, the lyrics of every song were printed in full. Inside with the record was a sheet of cutout novelties, figments of the Beatles' own comic-book childhood transformed to the last, or next, word in Pop Art—a jovial Victorian army sergeant picture card, a paper mustache, two badges, and a set of NCO's stripes.

One other feature of the cover passed unnoticed by EMI's lawyers, nor was it picked up by the keen eye of Lord Shawcross or Lord Goodman. In the foreground of the garden where Sergeant Pepper's band and their companions stood grew a flourishing row of what looked like marijuana plants.

The landmark events in each era, those strokes of history so monumental that people recall for ever afterward exactly where they were and what they were doing at the time, are generally tragedies. The outbreaks of world wars, the passings of sovereigns or statesmen, the from-nowhere annihilations of John F. Kennedy, John Lennon, and Diana, Princess of Wales, the wanton mass slaughter of 9/11: Such have been the moments that, for billions across the globe for their remaining life span, recall exactly the circumstances they were in, the clothes they wore, the faces that looked disbelievingly into theirs on first hearing the news.

Only the blessed sixties generation have such a moment to remember not marked by open-mouthed horror and incredulity but open-mouthed delight and exaltation: the moment in June 1967 when they first listened to the Beatles' *Sgt. Pepper's Lonely Hearts Club Band.* The memory in this case is uniform to all: how they rushed to their record store to buy it; how Peter Blake's cover dazzled and delighted them as no album design ever had before; how they first opened its booklike flap and drew out the disk with its shiny virgin grooves and green Parlophone label; how at the first play they simply couldn't believe it, and had to play it again and again and again.

Musically its conquest was total. It equally entranced the most avant-garde and most cautious, both fan and foe alike. The wildest acid freak, listening in his mental garret to "Lucy in the Sky with Diamonds," could not doubt that his mind had been blown to undreamed realms of psychedelic fancy. Nervous old ladies, listening to "When I'm Sixty-Four" in their front parlors, would never be frightened of pop music again. Sergeant Pepper's cabaret show, with its twanging mystery and workaday humor, its uppercut drive and insinuating charm, invited the elderly as well as the young, the innocent no less than the pretentiously wise. On drama critic Kenneth Tynan, the most rigorous cultural commentator of his age, and on Mark Lewisohn, an eight-year-old in Kenton, Middlesex, the effect was the same. Tynan called *Sgt. Pepper* a decisive moment in the history of Western civilization. Mark Lewisohn stood in the garden as it played, shaking his head wildly while trying not to dislodge the cardboard mustache clenched under his nose.

In America, where the album appeared one day after its U.K. release, critical hyperbole climbed to Gothic heights. The *New York Times* announced that *Sgt. Pepper* heralded "a new and golden Renaissance of Song." *Newsweek*'s reviewer, Jack Kroll, compared the lyrics with T. S. Eliot: "A Day in the Life," he said, was "the Beatles' *Waste Land.*" Some of the more woolly-headed American commentators classed the album as an almost religious experience and the Beatles as deities—this time with none of the fundamentalist backlash John had caused with his "bigger than Jesus" remark. "I declare," said Dr. Timothy Leary, high priest of hippiedom, "that the Beatles are mutants. Prototypes of evolutionary

agents sent by God with a mysterious power to create a new species—a
young race of laughing freemen. . . .They are the wisest, holiest, most effective avatars [God incarnations] the human race has ever produced."

Others saw things rather differently. By the time *Sgt. Pepper* was released the adult world had moved on somewhat from its initial amused
tolerance of the swinging one. Concern was growing about the use of
drugs among young people and the degree to which pop music encouraged, even exhorted it. A growing body of opinion now called on pop
stars to recognize their position as vastly influential role models and to
set a good rather than exultantly bad example to their millions of impressionable fans.

Before *Sgt. Pepper* there had been occasional controversies over pop
lyrics deemed explicit or suggestive, like the Rolling Stones' "Let's Spend
the Night Together." Now for the first time—thanks to the helpful provision of its lyrics in cold print—an album attracted as much notoriety
as a subversive eighteenth-century pamphlet. The BBC took the lead by
banning "A Day in the Life" for a list of overt references to drug taking,
some readily sustainable but others merely the products of overheated
bureaucratic imagination. Obvious fair game were the "man who blew
his mind out in a car," the references to "smoke" and "dream" in Paul's
middle section, and, of course, the mischievous cry of "I'd love to turn
you on." But the "four thousand holes in Blackburn, Lancashire," now
interpreted to mean mass heroin needle marks, had simply been John
using a news item that caught his fancy. Even the final "sound like the
end of the world," created by classical violinists in clown noses and gorilla paws, was accused of symbolizing an addict's first chaotic joy after
a fix.

More dubious subtexts were eagerly sought and quickly found on the
album's other tracks. Paul's "Fixing a Hole"—a song plainly about little
more than home maintenance—was condemned as another heroin alle-
gory. The Ringo track "With a Little Help from My Friends" caused such
a furor in America with its reference to getting high that Senator—soon
to be vice president—Spiro T. Agnew led a public campaign to ban it. In
"She's Leaving Home," the "man from the motor trade," in reality Brian
Epstein's car-sales partner Terry Doran, was thought to be a euphemism
for an abortionist. Even the tracks with no alleged narcotic subtext were
credited with a role in turning nice, normal teenagers into mumbling,
shiftless freaks. The ultra–right wing John Birch Society went so far as to

announce that the Beatles were part of a communist conspiracy and warned that *Sgt. Pepper* showed "an understanding of the principles of brainwashing."

But by far the greatest furor arose from the realization that "Lucy in the Sky with Diamonds" was a mnemonic for LSD. Since the song clearly could have only one author, it was John who received the bulk of the condemnation for advertising the substance that now dominated every media drug scare story and representing its effect in attractive terms of "tangerine trees and marmalade skies." John protested that the song had nothing to do with LSD, but had been inspired by a painting his son Julian had done at school. "What's that?" John had asked, and Julian had replied, "It's Lucy in the sky with diamonds." Had the story come from anyone without John's love of verbal jokery, it might have been more believable.

For the millions of hippies now dropping out across America, and their ever-increasing British brethren, *Sgt. Pepper* very quickly became more than a phonograph record. In their quasi-religion of love and peace, it became an almost sacred text, its random tracks elevated into a gospel more cohesive than even Paul McCartney had ever dreamed, its casual in-jokes and spur-of-moment sound effects interpreted as coded symbols, messages, and philosophical observations on the deepest matters of life and death. Even the fragment of electronic gibberish in the play-out groove was subjected to intensive analysis and eventually pronounced to be saying "Fuck me like a superman," whatever cosmic profundity that might imply.

If the Beatles had hated the mindlessly screaming fans of four years back, they hated the mystery- and message-seekers more. John, especially, denied with increasing bitterness that his songs had any hidden or mystical meaning. "I just shove a lot of sounds together, then shove some words on," he said. "We know we're conning people, because people want to be conned. They give us the freedom to con them."

A month earlier in the Beatles' fan magazine a correspondent had expressed the view of the huge other audience they still had. "I know that if Paul took drugs, I'd be worried sick," the letter-writer said. "But I know he's too sensible."

It was, however, the most cautious and image-conscious Beatle who, a fortnight after *Sgt. Pepper*'s release and on the eve of his twenty-fifth birthday, admitted to *Life* magazine that he had taken LSD. The admission was possible since acid had only recently become illegal. Paul, while stressing the pluperfect tense, spoke nonetheless as an enthusiast. "It opened my eyes," he said. "We only use one-tenth of our brains. Just think what we'd accomplish if we could tap that hidden part."

The outcry was even more ferocious than over Sergeant Pepper's alleged illegal pharmacopoeia. The Beatle who had hitherto been looked on as pop music's best ambassador was denounced, in the *Daily Mail*, as "an irresponsible idiot." Intercessionary prayers were offered by Dr. Billy Graham to prevent the world's innocent youth from rushing to emulate him. Paul, protesting he bore no such responsibility, did his best to disarm his attackers with good old Liverpool humor. Taking drugs, he said, was "like taking aspirin without a headache." On television he was asked if he didn't feel it irresponsible to broadcast that endorsement to such a huge audience. Paul very reasonably answered that the television company was doing no less by interviewing him in prime time. "It's *you* who've got responsibility not to spread this. If you'll shut up about it, I will."

Soon afterward came news of an even more unlikely acid-head. Brian Epstein, the Beatles' apparently well-bred and respectable manager, came forward with John and George in a supportive phalanx to admit having taken LSD about half a dozen times before it became illegal. Among those who read the news (oh, boy) was the Beatles' supreme idol Elvis Presley, soon to forsake Hollywood schlock and return to live performance. Once the standard bearer for rebellious youth, Elvis now looked with horror on the drug counterculture (in which he did not include his own massive narcotics intake, those all being supplied on doctors' prescriptions). Indeed, the King now sported the honorary badge of a federal narcotics agent and, later, would personally urge America's new president, Richard M. Nixon, not to let the Beatles into the country again.

Within a few days the whole controversy had been eclipsed by an event that established the Beatles as a literally astral presence as well as demonstrating the schizophrenic nature of the BBC. To demonstrate the ever-developing marvels of satellite broadcasting, the corporation initiated a program called *Our World*, made jointly by itself and TV networks in thirteen other countries and broadcast live as a symbol of international amity in tune with hippie love and peace. The same BBC that so recently had damned "A Day in the Life" as a drug addict's guidebook now saw nothing contradictory in presenting the Beatles as stars of *Our World*'s British segment, representing the corporation, the country, and the theme artistic excellence. And, however terminally pissed-off with the corportion they might feel, the Beatles could hardly resist such a showcase for a new song.

The broadcast took the form of a party—now more correctly called a happening or a love-in—in Abbey Road's Studio One. The Beatles in flower-power gear performed their specially written number perched on stools and wearing headphones as if caught in the act of recording. Among the privileged crowd who sat around them were Mick Jagger, Marianne Faithfull, Keith Moon of The Who, Eric Clapton of Cream, Patti Harrison, Jane Asher, and Paul McCartney's brother, Michael.

The new song was called "All You Need Is Love," a foot-stomping chant seemingly designed to contain no shades of meaning or hidden symbols or messages whatever. In a Scouse accent, of course, the crucial word came out as "loov," suggesting something rather more edgy and ironic than the usual bland flower-child articulation. "All you need is loov," sang John, between chews on a wad of gum, "Loov, loov. Loov is allyerneed . . ." A thirteen-piece orchestra was on hand to provide sound effects that included the opening trumpet fanfare of "La Marseillaise" and a sarcastic Lennon reprise of "She loves you, yeah, yeah, yeah." At the end, balloons and party streamers were showered onto the set, and members of the pop royalty present walked rather self-consciously up and down with placards saying "Love" in various languages while others danced a conga around the studio floor.

The performance went out to thirty-one countries and was watched by approximately five hundred million, a global audience destined not to be surpassed until the Live-Aid concert of 1985 and the death of a still unknown Princess.

That hopeful message to the world was unfortunately lost on the British police who, in response to mounting pressure from Fleet Street, parliament, and the Church, had chosen 1967 for an all-out assault on the drug-guzzling counterculture. Their intended victims presented invitingly soft targets, not least the group who had most outraged public feeling with their hairiness, surliness, sexiness, and refusal to mount the revolving platform on *Sunday Night at the London Palladium*. In February, an eighteen-strong police task force had raided the Sussex home of the Rolling Stones' lead guitarist Keith Richard while Mick Jagger, Marianne Faithfull, and a number of other upmarket underground figures were spending the weekend there. A thorough search of the premises and everyone present had revealed four illegal amphetamine tablets in the pocket of a coat belonging to Jagger. George and Patti Harrison had also been among the party, but had left just before the police arrived. It would later be alleged that the raiders had waited for them to get clear, because to bust a Beatle was still considered tantamount to defiling a national treasure.

The subsequent trial of Jagger and Richard, each for about the most minor drug offense in the book, gave a dark and ugly descant to that summer of flowers and bells and joss sticks and multicolored *Sgt. Pepper* satins, when "all you need is loov" seemed woven into the very sunshine. Tried and convicted at Chichester Quarter Sessions the following June, Richard was sentenced to a year's imprisonment and Jagger to three months, while Marianne Faithfull achieved notoriety as "the girl in the fur rug" who had allegedly been the centrepiece of a group-sex orgy. A rumor swept Britain that when the police burst in Jagger had been licking a Mars bar lodged in Marianne's vagina. Although there quickly proved to be no basis for the rumor, for a time it was the Profumo scandal all over again, just moved down an age group and a class.

The affair took on some of the qualities of an LSD hallucination when Britain's most pro-Establishment newspaper, the *Times*, rallied to Jagger's and Richard's defense, criticizing their vengeful public humiliation and plainly excessive sentences in an editorial headed by a quotation from William Blake, "Who Breaks a Butterfly On a Wheel?" Both Stones were freed on appeal, Jagger being then helicoptered to take part in a televised discussion with assorted Establishment grandees, including the editor of the *Times,* about "what today's young people really want." His next act was to join Richard and the other Stones in the studio to produce their own sarcastically Beatles-themed message to their late persecutors, a song called "We Love You" with anonymous backup vocals by John Lennon and Paul McCartney. The Beatles and Brian lent them further support on July 24 as signatories in a full-page *Times* advertisement calling for the legalization of marijuana.

In early August came another portent of how the Summer of Love's seemingly limitless sunshine was soon to turn rancid. The playwright Joe Orton, so nearly the scriptwriter of the Beatles' third film, was battered to death by his jealous lover, Kenneth Halliwell, who then himself took an overdose of sleeping pills. John Lennon's "A Day in the Life," about the "lucky man who made the grade," was Orton's funeral music.

Visiting Nat Weiss in New York that spring, Brian had felt a strong premonition of death. "He was sure his plane would crash on the journey home," Weiss says. "I persuaded him to take the flight—which, in fact, was delayed a long while on the runway at Kennedy." The jet finally took off, leaving Nat Weiss with Brian's last wish, scribbled in a note at the airport coffee shop. His last wish concerned the packaging of the Beatles' new album: "Brown paper bags for *Sgt. Pepper.*"

When Weiss came to London a few weeks later Brian was back at the drying-out clinic in Putney. The attorney drove to visit him with Robert Stigwood, his Australian heir apparent at NEMS Enterprises. According to Weiss, Brian now regretted his decision to let Stigwood buy control of NEMS. "Stigwood had the option to buy, but they were still joint managing directors. Brian was telling Stigwood to do things, but it was obvious that Stigwood had no intention of doing them.

"While I was with Brian, a big bouquet of flowers arrived from John Lennon. The card from John said, "You know I love you—I really mean that." When Brian read it, he just broke down.

"He begged me to stay on until he got out of the clinic, but I had to go back to New York. That was the last time I saw him."

Not even Nat Weiss could comfort Brian in the dread that had begun to torment him—the dread foreshadowed in early summer when Cilla Black announced her intention of leaving NEMS Enterprises. Cilla disliked Robert Stigwood; still more had she been offended by the loss of that feminine solicitude with which Brian had built up her career. The emergency cleared Brian's head. There were meetings with Cilla at Chapel Street: He apologized, was charming—from the haunted, drug-exhausted night-being, enough of the old Brian returned to persuade Cilla, at least, not to leave him.

But the greater, unassuageable dread remained. In October 1967, Brian's five-year management contract with the Beatles ended. He had reason—or thought he had—to believe it would not be renewed.

There had been signs for many months that Paul McCartney, in particular, was discontented with Brian's management. Their relationship, in any case, was never easy. Paul, with his looks, was the one Brian *ought* to have loved: He always felt he owed Paul compensation because he had chosen John. The worst moments of all for Brian, worse even than John's sarcasm, were when Paul decided, in his smiling way, to play the prima donna. "Paul could get to Brian the way none of the other three could," Joanne Newfield says. "Whenever I saw him put down the phone really upset, he'd always been talking to Paul."

At the beginning, it was always George, in his dour Liverpool way, who cross-examined Brian closest over business deals. As George absorbed himself in spiritual things, Paul took over, with more unsettling effect, as Brian's chief inquisitor. "He'd come into Chapel Street, doing his business Beatle bit," Joanne says. "That always worried Brian. They never had a row, but you could see he was uneasy when Paul was there."

Brian had hoped to please Paul, above all, in the new recording deal with EMI and American Capitol that he had negotiated the previous February. This replaced EMI's risible "penny per record" for a 10 percent royalty on singles and albums, rising to 15 percent after 100,000 and 300,000 copies respectively. In America, the royalty was 10 percent, rising to 17 percent. The deal, in fact, transformed the economics of the record industry. No longer would record companies be able to sign impressionable young men to miserly contracts with the excuse of its being standard practice.

But Paul, rather than giving Brian the longed-for congratulations, had instead been full of the new recording contract negotiated for the Rolling Stones by the manager who had taken over from Andrew Loog Oldham—a New York businessman named Allen Klein. Faced with the threat of losing the Stones to another label, Decca had agreed to pay an unheard-of advance against future royalties of $1.25 million. In all the years that the Beatles had been sending EMI's profits through the roof, it had not occurred to Brian to demand any money up front.

Paul was also mainly responsible for a feeling within the Beatles that they had now outgrown their need for a manager in the old proprietorial sense. Certainly, *Sgt. Pepper*, that multihued testament to their infallibility, had been made to a large extent against Brian's wishes. By now, too, rumors were beginning to filter out of NEMS, and through each Beatle's personal court, that even as that kind of manager Brian had made serious long-term mistakes. They were starting to hear about Seltaeb and Nicky Byrne; the 90 percent merchandising contract given to five strangers; the millions of dollars that had been allowed to blow away.

Brian, on his side, made strenuous efforts to prove that they did still need him. He took special trouble over the arrangements for Paul Mc-Cartney's first private trip to America. It was, ironically, the trip that Paul used to formulate much of a future for the Beatles in which there would be little room for anyone named Brian Epstein.

To one person, the impresario Larry Parnes, Brian finally confessed what he could still barely articulate in his own mind. "He told me the Beatles were leaving him," Parnes said. "He was losing Cilla and he was losing them. The Beatles were giving him notice."

His support of Paul in the LSD furor revealed how fervent was Brian's desire to stay at one with the Beatles. And, indeed, it brought him closer to them—certainly, closer to Paul—than for many months. Soon afterward, at Kingsley Hill, he threw a weekend party to which the Beatles and their women drove together, packed into John's psychedelic Rolls. When the Rolls stopped at traffic lights people crowded round to try to see through its darkened windows. It was a day that Cynthia Lennon was to remember with horror. Brian's party, at the house where Churchill used to meet his wartime chiefs of staff, turned into a mass LSD trip. Cynthia took some acid herself, for only the second time, in her fast-failing attempts to keep up with John. The result was a horrendously bad trip in which she almost jumped from a second-story window onto the heads of the beautiful people below.

In July, the Beatles began to think of leaving England and setting up in hippie-commune style on their own private Greek island. All of them and their wives took a lengthy boat cruise, looking at possible sites to buy. The plan went as far as negotiations with Greece's fascist military government and with the British Treasury—who gave permission in principle for them to transfer the purchase price abroad—before being dropped in favor of the next big idea. Brian took no part in the plan and pretended mild amusement at it. "I think it's a dotty idea," he wrote to Nat Weiss, "but they're no longer children, and must have their own sweet way."

The fatherly tone is poignant, considering the moment. His own father, Harry Epstein, the hardworking, straight-dealing, uncomplicated Liverpool businessman, had died suddenly of a heart attack, aged sixty-three. It was his second within only a few weeks. When news of the first one reached Brian, at a party, he did not think it sounded serious enough to return home immediately.

The bereavement, paradoxically, had a stabilizing effect: It forced him out of his own depression into concern for his family—in particular, for his mother, Queenie, widowed after thirty-four years of marriage. From the age of eighteen, she had known no existence other than as Harry's wife. After her religion, it was to her elder son that she turned for support. Brian was comforted to realize that someone in the world truly needed him.

He spent several days with Queenie in Liverpool, surprised to discover how a city that had once seemed so dully provincial now soothed and reassured him. After Harry's retirement, his parents had moved from their Queen's Drive house to a more convenient bungalow. Brian visited their old next-door neighbor Rex Makin and sat in Makin's garden, staring at the house with the sunrise over its front door, thinking of the father who had returned from the shop one afternoon to find him sent home from school, and whose angry words were still etched on his son's memory. "I simply don't know *what* we're going to do with you."

He wrote to Nat Weiss from Liverpool, mentioning his plan to come to New York on September 2. Weiss, as his agent, had arranged for him to present a series of talk shows on Canadian television. Brian was excited by this opportunity to test himself as a performer. In comforting his mother he had himself evidently drawn comfort from the Jewish religion. "The week of Shiva [mourning] is up tonight," his letter to Weiss continued, "and I feel a bit strange. Probably good for me in a way."

His mother came to London to stay with him on August 14. The idea was that she should move down to London permanently, to be near Brian and her sister, his aunt Frieda. For the ten days of her visit Brian forced himself to keep to a normal routine. Queenie would wake him each morning, drawing his bedroom curtains as she used to when he was small, and they would have breakfast together in his room. Brian would then work a conventional office day with Joanne. Each night, he stayed in, watching television with Queenie, rarely going to bed later than 11:00 P.M. Joanne had never seen him so quiet and apparently content.

Mrs. Epstein returned to Liverpool on Thursday, August 24. That evening, at the Hilton Hotel, sitting on a bedroom floor and staring devoutly upward, the Beatles embarked, three days prematurely, on their post-Brian era.

A letter to Nat Weiss was in the mail—a cheerful note concerning arrangements Weiss was to make for Brian's American visit, such as the chartering of a yacht and tickets to a Judy Garland concert. There was also mention of Eric Andersen, a folk singer whom Brian wanted to put under contract: "till the 2nd," the letter ended, "love, flowers, bells, be happy and look forward to the future."

Enclosed was a color snapshot, taken on the roof at Chapel Street, of a young man—hardly more than a boy—in striped trousers and a frilled shirt open to the waist. His hair was long; it fell in bangs over his eyes. Four days before his death, Brian at last became what he had strived hardest to be: a Beatle.

The new era took a form already long familiar to London Underground travelers. For it is on subway station walls that advertisements for Indian holy men and their spiritual crusades in Britain commonly appear. Among this bearded, cross-legged platform-wall fraternity the most clearly recognizable was the holy man named Maharishi Mahesh Yogi. In 1967, after a decade of regular visits, the maharishi—or great saint— could claim some ten thousand British converts to his doctrine of Spiritual Regeneration. A still larger number recognized him in the way they recognized chocolate vending machines, posters for Start Rite shoes, and illuminated signs to the Central or Bakerloo line.

It was, ironically, not George Harrison but his model wife, Patti, who brought the Beatles and the Maharishi together. Patti had joined the Spiritual Regeneration movement in February after hearing a talk by one of the guru's lieutenants. George, although immersed in Hindu religious study since his Indian expedition, had found no real direction as yet. He had been to San Francisco and—accompanied by Derek Taylor, now a fashionable Hollywood publicist—had strolled among the Haight-Ashbury hippies. There he found less love and peace than beggars and souvenir stalls. He had also been in contact with a Britain-based guru who persuaded him to go down to Cornwall and climb a hill, with equally disappointing spiritual results.

In the week before August Bank Holiday Patti Harrison read that the Maharishi Mahesh Yogi had come to London to deliver a single lecture before retiring from his crusade and devoting himself to a "life of silence" in India. The valedictory lecture was to take place at the mystic's hotel, the Park Lane Hilton, on Thursday, August 24. Patti made George contact the other Beatles and persuade them to attend.

Amid the small 7s 6d (37p) per head audience of the faithful, four Beatles garbed as flower-power aristocrats listened while a little Asian gentleman, wearing robes and a gray-tipped beard, described in his high-pitched voice an existence both more inviting and more convenient than mere hippiedom. The inner peace that the Maharishi promised, and which seemed so alluring to pleasure-exhausted multimillionaires—not to mention the sublime consciousness so attractive to inveterate novelty-seekers—could be obtained even within their perilously small attention span. To be spiritually regenerated they need meditate for only half an hour each day.

Maharishi Mahesh Yogi, despite a highly developed nose for publicity, did not know the Beatles were in his congregation until after the lecture, when they sent a request to speak to him in private. There and then, acting as a group, they offered themselves as his disciples. The holy man, for whom "tickled" would be an insufficient adjective, invited them to join him the next day on a course of indoctrination for the spiritually regenerated at University College, Bangor, North Wales. The Beatles said they would go.

They did subsequently contact Brian and ask him to join the party. He, too, had been showing some interest in Indian religion. Brian said he had other plans for the Bank Holiday weekend, but that he'd try to get down to Bangor later during the ten-day course.

The next day an incredulous mob of reporters and TV crews saw them arrive at Euston station and climb aboard the dingy blue and white train that now had to serve instead of their usual private jet. Also in the party, thanks to a spur-of-the-moment decision, were the country's favorite anti-Christ and scarlet woman, Mick Jagger and Marianne Faithfull. Cynthia Lennon missed the train; when she arrived at the barrier, the ticket inspector mistook her for just another fan and refused to let her through until after the guard's whistle had blown for departure. As Cyn sprinted vainly along the platform John leaned from his compartment window, laughing and calling, "Run, Cindy, run!"

It was the first journey they had ever made without Brian—without even the two protective road managers. John compared it to "going somewhere without your trousers." They all sat rather guiltily, wedged into one first-class compartment, afraid to venture so much as to the lavatory. They then had a second audience with the Maharishi, who occupied his own first-class compartment, squatting on a sheet spread over British Rail's green upholstery. He held up a flower—the first of many—and explained that its petals were an illusion, like the physical world. In a telling simile he compared spiritual regeneration to a bank, from which its practitioner could always draw dividends of repose.

It had become apparent by now that the Maharishi considered himself fully as great a star attraction as the Beatles, and believed the crowds and media attention to be on his account rather than theirs. As the train finally limped toward Bangor station, another frantic multitude and battery of television cameras came into view on the platform. The Beatles, with no shield of roadies to protect them, were all for staying on the train a couple of extra stops, then returning to Bangor by taxi. With his beatific smile, the Maharishi told them to stick close beside him and they'd be all right.

That night the Beatles' party found themselves ensconced with the Maharishi's three hundred other conference students, in the spartan bedrooms of a teacher-training college. Later they went out to the only restaurant open late in Bangor—serving Chinese food. Only after a long and rowdy meal did they realize they weren't carrying enough money between them to pay the bill. In London, any restaurant would have pressed the dinner on them gratis, but Chinese waiters in a remote North Wales seaside resort were clearly a somewhat different proposition. Things had begun to look decidedly tricky when George pried open the heel of one of his sandals and produced a wad of ten-pound notes he had secreted there.

The following day the Beatles used a press conference with their new guru to announce that they had given up taking drugs. "It was an experience we went through," Paul McCartney said. "Now it's over. We don't need it any more. We think we're finding new ways of getting there."

One of the journalists present was George Harrison, their old *Liverpool Echo* acquaintance—for Bangor is just in the *Echo*'s circulation area. Harrison was with them the next afternoon—Sunday—as, fully initiated into Spiritual Regeneration, they strolled around the college grounds.

"There was a phone ringing inside," Harrison said. "It rang and rang. Eventually, Paul said, 'Someone had better answer that.' He went in and picked up the phone. I could hear him speaking. Yeah,' he said. 'Yeah . . .' Then I heard him shout, 'Oh, Christ—*no!*'"

•   •   •

That Friday, Brian had suddenly asked Joanne down to spend the Bank Holiday weekend at his house in Sussex. He also told her to invite a mutual friend of theirs, the Scots singer Lulu. But he had left it too late: Both Lulu and Joanne herself had other arrangements. As Brian did not seem too disappointed, Joanne presumed he would be entertaining a large house party. "He went off on his own on the Friday afternoon. He seemed really bright and happy that day. He'd put the top of the Bentley down. He was waving to me as he drove off."

At Kingsley Hill, other disappointments waited. A young man whom Brian had hoped to get to know better that weekend would not, after all, be able to make it. Peter Brown had not arrived yet. He was still in London, trying to get Cynthia Lennon off to Bangor by car. Peter, and Geoffrey Ellis from the NEMS office, would be the only house guests. They were old friends and familiar companions. Brian, after two quiet weeks, had looked forward to more exciting company.

The three had dinner served to them by Brian's Austrian butler. Afterward, in an evidently restless mood, Brian began telephoning numbers in London that supplied what we would now term male prostitutes. But all were fully booked. Brian grew more edgy and irritable and finally announced he was returning to London. Peter and Geoffrey were not offended, nor particularly surprised. Walking out was a habit of Brian's. Peter went with him out to the Bentley and told him he oughtn't to drive after the wine he'd drunk with dinner. "Brian said I wasn't to worry. He'd be back in the morning before I woke up."

By this time, one of the agencies he'd contacted had found three boys and dispatched them on the sixty-mile journey to Sussex in a black London cab. But Brian was now well on his way back to London.

Geoffrey Ellis telephoned Chapel Street shortly after midnight to confirm that he had arrived safely. Up to then, Peter and Geoffrey had half-expected him to reappear at Kingsley Hill after a drive round the countryside. The call was taken by Antonio, Brian's Spanish town butler. Antonio said that Mr. Epstein had come in a little time ago and had gone straight upstairs. He tried the intercom to the master bedroom, but got no reply. Peter and Geoffrey were reassured. Brian had managed the car journey safely and had obviously succeeded in falling asleep.

When Peter and Geoffrey got up, late on Saturday morning, Brian had not returned. They thought of ringing Chapel Street, but decided to let him sleep. At about five that afternoon, the telephone rang. It was

Brian. He told Peter he had been asleep all day and was still very drowsy. Peter said that if he was returning to Sussex it would be safer to take the train. Brian agreed to telephone just as he was setting off so that Peter could collect him by car at Lewes station. Peter waited all Saturday evening for his call.

By Sunday morning, Antonio and his wife, Maria, were beginning to be worried. Brian was still in his room. The Spanish couple had heard nothing from him since breakfast time the previous day. Nor had he gone out, as was his habit, after dark. The Bentley was still as he had left it on Friday night. At the same time, they knew his irregular ways and how angry he could be. A lengthy discussion in Spanish ensued before Antonio decided to take the initiative.

He telephoned Peter Brown in Sussex first, but Peter had gone with Geoffrey Ellis to the village pub. He then telephoned Joanne Newfield at her home in Edgware. Joanne had helped cope with Brian's two suicide attempts: She had also seen several false alarms. She drove at once from Edgware through the Bank Holiday silence to Chapel Street. "The moment I walked in," she says, "I felt uneasy."

Ceaseless hammering on Brian's door and buzzing of his bedroom intercom brought no reply. Even then, they hesitated to break down his door. They had done so, unnecessarily, once before and Brian had been furious. By this time a doctor had arrived—not Brian's regular, Dr. Cowan, but another man who understood his case. Peter Brown had rung up again from Sussex and was waiting on the line for news.

Antonio and the doctor broke down the bedroom suite's outer double doors. Beyond the dressing-room lobby the curtains were drawn. Brian lay on his side amid the litter of documents and correspondence spread over the bed. Joanne approached and shook him. "Even though I knew he was dead, I pretended to the others that he wasn't. 'It's all right,' I kept saying, 'he's just asleep, he's fine.'

"The doctor led me out of the room then. Maria was there, screaming, 'Why? Why?' Peter Brown was still holding on on the phone.

"A little while after that, something really strange happened. We broke into Brian's room at about two o'clock. At three o'clock, the *Daily Express* rang up and said, 'We've heard that Brian Epstein's terribly ill. Is there any truth in it?' Only the four of us knew what had happened and none of us had contacted any press. It was never explained how the story got out to the papers."

Reporters and photographers were already massed in Chapel Street when Peter Brown and Geoffrey Ellis arrived from Sussex. Alistair Taylor, the NEMS office manager, had been sent for, and also Brian's lawyer, David Jacobs. Peter Brown got through to Bangor and broke the news to Paul. Then he telephoned Brian's brother, Clive, in Liverpool. Joanne heard Clive shout: "You're lying! You're lying!"

Brian's body was taken away in a makeshift police coffin. Joanne attacked a photographer who pointed his camera at it. "I just couldn't bear the thought of people seeing Brian in a thing like that."

By early evening, there were television pictures of the Beatles leaving the Maharishi's conference through forests of microphones and lights. "How do you feel," they were asked, "about Brian Epstein's death?" It emerged that they had been to see the Maharishi again and had been told that Brian's death, being of the physical world, was "not important." Their faces, even so, looked ravaged among the garlands and the bells. "He was a lovely fella," John said bleakly.

The story was told in full on Bank Holiday Monday in newspapers read at the seaside or in back gardens. "Brian Epstein Death Riddle: Valet Finds Pop King in Locked Bedroom." It was widely assumed—and still is—that he committed suicide. The story gained weight—not instantly, since Fleet Street still shunned the word—when his homosexuality became public knowledge. To the larger British public in 1967, that was reason enough to want to die.

The inquest, on September 8 at Westminster Coroner's Court, found that Brian had died from an overdose of Carbitrol, a bromide-based drug that he had been taking to help him sleep. That the overdose had not been all at once but cumulative, over two or three days, seemed to rule out the possibility of suicide. The suggestion was that Brian, in a gradually more drowsy state, had not realized he was exceeding the proper dose. The police inspector called to Chapel Street reported having found seventeen bottles of various pills and tablets in his bathroom cupboard, in his briefcase, and beside his bed.

Nat Weiss traveled from New York to attend the inquest, bringing with him Brian's last letter—the one that seemed so full of confidence in the future. The coroner, Mr. Gavin Thurston, recorded a verdict of accidental death from "incautious self-overdoses."

One person who knew him, and also knew well a particular burden he carried, remains convinced that Brian's death was neither accident nor suicide. According to this, necessarily anonymous, ex-associate, Brian was the victim of a murder contract taken out on him three years earlier in America after the Seltaeb merchandising fiasco.

In 1964, certainly, any number of American businessmen bore him a bitter grudge. The confusion over manufacturing licenses, and consequent cancellation by the big stores of seventy-eight million dollars' worth of Beatles merchandise, caused several manufacturers to lose a fortune. "One man even had a heart attack and died. I was at a meeting when Lisson said he was going to kill Brian Epstein. I thought it was just American bullshit. I said, 'No—wait until the courts have finished with him.' "

In August 1967, the courts had finished. The twenty-two-million-dollar lawsuit between NEMS and Nicky Byrne had been settled for a cash payment of ten thousand dollars to Byrne—enough to buy himself a yacht and sail off to start a new life in the Bahamas.

Just before he left New York Nicky Byrne received a mysterious telephone call. "This man's voice, very low, very polite, said: 'Mr. Byrne. I understand that your suit against Brian Epstein is settled, is that right?' I said: 'Yes, and what's it got to do with you?' But whoever it was just hung up.

"In August, I was in Florida—actually on my boat—and I got another call. That same very quiet, polite voice. 'Mr. Byrne,' it said, 'you're going to hear soon that Brian Epstein has met with an accident.' "

No one has ever explained those two telephone calls to Nicky Byrne, nor explained the curious fact that Brian's death was known in Fleet Street less than an hour after Joanne Newfield burst into his darkened room.

For the murder theorists there is one further and deeply significant detail. The signature on the Seltaeb contract—the signature that gave five strangers 90 percent of Beatles merchandise royalties, and so ensured the back-tracking litigation that followed—was that of Brian's lawyer, David Jacobs. In the autumn of the following year Jacobs was found in his garage hanging by a length of satin from one of the beams. The inquest verdict was suicide. But several of his friends and associates were later to remember that in his last weeks alive he had seemed profoundly upset and worried about something.

·   ·   ·

Brian's funeral, at Long Lane Jewish cemetery in Liverpool, was a private family affair. To his mother's distress he was not buried next to his father but in a separate avenue of undecorated memorials. The Beatles did not attend. George Harrison sent a sunflower that Nat Weiss threw into the open grave.

Five weeks later, a memorial service was held for Brian at the New London Synagogue, St. John's Wood. It was only a short walk from there to Paul's house and Abbey Road and the studios where Brian ushered in the Beatles to meet George Martin on that summer day long ago in 1962.

The Beatles did attend this time, as did George Martin, Dick James, and scores of people who were wealthy and well known only because of the young man who came down from Liverpool in his Crombie overcoat; who blushed easily and never went back on a promise; who could be ecstatic but never happy; who somehow caught the lightning and then somehow let it go. The rabbi's text was chosen from the Book of Proverbs: "Sayest thou that the man diligent in his business, he shall stand before kings."

Jewish cemeteries as a rule do not permit flowers. But after the funeral a tall, quietly spoken man visited the rabbi at Long Lane synagogue and obtained special dispensation to lay a small posy on Brian's grave each year on his birthday. It was Joe Flannery, his one-time companion in the nursery: the one-time lover who'd never fallen out of love with him.

PART FOUR

WASTING

SIXTEEN

"WE'VE GOT TO SPEND TWO MILLION OR THE TAXMAN WILL GET IT"

Since Brian had died without making a will, his whole estate passed automatically to his mother, Queenie. Nor was it worth anything like the seven million pounds commentators had estimated. Lush living had absorbed—even exceeded—a vast yearly income that had never been left to accumulate for one second into capital. What Brian did not spend on himself, on other people, or on the roulette table, he invested into offshoot companies and loss-making personal projects, like the Saville theater. Toward the end, shortage of ready money had led him to borrow heavily from NEMS Enterprises. His debt to his own company was found to be in the region of one hundred fifty thousand pounds. His final cash estate was realized chiefly through the sale of his two houses and his cars, paintings, and artworks. The residue, after death duties, was a little more than three-quarters of a million pounds.

Mrs. Epstein, bereaved within six weeks of both her husband and elder son, was in no state to face the complexities instantly arising from her inheritance. It fell to her younger son, Clive, to try to sort out Brian's tangled business affairs. Clive, as cofounder of NEMS Enterprises, took over the chairmanship, pending discussions on the company's future.

Tony Bramwell, George Harrison's friend, visiting NEMS a few days after Brian's death, found the half-dozen directors in a state of total confusion. No one at NEMS realized yet that Brian had virtually sold the company to his Australian associate, Robert Stigwood. "They were all squabbling about who was going to manage the Beatles," Bramwell says. "It sickened me. I just walked out."

Despite Brian's depleted personal wealth, his estate was liable to taxes, based on NEMS's current value, of some half a million pounds. Word quickly leaked onto the London Stock Exchange that to meet the estate duty the Epsteins would have no choice but to sell NEMS. It was rumored that an offer would be made, linking NEMS with Brian's 10 percent holding in Northern Songs, the Lennon-McCartney publishing company.

Since Brian's death the Beatles had had several further, apparently fruitful, sessions with the Maharishi. They were now full members of the Spiritual Regeneration movement and, as such, liable to pay a week's earnings per month to support it. They had also undertaken to visit their guru's academy in India to further their studies and ultimately to qualify as "teachers of Meditation."

At Buckingham Palace the same week, the Queen held a levée for the Council of Knights Bachelor, whose members included Sir Joseph Lockwood, chairman of EMI. As Her Majesty entered the room she called out to Sir Joseph: "The Beatles are turning awfully *funny*, aren't they?"

A few days after Brian's funeral the four of them met Clive Epstein at Brian's house in Chapel Street. Queenie, too, had insisted on being there. "All the boys turned up in suits, out of respect for Queenie," Joanne Newfield says. "We all sat around Brian's sitting room, having tea together. It felt so strange—as though nothing had happened at all. I half-expected Brian to walk in, just the way he used to, and join us.

"It was all too much for me. I just burst into tears. George looked at me very sternly and said, 'You're 'not crying for Brian. You're crying for yourself.' "

At that and subsequent meetings the Beatles agreed to accept Clive as Brian's successor, at least for the two months until their contract with NEMS expired. What they most emphatically did not want was any managerial relationship with Robert Stigwood. Lengthy consultations followed with Lord Goodman, the country's most eminent lawyer, who had recently acted for Brian as well as for EMI. As a result, Stigwood was persuaded to relinquish his option on NEMS. He departed with some five hundred thousand pounds, plus half the NEMS artists roster— among them the Bee Gees, Cream, and Jimi Hendrix—to set up, with spectacular success, on his own.

A new company, Nemperor Holdings, was formed to administer NEMS in what Clive Epstein promised would be "a program of vigorous expansion." Vic Lewis, the ex-bandleader, became managing director. Clive, as chief executive, commuted back and forth from Liverpool, conscientiously trying to fill his elder brother's shoes.

Peter Brown, at the Epstein family's request, lived on for a time at Brian's Chapel Street house. His resemblance to Brian, and the consequent reliance of Queenie Epstein on him, seemed to guarantee his accession to the role he had so long understudied. He took over Brian's desk and Brian's assistant—even certain of Brian's little executive affectations. "Brian used to have this habit of dropping all the music papers on the floor and saying, 'I've finished with these now,' Joanne Newfield says. 'A few days after he took over, Peter did exactly the same thing and used exactly the same words.'"

It was Brown who now had the direct line to all four Beatles and who, in a voice so very like Brian's, passed along the inter-Beatles message he had just received. Paul wanted to have a meeting, just among themselves, to discuss future projects and plans. Could they all meet up on September 2 at Paul's house?

The girls who stood outside Paul's Cavendish Avenue house had never been formally introduced. They knew each other only as syllables, breathlessly gasped out in the running and jumping and climbing and neck-craning of the campaign they pursued in common. There was Big Sue and Little Sue, and Gayleen, and Margo, and "Willie," and "Knickers." Others came and went, or were shooed away, having tried to preempt the space allotted by mutual agreement among those half-dozen perennials. Waiting there, day after day, night after night until dawn, as days turned into months, as months lengthened to years, they somehow never did discover one another's surnames.

They waited outside Paul's because he was their favorite Beatle, but also because his house, being only a short walk from Abbey Road studios, was the recognized listening post for all Beatles intelligence. Pilgrimages would be made at intervals to John's mock-Tudor Mansion in Weybridge or George's Esher bungalow. But always the trail led back to St. John's Wood and the big black double gates whose electric security lock, as time passed, grew less and less of an impediment.

Bored to distraction as the Beatles were by their female following, they could not help but marvel at the almost psychic power that enabled these hard-core fans to shadow or waylay them. At Paul's house or Abbey Road, or any ad hoc rehearsal or film-editing rendezvous, Peter Brown's secret call would bring the four together under the scrutiny of those same half-dozen rather red and breathless faces. "They used to shout at us, 'How did you *know*?'" Margo says. "Paul always called us the eyes and ears of the world."

Margo, a brisk, jolly, and otherwise deeply rational girl, worked as a children's nanny in Kingsbury, North London. Both job and location had been chosen for their convenience to the greater purpose that had brought Margo to London from the Lincolnshire seaside town of Cleethorpes. She arrived in 1968, looked after her two charges conscientiously for forty-eight hours, then made her way to St. John's Wood. For the next two years, with only the most necessary intervals, Margo stood and waited outside Paul McCartney's house.

The other Beatles had their own faithful followers, usually identified by a nickname: "Sue John" or "Linda Ringo." "We all respected John," Margo says. "We were a bit afraid of him, really. Ringo would come along and you'd never notice him until someone said, 'That was Ringo.' George always seemed to hate us. He'd push past us and even try to tread on our toes or kick us. He seemed very unhappy in those days."

The main objective, however, remained that Beatle who was not only the most irresistibly good-looking but also the most patiently amiable and accessible. Margo had first noticed this quality in 1964 while chasing the Beatles' limousine down Monmouth Street, when Paul leaned out of a window and shouted, "Run, girls, run!" There was also a time outside the Scala Theatre, during filming of *A Hard Day's Night*, when he emerged to talk to Margo and her cousin in one of his several disguises. "This man came up to us with blond hair and a clipboard. He told us where to go if we wanted to see the next day's filming. It was only when he said, 'Ta-ra' that we realized it was Paul."

So, every day of the week, Margot, Big Sue, Little Sue, Gayleen, "Willie," and "Knickers" waited on Cavendish Avenue with their hungry eyes and small Instamatic cameras. They photographed Paul in the early morning as he came out to walk Martha the sheepdog on Hampstead Heath. They photographed him late at night, returning from vacation, his sunburned nose shining eerily in the flashbulb glow. They photographed him driving out, with Jane or without her, in the Aston Martin or Mini Cooper; then, hours, even days, later, they photographed him driving back in again.

Paul, for his part, presented token discouragement. The front gates would be thrown open suddenly, and the Aston Martin would roar out and away up Cavendish Avenue. The girls were by then so fit, they could beat the car on foot over at least the distance to Abbey Road studios. "We all got very tough as well," Margo says, "through being thrown down the EMI front steps by Mal Evans, the roadie. But we understood that he was only doing his job. At other times he'd be concerned for us, standing out there in all weathers. At heart he was an incredibly gentle person."

The bulk of the snapshots, however, showed Paul, in his endlessly changing suits and shirts and scarves and waistcoats, pausing at an entreaty: turning and smiling. The face—in real life slightly asymmetric—became for the cheapest Instamatic what it was in the glossiest magazines. Frequently, too, he would be in a mood for conversation. One snapshot from the hundreds shows him playing with a monkey one of the girls had brought. It bit his finger a moment afterward. "We told him once we could see him from the back of the house, sitting on the loo," Margo says. "We stood him on a flowerpot to show him we were telling the truth."

Each of the girls, by tradition, brought Paul gifts of varying usefulness. "I gave him three peaches in a bag once," Margo says. "He'd eaten one of them by the time he got down the Abbey Road front steps. Another time, we shouted out, 'What do you want for your birthday?' He thought for a minute, then he said, 'I haven't got any slippers.' " The slippers were ceremonially handed over in front of massed Instamatics.

The vigil broadened in scope after someone discovered under which flowerpot Paul was accustomed to hide his backdoor key. Selected parties then began letting themselves into the house while he was absent, and moving from room to room in hushed wonder at the opulent chaos mingled with working-class formality: the lace-covered table, the Paolozzi sculpture, and the ranks and ranks of clothes. They would bring away some memento—small at first—a tea towel or a handful of toilet paper.

"The American girls were worst," Margo says. "They started nicking his clothes." The English girls, though refusing to pilfer, felt their scruples waver when offered a share in the booty. Margo acquired a pair of Paul's underpants and a spotted Mr. Fish shirt. Some Harris tweed trousers were also brought out as a communal prize to be worn reverently, in turn. The hems would be shortened for Little Sue, then lengthened again so that Big Sue could have a turn at wearing them.

Six months earlier, Paul had written a song, or the beginning of one, called "Magical Mystery Tour." It was to have been put on the *Sgt. Pepper* album: It had been arranged, rehearsed, even partially recorded before Paul conceded that it did not quite fit into Sergeant Pepper's cabaret show. The track was held over—indeed, it was forgotten until early September, and the meetings to decide how the Beatles were to begin the era after Brian.

The idea, like the song, was Paul's. He had been thinking in his whimsical way about little tourist buses, setting out with coy trepidation on Mystery Tours from British seaside towns. He had been thinking, too, of Ken Kesey's Merry Pranksters, an American hippie troupe that, two years earlier, had journeyed by bus through the Californian backwoods, buoyed up by LSD diluted into thirst-quenching Kool-Aid. Tom Wolfe's chronicle of their journey, *The Electric Kool-Aid Acid Test,* recorded, among other things, what visions the Pranksters experienced by taking acid during a Beatles concert in Los Angeles. So, yet again, something they had originally inspired came floating back to them almost unrecognizably as a new idea to copy and adapt.

Paul's plan was to rent a bus and set out on a real life Mystery Tour, as the Pranksters had, to see what adventure—what magic—would be extracted from the unsuspecting English countryside. They would take cameras and film it, Paul said, but this time direct the film for themselves. He showed the others the scenario he had written—or rather, drawn. It was a neatly inscribed circle, segmented with what were to be the visual high points. In one segment, Paul had written "midgets"; in another, "fat lady"; in yet another, "lunch."

The prospect, as Paul outlined it, was generally appealing. At last they would be able to make a film unhampered by Walter Shenson, Dick Lester, and all the petty restraints that had made *Help!* and *A Hard Day's Night* such tedious and disappointing experiences. Filmmaking, as they well knew, was easy enough. All you needed was money and cameras, and someone saying "Action!"

So exhilarating did the project—and other projects—seem that they decided to postpone their pilgrimage to the Maharishi's Indian ashram until early 1968. John and George gave their first television interview in two years, appearing on the *David Frost Show* to explain their newfound religious beliefs. Even about Transcendental Meditation they were pithy and funny: They seemed calm, cheerful, and restored to sanity. Best of all, they no longer incited Britain's gullible youth to experiment with

LSD. The *Daily Sketch* spoke for all in noting maternally, "It's nice to see the roses back in the Beatles' cheeks."

Certainly, it was simple enough to hire a luxury coach and commission the best graphic artists to design placards reading MAGICAL MYSTERY TOUR, though not quite so easy to make the placards stick to the coach's highly polished sides. It was easy to hire actors to play the characters specified in Paul's diagram—a fat lady, a midget, a music-hall funny man. It was easy to engage cameras, and three crews to operate them, and to persuade a sprinkling of journalists and NEMS employees to go along as extras. Forty-three people eventually boarded the bus that, early in September 1967, in a secrecy somewhat compromised by its insecurely fixed MAGICAL MYSTERY TOUR placards, headed out of London along the Great West Road toward a still unspecified destination.

Chaos set in from the beginning. The Magical Mystery Tour, far from floating off into a psychedelic sunset, labored sluggishly and all too materially around Britain's summer vacation routes, hounded by a cavalcade of press vehicles, surrounded at every random halt by packs of sightseers and fans. Encountering a sign to Banbury, they followed it, to see if Banbury had a fair. It didn't, so they turned round and headed for Devon.

The journey, it became quickly evident, held neither magic nor mystery: only poignant reminders of how things used to be when Brian Epstein looked after the travel arrangements. Aboard the bus, becalmed in traffic jams, or trying to register at hotels that were not expecting them, everyone realized at last what a protective shield had been wrenched away. Neil Aspinall realized it, trying to apportion overnight rooms among midgets and fat ladies squabbling over who had to double up with whom: "When Brian was alive, you never had to worry about any of that. You'd just ask for fifteen cars and twenty hotel rooms and they'd be there."

They reached Devon and started back, still vainly trying to extemporize quicksilver comedy from the all too mundane disorganization and bad humor. Nothing was explained to the actors or even the cameramen. The script was anything that anyone happened to say.

"We missed the tour ourselves in the end," Neil Aspinall says. "We were too busy driving. We drove all the way to Brighton and finished up just filming two people on the beach. What we *should* have been filming was the chaos we caused—the bus trying to get over this narrow bridge, with queues of traffic building up behind us, and then having to reverse and go back past all the drivers who'd been cursing us, and John getting off in a fury and ripping all the posters off the sides."

The climactic scenes were filmed on a disused airfield in West Malling, Kent. There, under Paul's direction, a scene was improvised with forty dwarfs, a military band, a football crowd, and a dozen babies in prams. The bus, by now looking decidedly careworn, swerved round the pitted runway with limousines in hot, but unexplained, pursuit. That was the finish of the Magical Mystery Tour.

It was the finish, that is to say, but for the editing, which took eleven weeks. "Paul would come in and edit in the morning," Tony Bramwell says. "Then John would come in in the afternoon and reedit what Paul had edited. Then Ringo would come in . . ." When not editing and re-editing they would stand in the cutting room, having singsongs with a toothless Soho street busker who carried a port bottle balanced on his head.

The print eventually passed by all four Beatles was then handed to NEMS Enterprises for distribution. NEMS's response was indecisive. "It was like giving your film to NBC and CBS and all the networks at once," Neil Aspinall says. "Everyone came up with a different comment. 'Couldn't you do it this way?' 'Couldn't you do it *this* way?'" NEMS eventually sold the British rights to BBC Television, even though the film had been shot in color and BBC TV, to all but a select handful, was still black and white. BBC 1 announced that it would be shown on Boxing Day, 1967.

The Beatles had been at Abbey Road since mid-September, recording material for an EP to accompany the film. Their pre-Christmas single, however, was a separate track, "Hello, Goodbye," written by Paul, in which a grandstand of overdubbed voices chanted a lyric so simple as to be almost inane and so inane it appeared subtly ironic. "You say good-bye and I say hello. Hello, hello. I don't know why you say good-bye, I say hello. Hay-la! Hey-hello . . ." By early December, "Hello, Goodbye" was number one in Britain and America. The Beatles continued to walk upon water.

Magical Mystery Tour was launched by a party whose lavishness showed no doubt of *Sgt. Pepper*–like success. The Beatles specified fancy dress. John came as a Teddy Boy, accompanied by Cynthia in Quality Street crinolines. George Martin came as the Duke of Edinburgh, Lulu as Shirley Temple, and Patti, George's wife, as an Eastern belly dancer. John, that night, made no secret of powerfully desiring Patti Harrison. He danced with Patti time after time, leaving Cynthia so disconsolate in her crinolines that Lulu was roused to sisterly indignation. The climax of the party was the moment at which a little ringletted Shirley Temple, clutching an immense lollipop, confronted the chief Beatle in his greaser outfit and berated him for being so mean to his wife.

Fifteen million British viewers, on the dead day after Christmas, tuned their television sets hopefully to BBC 1 and *Magical Mystery Tour*. Expecting a miracle, they beheld only a glorified and progressively irritating home movie. The four donned crude animal costumes to perform "I Am the Walrus," a song inspired by Lewis Carroll's nonsense poem about the "Walrus close behind us . . . who's treading on my tail." The Beatles themselves were only intermittently visible sitting among forty-three freaky passengers on the bus or as four red-robed wizards messing around in a chemistry lab. Paul, in one of the few professionally directed sequences, sang "Fool on the Hill" against a background of French Riviera mountains and sea. George, squatting Indian style, sang "Blue Jay Way," repeating the line "don't be long" twenty-nine times. A lengthy abstract interlude, devoid of its color, became merely puzzling cloud drifts and icebergs. The finale was one more idea that no one had quite bothered to think through. "Let's do a Busby Berkeley sequence," Paul had said. The Beatles, in white tailcoats, descended a staircase, singing "Your Mother Should Know" while ballroom dancing teams whirled in aimless formation beneath.

The *Daily Express* TV critic received front-page editorial space next morning to declare that never in all his days of viewing had he beheld such "blatant rubbish." The unanimous decision of the British critics was picked up by American papers like the *Los Angeles Times* ("Beatles Bomb With Yule Movie") and brought speedy cancellation of the film's U.S. television deal. The BBC, meanwhile, took belatedly old-maidenly fright at John's lyrics for "I Am the Walrus"—especially the references to "knickers" and "yellow matter custard," i.e., snot—and denied it any further airplay.

For the first time since they'd worn leather jackets at a Young Conservatives dance, the Beatles found themselves being collectively criticized in every newspaper they opened. It came hardest of all to the one who'd initiated the whole catastrophe, drawing a clock face and trusting to his Pied Piper magic to do the rest. Dusty Durband at Liverpool Institute Grammar School could have cited many similar instances long ago when Paul McCartney did insufficient preparation.

Now, too, it came home to them with full force what life was like without Brian to protect them and clear up the messes they made. "If Brian had been alive, the film would never have gone out," Neil Aspinall says. "Brian would have said, 'Okay, we blew forty thousand pounds—so what?' Brian would never have let it happen."

John Lennon's old schoolfriend, Pete Shotton, had long felt a distinct impression that John was trying to tell him something. Pete still lived in Hampshire, managing the supermarket John had bought him: on visits to John in London he could not but notice what larger business preparations were afoot. "I'd known John so long and had so many laughs with him, he could never come out with anything straight. He'd just grin across the room and say: 'When are you coming up here to work then?'

"Eventually he did come out with it. He said he wanted me to come to London and run a boutique the Beatles were opening. He said: 'We've got to spend two million or the taxman will get it.'"

Dr. Walter Strach, their chief financial adviser, had many times implored Brian to invest the colossal Beatle earnings simply left on deposit at various British banks. Socialism had as yet closed few of the Tory loopholes for channeling money abroad into tax-exempt trusts and companies. Brian would never do it, partly through a naive respect for capital, partly from a belief that to take money abroad was unpatriotic. "After the Beatles got their MBEs," Dr. Strach remembered, "Brian always insisted they had to be whiter than white."

It was therefore on "Uncle Walter's" advice rather than Brian's that individual Beatles made personal investments, such as John's Hampshire supermarket and Ringo's brief, unsuccessful foray into the building trade. On one occasion, all four came to Strach, eager to put money into a washing-machine company run by a bearded young tycoon named John Bloom. The doctor took credit for talking them out of involvement with one of the decade's more spectacular financial crashes.

Strach figured in the single attempt during Brian's lifetime to divert Beatles money from its huge liability under British income tax. In 1965, the proceeds from *Help!* were paid directly into a Bahamian company,

Cavalcade Productions, formed jointly by the Beatles and the film's producer, Walter Shenson, and administered by Dr. Strach as a temporary resident in Nassau. "That was why we shot part of *Help!* in the Bahamas," Shenson admitted. "It was a goodwill exercise to persuade the Bahamian authorities we were an asset to their business community." Unfortunately, the *Help!* proceeds were banked entirely in sterling. When Harold Wilson devalued the pound in 1967, Cavalcade Productions lost approximately eighty thousand pounds.

Toward the end of his life Brian had been considering more complex measures to protect the Beatles' accumulated fortunes. His concept was not much different in essence from that which would soon spectacularly emerge—a corporation built around the Beatles that would both lighten their personal tax liabilities and give them control of their own work at every level, from songwriting to recording, even of distribution, marketing, and retailing. Brian had also visualized a string of Beatles boutiques, or pop supermarkets, selling records and clothes.

In addition to their original company, Beatles Ltd., the four were now incorporated into a partnership, Beatles & Co. The maneuver took place in April 1967 as a means of providing each with some quick capital. Beatles Ltd. paid eight hundred thousand pounds for a share in the partnership. By this absolutely legal method of selling themselves a share in themselves, each Beatle received two hundred thousand pounds and, later on, a tax demand to match.

In 1968, they had joint reserves of around two million pounds that, after the taxman's punitive bite of 90-plus percent, would leave scarcely enough to buy them each a new Mr. Fish shirt. Far better, their advisers agreed, to write off the money as a business loss. And if they could have a little fun—even do a little good—in the process, so much the better.

Simon Posthuma and Marijke Koger were beautiful people from Holland. Couturiers and interior designers, famous for their Amsterdam boutique Trend, they had migrated to London in 1967, hoping to widen their activities to the theater. Among their first patrons were a pair of publicists named Barry Finch and Simon Hayes whose clients at the time included Brian Epstein's Saville Theater. By this means, Simon and Marijke gained access to the Beatles' circle, where their exotic clothes and dreamy, Dutch-accented hippie talk made an immediate impression. So successful were they, both as stage designers and Beatles friends, that they brought their former Amsterdam boutique partner, Josje Leeger, over from Holland to join them. The three, plus PR man Barry Finch, then formed themselves into a design group named The Fool.

All through the Summer of Love and the still-affectionate autumn that followed it, The Fool enjoyed the quasi-royal status of designers and couturiers to the Beatles. They made the costumes for the "All You Need Is Love" television sequence. They painted a piano and a gypsy caravan for John and designed a fireplace for George's Esher bungalow. They began to appear in newspaper fashion spreads as heralds of an era to follow wasp stripes, PVC, and miniskirts. "Simon," explained the *Sunday Times*, "is dressed to represent Water. His jacket is glittering Lurex in bluey, greeney colours; his trousers are blue velvet. Marijke is Nature, in blue and green, and has a pastoral scene on her bodice. Josje is Space, her midnight-blue trousers covered with yellow appliqué stars." To the *Sunday Times*, Simon explained that The Fool was a name with meaning beyond the obvious one. "It represents Truth, Spiritual Meaning and the circle, which expresses the universal circumference in which gravitate all things."

In September 1967, The Fool received one hundred thousand pounds to design a boutique for the Beatles and stock it with their own exotic garments and accessories. It was Paul, the most dandified Beatle, who announced "a beautiful place where you can buy beautiful things." It was Paul who strove to think of a name befitting the new boutique's ideal of chaste elegance, and who found inspiration in a Magritte painting he had recently bought as well as the general idea of a hippie Garden of Eden. The others agreed: they would call their boutique, simply, Apple.

The summer had produced another Beatles friend. His name was Alexis Mardas. He was a young, blond-haired Greek who had come to Britain knowing only two people: Mick Jagger and the Duke of Edinburgh.

Nicknamed Magic Alex by Lennon, Mardas was an inventor of electronic gadgets with ideas that, he believed, could revolutionize twentieth-century life. There was the transistorized hi-fi; the "scream" built into a phonograph record to prevent illicit taping; the force field around a house that would keep intruders at bay with a wall of colored air. His ideas appealed to the Beatles' thirst for novelty and their endless quest for protection against a cheating, importunate world.

Meanwhile, on Baker Street, a respectable eighteenth-century corner house, not far from Sherlock Holmes's mythical consulting rooms, was being transformed into a condition that might have baffled even Holmes. The Fool hired gangs of art students to help them cover the side wall along Paddington Street with psychedelic patterns whizzing and whirling around what seemed to be the face of an enormous Red Indian. Magic Alex was also there, designing floodlights.

All the Beatles relished the novelty of setting up a shop. The prettiest, swingingest girls—among them Patti Harrison's sister, Jennie—were recruited as staff. Pete Shotton left his Hampshire supermarket to oversee the arrival of oriental fabrics and exotic jewelry ordered in profusion by The Fool. "John would come in every day," Pete says. " 'You've got to put a partition over here,' he'd say. Then Paul would come in and say, 'What's that partition here for? Better move it over there.' "

The Apple boutique opened on December 7, 1967, with a lavish party and fashion show. "Come at 7:46," the invitations said. "Fashion show at 8:16." In the elegant, sweating crush, sipping apple juice, only two Beatles were visible: John and George. Ringo was abroad, playing a small part in the film *Candy,* and Paul had decided to go away to his farm in Scotland.

Within a few days the pattern of trading had been established. Hundreds of people came to Baker Street to look at the Apple boutique, and look inside it. There was no obligation to buy, or to consider buying. Garments began to leave the premises rapidly, though seldom as a result of cash transactions. The musk-scented gloom, where feather boas hung helpfully from bentwood hat-stands, was a shoplifter's paradise.

It was upstairs from the Apple boutique that the empire named Apple initially took root. On the second floor, in a snow-white office, Terry Doran, "the man from the motor trade," ran Apple Music, the intended nucleus of the Beatles' own independent publishing and recording company. On the next floor Pete Shotton administered Apple Retail, comprising the boutique and men's tailoring and mail order subsidiaries. Pete also did much of the hiring for the other Apple provinces springing up almost daily. For the empire, unlike its symbol, did not ripen at leisure. It appeared all at once, like a conjuring trick at the imperious clap of four multimillionaires' hands.

Its purpose—to begin with, at least—was clear and concurring in all four multimillionaires' minds. It was to be *theirs,* rather than administered on their behalf. It was liberation from the control of "men in suits," as John Lennon called the irksome powers at NEMS, Northern Songs, and EMI. It was to prove that people of less than middle age, without stiff collars or waistcoats, were capable of building and running an organization. Apple was to be the first triumphant annexation by youth's living apotheosis of all the power and riches that youth had generated. It was to be free and easy and openhanded; above all, in that poignant sixties word, it was to be "fun."

Magical Mystery Tour, in 1967, was the first production credited to Apple Films. Among future productions, it was announced, would be a film starring Twiggy, the model; possibly a screen version of the hippie world's most sacred text after *Sgt. Pepper,* J. R. R. Tolkein's *The Lord of the Rings.* Simultaneously there appeared an Apple Electronics division, run by Magic Alex from a laboratory financed by the Beatles. Alex was to design an entire recording studio for them; meanwhile, his Hellenic wizardry would be applied to such marketable novelties as luminous paint, domestic force fields, and plastic apples with miniature transistor radios inside.

In January 1968, Beatles Ltd. changed its name to Apple Corps Ltd. "It's a pun," Paul explained patiently. "Apple *Core*—see?" Neil Aspinall was appointed managing director and Alistair Taylor, general manager. The board of directors included Peter Brown and Harry Pinsker, head of Bryce, Hanmer, Brian Epstein's old Albemarle Street accountants.

The new divisions, and their newly appointed directors and managers, quickly spilled over from the Apple shop into a suite of offices on Wigmore Street, a quarter of a mile away. Here were established Apple Records, with Jane Asher's brother, Peter, as A&R man, and Apple Publicity, run by Derek Taylor, the idiosyncratic press officer whom the Beatles had wooed home from Hollywood for his second term of serving them. Also at Wigmore Street, Neil Aspinall exchanged his time-honored role as roadie for that of office manager, finally making use of his teenage accounting training.

In these early days a stark contrast emerged between friends of the Beatles, working for a moderate salary, and impressive outsiders, recruited to senior executive positions at almost any figure they cared to name. Pete Shotton, whose weekly take-home pay was £37 10s, found himself approving munificent salaries for Denis O'Dell, head of Apple

Films; Ron Kass, head of Apple Records; and Brian Lewis, lawyer in charge of Apple contracts. "As soon as they arrived," Pete says, "they started going out to lunch. I'd be left with a toasted sandwich from the café across the road."

In February, in the midst of Apple's blossoming, John and George, with Cynthia and Patti, flew to India to begin their much postponed religious studies under the Maharishi Mahesh Yogi. The advance party also included Patti's sister, Jennie. Paul and Jane followed soon afterward, with Ringo, Maureen, and a consignment of baked beans that Ringo had brought as insurance against the curry-eating weeks ahead.

The ashram to which their guru beamingly welcomed them was not devoid of worldly comforts. Situated in verdant foothills above the Ganges at Rishikesh, it was a settlement of stone bungalows, with English hotel furniture, telephones, and running water. A high perimeter fence and padlocked gate kept out sightseers, beggars, *sadhus*, wandering cows, and the clamor of everyday worship at the *ghats*, or holy bathing places, along the river bank. The Maharishi himself occupied an elaborate residence equipped with a launching pad for his private helicopter.

Apart from the Beatles an impressive netful of personalities had been trawled to sit at the Maharishi's feet. They included Mike Love of the Beach Boys; Donovan, the English folk singer, and his manager, "Gipsy Dave"; and the film actress Mia Farrow. All took off their pop hippie finery, the girls to dress in saris, the boys in *kurta* tunics, loose trousers, and sandals. At Mike Love's example, both John and George started to grow beards. John even experimented with a turban, though he could not resist the temptation to pull Quasimodo faces when wearing it.

The Maharishi took pains to ensure that ashram life would not be too stringent for his star disciples. The chalets were comfortable—like Butlin's, Ringo said—and the food, though vegetarian, was ample; there were frequent excursions and parties. The Lennons were presented with Indian clothes and toys for their son, Julian, and George's twenty-fifth birthday was celebrated by a seven-pound cake. Obliging houseboys would even smuggle the odd bottle of forbidden wine into the Beatles' quarters.

Even so, the schedule of fasting, chanting, and mass prayer quickly proved too much for Ringo Starr. He left Rishikesh with Maureen after only ten days, complaining that his delicate stomach couldn't take the highly spiced food and that he missed his son.

The others showed every sign of sticking out the course for its full three-month duration. Fleet Street journalists who had infiltrated the stockade reported seeing this or that Beatle seated contentedly at a prayer meeting, feeding the monkeys that inhabited the trellises, or aimlessly strumming a guitar. It emerged that they were holding a contest among themselves to see who could keep up nonstop meditation the longest. Paul led the field with four hours, followed by John and George with three-and-a-half each. They were also using the unwonted peace and immobility to write songs for their next album.

At regular intervals, Neil Aspinall would fly out from London to report the latest progress in setting up Apple, and the position of "Lady Madonna," the single they had left for release in their absence. Neil was also making arrangements for Apple Films to finance a production in which the Maharishi himself would star. "We had a meeting about it in his bungalow," Neil says. "Suddenly, this little guy in a robe who's meant to be a holy man starts talking about his two-and-a-half percent. 'Wait a minute,' I thought, 'he knows more about making deals than I do. He's really into scoring, the Maharishi.' "

Paul, who filmed most of his and Jane's nine-week stay, remembered their Rishikesh experience as being very like school, with the teachers delivering long, boring sermons and the pupils nudging each other and trying not to giggle. As he told John later, "We thought we were submerging our personalities, but really we weren't being very truthful then. There's a long shot of you walking beside the Maharishi, saying 'Tell me, O Master,' and it just isn't you."

It was in the ninth week, after Paul and Jane had decided to leave, that John himself began showing signs of restlessness. "John thought there was some sort of secret the Maharishi had to give you, and then you could just go home," Neil Aspinall says. "He started to think the Maharishi was holding out on him. 'Maybe if I go up with him in the helicopter,' John said, 'he may slip me the answer on me own.' "

By the eleventh week, despite trips above the Ganges in the Maharishi's helicopter, the answer still had not come. Furthermore, it began to be whispered that the Maharishi was not so divine a being as he had seemed. There was also a rumor that his interest in Mia Farrow might not be spiritual only. Even George, the guru's most impassioned disciple, seemed to be having second thoughts. So, to Cynthia's dismay, John decided they were going home.

He led the way into the Maharishi's quarters and announced his decision, characteristically mincing no words. The guru, for all his quick-wittedness, seems to have had no idea that the lights had changed. When he asked "Why?" John would say only, "You're the cosmic one. You ought to know." At this, he said later, Maharishi Mahesh Yogi, The Great Soul, gave him a look like "I'll kill you, you bastard."

John, in fact, was convinced for a long time afterward that the Maharishi would wreak some sort of transcendental vengeance. He told Cyn it was already starting when, on the way back to Delhi, their taxi broke down, and they both stood panic-stricken, trying to hitch a ride as the Indian dusk with its thousands of staring eyes closed in around them.

The Maharishi, his teachings and flowers and transcendental gurglings, were dismissed as utterly as last month's groupie or yesterday's Mr. Fish shirt. "We made a mistake," Paul said. "We thought there was more to him than there was. He's human. We thought at first that he wasn't." Into another airport microphone, George concurred: "We've finished with him." The holy man was left in his mountain fastness to cogitate upon a mystery as profound as any offered by Heaven or Earth. Had the Beatles, or had the Maharishi Mahesh Yogi, been taken for the bigger ride?

Last month's ashram-dwellers were this month's corporate executives, flying to New York with their numerous highly paid lieutenants to unveil Apple Corps to the most crucial of its prospective markets. The first board meeting was held aboard a Chinese junk, cruising round the Statue of Liberty.

At press conferences and on the NBC *Tonight show* John and Paul explained to Johnny Carson the revolutionary but also philanthropic motives that would guide the Beatles' business. "The aim," John said, "isn't just a stack of gold teeth in the bank. We've done that bit. It's more of a trick to see if we can get artistic freedom within a business structure— to see if we can create things and sell them without charging five times our cost."

Paul said that Apple's aim was "a controlled weirdness . . . a kind of Western communism." It was he who announced the newest subdivision: an Apple Foundation for the Arts. "We want to help people, but without doing it like a charity. *We* always had to go to the big men on our knees and touch our forelocks and say, 'Please can we do so-and-so?' We're in the happy position of not needing any more money, so for the first time the bosses aren't in it for profit. If you come to me and say, 'I've had such and such a dream,' I'll say to you, 'Go away and do it.' "

In other words, the Apple Foundation for the Arts would grant struggling unknown artists in every genre the finance and fulfillment they had been denied by a mercenary, unsympathetic, middle-aged world. Paul designed a proclamation to that effect, issued via full-page advertisements in the British music press. Alistair Taylor, Apple's general manager, was coerced into posing for a photograph weighed down with the impedimenta of a one-man band. "This man has talent!" ran Paul's caption. "One day, he sang his songs into a tape recorder and, remembering to enclose a picture of himself, sent the tape to Apple Music at 94 Baker Street. You could do the same. This man now owns a Bentley."

The response was as anyone but a Beatle might have predicted. An avalanche of tapes, of novels, of plays and poems and film scripts and synopses and scenarios, of paintings, etchings, sketches, lithographs, sculptures, designs, blueprints, working models, and other, less easily classified submissions fell at once, with a huge, soft, slightly deranged thud upon Apple's Wigmore Street office. Many were delivered in person, the artists electing to wait the short time necessary before they received their bursaries from the Apple Foundation for the Arts. The reception area all day thronged with creative, insolvent humanity, from ethnic bards to seaside Punch and Judy men, reminding Richard DiLello, a young San Franciscan working for the press office, of nothing so much as the VD clinics back home in his native Haight-Ashbury. Brighter even than hope of penicillin shone the belief that the Beatles meant it: that behind those very partition walls even now they were reading, listening, looking, nodding, and saying, "Yes. Go away and do it."

They were certainly there, though not engaged precisely as imagined. They had a big corner room in which open house was kept for the fellow rock stars and friends who dropped in continuously to wish Apple luck and drink, and smoke, its health. John and Paul each kept more or less regular office hours, enjoying the novelty of a fixed destination, a desk, and secretaries. John employed an astrologer named Caleb to cast a daily horoscope for senior staff and guide major policy decisions by consulting the *I Ching Book of Changes*. Paul's concern was that people arrived on time in the mornings and that there was enough lavatory paper in the Ladies.

It was pleasant, now that they themselves could rise no higher, to act as sponsors of new, young pop talent to join them on their very own Apple record label. Terry Doran had made the first signing—a teenage group named Grapefruit, and launched to the music press on an avalanche of Fortnum & Mason grapefruit in special presentation boxes. A second group, The Iveys, was Mal Evans's discovery. George had his own protégé, a fellow Liverpudlian named Jackie Lomax; in America, Peter Asher had found a raw-boned singer-songwriter named James Taylor. Twiggy the model also kept telling Paul about a sweet little Welsh soprano named Mary Hopkin, the longest consecutive winner of the television talent show *Opportunity Knocks*.

By June 1968, Wigmore Street could no longer contain all this bright, bustling activity and expansion. Neil Aspinall was given half a million pounds and told to find Apple a larger orchard.

Within a few days, Neil found 3 Savile Row, a five-story Georgian house standing deep in the heartland of custom tailoring and dealers in handmade cigarettes. The house knew something of show business: It had previously been owned by Jack Hylton, the theatrical impresario, who in latter days ran it as the Albany Club. On its left, Gieves, the military tailors, guarded the crevice into Regent Street. To its right stretched timbered casements displaying Royal warrants, in which elderly men with tape measures still toiled around the waistlines of peers and archbishops.

Savile Row was never to be quite the same again.

Throughout June and July, the Beatles' new business occupied them to the exclusion of almost everything else—including music. In the past six months, indeed, they had been to Abbey Road only to record a new single, "Hey Jude," and some tracks for a project about which they felt zero enthusiasm. The problem of what to do as their contracted third film for United Artists had finally been solved by a compromise that mercifully spared them from having to go in front of the cameras again. A cartoon feature film would be made, featuring their music and themselves as principal characters but with voices overdubbed by actors. The theme would be their song "Yellow Submarine," which since its 1966 release—despite its association with ochre-tinted pep pills—had become one of the best-loved melodies in Britain. Tiny tots were taught to sing it in kindergartens. Strikers chanted it on protest marches, changing "We all live in a yellow submarine" to "We all live on bread and margarine."

The Beatles' lack of involvement in the film was hardly conducive to enthusiasm in recording songs for its soundtrack and subsequent album. To be sure, they regarded it as a dustbin for second-rate tracks. "It'll do for the film," John would say whenever a song had not come up to expectations. Even after recycling "Nowhere Man" and "All You Need Is Love," they found they hadn't enough material for even one album side. So George went away for an hour and wrote "Only a Northern Song," a sarcastic reference to the publishing company and the low standard to which its product seemed to have sunk. George Martin in the end had no option but to make up a side two of Beatles songs scored as orchestral pieces by himself. For the first time ever, the Beatles had given short weight.

Surprisingly, however, *Yellow Submarine* turned out to be an artistic triumph. Scripted by Erich Segal—soon to hit the fiction jackpot with *Love Story*—it translated Beatles lyrics and Beatles allusions into a genuinely appealing and inventive fantasy about the inhabitants of a dream world called Pepperland and its oppression by killjoy invaders called Blue Meanies. Through it floated four little cartoon Beatles with the same characters and much the same childlike insouciance as in *A Hard Day's Night* and *Help!* and actors' voices that could easily have been mistaken for their real ones. The film opened in London on July 17. Though patronizingly reviewed and—amazingly—denied a general release, it proved popular with fans, restoring much of the goodwill that *Magical Mystery Tour* had lost.

At Baker Street, meanwhile, the Apple boutique was sliding into chaos. Its psychedelic mural had been scrubbed away after petitions by local tradespeople, leaving behind what was, after all, just another clothes shop, distinguished only by the ineptitude of its management. Despite their alleged boutique experience in Holland, The Fool seemed to have no idea how to run a business, and borrowed many of the choice items of stock for their own use. Shoplifting raged on, barely noticed by assistants, some of whom regularly swindled up to fifty pounds each week on top of their wages. A new head of Apple Retail, John

Lydon, was desperately trying to stop the rot. Stern memos went out to The Fool, warning them to take no more garments off the premises and forbidding any further expenditure without direct authorization.

At the end of July Pete Shotton was called to a meeting at Paul's house. "John told me, 'We've decided to close the shop down. We're tired of playing shops.' "

The Apple boutique liquidated itself on July 30 by the simple process of giving away its entire stock. A dozen policemen fought to control the riot in Baker Street as hundreds grabbed at Afghan coats, Indian beads, Art Deco ashtrays, and whatever shop fittings could be wrenched loose. The Beatles and their wives had already gone in privately for first pick, gleefully carrying off the choicer spoils with no sense that it was their own property they were plundering. To the media, Paul repeated John's remark, with an almost Napoleonic twist: "The Beatles are tired of being shopkeepers."

Bright, fresh, apple-green carpet now covered all five floors at 3 Savile Row. On August 11, Apple Records released four inaugural titles on the label whose logo was a perfect Granny Smith apple. Teams of photographers, designers, and typographers, not to mention fruit sellers, working in London and New York, had labored for six months, rejecting whole crops, to produce that stunningly crisp and explicit motif. When you turned the record over you saw the same apple, cut into a heart-shaped creamy half. As a final touch Alan Aldridge, London's highest-paid pop illustrator, contributed the copyright line message in hand-drawn italic script.

The Beatles' new single, "Hey Jude," was accompanied, in a shiny black presentation box, by three of the talents now under their wing: Mary Hopkin, Jackie Lomax, and the Black Dyke Mills brass band. Paul had produced Mary Hopkin's ballad "Those Were the Days," and conducted the Black Dyke Mills band's performance of his own composition, "Thingummybob." George had written and produced Jackie Lomax's song "Sour Milk Sea." The young press officer Richard DiLello was given the job of delivering one boxed set each to the Queen at Buckingham Palace, the Queen Mother at Clarence House, Princess Margaret at Kensington Palace, and the prime minister, Harold Wilson, at 10 Downing Street.

By far the greatest augury of Apple was the Beatles' appearance together on television, for the first time in two years, to perform "Hey

Jude" on the *David Frost Show*. The studio audience came and stood round them as Paul, at his piano, sang the wistful wounded ballad that turns, midway, into an anthem seven minutes long. At the Abbey Road session all of the forty-piece symphony orchestra had joined in that final, mesmeric la-la chorus. So did the studio audience—and much of the country—join in tonight. It was as though the Beatles were reaffirming their oneness with their audience and with each other, instead of just beginning their drift into chaos and bitter enmity.

SEVENTEEN

"YOUR FINANCES ARE IN A MESS. APPLE IS IN A MESS"

Cynthia Lennon knew there was no hope left for her and John. The marriage survived only because John could not be bothered to end it. For months, Cyn had been little more than a prisoner in the mock-Tudor mansion at Weybridge, with its miles of untrodden pastel carpet, its unused gadgets, its antique globe cocktail cabinet from Asprey's, its suits of armor and medieval altar pieces. By day she looked after Julian; at night she watched television, wondering if she would see her husband on it. She did yards of embroidery, and took up drawing and painting again. She slept alone in the huge master bedroom, often awakening to find only her half of the bed disturbed. She would then nerve herself to voyage through the house to look for John among the empty bottles, the scattered album sleeves, and the groggy, sprawling figures of whatever new strangers he had brought home at dawn.

Sometimes, at her embroidery when the house was quiet, Cyn would speculate on the type of woman John ought to have married. In this, as in all else about him, she faced impenetrable mystery. She could think only of Brigitte Bardot, his adolescent passion whom Cynthia herself had tried so hard to copy. And Juliette Greco, who was not at all pretty and who played the guitar and sang like a man. His unknowable strangeness used to disappear, at least, when they made love. But that had stopped happening more than a year ago.

Cyn knew John could suffer bouts of depression—desperation even—that were entirely separate from his outward success. One such trough had been in 1965, at the height of Beatlemania, when no one thought to ask why the idol of millions would write a song called *Help!* Another, still deeper trough came in 1967, in the months before he met the Maharishi, when John, under Dr. Timothy Leary's influence, tried to destroy his ego by expanding it to ludicrous proportion. He would arrive at Abbey Road dressed like Sabu the Elephant Boy in a cloak, curly slippers, and a turban. At a dinner party given by Jane Asher, a guest happened to ask for an ashtray. John crawled under the table and invited her to flick her ash into his open mouth.

Now, in early '68, Cynthia felt another trough beginning. So far as she could divine, it had something to do with student riots—the savage street warfare in Paris, West Germany, even London's own elegant Grosvenor Square. John, in some obscure way, felt himself a part of this worldwide change from lisping hippie love and peace to brick-hurling activism. The underground looked on him as a potential leader, to join Tariq Ali and Daniel Cohn-Bendit and the others whose charisma, was akin to that of rock stars. He had even written a song called "Revolution," but then, apparently, lost his nerve. One version said, "You can count me in"; the other said, "You can count me out." Part of him wanted to be a pamphleteer, a rabble-rouser, a street fighter. The larger part was still buttoned into his Beatle self, still forged to a corporate smile, still fearful of what his aunt Mimi might read about him in the press.

Occasionally, summoning up her courage, Cynthia would ask him if he had found someone else. John always vehemently denied it. He still did not think in remotely that way of the Japanese woman he had met two years earlier at John Dunbar's Indica Gallery, and who, instead of speaking, had handed him a card inscribed "Breathe." And yet, as the months passed, as his restlessness grew to match the outside world's, for some unfathomable reason he could not get Yoko Ono off his mind.

The woman whose name in English means "Ocean Child" was born seven years before John, in February 1933. On her mother Isoko's, side, she could trace her ancestry back through a line of wealthy bankers and aristocrats to a Japanese emperor. Her father, Keisuke Ono, was a talented classical pianist who had opted to abandon his dream of turning professional to work in a bank. One of Yoko's earliest memories was of her father spreading out her fingers to see if she might become the classical pianist he had wanted to be.

Keisuke's career prospered, and Yoko was brought up in sheltered luxury with her younger brother, Keisuke, and sister, Setsuko. Her mother was fanatical about cleanliness, often insisting that seats should be disinfected before Yoko was allowed to sit in them. At the same time her mother encouraged Yoko to be hardy and self-sufficient. As a tiny tot, if she happened to slip and fall, the household servants had instructions not to help her but to let her get up by herself.

Yoko spent World War II in Tokyo, frequently in terror from bombing attacks, though spared the horror of the atom bomb attack on Hiroshima that completed Japan's annihilation. Keisuke's bank job had taken him to America frequently before the war, and in 1945, when Yoko was twelve, he decided to move his family there permanently and settled with them in the New York suburb of Scarsdale. Yoko attended the highly respectable and conventional Sarah Lawrence College, where she studied art and musical composition. At the age of eighteen, she outraged both her family and Sarah Lawrence by marrying a Japanese musician and going off to live with him in a Greenwich Village attic.

Here she fell in naturally with the crowd of avant-garde painters, sculptors, and poets who collected around the anemic figure of Andy Warhol. Warhol's dictum that art should aim principally to surprise, or even shock, found a willing convert in Yoko. In direct lineage with his Campbell's soup cans, she became known for works seemingly designed to stir people into bewilderment, if not outright fury, that they should be presented as art at all. One of her creations was an "eternal time clock," showing only seconds and encased in a sound-proof Plexiglas bubble attached to a doctor's stethoscope. Another was a book called *Grapefruit*, a collection of cards bearing one-line "instructional poems."

She came to England in 1966 to attend a symposium entitled "The Destruction of Art." Swinging London was in full bloom, and ripe for events and happenings such as she had staged in New York. She settled in London, with her second husband, an American filmmaker named Tony Cox, and had a daughter by him, Kyoko. She received the mild notoriety the era so freely bestowed by photographing naked human bottoms and, later, wrapping the Trafalgar Square lions in white canvas. She had not, however, heard a single Beatles record until that night at the Indica when John Lennon walked in on her "Unfinished Paintings and Objects Show," and John Dunbar sent her across to sweet-talk as a likely sponsor.

Shortly after their first meeting she asked John to finance her next exhibition, at the Lisson Gallery in north London. This new Yoko Ono event was entitled "The Half Wind Show," because everything was in halves. There was half a chair, half a table, half a bed, half a pillow, half a washbasin, and half a toothbrush. Like the apple with its two-hundred-pound price ticket, the idea delighted John's sense of the absurd. He put up the money but recoiled in horror when Yoko suggested his name should appear in the catalog. Instead, the show was credited enigmatically to "Yoko plus Me."

She also sent John her book, *Grapefruit,* with its enigmatic messages, like "Bleed" or "Paint Until You Drop Dead." John, alternately puzzled and fascinated, kept the book at his bedside. While organizing yet another happening, entitled "Dance Event," Yoko sent him further message cards: "Breathe" or "Dance" or "Watch the Light Until Dawn."

John met her again at different galleries and again was unaccountably disturbed. He could not explain the disturbance: It occurred in an unused organ, his mind. It was unrelated to his inbred northern concept of servile womanhood. It was something he had only ever felt for men—for the tough, mad Liverpool Teds who could make even him defer and keep silent. Yoko Ono, quite simply, did things that John Lennon did not dare.

He began to look out for her across rooms. He would stand with her and simply listen while the little white face, in its clouds of black hair, poured forth ideas bent on only one purpose: to challenge and upset the conventional, complacent art world. "As she was talking to me, I'd get high, and the discussion would get to such a level, I'd be getting higher and higher. Then she'd leave, and I'd go back to this sort of suburbia. Then I'd meet her again, and my head would go open, like I was on an acid trip."

He did make one outright move on Yoko in this period, though unfortunately it had about as little finesse as propositioning a groupie in his Beatles touring days. "John had invited me to the recording studio," Yoko remembers. "He suddenly said, "You look tired. Would you like to rest?" I thought he was taking me to another room, but instead we went off to this flat—I think it belonged to Neil [Aspinall]. When we got there, Neil started to fold this sofa down into a bed. Maybe John thought we were two adults: we didn't have to pretend. But it was so sudden, so crude, I just rejected it. I slept on the divan, I think, and John went into another room."

He considered asking Yoko to join the pilgrimage to Rishikesh, but couldn't pluck up courage enough to do it. Instead, she went off to Paris, feeling—as she now says—"like we'd never get started." He wrote to her there from India—long, rambling letters like the ones he used to send to Stu Sutcliffe. Yoko replied with further message cards. "I'm a cloud," one card said. "Watch for me in the sky."

It was at Rishikesh, ironically, that Cynthia felt a small revival of hope for her marriage. She, at least, remained convinced that the Maharishi was a power for good and that only envious whispers were turning the Beatles against him. In India, John seemed calmer and happier than Cyn had ever known him. He began writing songs, about childhood and his mother, Julia, that Cyn could again understand. Then, on the plane back to England—still half-fearful of the Maharishi's revenge—he told Cyn something that caused her vast astonishment. He told her that, over the years, he had not been completely faithful to her.

Back in Weybridge, their estrangement deepened. Cynthia even suggested, rather wildly, that John would be better off with someone like Yoko Ono than with her. She begged to go with him to New York for the Apple launching, but he refused. In May, he packed her away on vacation to Greece with Jennie Boyd and Magic Alex. His old school crony Pete Shotton came down to Weybridge to keep him company.

"We were just sitting round together one night." Pete says. "John suddenly asked me, 'Don't you feel like having a woman around again?' Then he said, 'I've met this woman called Yoko. She's Japanese.' Yoko came over and John took her off to listen to his tapes. I just went to bed.

"When I got up the next morning John was sitting in the kitchen, eating boiled eggs. He said he hadn't been to bed. Then he said, 'Will you do us a favor? Would you get us a house?' I said, 'What do you want a house for?' 'To live in,' he said. "With Yoko. This is it.'"

When Cyn walked in to Kenwood unexpectedly a few days later, she found John and Yoko seated together, with the curtains drawn, in a sea of dirty cups and plates. Both looked nonchalantly up at her and said: "Oh, hi . . ." A pair of Japanese slippers, standing neatly on an upstairs landing, opened the gentle, nearsighted girl's eyes at long last.

The Beatles first became aware of Yoko at Abbey Road studios. They could hardly do otherwise. She did not stay, as was proper—as was womanly—in the control room. She came down onto the sacred floor of the studio, where none but Beatles and their closest male aides were allowed, and settled herself down at John's side. Paul, George, and Ringo exchanged eloquent glances but—for the moment—said nothing. They could not have survived so long as Beatles without a deep tolerance of one another's fancies and blind spots. They expected John to tire of this soon, the way he tired of everything. They tried not to notice Yoko, and referred to her obliquely as "Flavor of the Month."

She was still there, however, as Apple grew and its divisions multiplied. She had now left Tony Cox and her daughter, Kyoko, to live with John, at Kenwood first, then in London, at Ringo Starr's Montagu Square flat. Pete Shotton drove them around, glad to have been superseded as John's personal assistant. Such was Yoko's introduction to Sir Joseph Lockwood, the EMI chairman, at a boardroom lunch with all four Beatles, Neil Aspinall, and Apple executive Ron Kass. In the visitor's book after her name, John wrote "female." "This little white figure followed the Beatles in," Sir Joseph said. "She sat further down the table with my assistant, but hardly said a word all through the meal. Afterward, my assistant told me she'd had a tape recorder running all the time."

Her first night with John at Kenwood had begun an artistic partnership that was to perplex and enrage the world. When Yoko first arrived John played her all the experimental tapes he had made, knowing they were useless for Beatles albums. After the final tape Yoko said, "Let's make one of our own." It was only as dawn broke that they got around to first making love.

In the character that everyone believed so uninhibited and audacious, Yoko found bottomless wells of shyness and self-doubt, exacerbated by years of having to keep his mouth shut as a cuddly mop top. "He was a genius, but he had this huge inferiority complex. He was brilliant as an artist, but he didn't think he was capable of it. Like, when someone wanted to do an exhibition of his lithographs, he was just too scared to get started on the drawings. We both took mescaline, and then he tried. I told him, 'That's brilliant, it's beautiful.' John said, 'But it's only a circle, like a child would do.' I said 'Maybe it's childish, but it's still beautiful.' "

"It was the same when he was asked to write a sketch for *Oh! Calcutta!* [a soft porn stage show compiled by drama critic Kenneth Tynan]. 'What am I going to write?' John kept saying. I said, 'Write that thing you told me about when you were a boy and you used to masturbate.' He and his friends all used to masturbate, shouting out the names of sexy actresses—then suddenly John or one of them would shout, 'Frank Sinatra!' So he made that the sketch and it was marvelous."

The obsessive jealousy with which John used to guard Cynthia from other men was now passed on to Yoko. "Jealous! My God! He wrote a song, 'Jealous Guy,' that said it all," Yoko remembers now. "After we got together, he made me write out a list of all the men I'd slept with before we met. I started to do it quite casually—then I realized how serious it was to John. He didn't even like me knowing the Japanese language because that was a part of my mind that shut him out. He wouldn't let me read any Japanese books or newspapers."

Despite her seemingly unquenchable self-belief, Yoko had her insecurities, too. "When I met John I was self-conscious about my appearance. I thought my legs were the wrong shape, and I used to try to cover my face with my hair. He told me, 'No, you're beautiful, your legs are perfect, tie your hair back and let people see your face.'"

At other times, the compliments seemed more backhanded, although he seriously wanted to convey to Yoko he'd met no one with her toughness and audacity since the Teds at Garston's Blood Baths. "I used to tell him, 'I think you're a closet fag, you know.' Because he often said, 'Do you know why I like you? Because you look like a man in drag. You're like a mate.'"

In June 1968, their first collaboration went on public show. It was a sculpture consisting of two acorns, one labeled "John by Yoko Ono," the other "Yoko by John Lennon, Sometime in May 1968." The acorns, symbolizing peace and simplicity, were to be buried as an event at the National Sculpture Exhibition in the grounds of Coventry Cathedral.

John and Yoko, both dressed in white, drove to Coventry in John's white Rolls, accompanied by their newly appointed art adviser, Anthony Fawcett. Outside the cathedral they were met by a canon, who informed them that objects could not be buried in consecrated ground and that, in any case, acorns were "not sculpture." Yoko flew into an impressive rage, demanding that leading British sculptors be instantly telephoned to vouch for her artistic integrity. Someone actually got through to Henry Moore's house, but he was out. As a compromise, the acorns were buried on unhallowed ground, under an iron garden seat. Within a week, they had been dug up and taken by Beatles fans as souvenirs. Two more acorns were buried; a security firm mounted twenty-four-hour guard on the seat that marked the spot.

On July 18, a stage adaptation of John's book *In His Own Write* opened at the London Old Vic theater. The play had been heavily censored by the lord chamberlain's office for its blasphemous reference to "Almighty Griff" and disrespect to such world statesmen as "Pregnant De Gaulle" and "Sir Alice Doubtless-Whom." Fleet Street, by now perceiving a still racier story, were out in force in the summer downpour. When John arrived with Yoko and Neil Aspinall, he was surrounded by press raincoats and challenging cries of "Where's your wife?"

The girls who stood outside Abbey Road studios—and now also outside 3 Savile Row—made no secret of their instant hatred of Yoko. "Every time we saw her, we shouted awful things," Margo says. "'Yellow!' 'Chink!' Subtle things like that. We all felt so sorry for Cynthia. Once, outside Abbey Road, we'd got this bunch of yellow roses to give Yoko. We handed them to her thorns first. Yoko took them and backed all the way down the stairs, thanking us. She hadn't realized they were meant to be an insult. Nor did John. He turned back and said, 'Well, it's about *time* someone did something decent to her.'"

In July, John's first art exhibition opened in London, at the fashionable Robert Fraser Gallery. Its title, inspired by the hackneyed message on British street maps, was "You Are Here": It acknowledged its motive force with a dedication "To Yoko from John with love." It began with the release of 360 white balloons into the sky above Mayfair. Each balloon bore the printed message: "You are here. Please write to John Lennon, c/o the Robert Fraser Gallery."

To reach the exhibition one had to walk through a display of charity street collection boxes in the shapes of pandas, puppets, and disabled children. The only other items were a circular piece of white canvas, lettered "You are here" and John's hat lying on the floor, its upturned brim inscribed: "For the artist. Thank You." When some art students sarcastically contributed a rusty bicycle, John immediately put that on show also.

The critics were scornful. They said what was to be many times repeated: that if John had not been a Beatle, he would not have dared put such rubbish on show. In this, at least, the critics erred. So long as he was a Beatle, he never dared do *anything*.

Many people who picked up the white balloons responded to John's invitation to write to him. Their letters, for the most part, combined racial slurs against Yoko with advice concerning the sanctity of wedlock. "I suppose I've spoiled me image," John said. "People want me to stay in their own bag. They want me to be lovable, but I was never that. Even at school I was just 'Lennon.'"

Cynthia, meanwhile, had found herself ruthlessly cauterized from his life. Magic Alex was deputed to travel to Italy, where Cyn, her mother, and Julian were staying, and announce that John intended to divorce her. "Alex was waiting for me one night when I got back to the hotel. He told me John was going to take Julian off me and send me back to my mother in Hoylake.

"When I got back to England, I tried to have a meeting with him and discuss things. The only way I could get in touch with John was to make an appointment with him through Peter Brown at Apple. And when I finally did meet him, Yoko was there. He insisted she should stay while we were talking."

John, at the outset, intended to divorce Cynthia for adultery supposedly committed in Italy. Despite his own countless infidelities, he was still mortified—as he told his aunt Mimi—that Cynthia should have slept with someone else. The petition was dropped when it became clear that Yoko had become pregnant. Cynthia sued for adultery, and was granted a decree nisi in November 1968.

A few weeks earlier, as Cyn was alone and helplessly contemplating the future, Paul had paid her a surprise visit. With him he brought a song he had written on his way in the car—it was for Julian, he said, although the title was "Hey Jude." He gave Cynthia a single red rose, then said, in the old carefree Liverpool way, "Well, how about it, Cyn? How about you and me getting married now?" She was moved that Paul should think of her, and grateful for his gesture of friendship and encouragement.

Sometimes, in a surge of ecstasy, the girls on watch outside 7 Cavendish Avenue would approach the black security gates and buzz the intercom. As a rule, the voice that answered would belong to Jane Asher, Paul's longtime girlfriend. The voice was serious but tolerant and always polite. So Jane was, too, on the hundreds of occasions when she answered the front door. The girls appreciated that civility and patience. Far from resenting Jane, they felt their angelic Beatle was in deserving hands. They were Jane's admirers in a small way, as well as Paul's. They grew their hair long like hers, washing it only in Breck shampoo, because that was the brand Jane advertised on television, pressing it out straight on their mother's ironing boards.

Everyone close to Paul liked Jane and acknowledged her beneficial influence. For, in her clear-voiced way, she was as down-to-earth as any Liverpool girl. Alone of almost the entire female race she refused to pamper and worship Paul. If Jane disagreed or disapproved, she said so. She could curb his ego, his use of charm as a weapon—rather as John curbed the syrup in his music—and yet do it in a way that commanded respect and a maturing love.

That the relationship had lasted five years was due principally to Jane's skill in avoiding the worst of the Beatles madness, and her insistence on following her own successful film and stage career. When Paul and she met, it was with the freshness and appreciativeness of new lovers. Paul's farm, near Campbeltown, Argyllshire, was their usual retreat. Paul had done the painting and decorating, even threw together some rudimentary furniture. There, in the uncurious hills, they walked and rode; they talked and read by lamplight and washed in the kitchen sink, and Jane cooked appetizing vegetarian dishes. Each time they left she would pack the leftovers thriftily away in plastic bags.

For Paul, it was the best of two highly pleasurable worlds. His life with Jane provided domesticity, and the refinement and social standing he craved. In her absence, his life reverted to that of Britain's most hotly pursued bachelor. His casual affairs were conducted with such diplomacy and discretion that Jane never suspected anything. So it might have continued but for a theater tour that ended prematurely, and a witness who suddenly found herself with a legitimate reason to press Paul's intercom.

Margo Stevens, the girl from Cleethorpes, was just beginning her second year of standing outside 7 Cavendish Avenue. She preferred to begin her vigil late at night, when the picket was thinning or absent altogether. She would arrive at about 10:00 P.M., always with some gift for Paul—fruit or a miniature bottle of whisky—on the off chance of handing it to him as he came home late from the studios or a club. She had been standing there so long, Paul vaguely recognized her now. She knew how to open the security gates by kicking them, and had done so once for him when he could not find his key. Lately, on the recommendation of his housekeeper, Rosie, he had even trusted her to take Martha the sheepdog for walks on Hampstead Heath.

"It was a summer day: We were all standing there as usual," Margo says. "Jane was on tour with a play, and Paul brought home this American girl, Francie Schwartz. He waved to us as they drove in. Later on, another car turned onto Cavendish Avenue—it was Jane. She'd come back to London earlier than she was supposed to. We did our best to warn Paul. Someone went to the intercom, buzzed it, and yelled, 'Look out! Jane's coming!' Paul didn't believe it. 'Ah, pull the other one,' he said.

"Jane went into the house. A bit later on she came storming out again and drove away. Later still, a big estate car drew up. It was Jane's mother. She went inside and started bringing out all kinds of things that were obviously Jane's—cooking pots and big cushions and pictures.

"We all thought after that they must have finished with each other for good. But the next day, a whole crowd of us were in Hyde Park. Who did we run into but Paul and Jane. They were walking along, holding hands and eating ice lollies."

Early in 1967, Jane went on tour in America again with the Bristol Old Vic company. Apart from Paul's visit, to celebrate her twenty-first birthday, they were separated for almost five months. When Jane returned, she found Paul deeply involved in the creation of Sgt. Pepper and in LSD. She herself would have nothing to do with acid, and said so bluntly. Paul could not convince her of what she was missing.

Brian Epstein's death was a heavy blow to Jane. She, too, found comfort in the Maharishi: She went with Paul to Rishikesh and felt the experience to have been rewarding. With LSD banished, their understanding returned. Paul, at long last, made ready to commit himself. They announced their engagement at a McCartney family party on Christmas Day, 1967.

The following June, they were back up north for the wedding of Paul's younger brother, Michael. Jane opened in a new play that month and Paul, as usual, attended the opening night. All between them seemed normal until mid-July, when Yellow Submarine received its gala premiere. Paul arrived alone at the cinema and at the party that followed. Two days later, on a television talk show, Jane was asked a casual question about their wedding plans. She replied that Paul had broken off the engagement and they had parted.

"Hey Jude," the song that brought such comfort to Cynthia Lennon, was Paul's expression of his own deep personal unhappiness. The words, for once, were not facile and neat; it was a song written honestly, in pain. It moved even John as no song of Paul's ever had before. "Hey Jude, don't be afraid, you were made to / go out and get her," seemed to John to be a message of encouragement for Yoko and him. "I took it very personally," he admitted. 'Ah, it's me!' I said when Paul played it. 'No,' he said, 'it's *me*.' I said, 'Check. We're both going through the same bit.'"

The news that the most adorable and adored Beatle was now on the market again sent a seismic wave of excitement through the young womanhood of the Western world. Paul clearly could have his pick of anyone he wanted, and in a million hairdressers' shops and club powder rooms debate raged furiously as to which breathtakingly beautiful starlet or model would be the lucky one. In the event, his choice was to be almost as surprising as John's had been.

A year or so earlier, an American photographer named Linda Eastman had called at Brian Epstein's office to show her portfolio of rock star portraits in hopes of getting work from the Epstein stable. She was a coltishly built New Yorker with rather unkempt blonde hair and a dour, unsmiling face. Peter Brown, who dealt with her, knew her already as a regular backstage at American rock venues like New York's Fillmore East. "She was just an ordinary girl, like so many you saw around then. She'd arrived in London, saying she wanted to photograph the Beatles. I let her in on the *Sgt. Pepper* session, which was a big thing, because only fourteen photographers were allowed from the whole world's press."

Brown next met Linda one night when he was with Paul McCartney and some other rock figures at the Bag O' Nails Club. He introduced Paul to Linda and, as he remembers, "That was it. The two of them just went off together."

Linda Eastman did not belong, as many supposed, to the Eastman family whose enormous wealth derived from Kodak photographic film and Eastman color film stock. Her father, Lee, a New York lawyer, had taken the surname to replace one more directly announcing his Jewish immigrant antecedents. But for this gentrification, Paul's future wife as well as his late manager would have borne the surname of Epstein.

Lee Eastman had built up a highly successful New York practice, specializing in music copyright and also representing several of America's leading painters. His wife, Louise, was independently wealthy through her family connection with department stores owned by her family, the Linders. Linda and her brother, John, grew up in the affluent environment of a house in Scarsdale and a Park Avenue apartment. Linda became accustomed to mixing with the stars whom her father represented, among them the songwriter Hoagy Carmichael and the cowboy action-hero Hopalong Cassidy.

Louise Eastman died in an air crash when Linda was eighteen. Resisting all opportunities to exploit her father's social connections, she married a geologist named John See, moved with him to Colorado, and gave birth to a daughter, Heather. The marriage quickly failed, however, and Linda returned to New York with her baby daughter, by now determined to make her name as a photographer. She got a job with *Town and Country* magazine, Manhattan's equivalent of the *Tatler,* and became a familiar face backstage at the Fillmore East and at photo calls for pop bands flying in from Europe. Her abilities as a photographer were not rated very highly; she was known, rather, as a rock chick who used her camera to get on close—sometimes very close—terms with male pinups such as Mick Jagger, Stevie Winwood, and Warren Beatty.

She did not see Paul between the *Sgt. Pepper* session and May 1968, when he came with John to New York to inaugurate Apple. Linda was at the launch party with her journalist friend Lilian Roxon. On Lilian's advice, she slipped Paul her telephone number. They met at Nat Weiss's New York flat and afterward in Los Angeles. Paul returned to London, but a few weeks later telephoned Linda and asked her to come and join him.

He brought her home to Cavendish Avenue in his Mini-Cooper late one summer night. Margo Stevens was on watch by the gates, as always. "A few of us were there. We had the feeling something was going to happen. Paul didn't take the Mini inside the way he usually did—he parked it on the road and he and Linda walked right past us. They went inside and we stood there, watching different lights in the house go on and off.

"In the end, the light went on in the Mad Room, at the top of the house, where he kept all his music stuff and his toys. Paul opened the window and called out to us, 'Are you still down there?' 'Yes,' we said. He must have been really happy that night. He sat on the windowsill with his acoustic guitar and sang 'Blackbird' to us as we stood down there in the dark."

Linda was certainly a startling change from the carefully back-combed and immaculate Jane. Hers was the New York preppy style, still so unknown in Swinging Britain that it seemed like no style at all—shapeless dresses below the knee, flat-heeled tennis shoes, even ankle socks. Nor was she nice, the way Jane always had been, to the girls who eternally monitored Paul's comings and goings from Cavendish Avenue and the Apple offices. "We could tell that she viewed us as a threat," Margo remembers. "Every time they appeared together Linda would cling to Paul's arm as much as to say, '*I've* got him now.' None of us could understand what he saw in her."

For all her seeming unkemptness, Linda had an irresistible appeal to the social-climbing Paul—the aura of Manhattan's aristocracy that, in its way, is as rarified and exclusive as London's. She was certainly beautiful, with her finely-chiseled cheekbones and straw-blonde hair, though she always seemed utterly unconcerned about her appearance. Most important, she idolized and deferred to Paul as Jane had always firmly refused to do. Clinging to his arm, she would gaze up at him with awe and say what an honor it would be to bear his children.

Her daughter, Heather, helped to cement the bond between them. Paul had always adored children. His final parting with Jane arose from their disagreement over when to start a family. After meeting Heather, an insecure, rather lonely six-year-old, he insisted she be brought to live at Cavendish Avenue. He delighted in playing with her, reading stories and drawing cartoons for her, and singing her to sleep at night.

Linda, meanwhile, was bringing about changes in Paul that Margo and the other girls viewed with deep resentment. They knew, from their illicit journeys round the house, how fastidious he had formerly been. "He used to shave every day, he always wore fresh clothes, and he smelled delicious. Rosie, the housekeeper, told us he insisted on having clean sheets on his bed every night.

"We heard from Rosie how different Linda was. We hardly recognized Paul once she'd got hold of him. He started to put on weight— and he got so scruffy. I'll swear he didn't wash his hair for three weeks at a time. He never shaved, never wore anything but this old navy overcoat. He could go on the bus down to Apple, and no one would recognize him. Some of us thought we saw him in Oxford Street one day. We followed this real tramp in a navy overcoat all the way down Oxford Street, thinking he was Paul."

In May, the Beatles had met at Abbey Road to begin their first album for release on their Apple label. John and Paul between them had a backlog of some thirty songs, mostly written during their stay in India. George had been earnestly composing; even Ringo had a tune of his own to offer. With so much material in hand it was decided to use a format common enough in classical recording but unprecedented in pop. The collection would appear as two LP discs packed into a single dual-envelope sleeve. Not even *Sgt. Pepper* started in such an atmosphere of energy and abundance.

Things began to go wrong on the very first day, when John Lennon walked into Studio One, his arm protectively encircling a small, frizzy-haired figure, dressed all in white. He had not, it seemed, grown tired of Yoko Ono. He was, if anything, more obsessed by her. As before, Yoko showed no awareness of studio protocol. She settled herself among the Beatles, cutting herself and John off from the other three by the neck of his guitar. His hair center-parted like hers, his eyes aslant behind pebble glasses, he was even starting to look a little Japanese.

They whispered together, constantly and secretively, all through the session. Most unbelievably, when John took off his headphones, laid aside his guitar, and went off to use the men's lavatory, Yoko still trotted at his heels. "That wasn't me pursuing John, the way everyone thought," she says now. "That was John's terrible insecurity. He made me go out to the men's room with him. He was afraid that if I stayed in the studio with all those other guys, I might go off and have an affair with one of them."

The awkwardness deepened as John and Paul strummed over to each other the finished songs they proposed the Beatles should record. This interchange, so often the flashpoint for brilliance, now produced only noncommittal nods. To Paul, John's new music seemed harsh, unmelodious, and deliberately provocative. John, for his part, found Paul's new songs cloyingly sweet and bland. For the first time, Lennon and McCartney saw no bridge between them.

The album that resulted was, therefore, not the work of a group. It was the work of soloists: of separate egos, arguing for prominence. Paul and John each recorded his own songs in his own way, without advice or criticism from the other. George—apart from his own individual sessions—withdrew into a resigned neutrality. Ringo, in his acoustic hutch, bent his drumsticks as far as possible with the ever-changing currents. Sometimes, Ringo did not even bother to turn up.

From John came music equally full of resentment and defiance and lingering terror of opening his mouth too wide. "Sexy Sadie" was a satire on Maharishi Mahesh Yogi ("What have you done? You made a fool of everyone?") but heavily camouflaged for fear that the holy man might still be able to put some kind of transcendental hex on him. "Revolution" was a chant in sympathy for the student protests now breaking out all over the world, yet of two minds whether the composer himself was quite ready to take to the barricades. "Happiness Is a Warm Gun," inspired by an American firearms magazine, swiped in the approximate direction of the Vietnam holocaust. "Glass Onion" satirized overearnest Beatles fans with cross-references to earlier lyrics, even a false clue: "The Walrus was Paul." The straightforward rock pieces, like "Yer Blues," were one-dimensional and charmless, the playing turgid, the singing harsh and somehow vindictive. Nowhere was his conversion more evident than in the track called "Revolution 9," a formless length of electronic noise interspersed with vocal gibberish, which Paul—and everyone else—tried unavailingly to cut from the finished album.

Paul's tracks were neat, polished, tuneful and, in their way, as unbalanced and incomplete: "Martha My Dear," a song for his sheepdog; "Rocky Raccoon," an unfinished Western doodle; "Honey Pie," a glutinous twenties pastiche. In each, somehow, the most noticeable element was John's missing "middle eight." Only in "Blackbird," briefly and beautifully, did Paul's gift succeed in editing itself. "Back in the USSR," too, was totally successful, a Chuck Berry–style rocker with Beach Boy harmonies that briefly restored the old familiar grin to John's face. In that, as in a few more songs to come, their matchless combination somehow survived in an individual effort. Paul could have written John's song "Julia." It was his memorial, ten years too late, to the mother whose laughter gave the timbre to his own. But Julia in the song bore a second name: "Ocean Child."

It was while Lennon fought McCartney on "Ob-la-di, Ob-la-da" and "Revolution 9" that George Harrison suddenly and surprisingly gathered strength as a composer and performer. His tally of four songs on the finished thirty-track list was the highest John and Paul had ever permitted. As their joint control dwindled, so George's presence increased: His voice, gathering confidence, sounded somehow like John's *and* Paul's. His "Savoy Truffle" was, after "Back in the USSR," the album's best piece of rock 'n' roll. "Piggies," a nursery-rhyme-ish diatribe against meat eaters, was mordantly humorous. Best of all was "While My Guitar Gently Weeps," a heavy rock lament, with searing guitar phrases played by George's friend Eric Clapton of Cream. Clapton could not believe at first that the Beatles needed anyone but themselves.

All this happened amid a constant drip of argument and bad feeling that, strangely enough, took heaviest toll on the Beatle whose placid temper was so often a strength and rallying-point. Ringo, halfway through the sessions, emerged from behind his acoustic screens looking tired and morose. He was playing badly, he said, and generally "not getting through." To John first, then to Paul, he announced he was resigning. The others, tactfully, did not try to stop him. A week at home with Maureen and Zak and his new baby son, Jason, restored him to his old equanimity. When he returned to Abbey Road, Paul and George had covered his drums with welcome-back messages and flowers.

They had been working on the still untitled double album for five months. For all that time, by night as well as day, Margo Stevens and the other girls had waited and watched the Abbey Road front steps. "We stuck it out through all weathers," Margo says. "We were as tough as old boots in the end. When they came in to record, we'd sleep out on the pavement. People who lived in Abbey Road saw us when they came home from work at night. In the morning when they left for work, we were still there. I got so tough, I could sleep in all weathers. When I woke up one morning, there was snow all over me."

Margo, on these all-night watches, shared a sleeping bag with Carol Bedford, a Texan girl to whom George Harrison had once actually said "Hello." "Normally the Beatles would go in to record around midnight," Carol says. "They'd finish around four a.m. So we could count on at least four hours' sleep. But once they all came out suddenly at about two-thirty. Margo and I woke up—we tried to stand up but we couldn't undo the zipper on our sleeping bag. Both of us were hopping round the pavement, shrieking and trying to undo the zipper while the Beatles stood there, laughing at us."

George Martin had done all he could as adviser and editor. To Martin, the thirty songs, or song fragments, on tape reeked of the argument and self-indulgence that had gone into their making. Vainly he pleaded with John and Paul to drop the double album idea; to lose the scribble, like "Goodnight" and "Revolution 9"; to cut out all the linking, meaningless shouts and murmurs and pull the fourteen best titles together for a Beatles album like *Revolver,* packed end-to-end with quality. The answer was no. On that, at least, all four agreed.

"One night, we were all outside—we could tell they'd nearly finished," Margo says. "It got to about three in the morning. We could see John through a window, playing with a light cord hanging from the ceiling. 'Come *on*, boys,' we were all saying, 'it *has* been five months.' Then they all came out and down the steps. It was all over."

As a tribute to their five-month wait Margo and the others were then taken into the empty Studio One to hear a playback of "Back in the USSR" and to pick up and take home as cherished souvenirs the apple cores and crisp packets littering the floor.

The doorman at Apple was a thickset, heavily genteel young Cockney named Jimmy Clark. He was, so people said, a discovery of Peter Brown's. He wore a stiff collar, tight-fitting trousers, and an exquisitely cut dove-gray morning coat. On fine days he would bask on the Apple front step, his hands in his coattails, watching the girls who eternally watched the house. His job was to prevent unauthorized entry via the front door or the area steps to the basement studio. He would block the rush and repel it with his large, starch-cuffed, shooing hands. To the resultant boos and insults, Jimmy Clark would grin and bridle delightedly like a cat under the grooming brush.

It was, even so—as hundreds discovered—quite easy to enter the Apple house. Provided that one arrived by taxi and that one carried no banner or other sign of Beatles fanaticism, one was generally assumed to have legitimate business with Apple Corps. The girls fell back, unenviously. Jimmy Clark sardonically stood aside. The white front door yielded to a gentle push.

The front hall was much as in any half-million-pound Georgian house. To the right sat a receptionist, instructed, like all Apple staff, to believe in the bona fide of all visitors. Into a telephone, white as the *White Album,* she would murmur the information that so-and-so was here. She would then smile. "OK, you can go up. You know the way, don't you?" Everyone knew the way, up the green-carpeted stairs, past the framed gold records, too numerous to count, and the soft-lit oil painting of two honey-colored lion cubs.

One did not, if one were scrupulous, try any of the doors of offices on the second floor. One climbed on, past more gold records, to Derek Taylor's third-floor press and publicity office. This room, in the mornings, was bright with sun and fragrant with the scent of furniture polish.

In the late afternoon it grew dark and bewildering. The only light came under the window blinds and from two projectors that beamed a psychedelic light show of bright-colored, writhing spermatozoa shapes, traveling in perpetuity across the opposite wall. Though dark and filled with obstructions, the room was exceedingly busy. One crossed the projector beam, conscious of many shaggy heads turning, like anxious topiary hedges, in the gloom.

None but the specially important or importunate caller immediately approached Derek Taylor's desk. If one were merely a journalist, one sat initially on a small outlying sofa, behind Taylor's second assistant, Carol Paddon, and next to a tray of water into which several plastic birds endlessly dipped their beaks. Presently, one might move across to the small white button–backed sofa that led directly into Taylor's presence. Already, one would have been offered tea, Scotch, and Coke, a cigarette, or perhaps something stronger. As each of Taylor's visitors got up and left, one wriggled toward him another few inches. Eventually one would be seated immediately to the right of his huge scallop-backed wicker chair. The slender man with his neat hair and mustache and quiet, indiscreet voice, would lean over on the wicker arm that was to become split and broken with hours of leaning and listening.

Press officers by their very nature pursue journalists. It was Derek Taylor's unique accomplishment to be a press officer whom journalists pursued. Journalists from every newspaper, magazine, wire service, and radio and TV network in the Western world pursued him, as a means of access to the Western world's longest-running headline story. They pursued him also because Taylor, strangely enough, was not a monster. He was amiable, sympathetic, polite to a degree that would ultimately seem miraculous. As an ex-journalist himself, he believed that journalists should get their story. It was simply a matter of time, he always said, and of choosing a moment when one or another "Fab" would be amenable.

Two side doors connected the press office with other Apple departments. On Taylor's right was the door to a downstairs kitchen where two Cordon Bleu–trained debutantes supplied meals to the directors and executive staff, and refreshments to all. On the left was a walk-in closet, presided over by Taylor's hippie assistant, Richard, and popularly known as the Black Room. It had been used initially as a dumping ground for the entire—and entirely unread—cache of novels, poems, synopses, plans, and blueprints submitted from all over the world as projects deserving support by the Apple Foundation for the Arts. Several thousand manuscripts lay there, forgotten as absolutely as the nearby row of high-fashion shoes that Derek Taylor had brought home from Hollywood. What the Black Room principally contained were boxes of LP records by Apple artists, cases of wines, spirits, and soft drinks, and cartons of Benson & Hedges cigarettes.

Another amenity of the press office—as of almost every other office in the building—was drugs. The presence of the West End's major police station only a couple of hundred yards away did not prevent 3 Savile Row's staff from puffing joints as casually as they sipped tea. Upper and downer pills of every color, compounded by the costliest amateur pharmacists, were to be found in desk drawers, along with the envelopes, glue, and staplers. A certain secretary had been nominated to gather up the entire stock and flush it away in the ladies' lavatory if ever Savile Row's boys in blue should decide to pay a surprise visit (which, amazingly, they never did). Another female employee brought in regular consignments of hash brownies that she herself had baked at the home she still shared with her parents and grandmother. Finding some left to cool in the family kitchen, her grandmother innocently sampled one and remained unconscious for the next twenty-four hours.

"Press," under Derek Taylor's tolerant regime, was a term of almost infinite elasticity. It described virtually anyone who came to Apple with the ghost of an excuse for sharing in the Beatles' artistic Utopia. It encompassed the sculptress who wanted money to produce tactile figures in leather and oil; and the French Canadian girl, frequently pried from the basement windows, who wanted money to get her teeth capped. It corraled in the same potentially creative ambit a showman who wanted money to do Punch and Judy shows on Brighton beach and an Irish tramp who wanted money to burn toy dolls with napalm as an antiwar gesture in the King's Road.

It encompassed, most of all, the hippies, who simply wanted money and who flocked to Savile Row in every type of flowing garment and every degree of dreamy-eyed incoherence. Several times each week the call would come to Apple from Heathrow Airport's immigration department announcing that yet another beautiful person had arrived from California with beads and bells, but without funds or definite accommodation, to look up his four brothers in karma and Sergeant Pepper. At 3 Savile Row an entire San Francisco family, complete with breast-fed baby, waited to accompany John and Yoko to found an alternative universe in the Fiji Islands. There was also a mysterious Stocky, who said nothing, but perched all day on a press office filing cabinet drawing pictures of genitalia. He was harmless enough, as Derek Taylor always said.

The spirit of Apple in those days is best summed up, perhaps, in a moment when Taylor's desk intercom chirped yet again. "Derek," the receptionist's voice said, "Adolf Hitler is in reception."

"Oh, Christ," Taylor said. "Not that asshole again. OK, send him up."

It was a consequence of the hippie age's mingling superstition and vanity that young, fashionable people, in the young, fashionable music industry of the late sixties, endowed themselves freely with what amounted to psychic powers. Judgment of a person was made according to what vibrations—or vibes—he gave off by his presence and mood. So the people who came to 3 Savile Row were judged not by the legitimacy or sincerity of their purpose but by their good or bad vibes. A person visiting Apple in a beard and sandals, holding a lighted joss stick, portended good vibes. A lawyer, tax official, or policeman portended bad vibes. Colloquies of people, such as board meetings, created vibes proportionately stronger. It was mainly under the influence of these ever-changing, ever-unpredictable vibes that 3 Savile Row, during the next year and a half, alternately glowed with happiness and grew pale with fear.

To start with, the vibes were nearly all good. "Hey Jude," the Beatles' most successful single ever, had sold almost three million copies for their own Apple label. "Those Were the Days," by Mary Hopkin, the little Welsh girl Paul had taken up, was number one in Britain and number two in America. Apple's other new signings—James Taylor, Jackie Lomax, the Iveys, and, a prestige acquisition, the Modern Jazz Quartet—were all receiving an energetic and expensive launch as the Beatles' favored protégés.

There had been some bad vibes, admittedly, over the Apple boutique, The Fool and their extravagance, and the undignified scrimmage for giveaway merchandise. Nor were the vibes entirely amiable downwind of the house, among Savile Row's custom tailors and outfitters. Dukes and bishops in their fitting rooms looked on appalled at the daylong riot, the banners and chanting, the shrieks whenever a white Rolls-

Royce appeared. But, in general, the West End treated Apple with indulgence. The scene around the front steps made even passersby with bowler hats and rolled umbrellas smile.

Best of all were the all-powerful vibes given off by the Beatles' own frequent presence in the Georgian town house, directing their luscious new empire with a zest that infected each member of their ever multiplying staff. Though largely invisible within Apple, their presence was unmistakable. There would be the commotion on the first-floor landing, the tightly shut door to Neil Aspinall's office, or Peter Brown's. There would be the wakefulness surging suddenly through the press office as Derek Taylor answered his intercom. There were the familiar kitchen orders—a one-egg omelette for Ringo; cheese and cucumber sandwiches for George; for John and Yoko, brown rice, steamed vegetables, chocolate cake, and caviar.

Bad vibes from the outside made their first major strike on the afternoon of October 18. Laurie McCaffery, the deep-voiced telephonist who had followed NEMS down from Liverpool, put through a call to Neil Aspinall from someone who declined to give his name. In a moment, John Lennon's voice came on. "Imagine your worst paranoia," John said. "Well—it's here." He and Yoko were in police custody, charged with possessing cannabis.

They had been camping out at Ringo Starr's Montagu Square flat when the bust happened, shortly before midday. Six policemen and one policewoman had arrived with a search warrant and a sniffer dog, which had nosed out approximately one and a half ounces of cannabis. There was an additional charge of obstructing the officers during their search. John and Yoko were now being held at Marylebone police station.

Paul at once sought the help of Apple's most powerful ally, Sir Joseph Lockwood, chairman of EMI. "As soon as Paul contacted me, I rang Marylebone police station," Sir Joseph said. "John picked up the phone. ''Ello,' he said, 'Sergeant Lennon here.' 'Now stop all that,' I said. 'You've got to plead guilty. We'll get Lord Goodman on it. Oh no, we can't: He hates drugs. Anyway, you must plead guilty.' "

After a preliminary court appearance John and Yoko were released on bail. They emerged from Marylebone Magistrates Court into a forest of press cameras and a three-hundred-strong crowd. John's slight figure, hemmed in by scowling police helmets, hugged Yoko tightly to him. Though his martyrdom was self-inflicted and self-aggravated, there began to be something almost chivalrous in the way his slight body shielded Yoko's.

The case was due to be heard in full on November 27. That date had special irony for a press office bracing itself to deal with another John Lennon event whose vibes had already shown themselves practically combustible.

John had been determined from the start that Apple Records should be a medium for his and Yoko's experiments in avant-garde electronic music. The first album they had produced together was now ready for release. Entitled *Unfinished Music No. 1—Two Virgins,* it consisted mostly of the tapes they had made during the first night they had ceased to be virgins, at least with one another. Early in October, John had handed to Jeremy Banks, Apple's photographic coordinator, the picture he wanted used as the album cover. Banks immediately shut it in his desk drawer: for some days afterward, he could be seen surreptitiously peeping at it. The picture had been taken by John himself in the Montagu Square basement, on a delayed action shutter. It showed him with Yoko, their arms entwined, both—as word swiftly circulated—"stark bollock naked."

The vibes were precisely as expected. EMI flatly refused to distribute *Two Virgins* unless the sleeve were changed. John appealed direct to Sir Joseph Lockwood, but this time "Sir Joe" stood firm. " 'What on earth do you want to do it for?' I asked them. Yoko said, 'It's art.' 'In that case,' I said, 'why not show Paul in the nude? He's so much better looking. Or why not use a statue from one of the parks?' "

The eventual compromise was that EMI would manufacture the album but that it would be distributed by The Who's record label, Track, and the offending cover would be hidden inside a brown paper outer envelope. The same deal was done in America through a label called Tetragrammation. While thirty thousand copies sat in a New Jersey warehouse awaiting distribution they were confiscated as obscene material by the local police.

From here on, good and bad vibes bombarded Apple Corps with even greater capriciousness than the London weather.

On November 22, the double album was released whose enmities and unevenness faded in the breathtaking novelty and simplicity of its appearance. Originally, its cover was to have been created by Alan Aldridge, Swinging London's leading graphic entertainer and a popular figure in the circle that included the Beatles, the Stones, Jimi Hendrix, The Who, and Cream. Aldridge had proposed a design like an advent calendar, each window of which opened to show a scene from a song on the album—but the cost had been beyond even what EMI was prepared to spend. Instead, it was decided to go for stupendous understatement. The album would be packaged in pure, plain, shiny white, its only title a small, crooked die stamp, *The Beatles*. Each cover also bore a serial number, making a select limited edition of the first two million copies pressed. On opening the double sleeve one found only more tasteful austerity: a list of the thirty tracks on one side, four small, separate portraits of the musicians on the other.

The reviews were of snow-blinded ecstasy. In the *Observer*, Tony Palmer wrote that Lennon and McCartney stood revealed as "the greatest songwriters since Schubert." Palmer's review, more than any other, perpetrated the belief that the *White Album* (so its public soon renamed it) represented conscious artistic enterprise; that, by going to the opposite extreme of *Sgt. Pepper*, the Beatles had touched a new, stark, self-surpassing virtuosity. That *Sgt. Pepper*'s abiding quality was cohesion and that the *White Album*'s was disorganization quite escaped most critics' ravished ears. The quality most evident throughout, Palmer wrote, was "simple happiness." Even *Revolution 9* could not qualify his belief that the Beatles dwelt on "shores of the imagination others have not yet sighted."

The day the *White Album* was released, Yoko lost the baby she had been expecting. Her room at Queen Charlotte's Hospital had a second bed in which John himself lay, propped up with pillows. Throughout the emergency that ended in Yoko's miscarriage he refused to leave her. When the second bed was needed for another patient he spent each night in a sleeping bag beside her on the floor.

Their drugs case was heard a week later at Marylebone Magistrates Court. John pleaded guilty, assuring the bench that Yoko had nothing to do with acquiring or using the cannabis. He was fined £150, with £21 costs. On the charge of willful obstruction, no evidence was offered. His counsel, Martin Polden, asked for leniency for someone who had given pleasure to millions with his music. "An ounce-and-a-half of compassion," Polden said, was not too much to ask.

It was on that very same day that Apple, having no other choice, released the album that could not be advertised in any music paper and could be bought only like pornographic literature, in a plain brown paper bag. On its front cover the two virgins proclaimed their commitment to each other and their new agenda with full-frontal nudity; on the back, they stood hand in hand, looking over their shoulders and showing their bare bottoms.

The success of Apple Records was unquestionable. But what of the other divisions? Six months had passed since Paul had announced that wide-ranging creative prospectus. Apple Films had yet to make a film. The Apple Press had yet to publish a book. Apple Retail, after the boutique disaster, was virtually moribund. The Apple Foundation for the Arts was something people preferred not to recollect. Occasionally, when a press office employee went into the Black Room and pulled out another case of wine, the huge, unread pile of manuscripts would totter and slide a little, then once more settle to rest.

Numerous subsidiary projects had been floated on the seas of Beatles cash. As a rule, these represented the whim of an individual Beatle: They lasted as long, and no longer, than that Beatle's flickering enthusiasm. Paul had at one stage been keen on an offshoot called Zapple, a label that would release spoken word records by modish underground writers like Ken Kesey and Richard Brautigan. Kesey—the original Merry Prankster, progenitor of the *Magical Mystery Tour*—was brought to London, given an IBM golfball typewriter and invited to write a street diary of his impressions. By the time it was completed Paul's enthusiasm had moved elsewhere. There was no one else to read Ken Kesey's street diary; he returned to California, leaving his IBM typewriter at the front desk.

Apple's design consultant was Alan Aldridge, who would be called in to Derek Taylor's office several times a week and handed an outsize joint called a B-52 before being asked to come up with plans for an apple-shaped record player, an apple-shaped transistor radio, or a jokey letter-head for Taylor's own press office headed "Lies from Apple" and illustrated by a picture of a pear. "I also designed some wallpaper based on 'Lucy in the Sky,' Aldridge remembers. "The idea was to come up with colors that would make people get high just by looking at them."

Expenditure ran on at a dizzy rate that was, by Beatles standards, entirely normal. Only now, more than four people were spending and consuming. The tea, the coffee, the Scotch and Coke, the VSOP brandy, the

Southern Comfort, the Benson & Hedges Gold dispensed so liberally in Derek Taylor's office were but the visible, obvious part of the largesse poured out by Apple to its visitors and its staff. From a kitchen stocked by Fortnum & Mason endless relays of food came forth—hot meals, cold meals, cold wine, sandwiches, champagne. Junior staff shared liberally in the company picnic. A certain brand of vodka favored by the Apple high command could be bought only at a restaurant in Knightsbridge. Since the restaurant did no take-out sales, two Apple office boys would be sent there to eat an expensive lunch and bring back the vodka. One of the kitchen girls remembers a certain Friday afternoon when a sixty-pound pot of caviar had been ordered from Fortnum's for Yoko, who did not arrive after all. Two girls spread the sixty pounds' worth of caviar on a single round of toast, and ate a slice each.

Only after three Apple secretaries had had their pay packets stolen on the same day was it realized that Apple's openhandedness now extended to casual passersby. Security barely existed. That beautiful people, clad in kaftans and emitting good vibes, could stoop to theft simply did not seem possible. Meanwhile, LPs, hi-fi speakers, television sets, IBM typewriters, any movable part of the green-and-white decor continued to vanish, not through the back door—there wasn't one—but through the front door in broad daylight, before hundreds of staring eyes. Post office messengers who brought in the sacks of fan mail were methodically stripping off the roof lead and carrying it away in the empty mailbags.

The Beatles' accountants were still, as in Brian Epstein's day, Bryce, Hanmer Ltd. of Albemarle Street. Harry Pinsker, the head of the firm, supervised Apple's financial affairs and also sat on the Apple Corps board. When John and Yoko appeared nude on the *Two Virgins* album cover, Pinsker and four other directors resigned. Apple's day-to-day accounting was then delegated to a junior partner, Stephen Maltz. For a few weeks Maltz worked at 3 Savile Row, attempting to control its vast outgoings. He resigned in late October in a five-page letter to each of the Beatles, warning of dire consequences if they could not find a way to curb Apple's expenditures.

By that time, the company had gobbled up the £1,000,000 set aside to launch it. It had devoured a further £400,000, the second installment of the £800,000 that the Beatles had realized by selling themselves to their own company. All four had heavily overdrawn their corporate partnership account: John by £64,858, Paul by £66,988, George by £35,850 and Ringo by £32,080. All four, in addition, were facing personal income tax liabilities of around £600,000 each.

"As far as you were aware," Maltz wrote, "you only had to sign a bill and pick up a phone and payment was made. You were never concerned where the money came from or how it was being spent, and were living under the idea that you had millions at your disposal.

"Each of you has houses and cars . . . you also have tax cases pending. Your personal finances are in a mess. Apple is in a mess."

The Beatles by then could see that Apple was in a mess. They could even, however reluctantly, see why. They had all shared Paul's vision of Western Communism—of young people freed from turgid conventional business methods, managing their own affairs on the pure, simple dynamo of their own young energy. The lesson of the past six months was that young people were no less greedy, dishonest, avaricious, and incompetent than middle-aged ones. Maltz's letter and grim warning only confirmed a suspicion, growing even in John's mind, that turgid, conventional business might have something to recommend it after all. In particular, their thoughts turned toward the very concept that Apple had meant to disown: Someone, they agreed, had better become the boss.

At 3 Savile Row, despite all the high-paid executives in their elegantly appointed offices, no one was quite the boss. Ron Kass, the head of Apple Records, probably came the closest. But Kass did not have, as Peter Brown did, the direct hotline to all four Beatle hides. Peter Brown held expansive managerial lunches. But Neil Aspinall, who never ate lunch, held the post of managing director. Neil, their former road manager, was the Beatles' oldest, closest friend; it was his very closeness and trustworthiness that prevented him from seizing full executive power. He simply took on a workload that on several occasions caused him to be physically sick.

If Apple was to have a boss, the Beatles decided, it must be a big boss. It must be the biggest, bossiest boss that the land of business and bosses could provide.

As so often in such matters they sought guidance from the biggest boss on their horizon: Sir Joseph Lockwood, chairman of EMI. Sir Joe's advice was to bring in the head of a merchant bank. He himself offered to approach Lazard, one of the city's most powerful merchant banks, on their behalf. A meeting was arranged between Paul and the bank's chairman, Lord Poole, who at that time also happened to be giving financial advice to the Queen.

Sir Joseph accompanied Paul to the Lazard meeting. "He'd come along without a tie of course. So Lord Poole took off his tie and jacket and we sat down to lunch. At the end, Lord Poole said, 'I'll do it. And what's more, I won't charge you anything.' The Queen's financial adviser was offering to sort out the Beatles—for nothing! But the Beatles didn't bother to follow it up."

Another highly symbolic approach—by John this time—was to Lord Beeching, the man who reorganized British Railways by shutting down huge lengths of them. The legendary "Beeching axe" was not available to be wielded at Apple. Beeching, however, listened sympathetically to the tales of chaos and then offered one wise—and prophetic—recommendation: "Get back to making records."

Meanwhile, Christmas was coming. So were the Hell's Angels. The former was to be celebrated with a party for Apple employees' children organized by Derek Taylor in Peter Brown's sumptuous first-floor office. The latter were motorcycling heavies from San Francisco whom George Harrison had asked to drop in whenever they happened to be passing through London.

At first, it was rumored that the entire San Francisco chapter of the Hell's Angels had decided to take up this invitation. The deputation, however, proved to be limited to only two, though sufficiently terrifying, Angels, one named 'Frisco Pete, the other, Billy Tumbleweed. With them they brought two Harley-Davidson bikes—shipped from California at Apple's expense—and a harem a dozen strong. They and their retinue were reportedly en route for Czechoslovakia "to straighten out the political situation."

First, 'Frisco Pete and Billy Tumbleweed straightened out Apple, partaking of hospitality made still more liberal by the terror their looks inspired. Carol Paddon, in the press office, was one of several Apple girls who mastered the knack, when a Hell's Angel hand went up her skirt, of smiling with ghastly good humor. Naturally, it would have been discourteous, not to say dangerous, to exclude the two visitors from the Apple children's Christmas party.

The party, in Peter Brown's office, featured seas of jellies, blancmange, and a conjurer named Ernest Castro. Afterward there was to be a grown-ups' party, with John and Yoko officiating as Father and Mother Christmas. Of the lavish buffet that Apple's Cordon Bleu cooks had prepared, the centerpiece was a forty-two-pound turkey, guaranteed by its suppliers to be the largest turkey in Great Britain.

The party proved a fitting climax to Apple's Golden Age. John, sitting on the floor with Yoko, a white Santa Claus beard covering his dark one, was bewildered to find himself menaced by both 'Frisco Pete and Billy Tumbleweed. The Hell's Angels resented what they felt was unnecessary delay in starting on the largest turkey in Great Britain. When the music journalist Alan Smith tried to intervene, 'Frisco Pete felled him with a single punch. Smith's toppling body struck John as he was raising a teacup to his lips. Father Christmas sat there, protecting Mother Christmas, with tea dripping down his spectacles.

EIGHTEEN

"THE BEATLES ARE THE BIGGEST BASTARDS IN THE WORLD"

Until 1969, the British public at large had never heard of Allen Klein. They had heard only of Alan Klein, a young Cockney songwriter briefly famous during the early sixties for a number entitled "What a Crazy World We're Livin' in." To be sure, when the Klein named Allen first began to impinge on their consciousness, many people initially mistook him for the Klein named Alan, whom they remembered as young, wiry, and humorous, a kind of bargain-basement Lionel Bart. Not until Allen Klein's stunning coup had put him on every national front page did the realization dawn that he was in fact a thirty-eight-year-old New Yorker whose shortness, tubbiness, and total absence of neck gave him a more than passing resemblance to Barney Rubble in *The Flintstones.*

Klein did not originally set out to manage the greatest pop act the world had ever known. He was born in New Jersey in 1932, the son of an impoverished kosher butcher. His mother died when he was still a baby and his father, unable to cope, gave him and his sister into the care of Newark's austere Hebrew Shelter Orphanage. In later years, when his father remarried and his new stepmother proved unsympathetic, Allen was boarded out with an aunt. This fact was to prove crucial years later, during perhaps the most important business conference of his whole career.

His young manhood, as Klein himself liked to recall, was one of almost Dickensian hardship, endeavour, and self-denial. He worked as a clerk for a firm of New Jersey newspaper distributors, at the same time holding down two or three other part-time jobs to pay for a course in accounting at the Lutheran Uppsala College. As he sat in class there, he would often be so exhausted that his head would drop forward onto his arms. Yet whenever the teacher posed a problem in mental arithmetic, he would still always be first to rattle out the answer.

After graduating from Uppsala he married his college sweetheart and set up as the newest and hungriest of Manhattan's million-and-one accountants. His vocation made itself clear when he accepted a small retainer to handle the finances of Buddy Knox, a teenage pop idol who had a nationwide hit with "Party Doll" in 1957. Klein discovered that Knox's record company had failed to pay a substantial part of what they owed him in royalties. An equally interesting discovery was the mixture of guilt and confusion on the faces of the label executives when Klein confronted them with these discrepancies. The upshot was that Knox received what he was owed and Klein received three thousand dollars in commission, enough to buy him and his wife, Betty, their first-ever new car.

Klein thereafter specialized in clients from the pop music world, making each the same bluntly seductive offer: "I can get you money you never even knew you had." He would ferret it out in the same way he had for Buddy Knox, trapped in ponderously slow accounting systems, or in unpaid performance fees or miscalculated royalty returns. He would then confront the miscreant company in the role of avenging angel, threatening legal action or criminal prosecution if the deficiencies were not instantly made good. Even record companies who dealt conscientiously with their artists could not be sure that Klein wouldn't find something to stretch them on the rack. "If a corporation is big, it *has* to make mistakes," was his maxim. "There's no big organization in the world that doesn't have something to hide."

The technique worked with spectacular success for the singing husband and wife Steve Lawrence and Eydie Gormé, for Bobby ("Splish-Splash") Darin, and most notably Bobby ("Blue Velvet") Vinton, whom Klein approached at a mutual friend's wedding and asked, "How would you like to make a hundred thousand dollars?" Within just a few days that very sum in ferreted-out fees and back royalties was paid into Vinton's bank account. Among these grateful clients he became known as "the Robin Hood of Pop," though Klein himself never claimed such dashingly altruistic motives. Despite his general orthodoxy in religious matters, he chose as his desktop motto a slightly amended version of Psalm 23: "Yea, though I walk through the Valley of the Shadow of Death, I will fear no evil, for I am the biggest bastard in the valley."

In 1964, he took over the affairs of Sam Cooke, a talented soul singer then riding high on the Twist dance craze. Klein negotiated an unheard-of one-million-dollar advance for Cooke from the RCA label, though unhappily the singer did not live long to enjoy it. A year later, he was shot to death in a Los Angeles motel while in the company of a lady other than his wife.

When the Beatles conquered America in 1964 Klein looked on with the same hungry, helpless eyes as a hundred other indigenous agents and managers. A couple of months afterward, on a trip to London, he called on Brian Epstein to offer Sam Cooke as a support act on the Beatles' soon-to-follow second U.S. tour. During the meeting, with typical chutzpah, he also offered himself as their financial consultant, implying that the same huge sums in unpaid royalties could be pried from their record companies as from Bobby Darin's and Bobby Vinton's. Brian did not take the suggestion seriously. But Klein came away boasting that he would have the Beatles, even setting a deadline of Christmas 1965. Meantime, he occupied himself in sucking up other significant names from the so-called British invasion: the Dave Clark Five, the Animals, Herman's Hermits, Donovan. and, finally, the Rolling Stones.

Klein's acquisition of the Stones showed his unerring ability to spot the most vulnerable points in his prospective quarry. He had observed how the band's young manager, Andrew Loog Oldham, cast himself as a star equally glamorous as Mick Jagger, and also how much Oldham longed for wealth and status symbols to equal those of his one-time employer, Brian Epstein. Meeting Oldham in London in mid-1965, Klein's opening gambit was, as usual, devastatingly simple. "Andrew," he said, "whaddaya want?"

"I want a Rolls-Royce," Oldham replied.

"You got it," Klein told him.

The dazzled Oldham thereupon dropped his existing partner, Eric Easton, and hired Klein as his personal business manager, so giving the New Yorker effective control of all the Stones' financial dealings. The move, as it happened, came midway through Oldham's and Easton's negotiation of a new contract for the Stones with Decca Records, one that as usual promised royalty payments only after the records had been sold. Klein weighed into the negotiations with all the tactics that had made him feared in New York. The upshot was that a stunned Decca found themselves agreeing to pay the Stones an advance of $1.25 million.

Following this apparent huge coup on their behalf, the supercilious, supercool Stones were as enraptured by Klein as Steve Lawrence and Eydie Gormé ever had been. They were also impressed by his organization of their 1966 American tour and announcement of a three-movie deal aimed at making them just as big on the big screen as the Beatles. Not the least exhilarating feature of Klein's management was a rumored direct connection with the underworld, which Klein himself always firmly denied while being obviously not displeased by it. One of his closest associates, a promotion man named Pete Bennett, dressed just like a mafioso in sharkskin suits and shades, and was given to patting his left armpit as if a holstered handgun were secreted there.

The Stones naturally were not slow to extol the achievements of their new miracle man to their good friends, the Beatles. That wonderful $1.25 million Decca advance in effect quite eclipsed the new contract with EMI that Brian Epstein negotiated for the Beatles early in 1967, and further complicated the always fraught relationship between Brian and Paul McCartney. Ironically, in view of later events, Paul suggested that Klein be hired to do for the Beatles what he had for the Stones. Rumors spread of an impending merger between Klein's company and NEMS, negotiated by a so-called third man, which Brian angrily dismissed as "rubbish."

By 1967, Klein's control of the Stones was absolute and exclusive. Relations between the band and Andrew Loog Oldham, which had seriously declined during Jagger's and Richard's drugs trial, hit rock bottom as the Stones struggled to finish *Their Satanic Majesties Request*, the album intended to be their answer to *Sgt. Pepper*. One day, goaded beyond endurance by their slipshod playing and unfocused attitude, Oldham walked out of the studio, never to return. Klein subsequently bought out his management share for around one million pounds.

Brian's death might have seemed the perfect moment for Klein to move in on the Beatles. Yet he continued to bide his time and watch from afar the confusion among Brian's too many heirs apparent. Among the plans swirling round in late 1967 was an ambitious—and rather sensible—one whereby the Beatles and Stones would have shared the same UK front office and jointly financed their own recording studio at North London's Camden Lock. Mick Jagger approached Peter Brown to see if he would act for the Stones, as he did for the Beatles, as ambassador, fixer, and social secretary. But Klein violently opposed the idea, and flew straight over from New York to scotch it. There was a meeting, also attended by Clive Epstein, when Klein struck Brown as "a rather hysterical, unstable person. Then he realized I wasn't trying to take over the Stones, and calmed down a bit. As he walked out, he suddenly turned to Clive and said, 'How much d'ya want for the Beatles?' "

Across the Atlantic, meanwhile, Klein's reputation as a ruthless opportunist and wheeler-dealer was reaching new heights. He had recently acquired Cameo-Parkway, a record label once successful with Twist king Chubby Checker but now on the edge of bankruptcy. No sooner had Klein bought the label than its shares rose steeply in value, from three dollars to more than seventy-five dollars each. He was suspected of talking up Cameo-Parkway's share price by inventing rumors of impending lucrative takeovers or mergers with larger organizations, like the British music firm Chappell. As a result, the New York Stock Exchange suspended dealings in Cameo-Parkway shares and ordered an investigation by the Securities and Exchange Commission. Cameo-Parkway's stockholders also began legal proceedings against Klein, enraged, among other things, by the $104,000 per year salary he had awarded himself as chief executive. Klein denied any wrongdoing. In the event, Cameo-Parkway was to make only one significant acquisition: the Allen Klein accounting company. Klein took himself over in reverse, naming the resultant entity ABKCO Industries (the "ABK" part standing for Allen and Betty Klein).

As 1968 drew to a close, and Apple stood revealed as a bottomless financial pit, Klein's dream of winning the Beatles seemed as far away as ever. The Rolling Stones had extolled his genius to them time after time, without result. He himself had put in a telephone call to John Lennon, but John could not be bothered to accept it. They had also met briefly, in December 1968, when John and Yoko took part, with Eric Clapton, The Who, and other pop luminaries, in the Stones' Sgt. Peppery *Rock 'n' Roll Circus* film. But Klein, surprisingly, made no attempt to capitalize on the meeting, and John barely glanced at the tubby little man with his unfashionable greased-back hair, cardigan, and pipe.

Not until the following January did Klein's moment come—when he picked up *Rolling Stone,* the new intelligent music paper named after his first supergroup protégés, and saw the story splashed all over it. John had said that, if the Beatles carried on spending money at their present rate, he'd be "broke in six months."

•   •   •

With Paul McCartney, the need to breathe was scarcely more important than the need to perform. It was a need that transcended mere vanity and his love of his own bewitching, beguiling, melodic power. He would sing and play for as many, or as few, people as happened to be there when the impulse came that was as natural as breath. Once, on a car journey with Derek Taylor, he stopped in a Bedfordshire village and played the piano in a village pub. He would sing softly through the dark to the girls on watch outside his house. Late in 1968, he and Linda spent a week with friends in Portugal. His hosts noticed a phenomenon unchanged since a decade ago on Forthlin Road, Liverpool. Even in the lavatory, Paul could not stop singing and playing his guitar.

Paul had always felt that by giving up road tours and retiring into album work, the Beatles had broken faith with the public to whom, fundamentally, they owed everything. So he began arguing with renewed persistence after the *White Album* was finished. He had lately—at Linda's encouragement—grown a dark, bushy beard. It might have been a keen and determined young schoolmaster who sat in the Apple boardroom, urging the other three that their next project together ought to be a return to playing live concerts.

The chief deterrent, as Paul himself acknowledged, was simple stage fright. It had been more than two years since the Beatles last faced an audience together. In that time, only John had given anything like a live performance, in the *Rock 'n' Roll Circus* film. He had also appeared at the Alchemical Wedding, a Christmas rally of Britain's hippies, mystics, and dropouts, though that merely meant sitting with Yoko inside a plastic bag on the stage of the Royal Albert Hall.

Paul kept up the pressure, reminding them of stage fright successfully overcome in the past. Hadn't it been the same when they suddenly took a step up from Liverpool and Hamburg clubs to the grandeur of Leicester's de Monfort hall? And when they had made the quantum leap from the London Palladium to Shea Stadium? John and Ringo seemed persuadable but not George. Nothing, he said, could make him go back to the witless screaming and frantic running of the Beatlemania years. Paul agreed that going back on tour in the old way would be unendurable. They would play only a few, carefully selected live dates; perhaps only a single one. "But we've got to keep that contact somehow. And it's what we do best."

In the end, they agreed on a compromise. Rather than giving a live performance, they would make an album that was like a live performance—an album shorn of all studio artifice, reliant only on their abilities as singers and musicians, simple and powerful and honest enough to reach back over the years to their original, punching power in the Cavern Club. To underline the point, they went to George Martin—now a freelance producer, soon to launch his own independent AIR studios—and asked, or rather begged, him to work for them again. It was their obvious sincerity rather than any fee that persuaded Martin to put his new career on hold and try to re-create the spontaneity and honesty of the *Please Please Me* album. "They said they wanted to go right back to basics," Martin says. "They wouldn't use any overdubbing. They'd do the songs just as they happened."

The simple resolve of four musicians, however, was now subject to the complexities of Apple Corps, and its still unused subsidiaries, Apple Films and Apple Publishing. It was decided that the making of the album must be made into a film, and that film and record sessions should be described in an illustrated book to accompany each album. The climax of the film would be the live performance Paul wanted, at a location still to be decided.

The arrival of a film crew, led by director Michael Lindsay-Hogg, gave additional scope to Paul's ideas. At one point, with Lindsay-Hogg's encouragement, he proposed giving the concert in a Tunisian amphitheater; at another, he suggested making the whole album live in Los Angeles. George vetoed both suggestions as "very expensive and insane." Another of Paul's schemes was to record at sea, onboard an ocean liner. George objected that the acoustics would be impossible and that, anyway, they'd need two liners rather than one. As the argument flew back and forth, John was heard to mutter, "I'm warming to the idea of doing it in an asylum."

The project's working title—symbolic of their desire to rediscover their roots—was *Get Back*. At John's suggestion, they even posed for a photograph looking down from the same balcony as on the cover of their first chirpy, working-class LP.

Rehearsals began on January 2, 1969, at one end of a cavernous soundstage at Twickenham film studios. Michael Lindsay-Hogg's camera crew were already in position to film Mal Evans, the perennial roadie, carrying in amplifiers and cymbal stands, and Paul testing the grand piano, still in his hobo-ish tweed coat, a half-eaten apple before him on the polished lid.

The cameras ran on as Paul, each morning, strove to make the other Beatles forget their dismal surroundings, the unaccustomed daylight playing, and the constant, numb-fingered cold. His resemblance to a schoolmaster grew, even as the class grew more plainly recalcitrant. "Okay—right. Er—Okay, let's try to move on." He went and sat with George, as with a backward and also stubborn pupil, tracing with his arm the sequence he wanted George to play. "You see, it's got to come down like that. There shouldn't be any recognizable jumps. It helps if you sing it. Like this—"

Resentment was not yet in the open. Paul worked conscientiously to provide a falsetto counterpoint to John's "Across the Universe." John played chords as instructed to a pretty little Paul tune that would one day become "Maxwell's Silver Hammer." They even, spasmodically, enjoyed themselves. John got up, and Yoko did not follow him: Paul and he sang "Two of Us," burlesquing like teenage Quarry Men. When George played over "I Me Mine," a new song in turgid waltz time, Paul and Ringo tackled it gamely. John and Yoko, two white-clad figures in gym shoes, waltzed to it together across the cable-strewn floor.

As well as the new material, they continually ran through old songs from Liverpool and Hamburg: the Chuck Berry and Elvis and Little Richard songs they had always played to warm up before performing or recording. They even resurrected a Quarry Men song, "The One After 909," written by John and Paul on truant afternoons in Jim McCartney's sitting-room with the Chinese pagoda wallpaper and the *Liverpool Echo*s piled under the dresser. "We always hated the words to that one," Paul said. " 'Move over once, move over twice. Hey, baby, don't be cold as ice . . .' They're great, really, aren't they?"

Whatever glow these memories awoke soon died again in the cold and general discomfort. Nor did playing the old songs seem to bring the new songs any nearer to satisfying Paul. "We've been going round and round for an hour," he complained wearily at one point. "I think it's a question of either we do it or we go home."

As Paul talked to George, a row started. "I always hear myself—annoying you," Paul said. "Look, I'm not trying to *get* you. I'm just saying 'Look, lads—the band. Shall we do it like this?' "

"Look, I'll play whatever you want me to play," George cut in. His voice silting with resentment, he continued: "Or I won't play at all. Whatever it is that'll please you, I'll do it."

At lunchtime on January 10, George said he had had enough. He was tired of being "got at" by Paul. He was quitting the Beatles, he said. He got into his car and drove home to Esher.

It was a temporary flare-up, and recognized as such. George knew, and the others did, that he could never resign with an album half-finished. And, sure enough, when a business meeting took place at Ringo's a few days later, George turned up as usual. Work on the album resumed after Paul promised not to get at George or try to teach him the guitar. And, they all agreed, they had had enough of Twickenham studios. They decided to move straight into their own studio—the one that Magic Alex had been designing and assembling in the basement of the Apple house.

George Martin had already visited the basement but found the studio unready, lacking a console. It could be made fit for recording only by silencing the air conditioner, which thumped and wheezed in the corner, and by bringing in heavy consignments of rented sound equipment. This done, the Beatles and their film crew tried again. Billy Preston, a gifted American performer who was George's protégé, joined the sessions as organist. What with the film crew, and this or that friend and acolyte, there was scarcely room in the basement to move. Yoko sat by John, as always, reading or embroidering. When Paul arrived—managing to make an entrance even through that narrow basement doorway—he brought Linda's little daughter, Heather, riding on his shoulders.

The album that would finally be released as Let It Be in fact contained only the tiniest fraction of what the Beatles recorded in that crowded basement during January 1969. More than a hundred songs, by every artist they had ever admired or copied, and also from every epoch of their own career, piled up on spools destined never to be released, or even listened to, again. It was as if, to rediscover themselves as musicians, they were putting themselves through the kind of endurance test that Hamburg used to be, seeking to renew themselves with music that stretched back to their collective birth. They even recorded "Maggie May," the Liverpool sailors' shanty that John sang at the Woolton fete that day in 1957 when Paul McCartney cycled across from Allerton to meet him.

It was after they stopped jamming and returned to today's material that the breakdown always came. Determined to be "honest," to forsake all artifice, they still wanted from George Martin what he had always given them: a flawless final product. "We'd do sixty different takes of something," Martin says. "On the sixty-first take, John would say, 'How was that one, George?' I'd say, 'John—I honestly don't know.' 'You're no fookin' good then are you,' he'd say. That was the general atmosphere."

Ironically, the best and happiest song on the finished album was one that grew out of random studio ad-libbing. Paul gave it the shorthand name "Loretta": Only later did it receive the album's original title of "Get Back." Several versions of Paul's vocal were taped, including one that sarcastically made "Get Back" a warning to Asian immigrants in the tones of the racist lobby inspired by Enoch Powell. Another featured John as lead singer, giving the song a bitter drive and bite that even Paul's best version lacked. Halfway through the John version, both he and Paul suddenly tailed off into silence: It was Ringo, redeeming himself at last in George Martin's eyes, whose quick-witted drum solo forced them back again on target.

The film crew, with twenty-eight hours of footage, finally packed up and left. The Beatles themselves did so a few days later, leaving behind an aural rag-bag that not even Paul could face hearing, let alone editing down to fourteen songs. John was all for putting out the album as it stood: a confession of their own internal chaos. "It'll tell people, 'This is us with our trousers off, so will you please end the game now?' "

For the benefit of the film crew, they had already given their much debated live performance—not in Tunisia or L.A. or on an oceangoing liner, but on one arbitrarily chosen afternoon on the roof of the Apple house. In keeping with the atmosphere of reticence and self-deprecation, no one knew about the event but their own employees and a few close friends. They little realized they were creating yet another scene to be replayed, and many times imitated, in decades to come, as passersby stopped to stare up in amazement at the electric din erupting in the sky; as traffic between the custom tailors' shops ground to a halt; as policemen appeared, at last, from nearby Savile Row station; as the law decided it must put a stop to it, and a thickset sergeant crossed the road to knock sternly at Apple's white front door.

·   ·   ·

It was, in fact, a British music paper, *Disc,* that had first broken the story now blazoned all over American *Rolling Stone*: "John Lennon Says Beatles In Cash Crisis." *Disc's* editor Ray Coleman, a longtime Beatles follower and friend, later received an angry dressing-down from Paul on the stairs at Apple for having run the original piece. "This is only a small company and you're trying to wreck it," Paul shouted. "You know John shoots his mouth off and doesn't mean it." Coleman had been close to the Beatles long enough to recognize what was off or on the record.

So it proved when the world's press poured over the Apple threshold, asking for further and better particulars. John confirmed what he had told Ray Coleman—that Apple was losing some twenty thousand pounds a week to its myriad hangers-on, and that he personally calculated he was "down to my last £50,000." George, as a rule the closest one in money matters, was equally willing to talk. "We've been giving away too much to the wrong people—like the deaf and the blind," George said. "This place has become a haven for drop-outs. The trouble is, some of our best friends are drop-outs."

The story that the Beatles were going broke somewhat abated the Apple orgy. It also placed the honest, and rather underpaid, regular staff members under the same stigma as predatory Hell's Angels and larcenous visitors. Paul, in a thoughtful PR gesture, sent round a morale-boosting letter to all Apple artists and employees: "In case you're worried about anything at Apple, please feel free to write me a letter, telling me about the problem. There's no need to be formal. Just say it. Incidentally, things are going well, so thanks—love, Paul."

The news that Allen Klein, the Rolling Stones' manager, was in London and wanted to see the Beatles with a view to helping them, did not at first seem vastly portentous. When Klein's first call reached Apple, they were still immured at Twickenham studios, refusing to see anyone. It was simply another message from the hundreds left hanging in the psychedelic twilight of Derek Taylor's press office. "Allen Klein! What the fuck does he want, man?" "How the fuck should I know?"

That Klein's message should have reached John Lennon was surprising enough. What was still more surprising was John's instant agreement to meet him, as requested, at Klein's suite in the Dorchester Hotel. John went without telling the other Beatles, accompanied only by Yoko, and, as he later admitted, petrified with nerves.

Klein played the scene perfectly, meeting John and Yoko alone in his room, wearing a sweater and sneakers, the nearest to their hippie threads that he could muster. Having expected a one-dimensional businessman, John found a fan of more than usual devotion, for Klein knew by heart every Beatles song dating back to the very start of their career. He showed an instinctive grasp of the Beatles' peculiar problems, and had clear and forceful proposals for remedying them. He impressed John with his straightforward manner and the blunt New York wit that put him spiritually not far from a Liverpudlian. The fact that he, too, had lost his mother in early childhood and been boarded out with an aunt cemented the bond between them.

By the end of that first meeting John had made up his mind. There and then he wrote a note to EMI's chairman, Sir Joseph Lockwood: "Dear Sir Joe—from now on, Allen Klein handles all my stuff."

Sir Joseph read the note with a bewilderment shared by others to whom John announced his adoption of Allen Klein. For so far as their closest associates knew, the Beatles had already decided on the man who would rescue them and Apple Corps from chaos.

Late in 1968, Linda had taken Paul McCartney home to New York to meet her family. He had met her father, the elegant Lee Eastman, and her brother, John, a bright young Ivy Leaguer, already a partner in the family law and management practice. He had surveyed the list of show business VIPs and renowned painters whom the Eastmans represented, and tasted the high-caste Manhattan life that formed the highest rung of his ascent from a little row house in Allerton. By the time he returned to London, he had decided that Eastman & Eastman were the solution for both the Beatles' management and Apple.

Paul having prepared the ground on both sides, John Eastman flew to London to meet the other Beatles a few weeks later. They were not bowled over—first, because Lee hadn't thought it worthwhile to show up in person; second, because John came across as rather immature and overeager. No one was impressed by his efforts to make up to John and Yoko with arty talk about Kafka. Also, it was known to everyone inside the Beatles' circle, though not yet to anyone outside it, that the Eastman and McCartney families were soon to be joined by matrimony. Nevertheless, a letter signed by all four Beatles authorized John Eastman to act for them in contractual matters. By the time Allen Klein appeared, Paul's soon-to-be brother-in-law had begun an ambitious plan to consolidate their dwindling reserves.

NEMS Enterprises, Brian Epstein's original management company, still hung ghostlike in the Apple firmament. Under its new name, Nemperor Holdings, it continued to receive the Beatles' earnings and to deduct Brian's 25 percent before passing on the residue to Apple. Yet NEMS had long since ceased to exercise control over them as agents and managers. The bond was purely technical—and sentimental, since Brian's mother, Queenie, was NEMS's main shareholder and his brother, Clive, was chairman. The Beatles themselves still held the 10 percent share in NEMS allotted to them by Brian's tender conscience.

The Epsteins, on their side, while wishing to retain control of NEMS, still faced the bill for half a million pounds in estate taxes that Brian's cash assets had nowhere near covered. Clive Epstein, for all his dutiful efforts to expand NEMS, knew he had no ultimate course but to sell the company. What restrained him was his sense of obligation—to Brian's memory, to his mother, to the remaining Liverpool artists—to everything, in fact, but his own fervent desire to return to Liverpool's quieter business climes.

Late in 1967, Clive had received an offer for NEMS from the Triumph Investment Trust, a city merchant bank with a reputation for aggressive takeovers. At that stage, however, NEMS, transformed into Nemperor, was committed to a "programme of vigorous expansion." The expansion proved less than vigorous, and a year later, preempting a rumored bid by the British Lion Film Corporation, Triumph's chairman, Leonard Richenberg, made a second approach to Clive Epstein. This time, Clive was ready to accept Richenberg's offer.

John Eastman's plan was that the Beatles themselves should buy up NEMS, matching Triumph's offer of one million pounds. Sir Joseph Lockwood at EMI had agreed to advance the entire sum against future royalty earnings. Clive Epstein, feeling that the Beatles had a moral right to the company that Brian had launched on their name, notified Leonard Richenberg that the sale to Triumph was off.

It was at this point that John met, and adopted, Allen Klein. George and Ringo, who met Klein soon afterward, were struck, as John had been, by Klein's forthrightness and his thorough grasp of the Apple problem. They did not instantly accept him as their savior, but they were willing to listen. Paul was not. He attended only one meeting with Klein, and walked out soon after it had begun.

The plan agreed to by the other three was that John Eastman and

Klein should *both* work as advisers to Apple. Eastman was to follow up the NEMS deal while Klein looked into their financial position with special regard to EMI's one-million-pound loan.

The Eastmans, father and son, made no secret of the disfavor with which they regarded Allen Klein. They were quick to inform Paul—as Leonard Richenberg had independently discovered—that Klein was viewed with suspicion in New York because of the Cameo-Parkway affair; that some fifty lawsuits decorated the escutcheon of Klein's company, ABKCO Industries; and that Klein himself currently faced ten charges by the U.S. Internal Revenue Service of failing to file income tax returns.

To George and Ringo that was less important than the stunning promise Klein held out to them. He would go into Apple and clean up the mess. He would also make each of them wealthy in a way that even they, in their clouds of ready cash, had never imagined possible. He had a way of characterizing money as some dragonlike entity that had slain Brian Epstein, with his paltry seven-million-pound gross, but which Allen Klein, with his ABKCO sword, knew the secret of vanquishing: "You shouldn't have to worry about money. *You* shouldn't have to think about it. You should be able to say FYM—Fuck You, Money."

George and Ringo responded, as John had, to Klein's pungent fiscal imagery and down-to-earth manner. They liked him for the brusqueness he did not trouble to moderate, whatever the company. John Eastman, by contrast, wavered between urbane bonhomie and spluttering rage. It was a trait shared by his father, who had at length flown over from New York to meet the Beatles and Klein together at the Claridge Hotel. A few minutes after the meeting began, Lee Eastman rounded on Klein and began to shout abuse at him. The outburst was, in fact, skillfully engineered by Klein, to reveal Lee Eastman as a hysteric and himself as the stolid underdog. John, George, and Ringo naturally sided with the underdog.

Clive Epstein, meanwhile, had begun to suspect that selling NEMS to the Beatles was a process that might drag on for months. He therefore reopened negotiations with Leonard Richenberg and Triumph, though stressing he would still prefer to accept the Beatles' offer. He undertook not to sell for three more weeks to give them time to conclude their bid.

But the Beatles' advisers were by now bogged down in internecine warfare. Klein claimed that the Eastmans were blocking his access to vital financial details within Apple. John Eastman accused Klein of imperiling the deal by boasts that he could get NEMS "for nothing" on the strength of sums owed to the Beatles in back payments. Though the deadline had not expired, it clearly would not be met. Clive Epstein sold out to Triumph for a mixture of cash and stock on February 17.

John Eastman flew back to New York. The Beatles continued discussions with Allen Klein—minus Paul. Instead, Paul would send along his lawyer, a Mr. Charles Corman. The others were amused at first that such a personage was meant to fill Paul's place at the board table. They would ask Mr. Corman why he hadn't brought along his bass guitar.

On March 11, Apple's press office issued a brief communiqué confirming the rumor it had for weeks been vigorously denying. Paul McCartney *was* to marry Linda Eastman. The ceremony would take place the following day in London, at Marylebone Register Office.

The bombshell exploded, among other places, in a small house in Redditch, Worcestershire, where Jill Pritchard, a traveling hairdresser, was giving one of her regular customers a shampoo and set. "Even before I heard it on the radio," Jill says, "I had a sort of premonition it had happened. I remember looking at the customer's little girl and wondering how she'd react.

"It was just a short announcement on the BBC News. I finished the shampoo and set, then I drove straight home and packed a little overnight bag. I'd got a bit of money that I'd always kept put by for an emergency. I got a friend to ring up my mum later and tell her where I'd gone. Then I drove to New Street Station in Birmingham and left my car on a No Waiting sign. I bought myself a ticket to London—first class, so I wouldn't have to sit and cry in a compartment full of people."

Late that night, wet-eyed and still carrying her suitcase, Jill Pritchard walked up Cavendish Avenue and joined the large, stunned crowd that had gathered there. The first girl she spoke to was Margo Stevens. "Is *she* in there?" Jill asked. Thousands of girls throughout Europe and America found it similarly impossible to articulate Linda's name.

"We all knew it was going to happen," Margo says. "We even knew Linda was pregnant. We'd seen the prescription that Rosie, the housekeeper, collected for her. But we kept hoping Paul would get out of it somehow. He was upset because we were taking it so badly. He'd come out to the gates to talk to us earlier in the day. 'Look, girls,' he said, 'be fair. I had to get married some time.' "

Every British newspaper, the day after Paul's wedding, carried pictures of the same desolately weeping girl. It was Jill Pritchard, the traveling hairdresser from Redditch. Photographers whirled her this way and that for most of the afternoon, shouting, "Go on—cry. You'll be in the papers." When Paul drove back with Linda after the ceremony, grief began to turn to violence. The security gates were forced apart, the front door was kicked, and wads of burning newspaper were pushed through the letterbox. After that, the police appeared and told everyone to disperse.

Margo, Jill, and the other regulars, drained of all emotion, adjourned to the nearest pub. "We heard later from Paul's housekeeper, Rosie, that he was really upset about us," Margo says. "He was standing just inside the front door, saying, 'I *must* go out and talk to them again.' But when he did come out, none of us was there any more. He couldn't believe we'd all gone away, so Rosie said. When he came back into the house, he was almost in tears."

That same night, a squad of police officers raided George Harrison's Esher bungalow, and found a total of 570 grains of cannabis. George was in London, recording his friend Jackie Lomax; when he returned he found the officers sitting with his wife, Patti, watching television and playing Beatles records. By an unkind coincidence, the name of the sniffer dog was "Yogi."

Eight days later, at the British consulate on Gibraltar, John and Yoko were quietly married. John wore a crumpled white jacket, an apostle-length beard, and tennis shoes. Yoko wore a wide-brimmed white hat, a matching mini-dress, and outsize sunglasses that made her face as expressionless as a panda's. They had decided on marriage suddenly while on vacation in Paris, and chosen Gibraltar as being "quiet, friendly, and British." Peter Brown made the arrangements from London, and himself flew out to be best man. John and Yoko posed for pictures with the consulate staff, saw what little of Gibraltar there was to see, then flew back to Paris to own up to the international press. "We're going to stage many happenings and events together," Yoko said. "This marriage was one of them."

The Beatles' American fan club organizer issued an appeal for tolerance of what the whole world greeted as John's worst aberration yet: "I know this news is shocking. Please try to understand that we should at least give Yoko the same chance we are giving Linda, and that Maureen and Patti got. If it makes John happy, I suppose we should all be enthused too."

Their honeymoon was the first of Yoko's promised happenings: It also inaugurated their campaign to promote that much desired but fast-fading hippie commodity, Peace. To promote the cause of peace they announced they would spend seven successive days in bed, at the Amsterdam Hilton hotel.

Most of the press who instantly converged on Amsterdam believed that the newlyweds had actually offered to make love in public. To their disappointment, they found John and Yoko merely sitting up in bed, in a suite decorated with placards reading "Bed Peace" and "Hair Peace." Few papers could understand, any more than could their progressively exasperated readership, how two people cocooned thus in the casual squalor of rock star hyperluxury, had any relevance to burned babies in Vietnam or Biafra's living skeletons. Even calling it, with that so-fashionable suffix, a "Bed-in" could not avert savage criticism of "the most self-indulgent demonstration of all time." But the press was, as always, unable to deliver the ultimate rebuff. It could not stay away. "Day Two of the Lennon Lie-In," ran a British headline. "John and Yoko Are Forced Out by Maria the Maid."

They moved on to Vienna for the first television showing of their film *Rape*—an action they depicted being performed by reporters and TV cameras. Later, in the Sacher Hotel's sumptuous Red Salon, they staged a second happening. This time, the press found them crouching on a tabletop inside a bag. It was, so John said, a demonstration of "bagism" or "total communication," in which the speaker did not prejudice the listener by his personal appearance. More bagism, he suggested, would generate more peace throughout the world. The British *Daily Mirror* spoke for the whole world in mourning "a not inconsiderable talent who seems to have gone completely off his rocker."

The loss of NEMS Enterprises had not discountenanced Allen Klein. The episode, indeed, had served Klein by revealing shortcomings in John Eastman that even his brother-in-law seemed to acknowledge. For it was with Paul's tacit agreement, or nondisagreement, that Klein began a counterattack designed to extricate the Beatles from the hold of the Triumph Investment Trust.

A week after Triumph's takeover of NEMS Klein visited the bank's chairman, Leonard Richenberg. There followed what Richenberg subsequently described as "various vague and threatening noises." According to Klein, the old NEMS company owed the Beatles large sums in unpaid fees from road shows dating back as far as 1966. They would forget these arrears if Triumph agreed to give up its 25 percent of their earnings Richenberg had bought up with NEMS. Richenberg's response showed him a worthy adversary. He requested Klein in words of one syllable to go away. No more successful was Klein's offer of a million pounds outright for Triumph's stake in the Beatles. Richenberg merely repeated his request to his visitor to depart.

Sir Joseph Lockwood, chairman of EMI, was Klein's next point of attack. Sir Joseph, a few days later, received a note, signed by all four Beatles, requiring that henceforward their record royalties were not to go to NEMS-Triumph but were to be paid direct to Apple. The letter was timely, since EMI was on the point of paying out Beatles' record royalties in the region of £1,300,000.

Leonard Richenberg had received a similar notification. He wrote back to Neil Aspinall, tersely rejecting the Beatles' claim that their contract with NEMS had expired when the *management* agreement did, in 1967. There remained the nine-year EMI contract, signed in January 1967, under which all record royalties were to be channeled via NEMS. Triumph Investments were thus entitled to collect their 25 percent for seven more years.

At EMI, Sir Joseph Lockwood faced the uncomfortable alternatives of breaking a manifestly binding legal obligation to NEMS-Triumph or alienating the affections of the four individuals on whom his company's fortunes largely rested. Sir Joseph, with great wisdom, elected to do neither. Triumph then sought a high court order to freeze the £1,300,000 pending the obviously protracted legal battle over it.

The application was heard on April 2 in the high court before Mr. Justice Buckley. Counsel for Triumph, Jeremiah Harman, QC, said that the Beatles had "fallen under the influence of Mr. Allen Klein, an American of somewhat dubious reputation." The judge, though inclined to agree, refused to freeze the money officially since, he said, EMI themselves would obviously not release it until the dispute was settled.

It was therefore left to Klein and Richenberg—in an atmosphere now tinged by mutual respect—to slug out a deal between them. Richenberg agreed to relinquish Triumph's 25 percent of Beatles earnings in exchange for eight hundred thousand pounds cash plus a quarter of the suspended £1,300,000. Triumph would buy out the Beatles' 10 percent of NEMS for just under half a million pounds' worth of the bank's own very desirable stock.

Klein could thus go back to the Beatles claiming to have turned defeat into victory. If they had not managed to acquire NEMS, at least NEMS had no further control over them. He had bought them freedom, in other words, from one cabal of men in suits. The Robin Hood of Pop, in his crumpled white polo-neck sweater, was one deal up on his rivals in the Apple camp. And if Allen Klein knew anything, he would soon be two deals up.

Dick James was always first to admit that he was one of the luckiest men alive. Pure chance had brought Brian Epstein to his office that morning long ago in 1962. Pure chance had ordained that James be there in person, to soothe Brian's ruffled feathers and listen to the demonstration disk he carried in his briefcase. So by pure chance it came about, as the voices pealed round his dusty Denmark Street cubbyhole, that Dick James, the so-so crooner, average song plugger, and now struggling music publisher realized he was on his way to his first million.

He had seized on that luck, of course, with some prescient fair-dealing. As publisher of the early Lennon-McCartney hits he could have been greedy, and lost them. Instead, he looked to the long term. He saw not only quality but quantity. So Heaven whispered in James's ear, prompting him to offer Brian a deal unprecedented in Tin Pan Alley. He would set up a song publishing firm exclusively for Lennon-McCartney music. It was piquant to remember Brian's disbelieving gratitude when Northern Songs was formed: "Why are you doing all this for us?"

When the company came into existence in 1963 Dick James and his partner, Emmanuel Silver, between them owned 50 percent. John and Paul had 20 percent each and Brian, 10 percent. James administered the company through his own Dick James Music Ltd. Ironically, he himself only ever published two Lennon-McCartney songs—the first one he ever heard, "Please Please Me," and the B-side "Ask Me Why." It was as a middleman that he grew wealthy, husbanding a store of hit songs that piled up faster almost than an old-time Tin Pan Alley plugger could count.

The Beatles laughed at James for his tubby shape, his bald head, his constant pleas for more nice *tuneful* numbers like "Michelle" and "Yesterday." His knowledge of the music business and its manifold dodges merged into the invisible shield that Brian Epstein built around them. It was James who, on the eve of a new Beatles single, would contact every American record station with dire legal admonitions not to break the release embargo. It was James who, after the initial chaos, maximized their American impact by ensuring that other singers and groups did not cover Lennon-McCartney material to excess.

In 1965, Northern Songs had been floated as a public company. Twenty-five percent of its 2s (10p) shares were offered on the London Stock Exchange at 7s 9d (38p) each and all were instantly snapped up—in financial as well as Beatles terms an instant number-one hit. Three thousand shareholders henceforward would turn to the record charts as well as the *Financial Times* to check on the health of their investment.

After the flotation, Dick James and his partner held 23 percent of Northern Songs. John and Paul held 15 percent each; NEMS Enterprises held 7.5 percent, and George and Ringo between them, 1.6 percent. By 1967—the year when two Beatles albums, *Revolver* and *Sgt. Pepper*, between them brought profits near the million-pound mark—shares in Northern had quintupled their 1965 value.

For any investor, the company's pièce de résistance were the 159 Lennon-McCartney copyrights, and John and Paul's contractual commitment to keep on composing until 1973. James, however, worked hard to create a wider catalog. By buying up moribund firms like Lawrence Wright Ltd., Northern Songs acquired such diverse musical properties as "Les Parapluies de Cherbourg"; "Among My Souvenirs"; and the theme from television's *Coronation Street* soap. James, indeed, worked for Northern somewhat at the expense of Dick James Music Ltd. But he was happy. Everyone in Tin Pan Alley said so. He reminded himself all the time how lucky he was.

Just lately, Dick James had been a little less happy than before. It was not that Lennon-McCartney music had declined in quality. "Hey Jude," in 1968, became a publishing success second only in worldwide sales to "Yesterday." The trouble was the increasingly erratic behavior of one-half of the publishing credit, and its effects on that sensitive organ the London Stock Exchange. John Lennon's espousal of the Maharishi, his involvement with Yoko, his bagism, his nudity—above all, his drug conviction—each produced disquiet among Northern's shareholders and fluctuations in its share price. As John's song publisher, James could be tolerant. As managing director of a public company with three thousand shareholders to consider, he fretted.

Lately, too, his relationship with the boys had grown somewhat strained. The deal that had seemed so miraculous in 1963 had, by 1969, become a source of vague resentment. The Beatles felt, quite simply, that James owned too large a share in their music. Nor was their resentment assuaged by James's habit of sending out inexpensive Christmas gifts such as plastic DJM monogrammed playing cards. A frosty reception had greeted him when he visited Twickenham studios during the *Let It Be* sessions.

As Northern Songs grew in prosperity, Dick James had received many offers for his 23 percent. Of these, the most persistent came from Lew Grade, Britain's most famous showbiz mogul, whose ATV network was already a minority shareholder, and who, in the dear dead music-hall days, had been James's own theatrical agent. "He'd been romancing me to sell out to him ever since Brian's death," James remembers. "It was a standing joke between us. 'Oh *no*,' I'd say, 'not *that* again, Lew!' "

It was the addition of Allen Klein to an already unstable Beatles landscape that suddenly changed James's mind. In March 1969, without prior warning, he sold his 23 percent of Northern Songs to ATV for something over one million pounds.

That the deal went through in secret was, as James would later admit, "rather unfortunate." In fairness, both John and Paul were out of the country on their respective honeymoons. John read the news in the papers on March 28, during his Amsterdam Bed-in. Paul found out a few days later in America. The news by then was that ATV, with 35 percent of Northern Songs under its belt, had bid £9,500,000 for the rest of the company.

John and Paul contacted one another, united in fury that Dick James had sold them down the river. It would have been fruitless to point out—had anyone dared try—that Northern Songs had long ago ceased to be theirs, but was the legitimate prey of whichever shareholder could gain the upper hand. All they knew was that, behind their backs, a major stake in their music had gone to a man who, with his large bulk and still larger Havana cigar, epitomized the hated breed of men in suits. The conciliatory noises that Lew Grade was already making might just as well have been the snarl of an alligator on the banks of the Zambesi.

Allen Klein was recalled from vacation in Puerto Rico to formulate plans for the Beatles themselves to oppose ATV's takeover of Northern Songs. The Eastmans, though still advising Paul, figured little in the subsequent drama. Paul, once again, was willing to let Klein act for him, in the troubleshooting capacity that was still unconfirmed by any written contract.

Klein's strategy was that the Beatles, already owning 31 percent of Northern Songs, should publicly offer £2 million for the further 20 percent that would give them a majority shareholding. The money was to come partly from the Beatles' own coffers, partly from a merchant banker, Henry Ansbacher & Co. Two Beatles companies, Subafilms and Maclen, together scraped up almost £1 million. Ansbacher's would provide the remaining £1 million, on collateral furnished by Apple shares and John Lennon's entire stock holding in Northern Songs. Paul— though he had recently increased his own Northern shareholding—refused to pledge any shares as security. Allen Klein completed the bond by guaranteeing £640,000 worth of ABKCO Industries' share in the MGM film corporation.

There now began seven weeks of business meetings, long and tortuous enough to surfeit even Allen Klein, in the winding course of which John and Yoko drifted, like rumpled white wraiths, through the grim purlieus of Threadneedle Street. John—to begin with, at least—enjoyed the negotiations. "It's like playing Monopoly," he said, "but with real money."

A third element in the ATV–Apple struggle had by now shown its hand. This was a consortium of city broker firms that, over several months, had quietly built up its own stake in Northern Songs to 14 percent. To capture the company, ATV or the Beatles must buy out—or, at least, win over—the consortium. And from the beginning it was clear the consortium, which included the Howard and Wyndham theater chain, was inclined to favor the Beatles.

The main stumbling block to what might otherwise have been an instantly done deal was Allen Klein. For the Robin Hood of Pop was currently enjoying a spell of notoriety in London's financial world just as intense as his recent one in New York's. The *Sunday Times*'s Insight investigative unit had just published a lengthy piece headlined "The

Toughest Wheeler-dealer in the Pop Jungle," delving into Klein's recent exploits, from the Cameo-Parkway shares furor to his activities as the alleged savior of the Rolling Stones. Insight also revealed how the Stones themselves had begun to turn against him, complaining that only a small portion of the $1.25 million advance he had wrung from Decca two years earlier had yet found its way into their bank accounts. There was also an impending lawsuit against Klein from the band's ex-manager, Andrew Loog Oldham, over Oldham's £1,000,000 payoff. From having pressed Klein on the Beatles as their only possible hope, the Stones were now urging them to have nothing to do with him.

Klein filed suit against Insight, then did his best to reassure the nervous city consortium that if they joined up with the Beatles to purchase Northern Songs, he would personally play no part in either the negotiations or the company's administration. He gave the same assurance in typically salty terms at a press conference that, the *Financial Times* said, "must have set some kind of a record for unprintable language." This promise was repeated two days later in a message to Northern's shareholders from Henry Ansbacher's. If their takeover bid were accepted, neither Klein nor the bankers themselves would play any part in the company's management. The board would be strengthened by the appointment of David Platz, head of the powerful Essex Music Corporation, as chairman. As a further inducement, John and Paul would extend their songwriting contract with Northern beyond its present 1973 expiration date.

By mid-May, Lew Grade was ready to concede defeat. The Beatles had successfully wooed the consortium, both with assurances of Klein's nonparticipation and also with promises of directorships for the Howard and Wyndham theater faction. Then, at the very last minute, the pact dissolved. John pulled the plug on the negotiations, announcing he was "sick of being fucked about by men in suits sitting on their fat arses in the City."

The consortium melted into Lew Grade's open arms—if not as sellers yet, then as fully committed allies. On May 20, ATV achieved effective control of Northern Songs. Grade expressed delight at having acquired a cache of songs that would live forever and hopes for an amicable future working relationship with their creators.

That same day's papers announced that Allen Klein had now officially been appointed the Beatles' business manager. Earlier reports that he would receive 20 percent of their earnings were described as "exaggerated."

The agreement had been signed on May 8. It bore the names of only three Beatles: John, George, and Ringo. Paul still had not refused outright: He said he wanted more time—as Klein had repeatedly promised he should have—to go through the management document with John Eastman and his English lawyer. But the others, John especially, had lost patience with Paul. Klein now told them he needed the signed agreement urgently to take back to New York to present to his ABKCO board. When the four Beatles met at Abbey Road on May 9, the deed had been done. "I see you've outvoted me," Paul said.

So Allen Klein and ABKCO Industries Inc. moved into 3 Savile Row, W1. Shortly afterward within the house, a soft and regular sound became audible. It was the sound of Apple executives perishing under the ax. Ron Kass, head of Apple Records; Denis O'Dell, head of Apple Films; Peter Asher, head of A&R; Brian Lewis, head of the contracts department, all left the Beatles' employment with as much dispatch as if a medieval catapult had propelled them through the white front door. It was the first phase of Klein's promised economy drive against those he condemned as pampered and unproductive management figures. That Kass and Asher between them were responsible for selling some sixteen million records on the Apple label did not for one instant stay the hand of their turtlenecked executioner.

After unnecessary management figures on Klein's death list came friends and dependents. The scythe swept upward through Apple's subdivisions: through Magic Alex and his electronic workshop; through Zapple, the spoken word label; through Apple Retail, Apple Publishing, and the Apple Foundation for the Arts. In vain did the victims appeal to their good friends John, Paul, George, or Ringo. The Beatles had suddenly become as remote as Tudor monarchs after signing warrants of execution. So it was even when Klein fired Alistair Taylor, Brian Epstein's original NEMS assistant, and a longtime friend and fixer for each of the four. Taylor, when his sentence was pronounced, spent a whole day on the telephone, trying to reach John or Paul to have his dismissal confirmed first-hand. Neither was available to discuss the matter. "The Beatles," John would admit, "are the biggest bastards in the world."

Klein's original intention was that not a single Apple executive should survive to stand between the Beatles and him. He even succeeded, for a short time, in toppling their two closest aides, Neil Aspinall and Peter Brown. Both were on the Apple board of directors, itself a gallows mark. "I gave Klein the perfect excuse," Peter Brown says. "We were just coming up to the annual general meeting. I told him that all the directors had to resign as a formality and then be reelected. Neil and I both resigned, but we weren't reelected. We thought the Beatles wouldn't ditch us, but they did."

Here at least Klein had gone too far. The Beatles could not function without Peter Brown, their immaculate minister of court. And Neil Aspinall, their oldest, truest, straightest friend, proved invulnerable to the headsman's axe. For Neil, Klein's coming was ultimately beneficial: It removed the weight of worry he had shouldered as road manager to the whole Apple fiasco. At first, when the burden went, Neil could not believe it had gone. He dreamed strange dreams that only a road manager to the Beatles could dream: of running in fear from some unknown pursuer, with both arms full of precious silver fish. The more he ran, the more his pursuer gained on him; as tightly as he tried to hold the silver fish, they always slipped from his grasp.

Gone was the holiday atmosphere of 3 Savile Row. Rather than showing up for work and leaving whenever they pleased, staff were now expected to clock in and out just like any other wage slaves in the unenchanted world outside. The perks they had formerly enjoyed—the food, the drinks, the drugs, the free gifts, the unlimited taxi rides—were all terminated. Nothing could be bought for the company without a purchase order signed by Klein or his lieutenant, Peter Howard. Charge accounts that had nourished hundreds dried up all over the West End.

It was no more than the way most hard-nosed American businesses were run, but Klein had a special genius for making people afraid of him. Everyone, from secretaries upward, felt themselves under the same nervous compulsion: to prove simultaneously that they were essential to Apple and that they posed no obstacle or threat to Klein. Even those he moved upward carried a kind of stigma. Jack Oliver, Ron Kass's young deputy, found himself suddenly in Kass's job as head of Apple Records, yet with no feeling that he had been promoted. "I was told: 'You're shit, you know that don't you, but this and this needs doing so get on with it.'"

Klein had annexed Peter Asher's old office on the third floor, opposite Derek Taylor's press department. It only added to the terror felt throughout 3 Savile Row that this office remained empty for several days each week, while Klein was in New York dealing with ABKCO Industries business. Then at some unguarded moment in the late afternoon of a day when he appeared to be absent, he would return. Jimmy Clark, on the front doorstep, would hurriedly straighten a dove-gray back. The chauffeur-driven car would draw up and disgorge a squat figure that, even in its walk of a few yards to the front door, could not bear to break off its study of balance sheets or *Billboard* magazine. Margo Stevens and the other members of the doorstep brigade had already formed their own conclusions without seeing his scary sidekick, Pete Bennett. As the door closed on Klein one of them would dart forward and shout "Mafia!" through the letterbox.

Klein, in fact, despite the May 8 agreement, was still not absolutely sure of his position. How could he be until all four Beatles recognized him as their savior? John Eastman remained on the scene, representing Paul and supposedly cooperating with ABKCO Industries in what had been described to the press as a "warm, workable relationship." Riven as he was with contempt for Eastman, Klein recognized that the relationship, if never warm, if barely workable, had to continue for the present. Sooner or later, he hoped to pull off a coup major enough to dazzle Paul out of his new fraternal obligations, and so complete the equation of Klein's heart's desire. Meanwhile, he contented himself with responding to Eastman's many challenging and provocative interoffice memos in a tone of Groucho Marxist sarcasm. "Dear John . . . I am on a diet, so stop putting words in my mouth."

A still greater incentive to Klein existed in the three-year contract that John, George, and Ringo had signed with ABKCO Industries. This, indeed, gave Klein 20 percent of their income—but only such income as was generated after his management began. Benefits gained through the NEMS and Northern Songs deal did not fall within the scope of the contract. To earn his 20 percent, as well as prove himself to the Eastmans and Paul, he must make a major killing in the field where he had strewn so many earlier corpses. Klein's next targets, in other words, were the Beatles' English and American record companies.

Sir Joseph Lockwood was surprised, shortly afterward, to be visited at his EMI office by Klein and all four Beatles. They had come, Klein announced, to renegotiate the nine-year contract that Brian Epstein had signed with EMI in 1967. "I said: 'All right, we can talk about it,' Sir Joseph recalled. 'Provided both sides get some benefit, there's no harm in renegotiating.' Klein said: 'No, you don't understand. *You* don't get anything. *We* get more.' "

"I told them to get out. They went, looking very sheepish. Paul was pulling faces behind the others' backs, as if to say, 'Sorry, it was nothing to do with me.'

"My assistant was very worried. 'You shouldn't have sent them off like this,' he said. I said, 'It's all right. I recognize the sort of man Klein is. He'll be back in half an hour.' And sure enough, half an hour later he rang me to apologize."

At 3 Savile Row Klein and the Beatles—except Paul—went into conference again. Margo and the other girls were beginning to recognize those conferences by the lights burning late in the big top-floor window. In the press office Derek Taylor's light projector cast its wriggling colored shapes over the wall. Journalists, still waiting for interviews, strained to catch scraps of gossip among insiders who were now all far on the outside.

"—they're just puppets now. I took something in to John and he just said: 'Give it to Klein.' "

"—they've calmed down a bit. They're eating scrambled eggs."

"—you know what happened to that note you sent in? Screwed up into a ball and thrown across the room."

On May 26, in a suite at the Queen Elizabeth Hotel, Montreal, John and Yoko staged a second, even more ambitious Bed-in. They had meant to hold it in the Bahamas but they decided on Canada as being closest to the country at which their Peace campaign was chiefly aimed (and which John, through his drug conviction, was now prohibited from entering). The Montreal Bed-in lasted seven days: It included an extended visit from Dr. Timothy Leary, live broadcasts to Canadian and U.S. radio stations, a hook-up with insurgent students at the University of California at Berkeley, and an encounter with right-wing humorist Al Capp, whose racist digs against Yoko almost got him thrown out on his ear. The climax was the recording at John and Yoko's bedside of the newly written campaign anthem "Give Peace a Chance" with a chorus that included Timothy Leary, Murray the K, Tommy Smothers, a rabbi, and a troupe of bald-headed, bell-ringing, chanting Radha Krishna Temple singers.

It was the prelude to two months in which John, with Yoko at his side, consciously set out to saturate the media with their demonstrations, their slogans—above all, with themselves as a living slogan: "Mr. and Mrs. Peace." For John, the campaign was tinged with aggressive satisfaction. He was turning the tables on the press, exploiting them in precisely the way he, as a Beatle, used to be exploited. He said so in a voice that still incised through the curly apostle beard, the woolly thought, the inherent heart-sinking fatuousness of representing sitting up in bed in a luxury hotel as a political, humanitarian act. "The Blue Meanies, or whatever they are, still preach violence all the time in every newspaper, every TV show, and every magazine. The least Yoko and I can do is hog the headlines and make people laugh. We're quite willing to be the world's clowns if it will do any good. For reasons known only to themselves, people print what I say. And I say 'peace.' "

In June, the campaign moved to 3 Savile Row. The front ground-floor office formerly occupied by Ron Kass was commandeered by John and Yoko for their own company, Bag Productions, and their continuing saturation of a still-acquiescent press. In a rooftop ceremony, before a somewhat bemused commissioner for oaths, John changed his name, dropping the Winston his mother had given him as a talisman against Hitler's bombs, becoming, instead, John Ono Lennon. Yoko became Yoko Ono Lennon. John was delighted to realize that their combined names contained nine letter O's, since nine had always been his lucky number.

Ron Kass's elegant salon next to the front door took on the appearance of a hotel bedroom during a Bed-in. Hand-lettered peace slogans and Lennon drawings papered the paneled walls. Newspapers, dirty plates, Magic Markers and Gauloises packets submerged the chaste white telephones. In the Georgian fireplace a plastic doll that had somehow escaped the King's Road napalm holocaust, stood on its head in a mess of cigarette butts. Yoko sat at the large executive desk with John a little to one side of her. The journalists were brought in at fifteen-minute intervals.

Sooner or later, in each interview, the talk would turn from peace and bagism to a question far more deeply significant to Western civilization. Was John truly, as he had said, reduced to his "last fifty thousand pounds'? Yes, he said. "All that stuff about us being millionaires is only true on paper, you know. All we've really got is our houses, our cars, and this place. In the old days with Northern Songs, you used to get a check occasionally. There's a deal now where a certain percentage of our royalties is paid into this place. So I haven't had any income for about two years. It's all been bloody *outcome*.

"Allen's putting it right for us now. We've made a lot of mistakes, but we're still here. The circus has left town, but we still own the site."

The presence of John and Yoko downstairs gave a new complexity to the already complex "vibes" gripping 3 Savile Row. Fear of Klein required that clerical staff should look brisk and businesslike, and sit behind their IBM typewriters like stenographic mice. Fear, no less well-founded, of the chief and ever-present Beatle demanded their help in collecting acorns to be sent by John and Yoko as a peace gesture to all world leaders from President Nixon to the king of Yemen. Since early summer is not acorn season, a countrywide appeal had to be launched. One elderly spinster sent in two dried-up specimens she had kept for forty years in a silver box. An entrepreneur, well-versed in the principle of Beatles supply and demand, offered a supply at one pound per acorn.

His Peace Campaign, in fact, aroused John to a belligerence frequently vented on this or that awe-struck Apple employee, unable to tell him, for instance, how to plaster the whole of London with Peace slogans. Ever since the *Two Virgins* fiasco he had suspected the whole house of intent to sabotage his and Yoko's personal projects. He suspected it even more now that their second album, *Unfinished Music No. 2—Life with the Lions*, had gone on release. The cover this time showed Yoko in the hospital after her miscarriage, with John in his sleeping bag beside her bed. The tracks were screech and electronic scribble, and a few seconds' heartbeat from the baby that had not survived. John bitterly resented the fact that the album was not mentioned in Apple's current radio promo.

And yet none of the Beatles, however artfully approached, would let slip a word against Yoko. "People think they're mad, both of them," Ringo said, "but that's not Yoko. That's just John being John."

On May 30, Apple released a single that at once seemed to show the Beatles reconciled to Yoko, and Yoko herself to be capable of figuring in an art form that was quite intelligible. This was "The Ballad of John and Yoko," a diary of the pair's recent peregrinations from the Amsterdam Hilton, "talking in our beds for a week," and "eating chocolate cake in a bag" in Vienna, to "honeymooning down by the Seine" when Peter

Brown sent word that they could "get married in Gibraltar, near Spain." "*Christ*, you know it ain't easy!" ran the refrain, so guaranteeing worldwide bans on airplay. As a gesture of apparent unity, the song was credited to Lennon-McCartney and its performance to the Beatles.

In fact, "The Ballad of John and Yoko" had been recorded by John virtually single-handed. George and Ringo were both out of the country. The drumming, overdubbed later, was Paul's.

It had been a typical gesture by a personality that, though outmaneuvered, outvoted, and furiously affronted by the events of the past months, still followed its old vocation of presenting the Beatles as a united and invulnerable front. It was no less symbolic of Paul's belief that the Klein era must pass and that, meantime, there was one safe refuge from him. Not even Allen Klein could harm the Beatles in any sphere where they made music together.

Early in July, Paul asked Ringo to drive up and have dinner with him and Linda at Cavendish Avenue. He had by then given up trying to dissuade John or George from appointing Klein. Ringo was, perhaps, a different story. Ringo had gone along with the others, saying that Apple needed "a hustler." But Paul evidently still had hopes of the solid common sense that, in so many ways, had given the Beatles their inner strength and balance.

The evening, however, did not turn Ringo against Klein so much as against Linda. "It seemed that as soon as I started saying, well, maybe Klein wasn't so bad and we should give him a chance, Linda would start crying. In a few minutes, I'd be saying the same—well, maybe he *isn't* so bad—and Linda would start crying again. 'Oh, they've got you, *too*,' she kept saying."

Apple, Paul's brainchild, his living Magritte, his Western Communism, was now repugnant to him. London was becoming almost as bad. The girls outside his gates showed increasing hatred of Linda: They broke into the house not just to look now but to steal the new Mrs. McCartney's clothes and photographic prints. When money began to vanish, even Paul's tolerance became exhausted. One day, he and Linda pretended to go out, then kept watch on the house from a garden across the street. Unfortunately, it was the moment chosen by Margo Stevens, his longest-standing admirer, to leave a bunch of flowers on the front step. "Suddenly, Paul ran up and started shaking me. 'It's *you* all the time, isn't it?' he kept shouting. I was terrified. I said, 'No—I only wanted to leave some flowers.' I think he could see how much he'd frightened me. He stopped shaking me and started stroking my hair."

Late in July, Paul got in touch with George Martin. It was now five months since Martin had worked on the *Let It Be* album. According to Paul, no one had yet been able to face editing the hours of ramshackle playing. The book that was to have accompanied the record had been written, but then heavily censored in proof by EMI. The film, originally intended for television, was now to be a full-length cinema feature, and so impossible to release before early 1970. The album, when edited, must therefore be held over to accompany the film.

Then Paul made a surprising request. The Beatles, he said, wanted Martin to produce an album for them "the way we used to do it." Martin, remembering his latter experience, responded cautiously. "I said: 'If the album's going to be the way it used to be, then all of you have got to be the way you used to be.' Paul said: 'Yeah, we will. We promise. Only please let's do the album.' "

So it happened, in July and August 1969, as the decade began to wear out, that its chief creators agreed to turn back the clock a little way. John suspended his Peace Campaign. George broke off from recording the chants of the London Radha Krishna Temple. Ringo interrupted his burgeoning film career. Paul steeled himself to remain in London a little longer. The four Beatles met, for the last time, at Abbey Road.

NINETEEN

"EVERYBODY SAW THE SUNSHINE"

On July 22, 1969, a human being first set foot on the moon. It was an oddly anticlimactic moment. Fictive representations of the great event for half a century past had imagined a planet inhabited by bellicose little green men, not the dead white wilderness that later close study had revealed. Storytellers in print and film alike had failed to realize, too, that as rocket science advanced, other technologies would keep step with it. Consequently, no one expected that when a first moon landing finally came, it could be televised to the whole world exactly as it happened; that, shown on black-and-white screens for hour after hour, it would gradually lose its initial stupendous fascination, becoming commonplace and ultimately even boring; so that by the time the astronaut Neil Armstrong took his carefully scripted "One small step for [a] man—one giant leap for Mankind," he would seem less like history's greatest explorer since Columbus than a kind of intergalactic disk jockey.

So, in their expiring months, the sixties turned from the dusty feathers of the past and shuffled reluctantly toward a new world shaped by the myriad tools and byproducts of space exploration: computers, microchips, digital clock faces, digital typefaces, nonstick saucepans, moon boots, clingfilm, the expression "We have lift-off."

For millions of the young, paradoxically, that moon-shot summer was devoted to getting as close as humanly possible to earth. In August came the free Woodstock festival when, on a small farm in upstate New York, a four-day pageant of top American and British rock acts was watched by a nonpaying crowd of 450,000, their spirits undampened by periodic rain and the sketchiest of life-support facilities; good-humored even in their message to a government that still wished to export their young men as cannon-fodder to Vietnam. "There ain't no time to wonder why," sang the giant open-air chorus led by Country Joe and the Fish. "Whoopee! we're all gonna die."

After Woodstock, the exotic notion of playing music for nothing spread like wildfire through the small, mutually imitative top echelon of rock bands. Doing a free concert was an easy way of becoming patron saints to the hippie subculture, who would afterward buy their records by the million at full price; it also symbolized a widespread breakaway from the control of old-fashioned, money-motivated managers. London had seen its own pioneering free festival earlier in the month when Eric Clapton and his new "supergroup" Blind Faith performed in Hyde Park before a crowd estimated at 150,000. That event also passed off happily and peacefully, and was followed by news of one still larger and more impressive. The Rolling Stones would give a free concert, also in Hyde Park, on July 5.

It would have been hard to imagine a one-shot live performance more unlike the one the Beatles had given for thirty-odd people among the Apple chimney pots in biting January cold. Half a million Stones fans massed around Hyde Park Corner to watch the band give the most riveting show of its career to date, fronted by Mick Jagger in what seemed to be an Edwardian little girl's white party frock. The concert was also a rite of mourning for Brian Jones, their recently dumped instrumental genius, who had been found dead in his swimming pool three days earlier. Jagger read a funerary passage from Shelley's "Adonais"—the signal for hundreds of symbolic white butterflies to be released—before settling down to simulate fellatio with a hand microphone.

On August 31 came the most remarkable of all Britain's free rock festivals, convened on the sleepy, 1950s-ish Isle of Wight and headlined by Bob Dylan, whom the organizers had tempted out of Beatle-like seclusion by stressing the island's associations with his favorite poet, Alfred, Lord Tennyson. After what proved a short, disappointing performance, Dylan was helicoptered away to what the press knew only as "a destination near London." It was in fact Tittenhurst Park, the rambling stately home in Sunningdale, Berkshire, now occupied by John Ono Lennon and Yoko Ono Lennon. As Dylan and John greeted each other in the gusts from the rotor blades, it was hard to say which of them had changed more out of all recognition.

Thunderous with alfresco guitars, perfumed with joss and pot, sparkling with sunshine and acid, it was as if this last summer of the sixties truly could, and would, go on forever. Young people lying half-naked in the grassy heat, romping in water, foam, or mud to the free sounds, for hectare after hectare, had found *anno Domini*'s nearest equivalent to the Garden of Eden. Though their power was soon to dissipate, if it ever really existed at all, they could point to this one irrefutable achievement. Never again in their lifetime would youthful crowds of half a million and more congregate together without wanting to harm each other or smash up the environment.

But the season was already changing. And the great guiding beacon for harmless joy in the past six-year golden age was being appropriated for darker purposes. From Los Angeles came news of random multiple murder on a scale previously associated only with gangland violence. A young movie actress named Sharon Tate, the pregnant wife of the Polish director Roman Polanski, and six friends had been hacked to death at Tate's luxury home by a hippie named Charles Manson and his "family" of largely female disciples. With his vaguely artistic as well as criminal tendencies, Manson was exactly the type who, a few months earlier, might have come begging at Apple's still-open door. He was also the first fan-turned-fiend; the prototype of Mark David Chapman and George Harrison's future stalker, Michael Abrams. Under questioning, Manson claimed to have received "guidance" to commit his atrocities from two songs on the Beatles' *White Album*, "Piggies" and "Helter-Skelter," the latter title having been found scrawled on walls throughout Sharon Tate's home in her and her fellow victims' blood.

Not all Apple creatures had perished under Allen Klein. In the press office there were still plastic birds, dipping and dipping their beaks around a shallow watertray. The press office, likewise, continued to function, though at what inscrutable whim of Klein's Derek Taylor could not claim to understand. Sometimes in mid-afternoon, when his department became too crowded and the Scotch and Coke fumes too uproariously thick, Taylor would raise himself in his scallop-backed throne, push the hair off his eyes, and shout, "Clear the room now! I mean it!" After one such dismissal, wandering in the sudden space behind Carol Paddon's desk, he paused by the water tray and studied the nodding birds. "Those beaks are going moldy," he remarked gloomily. "No one told us they'd do that when we bought them. They cost us one pound each."

Derek Taylor was a frustrated writer. But, unlike most frustrated writers, he had talent. Often he would have dismissed his court simply for the purpose of fighting his way back the few inches across his desk to the typewriter that stood there. He wrote a great deal during Apple's last year: essays and soliloquies and memoranda to himself, all on a theme as constant as the pressure on him from above, below, and sideways. Why do I work for the Beatles? And why, of all the complex emotions produced by working for the Beatles, is the commonest one simple fear?

"Whatever the motivation," Taylor typed, "the effect is slavery. Whatever the Beatles ask is done. I mean, whatever the Beatles ask is tried. A poached egg on the Underground on the Bakerloo Line between Trafalgar Square and Charing Cross? Yes, Paul. A sock full of elephant shit on Otterspool Promenade? Give me 10 minutes, Ringo. Two Turkish dwarfs dancing the Charleston on a sideboard? Male or female, John? Pubic hair from Sonny Liston? It's early closing, George (gulp), but give me until noon tomorrow. The only gig I would do after this is the Queen. Their staff are terrified of them, and not without reason. They have fired more people than any comparable employer unit in the world. They make Lord Beaverbrook look like Jesus."

Then the music would begin again, and Taylor, and Mavis Smith, and Carol Paddon—who was afraid to go on vacation lest her job should vanish—each remembered why they were sitting here. The stagnant sea of journalists and TV men remembered, or almost did. Taylor said the same thing into the telephone a dozen times each day. "It's called *Abbey Road*. Yes—the studios are in Abbey Road. It's an album just like they used to make. They sound the way they sounded in the old days."

Something had stopped the elements diverging and restored them to their old unsurpassable balance. *Abbey Road* was John Lennon at his best, and Paul McCartney at his best, and George Harrison suddenly reaching a best that no one had ever imagined. It was John's anarchy, straight and honed. It was Paul's sentimentality with the brake applied. It was George's new, wholly surprising presence, drawing the best from both sources. It was a suite of glorious new songs, not warring internally as on the *White Album* but merging their irreconcilably different viewpoints into a cohesive and balanced whole, and performed with the tautness and unartificiality they had sought for so long. It was the moment, caught again and crystallized, even in the flux of an expiring decade. It was hot streets, soft porn, and hippiedom fading into a hard reality. It was London here and now, and Liverpool then, and the

Beatles, dateless and timeless in a sudden, capricious illusion of perfect harmony.

It echoed throughout 3 Savile Row on September 11, then a date just like any other, as the Apple house girded itself to face whatever ructions this day might bring, its green carpets vacuumed smooth, its still-empty upper suites savory with the aroma of furniture polish. Here was the opening track, "Come Together," with its hissing percussion and all-too-obvious echoes of the Lennons' bedroom. Here was "Maxwell's Silver Hammer," another cutie-pie Paul song, but this time with an undertow of viciousness: "Bang bang Maxwell's silver hammer came down upon her head / Bang-bang Maxwell's silver hammer made sure that she was dead." Here was the ritual Ringo track, a children's song called "Octopus's Garden," as happy and optimistic as Ringo somehow remained, yet still with a wistful subtext of longing for the Beatles to be "under the sea . . . knowing they're happy and they're safe." Here was "Because," featuring the sweetest and closest group harmony since "Here, There and Everywhere," from a lyric jotted down by John on the reverse of one of John Eastman's most reproachful interoffice memos.

In the ground-floor office of Bag Productions, the first visitors were led in to meet John and Yoko. They were not journalists; they were two blind, middle-aged Texan women in pink and orange taffeta ballgowns. Each was led across to touch John, then Yoko led them to the group of four Plexiglas cabinets blocking the fireplace. It was the hi-fi system that John had ironically christened The Plastic Ono Band, and even credited with the playing of "Give Peace a Chance." Each blind girl's hand in Yoko's touched the featureless robots hopefully, like a shrine.

Next came the day-long line of reporters, primed with questions about peace; about John's interest in the Tate murder case, but mainly about the two films he and Yoko had shown that week at the Institute of Contemporary Arts. The first was *Rape*; the second, entitled *Self-Portrait,* was a forty-two-minute study of John's penis both in partial and full erection. "Anything that gets a reaction is good," he told the *New Musical Express.* "People are just frozen jellies. It just needs someone to do something to turn off the fridge." Yoko sat beside him, eating brown rice from a bowl with a long wooden spoon. She interjected only to regret that no serious critical comment had been directed at their film of John's penis. Or, as Yoko innocently said, "The critics wouldn't touch it."

George and Ringo were both at Savile Row that day. For Ringo, the errand was straightforward. He had come in to give Peter Brown details of the house he wanted to sell, having bought it from Peter Sellers a few months previously. Now he was tired of its extensive parkland, its private cinema and sauna baths and wide frontage, with fishing rights, on the River Wey.

"Do you want some apple jelly?" he asked Neil Aspinall.

"Apple *jelly*?" Aspinall echoed suspiciously, as if it were code for some new narcotic.

"Yeah, we've got hundreds of apples lying round our orchard," Ringo said. "So Maureen's made pots and pots of apple jelly."

George arrived, accompanied by his assistant, Terry Doran, to do a photographic shoot for a German magazine named *Bravo*. He was suddenly in demand, thanks largely to the song that, by common consent, was one of *Abbey Road*'s very best. George had written it months before while sitting in his friend Eric Clapton's garden. Forgetting his mantras and sitars, he had entitled it "Here Comes the Sun," and in that simplicity at long last touched a chord of the mystical. Perhaps its ultimate accolade was that, on first hearing it, most people mistook it for a "John" song, lead-sung by John. In the same way, years of exposure to Paul's melodic gifts had borne fruit in a ballad called "Something," the first-ever George song chosen for a Beatles single as the A side.

Upstairs, the *Bravo* photographer was waiting patiently beside a set banked high with flowers in Hare Krishna yellow and orange. An elderly workman staggered in, carrying a box containing the disconnected components of an eight-armed Hindu deity. Between them the photographer and he began to assemble the figure, trying to figure out which arm went into which socket. Even George seemed impressed by the thoroughness of the preparations. "If I'd known it was going to be like this, I'd have washed me hair," he said. As the shoot was about to start, he decided that his blue denim shirt and jeans were not a suitable outfit. A press office secretary was sent to the nearby Mr. Fish boutique to buy half a dozen silk shirts for him to choose from. As he looked through them he tried to answer an English journalist's question, the same old one—how had Apple managed to go so wrong? "It was like a game of Chinese whispers, really," George said. "We said one thing, it was passed along among lots of other people, and what came back to us wasn't anything like we'd meant."

The Beatles ceased to exist that afternoon, when Anthony Fawcett, John and Yoko's personal assistant, picked up a ringing telephone from the debris of papers and plates. It was a Canadian entrepreneur asking if John and Yoko would attend a rock 'n' roll revival concert in Toronto the following day. John took the telephone from Fawcett: He would go, he said, but only if he were allowed to perform. Within hours, the Plastic Ono Band had metamorphosed from Plexiglas robots into an ad hoc supergroup consisting of John, Yoko, Eric Clapton, Klaus Voorman, and Alan White. A charter airliner was booked to carry them, if John got up in time and did not take fright at the last minute at the thought of appearing with an unrehearsed band before an audience of thousands.

In the studio, George was still being photographed by *Bravo* magazine in his chosen Mr. Fish shirt, against the Hindu idol and the banked yellow flowers. Ringo wandered in to say hello and, as a keen photographer himself, to check out the professional camera equipment being used. "You want to use a zoom lens through that prism," he advised the *Bravo* photographer.

"Do you fancy going to Australia to play?" George asked him in ironic reference to John's impending twenty-four-hour Canadian visit.

"When do we get back?"

"Tomorrow."

Two floors down, the press office was, as usual, plunged into darkness, speckly with psychedelic light shapes, crowded with expectant, seated figures, and reverberant with the aural sunshine of the *Abbey Road* album. In one corner, Mal Evans's discovery, the Iveys—now renamed Badfinger—sat, like very young pantomime pirates, awaiting news of their first release on the Apple label. Mary Hopkin, a sweet, frail, bewildered girl, passed through with her even more bewildered Welsh parents. Neil Aspinall came in to say that the Plastic Ono Band had got away to Canada on the second charter airliner asked to stand by after they missed the first one.

Now on *Abbey Road* the Apple house heard the voice that had first imagined it, and argued to launch it, and that had now abandoned it, leaving only a song lyric behind as explanation. "You never give me your money," sang Paul to the manager he would not recognize. "You only give me your funny paper." He had contrived to make the album that was an act of reunion serve also as an outlet for his bitter frustration, even though, being Paul, he could only do so in hints, between the smiles of one who still hated to admit any unpleasantness.

By late afternoon, after its umpteenth play, it was as though *Abbey Road* told the Beatles' whole life story in miniature, from the effortless good sex of "Come Together" to the finish of side two, where the narrative splintered into unfinished scraps and intros that led nowhere: the mystical "Sun King," the Sergeant-Pepper-ish "Mean Mr. Mustard," the Scouse wisecracking "Polythene Pam" ("she's the kind of a ge-erl who reads the *News of the We-erld* . . ."), the memory of some relentless groupie in "She Came in through the Bathroom Window." Here, if not in real life, Paul had the last word, with his tender cradle song "Golden Slumbers"; his little wink and nod ("Her Majesty's a pretty nice girl") to the monarch who would one day knight him; his coded warning to those who had beaten him that they would "carry that weight a long time." Here, prematurely, from Paul was an epitaph for the band that would never be bettered:

And in the end, the love you take
Is equal to the love
You make.

That September, in the heady aftermath of festivals and free concerts, Paul made one last effort to reunite the others on stage again. His idea now was that they should play at small clubs, unannounced, perhaps even in disguise. Ringo supported the idea and George, though noncommittal, did not refuse outright. But John told Paul bluntly he must be daft. "I might as well tell you," John continued, "I'm leaving the group. I've had enough. I want a divorce, like my divorce from Cynthia."

He had reached his decision while flying back with Yoko, Eric Clapton, and Klaus after their tumultuous welcome at the Toronto rock 'n' roll festival. Standing up there with Yoko and the robots, singing any words that came into his head, he had realized that ceasing to be a Beatle need not strike him blind. "Cold Turkey," his new song, named for heroin's withdrawal horrors, was written to renounce an even worse addiction. He would never again be hooked by "Yesterday" or "Ob-la-di, Ob-la-da." All that remained was to do what his idol Elvis Presley had never been able to, and "break out of the palace."

What restrained him was an urgent plea from Allen Klein not to jeopardize the deals Klein still hoped to do on behalf of the Beatles as a unit. For Klein, at that very moment, was on the brink of an unequivocal coup concerning their record royalties. Having failed to browbeat EMI he had set about browbeating their American label, Capitol. Bob Gortikov, Capitol's president, under pressure from Klein, was proving less inflexible than Sir Joseph Lockwood. But clearly, for John to announce his resignation would seriously weaken Klein's bargaining position. John, therefore, agreed to keep silent—even to the other Beatles—until the Capitol deal was done.

It was a promise he found impossible to keep when Paul, in another long boardroom wrangle, brought up the subject of live performing again. A furious row developed, with John railing bitterly at Paul for his "granny" music, especially "Ob-la-di" and "Maxwell's Silver Hammer," on the *Abbey Road* album, which John had particularly detested. He told Paul he was sick of fighting for time on their albums, and of always taking the B sides on singles. Then, rather tactlessly, he pointed at George as perennial victim of the Lennon-McCartney "carve-up." Paul replied that only this year had George's songs achieved comparable quality with theirs. George interrupted resentfully that songs he had recorded this year were often those he had written years earlier but not been allowed to release. He added that he had never really felt the Beatles were backing him. As John rounded angrily on George, Paul made a sudden, quiet plea to them to remember how they had always overcome disagreements in the past. "When we go into a studio, even on a bad day, I'm still playing bass, Ringo's still drumming, and we're still *there*, you know."

Paul could not believe that John's resignation was anything other than a fit of temperament—like George's during the *Let It Be* sessions. When the white Rolls-Royce moved off down Savile Row that afternoon, it had been agreed not to dissolve—for the time being. Not long afterward, a slightly stunned president of Capitol Records agreed to Allen Klein's demand for an unheard-of royalty of sixty-nine cents on each Beatles album sold in America. Derek Taylor spoke to Bob Gortikov shortly after Gortikov ended his last session with Klein. "We would have done the deal anyway," Gortikov said, "but did he have to be so *nasty* about it?"

According to Klein, the deal with Capitol swung Paul in his favor at last. "Paul congratulated me on the agreement. He said, 'Well, if you *are* screwing us, I can't see that you are.' " Paul's version, sworn subsequently in a high court affidavit, was that, on the contrary, he felt uneasy to think the Beatles had received a massive royalty increase at the very moment when their future together was so uncertain. Also, by that time, he had ceased to believe anything Klein said. The most public and PR-conscious Beatle retreated into complete seclusion, with Linda and their newborn daughter, Mary, on his farm in Argyllshire.

With the Capitol deal Klein was assured of his 20 percent. He could now turn his attention back to the five months' stalemate over Northern Songs and Lew Grade's ATV network. Grade, having gained effective control of Northern, now hoped to woo the Beatles into accepting him as a sort of supercharged Dick James. His plan was to buy out the Howard and Wyndham consortium's blocking 14 percent, but to persuade John and Paul to retain their 31 percent, and extend their songwriting contract beyond the present expiration date in 1973.

Late in October, ATV finally bought out its consortium partner, bringing Lew Grade's share of Northern to slightly more than 50 percent. Hours afterward, it was announced that John and Paul, and Ringo, were selling their combined 31 percent shareholding to ATV. The news, when it reached Apple—by a tip-off from the *Financial Times*—sounded very like defeat. Allen Klein, interviewed during his customary afternoon breakfast, claimed it as a victory. A threatened lawsuit against Northern for five million pounds in allegedly unpaid Beatle royalties helped to persuade ATV to pay cash rather than stock for the Beatles' holdings. Klein could thus congratulate himself on having enriched John and Paul by about a million and a half pounds each, and Ringo by eighty thousand pounds.

The American release of *Abbey Road,* together with Paul McCartney's disappearance, now produced one of Beatlemania's strangest and sickest by-products. A Detroit disk jockey claimed to have received a mysterious telephone call telling him that Paul McCartney was, in fact, dead, and that corroboration could be found in the *Abbey Road* cover photograph. This, though it might appear a somewhat unimaginative shot of the four Beatles walking over a St. John's Wood zebra crossing, actually, the mystery caller said, represented Paul's funeral procession. John, in his white suit, was the minister; Ringo, dark-suited, was the undertaker, and George, in his shabby denims, the grave-digger. Still stronger funereal symbols were divined from the fact that Paul himself walked barefoot, out of step with the other three, and smoking a cigarette right-handed. The clinching clue alleged was a Volkswagen car parked in the background, plainly showing its numberplate "28 IF"—or Paul's age *if* he had lived.

Picked up by other disk jockeys, elaborated by Beatles fanatics, the rumor swept America, growing ever more earnestly complex and foolish. One faction claimed that Paul had been murdered by the CIA. Another—the most powerful—claimed he had been decapitated in a car accident and that actor William Campbell had undergone plastic surgery to become his double. Scores of further "clues" to support this theory were discovered in earlier Beatles albums—in the scraps of gibberish and backward tapes; the fictional "Billy Shears" mentioned in *Sgt. Pepper*, and various macabre John Lennon lines from "A Day in the Life" and "I Am the Walrus." It was said that by holding the *Magical Mystery Tour* EP cover up to a mirror a telephone number became visible on which Paul himself could be contacted in the Hereafter. The number, in fact, belonged to a *Guardian* journalist, subsequently driven almost to dementia by hundreds of early morning transatlantic telephone calls.

In America, an industry grew up of "Paul is Dead" magazines, TV inquests, and death disks—"Saint Paul," "Dear Paul," "The Ballad of Paul," and "Paulbearer." It was all something stranger than a hoax: It was a self-hoax. Even when Paul himself surfaced on the cover of *Life* magazine, the rumors did not abate. Consequently, Beatles record sales in America in October 1969 rose to a level unequalled since February 1964. *Abbey Road* was to sell five million copies, a million more even than *Sgt. Pepper*. The Beatles, not Paul, had died; yet how could that be when they seemed bigger and better than ever?

John kept his promise to say nothing of the breakup. And in a strange way, his and Yoko's continuing notoriety served as camouflage. In November, he renounced his MBE, taking it from the top of his aunt Mimi's television set and sending it back to the Queen as a protest against Vietnam, the war in Biafra, and the failure of "Cold Turkey" to remain in the British Top Twenty. Though that final flippancy made the gesture futile, it was not without a certain coincidental irony. For the statesman who had bought his own popularity with that same small, pink-ribboned medal still reigned at 10 Downing Street. What Harold

Wilson had started with the Beatles he had continued less and less discerningly, showering MBEs, CBEs, knighthoods, and peerages on any cheap entertainer who might cadge him a headline or a vote.

All politicians had learned something from Harold Wilson. In Canada, Prime Minister Pierre Trudeau held talks with John and Yoko to hear their plan to turn 1970 into "Year One for Peace," commemorated by another vast open-air concert in Toronto. *Rolling Stone* magazine named John as "Man of the Year." "A five-hour talk between John Lennon and Richard Nixon," said *Rolling Stone,* "would be more significant than any Geneva Summit Conference between the USA and Russia."

In Times Square, New York, and prominent places in half a dozen other American cities, vast billboards carried a cryptic seasonal message. "War is Over if You Want it. Happy Christmas From John and Yoko." In London, the *Beatles Monthly* ceased publication. Princess Margaret attended the premiere of a new film, *The Magic Christian,* featuring Ringo in a small cameo part. In Campbeltown, Argyllshire, Paul put the final touches to an album he had tried to make already, with *Revolver, Sgt. Pepper,* and *Let It Be*—an album for no one but Paul.

Before 1970 had even arrived came an event foreshadowing the new face of rock music. The Rolling Stones decided to conclude their current money-soaking American tour by giving another free show, this time on a motor-racing track in Altamont, California. The event quickly turned into a nightmare, thanks to the drunken brutality of the Hell's Angels who had been hired as security. Its climax was the fatal stabbing of a young black spectator while Mick Jagger vainly appealed to the crowd to "cool out" and love one another. Good-bye Sixties; welcome to the future.

Three Savile Row already felt the vibes of the new decade. A house that had stood elegantly intact for two centuries before the Beatles' coming seemed to decide deep within itself that the effort was no longer worthwhile. The rear promontory began to subside, throwing an ugly crack slantwise across the Cordon Bleu kitchen wall. The apple-green carpets were scuffed and threadbare. The deep leather sofas were cracked and split. Most of the framed gold records on the staircase wall had been stolen. On the front stairs the oil painting of lion cubs was torn at one corner where someone had tried to wrench it from its frame.

Though the front door frequently stood wide open, no invaders seized the chance to stampede through it. The Apple scruffs in their front-step purdah had risen above such immature displays. Now they wore badges, denoting seniority and precedence; they had their own magazine, even their own notepaper, headed 'Steps', 3 Savile Row. Margo, their leader, had crossed the ultimate threshold on their behalf: She now worked inside Apple as a teamaker. She had served George with cheese and cucumber sandwiches and Ringo with a one-egg omelette. She had seen how ordinary, how rather pale and pockmarked, were the gods whom she had worshipped for the past three years of her life, in all weathers.

The press office continued functioning, but in broad daylight and a quiet that grew steadily more ominous. John had unilaterally fired the whole department, transferring his publicity arrangements to the Rolling Stones' press agent, Les Perrin. Derek Taylor had left, at George's kindly insistence, to finish the book he had been trying to start since 1968. Carol Paddon was fired for telling the *Daily Sketch* the truth, that Apple was "just an accounting office now." Mavis Smith, the ex–Ballet Rambert dancer, and Richard DiLello, the "house hippie," stayed on for the present. All around the room, on the desk supporting a scarlet torso; on the desk with the light-show projector; on the desk next to the nodding birds—one by one the telephones stopped ringing.

It was in such a dismal morning-after spirit that the Beatles' *Let It Be* project limped, at last, toward a conclusion. Klein had sold the film to United Artists, and expected it to open in London in late spring. The album tapes, recorded a year earlier, had been exhumed from Apple's now sepulchral basement studio. There remained only the job of making an LP from those uncounted hours of rehearsing, improvising, joking, jamming, and angry argument.

With the Beatles' consent, Klein had brought in the American producer Phil Spector to do that sifting and editing job that they themselves could not face. Spector's girl groups and "wall of sound" technique had been among their earliest and strongest influences: He was, at the same time, renowned for Gothic overelaboration and triumphant bad taste. His appointment to doctor what had begun as an "honest, no nonsense" Beatles album only confirmed the weary indifference they now felt to their music, as well as to each other.

Spector labored, and an album duly went to EMI for pressing. It was, inevitably, a strange, inconclusive affair. Half of it chronicled the sessions as they had happened, with tuning-up noises and parody announcements by John, amid sycophantic laughter from the film crew. The other half had been remixed and augmented by Phil Spector in his own inimitable way. An acetate went to each Beatle accompanied by a long letter from Spector, justifying what he had done but assuring them he would make whatever changes they wished.

When Paul played the acetate he found that his ballad "The Long and Winding Road" had been remixed, then dubbed with a violin and horn section and topped with a sickly celestial choir. Paul tried to contact Spector, but could not. He wrote to Allen Klein, demanding the restoration of his original version, but to no avail. It was the final affront of the Klein era that the most tyrannically particular and perfectionist Beatle should find he no longer controlled even the way he sang his own songs. Paul decided at last to stop fighting against fighting.

He had completed his solo album in Scotland, with no editor but Linda and no help but from Linda, that untried musician, on backing vocals. In March he returned to London and rang up John, breaking a silence of almost six months.

"I'm doing what you and Yoko are doing," Paul said. "I'm putting out an album and I'm leaving the group, too."

"Good," John replied. "That makes two of us who have accepted it mentally."

Paul then notified Apple, or what remained of it, that he wanted his solo album, *McCartney,* to be released on April 10. The date was vetoed by Klein and all the three other Beatles as clashing with the release of *Let It Be,* and also Ringo's first solo album, *Sentimental Journey.* Paul, suspecting Klein of sabotage, appealed directly to Sir Joseph Lockwood at EMI. Sir Joseph said he must accept the majority decision.

Ringo well-meaningly visited Cavendish Avenue to add his personal explanation to letters he had brought from John and George, confirming that Paul's solo debut would have to be postponed. Ringo, in his own subsequent high court affidavit, described his dismay when Paul "went completely out of control, prodding his fingers towards my face, saying, 'I'll finish you all now,' and, 'You'll pay!' He told me to put on my coat and get out."

The outburst showed Ringo, at least, what a gigantic emotional significance the *McCartney* album had for Paul. It is a testament to his eternal good nature that after Paul threw him out, Ringo went straight back to John and George and talked them into giving Paul his way. Ringo's *Sentimental Journey* LP was brought forward and *Let It Be* put back so that *McCartney* could appear, as Paul now agreed, on April 17.

Its release gave Paul the opportunity to do what John had been dissuaded from doing the previous October. Included with the album was a smiley yet barbed "self-interview" in which he made clear that he was leaving the Beatles—at least, as clear as Paul could make anything:

Q: Are all these songs by Paul McCartney alone?

A: Yes, sir.

Q: Did you enjoy working as a solo?

A: Very much. I only had to ask me for a decision and I agreed with me. Remember Linda's on it too, so it's really a double act.

Q: The album was not known about until it was nearly completed. Was this deliberate?

A: Yes because normally an album is old before it comes out. (Aside) Witness "Get Back."

Q: Are you able to describe the texture or feel of the album in a few words?

A: Home. Family. Love.

Q: Will Paul and Linda become a John and Yoko?

A: No, they will become Paul and Linda.

Q: Is it true that neither Allen Klein nor ABKCO Industries have been or will be in any way involved with the production, manufacturing, distribution, or promotion of the record?

A: Not if I can help it.

Q: What is your relationship with Klein?

A: It isn't. I am not in contact with him and he does not represent me in any way.

Q: What do you feel about John's Peace effort? The Plastic Ono Band? Giving back the MBE? Yoko's influence? Yoko?

A: I love John and respect what he does—it doesn't give me any pleasure.

Q: Are you planning a new album or single with the Beatles?

A: No.

Q: Is this album a rest away from the Beatles or the start of a solo career?

A: Time will tell. Being a solo album means it's the start of a new career and not being done with the Beatles it's a rest. So it's both.

Q: Is your break with the Beatles temporary or permanent, due to personal differences or musical ones?

A: Personal differences, business differences, musical differences, but most of all because I have a better time with my family. Temporary or permanent? I don't know.

Q: Do you foresee a time when Lennon-McCartney become an active songwriting partnership again?

A: No.

Q: Did you miss the Beatles and George Martin? Was there a moment, e.g., when you thought: "Wish Ringo was here for this break"?

A: No.

The announcement enraged John, who had longed to quit years ago but had always kept on in the band for the sake of their common good. Now here was Paul, self-centered as ever, not only walking out when he felt like it, but also making out he was first to want to. Or as John put it bitterly, saying he'd had enough long after everyone else had left the stage.

On May 20, *Let It Be,* the Beatles' last film and final appearance together, received its British premiere simultaneously in London and Liverpool. A large billboard had been erected over the London Pavilion, on which four faces, fenced off from each other, stared out with expressions of faint nausea befitting this one more perfunctory ordeal. In Liverpool, a civic welcome waited in the foyer of t he movie theater: the lord mayor, aldermen, dignitaries, and old friends. The train supposed to be bringing the Beatles pulled in to Lime Street, but they did not alight from it. Nor did they from the train after that. The civic welcome waited for the next train, and the next.

The Beatles were gone, but how could they be when the screen showed them as always: together, advancing? It was their last trick to make those tired, year-old scenes, at Twickenham studios and in the Apple basement, seem fresh and exciting, full of promise for the future that so obviously could not be. *Let It Be* was their sad fading; it was also the desperate sadness that they must fade. It was Paul and John singing "Two of Us," rather pale and subdued like marriage partners after a terrible row, admitting they had been "chasing paper, getting nowhere," but now seemingly in agreement about being "on our way home." It was Paul when he sang "The Long and Winding Road" in its proper version, with only Billy Preston's keyboard and himself on piano: his make-believe beard, his make-believe hobo suit, his great, round, regretful eyes. It was Paul again, singing "Let It Be," the mollifying phrase of a Liverpool mother to a fractious child, as if he forgave and had been forgiven and everything would get better now.

It was the scene in Savile Row when lights still filled every Apple window, and the big white cars drew up outside. It was the day when clamor split the Mayfair skies; when people came across rooftops and climbed down fire escapes to look, and people in the streets stared upward. It was the old soldier in a porkpie hat whom the film crew stopped and asked for comment: "Yus—well, the Beatles, what I say is, you can't beat 'em. They're out on their own. They're good people. I say, good luck to 'em."

It was the rooftop concert with their hair blowing into their eyes, with Ringo in a red plastic raincoat, George in green trousers, John in a ladies' short fur coat. It was four musicians playing together as no four musicians ever could or ever would again. It was voices singing "The One After 909," the way they used to on truant afternoons at Forthlin Road. It was slow-motion guitars in the biting wind as John summed up their gift to their generation, all those World War II babies who'd thought there was nothing ahead but grayness and rationing. "Everybody had a good time. Everybody had a wet dream. Everybody let their hair down. Everybody saw the sun shine." It was "Get Back" dying into discord as the police finally found their way up to the roof, as the drumbeat failed, the electricity was turned off, and the derisive Lennon voice speaking as if in mock humility to Larry Parnes, all those years ago at the Jacaranda Club:

"I'd like to thank you very much from the group and ourselves, and I hope we passed the audition."

PART FIVE

LASTING

TWENTY

"I JUST BELIEVE IN ME. YOKO AND ME"

The breakup, in fact, was to stretch over fifteen months, between September 1969, when John told the other three privately that he wanted out, and December 1970, when Paul confirmed the split unequivocally by beginning unilateral legal action against Allen Klein. It was an odd period of limbo, with all four Beatles leading determinedly separate lives and billions of fans still hoping, even praying, for their reconciliation.

John and Yoko initially went to ground at Tittenhurst Park, their Georgian mansion in Sunningdale, Berkshire. The house was equipped with its own private studio where John could set to work on a second solo album without fear of anyone objecting to his wife's presence or creative input. To work with him he summoned Phil Spector, who had put the chaotic *Let It Be* album into releaseable shape, albeit to Paul's unforgiving disgust. These Tittenhurst sessions included a simple voice-and-piano track that was to become John's post-Beatles masterpiece. "Imagine no possessions," he sang wistfully, forgetful of his rambling stately home and seventy-two-acre estate. It was also at Tittenhurst that the famous "Imagine" video was shot, with John seated at a white grand piano in a long, white room, and a white-gowned Yoko drawing back curtains as if on the vista of their new life together.

In March 1971, the British high court granted Paul's suit to remove the Beatles' partnership from Klein's control and place it in the hands of a receiver, meaning that the break between the four was now legal and irrevocable. The following September John and Yoko closed the white drapes at Tittenhurst Park for the last time and moved to America.

Their ostensible reason was to win custody of Yoko's seven-year-old daughter, Kyoko, from her former husband, the American filmmaker Tony Cox. Though originally well-disposed toward John, the eccentric Cox had undergone the first of a series of religious transfigurations, and now furiously execrated his ex-wife and her ex-Beatle spouse as ungodly dope fiends. When ordinary diplomatic methods failed John and Yoko resolved to snatch Kyoko from her father who, by a bizarre twist, had lately become a disciple of the Maharishi Mahesh Yogi. While Cox attended a course with the Maharishi on the island of Majorca, the Lennons abducted Kyoko from the children's nursery, but were forced to return her after spending some hours in police custody.

Their lawyers' advice was to seek legal guardianship of Kyoko in the American Virgin Islands, where Yoko had obtained her divorce from Cox. The order was granted, but could only be put into effect within the United States, where Cox, his second wife, Melinda, and Kyoko were now thought to be living. The Lennons therefore would have to take up residence in America.

It was meant to be only a temporary, pragmatic arrangement, but John had already made up his mind not to return to Britain. He had had enough of its intrusive media, its racist attacks on Yoko, and the business meetings he described as "rooms full of old men, smoking and fighting." America not only promised refuge and relative anonymity, but still had magic as the heartland of his musical first love, rock 'n' roll. He never forgot how, as a no-hope teenager, he would stand on the Liverpool Pier Head and gaze out over the gray waves of the Atlantic Ocean, excited to think that "the next place was America."

Going to the opposite extreme of Tittenhurst Park, he and Yoko moved into what was little more than a glorified studio apartment in New York's West Village. More than ever like twins in their matching convict crops and sunglasses, both were soon immersed in the harsh radical politics that had elbowed aside sixties-style love and peace. For John, it was as if the Statue of Liberty had reached down and touched him personally with her beacon. The image-fettered pop star who had once been scared to voice even mild criticism of the Vietnam War now publicly allied himself to Black Power revolutionaries like Malcolm X and Angela Davis, and icons of the yippie movement Jerry Rubin and Abbie Hoffman. The one-time male chauvinist who'd kept his first wife in child-rearing purdah became a vociferous convert to the feminist movement, writing a song based on Yoko's axiom "Woman is the nigger of the world" that would appear on his 1972 album, *Sometime in New York City.*

His songwriting style had changed absolutely, from the allusiveness of "Strawberry Fields Forever" and "A Day in the Life" to graffiti-simple political tracts like "Give Peace a Chance," "Power to the People," and "Happy Xmas (War is Over)," which was to top radio Christmas playlists forever afterward. He was determined to put his Beatle past, and all its monstrous highs and lows, totally behind him; to prove that, unlike Elvis Presley, he *could* break out of the palace. The message was hammered home by his new, acrid solo voice on an album with the Plastic Ono Band: "I don't believe in Beatles . . . I just believe in me . . . Yoko and me . . . and that's reality."

Another kind of exorcism was giving a marathon interview to Jann Wenner, whose *Rolling Stone* magazine had set new standards in thoughtful and analytical rock journalism. John's testament ran to thirty thousand words and was later published as a book, *Lennon Remembers*. In it, he declared he had outgrown George Martin ("he's more Paul's sort of music than mine") and alleged that some of the worst "shit" thrown at Yoko had come from Apple's managing director, Peter Brown, and—surprisingly—from George Harrison. Indeed, he largely blamed his and Yoko's recent resort to heroin on "what the Beatles and their pals were doing to us."

But Wenner's tentative question, "You were really angry with Paul?" brought a strangely muted response. "No, I wasn't angry," John replied. "I was just . . . shit! He's a good PR man, Paul. I mean, he's about the best in the world, probably. He really does a job."

Even so, his bitterness against Paul continued to fester, for reasons that even now are difficult to fathom. True, Paul had displaced him as head Beatle, but only at the very end, when he himself could no longer be bothered. As he half-told *Rolling Stone*, he was furious about Paul's public resignation from the band on the *McCartney* album when he himself had effectively quit six months earlier. Yet even this does not explain his later remark to Yoko that no one had ever hurt him the way Paul hurt him. He might have longed to get away from Paul, but he could never quite get over him.

Paul, too, had been far more wounded than he ever showed, and no longer cared about preserving diplomatic niceties. On the second McCartney solo album, *Ram*, was a veiled reference to John's having thrown away his talent by going off with Yoko ("You had your lucky break and you broke it in two"). John's *Imagine* album—despite the plea for universal peace and brotherhood in the title track—launched a thermonuclear strike back at Paul with "How Do You Sleep?" a title suggesting crimes almost in the realm of first-degree murder. The McCartney references were unmistakable and often cruelly unjust: "The freaks was right when they said you was dead. . . . The only thing you done was Yesterday." There was even a two-fingered gesture of contempt for Paul's new outdoor life with Linda on their Scottish farm. The *Ram* album's cover had shown him in rural outdoor mode, holding down a ram by its curly horns. Inside the *Imagine* album jacket was a postcard picture of John, playfully wrestling with a pig.

To his credit, John realized that his life in the Beatles, and before, had left him in serious need of psychiatric help. Before leaving Britain, he and Yoko had signed up for extensive sessions with the therapist Arthur Janov, whose primal scream technique encouraged patients to vent emotion with the same directness as babies and animals. Consultations with Janov in Los Angeles had plumbed the deepest sources of John's anger and anguish—the abandonment by his parents when he was a toddler; his relationship with his mother, Julia, when he was a teenager, only to lose her at the hands of a speeding motorist just a few yards from his aunt Mimi's house.

Primal scream therapy also finally overcame the stage fright that had built up in him throughout the late sixties—and had ultimately prevented the Beatles from making peace onstage together again. In August 1972, he gave a show at Madison Square Garden, dressed in military fatigues and letting loose all the emotions released by Arthur Janov in a song about Julia very different from the earlier ballad of that name. "Mother you had me . . . but I never had you." Half a lifetime later the filmed version is still almost too painful to watch.

America under the early seventies presidency of Richard Nixon was a very different country from the one that had welcomed and adored the Beatles in 1964. John's public support for the Black Panthers and the yippies soon engaged the attention of an FBI still under the control of the paranoiac J. Edgar Hoover (whose penchant for wearing women's dresses none then suspected). Following the earlier lead of Scotland Yard's Special Branch, extensive and often farcical FBI dossiers were compiled on the Lennons as potential subversives; they were covertly followed and their telephones were bugged. In March 1972, the U.S. Immigration Service declared John an undesirable alien on the grounds of his conviction for cannabis possession in 1968 and ordered him to leave the country within sixty days. His ensuing four-year battle, first against deportation, then for resident-alien green card status, confirmed his exile from Britain. For he knew that, were he to leave the United States with these matters unresolved, he would never be allowed back in again.

He also continued to devote himself to Yoko's pursuit of Kyoko, though now careful to give the immigration service no further ammunition against him. In 1972, Tony and Melinda Cox were found to be living in Houston, Texas, where Cox had applied for legal guardianship of eight-year-old Kyoko—now renamed Rosemary. When the Lennons flew to Houston and presented their Virgin Islands custody order, the court ruled Cox to be a more suitable guardian, though it did grant Yoko visitation rights. Cox, however, refused to give up Kyoko-Rosemary for even those prescribed ten days, and received an overnight prison sentence for contempt of court. On his release, he, Melinda, and Kyoko-Rosemary once more disappeared without a trace.

John and Yoko had by now exchanged their New York studio for an apartment in the Dakota, at the corner of West Seventy-second Street and Central Park West. With its Gothic towers and mildew-green roof, the place bore a strange resemblance to some grimly grand Victorian bank or orphanage back home in Liverpool. It was so named because at the time of its construction in the mid-nineteenth century, this corner of Central Park seemed to Manhattanites as wild and unfrequented as faraway North and South Dakota. Lately, with its forbidding exterior and relatively low rents, it had become an abode of Upper West Side bohemians, actors, and film directors. Before the Lennons' arrival it was best known as the location for the filming of Roman Polanski's urban horror classic *Rosemary's Baby*.

Despite their public inseparability, the Lennons' marriage was running into trouble. Though still obsessively jealous if he thought Yoko even noticed another man, John felt himself under no similar obligation to be monogamous. Women had always thrown themselves at him, and still did so now, undeterred by Yoko's constant proximity. His infidelities grew ever more blatant. One night, he and Yoko went out to a party at the home of a mutual friend. Within a few minutes of their arrival John was having sex with another woman in an adjoining room within earshot of everyone at the party, including Yoko.

At the end of 1973, she ejected him from their Dakota apartment, though in a way that only Yoko could have devised. Both of them, she suggested, needed a breathing space after having been together virtually nonstop for more than five years. It was arranged that John should go to the West Coast for an indefinite period, accompanied by a pretty young Chinese-American woman named May Pang who had recently begun working jointly for him and Yoko. John himself seems to have remained blissfully unaware of how his life was being regulated. "I'd been married since I was a kid. Now I was a single guy. All I thought was 'whoopee!' "

He was to spend something like a year in Los Angeles on what he would later call his "Lost Weekend" (after the 1940s film noir classic), living in Bel Air and hanging out with music cronies like Phil Spector, Harry Nilsson, Elton John, and Elton's lyricist Bernie Taupin. His favorite tipple was brandy Alexander, a mixture of cognac and milk that found its way to the real Lennon as surely, and rather more rapidly, than any primal scream therapy. "After two brandy Alexanders, John was wonderful," his TV reporter friend Elliot Mintz remembered. "You got all the old stories . . . he was hilarious . . . delightful. But after his third, he was just a plain ugly drunk." One night, he was thrown out of L.A.'s famous folk club, the Troubadour, for heckling the Smothers Brothers as they performed onstage. Another evening, mildly stoned, he provoked the kind of put-down he himself might once have delivered, by emerging from the Troubadour men's room with a Kotex sanitary napkin clamped to his forehead. "Do you know who I am?" he slurred at a passing waitress. "Yeah," she snapped back. "You're an asshole with a Kotex on his head."

Periodically he would get in touch with Yoko and plead for another chance, a campaign that intensified when he tired of L.A. and returned to New York, bringing the Lost Weekend to almost a year and a half. But thus far, Yoko had remained impervious. "I'd been married twice before and divorced," she remembered. "For me, that was what happened to marriages. They ended." She, too, returned to the life of a single, dating a man considerably younger than herself.

For Bernie Taupin, however, the stories of Lennon debauchery and desperation on the Lost Weekend have been much exaggerated. "All I know is that every time I went around with him, he was perfectly normal. I remember going with him to see Bob Marley at the Roxy, and we had a great night. . . . John was always very sweet and encouraging about the things Elton and I did, especially 'Your Song.' And he was incredibly modest about the fantastic things he'd done. He'd say things like, 'Er, I wrote this song called "Across the Universe." I dunno if you know it.' "

Elton John had by now become as massive a world attraction as the Beatles had been ten years earlier. But, for all his stature as a performer, he remained at heart an inveterate record fan whose greatest thrill was meeting the musicians who had colored his lonely boyhood in Pinner, Middlesex. The Beatles, above all, had inspired his earliest songwriting efforts with Taupin, often in outright *Sgt. Pepper* knockoffs with names like "Regimental Sergeant-Major Zippo." And, by a weird coincidence, the duo had been discovered by the Beatles' former music publisher, Dick James, proving that once-in-a-lifetime luck can strike the same person twice.

As Elton got to know John better, he was dismayed to see how his greatest idol's solo career seemed to be slipping into the doldrums. And, with the generosity and altruism that was to be a feature of his career, he decided to do something about it. The next Elton single was both an homage to John and a ruse to drag him back into the limelight. At Caribou studios, nine thousand feet up in the Colorado mountains, the ultimate seventies glam-rock star recorded the ultimate sixties spine-tingler, "Lucy in the Sky with Diamonds," set to a modish reggae beat but otherwise almost eerily reminiscent of John's 1967 version. The composer himself joined the backup rhythm section under a complex but easily crackable code name, "the Reggae Guitars of Dr. Winston O'Boogie." That December, it became Elton's third U.S. number one.

John so enjoyed working and playing with his superstar fan that when he returned to the studio to make the album that would become *Walls and Bridges,* he asked Elton in to sing backup vocals. The result of their collaboration was "Whatever Gets You Thru' the Night," a scatter-gun rocker equally infused with John's acidity and Elton's pub-pianist good humor. As they listened to the playback, John said jokingly that if it was a hit, he'd sing it with Elton live onstage. By November, "Whatever Gets You Through the Night" was at the top of the U.S. chart—and, it would prove, John's only number one outside the Beatles in his lifetime.

Elton's current sellout American tour was scheduled to end with a gala concert at Madison Square Garden on Thanksgiving night, November 28. It was the perfect moment for John to honor his promise, though the very idea scared him almost witless. He had not performed in public since a charity appearance two years earlier; in the meantime, his old enemy, stage fright, had come back worse than ever. A brief rehearsal with Elton and his band in New York did not do much to help calm his fears. He showed up at the Garden wearing dark glasses and a black suit more appropriate to a funeral parlor than dueting with glam-rock's answer to Liberace. Waiting backstage, he was so nervous that he went into the men's room and vomited. He even temporarily forgot the order of strings on his guitar and had to ask Davey Johnstone, from Elton's band, to tune it for him.

Just before showtime, a messenger delivered two identical gift boxes, one for him and one for Elton. Inside each was a white gardenia and a note: "Best of luck and all my love, Yoko." "Thank goodness Yoko's not here tonight," Lennon said. "Otherwise I know I'd never be able to go out there." He had no idea that, playing Cupid as well as Svengali, Elton had also invited Yoko to the concert, and that she was seated in the front row with her current date.

Midway through the concert Elton paused at the piano in his top hat decorated with outsize pheasant feathers. "Seeing as it's Thanksgiving," he said, "we thought we'd make tonight a little bit of a joyous occasion by inviting someone up with us onto the stage." In the wings, still hesitating, John turned to Bernie Taupin. "He said, 'I'm not going out there unless you go with me,' " Taupin remembers. "So I went forward a little way with him, then he sort of hugged me, and I said, 'You're on your own.' "

Also in the audience was Margo Stevens, the former Apple Scruff (George's name for the female fans who haunted the individual Beatle's front gates, EMI's studios, and the steps at 3 Savile Row) who had progressed from camping outside Paul McCartney's house to working as Elton's housekeeper. Margo has never forgotten the moment when John walked—or, rather, was propelled—onstage. The house lights went up and all sixteen thousand people present rose to their feet in a spontaneous cheer. Only Yoko felt the moment to be one of less than pure euphoria. "When John bowed, it was too quickly, and one too many times," she remembers. "And I suddenly thought, 'He looks so lonely up there.' "

The John-Elton set was brief and, progressively, brilliant. John sang "Whatever Gets You Through the Night," as promised, with Elton's backup vocals like a friendly instructor keeping him on track. Then Elton sang his revisited "Lucy," backed by John. Within a few minutes, his confidence was sufficiently restored to take a sly dig at Paul McCartney: "We thought we'd do a number of an old, estranged fiancé of mine, called Paul." The number was "I Saw Her Standing There," Paul's kick-off track on the Beatles' first-ever album, from the days when Lennon and Mc-Cartney songs were interchangeable and as perfect, in their way, as early Picassos. "Everyone around me was crying," Margo Stevens remembers. "John was hugging Elton, and Elton seemed to be crying, too."

After the show, Yoko and her companion came backstage for what was only supposed to be a friendly word with John and his own date that evening. "John and I started talking at once, each of us totally forgetting the person we were supposed to be with," Yoko remembers. "After that, he invited me to an art exhibition. We started dating all over again."

They settled down, as they thought, to grow old together in their rambling apartment on the Dakota's seventh floor. In October 1975, the U.S. Court of Appeals finally overturned the deportation order against John, ruling that the British law under which he had been convicted of drug possession in 1968 had been unfair by American standards, and paving the way for the green card that would allow him to stay in the country without further harassment. At the age of forty-one, despite the traumatic memory of three miscarriages, Yoko became pregnant again. On John's thirty-fifth birthday, she gave birth to a son whom they named Sean Ono Lennon.

The year had seen John release two further albums—*Shaved Fish*, a compilation of existing tracks, including "Instant Karma," "Cold Turkey" and "Mind Games," and *Rock 'n' Roll,* a nostalgic collection of four-chord classics from his boyhood in the Merseyside dance halls. He had also briefly found another songwriting partner in Elton John's main glam-rock rival, David Bowie. The result was "Fame," Bowie's first number-one single in America.

After Sean's arrival, quite spontaneously, John decided to opt out of the music business altogether and devote himself to parenthood. With Yoko's help, he said, he finally felt secure enough to function without the golden armor of fame. "My whole security and identity [had been] wrapped up in being a pop star. But Yoko told me, the same way she told me with the Beatles. That was one liberation for me. The other was that I didn't have to go on making records." He delighted in the symmetry of including Gene Vincent's "Be Bop a Lula" on the *Rock 'n'*

Roll album. For he'd sung that same song for the first time onstage at Woolton village in 1957, the day he'd first met Paul McCartney. He was leaving the business at exactly the same place he had come in.

From there on, he organized his whole life around Sean, feeding him, putting him to bed, establishing a routine for the little boy as settled and healthy as Aunt Mimi once had for him. He learned to cook and even bake bread—his triumph in his first successful loaf mingled with slight annoyance that it did not receive the kind of accolades he was used to. ("I thought, 'Well, Jesus, don't I get a gold record or knighted or nothing?' ") Having given him the child he had so much wanted, Yoko was content to play a secondary role with Sean. While John took on the role of "househusband," Yoko became their business brain, a role in which she proved highly, though perhaps not unsurprisingly, effective.

They began to buy up other apartments in the Dakota, including a ground-floor suite that they turned into their office, Studio One, and another merely to serve as storage space for their vast accumulation of files and videos. They also bought a harborside mansion on Long Island, a Florida mansion that once had belonged to the Vanderbilt family, and a farm with a collection of prize Holstein cattle in upstate New York. Even if they had elected to sit still and do nothing, there was no danger of John's bank account ever being down to its last fifty thousand pounds. Despite the feverishly changing fashions of seventies pop, Beatles albums and compilations still sold incessantly the world over. A vast annual royalty income was channeled to John from London via the Apple office—now merely a nest of busy accounting machines, supervised by the ever faithful and honest Neil Aspinall.

John's involvement with Sean also awoke guilty memories of Julian, the son by his first wife, Cynthia, whose childhood he had almost missed in the whirlwind of being a Beatle. Now in his early teens, Julian lived in the Welsh hill town of Ruthin with his mother and her new husband, an electrical engineer named John Twist. He was already showing an interest in music, singing and playing guitar. But, so far as he knew, he had left no mark on his faraway father other than as the alleged inspiration for "Lucy in the Sky with Diamonds."

Soon after Sean's birth John invited Julian to New York and, over the next few years, made concerted efforts to rebuild a relationship with him. One of the many presents that Julian brought home to Ruthin was a portable typewriter, given to him by Yoko. Cynthia took a certain grim pleasure in using it to write her autobiography, *A Twist of Lennon,* published in 1978. But the book itself was characteristically free of rancor, ending with words from the *I Ching:* No blame.

John's only other regular contact in Britain was Aunt Mimi, the resoundingly normal and conventional woman whose virtues he unconsciously carried within him, and who still could read him better than anyone else.

Since the late sixties, Mimi had lived alone in a waterside bungalow in Poole Harbour, Dorset. She had never wanted to leave Liverpool or, indeed, her old home on Menlove Avenue, but in the end the pressure of Beatles fans had made it uninhabitable. One night John arrived at Mendips to find the house under siege and Mimi, uncharacteristically, crumpled up in tears on the front stairs. Next day, he told her to choose a new house anywhere else in the country that she fancied.

Mimi being Mimi, the bungalow was several sizes short of the place he would have bought her without a thought. Inside, all was as neat and spotless as ever. On the television set stood a photograph of John in his Quarry Bank High School cap, the happy, sunny little boy Mimi preferred to remember. In a bureau drawer lay bundles of his childhood drawings and poems, not yet the stuff of sky-high Sotheby auctions. Beside the patio window stood an anomalously expensive and tacky object, a cocktail cabinet shaped like an antique globe from Asprey's, the Bond Street jewelers. Each Beatle rushed to possess such a globe in the first, free-spending days when, as Ringo said, Asprey's used to feel "just like Woolworth's." Mimi was keeping John's in case he should ever want it again.

Even this secluded reach of Poole Habour was not completely safe from lingering Beatlemania. Sometimes, to Mimi's annoyance, passing pleasure boats would announce "There's John Lennon's aunt's house" over the loudspeaker to their passengers. At regular intervals, groups of pilgrims would turn up on her doorstep from as far away as Japan and Australia. Mimi would give them a scolding, then invite them in, just as she once had Paul McCartney and George Harrison. A few even got to stay the night in the little spare-room bed whose history they did not dream. "This used to be John's bed, you know," Mimi would say casually when she brought their morning cup of tea.

As John moved into his late thirties, his regular telephone calls to Mimi began to show increasing signs of nostalgia about his childhood—even aspects of it that he'd detested at the time. He asked her to send him various family mementoes, including the Royal Worcester dinner service that used to be displayed in the front hall at Mendips, and a photograph of Mimi's late husband, his much loved Uncle George. Once, to her amazement, the one-time incorrigible school truant and outlaw asked for his old Quarry Bank cap with its Latin motto, *Ex Hoc Metallo Virtutem.*

Despite the five thousand miles between them, aunt and nephew could have furious rows. One of their worst—on the subject of repainting the bungalow—ended with Mimi hooting, "Damn you, Lennon!" and slamming the phone down. A little later, John rang back, anxious and contrite. "You're not still cross with me, Mimi, are you?" he asked.

New York has always allowed its large celebrity population a surprising measure of privacy and anonymity. John and Yoko became just another famous uptown couple in semidisguise, walking through Central Park, standing in line for pizza, or having birthday parties at Tavern on the Green. In a city then among the world's most violent, John said he never felt a moment's insecurity—though in late 1979, with chilling prescience, he and Yoko donated a thousand dollars to a fund to equip the city's police with bulletproof vests.

Where he had once seemed thoroughly Ono-ized, Yoko now grew increasingly Lennon-ized. After Sean's birth, John took to calling her Mother with a frisson of old-time northern comedians like Al Read. Yoko looked forward as much as he did to settling down before the television on Sunday evenings to watch public television's imported English classic serials like Daphne du Maurier's *Rebecca.*

In the daytime, when Sean was asleep and the latest batch of loaves were safely in the oven, he would put on a Japanese happi coat and lie before his ever flickering giant TV screen, reading or watching the Central Park trees outside his window change from the heathery palette of spring through summer's deep green to the russet and radicchio blaze of autumn. On the wall above his bed hung a state-of-the-art electric guitar that he'd bought just after getting back with Yoko but had hardly ever played. Next to it was the number 9 and a dagger made out of a bread knife dating from the American Civil War, as he said, "to cut away the bad vibes—to cut away the past symbolically." From time to time he would glance at the guitar and wonder if he'd ever hold it again.

He was certainly no recluse, as would later be claimed: each day he saw dozens of people and spoke to dozens more on the telephone. He made regular trips with Yoko to their other properties and took extended overseas vacations with her and Sean (sometimes traveling under the alias "Fred and Ada Gherkin"). But for most of his former friends in the music business, he had disappeared from the radar screen. When Mick Jagger moved into a Central Park apartment within sight of the Dakota, he dropped John a note, asking him to telephone. But no reply ever came. The only exception was Elton John, who continued to bask in the Lennons' gratitude for bringing them back together and whom they asked to be Sean's godfather.

Elton returned from his first visit to the Dakota complex acknowledging that the world now held an even bigger shopaholic than himself. "I couldn't believe it. Yoko has a refrigerated room, just for keeping her fur coats. She's got rooms full of those clothes racks like you see at Marks and Spencer. She makes me look ridiculous. I buy things in threes and fours, but she buys things in fifties. The funny thing is, you never see her wearing them. She's always got up in some tatty old blouse." Yoko bore no resentment for such observations, nor did she even when Elton poked gentle fun at her in a birthday card to John:

Imagine six apartments
It isn't hard to do.
One is full of fur coats
The other's full of shoes.

John was equally cut off from the Beatles' old circle, though the fate of Mal Evans, their former roadie, caused him a certain macabre amusement. In 1976, Mal died a bizarre death in Los Angeles, shot through a motel-room door by police who feared he was about to harm a young girl he had with him. His wife, Lil, who still lived in England, afterward received a bill from the motel for dry cleaning the carpet on which he'd died. Without reference to Lil, Mal's body was cremated and the ashes were mailed to her—but en route the package got lost. It was a sickly appropriate footnote, since Mal had been working for the post office in Liverpool when he first joined the Beatles' entourage.

The general mellowing of John's character finally encompassed even Paul McCartney. Though still nothing like a fan of Paul's solo output, he could not help but admire his old estranged fiancé's steely determination in creating a new band, Wings, in controversial partnership with his wife, Linda, and winning it a worldwide fame almost comparable with the Beatles' own in their heyday. Paul, too, had been mellowed, by matrimonial stability as much as by solo success and, around 1978, decided it was time to make up with John. The way John later told it, Paul took to showing up on his doorstep unannounced with a guitar, as if hoping to re-create their schoolboy songwriting sessions in Allerton twenty years earlier. John, however, had more pressing grown-up concerns, like putting Sean to bed at his scheduled time. "I'd let [Paul] in, but finally I said to him, 'Please call before you come over. It's not 1956, and turning up at the door isn't the same any more.' "

In fact, John and Yoko and Paul and Linda spent several evenings together, in a friendliness one would never have predicted for that uneasy foursome of the late Apple era. The McCartneys happened to be visiting one evening when *Saturday Night Live,* America's seminal TV satire show, turned its mocking gaze on the continuing multimillion-dollar offers for a Beatles reunion. Producer Lorne Michaels jokingly put up a fee of $3,200 if the four would reconvene before his cameras. John and Paul happened to be watching, and for a moment considered jumping in a cab and turning up at the *SNL* studios; then they decided they were too tired to bother.

John's retirement ended as impulsively as it began. He had been intrigued to see how the British punk rock movement of the late seventies had filled the charts with noises wilder than any he and Yoko ever had created on their private tapes. Postpunk female vocalists like Lene Lovich, Chrissie Hynde, and, especially, the keening and warbling Kate Bush, seemed to John to be "doing Yoko's act from ten years ago." The clincher, he said, came one night in a Bermudan dance club when he heard the B52s" "Rock Lobster." "I said to meself, 'It's time to get out the old axe and wake up the wife.' "

Pulling down the barely used guitar from above his bed, he began to write new songs at frenetic speed. But this was no longer the angry, insecure John of the early seventies, obsessed with making propaganda points and settling scores. It was a man approaching forty with most of his old demons apparently exorcised, celebrating the joys of parenthood, home, and monogamy as he had once so despised Paul McCartney for doing. "Beautiful Boy" was a song about Sean and all the bedtimes and bath times they had shared. "Watching the Wheels" was a view from his Dakota retreat, thankful he was "no longer in the game." "Woman" was both an apology and a tribute to Yoko ("after all, I'm forever in your debt") while "Starting Over" affirmed that for him their love was "still special."

They planned a double album of his-and-her songs, naming it *Double Fantasy* after the freesia John had seen in Hong Kong's botanical gardens. To symbolize the new beginning, he chose not to release it on the Apple label, as all his previous solo albums had been. Instead, he went to David Geffen, creator of the Asylum label and, later, the inspirational driving force behind the hugely successful Warner-Elektra-Asylum conglomerate. Geffen won John to his new, eponymous label, not with huge cash advances but with a guarantee of personal care and sensitivity.

With *Double Fantasy* set for release, the doors of the Dakota, shut and padlocked for so long, were thrown open wide. The journalists who stampeded there from every corner of the world were equally astonished and charmed by the new John. Yoko had got his weight down and—for Sean's sake—even persuaded him to give up his incessant Gauloises cigarettes. Posing for *Rolling Stones* star photographer Annie Leibovitz, he looked more youthful than at any time since Brian Epstein first buttoned him into a round-collared suit. Even Yoko, not one for idle flattery, was moved to exclaim, "Hey—you're even better looking now than when you were a Beatle."

To every interviewer, from *Newsweek* magazine to BBC Radio One, he sounded the same top note of reenergized optimism. "I am going to be forty and life begins at forty, so they promise. And I believe it, too. Because I feel fine. I'm, like, excited. It's like twenty-one—you know, hitting twenty-one. It's like, 'Wow! What's going to happen next?' "

The only middling sales of *Double Fantasy* did not dampen John's spirits. His fortieth birthday behind him, he and Yoko started work on a follow-up album at New York's Hit Factory studios—a home-away-from-home for the Lennons now that Yoko had decorated one of its rooms like an Egyptian temple. The backing musicians were expected to share John's new healthy regimen, exchanging their normal drugs, cigarettes, and booze for sushi, green tea, and shiatsu massages.

The evening of December 8, 1980, John had set aside to work on one of Yoko's new tracks at the Hit Factory. Ordinarily, he preferred to hop in a yellow cab to the studio, but tonight Yoko had called up one of the limousines she kept on permanent twenty-four-hour standby. Outside their building's Gothic front arch stood a little knot of the fans that John called "Dakota groupies." As he walked out to the car a pudgy young man in a Russian-style fur hat proffered a copy of *Double Fantasy* and asked him to autograph it. A bystander photographed John scribbling a signature while the pudgy young man looked on.

His name—henceforward destined always to be spoken in full like those of John Wilkes Booth and Lee Harvey Oswald—was Mark David Chapman. And his twenty-five-year life history, when it came to be written, would show he was almost as perfect an example as Charles Manson of the way the sunny, smiling sixties could turn bad.

Born in 1955, in Fort Worth, Texas, the son of an air force sergeant, he had spent a rootless childhood and adolescence living variously in Texas, Indiana, and Virginia. A lonely, introverted boy, mocked and bullied by his schoolfellows, he sought refuge in his imagination, inventing a world populated by "Little People" where he could enjoy both status and control. As a teenager, he got into drugs, experimented with LSD, and became a devout Christian. But what colored his mind above all was the music of the Beatles.

He was no graceless, hopeless nerd, as he would often later be portrayed. Despite meager academic qualifications, he became for a period a valued worker for the YMCA organization, helping to resettle Vietnamese refugees, or boat people, and spending a hazardous time in Beirut during the first stages of Lebanon's mid-seventies civil war. He received commendations for his work, and on one occasion had his hand shaken by President Gerald Ford. Settling in Honolulu, he was hospitalized for depression after a suicide attempt, but seemed to make a full recovery. In 1979—in an eerie unconscious emulation of his still-unchosen victim— he married a Japanese-American woman several years his senior.

John Lennon's emergence from retirement turned Chapman's former near worship of him into contempt first, then hatred. He felt personally betrayed that the man who had sung "Imagine no possessions" now had accumulated costly real estate and herds of prize cattle. His parallel obsession was with Holden Caulfield, the anarchic sixteen-year-old narrator-hero of J. D. Salinger's *The Catcher in the Rye*. The fantasy grew in his mind that once he had made an end to John, he would step into the pages of Salinger's novel, transfigured into Caulfield.

So, on the first weekend of December 1980, he said goodbye to his wife, Gloria, and flew out of the Hawaiian sun, bound for New York with a .38-caliber handgun in his baggage. He would later tell his interrogators he had intended to shoot John during their first encounter early on the evening of December 8. But John's niceness about signing his *Double Fantasy* album temporarily disarmed him.

John that night was in particularly good spirits, feeling that Yoko had at last begun to receive proper respect as a musician in her own right. When they left the Hit Factory and headed back to the Dakota, shortly before 11:00 P.M., he carried a tape of her new song, "Walking on Thin Ice." As he climbed out of the limo and walked under the Gothic arch, a voice softly called, "Mr. Lennon?" Mark David Chapman stepped forward with the leveled .38 and pumped five shots into his back.

Inside the Dakota's entrance hall, the night doorman, Jay Hastings, heard the fusillade of shots. A moment later John staggered in with "a horrible confused expression on his face," followed by Yoko, screaming, "John's been shot! John's been shot!" Hastings thought it was some kind of macabre joke until John collapsed onto the floor, scattering cassette tapes around him. Hastings tore off his own tie to try to use it as a tourniquet to stem the bleeding, but did not know where to begin. He dialled 911, then knelt beside John to give what comfort he could. Within minutes, three police squad cars were at the scene. Chapman still stood on the sidewalk, calmly rereading *The Catcher in the Rye* for the umpteenth time.

When no ambulance arrived, a police car was used to take John to Roosevelt Hospital at West 59th Street and Ninth Avenue. A few minutes after his arrival, he was pronounced dead.

Away across the time zones in Poole, Dorset, his aunt Mimi awoke, switched on the radio, and heard someone talking about him. Mimi's first thought, as so often down the decades, was, "Oh, Lord! What's he done *now*?"

Five months later, I walked into the lobby of the Drake Hotel, having just been interviewed about the Beatles on ABC-TV's *Good Morning America* show. Awaiting me at the front desk was a message to call a number I did not recognize. "Studio One," said the voice that answered. A moment later, another, so familiar, voice came on the line. "Hi, this is

Yoko. What you said about John was very nice. Maybe you'd like to come over and see where we were living."

I remember how glorious was that spring afternoon of what now must be termed New York's good old days. Balmy sunshine lightened even the Dakota's drab stonework and the heavy iron vases along its Central Park facade, cheerily planted with red geraniums. Outside the Gothic arch on West 72nd Street tourists with cameras lingered around America's most famous assassination site after Dealey Plaza. Another Liverpool-Victorian touch is a kind of small sentry-box with a coppery metal finish, from which a security guard keeps twenty-four-hour watch. Its occupant was bundled firmly inside it, as though too squeamish to look at the killing place, barely ten feet away.

Everything possible had been done to mitigate the pain and shame of this seemingly ultimate Manhattan tragedy. Despite psychiatric opinion that he might be schizophrenic, Mark David Chapman—arrayed in two bulletproof vests to protect him from tit-for-tat reprisals by Lennon fans—had pleaded guilty to second-degree murder. He was now serving twenty years to life in New York State's Attica Penitentiary where, seven years earlier, forty-three inmates had died during the worst riot in U.S. prison history. Ironically, one of John's first stage appearances after settling in America had been a charity concert for the Attica riot's bereaved wives and children.

I had not seen Yoko since the Apple era's final days—and, indeed, at first hardly recognized her. Grief had played the cruel trick it does on so many widows of making her look better than her years. The former cloud of black hair was now tied back as neatly as any lady lawyer's or Wall Street banker's. In place of miniskirts and hot pants were sleek black trousers, high-heeled boots, a black shirt, and a loosened tie. The face which once seemed so implacably humorless frequently softened into smiles, even when discussing the most painful things. The once flat little voice was full of John's sayings and phraseology, and cozy north-of-England usages like "cuppa" for "a cup of tea."

She admitted feeling that with John's death, his whole character had somehow been subsumed into her. Having enjoyed twenty-twenty vision all her life, she suddenly found herself as myopic as he used to be. She also developed his raging sweet tooth. "John was the one who loved chocolate; I hardly ever used to touch it. But on the day after he was killed, all I wanted to do was eat chocolate. Elton [John] was so sweet; he sent me an enormous chocolate cake. My diet went crazy for about a month—nothing but chocolate and mushrooms."

We talked for almost two hours in Yoko's office at Studio One, a long, high-ceilinged room decorated with small trees, white sofas, and pastel-shaded Art Deco lamps. She sat behind a huge inlaid desk, in a chair modeled on the throne of Pharaoh Tutankhamun. The ceiling was a trompe l'oeil panorama of lazily drifting clouds. "Above us only sky," I couldn't help thinking.

She still had not come to terms with no longer being hated—with having changed overnight from a figure of poisonous ridicule to one of monumental tragedy. As she told me, hundreds of messages continued to pour into the Dakota each day, a goodly number from women who as teenage Beatles fans had once screamed "Chink" and offered her yellow roses with the thorns uppermost, but who now wished to thank her for making John happy according to his wishes, and to sympathize in her inexpressible loss.

She could even smile bleakly at the horrible irony of John's being taken just as he was feeling so fit and rejuvenated, and new doors seemed to be opening on every side. "After all those years of not smoking and losing weight and trying to keep healthy by eating the right foods. . . . Since December, I've been telling Sean, 'Eat whatever you like. It doesn't matter.'

"And he was so happy. Both of us were. A few days before it happened, I remember thinking, 'This is all so good. I wonder how long it can go on being as good as this.' "

She referred to the other former Beatles wryly as "the in-laws," something else she must have picked up from John. There was no disguising her bitterness against Paul McCartney, though she said no more than repeating John's cryptic remark about how much Paul had hurt him. It had also deeply offended her that, after John's death, Ringo was the only ex-Beatle to fly to New York and offer her his condolences personally.

After our talk, Yoko sent me on a tour of the seventh-floor apartment where she and Sean still lived together. My guide was Fred Seaman, the same assistant who signed the polite turndown I had received when I first asked the Lennons for an interview. I remember thinking that he seemed the ideal factotum for someone like Yoko in her present circumstances: soft-footed, soft-mannered, infinitely attentive, caring, and trustworthy.

And so, five months later than I could have wished, I finally got to see where they were living. I saw the vista of high-ceilinged white rooms with their stunning view of skyscrapers set down as though at random among the Central Park treetops. From the Strawberry Fields memorial garden directly below came a succession of small glints and flashes as visitors used pocket mirrors and other shiny objects to heliograph messages of sympathy to Yoko.

I saw the kitchen where John had learned to bake bread, a cozy domestic nucleus no different from any other wealthy New Yorker's apart from the wall painting of himself, Yoko, and toddler Sean in Superman costumes, soaring upward hand in hand. I saw the room devoted to Egyptian relics, including a full-size gold mummy in a case, and the bentwood hatstand on which John had hung his old school cap, and the Yoko artworks and sculpture dating back to their first cautious, awkward encounters in London. A thin Plexiglas column supporting four silver spoons bore the inscription "Three spoons, Y.O. 1967." I remembered how John always used to say that what attracted him first had been the humor in her work.

I saw the little side room where he used to lie and "watch the trees change color," now empty but for some cardboard cartons and the giant-screen TV set he'd had specially shipped from Japan. Along the hall was a triangular-shaped room, full of circular clothes racks, and resembling some ghostly boutique. Here with the care of a museum curator—the last quality one would have suspected in him—John had preserved everything he'd ever worn since the sixties, from Swinging London military tunics and cloaks to agitprop fatigues, with their attendant floppy-brimmed fedoras, denim caps, boots, and shoes. I even saw, or fancied I did, the knitted scarf that Stu Sutcliffe, the fifth Beatle, had given him circa 1961. The same thought kept recurring as I followed Fred Seaman around: This is the only time I'll ever see all of this.

For the most part, Yoko played her new role as rock's most tragic widow with a restraint of which few had ever suspected her capable. Her replies to the grieving millions were limited to brief, dignified communiqués asking them to keep alive John's ideals of peace and brotherhood, and entreating some space to mourn him in private. She became a familiar, forlorn figure in Central Park, walking the paths she and John once had arm-in-arm, wrapped in a white fur coat and dark glasses to hide the tears none yet had seen, nor ever would.

Yet under the widow's weeds, the old performance artist had lost none of her compulsion to shock. Two years after John's death, she released a solo album called *Seasons of Glass* whose cover showed the bullet-shattered and bloodstained glasses he had still been wearing in his dying moments. Many were offended, though some were willing to interpret it as an extreme form of therapy.

Yoko had made it clear she was not willing to settle for merely being the guardian of the Lennon shrine, but that she intended to continue the careers in which John had so encouraged her. She put her artworks on display at leading galleries, few of which could now refuse her, and went on releasing albums. Without John to give them melody and accessibility—much as Paul McCartney had once done for him—their sales were never spectacular. In 1990, John's solo music was collected in a memorial four-CD set. When Yoko's collected work appeared soon afterward, the set ran to six CDs.

She made efforts to reinforce the new, favorable view of her, taking Sean on a trip to Liverpool in 1983 to visit Beatles landmarks like Strawberry Field, and returning in 1990 for a concert to mark the fiftieth anniversary of John's birth. More positive vibes were created that same year when, helped by Sean, she rerecorded "Give Peace a Chance" as a protest against the Gulf War. At other times, she seemed to show her old total disregard for public and media opinion, as when she allowed John's name to appear on a range of mugs, plates, and jigsaw puzzles. Uncomfortable echoes of *Seasons of Glass* were stirred at a Yoko exhibition in Los Angeles when a replica of John's broken and bloody glasses went on display.

But Yoko, too, was to learn something about being exploited. In the years immediately following John's death, a succession of one-time Lennon employees—aides, gofers, tarot-readers, and the like—produced trashy books on their lives with the Lennons, usually portraying Yoko as a scheming, manipulative virago. The worst betrayal came from Fred Seaman, the soft-footed young man who had been one of her two most trusted personal assistants. It later emerged that, just a day after John's death, Seaman had begun walking out of the Dakota with bags full of his diaries, drawings, and correspondence, and feeding them to an accomplice to be processed into a book. He was charged with theft, received five years' probation, and was prevented from quoting from any of the letters or diaries in the book he persuaded a New York publisher to bring out in 1991.

In 1988, Albert Goldman published *The Lives of John Lennon*, branding John as an epileptic, schizophrenic, autistic killer, thug, wife-beater, and recluse whose entire musical oeuvre had been founded on the tunes of nursery rhymes. A few weeks after the book appeared, despite all my expectations I found myself back in Yoko's Studio One office with the trees, the white sofas, and the chair like Tutankhamun's throne. Seated beside her was a teenage boy with oriental almond eyes but an unmistakable twist of Britishness around the mouth. I realized I was to be the first writer to meet Sean Lennon, now aged thirteen.

Yoko had made no attempt to sue Goldman for his many extreme references to her, nor to bring an injunction that would have removed the book from sale. Her nonreaction was seen as further evidence of her toughness and imperviousness to criticism. But to me she confessed the book had so devastated her that she'd seriously thought of committing suicide and had been held back only by the thought of Sean. Wasn't it a mistake, I asked, for her not to have uttered a single word of denial? "I am in the position of someone who's been punched five hundred times," she answered. "There are so many allegations against John, I could never deal with them all in one interview. If I answer just a few, people might say, 'What about the others? Maybe they are true.' "

I reflected, but did not say, that it seemed less than wise strategy from the many high-priced advisers at her disposal. Sean corroborated that, in his very clear memory, John had not been the volcanic domestic tyrant and recluse portrayed by Goldman, but a conscientious, loving, and laughing dad.

Yoko's main biographical service to John was authorizing the respected film director David Wolpert to make a documentary, *Imagine: John Lennon*, which had a worldwide cinema release also in 1988. Firmly suppressing all her own ideas about avant-garde filmmaking, she gave Wolpert a free hand to produce a clear and comprehensive portrait that unwittingly rebutted several of Albert Goldman's crazier allegations in *The Lives of John Lennon*. Goldman had asserted, for example, that John suffered from a total lack of motor coordination that amounted to autism. One of the film's early scenes shows him at work in the studio at Tittenhurst Park and, with lightning reflexes, catching a sheath of song sheets as it slips off his music stand. Yoko had told me that, in fact, he was double-jointed and could fold his limbs into the most demanding yoga positions without effort.

Wolpert's film also includes the touching scene when John confronts a young American hippie who has been found living rough in the Tittenhurst grounds. For about ten minutes he talks to the boy, trying to persuade him that there's nothing godlike about John Lennon nor mystical truth to be disinterred from his song lyrics. The encounter has an almost New Testament quality—Jesus this time preaching unbelief. Finally, he realizes that it's hopeless and asks whether the vagrant is hungry. The answer is a shamefaced nod. "OK," John says to the watching musicians and security people. "Let's give him something to eat."

Perhaps the saddest casualty was John's elder son, Julian, for whom all of this cruelly echoed what had happened to his father at the same age, seventeen. Having been given away by his mother as a toddler, John had just been getting to know her again when she was knocked down and killed a few yards from Aunt Mimi's front gate. In the same way, Julian had virtually lost his father in infancy and found him again as a teenager, only to be robbed of him a second time.

The Dakota apartment, when I first saw it, had photographs of Julian and Sean displayed in equal prominence. But with John no longer around, Julian could hardly expect the same treatment from his stepmother that she gave to her own son. Although Yoko made him an allowance and still invited him on visits, their relationship was clearly not an easy one.

A young man named Lennon who could sing and play guitar was something the recording industry could hardly pass up. Julian's debut album, released in 1984, revealed some songwriting talent and enough of the familiar Lennon vocal rasp to compel attention. His first single, poignantly entitled "Too Late for Goodbyes," reached number six in Britain, though, surprisingly, it failed to make the American Top Forty. He appeared in Chuck Berry's film autobiography, dueting with Berry on John's old favorite, "Johnny B. Goode," and in 1991 had a second U.K. number-six single with the proenvironment song "Saltwater."

After that, his career seemed to lose momentum. He knocked about the social scene with eligible young women in London, New York, and Monte Carlo, where he acquired a share in a harborside restaurant, La Rascasse. With increasing bitterness, he accused Yoko of withholding his rightful share in his father's estate, and at one point even threatened legal action against her. Though their financial differences seemed to have been settled quietly, Julian remained resentful that personal keepsakes like John's guitars had not been passed on to him. His next album, *Photograph Smile*, came out in 1998—ironically on the same day as *Into the Sun*, the debut album of his half-brother, Sean. The critics' view was that Sean's effort had the edge.

To mark the twentieth anniversary of John's death in December 2000, Julian put a message on his website, revealing undiminished pain and anger toward the father he almost never had. John's dedication to love and peace, he said, "never came home to me."

When the Rock and Roll Hall of Fame gave John a lifetime achievement award in 1994, Paul was chosen to read the citation. His speech was an open love letter to his old partner; at its conclusion, he embraced Yoko and Sean, symbolizing an end to all the old bitterness between their two houses. A significantly short time afterward came the Beatles' reunion on record, with Paul, George, and Ringo playing backup firmly to some John solo vocal tapes provided by Yoko, and the multipart TV documentary.

That year, 1995, found me back at the Dakota for a third time. Yoko by now had a permanent man friend, an amiable antiques dealer named Sam Havadtoy, and, at sixty-two, looked better than ever, though she had taken to chain-smoking thin, dark cigarettes. My ostensible purpose was to interview her about the album she had just made in partnership with Sean, now aged nineteen. But during our talk, by looks more than words, she made it clear that the reconciliation with Paul had been for the sake of business only, and that there was still bitterness between them.

Our conversation also touched on the subject of Kyoko, the daughter Yoko had lost at eight years old, and who had lost her as traumatically as John had lost Julia and Julian had lost John. After Kyoko's father, Tony Cox, absconded from Houston with her in 1972, the two had completely vanished. All John and Yoko's subsequent efforts to trace them had been in vain. Whatever her private feelings, the subject seemed to be a closed book with Yoko, although after John's death she continued to place newspaper advertisements each year on Kyoko's birthday, appealing to her to get in touch. "Basically," Yoko told me with a bleakly expressionless look, "we're not in contact at all."

Two years later, in November 1997, Kyoko finally contacted her mother by telephone from Denver, Colorado. Now thirty-three and married to a devout Christian, she had given birth to her first child, a daughter, only a few days before. As she was to explain later, "I didn't think it right to become a mother without at least letting my mother know I'm alive and well."

Kyoko's history in the intervening years had been a bizarre one. While she and her father were moving around the world as fugitives, Tony Cox had abandoned fundamentalist Christianity and joined an extreme doomsday sect known as The Walk. Kyoko had been submerged in the cult and taught that her mother and John Lennon were "the personification of evil."

It was to be no dramatic, sobbing mother-daughter reunion. For a year after her initial contact Kyoko kept her distance, speaking to Yoko only in phone calls initiated by her. By 1998, they had built up sufficient rapport for a face-to-face meeting. Not for three years more did Yoko get to meet her granddaughter, Emi—a name accidentally reminiscent of the Beatles' original record company. Photographs of the occasion showed Kyoko to be a cozy, uncomplicated-looking woman, and Emi a pretty and secure-looking child. The entranced Yoko reportedly indicated to friends that Emi would become joint heir to the Lennon fortune, along with Sean.

Not all visitors from the past were quite so welcome. In 2000, the world heard again from John's killer, Mark David Chapman, serving twenty years to life in Attica. Kept largely in isolation for fear of revenge attacks by fellow inmates, Chapman had received a nonstop torrent of letters that he never answered but nonetheless filed meticulously in his cell. Although most came from Beatles fans wishing him in Hell, a good proportion were from would-be celebrity stalkers saying they were "fans" of his, or women professing romantic interest and asking if they could visit him.

Having served the minimum of his sentence, Chapman was now eligible for parole. For an unreal moment, the possibility arose of his being back on the streets again at around the twentieth anniversary of John's death. His application was denied, however, after a press furor and a victim-impact statement from Yoko saying that she, Sean, and Julian would all fear for their lives if he were set free.

My most recent meeting with Yoko, in March 2003, brought this book to a full circle more neatly than I could ever have imagined. It was by that time four years since Paul McCartney's old family home, 20 Forthlin Road, Allerton, had been acquired by the National Trust, restored to its character during Paul's boyhood, and opened to the public as a site of historical interest. But for some reason, no such sanctification had been given to Mendips, the mock-Tudor villa on Menlove Avenue where John was brought up by his aunt Mimi. Though a magnet for Lennon pilgrims from all over the world, it remained in private ownership until 2002, when the death of its longtime owner finally brought it onto the real estate market. Various plans for the house were mooted, including one to turn it into a hotel with John's old bedroom forming part of the honeymoon suite. The idea so horrified Yoko that she bought Mendips for £150,000 and presented it to the National Trust. She also paid the £75,000 cost of its restoration and made an endowment to cover its operating costs and maintain a permanent live-in custodian.

One can now therefore belatedly examine every detail of the genteel home that that professed working-class hero never got completely out of his system. Here is the "morning room" with its defunct servants' bells where Mimi first put him as a baby, tying him into an armchair with a scarf. Here is the rather chilly formal dining room, the comfortable front lounge, the half-timbered hallway with its Spode and Coalport china plates, the glass front porch to which Mimi banished him for so many hours of solitary guitar practice. Here is the sub-baronial staircase to the seven-by-ten-foot room, with its red-quilted bed and pinups of Elvis and Brigitte Bardot, where he read alone for hours or drafted the first eccentrically spelled versions of songs and stories that one day would captivate the world.

Virtually everything is authentic. Family members to whom Mimi left furniture or ornaments in her will have been contacted by the Trust and persuaded to lend their bequests in perpetuity. Replicas have been needed mainly for the items that, in the last months of his life, John nostalgically asked Mimi to send to him in New York—for instance, an antique wall clock inscribed "George Toogood, Woolton Tavern" that belonged to his beloved uncle George. To replace it, Yoko commissioned a custom-made exact copy. When this did not quite meet her standards, another clock was made from scratch. The front door is also a replica, the original having been bought some years ago by a Lennon fanatic in Japan.

Our meeting took place when Yoko came from New York to perform the official opening of the house under its National Trust blue plaque, and show around a group of children from John's first school, Dovedale Primary. After previous conversations at the great white Dakota apartment and under Studio One's trompe l'oeil clouds, it felt ineffably strange now to be facing her in a couple of Deco armchairs in Mimi's old front lounge.

She had recently turned seventy, but looked a good twenty years younger, with her cropped, lightened hair, chic black trouser suit, and trendy thick-soled boots. In *Vanity Fair* magazine some weeks earlier the social commentator Dominick Dunne, covering the latest court hearing in the Fred Seaman saga, had gone so far as to call her "a dish." A far cry indeed from racist taunts of "Chink!" and "Yellow!" and yellow roses offered to her with thorns turned uppermost.

Naturally uppermost in Yoko's mind was the current war in Iraq—the long-delayed outcome of 9/11 and George W. Bush's King Lear threats—and how fiercely John would have hated and opposed it. She had responded, just as he would have done, with giant billboards in London and New York saying IMAGINE PEACE. There was also a sense of déjà vu, or déjà entendu, in the way some radio stations were currently banning "Imagine" from their playlists for fear of subverting the Anglo-American war effort. But nothing could stop John's voice from getting through—even at a Paul McCartney show. During his Paris concert the following night Paul was to be temporarily nonplussed by a spontaneous audience chorus of "Give Peace a Chance."

Even the spartan little bedroom upstairs, Yoko felt, could be another Lennon message to posterity. "A lot of young people might feel they can't do much on their own because they don't have a big enough room. But I'd like to say to them: 'John only had that small room, but it nurtured him enough to go out and change the world. Maybe you can do the same.' " A few weeks later she was to have her first ever American hit with a dance version of "Walking on Thin Ice"—the song on the tape that fell from John's hands as Chapman's bullets struck him. Almost his last words, indeed, had been to predict it would do well.

I once asked Yoko what most reminded her of John, apart from his picture or his voice on record. She replied that she thought of him every time she put on a loose-fitting shirt or T-shirt. This she always did as he had shown her, tucking it tight inside the belt, then raising both arms at once to make it billow out in symmetrical folds around the waist.

Love was ever made of such commonplace detail. Even for John and Yoko.

TWENTY ONE

"THE FREAKS WAS RIGHT WHEN THEY SAID YOU WAS DEAD"

The blandly indifferent smile that Paul McCartney turned on the breakup was merely camouflage for someone who hated showing weakness, betraying real emotion, or admitting the world was other than the happy-go-lucky, sunshiney place he portrayed in his music. Whatever he might pretend, it was a far more devastating moment for Paul than for any of the others.

He who for years had known nothing but golden success now seemed to be staring at comprehensive failure on every front. He had failed to make a success of Apple, failed to carry through his choice of a new manager for the Beatles, failed in all his efforts to steer the band past the fatal shoals of John's indifference, failed to keep control of his own music, failed above all in his lifelong vocation as Mister Nice Guy. The three individuals who were once closer than family to him had ganged up against him, outvoted, isolated, and sidelined him, and were now ranged against him in implacable hostility.

Typically, it would be years before Paul revealed what an effect all this had on even his seemingly boundless confidence and self-esteem. In 2001, during a television interview with his daughter, Mary, he finally admitted having felt that with the Beatles' disintegration "I'd lost the framework for my whole working life . . . I just didn't know what to do. I started staying up all night and staying in bed all day. I stopped shaving, I started drinking Scotch and I sort of went crazy . . . Looking back, I guess I nearly had a breakdown."

What pulled him through was the new family life he had established with Linda, their new baby daughter, Mary, and Linda's seven-year-old daughter, Heather, whom he had always treated as his own. For months the four of them remained virtually dug in at the farm near Campbeltown, Argyllshire, that Paul had bought in 1966 while he was still with Jane Asher. The unspoiled mountain country around the tract of water known as the Mull of Kintyre was the farthest possible extreme from the urban pressures and strife of the previous six years. Paul had no doubt that it saved his soul and, maybe, his sanity.

The received wisdom for years afterward was that, in the sniping between Paul and John, both on and off their respective solo albums, Linda played only a passive, involuntary role. While understandably prompting Paul to loosen all lingering matrimonial ties with the Beatles, she was thought to have stayed firmly apart from the spats between him on one side and John and Yoko on the other. However, a long handwritten letter from John, sent from Tittenhurst Park in 1970, reveals Linda to have been in the very thick of the feud. Pointedly addressed to "Dear Paul and Linda," it is a reply to a previous missive written by the couple in tandem, and is just as vitriolic toward her as toward him. "I was reading your letter and wondering what cranky, middle-aged Beatles fan wrote it. . . . I kept looking at the last page to find out. . . . What the hell—it's Linda!"

The letter ends on an almost schizophrenic note, signing off "in spite of it all, love to you both," then adding a furious P.S. and a line of dots and exclamation marks at the further slight John perceives in their letter not having been addressed jointly to him and Yoko.

To begin with, Paul's solo output showed little sign of missing John. The *McCartney* album and its 1971 successor, *Ram* (also billed as a "partnership" with Linda), each contained work as good as any he'd ever done inside the Beatles. In March 1971, he reached number two in the U.K. singles chart with "Another Day," a narrative song about a lovelorn spinster ("Every day she takes a morning bath, she wets her hair") evoking both "Eleanor Rigby" and "She's Leaving Home." The following August, he had his first American solo number one with "Uncle Albert/Admiral Halsey," a novelty number with some of the same northern music-hall atmosphere as *Sgt. Pepper*.

But having solo hits in the intervals of family and agricultural life was never going to be enough for Paul McCartney. As his spirits revived, so did his burning need to reestablish contact with the live audiences whose adulation he had been denied during his last four years as a Beatle. He had worked as unselfishly as he knew how to hold the Beatles together, and it hadn't worked. Very well then, he'd show them there could be life after the Beatles onstage as well as off, that a world-beating combo could exist that did not also feature John, George, and Ringo.

In 1971, he announced he had formed a new band with the Moody Blues' former guitarist Denny Laine, drummer Danny Seiwell, and Linda on keyboards and vocals. Its name—consciously evoking some thankfully liberated blackbird or butterfly—would be Wings.

Today, such a step by a musician only a hundredth as big as Paul was in 1971 would compel instant, comprehensive media attention. But the media back then remained still overwhelmingly obsessed by the Beatles—in particular by the notion that their differences were reparable and that, sooner or later, they would get back together. The idea of Paul McCartney in any other band was one that most music journalists found impossible to take seriously. The PR man he employed to drum up stories about Wings, rather than about recent Beatles history, found few takers up and down Fleet Street. It was as though he were starting all over again from the bottom.

Paul's response was one of extraordinary courage or hubris, depending on your point of view. If they wanted him to start at the bottom again, then he'd do it. But not just at the bottom represented by third-rate TV shows and concert venues. He'd go right down to the bottom the Beatles had got to know so intimately ten years before when they were still playing for small change, nurtured only by chips, beer, and impossible dreams.

Packing Wings and their virgin equipment into a single van, he headed north up the M1, determined to break them in by playing the same kind of small halls and clubs where the Beatles had originally honed their craft. It was done somewhat in the chaotic spirit of a modern Magical Mystery Tour, with no firmly planned route or set itinerary of gigs (but also, no doubt, a highly professional appreciation of its ultimate publicity value). One day, for instance, Paul saw a sign to Nottingham University and on a whim told his driver to go there. When they reached the university campus, a roadie was dispatched to find the secretary of the students' union. "I've got Paul McCartney and his new band outside," the roadie said. "Would you like them to play for you tonight?" It would have taken an iron-willed secretary to reply, "No thanks, I think we'll stick with our scheduled lecture on the place of the potato in Irish folklore."

Linda's inclusion in the Wings lineup had provoked universal disbelief and derision. To the residual millions of Beatle-Paul worshippers, it seemed yet further proof of her baleful influence and grim determination to advance herself by clinging tight to his coattails. Despite Paul's lavish tributes to her as a creative muse, she had so far been detectable only in the faint feminine coo that now shadowed his lead vocal—a "deified Scouse with unmusical spouse," as one British magazine called them.

Yet there she was with Paul onstage, filling the place once occupied by John Lennon, her blonde hair now cut in a modish seventies sheaf, dressed in gaudy glam-rock shirts and waistcoats, but still not smiling very much, even when waving puffy sleeves above her head to encourage audiences to clap along. In some Wings songs she took the vocal, closely backed by Paul; in others she played an elementary keyboard solo he had obviously taught her that was only a step or two on from "Chopsticks." Halfway through the show, he would introduce her in homely Liverpool style as "Our Lin," though to applause never more than polite.

In fact, as Linda later admitted, it was all Paul's idea that she should join Wings, mainly so that they wouldn't be separated when the band went out on tour. She said she never felt comfortable onstage and would always much rather have stayed at home with her children and animals. She did it only because it meant so much to Paul.

Despite its huge success and cozy family image, Wings was never to be a happy or stable band. As if in reaction to the old democracy of the Beatles, Paul proved an iron-fisted autocrat. A succession of talented musicians flocked to his banner, but soon left again, frustrated by his dominating ways and refusal to share the limelight with anyone but "Our Lin" and her Chopsticks solo. Even the talented and crucial Denny Laine was given no percentage of the band's earnings, simply receiving a wage of just seventy pounds per week (though Paul later raised this to seventy thousand pounds per year and paid off Laine's outstanding income tax). "It was inevitable," a former Wings associate comments. "You had a leader who was a multi-instrumentalist, a perfectionist—and a former Beatle. Other than John, George, and Ringo, he wasn't going to regard anyone else as nearly in his league."

On record, too, Wings had a bumpy takeoff. For their debut single Paul chose to air his Hibernian Catholic roots in an overt political statement whose title, "Give Ireland back to the Irish," could hardly have been worse timed. When the record appeared in 1972 the so-called Provisional IRA were escalating their campaign of sectarian murder in

Northern Ireland and were soon to extend indiscriminate mass murder to the British mainland. The simplistic sentiments of "Give Ireland back to the Irish" seemed all too much in tune with hooded thugs now bombing and knee-capping in the name of Republicanism. Like John Lennon with "I Am The Walrus" five years earlier, Paul found himself banned by the BBC and so deprived of any significant airplay within the U.K.

His heavy-handedly ironic response was to make Wings' follow-up single a song no one on earth could accuse of being politically controversial. This was the nursery rhyme "Mary Had a Little Lamb," in a setting that he had originally devised to sing to his daughter, Mary, while he put her to bed. "La-*La*" ran its chorus—then, by way of a change, "*La*-la". When Wings premiered the single on American television, there were sarcastic comments even from the talk-show hosts who introduced them. "Once upon a time, Paul McCartney recorded songs like 'Eleanor Rigby' and 'Hey Jude.' Now here he is with his new group and 'Mary Had a Little Lamb.' "

Wings' continuing struggle to be taken seriously was further illustrated that same year, 1972, when Paul agreed to provide a title song for the latest James Bond film, *Live and Let Die*. Having written the song, he went into the studio on his own to record it with Wings, using the Beatles' old producer, George Martin, to score and produce it. A justifiably excited Martin then played the result to the Bond film's American co-producers Harry Salzman and Albert "Cubby" Broccoli. "Great demo," they enthused. "Now . . . who are we going to get to make the *record*?" It took all Martin's powers of persuasion to convince them that Paul McCartney's imprimatur could take Bond to a new, younger market and that they shouldn't call up Shirley Bassey or Lulu. "Live and Let Die" became a Top Ten single for Wings and was rated the best Bond theme since John Barry's original one for *Dr. No* in 1962.

This breakthrough was consolidated by their 1973 album *Band on the Run*, whose packaging was both an oblique allusion to their spell as highway-wandering outsiders and a throwback to *Sgt. Pepper* in-jokiness. The cover showed a melodramatically slinking posse of cloaked "fugitives" including the Hollywood actor James Coburn, the television interviewer Michael Parkinson, and the gourmet-soon-to-be-Liberal-MP Clement Freud. Two tracks from the album, its title song and "Jet"—a number likewise hinting at bonds triumphantly burst and the accelerator now pressed down flat—each became huge-selling singles.

From here on, Wings would compete with David Bowie, Elton John, T-Rex, and Queen as the surest crowd-pullers of 1970s glitter rock. Their 1976 American tour sold out every venue, and found no chat-show hosts snickering now. For Paul it was an especially sweet triumph, coming as it did exactly ten years after the Beatles' farewell concert in San Francisco.

Although Allen Klein had retained managerial control of John, George, and Ringo until 1973 (as he did of the Rolling Stones until 1975), Paul had the further satisfaction of seeing "the Robin Hood of Pop" finally go down with an arrow in his back. In 1977, two years after Klein finally ended all connections with the Beatles, he was charged on six counts of income tax evasion by the U.S. Internal Revenue Service. Thanks mainly to incriminating testimony from his old associate, the scary Pete Bennett, he was convicted of failing to declare income made from the illicit sale of promo Beatles albums. He was fined five thousand dollars and sent to prison for two months.

From here on, the new brand of McCartney songs rolled forth in the new, faintly mid-Atlantic McCartney voice that had Linda's insubstantial harmony clinging permanently to its underside like barnacles to a ship's keel. They were always catchy, always pleasant, always empty of real content and lacking that extra effort and edge that used to come from John peering over his shoulder.

The honed perfection of a lyric like "Eleanor Rigby" or "Yesterday" was replaced by sloppy first drafts of half-thoughts: "Silly Love Songs," "Listen to What the Man Said," or "Let 'Em In," the latter merely a rambling name check—reminiscent of John's on "Give Peace a Chance"—from "Martin Luther" (King) and "Phil and Don" (Everly) to McCartney family members like "brother Michael" and Auntie Jin. Clunky rhymes got through that John would have mocked to the skies ("The county judge / held a grudge"). The relentless journey to the middle of the road that had begun with "When I'm Sixty-Four" took another less-than-giant step when he agreed that Wings should record the theme music for television's tackiest soap opera, *Crossroads*. To Beatle-Paul fans (now being fast overtaken by Wings-Paul ones) his *Crossroads* instrumental seemed the nadir—but they were soon to be proved wrong.

In 1977, inspired by the tract of water near his Argyllshire farm, and gratefully recalling its healing properties during his post-Beatles depression, he wrote a ballad entitled "Mull of Kintyre." Recorded at dirgelike tempo, with full bagpipe accompaniment, it seemed to have all the appeal of Fort William on a wet afternoon. Reviewers in the domestic pop press (who then still aspired to a degree of literacy) were unanimous in calling it the dreariest, blandest solo McCartney production yet. It stayed at number one in the U.K. for nine weeks, sold two million copies, and was to remain Britain's top-selling single until Band Aid's "Do They Know It's Christmas?" in 1984.

With Wings now triumphantly spread, Paul set up a publishing company, MPL (McCartney Productions Ltd). The organization was as small and low-key as Apple had been diffuse and flamboyant, operating from one unshowy office in London's Soho Square and another in New York. The New York end was run by Linda's brother John, with frequent recourse to the legal expertise of her father, Lee—the very management team, in fact, that Paul had once proposed should run the Beatles.

The new company was not long in pulling off a major publishing coup. In 1975, the song catalog of Buddy Holly, the Beatles' first great idol and inspiration, was put up for sale by Holly's former manager, Norman Petty. For a knockdown price of less than one million dollars, MPL snapped up the rights to Holly's music in the United States and Canada. So moved was Paul to have become the custodian of "That'll Be the Day," "Peggy Sue," and all the rest that he decreed an annual "Buddy Holly Week" of Holly-related concerts and events that was to be faithfully observed for some years afterward. Norman Petty himself came over from New Mexico to inaugurate the first Buddy Holly Week; at the celebration lunch, he presented Paul with the cufflinks Holly had been wearing at his death in a plane crash in February 1959.

That was just the beginning for MPL, whose body may have been small but whose mouth quickly proved as large and ever open as that of an angler fish. Over the following years, often acting on advice from Lee Eastman, it gobbled up the publishing for a succession of hit stage shows, including *A Chorus Line, Grease, Annie,* and *Hello, Dolly!,* as well as for innumerable standards and even TV theme music, notably that for Lucille Ball's 1950s comedy show, *I Love Lucy.*

Paul had always fought shy of the rock star's lifestyle. Now, as his new band rocked the world, as he found his wealth growing far beyond any he had ever known as a Beatle, his personal life became proportionally more modest. By the mid-seventies he and Linda and their growing brood had left London, keeping on his old St. John's Wood mansion as a pied-à-terre but settling permanently in a small house near Rye, Sussex. Given that those were far safer, less media-intrusive times, it was still an extraordinarily unpretentious and accessible roost for a multimillionaire ex-Beatle. It had neither security fences nor patrolling guard dogs; for many years, indeed, the entrance to its front drive did not even have gates. "It wasn't much more than a hole in the hedge," remembers one McCartney fan who trekked down for a look. "I used to think how many cars passed that gate each day without ever knowing Paul was there."

The interior was equally unshowy, save for Paul's growing collection of modern art. Ever the autodidact, he had developed a passion for twentieth-century American painters like Jackson Pollock and Willem de Kooning (the latter, fortuitously, a client of Lee Eastman's). The knack for cartooning that he himself had had since school days now developed into full-blown painting, though as yet for purely recreational purposes.

His house might look open and accessible, but Paul guarded its privacy as fiercely as if it were surrounded by razor wire and searchlights. Most people, and almost all journalists, thought he lived in the rather larger and more opulent mill house nearby that he'd turned into a recording studio. Even some of his closest professional colleagues never got to see inside his real home. A public relations man who worked closely with him during the late seventies remembers being kept firmly at arm's length in this way. When they needed to discuss something the PR man would drive down from London, wait in his car outside the house, and Paul would emerge and talk to him there.

After Mary in 1969, Linda bore two more children: Stella (born in 1971) and James (Paul's baptismal name, born in 1977). Together with Linda's daughter Heather, they grew up in an atmosphere of absolute parental love and security, with a father who could not have been more hands-on. Unlike most rock-star kids, however, none was in the least spoiled: all four were born in National Health maternity wards, attended local state schools, and were firmly inculcated with the old-fashioned Liverpudlian virtues of politeness, considerateness, and respect that their grandfather, Jim McCartney, had unknowingly bequeathed them.

Linda immersed herself in family and country life, proving to be a devoted mother and an increasingly skillful cook (witness that rather patronizing album track, "Cook of the House"). Under her influence, Paul became both a vegetarian and an animal rights enthusiast, proselytizing to the extent of hanging GO VEGGIE banners above the stage at Wings concerts—so fueling the worst fears of Beatle-Paul fans who'd wondered what "she" would do to him next.

From their Sussex neighbours, the couple won esteem for their refusal to come on like rock 'n' roll royalty and their obvious love and respect for the surrounding countryside. The only waves they made in the community came from their fierce opposition to the local hunt—and flat refusal to allow it to cross their land. When the district's only NHS hospital was threatened with closure, Paul stepped in and donated enough money to keep it going. Despite her crowded new domestic life, Linda persisted with her photography, snapping her husband, children, animals, and surroundings at every opportunity and putting together a Christmas calendar made from the best of her year's shots.

At some moment in the mid-seventies, British pop journalists ceased referring to Wings' front man as "Paul" and instead dubbed him "Macca." Though merely a contraction of "McCartney," vaguely evoking both his Irish and Liverpool working-class heritage, it perfectly fitted the new and very different persona that came more clearly into definition with each seven-league leap of solo success. Whereas Paul, in Beatles times, had suggested almost saintly softness and charm, Macca suggested something altogether tougher and more synthetic; a perhaps-not-too-distant cousin to Formica. Whereas Paul had been adept at concealing his prodigious vanity from the world, Macca sometimes let it show as helplessly as a "flasher" in a raincoat on Clapham Common. Whereas Paul had steered a largely trouble-free path through the minefields of pop stardom, Macca at times would seem almost hell-bent on blundering into the most obvious trip wires.

His and Linda's devotion to family values did not prevent them from still indulging the emblematic habit of sixties flower children. They used marijuana, both at home and while traveling with Wings. And, alas, there was now no magic shield to protect pot-smoking ex-Beatles from retribution.

John Lennon has gone down in history as the band's most reckless drug user; in fact, Paul in the post-Beatles years would be busted more times, and more spectacularly, than John ever was. It happened twice in 1972 for cannabis possession—first in Sweden, then on the McCartneys' Scottish farm. Another bust came in 1984 while they were vacationing in Barbados; the following day, when they and their children arrived back at Heathrow Airport, further cannabis was found in Linda's luggage.

But worst by far was the Tokyo bust of January 1980, an episode almost suggesting that the new Macca-Paul was bent on a subconscious course of hara-kiri. In the whole addle-brained history of pop stars and forbidden substances, it's hard to find anyone else who has acted so stupidly or paid so scary a price.

His reputation at that moment, ironically, was at an all-time high. A month earlier, he had organized a series of London concerts, headlined by Wings, to aid refugees in Kampuchea, formerly Cambodia—a gesture of altruism still comparatively rare among pop superstars that in effect prepared the ground for Bob Geldof and Live Aid four years later. Hence that breathless moment of almost Beatles reunion, with George and Ringo reportedly willing to appear onstage with Paul if it would send more milk and penicillin to the Kampuchean refugees, but John flatly deflating the whole idea and remaining firm even against pleas from the UN's secretary-general.

Wings then departed on a world tour, of which the high point was to be their first-ever performances in Japan. Despite Paul's huge fan base there, he had been repeatedly denied a Japanese visa as a result of his 1972 drug busts. Now, thanks to intense diplomatic and entrepreneurial lobbying, not to mention his current high standing with the UN, he was to be allowed in at last.

The celebratory atmosphere of the visit was to be short-lived. When Paul arrived at Tokyo airport, customs officers found 219 grams of marijuana in a toiletries bag placed on *top* of the clothes in his suitcase. He was arrested, charged with possession—an offense carrying a maximum seven-year sentence—and then thrown into prison. Only after nine days of further intense diplomatic activity did the authorities release and instantly deport him.

He arrived back in Britain more chastened than his public had ever seen him, pale, hollow-eyed, and visibly shaken by prison conditions that he compared, with a ghost of his old flippancy, to *The Bridge on the River Kwai*. About the offense itself he said nothing, so adding further fuel to a rumor that the marijuana had actually belonged to Linda and that he'd taken the rap for her, just as Mick Jagger had for Marianne Faithfull in the famous "Mars bar" bust of 1967.

The other members of Wings were understandably outraged at the worldwide notoriety their leader had brought down on their heads. After Paul, the band's main instrumental linchpin had been Denny Laine, an insouciant character who always seemed able to ride the Macca bossiness and egotism. But now even Laine had had enough and quit the band without notice—so making its breakup inevitable—afterward writing a song, "Japanese Tears," that attacked Paul in terms almost as bitter as John's "How Do You Sleep?"

After this traumatic and demeaning episode there would be no more glimpses of the real McCartney for a long time to come. Even the shock of John's murder, eight months later, produced no public sign of the devastation that he was suffering. "Yeah, it's a drag, isn't it?" he said to the besieging media pack as off-handedly as if it were something no more serious than a record slipping out of the Top Ten.

Words often come out wrongly at moments of anguish. No one could possibly blame him for not producing a polished sound bite to express what a huge part of his life Mark David Chapman's bullets had blown away. Just the same, there was something vital missing from his public response, just as there was from George Harrison's. The people whose greatest gift next to music had been the gift of the gab, who had always known just the right thing to say at any given moment, now astonished the grieving world with their gaucherie and gracelessness. More tellingly, neither appeared to think the tragedy sufficiently important to rearrange their lives for. Of the three remaining ex-Beatles, only Ringo immediately dropped everything and flew to New York as a public gesture of support for John's family.

From here on, Paul would seem intent on proving he didn't need Wings any more than he had the Beatles. And so his public seemed to reassure him. In 1989 and again in 1993, he undertook world tours, accompanied by Linda and an unnamed backing band, and dispensing with most of Wings' flashy glam-rock effects. Both tours combined brought him an ecstatic audience numbering around 2,500,000; on a single night in Rio de Janeiro during the first, he played to a crowd of 184,000.

No one better symbolized the dawning era of brotherhood and co-operation among rock stars—or was more adept at turning it to his personal advantage. During the early eighties, he recorded duets with two major black performers, in each of which he managed to express deference and respect to his covocalist while at the same time shamelessly hogging the mike. With the former Motown prodigy Stevie Wonder in 1982 he recorded "Ebony and Ivory," a plea for racial harmony with rhymes ("piano keyboard" and "Oh, Lord" for instance) that one would hardly have expected from the writer of "Eleanor Rigby." With Michael Jackson—soon to be as big to the eighties as the Beatles had been to the sixties—he recorded "The Girl Is Mine" (1982) and "Say Say Say" (1983).

Since the Family Way and Black Dyke Mills Band days people had been urging him to try his hand at writing classical music. In the early nineties, seemingly with no new pop worlds left to conquer, he decided the time had come. He may have had no formal training in classical theory or scoring—but he was Paul McCartney. The result was *Paul McCartney's Liverpool Oratorio,* drawing on recognizably the same childhood echoes as had "Penny Lane" and "Eleanor Rigby." It received its world premiere at Liverpool's Anglican cathedral in 1991, performed by a full symphony orchestra and chorus conducted by Carl Davis, who shared composing credit with Paul. Dame Kiri Te Kanawa headed a solo quartet that included Sally Burgess, Jerry Hadley, and Willard White. Though deserving no epithet much stronger than "pleasant," the *Liverpool Oratorio* was received with as much critical rapture as a long-lost work by Bach or Handel: It went on to play in London at the Royal Festival Hall and in New York at Carnegie Hall, and in other venues.

Not everything he touched, however, was to turn instantly to the gold of million-selling records. In 1984, MPL had moved into feature films with *Give My Regards to Broad Street,* a nine-million-dollar project inspired by the imminent closure of London's Broad Street railway station. As the lamely punning title (on *Give My Regards to Broadway*) suggested, it was Paul's pet project; like *The Magical Mystery Tour* seventeen years earlier, it revealed his fatal tendency not to think things through properly but believe he could just wing it on McCartney Pied-

Piper magic. He himself was said to have largely written the script, which concerned a famous pop star's picaresque quest for some lost demo tapes, but was above all a device for putting Paul McCartney, soft-focused to mid-sixties youth and prettiness, in the dead center of almost every frame. As in *Mystery Tour*, various accomplished actors and performers wandered in and out of shot, obviously wondering what the hell it was all about but still tickled beyond measure to be working in Beatle Heaven.

The subsequent reviews made *Magical Mystery Tour* seem like a smash hit by comparison and brought Paul his first public ridicule on British TV's *Spitting Image* puppet show. As a big-eyed Macca figure sat in a restaurant, his waiter announced "Your turkey, Sir!" and dumped a film can labeled *Give My Regards to Broad Street* onto his plate.

More successful MPL film projects were an animated feature about Rupert Bear and a television documentary on the Beatles' old idol Buddy Holly, released in 1985 and including the first ever intimate glimpses of Holly from his family, his fellow musicians, and his widow, Maria-Elena. Yet here again, Macca could not bear to stay off-camera: As well as introducing the film, he made several incidental appearances, including a lengthy—and poorly prepared—soliloquy on Holly's compositional methods. It was noticeable, too, that he chose not to be filmed in his own home but in the deliberately neutral setting of a hay barn. Even when talking of the music closest to his heart, he could not "open the door and let 'em in."

Supremely successful though he was on so many fronts, there remained one glaring gap among his myriad possessions, acquisitions, and holdings. This ultimate creative control freak might have the satisfaction of controlling everything from Buddy Holly's songbook to *Grease* and *I Love Lucy*. Yet, ironically, he did not control his own earliest work, the songs he had written for the Beatles under the democratically unspecific "Lennon–McCartney" byline. "I Saw Her Standing There," "Love of the Loved," "I Want to Hold Your Hand," "Do You Want to Know a Secret," "Eight Days a Week," and all the dozens more of John and Paul's perfect primitive paintings still belonged to Northern Songs, the publishing company Dick James had sold from under their feet at the height of the Apple crisis in 1969.

Northern's original buyers, Lew Grade's ATV network, had in turn sold the company on to the Australian mogul Robert Holmes à Court.

In 1985, it unexpectedly came on to the market again. Swallowing his ill-feeling toward Yoko, Paul contacted her and persuaded her of the wisdom of their making a joint bid. But while the two and their lawyers argued over strategy, Northern was snapped up in a $47.5 million deal—by none other than the eighties wunderkind Michael Jackson.

Even the canny Macca was stunned by the speed and duplicity with which his former recording partner, and supposed good friend, engineered the coup. He was later to give his own wry account of it, perfectly mimicking "Jacko's" childlike lisp. "Michael asked me one day how you went about buying a song catalog, and I gave him all kinds of advice. The next time I saw him, he said, 'I'm gonna buy *your* songs, Paul.'"

All of the former Beatles had attracted criticism for their seeming indifference to Liverpool's desperate economic plight during the recession-hit seventies and early eighties. With his well-founded reputation for being careful, to put it no stronger, Paul had always seemed the least likely benefactor of his home city or his alma mater, Liverpool Institute High School. During the late seventies his former English teacher, Dusty Durband, wrote to ask his support in a school reconstruction appeal. Mr. Durband was disappointed—and annoyed—to receive a cheque back for just one thousand pounds.

A radical change of mind came in the mid-nineties after it was reported that Liverpool Institute, already closed for some years, now faced actual demolition. Paul became the moving spirit in the old high school's thirteen-million-pound transformation into the Liverpool Institute for the Performing Arts (LIPA for short), a project that, perhaps more than any other, was to symbolize the city's economic revival and regenerated self-belief. It was opened by the Queen in 1996, with an unfamiliarly dark-suited Macca beside her. Not since 1964 had any Beatle made so triumphant a homecoming.

By this point, it seemed that the McCartney name automatically shed magic in whatever context it occurred. In 1995, Paul's younger daughter, Stella, graduated from St. Martin's School of Art and began an ascent in the couture world destined to be as meteoric as her father's in the musical one. Even more to Paul's satisfaction, Linda had at long last achieved recognition in her own right by skillfully blending her dietary principles with her prowess as "Cook of the House." The Linda McCartney range of vegetarian frozen foods with accompanying recipes, launched in

1991, now adorned major supermarkets throughout both the U.K. and America.

In the Queen's birthday honors of 1997 Paul became the third British pop singer to receive a knighthood (after the saintly Cliff Richard and Live Aid's organizer Bob Geldof). The award came in the dying days of John Major's sleaze-ridden and clapped-out Tory government, and could be seen as a desperate bid for popularity by playing the well-worn Harold Wilson card; even so, none could deny Paul had long been in line for some public recognition more substantial than his 1965 MBE. Significantly, his checkered history of drug busts and brief Japanese incarceration seem never to have been an issue when 10 Downing Street consulted with Buckingham Palace about the award.

Becoming Sir Paul was just one of the honors now showering on him thicker than jelly beans at an old-time Beatles Christmas show. His family home, the modest council house on Forthlin Road, Allerton, was acquired by the National Trust and opened to the public, creating a historic shrine of the little front room where John and he used to huddle with their guitars and Buddy Holly records after cutting school. He was invited to join leading politicians and diplomats as a weekend guest at Highgrove, the Prince of Wales's country seat. He even had a variety of rose named after him.

The whole rose-tinted idyll came crashing around his ears when Linda was diagnosed with breast cancer.

The disease is never other than cruel and arbitrary in its toll on women often still in the prime of life. And in this case, like so many others—and so much else in the Beatles' story—history was horribly repeating itself. Breast cancer had also struck down the other essential woman in Paul's life, his mother Mary, when he was only fourteen. Ironically, on Linda's public appearances with Paul she looked smilier and more vibrant than her hypercritical public had ever seen her before. Only the close cropping of the former luxuriant blonde hair gave a clue to the ordeal she was suffering.

Linda's greatest solace in those grim and increasingly less optimistic months was the explosive success of her daughter Stella in the fashion world. In 1997, just two years after graduating from St. Martin's School of Art, Stella joined the Parisian couture house of Chloé as chief designer in succession to Karl Lagerfeld. She was already becoming an international celebrity in her own right, with her peaky Paul face, her plunging necklines, and her penchant for walking hand-in-hand with female rather than male escorts. She designed clothes with a rummage-sale raggedyiness no sane woman would ever wear but which flew into the glossy fashion mags as instantaneously as her father had once burned up the Top Ten. At her first Paris show—arguably the most highly publicized since Yves St. Laurent's debut in the pre-swinging sixties—Linda and Paul were among the host of rock and movie celebrities cheering her from the catwalk side.

Linda died in April 1998 at the McCartneys' ranch near Tucson, Arizona, a retreat whose existence had been kept secret from all but their closest friends and associates. In a misguided attempt to preserve the ranch's incognito, Paul's spokespeople initially announced that Linda had died several hundred miles to the west, in Santa Barbara, California. The truth emerged only when Santa Barbara's municipal authority began asking why the death had not been registered with them.

It was barely seven months since Diana, Princess of Wales, had been killed in a Paris car crash, unleashing a wave of hysterical mourning throughout Britain. An appetite still remained for a blonde-haired female martyr, and Linda McCartney perfectly fit that bill. Forgetting their old hostility, the media extolled her campaigns for vegetarianism and animal rights in much the same terms as Diana's for AIDS and land-mine victims. For a brief, surreal moment, she became a kind of mini–People's Princess, lauded with the same crazy disproportion as she had formerly been denigrated.

For Paul, paradoxically, losing Linda meant stepping back into limelight brighter than any he had known for more than a decade. Rock, as a rule, tends to create widows; here was the music's first A-list widower. For the first time ever he showed pain and vulnerability to the world, which in turn responded with an affection greater than any he had received in all his previous decades of relentless winning. To one interviewer he recalled how he had comforted Linda's final hours by making her picture them both riding their favorite horses through their favorite countryside. To another he revealed that, in twenty-nine years of marriage, they had never spent a single night apart.

Two memorial services for Linda were held, one in London, the other in New York. It might have been expected that the widow of Paul's oldest friend and still much-missed partner might have been asked to the New York service, especially after the reconciliation he had so publicly proclaimed at the Rock and Roll Hall of Fame ceremony four years earlier. But Yoko was excluded from the list. An additional memorial was a Linda McCartney solo album, compiled by Paul in an obvious attempt to win her the musical credibility she'd been denied in her lifetime. Entitled *Wide Prairie,* it brought together various Linda vocal tracks from the Wings era, including "Cook of the House." Though it was widely and earnestly reviewed, not even the most ardently pro-McCartney critic could find much more to say than "nice try."

But the period of mourning was to end rather abruptly. Early in 1999, Paul began to be seen in public with thirty-two-year-old Heather Mills, a prominent figure in the now interdependent worlds of show business and charity. Though initially he smiled away their meetings as pure coincidence, the subterfuge was short-lived. That summer, while Heather was being interviewed on a TV talk show, Paul made a "surprise" appearance, took her hand, and announced that they were in love.

His new love's background was, to say the least, an unusual one. Born and raised on Tyneside, she was a self-confessed juvenile delinquent who claimed to have fled from a violent, tyrannical father to work on a fairground on London's Clapham Common and live rough "under the arches" at Waterloo station before turning her looks and spectacular figure to account as a glamour model and playmate of the Arab billionaire Adnan Khashoggi. As a teenager, she had been arrested for stealing jewelry, but had been let off with probation owing to her troubled family circumstances.

Her autobiography, *Step by Step,* recounted further traumatic youthful experiences—among them, being held prisoner as a seven-year-old by a pedophile swimming teacher and being almost murdered by a knife-wielding lesbian flatmate. She made an early first marriage, to a Middlesex businessman named Alfie Karmal, who had encouraged her to progress from Soho club waitress to pinup, a career in which she would later claim to earn as much as two hundred thousand pounds per year. She became pregnant but lost the baby through an ectopic pregnancy and, not long afterward, left Karmal for a Slovenian ski instructor. At the age of twenty-five, she was run over by a police motorcyclist who had been hurrying to a so-called emergency involving Diana, Princess of Wales. Her left foot was almost severed, and surgeons had no choice but to amputate the leg just below the knee.

Whatever might subsequently be said of Heather, no one could deny her courage or unstoppable determination. She designed her own prosthetic leg, with which she was soon able to run, dance, even ski with the same freedom she had before her accident. She would recall with hilarity how, on one early ascent in a ski lift, her prosthetic leg came loose and sailed down the slopes below with the ski still attached to it. Nor could her spirit be dampened even by the crushing advice of a female social worker immediately after she lost her leg. "You'll have to face it, dear," the social worker told her. "You're never going to be attractive to men again."

"I could lose both my arms and both my legs," Heather replied, "and I'd *still* be more attractive to men than you are."

In fact, she was always to maintain that men were never turned off by her leg and that every one of her boyfriends had asked her to marry him "inside a week." She was determinedly frank and open about the prosthesis, showing it to any interviewer who wanted to see it, once even whipping it off and waving it under the nose of American radio talk-show host Larry King.

Following her accident, she tried to make a career as a television presenter, appearing on various regional programs but never winning any permanent spot. Her involvement in charity work began at the same time, drawing directly and indirectly on the traumas of her own past. She became a campaigner for the homeless, for amputees, and—like Diana, Princess of Wales—for the victims of land mines left behind by wars in Asia and Africa.

A television colleague of that era describes her as "one of the shrewdest and most calculating women I've ever met. Whatever misfortune is being talked about, Heather has suffered it—from homelessness to ectopic pregnancy. But I have to admire her. Once, after she'd appeared on *The Richard and Judy Show* with a homeless girl, she had the girl to stay with her for about two weeks, even though her current boyfriend was coming over to see her from New Zealand. The three of them were together in Heather's house, plus her terrier.

"When she went to Cambodia to see land-mine victims with the Duchess of Kent, she met a girl who'd lost both arms and both legs.

Heather took the girl under her wing, and she's now working in the Anglia Television newsroom.

"Her attitude was that in her life she'd sunk to the very bottom, so she deserved only the very best. And Paul McCartney was the ultimate notch on the bedpost."

The new relationship had a galvanic effect on Paul, blowing away the clouds of sadness that had engulfed him since Linda's death. To escape media harassment, he and Heather took to spending weekends at a borrowed cottage on the Cliveden estate in Berkshire—the famous scene of John Profumo's first meeting with Christine Keeler, now transformed into a luxury hotel. Heather tempted him back to parties and even discos where—as one friend reported—"they danced together like a couple of teenagers." As proof of her beneficial influence, he declared he had even given up using marijuana for her sake.

The announcement that they planned to marry brought a sharp change to this initially friendly perception of Heather. To be sure, the ructions surrounding Paul's wedding to Linda, thirty years earlier, would sometimes seem mild by comparison. Heather was portrayed as an opportunistic gold-digger, out to stake her claim on a McCartney fortune that—after the phenomenal success of the Beatles' *1* album— was on course to make him pop's first-ever billionaire. (To this charge, she made the somewhat surprising reply that if she'd been out for money alone, she would have gone for someone "richer than Paul.")

The media pack quickly tracked down her former husband, Alfie Karmal, who did not need much persuasion to describe a "damaged" person who, he said, had left him without warning after their five-year relationship, trashing their home by way of farewell. The childhood friend with whom she claimed to have been held prisoner by the pedophile swimming teacher dismissed her account as "crap." Her stepfather, John Stapley, said that her memories of fairground life on Clapham Common were likewise part of the "fantasy world" she had created from her past. It was whispered that even the best part of her career, her work for land-mine victims, derived merely from an ambition to be seen as a substitute Princess Diana. Fellow campaigners questioned her claims to have been appointed a United Nations ambassador for land mines and even to have been short-listed for a Nobel Peace Prize. One of her former TV colleagues was surprised to see her on BBC2's *Ready, Steady, Cook* program, claiming to have been a vegetarian every bit as devout as Paul "for the past seventeen years." "When I worked with her a few years back, her diet used to be almost all protein," her ex-colleague says. "She used to tuck in to huge bits of steak."

Most crucially, Paul's children—particularly his three grown-up daughters—were said to be horrified by his choice of a former swimwear model to replace their mother (and one sharing the name of their mother's oldest child to boot). Paul himself dropped his sunshine mask sufficiently to admit there were difficulties about Heather within the family and that she could be "bossy" at times, but at the same time made it clear that these factors had no effect on his resolve to make her the next Lady McCartney. From then on, he became as determined to win acceptance for Heather as he had once been to win it for Linda. So that nobody around him should mistake his wishes, he granted her a power and influence of which even Linda had never dreamed. At his concerts, Heather became the first person in history to give him critical notes on his performance—and have them earnestly listened to.

She on her side showed little of the meekness and deference he had always been used to from Linda. Early in 2002, staff at a Miami hotel reported overhearing a furious row between them, in which Paul allegedly shouted, "I don't want to marry you any more." A hotel team equipped with metal-detectors was then mobilized to search the bushes below their room after Heather had apparently hurled her fifteen-thousand-pound engagement ring through its open window. Heather's explanation was that Paul and she had simply been "having a laugh" and playing catch with the ring.

The approaching nuptials brought further allegations of dissent and discontent among the McCartney children. Stella was reportedly furious at not having been asked to design Heather's wedding dress, her soon-to-be stepmother considering her clothes "too tarty." Instead, Heather announced, she would be creating her own Chantilly lace bridal gown with the help of London couturiers Avis and Brown. Mary McCartney, a rising portrait photographer—whose subjects had already included Tony and Cherie Blair—was said to feel equally slighted because she hadn't been asked to do the wedding pictures.

The ceremony took place on June 11, in Glaslough, County Monaghan, the part of Ireland from which Paul's maternal ancestors had originally sprung. Apart from the best man, his younger brother, Michael, it was a very different occasion from the simple register office ceremony at which he'd married Linda in 1969. This time the cost was around one million pounds and the setting was Castle Leslie, a medieval pile whose eccentric owner, eighty-seven-year-old Sir Jack Leslie, was famous for performing Madonna's "Like a Virgin" in local pubs. Offers of £1.5 million from *Hello!* magazine and £1 million from *OK!* for exclusive photo access had both been refused: Instead, a single color shot of the newlyweds was issued to the media, with all reproduction fees paid to Heather's principal charity interest, Adopt a Minefield U.K. The guests, including Eric Clapton, the Ringo Starrs, and Sir George Martin, were asked to donate one thousand pounds each to the charity in lieu of wedding presents.

Paul's stepdaughter, Heather, and his son, James, were both significantly absent from the celebrations. Stella and Mary did attend, albeit with the kind of stuck-on smiles in which their father used to specialize as a Beatle. It would later be claimed that the new Lady McCartney had expressed willingness to sign a prenuptial agreement limiting her claim on Paul's assets to twenty million pounds in the event of a divorce. But he had refused to consider it. Somewhat undermining the media-free atmosphere, the day's events were filmed for inclusion in a documentary about the bridegroom's ongoing American tour. With the slightly aggrieved tone that can flavor her public statements, Heather was to say that media attention—surely not unexpected either to her bridegroom or herself, and not always unwelcome—had made her wedding year "the worst of my life."

After their honeymoon, the couple settled in Brighton, where Heather had already lived for some years. Reports soon began to emerge of a besottedly attentive new husband, preparing hummus sandwiches for her packed lunches, being a perfect host to her friends at dinner parties, and "dancing around the room like Fred Astaire." In May 2003 Heather announced that she was pregnant.

To have written pop music's equivalent of the works of Shakespeare, to be a billionaire, a knight of the realm, a national monument, the name of a rose, and still, after all these years, among the half-dozen most famous faces on the planet might be thought more than enough to satisfy the most ravenous ambition. But it seems not to satisfy Paul.

Despite the almost incalculable pile-up of achievement behind him, he still works at being a star as though he has everything to prove, still churns out songs, still cracks the whip as unrelentingly over musicians and technicians at his recording sessions, still pushes, promotes, and hypes for all he's worth, and gets miffed when there's no phone call summoning him back on to *Top of the Pops*. The one-time master innovator scans the output of single-brain-cell rappers and ninth-hand boy bands hoping to pick up tips that will make his next product more appealing to modern teenagers. The all-time classic endlessly ponders and frets over how to be "contemporary."

From time to time he allows us to see how, even if you are as huge and rich and loaded with honors as Sir Paul McCartney, you can still be plagued by insecurities that no ocean of adulation can drown; old grudges and frustrations that poison the most golden triumph; little niggles that just never go away. Despite all that being a Beatle bestowed on him, he plainly continues to feel he received less than his proper share, in terms of both money and credit. In the mid-eighties he went to the band's old record company, EMI, and demanded a larger share of their collective royalties than that paid to his two fellow survivors and John's estate. George, Ringo, and Yoko joined forces to sue him and the matter was settled quietly out of court.

Someone else who had written a ballad like "Yesterday" and lived to see it challenge Irving Berlin's "White Christmas" as the world's most covered song might well feel only pride and satisfaction in that achievement. But not Paul. In 2000, while the hardcover edition of the *Beatles Anthology* was in preparation, he asked Yoko if the credits for "Yesterday" could be changed from "Lennon-McCartney" to "McCartney-Lennon" since he had written it without any input from John. He even claimed John's precedence on the credit meant the Lennon estate had received a greater share of the song's royalties.

Yoko's refusal to consider the idea put the Beatles-watching community, for once, unequivocally on her side, for it was an elemental part of Beatles history, and of their ineluctable charm, that songs were historically credited to "Lennon-McCartney," whichever of them had been the dominant or exclusive composer. The two had always been absolute creative equals no matter whose name came first; indeed, on the Beatles' first album and early hit singles like "From Me to You," their byline had appeared as "McCartney-Lennon." If John received an undeserved half-credit for Paul songs like "Yesterday" and "Let It Be," then so did Paul for John songs like "Norwegian Wood" and "Strawberry Fields Forever."

He had already received one chance to rearrange the credit to his liking when several of his Beatles songs were featured on the *Wings Over America* album in 1976. Another came in 2002 with the live album of his latest American tour, which included "Yesterday," "Eleanor Rigby," "Can't Buy Me Love," and "Hey Jude." On the Wings album he had simply reversed the credit; this time, as if to ram the point home, it read "composed by Paul McCartney and John Lennon." Even longtime McCartney fans expressed themselves dumbfounded by the pettiness of it. "He just can't bear anyone to think he didn't write 'Yesterday' or 'Let It Be' on his own," observed one. "And it was also a sign he doesn't care any more who knows his real feelings about Yoko."

Yoko had never publicly spoken a word against him, and had gone along with many of his schemes—such as his plan to reissue the *Let It Be* album in its intended raw state without the Phil Spector overdub that so offended him in 1970. But with his unilateral rewriting of the Lennon-McCartney credit, word came out of the Dakota that Yoko had had enough and was considering legal action against him. He responded with a seven-hundred-word statement claiming that the Lennon-McCartney formula had been agreed to by John and Brian Epstein behind his back, but with the half promise it might be changed sometime in the future. He also said that Yoko had initially agreed to let him rearrange the credit, but then had changed her mind.

The statement almost descended to inarticulacy in Paul's simultaneous determination to get his way, yet still keep the smile on his face. "This isn't anything I'm going to lose any sleep over, nor is it anything that will cause litigation, but it seems harmless to me after more than 30 years of it being the other way round for people like Yoko who have benefited and continued to benefit from my past efforts to be a little generous and to not have a problem with this suggestion of how to simply map out for those who do not know who wrote which of the songs." The inclusion in his stage show of a tribute song to John—allegedly written just after John's death—did little to moderate the widespread negative reaction. Even his fellow survivor, the normally tractable Ringo, expressed puzzlement and faint disgust: "I think the way he did it was underhanded. I thought he should have done it officially with Yoko. . . . It was the wrong way to go about it." The furor eventually persuaded Paul against any further interference with the credit.

The whole episode illustrated the extent to which, a generation after

John's death, Paul still feels driven to compete with him, still hankers for the dividend of love and esteem that John drew from their partnership. It has never ceased to rankle that from their earliest Beatles days John was typecast as the arty, avant-garde, intellectual one while he himself was considered merely the nice one. Every interview he ever gives fulminates against this gross misconception, stressing what difficult books and art he used to relish in those days, how he helped Barry Miles and John Dunbar put the trendsetting Indica Gallery together, how he was at the sixties' cutting edge in London while John was being a Nowhere Man in the Weybridge stockbroker belt.

In recent times, the focus of his ambition, perhaps even more than music, has been showing us how wrong we were all those years ago. Together with his songwriting, John won lasting fame as a poet and an artist. Damn it then, Paul will prove himself to be an artist and a poet of a hundred times the size. And if you are Paul McCartney, with unlimited fame and funds and nothing on your horizon but yes-men, you can do it.

His collected poems, *Blackbird Singing*, appeared in 2000, heralded by mobbed book signings and appearances at literary festivals, and greeted by plaudits from established poets such as Adrian Mitchell and Paul Muldoon. The poems dated back to 1965, with the most recent batch written during Linda's final illness. A few had the simple directness of his best song lyrics, seasoned by the wisdom of personal loss. But others demonstrated how an unfinished thought or half-coined phrase that may get by in a song lyric shrieks pure embarrassment from the printed page. "Tears are not tears," ran the most widely quoted lines, "They're balls of laughter dipped in salt."

His painting—long a private hobby and beneficial therapy—has been the subject of even more determined hype. In his authorized biography, *Many Years From Now*, an entire section was devoted to his views on Art, his formative influences as a painter, even the kinds of paints, canvases, and brushes he favors.

The 2001 Royal Academy Summer Exhibition included a blobby-blue and red Paul McCartney abstract in a kind of rock 'n' roll corner also featuring work by David Bowie, Rolling Stone Ronnie Wood, and the late Ian Dury. A year later, he had his first solo exhibition at Liverpool's Walker Art Gallery. Once again, no critic quite had nerve enough to spell out the differences between an amateur and a professional, though a glance at the Stuart Sutcliffe painting owned by the same gallery would have made the point well enough.

Echoes of John continue to turn up in McCartney music seemingly light years away from the Beatles. The title of his *Flaming Pie* album, for instance, was a quotation from John's long ago *Mersey Beat* article, "A Short Diversion on the Dubious History of Beatles" ("It came in a vision—a man appeared on a flaming pie and said unto them 'From this day on you are Beatles' "). Paul's appropriation of the quote caused extreme dismay to even hard-core Beatles loyalists. "He's achieved everything he possibly could as Paul McCartney," said one. "Why couldn't he leave that last little bit of John alone?"

For a long time he was reluctant to discuss the Beatles years, saying things like "Yeah, they were a good little band" with the same brand of studied understatement Earl Mountbatten used when he described being viceroy of India as "great fun." Now the story is a central part of every show and interview he gives, always in carefully sanitized form, with himself the focus of every scene. So familiar and formulaic have his anecdotes become that his fans refer to them by number. "Paul did number 21 and 37 on Parkinson last week," they will report to each other, or, "There was quite a good version of number 14 on Radio 2 on Saturday."

As a sexagenarian he remains enviably slim and youthful, though the still-abundant hair is now dyed (as Heather has confirmed) and the pixie face has begun to wilt around the jawline, turning him more each day into a facsimile of his father, Jim. His manner remains that of an ebullient boy next door, gazing on the limitless excitement and promise of Beatledom for the very first time, raising both thumbs into the air and chortling, *"Great!"* Indeed, he turned down a Lifetime Achievement award in the 2002 Brits, the biggest U.K. music awards of the year, because he said it would imply he was now old and past it, with all his best work behind him.

He spent most of 2002 on an American tour, filling major arenas across the continent and featuring more than ever previously "studio only" versions of Beatles songs such as "Blackbird," "Hello, Goodbye," and "It's Getting Better." The tour, by then subtitled "Back in the World," moved on to become his first journey through the U.K. for ten years, then on to Europe to venues including the Colosseum in Rome. It also included "Here Today," his tribute to John, and a version of "Something," played on George's beloved ukulele.

Before the tour, he had issued his American concert promoters a twelve-page list of backstage demands recalling the egomaniacal 1970s, when top groups would demand Napoleon brandy, can-can dancers in their dressing room, or dishes of M&M's consisting only of red ones. Though Paul's requirements could be classified as matters of conscience, stemming from his vegetarianism and animal rights beliefs, they still took superstar imperiousness into a new and surreal realm. The stretch limos provided for him must not have leather seats. The soft furniture in his hotel suites and dressing rooms must not have covers of real—or even artificial—animal skin. Not only must Sir Paul himself never be served with meat or meat by-products, but they also were banned from all the tour's production offices and backstage areas. The flowers in his dressing room must come only from "reputable florists," must include at least one arrangement of pale pink and white roses and another of Casablanca lilies as well as the star's own favorite freesias, and should avoid "weedy" things and pot plants with too visible trunks.

In February 2002, he became potentially the world's highest-paid entertainer when he was offered four million dollars to play in Las Vegas for a single night. The city was facing heavy losses after cancellation of the world heavyweight title fight between Mike Tyson and Lennox Lewis: In the whole wide world of twenty-first-century entertainment, there seemed only one comparable heavyweight, one name guaranteed to pay out the mega jackpot.

And did it make him happy? Who knows?

TWENTY-TWO

"IT DON'T COME EASY"

n December 1969, Eric Clapton set off on a British and European tour with his American protégés, the folk-rock duo Delaney and Bonnie. Among their backing group—billed simply as their "Friends"—was a rhythm guitarist whose bushy beard, wide-brimmed Stetson hat, and buckskin jacket gave him a more than passing resemblance to Buffalo Bill Cody. He seemed anxious to avoid attention, keeping always to the back of the stage, playing only essential chords on his state-of-the-art red guitar. Among the crowds who cheered for "the Great God Clapton" each night, few even recognized his shy, shrinking stage companion as George Harrison.

These were days long before rock superstars made elaborately modest "surprise" guest appearances in their friends' shows. Asking George out on tour was a pure act of kindness on Clapton's part, to take his best friend's mind off the turmoil within the Beatles and encourage his first steps in the solo career that now seemed inevitable.

So George, very reluctantly and nervously at first, joined the tour, traveling with Clapton and Co. at the back of their bus, staying at drab railway hotels, and each night, in Birmingham or Newcastle upon Tyne, becoming a little more used to facing a live audience once again. Most therapeutically of all, perhaps, in these far northern climes, Clapton proved to be far more instantly recognizable than he. One lunch-time, as the two sat together in a motorway café near Sheffield, a passing waitress stared suspiciously at Clapton, then turned to George. "He *is* famous, isn't he?" she queried. "Oh, yeah," George replied in his deadpan monotone. "That's the world's most famous guitarist . . . Bert Weedon."

After a few days of sharing Clapton's juvenile high spirits—food fights with the late-night hotel buffets, races with windup toys on their dressing-room floor—the gaunt, bearded face was beginning to look noticeably more cheerful. The buckskinned figure at the back of the stage was almost grooving, even reaching for single-string licks during the medley of rock 'n' roll classics that closed each show. "I'd forgotten what a gas it is to play live," he told Clapton gratefully. "That Little Richard medley is in E, isn't it?"

George may have been little more than a bystander, with Ringo, in the central battle for the soul of the Beatles, but he had still been deeply affected by the months of feuding and intriguing, the wearisome board meetings and tense recording sessions, and the final, unavoidable compulsion to side with one of his two former closest friends in outvoting and marginalizing the other. As he admitted in "Here Comes the Sun," "It's been a long, cold, lonely winter . . . It seems like years since it's been clear."

John and Paul each had a wife to go to when the group was no more. But George had no such anchor to his existence. His six-year marriage to the bewitching former model, Patti Boyd, was already running into trouble, largely the result of his serial infidelities and northern male arrogance. "He could be just horrible to Patti," remembers one of their friends. "George would say he was hungry, so Patti would make a wonderful meal . . . then he'd turn round and say he didn't want it." Patti, who genuinely loved him, stayed with him in the misguided belief that he might still one day change back into the lighthearted charmer who had wooed her on the set of *A Hard Day's Night;* he stayed with her mainly from inertia, and because he had other, more pressing problems to deal with than that of changing his woman.

It was in this insecure, restless frame of mind that his eye fell on the "Apple Scruffs," his own name for the female fans who haunted the individual Beatles' front gates, EMI's studios, and the steps at 3 Savile Row. Among them was Carol Bedford, the Texan girl who had arrived from Dallas to join the sisterhood a few months earlier and now lived in a shared flat not far from Abbey Road. In their brief doorstep exchanges Carol had impressed George with her humor, articulateness, and lack of sycophancy. She sensed they were developing a rapport—though never dreaming that the ultimate fantasy of every Apple Scruff was about to come true for her.

"One day, while I was at EMI studios, the roadie Mal Evans came up and asked me where I lived. I thought he might be the one who was interested, so I refused to tell him. Then later, while I was standing at the bus stop, George came along in his Mercedes. 'Fancy meeting you here,' he said, and offered me a ride home."

With all his experience as a Beatle, Carol expected him to be the smoothest and most nonchalant of seducers. Instead, she found he was almost as paralyzed by nerves as she was. "When we got to where I lived, George switched off the engine, then he pulled down his hat-brim, turned up his collar, and sank down low in his seat so that no one passing would recognize him. I tried to get out of the car but couldn't get the door open, so he had to lean over to do it for me. Then the scarf I was wearing got caught somewhere. As I was trying to pull it free, I accidentally hit George in the face and knocked his hat off."

She presumed that that first uncomfortable encounter would be their last one, but a week or so later, George overcame his seigneurial inhibitions so far as to call round at her flat. He gave no advance warning, however, and Carol happened to be out at the time. "When I came home, my flatmate told me this guy had been asking for me and that he seemed very shy and nervous. She didn't have to say any more for me to know who it had been."

Despite his nerves he tried again, and this time did find Carol at home. "He sat on my bed for about half an hour, and we talked. I kept thinking to myself, "He must have been in so *many* girls' flats, all over the world.' I offered to make him a cup of tea, but was so nervous that I dropped the box of matches all over the floor. George knelt down and helped me pick them up."

At the time he still had not fully recovered from a car accident some weeks earlier in which both he and Patti had been involved. "Patti had been hurt worse than George and was still having to stay home," Carol remembers. "I asked George how she was and he said, 'She's got to have plenty of peace and quiet, so I'm playing the drums really loudly in the next room.' That's when I realized what a rocky state their marriage was in."

Although obviously attracted to Carol, even in these private surroundings, George still made no move on her. What chiefly seemed to inhibit him was the risk of sexually transmitted disease—mild enough in that pre-AIDS era, but still a major deterrent for someone who'd been a musician on Hamburg's Reeperbahn. "He asked me if I'd ever had VD, or passed on NSU [nonspecific urethritis]. And he also got incredibly uptight when I told him he smoked much too much. If I'd had the pressures he did, he told me, I'd be a chain-smoker, too. He was telling me about his last medical checkup after the accident and what his doctor had said. He reminded me of a little boy who'd skinned his knee and was coming to his mother for comfort and reassurance."

His curb-crawling for Apple Scruffs was not the only bizarre infidelity Patti Harrison would have to endure. Not long afterward, the
couple visited Tittenhurst Park, the mansion in Henley-on-Thames that
Ringo and Maureen Starr had taken on after John and Yoko's departure
for America. Over dinner, George suddenly blurted out that he was in
love with Maureen. A few days later Patti came home to find him and
Maureen in bed together. For such a gross and meaningless betrayal of
two old friends, his only explanation was a shrug and the single word
"incest."

To musician friends like Eric Clapton, George compared his release
from the Beatles when it finally came to "recovering from a six-year
dose of constipation." At long last he was free of the Lennon-McCartney
stranglehold that had always kept his contribution to the band's oeuvre
so pitifully small. Never again would John patronize him or Paul try to
boss him or George Martin lead him to a studio piano and spell out the
solo he was expected to replicate on his guitar.

Certainly, in the immediate aftermath of the breakup, he seemed like
nothing so much as a brilliant genie, billowing forth from the bottle that
had confined him and towering triumphantly over those who had so
unfairly held him captive. His first solo project was no mere two-sided
album like John's and Paul's but a grandiose three-record set whose title,
All Things Must Pass, could be read either as a philosophical generaliza-
tion or as a heartfelt sigh of relief that the "long, cold, lonely winter" was
finally at an end. The album projected a completely new George, no
longer the grimly earnest sitar-bore of "Within You Without You" but a
lighter, more open-hearted character who seemed to have found the
perfect balance between his cherished Indian mysticism and high-
octane commercial pop. Its perfect synthesis was "My Sweet Lord," a
global chart smash destined for eternal life as an anthem to simple faith
that crossed all religious boundaries, equally valid whether chanted in a
Himalayan ashram, played on the organ of an English parish church, or
chanted at sundown by an imam from a minaret.

In the wake of *All Things Must Pass* came a chance to prove the gen-
uineness of his affinity with the Indian subcontinent and his exhorta-
tions to universal brotherhood. In the easterly part of Pakistan's two
separate segments, a secessionist movement had declared independence
from larger and richer West Pakistan, setting up a provisional govern-

ment and renaming their country Bangladesh. The Pakistani army had responded with genocidal cruelty, indiscriminately slaughtering college students, women, and children as well as independence fighters. In a land already awesomely impoverished, something like two million refugees were fleeing in panic to seek refuge over the border in neighboring India.

George conceived the idea of an all-star charity concert and live album to raise money for relief aid. As a Beatle, he doubtless would have turned the project over to his Apple minions to manage, or mismanage, as best they might. But in his new, can-do persona, he took over its organization personally, ringing up superstar friends to enlist their support, persuading hard-nosed managers and record companies to sanction the appearance of their multimillion-dollar talents, unprecedentedly, for free.

There were, in the end, two concerts for Bangladesh at New York's Madison Square Garden in August 1971, featuring George in company with, among others, Bob Dylan, Leon Russell, Ringo Starr, and Ravi Shankar. It was a historic event that gave rock the first inklings of dignity and altruism that would culminate with Live Aid fourteen years later. It was no less a personal accolade for George, demonstrating in what high regard he was held by the foremost names in the business. Rock concert audiences would never again be quite so high-minded, nor so overanxious to prove themselves just as au courant with Eastern mysticism as were their idols. During one show, as Ravi Shankar and his musicians finished tuning up for their sitar set, they were surprised to receive an earnest round of applause.

Ironically, the star management most difficult to square over the concerts for Bangladesh proved to be George's own. The high court–appointed receiver who—thanks to Paul McCartney—now administered the Beatles' partnership, was empowered to receive each ex-Beatle's solo earnings as well as their continuing income as a group (four million pounds in 1970). The receiver, James Spooner, was therefore less than thrilled to learn that George intended donating his royalties from the live album directly to the Bangladesh relief effort. Before the gift could be made there had to be lengthy enquiries to satisfy Mr. Spooner that it would not adversely affect the other Beatles' income tax situation. The individual permissions of John, Paul, and Ringo also had to be given in writing. It was to take a further high court ruling, seven months after the event, for George's spontaneous act of generosity to be finally sanctioned.

His humanitarian instincts were not confined to people far away. In 1972—a time when few British pop stars other than Elton John interested themselves in good works—he set up a charity called the Material World Foundation (named after his album *Living in the Material World*) that gave support to a range of causes, from the arts to children with special needs. He could be generous to friends, notably the Beatles' former publicist, Derek Taylor, whom he helped to acquire a mill house in Suffolk.

It was in every way a brilliant start to his new life in the new decade. But as time passed, a terrible truth slowly became apparent. "My Sweet Lord" and the other songs bountifully packed onto the six sides of *All Things Must Pass* had almost all been written by George from inside the Beatles, when the genius of Lennon and McCartney could not help but rub off a little on him. Without John and Paul to stimulate as well as frustrate him, he would never produce work even approaching such quality again. To make matters worse, with "My Sweet Lord" he was accused of plagiarizing a 1964 song called "He's So Fine" by an American female group, the Chiffons. Though George denied any conscious plagiarism, the three notes that made the central hook in both songs were clearly identical. The resulting litigation dragged on for years and took its most bizarre turn when Allen Klein, the Beatles' displaced manager, acquired the copyright of "He's So Fine," seemingly just for the satisfaction of prolonging the lawsuit against George.

Even more bizarre was the conclusion, reached years down the line, after a British court had decided against George and he had been obliged to pay a six-figure sum in compensation. He himself acquired the copyright of "He's So Fine," and so was free to plagiarize it or not, as he chose.

The Apple experience had not stifled his desire to have his own record label, on which he could both enjoy total artistic freedom and also foster new talent. In the mid-seventies, he finally found the right parent company in America's A&M, a label cofounded by Herb Alpert (of Tijuana Brass fame). So was launched Dark Horse Records, its name consciously congratulating a longtime outsider who was now the music industry's odds-on favorite.

Ironically, however, the establishment of Dark Horse saw his solo career begin a gradual and seemingly irreversible decline. His albums were critically panned, and sold in decreasing quantity. He began to alienate concert audiences by his self-importance and his heavy-handed attempts at lecturing and preaching. His 1974 American tour was a failure so resounding that he never again went on the road in America, nor any other Western country. He had the satisfaction, at least, of seeing "Something," his Abbey Road song, mature into a classic whose originality no one questioned and which over time would be covered by vocalists of every stamp, including Frank Sinatra and Shirley Bassey.

His continuing unhappy marriage to Patti, meanwhile, had produced one of rock's strangest ever love triangles. Eric Clapton had become infatuated with Patti years earlier but, as George's best friend, felt honor-bound not to pursue her. His classic song "Layla," on the pseudonymous *Derek and the Dominoes* album, was both a love letter to Patti and a lament for his own tied hands: "I tried to give you consolation . . . when your old man let you down. . . ." In 1974, Patti finally left George, subsequently divorcing him and marrying Clapton. Despite all this, the two guitar soulmates managed to stay friends; George even attended Patti and Eric's wedding. "If my wife's going to run off with someone," he said, "I'd rather it was with a guy that I love."

Thereafter, he seemed to content himself with the life of a landed gentleman-hippie, retreating into Friar Park, the 120-room Gothic mansion near Henley he had bought for two hundred thousand pounds in 1970. The house, built by an eccentric named Sir Frankie Crisp, would have made a perfect alternative school for Harry Potter, with its myriad sooty turrets, grotesque gargoyles, and light switches fashioned like monks' skulls. Although George went on releasing albums at regular intervals, he devoted himself mainly to restoring Friar Park's vast grounds, which encompassed a lake with stepping-stones set near the surface so that he could enjoy the feeling of walking on water. He also began a relationship with Olivia Arias, a secretary in the American office of his Dark Horse label. They married in 1978, a month after the birth of their only child, Dhani.

In 1980, he published *I, Me, Mine*, a limited-edition pictorial autobiography retailing at £175 per copy and including color facsimiles of his song lyrics as he had first handwritten them on sheets of hotel or office stationery; one even reproduced a burn he had made on it with his cigarette. Also reproduced was the check for one million pounds he'd had to write in August 1973 in part payment to the hated taxman.

John Lennon's murder in 1980 had a profound effect on George, although—like Paul—he was unable to react with more than inappropriate Merseybeat flipness. He said that a late-night phone call had woken him with the news, he'd gone back to sleep, "and when I woke up next morning, it was still true." With reflection he could only add the mock-tabloid cliché that he was "shocked and stunned." In fact, he was probably the worst affected of the three survivors, having never rebuilt bridges with John the way Paul and Ringo had. He knew, too, that John had been furious with him over the scant references to their early friendship he had made in *I, Me, Mine.*

He tried to make amends with a tribute song, "All Those Years Ago," which recalled his teenage hero-worship of John ("I always looked up to you") and hit out, rather too late, at those who had treated him "like a dog." It was, however, little more than a hasty doodle, sung at the anomalously cheerful tempo of a Boy Scout campfire song and not in the same league with the Elton John–Bernie Taupin Lennon tribute single, "Empty Garden," released soon afterward.

The main effect of the tragedy on George was to increase the secretiveness and suspicion that had always been so deeply embedded in his nature. From now on, he would be haunted by the fear that some Chapman figure—characterized as "the devil's best friend" in "All Those Years Ago"—might ultimately come gunning for him, too. He installed elaborate security systems at Friar Park and brought in his older brothers, Harry and Peter, as security chief and head gardener, respectively. "Before John's death, the front gates had always stood wide open," a former associate recalls. "But afterward, they were always shut and locked."

In the early eighties, a wholly unexpected new career beckoned, thanks to his friendship with Michael Palin and other members of the Monty Python comedy team. He was especially close to Eric Idle, whose post-Python fantasies included a 1977 documentary send-up of the Beatles called *The Rutles*. One scene parodied the plundering of the Apple house, with a TV interviewer speaking to Palin outside the front door while figures in the background gamboled off with TV sets and furniture. Demonstrating a little-suspected ability to laugh at himself, George took the role of the interviewer.

Idle, Palin, John Cleese, and company had since moved from television into cinema films with Monty Python's *Life of Brian*, a project originally financed by the Beatles' old parent company, EMI. Not until filming had begun in Tunisia did EMI's chief executive, Lord Delfont, realize he was funding a breathtakingly sacrilegious skit on the story of Christ. Delfont immediately pulled the plug, leaving the cast and unit marooned on location. Hearing of their plight, George weighed in to help them, mortgaging Friar Park to raise the four million pounds necessary for the film's completion. "Python helped keep me sane while the Beatles were breaking up," he told Idle and the others, "so I owed you this one."

The *Life of Brian* went on to make a fortune at the box office and bring George properly into the film business as part owner of a new company called HandMade. His partner was a former merchant banker named Denis O'Brien, to whom he had originally been introduced by the comedian Peter Sellers. Tall, dapper, and persuasive, O'Brien subsequently took over the financial management of both George and the Python team.

On the surface, HandMade appeared a spectacular success, releasing twenty-three films in ten years and taking most of the kudos for the British cinema's strong revival during the early and middle eighties. Their slate included lasting classics like *Mona Lisa, The Long Good Friday, Withnail and I,* Terry Gilliam's *Time Bandits,* and Alan Bennett's *A Private Function,* though there were also such notable turkeys as *Shanghai Surprise* starring Madonna. One of the more surreal moments in that era was seeing Madonna appear at a press conference with George—once a king of press conferences the world over—as her silent, scowling minder.

In 1987, his long-dormant recording career was suddenly revived by a collaboration with Jeff Lynne, formerly of the Electric Light Orchestra, a Birmingham band sometimes called "the Beatles of the seventies." From the *Cloud Nine* album, produced by Lynne, came a single, "Got My Mind Set on You," that took George to number one in America and number two in Britain. The following year, he and Lynne teamed with Bob Dylan, Tom Petty, and Roy Orbison as the Travelin' Wilburys, a kind of cornpone Sergeant Pepper band playing laid-back acoustic country-rock that they self-deprecatingly termed "skiffle for the eighties." The Wilburys released a hit album and brought Orbison back to prominence as a seminal rock artist in the last months before his death.

Meanwhile, HandMade Films was proving an even more painful financial experience for George than Apple Corps had been a decade and a half earlier. The company's projects were financed chiefly by bank loans supposedly guaranteed by him and his partner, Denis O'Brien. In fact, as he belatedly discovered, he was usually the sole guarantor. Most banks were happy to trust in the solvency of a former Beatle but then one—Barclays—demanded an audit of George's affairs and brought to light a deficit of something like twenty million pounds. In yet another eerie echo of Beatles history, George received the same warning John Lennon once had: If he carried on like this, he'd soon be bankrupt. The possibility even loomed of having to sell his beloved Friar Park. He launched a twenty-five-million-dollar lawsuit against Denis O'Brien, also adopting the now familiar Beatles tactic of pillorying him in a song ("Lying O'Brien"). But by the time the American courts had decided in George's favor and awarded him eleven million dollars, O'Brien had filed for bankruptcy. "George was traumatized by the HandMade experience," one former associate remembers. "It wasn't so much the money he lost as the feeling of personal betrayal. In fact, I'd go so far as to say that all the health troubles he suffered later really started here."

It was mainly George's urgent need of cash that helped bring about the Beatles' reunion on their 1995 *Anthology* project—although of the three survivors he proved conspicuously the least charming. Most bitterly did he seem to resent the fact that they had received no collective national honor beyond their MBE each in 1965. "After all we did for Great Britain, selling all that corduroy and making it swing," he sneered, "they gave us that bloody old leather medal with wooden string [*sic*] through it."

Charm was, indeed, the most notable deficiency in these later years. Despite his own late burst of chart success, he began to come across like some old curmudgeon in a chimney-corner, voicing detestation of new musical styles like rap and Britpop and affecting not to listen to anything recorded later than about 1976. He even spat some venom at Oasis, a band who made their adoration of the Beatles clear in almost every note they played. True, they released a track whose title unwittingly copied his *Wonderwall* album—but he, of all people, might have understood about that. Liam Gallagher, their volatile front man, became incensed enough by George's negative comments to vow to beat him up if ever they should meet.

Though private and publicity-shy he never became a recluse in the Howard Hughes mold, as would later be alleged. He followed Formula 1 racing and also became an obsessive fan of the 1940s musical enter-tainer George Formby, who used to sing in a squeaky northern accent, playing a ukulele. George took his own Formby-style ukulele with him wherever he went and frequently attended conventions of Formby soundalikes, though he always shunned equivalent gatherings of Beatles fans. "He was rubbish on the ukulele," remembers Mal Jefferson, an old school friend and fellow Merseybeat musician who occasionally met him at George Formby conventions. "I saw him play once, and then get slaughtered by a nine-year-old lad.

"Afterward, I offered to buy his uke off him and, to my amazement, he agreed. 'But I paid two grand for it,' he said. 'I've got to get back what I paid. I need every penny at the moment. I've just lost forty million with HandMade Films.' As a joke, I wrote him out a check for £2001— but George said, 'Thanks very much' and stuffed it into his pocket."

At the time of the *Anthology* came a brief period of rejuvenation, when he took to combing his hair back in the same Teddy-boy style that used to get him into such trouble at Liverpool Institute. But as time passed, he looked increasingly scruffy and unkempt in his old parkas and shapeless gardening hats. Despite his public reconciliation with his former Beatles colleagues, his bitterness toward Paul continued to fester. In a BBC Radio 2 interview during the late nineties he was heard grip-ing about how "Paul McCartney ruined me as a guitarist," still appar-ently unable to recognize the inestimable luck of having lived and worked alongside such provocative talent.

He remained a devotee of Transcendental Meditation and, despite all John's mockeries and fulminations, had never turned against Maharishi Mahesh Yogi. Despite losing the Beatles as figureheads, TM and the Ma-harishi had prospered in Britain; they now owned Mentmore House, the former country seat of the Rosebery family, where they were ru-mored to teach their followers to fly in rooms with shock-absorbing mattresses nailed around the walls. They had also produced a political wing, the Natural Law Party, that fielded a huge array of parliamentary candidates in the 1992 general election. They hoped that George himself might run, thereby guaranteeing at least one NLP MP in parliament. He declined, but showed his support by giving his first-ever solo concert in the U.K. and donating its proceeds to their election campaign.

His greatest asset proved to be his marriage to Olivia, not a rock star's cipher wife but a woman of character and compassion, who became deeply involved in charity work to help orphans in Romania. Though George no longer engaged in casual affairs, as he had when he was with Patti, Olivia still found life with him anything but a bed of roses. The rockiest moment occurred when a Los Angeles prostitute known only as Tiffany identified him as one of her clients, alleging that while a sexual service was performed for him, he was playing his ukulele and singing a George Formby song. But Olivia stood by him, becoming—in one insider's words—"the bedrock of his existence." Together they proved model parents, raising their son Dhani in comparative normality—and totally out of the media spotlight. Despite his ambivalence toward "the material world," George acquired several properties overseas, including estates in Maui and the West Indies, and traveled by private Gulfstream jet.

In 1997, while gardening at Friar Park, he noticed a lump had appeared in his neck. Its cause was found to be a cancerous tumor in his throat, the result—as he himself acknowledged—of a lifetime's heavy smoking. After an operation at the Margaret Hospital in Windsor followed by a course of radiation therapy at Royal Marsden in London, he was pronounced to have made a complete recovery. He himself told the media he was completely fit again and had taken to heart this warning never to smoke again.

On December 30, 1999, the "devil's best friend" he had feared for so long finally called on him. It was, indeed, an eerily exact replay of the December night seventeen years before when Mark David Chapman had murdered John Lennon. A similarly deranged Beatles fan, thirty-four-year-old Michael Abrams, broke into Friar Park, believing himself to be on "a mission from God" to murder George. His intended victim later recounted how his first instinct on coming unexpectedly face-to-face with Abrams was to shout his old sixties peace mantra, "Hare Krishna!" As the two grappled at the foot of the main staircase, Abrams stabbed George four times in the body with a knife. "I felt my chest deflate and the flow of blood to my mouth," George said later. "I truly thought I was dying."

So he certainly would have done but for his wife, Olivia, who, like an avenging angel, laid into Abrams with a poker and the base of a lamp while her husband lay bleeding and helpless on the ground. Her later testimony would uncannily recall Yoko's description of the "horrible confused" look in John's eyes after Chapman had pumped five shots into him. Olivia was likewise to remember how, as George lay bleeding among his meditation cushions, "he was very pale and . . . staring at me in a really bizarre manner." The struggle continued until police arrived and overpowered Abrams. "I should have got the bastard better," muttered the intruder as he was led away.

The Apple office, through Neil Aspinall, initially played down the seriousness of the incident. Not until Abrams's trial at Oxford Crown Court eleven months later was its full horror revealed. Olivia appeared as a witness, though George, still seemingly traumatized by his ordeal, was allowed to give evidence by written statement. After Abrams had been sentenced to be detained indefinitely in a secure psychiatric unit, a statement was read on George's behalf by his son, Dhani, now twenty-two and an almost exact replica of his father at the same age.

The attack inevitably deepened George's paranoia over personal privacy, to the point where he seriously considered leaving Britain altogether and settling in either America or the West Indies. Security at Friar Park was immediately strengthened, with guard dogs and, it was rumored, ex-paramilitary bodyguards added to the existing razor-wire fence, electronic front gates, and video surveillance system that had failed to stop Abrams from entering the house. His stable-door security mania even extended to the police officers who had rescued him from Abrams. Police Constable Matt Morgans, who had cradled him in his arms until medical help arrived, later gave an interview to the local newspaper, the *Henley Standard*. George was so incensed by the interview that he threatened an official complaint against his rescuer.

According to George's Henley neighbor, Sir John Mortimer, there was a sick aftermath to the episode—one which revealed how far Britain had traveled as a society from the loving, sunny sixties. A car full of people drove past Friar Park's gates, loudly cheering because George had been attacked. Other anonymous sickos sent flowers to his would-be killer in the hospital.

In March 2001, a routine checkup at the Mayo Clinic in Rochester, Minnesota, revealed cancerous cells in one of his lungs. He underwent surgery and was said by his doctors to have made "an excellent recovery." He himself assured the media, in his familiar mordant way, that he had "no plans to die." But he seems to have realized already that the writing was on the wall. Most of that following summer was spent in Switzerland, at a villa near Lugano's San Giovanni clinic, where he was receiving treatment from the world-famous oncologist Professor Franco Cavalli. Partnered by his son Dhani, he wrote and recorded a new song, "Horse to the Water," for inclusion on an R&B album also featuring Jools Holland, Van Morrison, and Sting. With typical graveyard humor, he copyrighted the song to "Rip 2001 Ltd." "He never felt sorry for himself," Dhani was to recall. "We took the view 'be here now' and made the most of our time. He used to say, 'Oh, you're going to have to finish all these songs.' I'd say, 'Well, not if you do it first. Get off your arse and finish them.' "

Aware that the end could now not be far away, he set about making arrangements for his departure and healing the two major emotional breaches in his life. There was a reconciliation with his older sister, Louise, now in her seventies, to whom he'd barely spoken since she lent her name to an Illinois bed-and-breakfast called the Hard Day's Night. He also got together with Paul McCartney, ending the chill that had never really abated since Paul had tried to boss him around on the *Let It Be* sessions. Hugging one another as they never had even as boyhood cronies, they agreed how little all such things matter in the end.

Nor did the eerie repetitiveness of Beatles history cease with his death on the last day of November. As with Linda McCartney three years earlier, the quest for privacy created some initial confusion about where the event had happened. Initially, it was reported to have been at the Laurel Canyon mansion of Gavin de Becker, a security consultant who specializes in providing safe houses for celebrities. On the death certificate, however, it appeared as "1971 Coldwater Canyon," an address that proved fictitious. The discovery brought faint echoes of a time when all Beatles output was thought to carry hidden subtexts and messages. For 1971 was the year of George's greatest triumph, the concerts for Bangladesh. As in Linda's case, too, the ruse brought a threat of official prosecution that hung over Olivia Harrison until she filed an affidavit stating the true address six months later.

In fact, the place where George died had symbolized a Beatles reunion perhaps more significant than any in the previous twenty years. He had been staying at 9536 Heather Road, Beverly Hills, a property owned by Paul McCartney and loaned to George as a last sanctuary that the media would never find. With him at the last, as well as Olivia and Dhani, were his two favorite Indian gurus, Mukunda and Shayamsundra, chanting the same Hare Krishna mantra that used to echo through

the lush carpeted corridors of the Apple house and up and down Oxford Street. Olivia requested a worldwide minute's silence as a mark of
respect. (One could imagine George somewhere fuming over the fact
that John got a full five minutes' silence in 1980.) At Varanasi, India,
hundreds gathered beside the River Ganges, expecting his body to be
brought there and cremated according to Hindu custom. But, like so
many watchers outside Apple in days of yore, they were doomed to disappointment. Cremation had been quietly carried out in L.A., immediately after his death.

His obituaries touched levels of hysteria and hyperbole remarkable
even for the early twenty-first century. He was lauded not only as a towering figure in popular music but also as a philanthropist, a visionary, a
mystic, even a messiah. On BBC radio, the former Traffic drummer Jim
Capaldi said that if Christ had been reborn into the world, He could just
have easily written the opening line of "While My Guitar Gently Weeps."

His estate was valued at £99 million, a figure said not to include his
properties in Hawaii, Switzerland, and Italy. Everything was left to
Olivia, in trust for Dhani. Neither his sister, Louise, nor his surviving
brother, Peter, received a penny.

On the first anniversary of his death his closest musical blood
brother headlined a memorial concert at London's Royal Albert Hall
that eerily re-created that 1969 concert billing of "Eric Clapton and
Friends." It also brought a further reunion of the Beatles' surviving, un-
contentious half, with Paul McCartney and Ringo Starr instantly agreeing to join Clapton's ensemble. Before the show, tickets with a face value
of £150 were changing hands for up to £1,000.

George was not great; just an average guitarist who got incredibly
lucky. But he was also an indispensable part of the greatest engine for
human happiness the modern world has known. The pity was that it
never seemed quite enough for him.

Of the four Beatles, Ringo Starr may have had the least natural talent
with which to sustain a solo career. But what he did have was an enormous fund of goodwill, both inside the music business and outside.
Whereas John, Paul, and George, in their different ways, all had to battle
to prove themselves as individual performers, there was general, unspo-
ken agreement that Ringo *had* to make it.

The conflict and bitterness of the breakup seemed not to have affected his essentially happy, optimistic nature nor in any way compromised the affection that all the other three still felt for him. Apart from that one atypical loss of self-control at Cavendish Avenue, even Paul had never shown him hostility nor said a bad word about him. Rather as divorcing parents worry about the children, so all three felt concern about how Ringo would fare without them around to look after him. To be sure, it was probably the one point on which they all agreed. The little unselfishness and team spirit they had left they focused on him.

Thanks to these helping hands from all directions, Ringo's post-Beatle career looked potentially bigger than either John's or Paul's. In 1970, following Beatles practice for some years past, he put out two albums: the country-flavored *Beaucoup of Blues*, recorded in Nashville, and *Sentimental Journey*, a collection of standards aimed mainly at pleasing his mum. The more than a little help from his superstar friends spawned two massively successful singles, "It Don't Come Easy" in 1971 and "Back Off Boogaloo" in 1972, both his own compositions, produced by George Harrison and warbled in the same chewy lead vocal style, as though he were simultaneously masticating egg and chips.

In 1973 came the *Ringo* album, which, amazingly, brought him two American number-one singles: "Photograph" and a cover version of Johnny Burnette's "You're Sixteen." The album's numerous celebrity sidemen included not only George but both other concerned "parents," John and Paul, playing on separate tracks. A year afterward came a third successful album, *Goodnight Vienna*, including a hit cover version of the Platters' "Only You." With George simultaneously triumphing in the American singles charts and John and Paul's relatively small impact there, the Beatles' long-eclipsed second division seemed to have turned the tables with a vengeance.

Following his droll cameo appearances in the Beatles' own films and Terry Southern's *Candy*, a screen acting career seemed to beckon even more alluringly than Ringo's musical one. Those early comparisons with Keaton and Chaplin seemed justified when, also in 1973, he costarred with David Essex and Adam Faith in *That'll Be the Day*, a nostalgic evocation of the seaside summer camps he used to play with Rory Storm's Hurricanes, before John rang him at Skegness and offered him Pete Best's old chair in the Beatles. The previous year had seen his debut as a documentary director with *Born to Boogie*, a film about his close friend the glam-rocker Marc Bolan. Then suddenly in the mid-seventies it was as if a turbojet had been removed from Ringo's back. His albums were recorded with ever-decreasing energy and conviction—like the spiritless *Rotogravure* of 1976—and sold in ever-decreasing quantities. He refused to appear in the sequel to *That'll Be the Day,* turning instead to Hollywood, which cast him in a series of increasingly dire potboilers. He became best known as a guest on TV talk shows, always jokily side-stepping the only question that interested his audience: what had it been like to be a Beatle?

His marriage to Maureen in the end lasted for ten years—though it probably never recovered from Maureen's fling with George—and by the early seventies the two of them were living separate lives on separate continents. In 1970, Ringo began a relationship with American model Barbara Bach, his costar in a risible movie called *Caveman.* Their marriage in 1981 was attended by Paul and Linda McCartney and George and Olivia Harrison, proof of Paul's and George's undimmed fondness for him and a symbolic act of togetherness in the aftershock of John's murder.

In the early eighties, Ringo's artistic fortunes sank to their nadir. Signed to the RCA label in 1981, he made an album called *Stop and Smell the Roses* that failed to register despite further fraternal contributions from Paul and George. Its follow-up, *Old Wave,* was considered too feeble for release either in America or Britain. Over the next decade his main public exposure would be on children's television and video as narrator of the Reverend W. Awdry's Thomas the Tank Engine stories.

As with so many of his contemporaries, decades of heedless rock-star life finally began taking their toll when he entered his forties. Even his buoyant spirits could not completely protect him against the slump in his prestige other than with juvenile steam-railway enthusiasts. Despite his delicate stomach, he had always been a heavy drinker; now his consumption of champagne and table wines increased to several bottles per day, with Barbara usually matching him glass for glass. In 1988, they entered a drying-out clinic together, which not only saved their health but also seemed to consolidate a marriage that few had expected to last.

Following this internal spring-clean, Ringo's enthusiasm for drumming returned, with a consequent small revival in his career. In 1989 he went back on the road, leading (shades of Rory Storm!) an "All-Starr Band," including distinguished sidemen like Billy Preston, Dave Edmunds, and Nils Lofgren, and featuring his own elder son, Zak, as backup drummer. A successful U.S. and Japan tour that year was followed by a less successful European one in 1992. The once modest and self-knowing character who, as George Martin noted, "couldn't do a roll to save his life," now billed himself unblushingly as "the World's Greatest Rock 'n' Roll Drummer."

His 25 percent share of Apple meant he never had to work again unless he wanted to. By the nineties, he had moved to the tax haven of Monaco, acquiring a top-floor apartment in a luxury sea-front building overlooking the famous Sporting Club. Barbara and he took a full part in the principality's jet-set social life, were received by its ruler, Prince Rainier, and could often be seen strolling along Avenue Princess Grace hand-in-hand, in matching black outfits, as if making their virtuous way to some Quaker meeting house.

Both Ringo's sons, Zak and Jason, went on to become rock drummers, both creditably refusing to exploit his celebrity to advance their careers and always working under their real family name of Starkey. Zak in particular turned out to be a brilliant performer, although, ironically, his role model was not his father but the manic Keith Moon of The Who. Far from resenting this, Ringo even arranged for Moon to give Zak lessons. And no one could have been prouder when, long years after Moon's death from suicidal alcohol and drug abuse in 1978, The Who recruited Jason to be drummer on some of their various comeback tours.

Perhaps the greatest surprise of all was Ringo's former wife, Maureen, the former mousy little Liverpool hairdresser who, after the divorce, might have been expected to sink into comfortably maintained obscurity. Instead, Maureen went on to marry Isaac Tigrett, the founder of the Hard Rock Café chain, and then to present Tigrett with a baby daughter, Olivia. Ringo remained on good terms with her and close to all three of their children. The original family not only survived but provided each other with crucial love and support in the double ordeal that was soon to come.

In 1995, Ringo and Maureen's fashion designer daughter, Lee, by then twenty-five, was rushed to a London clinic to have fluid removed from her brain. Diagnosed with a brain tumor, she underwent radiation treatment at the Brigham and Women's Hospital in Boston, Massachusetts, and, after several agonizing weeks for her parents and brothers, was pronounced to be in the clear. Late that same year Maureen herself

DAMAGE NOTED

was found to be suffering from leukemia. Again, the prognosis seemed favorable, especially after an apparently successful bone-marrow transplant from her son Zak. But by Christmas, the illness had shown itself to be incurable. Maureen died in January 1996 with Ringo and her children at her bedside.

In 2000, Ringo bought a property in Cranleigh, Surrey, mainly to be near Jason and his girlfriend Flora, who had by now presented him with two grandsons, Louis and Sonny. Coincidentally, their near neighbor in North London happened to be Paul McCartney's daughter Mary, herself the mother of a son, Arthur, by her TV producer partner Alistair Donald. The Beatles grandchildren were often to be found playing together, establishing who knows what early links for bands far into the future.

That November 5, the villagers of Cranleigh asked the newly arrived celebrity in their midst to be guest of honor at their Guy Fawkes night fireworks display. It must have seemed small stuff to Ringo, after all the red carpets that had been unrolled for him all around the world, but he turned out good-naturedly enough on the village green to give the signal for the display to start, then stood and watched the Catherine wheels, the Roman candles, the little rockets whooshing only halfway to Heaven. As he advances into his sixties, the only cloud on his horizon seems the health of his daughter Lee who, in late 2001, was reported to be having further hospital treatment in Boston for a second brain tumor called an ependymoma.

He may have been no more than history's most famous bit-part player, but still, his must be the last word about it all. Look at the *Beatles Anthology* television documentary, that laughably incomplete and doctored account. Fast-forward through show bizzy Paul and crabby George until you find Ringo, playing his usual cameo role on some sun-soaked L.A. balcony, his close-cropped hair and gray-grizzled beard giving him an almost uncanny resemblance to the Palestinian leader Yasser Arafat.

Not only is he the funniest, most honest, and self-knowing of the survivors; he is also the only one willing to show real emotion. Tears glisten in the big mournful eyes as he says that for him, above all, the Beatles will always be "just four guys who loved each other."

Which perhaps best sums up the whole story.

PHOTO CREDITS

First photo section, pages 1–8: John in garden, Mimi Smith, Julia—Hunter Davies. George and family—Freda Norris. Ringo as a boy, Ringo's parents, Mary McCartney, Michael and Paul—Hunter Davies. Quarry Men—Colin Hanton. Rory Storm and The Hurricanes—Keystone Press. Rooftop cowboys—Keystone Press. Stuart Sutcliffe, Astrid Kirchherr—Sutcliffe family (photographer: Astrid Kirchherr). John and Stuart on the beach—Sutcliffe family. At the Top Ten Club in Hamburg—Jurgen Vollmer. Mathew Street—Pix Features. Cavern Club—Dick Matthews. The band in suits—Albert Marrion. Recording "Love Me Do"—Rex Features (photographer: Dezo Hoffman).

Second photo section, pages 9–16: Wearing art student's clothes—Rex Features (photographer: Dezo Hoffman). Beatlemania—Rex Features. With Ed Sullivan in New York—Rex Features (photographer: Suomen Kuvapalvelu). *Royal Variety Show*—Rex Features (photographer: Dezo Hoffman). Ringo's wedding—Camera Press (photographer: Robert Freeman). George's wedding—Keystone Press. Press conference—Keystone Press. John with Julian at Kenwood—Keystone Press. Allen Klein—United Press International. Linda, Paul, Yoko and John—Camera Press (photographer: Bruce McBroom). John and Yoko—Iain Macmillan. John and Yoko—John Hillelson Agency (photographer: Tannenbaum). Yoko outside Lennon's house—Mercury Press Agency/Rex Features. Paul and Heather Mills—Rex Features. George with Olivia; Ringo performing—Richard Young/Rex Features.

Every effort has been made to acknowledge all those whose photographs have been used in this volume, but if there have been any omissions in this respect, we apologize and will be pleased to make the appropriate acknowledgment in any future editions.

INDEX

The **REAL** Book of **Real Estate**

The **REAL** Book
of **Real Estate**

REAL EXPERTS. *REAL* STORIES. *REAL* LIFE.

Robert Kiyosaki

PLATA®
PUBLISHING

Copyright © 2013, 2016, by Robert T. Kiyosaki

Published by Plata Publishing

All rights reserved. No part of this publication may be reproduced, stored in a retrieval system, or transmitted, in any form or by any means, electronic, mechanical, photocopying, recording, or otherwise, without the prior written permission of the publisher.

Printed in the United States of America.

Library of Congress Cataloging-in-Publication Data

The real book of real estate : real experts, real advice, real success stories/Robert Kiyosaki.
    p. cm.
    Includes index.
    ISBN 978-1-61268-079-8

1. Real estate investment. 2. Real estate business. I. Kiyosaki, Robert T., 1947-
HD1382.5.R33 2009
333.33—dc22

 2009008346

ISBN 978-1-61268-079-8

082016

"I'm not a genius. I'm just a tremendous bundle of experience."

—Dr. R. Buckminster "Bucky" Fuller

Dr. R. Buckminster "Bucky" Fuller at eighty-six years old with Robert Kiyosaki in 1981. Buckminster Fuller was an American architect, author, designer, futurist, inventor, and visionary.

Recognized as one of the most accomplished Americans in history, he dedicated his life to a world that worked for all things and all people.

Contents

PART 3: Creative Ways to Make Money in Real Estate

PART 4: Lessons Learned

Acknowledgments

For years I have been an advocate for financial education. While many other financial advisors are telling people what they should invest in, I have been telling people to invest in themselves—to invest in their own knowledge. That is what I have done, and it has made me rich. I have also been telling people to surround themselves with great teachers who are actively practicing what they preach. The creation of this book was made possible because of the people I consider my teachers. Each one has a lifetime of experience and a lifetime of knowledge. And each one knows the importance of continual learning.

The contributors to this book generously gave of their time and their talent so that you could see the possibilities, avoid the pitfalls, and understand the methods of building wealth through real estate. They have recollected their great achievements, and they have revealed their painful failures. I thank them for their openness. The lessons we learn from our own mistakes and the mistakes of others are the most powerful.

These people are not only my advisors, but they are also my friends. Together we have been through the ups and downs of the real estate cycle, ridden each wave, and made money doing it. These are the friends I run my ideas and my deals by. And because they are friends, I know that they will give me their honest opinions. I thank them for that, too.

Introduction: A Note from Robert Kiyosaki
Why a Real Book of Real Estate

There are four reasons why I think a real book of real estate is important at this time.

First, there will always be a real estate market. In a civilized world, a roof over your head is as essential as food, clothing, energy, and water. Real estate investors are essential to keeping this vital human need available at a reasonable price. In countries where investing in real estate is limited or excessively controlled by the government, such as it was in former Communist Bloc countries, people suffer, and real estate deteriorates.

Second, there are many different ways a person can participate and prosper with real estate. For most people, their only real estate investment is where they live. Their home is their biggest investment. During the real estate boom from 2000 to 2007, many amateurs got involved with flipping houses—buying low and hoping to sell higher. As you know, many flippers flopped and lost everything. In true investor vocabulary, flipping is known as speculating or trading. Some people call it gambling. While *flipping* is one method of investing, there are many, more sophisticated, less risky ways to do well with real estate. This book is filled with the knowledge and experiences of real, real estate investors—real estate professionals who *invest* rather than flip, speculate, trade, or gamble.

Third, real estate gives you control over your investments, that is, *if* you have the skills. In the volatile times of early 2009, millions of people were losing trillions of dollars simply because they handed over control of their wealth to other people. Even since the middle of 2008, the great Warren Buffett's fund, Berkshire Hathaway, has lost 40 percent of its value! Millions of people have lost their jobs, which means they had no control over their own employment either. The real, real estate professionals in this book have control over both their businesses and investments. They will share their good times and the bad times with you. They will share what they have learned *while* learning to control their investments and their financial destiny. The learning process is continual.

And, finally, here's my real reason for this book. I am sick and tired of financial experts giving advice on real estate, especially when they do not actually invest in real estate. After my book *Rich Dad Poor Dad* came out, I was on a television program with a financial author and television personality. At the time, in 1999, the stock market was red hot with the dot-com boom. This financial expert, who was a former stockbroker and financial planner, was singing the praises of stocks and mutual funds. After the stock market crashed in 2001, this man suddenly resurfaced with a new book on real estate, portraying himself as a real estate expert. His real estate advice was beyond bad. It was dangerous. Then the real estate market crashed and he dropped out of sight again. The last time I saw him, he had written a book on investing in solar energy and was claiming to be a green entrepreneur. If he were to write a book about what he really does, his new book would be about raising bulls . . . and selling BS.

There are other financial "experts" who know nothing about real estate, yet they speak badly about real estate and say it is risky. The only reason real estate is risky for them is because they know nothing about investing in it. Instead, they recommend saving money and investing in a well-diversified portfolio of mutual funds—investments which I believe are the riskiest investments in the world, especially in this market. Why do they recommend investing in savings and mutual funds? The answer is obvious: Many of these professionals are endorsed by banks, mutual fund companies, and the media. It's good business to plug your sponsors' businesses and products.

Commissioning this book gives the public its first chance to learn from real, real estate investors, friends, and advisors—people who have been through the ups and the downs and who walk their talk. This book gives them the opportunity to share the spotlight with the many media financial "experts" and speak the truth. These real estate experts are true pros, and you're about to move beyond the media hype. I hope you are ready. *The Real Book of Real Estate* is the *real* deal.

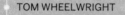

TOM WHEELWRIGHT

CHARLES W. LOTZAR

ROSS MCCALLISTER

R. CRAIG COPPOLA

GARRETT SUTTON

BERNIE BAYS

PART 1

The Business of Real Estate

The Business of Real Estate

Tom Wheelwright is a rare combination of CPA, real estate investor, and teacher. He has the ability to take the complex and often boring subject of tax and tax law and make it into something that's simple enough for a person like me to understand.

Tom understands the tax code. He actually enjoys reading the tax code, and because he is such a student of it, he understands this lengthy document better than anyone I know. Most CPAs focus on a very small part of the tax code. They focus on the part that lets you and most Americans defer taxes until retirement—the code relating to IRAs, 401(k)s, and other so-called retirement plans. Tom also pays close attention to the other, much lengthier part of the code that shows you how to reduce or eliminate your taxes permanently. The difference between Tom and other CPAs is that Tom understands the purpose of the tax code. It's not just a set of rules. It's a document that when followed is designed to reward certain behaviors through lowering or eliminating taxes. Does your CPA see the tax code this way?

I consider Tom to be a very moral and ethical man. He is very religious, raised in the Mormon faith. While I am not Mormon, I do share many of the values of the Mormon religion—values such as tithing, giving at least 10 percent to spiritual matters, and dedicating a number of years as a missionary. While I have never

*been a religious missionary, I have spent nearly ten years as a military missionary:
a Marine Corps pilot in Vietnam, serving my country.*

*One important lesson I have learned from Tom and others of the Mormon
faith is the saying, "God does not need to receive, but humans need to give." This
reminds me of the importance of being generous. It is my opinion that greed
rather than generosity has taken over the world. Every time I meet someone who
is short of money, or if I am short of money, I am reminded to be generous and to
give what I would like to get. For example, if I want money, I need to give money.
Having been out of money a number of times in my life, I have had to remind
myself to give money at times when I needed money the most. Today I make a
point of donating regularly to charities and causes that are dear to my heart. My
opinion is, if I cannot personally work at a cause near to my heart, then my money
needs to work there for me. Going further, if I want kindness, then I need to give
more kindness. If I want a smile, then I need to first give a smile. And if I want a
punch in the mouth, then all I have to do is throw the first one.*

*I asked my friend Tom Wheelwright to be a part of this book not only because
he is a smart accountant—a team player that anyone who wants to be rich needs
to add to his or her team—but also because he comes from a generous and sound
philosophical background.*

*Tom is a smart CPA who is an advocate of investing in real estate. Why?
Because he knows that tax laws reward real estate investors more than they
reward stock investors. He is a great teacher, a generous man, and, most
importantly, a friend I respect.*

—ROBERT KIYOSAKI

I was one of the fortunate few growing up. Unlike much of the rest of the
world—people who have been told to save their pennies and invest in mutual
funds—my parents taught me to invest in real estate and business. My father
had a printing business, and my mother handled their real estate portfolio.

So it was natural that once I had received my education, both formal and
work related, I opened my own business. (I had a lot of education before I
finally opened my own business—a master's degree in professional accounting,
thirteen years of experience with international accounting firms, as well as
experience as the in-house tax advisor to a Fortune 1000 company. I was a little
slow to realize the power of business.) When I started my accounting firm, I
did it like most people: I worked all hours of the day and rarely took a vacation.

When I did take a vacation, I still took calls from clients and colleagues. After all, business never rests, so why should I?

Several years into my business, we had experienced significant growth, but I was still working day and night and never taking a real vacation. And outside of my business, I had no substantial assets. That's when I read *Rich Dad Poor Dad* and first met Robert Kiyosaki. He helped me realize that I was thinking about business all wrong. It was not about how *hard* I worked, but rather about how *smart* I worked.

Like many of you, my first real experience with Robert was at a Rich Dad seminar. There I was, sitting next to my business partner, Ann Mathis, and her husband, Joe. Robert was talking about a subject near and dear to my heart—the tax benefits of real estate. Out of the blue, Robert asked me to come up to the front of the room to explain the tax benefits of depreciation, introducing me as his "other accountant."

I had come to learn about Robert Kiyosaki and Rich Dad only a few months earlier. One of my good friends, George Duck, had become the chief financial officer at Rich Dad and had introduced us. I'm not sure who was more nervous that first time I went on stage, Robert or me. Can you imagine putting an accountant on stage? Robert had no idea that I had spent my life teaching in one capacity or another, but he took the chance and put me up there anyway. This began a long and inspiring relationship between us, and it launched my journey toward financial freedom.

I remember one of the first times Robert and I worked together. He used me as "muscle." Robert had been asked by a reporter to give an interview for the business section of the *Arizona Republic*. The primary topic was how Robert could claim that he routinely received 40 percent returns on his investments.

I went as the authoritative backup to Robert's ideas. Someone might not believe a marketing genius (i.e., Robert) when he says he gets these levels of returns on his investments, but who wouldn't believe an accountant? When it comes to investing, numbers are everything, and who better to support the numbers than someone who spends his life documenting, reviewing, and analyzing them?

That was one of the first opportunities I had to explain the benefits of the leverage that comes from real estate. Not long before, I had started my own real estate investing. You would think that with parents who were real estate investors I would naturally become a real estate investor. I had even spent my career showing real estate investors and developers how to reduce their taxes.

But I didn't actually begin investing in real estate until after the first time I played Robert's game, CASHFLOW 101®. The game had a powerful impact on me. I saw the power of leverage in real estate with my own eyes. The game was so powerful that the next day after playing the game, I called one of my clients who had been investing in real estate for several years and asked him to meet with me to show me how I could begin my own real estate investing.

And then I began making serious changes to my business. My partner, Ann, a systems genius, created the systems, policies, and procedures in our firm so we could focus on running the business and not working in the business. It took a few years, but eventually we were able to step away from working for hourly professional fees and instead supervising and growing a business that worked without us.

Now I can take three weeks off each year with no e-mail or phone access, whether it's spending time in Hawaii with my sweetheart or taking a trip to the châteaux region of northern France with my son. I don't have to worry about my accounting firm or my real estate investments while I'm gone because they both run without my daily attention.

TIP Real estate investing is a business and should be run like a business.

Robert talks a lot about the CASHFLOW Quadrant, with each labeled as E, S, B, and I. He emphasizes that we need to move out of the E (employee) and S (self employed) quadrants and into the B (business) and I (investor) quadrants. I take this one step further. That is, to move all I-quadrant investing into the B quadrant.

Think about what you could do with the time you would have if you didn't have to worry about tenants, repairs, and cash flow. How would it feel to eliminate the frustration that comes from constantly watching your real estate investments and worrying about a tenant calling you in the middle of the night with a problem? You can eliminate all of this stress and free up hundreds of hours of your time simply by running your real estate investments as a B-quadrant business.

FIGURE 1.1 I've learned to take the quadrant a step further and free up hundreds of hours of my time simply by running my real estate investments like a B-quadrant business.

It's really not that difficult. You simply have to *start acting like a business* and apply fundamental business principles to your real estate investing.

BUSINESS PRINCIPLE NO. 1: STRATEGY

Every business should have a clear strategy. Your real estate investing business is no different. A strategy is simply a systematic plan of action designed to accomplish specific goals. There are seven simple steps to creating a successful strategy.

STEP 1: IMAGINE

Begin your strategy with goals. Imagine where you would like your real estate investing to take you. It may be a white sand beach in the Caribbean, unlimited time with your family, or working for your favorite charity. My favorite places in the world are Hawai'i, France, Arizona, and Park City, Utah. So my dream is to own a house in each of these locations.

Don't be afraid of being too aggressive. These are your dreams, after all, not some number that is artificially imposed by a financial advisor. Our clients frequently have dreams of financial freedom in as few as five to ten years. And with a good strategy in place, anyone can be financially free in less than ten years if they just *start by applying* these few basic business principles to their real estate investing. I already have properties in Hawai'i, Arizona, and Park City, Utah. France is next on the agenda for next year. Pretty aggressive goals, but I have been able to reach them in a very short time by applying basic business principles to my real estate and business.

STEP 2: FINANCIAL GOALS

Determine what it will take to realize these dreams in terms of wealth and cash flow. And commit to a date for accomplishing this goal. Then write down what you currently have available in terms of investable assets less the liabilities. This is your current wealth (also called net worth).

STEP 3: CASH FLOW TARGET

Of course, you will need to figure out the amount of wealth that it will take in order to create your desired cash flow. A simple rule of thumb for calculating this number is to multiply your desired cash flow by twenty. For me, I figured that I need $20 million in order to create an after-tax cash flow of $1,000,000 each year.

STEP 4: CURRENT WEALTH

Once you have your dream firmly in mind, the next step is to identify where you are today. When considering where you are today, list only your real assets, that is, those that are available to invest. Don't list your car or your jewelry. But do list the amount of equity in your home if it can be made available for investing through a home equity loan. Here is an example of what I mean:

TABLE 1.1

Liquid:	Long-Term:
Savings	Loans
Stocks & Bonds	Real Estate
Mutual Funds	Oil & Gas
CDs	Business
Other	Intellectual
Other	Other
Sub-Total:	Sub-Total:

These first four steps are the essence of a process referred to as "dreamlining," and I will use a simple illustration to show you what I mean. Here is what my dreamline looked like when I first met Robert and started down my road to financial freedom.

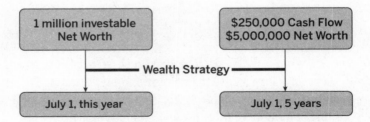

FIGURE 1.2 Tom's "Dreamline" When He First Met Robert Kiyosaki

STEP 5: VISION, MISSION, AND VALUES

After you have your dreamline in place, you can make a plan to reach those dreams. This plan should include your vision, mission and values, the type of real estate you will specialize in buying, and the criteria you use for choosing your real estate investments.

At this point, you may be wondering if I have truly lost my mind. After all, aren't vision, mission, and value statements only for true businesses? Exactly! And your real estate investments are a true business. At least they should be if you are going to reach your dreams in the shortest amount of time possible and with the least amount of work.

When creating your vision, remember that this represents your focus for the future, that is, what you want your life to look like when everything is in place. Your mission is simply a statement of how you are going to go about your investing business. And your values are the values that you insist everyone you work with in real estate share with you.

Tom's Personal Vision, Mission, and Values

Vision. My vision for financial freedom means having the time and resources to do what I want, when I want. I know I have reached financial freedom when I can travel anytime I desire, spend quality time with family and friends, and serve through charities I enjoy.

Mission. My mission to reach financial freedom is to invest in highly appreciating single-family homes by researching foreclosures, borrowing from banks and sellers, holding properties for five to ten years, and obtaining tax leverage through depreciation.

Values. My values are these: abundance—recognizing that there are plenty of resources and real estate deals to go around; caring—being kind and expressing gratitude; learning—taking the time to grow and improve my real estate knowledge; and respect—treating others the way I want to be treated.

STEP 6: INVESTMENT NICHE

Once you have your vision, mission, and values in place, you can begin looking at what type of real estate makes sense for you. Every successful business owner knows that you are always most successful when you focus your attention on something you enjoy doing and for which you have a natural ability. At my company, ProVision, we have a variety of tools we use to help people figure out which type of real estate they will enjoy the most—multifamily, commercial, industrial, raw land or single-family homes. My personal investment niche remains highly appreciating single-family homes.

STEP 7: CRITERIA

The final step in your strategy—determining your investment criteria—is something that few people take time to do. And yet, if you can determine your investment criteria as part of your strategy, you can avoid a lot of headaches, stress, and wasted time. You can also avoid making costly mistakes. And you will save a considerable amount of time and energy, enabling you to focus on only those investments that meet your criteria. As an example, here are my personal investment criteria:

TABLE 1.2 Tom's Personal Investment Criteria

Criteria	Decision
Minimum appreciation	10%
Minimum rate of return	50%
Cash flow or cash on cash return	-0-
Price range	$200,000-$600,000
Maximum amount of investment/deal	$60,000
Maximum time commitment	1 hour per month
Location of investment	Western U.S.
Price as a % of value	85%

You may be asking why you need to spend so much time and effort developing a strategy. We teach our ProVision clients about the importance of strategy by playing CASHFLOW 101® with them in a very specific way. If you have played the game, you realize that, on average, it will take two and a half hours. We instruct our clients that their team (the players at their table) must spend the first thirty minutes developing a strategy to win the game. This strategy includes the type of assets they will invest in and their criteria for investing. All members of their team, though playing as individuals, must follow the strategy precisely.

The result is astonishing. Each player gets out of the Rat Race and wins the game in less than two hours. So even though they have spent an enormous percentage of their allotted time developing their strategy (roughly 20 percent), they finish substantially earlier than they would have without their strategy. This happens every time, so long as each team member adheres to the strategy.

BUSINESS PRINCIPLE NO. 2: TEAM

Just as every good business has a strategy, every successful business owner has a very carefully chosen team of individuals and companies to help him/her succeed. Your team will add considerable leverage to your investing. You can take advantage of your team members' time, talents, contacts, knowledge, and resources.

TIPS FOR BUILDING A TEAM

Plan. Think carefully about what skills you need on your team. For example, you are going to need an attorney, an accountant, a banker, at least one property manager, and others. Decide on the skill sets you need before you decide on which people will fill those roles.

Referrals. The best team members almost always come as a referral from someone you trust. But make sure the person referring is also a real estate investor and is knowledgeable about your situation and needs. A trusted advisor, such as an attorney, accountant, mentor or wealth coach, can be a good source of referrals.

Agreements. Make sure you have good, clear agreements in place with each of your team members so they know what is expected of them and what they can expect from you.

Before we leave the concept of a team, let me give you my personal experience with developing a real estate team. Anyone who knows me realizes that I spend most of my day growing my business. This doesn't leave me much time for real estate investing. But I love real estate investing and understand completely the importance of it in my wealth strategy.

I estimate the time I spend each week on real estate to be no more than one hour because of the great team I work with and by applying the other business principles we have talked about in this chapter. This brings me to our next principle: accounting.

BUSINESS PRINCIPLE NO. 3: ACCOUNTING

You may wonder if I include accounting as a basic principle of business because of my accounting background. While I have to admit to a natural bias in favor of good accounting, I believe that if you were to ask one hundred successful business owners if good accounting (including good reporting) were critical to their business, at least ninety-five of them would agree.

Why? Because good accounting leads to good reporting, and good reporting leads to good decisions. If you don't have the information you need, how are you going to make good decisions, such as when you should sell a piece of real estate or how to know if your portfolio is producing the desired results?

Great entrepreneurs understand the purpose of accounting. Here are a few of my personal keys to great accounting.

KEY NO. 1: PURPOSEFUL ACCOUNTING

Accounting should never be done solely to satisfy the IRS. Accounting's primary purpose should be to provide accurate and useful information so that you can make the best decisions. Poor investors think that the only reason to keep records is so their accountant can prepare their tax return at the end of the year.

This is a huge mistake. Good accounting is critical to good decision making. Without current, accurate numbers, how are you going to make the decision to buy, sell, or refinance your property? And how will you know which property is doing well and which is doing poorly? You won't even know if your property manager is doing a good job or not.

Several years ago, Ann and I purchased a group of fourplexes in Mesa, Arizona. The price was good based on the information we had at the time. We kept

---

Real Life Story: My Team Took Care of It All

So how do I make time for real estate? You guessed it—I have a terrific team. They are so good, in fact, that the only time I have to spend is to quickly review reports, make decisions (which are pretty easy, since I have very well-defined investment criteria), and sign documents. I remember one time recently when I was speaking to my team leader and he informed me that a tenant had vacated a house unexpectedly and not turned off the water. My team leader, who is not the property manager, drops by all of my houses on a regular basis and noticed that the tenant had left. He rushed into the house only to discover that the pipes had broken (this was in Utah in the dead of winter), and the house was flooded. The cost of repair was in the neighborhood of $50,000.

My team leader immediately took action. After turning the water off, he called the property manager and the insurance agent. He arranged for the repair company to renovate the property, made sure the insurance accepted the claim (before spending any money), and went after the property manager and tenant for any damages not paid for by the insurance company. I did not have to worry about a thing. And I probably spent only thirty minutes total dealing with this mess (signing authorizations and talking to my team leader).

very close track of the cash flow and the income from these properties. But after a year or so, it became clear to us that these properties were not going to generate positive cash flow in the near future. At the same time, we noticed that cap rates (see Principle No. 4, p. 17) were going down. So, based on our numbers, we sold the fourplexes. Because of the decrease in cap rates, we were able to make a significant profit, and we stopped losing money each month.

KEY NO. 2: ACCURATE BOOKKEEPING

While good accounting should go far beyond mere bookkeeping, it begins with accurate and appropriate bookkeeping entries. Accurate bookkeeping is the basis for creating useful reports and analysis.

Bookkeeping is merely the process of entering the results of transactions into a record that can be used for reporting and analysis. My experience is that most people will save time (and money) by doing their own bookkeeping through on-line banking and a very simple accounting software program, such as Quickbooks.

KEY NO. 2A: CHART OF ACCOUNTS

Begin by setting up a chart of accounts (this is just a list of the accounts you are going to use to classify your receipts and expenditures). The accounts you use should be those that make the most sense to you. For example, one person may list printer paper as an office supply while another may list it in the more general category of office expense. It's simply a matter of how detailed you want your reporting to be. Just remember that if you did not create an account for it, you cannot create a report for it.

TIP Here's a little trick for you: You don't have to create a separate chart of accounts for every property. Instead, you can create a "class" for each property. This allows you to do all of the bookkeeping for your real estate business in one Quickbooks "company" while creating the detail and report options that you need in order to understand what is happening with each property.

If you need help setting up your chart of accounts, ask your accountant/ CPA—a critical member of your team—to lend you a hand. This person should be happy to help, and can do this fairly quickly for you.

KEY NO. 2B: DETAILED DATA ENTRY

Once you have your chart of accounts set up, you are ready to begin entering your data. Remember that you need to enter the details of every transaction. Most transactions will have some cash involved, so if you enter the details every time you receive or spend money, you will catch 98 percent of your transactions. Some transactions don't have cash involved, such as recording depreciation expense. These are done through journal entries. Since you will likely have some journal entries to do, I will give you a brief explanation of how to do these.

Understand that every transaction has two sides to it for accounting purposes; a debit side and a credit side (think left and right so the total of the left side always equals the total of the right side). Expenditures are always a debit to the expense, income, liability, or asset account (left side), and a credit to cash (right side). Receipts are always a credit to an income, expense, asset, or liability account (left side), and a debit to cash (right side). To increase an expense or an asset, you debit that account, and to increase income or a liability, you credit that account.

KEY NO. 2C: JOURNAL ENTRIES

When you enter a receipt or an expenditure into Quickbooks, the software automatically creates both the debit and the credit. But sometimes you will need to make a correction or adjustment to your books when there has not been a cash transaction. You do this with a journal entry. When you make a journal entry, you simply enter both a credit and a debit. Let's use our depreciation journal entry as an example, since everyone has to make this journal entry at least once a year:

Debit to Depreciation Expense in the amount of depreciation calculated for the period (usually based on tables provided by the Internal Revenue Service or your accountant). See Chapter 7 of my Rich Dad Advisor book, *Tax-Free Wealth* for more details about the Magic of Depreciation.

Credit to Accumulated Depreciation in the same amount (this account is an offset to the asset account for the asset you are depreciating, such as a building).

See? It's simple.

KEY NO. 3: CONSISTENCY

Learn to use the correct accounts, and use the same accounts for all similar receipts and expenditures. If you decide to put paper costs into office supplies, *always* put purchases of paper into office supplies. Don't put them into the office supply account one month and the office expense account the next month.

KEY NO. 4: FREQUENCY

Do your bookkeeping no less than once a week. Two problems happen when you get behind. First, it becomes overwhelming, and you will continue putting it off until the end of the year when it becomes urgent for your tax returns. This creates the second problem: Not having up-to-date bookkeeping means you cannot get good reports to make good decisions.

KEY NO. 5: ONLINE BANKING

I do my bookkeeping every Friday morning. It takes me less than one hour because I use the systems that are available to me, such as online banking and automatic bill pay. Quickbooks will automatically classify all of my online banking to the right accounts with a few clicks of the mouse. I actually find it quicker to do the bookkeeping myself using these systems than if I were to use an outside bookkeeper (I tried that once and found it took me more time to correct the bookkeeping than if I just did it myself using online banking).

The next principle I'm going to share with you is how to get good reports from your bookkeeping software. If you review these reports each month, you will be able to make good decisions about your real estate business quickly and effectively.

BUSINESS PRINCIPLE NO. 4: REPORTING

All successful entrepreneurs understand the importance of managing their business by metrics. Metrics are simply measurements of the day-to-day results of the business. Sometimes these measurements are raw numbers, such as cash flow. Other times they take the form of ratios. And still other times these measurements are comparisons, either to a previous period, to targets, or industry averages.

TIP If you don't know your numbers, you don't know your business.

REPORT NO. 1: STATEMENT OF CASH FLOWS

Let's start with the king of all raw numbers: cash flow. Unfortunately, it's rare that a real estate investor has a clear picture of his/her true cash flow. You should know the cash flow from each property as well as the overall cash flow for your real estate business.

There is a tendency among real estate investors to believe that all they need to know about cash flow is the difference in their bank account from the beginning of the month to the end of the month. But the real key to using cash flow as a tool is to understand where the cash came from and where it went. A standard accounting report that you can use to figure this out is the Statement of Cash Flows. This report, though rarely used among real estate investors, is the most important report of all.

It begins with operating income. Operating income includes rents minus normal cash expenses, including repairs, maintenance, and management fees. It then details nonoperating items such as financing transactions and investing transactions. Financing transactions include any money that flows to or from your business because of loans. These include your mortgage payments as well as any loans you take out or money you put it. Investing transactions include any money that flows to or from your business because of investing activities. These include down payments on properties and cash from the sale of a property.

The end result is the increase or decrease in the amount of cash you have at the end of the period (month, quarter, or year) compared to what you had at the beginning of the period. This report makes it clear how much of your positive or negative cash flow is coming from operations versus other activities, such as financing or investing. Wouldn't it be great to know this and be able to

TABLE 1.3 Tom's Statement of Cash Flow

Property A	Oct - Dec
OPERATING ACTIVITIES	
Net Income	-6,706.40
Adjustments to reconcile Net Income to net cash provided by operations:	
Escrow Accounts	-174.40
Security Deposits	800.00
Net cash provided by Operating Activities	-6,080.80
INVESTING ACTIVITIES	
Accumulated depreciation	6,790.00
Accumulated amortization	18.00
Net cash provided by Investing Activities	6,808.00
FINANCING ACTIVITIES	
Mortgage Payable	-258.34
Net cash provided by Financing Activities	-258.34
Net cash increase for period	468.86

find out this information at any time? Table 1.3 is an example of a statement of cash flows for one of my properties. I pulled this report directly from my Quickbooks.

This report tells me several things about this property. First, it tells me there was positive cash flow. Second, it tells me that there was a loss for tax purposes (net income was negative), producing additional cash flow for me through depreciation. Third, it tells me that I paid down my mortgage by $258, which is an additional benefit to me. If all I knew was that my cash had increased by $468 for the period, I would never have learned these other important benefits from this property and may have thought the property wasn't doing too well.

REPORT NO. 2: RATIO ANALYSIS

While raw numbers are helpful to know, serious analysis of your real estate business comes from ratios and comparisons. A list of the most common ratios used to analyze your results is found in Table 1.4.

TIP Two of the most important ratios are the cap rate on your properties and your return on investment (ROI).

TABLE 1.4 Most Common Ratios Used to Analyze Property Results

Ratio	Numerator	Denominator	Tells You
Cap rate	Net Operating Income	Property Value	How much the property is earning
ROI	Annual increase in value plus income	Cash invested	Total return
Cash on Cash return	Net cash from investment after taxes	Cash invested	Cash return
Current ratio	Current assets	Current liabilities	Ability to pay liabilities
Debt/equity ratio	Total debt	Net Equity	Leverage
Return on assets	Net operating income	Total assets	Profitability
Debt coverage	Net operating income	Annual debt service	Ability to service debt from cash flow
Loan to value (LTV)	Debt	Value of Property	Leverage
Internal Rate of Return (IRR)	Complex formula		Average annual return on investment

Ratio No. 1: Cap Rate

Your cap rate (or capitalization rate) is simply your net operating income divided by the value of your property. Remember that this figure represents the value of the property, not the cost of the property. Let's look at an example. Suppose your property produces $10,000 per month in rent, or $120,000 for the year. And suppose your operating expenses (remember, this doesn't include mortgage interest or principal payments, or depreciation) are $70,000. This means that your net operating income (NOI) is $50,000. If your property is worth $500,000, then your cap rate is 10 percent.

TIP You can use this information to make decisions. Let's suppose that you have a loan on the property with a 5 percent interest rate. If your cap rate goes below 5 percent, then you need to think about selling the property. Why? Because now you have what is called "negative leverage." Negative leverage occurs when your return is less than you are paying on your loan. At this point, it is actually costing you money to borrow because the cap rate is lower than your borrowing rate.

When Ann and I sold our fourplexes in Mesa, the cap rate had dipped down around 5 percent. The interest rate on our mortgage was 6.5 percent. So we were now into negative leverage. On top of that, we had negative cash flow. So it was time to sell the properties. And we did so at a substantial profit because we watched the cap rate. When we purchased the properties, the cap rate was around 10 percent. Though our net operating income never increased, our property value doubled simply because of the cap rate decreasing from 10 percent to 5 percent.

Ratio No. 2: ROI

Another ratio we review is Return on Investment, or ROI. ROI is the ratio of the money you recieve from the property annually divided by the amount of money you put into the property. This ratio tells us how a property is doing overall. It's critical to review this ratio on a regular basis. I know several investors who calculate expected ROI when buying a property but never again. Like the cap rate, your ROI can tell you if you should be holding on to the property or if you need to do something different with the property.

ROI is the ratio of the money you receive from the property annually divided by the amount of money you put into the property.

For example, one of my criteria for investing is an after-tax ROI of at least 30 percent. This includes cash flow from the property and the appreciation on the property plus my tax benefits from the property and principal reduction on my mortgage. A few years ago, I bought a property in Utah that looked like it would have an ROI of 35 percent over a five-year period. But it turned out that the property was very difficult to rent, so the ROI was less than expected. Once it was clear the ROI was going to fall below my 30 percent requirement, I sold the property and found another property that better fit my investment criteria. It should be obvious to you by now that a lot depends on coming up with the appropriate investment criteria. Many of your decisions will be based on these.

Working through your numbers and applying them to your criteria is where another member of your team—your wealth coach—will be critical. Everyone should have a coach for his/her business. Your coach should be someone well versed in real estate and in overall wealth strategies. Go to www.ProVision Wealth.com/wealthstrategies.asp for more information on wealth coaching.

REPORT NO. 3: COMPARISON REPORTS

The third type of reporting is comparison reporting. Comparison reports take the actual data from your real estate business and compare it to some other data, such as industry standards, past performance, or expected/budgeted performance. Let's suppose that when you bought your property, you expected that it would appreciate 10 percent per year. Suppose the actual appreciation is 15 percent.

Your appreciation report should show you not only your current appreciation, but also your expected appreciation and perhaps the average appreciation in the market. This gives you a good idea of how you are doing compared to the market and to your own expectations and whether you might want to consider buying more property in that market or selling what you have so you can buy other property that better meets your criteria.

Can you see how important it is to have good reports? It's not just the raw data you want; it's also the ratios and the comparisons. One of my biggest complaints about many property managers is that they produce terrible reports. Typically, they give you only the raw data, and frequently even that is impossible to understand. Let me show you the type of report my property manager gives me.

While it doesn't give me any analysis, at least it gives me the data in a way I can create my own analysis. I can see immediately that I have positive cash flow, which meets my criteria. I now need to take this information and put it into my reporting system (Quickbooks or something similar), and from that system I can create reports that give me cap rates, ROI, and other analyses.

TABLE 1.5 Real Life Example of
a Good Property Report

Property Address	Lease Rate: $1200/mo
Rent Collected:	$1200.00
Less 8% Management Fee:	$96.00
Expenses-HOA Fee:	$105.00
Amount to Owner	**$999.00**
Mortgage Payment:	$987.90
March 2009 Cashflow:	$11.10 +
April 2009 Projection:	$999.00

BUSINESS PRINCIPLE NO. 5: TAXES

If you want to make an immediate impact on the return on your real estate, you need to pay close attention to tax laws.

TIP The fastest way to increase your ROI on a property is to take advantage of the tax laws in place to encourage real estate investment.

The single biggest expense for most people is taxes. In the United States, which is routinely considered to be a low-tax country, the average business owner earning $100,000 pays more than 50 percent of his earnings to the government in some form of taxes. These include income taxes, property taxes, transfer taxes, sales taxes, employment taxes, and excise taxes, not to mention estate taxes.

Some ancient civilizations equated a 50 percent tax to being in bondage. Yet here we are in the twenty-first century paying more than 50 percent of our income in taxes and accepting this as okay. The good news is that if you are in business, and particularly if that business is real estate, you can easily lower this rate from 50 percent to 20 or 30 percent. In fact, many of our clients at ProVision who are serious real estate investors legally pay no income tax at all.

Think about what you could do with the extra money you would have if you reduced your income taxes by even 20 or 30 percent. How much more real estate could you buy? How much faster would your portfolio grow? I once calculated that someone in the 30 percent tax bracket could double his investment portfolio over seven years simply by maximizing his tax benefits from real estate and reinvesting these savings in more real estate.

When I tell people that they can legally reduce their income tax by 30 percent or more, they are immediately skeptical. They think I must be getting my clients into some tax shelter. They are correct. That tax shelter is real estate investing. And it doesn't matter whether it is residential, commercial, or industrial property. In the United States and many other countries, real estate is a highly favored investment under the tax laws.

TIP In the United States and many other countries, real estate is a highly favored investment under the tax laws.

So let's talk about what you can do to receive the maximum tax benefit from your real estate. We will focus on the laws of the United States, but keep in mind that many other countries have similar laws. So even if you don't invest in the United States, these tax reduction principles may apply to your real estate investments in Canada, Europe, or other areas of the world. Here are five ways to reduce your income tax by 30 percent or more.

TIP NO. 1: TAX STRATEGY

A good tax strategy is like a good business strategy in many ways. You have to look at the big picture, including not only your real estate but also any other businesses and investments you own. And you have to look at it from a long-term perspective. My personal tax strategy includes my two sons. One of my sons, Sam, enjoys business and wants to be involved in my business in the coming years. My other son, Max, has no interest in business and wants to write children's books. So my tax strategy keeps my sons' interests in mind. They both own parts of my business, but I have to structure their ownership differently, since one is actively involved and the other is not.

TIP A good tax strategist could really help here. So, another team member for you is a tax advisor who specializes in tax strategies.

Your tax strategy needs to be a plan that you can readily accomplish without making life too complicated. Of course, a good tax strategist could really help here. So, another team member for you is a tax advisor who specializes in tax strategies.

TIP NO. 2: ENTITY STRUCTURE

Which type of entity should you use? Should you use a limited liability company (LLC), a corporation, or a partnership? Or should you avoid using an entity at all? In some countries, where there is not a lot of litigation, you may not need a separate entity for your real estate. But in the United States, where 95 percent of lawsuits worldwide are filed, the proper entity is essential. Let's look at a quick overview of the tax entities available in the United States.

While every person's situation is different, let me give you a few pointers about which entity you may want to consider for holding your real estate investments. From an asset protection standpoint (discussed in detail in another chapter of this book), LLCs are frequently the best entity to use. One of the great things about LLCs is that they don't have any tax consequence. You can elect to tax an LLC anyway you want. An LLC can be treated as a sole proprietorship, a partnership, an S corporation, or a C corporation.

For most real estate rental properties, you will want to be taxed either as a partnership or a sole proprietorship. Don't make the mistake of putting your real estate rentals into an S corporation or a C corporation. This could spell disaster if you ever have to take the property out of the corporation to refinance it; you will be taxed as if the corporation sold the property to you at its fair market value. I had someone in my office recently who owned his investment property in an S corporation. We estimated the tax cost of refinancing to be in the neighborhood of $250,000 simply because of the entity structure.

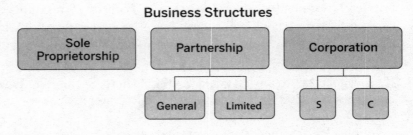

FIGURE 1.3 Overview of Entities

TIP Don't make the mistake of putting your real estate rentals into an S corporation or a C corporation. This could spell disaster if you ever have to take the property out of the corporation to refinance it; you will be taxed as if the corporation sold the property to you at its fair market value.

If you are a real estate dealer or developer, you may want to consider S corporation taxation. This includes those of you who want to fix and flip properties. The reason? You can significantly lower your social security taxes by owning your property in an S corporation. And since you probably won't need to distribute the property out of the company except when you sell it, you won't have the bad income tax consequences I spoke of earlier.

TIP NO. 3: TRAVEL, MEALS, AND ENTERTAINMENT

Remember that the United States and most other countries tax only the net income from a business. So any expenses that you can treat as deductible expenses lower your income tax. The most overlooked deductions in the real estate business are travel, meals, and entertainment expenses. The rule in the United States for meals and entertainment is that if you discuss business before, during, or after the meal or entertainment and the discussion is necessary and ordinary for your business, then you get to deduct the cost of the meal or entertainment.

I'm not talking about going to dinner with your real estate agent or your accountant (though I'm sure they would appreciate it). I'm talking about going to dinner or a sporting event with your partner. For most of you, your business partner in real estate is your spouse. My experience with business owners is that when they go to dinner with their spouses they almost always talk about business. And if you and your spouse are working on the real estate business together, I can virtually guarantee that you are talking about your real estate every time you go out to eat.

So stop paying for your meals out of your personal bank account, and start paying for them from your real estate business bank account.

Travel is a little more difficult to deduct, but not much. If you are traveling within the United States, you simply have to prove that your primary reason for the trip was business. You prove this by showing that you spent more than 50 percent of each eight-hour workday discussing or working on your real estate investment business. This could include your annual meeting or you could simply be investigating real estate opportunities in that location.

We had one client who applied these principles and ended up with a $1 million deal. He really liked to travel to New Mexico. Knowing that he had to look at real estate to deduct his travel expense, he set up a meeting with a local real estate agent to review land development opportunities in his vacation spot. He ended up finding a deal that netted him $1 million. And, of course, he got to deduct his travel expenses.

TIP NO. 4: DEPRECIATION

After Robert and I met with the *Arizona Republic* journalist to discuss 40 percent returns, we walked across the street to have lunch at a local restaurant. Robert asked me what I thought about depreciation. I told him I thought it was like magic. Where else can you get a tax deduction for something you didn't pay for and that is appreciating in value? Yet that is exactly what happens with depreciation in the United States, Canada, and many other countries. Here's how it works:

Say you pay $500,000 for a house that you are going to rent. You put $100,000 of your own money into the house, and the bank loans you $400,000. You get a deduction for a portion of the cost of the house each year—not just a portion of your $100,000, but of the entire purchase price. Let me show you the calculation for U.S. tax purposes.

Let's estimate that 20 percent (or $100,000) of the cost of the house was for the land. Even the IRS recognizes that land does not wear out, so we don't get to depreciate the land. But we do get to depreciate the remaining $400,000. At a minimum for residential property, we should get a deduction of 3.636 percent or $14,545 each year. And that's assuming that the entire $400,000 is allocated to the building. You can increase this deduction by doing what's called a cost segregation.

Briefly, here is what happens in a cost segregation. Your accountant or his engineer goes through your property and segregates (on paper) everything that could easily be removed from the building and is not necessary for its basic operation from the building itself. Those items that can be removed are called personal property or chattels. Personal property can be depreciated at 20 percent or more per year.

In our case, let's suppose that $100,000 of costs is segregated from the building. This would increase our annual depreciation deduction from $14,545 to $30,900—more than double. So while our property appreciates, we still get a tax deduction for depreciation of more than $30,000. This is the best of all deductions, since there is no cash outlay involved other than the down payment on the property.

So if our cash flow is $30,900 or less, we will not pay any income tax on our annual cash flow. And if our cash flow is less than our depreciation, then we create a tax loss from the property that we can use (with proper planning) to offset income from other sources. This is the primary reason many real estate investors are able to reduce their income tax by 30 percent or more and why some real estate investors pay no income tax at all.

TIP NO. 5: DOCUMENTATION

Last but not least, let's talk briefly about the importance of properly documenting our real estate transactions and expenses. Without good documentation, the IRS has the right to disallow your deductions. What a waste of good deductions! We have already discussed the most important form of documentation—good accounting.

In addition, there are other forms of documentation you must keep. For travel, meals, and entertainment, you must keep receipts, and you must note who you were with, where you went, what you discussed, the date of the event, and why you incurred the expense. For automobile deductions, you need to maintain a log of business versus personal miles driven. And for your entities, you need to write down minutes that detail all of your meetings and major transactions.

Documentation is not the most fun part of real estate, but it's not too difficult if you just take a few minutes a week to take care of it. Stay on top of it. If you don't know exactly what you need to document, consult with your tax preparer. Remember that if it isn't documented, then you probably cannot prove to the IRS that it was a legitimate deduction.

So there you have it—five easy opportunities to reduce your income taxes while making tons of money in your real estate business. Now you can see why smart business owners include tax planning as one of their keys to success. Applying these basic principles to your real estate business will enable you to build enormous wealth in a very short time. Remember to begin with a strategy, add a team, maintain good accounting, regularly review your reports, and minimize your taxes by creating a long-term tax strategy. The sooner you begin treating your real estate investing as a real business, the sooner you can stop working so hard and start reaping the profits that are there for all good real estate investors.

WAYS TO LEARN MORE

Tax-Free Wealth – How to Build Massive Wealth by Permanently Lowering Your Taxes — Tom Wheelwright's best-selling book for entrepreneurs and investors who want to permanently reduce their taxes.

ProVision Wealth Strategy U — a free resource at www.WealthStrategyU.com/

ProVision, PLC — An international CPA firm based in Tempe, AZ developing wealth and tax strategies for clients in all 50 states and worldwide.

ProVision School of Wealth Strategy — a monthly subscription to comprehensive training materials on building wealth. Includes courses on creating your wealth vision, building your wealth team, and designing your personal wealth strategy.

ProVision School of Tax Strategy — a monthly subscription to comprehensive training materials on permanently reducing taxes. Includes courses on designing your family tax strategy, involving your children in your real estate business, and getting the greatest tax benefits out of your real estate.

For more than 30 years, **Tom Wheelwright** has developed innovative tax, business, and wealth strategies for sophisticated investors and business owners across the United States and around the world, resulting in millions of dollars in profits for those clients. His goal is to teach people how to create a strategic and proactive approach to wealth that creates lasting success. As the founder of ProVision, Tom is the innovator of proactive consulting services for ProVision's premium clientele, who on average, pay much less in taxes and earn much more on their investments. He works with select clients on their wealth, business, and tax strategies and lectures on wealth and tax strategies around the world.

2

A Real Estate Attorney's View of Assembling and Managing Your Team

I first met Chuck Lotzar in 2001 or so when he was a senior partner in a national law firm. At Chuck's former law firm, I delivered a presentation to approximately ten attorneys that covered my rich dad's philosophy on money, wealth creation, and wealth management. Chuck seemed to be the only one out of the ten who understood or was interested in what I was saying.

In 2003, Kim and I used Chuck to finalize one of our biggest real estate investments. It was a zero-down deal that would put more than $30,000 a month net income in our pockets. If not for Chuck, this deal could have been our biggest nightmare. He found irregularities that most people, including most lawyers, would have missed. On top of that, after the deal was closed, Chuck offered to give us a discount on some of his firm's legal fees since he felt his firm did not work as effectively as it could have. Needless to say, we told him to bill us in full and keep the money. He had more than earned it.

In 2007, Chuck again came to our rescue, this time as our personal attorney against our former business partner. The lawsuit was the worst, most vile event in Kim's and my life. If not for Chuck, I do not know where Kim and I would be today.

The good news is that Chuck Lotzar has turned out to be far more than our real estate attorney. Through Chuck's guidance, the Rich Dad Company has emerged stronger, better staffed, and much more profitable. Personally, I have emerged more *mature, wiser, and less of a hothead, which is a miracle. Chuck has not only made Kim and me vastly richer; we have become better entrepreneurs and investors.*

The lesson again is this: It is often through our worst deals with the worst people that the best people emerge.

—ROBERT KIYOSAKI

I know attorneys see the world differently than most people. A working relationship isn't just a working relationship; it ideally should be a contract between two parties with built-in protections, limitations, and provisions, just in case the relationship goes south. A piece of real estate isn't just a piece of property; it's an asset that brings with it the need for appropriate entity structure, identification of risk, allocation of risk, mitigation of risk and liabilities, and a host of other legal protections and caveats associated with its development, management, and eventual sale.

I know you're thinking life is easier when you are not an attorney. You're probably right! But for me life as an attorney and particularly a real estate attorney is full of the excitement, the challenges, and the accomplishments that can come only from working with people so that they sleep well at night, have their family fortunes protected, and bring their dreams to life. It's a profession that keeps me continually learning, which I love. Real estate is a dynamic field that keeps every day at the office new and fresh.

The likelihood that you are reading the chapter written by an attorney first is slim, so I'll assume you've read at least a few chapters before mine. If you have, you've probably noticed that there are a number of references in them to team members: the professionals it takes to make a real estate deal actually happen. Many of the contributors list the types of team members that they need in the type of real estate work that they do and how they have helped.

Well, I will echo their beliefs. Team members are the deciding factors in spelling success or disaster for a real estate project. In my practice, I have seen teams that operate seemingly effortlessly and others that are clumsy and doomed to failure. So how do you assemble one that works effortlessly, and avoid the kinds that are disasters waiting to happen? The answer is, you can't. You can only try to do your best and know that the reality of your team— particularly as you are just starting out—will fall somewhere in the middle of those two extremes. Your job will be to assemble and manage a group of pros that makes its way progressively more efficient to close every deal you do.

My perspective on teams and team members is different from the views of many in this book because I am *one* of those team members. Many of the others in this book are the investors who drive the team. They delegate to team members who advise them. I'm the one they delegate to and who advises them on how to lead the team. That gives me a slightly different perspective. Combine that with my attorney's perspective and you have a chapter with three primary purposes:

1. To tell you who you need on your team and how to know you have a winner.

2. To identify known risks and make sure that they are properly allocated among other writing parties, including the members of your team.

3. To establish performance measures and deadlines, and to follow up to make sure that each of those performance measures and deadlines are met in a timely manner.

See, this is where my lawyer's mentality comes into play. I know your team will not be perfect, no matter how perfectly you follow this book's directions, how well you interview potential team members, or how ironclad their references were. Life and real estate deals are not that cut and dried. So what do you do? Well, quite simply, you do your best on the front end, and you attempt to protect yourself on the back end.

THREE RULES OF THE GAME

Before you say to yourself, "This team thing seems like more trouble than it is worth. For my project, I'll keep it simple and do most of the work I need alone. I'll keep the team small—as small as possible—and that will minimize my problems," understand that it is very hard to do anything in real estate alone. It is a team sport and as such, I have assembled my Three Rules of the Game.

Nowhere else will your team come into play more than when it is time to perform your due diligence. It's a necessary part of every real estate deal, and with the right team it can be your best friend and actually a lot of fun because you often find the hidden gems that can signal great opportunity. On the other hand, it can be the beginnings of a vivid nightmare you are living because you are the proud owner of a "problem-property," thanks to a team that missed something big during due diligence. Again, the first camp is the place to be.

You'll recall that the due diligence period is usually not less than sixty days in length. Its purpose is to discover any problems and opportunities with a property to determine whether you want to go through with the transaction, and if so with what specific stipulations. It's also designed to allocate and alleviate risk among various parties: the buyer, the seller, the lender, and the various third-party professionals on your team.

Chuck's Three Rules of the Game

Rule No. 1: Talent pays for itself. Accept that hiring a capable and talented real estate team to complete your transaction is in your best interest. Although there will be costs up front, your investment should more than pay for itself over time.

Rule No. 2: You are hiring folks' brains; let them use their brains to solve your problems. Allow teammates to give you their honest and complete assessment of any transaction given the circumstances presented—you want to know all of the problems so that you can craft solutions and quantify the costs of obtaining those solutions. Unfortunately, in some instances you will learn that the cost of continuing with the transaction outweighs the opportunity to be achieved, and you are forced to stop so as to prevent yourself from throwing good money after bad.

Rule No. 3: It is better to hire someone with outstanding judgment and wisdom than a person who has merely completed similar types of transactions.

As I mention in rule number two, when it comes to due diligence, you want a team that will be willing to learn the truth about the property and tell you the brutal facts. If your baby is ugly, you need professionals and advisors who aren't going to be afraid to tell you the truth to your face—before the acquisition takes place. So let's delve into the team members and their roles from a fellow team member and a lawyer's perspective.

Consider these your core team members, the ones you'll need for virtually every real estate deal you do. I believe that people generally fall into two categories: those who are relationship oriented and those who are transaction oriented. Although I have a law practice based on the ability to successfully complete transactions, I am a relationship-oriented person who generally seeks out other teammates who are also relationship oriented. I am willing to work with other teammates who are transaction oriented, but I do so recognizing that their ability and willingness to step up to solve a problem is limited, especially after the transaction closes.

REAL ESTATE ATTORNEY

Notice how I wrote *real estate attorney*, not just *attorney*. That's the first tip I will give you right up front. Real estate transactions are significantly different from other transactions, so it is critical to hire an attorney who understands and is experienced in real estate. Contract attorneys without real estate experience are not good enough.

The reason I am so emphatic here is because a good real estate attorney can take a lot of the pressure off you by acting as the quarterback and taking responsibility for coordinating the entire team. A good attorney is strong, experienced, and at the same time self-confident enough to know when he or she needs your input or help from a third party. There are times when a real estate transaction will have nuances that your lead real estate attorney—no matter how experienced—may not have ever encountered before. You don't want your attorney learning on your transaction; you want an attorney with a network of people, inside or outside the firm, that he or she can call on to bridge any gaps.

Often a good real estate attorney can be the master of the due diligence budget and calendar and keep all the other team members on track and on time with their deliverables. That means you'll want your attorney on board early, right at the very start, to handle the early documents, such as the term sheet or the letter of intent, to make sure that the allocation and assignment of risks are thoughtfully documented for closing.

Real Life Story

Every real estate opportunity is different, and it's the truly unique ones that sometimes cause your teams to expand beyond your expectations, even into the realm of the unbelievable.

Too often real estate investors become successful based on their ability to overcome numerous problems, and they become insensitive to the weight of certain problems that would otherwise thwart a transaction. I recall one group of clients who were prolific real estate investors. Although they were astute business people who accomplished a number of successful transactions in sequence, their history of success impeded their ability to walk away from a bad deal, even when they knew that there would be insufficient equity in a transaction and visible and invisible deferred maintenance issues with the heating and cooling system for the apartment complex, which needed replacement and caused the buildings to settle in the ground by more than one foot! No matter how successful you have been in the past, you need to replicate good habits for the diligence and closing with each new transaction.

Most often, however, your team will be highly predictable and consist of several core members. You will find that the more you work with them, the better you will all work together, which will increase your efficiency.

A good real estate attorney can be your greatest ally. I frequently find myself providing ideas and advice that will enhance my clients' transactions and their businesses as a whole. At our firm, we approach projects from a business-owner's perspective. Business owners want us to tell them the things that are standing in their way, of course. But they also want us to come up with innovative ways to transcend the problems and get the deal done. If you have an attorney who seems to be pointing out all the problems without posing solutions, that's a sign that you may need another attorney. If you have an attorney who conducts himself or herself in a manner that makes you uncomfortable, e.g., rudeness, or overly passive or overly aggressive under the circumstances, then that's another sign that you may need another attorney.

Specifically, it's our job to read and analyze all documentation, including third-party reports, title and survey, purchase and sale agreements, and loan documents. Sometimes, we may be requested to draft these documents along with corporate entity documents when dealing with equity investments and partnerships.

Hiring a Real Estate Attorney?
What to Look For, and What to Watch Out For

What to Look For

- Portability of past knowledge, wisdom, and judgment
- Availability of time to do the work
- An understanding of professional limitations
- Openness to engaging the assistance of other lawyers or law firms
- A willingness and ability to work as a team player
- Experience in various forms of real estate transactions
- Experience with complex finance structuring of real estate transactions
- Demeanor and approach to the practice of law, e. g., that's part gentleman, part pit bull
- The support of the law firm—how deep is the bench?

What to Watch Out For

- Any past malpractice claims
- Any past Bar complaints
- Experience with contracts, business, and litigation, but not in relation to real estate
- A personality and/or demeanor incompatible with the client's personality and/or demeanor

Your attorney can either bill you hourly for his or her work or provide a soft estimate for the scope of work. Should the scope of work exceed the estimate, the additional work is billed at the hourly rate. Another payment method is hourly against a hard estimate. These agreements generally have a large contingency built in for unforeseen events that is payable at closing. This type of contract can put the attorney and the client at odds. You want your attorney to find the unexpected—that can save you in a real estate transaction—but if you are worried that the work of searching for the unexpected will cost you more money, you may be thwarting your own success. In the best instances, the fruits of the deal, or the savings in terms of money and/or risk, a contingent fee that changes which party is in control will more than pay for any attorney fees. Many of our clients feel we have more than earned our fees, and that's ideally what both sides want.

Over the years I have focused a good portion of my law practice working on contingent-fee matters related to large revenue bond financings and tax credit projects. Whenever I have a contingent fee, I want to be the person with the most control over the ability to advance and close the transaction. However, a lawyer's compass needs to be completely aligned with the interest of his client, regardless of his fee arrangement.

How to Construct an Effective Engagement Letter

Most members of your team will require an engagement letter before beginning work. They may provide one, or you can. To protect yourself, make sure the following points are included:

- Spell out scope of work, particularly the roles of each party.
- Specify the nature and timing of payment, including timing of service and due date.
- Define the particulars of termination for both the contractor and you.
- Be specific on needs (software) and deliverables (eight copies of plans, etc.) due to cost and which party will bear the cost.
- Disclose conflicting relationships.
- Identify and allocate known risks.
- Dispute resolution.
- Limit liability.

REAL ESTATE BROKERS

Real estate brokers are important team members because they are the generators of opportunities. They can decide who sees a property that is coming on- line first and can be the bearers of great opportunities. What it takes is a broker who understands the importance of relationships and working as part of a team.

On the other hand, many brokers are transactional, living and dying by their fees, which naturally results in an eat-what-you-kill mentality. They will indiscriminately pose opportunities that are nothing more than distractions because they do not fit your business goals. What you really want is a real estate broker who looks out for your best interest, understands your needs, and seeks out opportunities that match them. That adds value.

Beyond this, the true role of a real estate broker is to bring a willing buyer and willing seller together, not necessarily to ensure his or her client gets the best deal. But the good ones do both. They work to execute the best possible transaction for their client from start to finish.

Sometimes a real estate broker will perform what is known as dual representation, which means the same broker will represent both the buyer and the seller. On the surface, this may seem like an opportunity to save some money in commissions; after all, typical transactions have two brokers who

Real Life Story: How to Know Your Real Estate Broker Is Looking Out for You

The dual brokerage relationship does not trouble me when I see sophisticated parties on both sides of a transaction. The broker frequently has problems when there is a mismatch of sophistication among the parties. I have had many conversations with brokers who had dual agency relationships that they regretted once problems arose.

I have found that the best real estate brokers have the clients' interests at heart. The best example I can give relates to my good friend and client, Craig Coppola, who was acting as my real estate broker in my attempt to buy an office building for my law firm. Although I had my heart set on buying a particular building, Craig was a good friend and professional broker who looked me in the eye and told me that it was not in my best interest to act and that I needed to be patient as the market was trending downward. Clearly, Craig's advice was in my best interest and not in his short-term interest since no commission would be paid.

must share the commissions. But dual representation can be tricky, and in the very least it requires full disclosure of all known facts and circumstances to avoid conflicts of interests.

While most people in business recognize the need to adjust to market changes, real estate brokers really need to moderate their styles as market conditions fluctuate. During the boom times of the mid 2000s, many real estate brokers, based on the volume of work, became more transactional as they tried to close as many deals as they could. But the best ones knew that booms also create busts, and it's the real pros who maintain relationships during the booms that have business during the down times. The best brokers also know that the height of the market is not the time to buy and provide that level of counsel to investor clients. They are market advisors as well as salespeople who are in it for the long term and know that no deal today is worth the loss of many deals tomorrow. That's the kind of broker you want.

ACCOUNTANT

I have found that almost all business is based on some form of mathematics, and it is important to have accountants who are well versed in the intricacies of real estate. In fact, much of the advice that I gave you with respect to establishing a relationship with a real estate attorney has equal weight to establishing a relationship with an accountant.

I have also found that one of the first folks hired internally by real estate investors is an accountant who will be charged with working cooperatively with an outside accounting firm. Frequently, the internal accountant is charged with a substantial amount of responsibility beyond accounting and feels pressure to limit the involvement of the outside accounting firm. If the internal accountant is strong enough, then there will not be problems. Unfortunately, problems frequently do arise based on lack of communication and sophistication.

A strong real estate accountant will understand the effect of changes in deal structure on the various tax attributes such as amortization, depreciation, and losses (which are inevitable during a construction phase since no money is being generated during the development and construction of the project). Additionally, a real estate accountant will know when it is in your best interest to obtain a cost segregation study to identify the component parts of the building(s) so as to allow for an accurate and possibly accelerated application of amortization and depreciation.

ARCHITECT

First of all, special thanks to Greg Zimmerman and Chris Ilg for sharing their knowledge on this subject. Architects are critical members of any real estate team because they have the ability like no one else to provide creativity, innovation, and magic that can transform an ordinary property into a showpiece. They also have the ability to create a lot of expense that sometimes isn't needed at all.

Good architect partners understand that while they may have the ability to turn a property into a project that provides accolades and acclaim, the project objectives may dictate otherwise. The project may require the architect make minor modifications that deliver big results. They are not exciting modifications, and they are often not very dramatic. They may not even be all that rewarding to do, but sometimes that's the nature of the project, and although the design work might be mundane, it can deliver a big payoff for the investors. And that is anything but mundane. While it's more fun to redesign an apartment building to create exciting loft living environments, a profitable, cash-flow-positive project may require only that the architect figure out how to fit a washer and dryer in each existing unit. This is actually one of the biggest challenges faced in the apartment industry. The trend is away from common area laundry rooms, and architects are challenged to make washers and dryers work in small spaces.

Design professionals are a lot like physicians or attorneys. They specialize. While there are excellent neurosurgeons out there, you don't want the neurosurgeon performing your heart surgery. And the attorney who makes a living in divorce court isn't the one you want handling the financial complexities of a real estate transaction. Just the same, you don't want the architect who designs million-dollar homes designing your mini-storage investment property. You want the architect who can design those structures in his or her sleep.

But the biggest reason why you want to work with experienced, specialized architects is because they know the ins and outs. National and local codes change almost daily. Only architects and their firms can keep up with it all. Even the slightest revision to any of the several codes could have a serious impact on a design. As an attorney, I have seen too many investors' projects get caught up in the complicated codes and laws of building, remodeling, and restoring a property. It wastes a lot of time and can get messy. It's never easy to fight city hall, and with the right architect who knows the laws and the regulations, you should not have to.

Let me elaborate on the word *experience*. Architecture is a lifelong endeavor, and it is not unusual for an architect to require years of experience before

Experience Is Everything

When you work with an experienced, specialized architect partner, you reap the advantages:

- Design moves along quicker.
- There is not a steep learning curve.
- You get a completed design that works with fewer surprises.
- Plans, although custom, are somewhat field-tested.
- Building is smoother because the plans have commonalities with past projects.
- He knows the ins and outs of building codes.

truly gaining the amount of competence required to guide the client through a highly specialized project. It's not necessarily just the design aspects that I am talking about. It's the peripheral know-how that cannot be learned in school but can come only from doing things like working through the political process. Working positively and effectively with federal, state, and city employees is a honed skill that only comes over time. And let's not forget the value of a keen sense for anticipating market trends. After all, the work you are hiring from an architect may be happening today, but it needs to be valued by customers for years to come.

Once you interview and select your architectural firm from these perspectives, you can also look at other important requirements like working relationship and costs. I won't elaborate too much on the fact that regardless of how skilled the architect, if that person can't work with the team or with you, you need to keep looking. Relationships are everything, particularly when it comes to the architect. Too often the design side of the project can put off the trades side of the project by being overly demanding about aesthetics and not being open to finding reasonable solutions that don't compromise the look and function of the project. It's extremely important to have a strong and collaborative working relationship between an architect and the general contractor. Forcing the architect or the general contractor to work with an architect or general contractor that they don't work well with leads only to trouble for the property owner.

When it comes to money, be prepared to fully spell out exactly what you are hoping to achieve—your objectives—and how you would like to achieve them. Share your budget both for the design aspects of the project and for how much you plan to put into the building process. You must be concerned at this point with the architect's fees, yes, but also the cost to build out the architect's design.

Again, having been involved in many real estate projects, I have seen architects create designs that are simply too costly to build under the predefined budget and profitability constraints. Those are severe mistakes that can cost time and money. Architects and contractors must communicate to avoid these kinds of problems.

The better the information that you give the architect up front, the more accurate his fee proposal should be. Understandably, it is difficult to have a handle on every issue surrounding a project; things do come up that are unexpected. But there are ways to protect yourself a bit from costs getting out of control. First of all, you may want to begin your working relationship with an architect by putting together an agreement for the due diligence and preliminary design/consulting work. There is nothing wrong with doing this, and as long as both you and the architect understand that further work is contingent on the success and outcomes of the preliminary work, you may find this is the best arrangement.

You can implement this kind of arrangement with either a phased contract or better yet, a time and materials contract with provisions for a subsequent contract using the American Institute of Architects (AIA) form B181, which is a standard agreement between an owner and an architect. You can find this form on the Internet when you search AIA B181. It may serve as a good reference for you.

The benefit of this arrangement is that you can move forward without a huge commitment and no real idea of what can be done. That's handy because most likely at this point, you won't have much idea of what can be done. That's why you need the architect. The benefit to the architect is job security. It's nice to know that if the due diligence is favorable, all further work, including time, designs, and working drawings will be developed in his or her office. That also is excellent incentive for the architect to work harder to find feasible design solutions that fit into the budget for the project. If he or she wants more work, then make the project work.

I've seen this approach work well quite often. One minor, but important, point is that the services you contract with the architect may require the services of other consultants. I recommend contracting with them directly to maintain knowledge and control over the outside service provider's work and progress.

Assuming the project moves forward, and you and the architect have executed the contracts, the next phase is all about communication. The best, most efficient projects I've been associated with have been ones where the design team holds weekly meetings and provides progress plans and updates for review. With so many moving parts to any design project, keeping everyone informed is always a top priority. When well executed, it speeds up the process and delivers far better outcomes.

Once the design and development phase is complete, the construction documents get under way. At this point, it is the architect who should control the consultants and keep the attorneys and lender informed of all progress. As a ring leader for the design and construction side of the project, all information needs to funnel through the architect to maintain control and ensure that no deviation to the schedule, scope, and of course, fees are made without his or her knowledge.

CIVIL ENGINEER

Civil engineers are frequently hired by your architect. They are responsible for locating existing utilities and developing the plans to connect to them or determine if and how to upsize the capacity. American Land Title Association surveys are part of this process, as is obtaining a "will serve" letter from the utility provider, which legally obliges it to serve the particular project with utility service.

Civil engineers are also responsible for such things as drainage, grading requirements, and in cases where canal irrigation is involved, that too. Your architect will inform you when and why a civil engineer is needed for a project.

Your architect will review all contracts for service from not only civil engineers but all related design consultants. And I recommend you allow your real estate attorney to review these documents as well, solely from a legal perspective. By contrast, the architect will review them to make sure the intent of the design is being met and to look for gaps and overlaps with the goal of a seamless scope of service.

You will want to execute the contracts once your real estate attorney and architect have reviewed them and given them the go ahead. Often these contracts contain contingencies or line items in them that are part of the contract, but which could be separately executed or deleted as needed. Your attorney and architect can point these out, but be aware that if these contingencies are executed in the course of work because of requirements in the field, they can and often will cost you more money.

In my experience, civil engineers are not known for adding on unneeded services, but rather omitting services. And it is very difficult as a property owner, particularly if you have not been doing this work for twenty years, to know what the civil engineer should have done until there's a torrential rain and you find half your parking lot is submerged in a murky brown puddle. Then you know more work should have been done regarding drainage. These things happen.

The challenges a civil engineer can solve go beyond the concrete world of grading, utilities, and drainage. I always recommend to my clients that they find civil engineering firms with a lead engineer or representative who is not only knowledgeable of civil engineering but knows how to walk the corridors of city hall. Political savvy is a huge value-added advantage. Knowing the people who matter and then presenting your case before city officials and a crowd of interested citizens without acting and sounding like a civil engineer is a real ace card to hold.

Three Most Common Pitfalls with Civil Engineers

1. Delivering in a timely manner.
2. Plans that do not have sufficient detail to match the existing utilities.
3. Plans that fail to adequately take into consideration the property's topography as it relates to water retention and drainage.

   Overcome these problems by holding your civil engineers to incentivized timetables and have your engineer, architect, and your contractor review the drawings with all those involved in advance.

PROFESSIONAL SURVEYOR

We've all seen surveyors standing in the middle of the street, gazing through their transits and taking measurements of the ground. This information is precisely what makes property owners and lenders sleep well at night, knowing that the properties they are considering during the due diligence phase are all that they have been stated to be. And best of all, they report this information with a very official document that bears all the appropriate seals and certifications. It's the real deal, and it becomes a matter of public record.

So what exactly are surveyors looking for, and looking at, through those tiny site scopes? When it comes to most projects, they are confirming or establishing the following:

- Easements. The surveyor is designating or verifying the access into and out of the property.
- Dimension and Location of Property. The surveyor is looking at and marking the property lines to determine the property's exact size and location in respect to other properties.

- Encroachments. The surveyor is looking at the property lines and determining if any structures belonging to another party are within your property line . . . or yours within theirs. This can affect the appraised value of a property and cost money to remediate.
- Location of All Buildings and Improvements. The surveyor is determining the exact placement of all buildings and improvements within the land parcel to assert that they are placed as specified and that they are within the constraints of local building codes.
- Nonvehicular Access. The surveyor is determining the exact placement of any nonvehicular access easements like pedestrian walkways that may exist on the property. These can impact building improvement and building placement plans.
- Traffic Calming Measures. The surveyor is looking at and indicating or planning the location of traffic-calming improvements such as speed humps, median plantings, etc., that slow traffic and improve the environment for residents, pedestrians, and bicyclists.

Of course, every project dictates what your surveyor will need to do, and every piece of land brings its own unique needs, too. In the mountainous, boulder-ridden terrain of Arizona—a state with strict laws related to indigenous plants and natural formations—surveyors indicate the location of every giant saguaro cactus, every palo verde tree, and any rock outcroppings that are to be preserved as natural space.

Ultimately, your title company and the surveyors themselves do not want there to be any gaps between adjacent properties. There are a lot of reasons for this when you think about it. One is ownership. Who is responsible to care and maintain the gap area? A second is liability. Are both owners, one or neither, responsible for a mishap that may take place in between property lines?

Another is property value. It can be really expensive to buy a small piece of land that your project may need in order to be compliant with development requirements related to setbacks, ingress, and egress, etc. Remember, just because you may need additional land to complete your project does not mean that your neighbor has to sell it to you.

HAZARDOUS SUBSTANCE SITE ASSESSMENT ENGINEER

This is a professional you want to bring on very early in the due diligence process because if he or she finds there are hazardous substances on the property, you may want to rethink everything. Your lenders will strongly advise and may even insist upon it. You simply must know the status of the property in terms of hazardous substances. There have been too many cases where—and these are the worst kind—entire housing developments have been built in areas that were later found to be toxic. Love Canal in New York is one of them. Cases that are far less dramatic, but still incredibly expensive, are those where a hazard exists but can be remediated. You never want to find yourself responsible for the first scenario; it is actually quite difficult, given the law and requirements for development and redevelopment today. But in the event of the second case, which is more likely to occur, at least know what kind of remediation costs you are in for.

When selecting an environmental engineer, begin by finding one who is fully accredited in the field. Having a trustworthy relationship with your mortgage banking professional is also key. The mortgage banker will know which environmental engineers are responsive and familiar with the reporting requirements of a broad spectrum of lenders. The lender may have a list of preferred providers that may at times take selection out of the borrower's hands. It is also important that while your environmental engineer is thorough so as to identify actual existing recognized environmental conditions, he does not create unnecessary work by requiring more expensive Phase II reports.

During due diligence, you must contract what is called a Phase I hazardous substance site contamination study. Among the many things the inspector looks at, he or she will perform a visual assessment of the site and surrounding properties; interview the owner, neighbors, occupants; and take a look at the site's history. The goal is to determine if any hazardous materials were ever manufactured, stored, or dumped there. At this stage the inspector doesn't take any samples.

Ideally, you will receive a clean Phase I report and not need any additional testing or a Phase II study in which the inspector takes samples of the discovered hazardous materials. This process can be costly and time-consuming because sometimes just getting the "samples" requires excavation and core drillings.

Interestingly, certain entities in the chain of title may have remediation responsibility should hazardous materials be found. In addition, they have a disclosure responsibility should they know of these hazards during the due diligence period. Lenders obviously are looking for a clean Phase I report so that there is no drag on their ability to seize collateral and liquidate, should the need arise. This action usually requires stepping into the chain of title, and it's best if there are no obstacles due to a history of hazardous materials liability.

Recently, engineers to prepare Phase I and II reports have sought to limit the amount of their liability to property owners by having their engagement letter or contract specify that damages are limited to the amount of fees paid to the engineer. Obviously, limitations of this nature do not afford the property owner the benefit intended when a professional engineer was hired to conduct the Phase I or II investigation and report.

ESCROW OFFICER/TITLE AGENT

The more real estate deals you do, the more you will get to know your escrow officer/title agent. This person acts as a neutral party who is attempting to carry out the express written instructions of the buyer, the seller, the lender(s), and in some cases the real estate brokers. They review and verify all documents and pass the documents along with the funds between the appropriate parties in the transaction. They are there at closing.

Again, my approach to this chapter is from a legal perspective. Where I have seen issues relating to this area is in title insurance. It is the title agent who issues the title insurance policy. Title insurance is insurance covering the past because it protects only against losses arising from events that occurred *prior* to the date of the policy. Coverage ends on the day the policy is issued and extends backward in time for an indefinite period. This is in marked contrast to property or life insurance, which protect against losses resulting from events that occur *after* the policy is issued, for a specified period into the future. A Title policy protects property owners and lenders from monetary losses that could result from ownership of a property's title, which may include fraud, liens against the property, or errors missed during the title search. Title insurance does not prevent loss of marketability due to a title claim, and that is important to know if you are going to assume ownership of a property.

In other words, a title insurance policy does not obligate the title insurance company to make corrections to your property's title if a problem is discovered; rather it simply provides a basis to receive monetary compensation for your loss at a maximum level specified by the title policy limits.

I am frequently surprised by a real estate investor's willingness to accept a title company's offer to "insure over" a known risk because the title insurance does not cure the apparent defect in the title; which may come back to haunt the property owner in the future.

The policy covers only the amount of the loan, so the policy's cost is based on this amount. It is best to obtain both a lender and owner's policy. The coverage extended to the owner is usually referred to as the ALTA policy, which must be based in part on a survey.

The talent associated with escrow and title officers varies widely. For that reason it is important to know who we are dealing with and their approach to solving problems. An effective escrow agent anticipates the demand of the transaction for all parties and is proactive. I am very loyal to escrow and title officers who I know have the capacity to close complex transactions in a timely manner. Unfortunately, I had to kiss a few toads in order to find folks who are keepers!

MORTGAGE BROKER

Selecting your mortgage broker is one of the most important decisions you will make. You want to find a mortgage broker, who like the architect you choose, specializes in your area of investment. You may not know this, but the brokerage industry is a specialty business, and few brokers possess the expertise needed to service all areas of the lending arena. I want a broker who is well versed in not only the execution of the loan but also very in touch with the local trends. If your proposed project is not well suited to the market, your mortgage broker should tell you outright or will facilitate the market telling you. Either way, you'll know because the process will be arduous and most likely not well received by lenders.

Almost anything can trigger lending difficulties. Perhaps the proposed project isn't right for the location. Or maybe the location is right, but the timing isn't right for the project. Sometimes the lender will raise flags because the plan and proposed product didn't go through enough feasibility studies or a satisfactory amount of market research to ensure the project is on target. Any investor who comes to a mortgage broker without having done his or her homework and as a result made the proper adjustments to the plan and design will find the underwriting will stall, and a loan will be next to impossible to attain. That's a failure by the investor.

A failure on the mortgage broker's side can happen, too. A good mortgage broker should guide you to the most appropriate lending vehicle and steer you clear of the ones that are not in your best interest. Too often I have seen or heard of mismatches between a product and the type of loan terms, even when the product has qualified for that kind of loan. A mismatch can impact a lot of things, not the least of which is the pro forma of the property. It can also contribute to reduced profitability. And loan vehicles such as city, local, and federal funding have stringent requirements so their cost-benefit is questionable, unless the fit is just right. Your mortgage broker should be very clear about every loan term so you can take full advantage of them and avoid the pitfalls. If there is something you don't understand, do whatever it takes to clarify it.

You also should ask your mortgage broker what they know about tax credit, HUD financing, and related agencies, and ask them to relate to you the advantages and disadvantages of these financing vehicles. Experience with them in addition to knowledge about them is a real advantage. The last thing you want is a mortgage broker who is learning on the job with your project. Look for a seasoned veteran.

In the absence of a good mortgage broker partner, some real estate attorneys— I am one of them—also specialize in obtaining the most favorable financing vehicles available. It is a service we provide, and I am sure we are not alone. Given that your attorney is looking out for your best interest, he or she will analyze the loan for more than just interest rates and amortization schedules. He or she will read the fine print and the finer points to discover any possible ways a loan, because of its terms, could come back to bite you years later.

INSURANCE AGENT

I won't go into big detail on this one except to make a few points. Have an insurance agent who specializes in real estate and development early on in the process to avoid easily avoidable pitfalls. The lender generally has the specific coverage required for your transaction. You should be able to rely on your insurance broker to easily interpret the requirements and deliver an insurance certificate covering the same within twenty-four hours.

Over the years, as lending has become more oriented to packaging loans for sale in the secondary market, lenders have dictated the types of insurance that must be obtained, as well as the limits that they believe to be appropriate. Your insurance agent should be able to provide you additional insight with respect to the suitability of the proposed forms of coverage applicability of the proposed limits.

There are probably entire agencies in your city or town that offer mostly real estate, construction, and development insurance. There are a number of things, based on your project, that will require insurance of one sort or another. Insurance is all about risk management and the question becomes how much risk you want to assume versus if you should pay a premium to have someone else assume it. If you know in advance the type of insurance you will need, you can factor it into your project budget and determine if the project is feasible and will deliver a solid return with these added costs. If it won't, then you may want to reconsider the project entirely.

1031 Exchange Intermediary

Every time a client presents me with an opportunity to participate in an IRC Section 1031 transaction, I insist that he or she has his or her accountants run the numbers to determine the effect of paying the taxes versus deferring the tax with an exchange. From my vantage point, the tax savings do not replace the need for a strong real estate transaction for the replacement property. I believe you make money buying real estate; which is best demonstrated when you sell real estate.

Many times, investors are working on a project that will be part of a 1031 Exchange. There's an entire chapter in this book about exchanges, but in a nutshell, a 1031 Exchange occurs when you sell one property and purchase another property under the tax code 1031 and minimize or avoid paying taxes on the gain. Anytime a 1031 Exchange is involved, you should have a qualified intermediary execute it. The reason is simple. If there is any misstep with the procedures of the exchange, you will not qualify and you will end up paying the taxes you were trying to avoid.

You want to know exactly how much the tax is and weigh the pros and cons of the exchange. A good test in my opinion, is asking yourself whether or not you would go forward with the transaction if an exchange was not involved. In other words, would you still consider this opportunity a good investment? Even if you answer yes to this question, I always make sure my client has discussed the exchange with me and his or her tax advisor so the entire plan can be viewed in light of the investor's bigger financial picture.

There are also nontax reasons for exchanges. Here are a few that you may not have considered:

- Exchange from fully depreciated property to a higher value property that can be depreciated.
- Exchange from non-income-producing raw land to improved property to create cash flow.
- Exchange to meet location requirements.
- Exchange from a larger property to several smaller properties, used to divide an estate among several heirs or for retirement reasons.

- Exchange from a tenants-in-common interest in one property to a fee interest in another property.

So what do you look for in a qualified intermediary? Exchangors must feel confident that exchange funds will be safe and available for the successful conclusion of their exchange. It is best to hire a qualified intermediary that, first, comes highly recommended by other real estate investors. You should also do your own due diligence to determine how the intermediary is investing funds it has on hand. Recently, a large intermediary was unable to fulfill its funding obligations because it had invested the bulk of its funds in auction rate securities, which became illiquid overnight! If you cannot understand the nature of the intermediary's underlying investments, then you should not let the intermediary hold your money!

Second, be sure to obtain a written guarantee for the exchange of funds. And, finally, verify that the qualified intermediary has fidelity bond coverage, preferably in the amount of $100 million professional liability insurance and employee theft and dishonesty coverage.

General Contractors

Nearly all real estate projects involve some construction or renovation. And for that reason, having a general contractor run the show is a good idea. Unless you are a general contractor yourself, you should never attempt to manage your own construction, no matter how well you think you can do it. If you are an investor, remain an investor.

It should almost go without saying that you want to be very careful which contractor you choose. Your decision will greatly impact the quality of your project. You can get excellent referrals from your architect who may even recommend one particular contractor. And if you have selected the right insurance agency in your city or town, the one that specializes in construction and does the bond work for all the contractors in town, you will be able to get some solid referrals from them as well. Other than that, you can ask your attorney, mortgage brokers, lender, and look around town at the projects that are currently underway. That will give you a good idea of which companies are the most reputable.

No matter how tempting it is to go cheap and hire a small-time player for your "small job," it is never a good idea to hire any contractor who isn't licensed and insured. As an attorney, I will never allow my clients to assume the astronomical risks that they are assuming when working with a contractor or any trades person who is not licensed and insured.

I think it is always a good idea to determine whether or not the general contractor can obtain a performance and payment bond. If you learn that the general contractor is unable to obtain a performance and payment bond, you should find out exactly why that is the case. If the general contractor is involved in its own development activities, bonding companies will frequently shy away from the risk. However, if the general contractor is not involved in development, then bonding companies should be more inclined to underwrite the risk associated with the general contractor's affairs. If a performance and payment bond is obtained, the general contractor will pass the cost on to the developer, which may be significant.

Your general contractor is responsible for carrying out the design plans to the letter, and for managing the trade contractors (subcontractors) who will actually do the work. General contractors seldom actually perform any of the trades themselves; they are simply very experienced project managers who know the process of construction and know the people and the companies that will get the work done. Pick a good contractor and you elevate your chances of having good trades people working on your project. You should look for general contractors who pay their subcontractors and material men in a timely manner and have a systematized manner of obtaining all of the required lien releases. Too often, general contractors who are struggling look to use subcontractors and material men as a form of working capital financing, as a result of the general contractor's failure to pay them in a timely manner. Ask for a list of references who are subcontractors from various trades and material men from various product lines.

How do you know you have a good contractor? First of all, look at their previous projects. Walk through them. Is the quality up to your standards of excellence? You can tell by looking at finishes and details. If the details are shoddy, one can only assume what lies behind the walls hidden from view isn't much better. Second, and perhaps even more important, is ask the tradespeople. Does the contractor pay them on time, or is the company always running way behind on payment? This could be a sign of cash flow problems. Stay as far clear of that as you can. What you don't want is to have construction loan draws that are meant to be buying your building materials going to pay off an old debt on another project.

And speaking of money, building costs—like anything else—can start out in one solar system and end up in a completely differently galaxy if not closely managed right from the time of the initial estimate. To set a price, you'll need a clearly defined budget, a clearly defined scope of work, and a clearly defined schedule.

From my vantage point, I believe that folks starting out in development should look to work with established general contractors who have obtained a performance or payment bond for the project. The additional costs associated with the performance and payment bond are substantially less than the potential downside.

Construction Risks That Can Cost You Money

As an attorney, I'm always concerned about risks, so here are a few that I have encountered, which you'll want to keep within your field of view. It will save you money.

- Poorly defined separation of functions between architect, engineer, and contractor.
- Scope creep that causes a small project to become a big one based on change orders.
- Project acceleration. This may be done as a way to provide an incentive for your contractor to complete your project prior to the original date for purposes of interest savings, favorable material pricing, or changes and deadlines for laws or regulations.
- Poor working relationships between parties that cause a lack of collaboration and inefficiencies.

Keeping your contractors happy is pretty easy. Mostly what they want is to be paid on time. They, in turn, have subcontractors to pay and paying them on time keeps their tradespeople happy. Pay on time and you have a happy worksite. Contractors also tend to take great pride in the work that they do and feel a great sense of accomplishment bringing a building out of the ground. And, finally, they value their relationships with owners, designers, and subcontractors. Work as a team, keeping all these things in good standing, and you'll have a general contractor who will become a valued asset to your real estate investment business.

A Few Final Words

Any real estate project is all about minimizing financial risk, time risk, design risk, and quality risk. It's about choosing the right people to help you achieve this and working collaboratively all along the way. If you are the type of person who seems to foster adversarial relationships, this will be difficult. That's not to say that there won't be times when being tough will be required. There most definitely will be.

You'll find as you go from simple projects to the more complex that your team will have to function at a higher level with greater cooperation and problem-solving abilities. In all instances, and with every project—big or small—that you do, have a good attorney looking out for your interests. Find the best one you can, and let him or her do the job you deserve.

Ways to learn More

www.lotzar.com

Charles W. Lotzar is founder of the Lotzar Law Firm, P.C., a diversified practice with representation of clients in commercial and real estate transactions, low-income housing, tax credit financings, administrative proceedings, and various forms of tax-exempt and taxable bond financings. A former senior partner in the national law firm, Kutak Rock LLP, Lotzar is involved in all phases of real estate development, including debt and equity financing. He has extensive experience in dealing with public contracts and issues related to public officials, and he has been involved in bond financings that have an aggregate value in excess of $5 billion.

3

Profits from the Ground Up

R oss is Ken McElroy's partner in their business MC Properties. Kim and I are often financial partners with Ken and Ross in a number of their projects and have done very well financially, even in tough economic times.

There are three primary reasons why our investments with Ross do so well. The first reason is that he is a builder. He understands the ins and outs of the construction industry. Second, he is a property manager. This is important because the key to long-term investing in real estate is professional property management. And third, Ross is exceptional at finance by managing the ratios between debt, equity, and expenses. When it comes to real estate investing, he is the complete package. On top of that, he is a great guy. He is fair and honest.

In 2002, when the Tucson apartment market was hot, Ross's background allowed us not only to do well buying existing apartment houses but also building new apartment houses. One of our first investments together was the purchase of an existing apartment complex his company was managing. This gave us an advantage because we knew the numbers were honest—which is important since most pro forma numbers provided by realtors are lies. Second, the property had an additional ten acres of vacant land. Once we bought the existing apartment house, our next step was to begin construction on an additional one hundred units on the vacant land. Then with the increased rents a few years later, Ross refinanced the property, and Kim and I got all of our initial investment money back. This means *each month we receive a check from the positive cash flow, and Kim and I have zero invested in the project. If you do the math, this means Kim and I have an infinite return on our money. In layman's terms, an infinite return is truly money for nothing . . . every month.*

This is why Kim and I love being partners with Ross McCallister and Ken McElroy.

—ROBERT KIYOSAKI

Perhaps you've already read and maybe even re-read *Rich Dad Poor Dad* by Robert Kiyosaki, as well as my partner Ken McElroy's book, *The Advanced Guide to Real Estate Investing,* and now you are ready to take the plunge and invest in real estate on your own. That's probably why you bought this book written by real estate professionals, each of whom have been earning their livings in real estate for decades.

There are pages in this book that are full of tremendous opportunities and innovative ways to make money in real estate. But one avenue of investment you may not have thought of and may want to consider is to develop your own project from the ground up.

The profits you have heard about from real estate development are mind boggling, and if you are like most people, the numbers leave you frothing at the mouth for a piece of the development pie. Yes, there is tremendous profit to be made from real estate development, but as with any high reward venture there is also the possibility of tremendous financial losses if you let your emotions override good judgment, or if you don't know what you are doing.

In this chapter I will outline some of the steps you need to take to evaluate a development opportunity, steps I've gleaned from my expertise in developing apartment communities during the past three decades and from some twenty-plus projects of about four thousand units. And because my experience is primarily in apartment development, that is what we will talk about. However, these fundamentals apply to any commercial development, such as office or retail, and to any size apartment community, be it four or four hundred units.

For me, development from the ground up is the most exciting way to invest in real estate. There are few professional accomplishments more rewarding than to see a project go from conception to reality. And it's even better when that project produces positive financial results. Yet, with that said, nothing can be more frustrating than working for years (yes, years!) to start your project and battling through environmental and governmental regulations, market conditions, financial institutions, and your own continuous questioning about whether all this frustration and risk is worth it. That side of the business is a reality, too, even for those of us who have many projects already under our belts.

I know you can see yourself as the owner of that "perfect" corner lot at Main and Better Main, graced with a structure and a monument sign bearing the name you have been dreaming about for years. Maybe it's (insert your dream name here!) in large letters on the monument sign in the front. You can see all the happy families living there, and you can hear the ka-ching of the cash register as the rents roll in every month. But before you build that sign or take that cash to the bank, let's talk about some of the decisions you must make first before you consider embarking upon this adventure.

TIP The main lesson I have learned in thirty years of apartment development is that each project is unique and different. Each will bring its own set of opportunities and challenges.

Before you call me when you are in the middle of your next development and say, "But Ross, you didn't tell me I would need an environmental impact study on the duck-billed humpback pygmy field mouse!" remember, I did tell you that something always comes up to make your project harder than you thought it would be.

A CLEAR VISION

From the beginning, for any project to be truly successful, you need to have a clear vision of what you want to build and how developing this property meets your own objectives. That means you also need to actually have objectives—or better said, you need a solid understanding what you want this project to achieve. One of the reasons MC Companies—the company Ken and I own—has been successful in development is that we have an infrastructure in place within our firm to develop, construct, manage, and profitably operate multifamily communities. We are careful to select communities large enough to support an on-site staff, earn economies of scale, and that fit within our investment model. We are careful to keep our egos in check and build for the market rather than for our own self esteem.

When we take on a new development, we draw upon each and every one of those disciplines—development, construction, and management—from inception to ensure that we make good decisions in the present because we know they will impact the future. This inclusive team approach is crucial to the successful development and operation of our multifamily communities. If you do not have expertise in all these areas, then it's in your best interest to create a team whose members do have the expertise in each of these fields before you venture into multifamily investments, whether you are building a duplex or four hundred units.

DEVELOP FOR THE LONG TERM

Without exception we build communities with the full intent of operating them once they are done. If the market is strong and the right buyer knocks on our door after the development is complete, we have an alternate option to make money on the investment, but we don't enter a project with this end in mind. It takes many months, or years, from the time we create the vision of our finished community to the time when we collect even a dollar in rent from the first tenant. To predict what the market will be like at the finish line is not always possible. But if you plan to own and operate the project after it is built and use those numbers in your pro forma, you begin with a more solid platform—a better business premise—from which to launch your development, lease it up, and operate the community profitably.

Let's look at the other scenario—from the point of view of building and selling rather than building and operating. What if the market changes from the time that you planned your development to the time it is built and ready for you to operate? If you have not planned on operating it from the beginning, the likelihood of you recognizing the changes, knowing how they affect your project, and then making the necessary adjustments are slim. In the end, you may find yourself holding an obsolete project or one that would require some serious adjustments to fit the new market conditions.

My examples are not entirely hypothetical. In the spring of 2006 the apartment market was hot, and any project completed could be sold for a big profit. Many developers began projects with the idea that they could cash in upon completion with an immediate sale. So, thousands of units were developed and built over the next two years. In 2008, banks had changed their qualification and ratios for loans, and their credit criteria changed dramatically, too. Investor money was not readily available, either. Economic conditions had deteriorated, resulting in higher unemployment and a tight economy. The market for new apartments was, at best, weak. Investors were demanding lower purchase prices to compensate for the slower economy.

Consequently, many developers found themselves sitting on their shiny new properties in a down economy, with cautious investors, reluctant banks, and a weak market for their product. All the assumptions they had made two years prior were based on factors that no longer applied. Because they didn't develop their projects with the idea that they were going to operate them, they created a scenario dependent on a sale and ripe for financial disaster!

Ken and I have avoided this situation because we plan from the start to operate the communities once they are completed, and we make sure all our actions are consistent with our investment objectives. Consequently, we have been able to adjust to market changes and ride out the difficult times, all the while building long-term value.

TIP I don't believe that it is possible to hit a real estate cycle perfectly. If you do, it's luck. Building value from real estate development over the long term takes skill and expertise. It also takes an operator's eye to recognize market shifts and a mind-set that is open to change.

YOUR MARKET NICHE FOCUS

Just as you simply must have your objectives for a development in place, you must decide which market niche your apartment project, or other project, will fill. Here are the basics I consider when looking for a market niche:

- What are the demographics of the area you are considering?
- What is the salary level of the area?
- Is there a college population looking for more off-campus housing, and is that the type of community I want to run?
- Where are the major employment centers?
- Are new businesses and employment being generated in the area?
- What other communities are in the area that a prospective tenant will consider, and are they the same class as the community you are developing, that is, luxury, blue-collar, or subsidized housing?
- What can I build, and how much rent can I charge?
- Will I enjoy owning and managing the community?

In 1999, we took over the development of an eighty-unit townhome community in a town with lots of retirees. Twenty-four units had been built, and only two had sold in more than one year. When we inspected the project, it was obvious why the sales weren't happening. Each unit had two bedrooms with a detached garage. When homeowners came home, they would park in the garage and would have to walk sometimes hundreds of feet through the property to enter their front doors. A review of other competing townhomes for sale in the area revealed they all had attached garages. Homeowners park, get out of their cars, and take a few steps right into their homes. Is it any surprise why an elderly buyer would prefer the competition?

When we took the project over, we bought the two sold units back and converted the entire community to an apartment project, offering it for rent, not to retirees, but to the people who worked in the town. We completed construction of the eighty units, leased the property to full occupancy within six months, and operated the project at a profit until we sold it four years later. That's understanding the niche and developing for it. The original developer of the townhomes clearly did not understand the market niche, which meant he did not understand the buyer.

The most beautiful project imaginable will not rent if it's built in the wrong place. A luxury apartment community may be your dream, but if you build it in a blue collar area, you won't be able to lease the community or be able to charge enough rent to make the economics work. Matching the needs of the community with the project you develop is crucial to your success. Research and know your demographics before you proceed. Only research will give you the perspective that you need before you take another step forward.

WHERE TO BUILD YOUR COMMUNITY

You've most likely heard it before in this book and likely everywhere else: location, location, location. As you are standing on that dusty lot, filled with years of accumulated trash, a couple of homeless camps, and overgrown weeds, envision where the main entrance to your community will be located. Pretend you are driving in and driving out. Look around you. What do you see? If the view is of an industrial complex across the street, a junkyard, or poorly maintained buildings, don't just brush it off. Signs like that generally mean the area isn't going to entice many people to choose your community no matter how beautiful you make it. On the other hand, sometimes negative factors like these can be minimized.

We developed an apartment project on a site where our due diligence revealed that a processing plant was located just half a mile away. The plant took used grease from restaurants and processed it to be reused. When the plant was operating, it stunk to high heaven. But the site was an excellent infill location in a good school district. The clincher was when we discovered that the processing plant was in the midst of implementing rigid pollution-control measures. We were able to pull off a really nice, affordable apartment community in an underserved area with confidence. Research paid off.

While a panoramic view of the mountains or ocean may not be possible, or even relevant to your community plans, don't forget to envision what residents will see and feel coming home. Is it welcoming? Does it feel safe? Would you want to call that home after a long day at work?

Before Beginning a Multifamily Development Project, Ask Yourself These Questions

Lifestyle and Convenience

- Will your community have good exposure to drive-by traffic? Heavy drive-by traffic is a plus when you are trying to attract potential tenants, but possibly a negative for residents concerned about traffic noise. On the other hand, the cutest, most affordable community in town could suffer high vacancy rates if it is located on a street no one can find, even with a blitz of advertising.
- How far from the major thoroughfares will your community be, and how easy is the access to them? Is that important for the type of community you are planning to build?
- How easy will it be for residents to get to work, school, shopping, the movies, etc.?
- Where are the schools in relation to your community? What is the reputation and rating of those schools? What are the transportation options to and from those schools?
- What are the employment opportunities in the area? What mass transit is available to help your residents get to work?
- Is the major downtown area easily accessible?

Social Amenities

- Are parks, movie complexes, theaters, arcades, and sports facilities an acceptable distance from your proposed community?
- What is the "flavor" of the part of town you are considering?
- How does your apartment community plan fit in with the area?

Neighborhood Amenities

- Is shopping in close proximity?
- Is a major grocery store nearby? It matters for those 10 p.m. milk runs.

DEVELOPMENT OF YOUR SITE

By this point, you understand that you must choose a site based on your demographic research. Now consider your site from the development perspective. How easy will bringing the project, literally, out of the ground actually be? This is perhaps the most critical analysis you will need to do, and it is the one that will have the biggest effect on your development costs. Is the site fairly flat, with a minimum of site prep work required? Or does the site have some geographical features that are interesting but challenging?

Flat sites are wonderful, and they typically will allow for the highest density. That is, they allow you to construct the most units per acre. Drainage becomes your biggest concern with flat sites because water will not flow off them without effort. On the other hand, a lovely, hilly piece of land can make for an interesting project. But on the downside, density will be a challenge, and the geography itself can run up the site development and infrastructure costs very quickly. Foundational structures like retaining walls can take a huge chunk of your development budget in the blink of an eye. The point is, each site provides its own set of challenges and opportunities. You need to understand how they affect the number of units you can build and at what costs.

When considering the location of your community, consult with your local governing bodies regarding zoning and other development requirements as soon as you can. Your local government development department can help you determine the required process for gaining permission to develop your project. Be wary, though. I've found cities and counties are notorious for seeing new development as a significant revenue source, and they look for opportunities to solve their problems and budget overruns at your expense. For example, some will make approval of your project contingent upon the city or the town getting concessions from you. You need to understand the law and the regulations, so you know what a government jurisdiction can and cannot legitimately require. Do not take their word as gospel without checking. And most of all, be prepared to do battle on every issue.

Can you tell that I speak from experience? During the approval process for one project we developed, the city initially required us to build a traffic median in the middle of a six lane street—the major highway through town—with the excuse that the median was required to provide safe access to the proposed apartment community. Medians are not cheap! We were going to incur several hundred thousand dollars in off-site expenses that threatened to jeopardize the entire deal. However, after many sleepless nights, a great deal of contemplation, and consultation with our development team, we were able to determine that, although we were required to augment the street improvements to provide safe access, we could do it by slightly redesigning the entrance to the project and re-striping the street, at a cost of only $3,000.

Just as important as knowing how to work with the city or town is knowing how to work with the utility companies. On your to-do list should be checking with the utility companies that will serve your community for availability of their services, hook-up fees, development fees, and monthly service rates. I've seen too many novices get surprised by utility access and hook-up issues. Another often overlooked detail is checking on the possible future infrastructure requirements of your site. For example, if your site is on a heavily traveled two-lane street, and the city decides to widen it to four or six lanes, you will be assessed for your portion of the cost, and you will lose part of your site for the right-of-way. Be prepared for these issues by knowing they can happen up front, then plan your development accordingly.

Oh, and let's not forget the remote possibility, which in some parts of the country isn't that remote, that your site could have archeological or environmental significance. Find out what rules are governing those discoveries in advance of even buying the land. Remember, finding out that your site is the home of those endangered duck-billed humpback pygmy field mice, or the next Machu Picchu, could either kill your development entirely or put it on hold for an indefinite period of time while experts complete expensive studies and develop mitigation plans.

Another tip that every developer must know is the value of checking for any riparian or wetland conditions on the property, as well as drainage, flooding potential, and soil conditions. You don't want your beautiful new community to be in a lake when the summer rains come. And you don't want to find your buildings slowly—or not so slowly—sinking into the ground because of poor soil conditions. When evaluating a site, you must consider all these factors. I know there are quite a number of them, and I can't stress enough that each site has its own nuances. As a developer you must be prepared to spend the money to do a proper evaluation. It's pretty easy to see the cost implications if you don't.

YOUR DEVELOPMENT TEAM

In our company, Ken and I have worked out clear guidelines regarding who will handle which areas of development and management, based on our respective professional backgrounds. At the same time, we constantly consult with each other and make joint decisions.

TIP You do not have the expertise to handle all the development, management, and construction phases for the community you want to build. You need to start by putting together a development team with the strongest expertise in each area you can find.

We're always certain to clarify up front and in writing who will be the team leader and who will make the final decisions. That holds people accountable and gives them ownership. It's fine to use people you know, but this is not the time to give your sister-in-law's cousin his first break in the development business!

Your Architectural Team

The next person on your team will be your architect. Ideally, this will be someone you have worked with in the past and have traveled a lot of rocky roads together. This person will have the experience and relationships with the governing jurisdiction to guide you through all the government requirements. He or she will also coordinate all the other design professions that you need, and will provide the site plan, design, and building elevations, unit plans, project amenities, and construction drawings with specifications.

Other members of your development team that your architect will coordinate include:

- Mechanical engineer who will design the plumbing and HVAC systems.

- Structural engineer who will design the foundations, the framing requirements, and the roofing system.

- Electrical engineer who will design both the underground electrical systems and the building electrical requirements.

- Civil engineer who will design the grading requirements for your site, including drainage, parking lot, and zoning compliances.

Your Contractor

The contractor will be the guy or gal who is going to take all these drawings, plans, and specifications and construct your community. Think of him/her as translating the two-dimensional plans into three-dimensional buildings, from overseeing the grading of the site all the way through handing over the keys of the finished units. You will want a general contractor licensed in the state in which you are building and who hires only licensed subcontractors in each trade qualified to do the work. Reputation and past performance of the general contractor will be your main guideline for this professional. Once chosen, you will want to have a signed contract between you as the developer/owner and the general contractor that will delineate the terms of the relationships including compensation.

Common Construction Contracts

- **Lump Sum or Fixed Price Contract**—In this type of contract, the contractor agrees to provide specified services for a specific price and receives this sum upon completion of the project or according to a negotiated payment schedule. If the actual costs of labor and materials are higher than the contractor's estimate, his profit will be reduced. If the actual costs are lower, the contractor will get more profit. Either way, the cost to the developer/owner is the same.
- **Cost Plus a Fixed Fee Contract**—In this contract, you as the owner/developer will pay the contractor the actual costs of construction plus a fee to the general contractor. If the actual costs are higher than the estimate, the owner must pay the additional amount. If the actual costs are lower, then the owner gets the savings.
- **Guaranteed Maximum Price Contract**—This contract states the owner/developer will pay for the costs like a Cost Plus contract, but the contractor will guarantee that the costs will not exceed a maximum amount. In the event that actual costs are lower than the estimates, the owner keeps the savings. As costs rise, the owner must pay for the additional costs up to the guaranteed maximum. Thereafter the contractor pays.

THE CONSTRUCTION TEAM

For as important as the general contractor is to the success of any project, understand that the success or failure of your construction relies heavily on the expertise of the entire construction team. I cannot stress enough the importance of hiring a qualified, financially stable contractor who employs a bright project manager, assigns experienced superintendents, and hires excellent tradespeople. Carefully scrutinize each person who will be involved with the construction of your project; not only is that your prerogative, it's your job. In addition to your general contractor being licensed in the state of your project, he or she must also be fully insured and be bondable. Another tip, and I know, everyone needs to get their start somewhere, but give careful consideration before you agree to allow your general contractor to break in a new superintendent or project manager on your job. His limited experience in the field may cost you money and may even jeopardize the quality of your finished product.

So just who constitutes a construction team? Your team should include a strong project manager. It is this person's responsibility, among other things, to decide which subcontractors will be awarded the contract for the project and to set the construction budget. The project manager studies the plans and specifications submitted by the architectural team and based on his or her experience will often suggest adjustments or changes in the plans. A few choice suggestions made by a perceptive and confident project manager can save you thousands of dollars in the construction budget without affecting the quality or the appearance of the finished product.

Each project has at least one on-site superintendent, based on the size and scope of the project. The superintendent is responsible for the day-to-day operations of all the subcontracting trades who will be working on the project at any given time. Superintendents set the schedule for the trades to ensure the proper flow of work. There is a sequential order to construction; for example, you don't want the painters arriving *before* the drywallers have finished putting up the walls. And you certainly want to make sure all the necessary site work—such as grading, compacting, etc.—is done before the concrete folks come to pour the building pads. This right-on-time kind of scheduling takes a person who has been around the block and knows how long things take to complete. It takes a person who knows what the demand is for the various trades and knows the appropriate lead times. It also takes someone who can forcefully, yet professionally, get you the best treatment from the subs.

Between the subcontractors, superintendents, and the project manager, this construction team is responsible for continued communication with the architect and engineers and for attending to construction methods and details that don't always show up on the drawings, yet become obvious as construction is in progress. They should also be in continual communication with the testing technicians, building inspectors, financial institution inspectors, and, of course, you the owner/developer! Remember, this is your baby, and you cannot deny the fact that you are ultimately responsible for the design and construction pros.

The project manager also has another very vital role, one you will come to appreciate. He or she is the person responsible for keeping a close eye on the construction budget. That involves closely monitoring if or when a particular trade is out of sync with the budget, and making adjustments before the close of the project. This is the person who looks out for your financial interests and communicates with you to discuss any overages. In construction, things often take longer and cost more than originally planned, so having a good project manager with good communication skills is a real plus.

Where does the general contractor make his money? When you get your first glimpse of a construction budget, you'll notice a line item built in for a specified percentage of the overall construction budget for the contractor's overhead and profit. Remember, construction costs are negotiated between you and the contractor, so you need to understand all the components of the construction budget, including direct costs for labor and materials, subcontractors, and general conditions, as well as profit and overhead.

Finally, you are part of the construction team, too. It is up to you to use every means available to make sure that the contractor builds the project correctly and pays his bills.

This includes hiring third party quality-control inspectors; requiring proof of payment for the materials and labor, such as lien waivers; and possibly requiring a payment and performance bond.

YOUR TITLE COMPANY

Title companies have been mentioned several times in this book, and here they are again. Just as they play a role in acquiring existing property, they play a role in new development, too. Here it is their job to hold all monies involved in the transaction of the land transfer in escrow. They also provide a title report and title insurance. The title company can help you by periodically checking to make sure that the contractor is paying his bills and that no liens have been filed against the project by a subcontractor. You don't want to have your buildings almost completed only to find out that there is a lien on the property from an unpaid sub. It happens!

YOUR PROPERTY MANAGEMENT COMPANY

Contrary to what you might think, you'll need a property management company, even before your project breaks ground. It is the property management company that will prepare the market analysis and determine the rents your community can reasonably charge. From there they help you prepare a realistic operating budget. The way management companies make their money is usually based on a percentage of anticipated gross annual rents. Having an experienced property management company has been a true key to our success. The market knowledge and expertise it provides is something we would never dream of doing without.

YOUR FINANCING PARTNER

Unless you are related to Daddy Warbucks or recently won the lottery (if that describes you, let's talk!), you will need to obtain financing for your project. You may qualify for various forms of financing from governmentally controlled financing, to commercial banks, to private money. All are viable and all come with certain requirements.

It is possible to qualify for governmental or commercial bank loans that offer development and construction financing. These lenders historically will lend from 65 percent to 85 percent of the total cost of the project. The credit crunch of 2008 has changed those lending percentages, and developers are required to have more of their own cash in their deal, but regardless of the amount, those capital sources are options. However, governmental or commercial bank lenders will have a first mortgage priority, meaning that in the event of a default, they get paid first. Their interest rates are based on the current market.

Another finance option is securing money from private lenders, meaning individuals wanting to invest in a real estate project as opposed to stocks or bonds. If you have a successful track record and a convincing business plan/ sales package for your proposed community, they will lend you the money with the condition that they receive an interest payment as well as a percentage of the profits from the operations of the completed project and any sales proceeds. Although private lenders are typically more expensive than traditional lenders, they are more flexible and may lend you a higher percentage of the project costs.

Given the scope of your project and your financial contacts, your funding may possibly come from a combination of these sources, depending on how you structure the financing. Most of the projects Ken and I work on are structured to obtain a commercial bank loan for approximately 67 percent of the total amount needed for the project, with the remaining 33 percent contributed as the equity, which may come from investors, our own funds, or both.

YOUR BUSINESS PLAN

Obtaining financing isn't as easy as strolling into a bank with a good idea. It takes much more than that. In reality, to obtain financing, you will need a business plan. Business plans come in many shapes and sizes, and you can find numerous templates for them all over the Internet. But let me cut to the chase and tell you exactly what banks want to see. This eliminates all the unnecessary fluff that they don't read anyway. Here's what you need to include in your business plan:

- Executive Summary, which explains the purpose of the project and gives a financial summary. You actually can write this first or last, but it's always the first few pages of your plan.

- Property Overview, which includes a description of the site, unit mix, floor plans, site plan, elevations, and pictures of the site.

- Market Overview, which presents neighborhood features, city economics, and the local apartment market.

- Financial Pro Forma, which includes development costs, construction costs, and projected operations income and expenses.

- Developer résumé which highlights your credentials.

- Development team résumés, which highlight the credentials of your architect, engineers, and property managers.

Those are the components lenders care about and are the sections they read. No amount of fluff or page volume will make up for a poor job assembling the details in these sections of the plan. Complete analysis and a realistic business case surrounding that analysis have a better chance of receiving funding. A sketchy plan based on incomplete research and analysis with blue sky projections won't. Not only is this document obviously important in your getting the financing for your project, the exercise of doing it helps articulate and establish your goals and objectives. It is the exercise that helps you determine if your project can ultimately be profitable, and let's face it, you should want to know that as much as the lender does.

WILL YOU QUALIFY FOR A LOAN?

Ken and I have spent our entire careers building our credit and financial standing, as well as building our network of contacts within banking and investing circles. These bankers and investors know our reputation and qualifications and are willing to entertain a development proposal that we present to them. Our track record and financial strength give banks and investors confidence that we can complete and operate a financially viable project. When searching for financing for your project, whatever your sources, you can count on them scrutinizing your background particularly in these areas:

- What is your financial strength? If you are building the community under the umbrella of a company, what is the financial strength of the entire company?

- What is your development experience? Have you successfully built numerous projects before, or is this your first time at bat? If this is your first development, what attributes and strengths do you have that will put to rest concerns about your experience?

- Have you had one or more previous projects fall through in some way?

- What are the backgrounds, experiences, and strengths of your development team? Are they all solid and strong, or are there any weak links that could potentially cause hesitation from the source of your loan?

- What is the source of the equity you will be bringing to the table for this project? How much of your own money are you willing to invest in the project?

The stronger your answers to each of these questions, the better the terms and rate of loan you will be able to qualify for. A lender will ask these questions regardless of the type of loan you are seeking—a construction loan or a permanent loan. And that leads us to our next subject.

SHORT-TERM LOAN VS. LONG-TERM LOAN

A construction loan is a short-term loan with a term length from six to thirty-six months, depending on the size of your project and construction budget. Construction loans usually have variable interest rates and are interest-only loans. The lending institution holds your project as collateral during the course of the loan. In the event of default, you will lose your property. Construction loans are also typically personally guaranteed by the developer, meaning the bank has recourse to your personal assets in the event of default.

Unlike with other loans, with a short-term construction loan the lender will not hand over to you the full amount of the loan all at once. Rather, you'll receive it in monthly payments based on the percent of completion of your project. This process is called a *draw*, and each month your construction team will submit an application to the lending institution. The lending institution will send out an inspector to verify the work is completed as stated in a workmanlike fashion and that all local government inspections are complete and approved. Only with the inspector's approval will the lender issue that month's draw.

After construction is completed, then you, the developer, will need to obtain a permanent loan. The permanent loan is long-term financing that will require a monthly payment for principal and interest. The proceeds of the permanent loan are used to pay off the short-term construction loan, and possibly repay a portion of your equity. Sometimes, a lender will provide a construction loan that will convert to a permanent loan upon construction completion. This has the advantage of reducing your financing risk. There's always the outside chance that you may have trouble getting long-term financing once the project is done. With a loan of this type, that financing is already in place.

Financing terms can be very complicated. Our company never takes on a loan without thoroughly reviewing the loan documents ourselves, as well as having the documents reviewed by an attorney who specializes in real estate financing. Be sure you understand what you are obligating yourself to.

A Few Final Words

You, the developer, will put yourself on the line for the money to fulfill your dream, but you won't see your profit until the project is completed and operational. While the rewards of a well-thought-out and well-constructed project are fantastic in the end, it is a long journey, and there is a lot of risk along the way. The processes I used for building my first home in 1976 for $29,000, and the communities we have built for more than $30 million are basically the same: lots of time, research, due diligence, expenses, and sleepless nights.

By the time we identify a site, analyze the market, hire the professionals, obtain financing, and start construction, we have invested huge amounts of time and money. Every day during the development process a new challenge presents itself. It is a major commitment and financial risk to take on an apartment development, with the prospect of financial reward in the distant future. The development process is complicated and frustrating but also exciting and fun. You cannot anticipate everything, but you can succeed if you approach your project methodically, get the best advice and help, don't cut corners, and never give up! The personal and financial rewards are unsurpassed.

Hang on for a challenging adventure. Watch out for the duck-billed humpback pygmy field mice and all the other bumps in this ride. You are either going to enjoy developing and building a new community as much as I do, or you will find that it isn't your cup of tea. Either way, I wish you much success!

Ross McCallister is a thirty-year industry expert in real estate/ development and finance. He is a co-partner of MC Companies and oversees investment analysis, development, construction, financing, business development, and client relations. He is a licensed real estate broker and a licensed general contractor. Ross has developed and constructed more than four thousand apartment units in Arizona and managed condominium conversions in Oregon, Las Vegas, and Arizona valued in excess of $300 million. Prior to founding MC Companies with Ken McElroy, Ross was president of The McCallister Company, a real estate syndication firm and property management company. Ross believes in "giving back" and has served the real estate industry on various boards throughout his career, including the Office of the Governor's Arizona Housing Finance Authority Board.

● R. Craig COPPOLA, CCIM, CRE, SIOR

4

Master Your Universe: Get the Lay of the Land

Commercial real estate is very different from residential real estate. Craig Coppola is recognized as one of the best commercial real estate brokers in the United States. That is why he is my partner in commercial real estate investments, and we have done extremely well financially.

When Kim and I began our transition from residential to commercial real estate, the first thing we had to do was let go of a residential real estate investor's mind-set. We had to see real estate investing through a different set of eyes. If not for Craig's experience, Kim and I might have lost a lot of money paying for our commercial real estate education. Craig is great because he is a tremendous teacher and takes the time to explain what we fail to see.

As an example, Craig's education of Kim and me began with our interest in a beautiful office building in a great location. It was a cute structure, built in the 1980s. The first thing Craig said was that there was not enough parking. He did not even look at the building. Since the 1980s, zoning laws had been passed requiring more parking spaces. If we wanted to improve the building, we would have to tear it down completely and rebuild from the ground up to comply with the new zoning law. The second lesson from Craig on the same building was that "Cute buildings attract cute businesses." He went on to say, "Rent to well-run businesses, not cute people running cute businesses. You'll have fewer headaches and earn more money."

Craig is the best organized person I know. He has his days planned to the minute. He is constantly studying and investing in his personal development— his business—yet time with his family takes the highest priority. Craig is a great family man and natural teacher, and he is priceless as a real estate partner.

—ROBERT KIYOSAKI

People who know me know that when I commit to doing something I generally jump in with both feet. And that is probably an understatement. It's not that I'm foolhardy about it; people would say I'm methodical and possibly relentless. I don't make rash decisions, and I don't give up. That's the way I approach my business goals, my personal goals, and my family goals. People would also say I'm consistent.

One of my passions in life has been baseball. I was an all-state high school and all-conference college player, and I was even drafted and played professionally with the Minnesota Twins organization. But after baseball, I knew I needed something that I could throw myself into 100 percent, something that I would love just as much and that would help me achieve my life goals.

Like so many people, my story of how I entered the real estate profession is a classic friend-of-a-friend story. I won't bore you with the details, but suffice it to say I did my share of paying dues. I didn't mind. My mentality then was no different than it is now and no different than it was playing baseball: Everything I do makes me stronger, smarter, and faster and gives me the only thing I ever ask for in life—an unfair advantage.

Yes, I want an unfair advantage and I do what it takes to get it—ethically. Getting the unfair advantage ethically usually means no shortcuts, lots of homework, discipline, and sacrifice. At least that is how it has been for me. When it pays off, those long days and longer nights of poring over real estate offering Memorandums, market comparables, and property financial data become distant memories that are replaced with cash, which flows into my mailbox on a monthly basis. It's a beautiful thing.

My career in real estate has afforded me spare time to do other things that I love; that was part of my plan when I got into this business. I wanted to be able to spend more time with my family, participate in my kids' lives, and pursue other passions in life such as running, Tae Kwon Do, and of course, baseball.

My passion for baseball took me to coaching a youth club baseball team— the Arcadia Rat Pack—and I approached that in much the same way I've approached everything else I've set out to do: with a startling amount of research, analysis, planning, and detail all in preparation for intense action.

I wasn't coaching a pro sports team, but regardless, I had batting lineups (based on who from the opposing team was pitching), training schedules, practice schedules, scouting reports, game strategies, substitution plans, even a plan for who was going to coach first base. Some of the parents, I'm sure, thought I was going a little overboard. After six years we finished first, second, or third in 16 out of 32 tournaments.

But to me "going overboard" was simply preparing the team to face every challenge in practice so that when those same situations came up in a game, they weren't new. I wanted to give those kids the unfair advantage, ethically. In essence, my role was to put those kids in a position to win.

That included mastering our universe and knowing the lay of the land. What teams were we going to be up against? What were their strengths and their weaknesses? How could we exploit those weaknesses and overcome their strengths? What do we do in a first-and-third situation? What's our bunt defense? How do we handle a "run down"? We studied, strategized, and practiced all this and more. We made it all the way to the state finals and were state runner-ups—that was victory to us. Sixteen wins and three losses. The team played great and came away with better and more confident kids. I want the same for you when it comes to commercial real estate investing. I want you to win! I want you to be the master of your universe before you even think about investing in property.

TIP In real estate, mastering your universe takes the form of knowing intimately your chosen area of city or town, fully understanding and enjoying your preferred type of real estate investment (also known as "asset class"), and being tuned in to the real estate cycle.

Once you've achieved all this, you are in a great position to begin considering properties. Here's your first pitch:

LET'S TAKE A RIDE

Even if you have lived in the same city or town your whole life and feel you know every road and every building, humor me, and still hop in your car and take a ride. This won't be a ride to simply look at buildings; it's a ride to help you look at your town or city with what I like to call "real estate eyes." Actually looking at the buildings is a minor thing at this point. This drive will help you to understand the lay of the land—the environment the buildings are sitting in—from many different perspectives. The drive is about location, location, location.

Start your drive with the goal of trying to understand the overall city from a real estate investment perspective. Be observant. What do you think is impacting real estate values in one neighborhood or another? Even if you think you know the area in which you want to invest, it's still a good idea to understand what's going on in other areas of your city or town. Those things will play a part in the value of the area you like best.

By now it is probably no surprise to you that I live by my schedule. My days, weeks, months, and years are open to change, but they are highly planned. Whether you are a heavy scheduler or not, if you really look at your life, you'll likely find that we are all creatures of habit. We drive the same way to work and the same way home, day in and day out. Not only do we miss the opportunities on that drive, but we never see the changes that are taking place in the other 90 percent of our community. So the first thing I recommend in order to get the lay of the land and master your universe is to drive a different way to work. If you normally take the highway, then take the residential streets. If you always stop at the same Starbucks for coffee, then go to a different coffee shop. Take in a variety of scenery and people.

TIP Recommendation No. 1: Master your universe by driving a different way at different times to work, and take in the world from a real estate perspective. You'll be surprised by what you see.

Once you think you know an area, travel there at different times of the day. How about evenings, weekends, and at night? Really take the time to see how people live in this area, how it is trafficked. You may be surprised. There are neighborhoods that not only have changed over time, but there are neighborhoods that change with the time of day. I've seen parts of town that are "happening" spots during the week and during lunch, but they are absolute ghost towns during the dinner hour and at night. If you're looking for a great building for a daytime business, this area of town could be the right place. But if you're looking for a building for an evening business, look elsewhere. Your goal here is to look at an area and "get it." That means you get what it's about, and you know what is a fit. Once you "get an area," you will begin to be able to see the future. This is a gut response that may be helpful to write down. You'll have an opportunity later to test how right you are when you talk to the experts who will eventually be on your team—appraisers, inspectors, attorneys, brokers, and builders.

Look for "The Path of Growth"

When it comes to understanding the lay of the land, I look for what real estate pros call "the path of growth" in the market. Even in cities that as a whole are not growing, there usually are areas that are. How do you recognize the path of growth when it comes to commercial real estate? Look for the areas where home builders are buying land, where new homes are being constructed, and where elementary schools are being planned and built. City governments are a great resource for this information because they tell you where they are planning to build new facilities and where infrastructure is going in. You can also get good insight from the economic development officials in your city offices. It's always interesting to see which projects they are the most excited about and what they see developing down the road.

TIP **Recommendation No. 2: Get to know your city officials and staff. Find out the projects that are underway that they are the most excited about. The more you talk with them, the more you'll come to know where the path of growth really is.**

City officials often can be very excited about urban revitalization projects that are underway and often help fund projects that jump-start the process. How exciting it is to think about being part of the solution to violence, crime, and urban blight! But here's my caution: These kinds of projects take time, lots of time. Not only is there the obvious planning, zoning, designing, and entitlement process that must happen; sometimes votes are involved. Then there is the intangible consumer acceptance variable that can take years. In my hometown of Phoenix, there were more than $800 million of revitalization projects built before I considered this area for investment, and the elapsed time to resolve them took more than twelve years. So stay cautious for a very long time because even neighborhoods marked for revitalization may remain in decline for years.

I should point out that some real estate investors make it their entire business to seek out declining neighborhoods. People who specialize in urban revitalization are just one example. That's not my area of interest or expertise, so for my specialty—commercial office space—I stay clear when I see a lot of graffiti or closed businesses. That seems obvious, but you'll be surprised how a quaint historic home that may have been recently rezoned commercial in a troubled neighborhood can still be compelling to emotional investors.

These buyers can easily talk themselves into a bad decision by thinking that purchasing this building will be good for the neighborhood, or by telling themselves they will live with the location because the building is so perfect. None of these arguments is good enough. Remember, it's location first, no matter how difficult the dwelling is to pass up.

It's Tough to Grow Your Way out of a Downhill Slide

The reason I'm such a stickler on this point is that it's really tough to grow your way out of a downhill slide. There's a difference between a declining area and an area that is going to be revitalized. When you get the feel that a neighborhood is going downhill, stay away. If it's on the upswing and that historic building is right in the center of it, don't let your preconceived beliefs about the neighborhood hold you back. There may be an opportunity. Understand they call it *real estate* for a reason. You're looking at the real estate first. That's the key underlying truth to all of this. The building is second.

To me an absolute must is to fully understand where the market is going, not just where it is today. It's all about feel and not getting in too early. What I mean by that is unlike some businesses where speed is everything, there is no need to be on the bleeding edge in real estate. You don't have to be first. You don't want to be first; leave that to the biggest players who can afford the risk. There's plenty of opportunity and money to be made by being second, third, and even twenty-third. Leave the bleeding edge to the big boys. In fact, if you're a small investor who is starting out, never be first.

TIP Recommendation No. 3: Do the homework it takes to fully understand where the market is going, not just where it is at this moment in time. You're investing for the future, so see the future as best you can.

Even though time flies, when it comes to real estate, I've been surprised by how long it takes the future to actually arrive. And if you're in a downhill slide, the future can't happen quick enough, believe me. You may find out that your grand vision for the property isn't two years away; it's actually twenty. This has happened to many real estate investors. The town of Fountain Hills, Arizona, was started by a real estate speculator in the 1970s. He built the world's highest fountain, which is powered by jet engines and shoots a huge plume of water 560 feet into the air. His goal was to attract curious people to the new community that at the time was out in the middle of nowhere. People came and marveled at the fountain, but not enough bought real estate. It took decades for the real estate in Fountain Hills to really take off. Today it is a thriving community, but it took almost thirty years for that to happen.

Is your view of the future too far ahead of the curve? My rule is to take my time and be patient. There's no need for excessive urgency at this point in the process. If there's room for one person to make money in an area, then there's room for more. In fact, I've found there are very few properties that are so special that if you miss them, you miss the deal of the century or even the decade. While those properties do exist, their owners know it and they typically overprice the properties anyway, negating the value of the deal. A good example is the Esplanade and Biltmore Fashion Park, both within the same city block in the highly sought after Camelback Corridor in Phoenix. Those properties are the types that are bought by huge institutions who want trophy properties where the look and the location are more critical than the solidity of the real estate and the return. For example, General Electric bought Hayden Ferry Lakeside in a prestigious area of Tempe, Arizona. MetLife bought the Esplanade in Phoenix. These are called core plus properties and are named such because they create a portfolio of foundation projects that entice other investors who are looking for glamorous investments.

TIP Recommendation No. 4: Real estate investing is about patience. There is no need to rush into an investment in any market.

KEEP YOUR REAL ESTATE EYES OPEN

As you look at neighborhoods, don't overlook the places that you think might be too expensive, too cheap, or that used to be blighted. Neighborhoods change. I know one investor who has made a ton of money improving the looks and performance of less-than-stellar buildings and increasing the property values. It takes a big commitment to do that, but she's doing it. Understand, too, that there are slum lords out there who have made big bucks owning very shabby properties. That's not something I encourage; part of what we can do as investors is create better spaces for all. But with that said, it's a free country.

Everyone always asks this: What are the warning signs of a declining neighborhood? That's easy, and if you go with your feelings, you'll know them instinctively. True story, I was driving one morning, checking out a few neighborhoods I hadn't been through in a while and drove right by a car on blocks with the tires missing. That's the classic bad sign, and there it was in all its glory. Other signs are multiple cars parked in the street at night and a tenant mix in a building that looks fly-by-night or that are in shady businesses. Finally, take a look at the general upkeep. If the properties are unkempt, that's not good either. You may even want to take a look at the police reports to see how much crime happens in the area.

The bottom line is you can modify your building, but you alone can't modify the neighborhood your building sits in. And about that quaint historic building in a seedy part of town: Sure it would make great offices for a trendy design studio, but if your employees are too afraid to work there or stay after hours, how wise was your decision? Open your eyes and think through what you're seeing, and listen to your gut. Write down what you feel—yes, what you feel— about every neighborhood. On the next page is a form that will not only help you know important considerations, but also will give you a place to record your impressions about the area.

TIP Recommendation No. 5: Look for the signs of a declining neighborhood, and don't be in denial about them. Unless you want to specialize in renewal projects, those signs matter.

LET'S TALK BUILDINGS . . . SORT OF

As I mentioned, the actual buildings themselves are practically the last things I look at when I'm getting familiar with a city and its neighborhoods. And even when it comes to a building, I don't initially see the vertical structure; I see the property it's sitting on. Are there enough parking spaces? Is it easy to get into and out of? In other words, does the property have good access? And looking at the building and the site it is sitting on, does it feel right? And can visitors find the location without getting lost?

From there I take a closer look at who is occupying the building. What are the tenants like? Are they quality, established companies or a little on the flakey side? A tenant doesn't have to be The Home Depot or Taco Bell to be acceptable. A local plumbing outfit that's been in a building for ten years is actually a good tenant—I have one like that—particularly when compared to let's say a start-up technology company that no one has ever heard of with millions in venture capital money and a burn rate of a million dollars per month with one customer and no profits. I also consider the tenant's position within their industry, the level of competition, and where the industry is going.

TIP Recommendation No. 6: Consider the building last and look at the location and property it's on first.

Drive Guide – The Neighborhood Environment

Below are the things you need to look for as you drive neighborhoods and look at environments. (Rating scale: 1 is poor, 2 is fair, 3 is average, 4 is good, 5 is very good.) Add comments to right.

Neighborhood Environment: _____ *(list area)*

Border: N_____ / S_____ / E_____ / W_____

(comments)

Overall upkeep	1	2	3	4	5 _____
General condition of buildings	1	2	3	4	5 _____
Quality/condition of cars in area	1	2	3	4	5 _____
Quality of businesses in area	1	2	3	4	5 _____
Traffic patterns	1	2	3	4	5 _____
Area landscape	1	2	3	4	5 _____
Overall visual interest	1	2	3	4	5 _____
Perceived prestige	1	2	3	4	5 _____

Would I buy here?   Yes   No
If yes, what product type? _____
On what street(s) would I own? _____

Your Feelings and Impressions

High points?   Morning   Noon   Night

          _____   _____   _____

          _____   _____   _____

Low points?   Morning   Noon   Night

          _____   _____   _____

          _____   _____   _____

Future Outlook

In 5 years: _____

_____

In 10 years: _____

_____

_____

Other impressions: _____

_____

_____

Questions I need answered: _____

_____

_____

FIGURE 5.1

One afternoon, a friend called me from her car as she was traveling in a small town some distance from her home. She said, "Hey Craig, I'm looking at a great building here that's all set up for a call center. What do you think?" For me the answer was easy. Call centers are declining in the United States with most companies shipping their operations overseas. I replied, "Unless you're in India right now, I'd pass." Much of this is really common sense and having some knowledge of where the trends are, not just in real estate, but also in the areas of business and life that affect real estate.

The tracking form on the next page is a tool you can use to record your first-glance view and impressions of a property. It's also a great idea to bring along a digital camera so you can take photos of buildings and attach them to the Driving Guide records. Pay special attention to these items and be sure to record your overall impressions as well.

COMMERCIAL ASSET CLASS OPTIONS

One of the most important decisions you as a real estate investor will have to make is in which area of the business you want to specialize. If reading this book tells you anything, it should tell you that there are a lot of ways to make and lose money in the world of real estate. Even within the commercial real estate sector, there are a number of different asset class options. You'll soon discover that they are each quite specialized with plenty of their own nuances and requirements. I believe it's important to see the commercial real estate sector in its entirety so that you get an accurate picture of how it is all interconnected because, even though the different asset classes are unique, they all do work together to create an environment within an area of a city or town. Here are the asset classes complete with descriptions and the risks and the rewards.

TIP Recommendation No. 7: No one can possibly be an expert in every commercial asset class. Choose the one you think you'll enjoy most and specialize in it.

Drive Guide – The Building

Below are the things you need to look for as you drive and look at buildings. You'll want one form for each building you view. (Rating scale: 1 is poor, 2 is fair, 3 is average, 4 is good, 5 is very good.)

Building Name: _____

Building Address: _____

(comments)

Location within area	1	2	3	4	5 _____
Curb appeal	1	2	3	4	5 _____
General condition	1	2	3	4	5 _____
Parking	1	2	3	4	5 _____
Lighting	1	2	3	4	5 _____
Access/entrance and exit	1	2	3	4	5 _____
Tenants	1	2	3	4	5 _____
Ease of finding	1	2	3	4	5 _____
Landscaping	1	2	3	4	5 _____
Fits with your needs/wants	1	2	3	4	5 _____

Your Feelings and Impressions

High points?	Morning	Noon	Night
	_____	_____	_____
	_____	_____	_____

Low points?	Morning	Noon	Night
	_____	_____	_____
	_____	_____	_____

Future Outlook

In 5 years: _____
_____

In 10 years: _____
_____

Other impressions: _____
_____
_____

FIGURE 5.2

MULTIFAMILY

The multifamily asset class includes everything from small duplex apartment buildings to entire apartment complexes with eight hundred units or more. The biggest risk in this asset class is oversupply because when people have lots of choices, rents can fall, affecting your property's operating performance and cash flow. Another risk with multifamily is that when interest rates are low, more people can afford to buy homes, so they don't have to rent. That leaves more apartment units vacant and competing for fewer residents. But on the plus side, when lending gets tighter and it becomes harder to qualify for a home mortgage, renting becomes the only option, and the demand for apartment homes increases. Investors have made a lot of money in this area of commercial real estate by buying right and managing efficiently. Like all commercial real estate, the value of a multifamily property increases based on increased operating performance. In other words, buying a property and then managing it and filling up the vacant space better than the previous owner can create an automatic bump in value.

RETAIL

Retail commercial space is something you know probably quite well: shopping centers, strip centers, malls, and stand-alone retailers. The benefit with retail property is that construction costs are high—often tens to hundreds of millions of dollars—making for a high barrier to entry by competitors. This keeps demand usually ahead of supply. As an investor, that's generally a good position to be in. But it's not all blue skies. Economic factors such as reports of inflation, recession, and declining consumer spending trends can trigger retailers to go out of business, and as a building owner you could lose a retail tenant. Competition can also turn a favored retail center into one that is second class. That's what I mean about knowing the lay of the land and seeing the future. You want to know what is coming, not just what is.

COMMERCIAL OFFICE

Office buildings and office condos are one of the largest real estate asset classes. Just look around. We all work somewhere, and offices house many of us daily from eight-to-five. Offices come in many shapes and sizes, so there is diversity and easy entry for new investors. Some offices are former residential buildings converted to office space. Others are conventional office buildings of all shapes and sizes. The benefit of commercial office space is that there is likely something in your town that will fit your budget whether you are a first-time or a seasoned investor and give you plenty of room to grow as you increase your wealth and your level of investment.

INDUSTRIAL

Just like commercial office buildings, industrial spaces tend to have longer leases and lots of options when it comes to investing. There are giant warehouses with upward of five hundred thousand square feet and smaller mixed-use spaces in the neighborhood of three thousand square feet, along with everything in between. Because of the many options available, industrial space is a classic first-time-investor property. One reason for industrial's popularity with first-time investors is that many have their own businesses and need this kind of space.

HEALTH CARE

This asset class in commercial real estate includes not just hospitals, but also nursing homes, medical buildings, and assisted living facilities. The benefit of this class is that recessions and economic downturns don't really affect it much. But it is prone to the ups and downs of the tenant. Medical practices are small businesses. Hospitals are big businesses. And business can fluctuate. Plus, the medical profession is one that is in a state of flux, and it will be so for many years to come. Through my experience in this area I know that not only is it important to have the right tenants in your space, but it's important to have the right *mix* of tenants in your space—the right practices and the right practitioners. Assisted living facilities, on the other hand, rely heavily on good management. Having a reputable management company that specializes in these kinds of communities is a must.

SELF STORAGE

Self storage spaces are those mini-warehouse consumer and commercial facilities that you most likely have seen in your town. You may even have some of your things stored in one of them. They are seemingly recession resistant, and that is a big advantage for you as an investor. Generally, the management is relatively easy. Believe it or not, corporations are actually the biggest users of storage facilities, and every year they pay billions to store excess files, records, and general stuff. The downside is that building self storage facilities is a low-cost proposition. That means it's easy for competitors to break into the market, charge a lower price, and erode your margins. When it comes to self storage, I always make sure there are lots of rooftops nearby as well.

HOSPITALITY

This asset class includes hotels, motels, casinos, bed and breakfasts, resorts, and vacation rentals. And like assisted care facilities, management is important. In general, it is the asset class most closely connected with the health of the economy. In periods of economic decline, travels for business or pleasure are early casualties of cost-cutting and penny-pinching. That affects the number of room nights booked, which means per-night room rates can fall as properties vie for fewer customers. This, in turn, erodes income and profitability, but in markets with a balanced supply-and-demand ratio, hospitality can be very lucrative.

Within each of these asset classes are subcategories. All these options may at first seem overwhelming, but in reality it's this diversity that makes commercial real estate so lucrative and why smart investors specialize. It's this specialization that enables us to have an advantage over other types of investments and over other types of investors who are trying to do it all.

THE ABCS OF COMMERCIAL SPACE

Just as you need to know the various asset classes and some of the nuances of each, it's a good idea to know the four classes of commercial space that refer to the quality of the property. Too often I have seen novice investors duped into believing that an office building is one class, when it is really a lesser class. Class matters because the better the class of building, the higher the rent per square foot. Here are the official class guidelines:

Class A+ (Core plus). Landmark quality, high-rise buildings with a central business district location. These are the best of the Class A buildings.

Class A (Core). Buildings that are one hundred thousand square feet or larger with at least five floors. The construction of these buildings is concrete and steel, and they were built after 1980. Buildings include business/support amenities such as cafés and banks, and they have strong identifiable locations and accesses.

Class B. Renovated buildings in good locations or newer buildings that are smaller in size. These can be wood frame construction in nonprime locations. Most first-time investors invest here.

Class C. Older buildings that are not renovated. They can be of any size, and are in average to fair condition.

Keep these qualifications in mind as you look at properties. They will help you know what you are looking at, and they will also help you recognize false advertising when you see it.

The Real Estate Cycle Revealed

Although you now know there are more kinds of commercial property than you could have imagined, you may still be surprised to learn that their performance over time is cyclical in whole and in part. What I mean by that is that each asset class runs through a cycle. And each asset class's cycle either flows before, flows with, or flows after another asset class's cycle.

For example, you'll find that growth in residential housing will fuel a similar but slightly lagging rise in retail. This pattern makes sense when you consider that new homeowners will want shopping centers, grocery stores, and other conveniences near where they live. The surge in retail then drives growth in the industrial and distribution sectors, so that means warehouse and mixed-use property development grows. Home development also drives some growth in commercial office space, but again commercial lags behind. That's why when housing development slows, it takes a few years for commercial to slow down, too. You've probably noticed that. When the news is reporting real estate declines, new commercial projects are still getting underway. Now you know why.

Real estate is about cycles and the inevitability of them. Once you know that and know how to pay attention to the cycles, you'll know the lay of the land in this regard, too, and you'll be in a position to make the best of the cycle by making the best decisions along the way.

TIP Recommendation No. 8: Understand the real estate cycle and watch for the indicators, and you will seldom be surprised.

Cycles are important, but in reality if you buy right, your real estate will do well, regardless of where in the cycle you bought. But if you are just starting out, buying right may not be as intuitive to you, so understanding the real estate cycle becomes golden knowledge. The following diagram shows the typical commercial real estate cycle and how it affects new construction and vacancy.

Let's walk through each quadrant. In Phase 1, the lower left quadrant, the market is in recovery phase. There is declining vacancy and no new construction. You know the market is in this phase when there is some growth in the market indicated by properties being rented and properties being sold. This uptrend can, and often does, last a long time, years in many cases. That's why I never feel like I need to rush into an investment. I also don't like surprises, so I generally let the bigger guys make the first leaps during this phase. Then I make my moves with solid knowledge that we are solidly in Phase one—the buying phase.

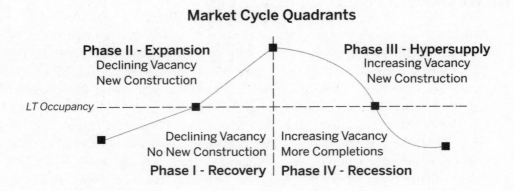

Market Cycle Quadrants

Phase II - Expansion
Declining Vacancy
New Construction

Phase III - Hypersupply
Increasing Vacancy
New Construction

LT Occupancy

Declining Vacancy
No New Construction

Increasing Vacancy
More Completions

Phase I - Recovery | **Phase IV - Recession**

TIP Recommendation No. 9: Phase 1 in the real estate cycle is the time to buy, and Phase 2 and 3 is the time to sell.

As you'll see in a minute when we talk about Phase 3 and Phase 4, declining markets aren't the time to take vacations. Doing lots of homework during those times will make you smarter and at the ready during a Phase 1 market when it *is* time to buy. When the other guys who bought poorly, or bought in the wrong phase of the market, have thrown in the towel, that's when I buy.

During Phase 2, you see the occupancy rates move below the Long Term Occupancy (LT Occupancy line on the diagram) for your market. (Long Term Occupancy means that owners typically need at least a minimum of five years of term remaining.) Every market is different, but in most cases, vacancy is very healthy when it is below 10 percent. Understand that new construction tends to start when vacancy rates drop below 10 and 15 percent, so during this phase new properties begin to be developed. Again, this phase of the cycle does not last days, weeks, or months. It tends to last a few years, so there is no hurry here. If and when I buy during this phase, I really make sure the numbers work and that the property meets my qualifications. There's no way of knowing exactly where the top of the market is or how long it will last, so caution is the rule. If you're going to sell, Phase 2 is when you do it.

TIP Recommendation No. 10: Phase 3 and Phase 4 are not the times to buy. They are the times to research and target properties to buy when Phase 1 kicks in.

In Phase 3, the market is in obvious decline. The guessing game, however, is how far the market will fall and how long it will take. If you bought in Phase 1, you may have bought yourself some strength. But when you are still seeing new construction underway and occupancy rates increasing above the LT Occupancy for your market, recognize the signs that you are in Phase 3. This is known as "hyper supply." Obviously, I never buy during this phase no matter how badly I want a building. I am simply not willing to ride the wave to the bottom, not knowing how far down bottom is. What's the point when I know that there will be plenty of time for deals that make sense in Phase 1? In fact, I'll be buying at bargain prices the properties others foolishly bought in Phase 3! You'll hear people say that there are buying opportunities in every phase. That is true. But it just depends on how strong your constitution is and how deep your pockets are.

Finally, Phase 4 signals market bottom. But there's good news in Phase 4, too. The darker it gets in Phase 4, the better the buying opportunities will be in Phase 1. So if you're on the buying side, relish Phase 4, and take the time to look at properties. Look a lot, but don't buy a thing. There's no way of knowing the bottom until it makes the turn upward. You'll know you're in Phase 4 when vacancy hits its high well above the LT Occupancy and buildings are no longer under construction. The cranes and bulldozers will be replaced by completed buildings sitting vacant. At this time, I do a lot of research so that when Phase 1 kicks in I have pinpointed some ripe buying opportunities. I have lined up investors and financing and spoken to lots of people and told them that when the turnaround happens, I'll give them a call.

While it is helpful to know that real estate is cyclical and in all cases interconnected by asset class, knowing where you are in a market cycle and predicting where it is going is key. Savvy investors can make money anywhere in the cycle, but it takes great skill and experience to make money on the right side of the line.

Further, understand that all real estate follows this pattern and that some asset classes will follow the curve earlier or later than others. For instance, residential real estate is always the first to decline and the first to rebound. Multifamily follows a little later, and retail and commercial after that. Commercial/ industrial is usually the last asset class to emerge from a down market; however it is usually the last to enter it. The more familiar you get with watching the real estate cycles, the better you will get at knowing where you are in them. Commercial real estate, for me, gives me plenty of warning to buy, sell, and hold.

THE LAST WORD ON MASTERY

Well, now you know how critical the lay of the land in terms of neighborhood, asset class, and the real estate cycle is to the success of your real estate investment career. But just like in baseball, there's a huge gap between *knowing* how to hit a home run and *hitting* a home run. That gap, of course, is technique, practice, and unfortunately, failure. Becoming master of your real estate universe will take all of those, too. It did for me. I've lived in Phoenix for more than twenty years, and I still drive around the market with real estate eyes. Things are always changing, and I need to keep up with those changes. I develop new systems to make me more efficient as I analyze properties and deals. And I'm not ashamed to say on my first deal I lost $15,000 and didn't even end up with the property! It never closed. These kinds of things happen to everyone, and they are what separate the serious investors from the novices.

The same goes for baseball. Every time the Arcadia Rat Pack stepped out on the diamond, they expected to win, but they also knew that losing was a possibility. Of course we did everything in our power to increase the odds of winning, but on those occasions when we didn't come out on top, our team learned what didn't work, what we had to do better next time, and what subtleties we missed. We didn't make the same mistakes twice, and that's the benefit of losing: the lessons.

Yes, knowledge is just part of the story. But action is the most critical part. All the information in this chapter and within this book as a whole is only as good as your willingness to take action on it. So make a pact with yourself to become master of your real estate universe. Step up to the plate. That first swing is yours to take.

WAYS TO LEARN MORE

CCIM Institute (Certified Commercial Investment Manager)
SIOR (Society of Industrial and Office Realtors)
CRE (Councilors of Real Estate)
NAIOP (National Association of Industrial and Office Properties)
ULI (Urban Land Institute)
LoopNet.com—a great place to learn about your market and research properties

 R. Craig Coppola is the top producing office broker in Lee & Associates' 35-year history, as well as one of the Founding Principals of Lee & Associates Arizona. Lee & Associates is the largest broker-owned Real Estate Company in the U.S. with over 50 offices nationwide.

Craig has completed over 3,500 lease and sale transactions in the past 30 years, totaling a value in excess of $3,500,000,000. He has a lengthy track record of representing companies on a national and international basis. His clients include Motorola, HDR, JDA Software, and more.

Craig has been awarded National Chapter President (the highest honor given by the largest real estate development trade association) for NAIOP (National Association of Office and Industrial Properties) and NAIOP Office Broker of the Year six times. He has also earned the top three designations in the real estate industry: CCIM, CRE and SIOR. Less than 40 people worldwide hold all three designations.

In addition to his Real Estate career, Craig is also the author of four books. His first book, *How to Win in Commercial Real Estate Investing*, won him the "Best First Time Author Award" from The National Association of Real Estate Editors (NAREE). As a follow up to his investing book, Craig published, *The Art of Commercial Real Estate Leasing* in December 2014. In addition to his two real estate books, Craig has also written *The Fantastic Life: How to Get it, Live it, and Pass it On*. His most recent book, *Chasing Excellence*, was co-written with Lee & Associates Founder Bill Lee.

10 Rules for Real Estate Asset Protection

*G*arrett *and I share a common love: the love of the game of rugby. Although we do not remember each other, we played against each other years ago on opposing teams at the Monterrey Rugby Festival. He played for the Hastings Rugby Club of San Francisco, and I played for the Navy/Marine Corps Flight School team from Pensacola, Florida. Unfortunately, we were not the better team, but it was a great game.*

In 2003, Garrett and I traveled to Sydney, Australia, to watch the Rugby World Cup. It is in our humble opinion that we witnessed the greatest game of rugby ever played. It was the final match between England and Australia. For as long as I live, I will always remember that game and feel honored to have been a spectator in the stands as we watched England beat Australia in overtime by a score of twenty to seventeen.

Besides being a rugby player, Garrett is an attorney. He is a very important attorney. He specializes in asset protection, which is a vital area of law because in today's world there are more attorneys who want to steal your assets than there are who want to protect them. One of the reasons why Kim and I can sleep soundly at night is because Garrett is an expert at making sure our assets are protected. This does not mean we are totally protected. This means Garrett has built legal firewalls around different assets. It means we might lose one or two properties, but we will not lose everything.

In today's litigious world, having a Garrett Sutton on your side is vital for anyone who wants to grow rich and get a good night's sleep, too.

—ROBERT KIYOSAKI

As a Rich Dad's Advisor, one of the questions I am most frequently asked is: "How can I protect my real estate?"

In answering this key question, a pattern of repetitive follow-up queries always ensues such that after several years I have been able to distill all of the issues and concerns into what I call the "10 Rules for Protecting Your Real Estate."

By knowing, following, and implementing these ten rules, you will not only properly protect your assets, but you will also avoid the many pitfalls placed in your path by the overpriced asset protection "gurus" and service providers out there who are more interested in your money than your situation. You will have the confidence to say "No" to these people because you will know more than they do.

Your important and easily acquired education lies ahead. Let's begin.

RULE NO. 1: INSURANCE IS NEVER A COMPLETE ASSET PROTECTION STRATEGY

Or: Never let a commissioned salesperson tell you how to protect your assets. At Rich Dad events around the country I am always confronted by the person who asserts that his insurance agent has assured him that asset protection is a hoax and that all that is needed is a good insurance policy. I have to laugh because there are so many instances of insurance companies failing to cover real estate investors and others under the provisions of their policies, that there is a whole area of law named after the situation. It is called "Bad Faith Litigation," as in the bad faith that occurs when insurance companies say they will cover you, collect your premiums, and then, heaven forbid, a claim arises and they find reasons not to cover you.

Never forget that insurance companies have an economic incentive not to cover you. As is clearly obvious, the less they pay out in claims, the more money they make. Also never forget that insurance agents receive a commission on all the policies they sell. So when an insurance agent says that all you need is insurance instead of asset protection, please remember where his incentive lies. It is also important to acknowledge that insurance agents are not licensed to give legal advice. You would have to question the motives of one who would do so.

Given my healthy skepticism of the insurance industry, you would think that I would advocate the exclusive use of asset protection entities without the use of any insurance at all.

TIP Insurance is the first line of defense when protecting assets. The proper use of asset protection strategies is this second line of defense.

But to the contrary, I believe that insurance is the first line of defense when protecting assets. Many insurance companies are forthright in their dealings and will honor their coverage commitments. Others, with the help of a legal nudge, will do the right thing. So I always advocate the reasonable use of insurance as a protection strategy. However, because we know that a certain percentage of insurance companies will use exclusions and find reasons not to cover you, you most certainly need another defense mechanism. The proper use of asset protection strategies is this second line of defense. As we will learn in this section, asset protection is not difficult or expensive, but it is required if you are to succeed at building real estate wealth.

Now that we know that insurance alone will not completely protect us, let's review further ways to *not* protect your real estate before we get to the promised land of beneficial strategies in later rules.

RULE NO. 2: THE TWO MOST COMMON WAYS OF TAKING TITLE TO YOUR REAL ESTATE DO NOT PROVIDE ASSET PROTECTION

Or: Why to avoid joint tenancies and tenants in common.
It is indeed ironic that the two most common and popular methods of taking title to your real estate provide you with the least protection. Joint tenancy is one of the most popular forms of holding title because it provides for a right of survivorship. This works such that if one party dies the other joint tenant becomes the sole owner by operation of law, meaning it happens automatically. Joint tenancy is popular with husband and wife couples. If the husband, for example, passes away first, then the wife has complete control of the property without having to go to court or file new deeds.

The problem for real estate investors is twofold. First, joint tenancies offer no asset protection. Suppose Peter, Paul, and Coco own a sixplex as joint tenants. If Paul gets sued, his creditor can reach Paul's joint tenancy interest. Peter and Coco now have a new partner in the sixplex, most likely someone, who after suing their friend and barging their way in, they don't like right off the bat. As well, this new partner can bring a partition lawsuit to force a sale of the property. It can get expensive in legal fees and messy in court.

Secondly, the right of survivorship feature that makes joint tenancies easy and attractive to married couples is the same feature that makes them so scary and abhorrent to investors. Let's take another look at the joint tenancy that holds Peter, Paul, and Coco's sixplex. Suppose Coco were to die in a fashion industry disaster. Her interest in the sixplex is automatically terminated. She can't pass her interest on to her heirs because Peter and Paul, by operation of law, are now the two remaining joint tenants on title.

Savvy investors will not invest with you if you propose taking title as joint tenants. The good ones know that you should never put yourself in a position where someone will benefit from your demise. That's what you are doing with joint tenancies. I will withhold comment on the state of marriage today and why so many knowledgeable spouses continue to use joint tenancies. But for investors it is not the right choice.

TIP Savvy investors will not invest with you if you propose taking title as joint tenants.

Similarly, but with one exception, taking title as tenants in common is not the best course, either. Again, there is no asset protection. In our example, if Peter gets sued, Paul and Coco can find themselves with a new and unwanted partner. Once again, the partner can bring a partition suit to force a sale of the property. As well, if there is a lawsuit involving the property (i.e., a tenant sues over a defective water heater) the individual tenants in common (or individual joint tenants, for that matter) can be held personally responsible. All of their personal assets can be exposed to such a claim. Holding title to any property as individual tenants in common does not make good sense in our very litigious world. In fact, it can make you more of a target.

The one exception for using tenants in common to hold title is when investors take their interest not as exposed individuals but with protected entities. In a TiC situation ("TiC" stands for tenants in common) investors come together from 1031 exchanges or with investment money to buy a large property. The large property is held as a tenancy in common with all the various investors holding their specific TiC interest through a protective entity such as a LLC (limited liability company).

A chart helps to illustrate:

**The Difference Between Individual Tenants in Common
and Tenants in Common (TiC)**

FIGURE 6.1

While I may have let the cat out of the bag (that LLCs are good entities for real estate), it is my belief that most of you may have already known this. Still, there are a few more rules involving what not to use before we get to positive asset protection territory.

RULE NO. 3: NEVER HOLD REAL ESTATE IN A C CORPORATION

Or: Fire the professional who even suggests such a thing.
One of the cardinal sins of real estate asset protection is to take title in the name of a C corporation. While there are certainly advantages to using a C corporation in business (which are discussed in my Rich Dad's Advisor book *Own Your Own Corporation*) there is a huge disadvantage to using a C corporation for real estate, which can be expressed in one word: taxes.

As you probably know, C corporations face a double tax. You pay taxes once at the company level and then again when dividends are distributed to shareholders. With an S corporation, LLC, or LP you pay tax only once at the company level. A chart graphically illustrates the difference between double taxation and flow-through taxation.

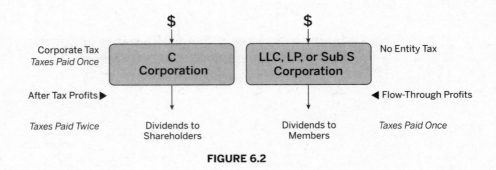

FIGURE 6.2

So what happens when you have a capital gain on the sale of real estate held by a C corporation? You pay a lot more in taxes.

Consider the situation in which a $500,000 long-term capital gain is realized on the sale of real estate held for longer than one year.

As the chart on p. 114 indicates, you will pay $144,500 more in federal taxes by using a C corporation instead of an LLC. Does Uncle Sam want you to use a C corporation? Of course. Will investors likely join your deal if you propose using a C corporation? Probably not. They'll know you don't know what you are doing. Avoid the professional who advises you to use a C corporation to hold any interest in real estate. They just don't know what they are doing—to your later detriment. Also avoid using on-line incorporation services. They won't even know what to ask.

C Corporation

$500,000	Gain
−170,000	Less 34% corporate tax *(35% for larger corporations)*
$330,000	
− 49,500	Less 15% tax to shareholder on distributions
$280,500	**Amount after tax**

LLC

$500,000	Gain
− 75,000	Less 15% capital gain tax
$425,000	**Amount after tax**

FIGURE 6.3

TIP Avoid the professional who advises you to use a C corporation to hold any interest in real estate.

We frequently have clients discuss how some asset protection "guru" or other promoter advised them to set up their structure as follows:

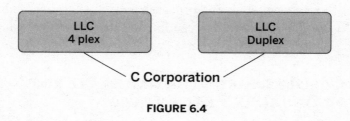

FIGURE 6.4

The rationale is that the two pieces of rental property are owned by the LLCs and each LLC is in turn owned by a C corporation. The gurus will state that all kinds of deductions can be taken with a C corporation. The problem is that, as flow-through entities, the profits flow from the LLCs to a double tax C corporation. You are still in a bad tax position.

If you are intent on using a C corporation in your entity mix (and please be cautious of promoters who overly tout the supposed glorious benefits of the C corporation) a better scenario is the following:

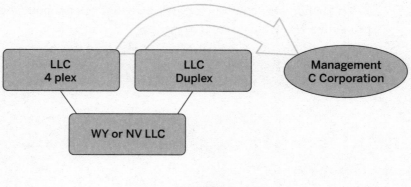

FIGURE 6.5

In the structure on page 73, the title-holding LLCs are held by an asset protecting Wyoming or Nevada LLC, thus providing flow-through taxation throughout the structure. For those desiring the write-offs of a C corporation, a management C corporation is used. Each title-holding LLC pays a management fee to the corporation so their benefits are obtained. But there is no ownership of real estate through the C corporation, thus avoiding the double taxation of profits we had in the first instance.

Please also beware of promoters who would have you set up more entities than you need. The management corporation may provide some benefits in later years when there is plenty of cash flow. But at the start, do you really need one? Probably not. So be very cautious of those promoters who want what is in their best interest and not yours.

RULE NO. 4: OFFSHORE STRATEGIES DO NOT WORK FOR ONSHORE REAL ESTATE

Or: What have you been smoking?

As you have probably noticed, throughout this chapter and in my other writings I have found the need to warn against the slick and salesy gurus and promoters with their incredible claims and come-ons. Certainly some of the most outrageous claims come from the offshore promoters who offer tax savings and absolute privacy. Of course, they never mention the existing United States rules and regulations that do, in fact, run contrary to their claims. In most cases, these people actually live on small Caribbean Islands or in European principalities beyond the reach of U.S. authorities. They can say what they want.

But as a U.S. citizen, can you afford to listen to those who intentionally misrepresent U.S. laws? Of course not.

To further your caution, let's review what can happen when offshore asset protection is used in attempt to protect U.S. real estate.

Real Life Story: John's Bad Day

John was a doctor in California. He had worked hard and paid his taxes. He owned a twenty-unit Roseville apartment building free and clear and a significant brokerage account. He felt as if he were doing well, but the combination of the malpractice and real estate litigation explosion and the ravenous demands of both the IRS and California's notorious state tax collector—the Franchise Tax Board—had led John down the path of considering offshore options.

A promoter from the Caribbean Island of Nevis held a seminar for doctors and dentists in John's hometown. The self-styled asset protection man with glowing testimonials and advanced degrees from schools John had not heard of, laid out a comprehensive and seamless case for using Nevis structures to protect assets. The promoter boldly claimed that by using offshore trusts John could obtain complete privacy and incredible tax savings. His strategy was graphically represented as follows:

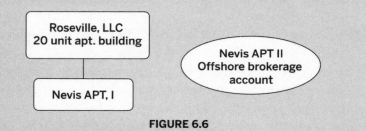

FIGURE 6.6

The promoter indicated that John would not have to pay any taxes. Because the apartment building LLC was owned by the Nevis APT ("asset protection trust"), profits generated from rents could pass offshore without taxes. The domestic LLC would simply file zero return. The promoter further stated that insurance was not needed on the apartment building because it was now in a bulletproof structure. As well, by moving John's significant brokerage account into the second APT, profits could be generated offshore without U.S. or California taxes. Better yet, the monies could be accessed by John, tax free, into the United States by simply requesting the Nevis trustee—who received $3,000 a year for the service—wire the money.

John followed the promoter's advice, paid the $25,000 for setting it all up, and in the first year his financial condition greatly improved. With his assets offshore and no onshore taxes paid, he was doing really well. He wondered why everyone didn't do this. Then, in one day, two problems arose. He was sued for malpractice by a patient and a tenant fell at the apartment building.

CONTINUED

When the tenant's claim was made, John informed the claimants that there was no insurance. When the tenant's lawyer indicated they would sue anyway, John calmly replied that the building was owned by a bulletproof offshore asset protection trust.

The lawyer laughed and said John needed to get a local attorney to advise him. When John did so he learned the bitter truth: You can't protect U.S. real estate with offshore entities. The apartment building was located in California and, as such, California courts had jurisdiction. This was the law in all fifty states. The tenant could bring a claim against the LLC, and with no insurance in place, the tenant could reach the entire free-and-clear equity in the apartment building. The fact that the LLC was owned by an offshore APT was of absolutely no consequence and offered zero protection.

John also spoke to his new lawyer about the malpractice claim. As a doctor, John was sued individually. But he felt protected because his brokerage assets were privately all held offshore. This was when the second shoe dropped.

The lawyer explained that if John had followed all the tax reporting requirements associated with offshore entities, a creditor could easily learn what John owned.

John was incredulous. The promoter had assured him that he had bulletproof privacy and asset protection without the requirement of taxes or even tax reporting. The lawyer had seen other professionals lured in before. He presented John with the following chart detailing all the reporting requirements:

John now realized that everything the promoter said was false. Given the IRS rules, there was no privacy, no tax savings, and no bulletproof protection. With the help of his new lawyer, John cleaned up the offshore mess by paying significant IRS penalties and fees. A demand to the Nevis promoter for the $25,000 John was lured into paying for worthless strategies and documents went unanswered.

TABLE 6.1

IRS Requirement	IRS Rule
U.S. persons must report all gratuitous and nongratuitous transfers to a foreign trust.	Section 6048, Section 1494
Foreign trusts owned by U.S. persons must file an annual tax return on IRS Form 3520-A. U.S. persons are subject to a 5% penalty against the value of offshore assets each year for failure to file.	Sections 671 to 679
U.S. persons receiving offshore distributions, whether taxable or nontaxable, must report them or pay 35% penalty.	Section 6677(a)
Foreign trusts owned by U.S. persons must appoint a U.S. agent so that the IRS may examine offshore records.	Sections 7602 to 7604

TIP Offshore strategies do not work for onshore real estate.

RULE NO. 5: LIVING TRUSTS OFFER NO ASSET PROTECTION

Or: Will you please stop listening to these guys?

Many of you have seen the ads touting the significant benefits of living trusts. Invariably, one of the great features mentioned is the ability of these trusts to protect your assets.

While living trusts do offer certain advantages it is very important to clearly recognize the one benefit they do not offer: asset protection.

Let's take a closer look.

Primarily used for estate planning, the key benefit of a living trust is to avoid probate. If you have only a will, or pass without a will, the distribution of your estate is supervised by a local probate court. The probate process is long and time consuming and a matter of public record, meaning that anyone can view the file to see what assets are involved, and perhaps challenge the distribution.

As well, the attorney's fees awarded for probate proceedings can be quite lucrative for the lawyers involved. For example, with a $1 million primary residence passing through a California probate, the court awards a statutorily set attorney's fee of $23,000. An executor is entitled to the same amount. These fees are due, even if the home is fully encumbered by loans, and thus without equity to pay the fees.

The solution is to set up a living trust, which is a trust document allowing you to use an appointed trustee, typically a surviving spouse or other family member, to distribute your assets without the need for probate court assistance or review. The several thousand dollars spent on a living trust can easily save many more thousands of dollars in probate fees.

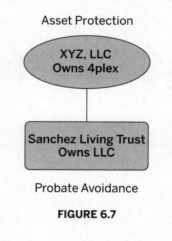

Asset Protection

XYZ, LLC
Owns 4plex

Sanchez Living Trust
Owns LLC

Probate Avoidance

FIGURE 6.7

The living trust also features a great deal of flexibility. It is a revocable trust, meaning you can change its terms and/or beneficiaries at any time. But that also means it does not offer any asset protection. Because it can be easily altered, a judgment creditor can get a court order forcing a transfer of any property from the trust to the litigation party.

Despite this factual lack of asset protection, living trust promoters continue to sell their services as offering such protection. When challenged, they will parse and narrow their overly broad claims to suggest that their living trusts help protect against creditor claims because they avoid the very public probate process. And this is true. But just as deciding not to sunbathe completely in the nude is not the same as the judicious use of sunscreen, avoiding a fully public probate is not the same as proper asset protection. By relying only on the former examples, you are going to get burned.

Real Life Story: Mario's Mistake

A client of mine named Mario came to me after titling all of his assets—his house, a rental fourplex, and a significant brokerage account—in the name of his living trust. The formal name for the trust—The Mario T. and Carmen O. Sanchez Revocable Trust dated June 10, 2004—was given to the county recorder and assessor for taking title to the two real estate properties. The Smith Barney broker took the same name for the Sanchez's brokerage account.

Mario indicated that the seminar promoter who set up his living trust assured him that his assets were now fully protected. But now he was being sued by a tenant who fell at the fourplex, and he wanted a second opinion.

It was not pleasant to inform Mario that his assets were not protected. By titling everything in his living trust's name, all of his assets were exposed to the tenant's claim.

When Mario asked if he could re-title everything into a more protective structure, it was even more difficult to explain that it was now too late to do so. Once you've been sued, or even threatened with suit, it is too late for asset protection.

The next question clients always have is: How do they combine the benefit of a living trust's probate avoidance with the necessity of asset protection? The answer is simple, and it is graphically charted in Figure 6.7: The LLC is on title with the county recorder as owning the fourplex. We have asset protection at this level. The living trust owns the membership interests in XYZ, LLC. If both Mario and Carmen die, the living trust document will dictate who owns the LLC without the need for court supervision. At this level we have probate avoidance.

TIP You can't rely on the LLC for probate avoidance, and you can never count on the living trust for asset protection, but in concert you can get both.

Properly structured LLCs and living trusts work well together and complement each other. You can't rely on the LLC for probate avoidance, and you can never count on the living trust for asset protection, but in concert you can get both.

RULE NO. 6: LAND TRUSTS OFFER PRIVACY BUT NOT ASSET PROTECTION

Or: Why privacy is not enough.

For many of the same reasons a living trust offers no asset protection, neither does a land trust offer asset protection. In fact, a land trust is very similar to a living trust. In both, you are transferring assets to a trust administered by a trustee for your benefit.

According to the seminar promoters, the big benefit of a land trust is its privacy. By using a trustee other than yourself, your name can be kept off the chain of title and public records. And while privacy is a good thing in this day and age, it is not a perfect substitute for asset protection. (Know that in some states, such as Arizona, the land trust beneficiary must be identified, thus defeating the supposed privacy benefits.)

It is important to understand the structure of a land trust in order to appreciate why asset protection is not inherent.

In our chart, Joe is identified on public records as being the trustee, but Jane, as beneficiary, is not anywhere identified. In this manner, privacy can be achieved.

But the land trust, like the living trust, does not protect Jane. If there is a lawsuit involving the fourplex, a judgment rendered is against the beneficiary. If Jane, as an individual, is the beneficiary, then any judgment is against her personally, and all of her personally held assets are exposed.

There are two better ways to handle it. In example A, we show the beneficiary to be an LLC.

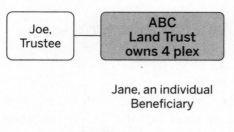

Jane, an individual
Beneficiary

FIGURE 6.8

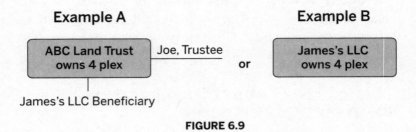

FIGURE 6.9

In this way, a judgment attained against the beneficiary is rendered against a limited liability entity. James's personal assets are not exposed.

Of course, this structure entails setting up two structures—the land trust and the LLC—as well as paying the trustee to serve every year. The same asset protection is attained by just setting up one entity, the LLC, as in example B.

TIP If privacy is important you can certainly have the manager of the LLC be a nominee, a person other than yourself.

If privacy is important you can certainly have the manager of the LLC be a nominee, a person other than yourself. Our firm charges $650 a year for this service. Others may charge more or less. But in this way you can achieve asset protection and privacy, without the need to set up a land trust.

For more on the fallacies of land trusts, see Chapter 22 of my book *Loopholes of Real Estate*.

RULE NO. 7: LLCS AND LPS ARE EXCELLENT ASSET PROTECTION ENTITIES

Or: Why you want the charging order.

So, finally at rule seven we are getting to the good stuff. But as I mentioned, there is so much misinformation out there that I felt it was important to first dispel the myths and outright lies. With all that completed, I can now state that LLCs and LPs offer excellent asset protection via the *charging order*.

Before reviewing the charging order, the difference between LLCs and LPs must be explained. With an LP you must have at least one general partner and one limited partner. The general partner, if an individual, is personally responsible for the LP's activities. To encapsulate that unlimited liability you must form a limited liability entity—a corporation or an LLC—to be the general partner. While you are now fully protected, it is important to remember that you have had to form two entities: first, the LP, and then second, a corporation or LLC to be the general partner of the LP. With the LLC you need to form only one entity, the LLC. Everyone is protected within the LLC. While LPs certainly have their place, due to the need for only one entity instead of two, we shall use the LLC example from here on out.

When it comes to protecting your real estate, we must also distinguish between attacks. A chart helps to explain:

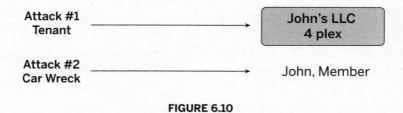

FIGURE 6.10

In Attack No. 1, a tenant sues the LLC over a broken stairway. If successful, the tenant can get what is inside the LLC—the fourplex—subject to any deeds of trusts against the property.

But if the tenant can get the equity in the property, you ask, why even bother with an LLC? Because without the LLC, the tenant could get everything John owns—his house and bank account and everything else. The LLC limits the tenant to just what's in the LLC and shields your outside assets from attack.

In Attack No. 2, John gets in a car wreck, his insurance company won't cover him, and a judgment creditor (the person who won in court; we'll call him Nate) is seeking to get paid. Because the car wreck had nothing to do with the real estate, Nate, the judgment creditor, can't sue John's LLC directly. Instead, Nate must go after John's membership interest in the LLC.

This is where the charging order comes into play. The charging order rule provides that Nate can't take possession of John's membership interest, his ownership in the LLC. If Nate could, he could then sell the fourplex and get paid. (And please note, this is what can happen with a corporation. The judgment creditor gets the shares and takes control and sells all the corporate assets. Nevada, to date, is the only state that has extended charging order protections to corporate shares in corporations with between one and ninety-nine shareholders.)

The charging order instead allows Nate to stand in John's shoes as a member and receive distributions.

But what if no distributions are made? Then Nate gets nothing. He has to wait to be paid. Attorneys, many of whom are on contingency fees where they collect on a percentage of the winnings, don't like to wait to be paid. They may be satisfied with the insurance payment and be done.

As such, the proper use of LLCs and LPs is an excellent deterrent to frivolous litigation. Not many people want to fight it out in court to not receive any money *and* have to pay taxes on the money. Using LLCs and LPs can be an aid in settlement discussions. They can even prevent a lawsuit from being filed in the first place.

TIP Using LLCs and LPs can be an aid in settlement discussions. They can even prevent a lawsuit from being filed in the first place.

Charging order rules vary from state to state. Nevada and Wyoming have the strongest laws. In those states, the exclusive creditor remedy is the charging order, even for single-member (one owner) LLCs. California has the weakest law. There are two California court cases allowing creditors to pierce through and sell off LLC and LP assets to pay the creditor.

So if you are going to buy property in California or one of the many other states with weak asset protection laws (including Georgia and New York), you may set up your LLC or LP in the state where the property is located or forming in Nevada or Wyoming, and then qualifying in the state where the property is located and then have that LLC owned by a Wyoming or Nevada LLC. The process of qualifying involves submitting, for example, the Wyoming LLC papers and appropriate fees to the California secretary of state's office. If properly done it is always granted and keeps you within the law.

The benefit is that if you get sued as in Attack No. 2, Wyoming or Nevada law applies, not California law. A judgment creditor has to hire a Wyoming or Nevada lawyer to fight a very uphill battle. This is what you want: a very strong reason for predators to leave you alone.

More information on this is found in my book, *How to Use Limited Liability Companies and Limited Partnerships* (SuccessDNA, 2009).

RULE NO. 8: SEGREGATION OF ASSETS IS GOOD

Or: Let's not put all of our eggs in one basket.

Since we've learned that LLCs and LPs are good entities for holding and protecting our real estate, the question then becomes: How many properties do I put in each entity?

This is a judgment call on your part. But consider these scenarios involving Liz, who owns twelve properties:

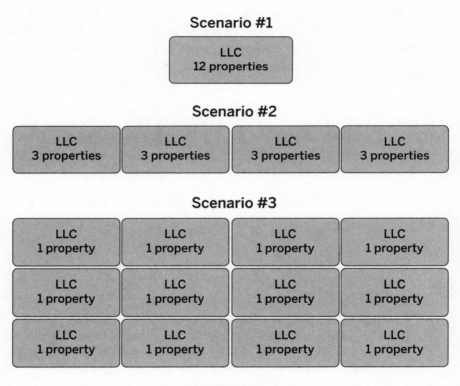

FIGURE 6.11

In Scenario 1, if a tenant sues over a problem at one property, the other eleven properties are exposed to the attack. In Scenario 2, with three properties in each LLC, only two additional properties are exposed if Liz is sued. Of course, in Scenario 3 with only one property in each LLC, only one property is exposed.

I would never suggest a client hold twelve properties in one LLC. With that many properties, your LLC is a rich target. In my experience, most of my clients choose somewhere between Scenario 2 and 3. As is evident, the best asset protection is obtained through Scenario 3. Only one property is exposed to any one attack.

But some clients don't want to pay the one-time initial set-up fees and continuing annual fees for twelve entities. In a state like California, where the annual fee is $800 per entity, $9,600 a year for twelve entities is rather daunting. So the choice of using one LLC to hold three properties is an option. It is your call. But once again, the fewer properties you hold in each entity, the better protected you will be.

Due to these issues, a new type of LLC is being touted to help reduce the number of LLCs you need to form, called the "Series LLC." Unfortunately, I cannot recommend this new creature. It attempts to place separate properties into separate series under one LLC, as follows:

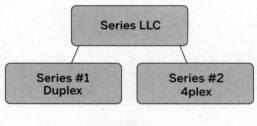

FIGURE 6.12

The supposed benefit is that by setting up one LLC you can independently protect two properties. The idea is that within the Series LLC there is an *internal liabilities shield* whereby a claim against the duplex in Series 1 does not affect the fourplex in Series 2. The problem is there is no guidance whether or not this supposed internal liability shield will be upheld. There are no court cases in the subject, and conceptually the strategy may be difficult for a court to uphold. Can two properties in the same state-chartered entity be protected from each other? As well, what if one series goes bankrupt? Will the other series be protected? No one knows.

The California tax authorities (the very aggressive Franchise Tax Board) have their opinion. If you are going to try and set up one series to hold two properties, they are going to charge you $800 per series, the same as if you had set up two separate LLCs to begin with.

Of course, by setting up two separate LLCs you have the certainty of separateness, rather than hoping that someday a court will miraculously rule that the muddled and imperfect concept of an internal liability shield actually makes sense.

TIP Stay away from promoters who would put you into this untested entity called the Series LLC.

Interestingly, the American Bar Association brought together the nation's brightest lawyers to review LLC developments. After looking at the Series LLC they declined to endorse the whole concept. Stay away from promoters who would put you into this untested entity called the Series LLC.

RULE NO. 9: TRANSFER TITLE INTO YOUR ENTITY

Or: What's the point if you don't?
All right, so you have set up one or more LLCs to protect your real estate. You have the articles properly filed with the state. You have approved and signed the operating agreement governing how the LLC will run. You have signed the minutes of the first meeting and issued the membership certificates. All the important documents are in one binder in a safe place.

And remember, if all these steps are not taken, you are not ready. Beware of promoters who will sell you the articles for just $99 but will not provide you with an operating agreement, meeting minutes, and membership certificates. Our firm charges $695 (or less if you are with Rich Dad) plus state filing fees for the complete package—binder and all—with all your documents prepared and finalized according to your specific needs, along with live phone support through the whole process. You have the certainty of knowing that everything is in order.

TIP You've formed the asset protection entity. The next step is to transfer title to the property into the LLC.

So assuming that everything is in order, now what?

Just because you have your asset protection entity in place, are your real estate assets now protected? No, not yet. You must take the next step, which is to transfer title to the property into the name of the LLC.

You must prepare a grant deed transferring ownership of your fourplex, for example, from John Jones, as an individual, to the Jones Real Estate, LLC.

Several questions arise during this process.

FIGURE 6.13

First, is this a taxable event? Will the IRS or my state taxing authority assess taxes when this happens? The answer is no. This is not a sale of the property—you are not receiving any money in this transaction. Instead, it is a transfer. You are transferring the property from yourself (as an individual) to yourself (your new 100-percent-owned LLC).

The property goes into the LLC at its basis, which is the amount you paid for the property originally. That basis, for tax purposes, remains the same once the property is in the LLC. So, for example, if you paid $250,000 for your fourplex, the basis of $250,000 remains once it is titled in the LLC's name. There is no gain in the transaction, and with no gain there are no capital gain or ordinary income taxes.

If John Jones added new members (owners) into Jones Real Estate, LLC before or after the transfer, there could be a taxable event. Be sure to consult with your advisors prior to any change in ownership.

The next question is: Are there any transfer taxes? The answer is: It depends.

Transfer taxes, a tax based upon the value of the property being transferred, vary from state to state. Many states have an exception to their transfer taxes. If you are transferring the property from yourself as an individual to yourself as an LLC, there is no tax. Check with your local advisors to understand your local rules.

Some states are very tricky, though. In Nevada, you are free to transfer title into your LLC. But if you transfer it from the LLC back to yourself there is a transfer tax. This situation occurs when you are refinancing and the lender wants title to be in your name when the new first deed of trust attaches. Resist the lender's attempts to require this. He will argue that he doesn't have security if title is in the LLC. That is nonsense. With title in the LLC, he will have your personal guarantee for the loan and a first deed of trust against the property, the same as if it was in your individual name. He is equally protected in either situation. Seek out lenders who are enlightened as to asset protection. They do exist.

One state is very costly when it comes to transfer taxes. Pennsylvania charges a 2 percent tax on the value of the property. So if you have a million dollar property with a mortgage of $950,000, you will still pay $20,000 (2 percent of $1 million) for the privilege of holding title in the name of your LLC. Ouch.

The best course in all of this is to take title in the name of your LLC when you first buy the property. With title in the proper entity at the start there is no need for a later transfer, thus no issue of transfer taxes. There are lenders who will let you take title at closing in the name of the LLC (or your LP). Speaking of banks and lenders, the next questions is: Will they call the loan if I transfer title? In dealing with clients, I have heard numerous times about the attitude of lenders regarding transferring title into an LLC. In their reptilian mind-set, they feel as if you are trying to hide assets from them and deny them their due. Of course, as mentioned, if the lender has your personal guarantee and a first deed of trust on the property, he is protected whether it is in your name or the LLC's name.

But that logic is lost on the functionaries at most lenders. They will argue that if you make the transfer they will enforce the due-on-sale clause, which states that the loan is due when you sell the property. Of course you haven't sold the property; you transferred it to yourself.

So what do you do?

In my experience it comes down to: Is it better to ask for permission or forgiveness? If you ask most lenders, as if by reflex, they will say no. But if you just go ahead and make the transfer without asking you can always say you are sorry later. The chances are good you will never have such a conversation. In my dealings, the lenders have never called a note. Will you be the first one? I don't know. But as long as you keep making the monthly payments, there is a very good chance that they are not going to call the loan. Why would they want to create such trouble for themselves, especially when they are being paid? If in some bizarre case they do, refinance with a lender comfortable with LLCs. It's not as if you are going to lose your property if they call the note.

The only group you do need to notify when you transfer title is your insurance company. It needs to know the policy is in your LLC name and not in your personal name. Otherwise, and this does happen, your friendly insurance company may claim it was insuring you as an individual, not your LLC, and use that as an excuse to deny any coverage in the event of a problem at the property. And while the insurance company may notify the lender of the change in insureds, that usually does not lead to due-on-sale threats.

A final question always arises as to why to use a grant deed instead of a quit claim deed to transfer the title. A quit claim deed merely transfers everything you claim you may own to the next party. A grant deed is a much more affirmative grant of property rights. As such, in many cases, title insurance coverage flows to the next party with a grant deed. Since you are essentially transferring property from yourself to yourself, it makes sense to give yourself the most complete rights you can. Use a grant deed.

RULE NO. 10: DON'T SET UP MORE ENTITIES THAN NECESSARY

Or: Beware of promoters telling you otherwise.

Several years ago I was at a real estate event in San Francisco. A lady approached me after hearing my speech, in which I argued that people should not go overboard and set up more entities than are needed.

I was shocked by her story.

Jane was looking to invest in her first duplex. She had previously attended a seminar on asset protection given by a self-styled asset protection guru. The seminar had been sponsored by a local real estate organization. She trusted that the group would provide her only with competent service providers.

The asset protection guy indicated that she needed the following structure for protection: (See Figure 6.14.)

Jane stated that the man convinced her that for the necessary protection she:

1. Needed the LP to hold her LLC. The LP was then, in turn, owned by the Nevada Asset Protection Trust and the Offshore Asset Protection Trust. These structures gave her extra layers of protection.

2. Needed an S corporation to manage the LP in order to achieve necessary asset protection.

3. Needed the C corporation to manage the LLC in order to achieve significant tax savings.

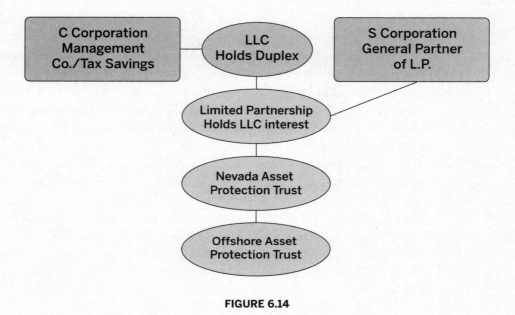

FIGURE 6.14

The cost of this structure was $20,000. The annual fees were more than $5,000 to maintain all the entities. Jane was in tears because after spending such a large sum of money for asset protection, she no longer had enough money for the down payment on her duplex.

I told her the truth. She had spent way too much money. The asset protection man's arguments were false. Extra layers of entities do not necessarily provide extra layers of protection. If you aren't making any money yet, you don't really need a C corporation to save on taxes. The structure they created was designed for their profit, not her needs. Jane asked me to give her a chart of what she needed to protect her duplex. It took five seconds to chart her strategy:

FIGURE 6.15

Jane was in shock. She asked how the local real estate group promoter, a person she trusted, could let such a snake in the door to present to them. I told her something that was an open secret in that business. The local promoter in many cases receives 50 percent of what the service provider sells. As such, there is a powerful economic incentive for local promoters to tout the value, integrity, and importance of the service provider, as well as the urgent need for the services offered. In Jane's case, the local promoter may have made as much as $10,000 for doing so.

Jane calculated that fifteen people had signed up for all this and figured the promoter must have cleared a total of $150,000 at the one asset protection event. She was furious and sickened by what had happened. She vowed never to invest in real estate. I tried to counsel her but could not. She had gone through a horrible experience and was adamant that her decision was final.

Do not let Jane's experience be yours. Real estate is an excellent way to build wealth, but at some points during your journey you will need to be able to navigate through shark-infested waters.

Important Tips

- Engage in critical thinking.

- Ask yourself if the "expert" really is such an expert.

- Ask yourself if the services are for your legal benefit or the expert's financial benefit.

- Use healthy skepticism and old-fashioned due diligence.

- Check around, and don't bite at the first supposedly "discounted" offer.
  These tips will work out to your advantage.

That said, asset protection, as we have seen, is important. You want to take the necessary steps to protect your real estate assets and your financial future. The correct use of entities will greatly assist you in achieving this goal.

Remember, asset protection is neither overly difficult nor outrageously expensive. And with critical thinking, never allow someone to tell you it is.

Good luck in all your asset-protected real estate investing.

Where to Learn More

www.corporatedirect.com
www.sutlaw.com

 **Garrett Sutton** is a Rich Dad's Advisor and is the author of *Loopholes of Real Estate, Start Your Own Corporation, The ABC's of Getting Out of Debt, The ABC's of Writing Winning Business Plans*, and *Run Your Own Corporation*. Garrett is an attorney with more than 30 years experience in assisting individuals and businesses to determine their appropriate corporate structure, limit their liability, protect their assets, and advance their financial, personal, and credit success goals. He has been featured in the *Wall Street Journal* and the *New York Times*, among others. His firm, Sutton Law Center, has offices in Reno, Nevada and Jackson Hole, Wyoming. He accepts new clients at (800) 700-1430.

How to Avoid and Handle Real Estate Disputes

Bernie Bays has been a friend of mine since the mid-1970s. He is also a fellow marine and rugby team member. If you go over his record, you can tell he is no ordinary marine, but a Force Recon Marine, the toughest of the tough. He is also no ordinary rugby player, playing for USC and for Stanford University on a national championship team. Small wonder he is such a smart and respected real estate attorney.

When I first started out in real estate, my deals were small, and I thought I did not need an attorney. Being naïve, I thought a real estate broker and a good appraiser were enough. On my first investment property—a small one bedroom, one bath condo on the island of Maui—my little dream bubble was popped. A few months after acquiring the property and putting a tenant in it, netting me a whopping $25 a month, the septic system in the condominium complex burst and flooded the apartment. The apartment went empty, I began to lose money, the homeowners told me the septic damage to my unit was my problem, not theirs. My first asset became a liability, and I learned a priceless but expensive lesson about real estate. Hire an attorney before you invest, not after.

Real estate is more than dirt, sticks, bricks, financing, and tenants. Real estate is also law, agreements, boundaries, and disputes. This is why Bernie Bays is not only a friend; he is the real estate attorney I call before investing in Hawai'i.

—ROBERT KIYOSAKI

One unfortunate reality of real estate deals today is that there is always the possibility that you can become involved in a dispute with other participants during the making of the deal. These participants can include sellers, lenders, construction and planning professionals, construction contractors, and buyers. Success in real estate means not only being great at picking properties, managing them well, and eventually selling at the right time, it also means knowing how to minimize the risk of becoming involved in a protracted dispute.

I have been representing clients involved in real estate–related disputes for more than thirty-eight years. During that time, I have observed that some participants in real estate deals are constantly involved in disputes. Others rarely get into disputes and when they do, they usually manage to resolve them relatively quickly. What's the difference between these two groups of people: the ones who seem to get into dispute after dispute and the ones who seldom do? How can you minimize your chances of being involved in a dispute?

Make no mistake about it. Disputes in real estate deals can spoil your party by diverting time, money, other resources, and, most importantly, emotional energy from what you are trying to achieve: a successful real estate deal. There are admittedly a few perverse individuals who occasionally come out ahead by picking fights in a real estate deal. And there are a few people who thrive on the negative emotional energy of disputes, even though they may not really come out ahead. You want to avoid these people in your real estate deals. But it's not always about the people. Sometimes it's the kind of real estate deals that are prone to disputes and you want to avoid those as well.

TIP Disputes in real estate deals can spoil your party by diverting time, money, other resources, and, most importantly, emotional energy from what you are trying to achieve: a successful real estate deal.

My objective here is to give you some simple guidelines so you can reduce your chances of becoming involved in a real estate dispute. I also want to give you some suggestions for how best to handle the disputes that you cannot avoid.

How to Avoid Disputes

The best defense against a dispute is to avoid the dispute altogether. Here's my list of how to keep yourself out of trouble.

WORK WITH A GOOD, EXPERIENCED BROKER

Always work with your own real estate broker on a real estate deal. Do not just work with the seller's real estate broker when you are buying a property. You want to select a broker who has the experience and good sense to look out for your interests rather than simply pushing you to close the deal at hand in order to get a commission. You want a broker who is in it for the long term and knows that there will be other deals to do with you if this one does not work out. You want a trusted broker who will advise you to walk away from the deal if that is the best thing for you to do under the circumstances.

I recently concluded a case for a client who had purchased a development property through the listing broker without using his own broker. My client initially told the broker that he could not buy the property because of the three-unit affordable housing requirement. The broker told my client that if my client would sell him three of the lots in the proposed subdivision at a reduced price, he would construct the affordable housing on the three lots and satisfy the requirement. My client allowed the broker's lawyer to draft the agreement regarding the three lots and proceeded with the purchase of the property. He did not have his own lawyer review the agreement, but instead just trusted the seller's broker. After my client purchased the property, he discovered that the affordable housing requirement for the project was actually five units, not three. Even more shocking, the broker said that he was not obligated to build *any* affordable housing at the site. "That was just something we discussed that I might do if it worked out," the broker said.

The broker then demanded that my client convey the three lots to him at the reduced price and threatened to sue. When my client came to me, we discovered that the agreement drafted by the broker's attorney provided for a sale of the lots to the broker at a reduced price, but said nothing about building the affordable housing.

My client did not have a legal leg to stand on. We were finally able to settle the case by conveying only two of the three lots to the broker. My client was left to satisfy the five-unit affordable housing requirement on his other lots. This case demonstrates how dangerous it is not to have your own broker representing you in a real estate transaction. It also demonstrates how dangerous it is not to have your own lawyer representing you in documenting your agreements, which is what the next section is about.

TIP Do not just work with the seller's real estate broker when you are buying a property. You want a trusted broker who will advise you to walk away from the deal if that is the best thing for you to do.

CONSULT WITH A GOOD, EXPERIENCED LAWYER EARLY AND OFTEN

I was giving a speech a few months ago to a group of real estate developers and joked that in real estate deals you should get a lawyer involved "early and often." I was joking, but there is a good deal of truth in what I said. The truth here is that an ounce of prevention in lawyer time spent drafting the deal contracts is worth a pound of cure in the form of costly litigation. So spend a little money on lawyers in the beginning to get clear contracts that protect your interests. It may save you a fortune in litigation costs later on. These are my suggestions to get the most value from your lawyer in a real estate deal:

- Find an experienced real estate attorney you trust and can afford.

- Keep him or her up to speed on pending transactions and request advice early and often.

- Specifically, have your lawyer involved in the preparation of any term sheets or letters of intent, even though they may be nonbinding. This is usually when the buyer and the seller agree upon important deal points that are difficult to change later on.

- Have your lawyer prepare any binding contracts.

- Do not try to save money by allowing the lawyer on the other side to prepare the first draft of the contracts. It is better to spend the money to have your lawyer prepare the first draft. It is often difficult to change a contract drafted by the other side. Once they have prepared and approved it, they tend to become wedded to it.

- Involve your lawyer in your due diligence process for any property you are buying. Skimping on legal due diligence to save money is a bad idea, a false economy. If a property is worth putting under contract, then it is worth spending the money on a thorough due diligence including legal.

TIP The truth here is that an ounce of prevention in lawyer time spent drafting the deal contracts is worth a pound of cure in the form of costly litigation.

INSIST ON CLEAR CONTRACTS THAT PROTECT YOUR INTERESTS

I handle real estate litigation that results when real estate deals go bad. Often these cases result from poorly drafted contracts that do not do a good job of protecting the legitimate interests of the parties. For example, I have had two cases in the last year or so where, believe it or not, the contracts really did not require one of the parties to follow through on his commitments to complete the real estate projects that were the subject of those contracts. Clearly the intent of the parties was to execute contracts that were binding, but the contracts they signed did not effectively do the job. In one case, the party financing the development just refused to proceed with the project, even though the market was good and the project would have been profitable. Unfortunately, the contracts did not explicitly require the investor to proceed. The developers had allowed the investor's lawyer to prepare the agreements without hiring their own lawyer, which turned out to be a very costly mistake.

In the other case, the investors gave the developer the money he said he needed to complete the development. Unfortunately the contracts did not really obligate him to finish the project, and the contracts also prevented the investors from replacing the developer, even if he completely failed to finish the project. The lesson here is to insist on clear contracts that obligate the parties to do what they have agreed to do and to have a lawyer represent you who is looking out for your interests and protecting your rights.

You are entitled to contracts that spell out precisely what you expect to happen in the real estate deal; contracts that reduce the uncertainty and keep ambiguity to a minimum. You also want to make absolutely sure the other parties are required to do exactly what you expect them to do when you expect them to do it. Spell out the consequences if the other parties do not do what you expect them to do. By the same token, you also want to know what the consequences will be if you do not or cannot uphold your side of the agreement. A good lawyer can help you define and limit your downside as much as possible in those situations. Later we'll talk about limiting remedies in more detail, but here's some legal advice: If you are not sure you can perform under the terms of the contract, then you should not sign it.

Beyond these words of wisdom, take the time to read and understand the contracts you are going to sign. In doing so, your real estate broker and your lawyer can give you all the help you need. Let them help you identify any risks that others will not perform or that you cannot perform, and make the necessary changes to fix the problems. Don't hesitate to have things explained again if you do not understand. And don't worry about looking stupid. The more you understand, the smarter you will get. The stupid thing is to sign a contract you really do not understand.

TIP You are entitled to contracts that spell out precisely what you expect to happen in the real estate deal; contracts that reduce the uncertainty and keep ambiguity to a minimum. You also want to make absolutely sure the other parties are required to do exactly what you expect them to do when you expect them to do it.

CAREFULLY SPECIFY AND LIMIT REMEDIES IN THE CONTRACT

Much of the uncertainty regarding real estate contracts can be eliminated by clearly specifying remedies. For example, real estate contracts often provide that the seller's only remedy if the buyer defaults is to keep the buyer's deposit. On the other hand, if you are a seller, you want to limit the buyer's remedy to just getting the deposit back and you want to specifically preclude the buyer from getting what is called "specific performance."

"Specific performance" is an equitable remedy that gives the buyer the right to legally compel the seller to sell the property to the buyer upon the terms in the contract. If the buyer is arguably entitled to specific performance, the buyer may have the ability to tie up the seller's property in court for years while the parties litigate their respective obligations under the contract and who did what. This could effectively give the buyer an option on the seller's property for years with only the deposit at risk. This is not where you want to be if you are a seller. If you cannot completely negotiate out specific performance, you want to limit the situations where the buyer is entitled to seek specific performance as much as possible.

TIP "Specific performance" is an equitable remedy that gives the buyer the right to legally compel the seller to sell the property to the buyer upon the terms in the contract. As a seller, if you cannot completely negotiate out specific performance, you want to limit it as much as possible.

Let me share with you a story of how powerful specific performance can be. I represented a large hotel chain in litigation that resulted from the failed sale of a trophy resort hotel in Honolulu. The buyer had failed to perform according to the exact terms of the contract, so my client finally canceled the deal and kept the buyer's $1 million deposit. The buyer had also spent more than $200,000 on a lengthy due diligence before my client canceled the contract. Had I been involved earlier, I would have recommended that my client give the buyer more time to perform and would have carefully positioned the buyer before canceling. But by the time the case got to me, the contract had been canceled, and the buyer had sued. We asked the court for summary judgment without a trial based upon the fact that the buyer had not met the time deadlines provided for in the contract. We got lucky and the federal court gave us summary judgment against the buyer.

After the hearing, I advised the top management of the hotel chain that we had been very lucky to get summary judgment, and that the court's decision might be reversed on appeal. I told them that they did not want a premier hotel tied up for years by the buyer's potential right to specific performance while the appeal got resolved. I recommended that they use this opportunity to settle with the buyer by returning some of the deposit. But warmed by the glow of victory, they refused to offer the buyer anything, and I was reprimanded by a senior partner for spoiling our victory with my dismal predictions about an appeal.

To make a long story short, I left the firm with some of my colleagues to form our own firm, and someone else handled the appeal. Years later, after the hotel had increased 50 percent in value, the appeals court ruled that the buyer should be allowed to proceed with the purchase of the hotel at the original price with full credit for the deposit the seller had retained.

TIP Here are some words of experience:

- Limit the buyer's right to specific performance whenever possible
- Always try to resolve the dispute instead of rolling the dice in litigation

In that case, the seller's failure to limit specific performance and insistence on keeping the buyer's $1 million tied up a premier hotel for years and resulted in the sale of an $80 million hotel for $55 million. Not a good outcome!

AVOID PROBLEM PEOPLE

Do not do real estate deals with people who are likely to be trouble down the road. Some people get into disputes with everyone. You want to do online litigation checks on people you are considering doing business with. If they have been involved in a lot of litigation you want to avoid them. This is also another good reason for you to avoid litigation; so that other people will not avoid doing business with you! Conversely, you want to do business with people who have a history and reputation for working things out when a real estate deal hits a rough spot. You want to have a mutual trust and respect for the other people involved in a real estate deal whenever possible, especially a real estate development project that will go on for several years.

TIP Do online litigation checks on people you are considering doing business with. Avoid litigation so people will do business with you!

Rough spots are sure to come up, and potential disagreements are certain to arise. You want to be involved with people who will work them out with you, not make a mountain out of every molehill. The last thing you want is someone who will blow up your deal in litigation to prove they are right.

AVOID PROBLEM DEALS

Some deals are just more trouble than they are worth. Some deals get more complicated, involved, and difficult as they progress. And the more complicated and difficult the deal becomes, the more likely there are to be disputes later on that will be difficult to resolve. So when the deal gets more and more difficult and the brain damage mounts, you need to ask: Is it worth it? Is this deal so good and so beneficial for you that it is worth the brain damage and risk that is inherent in complex, difficult deals? Some are worth it, and you may want to continue. Most are not, and you will be better off letting those go. Let someone else deal with all the headaches and problems if the potential benefit to you is really not worth the trouble. If the benefit is there and you decide to go ahead, then the help of a good lawyer and the need for clear contracts become doubly important. However, even a good lawyer can do only so much to overcome the risks inherent in a difficult deal.

TIP The more complicated and difficult the deal becomes, the more likely there are to be disputes later on—and problem people and problem deals often go hand in hand.

The purchase of a large ranch that I helped a friend put together several years ago was a deal that was just too difficult and complicated. A limited partnership owned the ranch and the general partner who originally formed the group that owned the ranch had sold his interest to a stranger who had gotten into litigation with the holder of the grazing license. In order to buy the ranch, my friend had to put together another partnership composed of some of the partners in the original partnership that owned the ranch and some new investor partners. We also had to get a federal farm loan, renegotiate the underlying ground lease to extend it to twenty-five years, settle the litigation between the general partner and the licensee, and resolve the disagreements among everyone as to how all this should be done. I was the person responsible for doing all of this. As I look back, the brain damage, work, and stress involved in trying to put this extremely complicated deal together clearly outweighed any gain. The deal finally collapsed of its own weight when the buyer went on a long-planned, month-long family vacation when the deal was supposed to close. Luckily, no one involved got sued; we just wasted a lot of time and money on a deal that was just too difficult and complicated.

Another point to consider is that problem people and problem deals often go hand in hand. Clear contracts can go only so far in controlling problem people in the context of a problem deal. The probability of serious disputes that will be difficult, if not impossible to resolve without litigation goes up exponentially. Some experienced real estate developers and investors would say that no deal is worth going through the brain damage, emotional drain, and risk of problem people and problem deals and would advise you to just walk away from them. I will just say that the problems will be more numerous and much worse than you expect so you need to be sure the deal is really worth it. A few deals are that good, but the vast majority are simply not worth it.

DO A THOROUGH DUE DILIGENCE, INCLUDING LEGAL DUE DILIGENCE

Due diligence is a period of time designated within a contract that allows a buyer to check out the property and the deal before committing to close. Usually the buyer's deposits are refundable until the buyer notifies the seller that the property and the deal are acceptable. At that point, the buyer's deposit "goes hard" (becomes nonrefundable) and the buyer is also usually required to increase the deposit so that the buyer will lose a substantial amount of money if the buyer fails to close. This nonrefundable deposit also gives the seller comfort that the deal will close.

TIP If you are a buyer and you think a deal is worth doing, then it is worth spending the money to do a thorough due diligence, including careful legal due diligence.

If you are a buyer and you think a deal is worth doing, then it is worth spending the money to do a thorough due diligence, including careful *legal* due diligence. If the deal is big, then you need to spend a substantial amount of money to check it out carefully before you agree to close. Many disputes can be avoided if you check out the property and the deal very carefully before you commit to close. If you discover problems or issues at the due diligence stage, you can insist that the contract be amended to fairly deal with the problems you have discovered. If you need more time to complete your due diligence, show the seller the effort you are making and the money you are spending on the deal and ask for an extension of time. You will usually get it if the seller is convinced you are proceeding in good faith. But sometimes the seller won't feel that way.

I recently had a development property in escrow and delayed the legal due diligence to save money. I instead focused a lot of time and money on planning the proposed subdivision and locating an adequate water source for the property. When I finally started the legal due diligence, my lawyers discovered an unusual legal restriction that prevented us from developing the subdivision project we had planned for the property. As a result, all the money we had spent on engineering and land planning was completely wasted.

How to Avoid Real Estate Disputes

Avoid disputes in your real estate deals by doing the following:

- Work with a good, experienced broker.
- Consult with a good, experienced lawyer early and often.
- Insist on clear contracts that protect your interests.
- Carefully specify and limit remedies in the contract.
- Avoid problem people.
- Avoid problem deals.
- Do a thorough due diligence, including legal due diligence.

HOW TO HANDLE REAL ESTATE DISPUTES

Even if you follow the steps I have outlined above, no contract is perfect, and conditions may change in ways that may make the deal more difficult for one or more of the parties. As a result, disputes can arise, even when you have clear contracts with decent people: One party may also just want to try to improve the deal after it is agreed upon. So how do you handle the disagreements that do arise in your real estate deals? The simple answer is that you should always do your best to work it out. In doing this, you may want to consider the following suggestions:

CONSULT WITH A GOOD, EXPERIENCED LITIGATION LAWYER TO AVOID LITIGATION

Strangely enough, a good litigation lawyer knows better than anyone that litigation in real estate deals seldom pays off and also knows the best ways to avoid it. While helping you avoid litigation, an experienced litigation lawyer can also put you in the best position possible if litigation cannot be avoided. He or she can also make sure you do not give up the farm or get bullied by the other parties. There is usually some middle ground between getting pushed around and doing your part to resolve disagreements. A good lawyer can help you find that middle ground.

But here is a fair warning. Litigation lawyers make a lot more money by representing you in litigation than they do in helping you avoid it. Some do not have enough work and may have a financial self interest in prolonging your dispute, or even aggravating it. Some lawyers also are just enamored with the litigation process and get carried away with protecting your position to the point they lose sight of the real objective, which is resolving the dispute for you as quickly and cheaply as possible. You do not want these unbalanced lawyers representing you. You want lawyers helping you who have the experience and good judgment to strike the right balance between protecting your interests and resolving your dispute.

TIP Experience warning: Litigation lawyers make a lot more money by representing you in litigation than they do in helping you avoid it. Choose carefully.

WHEN DISPUTES ARISE, DO WHATEVER YOU CAN TO WORK IT OUT

As I have said, disagreements may occur in real estate deals, even though you have had clear contracts prepared by a good lawyer. Generally, the more complicated the deal and the longer it lasts, the more likely there are to be disagreements. For example, a joint venture agreement to develop a planned community over a ten- to twenty-year period is almost certain to involve a number of disagreements, while the sale of a house in "as is condition" for cash to close in thirty days is much less likely to generate disagreements.

My advice is when disagreements arise, you should do your best to work out the disagreements as soon as possible. This can usually be done by respecting the other party's interests while protecting your own. There is no need to force the other party to live up to the letter of the contract if you can accommodate their legitimate interests without hurting yourself. You are almost always better off giving up a little ground, generating some good will, and resolving the disagreement before it becomes a serious dispute. Here are some suggestions:

- Respect the legitimate interests of the other party, and try to accommodate them whenever you can. There is usually a way to respect the other party's interests while protecting your own. For example, if you are selling a property, and the buyer wants to extend due diligence for thirty days, figure out a way to do it, maybe by getting a cash payment. This point is demonstrated by a case I handled several years ago for a very wealthy client whose name some of you would recognize. He was buying a large oceanfront resort property for development, and the seller refused to extend the time for due diligence in a situation where it was reasonable to do so. The seller's refusal to extend due diligence and abrupt cancellation of the sale precipitated a lawsuit by my client that tied up the seller's property for years and eventually led the seller to sell the property to my client for about $2 million less than the contract price, even though the real estate market had gone up. All this could have been avoided if the seller had just given my client a thirty-day extension for due diligence.

- Generate clear correspondence to the other side with the help of your lawyer. This will often help avoid litigation and, if not, this correspondence will be valuable evidence for you in any litigation.

- You can usually make substantial concessions to resolve disputes and avoid litigation and still come out way ahead. The cost of litigation is always higher than you expect. The case always costs more than you expect and there are hidden costs. The emotional cost of litigation can be overwhelming for many people and the lost time, energy, and opportunities can also be huge and may be more expensive than the direct costs of the lawyers and experts who participate in the case. The adage "avoid litigation at all costs" is only slightly off the mark.

TIP You are almost always better off giving up a little ground, generating some good will and resolving the disagreement before it becomes a serious dispute.

TRY MEDIATION

When you have tried your best and have been unable to settle the dispute directly with the other party, you may want to try mediation. Mediation is an abbreviated dispute resolution process where an experienced professional helps the parties reach a voluntary settlement of their dispute.

A number of years ago when mediation was first used, it had a very high success rate, between 80 and 90 percent. In recent years, the success rate is much lower. Today, the mediation process is only as good as the mediator.

Highly skilled, experienced mediators still maintain a high success ratio while less skilled mediators probably succeed in less than half their attempts. Mediation can work when you select the right mediator, and that is probably the most important factor in a successful mediation.

The second most important factor is a mutual desire by the parties to resolve the dispute in the mediation. Mediations used to take place in one day, but today a good mediator may work for as long as one or two months, going back and forth with the parties to resolve a dispute. A good mediator will put in whatever effort it takes to succeed. I was the mediator appointed by the court to resolve a series of interrelated cases that were estimated to use up one year of court time if they were not settled. That mediation lasted several months before I succeeded, but it saved a fortune in lawyers' fees and court time. It was well worth the effort I put into it.

TIP Mediation can work when you select the right mediator and when there is a mutual desire by the parties to resolve the dispute.

Another way to improve the odds for success in mediation is to begin the process with a comprehensive settlement offer that includes all the details of a settlement. You then want to insist that the negotiation of major terms take place within the context of this comprehensive agreement so you will know exactly what you are agreeing to.

Mediation is relatively inexpensive if it is successful and is much better than any other method of formal dispute resolution. However, if it is unsuccessful, then nothing has been accomplished, and the mediation will have been a waste of time and money. Because mediation can be so efficient and effective, many real estate contracts require mediation before arbitration or litigation. I recommend that you include a provision requiring mediation in most contracts.

Several years ago, I represented a client in a case that seemed ripe for mediation. The parties decided to pay a blue ribbon mediator $10,000 for one day, and we all flew to San Francisco to have him mediate the case. Although the mediator was very experienced and had a good reputation, he completely screwed up this mediation and failed to get any concrete settlement offer out of the other side. My client was so anxious to resolve the case that he made repeatedly lower offers to the other side without any counter offer, all contrary to the instructions his business advisor and I gave him repeatedly. The client negotiated against himself throughout the day and reduced his settlement offer from $500,000 (which was a fair deal for the other side) down to something substantially under $100,000, which the arrogant folks on the other side should have jumped at.

The case finally settled years later when the vice president of the real estate title insurance company (who was himself an attorney) called me directly and said we had to settle the case right then. He said that he could no longer take the amount the case was costing. He indicated his lawyer's fees had already exceeded $1 million with no end in sight. I recalled that his attorney had bragged after an earlier hearing in the case that he had "bought a new car" with the fees from the case. The title company finally agreed to pay my client $850,000 in cash to settle a case that could have been settled at the outset for less than $100,000 in the mediation. I estimate the total cost to the title company was well over $2 million, all because it did not accept my client's offer in the mediation. You should avoid making this mistake!

CONSIDER ARBITRATION

If settlement fails and mediation fails, you may want to consider arbitration as an alternative to litigation in court. Arbitration is a trial conducted by an experienced arbitrator paid by the parties instead of a judge or jury who are paid by the federal or state government. Many real estate contracts require arbitration instead of litigation. Where the contract requires arbitration, then the parties are required to resolve the dispute by arbitration, and any court litigation initiated by either party based upon the contract will be dismissed by the court in favor of arbitration under the terms of the contract.

The arbitrator hears the evidence and makes a binding and final decision based upon the evidence and the law. Your ability to appeal a bad decision made by an arbitrator is very limited. Arbitration used to be quicker and cheaper than litigation, but today it is unclear whether there is any net benefit to arbitration over litigation. Because the arbitrator is getting paid and a refusal to hear all evidence may be grounds to upset the arbitration decision, arbitrations can tend to go on forever, can become more expensive than litigation, and may not get the case resolved any quicker.

The quality of arbitrators can also vary greatly with some having difficulty deciding cases correctly. Because the benefits of arbitration are unclear, the trend toward requiring arbitration instead of litigation in real estate contracts has been curtailed to some extent. The arbitration requirement has now been deleted from some real estate contracts in favor of traditional court litigation. For example, the standard real estate "Purchase Contract" used by real estate agents in Hawai'i was recently revised to delete the mandatory arbitration requirement.

To me, arbitration and litigation are now a toss up with no clear-cut advantage to either. If your case is assigned to a good judge that your attorney has confidence in then you should stick with the judge. On the other hand, if your case is assigned to a poor judge and you can agree with the other side on a good arbitrator, then you may want to opt for arbitration. For example, both sides in a court case I handled recently agreed to arbitration instead of going through the litigation process. We selected a very experienced retired judge as the arbitrator, and my client just received a very fair award that the other side has paid in full. In that case, the arbitration was completed promptly and worked out very well for my client.

TIP Arbitrations can tend to go on forever, become more expensive than litigation, and may not get the case resolved any quicker. Because the benefits of arbitration are unclear, the trend toward requiring arbitration instead of litigation in real estate contracts has been curtailed somewhat.

LITIGATION IS YOUR LAST RESORT

If you are unable to resolve the dispute by negotiation or mediation and your contract does not require arbitration, then you are left with litigation. As I said earlier, litigation can be very expensive and emotionally draining. The direct cost—meaning cash—can be very high, and the indirect costs in terms of wasted time and emotional energy can be even higher. But there are also opportunities to resolve the dispute. The court will usually agree upon a request by either party to conduct settlement conferences in an effort to resolve the case early and without the expense of a trial. The court may also appoint a mediator to help settle the case. In my experience, a court-appointed mediator has a better chance of success than one without court backing.

In one case where I was acting as a court-appointed mediator, several of the parties were not even paying their own lawyers or returning their phone calls, much less contributing to a settlement of the case. Because I had been appointed by the court, I was able to get the presidents of those large companies on the phone and get their attention with some direct talk, and eventually I got their cooperation in contributing to a global settlement of a number of complicated interrelated cases.

There may also be opportunities to file motions to decide or limit issues in advance of the trial. However, generally things are not going well if you are embroiled in the litigation process. If you end up there, then you are left with no alternative but to do your best to win with the understanding that it will be very expensive.

A case earlier in my career demonstrates the financial and emotional toll that litigation can take. I recall sitting at the counsel table in court in the morning waiting for the trial to resume. The man on the opposing side was sitting at his table, waiting for his lawyer to arrive. I could not help feeling sorry for him; he looked so dejected. His lawyer had refused to settle the case, and he had been forced to go into this trial that was not going well for him. Things took a turn for the worse when the sheriff came in and served him with a complaint in a separate case that had been filed against him by his own lawyer to collect the fees he was owed. This caused a great deal of dissention between the client and his lawyer who arrived a few minutes later. The dissention lasted through the rest of the trial and probably contributed to the large monetary award the court made against this poor individual. Leaving aside the ethical problems with his lawyer, this graphically demonstrates the emotional and financial cost of litigation.

TIP The direct cost—meaning cash—of litigation can be very high, and the indirect costs in terms of wasted time and emotional energy can be even higher.

NEVER QUIT TRYING TO RESOLVE THE DISPUTE NO MATTER WHERE YOU ARE IN THE PROCESS

Always keep in mind that mediation, arbitration, and litigation are only means to an end: resolving a dispute. No matter where you stand in these processes, you should never quit trying to resolve the case on some basis you can live with. Never quit trying to work things out with the other side. Also never hesitate to take the initiative in trying to settle. Don't worry too much about appearing weak because you have taken the initiative. Only a fool would not want to settle a case if it is at all possible. The other side is probably not having any more fun than you are, and as both sides get progressively more fed up with the time and expense of litigation, they may be more willing to settle. So never stop trying to come up with alternative ways to resolve the dispute.

TIP Don't worry too much about appearing weak because you have taken the initiative to settle. Only a fool would not want to settle a case if it is at all possible.

Several years ago I represented the developer of the only large, new oceanfront hotel developed in Waikiki over the past twenty years. The owners and residents of the condominium apartment building across the street had opposed his project from the beginning through their association of apartment owners. They had contested the shoreline permit required for any oceanfront development in Hawai'i and had appealed the granting of that permit all the way through the court system. They also contested a number of zoning variances that the developer required for the construction of the hotel. To say that my client had a great deal of animosity toward these people would be an understatement.

I filed a motion in the case to have the variances upheld as a matter of law so that my client could proceed with the construction of the hotel. The argument before the judge went very well. We were well organized and made a clear, compelling presentation using visual aids, while our opposition made a sloppy, disjointed presentation. The judge also appeared receptive to our arguments. To observers in the courtroom, including my client, it looked like we were sure to win. I told my client after the hearing that I thought the judge's positive reaction was because of my favorable relationship with him, and that my intuition was telling me that we were going to lose the motion and the variances that would sabotage his plans for the hotel. My client was not buying it. He was at the hearing, and he was confident we were going to win.

Nevertheless, I started negotiations with the lawyer on the other side for my client to make a cash payment to the condo association in exchange for dropping its opposition to the variances. The association finally agreed to accept $150,000 to drop the case. My client refused, even though this case could sabotage his $100 million hotel project if he lost. He was also infuriated with me for wasting time and showing weakness by negotiating with his enemies. He told me to stop dealing with them and just wait for the judge's favorable decision. I got the judge to postpone his decision and continued to negotiate a reduced amount with the association. The client also rejected that offer and threatened to fire me. I continued to negotiate. Finally, the association agreed to accept $55,000 to settle the case. My client was very angry with me, but I kept calling and recommending that he accept the offer. I pointed out how small the amount was and how much was at stake. He told me never to call again about the offer. I continued to call. He again threatened to fire me. I did not let up, and he finally agreed to accept the offer and paid the $55,000 to settle the case. My client considered it a complete waste of money since he was confident he was going to win.

I went to see the judge after the case was settled, and he told me that he thought all the variances were wrong and that he was going to strike down all of them. Shortly after we settled the case on the variances, we won the appeal on the shoreline permit, and my client was able to proceed with what is now a beautiful oceanfront hotel owned and operated by another one of my clients. So this story had a happy and profitable ending, which is your goal in all real estate deals. The moral here is this: Keep trying to settle, and never take the risk of an adverse court decision if you can avoid it.

So, don't reconcile yourself to trudge down the path of seemingly endless acrimony in litigation if you can get a resolution you can live with. You are almost always better off settling than you will be by taking the risk of an uncertain outcome in litigation. Because of the complication of real estate deals and the limited remedies that can be provided by the court, in many situations a settlement is often a much better resolution for both parties than litigation, even for the "winner." In short, you may not be able to get what you really need from a court decision, even if you win.

How to Resolve Real Estate Disputes

Try to resolve the disputes you cannot avoid by doing the following:

- Consult with an experienced litigation lawyer to avoid litigation.
- When disputes arise, do whatever you can to work it out.
- Try mediation.
- Consider arbitration.
- Litigation is your last resort.
- Never stop trying to resolve the dispute no matter where you are in this process.

CONCLUSION

You are almost always better off settling your disputes in a reasonable, fair way that respects the interests of the other parties while protecting your own than you are having the dispute decided by an arbitrator, a judge, or a jury. And most of all, the best solution is to avoid disputes altogether by going into the right real estate projects, with the right people, the right mind-set, the right contracts, and the right legal representation.

 **Bernie Bays** is a partner in Bays, Deaver, Lung, Rose & Holma, a boutique real estate firm based in Honolulu, Hawai'i, and is one of the few attorneys in Hawai'i who is board certified as a civil trial specialist by the National Board of Trial Advocacy and the Hawai'i Supreme Court. During his thirty-eight year career, Bernie has represented clients in landmark real estate cases before the Hawai'i Intermediate Court, the Hawai'i Supreme Court, and the U.S. Supreme Court. His experience encompasses a broad range of business and real estate cases, including the representation of minority and majority shareholders, corporate proxy fights, antitrust representation of both plaintiffs and defendants, as well as litigation concerning real estate sales, commercial leases, land use problems, rent renegotiations, claims for economic loss and lost profit, property damage, general and limited partner disputes, condominium and subdivision problems, land valuation issues, and condemnation.

PART 2

Your Real Estate Project

Buy by the Acre,
Sell by the Foot
Understanding Real Needs, Financial Logic, and Asking Questions

Mel is my neighbor. We met at a neighborhood holiday party. I liked him immediately because he is a real estate developer and was a longtime owner of two professional sports teams. There is nothing like sitting in the owner's seat at a Phoenix Suns basketball game. The players, cheerleaders, and the action are much more intense at the court level. Usually I sit higher up and need to use binoculars to see the game.

One of the advantages of having a friend like Mel is that I get to find out where the next growth areas are going to be. Being a land developer, he is operating three-to-ten years out into the future. Not only do his developments expand the city, Mel and his high-profile team are responsible for bringing new life back into downtown urban areas.

Mel is a great neighbor, friend, and a real estate visionary. Whenever I want to know about the future and where to invest, I call Mel Shultz.

—ROBERT KIYOSAKI

Have you ever been driving around your city or town and passed by an open field and wondered if that field might be the only undeveloped land in the area? I asked myself that question many times, and actually found it pretty fascinating. I found it so fascinating, in fact, that the question itself actually jump-started my real estate career, and the discovery became my strategy.

Driving through your city or town can reveal a great deal about real estate. For instance, you may have noticed that houses tend to dot the interiors of most cities and towns while shopping, office, and other commercial properties generally run along the major streets. This all makes sense once you start to notice and make mental notes of how most cities and towns develop.

In the late 1970s, driving around seemed like a good way to find real estate. I didn't own any sophisticated tools other than maps and a car to explore opportunities, although I did buy one of the first giant mobile phones that looked and felt like a brick. Driving along the main streets of my city provided all the options needed to buy property during this time before instant information. When I saw larger parcels that were skipped over by development, yet were right in the path of growth or on the beaten path, it made sense to find out who owned these underserved parcels and inquire about the status. It seems pretty simple and obvious; however, there were ample spots that were ignored by most land buyers and developers. Finding the owners was just one call away to the title company. Once I found the owner's number, I handled it just like I learned in my insurance business training: pick up the phone and meet the prospect. These prospects were slightly different, though. Rather than the buyers I was used to calling, this time I was calling sellers, and I was offering to give people money rather than asking them to write checks.

Hard to believe, but it's always easier to buy something than it is to sell. Think about it. In your own life, you'll find it to be true. The problem is that the owner knows that what they own is valuable, so it's worth holding on to. On the other hand, the owner may not want to go through the process and the risk of investing the time and money it takes to plan and perform feasibility studies, as well as other land-use studies that may be required to develop the property.

Even though real estate can be very tax favorable, the process and final entitlement received on the land may negatively affect the tax status for some owners. We always discuss these kinds of tax issues with our tax advisors to be sure we are never crossing the lines, or if we are, to be fully informed of the negative tax implications. This is a complex part of the equation, and I absolutely recommend finding the best real estate tax counsel before even beginning to zone or make any changes to a piece of real estate. It is just as important to understand the tax and legal aspects at the beginning of a property transaction so you can get off on the right foot, as it is to understand these same implications when selling the property purchased. This cannot be emphasized enough. Talk to professional tax and legal experts.

I regularly hire and talk to CPAs and lawyers before getting too far down the road in real estate. My brother's law practice was the logical entry place for me. It is the oldest law firm in Arizona with expertise in all areas of real estate. I believed from the beginning that a portion of my investment dollars were to be earmarked, first for the land and, second for lawyers and other consultants who could better my chances for success.

The value of a team is self-evident. I always wanted to be the quarterback of our team at school. I knew the position was less about heroics and more about being sure the best support was in front of me. My job then was simply to remember the plays and throw or hand the ball to the best players.

TIP The *Dictionary of Real Estate Terms,* Sixth Edition, defines "entitlement" as this: The right to develop land with government approvals for zoning density, utility installations, occupancy permits, use permits, and streets.

MATCHING MARKET NEEDS WITH PRODUCT CREATION

Just because you buy a hotel doesn't mean it has to stay a traditional hotel. Just because you buy an apartment building doesn't mean it needs to stay an apartment building. Markets change, market needs change, and in order to be successful, you may find you have to change a property from one kind of product to another. Here are a few examples:

Converting a traditional hotel into a timeshare property.
Converting a rental apartment into a for-purchase apartment to the renter or another buyer.

These are examples of matching market needs with product creation. Space that already existed was transformed to create new revenue sources based on market demands.

When it comes to land, changes may involve simply splitting one larger lot into two or more residential lots or changing land permitted for one use to a different use that is usually better economically. Most often this requires the approval of the city or town (municipality) to consent to the proposed use change. This is called rezoning and/or the entitlement process.

Real Life Story: The Education on 32nd Street

In the mid 1970s, I bought a house on about five acres for $240,000. Within a short time, a friend asked if he could buy the home. His intent was to change the zoning from one house per acre to commercial/office use. He offered to pay triple my price with the caveat that the closing had to wait for up to twelve months. He figured it would take that long to convince all the residents on the north and south sides of the property to agree and the city to approve his rezoning plan. This was my first personal experience watching someone change the use (rezoning) of a property. I was in my mid-twenties, and it seemed worth waiting a year to make such a compelling profit.

Time passed; his rezoning was approved, and we closed the deal. This was an early eye opener. Suddenly, it hit me! I could add value by changing the use of the underlying land. I decided this was to be part of my new investment path.

Real Life Story: View from the Mountain

With confidence from my 32nd Street experience, I purchased the twenty-nine-thousand-square-foot McCune Mansion in Paradise Valley, Arizona. The monstrous mansion was built by oil tycoon Walker McCune in the 1960s for more than $3 million. The mansion sat on forty acres of hillside that overlooked the entire city and the spectacular Camelback Mountain. My plan was to change the use from a single home to a resort. The city fought the rezoning, so I decided to go with what they called preferred residential zoning, which included the "hillside ordinance." This is where I truly became a real estate developer and gained firsthand knowledge about the zoning process and lot layout. Each lot building pad had to meet complicated cut-and-fill requirements—how much you could cut into the mountainside and fill back in to create a building pad. I ended up on the committee with real homebuilders rewriting the town ordinances for slope-and-hillside cutting and refilling. In the process, I found a buyer who purchased the mansion for the price I paid for the entire forty acres and mansion. The sale included the mansion and five acres, which I carved out around the house. I then held onto the remaining land, which was now converted into twenty-eight one-acre-plus home sites. The lots sold from $200,000 to $600,000, and I had made my biggest profit yet. I retained one lot to build a home for my family, but the "desert snakes" were not my friends, so I made the decision to sell at a later time. Sales topped $10 million.

My early experience with the mansion on the mountain got me thinking about the economics of the land business. There's a story about Abe Lincoln's farm that makes the point about creative financial engineering better than I could ever make on my own. It seems Abe Lincoln bought his family's farm from his father, Thomas, when cash got a little tight as a way to bail him out. Eventually, after Abe became president and one of the great figures of our country, the friends of the Abe Lincoln Historical Farm near Lerna, Illinois, took on the ownership. It seems the owners of this land had a brilliant idea. They wanted to give people of Illinois and the nation the opportunity to own a tiny piece of American history in an effort to raise money for the owner's family. They planned to sell off small parcels of the estate to interested people. When they parceled out the designated acre, they had more than six million squares to offer the public. The net return on this is not known, but even with a low price for the land parcel, I am sure it was substantial.

This is the ultimate subdivision of land, almost beyond the scope of imagination. But I'm sure it won't be the last ingenious idea. If I had to start over today in the real estate business, what would I do? I can answer that question this way. In the late 1970s we would joke about a wealthy private lender and investor named Bill Levine. We'd say that if he were dropped out of a plane with a parachute on his back in the middle of China and with no money, within a few years he would be one of the wealthiest men in China or wherever else he happened to fall. Some people just seem to know how to create wealth. They are the true financial engineers.

TIP Starting is the hardest part of anything in life.

Starting is the hardest part of anything in life. In the early 1970s I had saved up about $5,000 from my life insurance sales commissions. A real estate firm in my building had several older, unoccupied houses it was trying to unload. Inside these old house bones lay bright red carpeting, purple-painted walls, and linoleum floors from the 1950s. Even the carpet stains were better than the original colors.

The cash requirement to acquire these homes was straightforward: pay closing costs, include a few hundred dollars in commissions, and assume the debt. I thought why not? I soon found that renting these showplaces was not easy because after I had purchased the properties I didn't have enough money to repaint and update the interiors, nor did I have the mechanical skills to do it myself. But somehow, enough renters were willing to take the houses and do their own fix ups. From the cash flow I received, I was able to buy more houses and sell some along the way, accumulating about $10,000 in cash. I didn't like the rent collection process much, so after selling my last house in 1973, I immediately moved on to something a little more sophisticated.

My first office building was just east of 24th Street on Thomas Road in Phoenix, Arizona, as were my second and third buildings. My logic was after buying my first building and not knowing where else to buy, it seemed like a good idea to go next door and buy those buildings, too. If it hadn't been for other opportunities that came my way, I may have just kept buying along the same major road in Phoenix. What did I know? These small office buildings were, for me, where it really all began.

After selling the first building and making $30,000, I began to get some traction. The next two were sold as a package with $130,000 in net profit. A California syndicator was looking for more buildings in Phoenix, and I liked the idea of negotiating the purchase and sale. My strategy was to buy and improve the properties, much like the houses I owned, except this time I wanted to be able to afford to hire contractors. After my house experiences, I learned to set aside cash up front for this purpose. The old painted white brick needed a modern look, so we put in new windows and doors, added beige-colored stucco to the brick exterior, new signage, and a parking lot. This clean, new exterior brought the building back to life. First impressions are lasting.

STARTING OFF WITH REAL ESTATE MATH

Getting started with basic real estate math is helpful to me. There are 43,560 square feet in one acre, and there are 640 acres in a section of land. The question arises regarding land uses and valuations. Commercial land is a higher economic use than a similar size residential-sized lot. In the course of planning, developers study the market demands and the appropriate use of a parcel of land and determine the best land use before buying. The planning and zoning process, which I learned after my house buying experience, incorporates the information learned along with the market demand to create the highest and best use. With that said, consider the math for a parcel of land. It may look something like this:

On the next page is a very simple illustration of buying in bulk at a "per acre" price and converting to a "square foot" price. Usually land owners sell large parcels of unzoned land in areas outside traditional development cores in bulk at a per-acre price. In urban areas, commercial or multifamily property is usually sold by the square foot. It's really a convenience because it all reverts back to the dollar amount paid for the land, the ultimate sales price, and profit.

Buying by the Acre, and Selling by the Foot

This example may help you see the potential of real estate in a new way.

The purchase price of ten acres is $50,000 per acre, or $500,000 total (zoned for ten houses).

The final plan for ten acres may be 250 apartment units, which may be worth $10,000 per unit or $250,000 per acre (after rezoning approval).

This equates to about $5.75 per square foot (43,560 square foot x $5.74 = $250,000 per acre).

Since the land was acquired for single family and changed to multifamily, the underlying use created an increased value of five times the original purchase.

This practice is convenient for both the buyer and seller. It's similar to the way we use inches as a measurement division of a foot. For example, rather than say it's one-quarter of a foot, we say say three inches, which is easily understood. Perhaps smaller measurement practices were used to influence a buyer's perception of the amount being paid for the product. It is like figuring out why gold is sold by the ounce and not by the pound. At the end of the day, it's perception.

Many other projects followed for me. I developed everything from business parks to large, master-planned communities. The lesson I learned through it all was to plan and divide the land, visualizing what a property could be and what it "wanted" to be. A residential community wants a compatible use like a grocery store, restaurant, pharmacy, or other convenience. That means forcing a property to a higher-return use doesn't make sense if it doesn't blend and fit into the surroundings. You've driven around your town and seen buildings that don't fit. The right products in the right places feel right and look right, and the neighbors know that. I saw how my friend, Joe Beer, went house-to-house to let the neighbors give input, to ask them questions, and most important, to listen as he petitioned for rezoning. This is a good practice particularly if you do this with forethought and patience and are willing to modify and compromise and be sensitive to the neighbors. You may actually find throughout the process that the land you bought by the acre may indeed be sold by the square foot.

Let me share a personal story. I was involved a few years back in the sale of a site for a post office. The buyer wanted an environmental report to ensure there were no hazardous substances on the site. This is very typical. But as my partners and I were working our way through the due diligence process with the buyer, an environmental problem came to our attention. Although the issue

> ## Three "Must Do's" to Buy by the Acre and Sell by the Foot:
>
> 1. Plan and divide the land thoughtfully.
> 2. Work with the neighbors in the community.
> 3. Always be willing to listen and compromise.

seemed to possess a very low chance of causing any real problem, the inspectors sent over a backhoe to test the area. During the test, a sample of soil showed a completely new problem: The sample contained oil. Impossible, we thought. So, they tested the same sample again with the same results. Perplexed and bracing ourselves for a costly soil remediation, which given the past use of the property seemed unfathomable, we decided to take a walk around the property. Thank goodness we did this. While we were walking by the backhoe, one of us noticed it had an oil leak. Upon further inspection, the oils matched up with the leaky equipment. Retested with a new backhoe, the soil turned up clean as originally expected. Walking the site can make all the difference. Hands on requires a physical look, not just reading a report.

TIP I have always enjoyed walking around the properties we are buying. For me, seeing is the difference between knowing and guessing.

WISDOM FROM THE FIELD

If you want to get involved in real estate (and not just when the economy is booming) then the following questions may come in handy:

HOW CAN I LEARN THE BASICS OF PROPERTY USES AND POTENTIAL CHANGES TO USE?

Each city and or municipality has its own ordinances and laws for permitted uses for property. Find a good zoning lawyer and inquire about current zoning and permitted changes. A planner or architect who has planned and designed other local projects is the best source for ideas. Real estate brokers are also an important part of determining potential tenants or other buyers and/or developers for parts or all of a properly thought-out land use plan.

WHO ARE THE KEY MEMBERS OF MY TEAM, AND WHAT DO THEY DO?

In addition to the zoning lawyer, the land planner or architect and the brokers (both leasing and sales) are critical. You'll need the following team members to help you along the way:

FEASIBILITY EXPERTS

This may include economists and often larger brokerage companies who gather and compile sector reports for vacancy, lease rates, absorption and other reports to help determine need for product type.

ACCOUNTANT

This person can put together a financial pro forma to estimate sales, costs, and potential profits so you can determine your offer price and capital/debt/equity requirements. The broker should provide sales input projections.

CIVIL ENGINEERS, SOIL EXPERTS, AND CONTRACTORS

These experts will help you determine the improvement cost estimates you will need to fully evaluate the property's potential from topographical and physical maps to understanding wet and dry utilities.

When you consider the many disciplines required to make all this come together you see why many avoid this aspect of real estate. It sounds harder than it really is. Although patience and knowledge are required, after the first few deals the process becomes clear. It is much like an NBA point guard or a quarterback on a football field. Most of your time is spent knowing where your teammates are and who to get the ball to. Rarely do you shoot or run; passing the ball is essential. You learn by doing, and starting with a simple lot split for a couple of houses is an easy way to experience the process firsthand.

HOW DO I FIND PROPERTY THAT CAN BE REZONED OR CHANGED TO BECOME A PROFITABLE VENTURE?

This is the bottom line of the whole exercise. Knowing the market needs and economics of the specific product that will ultimately be built on the site takes study and some imagination. Ask questions and write them down. The more questions you have, the better. A few, but important questions you could ask are these: What would improve the living quality and/or convenience for the people who live or work in the area?

How many people drive by this particular property each day?

How can I help people afford to live in the area or give them a better alternative for a retail shopping or dining experience?

What about better medical care closer to home or more convenient services in a certain area?

These questions stimulate the imagination and the possibilities. Most people ask too few questions. You can build a case for almost any business model if you ask enough of the right questions.

Bill Gates, founder of Microsoft, was interested in information at the speed of thought. Billionaire Warren Buffett considered simple businesses that are run well and provide capital to grow, as places to invest. These investment strategies have vaulted them to become two of the wealthiest men in the world. Mr. Buffett is the master of asking questions then boiling them down to the few most direct and succinct ones that become repeatable observations. True genius is when you can make the unnoticed concise. Ask and write down a few questions about land you have noticed regularly.

Why has this been skipped over by the path of development?
Who owns it?
What is the right use or fit for it?
How would the math look if it were used in a different way?
Who would buy or rent whatever I think should be built on this site?

After the experience of completing your first real estate process, you will have exercised your mind in a way that will help you look at land through new eyes. The fun for me is to drive by or walk into a project I have been a part of and know this was a piece of land few considered would ever be a place where people would want to live, work and play.

After thirty years of planning, negotiating, visualizing, building, and selling these ideas, I've learned that virtually anything is possible if you ask questions. Analyze and think through the answers, and take the steps to get your mind's ideas into pictures and then later into bricks. Remember, bricks are laid one upon another just like your thoughts. The hardest part is setting the first brick in place.

Mel Shultz cofounded JDM Properties, Inc., in 1983 as a full-service real estate firm that develops and manages quality properties in Arizona and Colorado, including upscale residential and commercial space, and business parks. A principal of JDMD Investments, LLC, Mel and his partners are developing the largest master-planned community in the greater Phoenix area for more than three hundred thousand residents. Mel was a general partner of the Phoenix Suns basketball team until the team sold in 2005, and he was one of the original general partners of the 2001 World Championship Arizona Diamondbacks baseball team. Mel led the design and build team for the five-thousand-seat Dodge Theatre in downtown Phoenix. The company's Web site is www.jdmpartnersllc.com.

It's All About Adding Value

I once accused Curtis of going "where white men fear to tread." He laughed out loud and said, "That's true." He went on to say, "I have basketball star Magic Johnson's philosophy of going into urban areas and bringing in development and businesses that lift the area up." Curtis then added, "Regardless of race, too many investors just suck the cash out of a neighborhood but never reinvest to improve it. I invest to reinvest and improve a neighborhood." This is why Curtis and his wife, Diana, are respected friends as well as fellow real estate investors.

Today, some of the most beautiful real estate is being boarded up as casualties of economic decline. It takes a special kind of investor to invest not only to make money, but to also bring an area in decline back up. I tried it once and did okay but not great. Truthfully, I was an outsider coming in, hoping to make a quick buck from a bad situation. Now personally wiser, I have a better appreciation for what Curtis does. It takes more than knowing about real estate. It takes knowing the people and the psychology of the neighborhood, and, most importantly, having a desire to be a part of the community. This is what I have learned about real estate from Curtis and Diana.

—ROBERT KIYOSAKI

As a successful real estate agent, investor, and developer, I've shared a stage as a presenter with Robert Kiyosaki, who is a personal mentor to me. His ideas and guidance have been instrumental in much of my success. I have presented seminars with Donald Trump, as well as coauthored with him an audio CD entitled *Three Master Secrets of Real Estate Success*. At this writing, my wife and I are renovating a multimillion-dollar home in an exclusive San Francisco neighborhood. To boil it all down, I have achieved all of this by following a simple mantra, one that anyone can understand and apply to achieve similar real estate successes: Profit from problems. There are two foundational things that have been a constant for my wife, Diana, and I throughout our process: knowledge and faith.

"My people shall be destroyed because of a lack of knowledge," *Hosea 4:6*.

"Faith is the confidence that what we hope for will actually happen. It gives us assurance about things we cannot see," *Hebrews 11:1*.

TIP Your mantra should be this: Profit from problems.

A pristine property with affluent tenants sounds wonderful, doesn't it? No huge maintenance issues, little problem collecting rents, and so on. Yes, these types of properties are easy on the mind, *but they also have a significant cost and little chance to appreciate.*

A problem property, on the other hand, has an amazing, and fast, upside potential. For example, let's say that the going rate for a building in a certain area is $200,000. The problem property might be worth $140,000. Once the problems are fixed, however, its value will zoom to the going rate for similar properties: $200,000. Likewise, rents in a problem building might be low. After you improve the property, however, you can raise rents—increasing your amount of income.

This is the concept of "forced appreciation," which occurs when an investor purchases a property that's less than the going market value (usually due to inherent problems, such as high vacancy rates, severely deteriorated buildings, environmental problems, etc.), then fixes the problems that "force" substantial appreciation in value back up to the current market value. I also call this the value-added approach, where you take an asset, make various improvements, and have the asset increase in value. Forced appreciation provides you with a short-term paper profit, which you can then use to your advantage in a variety of ways. This value-added approach has helped many, many real estate investors build everything from small nest eggs to multibillion-dollar fortunes.

TIP I never focus on or count on appreciation when analyzing whether or not to purchase a property. To me, market appreciation is always a bonus: if it happens, great, but if the property doesn't go up in value based on the market, that's okay, too, because I know that I am making what I need to make on the property in terms of cash flow and depreciation. Likewise, when someone says that they have an investment that will provide capital gains, thank them, then turn and run in the other direction! Why? Capital gains are based on the speculation that something "might" happen in the future to drive up the value of that investment. The key word here is speculation; something might happen. By focusing on a value-added approach to real estate investing, you have much greater control over a property's ultimate value.

If you resolve to become a problem solver—someone who embraces rather than runs away from problems—your chances of achieving success in real estate investing will dramatically increase. The next step becomes finding appropriate problem properties.

My Story

I purchased my first home in Philadelphia, Pennsylvania, in 1979 for $27,800. I used the G.I. Bill, which meant I had 100 percent financing. I had an adjustable rate loan with an interest rate of 17.5 percent. That's obscene by today's standards, but at the time I didn't care. I was thrilled to be a new homeowner, period. This also was my introduction to leverage, which is using a small amount of money to purchase a large amount of something else (in this case, real estate). I began to buy properties as long as I didn't have to put much money down. I didn't care what the interest rate was; as long as I had a positive cash flow, I bought.

My life as a real estate entrepreneur took another big leap in 1982 when I resigned from my government job for the Naval Aviation Supply Office. From the beginning, I specialized in value-added properties. In Philadelphia, boarded-up houses were practically everywhere, and that's what I looked for. Buying and then turning was easy because I could buy a property for between $5,000 and $30,000 and then decide to either rent or sell.

I had an uncle who came to visit me from San Francisco, California. Every time he came to visit, he would go on and on about the San Francisco real estate market. In 1985 he finally convinced me to move to San Francisco to invest in value-added real estate. However, little did I know that my Philadelphia success in renting and flipping houses couldn't be duplicated in San Francisco. Why? Simply because property was so much more expensive. The average duplex at the time was $250,000. These prices sent my nervous system into shock and fear. While I had accumulated some funds to invest, I needed a lot more information about California real estate before I could begin.

TIP I've had my share of challenges and problems. But with patience and the right approach, value-added real estate investing can work for you, too.

In the meantime, the cost of living and real estate school was beginning to deplete my investment nest egg. What's more, this fear of potentially losing everything held me captive. I wouldn't do a deal if I saw one! I finally got my real estate license and immediately went to work in an area in San Francisco to duplicate my success in Philadelphia. However, in Philadelphia it was relatively easy to identify value-added real estate. Just find a boarded-up house at a cheap price, fix it up, and sell it. In San Francisco, however, there were no boarded-up houses. I had to figure out how to add value in other ways. I finally found the area and the niche. The area was called Bayview Hunter's Point, and the niche was called "in-law apartments." So I went to work buying single-family homes (which were selling, at the time, for $50,000 to $75,000) and adding in-law apartments in the rear of the garages for rental units. Once construction was completed, I could sell the house for between $175,000 and $199,000. I had a full-time construction crew, and we were rehabbing and flipping, and life was good. Now, there are potential pitfalls—I've had my share of challenges and problems. But with patience and the right approach, value-added real estate investing can work for you, too.

FINDING THE RIGHT PROPERTIES

Now we've come to the exciting part, right? Right! Finding the right properties to invest in is obviously at the heart of long-term and sustained success in real estate investing. It's the area that will tap all of your knowledge and creativity, and where over time you'll build experience and expertise. You'll come to rely on this time and time again. Finding the right properties is equal parts knowledge and your ability to creatively "see" a property's potential. In short, here's where we marry your brain with your intuition to achieve a complete solution (wholeness).

First, let's review property types and property classes.

PROPERTY TYPES

The three types of buildings I'd like to focus on in this chapter are as follows:

Residential. Users live in one to four units. Can be various types, such as single family, duplex (two units), triplex (three units), and fourplex (four units).

Commercial. Five or more business units, such as an office building or a strip mall.

Mixed Use. A single building with both residential (people live there) and commercial (businesses) options.

If you are just starting out investing in real estate, I suggest that you begin by purchasing a two-or four-unit property. This way, you can begin small, leverage your way into a property, learn all you can, and then move up to a larger property when you have experience and a positive cash flow.

PROPERTY CLASSES

There are four classes of properties:

Class A. A property less than ten years old, in excellent condition, and with desired amenities, such as a pool or workout center. Class A properties can ask for, and receive, high rents, generally have a better quality of tenants, usually have lower maintenance costs, and are easier to manage. These properties are usually held by (owned by) investor groups and have a lower rate of return. They are the most sensitive to any downturn in the local or national economy.

Class B. Buildings that are ten to twenty years old and in fairly good overall condition. Class B properties are considered the most stable of the different property classes, and are usually located in well-established, middle-income neighborhoods. They are new enough to offer amenities, yet still old enough to be affordable to the average investor and tenants.

Class C. Buildings between twenty and thirty years old with limited or nonexistent amenities. Both ongoing and long-term maintenance costs are higher because of aging and the general need for a cosmetic "facelift." They have a lower quality of tenants, including those on government assistance. Value can be added by updating the property.

Class D. Buildings more than thirty years old that need substantial capital improvements. Usually located in declining areas, Class D properties usually have substantial deferred maintenance issues, such as the need to replace the roof, the electrical system, the HVAC system, etc.

TIP For beginning investors, I suggest that you focus most of your attention on finding *undervalued Class C buildings*.

You can look for undervalued properties in any of the four classes. However, please note that for Class A properties, the velocity of your money—the amount flowing to you—will slow down simply because there is less upside potential. For beginning investors, I suggest that you focus most of your attention on finding *undervalued Class C buildings*.

STARTING YOUR SEARCH

Here are the steps I recommend to find undervalued properties.

STEP ONE: BECOME AN EXPERT IN A PARTICULAR AREA

This generally is the area in which you live. Attempting to become an expert in a city outside of the state in which you reside, for example, would be time consuming and costly. Do as much as you can to study the area. Read the real estate sections in the local newspapers, drive around, and attend open houses.

This area should be large enough to have diverse neighbors. For example your initial area might be San Francisco. Over time, once you feel that you've mastered this particular area, then move on to another area.

Here's an example:

1. Select San Francisco as your area
2. Explore it, study it, drive around, etc.
3. "Master" this area
4. Then select another area such as Oakland

STEP TWO: SEEK OUT THE LEAST EXPENSIVE SECTIONS WITHIN THAT AREA

Again, you want to find problem properties and then solve the problems. You'll find the juiciest problems—and thus the potential for the largest returns—in the least expensive sections of your focus area.

STEP THREE: LOOK FOR PROBLEM PROPERTIES

Once you've become an expert in a particular area and identified the least expensive section within that area, the next step is to begin hunting for problem properties in that least expensive section.

How do you identify problem properties? They're usually the eyesore on a street or block. Signs to look for include buildings with one or more of these attributes:

- vacant
- boarded up
- tall grass / weeds
- trash strewn about / overflowing trash cans
- broken windows
- peeling paint
- general poor appearance

You also should be alert to potential property changes, such as:

- building owner wanting to retire / leave
- foreclosures
- probate
- code violations
- zoning variances not renewed or up for re-hearing
- a big-box tenant just left a strip mall

Please note that searching for real estate investment opportunities can be extremely fun, but it also can be an extremely frustrating process.

Tips As You Begin Your Property Search:

- **Stay positive.** Searches take time and involve walking around neighborhoods. There will be missteps and false alarms. Stay positive and have fun, and you'll be in the right frame of mind when the right property appears.

- **Be present and focused.** As much as possible, shut out past failures, negative thoughts ("The market hasn't bottomed out yet"), fears of failure, fears of success, and all other factors that might prevent you from seeing—really seeing—an opportunity. Those who are present and open to opportunities are almost always the people who are able to grab a new opportunity when it comes along.

- **Put in the time.** There's a saying in the writing world: To write a book, apply the seat of your pants to the chair. The same is true when searching for real estate investment opportunities. You must get out and look for the opportunities. You have to study the newspapers, drive around town, and network with real estate agents and lenders.

- **Don't be put off by market conditions.** Rarely will you find "perfect" market conditions when making any investment. There are always problems and potential pitfalls. Know this and accept it. Don't let the media, friends, or anyone else discourage you from seeking opportunities.

This last point bears repeating—never be discouraged by fluctuating market conditions. Interest rates will always go up, unless they happen to be going down. Property values will continue to decline until they hit bottom, and then they will rebound. And so on.

TIP This should be your "Real Estate Opportunity Search" mantra: In *any* market, at *any* time, I can find a great deal.

TIP Here is your "Never Give Up" mantra: Diligence leads to destiny.

You should actively search out potential deals. As well, you should create networks of people, tools, and resources to send potential deals your way. Here are ways to create a flow of deals—or at least whispers about potential deals:

- www.loopnet.com
- other investors
- real estate agents and brokers
- real estate lenders
- attorneys
- CPAs
- property management companies

TABLE 10.1 Personal Reflections

Brainstorm and list who else might be a "deal source" for you:	

Property Criteria and Analysis

Once you've identified a potential investment property, it's time to closely study the property for both short-term and long-term opportunities. You will want to put each prospective property through a rigorous review, using the following criteria:

1. Guiding Investment Principles
    a. Leverage
    b. Cash Flow
    c. Cash-on-Cash Return
    d. Capitalization Rate
    e. Gross Rent Multiplier
2. S.W.O.T. (Strengths, Weaknesses, Opportunities, Threats)
3. Trends
4. Demographics

Now, I could write an entire book about these four key areas of property analysis. Here, though, let me summarize each of these points quickly.

Leverage

Leverage simply means that you want as little of your money as possible used to secure the biggest opportunity possible. The less money you have to invest in a property, in other words, the larger the opportunity for a big payoff. When analyzing a property, know exactly what you will initially need to invest.

Positive Cash Flow

A key to building my real estate fortune over the years has been cash flow. We call cash flow "king" because having cash is always our primary objective. Positive cash flow creates and maintains your investment's momentum. It also has significant financing and lending implications. For example, when purchasing an apartment building containing more than five units, the bank will base the amount it will lend you on the building's cash flow abilities. (Your credit score is secondary.) Cash flow also is a significant factor in the building's overall value. A building with poor cash flow will appraise much lower than another comparable building in the same area that has a stronger cash flow. Never forget that.

Double Digit Cash-on-Cash Return

This is the velocity of your money. In other words, you want to know at the beginning of an investment how long it will take the money you invest (primarily the down payment) to come back to you. This is critical because you want to invest that down payment over and over again in other investment properties, so the quicker that you're able to receive back that initial payment, the quicker you can apply it to another opportunity.

TIP Cash-on-Cash Return defined: This is the amount of cash you receive from a property investment in a specified time period as a percentage of your initial investment in that property.

TABLE 10.2

Down Payment	Yearly Cash Flow	Years to Pay Back Down Payment	Cash-on-Cash Return
$20,000	$20,000	1	100%
$20,000	$10,000	2	50%
$20,000	$6,000	3	33%

Here are several examples using the same down payment amount ($20,000) but different cash flow amounts per year.

As you can see, this table shows how many years it takes for your down payment to come back to you. In the first scenario, it takes one year. In the second scenario, it takes two years, and in the third, three years. Your cash-on-cash return is 100 percent, 50 percent, and 33 percent, respectively.

Your goal as an investor should be a cash-on-cash return in the 10 percent to 20 percent range. Anything above 20 percent is considered an exceptional cash-on-cash return.

CAPITALIZATION RATE OF 7 PERCENT OR HIGHER

The cap rate measures a building's performance without considering the mortgage financing. If you paid all cash for the invest property, how much money would it potentially make? What's the return? A high cap rate usually means a higher risk investment and a low sales price. High cap rates are typically found in poor, low-income areas. A low cap rate usually indicates there's less risk and a high sales price. Low cap rates are generally found in middle-class to upper-income areas. If you know the net operating income (NOI) and the cap rate, you can calculate what the sales price should be using this formula:

NOI / Cap Rate = Sales Price

TIP The Cap Rate measures a building's performance without taking into consideration the mortgage financing. It is the Net Operating Income divided by the sale price.

GROSS RENT MULTIPLIER OF 9 OR LOWER

Gross Rent Multipliers (GRM) are used as a measure to compare income properties within a particular area or neighborhood. For example, for three properties within a similar area of town, you could calculate the gross rent multiplier for each, then compare the three. If all other factors were equal, you would select the property with the lowest GRM. In general, as the gross rent multiplier decreases, cash flow increases. And conversely, as the GRM increases, cash flow typically decreases.

TIP Gross Rent Multiplier is the ratio of the price of a real estate investment to its annual rental income. The lower the ratio, the better.

S.W.O.T.

S.W.O.T. stands for Strengths, Weaknesses, Opportunities, and Threats. A common business evaluation tool, S.W.O.T. also applies to investment real estate simply because each property will have its own unique strengths, weaknesses, opportunities, and threats. The savvy real estate investor—the one seeking guaranteed success—will put each property through a detailed S.W.O.T. analysis.

Please note that generally speaking, this is a subjective analysis. In other words, there are no "right" or "wrong" answers. Likewise, many factors are interconnected. For example, a property's weakness—such as needing a fresh coat of paint—might also be an opportunity—a fresh coat of paint can quickly increase the overall look of the property, and thus its value.

TRENDS

Part of your property-seeking work should be to pay close attention to trends, or similar new tendencies displayed by a large number of people. For example, in the past, many city dwellers moved out of the city into the suburbs. Over the last several years, however, the trend has become the opposite. Because of rising gasoline prices and other factors, people in cities are "cocooning"—they want to live within walking distance of work, stores, restaurants, and so on.

Learning about new trends through the media and other information outlets is important. An investor will have become exposed to even more opportunities if he "sees" a new or developing trend before it becomes known and published through the media.

How can you spot new trends as they begin to develop? It's a bit of an art, but generally speaking you can:

- **Observe what's going on around you.** Pay particular attention to what people are doing differently. For example, eight or ten years ago, SUVs were all the rage. It seemed like everyone had one. Over time, however— again, because of rising gasoline prices and other environmental issues— SUV purchases declined, and a new type of transportation emerged called hybrid cars.

- **Read, read, read.** Read as much as you can: newspapers, magazines, local real estate magazines, and so on. And vary the sources and subject matter. What do I mean by "varied"? Every so often, read something different, a newspaper or periodical that you normally wouldn't read. As well, do a little Web surfing. What are people discussing on blogs in your community? What new Web sites are popping up on housing, community life, and other related topics? The more that you can broaden the information you take in, the more you can begin to see emerging trends and other issues. This is known, generally, as "connecting the dots." Become a dot-connector.

- **Listen, listen, listen.** Get out in the world, and then listen to people. What are they doing differently? What are thinking about doing differently? What are they interested in? Excited about? Fed up with? Your friends, family, neighbors, and business colleagues are a fantastic wealth of information regarding what's going on in the world. Ask questions, then listen to them.

DEMOGRAPHICS

A final part of your property analysis should be demographics, or statistical data about a particular population, such as the people in the city in which you want to invest. Demographic research provides a snapshot of population, income, industries, biggest employers, and other economic details for a particular city or area.

Demographic information can be found at libraries, city and county government offices, and of course the Internet offers an abundance of demographic information. Suggested Web sites to locate demographic information include:

- www.freedemographics.com
- http://realestate.yahoo.com/Neighborhoods
- http://realestate.yahoo.com/Homevalues
- www.elook.org
- www.economy.com (fee site)
- www.city-data.com
- http://quickfacts.census.gove/qfd/

Demographics That Favor Investing

When reviewing demographic information and trends, watch for these characteristics that are generally favorable for investing in a particular property:

- More females than males (females tend to "nest")
- Higher percentage of singles vs. married (singles rent apartments)
- Higher percentage of younger and older people versus middle-age (middle-age people buy homes).
- Annual income at or lower than $40,000 (home prices push them to rent apartments)
- The stability and profitability of the area's largest employer

---

Key information you also want to review regarding the property's physical location include the following:

- How close is it to public transportation?
- What's the city's plan for that particular area?
- How close is it to a park?
- How close is it to a school?
- How close is it to shopping and restaurants?

Finally, you should ask yourself a simple question:
Do you want to invest in this area?

KEY SUCCESS PRINCIPLE: HAVE A GREAT TEAM

As my wife, Diana, and I began to acquire what become more than twenty cash-flowing properties in San Francisco, we eventually put together a team to begin tackling larger problems. Our most successful team consisted of attorney Elizabeth Erhardt, who specializes in evictions, and Sia Tahbazof, whose engineering and architectural brilliance could always see the intrinsic value that others often could not see on adding value to a property. Diana and I would buy buildings in San Francisco with brick foundations or with difficult tenants paying very low rents under rent control, and we would quickly pull the trigger and close the deal. Our goal was to add value by completely remodeling all the buildings we purchased. Liz would negotiate deals with the tenants, and Sia would get all our plans quickly through the planning process. On most of our projects we used a 1031 Exchange to acquire larger properties and others we rented. They all cash-flowed, but what was even better was that for most of the properties the value tripled and not because the market went up or down.

Here's an important point: The relationship we had with our team was far more important than all of the money we ever made. There will never be a deal that is more important than the relationships. Today, Liz Erhardt is one of San Francisco's top attorneys regarding tenant/landlord issues. We are still very good friends; she will take my call and we go on and on about our "war stories" from the trenches fifteen years ago. Sia Tahbazof is semi-retired and works only on his own projects these days, but we are still very good friends. To this day Diana and I work exclusively with Sia Consulting Engineering on our local projects.

TIP The relationship we had with our team was far more important than all of the money we ever made. There will never be a deal that is more important than the relationships.

I believe a large part of our success as a team was based on the saying, "Everyone stay in their lane." (I remember running anchor at the Penn State relays in middle school and the track coach always saying, "Stay in your lane!") Staying in your lane shortens the race. Curtis's lane was to be in charge of the demo and rough work, and Diana's was in charge of the finishes; Liz was in charge of tenants; and Sia was engineering, design, plans, and the city's approval.

Always be thinking about how you can build the best team possible to support both your short- and long-term efforts.

TIP I believe a large part of our success as a team was based on the saying "Everyone stay in their lane" because staying in your lane shortens the race.

PROBLEMS . . . OR OPPORTUNITIES

If you resolve to become a problem solver, your chances of success in real estate investing will dramatically increase. The key question then becomes: What is your tolerance for problems?

You see, opportunities are never easy. Problems, challenges, and setbacks almost always occur. Those who shy away from the hard work needed to embrace opportunities fail. Over the years I've had friends and acquaintances come to me wanting to partner with me on various real estate projects. Often they back out. Why? It's like a rope strung across the two sides of the Grand Canyon. They see a tightrope; I see a bridge.

What can we do to strengthen our faith so that we can embrace and overcome more problems? That answer is easy. Take more chances. Truly successful people pursue opportunities based on faith. They don't let fear get in their way. Successful people—the Donald Trumps of the world, for example—also are constantly strengthening their faith. They are admitting their fears but pursuing opportunities anyway. When we let fear rule our lives, we don't take chances. When we live by faith, we pursue opportunities and take controlled risks.

When I was younger, I left my government job, where I was earning $60,000 a year, to become a real estate agent and investor. I was excited. I had recently read Napoleon Hill's *Think and Grow Rich* and was ready to set the world on fire—and to do so immediately. But things didn't happen so quickly. In fact, for several months, no opportunities materialized. Zero, none, *nada*. My savings began to dwindle. And then do you know what happened? My mind, which had been positive and focused on possibilities, began to worry. My dreams turned—mentally—from delights to disasters.

Eventually I overcame this initial slow time, and my investing took off. Only those who have the courage and the tenacity to never give up *in the face of setbacks and other obstacles* will achieve success.

Success then isn't a straight line; it's a series of starts and stops, two steps forward, and then one step back. Here's what I thought success would look like:

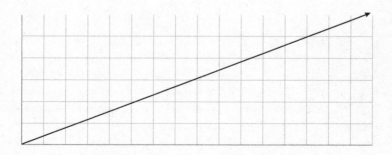

FIGURE 10.1 What I Thought Success Would Look Like

And here is what it actually did look like:

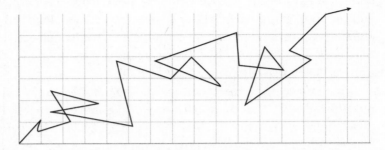

FIGURE 10.2 What the Path to Success *Really* Looks Like

TIP Only those who have the courage and the tenacity to never give up *in the face of setbacks and other obstacles* will achieve success.

If you have the patience to pursue and overcome problems, your chances for real estate successes will skyrocket. Remember your mantra:

Profit from Problems

You see, I believe that this concept of adding value to real estate can carry over into your life in many, many other ways. For example, too often I see and meet people who are focused on making less of other people or things. Instead, I want to encourage you to make more of every person you come in contact with. Avoid labels; there's no real right and wrong, just different points of view. Regardless of where you are in life right now, you can make the decision to reach up and out in your life and help others do the same.

Curtis Oakes has been a top-performing realtor for Coldwell Banker in San Francisco for more than two decades, placing him in the top 3 percent of all Coldwell Banker agents nationwide. In 1994, Curtis and his wife formed the Oakes Group, specializing in San Francisco Bay Area real estate sales, investment, and development. His passion for helping others has permeated his real estate practice, and he's helped countless individuals realize their dream of home ownership and investment property acquisition. Through his proprietary Oakes Group Mentoring Program, he teaches wealth building through real estate.

Analyzing the Deal, or Adventures in Real Estate

I have known John for more than thirty years. He and I were both Marine Corps officers and played on the same rugby team in Hawai'i. He is known as the Burger King of Hawai'i because he brought the franchise to the islands. Although he no longer owns the franchise, having sold it a number of years ago for a stunning profit, he is still known as the Burger King of Hawai'i because the name fits. John is the king of using fast food franchises to acquire priceless real estate.

In my book Rich Dad Poor Dad *I wrote about Ray Kroc, the person who made McDonald's famous and built it into a multibillion-dollar enterprise. In the book, Ray asks a group of students from the University of Texas, "What business am I in?" The response from the students was, "You're in the hamburger business." Ray shook his head and said, "No, I'm in the real estate business." Today, McDonald's owns the most expensive real estate in the world. Ray's formula was to use a McDonald's franchise to pay for the real estate.*

John, the Burger King of Hawai'i, uses the same formula, the formula of using a business to buy property. I too use the same formula today. Today my apartment house business, fitness club business, and office rental business pay for my real estate. It is a formula used all over the world. The formula of your business buys your real estate.

—Robert Kiyosaki

I have always been intrigued by the acquisition, ownership, and sale of real estate. For the majority of my professional life I've been advising people and making personal decisions about whether or not I should acquire real estate, how to acquire a particular piece of real estate, and finally whether to sell it, develop it, or simply hold it. That means as a practicing attorney and a private investor, I've reviewed hundreds of real estate transactions with a "stop or go" decision point. And the projects are varied. I have developed and sold office and residential condominiums (small and large); acquired and operated ranches and farms; developed and operated warehouse complexes; and financed, developed, and refinanced myriad other real estate–related business ventures.

However, my principal focus today and over the last forty years has been the consistent financing, development, and operation of quick-serve (fast-food) restaurants and convenience stores under franchise agreements with national franchise companies. It's fascinating work acquiring sites and handling the financing and development of those properties. It's also been fascinating to own, operate, and sell nearly one hundred of these quick-serve establishments over these past forty years. My efforts have taken me all over the western United States, Guam, Hawai'i, and Russia.

With this kind of background, analyzing deals has become second nature. And that's what this chapter is all about: "Analyzing the Deal" as it relates to the intelligent acquisition and operation of fast-food restaurants, convenience stores, and related franchise businesses. However, don't be mistaken that the principles set out here will apply only to quick-serve restaurants and convenience stores. That couldn't be further from the truth. The principles here are fundamental and will apply to entrepreneurial ventures of all kinds, particularly if they involve real estate.

Time and again, having a law background has helped when it comes to analyzing the deal at hand. But the true tempering of my deal-related judgment comes from my involvement in building and operating fast-food companies in Hawai'i, Guam, Nevada, Colorado, and Russia. The scope of my experience includes the location, financing, development, and operation of Burger King restaurants, Carl's Jr. restaurants, El Pollo Loco restaurants, Subway sandwich restaurants, Circle K convenience stores, and 76 gas stations, among others. This involvement in franchise deals has necessarily brought me in direct contact with major national brand franchisors with whom I have had extensive negotiations. Most of these franchise opportunities have proved successful, but there were a couple of spectacular exceptions, which I will get into later. In every case my experience in analyzing the deal at the outset proved to be a key to success or failure.

In this chapter, I will set out the principles that you can use in your own pursuit of workable, profitable real estate deals that meet your expectations. I am always suspect of people who talk only of their successes but not of their failures. The reality, as you and I know, is that no business endeavor is perfect. Heartache and despair happen from time to time. That's par for the course for someone who is truly driven by and committed to success. So don't expect all blue sky success stories; I will share with you some significant failures I have experienced as well. They were important learning opportunities for me, teaching me lasting lessons about this field. I know they will be important for you, too, because in most cases these costly mistakes resulted from my failure to analyze the deal correctly at the outset.

My goal is to provide you with a basic construct to direct your analysis of real estate and other deals, and to aid you in making intelligent stop-and-go decisions concerning these deals. It's critical to put some meat on these "bones of wisdom" so that you will be able to address any deal presented to you with practical and useful guidelines. These guidelines to intelligent deal analysis are particularly relevant in a tough economic climate, but they are also foundational and have stood and will continue to stand the test of time.

THE REAL WORLD OF ME

At the very outset of any deal consideration, one needs to engage in some serious introspection. Is this deal (job, purchase, career, etc.) what you really want or need? Does your self-image allow you to be passionate about the basic endeavor you are considering? Does the deal with its projected result produce the kind of monetary and emotional return you are looking for? Does "doing" the deal involve a sacrifice of time and/or require relocation, thereby effectively preventing you from pursuing more important life goals such as good and involved parenting, active and healthy lifestyle choices, team sports activity, church or civic leadership, continued or advanced formal education, personal relationships, or living in a safe and attractive home environment. In other words, if doing the deal, no matter how successful, will make your life or your family's life miserable, then keep moving. It's not for you.

TIP You don't need to do the first deal you see, nor do you need to pursue every deal that seems halfway good or reasonable. Wait for the deal to come down the track that is really for you.

My former partner, Robert Pulley, used to frequently say that deals are like streetcars since there's always another one coming down the track. Over time I have come to realize how true this postulate is. I used to pursue to thoughtful decision almost every deal that came across my desk regardless of what it was, where it was, or what it cost. By allowing my curiosity to take charge, I spent too much time spinning my wheels rather than focusing on realities. That curiosity and arrogance concerning my personal entrepreneurial capacity (I thought I could finance and manage anything) got me into some bad business spots, literally and figuratively. My experiences in Russia and in the nightclub and cemetery businesses (discussed later) represent painful memories that have stayed with me.

The fact is, you don't need to close on the first deal you see, nor do you need to pursue every deal that seems halfway good or reasonable. Wait for the deal to come down the track that is right for you. Your time is your most valuable asset, so spend it wisely. Let the obvious impracticalities of any deal you consider speak to you loudly. This is true no matter how apparently lucrative any deal may seem. Just because the latest and seemingly hottest franchise deal is available in your city doesn't mean that it's right for you. If flipping hamburgers in Detroit, selling cemetery plots in Guam, or polishing cars, creating signs and banners, or teaching math to preteens doesn't really fit you or create a passion within you to succeed, don't do it. Just fold up your cards and wait for a new hand to be dealt. Don't let your current circumstances, no matter how unsatisfying, chase you into a situation where you will work harder, go into debt, and actually lose money doing something you hate.

The Real World of Me

- Engage in serious introspection.
- Ask yourself, "Will doing the deal prevent me from achieving my personal life goals?"
- Deals are like streetcars since there's always another one coming down the track.
- If the deal doesn't fit, don't submit!

Spend some quality time on "the real world of me" before you invest your time chasing a deal that just doesn't suit you or takes you to places that will ultimately make you unhappy, even if you are successful.

WILL THE DOGS LIKE IT?

You've taken the time to be introspective; it's now time to look hard at the deal that's in front of you. You know, the one that looks, smells, and feels right for you.

A very astute Hawai'i-based Chinese businessman, whom I had the pleasure to work with in my early legal career, used to have a favorite saying to characterize any deal. He applied this saying to the many, many deals he considered. He would pause after reviewing the deal situation and ask, "But will the dogs like it?"

He meant that if a deal looks good, is workable, is affordable, and is in a good location, then the customers (tenants, purchasers, etc.) still have to show up to make it happen. He insisted at the outset that just because something may look right to you, it may not be quite so right to the man or woman on the street. You and your wife (partner, friend, banker, college business professor, etc.) might think you have the newest take on sliced bread; however, you must take off the rose-tinted glasses and look at the deal high and low. In other words, strive for total objectivity in your deal analysis.

TIP Just because something may look right to you, it may not be quite so right to the man or woman on the street.

A couple of deals from my past point out the usefulness of being truly objective. In 1977, my partner, Robert Pulley, and I opened the first Burger King restaurant in the state of Hawai'i, right across the street from a busy and well-located McDonald's restaurant. At that time in Hawai'i, McDonald's was pretty much the whole ballgame in terms of branded quick-serve hamburgers. After sampling Burger King's food and visiting existing Burger King restaurants on the mainland, we both agreed that the concept would work well in the Islands. And, even before we opened in Honolulu, we had customers banging on our restaurant doors to get in while we were still obviously under construction. We realized that we had a real winner on our hands. The "dogs" really liked our hamburgers. We set first day, first week, and first month sales records for gross sales for the entire Burger King chain. In fact, our drive-through service lane routinely filled up and cars backed up on the very busy Beretania Street for more than a mile. We had to hire off-duty policemen to control and direct traffic for seven months before we got things under control.

Our customers fell in love with Burger King. We had a very good product that was absolutely unique to Hawai'i at that time. There was a pent-up demand for fast-food hamburgers other than McDonald's hamburgers. To my partner's credit, we obtained a "bulletproof" location right across from a key competitor that we knew was very successful. And, we delivered good food fast. We had analyzed the deal objectively based on good information. In fact, as it turned out, we underestimated how much the dogs would like it.

On the other hand, I had the opposite experience with the introduction of the El Pollo Loco restaurant chain into Hawai'i some years later. I, along with my key employees, had eaten at El Pollo Loco in Southern California. The El Pollo Loco concept essentially involves charbroiling fresh and big fryer chickens to golden brown and serving the charbroiled chicken with tortillas, beans, and rice. The "dogs" really liked this product in Southern California where there is a strong Hispanic tradition. People there of all types are quite familiar with tacos, tamales, and tortillas, and fajitas. They viewed El Pollo Loco as a good Mexican food concept and made it very popular.

In addition to knowing the food was good and popular (in Southern California at least), we had the money and expertise to develop the chain in premier locations in Hawai'i. So we obtained the area franchise, and with the success of Burger King in Hawai'i encouraging us, we felt sure we could create another major quick-serve restaurant success. We opened two El Pollo Loco locations at about the same time. Imagine our disappointment when we found that the dogs didn't like the product in Hawai'i. Imagine our financial losses.

The El Pollo Loco concept depended on some customer familiarity with Mexican food preparation and service. What seemed routine in terms of Mexican food service to Southern Californians mystified many (if not most) of our good Hawaiian customers. The concept involved the simple act of pulling the chicken meat off the half-chicken serving and wrapping it in a warm tortilla with beans, rice, and salsa, thereby creating a world-class chicken fajita. In Hawai'i, the customers did not combine the ingredients (despite clever and instructive graphics on every table and menu); they typically ate the chicken serving, which was delicious, picked at the rice and beans, and threw the beautiful, warm flour tortillas away. We were stunned.

There was already *huli-huli* (flame-broiled) chicken all over the island of Oahu, which was a popular and long-standing fund-raising vehicle. Typically, community groups involved in fund-raising would set up huli-huli wagons in parking lots on weekends at several locations on the island. They would build charcoal fires in the huli-huli wagons and proceed to prepare and sell tasty flame-broiled chickens (whole and halves) to the public at relatively inexpensive prices. So in addition to our customer's failure to grasp the El Pollo Loco concept, we had a serious competitor that we never considered until it was too late.

> ## Will the Dogs Like It?
> - Is the product something that you would personally buy at the likely asking price?
> - Is the product unique or better than the comparable products sold by competitors?
> - Is the product too complicated or too much trouble for your customers?
> - Take off your rose-tinted deal glasses and look at the relevant market objectively.

Without the customers' grasp of the chicken fajita preparation, the El Pollo Loco chicken was simply good chicken. It wasn't really very unique, and it was pretty expensive compared to huli-huli chicken. We actually didn't fail completely, but our losses forced us to sell out to Kentucky Fried Chicken. KFC wanted to get rid of El Pollo Loco on the Islands, and our modest success was hurting their business. So we took the easy way out with a lesson well learned.

GARBAGE IN, GARBAGE OUT

Projected financial results, as you can imagine, are the primary concern in analyzing any deal, and when it comes to the numbers it's garbage in, garbage out. Essentially, if your sales projections or your cost projections are bad going in, the resulting projected bottom line (profit and cash flow) numbers are not only unreliable but outright dangerous to your financial well-being.

Up until now, everything we have discussed has been preparatory to real deal focus. Now it's time to get to the heart of our task. As you've seen, the numbers aren't the only consideration, but they certainly are most critical to the stop-or-go deal decision. With my focus on the development of franchise deals, I often had access to very reliable historical sales data from other franchise operations in comparable demographic areas. Typical numbers relating to fast-food operations, convenience stores, gas stations, and other similar operations are often made available to the prospective franchisees in the mandatory disclosure document that each prospective franchisee must receive under the Uniform Franchise Act enacted in most states. These "pro forma" (projected) numbers are useful in analyzing the deal—and other deals involving the same or similar product delivery—in most franchise opportunities.

Of course, using pro forma numbers to analyze a potential deal amounts to, at best, intelligent guesswork. In every case, one has to massage these pro forma numbers to fit the situation at hand. The pricing construct has to be adjusted up or down to fit the intended location. Additionally, an equally important concern is to evaluate the relevant market (assuming the dogs like the product) to arrive at reasonable projected transaction counts and customer counts.

Counting "heads" is the first step in evaluating a fast-food location. I have spent many hours personally counting every vehicle passing by my target location. In tourist locations, I often count the people who walk by every hour in high- and low-traffic periods. Getting a good handle on real numbers of potential customers who have direct exposure to your location is really chapter one in the sales number guessing book. So don't skip actually doing a thorough, realistic head count or traffic count.

Of course, what your closest and most relevant competitor is actually achieving in gross sales is also absolutely key to your analysis of projected gross sales. And if you don't have a close competitor you are either really lucky or more often than not, in the wrong location altogether. I don't care how you get these competitor numbers, but you must get them. This sales data can often be discovered through a review of public tax filings (i.e., gross excise tax data) or by simply interviewing your competitor's former employees or managers. You might want to hire them anyway, so you certainly can interview them. In summary, you must get solid and realistic projected gross sales numbers to avoid creating garbage in, garbage out projections.

Projected sales are only half the story. Projected expenses are equally important when it comes to developing usable bottom-line projections. Projected expenses can almost always be estimated reasonably with hard work. We are fortunate in the United States to have the remarkably efficient distribution of goods and services at comparable and fair pricing (assuming you pay your bills on time). With the exception of utility costs and gas, which historically can make dramatic moves to the upside, your costs for food, paper, products, produce, and people tend to be relatively stable. In quick-serve restaurants, gas stations, and convenience stores, you can move your pricing daily if necessary so you can preserve your profit margins as costs move up. Of course, you are always limited by the competitive atmosphere, but given a product or products the dogs like, reasonable pricing, and a good location, you can come up with projected financial results that are sensible enough to make a deal decision.

If you have hit your mark in projecting future gross sales and have a good understanding of your expenses, you should be able to derive some fairly good and usable guesses at cash flow and profitability numbers. When I have really done my homework, I have been able to avoid the garbage in, garbage out syndrome that turns business projections into birdcage lining. When I didn't do the work of counting vehicles and heads, or failed to research the success or failure of my closest competitors, my deal analysis was faulty. If I failed to be diligent in projecting reliable expense numbers, I had garbage or unrealistic expense numbers to factor into my profitability formula. Sometimes I got lucky and things turned out better than I had hoped for. However, you can't rely on luck and the mistakes that are burned into my brain resulted from overly aggressive sales projections and garbage out at the projected bottom line.

TIP **When I have really done my homework, I have been able to avoid the garbage in, garbage out syndrome that turns business projections into birdcage lining.**

Years ago, I along with my partner, Robert Pulley, built a Burger King restaurant in the heart of Waikiki in Honolulu, Hawai'i. Although the site was on the ground floor in the front of the popular Kings Village shopping center, the actual walk-by traffic seemed a little thin for this very expensive location. However, one-half block away on Waikiki Beach were absolute throngs of tourists, mostly milling about at the popular corner of Liliuokalani and Kalakaua avenues. My personal tourist head count revealed several thousand potential customers passing through this adjacent and very popular intersection every hour.

The downside of this location was that the view from this key corner to my target restaurant site was largely blocked by a ticket and information booth. A bad deal! So if I was going to choose this site, I'd have to adjust my sales projections way down. After all, they were based on actual walk-by traffic at the time. The obstruction by the ticket booth meant there was nothing to draw customers our way from that busy corner. My partner and I fortunately engaged in some "what-if" analysis before passing on this potentially great site. Our conclusion was that if we could create unobstructed sight-line visibility from this major tourist corner to our site, the deal would work. So I made a last-minute potential "deal-breaker" demand to the landlord that the offending ticket booth be removed to clear up the sight line. Fortunately, the landlord agreed. They wanted us in the center. So we ended up with probably the most successful quick-serve restaurant I have ever built. The dogs liked us, now they could see us, and there were plenty of dogs! Our first-year sales were more than $2.7 million out of less than twenty-seven hundred square feet. These are hall of fame numbers for fast food.

On the other hand, I once developed a cemetery on a parcel of land that my then partner, Bernard Bays—also a contributor in this book—and I had acquired to develop high-end residential condominiums. How did a parcel of land go from high-end condos to burial plots? Simple answer: Hurricane Iniki and ancient but unmarked graves on the property. As you can well imagine, everyone I knew razzed me with the old joke, "Hey John, I hear people are dying to get into your new project." Yeah, wrong kind of dying. All joking aside, the gross sales potential on paper from any new cemetery is just phenomenal. Anytime you can convert, as an example, six acres into six thousand saleable grave plots in a major metro area, your potential ultimate sellout can be as high as $15 to $20 million! Since our land was already paid for, I had only to face cemetery approval and development costs, which I had a pretty good handle on. So I constructed some very elaborate and detailed sales and cash-flow projections that convinced Bays, myself, and several of our associates that we had a winner indeed, even if it wasn't via condo development. The cash flow-to-cost ratio was very favorable on what seemed to be ultimately reasonable sales projections. Our deal analysis looked really good, but it was very wrong.

Unfortunately, I grossly overestimated how quickly people would buy burial plots in the cemetery. We had originally built the cemetery with the thought of selling it to a major company involved in the funeral home/cemetery business. In fact, we had a basic agreement that this company would run the cemetery and ultimately buy the operation and property at a price yielding a substantial profit to our group. So, even though we really had no experience actually operating a cemetery, we proceeded to develop it anyway. We wrongly assumed that our deal to sell to the pros would go through before we actually had to operate the cemetery business. The projected cash flow made us confident of closing such a sale. Unfortunately, our prospective buyers went into bankruptcy a short time after completion of the cemetery. There I was a fast food impresario, taking over cemetery operations.

I was stuck with the job as head "cemeterian," which I knew little about and greatly disliked. I soldiered ahead because our projected numbers still looked terrific. We still had millions of dollars in unsold inventory already paid for and waiting to be sold. I just didn't figure that it might take my lifetime to sell this inventory. Talk about garbage in, garbage out. I would likely be buried in this cemetery, and there still would be more than half the plots left to sell!

Many years later after investing countless and thankless hours learning about and actually running the cemetery, I finally ended up selling it at a loss. My partners and I are now much older and wiser. My projections of cemetery plot sales were based on selling significant numbers of plots from the get-go. We did finally begin to see significant sales of plots every month. However, this sales tempo took years to achieve. What I did not factor into my projected plot sales was the essential attribute of "heritage," which every new cemetery must gain slowly if at all before significant plot sales can be achieved. This is particularly true in smaller cities with more limited population bases.

The simple truth is that it is hard to get families to bury their deceased loved ones in new places. If aunty and uncle are buried in the public cemetery, the rest of the family will also likely want to be interred there no matter how "seedy" the old town cemetery has become. People will come to a new cemetery, but it takes time. They are dying to get in but just not fast enough at a new cemetery. So my decision to proceed to build a cemetery was driven by sales projections that were honestly derived but simply too aggressive for this kind of business. This was particularly true since we lost our major cemetery consolidator/operator at the very outset. My deal analysis was faulty because of overly aggressive "garbage" sales projections.

Garbage In, Garbage Out

- Access and use sales numbers from the best sources available (franchisor standard disclosures and competitor numbers, for example)
- Count the "heads" and/or traffic personally
- Do your homework when you work up expense projections
- Ask the "what-if" question before passing on a deal
- If you build it to sell, you better have a "bulletproof" buyer

BUILD IT AND THEY WILL COME (OR NOT)

Now that I have discussed some practical concerns that will prepare you for getting into a deal and shared some stories and my opinion about the relevance of numbers to every deal, it's time to focus on the question of location. Although I have related most of my discussion to quick-serve restaurants, convenience stores, and related businesses, the location question is central to analyzing *any* real estate deal.

It is often said that the three most important aspects of any real estate deal are location, location, and location. This is true, true, and true in any fast-food-type deal, but it is also the compelling issue in most real estate deals. Certainly, it is the central issue in the real estate deals I am referring to in this chapter.

Choosing the right locations for fast-food, quick-serve, gas, and convenience store businesses becomes an art after you have done it time and again and enjoyed success and experienced failures. I discussed above in the numbers analysis section the importance of counting heads and checking competitors' sales. I also stressed that the visibility of any site is a key part of this location issue. And finally I emphasized being in an area where the demographics support your product, where it is both needed and wanted by the people. Remember, will the dogs like it? For as simple as those concepts seem, be assured that you cannot properly analyze any real estate deal involving commercial sales to the public without paying close attention to these basic principles of site selection. Take it from someone who has learned these lessons the hard way.

In most cases, the location you want and are sure of is easy to figure out but is unavailable because of zoning, expense, public ownership, size (too big to afford or too small to be workable), and/or access. The locations that are available often are available because no one wants them or can afford them. This is especially true in major metro areas. If the site is available, you'd better go slow because usually there is something wrong with it. Never assume your competitors are dumb or lazy. Proceed with caution or you will build the perfect store and nobody will come.

I can't tell you how many times I have fortunately passed on real estate deals that were just about right, meaning just about in a great location, but were slightly off for one reason or another. Maybe the site was just interior from the key dominant corner or was in a perfect corner location but on the second floor or down a half-flight of stairs. Or the site was blocked by a huge banyan tree, ticket booth, adjacent building, or some other obstruction so you couldn't see it from the "coming home" side of the road. I will assure you that you can't build or manage your way out of a poor location, no matter how hard you try or how much you spend. I refer here to my area of expertise involving quick-serve restaurants and convenience/gas facilities; however, I believe this location issue is at the heart of every deal that involves sales to the general public.

TIP You can't build or manage your way out of a poor location, no matter how hard you try or how much you spend.

Aside from location visibility, access for your customers is another important consideration. I have thankfully passed on a number of sites that seemed perfectly located but suffered from limited access because of traffic, traffic controls, or limited parking. If it's not convenient the "dogs" will pass on by to someplace that's easier to deal with. So, if you build on a location that your customers can't get to, they won't come.

My partner, Robert Pulley, and I had some fantastic successes by securing locations that were seemingly unavailable or unattainable for our quick-serve hamburger restaurants. I mentioned above the Waikiki location with the problematic ticket booth. Once we got rid of this visual impairment we had an absolute grade "A" location. We had many other successes that I like to think were enabled by creative thinking and action.

When I was looking for deals that would compete favorably with my number-one competitor, McDonald's, I had to be creative since this competitor had seemingly tied up all the available, really good locations. I always laughed when a real estate broker would tell me that I was ahead of McDonald's on any particular site or that I was being offered the site first. I assumed, usually with complete accuracy, that any site McDonald's wanted in my city would end up in their hands no matter who else was interested. They were definitely the "big kahuna" in my development area, and they usually got the first right of refusal on any newly available sites. I guess it's good to be the real boss.

So I, along with my partner, had to think creatively if we were going to grow and succeed. Our deal analysis on sites had to be not only accurate but innovative. This creative mind-set led us to open the first nationally branded fast-food outlet ever in a U.S. military installation at the Navy Exchange at Pearl Harbor, Hawai'i. (We lost this location some years later when we sold out to a Japanese company, but that is another story.) We opened, with great success, the first fast-food restaurant with a partner in the Honolulu International Airport, and we opened the first national fast-food franchise operation in a Hawai'i public park at Ala Moana park in downtown Honolulu. We actually retrofitted part of a YMCA building to create a Burger King restaurant next to the University of Hawai'i, which was another first.

We definitely had to be creative in our site selection to survive and grow our company. We actually built five or more of the most successful restaurants in terms of sales volume in the history of quick-serve restaurants. In every case, the successful location was equal or superior to our competitors' locations or was uniquely situated to avoid any competition. In every case, the location was the key to our success. Our deal analysis was spot-on in these unique locations.

However, I would be less than honest if I didn't tell you about a couple of bad experiences I've had because of poor site selection. By that I mean, I built it and they didn't come. The first example involved building a very fancy and expensive Burger King restaurant on the ground floor of a high-end residential condominium that my partner had developed in Waikiki. Honestly, my site (deal) analysis was skewed by the ready availability of this commercial site, which my partner had in his back pocket as the condominium developer. What I didn't see were some major problems with this "captive site," although it was located on a busy Waikiki corner. First, the dogs didn't like it. The homeowners were less than enamored by a fast-food hamburger restaurant at the entrance to their new, exclusive, and expensive condominium complex. To add further insult, a fellow high-end restaurant tenant sued to stop our restaurant's construction as a violation of his exclusivity clause. But the real oversight in our deal analysis was that our location was on the busy corner but one-half floor below street grade. The walk-by traffic didn't seem to find our location because it was below their sight line. A final straw was that, even though there were hundreds of cars passing by every hour, there was no parking.

Here's a lesson I learned that is for everyone: If you are in the convenience food/store business you had better be convenient and readily accessible. I have never had much success in this quick-serve/convenience area when I locate below or above street level. So in analyzing site locations, don't count on too much tenacity or insight on the part of your customers—they just don't care that much.

TIP In analyzing site locations don't count on too much tenacity or insight on the part of your customers—they just don't care that much.

My experience in developing, owning, and operating a nightclub was equally painful. In this instance, a close personal friend, Robert Mardian Jr., had given me some solid advice against building this club on the Big Island of Hawai'i. He was in the club business there, as well, and knew the ropes. Unfortunately, I ignored that good advice and proceeded with the nightclub development. My reason for going forward was simply that I had space in a warehouse complex that I owned, which had already been substantially built out as a nightclub at great expense. I recaptured the space after my tenant defaulted (that should have been my first clue), and I decided the best idea was to finish out the club and operate it. So I spent hundreds of thousands of dollars building a state-of-the-art nightclub that opened with considerable fanfare. Unfortunately, I soon found out that, even if the dogs liked the club, they wouldn't come if they couldn't find it.

TIP Another important and costly lesson I learned is that you can't turn a sow's ear into a silk purse.

I made two major mistakes here concerning location. I had failed to heed the clear and sound advice from a knowledgeable consultant who advised me that the club would fail because of location. Also, I should have known that no matter how much money you spend, you cannot build yourself out of a bad location. This just wasn't appropriate space for a nightclub because it was in the back of an industrial warehouse that was off the beaten track. People who actually wanted to come couldn't find it. I used to joke that people just needed to drive until they heard gunfire (this was a rough area late at night). I ended up disliking the nightclub business as much as the cemetery business.

By now I think you get it. Deals where the location is "bad, bad, and bad" won't work no matter what you do. We finally tore out the nightclub improvements and returned it to warehouse use. The entire complex has been full since. Another important and costly lesson I learned is that you can't turn a sow's ear into a silk purse.

Build It and They Will Come (or Not)

- Location, location, location is true, true, and true.

- Count heads, review access and visibility, and check out the competition.

- If the site is readily available there is probably something wrong with it.

- Think "outside the box" to get unique locations.

- If you are in the convenience business you'd better be convenient.

- Seek out and listen to the experts.

- Don't try to turn a sow's ear into a silk purse.

TROUBLE WITH TRAVEL

With any deal you are considering, you simply have to ask yourself, "Can I manage the deal effectively? If the deal is located more than one day's travel from your home, you'd better ask (and answer) some serious questions about your personal span of control. You can't manage the type of deals I have been discussing by staring at a computer. You need to be at the site at least weekly if you are the majority partner. Or you'd better have a good, capable, and trustworthy operator/partner.

And that leads to an important point. One of the most important considerations in analyzing whether to proceed with any real estate deal or development is the availability of good management. And usually the key to good management is your personal involvement in the development and operation. Having good partners can solve many of the concerns about good management; however, if your own money is at risk in any deal it will require your personal attention. The question then is whether realistically you will actually be able to devote sufficient time to a deal to make it successful.

TIP One of the most important considerations in analyzing whether to proceed with any real estate deal or development is the availability of good management. And, usually that means you, with direct personal involvement in the development and operation.

I have found if a deal or operation is located too far from my home base or is difficult to get to, I won't pay enough personal oversight and attention to the situation to ensure good management. I have also found that it is very rare to see any deal run on its own without major problems. If I have to get on an airplane or drive several hours to a location, you are not going to see me very often. It really amounts to the trouble with travel.

I once stretched the limit concerning my effective span of control by agreeing to be a founding member of a company formed to develop Subway sandwich restaurants in the old Soviet Union. Before we got the first restaurant built, the Soviet Union imploded, so we had to be satisfied with the nation of Russia with only 300 million people or so. My major point here is that you don't need to travel to the other side of the world to find trouble. You can usually find plenty of trouble right at home.

How I ever got involved in Soviet Subway restaurants is a story of seduction. I was intoxicated by the sheer potential magnitude of a deal that involved an entire nation, despite the fact that it happened to be Russia—a mere 12,500 miles from my home. The prevalent "kleptocracy" that seemed to be the dominant ideology in the early nineties in Russia should have raised a cautionary note in my Russia deal analysis. The fact that I would have very little to do with day-to-day management of the restaurants should also have raised my personal red flag. Despite these serious road blocks to good deal formation, I along with some other U.S. partners built the first Subway sandwich restaurant in Russia on Nevsky Prospect in St. Petersburg. It took some real creativity and out-of-the-box thinking to build a workable and visible restaurant in a two-hundred-year-old building.

The restaurant was a rousing success primarily because I sent one of my very best partners from Hawai'i, Steve Brown, along with his wife, Roberta, to build and run the Russian Subway operations. Of course, Steve was also enamored with the prospect of owning part of the hundred or more Subway Restaurants we intended to build throughout Russia, so I am not entirely to blame for disrupting his life. Shockingly, we were taking in wheelbarrow loads of rubles (literally) and lots of hard currency (dollars, marks, etc.) from the very start of operations in St. Petersburg. Under Steve's management with some help from me and the other three principals, we had one of the most successful Subway sandwich restaurants in the world—for about three months.

After weeks of hard work and success, Steve and Roberta finally took a short trip out of Russia to decompress, leaving one of our partners in charge as the managing director, which was required by Russian corporate law. Call it confusion about travel plans and return dates, but we had literally one day without a so-called managing director in charge of operations in St. Petersburg. Our Russian partner, whom we took on at the outset of our plans because of his apparent control over some key real estate and his political connections, chose that day to make his move. He had been sitting on the sidelines as we operated for ninety days without any active part in management. He expressed great frustration that we were banking all our net receipts to pay start-up bills before making any partner distributions. What we didn't realize at the time, was that our partner had some very bad characters who had control over him and were part of a major Russian mob.

Under mob instructions (we think), he was waiting for his chance to gain control over the restaurant as managing director. He seized that one day's opportunity. When Steve Brown returned from Russia a day later he found our Russian partner's security people (formerly our security people, ex-KGB apparently) in charge. They literally ran Steve out of the restaurant at gunpoint! So we lost control of the restaurant and the backing we had lined up to build many more restaurants. And our Russian "partner" soon ran the existing restaurant into the ground. Talk about a mess!

> ## The Trouble with Travel
> - The trouble with travel is that it reduces your span of control.
> - Will you actually go there after you have built it?
> - Deals don't run on their own.
> - Foreign countries are especially dangerous turf.
> - You don't have to leave home to find trouble.

Despite the fact that our company finally got the restaurant back years later, we all lost most of our investment in this deal. Now we may ultimately get back some of our money as my old U.S. partners continue to build Subway sandwich restaurants through franchise agreements in Russia under the auspices of our former company. However, I have often reflected on my poor decision in getting involved in a deal so far from home and on hazardous turf we knew little about. I can't help but repeat that you don't need to travel halfway around the world to invest your way into trouble; there are plenty of landmines to step on right here at home.

DEALS ARE LIKE PARACHUTES

So far, we've covered many of the considerations involved in analyzing and negotiating good deals. Now let's discuss the importance of getting out of a bad or marginal deal. Think of deals as if they were parachutes. If you're freefalling or sinking fast, you need to be able to pull the rip cord to save yourself and get out of a deal that's simply not working. That means first and foremost, determine whether you can negotiate an "out" clause in your initial deal analysis. If you don't succeed in obtaining this concession from the landlord/seller you may want to pass on the deal.

When I first started building restaurants, my partner and I routinely signed personal guaranties on leases for long-term leasehold properties. We were reaching to obtain the best real estate available and believed, in many cases correctly, that we had no chance to obtain these superior sites without "kissing the paper," which is another way of saying signing personal guaranties. We ultimately stopped doing this since a personal guaranty on a long-term lease is like a life sentence. If the lease term is long enough you have to worry about whether the lease rent is being paid for the rest of your life. This is especially true if you have assigned this lease to someone else.

Although we ultimately got our names off most of these guaranties when we sold the restaurants and assigned these long-term leases, in some instances we could not get releases because the landlords were just too tough. And, our marker (guaranty) was called in a couple of times by landlords who we had no dealings with for years. So, if a personal guaranty is demanded, you must carefully consider whether you want to accept this liability for the term of the lease (or loan). This extra liability greatly burdens the benefit of any potential deal and should be factored into your deal decision making.

TIP If a personal guaranty is demanded, you must carefully consider whether you want to accept this liability for the term of the lease or loan—a potential life sentence.

After a couple of bad experiences, I not only stopped giving my personal guaranty on lease deals, but I began to insist on "rip cord" clauses to get out of leases that proved to be for marginal locations. In most instances, landlords met this demand for an "out" of a long-term real estate lease with stiff resistance or refusal. My resolve to leave a partially open door to get out of a bad deal was equally strong. My negotiating stance was to point out that I would be fronting significant improvement costs at the outset, which I would not walk away from without a really compelling reason. Sometimes I was able to negotiate only a qualified release from my personal guaranty, which was better than nothing. For example, my personal guaranty would go away after the rent had been paid for a short term of three to five years or on payment of a lump sum. But I was always prepared to walk away from

> ### Deals Are Like Parachutes
> - A long-term personal guaranty can amount to a "life-sentence."
> - Negotiate a "rip cord" clause in long-term leases if possible.
> - Be prepared to "walk" if terms are too tough.

deals that were just too tough in terms of personal guaranties or long-term lock-ins.

MAKE MY DAY, MAKE MY LIFE

At some point in every viable real estate deal you have the opportunity, or at least the consideration, of whether or not to sell. In my experience, the decision to sell or not to sell is usually an easy or obvious one. If the price is right, everything is for sale. The analysis issue is which course of action—sale or retention—will optimize the return from your deal. I have personally made some great selling decisions and also some pretty bad decisions that irk me to this day.

Generally speaking, there are certain rules of thumb that are commonly used in the sale of operating businesses. Of course, these rules can be warped in a hundred different ways to accommodate the unique features of every different deal. Fast-food restaurants often sell based on a ratio of annual (trailing twelve-month) cash flow. Six times annual cash flow is generally considered at the high-end while four-and-a-half times cash flow is considered at the low-end of selling prices for such operating businesses. And, my reference to cash-flow really more correctly refers to earnings before interest, taxes, depreciation, and amortization, or EBITDA. There are other variations of this cash-flow acronym, but this is the one I use.

TIP There are certain rules of thumb that are commonly used in the sale of operating businesses. Of course, these rules can be warped in a hundred different ways to accommodate the unique features of every different deal.

Of course, operating businesses are sold for all kinds of reasons and all kinds of prices. I remember an old legend concerning the sale of a gas station/

convenience store. Essentially, the owner of this business was a sharp operator who was trying to push the sales price beyond normal cash-flow rules of thumb. So every time a potential buyer was due to inspect the business, the owner would dump trash around the buildings, leave the restrooms in a mess, and generally present an untidy, dirty appearance about the business. Then when the buyer showed up, the owner would take him aside and point out the seemingly obvious fact that if someone would "just run the business properly" sales and profits would soar. It is also common for the owner/seller and spouse to add back to the cash flow their salaries (car allowance, expense account, etc.) to pump up the cash flow. This is true, even if the owner/seller and spouse are the very heart of the business management and operation. Owners play all kinds of games with the sale of operating businesses. More sophisticated buyers and sellers will rely on industry norms concerning cash flow and a real objective analysis of the numbers to arrive at a price.

Robert Pulley and I sold our Burger King restaurants in Hawai'i at a price that approached one times the gross sales, which probably doesn't happen very often. However, we had a business in the seemingly terrific state of Hawai'i, we had good management and good locations, and we had enthusiastic foreign buyers. The analysis of whether to sell or not in our case was an easy yes. I have sold restaurants at other times on the six-times cash flow multiple, but I personally have not seen another deal with a price approaching parity with gross sales.

Analyzing the deal in raw land sales, presuming one has staying power to hold on to the land, relates basically to the greed factor. How much gain is enough? There are no real rules of thumb concerning the sale of raw land or development land. You need to make the hard decision of whether holding the land or the further development of the land will justify holding costs. Of course, these decisions to sell raw land are often driven by the owner's inability

Make My Day, Make My Life

- Utilize common "rules of thumb" to reach a realistic valuation decision.
- Cash flow rather than assets determine sales prices (usually).
- Unless you have a "crystal ball," you can get burned on market directions (up or down).
- If you can't afford the deal you need to sell it.
- Don't miss a once-in-a-lifetime opportunity to sell; i.e., the "make my day, make my life" decision.

to continue to pay carrying costs. In cases where you are going to lose the property otherwise, selling becomes an easy decision.

My most memorable mistakes in terms of selling prematurely involve selling houses in Hawai'i that practically doubled in value a year or two after my sale. We all have had or know of examples of seller's remorse in personal house sales. This was particularly true in many areas of the United States that were experiencing explosive increases in house prices. I, along with lots of other sellers, failed to judge the rapid upward move of the market.

Of course failure to sell during market peak can be an equally grievous error. We also have become familiar with holding strategies that lead to dramatic losses in rapidly declining residential and commercial real estate markets.

There are factors other than price that may impact the decision to sell or to buy. You might decide to sell if you no longer are able to manage a business or take care of a house. You may know of planned major infrastructure changes that will impact the relevant market negatively or positively. You might want to sell to key employees to avoid losing them. In every case, the analysis of the deal, or the sale, requires every bit as much consideration as a deal to build or acquire.

Ways To Learn More

Look for future writings by John Finney on the adventures on real estate.
   Rich Dad Poor Dad, by Robert Kiyosaki
   ABC's of Real Estate Investing, by Ken McElroy

John Finney is the current president of Industrial Income Properties, Inc., a company he formed to find, develop, own, and operate real estate, ranging from residential and office condominiums, cattle ranches, fast-food restaurants with adjunct convenience store and gas facilities, single family residences, farm properties, nightclubs, and other real estate ventures in Hawai'i, Guam, and the western United States. Prior to that, he and his partner Robert W. Pulley secured the Burger King franchise rights in Hawai'i and in ten years opened thirty-five stores and sold them in one of the biggest deals in Burger King history. And each has had many other real estate ventures in the United States. John is an attorney and a graduate of Stanford Law School and a former U.S. Marine.

10

Real Estate Due Diligence

I met Scott in 1999 at the Phoenix Open golf event. I knew of his reputation as one of the biggest mortgage bankers in Arizona, but I did not know that he knew me. Smiling as he walked up, he said, "I'm glad you're saying what you say about stocks and mutual funds. They're terrible investments."

At the time, I was under blistering attacks from financial planners and financial magazines that were supported by mutual fund company's advertising dollars. You may recall that in 1999, the stock market was red hot and people believed they were making billions in the new economy of the dot-com world. So to have a person of Scott's reputation back up my philosophy that stocks and mutual funds were risky investments was a welcome relief and validation. His pat on my back made watching the Phoenix Open even more enjoyable.

Today Scott is one of the three mortgage bankers I call when I need the straight story about real estate financing. It was Scott who, years ago, warned me of the real estate bubble being formed by the sub-prime mortgage fiasco. It was because of Scott that my wife, Kim, and I became more conservative in our real estate investments while others became real estate gamblers.

I'm an advocate for financial education because when you get smarter, you minimize risk. That's what this chapter is about. Scott has made me smarter, and the knowledge he has shared with me minimizes my risk with every new investment I make. His wisdom in this chapter will do the same for you.

—ROBERT KIYOSAKI

When talking about the subject of real estate due diligence, you are really talking about nothing more than a team effort of discovery and verification. That's what due diligence is, and every real estate transaction you do, whether it is a single family home purchase or a very complex commercial real estate development, will require the buyer to take certain fundamental steps of underwriting. Only through that process can a buyer fully assess all aspects of the property he or she is purchasing. And if you are the buyer, you'll want to make sure you are diligent about due diligence.

TIP Benjamin Franklin once said, "Diligence is the mother of good luck."

When you as a real estate investor have identified a property that you want to purchase, you have come to the conclusion to buy it based on a series of somewhat superficial facts. You have usually seen the property, and generally have reviewed some of the financial information that the seller or broker has provided you. And based on this information and your belief that the property fits your business plan, you make an offer to purchase. Once the seller has accepted your offer, your work—or should I say your team's work—has just begun!

I am a real believer in putting together a very strong team when you approach a real estate acquisition. Many of the authors in this book have stated the exact same thing in their chapters. The fact is, most highly successful people or companies are built using a team approach to getting things done. No one can be an expert on every aspect of real estate, and frankly if you are investing on behalf of other people and are using their money, you should *always* seek competent third-party input.

In this chapter, I am going to walk you through a due diligence process and give you an overview of why the various members of your team are important. I am also going to include my Eight Tips and some real-life examples of why securing qualified and unbiased advice on your proposed acquisition is so critical.

To me, assembling a team to assist you with your due diligence is just like putting a puzzle together. Each of the team members have separate and specialized disciplines, but when they are brought together by you as the leader, the pieces come together, and all of a sudden the full picture comes to life. You can see what you are really buying!

I have separated the due diligence process into five main categories: physical review, legal, title, third party reports, and accounting tax. Let's start with the first one on this list.

PHYSICAL REVIEW

During the physical review, you and your team inspect the property to see if it falls in line with your business plan and your expectations. Let me expand a bit on this. As an example, let's say that you are planning to buy an apartment building and then do some slight renovations to the units that will allow you to increase the rents over the next couple of years. So how does the process start?

> **Due Diligence Process Categories**
> - Physical Review
> - Legal Review
> - Title Review
> - Third Party Reports Review
> - Accounting and Tax Review

Before you make your offer to purchase the property, you will want to interview and select a property management company to help you prepare your operating and renovation budgets for the property. The key word here is *before*! This is not something you want to do after you make the offer. The results of this work will help you decide whether the property is worth making an offer at all.

TIP If you are going to be a professional real estate investor, have your team lined up *before* you make the offer!

A successful and competent property management company can go over your operating and renovation budgets to make sure they are realistic and give you credible feedback on all the previous assumptions you may have made on the property—assumptions such as operating expense savings, new income opportunities, and even cash flow projections. They can look at your business plan and give it a thumbs up or a thumbs down and help you adjust it so it is attainable and realistic. Remember, you will rely on a property management company to make your business plan work, so you had better make sure you are both on the same page from the beginning.

The property management company will have its own sub checklists for its own due diligence process. The people in the company will walk through every apartment and check the condition of the property in a multifamily project, for example, and bring in the sub-trades such as roofing companies, landscape companies, etc., that can provide detailed reports on the condition of the property.

In addition to spearheading the physical inspection, the property management company will also review all the rent-rolls, the operating statements, and tenant profiles, all in an effort to gain an understanding of the true, current operating income of the property. Usually it will present you with a summary of the findings.

TIP The property management company is a critical member of your team. Find the best one you can and work closely with it.

I cannot tell you how many times during my career that this work and the report that it generates has helped buyers make the right decision about a property. Let me give you an example from two perspectives. I was involved in a twenty-unit apartment community that I was going to buy and convert to for-sale condominiums. When we did our walk-through, my property management company brought along several contractors who were going to do the work on the project once I closed.

To convert the apartments to condominiums, I planned to put about $20,000 of renovations—including adding a washer and dryer—into each unit. This was a non-negotiable expense since my market study indicated that other condo projects in the market all had washers and dryers. We needed to be competitive.

After the inspection, the owner of the property management company called me and said that everything checked out and there were no real surprises, except one. I asked, "What would that be?" He proceeded to tell me that his plumber and framer felt that because of the existing plumbing and stairwell configuration, putting in the washers and dryers would cost an additional five thousand dollars per unit. That added up to an *additional* $100,000. OUCH!

Well clearly, that unexpected expense was not in my budget, so I went back to the seller to renegotiate the terms of the deal. Specifically, I agreed to remove all contingencies after the completion of my due diligence, and in exchange I requested that the seller reduce the price by $100,000. He agreed. Having an expert in the room saved me $100,000! For as valuable as the property management company was in finding a potentially deal-breaking hidden cost, a property manager can also add strong value by reviewing the rent-roll and tenant profiles.

Here's my story: I was financing an acquisition of a large apartment building in Scottsdale, Arizona, that had been grossly undermanaged. My client was going to buy the asset and renovate the units and gradually raise rents. He thought the quoted street rents for this property were below market for the submarket and felt he could increase them once he renovated the exterior, improved the amenities, and did some minor interior work.

What the property management company reported after reviewing the rent-roll was both startling and exciting. They discovered that more than 25 percent of the existing tenants had not received a rental increase since they signed their original leases! Two tenants were actually paying the same rent they had paid when they moved into the property the day it opened . . . fifteen years prior! This news meant that the property's net operating income would indeed increase significantly simply by raising the old rents to the current market rates and once the additional rent kicked in, based on the planned property improvements. The property management company earned its keep that day.

LEGAL REVIEW

Hiring a lawyer that practices real estate law is a must. I am not advocating that you spend an incredible amount of money on legal fees, but with complex issues regarding title, contracts, entitlements, lender documents, and other items that you are certain to run into, you'd better have a good lawyer on your team. If you are an experienced real estate investor and you are buying a home or something without too many issues, maybe you can handle the transaction on your own. But regardless, the legal review phase is not the place to save money on professional fees.

In my experience, if you have a good lawyer who is a "deal maker" you should get him or her engaged on the issues he/she knows best. I have seen some problems arise when the lawyer becomes the negotiator for the transaction. Remember you are the team leader, and all of the members should be reporting to you. That's when a lawyer, as well as all your other team members, can really add value. There are many examples of how lawyers have added value in the numerous transactions in which I have been involved. Let me share a favorite.

I was financing both the debt and equity for a condo developer on a property in Portland, Oregon. My borrower hired a much-respected lawyer in Portland to review all title and entitlement documents regarding the property. He discovered during the title review that one of the owners had recorded a document requiring his approval before a property could be converted to condominiums. Without this owner's approval there was no way to get the state real estate approval to sell the units individually, and no way to deliver clear title to the buyers!

My borrower could not close the transaction without having this provision removed from the title. The only solution was to go back to this previous owner and get that person to remove the provision. Guess what? The previous owner was willing to comply, but for a price. My buyer was paying $48 million for a property that he was going to convert to condominiums and that he now discovered would not close until this provision was cleared up.

In this case, our seller and the previous seller agreed to a settlement, and we closed the transaction at no additional cost to my buyer. Thankfully, my client's lawyer had reviewed the documents thoroughly and was on top of this issue. This is the purpose of legal due diligence: finding the problems before they become insurmountable and providing you with the knowledge you need to make a go/no-go decision based on the findings and the proposed solutions. Just think if my buyer had closed on the property and *then* found out that he could not convert the property at all. Or worse yet, imagine the cost to remove the restriction post closing! My buyer would have been at the complete mercy of the previous owner.

TIP I do recommend strongly that if you are getting into larger and more complex transactions that require new debt or joint venture equity that you get legal representation at all times.

I am primarily a commercial mortgage broker. I provide debt and equity for commercial real estate transactions around the country. I can tell you that loan documents and joint venture agreements are extremely complex, and you do need someone who can thoroughly understand them and explain them to you.

TITLE REVIEW

Just as it's important to work with a lawyer you know and trust during the legal due diligence review, it's just as important to work with a title company you know and trust for this part of the process. In any deal I do, I try to control the title company choice in the purchase contract if at all possible. I find it best to go with a larger firm that has the capacity to provide a satisfactory level of insurance coverage for all parties.

TIP Using a title company that you know and one that is acceptable to your lenders and lawyer will save you a lot of time and effort.

I also like to use title companies to search comparable sales, foreclosures, or other owners in a particular area to help give you a feel of what is going on in the vicinity around the property. This is important intelligence you'll need as you formulate your marketing plans and your forecasts for a particular property.

Lawyers aren't the only ones who can save the day when it comes to due diligence. Let me give you an example of how a title company made me a quick profit on a house I was buying. The year was 1987, and the home was in Paradise Valley, Arizona. It was kind of a hidden jewel. I saw a sign on it one morning when I was jogging and decided to make a call. The house was small, but sat on two and a half acres surrounded by four other houses on five acres. I knew homes with that kind of acreage were not common, so I thought there might be value in this property.

When I got the broker on the line, he said his mother had passed away and they needed to sell the house quickly. They were asking $225,000 and would carry some amount for a quick close. I offered $185,000 that day, and they accepted my offer. That gave me thirty days to close and find the money!

Working with the title company, I asked them to pull up all the sales in the surrounding area so I could see who my neighbors were and how much they paid for their properties. What I discovered was that about five of the ten surrounding properties had changed hands in the last twelve months. Then I noticed something even more interesting about the sales. Each one was in a different name or entity, but they all had the same mailing address for the tax bills.

BINGO! The light went on that someone had been assembling these larger properties. I went to the address on the tax rolls and found out the entity was a land development company in town. Furthermore, I read in the paper that this land development company had just signed the Ritz Carlton and was going to announce a resort hotel development shortly!

Thanks to the information from my title company, I now knew that I was just about to close on a piece of property that the land development company needed to complete the assemblage for their planned resort development. After I closed on the house, I set up a meeting with the development company and subsequently sold them the property for $375,000. A whopping $150,000 more than I paid for it! On top of that windfall, I negotiated free rent to live in the house for one year. Remember what wise old Ben said: "Diligence is the mother of good luck."

THIRD PARTY REPORTS REVIEW

This is another crucial part of the due diligence process. The third party reports that I am talking about are primarily the Environmental, Property Conditions, Appraisal, and Market Study. You may or may not need them based on the type of property you are buying, but in most cases they are good to get and even may be required by your lender. Let's start at the top of the list.

ENVIRONMENTAL

I would highly recommend that you hire a company to provide you with an environmental study on the property. This report looks at soil composition, hazardous materials, and the like. Typically you contract for a Phase 1 report, which is affordable, approximately in the $2,000 to $3,000 range. This report is well worth the expense if the company turns something up like toxicity in the soil or some other hazardous materials.

TIP The downside risk is way too large not to spend the money on a Phase 1 environmental report. Do one, no matter what.

If you are using a conventional financing source, your lender will require a Phase 1 report. They often have an approved list of vendors, so I recommend that you check with your lender before you hire a provider to do this work. If you do not have a lender yet, you should hire a national company that has affiliates in your region, then ask them for a list of lenders they have done business with.

PROPERTY CONDITIONS REPORT

A property conditions report does just as the name states. It will call out issues with the property's condition that the inspections reveal. This would include structural issues, roofs, asphalt, sewer, and other building systems. The report also will give you an estimated useful life for those items. This is very important when you are capitalizing your budget.

TIP The property conditions report gives you a second opinion on the condition of the property and can either affirm/dispute the inspection findings that you and your property management firm did earlier. Or it can find something you both have overlooked. That's important to know.

When it comes to costs, property conditions reports can be all over the board, but this is no place to skimp. Not only do you want a firm that is experienced and knowledgeable, you want to hire a firm that has a national presence and is acceptable to your lender if you know who that is. As I mentioned earlier, if you have not yet chosen a lender, your inspection company may be able to help with a recommendation.

The other benefit of having a property conditions report is that it is a third party report and completely unbiased, in contrast to the report compiled by your property management company. If you go back to the seller with your property management report, asking the seller to pay for something that is wrong with the property, he or she may feel that the report is biased in your favor. That's hard to do when you are also holding a third party property condition report that reflects the exact same issue. This report gives you much more credibility and negotiating power.

APPRAISAL

Depending on how sophisticated a real estate investor you are, you may not think you need an appraisal. My advice is almost always to get one. If you are financing your project, you will need one anyway, and why not be sure that the property is valued where you believe it to be? It validates your own assessments, or in some cases refutes them. Either way, the knowledge is good to have.

As the borrower, it can get a little dicey if you hire the appraiser. Federally chartered banks have guidelines that they must adhere to. One of those guidelines is that the borrower cannot order the appraisal. Most banks and nonbank lenders are more comfortable making the decision on whom to hire. What I do in those instances is let the mortgage broker hire the appraiser or go to the lender with an appraiser in mind and let him hire that person. I generally want some say in the appraiser.

The mistake I see the most is when appraisers are hired and they are inexperienced in the type of property the buyer is purchasing. I run into this quite a bit with banks. They just send out a bid sheet to three appraisers and hire one not necessarily based on his expertise but on his time availability and price. A bad appraisal can bring the entire transaction to a standstill in a second.

To avoid this I always suggest having one or two appraisers that are good at what they do and qualified in your type of property that you can recommend to the bank. I also recommend that you take the time, or let your mortgage broker take the time, to share your vision of the property with the appraiser. If the appraiser does not see the value that you currently see or are going to create, you are toast. Finally, be proactive with him and provide him with as much information as you can.

TIP Remember an appraisal is an opinion of value. You may have, and are entitled to have, your own opinion, but you'd better be ready to back it up.

MARKET STUDY

Usually the appraisal will contain a good discussion of the market for your type of property. However if you are planning to do something a little more on the edge or something that is complex like a condo conversion, hotel, golf course, or some kind of unique single family project, for example, you may need an additional market study not only for your own knowledge but to help move your ideas forward with the people around you.

There are companies, both regional and national, that can do market studies geared directly toward your kind of project and just about any other kind of project including ones I mentioned in the previous paragraph. Consider engaging them to do the report and show it to everyone who you think needs to see it. What I mean by that is show your market study to clarify and support your vision and to defend your position.

TIP Show your market study to clarify and support your vision and to defend your position.

Warning—these market reports can be expensive. It is common to see them run in the $10,000 to $30,000 range. But at times, they are worth their weight in gold. I have successfully used these types of reports to argue the assumptions used in an appraisal that came in low. Again, it is much easier to argue your points on absorption, price points, rents, etc., when you have a credible third-party report supporting you.

ACCOUNTING AND TAX REVIEW

This is the last review on our list, and it is the one that can make you very happy at tax time. Having an excellent real estate and tax accountant on your side is critical. You are going to have to make decisions prior to closing the transaction and post closing, and the advice you need can come only from people who make their living understanding and staying on top of complex tax code. Prior to closing, they can work with your lawyer to develop the best ownership structure for you and/or your partners. Is it an LLC? A corporation? And how should it be structured? It matters because as you learned in the chapter on entity structures in this book, these decisions have tax implications. Post closing, your tax accountant can file the K-1 forms (the form used to report each owner's share of income and certain expense items) and perform audits if necessary.

TIP **If you do not have a good real estate and tax accountant, get one.**

One of the great benefits of being in the mortgage brokerage business is that I get to see amazing real estate projects and have the privilege of helping very creative entrepreneurs put those real estate projects together. I have learned much more from their good practices and bad decisions than I ever did in school or in my own real estate investment career.

Real estate is a magical way to use leverage to your advantage and develop sustainable wealth. With that as a premise, it also requires you have a professional focus that not only sees the big picture or vision but also forces you to pay attention to the details.

All real estate involves taking risks. The difference between the professional investor and the amateur is that the real professional tries to manage this risk by surrounding himself or herself with an incredible team that adds value at every turn. Property due diligence is one of those turns and it is too critical to just roll the dice!

 **Scott McPherson** is a principal and cofounder of a highly specialized real estate finance company called Capital Advisory Group, LC. Established in 2001, the firm has successfully closed around $3.5 billion of structured debt and equity in the United States. Scott has financed everything from raw land to high-rise condominium towers from Portland, Oregon, to Tampa, Florida, and has successfully sourced and closed multiple projects in excess of $100 million in cost. For more information, visit www.capitaladvisorygroup.us.

● Kim DALTON

11

Creating Value from the Inside Out

I often refer to Kim Dalton as the chameleon. She is the interior designer my wife, Kim, and I hired to be a member of our design team—a team of professionals that included our architect, general contractor, landscape architect, and interior designer. I describe Kim Dalton as a chameleon because there were days I did not recognize her. She would show up at the job site completely transformed with a totally different look and a totally different energy. She would change as the nature of the project changed. She was that flexible, and design flexibility is essential for an interior designer.

Today, when people walk into our home or our business offices, they often say "ooooh" and "aaaah" because the impact of Kim's work is powerful, yet subtle. Kim's input to our projects is priceless. Not only does she increase the immediate sales value of our projects, her work gives our home and business environment warmth. Her work increases our desire to stay at home and also to be at work.

As a professional real estate investor, I think there is nothing worse than a multimillion dollar project that goes cheap on interior design. I have been in homes, condos, and commercial projects where the developer went cheap or went boring, leaving the interior design up to him or his wife. Rather than inspire a sale, cheap and tacky interior design can drive buyers away. You'd be surprised how inexpensive coats of paint in different or unique shades can make a $100,000 *project look like a million dollar project. That is why Kim Dalton's professional design touch is essential to our success in real estate.*

—ROBERT KIYOSAKI

Perhaps I'm biased, but I consider interior design to be an essential part of real estate investing. Whether you are planning a spec home, preparing an existing home for resale, rehabilitating a multifamily complex, or renovating a commercial property, appropriate interior design can always help to increase the value of a property. It can also dramatically shorten your sales cycle. Thoughtful interior design will carefully organize space while integrating color, light, pattern, and finish in order to supplement function, flow, and performance.

Don't be confused. Interior design is not home staging, which was developed years ago to help homeowners sell residential properties. Staging specialists are trained to maximize the perception of space and light using principles that appeal to a broader audience of potential buyers rather than family, friends, and guests. Interior designers do all that plus include the elements of aesthetics, temperature, sound, smell, balance, and harmony. All of these are value-added elements that will help your property sell quickly and easily. They are certainly worth your consideration as an investor and could very well be the difference between selling a property and getting top dollar for a property.

ASSEMBLING YOUR TEAM

Although you may see putting together a team of professionals for your real estate project as a costly and unnecessary expense, in reality it can be the smartest investment you make beyond the investment in the property itself. Strongly consider any or all of the following professionals to help you make the most of your investment project. I am and have been very careful with my team selection. I started my business by aligning myself with a great architect and that relationship has lasted for more than twenty years. I know that the way my team collaborates is instrumental in the outcome of any project I undertake. Your team should include an architect, interior designer, general contractor, landscape architect, engineers, and appropriate subcontractors. Your architect and general contractor will usually recommend engineers and subcontractors with whom they work, but it never hurts to have a few in your back pocket.

How to Select Your Team

1. **Interview.** Ask the tough design questions, but also try to get to know the person to understand how he or she works.
2. **Conversations with references.** Ask about the outcome of the project, but also listen for clues about work habits and service philosophy. Always ask the question: "Would you hire this person again?"
3. **Site visits to similar projects.** Visit and view the end result to assess if the final product lives up to the words.
4. **Willingness.** How willing is this person to work holistically to achieve a common goal, that is, a profitable product that sells quickly and easily? If a potential team member balks at the collaborative approach, it may be best to move on.

Assemble your team right at the start because early involvement will benefit both the process and the outcome. Delivering value is key, so the sooner the team is assembled, the sooner everyone can begin contributing. The earlier in the process those ideas surface, the more likely it will be that they can be implemented.

Real Life Story: Having a Team You Can Count On Really Counts

We have a wonderful client who has several homes. Some time ago, we were awarded an elaborate remodel of their vacation home in Santa Fe. Because we were based in Scottsdale, Arizona, we thought it might be more cost effective to hire a local contractor to handle the details for phase one of the project. We learned the value of a cohesive team the hard way.

Although we made several trips to check on the project and oversee the construction, we hit a few roadblocks. The contractor had challenges he could not handle with the team he had assembled, and communication was difficult from the get-go. When we embarked upon phase two of the project, we decided to use our Arizona-based team to handle the project. Instantly, our communication improved and we were able to solve problems much more quickly than before. Moreover, because our tradespeople had worked together so often in the past, they were able to effectively collaborate and avoid potential pitfalls even when they were on site without us.

Teams make great things happen. One day several years ago, Robert Kiyosaki stopped by to visit me in my office. He wanted to discuss a new project he had for me. My excited staff gathered around to hear all about it. Robert humbly mentioned that while he was not a very knowledgeable man (highly debatable by many), he did consider himself to be excellent at assembling a team of experts in their respective fields. He considers that to be of utmost importance when embarking on a project of any type. He has come to call that team his "trusted advisors," many of whom appear in this book.

Now let's get to the people you'll want on your team.

TEAM MEMBER NO. 1: THE ARCHITECT

The right architect can be invaluable in providing not only a set of drawings for construction but also insight into current trends in construction, engineering, lighting, and environmentally friendly design. I don't do anything today without an eye toward green sustainable design. Depending on the size and scope of your project, you can look to an architect to help guide the planning, design, documentation, and construction administration of your project.

The architect on any project is usually considered the team leader. Not only will he or she be able to provide a wealth of recommendations for other team members, the architect will also be instrumental in keeping the project on track, both from a budget standpoint as well as in terms of scheduling. Additionally, because of the nature of their work, architects must be up to the minute on current building codes and requirements. Building code violations can severely impede the construction process by the assessment of fines and a significant disruption in schedule. A good architect can also be an invaluable asset when applying for building permits.

You'll want to select an architect who will assume the role of team leader, while allowing his or her team to flourish under his guidance. Again, collaboration is the key here. While an architect is valuable for many parts of the project, he or she must rely on team members for their respective talents. Of course, basic chemistry is always a good barometer. Trust your intuition. Is this someone whom I could trust with my project? Remember, the whole idea of assembling a team is to allow you to achieve something you do not have the experience or expertise to accomplish yourself.

When it comes to money, architectural fees vary with the project scope and needs. Most architects will prefer to work on a fixed-fee basis with a defined scope of work, or on an hourly basis with a "not to exceed" fee limit.

TEAM MEMBER NO. 2: THE INTERIOR DESIGNER

The right interior designer is the one who not only shares your vision but enhances it. He or she is the next necessary addition to your team. An interior designer differs from an architect in many ways. While an architect is concerned with the structure of your space, the interior designer helps you create spaces that work and that flow in a logical and functional way.

Because an architect's role encompasses several aspects of the design and construction process, the interior designer can focus on realizing the overall vision of the project. Several years ago, I was hired to design a home on the coast of Oregon for a longtime client. Luckily, I was brought on early in the project to work with the client and the architect before they had completed the plans. We traveled to Oregon, walked the site, and talked for hours about what the house was to be. From those many discussions, we developed a set of rules for the house. This would allow both the architect and me to adhere to those rules and keep the design intent consistent. It becomes the designer's job to ensure the interior of the space will function as the team intends. Finishes, lighting, and furniture are all integral parts of a successful project. The interior designer can assist in any or all of these areas as well as in accessorizing and art placement.

The same rules for selecting an architect apply to selecting a designer. Fortunately your architect can often recommend a designer or two from his own team who would be ideal for your project. That's how I began working with Robert and Kim. Several years ago, they bought a very tired, but charming home with the intent of lovingly restoring and adding on to it to make it their own. They hired an architect who referred a general contractor. They also hired an interior designer referred by a friend to complete their team. While Kim and Robert are very easy to work with, the process did not go smoothly. A second designer was hired with similar results. She simply did not share the vision the team had. This is in no way a reflection on those designers or their capabilities. It is simply a reinforcement of the importance of the team as a whole. Nevertheless, the contractor arranged a meeting between the team and me, and the rest is history. The team certainly faced its challenges along the way, but we all shared the same vision, had a common goal, and were determined to produce the best project possible.

TEAM MEMBER NO. 3: THE LANDSCAPE ARCHITECT

The landscape architect is in charge of site design, and this is the one person, more than any other, who will set the property's first impression. When you think landscape architect, think curb appeal, and if you've bought or sold a home, you know the importance of that. Look to a landscape architect for regional neighborhood context design, site planning and furnishings, and high-impact features with low maintenance. You want a design that enhances the overall quality of the building or development and mixes well with the environment. Here's what I mean.

I recently completed a facelift for a twenty-year-old office building. The owner wanted to sell and felt a fresh look to the building would speed up the process. Without a huge budget, we knew we had to rely on color and landscape to do the trick. We selected exterior paint colors to work with the existing natural stone and brought in a landscape architect to accentuate the building's best attributes. He suggested we clean up the entry by reducing the number of overgrown plants, replacing them with smaller, easily maintained varieties. This gave the building a cleaner aesthetic as well as an enticement to potential buyers who were looking for less exterior maintenance. He also worked to accentuate the main entries of the building, leading tenants and visitors to the entrances with ease.

TEAM MEMBER NO. 4: THE GENERAL CONTRACTOR

Very often, team members will recommend a general contractor with whom they have successfully collaborated. If not, please refer to your local state agencies to assist with the selection of a qualified contractor. When choosing a general contractor, I look for a company or a person with whom I would enjoy socializing. I know that sounds strange, but remember, this will be the team member you will see most often. Of course, this person must meet all the other criteria as well, but you really must have a good relationship with your contractor. After all, he will be responsible for spending your money. Whenever Robert and Kim embark on another project, we all look forward to the reunion of our team, knowing the general contractor will ensure we get the project done with minimal problems.

Many investors opt to handle the oversight of a project on their own. While this can work well, it more often than not goes badly, particularly if the person is inexperienced. My advice to clients is to always consider the scope and complexity of the job before making that decision. Think about it. Do you have another career that will keep you away from the jobsite? What is your time worth compared to a contractor's fee? Are you familiar with the local building codes, construction methods, backup trades if necessary? Do you have strengths in scheduling, budgeting, and managing people?

The value of an experienced contractor to manage the project and tradespeople is often a smart investment. On the other hand, if your remodel includes little more than paint and carpet, you may be fine managing the project. A brief consultation with an interior designer can help you select materials and provide recommendations for appropriate trades. Bear in mind, however, sometimes small projects lead to bigger ones. I've witnessed the discovery of problems that are bigger than any owner can handle.

Eventually, the more you work with your team of experts, the more they will become your trusted advisors, and you'll consult them for projects big or small. The more longevity you have with your team members and the more your rapport and working relationship with them grows, the better your outcomes will be. I've found that projects become easier, move quicker, and deliver better results the longer I work with my team. Robert understands this, and that is one of the benefits of this book. His trusted advisors—his team—can now be your team through the pages of this book.

As a real estate investor, you will want to maximize your return. And just as good property management plays a huge role in a property's value, so does the design of that property. But how do you know what design will bring in the bucks and what will just be another expense that lowers your bottom line return? Here are the guidelines I use for different types of real estate endeavors.

EXISTING HOME STRATEGIES THAT SELL

The trend of purchasing an existing home, remodeling, and selling it has made the need for staging unavoidable. Everyone wants to buy a home that looks like a builder's model. This concept was first developed by Barb Schwartz in 1972 and has grown over the years to become a widely used selling tool. It's all about merchandising the rooms to make them look like much more than just four walls.

TIP The goal of interior design for a residence is to personalize the space according to the tastes and preferences of the homeowner. Staging is the opposite. The professional stager's job is to depersonalize the space and allow potential buyers to imagine themselves living there.

As I mentioned before, professional staging is often confused with interior design and actually, the two couldn't be more different. Let's talk about staging for a moment because it is crucial to selling an existing home. When you decide to sell, agree that you will live there in a much different way. In fact, you'll want to get packing early because all the personal effects in your home must go. Precious collections, photos, mementos, all the things that are "you" will say to prospective buyers that this is your home, not theirs. So if you hire a stager or do it yourself, get serious and get rid of the clutter. It's all about vision.

As an interior designer of both residential and commercial spaces for more than twenty years, the last thing I thought I needed when preparing to list my home for sale was a stager. My realtor tactfully suggested that I meet with her stager, "It can't hurt," she said. I grudgingly agreed. I will warn you, this is a humbling experience. It's unsettling to have someone tell you that your collection of exquisite Chinese foo dogs may be best placed in a box in the garage. My advice is to listen and obey. I had spent seven years working to create a cozy space out of a large, open tract house. She told me I had succeeded. That, however, is not what the typical homebuyer is looking for. Light, bright, and airy still seems to be the best rule of thumb when preparing to sell a home. Also, clean, uncluttered rooms provide the most appeal.

In tough real estate markets when nothing is selling, the staged house will nine times out of ten be the one that sells first. So, as much as you won't like them, here are the five C's of successful staging:

1. **Clean.** Everything should be immaculate. That means carpets, floors, walls, counters, and bathrooms should look model-home perfect.
2. **Clutter Free.** Make counters, tables, and shelves ready for the buyer's favorite things, not yours. Remove everything, and then some more.
3. **Color.** You may have loved it wild and crazy to match your purple sofa, but buyers want to picture their own furniture and colors. Hot pink walls make that difficult.
4. **Creativity.** Give buyers something to talk about and remember. They'll be looking at a lot of homes that eventually all blend together. Make yours unforgettable.
5. **Compromise.** Stagers will tell you to do it all, and you may find that you'll only go so far. No problem. Compromise and do those things that matter most.

Did you know that most buyers make their buying decisions within the first fifteen seconds of seeing a property? That's a prevailing rule in real estate that I believe to be absolutely true. What does that tell us? First impressions are everything. It's worth spending extra time and money on curb appeal or the wow factor of the house.

Sell That House in Fifteen Seconds or Less

First impressions are everything and buying decisions are made in the first fifteen seconds. Here are the top five areas to spruce up:

1. **The front yard,** including lawn, trees, walkway—clean, sweep, and plant flowers with lots of color.

2. **The front door** and entryway—Give your door some color, or at least remove the cobwebs, and then be sure the first few steps inside the home are memorable.

3. **Exterior and interior paint**—nothing freshens a home more than new paint.

4. **Flooring,** including carpets, tile, etc.—no stains, no worn carpet, no dirt allowed.

5. **Healthy green plants**—emphasis on healthy, shiny plants without dead or dry leaves, dust, messy pots or water stains. Placing plants and trees near windows will blur the gap between inside and out, thus making the space feel larger and more connected to nature.

Staging will make your property look so good that, if it is your own home, you'll wonder why you lived in it the way you did for all those years. I advise everyone, particularly after my own experience, to hire a stager to help you weed out the clutter. It takes brutal honesty, and stagers are known for it. Stagers will rearrange furniture to maximize the appearance of space as well as downplay less desirable features. If you want to take things to the next level—and in tight markets you may have little choice—hire a professional stager and allow him or her to use their existing inventory of accoutrements to enhance your home.

If you are selling a home that is unoccupied, don't listen to people who say an empty home sells better than one that is furnished. If that were true, no builder would ever furnish a model home, and most all of them do. Stage the home as best you can within your budget. If you can't rent furniture from a stager for the main rooms, set up small vignettes within the home. This can be as simple as adding a few wall hangings, live plants, towels in the master bath, and soft music. You'll be surprised at the results.

The tangible aspects of a home are important, but there are intangibles as well that you must consider. Have you ever walked into a space and immediately felt uncomfortable, but had no idea why? That's energy flow, and all spaces have it. That discomfort usually comes from stale or bad energy in a space. There are consultants who specialize in clearing spaces of this negative energy. The ancient art of feng shui incorporates these principles and has done so for more

---

Real Life Story: It's All About Experience

Recently my real estate agent, Joanne Callaway, related a staging success story to me. She had been trying for months to sell a seemingly marketable home. The only problem area was the dining room. It had one red wall to match the homeowners' linens. I was surprised that this was the problem area as I often paint dining rooms red. Nevertheless, Joanne called upon the services of her favorite stager who immediately had the wall painted, changed the linens, added cushions to the dining chairs, and the house sold in one week!

---

than three thousand years. Listed at the end of this chapter are Web sites that will help you understand energy flow and how to improve it in your home.

Believe it or not, your own energy will either add to or detract from your home. A positive attitude will create better energy in the space. Instead of worrying about how long it will take you to sell the house, imagine how great those precious foo dogs will look in your *new* home.

I know this all sounds like a lot of effort, but consider the statistics—having homes properly staged significantly shortens the selling cycle as well as brings a higher selling price.

There are lots of helpful resources to learn more about staging, such as home stagingresource.com and stagedhomes.com. Perhaps the best book on staging is by the creator of staging itself, Barb Schwarz. Her book, *Home Staging: The Winning Way to Sell Your House for More Money* is the bible on the subject. And she's right about staging paying dividends. Homestaging.com. sites a recent HomeGain Survey that shows home staging delivered as much as a 169 percent return on investment. That's a significant figure, making staging well worth the time and effort.

MAKE YOUR MULTIFAMILY HOUSING PROJECT A WINNER

Just as selling your own home is less about you and is all about the buyer, when investing in multifamily housing, it's all about the target resident. Ask yourself, "Who is that person, and what will he or she want or expect from this property?" Then, how can you take those expectations one step further to truly wow them? Whether you developed the project from the ground up or are rehabilitating an existing property, spend your money on the things that will count in the eyes of the target resident. Of course, you'll want to contain your ambitions to a reasonable amount in proportion to the potential rent you can collect, but you will need to focus on those things that will leave a lasting impression. If a property isn't special in some way, it will not be easy to rent. Ask yourself, "Why would someone rent this property instead of the one down the street?" Consider these factors when preparing a multifamily project:

1. **Curb appeal.** Clean up the trees, bushes, add a fresh coat of paint, dress up the windows with awnings or shutters, repair steps and walkways, re-sod the lawns, and plant flowers, lots of flowers.
2. **Accessibility.** Make sure you purchase properties with ample parking for residents and guests. Inadequate parking is next to impossible to change. The property should be ADA (Americans with Disabilities Act) compliant, or you may have to make it that way, which can be costly.
3. **Location.** This is real estate, after all, and location is everything.
4. **Security and safety.** Walls, security gates, security alarms, and security cameras all add up to making residents feel safer, and can also justify higher rents for very little up-front investment.
5. **Durable finishes.** If you are rehabbing the property, use the best finishes you can afford and still maintain your profitability projections. Check your competition in the area. If they have tile counters, you may need to have tile counters.
6. **Neutral finishes.** This is so important in multifamily projects. Choose colors that work for everyone, which usually means light, light, light.
7. **Common area aesthetic.** Is there a pool? Is there a clubhouse? Is there a courtyard or garden? If so, it should look picturesque, clean, and be a true amenity, not an eyesore. Make it a point of difference.
8. **Views.** People buy views, and views can be big wow factors. Even if your project doesn't look out to rocky mountain majesty, be sure it doesn't look out on the dumpster or an unkempt parking lot. If you are building, plan for internal views to gardens or pool areas.

Showing a rental property is no different than showing a home. Here we go again! Yes, you'll want to furnish a model if you can. Rental spaces are usually small and look even smaller without furniture. Once furniture is in place, however, spaces look bigger, and people can visualize living in them. They can see that the space isn't small after all. It is cozy, livable, and oftentimes just right.

Senior living properties are another type of multi-unit housing. As the baby boomers age, the concept of the traditional nursing home is changing rapidly and drastically. Independent living facilities are being built all over the country, and there are new requirements for them, not all of which are coming from government regulations. I'm talking about buyers' requirements. This aging population demands a much higher level of design than the generation preceding it and they are willing to pay accordingly.

I am currently working with a developer on a number of senior living communities. Think twenty-first century; they in no way resemble the nursing homes of the past! These independent living communities are based on the desire for an active lifestyle with minimal constraints from the residents' pasts, i.e., home maintenance, yards, housekeeping, etc. These communities focus on the active lifestyles of this population with the utmost attention placed on comfort, autonomy, and quality of life. Obviously, we are working to respect and deliver on the changing needs of this population as it ages, but research has proven that it can be done with good design and thoughtful planning. One project will be set on the side of a mountain, and the hilly terrain obviously presents potential obstacles for an aging population. The architects and landscape architects have worked on a site plan that will take advantage of the scenic views and the wonderful climate by means of a series of covered breezeways and no stairs. This is just one example of how we can maximize accessibility without calling attention to potential limitations.

COMMERCIAL SPACES THAT STAND THE TEST OF TIME

As you venture into the world of commercial real estate, many of the principles we already talked about still apply. But first and foremost, you still need to take the target tenant into account first and create a fantastic first impression. After all, people want to be proud of where they work, and they want that space to be functional and comfortable. That charge isn't always easy because commercial properties can often be quite large, quite complex, and rather impersonal. The key is creating personal, more intimate spaces inside or outside a large building to add that personal touch and provide respite from a busy day. It doesn't take much. A shady tree, a fountain, or a comfortable bench away from the hustle and bustle can achieve this important goal. Alcoves within a lobby space with nice art and comfortable furniture can work, too, while they welcome visitors and provide a gathering place for tenants.

If your project is new construction, get an architect and an interior designer on board right from the start. An architect's primary role is creating the structure itself. An interior designer's role is to design the interior spaces. Unless you do this for a living, creating the design by yourself will not work. I've seen the aftermath of do-it-yourself commercial projects, and many of them are beyond hope or beyond the pocketbooks or the profit potential of most buyers to rehabilitate.

Lifecycle costs (meaning how long do you want these materials to last, will a new tenant mean new finishes?) and total budget are great places to begin your discussion with these professionals. They'll want to know who your target market is because they will design differently for a medical building than they would for a day care center, for instance. You've probably heard this phrase before: "form follows function." Well, this is what they mean by it.

While form and function are absolutely critical to good commercial space, so is using the natural environment as a guide to design. In fact, it has and, I would go so far to say, always will be a failsafe guide for many interior designers and architects in their quest for interiors and structures that stand the test of time. That's why certain styles of design and architecture are common to certain areas of the country and, indeed, the world. Suitable architecture and design respond to the environment rather than fight it. By using the natural environment as a guide, interior designers and architects establish rules to help guide the design process. And it's best to stick with them.

Unfortunately, rules get broken, and not always in a good ways. One building comes to mind in Phoenix—a desert city with desert mountains surrounding it and very bright sun most days of the year. Smack in the midst of mostly stucco buildings is a dark, wooden, modern for its circa-1970 construction structure that looks like it should be in the middle of the Rockies in Colorado. Interestingly, when I look at this building in Phoenix, it seems terribly out of date and out of place, but if I picture it among the pines and aspens in Colorado it would be spectacular. That's what I mean. The architect and designer of this project did not look to the environment and, therefore, the building design did not last.

So when I hear the common question when starting a new project, "Will it be outdated in five years?" I always have the answer: "Not if we build in harmony with the environment." The best way to avoid the problem of short-lived trends is to use materials and color palettes derived from the surrounding environment. The natural environment will not change drastically, and that means a timeless aesthetic to your building.

The only time this doesn't work is if the design is for a high impact space that needs an extreme reaction to attract tenants or visitors. These projects tend to be controversial and often get early press attention because one group or another loves or hates the design. But once completed they often become well-known and admired landmarks. Projects that fall into this category could include an art museum or a high-end jewelry store.

TIP The best way to avoid the problem of short-lived trends is to use materials and color palettes derived from the surrounding environment. The natural environment will not change drastically and that means a timeless aesthetic to your building.

Renovating a property requires a different tack because there are subtle trends in design that when followed will improve your chances of success. For instance, color preferences change from decade to decade, and you absolutely want to be up to date, not a throwback from the last century, unless your property is historic and then you'll want to go two centuries back. But kidding aside, color is critical. We've all seen buildings or been in offices with outdated colors of walls, cabinetries, floors, and carpets. They don't look like places with companies poised for future growth; they look like places where companies go to stagnate and die. It's amazing how interiors drive our impressions, but right or wrong, they always do.

To find out what colors are trending up, take a walk through some of the newest retail centers—the highest-end ones you can find—and you will see many examples of colors and materials. Locations that come to mind are Kierland Commons in Phoenix or La Encantada in Tucson—both Westcor properties. The Power & Light District in Kansas City, The Palazzo in Las Vegas. There are many others.

Of course, you will have a plan for the revitalization of your commercial building, and it will be based on projected net operating income and cash flow. But some designers don't relate to the numbers side of the business and can develop designs that spiral costs out of control. Choose a designer that understands the business fundamentals of an investment property and be critical when evaluating a proposed plan to update a building. Believe it or not, simple things like paint, landscape, and signage can go a long way when sprucing up an existing property.

As with the other types of properties, commercial buildings require balance and harmony, too. Office buildings are meant to house large numbers of varying businesses in the same overall space. When you utilize the principles of balance, harmony, light, and accessibility, it can only enhance the workplace experience.

Commercial Building Must Have's

1. **Accessibility.** ADA compliance is a must, as is ample parking and easement access.

2. **Ease of circulation, both internal and external.** Well thought-out placement of elevators, doors, lobbies, signage, etc., go a long way.

3. **Intuitive way finding.** Buildings and office spaces built like mazes are not fun. They leave guests lost and sometimes even embarrassed. In emergencies they can be dangerous.

4. **Customization.** What is the unique wow factor for this building? There should always be one.

5. **Familiarity.** Way finding is a method people use to intuitively navigate a space. Using landmarks like the big painting or the blue floor or the potted plant to remember the way lessens any anxiety about being in an unfamiliar place.

6. **Smell.** Some people are going so far as to run scent through their ventilation. Scent matters because our sense of smell affects our mood and is closely tied to memory centers in the brain (UPI, October 17, 2008).

7. **Sound.** If you can hear the quiet, break the silence with soft music that fills the room. Match the music to the mood you are trying to convey and you'll have a winner.

8. **Location, location, location.** When it is all said and done, location is the key.

SUSTAINABLE DESIGN

In recent years we have seen an enormous push toward sustainable or green design. Sustainable design means using our resources efficiently while creating healthier buildings. A green building is one that is designed, built, renovated, operated, or reused in an ecological and resource-efficient manner. You may think that green building design is more expensive than conventional building practices, yet while some up-front costs may be higher, the long-term benefits, both financially and environmentally, generally outweigh the initial costs. Proper design can significantly reduce operating costs over the life of the building while helping to preserve natural resources and minimize waste.

The first stop for anyone interested in green design, and today that should be everyone, is the Green Building Council and its Green Building Rating System called LEED, Leadership in Energy and Environmental Design. This rating system is the nationally accepted benchmark for the design, construction, and operation of high-performance green buildings. LEED process certification provides building owners and operators with the tools they need to have an immediate and measurable impact on their building's performance. LEED principles have now been adapted to a variety of residential and commercial building types.

The city of Scottsdale, Arizona, was one of the first in the country to adopt a voluntary Green Building Designation Program. Those homeowners, developers, and builders wishing to participate must complete a detailed checklist based on a point system. Points are given for meeting or exceeding environmentally considerate building materials and practices. Applicants must meet the point total necessary for certification. These categories range from recycled building materials to the use of indigenous materials, which cuts fuel consumption, to energy use.

Green Building Check List

Use this checklist when developing your green design plan.

1. **Sustainable site.** Opt for an existing site rather than undeveloped land.
2. **Water efficiency.** Think about adding on-site infiltration systems and storm water management.
3. **Energy and atmosphere.** Consider the location of the building as it relates to natural light, and explore the use of solar power.
4. **Materials and resources.** Always research the possibility of using reclaimed construction materials.
5. **Indoor environmental air quality.** Reducing off-gassing from furniture and finishes can lead to improved overall indoor air quality.
6. **Research.** Do your homework to ensure you have carefully considered all viable options to help ensure the completion of a sustainable project.

Once you get your green designation from the city or town, you'll be in a position to take advantage of it. Here are just a few of the benefits of green building:

1. Social and economic revitalization of depressed or disadvantaged neighborhoods and renewed sense of community pride

2. Greater market demand for the project

3. Water conservation and lower costs

4. Reduction of air and water pollution

5. Great energy and power reliability and reduced dependence on the local power grid

6. Reduced waste clogging up our landfills and conservation of new resources

7. Improved health of construction workers and building occupants

8. Superior indoor air quality

All these add up to a better, more responsible working environment that people can be truly proud of, enjoy working in, and feel better about. That signals more productivity.

Of course anyone doing any new building, remodeling, or revitalization knows that the quicker you can get through the city planning and zoning review process the better. Plan reviews can often take up to several months, and you know what they say: "Time is money." But some municipalities are providing incentives. For example, builders who participate in the Scottsdale Green Building Program projects receive "fast track" plan review service. This means green building projects receive building permits in half the time as regular projects, depending on the degree of complexity.

On the other hand, site inspections tend to be more thorough, scrutinizing environmentally sensitive aspects of the building to make sure they measure up to the standard. The city also provides Green Building site signage, which tells the world that this owner is willing to invest in the protection of the environment. Anyway you slice it, that adds up to good public relations as well as responsible development.

Government agencies in Arizona have become involved in enticing companies to "go green" by offering sales tax exemption for the purchase of solar energy devices. Also, local power companies offer rebates to those companies willing to invest in solar power. I fully expect to see tax concessions on the use of environmentally supportive or recycled materials in the coming years.

THE FINAL WORD

Design, whether it be green or any other color in the rainbow has the power to add value to your property. From residential to commercial, every property can benefit from good interior design, and it can save you from making costly mistakes that, once made, are hard to correct. The key is maximizing the space and the light, and working in harmony with the environment. Hire the right professional to pull all this together and you'll have a timeless building that you'll enjoy or will generate income for you for years to come.

Ways to Learn More

www.epa.gov/brownfields
www.epa.gov/owow
www.energycodes.gov
www.ashrae.org
www.asgbc.org/resources
www.spiritualclearing.com

Kim Dalton is an award-winning interior designer with more than twenty years of innovative interior design experience. She has the unique ability to transform clinical and institutional spaces into supportive, healing environments that are cohesive, economical, and timeless. Since founding Dalton Interiors in 1990, Kim has designed significant real estate projects, including Phoenix Children's Hospital, Del E. Webb Memorial Hospital, Christ Church of the Valley, and suite renovations at Chase Field in Phoenix.

Scott D. McPHERSON

12

Financing for Real Estate Investors

*S*cott McPherson is the mortgage broker I go to when I want to know the straight story about what's going on in real estate financing. He's more than just a mortgage broker; he is an investor, and, again, like all the others in this book, he lives what he teaches.

I can count on Scott to be a part of teaching the classes I hold on finance. He donates his time, just like he did to contribute to this book, to teach others how to be smarter with their money and with their investments. He has years of wisdom, is smart and experienced, and is an excellent resource particularly during times of economic chaos.

I met Scott in an unlikely place at the Phoenix Open Golf Tournament in 1999. His reputation preceded him; I knew him, but I did not think he knew me. When I discovered he agreed with my position on stocks and mutual funds, I felt relief and affirmation. Few agreed with me at the time, and I was under attack. Now people are learning otherwise, and they are seeing their stock and 401(k) portfolios slashed. The critics aren't so loud anymore.

From that day forward, Scott has been a great friend and a trusted advisor to Kim and me. He has the ability to see what's on the horizon. He has saved Kim and me a lot of money and saved us from a few investments that would have been *mistakes. I cannot emphasize the importance of having trusted advisors around you. If you can find a mortgage broker like Scott, you're very lucky.*

—ROBERT KIYOSAKI

I have always believed from early on, that there is no substitution for actual experience, no matter what you take on in your life. I can tell you that I am not a professional writer, but I am very active in the real estate finance business.

The principles of real estate finance are basically the same whether you are buying a single family home to rent or you are converting three hundred rental apartments to for-sale condominiums in Scottsdale, Arizona. The key to understanding real estate financing is really not a secret; it is just how to ask yourself some basic questions and follow some very simple steps along the way.

What I want to do in this chapter is walk you through the fundamentals of real estate finance and give you the pathway to apply them to your particular situation or requirements.

BEING BORN WITH A SILVER PAINT BRUSH IN HAND!

When I was studying real estate and finance at Arizona State University, I thought I had the world by the tail and could hardly wait to get out and carve my niche in the real estate business. I was living in an upscale apartment near campus, driving a nice car, and was doing well in my classes. I became the president of the Real Estate Club on campus, and at that point no one knew more about real estate (at least in my mind) than me.

That all changed when my father, Douglas McPherson, who was a successful real estate investor and owner of a prominent commercial real estate brokerage firm, sat me down and said, "Look, you think you know a lot about real estate, but it has only been from textbooks with no practical experience. If you really want to get in the business, you need to step up and buy something!"

I was planning on going to work after school for my father's company, but I did not know that it was predicated on me actually going out and buying some property. That twenty-minute discussion with my father was probably the best advice I have *ever* received in my career, and here is why.

I went to work trying to find a single-family home to buy, live in, fix up, and rent in order to get into the game. I got the newspaper out and suddenly realized I did not know where to even begin. After a couple of weeks looking at homes in locations that I wanted to live in, I quickly realized I was way out of my affordability range and unsure what to do next.

It was very hard for me to accept that I was about to get a degree in real estate and finance from a major university, and I was not prepared to buy a house!

I asked my father for help, so he spent two weekends with me, driving neighborhoods and reading want ads in the newspaper. We finally found something that sounded interesting. It was a small ad by an attorney who represented a widow that wanted to sell two houses for $15,000. AS IS. We went and looked at them, and I was completely not interested. They were in an older neighborhood in Phoenix and needed lots of clean-up work.

My father and I went to lunch, and he proceeded to tell me what a great deal this was. He pointed out that the properties were below replacement costs, and were in good rental neighborhoods. My problem was I could see these homes only as places for me to live and not as a real estate investment!

The other benefit of this deal was that the seller would carry her own paper or mortgage back because of the property's condition. I had no idea what this meant at that time, but I quickly learned that it was the key to becoming a real estate investor. I bought the property for $15,000 with $1,000 down, and the seller carried the mortgage of $14,000. I was on my way!

My father made me put together a budget for the property acquisition and renovation along with a stabilized pro forma once rented. I cannot stress enough how I struggled trying to figure out if this was a good deal or not. My father put up half of the down payment; $500 for half of the profits and turned me loose.

I really struggled at first, but I realized I had to make this work because my whole career was on the line. I spent a year fixing up the properties and leasing the homes and eventually sold the properties for $25,000 in eighteen months. During that time, I learned about basic property renovation, negative cash flows, property management, partner issues, tenant lease issues, and how to develop an exit strategy for my investment.

I learned more about real estate from owning two fix-up homes in a rough area of Phoenix than I did my entire time in college.

TIP I went on to purchase twelve houses over the next two years and I found one common thread in all my purchases: Understanding the financing was critical.

I was now addicted to real estate investing! I went on to purchase twelve houses over the next two years and I found one common thread in all my purchases: Understanding the financing was critical. Just like the first two homes that I purchased, I almost always had sellers carry the mortgages for me. This did two things: One, it allowed me to get much better leverage and financing terms than a conventional lender would or would not give me; and, two, it allowed me to close very quickly without appraisals. When an owner wants out, he or she wants out fast.

I quickly realized that having a good knowledge of how to finance these homes was paramount in my business plan. I actually enjoyed trying to come up with some pretty creative ways to get someone else to put up 80 to 100 percent of the capital to make my business plan a reality.

THREE BASIC STEPS TO UNDERSTANDING AND OBTAINING FINANCING

HAVE A BUSINESS PLAN!

In my business, it is a pleasure to come to work and see very creative real estate transactions and hear the sponsor's or developer's vision. I can tell in the first fifteen minutes of our discussions if this person is really someone we can finance and is truly a real estate investor. I have a policy that we promote internally in my office that if we (being the mortgage broker) are steering or making too many of the decisions for the borrowers, it is time to rethink their abilities.

Business plans can be very simple or complex based on the amount of moving parts, issues, or challenges your particular real estate transaction might have. All of this has significant impact on the type of financing that you should pursue.

I would encourage you to ask yourself the following questions:

Why am I buying this real estate?

Shelter. You need a place to live? If that is your motivation, then how much can you afford on your own, or should you bring in someone to help you with the down payment, or be a tenant?

Investment. What kind of investment? Short-term trade? Long-term hold? Buying for income? This can be very complex because everyone has different reasons for investing. The reason this is so important is that you need to match the appropriate financing with your correct business plan.

Real Life Story: Two Properties . . . The Financing Was Not Created Equal

Let me give you an example of how different the financing can be for the same type of real estate with two different buyers who had two different business plans.

When my son was born, I purchased a two-bedroom condominium in a complex that I had placed the financing on for a developer client of mine. **I purchased the condominium for the sole purpose of having someone else fund my son's college education through rent!** I set up the financing such that it was amortized more than twenty years and coupled it with enough down payment that a tenant's rent would cover the mortgage payment and the HOA dues.

I then leased the unit and let another person just gradually pay the loan down monthly though his rent. I was not concerned if the property appreciated one dollar. I just wanted the property to be free and clear when my son was ready to go to college.

Another friend of mine purchased another unit in the same complex and wanted to hold it for six months and sell it. He borrowed as much as he could and paid a higher interest rate than I, but he was able to pay the loan off in six months when he sold the property for a profit, without any prepayment penalties. He used leverage to his benefit.

Both of these loan structures were appropriate for the investors; however, they were very different in structure and actually had two different types of lenders.

How much risk am I willing to take?

You need to ask yourself how much risk you are willing to take. Ask some tough questions of your personal finances and lifestyle. If you are a financially capable, sophisticated real estate investor then leverage and debt can be your best friend. If you are not in that category, be honest with yourself and borrow less or spread your equity risk by bringing in a partner.

TIP One of the strongest traits that I see in my business is that successful real estate investors know their risk tolerance levels.

A good example of this was when another customer of mine wanted to build 400,000 square feet of speculative industrial space in the Phoenix metro area. This would be the first development for this client in the Phoenix market. He has done similar projects throughout the other southwestern states.

He hired me to find an equity joint venture partner and a construction loan. We spent quite a bit of time talking about how to finance the development, and he decided that he wanted a low-leverage construction loan and a large institutional partner that could weather any bumps in the road.

I brought him a pension fund that put in all of the equity and had a very long-term investment strategy. My client was very happy to get his first Phoenix project started with minimal equity requirement from him. This client could have easily done the project all on his own but decided to reduce some risk. This is probably why he has been in business forty years!

DEVELOP MULTIPLE EXIT STRATEGIES

For your piece of mind, your investors, and the lender's, please know how you are going to get your money back, along with everyone else's!

When I look at any real estate investment, I always start by asking how am I going to get out of the deal. You may have the greatest idea in the world for buying, building, or converting something, but with no clear way to get your capital along with a lender's capital back, you will never attract anyone to the deal!

TIP When I look at any real estate investment, I always start by asking how am I going to get out of the deal.

BUILD A CREDIBLE TEAM

It does not matter how talented you think you are, you need to surround yourself with a very good team! As I pointed out earlier, my father really jumped in and became my team when it came down to actually buying something.

Try to sit down and put together a list of people to hire to help you execute your business plan. Here's the short list:

Real Estate Broker
Appraiser
Property Manager
Mortgage Broker
Accountant
Real Estate Attorney
Contractor
Property Conditions Reports
Environmental Consultants

Your Exit Strategy Options

Exit strategies can be very easy, depending on the type of real estate project you are doing. Here are the options:

No Exit. If you are buying a home or duplex to live in, your exit is you! Very simple. However, just be sure you and your lender understand that.

Refinance. Maybe your plan is to renovate one hundred apartments that have been neglected and raise rents. If so, put together a forward-looking proforma with your team (more on this in step two) and show your investors or lenders how a refinance will get their capital back.

Sale. If the plan is to buy and then re-sell the property, then you must show how, when, and why that will occur. If your plan simply is to buy and let the market make you money, you are going to have a tough time just relying on that unless you made one incredible buy.

Let me give you an example of how and when I would use these team members. For this example, I am going to use a twenty-unit condo conversion project that I purchased in Scottsdale, Arizona. The property was a tired twenty-year-old property in a transitional neighborhood and needed major renovations before we could convert it to for-sale condominiums. Prior to closing:

- I interviewed (more on that process later) residential real estate brokers who gave me the condo market resale analysis and pricing matrix for the individual units once I had them completely renovated. I also asked them to provide me with a timeline for getting them sold. *Remember the exit strategy!*

- I hired a well-known appraiser to value the individual units as if they were fully renovated.

- I interviewed and hired a property manager to audit the existing operational statements and to create HOA budgets and run the HOA when it was turned over to the homeowners.

- The mortgage company interviewed and hired me! The reality would have been to interview a mortgage broker who has successfully financed condo conversions and could help me structure my debt and equity requirements. I did hire a residential mortgage broker to provide take-out loans for the buyers. *Remember the exit strategy!*

- I used my accountant to minimize our tax liability.

- I hired a very experienced attorney to set up our ownership, HOA, and condominium subdivision documentation.

- Since this property required about $35,000 per unit in renovations, I wanted to be sure my contractor did not miss anything. I matched his scope of work with my property conditions report along with the required finish levels that my residential real estate broker developed. *Remember the exit strategy!*

- I also engaged a property conditions report to backstop my contractor and to make sure I had a sound building. I coupled that with an environmental report to point out any environmental issues I needed to deal with.

When I assimilated all of this information and hired all of my team, I looked like the best condo converter that walked the planet! My goal was to fully understand what I was getting into before I went to a lender or investors to get the capital needed to do this conversion prior to closing on the property.

By hiring the best team you can, you have demonstrated to yourself, your lender, and your investors that you recognize areas that you need some support with. You also will potentially eliminate the "oops!" factor down the road that can become extremely costly in terms of profits and credibility.

How to Hire Your Team Members

How do you hire team members? My answer is very simple, once you locate them through referral or other means. Please go meet with them and ask these tough but basic questions:

- Have you done this type of work before?
- How many of these have you done?
- Would you mind if I spoke to one of your clients about your abilities?

If they stumble on any of these questions walk away. You have too much at risk not to get the "A" team because they are out there for you.

SHOW ME THE MONEY!

You now have found a property, created a business plan, and assembled your team. Now where do I get the money?

Most people when asked where they will go to get money for a real estate transaction will say "to the bank, of course." Clearly the local, regional, and national banks are a source for capital, but by no means are they the only place you should look. Have you considered any of the sources at the right?

All of these lenders will not fit all types of financing requirements. That will depend on size, risk, or property type, but you should be aware that there are many ways to find the debt and the equity to do your transaction.

I have done many multimillion dollar financing deals with a borrower that had marginal financial strength. What he did not have in financial net worth he made up for in a very strong business plan and an incredible team.

Remember this, lenders want to make you a loan or provide you with equity. They make money only when they loan money out. It turns from a liability to an asset on their books.

They also want to do business with people they have confidence in and who can repay the loan at some point in the future. *Remember the exit strategy!*

Capital Sources Other Than Banks
Credit Companies
Life Insurance Companies
Real Estate Finance Companies
Mortgage Funds
REIT's Thrifts / Industrial Banks
Investment Banks
Hedge Funds
Pension Funds
Credit Unions
Private Debt / Equity
Opportunity Funds
Mezzanine Debt Funds
Offshore Investment Funds
Friends and Family
Angels
High Net Worth Investors

How Do I Obtain Access to These Lenders?

If you are an experienced real estate investor, you may have some access to these types of lenders already. Unfortunately, if you are not on top of these lenders on a daily basis they may be out of the market when you need them.

If you're starting out and want to do this financing on your own you can talk to *successful* real estate brokers for the particular product type and ask for a referral. You can search the Internet and real estate finance publications. You can also go directly to some of your local banks to see what they can do.

I suggest you hire a competent mortgage broker. It may sound a little self serving, but here is why.

First, when you go to hire a mortgage broker you need to be sure you are really hiring someone who knows how to help you and adds value. If you are buying a single-family home, you should go to a good residential mortgage broker that can help guide you through the various programs that she or he can deliver. If he works for a bank and can deliver only limited programs offered by that bank, you move on because you are not being exposed to all the financing products you may need.

On the commercial side of the business, it is also very important to interview several commercial mortgage brokerage firms and ask the tough, but basic questions we talked about before:

- How long have you been in the business?
- How many financings like this have you done?
- Could I see one of your loan submission packages?
- I would like to talk to someone you have done similar business with.

A credible and competent mortgage broker should not have any hesitation in answering these questions.

Hire a Good Mortgage Broker First

I recommend hiring a good mortgage broker before you go looking for properties for these reasons:

- He can give you a realistic view of the capital markets for your type of transaction. This is extremely important to you as you are preparing an offer to purchase the property.
- He can provide another set of qualified eyes as to your underwriting assumptions and financial modeling of the property and the market.
- He can suggest credible team members to join you such as contractors or lawyers.
- He can package you and your property properly, so it will be presented in the best light to potential lenders.
- And, finally, he should be able to present your property to a wide variety of lenders that never would have access to, hopefully giving you multiple options to choose from.

Financing for real estate investors is really a blending of using good common sense and surrounding yourself with the best talent possible. I started with one team member—my father—and have developed additional members over the years as needed.

I encourage you to find the opportunities that are out there in the real estate market today. Go after them, knowing that there is a way to secure the appropriate capital for the transaction regardless of current market conditions.

WAYS TO LEARN MORE

The best way to learn more is from the professionals you surround yourself with. Seek them out. Ask them questions. Be an active learner.

 **Scott McPherson** is a principal and cofounder of a highly specialized real estate finance company called Capital Advisory Group, LC. Established in 2001, the firm has successfully closed around $3.5 billion of structured debt and equity in the United States. Scott has financed everything from raw land to high-rise condominium towers from Portland, Oregon, to Tampa, Florida, and has successfully sourced and closed multiple projects in excess of $100 million in cost. For more information, visit www.capitaladvisory group.us.

Lease It and Keep It Leased

C *raig is the most well-organized person I know. Not only is he one of the most highly regarded commercial real estate brokers, but he is also an investor in his own right, and together, he, Kim, and I have done several deals together. I say that Craig is organized, but I really mean he is very goal oriented. He has accomplished more in his life than many of us could achieve in several lifetimes. He attributes this to goal setting and prioritizing what he really wants from life. Craig is one of those rare people who chooses what he wants carefully, then goes after getting it with a vengeance.*

He has his days planned to the minute and is constantly self improving. He studies and invests in his personal development on a regular basis. Yet, his family takes the highest priority, and he is very involved in his children's lives. Again, what I learn from Craig beyond just about everything I know about commercial real estate is priorities.

Craig has a lot of designations after his name, but I don't need them to know that he knows what he's talking about when it comes to commercial real estate investing, leasing, and brokering. His track record and his guidance speak loud enough. He has shown us that commercial real estate takes a different set of eyes than the ones we have as investors in multifamily residential properties.

Whenever Kim and I see a commercial building that we think looks interesting, we call Craig. It usually only takes a few answers to a few questions that Craig asks us before he tells us whether the property is worth any more of our time or if we should keep driving the deal. He's that good.

He takes the time to teach with every deal, and he actively teaches and mentors others in his profession. Like the other contributors in this book, Craig practices what he preaches. He lives the real estate life he talks about.

—ROBERT KIYOSAKI

If you build it, they will come. And if you own it, they will lease it from you. No they won't! On both counts. As much as you may like to think that everyone will be as excited about your real estate investment as you are, this simply is not the case. In most markets, there are several buildings for rent and lots of choices for business owners regardless of whether they are looking for a Class A high-rise for their $500 per hour law firm partners, or a master carpenter looking for multiuse workshop space to create custom furnishings, and everything in between. Choices abound, as they say.

So what does it take to lease your building and keep it leased? It takes attracting good tenants. It takes professional management that makes the experience of being in your building an exceptional one. And it takes understanding the difference between a leasing company and a management company. There is a big difference.

I see so many first-time commercial property owners, and even those who should know better, think they can lease their properties themselves. While many of them know they don't want to *manage* the properties themselves, after all the thought of the Friday 5 p.m. toilet clog is enough to tame that crazy notion, I'm always surprised when people say they want to do their own leasing. My only conclusion is that they don't realize what is involved. I know from experience if they are not set up for leasing—and most building owners are not—it is nearly impossible to successfully lease a building. Building owners may also rationalize by asking why should they pay a commission to an agent when they can do the leasing themselves.

In my book, right up there with being able to analyze a deal and performing good due diligence is leasing your property. Why is this so important? Because leasing drives your cash flow. And cash flow is a significant definer of property value.

The Types of Leases Available

You may have heard terms like "triple net" or "full service" when it comes to buildings. This is the language of leasing, and there are four kinds of leases in all. The type of leases that you have for your tenants will dictate the amount of involvement that you and your property managers will have maintaining and paying for upkeep to your properties.

The decision to go with one lease or another depends on the market and what tenants are accustomed to paying in that market. In Chicago or New York, for example, it's called triple net for office space, whereas on the West Coast it's called "gross." Even within a single building there can be different tenants signed to different types of leases.

Here are the types of leases that are out there. Get to know them. They will become your language as you continue along your path as a real estate professional.

- **Gross.** Gross means full service. You as property owner would pay for all utilities, upkeep, and maintenance. The tenant pays for everything in one check to the owner.

- **Net.** This can mean a number of things, but generally it means the tenant pays for one or more aspects of the property's utilities, upkeep, and maintenance. For example, "net utilities" means the tenant will pay for utilities. "Net janitorial" means the tenant will pay for janitorial.

- **Triple Net**. In this type of lease, the owner is responsible for structure, roof, parking, etc., or maintaining capital elements to the building. But the tenant covers all other expenses it takes to operate the building, including utilities, taxes, utility repair, and maintenance. Companies like Walgreens and Jack in the Box, for example, typically sign triple net leases. Triple net is designated NNN in the industry, and you'll see it often on sales literature.

- **Absolute Triple Net.** Here, the tenant pays everything—real estate taxes, janitorial, and all capital improvements, including if the roof caves in. This is the least amount of work for you, but you'll find these leases are typically in single-tenant buildings where the tenant almost owns the building. They are typically long-term leases, and sometimes they are known as "sale lease back" deals in which a tenant owner sells their own building to an investor then leases it back for a long-term agreement.

LEASING IS MARKETING

The reality is that in most cases investors can't lease the building themselves because it takes leasing and communications knowledge most investors don't have. Leasing is actually marketing, and unless you know this specialty, investors' efforts are trial and mostly error. I am an investor, but I am also a leasing agent/advisor and have been for more than two decades. I know through my own successes and failures how to effectively lease a building. And I know that leasing a building starts with a good marketing plan. You may think that all there is to leasing a building is putting a sign out front and praying, but there's a lot more to it. In fact, when I am working with a client, we develop an entire marketing plan that is designed to generate awareness of the building and interest in its features and benefits.

Our basic approach is two-pronged. First we go business-to-consumer, meaning we market directly to those persons or companies that may be in a position to lease. And second, we go business-to-business within our trade, so that every other leasing agent/advisor is aware of the property, its particulars, and its availabilities. A good leasing agent/advisor knows how to work his or her industry and knows how to create buzz about a property. He or she knows how to position your property as more lucrative than others to these fellow leasing agents and advisors. They know how to steer them toward you and away from your competition.

The truth about leasing is that the space always follows the business. By that I mean that business owners look for space that reflects what the business does and how it operates and how it succeeds. A creative advertising business, for example, would not seek out a plain-Jane, white-walled shell with a sea of built-in cubicles. No, a creative business like that would look for space that is interestingly designed with unexpected hallway angles, unique finishes, and moody lighting. How many of those spaces exist? Not many. That is why so much of leasing is looking at a space for what it can become, not what it is at the moment. It takes a very skilled leasing agent and advisor to have this vision and then be able to communicate it to the client. If the company doesn't see itself in the space, then that's it. No deal.

TIP The truth about leasing is that the space always follows the business.

A funny thing about this business is that every building owner thinks his own space is not only wonderful, but that everyone will want it. Owners tend to think that it will lease or sublet very easily because it's so perfect. They are always surprised when no one shares their enthusiasm. But they shouldn't be. The building and the space is a fit for the owner or the existing tenant, but not necessarily a fit for anyone else. It happens all the time, so be prepared to either have a lot of vision or hire someone who does, and then knows how to market the sizzle along with the space.

LEASING IS SELLING

Leasing is marketing, but leasing is selling, too. And that's the part that surprises many property owners. I'm not exactly sure why. When I am working with a property owner, the sales and negotiation process is time consuming and takes experience and expert knowledge of selling and the market. It takes professionals years to discover what works when it comes to positioning the benefits of a product, minimizing the shortcomings, and overcoming objections.

It's also taken me years to get that gut instinct about a prospective tenant. And as much as I wish I could teach you that in this chapter, I can't. I can tell you a horror story, however, about a project in my market and an owner who decided to go it alone and lease the rest of his building after the first two floors were leased by a broker. He had found and placed in those spaces excellent businesses that were growing and successful—upstanding, too. The top floor of the building was being saved for one big tenant that had the type of business that would value the exceptional views the nearly floor-to-ceiling windows afforded, and who could handle the pricier rent.

Well, the building owner got a little impatient and got a little greedy, thinking he could do this himself. After all, leasing doesn't seem that hard. Why should he pay a leasing agent/advisor for something he could do himself? He fired his broker. Within no time, the building owner had a tenant. The problem was, the tenant wanted only a portion of the top-floor space, so the building owner figured what the heck and leased it. That was a bad decision. Another bad decision was that the tenant was a medical practice for transgender surgery. Everyone is entitled to his own life choices, but let me to tell you what happened to the building.

Within a year, the quality business tenants in the lower floors had moved out, and on the top floor near the medical practice a hair club for men moved in. It was all downhill from there. In less than a year, a solid class-A property with a quality tenant mix became an undesirable property to all but a few fringe businesses. Quite a shame. Professional leasing agents/advisors know what can happen if you lease to the wrong kinds of tenants. Little did this guy know we turned down the businesses that he naïvely signed. You get what you pay for.

In my experience, the best leasing folks are the ones who know how to provide the vision that the client wants to hear. But they don't do this out of thin air or try to stuff ten pounds of potatoes into a five-pound bag. They do it by knowing the client and understanding the needs and the business. They have a feel for the kind of space that will really excite. The best leasing people know how to create a match between client and space, and then they have the ability to sell the vision, even if it is not completely obvious.

TIP The best leasing people know how to create a match between client and space, and then they have the ability to sell the vision, even if it is not completely obvious.

But the vision is more than just how the space looks—or can look—on the inside. There are many more variables, which we will get to shortly. And many of them are just as important, if not more so, than the interior space itself. No building is perfect, but it is the job of the leasing agent/advisor to assemble the top picks, inspire, and close the deal.

LEASING IS DETAIL WORK

Leasing a building is seldom easy; actually it is quite the opposite. That's becoming obvious. It's generally very labor intensive. When we're doing a marketing plan for a building, we begin by looking at the property and effectively positioning it in the market. That requires us to do an intense market study of all competing properties—both the ones that are already there and the ones expected to be completed in the coming months or year. By understanding the market, we can find the gaps that will make the property we're representing far more desirable and therefore more leasable.

But our work doesn't stop there. We look at all the comparables and analyze each deal to understand the specifics and find the clues we need for our own success. We even look at the transaction activity rate within the vicinity of the property we are representing to see any trends up, down, or sideways. We don't stop until we have a full picture of the market. From these details we formulate the true value of a building or a space, and that enables us to set the rental prices and all the terms that accompany a lease. This includes operating expenses, tenant improvements, free rent, other concessions, parking terms, security deposits—I could go on and on. It's pretty extensive.

Often, I see people who are doing their own leasing and end up pricing a space out of the market. The first reason they do it is that, as you recall, their space is perfect and everyone will want it, right? We know that argument doesn't hold any credence. The other reason is that they have not done their homework or they have done it poorly. Often they are comparing their building or space to space of a higher quality or class. The final reason they overprice is that they are setting the price based on how much they paid for the building itself. How much you pay for a building has nothing to do with how much you can charge tenants for rent.

TIP An important lesson of leasing: The market sets the rental prices, not you.

As with any good sales function, eventually prospecting begins. From lists and sources that we have developed over time and others that we would develop specifically for the project at hand, we send our literature and make cold calls to gauge interest. We work inside and outside the target location, and we even do out-of-state prospecting, targeting companies that are coming into town. We give a lot of presentations to tenants in other properties that are in our target size and business range.

As I mentioned earlier, we'll also work within our industry and communicate regularly with the other agents/advisors in the community. We identify which ones specialize in buildings like the one we are representing. We do our presentations to their offices and their staff. We use e-mail, direct mail, and host parties to keep others informed about the properties we represent.

And, of course, we use the sophistication of the Internet to help us target those business prospects who are using the Web to troll for new office space. Our sophisticated Web sites are searchable and detailed. We are connected directly to listing services, and our user interface is the result of more than ten years of improvements. Clearly, you're beginning to see that a lot goes into finding the right tenants and getting a lease signed sooner rather than later.

Once we understand how we're going to market the property and to which companies, we create a development strategy that will outline our plans to fill the building. This is a complete plan that includes rent rates, leasing terms, expense stops (the maximum expenses per square foot for the building), tenant improvement limits, other concessions, even commissions.

The sign in front of the building may be the most visible part, but it is the smallest part of the marketing efforts for a building. If only it were as easy as hammering a sign into the ground and answering the phone. The truth is, experience is everything in the process. There are literally an unlimited number of pits that the novice can fall into. Over our careers, we have fallen into them all. That's another reason leasing agents/advisors are so valuable; they've already taken the falls for you.

THE DEAL MAKERS AND DEAL BREAKERS IN LEASING

Earlier in this chapter, I mentioned that it takes more than the vision of great space—space that matches the business—to actually get the business. There are more variables that come into play. I believe there are numerous variables that every client will consider before signing on the dotted line. Here's my top-twenty list:

1. **Rates.** Of course every client is going to be concerned with the rent and the cost per square foot because most every client has a budget. He knows how much his business can allocate to this expense-line item. I work to stay within my clients' budgets, not trying to oversell them. It is in everyone's best interest to have a client who pays on time every month. Rental rate is one of the most important considerations on the list.

2. **Term.** The length of the lease agreement is another important factor. Sometimes my user clients are looking for a short-term fix, and sometimes they want the lease agreement to run longer in exchange for some other consideration. This can be a highly negotiable variable, and the match is made when the term connects with the client's objectives.

3. **Free Rent.** Many building owners offer free rent for some length of time as part of the negotiated agreement. What's negotiated is the number of months and what is included. Is it just the rent, or does it cover common area maintenance fees, parking fees, etc.?

4. **Tenant Improvements.** Many lease agreements have negotiated into them some allowance money for tenant improvements, or "TIs" as they are called. This can be a lot of money or a little money. A good leasing agent/advisor will know the current market and know what is a realistic, yet generous, amount to request. A rookie can really mess up an otherwise good deal by demanding too much, or cause a client to overpay by not asking for enough.

5. **Layout.** This refers to the interior floor plan and the shape and size of the space. Sometimes square or rectangular spaces are a plus, and at other times oddly shaped space is what a client is looking for. It all depends on

the client and the business. Again, when I know a client's objectives, I know what space configurations will work and which ones won't.

6. **Quality of Building.** The building exterior on a commercial property is like the curb appeal on a residential property. It says a lot about your business, just as a home says a lot about you. A prestigious building with excellent upkeep and landscaping says to the world that this company is a player. That it is reputable and can handle my business. A shoddy-looking building tells the world that a company might be fly-by-night, not very progressive, or just plain cheap. If "the clothes make the man" as the saying goes, the building exterior makes the business.

7. **Parking Type and Ratio.** I've walked away from buildings as an investor and as a leasing advisor because the property is under parked; in other words, the number of parking spaces for the size of the building is light. I know my client's customers will not be happy if every time they visit, they have to allot an extra ten minutes to search for a place to park. Nothing is worse than a building that doesn't have enough parking, and in most cases there is little that can be done about it.

8. **Parking Location.** As bad as it is to not have enough parking spaces, clients also don't like having to park far away from a building. The reasons are obvious with safety concerns being one of the biggest. No one likes the idea of walking a great distance through a dark parking lot or alleyway to get to the car. And it's no fun to walk a distance—briefcase, workout bag, coffee cup, and cell phone in hand—to get into the building in the morning. We won't even talk about rain, snow, and ice. Parking should be easy and safe.

9. **Efficiency.** Clients look for generally efficient buildings, meaning that they are easy to find, get into, walk through, locate the businesses in, and find the restrooms, etc. Some buildings—and you probably can think of a few yourself—are just poorly designed. It's hard to find the entry, it's hard to find the elevator, it's hard to find the office numbers, it's hard to get to the restrooms, and the list goes on.

10. **Access.** Here's a big one. Accessibility means how easy it is to get into and out of the building site. Some buildings have excellent access, and others do not. I just moved one company because the business owner hated making an unprotected lefthand turn across a very busy street every time he turned into the building. While we were looking for his new space, he would joke that he was going to hold me personally responsible if he got into a wreck

while he impatiently waited! We found him space with better access, and he is much happier.

11. **Signage.** Some businesses need very visible signage, and others do not. This is one of the negotiation points that is critical for businesses that rely on either walk-in business or that want to use their building signage as awareness advertising.

12. **Amenities On Site.** Some buildings have shopping, banking, places to eat, dry cleaners, and more perks right on site in lobbies or in underground retail centers. To some of our clients, these conveniences matter. I know one person who leases in a building on a small municipal airport runway that has hangar space for corporate jets. That's a big amenity for some business owners.

13. **Amenities Off Site.** Then there are some buildings that seem to be on an island all their own. There's no place to go for lunch, there's no grocery store nearby, there's little to nothing around. Sometimes this is the nature of new development—retail and restaurants have not moved in yet—but sometimes it's just the way it is.

14. **Property Management.** Good property management is like a gourmet meal that has great presentation, tastes amazing, and completely satisfies you. And best of all you never have to be concerned with any of the details. It's just there for you to enjoy. Bad property management lets you know it's there at every turn. To go back to our gourmet meal, you have to ask for the salt, your silverware isn't clean, the food looks overcooked, and, in general, the whole experience is unpleasant. All you see are the details—the missed details.

15. **Ownership.** The ownership matters as much as the property management. Some owners can be terrific landlords, and others have baggage. One friend of mine leases space in a building advised by our company. The building owner is a very successful entrepreneur who makes his rounds every so often to his tenant businesses just to see how things are going and to catch up. He's a good guy, a welcome visitor, and a friend to those who lease from him. There's another building owner down the street who jets off for Cabo every other week and is incredibly unresponsive.

16. **Americans with Disabilities Act Compliance**. To many businesses, this is a very important consideration. It is critical that those who use wheelchairs have easy and safe access to all areas of the building and grounds.

17. **Location, Location, Location.** Some space has views of beautiful vistas, and other space has no view at all. Some space is visible right off the elevator, and other space is tucked back in some insignificant hallway corner. The location within the building matters. It says a lot about a business.

18. **Location of the Building Itself.** This is the most critical requirement, and that's why it is not just number 18 on our list, but 19 and 20, too. The right location is one of the absolute musts.

WHAT TO LOOK FOR IN A LEASING AGENT/ADVISOR

My hope is with the stories and the work load described in this chapter so far that I've convinced you to at least consider the value of having a leasing agent/advisor working on your side. If that's the case, then I should also point out that not all leasing agent/advisors are created equal. There are leasing agents out there who don't do their homework and say "yes" to shaky businesses all the time. There are leasing agents who don't know the market, leasing agents who are terrible negotiators, and leasing agents who simply can't sell. If you're going to hire a leasing agent, and I suggest you do, hire a good one, a true advisor. Aside from the obvious qualities like experience, motivation, organization, intelligence, expertise, and integrity, here's what else to look for:

RELATIONSHIP VS. TRANSACTION

Although real estate seems like a huge industry, it really is a small local industry. Each city or town has a small, tightly knit, and very intertwined real estate community. It is critical to find a leasing broker/advisor who sees his or her job as one of relationship building, not just completing transactions. I have spent the last twenty years doing deals and in the process building excellent relationships with the real estate professionals where I live and work. And this effort pays off for me and my clients every day.

The reality is that most transactions happen through other leasing agent/advisors. The opportunities come in through them, and we market our owners' opportunities outbound through them. How eager would they be to bring to me top-quality tenants, or even be interested in looking at space I pitch to them, if I had a reputation for win-lose arrangements where I win and they lose? Not very.

As a rule, I put a great deal of time and energy into providing lots of information to prospects and clients. Even if there is no agreement for representation, I generally am eager to help because I know that's how to build a relationship. And experience has proven to me that relationships eventually pay off. One story I recall was when a large healthcare insurance provider was moving into town. A high-powered agent came in from New York and called our office and said she was coming in to look at space. I asked if she needed local representation, and she said no. Regardless, I told her I'd get her a list of available buildings by the next day.

We met, and during that meeting I helped her in any way that I could. When she returned to New York, she told her boss she met an agent who could really help and who she wanted to work with. He said no, but she insisted. Long story short, she got her way, and I ended up doing not one but nearly fifty transactions with that company. Had I not been willing to freely give of my time and knowledge, I would not have been on the receiving end of that lucrative piece of business.

RAPPORT WITH YOU

This whole leasing effort has to be a partnership. There has to be a good rapport. A good leasing agent/advisor understands your objectives, and then works to match the right space and the right tenants. Plus, a good leasing agent/advisor willingly takes on even small businesses or buildings and educates clients as they grow into bigger businesses. I found space for one software company many years ago. It was their first space when they were just three people strong. I think the office was all of twelve hundred square feet. At the time, I was doing much bigger deals, but to me that didn't matter. We developed rapport and within a few years, I handled the transactions surrounding their 137,000 square foot corporate office and their more than forty-four offices worldwide. It happens.

LOCATION KNOWLEDGE

Any leasing agent/advisor you work with must have not only a versed knowledge of the metro area, but also intimate knowledge of the submarket area where your building is located. This comes back to the fact that real estate is really a small, localized industry. The best leasing agents/advisors are hands down the most knowledgeable people around, not about the whole city or town, but about one square mile. Find this person, and you'll be in good shape. It's not hard; just drive around and look at whose name appears on the leasing signs most frequently.

DEAL MAKER VS. PROCESSOR

There are leasing agents out there who are not advisors. They are the people who do little more than play middleman and parrot messages back and forth between prospect and building owner. That's not the type of representation you want. You want an agent/advisor who will add value by working for you and negotiating on your behalf. Anyone who has some training can relay information and process paper; that's not what you are paying for. You want to find a true advisor who can weed out the ridiculous and the no-chance-in-you-know-where offers and deal points to get to the end game quickly and efficiently.

REPUTATION

Finally, and this probably goes without saying, you want a leasing agent/advisor with a solid reputation in the community. How can you be sure? You ask around. You talk to other building owners and talk to other business owners who have worked with the person you are considering. It's worth the extra time and the effort to do this and can be the first step to developing a leasing agent/advisor partner for life.

These are the qualities I have developed in myself over the years, and they are the same qualities that I work to foster in young people who are entering this profession. Not all can cut it. The requirements are demanding. And if they can't cut it, they either get out of the business altogether or move over to my competition. Either is okay with me.

Choosing your leasing agent/advisor partner is one of the most important decisions you will ever make. It can mean the difference between a property that generates positive cash flow and one that doesn't. It can mean the difference between owning an asset or a liability. A good leasing agent/advisor can actually enhance the reputation and standing of your business within the community and bring you more business along with more profitability.

The Last Word: Coppola's Five Rules of Leasing

I will not need every deal.

I will discuss challenges with the client immediately.

I will not allow a commission to drive any transaction.

I will consider long-term relationships more important than any fee.

I will develop a professional profile that provides me access to all decision makers.

WAYS TO LEARN MORE

SIOR (Society of Industrial and Office Realtors)
CRE (Councilors of Real Estate)

R. Craig Coppola is the top producing office broker in Lee & Associates' 35-year history, as well as one of the Founding Principals of Lee & Associates Arizona. Lee & Associates is the largest broker-owned Real Estate Company in the U.S. with over 50 offices nationwide.

Craig has completed over 3,500 lease and sale transactions in the past 30 years, totaling a value in excess of $3,500,000,000. He has a lengthy track record of representing companies on a national and international basis. His clients include Motorola, HDR, JDA Software, and more.

Craig has been awarded National Chapter President (the highest honor given by the largest real estate development trade association) for NAIOP (National Association of Office and Industrial Properties) and NAIOP Office Broker of the Year six times. He has also earned the top three designations in the real estate industry: CCIM, CRE and SIOR. Less than 40 people worldwide hold all three designations.

In addition to his Real Estate career, Craig is also the author of four books. His first book, *How to Win in Commercial Real Estate Investing*, won him the "Best First Time Author Award" from The National Association of Real Estate Editors (NAREE). As a follow up to his investing book, Craig published, *The Art of Commercial Real Estate Leasing* in December 2014. In addition to his two real estate books, Craig has also written *The Fantastic Life: How to Get it, Live it, and Pass it On*. His most recent book, *Chasing Excellence*, was co-written with Lee & Associates Founder Bill Lee.

The Perils of Careless Property Management

O ne of the great pleasures in my life is having best friends as business partners. In my life, Ken McElroy is one of those rare persons. On top of that, Ken has made me a millionaire many times over.

There have been many valuable lessons I learned from my rich dad. One lesson is "Out of every bad deal comes a good person." This lesson has been priceless because it makes me less hesitant about having business deals go bad. Explaining further, I will often go into a deal, even if I do not trust the people. I go in because I know that I will probably meet a good person along the way, even if the deal goes bad.

I met Ken in a deal that went bad. In fact it was a horrible deal. The person who put the deal together—a young man I will call George—eventually went to jail. The Securities and Exchange Commission (SEC) eventually shut his operation down. Unfortunately, George was married with three kids.

Ken and I smelled a rat early on and did not participate in George's investment scheme. We almost invested, but we passed on his bogus opportunity. The good news is I met Ken, just as my rich dad's lesson taught me.

Today, Ken is a Rich Dad Advisor, writing on real estate. His books, The ABCs of Real Estate Investing, The Advanced Guide to Real Estate Investing, and The ABCs of Property Management are must reads for anyone who is interested in *real estate investing. He also has a priceless product entitled,* How to Increase the Income from Your Real Estate Investments. *It includes a due diligence checklist, which is an essential checklist that every investor should go through before buying a property.*

The thing I like most about Ken is that he is extremely generous with his knowledge. He and I have traveled to many parts of the world to speak about our favorite subject: investing in real estate. He is also the author of the book The Sleeping Giant.

He and his wife, Laura, are two of Kim's and my favorite friends. We have a great time together, teaching, sharing knowledge, and supporting each other's families in becoming richer and more financially secure in a financially volatile world.

—ROBERT KIYOSAKI

Of all the subjects in this book, property management might be the most misunderstood. The reason for this is simply the fact that in order to be a successful real estate investor, you don't necessarily have to be a successful property manager.

That statement might seem a little odd to you at first, but if you think about it for a second, you'll know it's true. You can have tremendous instincts and ability to find, analyze, and even take down phenomenal real estate deals. You might have an extensive network of equity sources and solid and trusted investors waiting for your next deal. You can have a solid team of lawyers, mortgage brokers, and general contractors. All of these things will enable you to be successful at finding and investing in real estate. But they are all transactional. By that I mean they are needed to *invest* well in real estate. This is often the focus of many real estate investment books. None of these things, however, will make your investment successful once you actually *own* it.

One of the things I appreciate about Robert Kiyosaki and the Rich Dad team is that they understand that being a successful real estate investor goes beyond just finding and acquiring quality deals. They know you have to manage those deals effectively to realize their full wealth-making potential. That is why I'm so glad that Robert contacted me to write this chapter. Mark my words, you can have the most incredible real estate holdings in the entire world, but if they are mismanaged they could quickly become worthless. Why is this? Because in order to be a successful real estate investor, the first rule you have to remember is that real estate values are typically based on performance, *not* on the asset itself. And in order for your real estate portfolio to run at its maximum potential you need to manage your property professionally.

TIP The first rule you have to remember is that real estate values are typically based on performance, *not* on the asset itself.

In this chapter I'll show you why property management is so vital to the health of your investments. The topic of how to manage a property effectively, while an important thing to know as a real estate investor, is much too large a topic for the space I've been given here. Rather than try and give you a crash course on how to manage properties effectively, my efforts here will focus on:

1. Why professional property management is essential for success

2. What successful property management entails

3. How to find an exceptional property manager for your assets

I guarantee that a fuller understanding of the importance of property management will make you a more successful real estate investor. In fact, I would venture to say that it's essential.

AN OUTSIDER'S PERSPECTIVE

Just like you, I didn't begin my career as a successful real estate investor. I have people like Robert and the Rich Dad team to thank for opening my eyes more fully to the immense wealth-building potential that real estate investing affords. Well before I began investing in real estate, I made my living by managing other people's assets. In the process, I've built some of the largest and most well-known property management companies in the southwestern United States.

In the course of managing more than 25,000 apartment units, I saw firsthand how poor property management can cause untold damage to a property's value and to the net worth of an investor.

I still remember the day when John called me at my office. John was part of a group of investors in Colorado who had purchased a multifamily property in Phoenix, Arizona, and he was in a bit of a panic.

"What can I do for you, John?" I said over the phone.

"I think we have a bit of a problem with one of our properties," was his response. "I was wondering if you could help us out with our operations."

As it turned out, John had more than a just a *little* problem. His company's property was literally in shambles. What brought them to this point was a series of mistakes that, in the course of my career as a property manager, I've seen over and over again.

John's first problem was that his group purchased a large multifamily building with very little research, which is commonly called due diligence, and they had little knowledge of the local real estate market since they were based in Colorado.

John and his partner's second problem was that they decided to be cheap. In an effort to save some money (or to make money off the property), they gave the task of managing their property to someone in their office, who was located in Denver, and who had no experience in property management. This person flew down about once a month, if that, to see how things were going. Why an investment group of very smart individuals would trust a multimillion-dollar asset to someone with no experience is a mystery to me.

I knew things had to be bad because John was basically firing himself for poor performance, and things are usually in pretty bad shape for this to happen. In fact, things had gotten so bad that they were having trouble making their mortgage payment.

I reluctantly told John I was willing to help him. After hanging up the phone, I shook my head. I knew the property he was talking about, and while it was in a good location and in a great neighborhood, the property itself was known for having high turnover of residents and high crime. Drug activity was prevalent at this property, and members of local drug cartels were actually living in some of the units. In the first week that we took over, one of these problems came to a boiling point when one resident, a local drug dealer, was shot down in cold blood inside his unit right in front of his girlfriend. It was well known that this was a gang-related incident because the man's hands were tied behind his back, and he had been shot point blank in the head, execution style. His girlfriend was unharmed and is now in the witness protection program. So, as you can see, this was definitely not a *little* problem.

You're probably asking yourself: What kind of property was this? What a terrible neighborhood! I can tell you that this property was in an upscale area near major employers, a school, and an upscale regional mall. This kind of thing can happen anywhere.

When my team surveyed the 250-unit property, we were shocked at its condition. We already knew its reputation, and we were expecting it to be bad. What we didn't expect was just how poorly the asset itself had been maintained—the physical condition of the property was astonishingly bad. The landscaping was completely shot, decks were rotting through and posed potential safety risks, and more than 20 percent of the interiors of many units were so rundown that they were not rentable. The result was that while comparable nearby properties were enjoying occupancy levels in the mid-90 percent range, this property was collecting less than 70 percent of the potential income. This, of course, is because many units were vacant, and many of the current tenants were not paying their rent.

Beyond that, people were leaving the property in droves because they were worried about their own safety and disgusted at the condition of the property.

So, the owner's problem was twofold: They couldn't rent to new residents because they did not have the money to fix up the property and the existing vacant units; and many of the current residents were moving out, citing health and safety reasons. As a result, the financial performance of the property was very poor.

We quickly realized we had a lot of work on our hands. Thankfully, my company has tremendous experience in turning around poorly performing properties, and we were eventually able to get this property in good condition. But it took a lot of time and a lot of money. In the end, the poor decision to "save money" cost John and his partners millions of dollars. But the damage to their partnership was irreparable. The tensions boiled over, and their partnership came unglued. Harsh words were spoken, friendships were destroyed, and John's reputation was severely damaged.

I had little pity for John and his partners. While it is unfortunate that they lost so much money, those losses could have easily been avoided if they had retained a quality property manager to partner with them in both the due diligence process when purchasing their property and to help them manage it effectively after they acquired it.

KNOWLEDGE: THE KEY TO SUCCESS

You may be thinking that this is just a severe, isolated case of stupidity. I assure you it is not. Every day, smart investors become idiots because they lack knowledge of the importance of property management and underestimate the work involved in managing a property well. I now make my living by capitalizing on situations just like John's. Because of my years of experience in property management, I buy deals just like John's at a significant discount from their market value and turn them around and reap huge returns for my partners.

Here's the good news. If you take the time to understand the importance of property management and to attain a thorough knowledge of how successful property management is achieved, you too can find the key to success as a real estate investor.

So this begs the question: What does successful property management look like?

THE TRIPLE THREAT

In my experience, successful property managers know how to improve the value of a property in three general areas—what I like to call the "triple threat" of property management: **income**, **expenses**, and **systems.**

TIP Property managers know how to improve the value of a property in three general areas, which is what I call the "triple threat" of property management: **income, expenses, and systems**.

INCOME

As I stated earlier in this section, the value of a property is not based on the asset itself, but rather on its financial performance. The number one misconception that can turn a good real estate investment into a bad one is by not understanding that real estate is a business, not just an investment. As such, the most important aspect of your investment is not how it looks, where it's at, or even how much it costs. While those things are important, they pale in comparison to the importance of the bottom line. In order to be a successful real estate investor you must understand that the value of your property, just as with any business, is based on how much *net operating income* it produces, that is, income after expenses.

Income - Expense = Net Operating Income (NOI)

And when it comes to maximizing your property's NOI, nothing is more important and easier to control than the actual *total income* your property produces.

In investment real estate, total income is determined by a number of factors. They are:

- rent
- occupancy
- other revenue opportunities

RENTS

One clear indication that a property could be mismanaged is when its rents are obviously substantially less than what the rest of the market is charging. I come across this frequently when I'm looking at a potential acquisition, and it excites me. As an investor, buying a property with low rents is a substantial opportunity.

In order to understand the importance of getting your rents right, you need to understand a little bit about how an investment property is valued.

TIP **The value of a property is not based on the asset itself, but rather on its financial performance.**

The most common way to value a property is by using a capitalization (cap) rate. In any given market, cap rates will vary. You don't have to worry about how to figure out what a market's cap rate is; you can get that number from a knowledgeable broker. For our purposes, you do have to understand how cap rates are used to estimate the current value of a property. The equation looks like this:

Net Operating Income (NOI) ÷ Market Cap Rate = Value

What Does This Look Like?

For simplicity sake, let's assume we are looking to buy a 200-unit property that makes $500,000 in annual Net Operating Income (NOI). And let's assume the market capitalization rate is 7 percent. That would mean the estimated value of your asset in that market would be $7,142,857.

$500,000 ÷ 7 percent = $7,142,857

Now, let's look at why keeping a close eye on your rents and making sure that they are in line with comparable properties is so important and, quite frankly, the easiest way to add value to your property.

How NOI Affects a Property's Value

Let's assume our property has an average rent of $800. During our due diligence, we find out that the average market rents for comparable properties is $900. That would mean that the current ownership, with absentee management, is realizing a rent loss of $20,000 per month (two hundred units times $100), which equals out to $240,000 per year in lost potential income. That would mean that instead of an annual NOI of $500,000, our property should be making $740,000 per year. Let's see how that affects the value of our property:

$740,000 ÷ 7 percent = $10,571,428

Amazing, isn't it? While it takes time to increase everyone's rents by $100 per month, it is worth it because by doing so, as shown in this example, we have created an additional $3,428,571 in value. The best thing about this is that I am creating value through good property management of the existing property and with the existing residents, so my business plan is not just based on relying on market appreciation, but I usually get that, too!

That's the power of effectively managing your property's income and the reason why keeping a close eye on not only your rents but the market rents is so vital to your property's financial health.

OCCUPANCY

Another great way to add value is to increase the occupancy. Remember, the Net Operating Income determines your value, so any and all income is very important. One very basic method to create better occupancy is have a good base of residents who take good care of your property and who do not move often. This is done by properly screening every occupant.

It is typical for many property managers to not run credit and criminal background checks for every occupant—a practice that every professional property management company does. It doesn't take a rocket scientist to explain the potential problems of renting to someone who cannot pay the rent or who creates problems in your property, but in a rush to fill vacant units, this basic function is often overlooked.

Problem residents can, and do, create vacancy and decrease your occupancy and can cause damage to the property itself. They can drive out good paying residents, which lowers occupancy, and many times they end up on a delinquent list, creating more work for the owner, eventually to be evicted, which also lowers your occupancy. Higher vacancy creates higher expenses with increases in maintenance, advertising, payroll, and supplies.

There are countless other ways that a good property manager can increase your occupancy; get him on your investment team and you will see the results.

OTHER REVENUE OPPORTUNITIES

In addition to rents, a property can realize substantial income if you look for numerous other revenue opportunities. These would be things like utility submetering, adding washers and dryers, charging pet rent and large pet deposits, charging rent premiums for prime locations . . . there are literally dozens of ways to increase your property's income like this. The problem is that most people don't know that these opportunities even exist, let alone charge for them.

A Real Life Story: How 288 Washers and Dryers Netted $1.9 Million

My partner, Ross, and I recently purchased a 288-unit building in Tulsa, Oklahoma. One of the strategies for our investment was to add a washer and dryer in every unit. This property already had small laundry rooms with all the electrical and plumbing in every unit. All we had to do was purchase the machines and install them. Before we did this we checked the local market to determine what additional rent we could get for a washer and dryer. As it turned out, many of the residents were already renting them, in many cases, for $40 to $50 per month.

We decided to buy 288 sets of washers and dryers and install them in the first year of operation. We budgeted a $40 increase to be realized over a two-year period. Let's look at the value we created for our investment.

288 units x $40 per month = $11,520 per month

$11,520 x 12 months = $138,240 in potential annual NOI

$138,240 NOI ÷ 7 percent cap rate = $1,974,857 added value

There are many revenue opportunities that may be great ideas to you but are considered ordinary for a professional property management company.

EXPENSES

When it comes to property management, expenses are generally the factor you have the least control over. The reason for this is that they are most often dictated to you. Typical expenses are for advertising and marketing, repairs and maintenance, management fees, payroll, utilities, property taxes, and insurance.

Property taxes, insurance, and utilities will be the biggest expenses a property will face. To a large extent, these are costs you simply can't control.

However, there are a few things you can do. For instance, a professional management company might have better purchasing power when it comes to insurance premiums and can get a better rate than the average person because of the size of its account, and you can also negotiate the property limits and the deductibles. A good property manager will utilize a tax consultant to analyze whether he might be able to challenge the property tax for the property.

Remember talking about running credit and criminal background checks? Well, let's examine the expense side of this. The actual credit check itself is paid for by the potential renter, so the cost, which is usually less than $50, is not paid by you. If you have ever bought or refinanced a house, you know that you pay for your own credit check.

TIP The cost of *not* running a credit report and a criminal background check is very high. Eventually, you will get burned.

The cost of *not* running a credit and criminal background check is very high. Eventually, you will get burned. Here is a typical scenario. You spend your hard-earned money getting a unit rent ready from the last move out, let's say $500 for cleaning, painting, making minor repairs, and cleaning the carpets. A bad resident moves in. You now have a renter who does not pay you. You are losing revenue because you cannot re-rent this until they move or are evicted. The cost to serve notices and to evict varies by state, so let's say it costs about $500. Eventually they move out, owing you rent plus legal costs, plus damages. You now must get the unit ready to rent, again which costs you another $500.

Don't get caught up in the estimated amounts; the point in this scenario is that you learn a lesson to run background checks. So far, you would have spent $1,000 to get the unit rent-ready two times. Legal fees were $500. Unpaid rent, late charges, etc., are estimated at $800. All in all, this mistake cost you $2,300. There was $1,500 in actual expenses, plus your time and lost rent until you could rent the newly vacant unit.

I think you realize that this story concerns just one unit. Imagine if this were happening on a two-hundred-unit property. These additional expenses resulting from high turnover due to poor management can and will lead to a lower overall property value.

SYSTEMS

In our discussion here about systems, I want you to think back to the story about John and his investors. While they were facing management issues surrounding both income and expenses, they were also facing serious issues regarding their property's systems. They didn't have any. What I mean by this is that due to poor management, they allowed a horrible resident base to move into the property, and the property itself was in serious disrepair due to deferred maintenance issues. All of these things added up to major losses for John and his partners.

Had they had solid management systems in place, that management would have used strict occupancy standards for potential residents. They would have performed extensive background checks, verifying the potential resident's income, job history, and rental history. They would have trained staff that would handle the daily reports to the management company and perform daily maintenance. The property would have been following an approved operating budget with monthly goals. The vacant units would have been "rent ready" within three days of the prior move-out. The lack of all of these systems or policies and procedures equaled lost income.

Do You Feel Lucky?

I've only scratched the surface of how property management, whether good or bad, can affect the value of your investment. Needless to say, there are hundreds of other factors that go into effectively managing a property. And the margin of error is very small. One seemingly minor oversight can end up costing you hundreds of thousands, if not millions of dollars. It should go without saying that managing a property is a full-time job, requiring an inordinate amount of time and expertise.

> ### Ken's Top-Five Words of Wisdom
> 1. Use your team
> 2. Trust, but verify
> 3. Find the right fit
> 4. You get what you pay for
> 5. Money matters

So the question you have to ask yourself is "Do I feel lucky?" Well, do you? Do you feel confident that you have the expertise and the time to effectively manage your hard-earned investments? If so, then this chapter should be a reminder and a catalyst for you to further increase your property management knowledge and to go back and reevaluate how effectively you are managing your properties. A timely review of your practices, and a little time spent furthering your property management knowledge could net you even more income than you are already realizing.

If you don't feel confident in managing your own properties, or don't feel that you have the time available to do it effectively, then by all means, find a good, professional property manager and hire him as soon as possible. It will be one of the best business moves you will ever make.

Finding a good property manager is not as simple as picking up the yellow pages and calling the company that sounds the most professional. Given the information we've covered already, it stands to reason that choosing your property manager will be one of the most important decisions you'll make in regards to your investment. Here are some helpful to-do's for finding the right fit for your property. This is by no means a comprehensive list, but it will get you thinking in the right frame of mind. For a more comprehensive discussion on this topic see my book, *The ABC's of Property Management*.

1. **Use your team.** As Robert Kiyosaki says, "Business and investing are a team sport." If you don't know of a reputable property manager that you can trust fully with your investment, then ask the members of your team. Chances are they will be able to refer you to an excellent company. But don't take their word for it. As I always say, "Trust, but verify."

2. **Trust, but verify.** If you were smart, you conducted a thorough due diligence on your property before you purchased it. You probably dug into every financial, scrutinized every lease, and walked every unit. You need to perform the same level of due diligence when looking to hire a property manager. Get a full client list, and interview the existing clients of the management company in question. Do they like the service they receive? Have there been any obvious mistakes or blunders you should be concerned about? Ask how the property management company has increased the value of the owner's property. Also, interview the employees of the company and the potential on-property manager for your property. Make sure they are upbeat, knowledgeable, and a good fit for your personality. You will have to interact with these people on a continual basis.

3. **Find the right fit.** There are tons of different types of management companies out there, each with their own specialization. Some companies will specialize in commercial property management, while others will specialize in apartments. Some companies will be better suited for large properties; others will be a perfect fit for smaller properties. The point is that, even if you do find a good management company, they might not be good for you and your needs. You wouldn't want to hire a large property management company that specializes in large apartment buildings to manage your duplex. They might be awesome at what they do, but your property would get lost in the fold—it would be too small for them to give it full attention. On the other hand, a smaller, local property management company would jump at the chance to manage your asset, and they would give you personalized service and attention.

4. **You get what you pay for.** Too often, people want to save money, and they balk at the fees a management company charges. Don't. Management fees vary by market and property type and size. But I will say that if a fee looks too good to be true, it probably is. Every investment in the world, if it is managed, costs you money. The beauty of property management is that you at least know what the fee is. Often, with investments like mutual funds and stocks, the fees are hidden (and substantial) so you don't feel them. You know what they say, "Ignorance is bliss." But with property management, the fees should be clearly explained and spelled out up front. I guarantee that if you find a good company, it will be worth its fees. In just a few simple (and common) examples, I've shown you how much income an effectively managed property can pull down.

5. **Money matters.** Make sure that any company you retain has a very good accounting department. When it comes to managing your investment, proper accounting is a must. You want the company that you use not only to understand what is going on with your property's operations, but also what's going on with your property's finances. Also, make sure that your property's money will be held in a separate account.

In Conclusion

Nothing is more important to the success of your investment than good, knowledgeable property management. Oftentimes it is the difference between meeting your investment goals and losing untold amounts of money. Whether you manage your property yourself, or have someone else do it for you, don't try to "save money." That always leads to disaster and loss.

The good news is that now you know. And if your investments aren't being properly managed, the solution is easy, and the ability to increase the value of your assets almost instantly is right in your hand. So, take the plunge. I promise you won't be disappointed.

WAYS TO LEARN MORE

Knowledge is the key to success. So, here are some of my suggestions on how to find property managers and how to increase your property management knowledge.

www.irem.org

www.naahq.org

www.kenmcelroy.com

The ABCs of Real Estate Investing, by Ken McElroy

The Advanced Guide to Real Estate Investing, by Ken McElroy

The ABCs of Property Management, by Ken McElroy

How to Increase the Income from your Real Estate Investments (audio book), by Robert Kiyosaki and Ken McElroy

How to Find and Keep Good Tenants (audio book), by Robert Kiyosaki and Ken McElroy

The Sleeping Giant, by Ken McElroy

The Property Management Tool Kit, by Mike Beirne

As copartner of MC Companies, www.mccompanies.com, **Ken McElroy** currently owns and manages 10,000 units of multifamily asset. As host of WS Radio's weekly *Entrepreneur Magazine's Real Estate Radio* program, Ken interviews experts in the real estate, finance, and legal arenas. He is a popular speaker at industry events, and his accomplishments as an author include *The ABCs of Real Estate Investing*, *The Advanced Guide to Real Estate Investing*, *The ABCs of Property Management,* and *The Sleeping Giant*.

PART 3

Creative Ways to Make Money in Real Estate

● Gary GORMAN

15

Getting from A to B Without Paying Taxes

T axes are our greatest expense. Today the average person is paying more than 50 percent on income taxes and hidden taxes. One of the beauties of real estate investing, when compared with investing in stocks and mutual funds, is the ability to pay nothing in taxes, legally. As far as I know, this real estate loophole is the biggest and best legal tax loophole remaining, and that is why Gary Gorman is my friend and advisor. Gary has both saved and made Kim and me a lot of money.

While this tax loophole has saved a lot of people money, it has also caused people to lose a lot of money. Many people lose money because they sell a piece of property, deferring their tax bill, but fail to plan their next real estate purchase. This failure to carefully plan their sell and their next buy causes them to either pay the capital gains tax anyway, or purchase a bad piece of property just to avoid the tax. Often, rushing to buy a bad piece of real estate is worse than paying the capital gains tax.

Today before I sell or buy a property, I call Gary Gorman's company for strategic advice. I call Gary before I call a real estate broker.

—ROBERT KIYOSAKI

One of the last great tax shelters left in the United States deals with the ownership of real estate, and more importantly, with how it's taxed when you sell it. There are essentially four different classes of real estate: property you own for development, property you own for a short time (less than one year), your personal residence, and investment property you own for an extended period of time (at least a year). Each is taxed a little differently. Here's a quick overview.

First, property you own for development is subject to ordinary income taxes, as well as self-employment tax (the self-employed equivalent of FICA). Short-term property, by contrast, is subject to short-term capital gains tax, which is typically taxed at the same rate as your salary and other ordinary income. There's no self employment tax. Your personal residence is treated differently, too. It qualifies for a gain exclusion of different amounts, depending upon whether you're single or married. That leaves us with *investment property that you've owned for at least one year*, and this is where real tax shelter advantages kick in.

Four Property Types and How They Are Taxed

1. Property owned for development—is taxed as ordinary income.
2. Short-term property—is taxed as short-term capital gains.
3. Personal residence—qualifies for a gain exclusion based on marital status.
4. Investment property—is the place where real tax shelter advantages kick in!

The government actually wants you to invest in long-term, investment-type real estate. So to encourage you to make this type of investment, it offers you a couple of tax benefits: The first is that you are allowed to write off the cost of the property, over a predetermined period of time, through annual *depreciation deductions*. The benefit of this depreciation deduction could be used to offset other income that you've earned.

For those of you who want to sell your property, you'll pay long-term capital gains tax, which is at a much lower rate than ordinary tax rates. Another author in this book, Tom Wheelwright, does a great job of discussing these benefits in Chapter 21 of this book. My chapter, however, is about my favorite tax benefit, which is available only with long-term investment property, and that is your ability to roll the gain from your old investment property over to your new property. This is called a 1031 Exchange because Section 1031 is the Internal

Revenue Code section that allows you this benefit. The 1031 Exchange is a beautiful thing.

All sophisticated investors include 1031 Exchanges as a critical technique in their bag of investment tools, and if you're not using this tool, you need to learn how powerful it can be to the creation of your personal real estate wealth. Start by understanding how an exchange works: When you sell your old investment property and buy a new investment property, you can roll the gain from the old property to the new one without paying the tax until some time way in the future. Investors who are experienced with this tax code section often can actually pick the amount of tax they want to pay, and when in the future they want to pay it. The obvious benefit of doing this is that you don't have to write a check to the government every time you sell a property. An even bigger benefit is that it allows you to buy a bigger property, which will result in more cash for you somewhere down the road.

To illustrate this, let's say Fred and Sue are selling their rental property, and the tax on their gain would be $100,000. Fred and Sue decide to do an exchange instead so that they'll be able to plow this money back into their new property. Because they are getting a 75 percent loan on their new property (which means that their lender will loan them three dollars for every one that they put into the deal, or $300,000 to their $100,000), Fred and Sue are able to buy $400,000 *more* property than they would have if they had paid the tax and not done an exchange.

$$\$100,000 + \$300,000 = \$400,000$$

Let's say a few years go by and their new property doubles in value, and they sell it. The *additional* $400,000 of property they bought with the 1031 money is now worth $800,000. After paying off the $300,000 loan they used to buy this additional property, they have the balance of $500,000. In other words, by doing an exchange, Fred and Sue were able to leverage the $100,000 tax check they would have written to the government into a half-million dollars' worth of cash in their pocket (before taxes of course)!

TIP 1031 Exchanges are a great way to build wealth!

So, what must you do to have a successful exchange? Well, there are six basic rules to an exchange (which is another way of saying that there are six things that the IRS will look at if it audits your exchange). Speaking of the IRS, and before I start, let me clarify that because Section 1031 is an IRS code section, the

Real Life Story: How $5,000 Grew to $200,000

About ten years ago, I bought a small, two-bedroom condo for $55,000 by putting $5,000 down and borrowing the rest. I rented the bedrooms to my son and daughter while he was going to college and she was finishing law school. After they were out of school, I sold the condo at a profit and exchanged into a very nice condo unit at the top of a building in downtown Denver that had beautiful views of snowcapped mountains. I have great monthly cash flow off this unit, I've gotten my original investment back many times over through cash flow, and my $5,000 equity has grown to about $200,000—just because of the exchange I did. There are two lessons to this story: The first is that you don't have to be Robert Kiyosaki or Donald Trump to do an exchange. Exchanges hold equal power for everyone. The second lesson is that exchanges are a great vehicle to pyramid wealth and build cash flow.

IRS must allow you to do an exchange. However, Section 1031 is a *form-driven* code section. That means that you really do have to dot the i's and cross the t's, and the tiniest misstep could get your exchange disallowed. Keep that in mind as you read the six rules.

The Six Rules of 1031 Exchanges

1. Hold property for investment
2. Adhere to the forty-five-day identification period
3. Replace the property within 180 days
4. Use a qualified intermediary
5. Follow the title holding requirement
6. Buy equal or up, and reinvest all the cash

RULE NO. 1: HOLD FOR INVESTMENT

Section 1031 applies only to property held for investment, but if you meet this rule you can sell any type of investment property and buy any other type of investment property. In other words you can sell a rental house and buy a duplex; you could also buy an office building, an apartment building, a warehouse, or bare land. We have clients who sell bare land, which is not income producing, and then buy rental properties, such as apartment buildings, which do produce income. In other words, they use an exchange to create cash flow. We also have clients who sell one income-producing property and buy another in order to increase their cash flow, and we have some who sell income-producing properties, generally apartment buildings, and buy bare land in order to get out of the hassles of managing their property; they use an exchange to simplify their lives.

TIP 1031 Exchanges are a great tool to help you accomplish your investment strategy.

A common misconception that people have about 1031 exchanges is that if you sell a purple duplex, you have to buy a purple duplex, and this is not the case; simply put, both your old property and your new property have to be *held for investment*.

One of the ongoing debates is whether vacation homes (or second homes), qualify for 1031 Exchanges; many of you own these type of properties. The debate is whether or not vacation homes are investment properties (which *do* qualify for exchanges) or personal-use properties (which *don't* qualify for exchanges), and since vacation homes by their nature fall somewhere in-between, the debate has raged for years. We do a lot of counseling with our vacation home clients to make sure that they are doing everything they can to protect their rights to exchange their property, and if this is the kind of property you have, I suggest that you work with a good intermediary (which I'll define in a moment) to make sure that you follow current law. Current law, by the way, allows you to exchange vacation homes if you follow very strict guidelines.

One of the things that Section 1031 does not allow is the exchanging of property held for resale. The IRS, however, does *not* define the terms *held for investment* and *held for resale*. Guidelines for these terms have arisen from a series of court cases that give us a pretty good understanding of what an investment property is versus a property held for resale. I expect that as time goes on, the court will continue to refine these definitions, but for now a property is held for investment if you hold it as such for at least one year and one day before you try to sell it. Property that you try to sell within the year after you bought it is generally considered to be held for resale. While a defined holding period is not mentioned in the code section, most exchange professionals are comfortable with a holding period of more than one year because one year is the required holding period to get long-term capital gain treatment if you sold the property and did not do an exchange.

A classic example that defines the term "properties held for resale" is the "fix-and-flip." A fix-and-flip is where you buy a "fixer-upper," clean it up, and then put it back on the market. Because your intent is to sell the property right away, the property does not qualify for an exchange, even if you have trouble finding a buyer. Does this mean that you can't buy a property with the intent to fix it up? No, you just have to hold the property for investment. How do you do that? The best way is to hold the property for at least one year and one day before you put it back on the market.

TIP Hold your investment properties at least one year before you try to sell them.

In the past, I've bought fixer-type properties, but I always make sure that I hold them for at least one year before I try to sell them. I might fix the properties up, rent them for at least one year, and then sell them, or sometimes I will rent them for at least one year and then fix them up before I sell them. Regardless of the process, the important lesson here is that I always make sure that I hold them as an investment for at least one year before I sell them.

One last thing before I go to rule number two is that, obviously, if your old property is real estate, you have to buy real estate as your replacement property, and anything that is land, or attached to it, or part of it, qualifies as real estate. Timber rights, water rights, and mineral rights are all examples of real estate. I sold a property several years ago, did a 1031 Exchange into another property, but had about $100,000 of cash left over after the purchase (which I did not want to pay tax on). I took the cash and bought some oil and gas interests to complete my exchange. The oil and gas interests provide a nice, consistent, monthly cash flow without my having to manage the investment.

RULE NO. 2: FORTY-FIVE-DAY IDENTIFICATION PERIOD

Starting the day you close the sale of your old property, you have exactly forty-five calendar days to come up with a list of properties you might want to buy. On this list you may place up to three properties with no limitation. For example, if you sold your old property for $100,000, you could list three properties for $10 million each, for a total of $30 million. While this may seem like a strange example, I actually had a client with this exact scenario several years ago. He was in the market to buy a shopping center and was actually looking at three different properties. Before he could complete his purchase, he got a call from a tenant who wanted to buy a small condo that he owned. Since my client was going to buy one of the shopping centers anyway, he threw the sale of the condo into the mix and did a 1031 Exchange so he wouldn't have to pay tax on it. It was just lucky timing for him, and he was able to sell the condo without a tax liability, even though it was insignificant to the overall transaction.

You may put more than three properties on your list, but if your list has more than three properties the IRS will subject you to an additional set of rules that says, in effect, that the combined purchase price of everything on your list may not exceed twice the selling price of your old property. This is called the 200 percent rule. Going back to my example above (where you sold your old property for $100,000), if you had put four or more properties on your list, the combined purchase price of everything on your list would be limited to twice ($200,000 in my example) the selling price of the old property. In other words, you could list three properties for $30 million or more, but once your list exceeded three properties your whole list is limited to $200,000 (twice the selling price). My advice: Keep your list to three properties or less.

TIP Keep it simple—keep your forty-five-day list to three properties or less.

As I said, the forty-five days are *calendar* days, starting the day you close the sale. This means that if the forty-fifth day is a Saturday, a Sunday, or a holiday, that is the date that your list must be completed, and you don't get until the following business day to complete your list. And no, you cannot get an extension of this time limit.

When you make your list, you have to identify the properties clearly enough that if you get audited the IRS agent could look at your list and go directly to the property. In other words you have to state: "123 Main Street, Phoenix, Arizona." You *cannot* say "a three-bedroom, two-bath house on Main Street in Phoenix."

You then give your list to a person called a qualified intermediary, which I'll discuss in rule number four.

RULE NO. 3: 180-DAY REPLACEMENT PERIOD

Again, starting on the day of closing of the sale, you have exactly 180 calendar days in which to purchase your replacement property, but whatever you buy has to be on your forty-five-day list. You can buy one of the properties, two of them, or all three if you wish, but whatever you end up buying has to be on your forty-five-day list, and it has to be closed by the 180th day.

As with the forty-five-day requirement, these are calendar days, which mean that if the day falls on a Saturday, Sunday, or holiday, that's the day, and barring an emergency declaration by the president, there are no possible extensions. Note that your timeframes are forty-five and 180 days—not six weeks and six months. Both the forty-five and the 180-day requirements are cast in concrete. You either meet them, or your exchange is toast.

TIP The time limits are very critical. Obey them.

RULE NO. 4: QUALIFIED INTERMEDIARY REQUIREMENT

You are not allowed to touch the money from the sale of your old property during the time between that sale and the purchase of your new property. The law requires that you use the services of an independent third party, called a *qualified intermediary*, to hold these proceeds and to prepare the documents the law requires to document your exchange.

Despite the implication that by being *qualified* the intermediary has been somehow approved by the IRS, qualified intermediaries are essentially ungoverned. They're not required to pass any tests of their knowledge and abilities, and for the most part, they may do as they wish with your money while they hold it. In most states, anybody with enough money to print business cards can hold themselves out as an intermediary.

There has been a pattern in the exchange industry of periodic losses of exchange proceeds by intermediaries who have used the funds for their own purposes or have made bad investments with the funds. Some of these bad intermediaries have been attorneys, some have been successful business people with successful track records, and some have been title companies. These losses have ranged from the comparatively small to the spectacularly large, but they all stem from the practice by the intermediary of *commingling* (or *pooling*) the funds of their clients. In other words, they put all clients' funds into one pool or account.

Intermediaries hold their clients' monies in one of two ways: Either they commingle all the funds into one account, or they set up a separate bank account for each client. Every problem that has arisen from intermediary theft stems from commingled accounts. Despite this fact, approximately 95 percent (from my informal poll) of the intermediaries commingle funds.

California, Nevada, and Idaho are the only states that at this point have adopted statutes designed to regulate intermediaries and protect consumers. A number of other states have proposed legislation to protect their citizens, but not surprisingly, the intermediary industry has strongly resisted any type of regulation. So, the bottom line is that you are on your own to protect your money.

Since you are required to use an intermediary to handle your exchange, what should you look for when you pick one? First, make sure that your money is not commingled, but placed in a separate account with your name and tax identification number associated with it. Call the bank frequently to make sure that the funds are still in the account. One of the intermediaries that failed had led their clients to believe that they had separate accounts, when in fact, the monies were commingled. So when you call the bank, keep a record of when you called and whom you talked to.

TIP Make sure your money is placed in, and stays in, a separate account for you.

Second, make sure that they know what they are doing. Many intermediaries have little or no background in tax law, real estate law, or 1031 law, yet they are all too happy to handle your exchange and hold your money (these intermediaries are easy to spot by the low fees they charge). Ask them how many exchanges they've done? How big is their staff? Will they give you a list of referrals? Have they ever had a complaint filed against them? Don't get hung up on who they are or what their degrees are—it's your job to protect your money because no one is looking out for you.

When you watch the news at night and some reporter is interviewing a fraud victim, the victim never says, "It doesn't surprise me that he ripped me off. I never trusted him; he just seemed like a crook." No, they never say that. Instead they always say, "I can't believe that he ripped me off. He was the nicest, most trustworthy person. My kids go to school with his kids; we go to the same church; his wife is so sweet; I just can't believe he could do this to me." So, if you can't trust the people you *can't* trust, and you can't trust the people you *do* trust, who do you trust? Nobody but yourself! You are the only one who is responsible to safeguard your money.

TIP When it comes to your exchange funds, if you can't trust the people you *can't* trust, and you can't trust the people you *do* trust, who do you trust? Only yourself!

RULE NO. 5: TITLE HOLDING REQUIREMENT

Section 1031 deals with the *taxpayer* who owns the old property, sells it, and does an exchange. That same taxpayer is the one who has to do the exchange, report it in their tax return, and buy the new property. A lot of our clients want to change the title to the property midstream, which as a general rule you can't do.

TIP You have to complete the exchange using the same taxpayer that sold the old property.

Let's say that Fred and Sue Jones are selling their purple rental house, which they own in their names, and want to have Jones Investments, Inc., the corporation they own, take title to their new property. Since the corporation has a different tax identification number, this would not be a valid exchange.

Since that won't work, what if Fred and Sue transferred the ownership of the rental house to their corporation right before the sale closed (that way the seller of the old property and the buyer of the new would be the same entity)? This won't work either because, if you remember from rule number one, you have to hold the property for at least one year and one day for it to be investment property. If Fred and Sue transferred ownership right before the sale, the IRS will argue that the corporation owned the property for resale rather than investment because it sold it right after it got title to it.

TIP The best time to structure the sale of your property to minimize the tax is when you first buy it.

The main reason that our clients want to transfer ownership to another entity in the middle of the exchange is that they want to own their new property in an entity that limits their liability. I fully agree with what they are trying to do, but doing it in the middle of the exchange is the wrong time to do it. There are ways to accomplish what Fred and Sue are trying to do—ways that are beyond the scope of this chapter. Call us and we'll walk you through your options to accomplish this, but the best advice I can give you here is that the best time to structure the sale of your property to qualify for a 1031 Exchange is when you first buy it.

RULE NO. 6: YOU MUST BUY EQUAL OR UP, AND YOU MUST REINVEST ALL OF THE CASH

In order to pay *no* tax on your exchange, you have to do two things: you have to buy equal or up, and you have to reinvest all of the cash.

Let's go back to Fred and Sue selling their purple duplex. Let's say that they sell it for $100,000, there is an unpaid mortgage, and closing costs associated with the sale total $40,000. This means that if I was their qualified intermediary I'd receive the balance of the proceeds of $60,000. If Fred and Sue then buy their replacement property for $90,000, they'd pay tax on the *buy-down* of $10,000 (they sold for $100,000 but bought for only $90,000, hence the $10,000 buy-down). Note that the buy-down does not toast their exchange; they simply pay tax on it. And note also that the whole buy-down is taxable—they can't offset any of their tax basis against the buy-down gain.

Let's change the example—Fred and Sue still sell the purple duplex for $100,000, but instead they buy the new property for $150,000, so in this case they bought up from $100,000 to $150,000. To pay for this purchase they plan to get a mortgage of $100,000, which means that they need only $50,000 of the $60,000 in funds that I'm holding to close the sale. So what happens to the unspent funds of $10,000? They are taxable; and again, the entire $10,000 is taxable.

TIP In order to pay *zero* tax on your exchange, you have to buy equal or up, and you have to reinvest all of the cash.

To recap this last rule, in order to pay no tax on your exchange, you have to buy equal or up, *and* you have to reinvest all of the cash. In these two examples, my implication is that Fred and Sue inadvertently ended up in taxable situations. Some of our clients actually want to buy down and are willing to pay the tax, or more typically they want some cash from the sale to buy a car or pay off a credit card.

If you are one of those people who want some cash from your exchange, there are a couple of ways to approach this: If you don't want to pay tax, you can wait and borrow from the new property after the closing. Let's go back to my second example above, where they're selling for $100,000 and buying for $150,000—by getting a loan for $100,000 they end up not spending all their cash. Remember, they have $10,000 left over. That's the taxable amount.

But what if they want the $10,000 in proceeds? Is there a way they can get that money without paying tax? Yes, if they buy the property for the $150,000 using all of the proceeds I'm holding (meaning their loan is only $90,000), they've completed their exchange and they can then refinance and pull proceeds from the refinance without paying tax. How long do they have to wait after the purchase to refinance tax free? One *nanosecond*! Yes, it's true! They can refinance the new property immediately. I say refinance, but a good intermediary can show you how to set up the loan on the purchase of the new property so that you can walk away from the closing with cash without having to get two loans. There is one caveat, however: The refinance has to be on the new property—if you try to do it on the old property before you sell it, the IRS could argue that you've violated rule number four and touched the money.

Refinancing tax free works great if you are buying equal or up, but what if you are buying down? When do you get the proceeds from the buy-down? Go back to my first example; Fred and Sue sell for $100,000 but are buying for $90,000. When do they get the cash from the buy down? There are actually two places that they can get the $10,000. The first place is at the closing table when they sell the purple duplex, and the second place is after the 180 days when their exchange has ended. If you know that you want cash from the sale of the old property, you have to convey that to the intermediary before the closing takes place so that the intermediary can prepare the exchange documents to allow this. Otherwise your money will be tied up until the end of the exchange period. Once the transaction closes and the intermediary has your proceeds, you cannot touch them until the exchange period has expired.

One last thing before I finish this chapter: I did *not* say that you have to have debt on your new property at least equal to the debt on your old property. This simply is not the case, even though a lot of intermediaries and most CPAs and attorneys seem to think so. If Fred and Sue sell the purple duplex for $100,000, netting $60,000 in proceeds, and then buy their replacement property, also for $100,000 by using the $60,000 that I'm holding, the balance of the purchase funds can come from any source: a savings account, a loan on the property, or some combination of the two. For example, they could use the $60,000 I'm holding, take $20,000 from their savings account, and get a loan for the balance of $20,000.

Now that you've finished this chapter, sit back for a moment and see the big picture: 1031 Exchanges are a great way to get from A to B without paying taxes. The place to start is with this question: "What are you going to do with the money when you sell your investment property?" If one of your possibilities, even with part of the money, is to buy another investment property, then you want to take advantage of this great code section.

Gary Gorman is a well-known educator and published author on the subject of 1031 Exchanges. He has written *Six Basic Things You Need to Know about 1031 Exchanges* and *Exchanging Up!* With more than thirty-six years of real estate tax experience, Gary is recognized as an expert witness in the federal courts on 1031 tax issues. Revolutionary exchange systems such as 1031Connexions.com, 1031 TaxPak, and 1031Access have all been developed by Gary to benefit the industry.

16

No Down Payment®
Using Other People's Money

*C*arleton is a legend in the world of real estate. He has single-handedly taught more people about real estate than anyone else I know.

Years ago, when I was just starting out, I was watching Carleton's television infomercial on real estate. I bought his program, and it is one of the smartest investments I have made.

Carleton and my Rich Dad are cut from the same bolt of cloth. They come from the same philosophy. They believe in cash flow and see value that most people overlook. They are not afraid of investing in distressed areas. They understand the need for a roof over a person's head, regardless of how much money the person makes.

Today, Carleton and I work together with the Professional Education Institute. PEI supports Carleton's work through his real estate coaching program, and supports me through all of my Rich Dad coaching programs. Regardless of which coaching program you select, PEI does a fabulous job for anyone who is serious about their financial future.

—ROBERT KIYOSAKI

In my many years of teaching people how to build wealth by investing in real estate, probably the most common objection I hear is this: "But I don't have any money to get started." That one common misconception has kept so many people sitting on the sidelines rather than pursuing their dreams.

TIP Lack of ambition (not lack of money) will lead to failure.

I could have been one of those people, but something happened that changed my life forever. After graduating from college, I started working in the private sector, working for one company eight years and then another for eighteen months.

I was pretty aggressive in trying to climb the corporate ladder, and as I look back I honestly think that I exceeded my capabilities. I was fired from the second company. I toyed with the idea of going into business myself, but I suddenly had a revelation. I realized that I had moved four different times with those two companies, and that each time I bought and sold a home I had made $5,000 to $8,000. That was a world of money back then! So I thought, why not go into real estate? However, I had very little money and no credit.

The "no credit" mind-set was a carry-over from my conservative midwest upbringing where my parents had instilled in me this philosophy: Never borrow money except to buy a home; otherwise pay cash. And since all of the money I had made from selling my previous homes had been reinvested in larger and more expensive homes, I needed to find something to support my family and enable me to make mortgage payments and to pay for all of the other expenses of everyday living.

So, I decided to become a real estate investor. I went back to school and attended seminars. I read books and studied courses. I sought out other investors and brokers who could advise me. The good news is that I quickly learned that you don't need a lot of money or perfect credit to successfully invest in real estate. What you *do* need are the time-tested and proven creative techniques to invest in real estate the smart way—by using other people's money.

When you think about it, this concept is used in business all the time—but with different terminology. When a large corporation changes hands, it is often the result of a "leveraged buyout." In essence, this simply means that the buyers used leverage instead of their own cash to accomplish the transaction. In other words, they used other people's money. But can this method work for you? The answer is "Yes!" The only major difference between the leveraged buyout of a huge corporate enterprise and purchasing a single-family home using other people's money is the number of dollars.

TIP The basic concept is this: Use other people's money.

You might ask, "What people, and where can I get this money?" These are legitimate questions, and I'll share a number of answers with you. It all depends on which creative techniques will work in a given situation. For example, some techniques involve the seller, some use partners, and still other techniques bring in additional investors.

The techniques that I am going to share with you are timeless; they work in any market: markets with high interest rates or low interest rates, boom markets such as in 2003–2005, and down markets as in 2008–2009. But they're not one-size-fits-all. Each investor has his or her own unique goals and circumstances and skills, and each property he or she analyzes will have a different set of circumstances. That's the beauty of these creative methods! You can pick and choose whichever techniques are best suited for each situation. As you learn the details of each strategy, you will recognize certain elements that will not work for you, while other elements will be a perfect fit. Control of the situation is in your hands, and once you've learned the ropes you will know precisely what to do when opportunity knocks.

THE SELLER CAN HELP YOU FINANCE YOUR PURCHASE!

One of the most obvious sources for funding to consider when purchasing a property is the owner. After all, who has a more vested interest in seeing that a sale occurs? The seller is the person who will answer either yes or no when you ask, "Are you open to financing arrangements?" or "Are you willing to take a promissory note?"

TIP Always remember that the seller has the most invested in making sure the deal happens.

Depending on how motivated the seller is, he or she may have a very attentive ear when you offer to pay the asking price—in return for working cooperatively with you to make the sale happen.

One of the key words to consider here is "motivated." Motivated sellers are those who don't just want but need to sell the property and may not have the time or patience to sell it the "traditional" way—that is, listing the property for sale, waiting for a qualified buyer, negotiating price, then finally selling the property months after they listed it. Sellers may be motivated for any number of reasons, including divorce, foreclosure, job relocation, or even a death in the family. These sellers are not "down and out"; they are just in a position where they are anxious to move on.

When you use creative financing, you can make the situation a win-win for both buyer and seller.

Ways to Use the Seller as a Source of Financing

There are many ways you can utilize the seller as a source for financing. You can:

- Ask if the seller will hold a second mortgage, in lieu of a down payment. For example, obtain a 70 percent loan from a lending institution or through partners, and ask the seller to hold a second mortgage note for 30 percent.

- Ask if the seller would give you credits at closing for repairs. For example, negotiate a $5,000 credit at closing for roof repairs and new carpet allowance. The credit will appear on the closing statement, and you may even get money back at closing.

- Ask if the seller would consider a lease option or a land contract. (I'll talk more about these techniques later.)

- Ask if the seller would trade services for a discount on the property. The key is: Don't be shy!

You may feel uncomfortable asking someone to help you finance the sale of his own property, but this will get easier for you in time and when you know the facts. You will feel more confident in your offer and be able to explain the win-win scenario to the seller. These suggestions are only the beginning. You are limited only by your lack of creativity when problem solving.

Using these tools will also help you educate buyers when you become the seller!

THE PROPERTY ITSELF CAN HELP FINANCE YOUR PURCHASE

Every property has worth. The value lies not only in the actual value of the house and land itself, but in other areas as well. Trees and mineral rights may have cash value. A vacant lot next door or furniture left on the property may also provide a source for cash.

TIP Online valuation services, and even some comparable market analyses from a real estate professional, usually don't include the value of trees or mineral rights. Check with a realtor or city or county office before you purchase a property. Educate yourself as to what local code enforcement or zoning will allow. Don't be afraid to ask questions, and always do your due diligence.

A property's value is often calculated by the sales of similar properties in the same neighborhood. You can research this information yourself or have a realtor help you. For a ballpark valuation, you can look online at a number of Web sites, including www.zillow.com, www.realestate.yahoo.com/homevalues, and my favorite, www.netronline.com. Visit www.CarletonSheetsRealBook.com for up-to-date links and resources.

Real-Life Story: Carleton's Success Story No. 1

Some time ago, I bought a forty-eight-unit apartment building creatively with very little money down. I then converted the apartments into condominiums and sold them in blocks of four and five to individual investors at nearly twice what I had originally paid on a per-unit basis. While the use of the building did not change, the legal framework did and, by doing this, I was able to make a huge profit.

INVESTORS ARE ALWAYS INTERESTED IN REAL ESTATE

People seem to have no problem putting money into the stock market. However, it can be risky and difficult to figure out exactly what to invest in. For example, when you buy a piece of rental property, you can reasonably anticipate what the future rents and expenses will be. But if you buy a stock, the value of the stock could drop in half almost overnight, and its dividend could be totally eliminated! Real estate, by contrast, is a much safer investment. Moreover, you will find that investing in real estate becomes easier and easier as you acquire more properties. In fact, once your friends and acquaintances see how you're amassing properties, they'll often ask if they can "get in on your next deal." When investors don't have the time, but do have the cash, they will frequently loan money to you at a good rate of return, or perhaps even agree to share in a portion of the profit upon resale of the property.

Where can you find investors? Check your local newspaper for "money lenders," or do an online search. It may even be as simple as a friend who isn't happy with his or her return in the stock market and is willing to lend you a large sum to purchase the property, while they hold the mortgage, and make a good return on their investment through your monthly payments. And if you have an investor willing to loan you only a portion of the purchase price, be sure to find out what your lender's requirements are before you structure a deal.

> ## Real-Life Story: Student Success Story No. 1
>
> Lupe began building her reputation by purchasing and rehabbing condos, one by one, in a run-down complex in her town. Her reputation spread by word of mouth, and, before long, investors were approaching her to get a better return than their 401(k)s were paying. These investors didn't have the time or knowledge of investing in real estate, but they did have some money they were willing to invest.

PARTNERS WILL PUT MORE SKIN IN THE GAME

Partners may sound like just a synonym for investors, but actually there is a distinct difference. Partners are people who will actually be purchasing property *with* you, not simply financing a loan for you.

TIP Partnerships are a great way to get started. A partner can help expand your portfolio and borrowing power, while sharing the work load. There are many types of partnerships, and I suggest you investigate each type and tailor yours to fit your individual needs. Seek professional help if you are unsure.

Where will you find your partners? For starters, ask family members who have the foresight to realize the relative safety and potential of investing in real estate. Over a period of time, you may have a dozen or more partnerships comprised of family members, friends, and business associates. Each partner will have put up cash (or services) in return for an equity position (ownership) in the property.

Real-Life Story: Carleton's Success Story No. 2

When I first started in this business as a real estate agent, my first listing was an apartment building. I kept wondering why it had not sold. It seemed like such a good investing opportunity. One of the seminars I had attended had focused on the benefits of partnership investing: accomplishing with others what you cannot do by yourself. I had learned some very effective techniques from the instructor who had a solid background in forming syndicates or partner groups, so I decided to acquire the building. I put together a partnership that consisted of two investors who contributed 100 percent of the required cash down payment, with the seller financing an 80 percent first mortgage. I contributed my "expertise," and we were off to a profitable start and, I might add—the beginning of a career that has spanned more than four decades.

But be aware: Partnerships can be a double-edged sword. Partners might see their responsibilities, duties, and partnership goals differently, which could lead to conflicts that can destroy the partnership. Make sure that all partnership agreements are in writing. Go to www.CarletonSheetsRealBook.com to find out more about my program that is devoted entirely to partnerships. As always, consult an expert for legal advice when necessary.

BORROW THE BROKER'S COMMISSION, SERIOUSLY!

Sometimes when a property listed is by a broker, it requires just 10 percent down. The reality is that the seller just wants to receive enough cash at closing to cover the broker's commission and closing costs.

The typical broker's commission ranges from 5 to 7 percent. In a real estate transaction, there are usually two brokers—the "listing" broker who listed the property on the MLS and represents the seller's interests, and the "buyer's broker" who represents the buyers and sells them the property. If one broker both lists the property and sells it, he or she gets all of the commission (subject to state law and the commission-splitting arrangement that the broker may have with the brokerage company he or she works for); if one broker lists the property and another broker sells it, the two brokers split the commission.

TIP What is the MLS? MLS stands for Multiple Listing Service. It is a regional or local (depending on where you live), fee-based service whereby members of the Board of Realtors exchange their listings.

For a real estate investor, the best opportunity to "borrow" the commission to use as the down payment is to negotiate with the listing broker, because he or she is in a position to receive up to 100 percent of the commission.

TIP It is helpful if you work with a real estate broker or realtor who is also an investor. They understand creative financing and using other people's money, and they may be more apt to loan their commission in the form of a note against the property.

Building rapport and credibility with brokers is crucial. Brokers may be reluctant to consider delaying receipt of their commission, but that reluctance can be tempered by an offer in which you give the broker a note for an amount higher than the commission, for example, $3,500 for a $3,000 commission. The premium price is offered for the broker's cooperation in accepting a note in lieu of full payment at closing.

YOUR OWN SERVICES, SKILLS, AND RESOURCES

Here's a technique that most people never even think of, and yet it's a great way to buy property without putting a lot of money into it. Many properties won't interest conventional buyers and investors because of needed maintenance or repairs. Sanding, painting, replacing—all of these "needs" have a dollar value. However, without having to put up actual dollars, you or a partner may be able to convert services or skills to dollars by identifying and meeting these needs. And you could negotiate a credit to be paid to you at closing to reimburse you for the cost of performing these repairs. The credit will appear on the closing statement and will decrease the amount of cash you need for closing (or will increase the amount of cash you receive back at closing).

TIP Negotiating repair credits at closing can be enough to cover the down payment.

Do you have something of value, say, a boat, jewelry, a 401(k), or an insurance policy that you can borrow against? Tapping into the equity of these assets by using a line of credit can be a great way to leverage a piece of property. Caution is advised, though. You will have to pay back a line of credit, usually through monthly installments, and you may not be able to deduct your interest expense. Again, consult an accountant to understand the specifics in your situation. Make sure that you can afford to make these payments. Alternatively, you could arrange a private loan from an investor using one of these assets as collateral.

> ### Real-Life Story: Student Success Story No. 2
>
> Some investors use the actual asset itself as a down payment. Scott is one of my students who sold sixteen of his properties as a package. His buyer purchased them by trading a condo and a lot the buyer owned "free and clear," as his down payment. A bank financed the balance of the $1.6 million transaction. So at closing, Scott received a mortgage-free lot and condo, and he also gained a monetary profit from the sale.

THE MOST TIMELESS TECHNIQUE OF ALL: THE LEASE OPTION

I'm often asked which is my favorite technique for buying or selling real estate. Well, my program is filled with dozens of great techniques I have enjoyed using successfully over the years. One that has performed particularly well for both buyers and sellers, especially since the real estate "meltdown" that began in mid-2006, has been the lease option.

TIP A lease option works in any market!

In simple terms, a lease option is a contract between a buyer and a seller that gives the buyer tenancy in a property, as well as the legal right to purchase the property at a predetermined price, or formula for price, on or before a specified future date. When you enter into a lease option with a seller, you promise to lease the property for a certain period of time and to make specified monthly payments. In return, the seller is obligated to sell the property to you under terms specified in the lease option agreement if you choose to exercise your option.

At first glance, it appears that a lease option benefits only the buyer. After all, the buyer is not obligated to buy the property. But if he or she does choose to buy the property, the seller is required to sell. If the lease option is carefully structured, however, it can be good for both the buyer and the seller.

When a buyer enters into a lease option with a seller, he or she is betting that the value of the property on a specified future date will be greater than the

TABLE 18.1

Benefits for the Buyer (Optionee)	Benefits for the Seller (Optionor)
The risk is low, and the financial leverage can be high.	The agreed-upon price of the property is frequently at the top of its current market value range.
The buyer receives control and possession of the property.	The option money that the seller receives is tax-deferred until exercised or expired.
Very little, or no, initial closing costs.	The option is forfeited if rent is not paid on time.
The buyer can walk away from the contract if the value of the property on the specified future date does not justify its purchase at the agreed-upon price, or the buyer can attempt to renegotiate the price or terms of the purchase.	The seller receives all the equity buildup (amortization) on the mortgage during the option period.
	The tenant has pride of ownership and, therefore, an incentive to take good care of the property.
	The rent, including the amount, if any, that is applicable to the option purchase price, is at the top of or above the fair market rental range.
	The ability to regain possession and control of the property in the event of the optionee's default in meeting the terms of the agreement.

agreed-upon purchase price. Even if this doesn't happen, considerable equity may still be achieved as a result of the credits of some or all of the monthly payments from the purchase price. As a result, there is a high chance that by purchasing the property at the specified date and price, he or she will gain instant equity. If, however, the value of the property on the specified future date is less than the specified purchase price, the buyer can walk away from the contract or attempt to renegotiate the price.

The seller is free to keep any option consideration (something of value, usually money, given as an inducement to enter a contract) that may have been paid and realize the gain from a monthly rental income. And if the buyer walks away, the seller is also free to start the process over—to either sell or rent or lease option the property.

TIP Over time, the real estate market is bound to change. The lease option technique allows both buyer and seller to take advantage of any market change and "bridge the gap," so to speak, with minimal risk.

Lease option contracts can be written to include several options—for both buyer and seller. These can include the following:

- Lease optioning a property with the intent to sublease to another person with a purchase option (sandwich lease).

- Lease optioning, then selling or assigning your position to a third party.

- Lease optioning a property requiring a modest rehab to sell to an end user or keep as a rental.

The lease option can be used on commercial investment properties as well as residential or investment properties.

Real-Life Story:
Student Success Story No. 3

This lease option was negotiated a number of years ago. The numbers may seem low, but the principles and the economics of the transaction are very much applicable in any market. The buyer (my student) owned a house worth roughly $100,000. There were a fair number of rental homes in the area; most of them rented in the $500 to $700 range.

Seeking to find a substantially nicer home, the buyer sought out a nearby upscale town where the home values exceeded $200,000. Rentals in this upscale area were fairly scarce. The buyer found a home for sale for $220,000, and it appeared to be reasonably priced. The seller was very anxious to sell since he had already moved out of state, and the home had been on the market for several months. The buyer proposed a lease option, and they ended up agreeing to a four-year option at the asking price of $220,000. The monthly rent was $900 (low for this particular house, but high in comparison to almost all other rentals in the surrounding areas), and the buyer received a 50 percent rent credit ($450 per month) toward the eventual purchase. The seller was to pay taxes and insurance during the option period, and the buyer agreed to pay for all of the maintenance (an inspection revealed that the house was in very good shape). The buyer put down $3,600 as a nonrefundable deposit for the option consideration, which was equivalent to less than 2 percent of the option purchase price!

The buyer was amazed when he figured out the "effective" interest rate that he was paying. He realized that, of the $900 a month he was paying, only $450 was the true "cost" of owning the house. From that, he subtracted the cost of taxes and insurance (which were $340 per month—an amount he would have had to pay had he owned the property) to yield a net "cost" of $110 a month. This worked out to an incredible effective interest rate of 0.6 percent ($110 times twelve months equals $1,320, divided by $220,000, which equals 0.6 percent). *That's less than 1 percent!*

After three years, the buyer was certain that he was going to exercise his option at the end of the four-year period (because, among other reasons, property values had been increasing very nicely in this area—at about 7 percent per year), but he figured it was worth the effort to see if the seller would be willing to extend the option in exchange for some additional consideration. The buyer and seller ended up agreeing to extend the option for one additional year in return for the buyer paying $10,000 of additional option consideration (which meant that it would be fully applied to the purchase price, but it would be forfeited if the buyer did not buy the house). Was this a good move? I sure think so. Even if it cost the buyer 10 percent interest to borrow the $10,000 for a year (which is $1,000), it was a small price to pay for another year of ownership at the effective interest rate of less than 1 percent.

After the five-year period, the buyer exercised the option and obtained the necessary funds by simply securing an owner-occupied loan (loan programs specifically designed for owner-occupants) for $179,400, which was the total amount due to the seller ($220,000 less the deposit of $3,600, less the additional consideration of $10,000 paid in year four, and less the rent credit of $27,000, which is equal to $450 for sixty months or five years). The property appreciated, and it appraised for $290,000; thus, the new loan was for only 62 percent of the property's fair market value. (By the way, the buyer eventually sold this house about a year later for $320,000 and, you guessed it, has since moved on to an even nicer home!)

The buyer's "profit" on his initial investment of $3,600 was $90,000—based on the property appreciation of $70,000, and the $20,400 savings of not paying taxes and insurance while living in the house. Under a lease option like this, the buyer (and seller, in this case) benefited in that the real estate taxes remained fairly steady throughout the five-year period because there had not been a reported sale of the property.

The action that the buyer took at the end of year three (asking for and getting the seller to agree to an additional year's extension) is an excellent example of the power of creative thinking. This would have been a great investment even if that had not occurred, but by thinking creatively and being willing to ask questions, the buyer turned what was already a great investment into one that was even better!

Let's take a look at how the buyer and the seller fared over this five-year deal.

TABLE 18.2 Benefits for the Buyer and the Seller

Benefits to the Buyer	Benefits to the Seller
Flexibility of option to purchase any time within a four-year term (this option was additionally extended for one more year).	The seller received full asking price.
Out of the total monthly rental payment of $900, $450 is credited toward the purchase, which makes the cost of occupancy $450 a month.	The seller is relieved of all maintenance responsibility and cost associated with the property.
Initial down payment of $3,600 and subsequent option extension of $10,000 are credited directly against the purchase price.	The seller receives sufficient income to cover the property taxes, insurance, and the principal and interest payment on the existing mortgage, plus a monthly profit.
The buyer had the advantage of time to put himself in the position to buy a home that he may not otherwise have been able to afford.	The seller receives a nonrefundable deposit up front.
Based on appreciation of approximately 7% per year, the buyer will enjoy instant equity of $110,600 ($290,000 fair market value minus $179,400 option purchase price balance).	The seller retains the $54,000 in rent payments ($900 per month) and the $13,600 total option deposit if the buyer fails to exercise the option. If he exercises the option, the seller credits back these amounts against the purchase price.
The buyer will have a much easier time obtaining favorable loan terms with $110,600 in equity in the property and therefore needs a mere 62% LTV (loan-to-value) to pay off the balance of the option purchase price.	The seller enjoys the reduction of the loan principal, which increases the amount the seller will cash out at closing or the equity the seller will have in the property if the buyer does not complete the transaction.
	The seller enjoys the deferment of taxes on the portion of money applied to the option purchase price (including the $3,600 and the $10,000 consideration) until the option is exercised or abandoned.
	The seller has the peace of mind of knowing that the property is under contract and is being maintained by someone motivated to take good care of it because, hopefully, he will soon own it.

This story is a perfect example of how a lease option can be very powerful for the buyer, and yet still represent an attractive proposition for the seller.

To learn more about lease options, and many other creative techniques to purchase property, go to www.CarletonSheetsRealBook.com to view my free online programs.

PUTTING IT ALL INTO ACTION

These are powerful techniques, but there is still one additional step that you need to take: learning to negotiate and structure offers. The best creative financing in the world won't gain you anything if you don't use it as part of a well-planned strategy with terms that are favorable to you. It's not really as difficult as it may seem. You might even discover that you are a better negotiator than you thought you were.

For me, it all begins with trust and credibility. For starters, keep in mind that people are naturally suspicious when it comes to conducting business with strangers. Yet in more cases than not, we find ourselves (as either buyers or sellers) negotiating with people whom we are meeting for the very first time. The number-one question on both parties' minds, therefore, is "Who do I trust?"

TIP Use the seller's name in conversation.

I once read a book that made the case that people are successful in life only to the degree that they are able to make people like and trust them. This is certainly true in negotiating. When talking to a seller, take a few minutes to establish a rapport. This builds a trusting relationship that is so essential to negotiating. If sellers feel comfortable with you, they often will be more forthcoming with important information, such as their true needs.

So how do you convince a seller that you're on the up and up? How do you establish that magical relationship based on rapport? One of the simplest techniques is a very basic one. When you get the person's name, remember it! Write it down, and be sure to get the right spelling. Then, when engaging him or her in conversation, be sure to use it. It isn't, "I'll tell you what," it's "I'll tell you what, Joe." That's a quick and easy way to begin building a rapport with the seller.

TIP Avoid being overly critical. You'll seldom, if ever, force the seller into lowering the price or terms by harsh criticism.

Another important element of rapport and trust building is being a good listener. As you talk to the seller, remember to always be an empathetic listener. Imagine yourself in his or her situation and try to experience, emotionally, what the seller is experiencing. By doing so, you might gain a new perspective on the negotiation and be able to make an offer that the seller is more likely to accept. People like to know that they're being listened to.

Using Nonessential Contingencies

Establishing a good rapport with someone is not in and of itself a negotiating strategy. It is merely one component of your overall approach. Compromise is what negotiations are all about. If you enter negotiations with an open mind, the seller is more likely to have an open mind, too. This mind-set allows both of you to create a win-win situation.

During negotiations, both parties must give something to get something; therefore, good negotiators always use nonessential, but purposeful, contingencies as negotiating tools. In other words, when you use a nonessential contingency—such as requesting that the seller include some, or all, of the furniture—you ask for concessions that you do not necessarily need or even want (concessions you are willing to "negotiate away"). In return, the seller concedes on a point that is important to you.

By using nonessential contingencies, you will arm yourself with effective negotiating tactics. You might only want the seller to pay all of the closing costs, for example, but by adding the other nonessential contingencies, you have some extra items that you can "give up" to get the one that you truly want.

Making Multiple Offers Simultaneously

The "traditional" way that people make offers on real estate is to make one offer, wait for the seller to counteroffer, go back and forth once or twice on terms or price, and then come to an agreement. By making more than one offer simultaneously, you will be able to pinpoint what the seller's needs are, and how your offer can meet his or her needs.

You may want to consider using a letter of intent when making multiple offers (or, for that

Multiple Offer Options:

A cash offer at a deeply discounted price.
An offer that incorporates seller-financing.
A lease option.
Make sure all amounts are clearly stated.

matter, with any type of offer you are making). A letter of intent is a letter stating a buyer's intent to make an offer to acquire a certain property. It is not a binding contract, but it shows a good-faith desire to own the property, and it can be a real time saver compared with filling out a formal contract offer to purchase. If a seller responds in a positive way, it could be the basis for further negotiations. If you are proposing a creative way to purchase the property, it may be helpful because you can show exactly how the transaction will benefit the seller by using a letter of intent.

In your letter of intent, you can bullet point two or three different scenarios that would work for you in purchasing the property. Make sure the seller understands that he or she cannot combine the offers. If you are filling out a formal offer to purchase, you will have to fill out one per offer with the creative details in the addendum.

To view a sample letter of intent, as well as many other forms, log on to www.CarletonSheetsRealBook.com.

TIP If you are working through a real estate agent, request to be present when your offer is presented to the seller. You will be able to explain any questions that the seller may have, as well as establish a sense of professionalism and build rapport.

It should also be noted that these negotiating skills work equally well when you are either the buyer *or* the seller. As real estate investors, we tend to always think of ourselves as the buyer, but this is not necessarily true. In fact, in many instances, one of the best ways for you to turn a profit is by knowing when to sell one of your properties. This is especially true when you have bought a fixer-upper with the intention of flipping it for a significantly higher amount of money. Knowing how to use other people's money in creative ways can make it much easier for you to find buyers. And the negotiating tactics we've been discussing will come in handy for you when you are the buyer as well.

SOME GOOD ADVICE—BASIC DO'S AND DON'TS

I'm often asked for advice from my students, such as, "Should I do this deal?" But mostly it's, "How do I get started?" Well, it's difficult to answer everyone's questions, personally. But I've adhered to some guidelines over the years that have helped me—and may help you get started.

TABLE 18.3 Carleton's Do's and Don'ts

DO	Keep an open mind	New ideas always seem strange at first. Imagine what it must have been like for the Wright brothers when they told people that they could fly! But new ideas can lead to a wonderful new way of life. And when it comes to real estate investments, the person with an open mind, who is always willing to entertain new ideas, is the kind of person who is most likely to succeed.
DO	Write down your goals	It's amazing what a difference a piece of paper can make. Once your goals are committed to paper, you are much less likely to veer from your plans or to be distracted. Writing down your goals will also make you better organized and help you to maintain your focus. Having dreams and aspirations is a good thing. In fact, I strongly encourage it. That doesn't mean, of course, that you should keep your head in the clouds. Be a down-to-earth, practical and realistic dreamer. Set achievable goals for yourself, and then enjoy the ride as you achieve them one by one.
DO	Commit yourself 100%	Making goals is not enough. You must commit to achieving those goals. Set aside a reasonable amount of time and energy per day or per week to pursue your real-estate-related activities. Stick to your schedule, and don't be distracted. Small steps add up and you will be surprised how much you have learned and how far you have progressed in a short amount of time.
DON'T	Listen to nay-sayers	As we all know, there are positive people in our lives and negative people, some who want to see us succeed and others who would be jealous of our success. Negative people will always find reasons to tear you down and criticize what you're trying to do to improve your life. Do not listen to these people or let them influence you. They are not being your friends and will only hurt your chances for success.
DON'T	Be afraid to fail	The most successful people in the world have had more than their share of failures. They know all about the concept of trial and error. Don't be afraid of making mistakes. Instead, allow every failure to teach you a valuable lesson. However, always make sure that your "worst-case scenarios" are something you can afford to live with. If not, then the risk is too great and you should move on to the next opportunity.
DON'T	Get emotional about a property	I realize that homes are often more than just buildings; they have emotional and sentimental value for the people who live in them. However, as an investor, you need to always keep in mind that this is a business—your business—and everyone involved in buying or selling real estate has a right to profit from each transaction, as long as it is conducted in an honest and ethical manner.

THE WAVE OF THE FUTURE

I've been involved with real estate investing for many years, and one thing I can say for sure is that the market is always changing and evolving. What might be true today may not be true tomorrow. As you know, there are buyer's markets and there are seller's markets (compare 2005 to 2009!). That's why success takes more than just learning a set-in-stone collection of rules. You have to be flexible and take into account the cyclical, ever-changing nature of the real estate market.

All of the sources and techniques I've outlined in this chapter will work for both buying and selling properties. You have to determine which techniques will work best for you in a given situation and market.

The United States recently experienced a sharp increase in the number of homes in foreclosure. This is a tragic situation for many homeowners. It happens for a variety of reasons; in short, people get into financial difficulties and can no longer afford the mortgage on their homes. For the investor, however, this means a large pool of highly motivated sellers. One of the most popular techniques involving foreclosures is known as a short sale. A short sale takes place when the lender agrees—with the homeowner's approval—to accept less than the amount owed on a piece of real estate.

A short sale could happen for a few different reasons, but the most common is the value of the property has declined below the value of the loan. This could be due to the property being in distress, or it could simply be that values in the area have significantly declined since the property was purchased.

Although foreclosures seem to be the "buzzword" between the years 2008 to 2009, don't overlook estate sales, tax liens, or tax deeds (depending on your state) or "for sale by owner" properties for leads to motivated sellers. That's one of the many things I love about real estate—you can find your own niche that best fits your goals and your level of risk.

TIP To learn more about how to invest in foreclosures, visit www.CarletonSheetsRealBook.com for my complete foreclosures program, which is absolutely free.

Another definite trend of the future—if you're not already using it—is using the power of the Internet. More than ever before, people have information at their fingertips. And they can demand answers at the touch of a "send" button. Almost any resource an investor would need is available almost instantaneously by searching the Internet. Using the Internet, you can:

- Search for local investment clubs for networking opportunities. For example, take a look at www.reiclub.com, or www.creonline.com.

- Market your properties through online advertising, or build your own customized Web site. Check out www.fsbo.com, or www.forsalebyowner.com for "by owner" opportunities. To build a specific Web site inexpensively, try www.yahoo.com, or www.networksolutions.com. However, if you are looking for a pre-built Web site designed specifically for real estate investors, consider www.investorpro.com.

- Pinpoint properties that fit your investing profile through a variety of online service providers, including www.realtytrac.com, www.realtor.com, and www.fsbo.com.

- Search the public records online to find past sales prices and owner information (or even to find out how much neighbors, friends, or family paid for their homes). I recommend www.netronline.com for links to local county records.

- Find lenders. Try www.lendingtree.com, or search "money lenders" on your favorite search engine.

Go to www.CarletonSheets RealBook.com to access any site I have mentioned. The possibilities are endless, and this is by no means a comprehensive list. But my point is that it has never been as easy to find information—and all from the comfort of your own home.

You Can Make Money in Any Market

No matter what the market dictates, one fact remains constant: people still need a place to live. Whether they are renting or owning, there will always be situations where a growing family needs to upsize, or a retiree needs to downsize. The real estate market is never totally stagnant. And any market can be a good market to invest in—as long as you know how and when to apply the techniques I've given you.

TIP You can tailor your real estate investing techniques to mirror market conditions. When the market is good, consider flipping properties. When the market is slow, consider buy-and-hold strategies—it's all up to you!

The changes that have taken place in recent years, within both the real estate market and the banking industry, are actually very good changes for the savvy investor. And using my creative financing methods is likely to become even more necessary to succeed in real estate in the future. Banks now have lending requirements that are stricter than in the past—which potentially impact both buyers and sellers. When participants on both sides of the transaction have an even greater incentive to do things in a more innovative way, they will consider creative options that they may not have even thought of before. Ultimately, that sort of creativity is good for the market and can keep it a dynamic, ever-changing arena where good ideas and strong visions are handsomely rewarded.

Ways to Learn More

Visit Carleton Sheets on the Web at www.CarletonSheetsRealBook.com. This site is your source for all things real estate. You'll find many of Carleton's best-selling real estate programs online for free, as well as links to Web resources, current trends and real estate news, blogs, products and services, and a forum for networking with other investors nationwide.

Carleton Sheets is recognized as the best-selling author of the *No Down Payment*® home study course as well as other successful real estate books, video, and audio programs. He has sold more than three million copies of his programs in the United States alone. In 1984, Carleton partnered with the Professional Education Institute to distribute his message nationally about creative real estate investing. His *No Down Payment* television program is now accredited as being the longest-running program of its kind, spanning twenty-five years. After thirty years of successfully selling his programs, Carleton began sharing his real estate programs online at no charge. His wish is to reach as many people as possible to help them achieve their dreams—as he has achieved his—with real estate. Today, on his own or with partners, Carleton has bought and sold more than $50 million of commercial and residential income-producing real estate.

● W. Scott SCHIRMER

17

Entitlements
The Sleeping Giant of Real Estate Profitability

Scott is my neighbor. He lives directly across the street from Kim and me. Every year, our neighborhood has a number of parties, and at every party I look forward to seeing Scott and asking him for his views on the world of money, real estate, and investing. Not only is he a neighbor, but he is a great friend, and someone I look to when I need more sophisticated information on the subject of real estate.

One aspect of real estate is politics. Being a developer, Scott needs to be tuned in to the local politics of the areas he is developing. Being a developer means he must be looking years into the future, years before he breaks ground. As some of you know, many times a worthy project—a project that will lift the value of the area—will be shot down by local neighborhood organizations that are resistant to change. This is where politics comes in.

I do not care where you live, politics and real estate go hand in hand. Local politics and politicians can improve or destroy the value of the real estate in an area. For example, at our last Christmas party, I was asking Scott about a local Arizona politician and that person's relationship to the police department. It was Scott's point of view that this politician and the police did not see eye to eye. That is why the crime in this one area was increasing and values of the property were going down. I did not invest in the area based on Scott's view of the future of this area of town. Today, many people who did invest in that once-friendly *neighborhood are losing financially as crime infects the area. This means, when I talk to Scott, I am often talking politics, but really I am discussing real estate.*

If you are to become a professional real estate investor, you must, and I do mean must, have a person like Scott who you can talk to about local politics and then talk about real estate.

—ROBERT KIYOSAKI

TIP *The current financial crisis in the United States is likely to be judged in retrospect as the most wrenching since the end of the Second World War.* —ALAN GREENSPAN, FORMER U.S. FEDERAL RESERVE CHAIR, MARCH 17, 2008

Missing from Mr. Greenspan's assessment is the other side of the coin: Those getting into a critical aspect of real estate now, who prepare for the eventual upturn, will be among the most successful in gaining wealth and security. How can that happen? This chapter will show you how to add value to real estate today—often without even owning or developing it—to capitalize on large returns tomorrow.

Whether you want to work in the area of entitlements or not, it is important that you understand this critical area of real estate. The knowledge can make you money, and it can make your life easier. Ask yourself a question: When you drive around your state or across the country, do you ever wonder who owns those acres and miles of raw land? The answer is that someone possesses every square inch of it, and it is owned by the federal government, the state, the county, the city, the Indian Nation, or a private party such as a company or an individual. Most people believe that private parties are the biggest property owners of our country. But this is not necessarily true. In Arizona, for example, only 15 percent of the land is privately owned.

Another illusion when it comes to real estate is if you own land as a private property owner, then you can do what you want with it. You own your property, you pay taxes, you buy insurance for it, and you maintain it. You own the right to do all that. But what you *do not own* is the right to do anything you want with the property. Surprised?

This is where the term *entitlement* enters the equation, and it is not a complicated concept. It simply means what you are entitled (or *"allowed"*) to do with your property as defined by the city, county, or state in which the land is located with regard to development. Those decisions are controlled by entitlements granted by the federal, state, county, or local government agencies. These agencies tell you whether your land is useable for agricultural, commercial, residential, or industrial uses. They tell you how much you can build on your property; whether you can remove vegetation; how to mitigate wildlife disturbances that exist on your property; whether you have rights to access streets, water, or sewer; and whether a septic system is permitted, along with many other governmental controls.

TIP Here is an old adage that will serve you well today and tomorrow: In reality, *owning* an asset is not as important as *controlling* an asset. And those who *entitle* an asset have the potential to obtain great profits from their endeavors.

LOVE THY NEIGHBOR?

Today, one of the most unquantifiable controlling factors that involves the use of your property is your neighbor—a factor that has historically caused owners and developers much grief. Neighbors have always held that they should have a say about what is done with the vacant lot they view over or visit, now and forever. Today more than ever, neighbors believe they have an inherent right to use a parcel of land as *they* see fit: parking, playing, cycling, jogging, walking, dumping, and controlling it, even if that vacant lot now happens to be *your* property.

Neighbors feel that when it comes to your property, whether vacant or with existing structures on it, you, the property owner, should abide by their rules and wishes. Because I've heard these complaints so often, I've given them their own name and formalized the list into: "The Top-Twenty Neighborly Complaints for Nondevelopment." Are these complaints fictitious? Believe me, I could never make this stuff up. Each one is based on a real-life situation I have experienced, and I marvel at the list every time I read it.

All developments, whether residential, commercial, or industrial, have many of the same neighborhood concerns. Commercial development adds the apprehension that you may be bringing people from other areas of the community into their neighborhood. Industrial development embodies fears about pollution and the potential hazards of large vehicles in the area. These neighbor issues have always been present but to a lesser degree than what they are today. There are two reasons for this increase in neighborly concern:

1. There has been a shift of political thought in the country from an attitude of self-reliance to an attitude of rights and entitlements. Your project might be

The Top-Twenty Neighborly Complaints for Nondevelopment

Do not change the height of the existing building, for it will hurt our privacy.

We have always walked across the land and must continue to do so.

You will disturb the habitat of existing animals, and this you must not do.

We will not be able to see over or across the land, for you will block our view.

You will create traffic, and that is unacceptable to us.

Development will overburden the number of children in the schools.

You must not change the character and compatibility of the neighborhood.

The old building that is on your property is historic; do not touch it.

There are rare biological plants that must be nurtured forever.

The apartment complex you want to develop will bring in undesirable people.

Your development will import crime into the neighborhood.

Whatever you do will not be environmentally friendly, so you may not do it.

The developer is out of state, and we are wary and suspicious.

The developer is greedy, and we are not. End of discussion.

If we let the owner develop, it should be with less density.

The owner should take less money for the property.

Any development will increase noise, and that is not good.

The lights from the development will destroy the night sky.

The city is too crowded, and we do not want anyone else in our neighborhood.

If we refuse to let you to build the roads, people will not come, and that is good.

the proper development for the site, but the neighborly feeling is, "Not in My Back Yard." (Such people are commonly referred to as NIMBYs.)

2. There has been an increase in the ability for a small group of NIMBYs or activists to organize a vocal minority of people through the Internet. The Internet has changed the political landscape. What has not changed is the axiom that a squeaky wheel does get the oil, and on the Internet a little squeaking goes a long way in creating an adverse situation between neighbors and owners.

Our society has evolved in a way that is less social in nature and more segregated geographically in political thoughts and beliefs. As someone who grew up in the Midwest, I knew all of our neighbors. We watched out for each other. I had a feeling of self-reliance, but I knew my neighbors were there for me if I needed help. And I was there for them. It was a close reflection of the Ozzie and Harriet Nelson society.

Moving to the West, I find our communities are developing in a way that segregates people. Neighbors are transient. They don't know each other. There is little feeling of community and of looking out for each other. It has forced people to push what they perceive as their "rights" onto others. The Nelsons have given way to *The Simpsons* and *Married . . . with Children*.

Assembling this disenfranchised group is easy through the Internet because it provides empowerment, and it offers pervasive access to large numbers of people almost instantaneously. This, in turn, creates a purpose for social gathering, often led by a vocal resident who feels validated to carry the cause: the self-appointed squeaky wheel.

Why have I spent time talking about this? Because whether you realize it or not, it is not your desires but the vote of the politicians to whom you present your product for approval that determines the use of your property. And it is the NIMBYs who elect and therefore influence those politicians who hold the cards.

TIP "All politics is local." —REP. TIP O'NEILL, LATE SPEAKER OF THE HOUSE

THE WORLD OF LOCAL POLITICS

Is it just me, or have politicians changed over the years? "To better serve your community" is no longer a motivation to run for office; it has become a campaign slogan void of reality. It seems that a large number of elected officials are in political office for their own personal gain. They want the office as a career; indeed, they feel as entitled to it as the neighbors who embrace a personal ownership of the property *you* own. Once such politicians have tasted the power, control and benefits of their positions, they will do whatever is necessary to keep their positions. Therefore, a small group of vocal voters do make a huge difference in the outcome of your project.

Real Life Story: The Politician Who Wasn't

As young people starting out in real estate development, my colleagues and I assembled one hundred adjoining parcels in a rundown area of Phoenix and presented a master plan for redevelopment to the Phoenix City Council for

CONTINUED

CONTINUED

approval. Two hundred people showed up to rally against the redevelopment. I remember Mayor Margaret Hance standing up in front of the angry crowd and wagging her finger, telling the crowd how good this was for the city. The project passed over neighborhood opposition. Mayor Hance was a leader, not because she voted for a project I was involved in but because she took a stand in support of a project that may have been against her own personal political interest, but that was nonetheless good for the city. She was a popular mayor in Phoenix, in part because she was recognized for her caring about the city. She was also an exceptional politician because she didn't act like one. Most of the time, you will not be dealing with that kind of leadership. You'll be dealing with quite the opposite.

Real Life Story: The Politician Who Was

Recently, I made an application for a mixed-use residential development in the city of Phoenix for my firm, M3 Companies. There was NIMBY opposition from a group that elected a councilman from the district in which this parcel was located. Before city council heard the application, this councilman announced he was against the development. He said he needed to take an early stand; that he was showing leadership. In this case, he was afraid to do what was best for the city. He wanted to appease the vocal NIMBYs for his own political gain. I'd like to say this is a rare occurrence, but it is not. You will find this behavior to be very common in today's political landscape.

ENTITLEMENTS = PROFITS

Are entitlements difficult to secure? The answer is yes. Then why not purchase property that has already been entitled? You can, and most developers do. But you can make a lot of money by entitling property for yourself or for others without the financing or capital risk that other areas of real estate require. Entitlement can be a profitable area of real estate just by relying on your learned skills. Your profits have nothing to do with how much money you have to buy real estate.

There are three secrets to entitlements that lead to success and great profitability. You will hear them from me more than once in this chapter. Please remember:

1. Knowledge
2. Knowledge
3. Knowledge

How do you obtain this knowledge? To quote from J. R. R. Tolkien (with apologies to *The Lord of the Rings*), "The tale grew in the telling." The way I gained my knowledge was by starting slowly and deliberately, and from there I worked my way to a comfort level where I could begin to take action. You can start and grow this way, too. Only I'm going to make it easier for you with my reality-based Detailed Entitlement Process. Each area is based on what I've learned, and these guidelines continue to serve me well. The remainder of this chapter is about the *Process* and it contains everything I do to profit from entitlements.

You'll find this Process to be a huge advantage as you learn. But, it will be only as valuable as your willingness to put in the time and rely on self-motivation and determination. There are no shortcuts to building a knowledge base, but there are long-term gains to be made. Give yourself at least six months to acquire the foundation necessary to succeed.

SCOTT'S DETAILED ENTITLEMENT PROCESS

KNOW YOUR CITY OR COUNTY PLANS, ORDINANCES, AND WAYS OF DOING BUSINESS

Become knowledgeable with your city's or county's goals and planning. This will help you understand what the city or town is doing or plans to do and why. You also need to understand how business is conducted to avoid rookie mistakes. Trust me, I have made them.

Your mission:

- Study the general plan for your city or town.
- Read the zoning code and ordinances.
- Learn how the "game" is played.
- Think in terms of how you can benefit the politicians, not the other way around.

BE ON TOP OF CITY AND TOWN POLITICS

Learn the political structure. Every city or town is governed by elected and staff individuals. (I will get to them in a minute.) Developing relationships is important. And believe it or not, mayors and council members are approachable.

Why? Because they are always looking for new people to help secure their positions and advance their self-interests. This is not cynicism; it is the way of the world. A lifelong friend of mine, Dr. Mark Horowitz, is both a businessman

Real Life Story: When a Hole Is Not the Whole

I acquired a twenty-acre piece of property that was in a great location but was a massive hole. It was an eyesore to the community and was preventing a major road from being built in the area. This property would require six hundred thousand cubic yards of compacted, clean dirt to fill the hole. For reference, a large dump truck carries about eighteen cubic yards of dirt, so when I say it was a big hole, I mean it. It would take about thirty-three thousand dump truck loads to fill it!

I wanted to develop a commercial shopping center on the property, which would require that I change the zoning from residential to commercial. The city was enthusiastic and said it would support my application. I deeded the right-of-way the city needed to allow for the development of the road. That was my first major mistake. Then I made the application to rezone the property. The process would take six months. Immediately after applying for rezoning, a contractor approached me with a request to dispose of dirt from a nearby canal project he had been awarded. He would fill the hole in my property with clean, compacted dirt at no cost to me. Naturally, I thought I had hit a homerun since I would not have to pay to fill the hole.

It took the contractor three months of night-and-day hauling of dirt to fill the property. The property looked great when it was completed! That was my second mistake. Timing is everything, and as fate would have it, my rezoning request was heard before the city council a month *after* I had filled the unsightly hole. I was thrilled! I had held up my end of the bargain. As fate would also have it, at the city council hearing a number of NIMBY residents turned out to protest my application. They didn't want commercial zoning in their neighborhood.

Astonishingly, the politician who promised me his support (pre-right-of-way and pre-hole) suddenly had a change of heart and led the charge *against* my rezoning request. It turned out that with the roadway and hole problems solved in his district, he was now worried only about votes. Thanks to my fine work, he had the right-of-way for the city road, *and* he had the "eyesore" problem solved. His job was done. He had the whole enchilada!

Lesson Learned: Make sure that you receive what is promised to you *before* you perform your end of an obligation with a politician.

and a scholar of early Tudor England who has spent much of his life researching and understanding the relationships between those in power and those who benefit from the powerful. In a special issue of the journal *Historical Research* commemorating the five hundredth anniversary of the death of the first Tudor king (1509–2009), Mark defines *politics* as "the pursuit of self-interest and self-preservation through the use of power." Henry VII is a model for all leaders and for those seeking benefits from them when it comes to cultivating relationships for "political" ends. Half the battle is simply showing up.

The same is true for you. For example, on Tuesday go to the planning committee meetings, and on Thursday the council meetings. In between, hold meetings with staff members and make appointments with developers. Go to their functions, help them, learn about them, and become known to them. Position yourself positively. When it comes time for you to make an application, they will all know you, which will go miles in helping you get your project approved.

TIP Remember: Those in power are motivated by self-interest and self-preservation, and they are looking for new faces and new ideas to help them with both!

These are the critical players in any city or town that you will want to get to know and that you will want to know you.

THE STAFF

The staff in the planning departments are a constant. They are government employees until they retire. Politicians, on the other hand, are elected every two or four years. Politicians and elected officials come and go. The staff in the planning department stay year after year. They play a very important role in the political support for your project.

Your mission:

- Meet the planning staff. Get to know them personally. Take them out to lunch, a cup of coffee, or play golf with them.
- Ask for their help. Make your project their idea. (Self-interests, remember?) Understand how they think.

APPOINTED BOARDS OR NEIGHBORHOOD GROUPS

Even though these groups may be informal and volunteer-based, they are powerful and should not be underestimated.

Your mission:

- Go to every neighborhood meeting.
- Get on neighborhood boards.
- Determine the leadership structure and who the decision makers are.

PLANNING COMMISSION

This usually consists of a board whose members are appointed by the elected members of the city council. Their decisions are usually advisory only, but they serve an important role as political cover to members of the city council.

Your mission:

- Go to every planning commission hearing and meet every planning commission member.
- Get to know them and learn their backgrounds.
- Make friends with them.
- Understand how they vote and determine which of them are business-friendly and which are neighborhood-friendly.
- Understand the alliances they form and why.
- Determine whose vote you need to pass your project through.
- Support their ambitions and causes.

CITY COUNCIL

This is the ultimate voting body. It will make or break your project, and it has the power to hold it up indefinitely.

Your mission:

- Go to every city council hearing.
- Meet the mayor and every city council member.
- Support them politically.
- Become their friends.
- Get to know all members and what their hot buttons are, and try pushing a few.
- Become known and trusted by them.
- Understand how they vote, and know which ones are business-friendly and which are neighborhood-friendly.
- Understand the alliances they form and why.
- Determine whose vote you need to pass your project through.

- Work on political campaigns and attend political functions.
- Go to events where they are present and make yourself visible.
- Find out the local election dates and when different members of the city council are up for re-election.

TIP When it comes to politics, you do not want to bring a controversial case before the city council within twelve months of the election of any member of the city council whose vote you will need. The politician's desire to be re-elected will work against you every time.

Does all this homework, knowledge-building, and cultivation of relationships guarantee success? The answer is yes and no. Yes, it will lead to great successes for you, because you are way ahead of the curve and therefore ahead of your competitors who do not make the time or the effort. But no, like all of life, there will be some setbacks. It is therefore important to know when to cut your losses, and I am the first to admit that despite all my success in the realm of real estate and entitlements, some things are beyond my control.

Real Life Story: Crack the Code to Corner Your Market

Some time ago, I was trying to purchase a corner that was zoned properly for the commercial retail center I wanted to develop. I had a major grocery chain interested in leasing part of the property, but the grocery store representative wanted to have a meeting with the head of the city planning department before moving forward.

At that meeting, the head of the city planning department asked the grocery store to locate to another property that was miles from my site, stating that he believed the trade area my site was located in was already adequately served, and the property he was offering had a trade area that was underserved. This is city "code" for saying that the city can generate more income from sales tax revenue by locating a business in one area over another. The city views each piece of property based on varying degrees of revenue-producing potential. Luckily in this case, the sales pitch didn't work, and the grocer ultimately located on my site due to the stability of the trade area.

Lesson Learned: Altruism usually isn't. Crack the code, and you'll understand the real motives.

STAY AHEAD OF NEIGHBORHOOD OPPOSITION

No matter what project you propose for a neighborhood, there will be neighborhood opposition. Indeed, I began this chapter giving you the Top-Twenty Neighborly Complaints. Expect these opposing views and build them into your plan. Again, knowledge is power. But as you are planning, be proactive.

Your mission:

- Study the leaders of the neighborhood opposition.
- Is it the same person or group of people who show up for every entitlement case? What are their backgrounds?
- Are they NIMBYs responding only to issues next to their neighborhood or are they full-fledged activists on zoning issues with the community at large?
- Talk to them. Listen to their issues. Become their friend.
- Do they use the Internet to communicate with one another? See if you can get on their e-mail list.
- Try to get hold of the database to be able to communicate with all of the neighbors. Then when it comes time to present your project, your message will be heard directly from you, without filtering.
- Go to every neighborhood meeting. Get on neighborhood boards.
- Set up your own Internet Web site as a proactive approach to groups or individuals both for and against your project.
- Use your Web site to educate the public about your project. Include testimonials and quotes from supporters of your project, especially neighbors. This will be a counterweight to NIMBY Web sites and help you control your message.

Most important, do not view NIMBYs as your mortal enemies, although they clearly can have an impact on your aspirations and your billfold! I approach them as citizens who want to be heard for some reason, and not necessarily the reason they may be voicing. Sometimes it can be a gripe or grievance that can be addressed without any harm to your project. Treat them with respect, and some can even be turned around to your point of view.

HAVE A TIMETABLE AND PATIENCE

Depending on the jurisdiction in which you are working, entitlements can take anywhere from six months to many years. Here is the short and the long of it:

- **Short timetable:** This comes into play only if you have the full support of all parties; it is just the actual process itself that takes time.

> ## Real Life Story: Turning a Mountain into a Mole Hill
>
> One project I developed early in my career involved a residential community. The owner of the property adjoining mine believed that my property would stay vacant forever. (See Complaint No. 2 in the Top-Twenty List.) Now that I had arrived, he feared that my development would impede his view of a mountain. We talked about his concerns at length and after some homework I came back to show him how I could reorient the houses to maintain his view. (See Complaint No. 4 in the Top-Twenty List.) In effect, I converted an adversary into an advocate and the project went through.
>
> **Lesson Learned:** Compromise can turn NIMBYs into allies.

- **Long timetable:** If you encounter opposition to a project and/or if you have developmental issues (e.g., water rights, environmental, access, etc.), your timetable will be extended.

Realistic timetables are critical to your success for several reasons:

- You don't want your case to be heard in an election cycle.
- If you are working with a landowner and you are purchasing the property subject to receiving entitlements by a fixed date, you don't want to run out of time with your seller and be unentitled: You will have invested too much time, effort, and money to get to this point.
- The market cycle in real estate may pass you by.
- The capital markets change. The supply of money, interest rates, and underwriting criteria may change.

GET TO KNOW THE DEVELOPERS AND BUILDERS

Just as you have met every staffer and every committee and council member at city hall, meet every developer and builder that makes an application. Call them on the phone and make an appointment to learn about their projects. Meet them at all hearings. They will be enthusiastic to tell you about their projects because they will want your support.

Your mission:

When you speak with the developers and builders, seek to answer the following questions:

- What are the opposition's issues, and how are you, the developer or builder, overcoming those objections?

- What third-party vendors are you using? These may include the following: land planner, architect, civil and structural engineer, zoning attorney, traffic engineer, contractor, and their subcontractors.
- Who does your soils report, and who performs your environmental studies?
- What title company and escrow officer do you use?
- What real estate broker are you using?

After attending a number of meetings, you'll have a good idea of the vendors who do quality work and can perform on time. These vendors will become invaluable to you when the time comes to put your own team together. Think of the education you will be getting from actual practitioners. And it's free!

UNDERSTAND WHAT DEVELOPERS AND BUILDERS WANT

To repeat: *Knowledge* is your most important asset. I made getting it a point early on in my career and continue it to this day. When it comes to developers and builders, I try to find out everything I can from each type. I want to know as much as I can about single-family, multifamily, retail, office, industrial, or mixed-use development. These developers and builders are putting their knowledge, reputation, and capital on the line. Why not learn as much as you can from them? All of these resources are coming to the city seeking approvals. It's a "knowledge vein" that is yours for the mining and is much better than school-based education. This is the real world, and that is where money is made. Your only impediment to success is your own lack of effort in mining this knowledge.

TIP Builders want to acquire *entitled* property! Hence, you are of great value to them, and they will pay for that value.

Entitlements involve all types of real estate: apartment buildings, residential, commercial, medical, mixed use. The key is to be aware of the specific requirements of each and understand the differences. Then, learn as much as you can about similar projects and how they have been entitled.

Here are the questions that I have asked of developers and builders. This will get you started and will help expand your knowledge base for planning your first project.

Your mission:

Ask residential builders these questions:

- What size lots do you want to develop. Why that size?
- What are the setback distances from the front, back, and side yards?

A Few Truths About Buyers and Builders

- A new home buyer is sold on a home before he or she walks in the front door.
- The streetscape of the subdivision, landscaping, and the elevation of the home are most important for the sale.
- School districts matter. Locate your residential developments in the best ones.
- Cities with the best images may be more expensive but create the most security for your investment.
- See if the builder will share his infrastructure costs with you. Find out:
  - On average, how much is the cost to engineer the subdivision to a recorded plat? This is called "paper lots."
  - How much does it cost on a per lot basis to construct the streets, sewer, water, common area amenities, and landscaping?
- It's good to know how much it will cost a homebuilder to improve a single family lot. Builders will pay 20 to 25 percent of the sales price of the home for an improved lot.

- What are the sizes of the homes you are building?
- How many phases do you plan for? How many lots per phase?
- How many lots do you need in order for you to develop a model home complex? Where do you like to locate your models within the subdivision? Why?

Beyond just asking questions, visit their subdivisions. Go through their model homes. Talk to the salespeople. Find out what are the most sought-after home features buyers ask for, and why. By knowing the kind of product they build, you'll be in a better position to provide them the entitled land they are looking for down the road.

Your mission:

Ask apartment builders these questions (the same as above, plus these additional):

- What density do you like to build? Usually it is fourteen to twenty-one units per acre, depending on the city and projected rental rate of the project.
- How many units does it take to make a project operationally feasible?
- What do you pay per unit (referred to as per door) for a piece of property that is entitled?
- What unit mix—one-, two- or three-bedroom units—are best for the market?
- What size—one-, two-, or three-bedroom units—do residents want most? What is the best mix?

- What rental rates does the market accept?
- What amenities are being offered and why?
- How many parking spaces per unit does the city require versus the market demand?
- What is the land size necessary for the density needed to operate and park properly?
- Are there any specific lighting, trash locations, and noise abatement issues?
- What kind of vehicle and pedestrian integration into the adjoining neighborhoods is needed?
- What about schools and crime?

YOUR FIRST PROJECT AND JUMP-START GAME PLAN

After six months of hard work, you now possess the three secrets to entitlements that can lead to great success, and you should be able to rapid-fire repeat them by now:

1. Knowledge
2. Knowledge
3. Knowledge

Gaining these assets has brought you to this point, and no one can take your knowledge from you. You can succeed or fail using other types of "capital," but your best chance of success in entitlements is directly proportional to your knowledge "capital."

TIP Principal Rule: Use your knowledge base as capital to create value.

Your mission:

Put into action my Jump-Start Game Plan to get your first project off the ground.

SCOTT'S JUMP-START GAME PLAN

1. From the knowledge you have gained, you can put together the best team of third-party vendors, such as surveyors, land planners, environmental companies, etc. Quality and reliability are key.
2. You know which areas of the community are sought after the most. Ask your real estate broker to map out vacant land or redevelopment opportunities in this area. Try to locate in a popular school district.

3. Compare your prospective sites to the city's general plan.

4. From your learned knowledge, work with your land planner in developing a plan which will be marketable to a buyer upon receiving entitlements.

5. Because you learned from the builders what they are willing to pay for entitled property, apply that number to the value of the property.

6. From that price, subtract the following:
   - The cost of the land.
   - Unusual or extra costs of construction required for the property you are considering. This might include rocky or expansive soil conditions, bringing in utilities to the property, undergrounding power lines or irrigation ditches.
   - The cost of your team's work to entitle the property.
   - Your cost of resale, brokerage fees, and title work.

7. If you are successful in entitling the property, this total will be the profit you earn for your knowledge and hard work. Determine if that bottom line is acceptable to you for your time and effort and cost of planning.

8. Meet with the people you are now familiar with in the city's planning department. Ask what use and density they would recommend for each property you have potentially selected. See if it matches your estimate.

9. Narrow the scope of your search to the most profitable properties if they were entitled for what you want and what the city staff would recommend.

10. Work with the landowner of the property you want to purchase. The landowner already has his capital in the land. Find out the motivation behind the landowner's desire to sell. If you can meet the seller's need, you might be able to get enough time to purchase the property subject to getting it entitled. Again, your profit is the value you create through entitlements.

Real Life Story

Be prepared for unusual requirements or actions that often defy logic. You will be exposed to every imaginable roadblock for your project, from underground mice to crashing airplanes! Do not be discouraged. I have encountered the most outrageous hurdles. Approach them with tenacity, and later you'll have great stories that will keep everyone laughing.

Hurdle No. 1, or the Mouse That Roared We were working on a master-planned development in Colorado. The fish and game department was concerned that an endangered animal known as a Preble's mouse might exist on the property.

CONTINUED

CONTINUED

Unfortunately, the only way to prove that supposition was to catch mice, kill them, and check their DNA for a match, thus potentially endangering the endangered species in the process. The department decided that we needed to set aside property within the development to provide habitat, just in case the mouse existed. Moreover, they told us that we had to impose a ban on the ownership of cats by residents since they might hunt and kill the mouse, should it exist. (This is no joke!) Through negotiations, we were able to change the department's requirement from forbidding cats entirely to making it a requirement in the Convenants, Conditions and Restrictions (CC&Rs) of the community that any cats residing in our community would have to remain indoors. We complied, fully realizing that this was the political solution to a problem. Commissioners, developer, residents, and mice were all happy campers.

Hurdle No. 2, or Sinking the Boat to See If It Floats We wanted to subdivide 620 acres in Santa Barbara County, California. It was an area where water was scarce and permits were rationed for homes. However, we had three wells on the property, and the hydrology reports concluded that there was more than enough water for the development. The county determined the reports to be insufficient and decided that, despite the scarcity of water in the area, they would need to measure the water in the wells by letting the water run into ditches . . . for an entire year! At the end of the year, and at great cost and enormous loss of water, it was determined that in fact there would be sufficient water for the development.

Hurdle No. 3, or Playing It Straight For a seemingly simple single-family residential subdivision with improved lots, we proposed a layout that was a little out of the ordinary. It involved adding curves to roads rather than creating a straight grid plan where houses lined up like barracks. The staff for this city said the plan was unacceptable. "Why?" we asked. It was then that the city informed us that elderly people who might not be able to make the subtle turns could be driving the streets. They could run off the road. (We call this protecting every issue that isn't an issue.) We countered by saying that elderly people can make a subtle turn, and that if they cannot they shouldn't be driving. Moreover, like the mouse in Colorado, no one knew if in fact there was a problem to begin with, in this case regarding the street design. The staff would not compromise, and the streets were built perfectly straight. In fairness, we believe no elderly people have run off any of the roads to date.

Hurdle No. 4, or It's a Bird! It's a Plane! It's You're Kidding, Right? A vacant piece of land was already developed on three sides. The fourth side fronted on a major road. We designed a small residential subdivision with one access point. The city didn't like this plan because they wanted two access points, which in fact was physically impossible to accomplish. Why two access points? One city staff member offered this explanation: "What if an airplane crashed in the entryway of the project? How will the fire department get in and save the people?" My response was plain and truthful: "They wouldn't get in, and everyone would die." Of course, it is an absurdity to think that you can plan or respond to every event that more than likely will never happen. Moreover, even with two access points, the fire department, under these circumstances, wouldn't be able to save anyone anyway. The result: We took the staff's objection and went to the city council, which overruled the staff and approved the subdivision. Indeed, they saw the logic to our plan. I am happy to report that after thirty years, maybe a few birds, but no airplane has crashed into the subdivision. No meteorites have, either.

Lesson Learned: Prepare to get very good at jumping hurdles . . . calmly.

KNOW THE POWER OF CONTROL VS. OWNERSHIP

Remember, control of a piece of property is as effective as owning it, with the additional benefit of minimizing your risk. If you purchase a piece of property before it is entitled, you will need to think about the following factors that could impact your investment:

- Capital. You'll need either your own or your investors to purchase the property.
- Risk. You risk the capital invested if your entitlements are unsuccessful.
- Unprofitability. Your cost of capital and interest may eliminate any potential future profits.
- Marketability. You now have an unentitled property that you may not be able to sell.

You may be wondering why would a seller give you the time to go through the entitlement process without risking any money. There are some very valuable reasons. First, you can offer the seller more money than his property is presently worth, which is obviously appealing. You can do this because, remember, if you purchased the property outright, you would be paying interest on the capital used to purchase the property so you might as well give that to the seller in the form of an increase in price.

Another reason a seller would allow you the time needed to gain the entitlements relates to taxes. If the seller sold the property, most likely he or she would pay capital gains tax on the sale (currently 15 percent federal tax, plus state tax). Then, when that money is reinvested and earning interest, that interest would be taxed as ordinary income (up to 38 percent under current law for federal income tax plus state and local taxes). If you offered the seller more money for their property to "buy" the time to get the entitlements and close the deal thereafter, the seller will be paying tax at the much lower capital gains rates instead of the higher ordinary tax rates.

Another incentive is offering to give the seller the survey, environmental report, soils report, traffic study, utility study, land plan, and title work you are doing as compensation for the time if you are not successful with entitlements and do not purchase the property. The seller will need those studies anyway with another buyer, and that information will decrease the time and up-front money needed by a new buyer. This information is worthless to you if you are not successful.

You can even find out if the seller will pay for the reports mentioned above. You can offer the seller an increased price for the land and a percentage of the increased value you are creating from your knowledge and entitlement work. Since you don't have to pay for the reports, now you don't have any capital at risk and only upside potential with the increased value you will be creating through entitlements. This is the best real estate position to be in.

Time can also be a blessing when a seller wants to find an exchange property before closing the sale of the current property, so there is no exposure to the strict time constraints for a 1031 Exchange. By giving you time to get the entitlements, the seller gets more time to search for another property investment. Exchanges must be executed within a specified period, and this allows the luxury of time most sellers would love to have.

Finally, a seller may want to be a part of the development on his property. The property may have been in the family for generations. There may be family pride regarding what is developed on the land. The motivation of a seller will either be monetary or family legacy.

AN AGREEABLE AGREEMENT—FOR YOU

Have your real estate attorney draft a standard Letter of Intent (LOI) for you to use with each seller. An LOI outlines the terms and conditions of a sale, is usually a nonbinding agreement but is used as a "gentlemen's handshake."

Once you have an executed LOI, ask your attorney to draft a purchase agreement for execution using the signed LOI as your guide. Make sure you have the right within the agreement to rezone the subject property for your intended use. Once the purchase agreement is signed, you have the property under your control. I repeat: It is not what you own that leads to wealth generation, it is what you control.

Once the purchase agreement is signed by all parties, open escrow with the title company and escrow officer you have learned to be the most reliable. Have the title company give you a title report with all recorded easements and liens and the requirements for an extended or lender's title policy.

Your mission:

- Have your real estate attorney draft an LOI.
- Execute the LOI with the seller.
- Have your real estate attorney draft a purchase agreement with the appropriate provisions from the LOI, particularly the right to rezone the property.
- Get the agreement signed. You now control the property.
- Open escrow and get the title report.

SOME DILIGENCE IS DUE

It is important to continue growing your knowledge base to protect your investment and avoid unwanted surprises. Consider these steps:

Your mission:

- Review your title report with the help of your title company. Make sure there are no recorded Covenants, Conditions or Restrictions (CC&Rs) recorded against the property that would affect your intended use.
- Check for deed restrictions that would affect ownership or use of the property.
- Read the recorded easements and understand who has the right of access. Make sure you have legal access to your property.
- See if there are any assessments recorded against your property that you will become responsible for.
- Study who has the rights to the minerals on the property.
- Give the title report and all recorded documents to your civil engineer to create an ALTA Builders/Lenders Survey.
- Once you have control of the property, have your team's real estate agent contact potential buyers for the property subject to your acquiring the entitlements. Don't think of a good real estate broker as a cost. Rather,

he or she is a valuable member of the team. A good broker has developed creditability over many years with builders and buyers. This will help ensure your success. If the deal can't afford the real estate fee, don't do the deal.

- Work with that builder/buyer in the planning process. Do not plan your property around one buyer unless that person has paid you a sizeable, nonrefundable deposit if you are successful in entitling your property and he does not perform. If planned around one buyer, you might ultimately receive the entitlement but no one else can use the plan.

Real Life Story: Removing Rocks from Your Soil May Be Mining

Recently, M3 Companies were involved in moving 6 million cubic yards of dirt on one of our two-thousand-acre master-planned communities. We were not selling the dirt or rock during the grading process but simply sifting the dirt to eliminate rocks for the golf course. We also crushed the larger rocks on site to a more manageable size.

By chance, a representative of the Bureau of Land Management (BLM)—a federal governmental agency—was driving by the site and noticed what we were doing. When he returned to his office he wrote us a letter saying we owed the BLM a royalty right for mining the minerals on the property since it owned these rights from the original governmental patent.

Almost every development crushes rocks on site and moves earth materials and screens soil. We explained that we weren't moving any material off-site or selling it, and therefore we did not believe we were mining minerals on the property. They replied to our argument that if we picked the rocks out of the soil by hand, instead of using machines, they don't consider it mining. The rocks were far too big for that.

Never before had they imposed this requirement on any other development of this scope. We ultimately negotiated a settlement with them to avoid the costly delays in construction and litigation.

Lesson Learned: Expect the unexpected, and bone up on your negotiation skills.

SURVEYS AND REPORTS

The next step is securing a lender's survey, which shows all of the recorded title report issues such as easements, property lines, and net/gross acreage/ square footage. It also outlines unrecorded roads and encroachments, legal descriptions, etc. It is used as the basis for all other planning on the property.

Your land planner will use the survey's information for computing acreage and for laying out everything that you do. It is your foundation. Below is a guide you can use during this important phase.

Your mission:

- Review your survey to see if there are any encroachments such as fences, structures, etc., that your neighbors have on your property or you have on theirs.
- See if anyone is using unrecorded access points on your property or unrecorded paths and roads across your property that may be a claim for adverse possession by the using party. This may restrict financing and ability to develop.
- Determine if there are any power and gas line easements and how that may affect the usability and marketability of your property.
- Make sure your engineer includes floodplain information on the survey.
- Give the survey to your land planner to help you develop a land plan and layout.

I never rely on my land planner's input only. I've found my learned knowledge and research is just as important to the final product. There is a belief, with some merit, that you design for a plan with a greater intensity and density than you really need so you can cut back at a later date. Why? So that the NIMBYs and politicians can feel they have pushed the developer back and got their way. You are catering to today's political correctness.

Your learned knowledge will tell you whether you should bring in a representative of the NIMBY group to be part of the land planning process. It is always better to have the NIMBYs as part of the planning process.

- Be prepared to cover your third-party vendors with liability insurance when they go upon the land of your seller to do their work. I would recommend that you provide at least $1 million of coverage. This insurance is relatively inexpensive.
- In addition, get these reports done up front. There's no point in waiting.

A SOILS REPORT

A soils report determines if there are any soil conditions that will increase the cost to build on the property and therefore lessen the price someone can pay for the property. Some sites have expansive soil that would increase the cost of construction. Some sites have hard rock and may need to be blasted. That would increase cost, too. If you were going to use septic tanks instead of city sewers, your soil condition might not meet the peculation requirements. Some sites even have underground fissures that are not readily determined. How important is a soils report? I have a true story.

Real Life Story: Low-Cost Property Can Be Very Costly

During the frenzy of the recent soaring real estate cycle, a buyer purchased nine hundred acres of land at a low price with the intent to "flip" it for a profit. The buyer came to me to help him after he had bought the property. The buyer did not order a soils report during the due diligence period prior to him buying the property. If he had, he would have realized that the soil was very expansive. That particular soil condition would make the foundation work for each house so cost-prohibitive that the homes would have been priced out of the market. Sadly, although the land was acquired at good price, the actual cost of the property was very high due to the increased development costs to mitigate the poor soil conditions. There wasn't much I could do. The buyer could have avoided all this by doing homework . . . and getting a soils report!

Lesson Learned: Soil matters. Never skimp on things that cost little and can save you a bundle.

A PHASE I ENVIRONMENT REPORT

This report will show you if your property is located within a Superfund site area, or if there are any environmental issues recorded on adjoining properties that may affect your property. It would include such things as a previous gas station on the adjoining property that had a fuel tank leak, which is now flowing under your property.

If any issues are discovered, you'll receive a recommendation to do a Phase II. This is more expensive and extensive. Laboratory testing will determine if contamination exists and what remediation methods need to be used. The remediation of environmental issues is often next to impossible to quantify. If your Phase I report comes back with a recommendation for Phase II, back away from the property . . . do not look back, and most of all *do not* move forward on any property with environmental issues at this stage of your career. And one more thing. If your proposed property is in a rocky, granite area, you should have your environmental engineer do a radon gas study to see if there is a need for mitigation.

A CONSTRAINTS REPORT

Besides doing the survey, have your civil engineer prepare a constraints report on the property. This will be a study of all the utilities to service the property. It will include water, sewers, telephone, gas, electric, cable, fiber optics, and storm sewers.

This study will show the location, capacity, water pressure, service providers, and methods of access to these services. It will also ascertain whether you are going to incur extra development costs by resizing existing utilities to serve your development or extending utility lines to provide these services to your property.

Have your engineer provide any Utility Development Fees and Utility Recovery Charges/Agreements in their report.

A DRAINAGE REPORT

This report will determine if you have any 404 issues. These are federal regulations by the Army Corp of Engineers on all navigable waterways. Don't think you need a stream on your property to come under this jurisdiction. It may be only an irrigation ditch. You also want to determine if there are any excess costs for retention, detention, or runoff of water from your property.

ARCHEOLOGICAL STUDY

If you are in an area that has artifacts or where artifacts are believed to exist, you should do an archeological study. Just because you are far away from a colonial settlement or an ancient Native American village does not mean that "something" may not be buried on your property.

Real Life Story: Unfortunately the Builder Didn't Strike Gold

A home builder was well into the development of his project when he discovered artifacts while digging water and sewer lines. The project was immediately put on hold—for eighteen months—while archaeologists, tiny picks and brushes in hand, meticulously uncovered and retrieved the artifacts. It almost bankrupted the builder because his capital costs, debt payments, contracts with vendors, and other cash outlays were dependent on his completion of the project on time. An archeological study in advance of development may have prevented this calamity.

Lesson Learned: If it *can* happen, it just might. Don't tempt fate.

FAA (FEDERAL AVIATION ADMINISTRATION) REVIEW

> Make sure the FAA has not imposed any restrictions on your property. Is it located out of the noise zone and flight paths? It's a good idea to be sure.

WELLS

> Check to see if there are any water wells on the property and if they have been properly recorded with the State Department of Water Resources. Also check to see if there are any historical records on the depth of the well, pumping capacity, and draw down of the water table. Make sure all abandoned wells are closed properly.

THE APPLICATION

> We're getting close now. You can begin to see the light at the end of the tunnel, assuming that all your reports came back positive and you didn't have to "back away from the environmental hazards" or anything else. It's time to make an application for the entitlement you are requesting. Every jurisdiction has different requirements. Some may require a traffic study, drainage study, landscape design, or letter from the school district on the impact of your proposed development on schools. Spend money only on the reports as are necessary.
>
> Your mission:

- Take your plan door to door and give every neighbor within six hundred feet of your project a personal presentation of your plan. Bring with you:
    - A full-color site plan and renderings of your development.
    - Traffic information generated by your development.
    - Letter of support from the school district.
    - Your business card and contact information.
    - A petition for the neighbor to sign in support of your project.
    - Printed cards giving the location, times, and dates of hearings, and the names, phone numbers, and e-mail addresses of the mayor and city council members.
- Start your presentation with the neighbors farthest from your project. They may be the least interested. You will have a better chance to get their signature on a petition of support.
- Use those signed petitions of support when asking the next neighbor for his support. Keep building those support petitions for your presentation to the neighbors that are closest to the project and to show to members of the city council. Give only those supportive neighbors your printed cards with the times and dates of the hearings.

How to Talk with the Neighbors

It's easy to make mistakes when talking with neighbors. Follow these guidelines and you should come out without incident:

Things You Should Do

- Dress neatly and be enthusiastic about your project.
- Always be polite.
- Present facts and be honest.
- Be prepared to answer objections.
- Listen. Don't debate.
- Make friends and develop relationships.
- If you do not know an answer to a question, return to personally give an answer. It gives you another chance to develop a relationship.
- Be proud of what you are doing.
- Ask for support and get contact information.
- Communicate with your neighbors.
- Ask supportive neighbors to invite their friends to a small meeting so you can explain your project.
- Get petitions of support signed. Ask supportive neighbors to be at the hearings. Have dates, times, and locations of meetings ready as a handout that you can distribute.
- Ask for them to e-mail and call city council members expressing their support. Have that information available to give to them as a handout.
- Get the support of the Chamber of Commerce, Homebuilders Association, and Board of Realtors.

Things You Should Not Do

- Do not leave any project information behind except for your business card and hearing information, and give it only to supportive neighbors. You may need to change your site plan while you are going through the process. If you leave your initial site plan behind, you will be accused of being deceitful by your neighbors if it changes in process.
- Do not exaggerate your project.
- Do not have group meetings initially. Group psychology is more difficult to cope with than handling individual concerns.
- Do not allow your differences with neighbors to become a matter of principle.
- Do not threaten neighbors with alternate uses, but point out to them the range of possibilities for which the land could be developed.

AT THE SAME TIME . . .

Continue to call upon all of the people you have met over the previous six months, including your friends on the city planning staff, on the community boards, the planning commission, and the city council. Try to get the leaders within each group to support your project. Use that support and visit with every member of each group. This is very important.

Politicians you have developed relationships with want to help you, but you need to give them the political reasons to support you, including narrowing the objections of the NIMBYs. Let the politicians know if there is neighborhood opposition, what objections they have and what you are doing to resolve their issues.

A politician always needs to understand why it is in his or her political interest to support you in the face of opposition: self-interest and self-preservation! Being prepared for this through your previous six months' worth of studying how the politician has reacted to other cases before you made your application, you will have insight into the right answer almost instinctively.

Remember, the vote that counts is the vote of the city council. Know that you have the votes that are required for approval before you allow your application to be heard for a final vote. Postpone the hearing until you have the votes committed.

THE END GAME

What are the best-case scenarios for all your hard work?

- Your acquired knowledge and relationship-building will help you obtain the right to purchase property you will entitle.
- You will get your property entitled, creating value.
- You will have a builder buy the property, with you profiting from the difference between the negotiated price from the landowner and your markup for entitling it.
- You will have succeeded by applying your knowledge, and not your capital.

TIP Remember: *You don't have to own a piece of property; you just have to control it.*

KNOWLEDGE, KNOWLEDGE, KNOWLEDGE

Starting small is the way to learn. But what you'll soon discover is that the size of the project is meaningless. You will go through all of the same steps for a small project as you would for a large project. That means the bigger projects have the potential to net you more money with the same amount of effort. It's just a matter of building confidence.

The M3 Companies have taken this direction, using our expertise in the planning, entitlement, and execution of master-planned communities from our learned knowledge over four decades of work. From developing a 610-acre American Ranch community in Prescott, an 1,100-acre Prescott Lakes community, and the 2,100-acre Wickenburg Ranch community (all in Arizona), to the 2,000-acre American Ranch Sandstone community outside Denver and our 6,000-acre community in Eagle, Idaho, we have taken advantage of our entitlement knowledge to succeed.

But make no mistake—you will make a lot of mistakes. Everyone does. Cut your losses short and let your gains run. Your own drive is the only limit to your success.

THE FUTURE

What is the future for someone who specializes in entitling real estate? We can count on governmental bodies to continue to impede property rights with each new law, regulation, ordinance, and environmental mandate. It becomes harder and harder each year to navigate through this minefield, and there are fewer people willing to make the attempt. Yet the demand from development companies and builders for entitled property increases each year: In adversity there is advantage and opportunity for those willing to pursue entitlements.

And what is the key? Knowledge. It is the knowledge you will gain that will make you one of the most sought after "properties" in the real estate industry. You can work for yourself, consult for others, or be in an executive position with a development company. Entitlements are the future of real estate. This chapter has given you the tools to create that future for yourself.

Knowledge is your capital when it comes to entitlements. But unlike other forms of capital such as cash, equity, or debt, *your capital* can never be taken away. And it can only grow and help you succeed.

Most important: Your capital is most valuable when the economy is in a recession. Sellers of properties are more receptive to giving you the time to entitle their property. Lenders who have taken properties back need someone with the knowledge to prepare their properties for resale. Why? Because you can *add value* to property that is losing value in the marketplace. That makes you indispensable, sought after, and in a very profitable position for yourself.

It takes many months to entitle a piece of property for development or for resale. Use the downtime of a recession to entitle a property. When the recession ends, as it always does, you will be ready immediately to take advantage of the recovery because your property is ready for development. It is called *great timing*.

Friends in High Places During Low Times

During a recession, you can process your application more quickly because the city staff has very few applications to process. Furthermore, it is more difficult for political leaders to turn your project down in the face of growing municipal deficits. Don't forget, landowners are willing to give you the time to work on entitlements. They need you!

My last words of wisdom are these: Be a contrarian. In a recession, people focus on their jobs, the economy, and the stock market. They rarely see an opportunity to take advantage of what only appears to be a dismal situation. When no one is investing money, when no one can borrow money, and when equity is disappearing on properties, keep this in mind: You have the most valuable capital during this period—your knowledge.

Let others spend their time looking backward and protecting their current declining assets. You will be using your time pursuing the Sleeping Giant of real estate profitability: entitlements. It's time to get going.

W. Scott Schirmer is a managing partner for M3 Companies. M3 Companies' core competency is developing master-planned communities that honor and advance the timeless heritage of the West. Schirmer is president of Schirmer Ball Company and CEO of SMDI Company. Since he began working in Arizona real estate in the late 1960s, he has entitled, acquired, syndicated, financed, developed, managed, and brokered real estate in Arizona, California, Idaho, Illinois, Oklahoma, and Utah. Schirmer and the M3 Companies charities are children-based, giving support to Childhelp, The Boys and Girls Club of Scottsdale, SARC, ANOZIRA Foundation, and The Solid Rock Foundation.

18

The Tax Lien Investment Strategy

T om Wheelwright is one of those people who is not just an expert in a very important aspect of investing, he is an investor himself who practices what he preaches. I like to surround myself with people like Tom because they don't just talk about what others should do; they actually do what they say. Tom is a CPA—a tax strategist who knows that the government rewards people who know the tax code and play by its rules—and he is also a real estate investor.

Tom has spent more than twenty-five years working with sophisticated investors to help them develop innovative tax, business, and wealth strategies. Tom is a teacher at heart, and even in his early days when he worked for a Big 4 accounting firm, he managed the training for thousands of CPAs. He makes the complicated simple, and that is no easy feat because, in order to do this, it takes a complete understanding of your subject and an ability to boil down the details to the ones that matter. Tom's skill comes from his years as a trainer and from his firm grasp of taxation and tax strategies.

But Tom has influenced my life in a much more profound way than just through his knowledge of wealth strategies. If you read my introduction to Chapter 1, Tom's first chapter, then you know I mentioned his Mormon faith. Through Tom and others like him, I have learned much about the beliefs of this faith. His religion has many important lessons to share with a world that is in financial turmoil. One *lesson that comes from the Mormon faith and that seemed odd before, now doesn't seem quite so odd. That lesson is the Mormon practice of storing enough food, water, and money to survive for at least one year. Many of my Mormon friends do this, and so do my wife, Kim, and I. We put these necessities away in case of economic disaster, or worse, financial collapse. How close did we come in 2008?*

We are all used to a world of plenty and don't think twice about what we would do for food and other necessities in an emergency. As many of us know, our supermarkets only have enough food to last three days. And if you have ever lived in an area that is hurricane prone, and the forecast is predicting a storm on the way, you know how quickly the most critical supplies are snatched up. Water, bread, canned goods, batteries, and other vital supplies vanish from the store shelves in a matter of hours.

In 2008 the world came very close to becoming a world of collapsed credit cards. Think about this for a while: What would happen if the world stopped accepting credit cards? What could you buy with only the cash you have on hand, the money in your wallet, the change in that jar? Not much. I believe the world would shut down.

Of course I don't wish for financial disaster, but Tom has taught me about preparation. And being prepared allows me to keep my mind free of worry, to think clearly, even as we enter a period of economic chaos, and to seize the opportunities. These are the times when fortunes are made.

Tom has been an influence to me on many levels, and I honor his integrity. This chapter and the knowledge he shares is a must read for anyone seizing investment opportunities now and in the future. I greatly value him personally and professionally. He is a true friend.

—ROBERT KIYOSAKI

If you have even taken a quick glance at the chapter titles in this book, or considered its sheer size, then you are probably realizing there are as many ways to invest in real estate as there are models of homes. The key, of course, is to invest in the type of real estate that best suits you and your personal investing preferences. Your investment preferences may include risk level, tax advantages, and simplicity, among others.

For example, some people prefer investing in single-family homes because they like the simplicity, and there isn't a lot of management involved. Others prefer commercial real estate so they have to manage only a few properties and can deal with business owners as tenants instead of dealing with families. Still others prefer to invest in apartment buildings where the loss of a single tenant doesn't make a major impact on the overall cash flow from the investment. And then there are those who prefer to invest in raw land where there are no tenants at all.

So before you begin investing in real estate, take some time to figure out which type of real estate is best for you based on your personal investing preferences. You are likely to be more successful by doing something you enjoy. And, of course, it makes life a lot more fun!

The question I get most often from investors just starting out in real estate is how to decide which type of real estate investing is right for them. Again, remember to focus on your personal investment preferences. For a complete list of the personal investment preferences we review with our clients, go to our ProVision School of Wealth Strategy at www.WealthStrategyU.com.

Once you have figured out your personal investment preferences, it's time to figure out which type of real estate investing most closely matches these preferences. This book is a great place to do some initial analysis of the different types of real estate investing.

One of the least known and most lucrative real estate investments is known as tax lien investing. Some of the best bargains in real estate are found through these tax liens. At ProVision, we have several clients who have made millions of dollars investing in tax liens. Let me start by giving you a brief explanation of how tax liens work. Then, we can discuss whether tax lien investing is right for you and if it is, which tax lien investment strategy might work best.

WHAT'S TAX LIEN INVESTING?

Tax liens are investments made possible by state law. Governments love to use tax money, but they really don't like being in the tax collection business. And they especially don't like to be bankers. Governments want their money now, so they can balance their budgets. So they have a serious challenge when a taxpayer, for whatever reason, decides not to pay his property taxes on a particular parcel of real estate. In fact, sometimes it takes years to collect the taxes from the owner of the property, and sometimes the owner never pays the taxes owed. As much as governments hate being the bank, they hate being property owners even more. What they really want is the cash, and they want it now.

So instead of becoming a creditor of the property owner and waiting for the money until the taxpayer ponies up, many local governments (usually counties) have figured out how to get their money immediately. It's called a tax lien. In the simplest terms, here's what happens:

1. The government assesses taxes on a piece of property, which is called a parcel. In most cases, the owner will simply pay the taxes that are due.

2. But what if the owner of the land decides not to pay the taxes on time? Then what happens?

3. The government puts a lien on the parcel for back taxes.

4. Then the government sells the lien to an investor, such as you or me. The lien is sold at a public auction with an opening bid made up of the amount of back taxes and other costs.

5. If the lien is sold at auction, multiple investors bid on the lien. Although variation exists among tax lien states, there are some general similarities. First, all primary sales must be held in a public auction and ordinary citizens like you and me may take part in the sale. Some states use a process in which the price of the lien is bid up (i.e., increased) based on competition for the lien. In this situation, the price paid for the lien may be bid higher, but the interest rate earned on the tax lien remains fixed and does not fluctuate due to the bidding. Other states use a bid down system. In this situation, the interest rate earned on a tax lien is bid down by the bidders. The standard interest rate on tax liens varies among states but can be as high as 18 percent.

6. The lien earns simple interest based on the standard rate or auction final bid rate.

7. The interest "accrues" (accumulates) until either the taxpayer or another lienholder (such as a bank holding a mortgage) ultimately pays the interest and the back taxes to the investor in order to have the lien on his property removed.

8. After a certain period of time if the lien is not paid, the investor can foreclose against the property and can end up owning the property outright for only the price of the back taxes and foreclosure/legal fees.

TABLE 21.1 Summary of a Tax Lien

Step 1	Property owner does not pay taxes due on the property (parcel)
Step 2	The government places a lien on the parcel for back taxes
Step 3	The lien is offered for sale at a fixed interest rate or at auction
Step 4	If lien is sold at auction, multiple investors bid on the interest rate of the lien
Step 5	The lien earns simple interest based on the standard or auction rate
Step 6	The interest accrues until the property owner or another lienholder pays the back taxes
Step 7	If the lien is not paid, the investor can foreclose against the property and own the property for the price of the back taxes

The great thing about foreclosing on a tax lien is that a tax lien supersedes nearly all other liens. So if you are able to foreclose on a tax lien, you get the property for the cost of the unpaid taxes, and in the majority of situations, any other liens are wiped out. Pretty cool, huh? Well, at least it *can be* in the right circumstance, but more about that later. In any case, there are several important steps to investing in a tax lien, and we are going to take them one at a time.

STEP NO. 1: YOUR TAX LIEN STRATEGY

So there are two possible outcomes of investing in a tax lien. First, and most likely, is the outcome that you will earn interest at a stated rate that can be as high as 18 percent. The other possible outcome is that the lien is never paid off (redeemed) and you get the property. These two outcomes are the basis for the two different tax lien investing strategies.

TABLE 21.2 Possible Outcomes

A	You earn interest at a stated rate, or
B	The lien never gets paid and you get the property

While it may seem to be the luck of the draw whether a tax lien is redeemed or not, in fact there are several factors that can give a strong indication of which outcome is likely to occur. Because of this, anyone investing in tax liens should first decide how tax lien investing fits into his investment strategy. Do you want the interest, or is your goal the underlying property?

TABLE 21.3 Investment Strategy

Strategy A	Strategy B
☐ I want interest paid	☐ I want the property

You really must decide what you hope to get out of your tax lien investment up front because this decision will affect everything else you do pertaining to tax lien investing. Why? Primarily because the type of property for which you are willing to buy the lien is going to differ based on the interest rate investment strategy versus the property acquisition investment strategy. The type of property owner will also be a factor, since some property owners are more likely to pay their liens than others. So let's look at why you would choose one strategy over the other.

THE INTEREST RATE INVESTMENT STRATEGY

In actuality, interest rate investing and property acquisition investing are almost completely opposite investment strategies. The interest rate investment strategy is a fairly short-term, cash-flow strategy with little or no possibility for long-term growth. This may be a good place to park some cash at high interest rates while you are waiting to make another investment. Or you may have accumulated a lot of assets and you just want the pure cash flow as "mailbox money" (money you get in the mail with no effort other than the initial investment and a little monitoring). This can also be a good investment strategy for money you have accumulated in a retirement plan, such as a pension plan, 401(k), or IRA (superannuations or RRSPs for you Australians and Canadians). The interest will be tax deferred, and there won't be any real tax or leverage benefits to holding an interest rate tax lien outside of a retirement plan.

TABLE 21.4 Interest Rate Investment Strategy

Considerations
☐ Short/mid-term investment
☐ Desire cash flow (mailbox money)
☐ Little or no possibility for long-term growth
☐ Good use of extra cash while waiting to make another investment
☐ You have retirement money to invest

PROPERTY ACQUISITION INVESTMENT STRATEGY

A property acquisition investment strategy is completely different from the interest rate investment strategy. Rather than looking for quick cash flow, you are hoping for the opportunity to foreclose and own the underlying property for a long-term investment. This could be part of a long-term land hold strategy or a development strategy for property that you expect to be in a redevelopment zone.

While it is possible to do property acquisition investing in a retirement plan, in most countries there are real tax benefits to holding property outside of a retirement plan. It could be, as it is in the United States, that the gain on the sale of the property would be taxed at preferential capital gains rates. Or you may be able to do a like-kind exchange and not pay taxes at all.

Furthermore, if the underlying property is improved, you could receive depreciation benefits from holding the property. Or you may find yourself with significant equity in the property, and you may want to refinance to take advantage of the leverage opportunities of real estate. These opportunities typically are substantially restricted inside a retirement plan. These and other reasons point to holding this investment outside of your retirement plan in the eventuality that you end up owning the property.

TABLE 21.5 Property Acquisition Investing Strategy

Considerations
☐ Long-term investment
☐ Desire to foreclose and own the property
☐ Property could be in a redevelopment zone with good appreciation potential
☐ Like-kind exchange into more desirable investment property is possible
☐ Depreciation or leverage opportunities

STEP NO. 2: YOUR TAX LIEN INVESTMENT CRITERIA

Once you have your strategy in place, you can begin creating your criteria for the tax liens you want to acquire. Let's look at the interest rate investment and property acquisition investment strategies separately.

INTEREST RATE INVESTMENT STRATEGY CRITERIA

When you think about investing criteria, think about what's essential for a specific investment to meet your standards. What rate of return do you want? What level of risk are you willing to assume? In the case of tax liens, how much are you willing to risk that you will end up with the property? How long are you willing to hold the lien until it is eventually redeemed?

TABLE 21.6

Interest Rate Investing Criteria	Your Standards
Rate of Return	
Level of Risk	
Amount willing to risk to take hold of the property	
Length of time to hold property	

As with any investing strategy, the clearer your criteria, the easier the investment process. With clear criteria, you can easily eliminate most of the available tax liens and concentrate solely on those that meet your specific needs. A little later on in this chapter, we will look at how to determine whether a particular tax lien meets your criteria.

PROPERTY ACQUISITION INVESTMENT STRATEGY CRITERIA

When your goal is to acquire the underlying property, you start looking at your criteria much differently. Here are some of the questions you need to ask yourself:

- How likely are you to be able to foreclose on the property?
- What is the likelihood that the owner or another lienholder will pay off the lien before you can foreclose?
- How many years will you have to wait to foreclose?
- What are the property taxes that you will have to pay in the future (before your foreclosure waiting period is up)?

TABLE 21.7

Property Acquisition Investing Criteria	Your Standards	
Likelihood of foreclosure on the property		
Likelihood the owner or other lienholder will pay off lien		
Years you prefer to wait until foreclosure		
Property taxes you may have to pay in the future		

And then you have to look at all of the criteria you have for your property investments, including the following:

- Does your investment strategy call for investing in raw land or improved property?
- Are you going to develop the underlying property?
- If improved, what type of improved property is within your focused investment strategy?
- Is it industrial property, commercial office buildings, multifamily housing, or single-family homes?

To be a focused real estate investor, you must be able to focus on a single type of real estate. This is the only way you can become an expert in a particular type of property investing. Once you have this focused strategy in place, you can look at the specific criteria for your tax lien investing.

TABLE 21.8

Criteria for Property Investments	
☐ Raw Land	
☐ Develop the underlying property	
☐ Improved property	Type:
☐ Industrial	
☐ Commercial	
☐ Office Building	
☐ Multifamily Housing	
☐ Single-family Homes	

- What is your criterion for rate of return?
- Do you want the property to cash flow?
- And if so, how much cash flow is required?
- Do you have a particular location of concentration?
- What about the expected appreciation of the property?
- What is your maximum holding period for the property?
- What tax benefits are you expecting from the property?

TABLE 21.9 Real Estate Criteria

TYPE OF REAL ESTATE CHOSEN:	
Specific Criteria for Tax Lien Investing	**Your Standard**
Rate of return	
Cash flow (if so, how much)	
Geographic location	
Expected appreciation	
Maximum hold period	
Tax benefits expected	

STEP NO. 3: EVALUATING THE TAX LIEN INVESTMENT

With your criteria in place, you can now begin looking at tax liens and evaluating whether they fit within your criteria. Between two weeks and one month before the tax lien auction, the county will release the information on the properties with tax liens that will be available for purchase. Begin your evaluation by determining which of the available tax liens will fit within your investment strategy.

INTEREST RATE INVESTMENT STRATEGY EVALUATION

Interest rate investors should look for properties that are less likely to be abandoned by the owner. Properties less likely to be abandoned include:

- improved property
- owner-occupied property
- property with other liens, such as a mortgage
- property that has a lien because the tax bill was sent to the wrong address

PROPERTY ACQUISITION INVESTMENT STRATEGY CRITERIA

Property acquisition investors should look for liens on properties that are more likely to be allowed to go to foreclosure, including:

- properties that have been abandoned by the owner
- properties where the owner has died, so the property is in probate or has passed to an estate or trust
- property where ownership of the property is free and clear of other liens
- property that has several years of unpaid back taxes
- property owned by someone living out of state

Once you have narrowed down your investment possibilities to those that fit within your strategy of interest rate investment or property acquisition investment, you need to further focus on which liens you should go after in the bid process.

If you are an interest rate investor, you'll want to understand exactly how the interest rate is applied in the state where you are investing. Once you determine this, find liens that are less likely to have multiple bidders or that are located in a state where the interest rate remains fixed at the auction. In a state where the interest rate is "bid down" at auction, look for properties that are likely to have the tax lien redeemed, but they have some attributes that might scare away other investors. These liens will retain the highest interest rate because they will have the least amount of interest in the bidding process. Look for tax liens with the following attributes:

- The property is located in a remote area of the state
- The property is small or an odd shape
- The property has other undesirable features

If you are a property acquisition investor, you'll want to find liens on properties that you want to own. Begin narrowing down the properties by researching only those properties that meet your criteria. For example, suppose you want to invest in raw land, which, by the way, is the most likely property to be available for foreclosure. Suppose also that you want land that is likely to be developed in the near future. In this case, you would want to find liens on property that

- is near other developed property
- is in a redevelopment area
- is in an area that will likely be developed in the next few years due to the growth patterns of the county
- does not have restrictions that could hinder development

A ProVision client purchased a tax lien on a 1.5-acre parcel a few years ago in a bad part of town. Across the street from the property was a lot of industrial junk. But the area was on the verge of being redeveloped. There were ten years of taxes owed on the property, so the liens were not likely to be redeemed. And the client noticed that the owner of the property was an estate. This client purchased the tax lien for the current year and then went back to the other tax lienholders and redeemed all of the other tax liens. The total cost of ten years of tax liens was $7,000.

The client then went to the owner of the property and asked if he wanted the property. The estate was willing to deed over the property just to get rid

TABLE 21.10 Summary of Evaluation for Tax Lien Investments

Interest Rate Investment	Property Acquisition Investment
PROPERTIES LESS LIKELY TO BE ABANDONED	**PROPERTIES MORE LIKELY TO FORECLOSE**
☐ Improved property	☐ Abandoned properties
☐ Owner-occupied property	☐ Death of property owner
☐ Property with other liens	☐ Property is clear of other liens
☐ Liens due to tax bill sent to wrong address	☐ Property has several years of back taxes
	☐ Out of state owner
Bid Process	
LESS LIKELY TO HAVE MULTIPLE BIDDERS	**PROPERTIES YOU WANT TO OWN**
☐ Property is in remote area of state	☐ Property near other developed property
☐ Property is small or odd shaped	☐ Property is in a redeveloped area
☐ Property has undesirable features	☐ In an area that will likely be developed

of it and not have the headache of the tax liens or the cost of a foreclosure. Six months after purchasing the tax liens, a developer approached the client about buying the property.

The developer wanted to consolidate several parcels of land in the area to do a large commercial development. But he didn't want to deal with the legwork of the tax lien process. So, once the liens were all cleared, he approached our client and made an offer of $197,000 for the property. The result? Our client made a profit of $190,000, after owning the property for just six months.

STEP NO. 4: DUE DILIGENCE

Once you have decided which properties fit within your strategy and your criteria, it's time to do the due diligence on the properties. Due diligence is the process of assessing the risks of both the tax lien and the underlying property. At this point, you should have already assessed the risk of the lien being redeemed. But there are other risks to the lien that you will need to consider. And let's not forget about the underlying property. You need to assess the risks of that as well.

LIEN RISKS

Tax lien risks can be separated into two categories: property owner risks and tax lien process risks. Let's go over each one.

PROPERTY OWNER RISKS

The biggest risk with respect to the property owner is a property owner's bankruptcy. If the property owner files bankruptcy, you will not be able to foreclose on the lien until after the bankruptcy is resolved. Of course, bankruptcy courts normally respect property tax liens and give them a high priority when the bankruptcy is resolved. However, in a Chapter 7 bankruptcy, the bankruptcy trustee could have the tax lien subordinated to administrative expenses. In this case, the tax lienholder could become an unsecured creditor and wind up with little or nothing. Luckily, there are steps you can take to guard against this.

A very small percentage of properties may have mortgages held by a bank now administered by the Federal Deposit Insurance Corporation (FDIC). When a bank fails due to insolvency (i.e., not enough money), any loans owed to the bank are administered by the FDIC. If a loan administered by the FDIC is attached to a property on your list, it could mean delays during the foreclosure. The good news is that it is easy to check for FDIC-held loans. With a few simple steps, the risk of a delayed foreclosure due to an FDIC-administered lien is quite remote and easily avoidable.

Another risk is that the owner is in the military. It's very difficult to foreclose on an active member of the military. Another difficult owner to deal with is an owner who lives in a foreign country. In this case, the difficulty lies with finding the owner and serving him or her with the foreclosure papers. Yet another risk is that a minor or a mentally disabled person owns the property. This could cause delays in the foreclosure process and additional litigation costs.

Finally, there is the off chance that the lien is on government-owned property. Since the government is normally exempt from property tax, once the lien is corrected, the investor will likely receive his/her investment back but may not receive any interest. Good research will prevent this and other owner problems because you can easily determine the owner of the property and avoid buying the lien. Researching the owner is not as difficult as it may sound. The owner of the property is public information that is typically available at the county assessor's office. You can then go to the county recorder, county treasurer, and bankruptcy court to find out additional information about the owner, including other liens he may have outstanding and whether he has filed bankruptcy. A quick search on the Internet about the owner may also turn up helpful information.

TABLE 21.11 Lien Risks – Property Owner Risk

Risk 1	Property owner files bankruptcy
Risk 2	Property owned by an active member of the military
Risk 3	Property owned by someone who lives out of the country
Risk 4	Property owned by a minor
Risk 5	Property owned by a mentally disabled person
Risk 6	Property owned by the government

Real Life Story: Research Paid Off

While owning property can be a risk, it can also be a great opportunity. My client, Ellen, acquired a tax lien a few years ago that was owned by a hotel chain. In her research, Ellen discovered that the hotel chain had changed its strategy and no longer was interested in the community where this property was located. So she purchased that tax lien for $7,000. Less than three years later, Ellen sold the property for $360,000. In this case, the property owner's intentions almost assured Ellen of a great investment so her research about the property owner really paid off.

TAX LIEN PROCESS RISKS

Several risks can arise due to the lien itself. These are risks that typically involve litigation costs or delays in the foreclosure process that increase the cost of ownership. They can arise because of disputes over property ownership, disposition of other liens, and getting clear title to the property after foreclosure. In addition, there is the risk of too much success. How is that? What if you successfully acquire a property that needs a lot of fixing up? Are you prepared to invest the additional money required to get the work done? And will it be in your best interest? The key to minimizing these risks is evaluating the potential of the property, quantifying the potential additional costs of litigation or improvements, and determining whether the tax lien meets your criteria, including the possible additional costs to complete the foreclosure process.

TABLE 21.12 Lien Risks – Tax Lien Process Risk

Risk 1	Litigation costs
Risk 2	Disputes of ownership
Risk 3	Disposition of other liens

Real Life Story: More Due Diligence Was Due

Andy purchased tax liens against all of the condominium units of an apartment building. During his due diligence research, Andy had learned that the out-of-state owner was no longer interested in the property. Andy foreclosed on the property, only to find out that it needed $300,000 of repairs to a building that was worth only $200,000. More due diligence would have saved Andy from this disaster.

PROPERTY RISKS

Once you have evaluated the tax lien risks and have concluded that there are a number of liens that meet your criteria, you can then evaluate the underlying property. Some of the risks to evaluate are as follows:

ENVIRONMENTAL RISKS

Perhaps the biggest risk in any property investment is that there is an environmental hazard that will be expensive to clean up. Reviewing the history of the property and contacting the EPA and state department of environmental quality about possible environmental problems is essential in any property investment, but particularly in a tax lien investment. An environmental problem could be the very reason that the owner has not paid the taxes.

VALUE OF THE PROPERTY

The most obvious risk, of course, is that the property will not be worth the cost to buy the lien (and other tax liens, both previous and subsequent to your lien). Include in your analysis the administrative costs of foreclosing on the property and getting clear title to the property.

STEP NO. 5: FORMING YOUR TEAM—THE REAL KEY TO REAL ESTATE INVESTING

At this point, you may be thinking that all of this is just too much work. As I was writing this, I had the same initial reaction. But remember that you don't have to do all of the work yourself. In fact, we like to say at ProVision that the three most expensive words in the English language are, "Do It Yourself."

While some of you will enjoy the research and the details, others will be content with a little lower return and a lot less work. The answer to this is to build a Tax Lien Team. You can reap the rewards of tax lien investing without doing all of the legwork yourself. Rather, hire others to do the work for you.

You already have determined the criteria for your tax lien investing. And you know the risks associated with tax liens that you are going to have to consider with every tax lien investment. You just don't want to spend all of the time and effort on the details of going through the various liens and the properties all by yourself.

Remember that there are lots of people who are looking for employment and are very competent at research and details. I know this; I hire these people myself, both for my accounting firm and for my real estate investing.

If you have clear criteria and create good procedures to follow for doing the due diligence, you can turn it over to someone else to do. I suggest you pay these people primarily based on results, but you can also pay them a small hourly wage. I like to give my team members large bonuses for success. Let's take, for example, the tax lien that my friend Jim acquired several years ago.

Jim found a property with twelve years of taxes owed. The property consisted of eighty acres of raw land located in a floodplain near a power plant. Most people would pass this property by, but Jim noticed that the property was not far from developed property and was zoned for industrial use. (Industrial zoning usually means that just about any buyer could use the property. It's normally fairly easy to rezone industrial property to a more conservative use of the property, such as commercial or residential.)

After doing all of his due diligence, Jim acquired the current year tax lien and then went to each of the prior lienholders and acquired their liens as well. Because he now owned all of the old tax liens, he could foreclose immediately. The total of the tax liens was $40,000. That's $500 per acre for property that was close to developed property.

A few years after buying the property, a solar energy company came to Jim and asked to purchase the property. Jim negotiated a price of $9,500 per acre for a total sales price of $760,000—a profit of $720,000!

The due diligence and research into this tax lien took Jim a lot of time and effort, which he was happy to do. But suppose he didn't want to do the work himself. What if he had hired someone to do the research for him? He might have paid this person $10 to $12 per hour plus a bonus when the property sold. Suppose he offered a 10 percent bonus on the increase in value from the total cost of investment. The researcher would have received a bonus of $72,000. Knowing that this type of bonus was possible, you can bet that the researcher would have been very diligent in his or her research and would have made sure to find only the best properties.

Some of you are thinking, "Wow! What a high price to pay for research." But think how many properties you could find if you had multiple researchers doing the work for you. And it really costs you very little. You have a small out-of-pocket cost for the initial wages, but you have no risk for more than that. Yes, you give up 10 percent of the profit, but that's a small price to pay for 90 percent of the profit that you didn't have to work for!

Now let me tell you the rest of the story of this property. When Jim sold it, he did a tax-free exchange for a sale/leaseback on a fast food restaurant location. This property came with a twenty-year lease with options for an additional twenty years. It is paying Jim $4,300 per month of lease income. In addition,

TABLE 21.13 Example of Tax Lien Team Members

1	Someone to research the available tax liens
2	Someone to identify the tax liens that fall within your tax lien strategy
3	Someone to evaluate the tax liens that fall within your tax lien strategy
4	Someone to complete the due diligence (risks) on the tax liens that fall within your tax lien strategy

Jim had $80,000 left over from the sale that he put into another piece of land—all because he found the right tax lien on the right piece of property.

Just think, if Jim had not had to do all of the work himself, how many more tax liens he could have found and how much more property he could have acquired.

What other team members do you need? Here is a list of possible positions:

1. Real estate appraiser to determine the value of the underlying real estate
2. Real estate banker/mortgage broker so you can refinance the real estate once you acquire it
3. Real estate attorney to assist with foreclosure proceedings and other legal matters throughout the lien process
4. Tax lien auction bidder. If you don't want to handle the auctions yourself, in most instances you can outsource so long as you provide proper guidance to the bidder.
5. Bookkeeper. You will need to keep good track of the properties you acquire and the costs to acquire each property for tax and investment analysis purposes.
6. Property manager if you plan to acquire improved property
7. Real estate broker to handle the sale of your acquired real estate
8. Banker to handle financial transactions
9. CPA to assist with the tax aspects of tax lien investing and property transactions, including like-kind exchanges of acquired property for desired property
10. Foreclosure assistant to follow through on all of the details of foreclosing on tax liens and obtaining clear title
11. Wealth coach and mentor to help you create your tax lien investment strategy and to keep your investing moving

STEP NO. 6: SETTING UP TAX LIEN INVESTMENT SYSTEMS

Like any good investment strategy, tax lien investing should be set up as a business. This includes setting up your team in Step No. 5 and determining a good strategy. It also includes setting up the systems to make your investing efficient and effective. In order to maximize your investing while minimizing your time and your risk, consider setting up the following systems:

DUE DILIGENCE SYSTEM

This will include a due diligence checklist, a list of your investment criteria and reports from your due diligence team members to let you know their progress so they can ask you questions.

INVESTMENT REPORTING SYSTEM

This will include reports monitoring the progress of the tax lien investing as well as reports indicating the returns on your investments. There are some good software packages available to track and monitor your tax lien investments, including rate of return and deadlines.

AUCTION SYSTEM

This includes policies and procedures for your auction bidder to follow when attending tax lien auctions.

FORECLOSURE PROCEDURES

Make a complete list of the steps for your foreclosure assistant to follow in beginning, handling, and completing the foreclosure process and obtaining clear title to the property.

SALES PROCEDURES FOR REAL ESTATE

Make a complete list of steps for your real estate broker to take in order to market and sell or exchange your properties.

Now you know about tax lien investing, which is a lucrative way to participate in real estate. And you have the strategies, steps, and checklists you need to begin exploring it if you so choose. As I mentioned in the beginning of this chapter, whichever real estate investing opportunity you choose, it should

TABLE 21.14 Steps for Tax Lien Strategy

Step 1	Determine Your Tax Lien Strategy
STRATEGY A INTEREST RATE INVESTMENT	
STRATEGY B PROPERTY ACQUISITION INVESTMENT	
Step 2	Identify Your Tax Lien Investment Criteria
Step 3	Evaluate the Tax Lien Investment
Step 4	Complete Your Due Diligence
Step 5	Form Your Tax Lien Team
Step 6	Set Up Your Tax Lien Investment System

be one that meets your objectives and one you really enjoy. That one factor alone will increase your chances for success considerably.

AUTHOR'S NOTE

I would like to thank Mark Manoil, Esq., for his assistance with this chapter. Mark is the foremost authority in Arizona for tax lien investing and his book, *Arizona Property Tax Liens*, was the source of much of the technical information included in this chapter. Mark was also gracious enough to spend some of his valuable time giving me his personal insights into tax lien investing.

I would also like to thank Darius Barazandeh, Esq., for his assistance with the state variations and subtle nuances of tax lien investing. Darius is an expert in the field of tax lien investing and his training, *Attorney Secrets to Investing in Tax Liens*, covers the subtle yet vital variations among states for those wanting to use a multistate investing strategy.

WAYS TO LEARN MORE

Please go to www.ProVisionWealth.com for more information regarding the wealth strategy information contained in this chapter.

For more than 30 years, **Tom Wheelwright** has strategically developed innovative tax, business, and wealth strategies for sophisticated investors and business owners across the United States and around the world, resulting in millions of dollars in profits for his clients. His goal is to teach people how to create a strategic and proactive approach to wealth that creates lasting success. As the founder of ProVision, Tom is the innovator of proactive consulting services for ProVision's premium clientele, who on average pay a lot less in taxes and earn much more on their investments. He works with select clients on their wealth, business, and tax strategies and lectures on wealth and tax strategies around the world.

19

How to Create Retail Magic: A Tale of Two Centers

Marty De Rito is an expert on retail real estate—shopping centers and retail properties. As you know by now, there is a difference between residential, commercial, office, raw land, and other niches of real estate investing. When I want information on retail real estate, Marty is the person I call.

For years, no matter where I would go to in Phoenix, I would see Marty's company's signs—DeRito Partners—everywhere, but I had never met the guy. One of my bigger commercial properties is right next to a shopping center that Marty manages. I knew the owner of the property and some of the tenants, but still I had never met Marty.

After a while, my imagination began to take over. I pictured that De Rito Partners was an old firm and that Marty was some old guy who had started the firm but was no longer active in the business. Then one day, I met him in the gym and was surprised to meet a very young person! After talking to him, I realized that the reason I had not run into him was that he is a very busy, ambitious young man.

Today, Marty is taking on some of the biggest and most ambitious retail real estate projects in Phoenix. He's got guts. Talking to him is invaluable because he has insights into the world of business seen only from the world of retail. In other words, he focuses on what shoppers are buying and where, along with how well the shopper is doing financially. When I want to find out what is hot and what is not

with shoppers, Marty is the guy. He has insight into the local economy and what
parts of the city are growing and what parts are dying because he is on the front
lines of consumerism—just by knowing how retailers in the area are doing. This is
why Marty's knowledge is priceless.

—Robert Kiyosaki

In your city or town, I'm sure there is one retail center that is simply the place to see and be seen. It is the center where people congregate, where people take their out-of-town guests, where they shop, and where they go for fun. And it is the center that you as an investor might be interested in owning one day, it is the center that you as a developer may want to emulate, and it is the center that you as a business owner would put at the top of your list when looking to lease space. No matter what your interest is in retail centers, this chapter will provide you with experiences and truths that you will want to know before entering the retail arena.

Generally speaking, centers like the one we are describing are no different from any other retail center; after all, retail centers are simply a collection of stores and eating places with parking spaces, signs, and landscaping. But somehow certain centers seem to be the ones that have won the popularity contest. They have become the winners in the battle for the shoppers' time, attention, and almighty dollar.

In the early days of my career, I admired the great minds who could pull together such amazing opportunities and then shape them into retail developments that didn't just hit the mark—they nailed the mark. Heck, they invented the mark, and then they nailed it! Now I admire those people even more because I know what it takes to make that kind of magic happen. Now I, along with the help of my team, have waved the magician's wand a few times. Experience has taught me, though, that it takes more than a wand, and there is little magic involved. Developing a premier shopping center takes three potent ingredients:

Great relationships
Great real estate
Great attention to detail

Now you may be thinking, "Marty, of course it takes those things. I've read a few other chapters in this book, and that seems to be what lots of successful real estate pros are saying." Good. I'm glad the other authors are reinforcing my message. Great relationships, great real estate, and great attention to detail are universal truths, and anyone who wants to achieve any level of success in real estate simply must put every ounce of effort into each one because any two without the other isn't good enough.

In my years, I've known real estate pros who have tremendous relationships with some of the biggest and best retailers. They can get the appointments when no one else can. They have their foot in the door. I've seen them have tremendous retail locations—at the proverbial corners of Center and Main with high traffic and plenty of customer potential. But then, I've seen them completely blow it when it came to the details. The architecture is off, or the economics of the center aren't right or the visibility is impaired or . . . the list goes on and on. It takes excellence in all three of these ingredients for success.

But what does excellence look like when it comes to retail centers? It's a very different animal when you compare it to other forms of real estate, and as you read further in this chapter, you'll come to see why. So whether you are considering venturing into the world of retail centers, thinking about buying a retail center, or even thinking about leasing space in one for a business venture, I'll show you what excellence means so you can recognize it when you see it.

It has taken me decades to learn what I am sharing with you. I was fortunate to handle the leasing and sales of hundreds of centers when I was a retail leasing agent at Grubb and Ellis Company and on my own at De Rito Partners, Inc., and the lesson has cost me plenty. About ten years into my real estate career, approximately seven years after I left Grubb and Ellis Company on good terms to start my own shopping center leasing and development company, I recognized a great piece of real estate—the 1-million-square-foot Christown Mall. It was more than thirty years old and needed a significant rehab to accomplish a drastic change in the tenant mix. My idea was simple. Add large power center retailers (Walmart, Costco, Target, etc.) into an enclosed mall setting. The previous standard department stores had either left or were leaving to go to the newer mall near the freeway. But my research showed Christown Mall still had significant traffic counts on the arterial street, there was a good density of customers who wanted discount stores, and the existing owner already had Walmart in the center but it wanted to expand to a supercenter.

It all sounded like I was well on my way. My mistake was in choosing a partner to purchase and redevelop the shopping center. The firm I chose had a net worth at the time that was equal to the size of the transaction. In development, nothing ever goes 100 percent right; working through a project takes time, persistence, and staying power, and by that I mean cash. The minute we hit some major obstacles, my partner wanted out. To make matters worse, when my partner entered the transaction, he sold a portion of his ownership to a "hard money" lender. I didn't know about it until it was already done. I knew if trouble were to occur, hard money lenders had no interest in giving me more time to work out the obstacles. Their business plan would be to push me out and force me to live up to the financial guarantees that I had given my partner, who I knew very well.

The lesson I learned was never enter a partnership if you are the sweat equity unless your financial partner has a significant net worth. Find a financial partner who has a net worth or financial means that is at least five times the opportunity. Additionally, never allow your partner to sell all or a piece of his ownership without your written approval and/or a first right of refusal. My little mistakes cost me $7 million dollars in cash.

That was eye-opening to me, and eyes once opened must never close again. I became far wiser after that, and so will you with every project. But my goal with this chapter is to make you wiser from the beginning *before* your money is on the line. I guarantee you'll never look at a retail center the same way again, whether you are looking at it as an investment or simply as a shopper. You'll see it in a whole new light.

I called this chapter "How to Create Retail Magic: A Tale of Two Centers" because I will be using two separate centers as examples throughout. The first center, called Casa Paloma, is one I built from the ground up, and it has been completed for about ten years. The second center, the Scottsdale Pavilions, is an acquisition, and we're in redevelopment right now, but the work was probably about ten years overdue. I chose these two centers for this chapter because in ways you will come to see, they are living, breathing examples of my three key ingredients for success: great relationships, great real estate, and great attention to detail. Let's dive in and define what these mean more specifically.

INGREDIENT NO. 1: GREAT RELATIONSHIPS

Years ago, I had the privilege of meeting Mel Simon, the largest owner of retail properties in the world (NYSE: SPG), and he said something I'll never forget: "Make a friend today and a deal tomorrow." Those were profound words, particularly in retail real estate where you may find yourself working with those same "friends" your entire career, particularly when it comes to leasing space to these tenants.

Unlike some areas of real estate—commercial office for example—where you may do a deal with a tenant company once and then never again, or at best maybe five or ten years later, retail real estate is often the opposite. You may find yourself doing one leasing deal, two, five, ten or more a year with a company like Subway, McDonald's, or a grocery store, for example. These companies and their real estate teams become regular customers, and, like anyone else in sales, I believe our product provides better value and adds to their bottom lines. In other words, almost on a daily basis, our reputation and our relationships go hand in hand. Weak performance is not an option.

Relationships, I've found over the years, come in a variety of flavors.

RELATIONSHIPS WITH TENANTS

I can't tell you how many times the great relationships I've earned with retailers on one project have helped me on another. For instance, at our Casa Paloma center—a wonderful upscale, mixed-use shopping area—our tenants there appreciated us because we created an exceptional property with significant retailer sales per square foot, and we worked to bring in the best of the best retailers creating a strong tenant mix.

TIP I can't tell you how many times the great relationships I've earned with retailers on one project have helped me on another.

Scottsdale Pavilions is a recent acquisition that we have always seen as a center with huge potential. It had been neglected by its previous owner, and currently it is about 20 percent vacant. The retail tenants didn't like the previous owner very much, but they are beginning to like us a lot because we are making a difference. We're infusing huge dollars into improvements that will make the center more desirable to both retailers and shoppers. And we are working with them to redefine the right mix of tenants and create significant customer demand so that everyone can make money. That's what relationships are all about.

This opportunity to completely redefine the tenant mix and remerchandise the Scottsdale Pavilions is good news for everyone. Guess where we will go to find new tenants? You got it, to the people and the companies who believe in us, who are partners with us in our other centers, and who are our friends. Of course, there will be retailers we've never worked with before in the Scottsdale Pavilions, too. Our existing relationships will even help us forge those new relationships. We have a ready, willing, and able group of friends who not only want their own brands to succeed, but they have us as well. And they know that partnering to create a great tenant mix is one of the ways success happens.

RELATIONSHIPS WITH SHOPPERS

Just as it is important to have great relationships with tenants, it's equally important to foster great relationships with shoppers. In retail, relationships come in the form of giving shoppers what they want. Later we'll get into the details of exactly what that is, but for now, let's focus on the relationship itself. When De Rito Partners, my Arizona-based company, bought the Scottsdale Pavilions, we knew it had a bad relationship with shoppers. How? Well for starters, business was dwindling year after year. It was an errand center, meaning it was a place where shoppers would come to stop at one store and then leave as quickly as possible.

In retail, the goal is to get the shopper to stay at your center as long as possible. Think about it; if you stay at a retail center an hour longer than you intended, you'll probably spend more money. We all do it, either on food or on some luxury that suddenly transformed into a necessity right before our eyes. That's the psychology of shopping (there's more, so keep reading), and each of us brings it to life every time we enter a Costco, a Saks, or any other retailer. But getting people to stay longer isn't as easy as it may seem. It takes the right combination of convenience, entertainment, and ambiance to make it happen.

TIP In retail, the goal is to get the shopper to stay at your center as long as possible. Think about it; if you stay at a retail center an hour longer than you intended, you'll probably spend more money.

That's where relationships come in. Call me a ladies' man, but I try to have great relationships with women. No, not in that way, but in the sense that women comprise two-thirds of all shoppers. With men making up 95 percent of retail center developers, it's critical that anyone in this business understand what women want. Before I began developing Casa Paloma, I asked my wife why she was traveling twenty miles north to shop at the retail centers in Scottsdale, rather than going to the ones closer to where we lived. She looked at me with an expression that seemed to say, "You don't know?" and then began to explain. "The centers here don't have the right stores. There's no Banana Republic, or Chico's or Ann Taylor. There are no good restaurants and no A.J.'s Fine Foods [a higher-end grocery store]. There's nothing upscale. It's just more fun to go shopping in Scottsdale and more convenient because there are lots of other stores nearby that I can stop in to pick up little things here or there."

"Oh," I replied, my wheels turning. I know she left thinking, duh, or some more adult equivalent of that expression, but the truth was I wanted to hear the truth from her. And then, I asked the same question of her friends. From them I got similar looks and similar answers. That led me to my lifelong relationship with female shoppers, and it's paid off in big numbers. Casa Paloma remains today one of the top-grossing centers in the state.

The Scottsdale Pavilions, by contrast, had forgotten about its shoppers. It was a hot property when it first opened up twenty years ago, before there was much competition in the area. But then the trade area began to grow. Other retail developers began forging relationships with shoppers where the Scottsdale Pavilions didn't bother. Business began to trail off, and before too long the Scottsdale Pavilions was in a downward spiral. When I bought the center, one of the first things we did was send a questionnaire to six thousand homes in the surrounding community. We told our neighbors that we were going to reinvigorate the center, and if they would kindly tell us what they would want there, we'd give them two free movie tickets. We had a flood of responses, not because of the free movie tickets alone, but because people were honored to have been asked their preferences. It was the beginning of our relationship with the shoppers in the trade area.

What Women Want

Women make up two-thirds of all shoppers, so it's a good idea to deliver what they want:

- convenience
- variety
- atmosphere
- fun—entertain me
- ample, easy parking
- security
- one-stop shop
- the right stores
- value for their dollar
- cleanliness

INGREDIENT NO. 2: GREAT REAL ESTATE

Ah, here it is again. You're thinking location, location, location. You've heard that before, but in retail, the word "great" means several things beyond just location, and they are critical. They are nonnegotiable. They are the differences between success and failure, between happy tenants and problem tenants. Here's my list:

GREAT MEANS VISIBLE

Let me say it again: great means visible. Shoppers can shop only in stores that they know are there, and that's all there is to it. A store that is hidden is a store that is empty. Or a restaurant or a newsstand or a health club or an oil and lube shop for that matter. Being seen from the street and visible to customers is *numero uno*!

TIP A store that is hidden is a store that is empty. Being seen from the street and visible to customers is *numero uno*!

One of the classic breaches of this rule happened a number of years ago in downtown Phoenix. The development was positioned on a busy corner a few blocks east of the city's main thoroughfare. It was an expensive center with beautiful Spanish Mission-style architecture and stucco walls. It was touted as a destination for shoppers downtown and the perfect venue for free community-building events. Add to the project that a very prominent, newsworthy group of investors were behind the development and you have the makings for a real success, right? Wrong.

The developers forgot two important rules: visibility and shoppers. Allow me to elaborate. The center was built in an open-air courtyard-style with its focus facing to an inner courtyard on all four sides. From the north/south and the east/west streets, drivers saw only the sides of the buildings. Sure there were some signs that faced outward, but they were not prominent and couldn't have been any more so without compromising the mission feel of the architecture. From inside the center, the feel was quite nice, with good intimacy and ambiance. But there were a few other problems. First, the center didn't have an anchor tenant to support its size and draw enough people to the destination. That was a big mistake. The second problem was that too few people ever actually experienced the courtyard ambiance because the center's design wasn't inviting. And the third problem was there simply weren't enough people living in the trade area to support the businesses that leased there. The economics didn't work.

The center struggled to attract retailers and shoppers, and within a few years it became office space and classrooms. It is a classic example of retail developers getting too focused on a vision for a retail center and forgetting the most critical rule of retail, which is visibility and shoppers.

I see the visibility and shoppers rule broken all the time, and I've seen retailers pay the price. Look around and you'll find otherwise successful retail brands and restaurant concepts unable to make their numbers work because there simply aren't enough customers walking through their doors. You'll begin to notice centers that just churn tenants every two to five years because no one can last. And you'll hear shoppers peg centers or specific storefronts as jinxed because nothing can ever survive there. I'm sure just as you have the winning centers in your city or town, you have the centers that just can't seem to get things going. Nine times out of ten, the problem is visibility.

I admit, the Scottsdale Pavilions has a visibility problem, but thankfully, it is one that can be corrected. When the center was first built, the front of it was designed to be along a soon-to-be constructed freeway on the center's west side. Large signs and landscaping water features, complete with the annual migration of Canadian geese, flank the west side of the center to this day. The signs are very visible, and anyone driving by can't miss the destination. Sounds great, right? The problem is that a few years after the Scottsdale Pavilions was built, the community had a change of plans and decided to build the freeway on the *east* side of the center, not the west. So now, the center's backside is facing the valuable freeway drivers. And let's face it, the backside doesn't have the water features, it doesn't have the landscaping, and it certainly doesn't have the geese. Our backside is not our best side. So part of the plan is to literally make over the center so that the back is no longer the back and the visibility from the freeway will be glorious, including new pylon signs.

GREAT MEANS THE RIGHT DENSITY
OF THE RIGHT SHOPPERS

But all the visibility in the world won't buy you anything if the right people—and the right quantity of the right people—aren't in the vicinity of the center. This is called demographics, and every center lives and dies by the density numbers. It takes the right number of people within your center's target demographic to create a winning project.

Retailers, restaurants, etc., are all interested in demographics. They count rooftops, they look at census numbers, and more, all to arrive at the ideal location profile for their stores. From the developer's perspective, density and demographics define which retailers will succeed in a center. For example, at Casa Paloma there was a high density of people who were perfectly suited to upscale retail. Our preliminary research showed that. So it made sense for us to skew the center that way. We were a fit for the higher-end retailers we targeted, and they were a fit for our shopper demographic. And the right density of those shoppers meant we could be confident that we would have enough traffic.

In some areas, density and demographics dictating the type of center is obvious. For instance, there is no point putting a check cashing service into a center that is sitting in the midst of million-dollar homes. But some areas are in transition, and the demographic makeup isn't always obvious. That's where research comes in and plays a critical role. In planning the Scottsdale Pavilions retail tenant mix, we know the higher-end customer density is there, and we have identified a number of demographic needs that are not being served. Our key priority will be matching those needs with the center, its retailers, and its customers.

GREAT MEANS CONVENIENT

My wife and her friends taught me this truth years ago when I was doing my research for Casa Paloma. Convenience is everything, and it came up over and over again in the list of what women want in a shopping center. If I sound sexist, I don't mean to be. Anyone getting into retail needs to always remember that most shoppers are women, so let's just say it: we are catering to women's needs, not the needs of men.

Convenience to women means several things. It means "on the way" to somewhere else. The center's location has to be on the way to or from work, school, the gym, the day care center, the salon, or some other destination. And better yet, if it is on the same side of the road she is traveling, all the better. Ask women and they will tell you that all things being equal, they are more inclined to stop at a store on the right side of the street than they are to stop at a store on the left side of the street. Crossing traffic is an inconvenience and can be dangerous.

TIP Convenience is everything, and it came up over and over again in the list of what women want in a shopping center.

Convenient also means easy and ample parking. Searching up and down rows of cars for a parking space is the last thing shoppers of any gender want to do when they are in a hurry; and who isn't in a hurry today? Shoppers tend to give a center a few chances when it comes to parking, but if the problem persists, shoppers will mentally label the center as "a hassle," and they won't come back. There are simply too many other choices today, including "stores" on the Internet where parking is never an issue.

At Casa Paloma, we knew shoppers' feelings about parking, so we made sure it was plentiful by building more parking than a center typically requires. But how many times has plentiful parking been an inconvenience all its own? Sometimes an over abundance of parking can cause the parking to be so far away from the store entrance that it is all too easy for shoppers to think, "I'll do this another time." Parking that is too far away from the store is inconvenient. Knowing this, when we built Casa Paloma, we built it with a parking configuration that extends wide instead of deep in relation to the store fronts. In other words, the walk from a parking spot to the center is a matter of at most twenty yards versus fifty or more. The perception is we're convenient, and convenient means great real estate.

GREAT MEANS HAPPENING

Another important aspect of great real estate is that it happens to sit in an area that is vital and alive. That doesn't mean it needs to be in the nightclub district. What I mean is that great real estate has (or has had) other great real estate projects happening around it. Take for example the Scottsdale Pavilions. One of the reasons I acquired it is because it is sitting right in the middle of two huge development projects, both of which are compatible to retail. On the east side is a $450-million casino resort under construction. It will bring convention business to within a quarter of a mile of the center. On the west, less than two miles away, is the $1-billion Ritz Carlton Hotel and high-end community slated for development. Beyond that, commercial office space is springing up all around, and the center itself sits on a road currently under construction— translate that in the process of expansion—to carry a heavy load of east- and westbound traffic. Add this action all up and you have a happening location.

TIP Great real estate has (or has had) other great real estate projects happening around it.

This location with all its opportunity seems extraordinary. But sometimes happening locations are far less obvious. I've seen small neighborhood centers be very happening spots for the right tenant mix. They seem to be where people congregate or where people go to eat out or shop. It's all relative. Sometimes a happening center in a small town would be a failure in a bigger city. You can feel which centers are happening and why they are happening.

The key is knowing which ones are going to become happening and which ones are going to stay happening.

We placed Casa Paloma in an area that had higher incomes, lots of families, strong high-tech employers, along with a strong and growing population density. The trade area wasn't providing places for these people, or others with similar demographics, to shop and eat. They wanted a high-end grocery store such as A.J.'s Fine Foods and upscale shopping for the family such as Gap, Banana Republic, and Talbots. Additionally, they wanted higher-end restaurants, which included Z Tejas Grill, Fleming's Prime Steakhouse, and Roy's Pacific Rim Cuisine. Casa Paloma delivered, and the center continues to be a success.

GREAT MEANS AFFORDABLE

Arizona has some of the most beautiful retail shopping in the world. I'm not biased about this; we simply do. We're a tourism state, and the Phoenix metro area is a tourism area, so my opinion stands to reason. We'd better cater to the tourists and provide great experiences, or they will simply take their travel dollars elsewhere. There are lots of wonderful travel destinations in this world.

But in an effort to create the most amazing shopping experience, it is easy for developers to overspend on a project, particularly with today's building costs. Elaborate building designs, costly façade work, expensive hardscapes and water features, high-maintenance landscaping, and high-dollar necessities like parking areas and garages can inflate the costs of a retail project very quickly, sometimes to the point where the economics just don't add up. Here's what I mean.

For the most part, all developers want to build the most beautiful shopping center that garners accolades from peers, family, and friends. However, your cost per square foot must be met by what your target retailers can afford to pay. A retailer whose rent factor, which is ideally less than 10 percent of sales, must have the appropriate sales volume from "their" customers. If the retailer can't justify the sales volume to meet the rent, they will not lease space at your shopping center. For us, we start with what we think the retailer can afford in rent, and then we back into what we can spend to develop or redevelop the shopping center.

If cash flow is king, as Robert talks about often in his books, then profitability is the king royale. Any center with economics that are so out of line that proven retailers cannot turn a profit will not stay in business long. Actually, when this pattern plays out, the center will go bankrupt and a second owner will buy it for cents on the dollar. Second owners do stand a better chance of getting the economics in line because their baseline costs are lower. But sometimes the damage is done, the shoppers' patterns have been established elsewhere, and there's no turning the center around.

As tempting as it is to want to build or even be a part of the most beautiful and best center in town, really examine the cost per square foot and sales per square foot spread. Even if you are looking to lease space, this rule applies. Affordability equals success.

TIP As tempting as it is to want to build or even be a part of the most beautiful and best center in town, really examine the cost per square foot and sales per square foot spread.

GREAT MEANS A SUPERIOR TENANT MIX

Way back at the beginning of this chapter, I asked if there was a center or two in your community that just seemed to be the winner. My guess is that at least one and maybe two came to mind. Well, while all these other great real estate requirements help make centers successful, the right tenant mix is a big part of the magic.

Is it an art, or is it a science? Creating the right tenant mix is as much about understanding the shoppers' psyches as it is about discovering the retail options, building the relationships, and knowing how to negotiate the deals. It takes being able to visualize a center before it comes out of the ground or before it is revitalized. That's the art part. I am fortunate to have great people around me, and we all work together to create a vision for a center. It is truly the most exciting part of my job and makes all the tough stuff worth it.

TIP Creating the right tenant mix is as much about understanding the shoppers' psyches as it is about discovering the retail options, building the relationships, and knowing how to negotiate the deals. It takes the right mix of stores that create the highest pedestrian traffic that lead to higher sales.

I mentioned earlier about the importance of keeping shoppers at your center longer. I always think of Las Vegas when this subject comes up. That's the key to success there. The casinos do everything in their power to keep people from walking out the door. They offer food, they offer drinks, they have shows, they have a variety of games to play, and many of the newer properties have spectacular attractions like elaborate gardens, water shows, and nightclubs. If a Las Vegas casino were a retail center, what I just described would be called "the tenant mix."

So using a casino as a model, what does that example say about tenant mix in a retail center? To me, it means making sure we have the right "something" at the right time for our shoppers. It's not about having "something" for everyone; I don't want *everyone* at our centers. I want only the people the center is designed for. But when those right shoppers are there, I want to satisfy their every need. I want to feed them. I want to entertain them. I want to make them beautiful. I want to make their lives easier. I don't want them going to the next casino—or retail center—if I can keep them at mine.

A retail center is about more than just shopping, and a good tenant mix delivers it all with a blend of shopping, eating, dining, entertainment, and attractions so that even an errand can become a fun excursion. A great example is Casa Paloma. It has a fantastic tenant mix that satisfies shoppers' needs all in one location. There's no need to drive from center to center wasting time, fuel, and effort.

> ## Casa Paloma Tenant Mix
>
> Great real estate has a superior tenant mix that satisfies a shopper's every need.
>
> **Food**
>
> A.J.'s Fine Foods
>
> Cold Stone Creamery
>
> Z Tejas Grill
>
> Pei Wei Asian Diner
>
> Tomaso's Italian
>
> Fleming's Prime Steakhouse
>
> **Fashion**
>
> Ann Taylor
>
> Banana Republic
>
> Chico's
>
> Francesca's Collections
>
> Coffin & Trout Fine Jewelers
>
> Gap Woman/Gap Body/Gap
>   Kids/Baby Gap
>
> *CONTINUED*

GREAT MEANS ATTRACTIONS

Over the years I have learned I can't always address every shopper's need through my retail tenants. Sometimes it takes a bigger attraction to make that happen. And if we think about our Las Vegas casino example again, we know that big attractions have the power to keep people engaged longer, sometimes for hours, and sometimes for days.

TIP We know that big attractions have the power to keep people engaged longer.

Paris Paris
Talbots
White House/Black Market
Furnishings
Creative Leather
Ritz Camera
Showcase Home Entertainment
Sur la Table
Gifts and Accessories
Urban
Paper Soiree
Personal Services
Rolf's Salon
Alltel
Bath & Body Works
Cool Cuts 4 Kids
Philosophy
Postal Annex
American Laser Center
Valley Nails

I'm proud to say that our new Scottsdale Pavilions acquisition is the home of the longest-running auto show in the United States. Every Saturday, car enthusiasts come to the center and show off to other car lovers and spectators more than four hundred of their classics: Camaros, Chargers, Corvettes, Cobras, and more than a few Mustangs. It draws hundreds and hundreds of people every weekend. That's an attraction.

The show's beginnings were humble. The center's McDonald's franchisee, a car buff himself, started bringing his three collector cars to the center every week. They would attract attention, draw people to his restaurant, and in the process he would talk with other enthusiasts when the opportunity arose. Little by little, this passionate, enterprising franchisee began inviting others to bring their cars, too. Now the show is a landmark, and because of it, so is this center.

Alcohol can be an attraction. What do I mean? The Scottsdale Pavilions is part of a Native American community, which currently doesn't allow alcohol at retail shopping centers. This makes it very difficult to get sit-down family restaurants such as Chili's or Macaroni Grill. Eating is a form of entertainment and keeps people shopping longer. The community now recognizes this and recently voted in favor having alcohol served at these restaurants.

I've seen centers offer everything from merry-go-rounds to wade-in fountains (a big attraction in Arizona in July), and everything in between. The key is finding the right fit for your target shopper. Is the car show the right fit for a shopping center when it attracts mostly men? Especially since we know women do most of the shopping? At first glance, you may think not. But consider that a lot of those men bring the women in their lives along with them to the car show. Some of the women enjoy the car show, while others do their shopping as the men talk cars. The show is actually a terrific attraction for men and women shoppers alike. It certainly doesn't hurt McDonald's or other restaurant business either; the show practically surrounds the restaurant.

Another important kind of attraction is architecture. Exceptional design and architecture will draw people from all over if for nothing else than the experience. Of course, everyone knows a positive experience requires something to remember it by, so most people who visit will buy something, which is the point of all this. People like to shop, dine, and in today's world, even run errands in pleasant environments. That's one of the reasons why at the Scottsdale Pavilions, we are embarking upon a major renovation.

TIP Another important kind of attraction is architecture. Exceptional design and architecture will draw people from all over if for nothing else than the experience.

When the center was built twenty years ago, it was considered aesthetically pleasing. But after twenty years of neglect, when we bought it, it looked tired and out of date. The appearance absolutely affected everything, including leasing, customer count, and sales. Particularly when newer, more exciting competition popped up during the last boom real estate cycle.

Great architecture can stand the test of time. It can grow better with age, and it can help you establish your center or business as the place to go with shoppers. That was the case with Casa Paloma. Yes, we have a good tenant mix, but architecturally, the center is a winner. Not only does it look up to date in terms of style and color, but there are no flat storefronts. The center itself moves in, it moves out, and each store is separate and distinct architecturally. It is not a long box with window fronts. Why? Because in the science of shopping, when the eyes get tired, the eyes leave. We have to keep things interesting. And the more interesting the storefronts are, the more shoppers lose track of how far they have walked. If I can get a shopper to walk into one more store, they will buy something. Malls employ this psychology, so why shouldn't retail centers?

TIP Architecture to a shopping center developer is like store design to a retailer. Keep it interesting because when the eyes get tired, the eyes leave.

And speaking of malls, Casa Paloma was able to lock in concrete consumer shopping patterns before the big regional mall opened up, three years later, about eight miles away. Today, that mall has not impacted our business because we serve shoppers' needs in terms of offerings, and we are more convenient,.

So whether you are considering investing in a shopping center, looking to develop a new one, or lease a space for your business, find a center that fits the bill when it comes to this very important second ingredient: great real estate. You will make your life exponentially easier if you do.

INGREDIENT NO. 3: GREAT ATTENTION TO DETAIL

The business of real estate is a detail business. From the very beginning of a real estate deal to the very end of it and beyond into management and eventual sale, the best real estate is planned and managed to the very last detail all along the way. So what does that involve? Well, aside from a long to-do list, for me attention to detail is all about time management.

Yes, it is the ability to effectively manage your time, which will allow you the luxury to pay attention to the details, and there are lots of them. For example, if there are five thousand retailers out there, I can spend ten years meeting them all, or I can spend three. I choose to be efficient with my time and do it in three. That means I need to have more appointments, more meetings than others, and not waste any time.

Do you know why Napoleon won so many battles? Because, as historians recount, he "saw the value of one minute." For Napoleon it was all about operating more efficiently than his enemy operated, and he squeezed productivity out of every minute. If you can adopt this mind-set, then you will have time for the details. If you don't, you won't. Not because there aren't enough hours in a day, days in a week, and weeks in a year, but because in real estate, you are in a race against the clock with just about everything you do. Whether you're deep into your sixty-day due diligence period and must meet your contractual obligations, or you are completing construction on a center and are neck-and-neck with a competitor down the road, or whether you are working to get your spaces leased, the race is against the clock.

At De Rito Partners, we have a Monday morning development meeting that lasts three hours. You may say that doesn't sound like an efficient meeting, but allow me to elaborate. In that meeting we go over each and every development project we have underway, and we clearly define exactly what we must accomplish that week and who is responsible for doing it. There is no question about our path, and there is no hiding under a rock. Everyone steps up, and everyone is held accountable. But at the same time, everyone is allowed to do their jobs. It's a simple process, and it works.

I believe one of the reasons why the details are so important is that in real estate development—again, whether you are developing something from the ground up, buying an existing property, or searching for the right leasing opportunity—you must be thinking ten years out. You have to look at who the shopper is, what retailers that shopper will want now, and what they will want ten years from now. You have to understand the real estate cycle trends and be able to predict where they will go in the next five years and in the next ten years (see Craig Coppola's chapter in this book). Then you must have the guts to leap early enough to get the jump on your competition, solid plan in hand.

THE LIST

A book I read many years ago had a long list of everything a developer had to do when developing and managing any kind of real estate project. We have adopted it as our detail list. Of course, within each of the items on this list are sizeable lists of actions as well. But this will give you the start you need to understand the definition of the word *details*. We don't miss a single one of these as we plan and execute a retail center project. We talk about them at our Monday meetings, and we feel a tremendous sense of accomplishment when we can cross completed items off the list. I see the world in terms of goals, objectives, and accomplishments, and this list is the cornerstone of what we do. Here it is from A to almost Z.

The List

Consider this your to-do list for developing and managing a retail real estate project.

A. Establish your development criteria and objectives

B. Analyze and identify your market

C. Develop and prepare preliminary site plans, concept design, and strategies

D. Oversee the entitlement process, and prepare the legal documents required by your city or town

E. Establish a construction team, a construction manager, and consultants

F. Perform your preliminary feasibility studies and financial pro formas

G. Negotiate any joint venture agreements, development agreements, and construction loans

H. Set up your legal documents such as leases, utility contracts, easements, CC&Rs, etc.

I. Create and maintain your project schedules

J. Develop your construction and operating budgets

K. Negotiate construction contracts and manage the bidding

L. Hire your brokers and manage your marketing/leasing programs

M. Negotiate your consultant contracts

N. Manage your development team regularly

O. Organize and hold on-site construction meetings regularly

P. Manage project accounts payable and watch costs

Q. Approve all invoices and submit for payment through loan draws

R. Review your change orders and lien waivers

S. Develop your monthly joint venture reports complete with financials, marketing, and budgets

T. Establish your property management plan, and management guidelines/procedures if self-managing

U. Manage tenant turnover, punchlists, and occupancy

V. Select a mortgage company, and negotiate the terms and conditions of the first loan

W. Work with the utility companies and the city or town to secure a certificate of occupancy

X. Negotiate and manage any sale of the property to a new owner

Y. Be persistent, honest, positive, and work hard

THE RESULT

When you pay attention to detail, the result is a center that works. It's a center that feels good to be at and is an enjoyable experience from the moment shoppers drive in, to the moment they leave. Perhaps you have a center or two like that in your community. You know the ones that I'm talking about. They are the ones that are easy to get into. There is no driving five hundred yards past the entrance, making a U-turn to double back, and pulling in. Access is truly easy. Convenience is a given from the first turn of the wheel.

Another telltale sign that a developer paid attention to detail is good parking. I can drive into a center and within a moment know whether the developer got it right. Are there enough spaces so that shoppers aren't searching and searching, wasting time, and causing aggravation? Or is there too much parking, causing a center to lose its intimacy and for shoppers, particularly female shoppers, to feel insecure at night? These things matter. You can do everything else right, but botch the parking and you can be in trouble. I could cite pages of other signs.

Ultimately, the magic all comes from bringing everything together—design, architecture, shopper needs, tenant mix, convenience, feel, legal aspects, construction, parking, the list goes on and on—and ending up with something that is uniquely suited for the market and the moment. From there, magic becomes lasting by having the foresight and the plan to grow the center into maturity.

I love the complexities of retail real estate, and I love the challenge. This business taps into every aspect of who you are and every talent you have or think you have. It confronts your weaknesses head on and forces you to find solutions and resources to overcome them. It puts you in front of and beside some of the most amazing people in the world who possess talent and perseverance beyond compare. And in the end all the hard work produces a product that satisfies people's needs but, more important, provides the escape and enjoyment that makes life all it can be. For me, retail centers are more than just bricks and mortar; they can be and often are magic—a magic that requires hard work, integrity, dedication, and a healthy dose of life-long passion.

WAYS TO LEARN MORE

www.icsc.org
www.uli.org
www.ccim.com
Zeckendorf: An Autobiography of William Zeckendorf, by William Zeckendorf
Threshold Resistance: The Extraordinary Career of a Luxury Retailing Pioneer, by A. Alfred Taubman
Trump: The Art of the Deal, by Donald J. Trump
Trammell Crow, Master Builder: The Story of America's Largest Real Estate Empire, by Robert Sobel
Crossing the Road to Entrepreneurship, by Bert L. Wolstein
Sharing The Wealth: My Story, by Alex Spanos
Maverick Real Estate Investing: The Art of Buying and Selling Properties Like Trump, Zell, Simon, and the World's Greatest Land Owners, by Steve Bergsman.

Marty De Rito is the CEO of De Rito Partners, Inc., and De Rito Partners Development, Inc.—brokerage, management and commercial development companies based in Phoenix, Arizona. He has more than twenty years of commercial real estate experience, specializing in the sale, leasing, and development of retail properties, including shopping centers and automotive parks. De Rito has been successful in providing top-quality aggressive leasing and management expertise combined with conservative development expertise. The development company has developed over 5.5 million square feet and acquired 1.1 million square feet of retail and automotive properties. De Rito Partners, Inc., is the largest retail brokerage company in the state of Arizona based on the number of exclusive listings. The firm has thirty retail agents and exclusively represents and provides leasing services to sixty-two retailer accounts. The company has leased more than 11 million square feet, and has listed for lease approximately two-hundred- and-thirty shopping centers totaling more than 14 million square feet.

PART 4

Lessons
Learned

20

What One Property Can Teach You

What can I say? I got lucky. Kim is beautiful on the outside, and even more beautiful on the inside. On top of that she has courage and is very smart. She learns quickly. And I know she did not marry me for my money because when we met, I did not have any money. What we had was our love and a dream of becoming a rich couple together.

In 1987, the stock market crashed. The savings and loan industry went bust, and the real estate market crashed. This is when I said to Kim, "Now is the time to invest."

She often states that, back in the 1980s, she had no idea what investing was, especially investing in real estate. On top of that, most people around us were crying the blues and complaining about the bad economy. Fear and pessimism were everywhere. In spite of that, she trusted me, and we began looking at distressed properties.

Our plan was simple. We would buy two houses a year for ten years, which meant we would have twenty homes to provide us income. She studied, did her research, and looked at house after house. Finally she bought her first property. That investment changed her life. Within eighteen months, she had achieved her ten-year goal of twenty properties. She has never looked back. She took to investing like a duck takes to water.

Today Kim is an investment partner in more than 4,000 rental units. Even as the economy crashed in 2007, her properties delivered positive cash flows while many other real estate investors were losing everything. In fact, her investment income went up as more people became renters.

She is, as the title of her book states, a rich woman. But more than money rich, she is financially smart. She is a financially independent woman who does not need me or any other man to take care of her.

That is why I am so proud of her and love her with all my heart.

—ROBERT KIYOSAKI

It is amazing the number of life lessons as well as the amount of hands-on knowledge you can learn from one single investment property. I'm not just talking about your first two or three investment properties as you're starting out; those almost always deliver a steep learning curve. I'm talking about the lessons I continue to learn after years of real estate investing. Every property teaches me something new that I didn't know before. Here is the story of one property that to this day remains one of my greatest teachers.

MIAMI, FLORIDA

In 2003 my husband, Robert, and I were in Miami, Florida, attending an investment conference. At one of the breaks during the first day, a young real estate broker, Matt, introduced himself to us, and we spent a few minutes chatting. Being the good salesman that he was, he couldn't help but tell us about a real estate property that he had some inside knowledge of. The property was not on the market, but the two owners were entertaining offers if the buyers were serious. My first response was understandably skeptical. I didn't know this guy, and I didn't know if this was just a hyped-up sales pitch. In any event, it was a good pitch, and we had a couple of hours free that afternoon, so we drove with Matt to take a look at this property. Of course, according to Matt, it was the best deal he'd seen in years!

About twenty minutes later, we pulled into an attractive strip mall with a few shops and restaurants. The mall was less than two years old, and some buildings were still under construction. At one end of the mall was a large health and fitness club. The building was about thirty-eight-thousand square feet with parking spaces allocated for the club. The property for sale was the building occupied by the one tenant (known as a single-tenant property): the fitness club. This particular piece of property was a triple-net lease investment. This means that the tenant—the fitness club—pays the property taxes, insurance, and all repairs and maintenance. There is very little management on the owner's end. It is a very appealing type of investment, given the right terms. We wanted to know more.

The First, of Many, Lessons

One of the first things that struck me on this visit was the potential risk. Since there is only one tenant, this means that all of our income on the property would be dependent on this one tenant. Therefore, the ultimate key to the success of a triple net, single-tenant investment property is, very simply, the quality of the tenant. Our income, our cash flow, and the value of our property would all depend upon the tenant's ability to pay us every month until the end of the lease. You can see the implications here. With any single-tenant building, you want to make sure that the tenant is financially strong and has a solid business foundation. In other words, Microsoft is a quality tenant, Martha's typewriter repair shop probably is not. The reason why you want an A-list tenant is that if the tenant leaves, so does all your income, and then you're left with an empty building that was designed for the tenant who is no longer there.

TIP One way to protect yourself from your only tenant vacating your property is to set up a reserve account. This is an account that you add to every month from the cash flow of your property. To sleep well at night, I'd recommend at least one year of reserves that allows you to pay the mortgage and any expenses associated with the property, while you look for your next better-quality tenant.

The Good and the Bad

With any single-tenant property there is the risk of the tenant moving out early and leaving the property vacant with no income. However, associated with that risk we discovered another risk that was unique to this property. The mall where the fitness club was located was adjacent to a gated neighborhood community. Ordinarily, that might be a good thing, but in this case, an agreement between the owners of the fitness club building and these neighbors was in force. The agreement stated that any changes to the building must get approval from the neighbors. What would this mean for us? It meant that if the fitness club tenant moved out, then the neighbors would control what we were allowed to do with the property. They would control who and what could move in there. The neighbors, not the owner of the property, were in charge. This was a stumbling block. Of course, Matt, the broker, didn't see this as much of a problem. Robert and I did, though. If we were to move forward, we would want this agreement closely reviewed.

On the plus side, this property was in a prime location. It was just around the corner from a prestigious country club, and it was on a high-traffic main street. The property was newly built, and the financials, at first glance, made sense. Based on the numbers shown to us, we would receive a healthy cash flow of about 18 percent.

TIP Lesson Learned: The financials given to you by most brokers are *projected* numbers not *actual* numbers. Projected numbers are typically the best-case scenario, and they present a better picture than how the property is *actually* performing.

Matt drove us around so we could get a feel for the area. There was quite a bit of new construction going on, and the number of people moving into the area was on an upswing. All good signs. We gathered up all the information he had and flew home to Phoenix. On the plane trip home, Robert and I discussed the pros and the cons of the property, at least what we knew of it in the brief time we had. By the time the plane touched down in Phoenix, we had decided we would make an offer on the Miami property and pursue it further.

The next day, I phoned Matt and put in our offer. We went back and forth with the owners and fairly quickly came to an agreed-upon price. Now the work began, otherwise known as the due diligence period. This is when you perform a very thorough check of the property to make sure that what you think you're getting is what you're actually getting. And this is when my problems began.

FROM THE BEGINNING

From the outset, this property had challenges. First of all, I live in Phoenix, Arizona. The property is located in Miami, Florida. Phoenix is nearly two thousand miles from Miami—quite a distance. There was no way I could just drive down the street to check on the property. If a problem arose, I'd have to get on a plane, spend all day flying, rent a car, stay overnight in a hotel, and then spend another day flying home—a lengthy and costly affair.

Second, this was the first triple-net commercial property I had ever pursued. Most of the properties I owned were apartment buildings with many tenants. This was a whole new animal in a whole new area. I immediately started telling myself how much I *didn't* know about this type of deal. And my feet were already cool from the start. I heard these words repeated in my head, "What if I lose money? What if I make a mistake? Do I know what I'm getting into?" My self-doubt was strong and loud. Then someone suggested, "You should hire an attorney to review the agreement." "Aha!" I thought. "That will solve my problems." So I got a referral for an attorney in Tucson, Arizona, and I hired him.

That decision led to my next problem, which I didn't understand was a problem until later. The lawyer I had hired was not a real estate attorney; he was a business attorney. He understood contracts but didn't understand a real estate investment. There is a big difference.

So the due diligence continued on. Now my attorney was talking to their attorney. And neither attorney thought the other knew what he was talking about. They didn't like each other. They did not respect each other. Whatever my attorney suggested, their attorney rejected, simply because it was my attorney's idea. And whatever their attorney recommended, my attorney said no to for the same reason. We were getting nowhere quickly, and the fees were mounting.

My attorney, being from Arizona, began arguing on issues that were not relevant to this Florida property. It was as if they were bickering over what remedies we'd have in place if a blizzard hit Honolulu—highly unlikely. Our attorney wanted guarantees on absolutely every single thing that could possibly go wrong.

TIP Lesson Learned: Out of this ordeal came a real estate (and business) rule that I now follow closely: Do not allow an attorney to negotiate your deal for you. An attorney's job is to point out potential problems, and options to those problems, and then it's up to you to decide what to do. It's up to you to negotiate the deal.

ON A PLANE

My attorney lesson was a major one. This back-and-forth dogfight went on for three months, and we did not even have an agreement yet! All we had was an agreed-upon purchase price. That was all. My attorney would call me every day with a new wrinkle in the deal. Finally, after weeks and weeks of this, Robert and I decided we needed to get on a plane and go meet face-to-face with the owners to work out the final four or five issues that were still unresolved.

We flew to Miami, rented a car, drove to the property, and sat down with the owners to discuss the final points. Within thirty minutes, all issues were resolved and agreed to. It was that fast when we met buyer-to-seller (another lesson learned). The seller went back to his attorney to draw up the final contract. Robert and I flew home. I called my attorney and explained what we agreed to and that a new agreement was on the way.

The new agreement arrived, and every point we and the seller had agreed to in our conversation was different than we had discussed. Had the seller or the seller's attorney revised the deal points? I didn't know. The two attorneys went head-to-head once more. This whole process was not just frustrating, it was exhausting.

The PHONE CALL

We had been working on this deal for three months, and there was still no agreement. Just when we thought we had the final issue resolved, a new one would appear. We'd take one step forward and then two steps backward. Would we ever close this deal?

Then my answer came.

It was 10 p.m. on a Thursday, and Robert was out of town. The phone rang. It was Matt, the broker. "The deal is off the table," he said.

"What?" I responded. "What do you mean it's off the table?"

Matt went on, "The owner decided it's just been too difficult, and he's pulling the property off the market. He's going to hold on to it for now."

I was stunned. "But we've been working on this for months! How can he just walk away?"

"He just did." Matt said. "I'll stay in touch since I'm sure there's another good deal out there. Bye."

I hung up the phone, and I sat in silence for what seemed an hour. It was probably five minutes. "I know how I can save this deal," I said to myself. "I'll call the owner and talk to him directly." Not paying attention to the time difference I phoned the property owner; and thank goodness he was a late-night guy because he answered the phone. He graciously spoke with me about his decision for about fifteen minutes, but it became clear that I was not going to change his mind. We said our good-byes, wished each other well, and hung up the phone.

WHAT THE HELL HAPPENED?

Again, I was stunned, and now I could feel the anger building inside of me. I thought to myself, "I have spent months on this one deal. I've ignored every other deal that's come to me. What a waste of time! Flying back and forth, all the phone calls, all the arguments, all the time! And to end up with nothing!"

Then, still fuming, I started to ask myself some questions: "Why did I hire a Tucson attorney for a Florida property? Why didn't I call Dan and Steven, my two friends who understand this kind of deal? Why did I act as if I know nothing about real estate? I know how to put a real estate deal together. Why did I let it drag out for so long? Why didn't I just talk to the owner, instead of going through attorneys?"

"What was I so afraid of?"

My anger was now near explosion. At first, my anger was directed at the owner for pulling out of the deal. I was furious with my attorney. I was furious with their attorney. I was mad at Matt for not holding the deal together. But then the truth hit me. My real anger wasn't at any of them. My anger was with myself. The truth was, the owner, the attorneys, and the broker didn't cause this deal to fall apart, I let this deal fall apart. Why? Because I was afraid I would screw up. I was afraid I would make a huge mistake and I'd lose our money. This was the biggest deal I had done up to this point. We were going to put $1.5 million cash into this deal. "What if I lost it?" I kept asking myself.

The bottom line is that I didn't trust myself. I didn't trust what I knew to get this deal done. After fifteen years of doing real estate deals I *still* didn't trust myself. And that's what really set me off because I *did* know what to do. At that moment, I knew exactly what I should have done to get this deal closed, and I didn't do it. Why? Because I let fear take over. I let my own fear beat me. I stepped up to the line, and I quit. At that exact moment I knew that I quit, and I was furious with myself.

NOW WHAT?

By now it was about one in the morning. I don't even know if I was talking silently to myself or if I was yelling out loud. I was nearly psychotic by this time. I don't even know how I got from the living room of my house to my home office in a separate building, but there I was standing in my office. I glanced at my desk, and on the corner was a stack of real estate investment offerings. I began to calm down. One of the things that upset me so much was the amount of time I spent on this deal only to wind up with nothing, when there were probably several other investments I could have been pursuing. I picked up the pile of pro formas, each with a description and some financial information on a property, and I started to look through them. Most of the properties were apartment buildings since that is primarily what I invest in, and the brokers I dealt with knew what I was looking for.

Then I came across an offer that made me smile. Craig Coppola, a commercial real estate broker in Phoenix who has since become a very good friend and contributor to this book, had presented this particular property to me when he heard about the Miami property I was looking at. But I was too engrossed with that time-consuming deal to pay attention to what he was showing me. At the time, I figured he was just looking to make a commission. Now that my mind had cleared enough to see what was in front of me, I recalled some of his conversation: "You should take a look at this property. Better deal. In Phoenix." I spent the next hour with my calculator, reviewing this offering and writing down questions. I went to sleep that night with one all-important question on my mind, the answer to which had to be "yes."

THE MORNING AFTER

I knew that Craig was an early riser. He's very driven and is always one of the top commercial brokers in Arizona. At 7 a.m. I called his cell phone. "Hello, this is Craig." he answered.

"Hi Craig. It's Kim Kiyosaki," I replied.

"Hey Kim. What can I do for you?" he asked.

Then I asked the all-important question, "Craig, remember that property you talked with me about when I was looking to buy the Miami property?"

"Yes. I remember you weren't too interested," he reminded me.

I held my breath and asked, "Is it still available?"

Craig responded, "That was months ago. They never actively listed it. They only wanted to talk to truly serious buyers. Are you interested in it?"

"I am," is all I said.

"Seriously interested?" he asked.

"Very seriously," I replied.

"Let me call them and see what the status is. I'll call you back as soon as I talk with them," he replied.

"Thanks, Craig. The sooner, the better," I said anxiously.

The next thirty minutes seemed like forever. I had my cell phone by my side every second, glancing at it every few minutes. Finally, my phone rang, and I saw it was Craig. "Hi, Craig. Did you get ahold of them?" I impatiently asked.

"I did," he said.

"And?" I asked holding my breath.

"It's still available. It's not on the market, but they will consider a serious offer."

I took a deep breath, more of a heavy sigh of relief. "Are you still there, Kim?" Craig asked.

"I'm here," I answered. "How much are they asking?"

"Their price is $7.2 million," he replied.

"What's it worth?" I asked.

Craig laughed. "Honestly, I think it's worth at *least* $7.2 million. I still love this deal."

I was elated.

"Craig, tell them I'll give them full price, $7.2 million."

Craig asked, "Do you want any special terms such as subject to you obtaining financing or specific terms of the due diligence period?"

I replied with confidence, "No. Full price. We have our due diligence period, and if all is as they say it is, we'll close in sixty days."

Craig questioned, "That's it?"

"That's it," I said.

It's a New Deal

Craig called me back less than an hour later. "It's done," he said. "Now it's time to get to work. I have to ask you, though, when I first showed you this deal you wanted nothing to do with it. Why are you so confident about this property now? What changed?"

I explained, "Craig, for the past three months I have been pursuing this health club building in Miami. I know more than I ever wanted to know about this type of property. I've learned about the business itself, about what's important to obtain financing, as well as what's an issue and what's not an issue related to a health club property. So even though the Miami deal fell apart, I realized I was simply paying my dues—and getting an education."

I laughed and continued, "Craig, the beauty of this Phoenix property is that it is a health club, almost identical to the Florida property. The purchase price is less, and the amount of down payment is less than the Miami deal. Plus the cash flow is greater in percentage and in actual dollars. But the most ironic thing of all is that instead of being located in Miami, this property is four blocks from my house! I think I know this area pretty well."

Sometimes your best opportunities are, literally, right around the corner.

THE CLOSING

We spent the next two months going through our due diligence, putting together the financing, and drawing up the agreement. In sixty days, the deal was closed without a lot of effort. Today that Phoenix property is one of the best-performing properties I own. Had I not gone through the process—the drama, the headaches, and the learning—of the Miami property, I would have never noticed this Phoenix property, and I would not be enjoying the beautiful cash flow this property delivers.

The biggest win for me out of this entire process was learning that the reason I lost the Miami property was because of my own fear. It was my own fear that caused most of the stumbling blocks to getting this deal done. I could blame everyone else, but in reality it was my own fear that was to blame: fear of making mistakes, fear of losing money, fear of looking stupid, all of it. When I dug a little deeper, I came to the conclusion that, yes, I probably will make mistakes, and I may lose money, and maybe I'll look like an idiot if things go sideways. But the fact is, I know how to do a real estate deal, and if I do my homework, do my due diligence, get good terms and financing, and dot the i's and cross the t's, then my chance of success is pretty good.

My greatest win from the Miami deal is that it took away most, if not all, of my fear and self-doubt regarding real estate investing. Emotions would now take a back seat to the facts, the figures, and the future potential of a project. This also frees up my creativity which is often needed to make a real estate deal work. Miami reminded me of what I *do* know and that I will always learn more.

THE PROPERTY THAT KEEPS ON TEACHING

Today, the learning hasn't slowed. Here are a few more behind-the-scenes stories and the valuable lessons I've learned.

Money? What Money?

Have you ever said to yourself, "That (*fill in the blank*) is too expensive. I can't afford it." And you walk away somewhat relieved that you don't have to put yourself in the uncomfortable position of buying something that will stretch your limits. I understand. I've done the same thing many times. The problem is, when it comes to real estate, if you automatically say, "I can't afford it," you take yourself right out of the deal . . . and it may be an exceptionally good deal you're walking away from.

One of many things I've learned from Robert's Rich Dad is that instead of saying "I can't afford it," ask yourself "How can I afford it?" By asking yourself that question, it forces your mind to think. And it's amazing the number of solutions you will come up with. So that's what I do with almost every real estate I pursue.

There was a time when I was just beginning in the world of real estate investing when I simply did not have the money because Robert and I were building our business, and we were broke. We barely had enough money to pay the bills—actually we didn't even have that much. So if we were going to purchase rental properties we *had* to get creative, we had to come up with inventive ways to finance our down payments.

Today, when I come across a good real estate deal, Robert and I rarely have the money we need—not because we're broke but because our money is always invested. It would be easy to say "I don't have the money" and pass on the property, but it's more challenging and makes me smarter if I have to figure out how to come up with the money that I need.

That was exactly the case with the health and fitness club property. I pursued the property first. Once I decided that I intended to purchase the property, only *then* did I begin to figure out how we were going to come up with the down payment. On the Phoenix property, the time frame was short from the time I said, "I'll take it!" to the day we actually closed. I had only about two weeks to create the cash funding needed.

Fitness clubs, in general, at the time were not considered grade-A tenants simply because of the number of clubs that had gone out of business throughout the years. The industry as a whole had a lower ranking when seen through the eyes of a lender because they were viewed as a higher-risk tenant. Because of this, the lender required an even greater down payment than an apartment building lender might require. So not only did I not have the money for the typical down payment, but also I had to come up with an additional 10 percent to get this deal done.

TIP Lesson Learned: When it comes to a single-tenant commercial property, not only is the buyer concerned about the quality of the tenant, but the lender is even more cautious.

The deal did get done. The down payment was a combination of cash we had on hand, a loan from our business, and a third-party private loan. The loans were just that, loans paying interest. No equity in the property was given up for these loans. The icing on the cake is that the rent on this property has increased annually as per the agreement, so every year the cash flow increases, the cash-on-cash return on our investment increases, and, as a result, the overall value of the property has greatly increased. It is an outstanding performing property.

Yet, when all the papers were signed, the cash changed hands, and we took ownership of this property, I made one more unbelievable mistake.

The *Really* Big Mistake

As we were leaving the law office where the closing took place, Craig, the broker, reminded me of something I had forgotten. He said, "Just to let you know, I told you several weeks ago that the seller of this property you just bought owns the exact same property in a location up north. It's still on the market if you want to make an offer." After all I went through in the past few months, and then scrambling to find the funding for this property, I was just so relieved to get the deal closed that I laughed at him and without thinking said, "Not right now, Craig. I'm tapped out. *I can't afford it.*" And that was a very big and costly mistake.

Instead of taking a step back and looking at the opportunity in front of me, I fell into the "I can't afford it" trap and let a fantastic opportunity slip through my fingers. Had I taken the time and asked myself, "How can I afford it?" and put my mind to work, today instead of *one* great-performing health club property I could have *two* great-performing properties. It was a costly, but priceless, lesson.

Your Property Is Only as Valuable as the Quality of Your Tenants... in Writing

Seek out real experts, because the money is often found in the details.

Attorneys are often the butt of many jokes... and I'm sure you've heard some of them:

> *How can you tell when a lawyer is lying? His lips are moving.*
>
> *What's the difference between a dead dog in the road and a dead lawyer in the road? There are skid marks in front of the dog.*
>
> *Why don't sharks attack attorneys? Professional courtesy.*

But there are also attorneys who are worth their weight in gold. As your real estate deals get larger, you'll want to have a great attorney on your team. The two attorneys who were working the Miami deal did nothing to endear me to lawyers. Yet, out of every bad deal comes something good. In this case, his name was Chuck.

First, I learned my lesson, and through referrals from a few successful real estate professionals, Robert and I met Chuck, whose expertise was real estate contracts. And he was in Phoenix, not Tucson or Miami.

Chuck taught me a priceless lesson. As he was making some necessary revisions to the purchase agreement with the seller and the lease agreement with the fitness club, he red-flagged one crucial item that I was not aware of. Chuck asked me, "This being a single-tenant property in a 44,000 square foot building, sitting on 5.2 acres, what's your biggest concern?"

"Simple," I responded. "My biggest concern is that tenant might move out before the lease is up—and I'm left sitting with an empty building that I'm still making loan payments on."

"Exactly," he replied. "So who would be a better tenant...a large national well-established chain or an Arizona company with one fitness club—yours?"

"The large national chain," I answered.

"Why?" he asked.

I thought for a moment and said, "Because the likelihood of a successful national company making its rent payments is greater than the small, one-club local company. It's easier for the smaller business to default."

"Yes, and let's take it one step further." Chuck explained. "If your lease is with a small Arizona company and they wanted to break their lease, they could simply declare bankruptcy and walk away. For a national chain to walk away from this lease, they would have to declare bankruptcy of their entire national chain. They cannot say that these five clubs are bankrupt, but these three are not. They would have to walk away from *all* their properties. You want the national chain as the lessee for your protection against something like this."

"That makes perfect sense. But the lease *is* with the national chain," I said.

Chuck just smiled, "Look again."

When I relooked at the agreement the lessee had a name similar to that of the national chain but, at closer look, it was actually an Arizona entity. The lease was with a subsidiary of the national chain, not the national company itself.

I was stunned. "Oh my gosh! That could have been a huge mistake!"

"That's why you bring me in. This is what I do."

Chuck went on to untangle the original lease agreement to include the national chain as the tenant of our property, and to get all parties to agree. Not an easy task, but a critically important one...and in the short time allotted.

That is the value and priceless benefit of having expert legal advice. That one item alone helped to increase the value of this property. Again, seek out real experts, because the money is often found in the details.

TIP Lesson Learned: When legal advice is needed on a real estate transaction, seek out a well-qualified expert. And don't be afraid to pay well for it. Cheap advice is usually just that: cheap. And in my experience, whenever I go cheap it ends up costing me more in the long run.

THE DEAL MUST MAKE SENSE

There is a small strip mall adjacent to our property. It sits on an extremely desirable corner in Phoenix. It's about two acres with five tenants, primarily restaurants. We knew from day one that we would be the natural buyer for this property if it ever came up for sale.

There is also a second commercial property adjacent to our property that we would be interested in purchasing as well. Knowing this was our long-term plan from the start, we offered Craig a small equity position in our property in exchange for managing any problem or issues that might arise and, more importantly, for keeping us abreast of what's happening with these two adjoining properties.

One key point I've learned is that when you find great real estate advisors, brokers and partners, be more generous, not less. Relationships, not transactions, are the key to any successful business or project. Too many people focus only on the transaction—making the most money, paying the least in commissions, or reneging on agreements in order to put more money in their pockets. They wonder why they don't get the best deals or why people don't want to work with them. Our real estate partners and associates are people we trust and who we want to see succeed...and vice versa. We are in the relationship for the long-term, not just a transaction.

Through Craig, we got to know the owner, James, and told him of our interest in purchasing the property if he ever wanted to sell. His father bought the property years ago and had since passed. The property is owned free and clear and the healthy cash flow it generates is split between James and his two sisters.

In 2014, James decided it was time to sell. He was tired of managing the property.

We met several times to discuss the terms of the purchase. James, of course, wanted quite a bit more than we felt the property was worth. Learning from my past mistakes, I took this deal to two different and highly successful commercial investors and operators for two reasons. One, I wanted to see how they would approach this deal; and two, I wanted to know if my analysis of this property had merit. Both parties I showed this deal to said the same thing:

> 1) James' price was highly overvalued. At that price we would lose money every month.
>
> 2) James just signed new 10-year leases with every tenant. Which means we either had to sit on the property and do nothing for ten years or buyout the tenants from their leases, which could be very expensive.
>
> 3) Although the tenants all had a very good reputation in Phoenix they were not A+ tenants. They were small business owners and could easily walk away from their leases.
>
> 4) Bottom line: the two investors valued the property 40% below what James was asking.

My analysis matched theirs precisely, except for one thing: I valued the property at 30% less than James' price. There may have been just a *hint* of emotion creeping into my price.

Here was my lesson. I had been patiently tracking this property for years. We were the perfect buyers for this property, since our property bordered two of the four sides of the strip center. It would give us over seven acres on one of the best corners in Phoenix. I wanted this property. *But*, as much as I wanted it, the numbers still had to make sense...and they did not. I didn't *need* the property, but I *wanted* it. And, sometimes, if the numbers don't work, you just have to walk away.

By the way, the property did sell. At the same time we were doing our analysis, we were unaware that James was talking to another potential buyer—a Goliath with money they needed to place. The result? Goliath paid 40% *over* James' asking price! I trust they have a better plan than we did. Otherwise, we may have another shot at this property down the road.

HIGH NEED, LOW POWER

Today, as I write, we have more new developments. This is definitely the property that keeps on giving.

Our tenant, who has 11 locations in Arizona, was recently acquired by the largest fitness chain in the United States. The first thing the new company announced when they took over was that they would be closing several of the existing fitness clubs. We knew our site was a great performer with a great location, so we were not too concerned, however you never know what a company is planning. The list of clubs slated for closure was announced and we were happy that our property was not on it.

However, even if it were, we already had many options in play. We all know the saying, "Don't put all your eggs in one basket." I would add. "And don't bet all your cash flow on one strategy." We have a series of contingency plans for the various scenarios that could play out.

So, for now, the future plan of our property is a bit unclear. Will the new club owner pull out at the end of their lease, three years from now? Will they want to renew? If they don't want to renew, is there another club that will want to lease this location? Or do we find a buyer for this property and sell?

Right now I feel like I'm in the middle of our board game, *CASHFLOW*. Do we negotiate a new lease with the new company or another fitness company and continue to receive cash flow or do we sell to any one of a number of potential buyers who have already stepped forward without any prompting from us? Is it cash flow or cash out?

And if we cash out, what new asset do we move our money into?

One lesson I learned early on from Robert's rich dad was that in a negotiation if you are in *high need*, meaning you must make this deal because your other options suck, then you've put yourself in a negotiating position of *low power*. High need = Low power.

When going into a negotiation, you want to be in a position of *low need*, which equates with *high power*. In other words, you want them to need you more than you need them. Currently, as we look at our choices to cash flow or cash out, we have numerous options. Being the queen of cash flow, I love the idea of keeping this property leased with a great tenant. Which is one option. We could lease this property to the new fitness company or to another fitness club—several of which we've already identified. And if that does not come to fruition, we can find a different category of tenant. Again: a list is in place. Or we can sell the property since it is in a super-prime location with a variety of possible uses. Buyers are already knocking on our door. Or we could even develop the property ourselves. Given that we have all these options, plus a few more, it puts us in low need of having to land any one deal. This puts us in high power as we negotiate through our various options.

We will see where this glorious property—the property that keeps on giving... and keeps on teaching—takes us next.

IN SUMMARY

When it comes to successful real estate investing, the learning never stops. Oftentimes, the key with real estate is not so much what's happening today but what you see coming in the future. This is where studying and understanding the market and the trends can give you the upper hand. Otherwise your real estate investment could become one big fat liability, instead of the asset you had intended.

Look at what happened to so many investors in the subprime 2007 and 2008 real estate fiasco. They weren't paying attention to the signs and it ended up costing them dearly. Why? As the market was surging and prices were soaring, many people jumped on the "prices will keep going up... forever!" bandwagon. As we all saw was this: What goes up must eventually come down. And come down hard it did.

I'll never forget the conversation I had with Ken McElroy, our investment partner and Rich Dad Advisor on real estate.

It was toward the end of 2005 and Ken called me. "Kim, get ready for the market to turn. Housing prices are about to come down."

"Why do you say that? What's happening?" I asked.

"Because," he said, "things are just not making sense."

He continued, "You know something is screwy when a husband and wife walk into our leasing office and fill out an application to *rent* an apartment. We run their credit report and we end up turning them down because their income is too low to qualify for the $650 rent they'd have to pay. But then they walk across the street to a condominium complex, and with the same income figures they miraculously qualify to *buy* a condo with payments twice as high as our rent! This can't go on for long. The market is about to turn, big time."

So Ken, Robert and I were already preparing for this mortgage crisis two years before it occurred, because of a trend Ken saw occurring with our own properties.

When the real estate market changes, it forces us to get smarter and more creative in order to use those market shifts to our advantage. Every property is a teacher to me in some way. If I learn my lessons well, I get a high grade. If I don't, it's a low grade. And my grade is determined by my primary reason for becoming a real estate investor: *cash flow*—my two favorite words in the world of investing.

Kim Kiyosaki began her real estate investing career in 1989 with the purchase of a small, two-bedroom, one-bath rental property in Portland, Oregon. Today Kim's real estate holdings include over 4,000 apartment units, commercial properties, golf courses, a resort, and land, and she continues adding to her property portfolio. With a passion for educating women about money and investing, Kim draws on a lifetime of experience in business, real estate, and investing in her mission to support financial education. She is a sought-after speaker, radio show co-host, television and radio talk show guest, and the host of a PBS *Rich Woman* show. She is a self-made millionaire and a happily married (but fiercely independent) woman. Her first book, *Rich Woman: A Book on Investing for Women*, hit the *BusinessWeek* best-seller list the month it was released and has held a spot there for the past eleven months. *Rich Woman* is a best seller in Mexico, South Africa, India, Australia, New Zealand, and across Europe. She is also the author of the book *It's Rising Time!* Kim has used the international forum of the Rich Dad brand to showcase the startling statistics related to women and money, and through her endeavors, she has created a global community where women can learn and grow and seek their own financial security and independence.

21

In the Beginning . . .

Much of the world has heard or seen The Apprentice, *Donald Trump's long-running television program. By writing a book together, I have had the benefit of being sort of an apprentice to Donald. Spending time writing* Why We Want You to Be Rich: Two Men One Message, *I learned a lot about him personally, his business philosophy, his real estate philosophy, and why he is as successful as he is.*

—ROBERT KIYOSAKI

MY FIRST BIG DEAL

I was still in college when I did my first big deal. I spent my spare time in college reading the listings of federally financed housing projects that were in foreclosure. I knew my colleagues might be reading the sports pages, but real estate truly was my focus even then, so I would devote my time to studying everything I could to learn about it.

One day I came across Swifton Village, which was in Cincinnati, Ohio. It was in big trouble with eight hundred, out of twelve hundred, vacant apartments. The developers had faltered. The government had foreclosed, and it wasn't looking too good. In fact, it was a mess. It was such a mess that there were no other bidders.

This did not discourage me because I saw it as a big opportunity. I presented the situation at Swifton Village to my father, and we bought it together for less than $6 million. The project had cost $12 million two years earlier. We got a mortgage for what we paid, plus about $100,000 that we used to fix up the property, which it badly needed. In translation, this means we got this project without putting down any of our own money, and it would be possible, from the rent proceeds, to cover the mortgage.

As a college student, I found this to be very exciting stuff. I knew it'd be a challenge, and it was, but my enthusiasm was there because I could so clearly see a success coming out of it. I had done enough research to know it had great potential—potential as well as immediate problems.

This complex had a reputation for having "rent runners"—tenants who would rent a trailer and in the middle of the night would pile their belongings into it and disappear. This happened on a regular basis, so I realized an immediate action would be for me to hire someone for 24/7 patrol, which I did.

The other thing that had to be addressed quickly was the state of the buildings themselves. Disrepair is one thing, dilapidation is another, and this complex had a high proportion of both conditions. We estimated it would require at least $800,000 to make an effective difference. One good thing is that we were allowed to increase the rents immediately, which we found much easier to do in Cincinnati than in New York.

The buildings were red brick, and we put white shutters on all the windows, which made a huge difference aesthetically. We fixed up the grounds. We replaced the very unattractive aluminum front doors on the apartments with white colonial doors, which, combined with the shutters, made a big difference. We didn't take shortcuts, but we made sure our improvements would be noticeable, and they were. Swifton Village had a new look, and people were impressed. We ran ads in the Cincinnati papers, and in less than a year it was completely rented.

We soon realized that we needed a permanent project manager. This was a big complex, and we'd already been through a few who hadn't worked out. I finally found a guy who has left a permanent impression on my memory. He was a con man from the inside out. He didn't try to hide that fact, and he had close to zero social skills. He was insulting, brash, and as politically incorrect as you could possibly be. But I noticed that he had the ability to get things done, to get them done quickly, and that he was effective as a property manager. The other guys I had might be more likeable or more honest, but they were not as competent when it came to their job. I had to keep my eye on this particular guy, but in the long run it was worth it to have the complex running well.

This property became a great success, and it didn't require me to be there very often. The property manager ran the place well, and there were no more rent runners. All was well until a few years later when I visited and spoke with a tenant who had become a friend. He told me that the neighborhood had changed, and that I should get out. Swifton Village was fully rented, and there were no complaints about the management, but I respected his insights enough to spend a few days in Cincinnati and check it out for myself.

I discovered that he was right. It was quickly becoming a very rough neighborhood. I decided to put Swifton Village up for sale, and it didn't take long to find a buyer. We sold it for $12 million—$6 million more than we had paid for it a few years earlier. For a first deal, it was a good one, and I learned some great lessons about human nature in the process. I also learned that foreclosures were not going to be my niche—but this first venture helped to fund my ultimate goal, which was to be a developer in Manhattan and to build my own buildings. I wasn't dabbling—my focus was intact.

Another lesson was the importance of delivering quality. I made sure the buildings were clean, safe, and well presented. We didn't have marble floors or gold fixtures, but the simple steps of making the grounds appealing, along with the addition of white shutters and attractive front doors went a long way to establishing my name with excellence. That's something to always keep in mind, whether your name is on the building or not. Learn to distinguish yourself in everything you do.

ARRIVING IN MANHATTAN

Starting out in Manhattan was definitely a challenge. One big New York real estate guy was quoted as saying, "Trump has a great line of s—t, but where are the bricks and mortar?" It wasn't exactly a warm welcome, but at least I knew what I was up against. Looking back, I think perhaps they didn't know who *they* were up against. I'm the guy who would eventually write *Never Give Up* and actually mean it. I'm still here and going stronger than ever.

That wasn't the case in the early 1970s. I was a newcomer, and the city was in debt. I even heard people talking about the city going bankrupt. It wasn't a nurturing environment for a budding developer. But my focus was so clear that I wasn't discouraged. I knew there were still opportunities even in a so-called

Quotable Quotes by Donald Trump

"Big problems can equal big opportunities."

"If you don't have major problems, you're probably not doing something major."

"Adversity is a fact of life. Accept that, and you will be prepared."

"Business is an art, whether it's real estate or anything else. Treat it that way by developing your technique, being tenacious, and remaining passionate."

"My father's four-step formula is one I've always used because it works: get in, get it done, get it done right, and get out."

"When you are confronted with a problem, ask yourself this question: Is this a blip, or is it a catastrophe? That will align your thoughts and your reactions to where they should be."

"Reaping and sowing are directly related, but you need to know which comes first."

"Resilience is part of the survival of the fittest formula—make sure you remain adaptable."

"Real estate has a way of evening itself out. There are always ups and downs, and that's a fact, not an aberration."

"Don't depend on anyone else for providing your financial security."

terrible market. In fact, it was a terrible market at that time. But my determination was such that I refused to give in to the facts and continued to work my way around them. There was no place like Manhattan—and I intended to stay.

My first real estate interests in the city were the abandoned railyards along the Hudson River, at 34th Street and 60th Street, which was about one hundred acres. I then tried to convince the city that the site for the new convention center (now known as the Jacob Javits Center) should be built where it is on West 34th Street, instead of where the city wanted to build it, all the way downtown in Battery Park. As I said in my first book in 1987, *The Art of the Deal*, "We won by wearing everyone else down. We never gave up . . ." in referring to this 1977 battle. In 1978, the city finally decided to build on West 34th Street, which was a victory for me.

However, the city and state decided they would oversee the job. My offer to manage it was rejected, and as a result they went close to $700 million over budget. A lot of money was wasted, and today we are seeing how quickly the center has deteriorated. But at the time, I focused myself on the far more exciting prospect of the 60th Street railyards that I had. I wanted to make it a residential haven that faced the Hudson River. I knew I'd face a lot of opposition there, between zoning and the adjacent community, as well as from a city that was in financial crisis. It was in 1979 that I allowed my option on the 60th Street railyards to expire—but somehow I knew I'd be involved with them again later, which has proven to be true. Trump Place now proudly stands on those former yards, and is still being completed, almost thirty years later. But that's another story.

During this time with the railyard property, I was still looking around at other opportunities in Manhattan. The old Commodore Hotel, which was situated next to Grand Central Station, was having a hard time of it. The whole area was having a hard time, in fact, and it looked like it. It had become a crummy neighborhood that everyone tried to avoid—certainly much different than it is today.

I set out to try to acquire the Commodore Hotel and change it for the better. Once again, I wasn't met with great enthusiasm. Even my father said, "Buying the Commodore at a time when even the Chrysler Building is in bankruptcy is like fighting for a seat on the Titanic." He was well aware of the risk involved.

While I was aware of the risk, I also saw it as a way to get the city back to a flourishing condition, not just limping along, which is what was happening. The neighborhood had become dilapidated, and this was a good way to get it back on track again, along with providing some jobs. There are always several ways to view a situation, and it's a good idea to have your vision intact enough to withstand opposition.

At the time that I was interested in going into negotiations for the hotel, they owed $6 million in back taxes, had recently spent $2 million in renovations (which was obviously not enough), and they wanted out. In order to purchase the hotel for $10 million, I would need a tax abatement from the City of New York, financing, and a commitment from an experienced hotel company. In addition, I would have to structure a deal with other interested parties, and that was certain to be complex. Complicated is an understatement for this situation, and it took several years of negotiating to work it all out.

One of the first things I did was to find a designer who knew what I wanted to do and had the same enthusiasm for the project. I found a young architect named Der Scutt who was a perfect fit—he understood what I wanted to do, which was to wrap the building and make it a reflecting façade for the buildings surrounding it. It might have been premature to find a designer before I knew the deal would even go through, but I'm a strong believer in following your vision and working from there. I also had a compatriot in vision who believed in my plans as vividly as I did.

I also needed to find an operator, one with a lot of experience. I realized that a lot of big hotel chains had a presence in New York, but the one that I liked the most, the Hyatt, didn't. I called to see if they were interested, and they were. We made a deal quickly and announced it to the press in May of 1975. So I had a hotel partner.

What was left was still monumental—I needed to get financing and a tax abatement from the city. I decided to hire a real estate broker who was in his sixties and had a lot of experience. I was twenty-seven at the time, and I thought having a broker on board would look good, which it did. With an architect, a hotel partner, and an experienced broker lined up, I was ready to go for it.

We hit a brick wall, and fast. Without financing, the city wasn't about to consider a tax abatement. Without a tax abatement, the banks weren't very interested in financing. It was a classic catch-22 situation. While discussing this, we decided we'd bring up the obviously hurting and decaying city and hopefully make the bankers feel guilty for looking the other way when we were obviously trying to do something constructive. Well, that didn't work. But we kept trying, and we finally found a bank that appeared to be interested.

After spending many hours of time and effort with them, one guy suddenly just changed his mind. He brought up ridiculous and unimportant issues and was obviously trying to kill the deal. We tried everything, but he was set in a negative groove and couldn't be convinced to change his mind.

It was at this point that I wanted to give up. Literally, I was worn out. It was my lawyer, George Ross, who convinced me to keep trying, and he made it clear that I'd already spent so much time on this project that I shouldn't just walk away from it. So I decided to approach the city, even without financing, to explain the situation. It was clear that the Hyatt Hotel organization was enthusiastic about coming to New York, and they'd do a great job, but the costs were just too high. We needed a break on property taxes or nothing would be done. I also pointed out how the new hotel could work as a catalyst for sparking up the whole Grand Central area into renovation and rejuvenation.

It worked. The city agreed, and it was a deal that would make us partners, and a deal that would benefit everyone. I would receive a property tax abatement for forty years, and I would buy the Commodore for $10 million, with $6 million going to the city for back taxes. Then I would sell the hotel to the city for one dollar, and they would lease it back to me for ninety-nine years. As a result, we got financing from two institutions.

None of this was easy, and when I look back I realize I had great fortitude to hang in there for so long. But it was worth it. The Hyatt at Grand Central started the revitalization of the whole area, and today it's a thriving and beautiful hub of New York City. The hotel itself reflects the architecture of the area in the four exterior walls of mirrors that replaced the formerly dingy façade of the Commodore. This project did not have my name on it, but I can tell you that every detail mattered. The quality was there, the vision was there, and the results are still there.

Ten Small Steps to Big Success

1. Find out what you love to do. Trust yourself enough to find out what is best for you, and what you're best at doing. For great success, you need great passion, but make sure it's well directed.

2. Learn everything you can about what you're doing: Be an expert.

3. Ask yourself questions. For example, ask yourself, "Is there anyone else who can do this better than I can?" It's another way of saying know yourself, and know your competition. That can simplify things quickly.

4. Know the world. See the world as an emerging market. Study it—daily. That's a requirement, not an elective.

5. Focus, and make sure it's a 100 percent focus—nothing less.

6. Know your own blind spots. Ask yourself, "What am I pretending not to see?"

7. Set the bar high—do the best you possibly can.

8. Think positively. Zap negativity immediately. Focus on the solution, not the problem.

9. Be persistent, tenacious, and alert—every single day. Get this momentum going daily and don't let up.

10. Never give up. Never, never give up—that is the best advice I can give you.

Donald Trump is the chairman and president of the Trump Organization, a privately held company in New York. The Trump Organization encompasses global real estate development and global licensing, sales and marketing, property management, a hotel collection, golf course development, product licensing and brand development. In a departure from his real estate acquisitions, he is a best-selling author and produced and starred in the hit television reality show *The Apprentice*, which had a record breaking fourteen seasons. His golf course portfolio has expanded nationally and internationally to include eighteen extraordinary championship courses, and Trump Hotels, a collection that spans the world, has met with equal acclaim worldwide.

22

What Is the Most Important Thing You've Learned from your Father About Real Estate?

DONALD TRUMP JR.

Don Trump Jr.'s father and I are the same age. The famous Donald Trump, one of the greatest celebrity real estate developers in the world, is a valued friend and mentor to me. Having Donald Trump as a coauthor and friend has been one of the greatest blessings in my life. Another blessing has been getting to know Donald's two sons, Don Jr. and Eric.

One night, Donald Trump and I were guests at the Quill Awards, an evening similar to the Academy Awards, but rather than recognizing Hollywood stars, the Quill Awards recognizes great authors. Donald Trump and I were there to present the award to the best business author.

At the awards dinner, I got to sit next to Don Trump Jr. and his gorgeous wife. For some reason, our discussion got around to the subject of big game hunting. At that dinner, I found out that Don Jr. along with his brother, Eric, is not only a hunter, but a gun collector, just like me. Now I know that guns and hunting are not politically correct subjects. So it was refreshing to find a young man, actually two, who shared the same passion in life, a subject I tend to be secretive about—even to my wife, Kim, who is an animal rights activist and person who is not particularly fond of guns. Kim, like Donald Trump, prefers the golf course to the wilds.

Over the years, I have gone hunting with Don Jr. and Eric a number of times and have gotten to know them personally. They have it all. They are rich, famous, good looking, and perfect gentlemen. They are not spoiled brats as many rich kids are. They are driven, smart, experienced, and market savvy. I learn a lot about real estate and life on every hunting trip we take together.

Their father and mother can be very proud of these two young men.

—Robert Kiyosaki

This simple statement seems so obvious, but I am always amazed by the number of people who miss out on incredible opportunities because they're too afraid to simply ask. Ultimately, these people fear rejection. They are afraid of the word "no." They are either shy, weak, or too proud to ask for something or to negotiate the things they want in life. The world of real estate is no place for people who fit this description. So here's your chance to buck up.

TIP In life and in business you never get anything you don't ask for: always negotiate!

Shrinking from the task of negotiating, by being afraid of simply asking for what they want, people from all walks of life, not just real estate, miss a fundamental opportunity to do what all great business people try to do: buy goods or service at a better price. I learned from my father at a very early age that in business you must take advantage of every easy opportunity. He didn't sit me down and explain this lesson. Rather it was one that took me two summers of very hard work to figure out.

My first job was as a dock attendant at a marina we owned as part of what was at the time Trump's Castle Casino in Atlantic City, New Jersey. I was fourteen years old and living away from home for two months tying down boats, and hooking up electrical and water systems and anything else that I could be persuaded to do for minimum wage plus tips. Everyone should work for tips at some point in their life. Nothing puts life, service, and work ethic into such clear perspective as that. Working for tips was a great lesson in and of itself.

After two summers of dock work, it was time for me to start working as a landscaper at one of our properties. The position had a lot more responsibility and required more skill. I ran tractors, I operated chainsaws, and I performed the hard labor required to keep the property looking pristine. I was making minimum wage at this job, too, but there were no tips from the drunken boaters who occasionally let a twenty slip through their hands. My salary was minimum wage and nothing more.

At first, I said nothing about the pay structure of this job. I didn't want to seem greedy, and I suppose I was too proud to ask for more money. But toward the end of summer, I finally went to my father and asked him why I had not gotten a raise when I took this more skilled position. Especially since the tip component of my salary was now nonexistent. His answer was very simple, "You did not get a raise because you did not ask for one. Why would I pay you more than you were willing to work for?" Well, that did it for me. It was a hard lesson, and one that in hindsight seems so obvious. But the bottom line was that I had let my emotions, my fears, and my pride get in the way of what I wanted to achieve.

Since then, I always make a conscious effort to never put myself in the same position again. The hard work that summer didn't bother me, but I felt like I had wasted an entire summer working a job that paid minimum wage when I could have been earning more if I had only asked for it. That lesson has stuck with me to this day.

As is often the case, the hardest lessons are the best lessons, and my summer as a minimum wage landscaper certainly drove the message home. Thankfully, I learned it before the stakes got too high. If you're going to lose income, it's always better to do it when playing with low numbers. Learn your lessons like I did, before too many zeros get into the mix.

I no longer let the fear of "no" overpower me. Instead, I make a game of negotiations. Here's how I play it, and you can do it, too. At every opportunity, I ask for, negotiate, and almost always get something above and beyond where I started. To me anytime I save a few dollars or get an extra "something" thrown in—whatever that "something" may be that I am asking for—I have created additional value. And here's a universal truth: Creating value is what business is all about!

When it comes to real estate and life in general, don't be afraid to ask. The worst that can happen is that the person you ask says, "No." And in that case, you're no worse off than you were when you started. Asking is quick, it takes two seconds, and believe it or not, good businesspeople expect it. By simply asking, you give yourself and everyone else the time and the opportunity to put themselves in a better financial position and add value. Even if you get the dreaded "no" at first, it's not so bad. Sure, you may not get exactly what you wanted, but often you can split the difference and end up somewhere in the middle with each side giving a little and getting a little. That's the power of negotiation. Even in that scenario, you end up ahead.

The reality that I learned all too well is to just keep asking and pushing. No one in his right mind will refuse to sell you something at his original price simply because you tried to buy it cheaper. The worst case scenario is that you end up exactly where you started. Eventually, you will come to realize that hearing "no" is not the worst thing in the world after all. It becomes part of the game, and hearing "no" actually makes it easier for you to ask in the future.

Eventually, you'll get bolder. You'll discover when you ask for something egregious that you think the other person can't possibly deliver, often the compromised position ends up more in your favor than you could have ever hoped for. In some cases the person may agree to your crazy question and take the bait, hook, line, and sinker. When playing the game, try not to fall out of your chair when this happens (and it will) because the last thing you want is the other person to realize is that he made a mistake. He may try to renegotiate for a better deal, leaving you snatching defeat from the jaws of victory.

The same holds true if a seller gives you a quote that you find completely thrilling. Don't accept the proposal as is. Go through the exercise of back-and-forth negotiation. Even after the back-and-forth seems to be over, ask him to do a bit better just so he feels he got the most out of you. It's how the game is played, and it will ensure the deal closes. There will be time for exuberance, but it is not when you are at the table. Practice restraint so the other person feels they got the best of you, not the other way around. Do that and you set the tone for future negotiations, and you set yourself up to win again and again and again.

Finally, the more you ask, the easier it becomes to ask in the future. Hearing "no" becomes no big deal. You'll find the habit of asking and the skill of pushing creates a positive cycle of circumstances that can create benefits for you and the projects you apply the techniques to. Try to negotiate at every opportunity, I mean every opportunity. You'll be surprised where you'll find results. I even try negotiating at retail stores. When the regular clerk who is checking me out says, "No," I ask to speak to his manager. Do this and you're almost guaranteed a 10 percent break if you push a bit. Sounds crazy? Try it and see. A 10 percent savings is 10 percent earned.

When you build up confidence in your negotiation techniques, become flexible in how you argue your points, and can adjust your style, you'll find the negotiating game becomes easier. Give it a go; you have nothing to lose and a lot to gain.

Donald Trump Jr. is an innovator and leader in today's young business world. As an executive vice president at the Trump Organization, Donald Jr. works in tandem with his siblings Ivanka and Eric to expand the company's real estate, retail, commercial, and hotel interests nationally and internationally. His extensive real estate development experience, rigorous education, and inherent business sense add a level of detail and depth to the management of all current and future Trump projects. In addition to his real estate interests, Donald Jr. is an accomplished and sought-after speaker and has been featured as an advisor on the highly acclaimed NBC show *The Apprentice*.

ERIC TRUMP

I am afraid to say my wife, Kim, is in love with Eric Trump. While she is very fond of Ivanka and Donald Trump Jr. Eric has a special place in her heart. She loves him because he is an especially kind person—just like her—and good-looking. He is the youngest of three children, just like Kim who is the youngest of three daughters. While all three Trump children have that celebrity magic, to Kim, Eric is special.

One of the most memorable times in my life was when Don Jr. and Eric invited me to hunt pheasants at their club, an hour out of New York City. At the time, I did not really know the two young men. Spending the day in the mud and the cold, slogging through knee-high water, and chasing pheasants with dogs, let me know how truly special and unique they are. I got to see them outside of the high-rise offices next to the Plaza Hotel and Central Park on Fifth Avenue.

One of the first things I noticed is both young men shoot and collect the same antique shotguns I collect. They are old shotguns—about seventy-five years old—from Belgium made by Francotte, a family of gunmakers few people have heard of.

The next thing I noticed was how kind and respectful Eric and his brother were to everyone. They were not snobbish or arrogant. They were not even phony gentlemen. They were truly kind and respectful. It did not matter if the people were members of the club or workers of the club, all people were treated with the same warmth and respect.

Later, as we drove back to New York City, we stopped by an old village inn, possibly two hundred years old, to have a meal. Again, both young men went out of their way to greet and say hello to the staff of the restaurant. While the patrons gawked and stared at the two young celebrities, Eric and his brother went behind the counter into the kitchen to say hello to the kitchen staff. I gained a new level of respect for each of them on that day. Their kindness is extraordinary.

In 2008, I invited both young men to a private island in the chain of Hawaiian Islands for a hunt. As we drove to the helicopter pad, Eric was texting his sister, Ivanka, a special family recipe. When I asked him if he knew how to cook, he and his brother chimed in saying, "Of course." When I asked them how they learned to cook, both young men explained that they saw their family service staff as servants for their mom and dad, not servants for them. Rather than become spoiled kids who expected to be waited upon by their parents' servants, they learned to cook and take care of themselves and each other. I can say that all three children truly love each other.

Today, I see all three kids as incredible role models for the next generation, just as their dad and mom were role models for my generation. It is with personal gratitude that my life's work has put me in contact with the Trump family and the people of the Trump Organization.

—ROBERT KIYOSAKI

For as long as I can remember, every morning started out the same way. I would make my way to my father's bedroom before school and kiss him goodbye. As I was leaving, he would always say, "And remember, Eric, never trust anyone." These certainly are not the words you typically hear a father say to a son who is heading off to kindergarten, and the true meaning of the words didn't quite resonate until adulthood. Today, however, as I grow our business, my father's lesson is more relevant than ever.

I first learned the meaning of my father's words from my older brother, Don, who is not only my best friend, but also a mentor to me to this day. After school, Don would always suggest that we trade the coins in our piggybanks: I would happily exchange my quarters for several of his shiny pennies, thinking that the quantity I was receiving far outweighed the actual value of my coins. One day, I walked into my father's room with my pile of pennies to show him what a great investment I had just made. Noticing how Don was conning his little brother, my father looked at me, explained the concept of value versus quantity, and exclaimed, "Eric, what did I tell you? Never trust anyone!" Suddenly, I remembered his daily admonition.

Today, as executive vice president of Development and Acquisitions for the Trump Organization, I encounter situations on a daily basis that make me reflect on my father's words and advice. I've realized that self-reliance is a businessperson's most essential tool. Take one particular instance. I was negotiating a mutual partnership to bring an ultra-exclusive restaurateur into one of our projects. After months of tedious negotiations, the night before we intended to sign the deal, I learned, through a slip-up made by one of the restaurateur's architects, that they had been instructed to build a restaurant far exceeding all our agreed-upon budgets.

Shocked by the dishonesty and fraudulent intentions exhibited by my would-be partner, I immediately cut off all negotiations and ended the deal. I am a firm believer that everything happens for a reason, and despite being upset over months of wasted efforts, today I have a smile on my face knowing we made the right decision, went with a different restaurateur, and now own the most successful restaurant in the city.

In a similar instance, my father knew a successful businessman who pledged to donate $40 million, to be paid in four equal installments, to his alma mater. After paying the first two installments, the businessman ran into severe financial difficulties and asked the college for additional time in which to pay the remaining $20 million. Instead of being grateful for the $20 million that it had received, the college sued this man for both nonperformance and breach of his contractual obligations. Eventually, this individual was forced to file for bankruptcy and, though he ultimately made a full financial recovery and was able to come back even stronger than before, he vowed to never give another cent to the college.

I have been fortunate to have lived a privileged life and am sincerely grateful for my family, education, and upbringing. However, make no mistake that with this lifestyle I also faced difficult challenges. It is human nature to be envious of what other people have, however oftentimes such envy creates a variety of rationalizations for bad behavior. As a child, you do not necessarily see or know that you are privileged or underprivileged, and therefore you can be an easy target for people who may have ill intentions. That was me. But my father's words helped me to see the world as it is and learn that people usually act in their own self interest, even to the detriment of others at times.

This belief is a fine line to walk because I typically like to give people the benefit of the doubt but, as I grow older, I often tend to expect the worst from people so I can avoid being taken by surprise or being disappointed. It is an unfortunate, but necessary stance. However, it gives me a new appreciation and insight into what my father was trying to instill in me as a young child: Discernment comes with experience.

In business and in life there is simply one reality: There are good people and bad. There always have been and always will be. The simple lesson to learn is trust yourself, not others, keep your head out of the clouds, and you will always succeed.

As an executive vice president of Development and Acquisitions for the Trump Organization, **Eric Trump** is actively involved in all aspects of real estate development, both nationally and internationally. From the initial acquisitions and development partnership to the final design, construction, sales, and marketing functions, he plays a pivotal role in Trump projects around the world. Eric appears as a keynote speaker for real estate conferences nationwide, as well as in various press outlets such CNBC, Fox, NBC, and the *New York Post*. Along with his work with the Trump Organization, he works fervently to aid children in need, having started the Eric Trump Foundation for St. Jude Children's Hospital.

Overcoming the Fear of Failing

For years I have traveled the world, speaking on entrepreneurship and investing. My intent is to highlight the importance of financial education and how financial education is essential to financial freedom and financial security. When asked what I personally invest in, I say, "I became financially independent investing in real estate."

Regardless of where I am—the United States, Australia, South Africa, Europe, or Asia—or to whom I am speaking—rich or poor—what I hear back are similar responses to the idea of investing in real estate. Here are a few choice comments:

"I don't want to fix toilets."

"I don't have any money."

"I don't have the time."

"Real estate is risky."

"What if I lose money?"

"You can't do what you do here."

It is my opinion these responses are simply excuses. Excuses that mask a deeper, darker, hidden, unexpressed reality. In my opinion, most people who use these excuses are:

1. Not educated in real estate.
2. Lazy.

3. Afraid of failing.

4. All of the above.

I say this because most people want to be financially free. Most people would love to have financial security. Most people would love to have money coming in regardless of whether they worked or not. Many people would love to stop working and do something they really wanted to do.

To me, real estate represents freedom. Real estate means control over my life and my future. I am not depending upon a retirement plan filled with stocks, bonds, and mutual funds—investments that someone else manages. I want control of my financial destiny.

This is why when I hear such excuses as "I don't have any money" or "I don't want to fix toilets." I know these excuses are just that. I know people are looking at the journey, not the destination. A friend of mine has two sayings about this human failing. His first saying is, "Everyone wants to go to heaven, but no one wants to die." His second, "Many people will not start the journey until all the lights are green."

TIP Unfortunately, too many people allow their excuses to get between them and the life they would love to live.

Unfortunately, too many people allow their excuses to get between them and the life they would love to live. Rather than look beyond real estate, looking at what becoming a real estate investor can do for their lives, most people are blinded by their own excuses. They see what they are afraid of rather than what they want in life. Fear and laziness blur their vision, limiting the boundary of their lives.

The following are my points of view regarding the four excuses.

EXCUSES OF THE POOR

EXCUSE NO. 1: NO EDUCATION

Most people are smart enough to invest in real estate. Investing in real estate is not that tough. Anyone who has bought a home or rented a place to live has invested in real estate. So investing in real estate is not tough. Making money in real estate is another matter. Making money in real estate takes real, real estate education.

When I speak of making money in real estate, I am speaking of *cash flow*. Cash flow is income coming in every month, regardless of whether I work or not. I am not talking about *capital gains*. When people say their house has appreciated in value, or they flipped a property—buying low, fixing it up, and selling it—they are speaking of capital gains. There is a tremendous difference between cash flow and capital gains. In my opinion, capital gains are easier to achieve than cash flow. Achieving sustainable cash flow requires a higher degree of financial education. The good news is you do not have to go to college for four years to get this education. A three-day seminar is sufficient, if it is a good seminar. The Rich Dad Company offers beginning and advanced courses in real estate investing.

In 1997, when *Rich Dad Poor Dad* was published, I wrote about the difference between *assets* and *liabilities*. My rich dad's definitions were simple: *assets put money in your pocket* and *liabilities take money from your pocket*. In the book I stated, "Your house is not an asset. It is a liability." In other words, for most people, their biggest real estate investment, their house, cash flows out, not in. I received hate mail for years because of this one point. After the subprime mess, massive foreclosures, and declining home values, millions of people now realize that real estate can be either an asset or liability.

For most people, their home is a *liability*, even if the mortgage is paid off. Most homes are liabilities because most homes do not produce any income. Most homes cost money: for insurance, property tax, repairs, and other expenses. If a person sells his or her home and the sale puts money in that person's pocket, at that moment the home is an asset. Until then, it is a liability.

TIP To be financially free, your real estate must produce income in good or bad economies. Once you learn to do that, you are free for life. This is why a little financial education is important.

EXCUSE NO. 2: LAZINESS

Laziness is a personal matter. I know I am lazy. I battle the lazy boy inside of me on a daily basis. For example, when I wake up, I know I should go to the gym, but the lazy boy says, "Oh, you can exercise tomorrow. Why not make a cup of coffee and read the paper." By the age of two, most people are experts at making excuses.

When I hear people say, "I don't want to fix toilets" or "I don't have enough money," I know these are excuses from a lazy person because I use the same excuses. When I hear someone repeat to me the same excuses I use myself, I want to say, "What makes you think I want to fix toilets?" or "What makes you think I have money?" But what I really want to say is, "It's because I don't want to fix toilets, and it's because I want to have a lot of money, that's why I invest in real estate."

Rich dad often said, "Many lazy people are hard-working people." At first, I did not understand what he meant. As I got older, I began to understand his words more clearly. Growing older, I also found it easier to be busy at work than it was to do what I needed to do. Today, I still use excuses such as, "I'm busy" or "I have too much work to do" or "I need a break." Today, I meet many hard-working people, hiding behind the curtain of hard work, yet deep down, they are too lazy to get rich. So they invent an excuse.

When I was in high school, my poor dad often said to me, "I can't go to your football game because I've got work to do." He never attended a game in the three years I played high school football. He also said the same thing about becoming rich or at least financially free. He was always busy. In my opinion, he often used hard work as an excuse to hide from life. He was a good, hard-working, high-income, poor man.

My rich dad was a rich man because he did not work hard for money. Instead, he worked hard at having his money work hard for him. The harder his money worked, the more money he made, and the more free time he had. The more free time he had, the more money he made.

This drove my poor dad crazy. My poor dad often called people like my rich dad, "The idle rich." Rather than have his money work hard, my poor dad put his money in the bank. My poor dad believed in saving money. This drove my rich dad crazy. He would say, "Your father works hard because his money is lazy. All your dad's money does is sit in the bank. I come along, borrow your dad's money, buy a piece of real estate, and put your dad's money to work for me."

TIP Professional education is all about learning to work for money. Financial education is all about learning to have money work for you. So the question is, "Who works harder? You, or your money?"

EXCUSE NO. 3: FEAR OF FAILING

Fear is often a combination of lack of education and laziness. The acronym F.E.A.R. stands for *False Evidence Appearing Real*. Because of fear, many people see only what can go wrong. Due to lack of education, they cannot see what can go right.

When I am asked, "How does a person overcome the fear of failing?" I simply reply, "Get some education, gain some experience, find a mentor, and get off your butt." In other words, improve your vision. See what most people cannot see. See the opportunities most people cannot see because of fear. See the destination and the journey.

TIP One of the reasons I have a team of advisors when I invest is simply that each person sees something different. After listening to what each person has to say, I then make up my mind.

Most great investments are right in front of you. The problem is seeing them. The reason most investments are hard to see is that great investments are seen with your mind, not your eyes. Years ago, I wanted to buy a piece of ranch-land. My dream was to build a remote mountain cabin in the woods. I also wanted it for free. After challenging my mind, I went looking for my dream. A few months later, I came across a spectacular piece of property. It was approximately eighty acres, including an old rock house built in the 1880s. The asking price was $115,000. I believe I put $10,000 down—with the terms of no interest and no payments—and asked for one year to pay off the balance. After fixing the house, I subdivided the property, sold thirty acres with the house for approximately $215,000. I put some money, about $75,000, net in my pocket and still have the fifty free acres today.

After the transaction was completed, a neighbor who lived in a remote cabin a few miles away came by and was upset that I made money and got fifty acres for free. She had watched the property for years, but did nothing. She had a similar idea but failed to buy the property because she was afraid of failing. "What would you have done if you had failed?" she asked. "What if the property had not sold?"

"I still would have had my dream," I replied. "It would not have been for free, yet I would still have my dream."

"But what if you had failed?" she demanded.

Taking a deep breath I replied, "I knew that if things did not work out, I would have been creative and tried something else. Every failure would have made me smarter and eventually more successful. You can fail only if you do nothing."

She looked back at me and said, "And I did nothing, so I failed."

Shrugging my shoulders, I said softly, "I leave that decision up to you."

The Deadliest Word

One of the most deadly words in the English language is the word "try." When someone says they will "try" to do something, I know they will probably not do it. There is a world of difference between the statements, "I will try to do it" and "I will do it." The difference between the two statements is the word "commitment."

My favorite way of describing the word commitment comes from the following question and answer:

Question: What is the difference between bacon and eggs?
Answer: The chicken is involved but the pig is committed.

If you want to become financially free, don't be a chicken. Get committed. Forbid yourself from using the word "try." You either will or you won't.

THE POWER OF EDUCATION

About twenty years ago, I took a simple two-day course on creative financing. I believe I paid about $350 for the program. I think lunch was included. If it hadn't been for that course, I would not have seen the free land opportunity. My neighbor, who did not take the course, could not see what I saw. All she could see was failure.

As most of us know, we are in the Information Age. The problem is, there is too much information. The reason education is important is that education trains our brains to selectively take in information and turn information into meaning. Due to a lack of real estate education, my neighbor was overwhelmed with information, most of it negative. Her brain was not trained to focus, process information, and turn it into positive meaning. That is why a little real estate education can be priceless.

RICH PEOPLE AND COWARDS

Fear is a very powerful human emotion. How we handle fear determines if we become rich people or cowards. When it comes to money, *fear* turns most people into cowards.

Is it okay to have fear? While fear causes most people to do nothing, fear causes other people to take action. Since I do not want to fail and lose money, I take real estate education classes and read books on real estate. I did it twenty years ago, and I am still learning today. That is why I could ask my brain to find me a piece of land that I didn't have to pay for, and why I continue to invest today. Buying the eighty acres, or any investment, I still have fear. I still fear losing. I just use my fear to take action and get smarter. I know that if things do not go right, I will use my creative mind and gain wisdom in the process. Many people use the fear of failing as a reason to do nothing.

TIP Fear causes most people to do nothing; fear causes other people to take action. I still have fear. I still fear losing. I just use my fear to take action and get smarter.

Then there are people who attend real estate classes, study hard, and they still let fear stop them. One reason is due to analysis paralysis. That means they study too much. When it comes time to put their money on the line, the coward in them chimes in and gives them all the reasons why the deal will not work. Just before they sign the papers, Chicken Little pops into their head and begins to shout, "The sky is falling! The sky is falling!"

Just as I battle the lazy boy in me, I also do battle with my own resident Chicken Little. One of the beauties of real estate is that you have time to think. There have been many times that I have found a piece of property, put in an offer, had the offer accepted, and then I began my research—a process known as due diligence. It is during this due diligence period, a period that can be as short as a week or as long as six months, that I bring in my team of advisors and mentors. When I make the final decision either to buy or back out, I make it as a member of a calm, rational, educated, and experienced team—like the team who contributed to this book.

Due diligence periods do not guarantee success. There can still be unforeseen problems. If a problem arises, again I call on a team to assist me with problem solving, and it is that problem solving that increases my wisdom, wisdom that I can use on the next investment. At minimum, even if I lose some money, I will be smarter than someone who did nothing. It is with this philosophy that I invest, in spite of my fear.

EXCUSE NO. 4: ALL OF THE ABOVE

All of us are human. All of us need more education. All of us can be lazy. All of us are afraid of failing. The difference between all of us begins with all of the traits that make us human. The difference between all of us begins with how we address our excuses.

The following are some of the ways I personally address the four excuses.

ADDRESSING EXCUSE NO. 1: NO REAL ESTATE EDUCATION

My financial education began with the game of Monopoly. Rich dad would play that game with his son and me, over and over again. When I asked him why we played the game so often he said, "Because the formula for great wealth is found in this game." Most of us know the formula, which is this: Four green houses turns into one red hotel. At the age of nine, I realized that I could be rich if I followed this simple formula and turned a game into real life.

To show us the game being played in real life, rich dad took his son and me to see his green houses. Ten years later, when I was nineteen, rich dad bought his red hotel on Waikiki Beach.

When I returned to Hawai'i from the Vietnam War, I asked my rich dad how I could get started in real estate. His reply was, "First get educated. I've taken you as far as I can go. You need to take the next step." A month later, I was watching television and saw an infomercial for a real estate course. I purchased the course for $385, which was a fortune at the time, since I made only about $600 a month as a Marine Corps pilot.

It was after the course ended that my real education began. Everything the instructor taught us came true. He said, "The first problems you will run into are real estate agents. Most real estate agents are salespeople, not investors. They would not know a good investment from a bad one." This is true today. For months, all I heard from real estate agents is, "You can't do that. Those deals do not exist."

The next thing the instructor said was, "Find a mentor, someone who did invest in real estate." Since my rich dad was already my mentor, I went immediately to him. Rich dad's first words were, "How can I teach you something until you do something?"

TIP "How can I teach you something until you do something?"—RICH DAD

For the next few months, I drove around in my spare time, looking at properties, talking to real estate agents, finally doing something as my rich dad had suggested. After I finally put an offer in on a property, I ran back to rich dad and proudly showed him the offer. As you can already guess, he ripped it to pieces. Although it was painful to find out how little I knew, that experience was priceless because I was finally doing something.

The deal I brought him was a low down payment deal. The problem was I lost money every month; it was a negative cash flow investment. Rich dad's lesson was, "How many investments can you afford if you lose money every month?"

Obviously, my reply was, "Not many."

His next question was, "Why do you want to pay money to lose money?"

"Because the real estate agent said the price would go up and I would make my money back," I replied.

"Will the real estate agent guarantee that?" rich dad asked.

"I don't know," I replied. "He just said I would make a lot of money when I sold it."

"Will he guarantee that?" asked rich dad again.

"I don't know," I replied again.

He then said, "Rather than lose money, how many investments can you afford if you make money every month?"

Thinking for awhile, I replied hesitantly, "As many as I can find?"

Rich dad smiled and said, "Go out and find investments you can make money on. Never bring me an investment that you pay to lose money on. Never bet on a property going up in value."

It was back to the streets. As rich dad said, "How can I teach you something until you do something?" I was beginning to learn something.

My next lesson was learning to handle discouragement. As time dragged on, I became more and more discouraged. Everything was too expensive or would have cost too much money in repairs. Dragging my tail between my legs, I went back to rich dad for some sympathy, and as you can guess, he gave me none.

When I complained about not having enough money, rich dad just laughed. His lesson was, "When you find an investment that makes money, you will find the money."

A month later, I found a one-bedroom, one-bath condominium on the island of Maui, one block from a gorgeous white sand beach. I was excited that I finally found a great investment. I bought three of them, with credit cards and seller financing. Each month, I made a net $25 per unit. I was making money, not losing money. Rich dad was correct. When you find a great investment, you will find the money.

TIP **When you find a great investment, you will find the money.** —RICH DAD

For your information, even if $25 does not sound like much, it is one of four sources of income. In real estate, the four sources of income are:

1. **Cash flow.** In this example I was making $25 a month.
2. **Amortization.** Each month, a little bit of my loan was being paid off. If I held the property to the end of the mortgage, technically my tenants would have paid off my mortgage.
3. **Depreciation.** Accounting and tax rules allow me to depreciate my property, which means I am making money but it looks like I am losing money. I am making money because I am legally allowed to pay less in taxes. So this is money coming in because less money is paid out in taxes. It is also known as *phantom cash flow*.
4. **Appreciation.** This is the price of the unit going up in value. Appreciation is also known as capital gains. Most people invest for appreciation. During the last real estate boom, flippers were buying and then selling for a profit. This is investing for appreciation (capital gains).

These four sources of income are also known I.R.R.—an internal rate of return. Being able to see these four different incomes gives me a lot more confidence.

As I said earlier, I don't invest for appreciation, I invest for cash flow. In fact, one of the reasons why I do not like to flip property is that I like all four of these income opportunities and it takes such a long time to find a great property.

Another reason why I do not like to flip a property is that I can gain access to my appreciation without selling the property. For example, let's say I buy a property for $200,000 and a few years later it goes to $300,000. Rather than sell the property, I would rather borrow out the equity and continue to let the tenant pay for my second mortgage. Obviously, I borrow only if my rent can cover the increase in monthly payments.

I learned the hard way about selling or flipping a property. Here's the story.

MORE THAN FIXING A TOILET

I wish I could say my education was complete after I bought the three units. Little did I know that the next phase of education was about to begin, an education in property management. After owning the three condos for a few months, the septic system on the entire development burst, and the sewage run-off ran into one of my condos. Next on my real estate education curriculum was how to deal with developers, homeowners associations, lawyers, and a smelly rental unit.

My first plumbing problem was a much bigger than fixing a toilet.

SELLING OUT OF THE PROBLEM

The good news is, even though I was losing money because the tenants moved out, the Maui real estate market was taking off. A real estate agent, the very type of person I was warned to be wary of in my real estate course, offered me $48,000 per unit. Since my base cost was only $18,000 a unit, my gross capital gains would be about $30,000 a unit. The money and the septic system went to my head. I sold.

Immediately after I sold and put the money in my pocket, the real estate agent sold the units for $65,000 a unit a few weeks later. The lessons were piling up. I made money, but I was really losing money. The septic system caused me to think emotionally rather than rationally.

In real estate investor terms, the septic system made me a perfect candidate for another investor. I became known as a "don't wanter." A don't wanter is someone who does not want their property. They want out. They are emotional and irrational. Soon after the subprime mortgage mess hit in 2007, the market was filled with don't wanters. Great investors love don't wanters. If you want to become rich, look for don't wanters, and then look at the real estate they don't want.

THE BIGGER PROBLEM AND BETTER LESSON

Another lesson I gained from that first experience is this: "If just starting out, make sure the real estate is less than an hour's drive away." Since these properties were on another island, when there was a problem I had to take time off from work, drive to the airport, park my car, take a flight, rent a car, drive an hour to the property, work on the problem, and then hurry back home, missing a day's work. That was expensive. Today, I can handle properties far away, but when I was just starting out, I should have found a property as close to home as possible, less than an hour's drive away. After you have purchased at least ten properties, because each property will have a new lesson, then you can start expanding your operational radius.

MORE PROPERTIES—MORE PROBLEMS— MORE MONEY

Next on my educational curriculum were capital gains taxes. Selling the three units put a lot of money in my pocket, and I spent it. The next year, I found out what capital gains taxes were. I had made money, and now I had tax problems. I found out that the government tax collectors do not like excuses.

Every property comes with different problems and different lessons. Each lesson caused me to seek further education and gain more real life experience. This is how I got smarter, wiser, and richer. I got richer by failing. I found out that people who do not fail also do not succeed.

TIP I got richer by failing. I found out that people who do not fail also do not succeed.

Today, my wife, Kim, and I own approximately fifteen hundred apartment units and earn more money in a month than most people earn in years. While the education and experiences have not stopped, the financial rewards have gone up. Even during the subprime mortgage crisis, our properties have continued to do well. No matter how tough times get, most people want a roof over their heads.

As far as mentors go, the real estate professionals in this book are our mentors. Whenever Kim and I have a question, these are the people we call. Simply said, our education never ends because the problems and challenges we face never end.

So how does one overcome the fear of failing? My answer is grow up. Since failing is part of learning, start with baby steps. Babies crawl before they walk and walk before they run. Babies fall many times during the learning process. That is why it is good that babies are short when they start out. They do not have far to fall.

Our educational system makes two big mistakes when teaching people. The first mistake is that it punishes students for making mistakes. If you make no mistakes, you are an A student. If you make too many mistakes you are labeled a failure. This is why so many people who did well in school do not do well in real life. The second mistake is that in school, you have to take tests on your own. If you cooperate with your classmates during test time it is called cheating. One of the reasons I make more money than many A students is because I make more mistakes and I cheat—meaning that I cooperate. This book is written by the people I cooperate with at test time.

How to Find Great Advisors and Mentors

A question I am often asked is, "How do I find great advisors and mentors?" My reply is, "In fairy tales and in real life, you kiss many frogs before you find a prince or princess, so start kissing."

One valuable lesson I have learned is, "In every bad deal I meet good people." For example, I was working on a deal with a person who talked like and looked like he knew what he was doing. "Joe," (not his real name), had the credentials and the diplomas. Then the deal we were working on went bad, and his true personality, his dark side, came out. The good thing was that I met Ken McElroy through the process. I do not know where "Joe" is today, but Ken and I have become great friends and have gone on to make millions of dollars together.

Today, I am not afraid of deals going bad because I know that through bad deals I meet good people. In other words, when deals go bad, the true character—the good or the bad in a person—comes out from behind the curtain.

HOW DO YOU OVERCOME THE FEAR OF FAILING?

Here are ten things you can do right now:

1. **Take classes or read books before starting.** If you have no money, go to the library. Remember, your mind is your greatest asset. Invest in that first.
2. **Avoid taking advice from losers.** Stay away from people who say that something cannot be done. Be aware of real estate sales people who give investment advice but who do not invest in real estate.
3. **Find mentors, people who have already gone to where you want to go.**
4. **Look at a minimum of one hundred investments before buying anything.** Take a new route home from work and look at different neighborhoods. Jog or ride a bike in new neighborhoods. Observe if neighborhoods are changing, going up, or going down. Talk to people who live in the area to find out what is going on. Once you find an area you are interested in, become a five-block expert. Become the smartest person in one square mile. When you begin to see investments that make money, the money will find you.

5. **Start small.** Know that you will make mistakes. My rich dad often said, "When someone does something to make a killing, they get killed." Invest in property less than an hour from where you live.

6. **Stay humble.** When people make money, they often get cocky. When people get cocky, they make foolish mistakes. It is through humility and humor, being able to laugh at our successes as well as our failures, that we learn best. In other words, don't take yourself too seriously. The septic system blowing up and flowing into my first condo still causes me to laugh. Today, I am cautious about investing in anything that is downhill from something else. Today, I do know exactly what rolls downhill!

7. **Dream big.** The only difference between my first investment and my investments today are zeros. My dream was not real estate. My dream was financial freedom, and each property, good or bad, was a stepping-stone to that dream.

8. **Remember, the world is filled with hard-working poor people.** Many people today are slaves to money. Today, many people will have to work for money all their lives. So, every day, remind yourself not to be one of them. Work hard at having your money work hard for you so you do not have to work hard for money.

9. **There are no perfect investments.** Each investment comes with problems. Each investment will challenge you. Each investment will teach you something new. If you *do nothing*, you *learn nothing*. If you learn nothing, you remain poor. So remember, the only way you can fail is to fail to do something.

10. **And no, I do not fix toilets.** If I knew how to fix toilets, I would, so I never learned how to fix them. Instead, I learned how to hire and fire professionals such as real, real estate agents, accountants who know the tax advantages of investing in real estate, mortgage bankers who personally invest in real estate, lawyers who understand real estate law, property managers who love taking care of property, contractors whose passion is building or fixing real estate, and other specialists whose business is to be the best at the business of real estate. So I do not know how to fix toilets, or how to do accounting or real estate law, but I do know who does.

As the years go on, you will get smarter and so will your team of professional advisors. Ultimately, real estate is not your asset. Real estate alone does not make anyone rich. Investing in real estate offers you the opportunity to get smarter. It is your education, good and bad experiences, lessons learned, wisdom that comes with time, and your team, a team like my team that contributed to this book, that will ultimately become your greatest assets.

TIP If you do not have enough money for an investment, remind yourself that if you *do not* solve that problem, you will have money problems all your life. My rich dad said, "If you can solve the problem of *not having money*, you will *have more money* for life." Henry Ford said, "Thinking is the hardest work there is. That's why so few people engage in it."

Real Life Story: Why Waste a Priceless Mistake?

During this last real estate bubble, a friend bought one property, flipped it, and made some money. That first easy success went to his head. He now thought he was Donald Trump's long lost brother. As the property bubble continued to inflate, he went on a buying spree, buying properties in Las Vegas, Miami, San Francisco, Mexico, London, and Phoenix. Today he is bankrupt and blames real estate for his problems. His problem was he knew only one type of market, a market bubble. He now knows what a real estate bust looks like. Since he blames real estate rather than himself, he has not learned much. He has wasted priceless mistakes. He fails to learn that it is after the bubble bursts that the real, real estate investors come out, and the real killings are made. The killings are made from foolish investors who got killed.

TIP The reason there are more poor people than rich people is that it is easier to say, "I can't afford it," rather than ask the question, "How can I afford it?" The moment you ask yourself the question, "How can I afford it?" your most important asset, your mind, goes to work. If you use the excuse, "I can't afford it," your mind goes back to sleep and you get back to working hard as a slave to money.

So please do not allow the *fear of failing* to come between you and your *financial freedom*. Failing is essential to success.

TIP If you *do nothing,* you *learn nothing*. If you learn nothing, you remain poor. So remember, the only way you can fail is to fail to do something.

Index

From the
Rich Dad
Series
of Books

RICH
DAD
POOR DAD

Best #1 Personal Finance Book of All Time! Seller

WHAT THE RICH TEACH THEIR KIDS ABOUT MONEY –
THAT THE POOR AND MIDDLE CLASS DO NOT!

ROBERT T. KIYOSAKI

RICH DAD'S
CASHFLOW
QUADRANT
GUIDE TO FINANCIAL FREEDOM

E B
S I

ROBERT T. KIYOSAKI

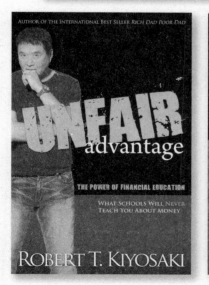

AUTHOR OF THE INTERNATIONAL BEST SELLER *RICH DAD POOR DAD*

UNFAIR
advantage
THE POWER OF FINANCIAL EDUCATION
WHAT SCHOOLS WILL NEVER
TEACH YOU ABOUT MONEY

ROBERT T. KIYOSAKI

RICH DAD'S
GUIDE TO
INVESTING
WHAT THE RICH INVEST IN, THAT THE POOR
AND MIDDLE CLASS DO NOT!

ROBERT T. KIYOSAKI

SECOND
CHANCE
FOR YOUR MONEY, YOUR LIFE AND OUR WORLD

ROBERT T.
KIYOSAKI
Author of the International Bestseller *Rich Dad Poor Dad*

Notes

From the Rich Dad Advisor Series

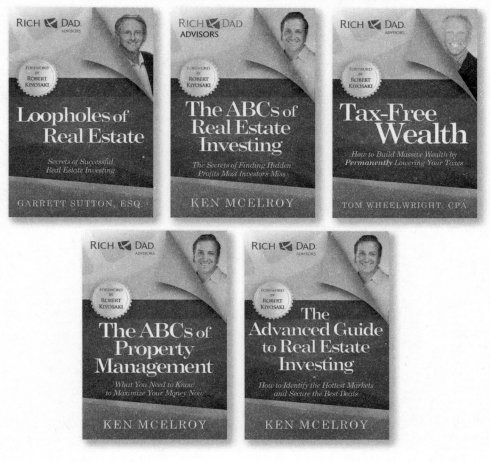

From the Rich Dad Library Series of Books

Notes

Credits

Chapter 1, "The Business of Real Estate," copyright © 2009 by Tom Wheelwright is used by permission of the author.

Chapter 2, "A Real Estate Attorney's View of Assembling and Managing Your Team," copyright © 2009 by Charles W. Lotzar is used by permission of the author.

Chapter 3, "Profits from the Ground Up," copyright © 2009 by Ross McCallister is used by permission of the author.

Chapter 4, "Master Your Universe," copyright © 2009 by Craig Coppola is used by permission of the author.

Chapter 5, "10 Rules for Real Estate Asset Protection," copyright © 2009 by Garrett Sutton is used by permission of the author.

Chapter 6, "How to Avoid and Handle Real Estate Disputes," copyright © 2009 by Bernie Bays is used by permission of the author.

Chapter 7, "Buy by the Acre, Sell by the Foot: Understanding Real Needs, Financial Logic, and Asking Questions," copyright © 2009 by Mel Shultz is used by permission of the author.

Chapter 8, "It's All About Adding Value," copyright © 2009 by Curtis Oakes is used by permission of the author.

Chapter 9, "Analyzing the Deal, or Adventures in Real Estate," copyright © 2009 by John Finney is used by permission of the author.

Chapter 10, "Real Estate Due Diligence," copyright © 2009 by Scott McPherson is used by permission of the author.

Chapter 11, "Creating Value from the Inside Out," copyright © 2009 by Kim Dalton is used by permission of the author.

Chapter 12, "Financing for Real Estate Investors," copyright © 2009 by Scott McPherson is used by permission of the author.

Chapter 13, "Lease It and Keep It Leased," copyright © 2009 by Craig Coppola is used by permission of the author.

Chapter 14, "The Perils of Careless Property Management," copyright © 2009 by Ken McElroy is used by permission of the author.

Chapter 15, "Getting from A to B Without Paying Taxes," copyright © 2009 by Gary Gorman is used by permission of the author.

Chapter 16, "No Down Payment," copyright © 2009 by Carleton Sheets is used by permission of the author.

Chapter 17, "The Sleeping Giant of Real Estate Profitability," copyright © 2009 by W. Scott Schirmer is used by permission of the author.

Chapter 18, "The Tax Lien Investment Strategy," copyright © 2009 by Tom Wheelwright is used by permission of the author.

Chapter 19, "How to Create Retail Magic: A Tale of Two Centers," copyright © 2009 by Marty De Rito is used by permission of the author.

Chapter 20, "What One Property Can Teach You," copyright © 2009 by Kim Kiyosaki is used by permission of the author.

Chapter 21, "In the Beginning . . . ," copyright © 2009 by Donald Trump is used by permission of the author.

Chapter 22, "What Is the Most Important Thing You've Learned From Your Father About Real Estate?" copyright © 2009 by Donald Trump Jr. and Eric Trump is used by permission of the authors.

Photo Credits: Donald Trump Jr. photo by DouglasGorenstein.com.